D0104747

Discover
Europe

Experience the best
of Europe

This edition written and researched by

Oliver Berry,

Alexis Averbuck, Mark Baker, Kerry Christiani, Mark Elliott,
Duncan Garwood, Anthony Ham, Virginia Maxwell, Craig
McLachlan, Andrea Schulte-Peevers, Ryan Ver Berkmoes,
Nicola Williams, Neil Wilson

Britain & Ireland p51

Germany p553

The Netherlands & Belgium p485

Austria, Switzerland & the Czech Republic p627

France p175

Spain p293

Italy p383

Greece p731

● Britain & Ireland

Highlights 54
- Tower of London
- London's Nightlife
- Stonehenge
- Bath
- Edinburgh Castle

● France

Highlights 178
- Eiffel Tower
- Versailles
- Chambord
- Pont du Gard
- Côte d'Azur

● Spain

Highlights 296
- La Sagrada Família
- Museo del Prado
- Alhambra
- Flamenco
- Cuenca

● The Netherlands & Belgium

Highlights 488
- The Rijksmuseum
- Amsterdam's Canals
- Kinderdijk
- Bruges
- Brussels

● Germany

Highlights 556
- Cold War Berlin
- Berlin's Tiergarten
- Neuschwanstein & Hohenschwangau Castles
- Munich's Beer Gardens
- Cologne Cathedral

● Austria, Switzerland & the Czech Republic

Highlights 630
- Salzburg
- The Matterhorn, Zermatt
- Vienna's Coffee Houses
- Prague Castle
- Jungfraujoch

Contents

Discover Europe

France 175

Highlights 178
Best... 180
Itineraries 182
Paris 184
Normandy 217
Brittany 225
Champagne 227
Alsace & Lorraine 234
The Loire Valley 237
Burgundy & the
Rhône Valley 241
The French Alps
& Jura 249
The Dordogne 253
The Atlantic Coast 255
Languedoc-
Roussillon 260
Provence 263
The French Riviera &
Monaco 272
Survival Guide 286

Spain 293

Highlights 296
Best... 298
Itineraries 300
Madrid 302

Castilla y León 321
Castilla-La Mancha 324
Catalonia 327
Barcelona 327
Basque Country 350
Navarra 355
Valencia & Murcia 356
Andalucía 359
Survival Guide 377

Italy 383

Highlights 386
Best... 388
Itineraries 390
Rome 392
Northern Italy 422
Venice 429
Tuscany 446
Florence 446
Southern Italy 468
Pompeii 446
Amalfi Coast 474
Survival Guide 478

The Netherlands
& Belgium 485

Highlights 488
Best... 490

Itineraries 492
The Netherlands 494
Amsterdam 494
The Randstad 508
Belgium 520
Brussels 520
Flanders 530
Survival Guide 545

Germany 553

Highlights 556
Best... 558
Itineraries 560
Berlin 562
Dresden & Saxony 582
Weimar & Thuringia ... 587
Bavaria 589
Munich 589
Bavarian Alps 597
Romantic Road 600
Nuremberg 605
Stuttgart & the
Black Forest 608
The Rhine Valley 609
Moselle Valley 611
North
Rhine-Westphalia 614
Cologne 614
Hamburg 617
Survival Guide 622

Contents

Plan Your Trip

This is Europe	6
Europe Map	8
Europe's Top 25 Highlights	10
Europe's Top Itineraries	32
Europe Month by Month	42
What's New	46
Get Inspired	47
Need to Know	48

Discover

Britain & Ireland 51

Highlights	54
Best...	56
Itineraries	58
London	**60**
Windsor & Eton	96
Canterbury	97
Brighton & Hove	98
Bath	102
Stonehenge	104
St Ives	109
Oxford	111
Stratford-upon-Avon	113
Cambridge	116
York	118
Manchester	123
Liverpool	128
Wales	**131**
Cardiff	131
Snowdonia National Park	135
Southern Scotland	**135**
Edinburgh	135
Stirling	146
Loch Ness	147
Glen Coe	147
Ireland	**150**
Dublin	151
Cork	158
Cliffs of Moher	162
Galway	163
Survival Guide	**164**

Italy

Highlights	386

- Colosseum
- Florence
- Venice's Canals
- Pompeii
- Amalfi Coast

Greece

Highlights	734

- Acropolis
- Acropolis Museum
- Meteora
- Knossos
- Santorini

In Focus | ## Survival Guide

●●●

Austria, Switzerland & the Czech Republic 627

Highlights **630**

Best... .... **632**

Itineraries **634**

Austria **636**
Vienna 636
Salzburg 656

Switzerland **672**
Geneva 672

Czech Republic **696**
Prague 696

Survival Guide **719**

●●●

Greece 731

Highlights **734**

Best... .... **736**

Itineraries **738**

Athens **740**

Peloponnese **756**

Cyclades **758**
Santorini (Thira) 761

Crete **764**

Dodecanese **770**

Ionian Islands **774**
Corfu 774

Survival Guide **778**

Europe Today **784**

History **786**

Family Travel **793**

Visual Arts **795**

Architecture **798**

Food & Drink **801**

Sports & Activities .. **808**

European Landscapes **812**

Directory **816**
Accommodation 816
Business Hours 816
Customs Regulations 816
Climate 817
Discount Cards 817
Electricity 817
Gay & Lesbian Travellers 818
Health 818
Insurance 818
Internet Access 819
Legal Matters 819
Money 819
Safe Travel 820
Telephone 821
Time 821
Tourist Information 821
Visas 821
Weights & Measures 822

Transport **822**
Getting There & Away 822
Getting Around 822

Language **827**

Behing the Scenes ... **829**

Index **830**

How to use this book **845**

Our writers **848**

This is Europe

Whether you're cruising along the French Riviera, punting down the canals of Venice, speeding down the slopes of the Alps or sipping coffee in a Viennese cafe, Europe offers more iconic experiences than practically anywhere else on the planet.

History is undoubtedly one of Europe's major draws.
From Neolithic sites and Grecian ruins to Gothic cathedrals and crumbling castles, taking a trip across Europe can feel like stumbling into the pages of a history textbook. While in many ways one of the world's most forward-looking regions, Europe's past inevitably informs its present and its future. Understanding this continent's turbulent history is essential if you want to get to grips with what makes it tick. Thankfully, there's no shortage of amazing museums to put it all into context, from the palatial Louvre and British Museum to Amsterdam's Rijksmuseum, recently reopened after a decade-long renovation.

Europe also understands the finer things in life.
And it's never shy about letting you join in the party. It's a place where you can indulge your taste buds, stretch your muscles, shop till you drop and dance into the small hours – all in the same day, should you so desire. Best of all, the next country is never more than a quick trip away. In a few hours you could swap the glittering Mediterranean for Berlin's bars, Rome's ancient ruins or the Alps' snow-capped peaks. Few places on earth can offer such a wealth of experiences and adventures. But don't be in too much of a hurry; the journey is an essential part of what makes exploring Europe such fascinating fun.

Wherever you end up, you're in for an unforgettable trip.
So *bon voyage, sichere Fahrt,* happy travels. And don't forget to send us a postcard.

> ❝
> Europe offers more iconic experiences than practically anywhere else on the planet
> ❞

Neuschwanstein Castle (p602), Germany

25
Top Highlights

1. Rome
2. Eiffel Tower, Paris
3. Nightlife, London
4. Vienna
5. Venice
6. Dublin
7. Berlin
8. Amsterdam
9. Prague
10. Alhambra, Granada
11. Bath
12. Jungfraujoch
13. Champagne Vineyards
14. La Sagrada Família, Barcelona
15. Matterhorn
16. Athens
17. Salzburg
18. Giant's Causeway
19. Skiing, Chamonix
20. Slow-Boating the Rhine
21. Beer & Chocolate, Brussels
22. Beer Drinking, Munich
23. Edinburgh
24. Santorini
25. Tuscany

25 Europe's Top Highlights

Ancient Rome

From the crumbling Colosseum to the ancient Forum and the Appian Way, few sights are more evocative than the ruins of ancient Rome (p393). Two thousand years ago this city was the centre of the greatest empire of the ancient world, where gladiators battled and emperors lived in unimaginable luxury. Nowadays, it's a haunting spot; as you walk the gravel paths you can almost sense the ghosts in the air. View of the Colosseum (p394) from the Roman Forum

1

IZZET KERIBAR/GETTY IMAGES ©

TRAVELPIX LTD/GETTY IMAGES ©

2

Eiffel Tower, Paris

Seven million people visit the Eiffel Tower (p189) annually, and this is one icon that definitely lives up to the hype. There are several ways to the top: masochists can hike up 324m of staircases to the summit, while everyone else pays to catch the lifts. Either way, the Parisian panorama that unfolds is simply staggering – aim for a twilight visit, when the crowds are fewer and the City of Lights is at its twinkly best.

London's Nightlife

World-famous theatres, landmark cinemas, iconic venues, underground clubs – London's at its liveliest after dark, when there's no better time to take the cultural pulse of the UK capital (p60). Catching a musical or a play in the West End is on most people's itinerary, but that's just the beginning of London's nightlife: you could join the groundlings at Shakespeare's Globe Theatre, watch a blockbuster on Leicester Sq, or experience high culture at the Royal Opera House. The only trick will be finding enough time to sleep. London's West End

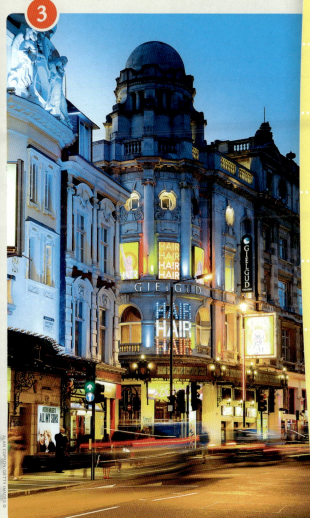

The Best...
City Views

PALATINE HILL, ROME
Gaze across the Italian capital from this iconic hill. (p393)

BASILIQUE DU SACRÉ-CŒUR, PARIS
The whole of Paris unfolds below you from this Montmartre landmark. (p195)

THE SHARD, LONDON
London's soaring new skyscraper has a bird's-eye view. (p72)

THE CAMPANILE, VENICE
Climb Venice's tallest building for a panoramic perspective. (p435)

THE BELFORT, BRUGES
This medieval bell tower looks over Bruges' most beautiful square. (p537)

The Best...
Royal Residences

VERSAILLES
Louis XIV's jaw-dropping statement of architectural excess. (p218)

BUCKINGHAM PALACE
Look for the Royal Standard above the palace to see if the Queen's at home. (p64)

SCHLOSS SCHÖNBRUNN
The Habsburg's rococo summer retreat in Vienna. (p637)

PALACIO REAL
Wander through the 50-odd rooms on show in Madrid's 2800-room palace. (p303)

PRAGUE CASTLE
The Czech monarchs are long gone, but their castle dominates Prague's old city. (p701)

4 Imperial Vienna

The monumentally graceful Hofburg (p643) whisks you back to the age of empires in Vienna as you marvel at the treasury's imperial crowns, the equine ballet of the Spanish Riding School and the chandelier-lit apartments fit for Empress Elisabeth. The palace, a legacy of the Habsburg era, is rivalled in grandeur only by the 1441-room Schloss Schönbrunn (p637), a Unesco World Heritage site, and the baroque Schloss Belvedere (p642), both set in exquisite gardens. Dining room of the Hofburg (p643)

GONZALO AZUMENDI/GETTY IMAGES ©

5 Venice in Winter

Venice (p429) is unquestionably one of the world's most bewitching cities, but its beauty has one drawback – crowds. Venice can feel swamped in summer, but in winter it's a different story: there are far fewer tourists, the light is sharp and clear, and the city is at its most atmospheric. Wander Dorsoduro's shadowy back lanes, then visit two of Venice's top galleries: the Galleria dell'Accademia and the Collezione Peggy Guggenheim.

JEAN-PIERRE LESCOURRET/GETTY IMAGES ©

Dublin

Whether you're wandering the leafy Georgian terraces of St Stephen's Green or getting acquainted with the past at Kilmainham Gaol, in Dublin (p151) you're never far from a literary or historic sight. And then there are the city's pubs: there are few better places to down a pint than Dublin, and you can even make a pilgrimage to the original Guinness brewery on the city's outskirts. Either way, you're bound to make a few Irish friends along the way. Kilmainham Gaol (p153)

DESIGN PICS/LM PHOTO/GETTY IMAGES ©

JOHN FREEMAN/GETTY IMAGES ©

Berlin, East & West

More than 20 years since the fall of the Berlin Wall, it's hard to believe that this most cosmopolitan of cities (p562) once marked the frontier of the Cold War. But reminders of Berlin's divided past still remain: whether you're passing the Brandenburg Gate, gazing at graffiti at the East Side Gallery or soaking up the history at Checkpoint Charlie, it's an essential part of understanding what makes Germany's capital tick. East Side Gallery (p570)

Amsterdam's Canals

To say Amsterdammers love the water is an understatement. Sure, the city (p494) made its first fortune in maritime trade, but that's ancient history. You can stroll next to the canals and check out some of the 3300 houseboats. Or, better yet, go for a ride. From boat level you'll get to see a whole new set of architectural details, like the ornamentation bedecking the bridges. And when you pass the canalside cafe terraces, you can look up and wave.

FRASER HALL/GETTY IMAGES ©

8

The Best...
Places for a Drink

A PINT IN A IRISH PUB
Dublin wouldn't be Dublin without its pubs. (p156)

FRENCH VINEYARDS
If you want to learn about the fruits of the vine, head for a Bordeaux vineyard. (p258)

GERMAN BEER GARDENS
Trying the local brews at a Munich beer garden is a great way to meet the locals. (p596)

SCOTTISH WHISKY DISTILLERIES
Many of Scotland's distilleries conduct tours, but Edinburgh is a good starting point. (p143)

Historic Prague

Emerging from behind the Iron Curtain, where it slumbered for decades, the capital of the Czech Republic is now one of Europe's most alluring and dynamic places. In some parts Prague (p696) has hardly changed since medieval times – cobbled cul-de-sacs snake through the Old Town, framed by teetering townhouses, baroque buildings and graceful bridges. And if castles are your thing, Prague Castle is an absolute beauty: a 1000-year-old fortress covering around 7 hectares – the world's largest castle complex. Old Town and Prague Castle (p701)

The Best...
Sacred Spaces

NOTRE DAME CATHEDRAL
See light filter through the rose windows in Paris' Gothic wonder. (p190)

THE MEZQUITA
Muslim and Christian architecture collide in Córdoba's mosque-cum-cathedral. (p367)

ST PETER'S BASILICA
The Vatican's largest church is among the holiest sites in Christendom. (p403)

WESTMINSTER ABBEY
British monarchs have been crowned at London's Westminster Abbey since 1066. (p61)

ANCIENT DELPHI
Where the oracle sat at the centre of the ancient Greek world. (p755)

RICHARD NEBESKY/GETTY

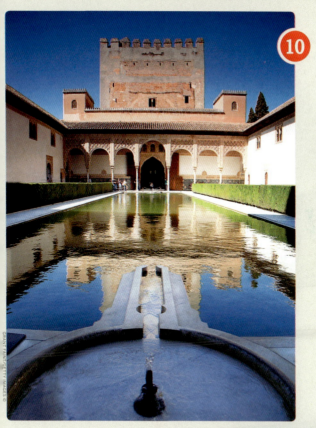

10 Alhambra, Granada

The palace complex of the Alhambra (p372) is perhaps the most refined example of Islamic art anywhere in the world. It's also an enduring symbol of 800 years of Moorish rule in a region that was then known as Al-Andalus. From afar, the Alhambra's red fortress towers dominate the Granada skyline, set against a backdrop of the Sierra Nevada's snow-capped peaks. Up close, the Alhambra's perfectly proportioned Generalife gardens complement the exquisite detail of the Palacio Nazaríes. Put simply, this is Spain's most beautiful monument.

Bath's Architecture

Britain boasts many great cities, but Bath (p102) is the belle of the ball. The Romans built a health resort here to take advantage of the hot water bubbling to the surface; the springs were rediscovered in the 18th century and Bath became *the* place to see and be seen by British high society. Today, the stunning Georgian architecture of grand townhouses, sweeping crescents and Palladian mansions (not to mention Roman ruins, a beautiful cathedral and a 21st-century spa) mean that Bath will demand your undivided attention. Roman baths (p106)

PETER RICHARDSON/GETTY IMAGES ©

12

Jungfraujoch

Travelling through Switzerland often feels like one nonstop scenic adventure, as every bend in the road opens up a new panorama of mind-boggling views. But if it's the ultimate alpine view you're after, then Jungfraujoch (p688) is guaranteed to fit the bill. A gravity-defying train chugs up to Europe's highest railway terminus (at 3471m), opening up an unforgettable vista of icy pinnacles, knife-edge peaks and gleaming glaciers. Dress warmly, don some shades and don't forget the camera.

SLOW IMAGES/GETTY IMAGES ©

13

Champagne Vineyards

For a celebratory tipple, there's only one drink that'll do – and that's a bottle of bubbly. The rolling vineyards around Reims and Épernay in Champagne (p227) are littered with prestigious names, including Mumm, Mercier, De Castellane, Moët & Chandon, most of which offer guided tours and *dégustation* (tasting) in their musty old cellars. There are also over 5000 small-scale *vignerons* (wine makers), all producing their own distinctive champagnes.

La Sagrada Família, Barcelona

Barcelona is famous for its Modernista architecture, much of which is the work of visionary architect Antoni Gaudí. His masterwork is this mighty cathedral (p332), which remains a work in progress more than 80 years after its creator's death. It's a bizarre combination of crazy and classic: Gothic touches intersect with eccentric experiments and improbable angles. Eight decades into its construction, no one is entirely sure when it will be finished; but even half-completed, it's a modern-day wonder.

The Best...
Ancient Monuments

STONEHENGE
The world's most iconic stone circle is also one of its oldest. Some sections date back to 4500 BC. (p104)

THE ROMAN FORUM
Exploring the streets, markets and temples of ancient Rome is unforgettable. (p393)

THE ACROPOLIS
Athens' ancient temple complex remains an architectural inspiration, more than 2000 years after it was built. (p742)

THE ALIGNEMENTS DE CARNAC
These Neolithic stones stretch for miles across the Breton countryside in France. (p230)

The Best...
Mountain Landscapes

THE FRENCH ALPS
Gaze up to Mont Blanc, Europe's highest mountain. (p249)

THE DOLOMITES, ITALY
This spiky chain of mountains is home to Italy's wildest scenery. (p445)

PICOS DE EUROPA, SPAIN
Remote Spanish mountains popular with hikers and wildlife spotters. (p356)

THE SCOTTISH HIGHLANDS
These barren hills straddle northern Scotland, including Britain's highest, Ben Nevis. (p151)

HOHE TAUERN NATIONAL PARK, AUSTRIA
The largest national park in the Alps, with many 3000m peaks. (p671)

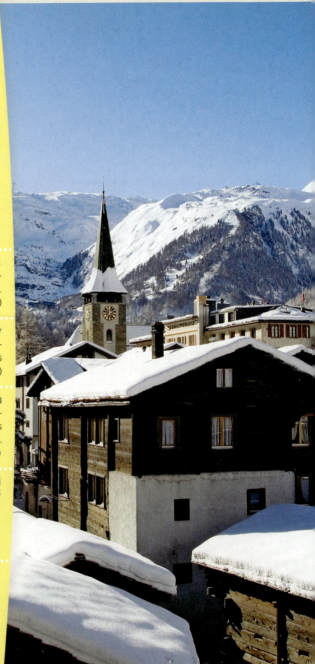

15

Matterhorn

It graces chocolate-bar wrappers and evokes stereotypical *Heidi* scenes, but nothing prepares you for the allure of the Matterhorn (p681). This mesmerising loner looms above the timber-chalet-filled Swiss village of Zermatt. Gaze at it from a tranquil sidewalk cafe, hike in its shadow along the tangle of alpine paths above town, with cowbells clinking in the distance, or pause on a ski slope and admire its craggy, chiselled peak. Left: The Matterhorn behind the village of Zermatt (p680); Above: Cable car

LEFT: MARTIN MOOS/GETTY IMAGES © RIGHT: BRUCE YUANYUE BI/GETTY IMAGES ©

Athens' Ancient Monuments

History looms around every corner in Athens (p740). This 2500-year-old city is awash with architectural reminders of the majesty of the Greek Empire. The grandest of all is the Acropolis, thought by many scholars to be the most perfectly proportioned building ever constructed. Elsewhere you can visit the Ancient Agora (marketplace), make a pilgrimage to the Temple of Olympian Zeus, and browse ancient artefacts at the Acropolis Museum. Acropolis (p744)

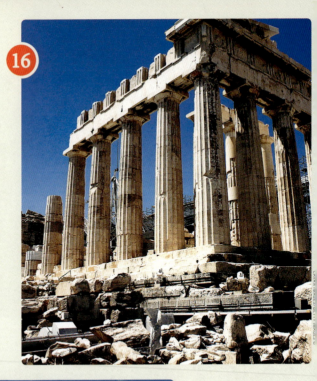

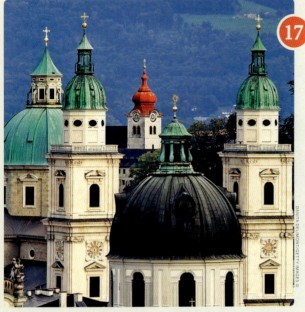

Baroque Salzburg

A castle on a hill, 17th-century cobbled streets, Mozart, the ultimate singalong – if Salzburg (p656) didn't exist, someone would have to invent it just to keep happy all the acolytes who visit Austria each year. It's hard to say what's most popular, but this is definitely *Sound of Music* country; faster than you can say 'do-re-mi' you will be whisked into gorgeous, steep hills that are alive with tour groups.

Giant's Causeway

This bizarre geological formation (p165) in Northern Ireland consists of more than 40,000 basalt pillars that emerge from the sea on County Antrim's northeastern coast. They're awash with legends (locals claim they're the work of an ancient giant), but were actually caused by a huge volcanic eruption that occurred between 50 and 60 million years ago. Nearby, you can test your nerves on the famous Carrick-a-Rede rope bridge, which dangles 30m above the foaming waves of the Irish Sea.

18

The Best...
Artistic Icons

MONTMARTRE, PARIS
This Parisian village inspired Toulouse-Lautrec, Dégas, Utrillo and many other artists. (p199)

FLORENCE
The home of the Italian Renaissance. (p446)

MONET'S GARDEN AT GIVERNY
Here in rural Normandy, Claude Monet created his *nymphéas* (water lily) paintings. (p271)

PROVENCE
Paul Cézanne and Vincent van Gogh were both inspired by Provence's landscapes. (p263)

MUSEUM HET REMBRANDTHUIS
Visit Rembrandt's original Amsterdam studio. (p501)

SISTINE CHAPEL
Michelangelo's masterpiece decorates the ceiling of this Vatican chapel. (p402)

Skiing in Chamonix

19

James Bond did it and so can you: France's Vallée Blanche is a once-in-a-lifetime experience. You'll never forget the five hours it takes to ski the 20km off-piste descent from the spike of the Aiguille du Midi to mountaineering centre Chamonix (p249) – every minute will pump more adrenalin through your body than anything else you've ever done. Craving more? Hurl yourself down Europe's longest black run (16km) at Alpe d'Huez.

CHRISTIAN ASLUND/GETTY IMAGES ©

The Best...
Natural Wonders

ALETSCH GLACIER
The largest glacier in the Alps, covering 120 sq km. (p685)

DUNE DU PILAT
Europe's largest sand dune, on France's Atlantic coast near Arcachon. (p260)

DACHSTEIN EISHÖHLE
These ice caves extend 80km into the mountains near Obertraun, Austria. (p667)

SAMARIA GORGE
The walls of this 13km canyon on the Greek island of Crete reach an amazing 1100m. (p770)

AIGUILLE DU MIDI
Enjoy a lofty lunch from this 3842m pinnacle in Chamonix, France. (p251)

20 Slow-Boating the Rhine

Catching a cruise boat along this mighty river (p609) is a must-do. As you sit back on deck, glorious German scenery drifts slowly past like a magic lantern: vineyard-clad hills, sleepy riverside towns and, every now and then, the ruins of a medieval castle. Stop off for a meal of sausage and sauerkraut, try a few of the local wines, and spend an hour or two wandering round a half-timbered village – the Rhine is a guaranteed highlight.

View of St Goarshausen from the beach of St Goar (p610)

OLIVIERO OLIVIERI/GETTY IMAGES ©

Belgian Beer & Chocolate

Belgium (p520) has a brew for all seasons. From tangy lambics to full-flavoured Trappists, the range of beers is exceptional, and there's no shortage of places to try them, from the breweries of Brussels to the riverside cafes of Bruges and Ghent. Sweet tooths will find plenty of shops selling the delicious chocolates (p529) for which Belgium is famous, including melt-in-the-mouth pralines to boozy choc laced with liqueurs.

21

22

Beer Drinking in Munich

It's not so much that you can drink beer in Munich (p596) – everybody knows you can. It's the variety of places where you can drink that makes this city heaven for beer afficionados. There's Oktoberfest, of course, and then there are the famous beer halls, from the infamous Hofbräuhaus to the wonderful Augustiner Bräustuben. And why stay inside? You can drink your lager in a park in Munich's city centre, or just about anywhere.

Edinburgh

Edinburgh (p135) is a city of many moods, famous for its amazing festivals and especially lively in the summer. The Scottish capital is also well worth visiting out of season for the sights. View the castle silhouetted against the blue spring sky or, for the atmosphere, fog snagging the spires of the Old Town, rain on the cobblestones and a warm glow beckoning from the window of a pub on a chilly December morning.

View of Edinburgh Castle from Princes St Gardens (p135)

The Best...
Shopping Experiences

PARIS' FLEA MARKETS
Paris' *marchés aux puces* are packed with vintage fashion and antiques. (p213)

NUREMBERG'S CHRISTMAS MARKETS
Festive *Christkindlmarkts* are held all across Germany, but Nuremberg has the best. (p606)

PORTOBELLO ROAD MARKET, LONDON
Forget Oxford St – this west London street market has the good stuff. (p93)

MERCAT DE LA BOQUERIA, BARCELONA
Shop for Spanish goodies at the gorgeous Boqueria food market. (p327)

GALERIES ST-HUBERT, BRUSSELS
Shop for dainty lace and handmade chocolates. (p520)

Santorini

The idyllic Greek island of Santorini (p761) will grab your attention and won't let go. The submerged caldera, surrounded by lava-layered cliffs topped by villages that resemble a sprinkling of icing sugar, is one of nature's great wonders. It's best experienced by a walk along the clifftops, from the main town of Fira to the northern village of Oia. The precariousness and impermanence of the place is breathtaking. Recover from your efforts with an ice-cold Mythos beer in Oia, as you await its famous sunset.

24

The Best...
Weird Buildings

CENTRE POMPIDOU, PARIS
An 'inside-out' building, with pipes and girders on the outside. (p195)

KUNSTHAUSWIEN, VIENNA
An architectural mishmash of uneven floors, wonky windows and industrial materials. (p644)

LA PEDRERA, BARCELONA
Rooftop sculpture and organic lines from the imagination of Antoni Gaudí. (p331)

LEANING TOWER OF PISA
Tilting in Tuscany since 1173, it still hasn't toppled over. (p461)

ATOMIUM, BRUSSELS
The 102m-tall Atomium has escalators in its connection tubes. (p525)

25

Tuscany

The gently rolling hills of Tuscany (p446), bathed in golden light and dotted with vineyards, sum up Italy's attractions in a nutshell. Battalions of books, postcards and lifestyle TV shows try to do this region justice, but nothing beats a visit. Here, picture-perfect hilltop towns vie with magnificent scenery and Italy's best food and wine – so it's hardly surprising that this is a tourist hotspot. Visit in spring or autumn to see it at its calmest.

Europe's Top Itineraries

London to Galway
England to the Emerald Isle

5 DAYS

This tour begins in Britain's nonstop capital, London, before hopping across the Irish Sea to visit two gems of the Emerald Isle, Dublin and Galway.

1 London (p60)

Samuel Johnson famously quipped that when you're tired of London, you're tired of life, and this is certainly a city that's brimming with unmissable sights. Begin with the British Museum and its treasure trove of artefacts, then mosey around Covent Garden en route to St Paul's Cathedral. Nip across the river to Tate Modern before seeing a play at the Globe Theatre, the rebuilt theatre where Shakespeare premiered many of his plays. On day two, head for Trafalgar Sq, browse the priceless artworks of the National Gallery, snap yourself outside the Houses of Parliament and Westminster Abbey, then picnic in Hyde Park. Finish with dinner and a show in the West End.

LONDON ⊃ DUBLIN
✈ 1½ hours

2 Dublin (p151)

Ireland's capital city makes a fascinating contrast after London. It's an altogether more laid-back city, known for its literary sights and riverside scenery. Among the must-sees are the city's historic seat of learning, Trinity College, the art-filled National Gallery and the impressive main boulevard of O'Connell St. Ale aficionados will definitely want to make time for a visit to the Guinness Brewery before investigating the countless lovely pubs dotted around the Liffey River. It's worth spending a couple of days in Dublin to soak up the vibe, and if you can spare a bit more time, the Neolithic site of Brú Na Bóinne makes a fascinating day trip. Many scholars consider it as archaeologically important as Stonehenge.

DUBLIN ⊃ GALWAY
🚗 **2¼ hours** It's 215km along the M6.

3 Galway (p163)

On the opposite side of Ireland, Galway City is known for its rich musical tradition and lively gig scene. If you want to hear some traditional Irish music, this is definitely the place to do it: most of the city's pubs host live music several nights a week. Elsewhere around Galway are the fascinating archaeological remains of the Hall of the Red Earl and a host of excellent restaurants where you can try some cutting-edge Irish grub.

Trinity College (p151), Dublin

5 DAYS

Paris to Bruges
Northern Highlights

This adventure heads from France into Belgium, via princely Paris, stately Brussels and beautiful Bruges. Taking the train is the most relaxing way to travel, with good rail links between all the stops.

THE NETHERLANDS

BRITAIN

ANTWERP

4 BRUGES

3

BRUSSELS 2

BELGIUM

English Channel

FRANCE

1 PARIS

❶ Paris (p184)

The City of Lights is a wonderful beginning to this whistle-stop tour. Devote the first morning to the Louvre, wander around the Jardin des Tuileries, then travel down the Seine to Paris' Gothic masterpiece, Cathédrale de Notre Dame – don't miss the panorama from the gargoyle-topped towers. The lively Marais is a great area to explore after dark. On day two, spend the morning on the Left Bank, factoring in a trip up the Eiffel Tower, a walk around the Jardin du Luxembourg and some window-shopping along stylish Blvd St-Germain. Follow up with Impressionist art at the Musée d'Orsay or catch the metro to bohemian Montmartre.

PARIS ⟶ BRUSSELS

🚃 **One hour 20 minutes** Via high-speed Eurostar trains. 🚗 **3¼ hours** It's around 320km between Paris and Brussels via the motorways.

❷ Brussels (p520)

Belgium's capital is best known these days as the centre of the European Union, as the European Parliament is based here. But the city has plenty of other attractions. At its heart is the magnificent Grand Place, not only Belgium's finest public square, but one of Europe's grandest. Leave some time for shopping around the elegant arcade of Galeries St-Hubert, where you can pick up delicious pastries, delicate lace and delicious Belgian chocolates.

BRUSSELS ⟶ ANTWERP

🚃 **30 to 45 minutes** 🚗 **45 minutes** It's 45km on the A12 motorway.

❸ Antwerp (p530)

Belgium's second city is often overlooked, but has plenty to recommend it. The Grote Markt is lined with attractive brasseries and cafes, but for most people Antwerp's essential sight is the Rubenshuis, the 17th-century studio of Pieter Paul Rubens, which has been carefully restored and houses 10 of the painter's canvases.

ANTWERP ⟶ BRUGES

🚃 **70 minutes** 🚗 **1¼ hours** On the main E34.

❹ Bruges (p537)

Belgium might not have any big mountains or superstar beaches, but it does have charming towns aplenty – chief among them being Bruges, an impossibly pretty package of cafe-lined squares, cobble-stone streets and romantic canals. The essential activity here is a trip to the top of the Belfort (bell tower), one of Belgium's most recognisable landmarks. After dark head for one of the city's cosy pubs, where you can try some of the beers for which Belgium is famous. Nearby Ghent is another waterfront town you'll find it hard not to fall for, and makes an easy day trip from Bruges.

Jardin du Luxembourg (p185), Paris
PHOTOGRAPHER: EURASIA/GETTY IMAGES ©

10 DAYS

Barcelona to Florence
Riviera Cruising

This trip tracks the glittering Mediterranean, and takes in some of its key cities including sexy Barcelona, fragrant Nice and stately Monaco, before heading over the Italian border to Pisa and Florence.

① Barcelona (p327)

Start the tour in Spain's most bewitching city, Barcelona. The classic areas to wander are the shady lanes of the Barri Gòtic and El Raval, the city's lively waterfront and the gardens of Park Güell. Don't miss Barcelona's celebrated modernista buildings, including the playful Casa Batlló and the outlandish (and unfinished) cathedral, La Sagrada Família.

BARCELONA ➡ MARSEILLE
🚃 **Seven hours** With a change at Narbonne. ✈ **1¼ hours**

② Marseille (p263)

This old port makes a great place to soak up the sights and sounds of the French Riviera. The heart of the action is around the Vieux Port (Old Harbour), where the city's chaotic fish market takes place, and Le Panier, lined with tempting shops and food stalls. Have lunch at one of the harbourside restaurants, then take a boat trip to the island fort of Château d'If.

MARSEILLE ➡ NICE
🚃 **2½ hours** 🚗 **2¼ hours** Via the A50 and A8.

③ Nice (p272)

The original Riviera resort, Nice is perennially popular (even if its beaches are pebbly). The street market on cours Saleya is one of France's liveliest, while Vieux Nice is a photogenic tangle of shady alleyways and colourful houses. There are top views from the Parc du Château, at the eastern end of Promenade des Anglais.

NICE ➡ MONACO
🚃 **20 minutes** 🚗 **30 minutes** It's 20km via A8, 25km to 30km via the roads.

④ Monaco (p282)

A breakneck spin along the corniches (coastal roads) takes you into the millionaire's playground of Monaco, where Europe's high-rollers gamble away fortunes at Monte Carlo casino. If it all gets too much, Monaco's aquarium and hilltop exotic gardens are a peaceful refuge.

MONACO ➡ PISA
🚃 **Five hours** Change in Ventimiglia or Genoa.
🚗 **4½ hours** About 350km via A10 and A12.

⑤ Pisa (p460)

Monaco sits on the Italy border, and nearby Ventimiglia has train links across Italy. Pisa is an essential stop, with its beautiful piazza and, of course, the famously wonky leaning tower. It's worth booking your ticket online to make sure you dodge the inevitable queues.

PISA ➡ FLORENCE
🚃 **1¼ hours** 🚗 **1¼ hours** It's 88km via the SGC Firenze.

⑥ Florence (p446)

Florence is where the Italian Renaissance began, and architectural landmarks abound, including the Gothic Duomo and the 14th-century Ponte Vecchio. The city is also renowned for its fabulous artworks, most of which are housed in two renowned galleries, the Galleria degli Uffizi and the Galleria dell'Accademia.

Duomo (p446), Florence
PHOTOGRAPHER: WESTEND61/GETTY IMAGES ©

10 DAYS

Bruges to Salzburg
Old Europe

This multicountry trip takes in the best of Belgium, the Netherlands, Germany and Austria. It's doable in 10 days, but will be more fun if you can factor in a bit more time for side trips.

NORTH SEA

THE NETHERLANDS

BERLIN ③

② AMSTERDAM

① BRUGES

GERMANY

BELGIUM

NUREMBERG ④

FRANCE

SALZBURG ⑤

SWITZERLAND   AUSTRIA

① Bruges (p537)

Start off with a leisurely day in Belgium's quintessential canal town, Bruges. It's a compact and relaxed place that's made for aimless ambling: mosey around the medieval centre, climb the Belfort, wander along the waterways, then round the day off with a bowl of *moules-frites* washed down by boutique-brewed Belgian beer.

BRUGES ➲ AMSTERDAM
🚆 **3½ hours** Via Brussels.

② Amsterdam (p494)

Regular trains run from Bruges to Brussels – another stately city that's worth a stop – but for this trip we're heading straight to Amsterdam, a city so laid back it's practically horizontal. Amsterdam's compact size means you can cover the centre in a day, squeezing in the Van Gogh Museum, Anne Frank Huis and Rembrandthuis, followed by a canal cruise and a visit to the Red Light District. Two days would allow a day trip to Leiden or Delft.

AMSTERDAM ➲ BERLIN
🚆 **6½ hours** Direct. ✈ **1 hour**

③ Berlin (p562)

Germany's capital ranks alongside London, Rome and Paris in the must-see stakes. You'll need two days: day one for the West, including the Reichstag, Holocaust Memorial and Tiergarten, and day two for the East, including a Berlin Wall tour, Checkpoint Charlie, the DDR Museum and Potsdamer Platz. With another day, add the landscaped gardens of Park Sanssouci in Potsdam.

BERLIN ➲ NUREMBERG
🚆 **Four hours** Direct. 🚗 **4¼ hours** About 435km via A10, A9 and A3.

④ Nuremberg (p605)

Since the dark days of WWII, Nuremberg's Altstadt has been impeccably restored and now hosts one of Europe's most beautiful Christmas markets. The city also has a fine castle, the Kaiserburg, and some excellent museums that confront its troubled past. Best of all, the rest of Bavaria is right on your doorstep, with the dramatic castles of Neuschwanstein and Hohenschwangau just a short drive away.

NUREMBERG ➲ SALZBURG
🚆 **Three hours** Change at Munich.
🚗 **3½ hours** 300km via E45, E52 and E60.

⑤ Salzburg (p656)

Across the Austrian border lies Salzburg, a baroque blockbuster chiefly known for its musical connections: Wolfgang Amadeus Mozart (born here) and *The Sound of Music* (filmed here). The town is at its busiest during the annual Salzburg Festival and Christmas markets, but the Altstadt is always animated – and the Alps are only a quick skip away. All together now – *the hills are alive...*

Christmas market, Nuremberg (p605)

2 WEEKS

London to Athens
The Grand Tour

This is the big one – end to end, top to bottom and back again. You're covering all four corners of Europe, so travelling times are long, but apart from a few flights, you can mostly let the train take the strain.

① London (p60)

Two days isn't much time in London, but you should still be able to do the highlights: the Tower of London, Tate Modern, Big Ben and Buckingham Palace, with an extra day for discovering some of the shops, restaurants and theatres of the West End, and perhaps a trip downriver to Greenwich.

LONDON ➡ PARIS
🚆 **Two hours** On the Eurostar ✈ **One hour** From Heathrow or Gatwick to Roissy Charles de Gaulle.

② Paris (p184)

A high-speed Eurostar train whisks you via the Channel Tunnel to Paris. It's a city you've seen a million times in movies, but somehow nothing prepares you for your first sight of the Eiffel Tower appearing above the rooftops – and that's before you even get started on the Arc de Triomphe, the Louvre and Montmartre.

PARIS ➡ MADRID
🚆 **Eight hours** Via the high-speed TGV line
✈ **Two hours**

③ Madrid (p302)

There's nowhere better to experience Spain than Madrid – whether that means dining out on tapas in one of the city's squares, heading for a meal at a top-class *taberna* (tavern), watching authentic flamenco at a traditional tablao, or surveying the national art collection at the Museo del Prado.

MADRID ➡ ROME
✈ **Two hours**

④ Rome (p392)

The Eternal City; it is said a lifetime isn't enough to know it. During two days' sightseeing in Rome, choose from among the attractions of the Colosseum, Vatican City, Pantheon, Spanish Steps and the Trevi Fountain. For the perfect pizza, you'll want to head for the *centro storico* (historic centre) or Trastevere.

ROME ➡ VIENNA
🚆 **13 hours** Via direct night train; other trains require change at Bologna, Venice or Florence.
✈ **Two hours**

Temple of Olympian Zeus (p741), Athens
PHOTOGRAPHER: HUBERTUS BLUME/GETTY IMAGES ©

7 **Berlin** (p562)

Another train trip transports you to the sights of Berlin, where you should spend a couple of days investigating the Berlin Wall's memorials and museums, plus new city sights like the Sony Center and Museum für Film und Fernsehen. To experience the city's famous nightlife, Kreuzberg is the alternative hub, while Prenzlauer Berg is smarter.

BERLIN ⬿ ATHENS
✈ **Two hours**

8 **Athens** (p740)

Finish with a cross-Europe flight to Europe's easternmost capital, Athens. The city is an Aladdin's Cave of ancient ruins: the Temple of Olympian Zeus, the Ancient Agora and the Theatre of Dionysos are all haunting in their own way, but it's the Parthenon that is guaranteed to stay with you long after you leave for home.

5 **Vienna** (p636)

Catch the overnight sleeper train direct to the imperial city of Vienna, where you'll spend a couple of days visiting the monumentally graceful Hofburg, watching the Lipizzaner stallions and whiling away hours over coffee and cake in one of Vienna's many grand cafes.

VIENNA ⬿ PRAGUE
🚌 **4½ hours** Direct; longer with connections.
🚗 **Four hours** It's 335km via E50.

6 **Prague** (p696)

Even after decades behind the Iron Curtain, Prague has managed to cling to its rich cultural and architectural heritage. This isn't just the Czech Republic's loveliest city, it's also one of the loveliest in Europe, with iconic buildings such as Charles Bridge and Prague Castle contributing to a truly dreamy skyline.

PRAGUE ⬿ BERLIN
🚌 **4½ hours** Direct. 🚗 **3½ hours** It's 350km via A13.

Europe Month by Month

Top Events

🔒 **Christmas Markets**, Germany & Austria, December

🍷 **Oktoberfest**, Germany, September

✳ **Venice Carnevale**, Italy, February

⭐ **Edinburgh International Festival**, Scotland, August

✳ **Notting Hill Carnival**, England, August

February

Carnival in all its mania sweeps the Catholic regions of the Continent. Cold temperatures – even in Venice – are forgotten amid masquerades, street festivals and general bacchanalia.

✳ Venice Carnevale

In the period before Ash Wednesday, Venice, Italy, goes mad for masks. Costume balls enliven the social calendar in this storied old city like no other event. Even those without a coveted invite are swept up in the pageantry.

March

Let's hear it for the crocus: the tiny bulb's purple flower breaks through the ice-crusted soil to let Europe know there's a thaw in the air and spring will soon come.

✳ St Patrick's Day

Celebrations are held on 17 March in Irish towns big and small to honour the beloved Saint Patrick. While elsewhere the day is a commercialised romp of green beer, in his home country it's time for watching a parade with friends and family.

April

Spring arrives with a burst of colour, from the glorious bulb fields of Holland to the blooming orchards of Spain.

✳ Semana Santa

Parades of penitents and holy icons take to the streets of Spain, notably Seville, during Easter. Thousands of members of religious brotherhoods parade in traditional garb. Look for the pointed *capirotes* (hoods).

February Venice Carnevale

Settimana Santa

Italy celebrates Holy Week with processions and passion plays. By Holy Thursday Rome is thronged with the faithful and even non-believers are swept up in the emotion and piety of the hundreds of thousands thronging the Vatican and St Peter's Basilica.

Feria de Abril

Hoods off! This is a week-long party held in Seville in late April to counterbalance the religious peak of Easter. The many old squares in this gorgeous city come alive during Spain's long, warm nights.

Koninginnedag (Queen's Day)

Celebrations are held nationwide in the Netherlands on 30 April, but especially in Amsterdam, which is awash in orange costumes and fake afros, beer, balloon animals, beer, dope, Red Bull, beer, leather boys, skater dykes, temporary roller coasters, clogs, beer, fashion victims, grannies...

May

Expect nice weather anywhere but especially in the south where the Mediterranean summer is already full steam ahead. Yachts prowl the harbours, while beautiful people ply the sands.

Cannes Film Festival

The famous, not-so-famous and the merely topless converge for a year's worth of movies in little more than a week in Cannes, France. Those winning awards will be sure to tell you about it in film trailers for years to come.

Brussels Jazz Marathon

Around-the-clock jazz performances hit Brussels, Belgium, during the second-last weekend in May (www.brusselsjazz marathon.be), when the saxophone becomes the instrument of choice for this international-flavoured city's most joyous celebration.

June

The huge summer travel season hasn't burst out yet but the sun has burst through the clouds and the weather is gorgeous, from the hot shores in the south to the cool climes of the north.

Glastonbury Festival

Glastonbury's youthful summer vibe peaks for this long weekend of music, theatre and New Age shenanigans (www.glastonbury festivals.co.uk). It's one of England's favourite outdoor events and more than 100,000 turn up to writhe around in the grassy fields (or deep mud) at Pilton Farm.

July

Visitors have arrived from around the world and outdoor cafes, beer gardens and beach clubs are hopping. Expect beautiful – even steamy – weather anywhere you go.

Il Palio

Siena's great annual event is the Palio on 2 July and 16 August, a pageant culminating in a bareback horse race round Il Campo. The Italian city is divided into 17 *contrade* (districts), of which 10 compete for the *palio* (silk banner), and emotions explode.

Sanfermines ('Running of the Bulls')

Huge male bovines and people who want to be close to them invade Pamplona, Spain, from 6 to 14 July, when the town is overrun with thrill seekers, curious onlookers and, oh yeah, bulls. The *encierro* (running of the bulls) begins at 8am daily. Anything can happen, but it rarely ends well for the bull.

Bastille Day

There's fireworks, balls, processions and more for France's national day, 14 July. It's celebrated in every French town and city: go to the heart of town and get caught up in this patriotic festival.

🎇 Notting Hill Carnival

Held over two days in August, this is Europe's largest and London's most vibrant outdoor carnival, where London's Caribbean community shows the city how to party. Food, frolicking and fun are just a part of a vast multicultural celebration.

⭐ Edinburgh International Festival

Edinburgh, Scotland, hosts three weeks of drama, comedy, dance and music from around the globe (www.eif.co.uk). For two weeks the International Festival overlaps with the Fringe Festival (www.edfringe.com), which also draws innovative international acts. Expect cutting-edge comedy, drama and productions that defy description.

📅 September

It's cooling off in every sense, from the northern countries to the romance started on a dance floor in Ibiza. This may be the best time to visit: the weather's still good and the crowds have thinned.

⭐ Venice International Film Festival

The Mostra del Cinema di Venezia is Italy's top film festival and one of the world's top indie film fests (www.labiennale.org). The judging here is seen as an early indication of what to look for at the next year's Oscars.

🍷 Oktoberfest

Germany's legendary beer-swilling party (www.oktoberfest.de) starts mid-September in Munich (don't ever tell anyone you turned up for it in October, even if you did). Millions descend for litres of beer and carousing that has no equal. If you haven't planned ahead, you'll sleep in Austria.

⭐ De Gentse Feesten

Belgium's Ghent is transformed into a 10-day party of music and theatre, a highlight of which is the vast techno celebration called 10 Days Off (www.gentsefeesten.be). This gem of the low country is high on fine bars serving countless kinds of beer.

📅 August

Everybody's going somewhere as half of Europe shuts down to go enjoy the traditional month of holiday with the other half. If it's near the beach, from Germany's Baltic to Spain's Balearic, it's mobbed.

⭐ Salzburg Festival

Austria's renowned classical music festival, the Salzburg Festival (www.salzburgfestival.at) attracts international stars from late July to the end of August. That urbane person sitting by you having a glass of wine who looks like a famous cellist probably is.

Festes de la Mercè

Barcelona knows how to party until dawn and it outdoes itself during the four-day Festes de la Mercè (around 24 September). Head for concerts, join the dancing and marvel at *castellers* (human-castle builders), fireworks and *correfocs* – a parade of firework-spitting dragons and devils.

November

Leaves have fallen and snow is about to in much of Europe. Even in the temperate zones around the Med, it can get chilly, rainy and blustery.

Guy Fawkes Night

Bonfires and fireworks erupt across Britain on 5 November, recalling a failed antigovernment plot from the early 17th century. Go to high ground in London to see glowing explosions all around. It's hard to imagine what might have happened if Fawkes had succeeded.

December

Christmas is a good excuse for warm cheer despite the weather in virtually every city and town. Decorations transform even the drabbest shopping streets and every region has its own traditions.

Christmas Markets

Christkindlmarkts are held across Germany and Austria. The most famous are in Nuremberg and Vienna but every town has one. Warm your hands through your mittens on a hot mug of mulled wine and find that special (or kitsch) present.

Natale

Italian churches set up intricate cribs or *presepi* (nativity scenes) in the lead-up to Christmas. Some are quite famous, most are works of art and many date back hundreds of years and are venerated for their spiritual ties.

Far left: July Il Palio (p464), Siena
Left: December Christmas market, Salzburg

What's New

For this new edition of Discover Europe, our authors hunted down the fresh, the transformed, the hot and the happening. Here are a few of our favourites. For up-to-the-minute recommendations, see lonelyplanet.com/europe.

1 RIJKSMUSEUM, AMSTERDAM
It's taken 10 years and an eye-watering budget of €375m, but the Netherlands' foremost museum is finally open once again – and it's receiving rave reviews. (p496)

2 THE SHARD, LONDON
Spiking up from the South Bank beside London Bridge, this controversial needle-shaped skyscraper is now officially Europe's highest structure at 310m high. The view from the top is really amazing – and really expensive. (p72)

3 LOUVRE-LENS, FRANCE
An offshoot of the landmark Louvre Museum in Paris, this architecturally ambitious art gallery has opened just outside the little town of Lens, and hosts revolving exhibitions of contemporary and modern art. (p236)

4 STONEHENGE VISITOR CENTRE, ENGLAND
After years of debate, discussion and legal wrangling, the experience at Stonehenge is finally getting a long-overdue overhaul, including a new visitor centre, cafe, gallery and exhibition space. And importantly, the nearby road is due to be grassed over by the end of 2013, and eco-friendly shuttle buses will replace the incessant drone of traffic. (p104)

5 GALLERIA DEGLI UFFIZI (UFFIZI GALLERY), FLORENCE
A major refurbishment programme is underway at Florence's most famous gallery. Nine new exhibition rooms are already open, and it's planned that the total floor space of the gallery will more than double to around 12000 sq metres. (p447)

6 HIGH-SPEED TRAINS FROM PARIS TO BARCELONA
The completion of a new high-speed rail link now means it's possible to zip the 788km between the French and Spanish capitals in less than eight hours. It's a brilliant journey, and you'll see a whole lot more scenery than you would through a plane window.

7 VIENNA'S HAUPTBAHNHOF
Vienna's shiny new central train station makes a suitably grand introduction to the imperial city. By 2014 most trains in and out of Vienna will arrive here, although for now the building is still a work in progress.

8 KENSINGTON PALACE, LONDON
This regal red-brick palace has been the home to many great royal names down the centuries, most recently the Duke and Duchess of Cambridge, and looks all the grander following a recent £12m renovation project. (p77)

9 VAN GOGH MUSEUM, AMSTERDAM
Amsterdam's second-most famous art gallery is drawing in the visitors again after a seven-month refit, and its world-beating collection of van Gogh's works are as impressive as ever. (p495)

10 BERLIN WALL PANORAMA
In 2012, Berlin-based Yadegar Asisi installed this fascinating fresco next to Checkpoint Charlie. Measuring 15m high and 60m in circumference, it depicts Berlin life on the day when the wall fell in 1989, and provides a timely reminder of the city's divided past. (p564)

Get Inspired

📖 Books

Neither Here nor There: Travels in Europe Hilarious travelogue by best-selling author Bill Bryson, retracing his European backpacking trip of 20 years before.

Europe: A History Professor Norman Davies' sweeping overview of European history.

In Europe: Travels through the Twentieth Century Fascinating account of journalist Geert Mak's travels.

Philip's Multiscale Europe Plan your European road trip with this continent-wide travel atlas.

🎥 Films

The Third Man (1949) Classic tale of wartime espionage in old Vienna, starring Orson Welles and that zither theme.

Amélie (2001) Endearing tale following the quirky adventures of Parisian do-gooder Amélie Poulain.

Shaun of the Dead (2004) Typically quirky British zombie comedy, set in London's streets.

Vicky Cristina Barcelona (2008) Woody Allen rom-com makes use of a beautiful Barcelona backdrop.

🎵 Music

The Original Three Tenors: 20th Anniversary Edition Operatic classics courtesy of Pavarotti, Carreras and Domingo.

The Best of Edith Piaf The sound of France, including a selection of the Little Sparrow's greatest hits.

Gipsy Kings: Greatest Hits Sexy Spanish rhythms married with folk, flamenco, Latin and gypsy tunes.

Arctic Monkeys: Whatever People Say I Am, That's What I'm Not Spiky tunes from northern British songsmiths.

🖊 Websites

Visit Europe (www.visiteurope.com) Extensive resource of the European Travel Commission.

The Man in Seat Sixty-One (www.seat61.com) Hands-on advice for European train travel.

Eurocheapo (www.eurocheapo.com) Budget-friendly ideas for hotels, eating, flights and sights.

Auto Europe (www.auto-europe.com) Cheap car hire from all over Europe.

Short on time?

This list will give you an instant insight into Europe.

Read *The Europe Book* is a sumptuous Lonely Planet photo-book packed with images of Europe's greatest sights.

Watch *Cinema Paradiso* (1988) tells the heart-warming tale of one boy's cinematic love affair in rural Italy.

Listen Soundtrack your own *Magical Mystery Tour* courtesy of The Beatles.

Log on Visit www.raileurope.com for the info to plan your pan-European train trip.

Gondolas and gondoliers, Venice (p429), Italy
PHOTOGRAPHER: RUTH EASTHAM & MAX PAOLI/GETTY IMAGES ©

Need to Know

Currency
Pound sterling (£) and euro (€)

Languages
English, French, German, Italian, Spanish

Visas
Not required for citizens of EU, USA, Canada, Australia and New Zealand staying up to 90 days.

Money
ATMs widely available. Major credit cards accepted in shops, restaurants and hotels.

Mobile Phones
Local SIM cards will fit most modern mobile phones. Beware high roaming charges.

Wi-Fi
Common in most hotels and cafes; usually free, but sometimes available for a small charge.

When to Go

Dry climate
Warm summer, mild winter
Mild year-round
Mild summer, very cold winter
Cold climate

Britain & Ireland
GO Apr-May

Germany
GO Apr-May

Austria, Switzerland & the Czech Republic
GO May-Jul

France
GO Apr-Jun

Italy
GO Mar-Jun

Spain
GO Sep-Nov

Greece
GO Sep-Nov

High Season
(Jul & Aug)
- Hotel prices take a hefty hike in summer
- Ski season in the Alps is December to early March
- Accommodation can be hard to find around Easter

Shoulder Season
(Apr–May & Sep–Oct)
- Weather is warm and settled across much of Europe
- Crowds are lighter, but some attractions keep shorter hours

Low Season
(Nov–Mar)
- Look out for cheap deals on flights and accommodation
- Some hotels, sights and activities close completely for the winter

Advance Planning

- **One month before** Book train tickets. Most train companies offer substantial discounts for advance bookings.

- **Two weeks before** Reserve tickets online for popular sights, such as the Alhambra in Granada, the Louvre in Paris and the Colosseum in Rome.

- **When you arrive** Look into buying a travel pass for public transport in major cities; some passes also offer free or discounted admissions.

Daily Costs

Budget Less than €100

- Double room in a budget B&B: €60
- Cheap bistro lunch menu: €15
- Museum ticket: €10

Midrange €100–220

- Double room in a midrange hotel or B&B: €80–120
- Restaurant meal with a glass of wine or beer: €20–30
- Museum admission and one-day travel pass: €15

Top End More than €220

- Night in a luxury hotel: €150
- Three-course gourmet meal including wine: €35–45
- Admission costs including guided tour: €25
- Taxi fares: €10–15

Exchange Rates

Australia	A$1	€0.77	£0.65
Canada	C$1	€0.76	£0.65
Euro	€1	–	£0.85
Japan	¥100	€0.76	£0.64
Swiss	Sfr1	€0.81	£0.68
UK	£1	€1.18	–
USA	US$1	€0.78	£0.66

For current exchange rates see www.xe.com

What to Bring

- **Passport or EU ID** Remember to bring your driver's licence if you're hiring a car.
- **Travel adaptors** EU countries use two-pin sockets; the UK uses three-pin sockets.
- **Sturdy shoes** You'll be doing a lot of walking, so good soles are important.
- **Rain gear** In case the weather turns bad.
- **Travel insurance** Check the policy wording on winter sports and flight delays.
- **A corkscrew** Essential for picnics.
- **Travel dictionary** Choose one with a good food section for the country you're travelling to.

Arriving in Europe

- **London** Trains run from Heathrow to London Paddington (20min), and from Gatwick to London Victoria (20min). Piccadilly tube line runs to Heathrow terminals.
- **Paris** Regular buses (1hr) and trains (30min) run from Charles de Gaulle and Orly to Paris.
- **Berlin** TXL bus connects Tegel with Alexanderplatz (40min).
- **Madrid** Line 8 of the Metro (15min) and the Exprés Aeropuerto (40min) run to the city centre.
- **Amsterdam** Regular trains (20min) from Schiphol to Centraal Station.
- **Rome** Buses (1hr) and trains (30min) run from the airport to the city centre.

Getting Around

- **Car** Huge network of motorways and major roads throughout Europe. Motorways in many countries incur a toll, and petrol is expensive. Rental cars are mostly manual shift.
- **Train** High-speed trains connect major cities throughout Europe; slower trains serve regional towns. Can be faster and cheaper than flying.
- **Air** Internal flights with budget carriers are numerous, but often don't land at major airports.
- **Bus** Useful for smaller towns and rural areas.

Sleeping

- **Hotels** There's a huge choice available, ranging from basic city digs to full-blown luxury.
- **B&Bs** Generally have fewer facilities than hotels, but more local character.
- **Hostels** Nearly every major city has at least one hostel, with a choice of communal dorms or private rooms.
- **Camping** Sleeping under canvas is very popular in Europe, and you'll find plenty of sites to choose from.

Be Forewarned

- **Holiday seasons** Prices skyrocket and accommodation can be hard to find in July and August. Easter is also busy.
- **Pickpocketing** A problem in many cities, especially on public transport and around major attractions.

Britain & Ireland

Few countries are as plagued by cliché as Britain and Ireland. On one side of the Irish Sea, it's all shamrocks and shillelaghs, Guinness and 40 shades of green; over in Britain, it's double-decker buses and red telephone boxes, buttoned-up emotions and stiff upper lips. Yet, while some of the stereotypes are still true, these ancient next-door nations seem to have sloughed off most of the old clichés and turned their gazes firmly towards the future.

Whether it's ancient history or contemporary culture that draws you to Britain's shores, you'll really be spoiled for choice. Travelling around these pocket-sized islands is an absolute breeze, and you'll never be more than a train ride away from the next national park, tumbledown castle, world-class gallery or stately home. There are museums aplenty, galleries galore and mile upon mile of some of the most stunning coast and countryside you'll find anywhere in Europe. So, buckle up – you're in for an awfully big adventure.

Castle Howard (p121), England
KARL BLACKWELL/GETTY IMAGES ©

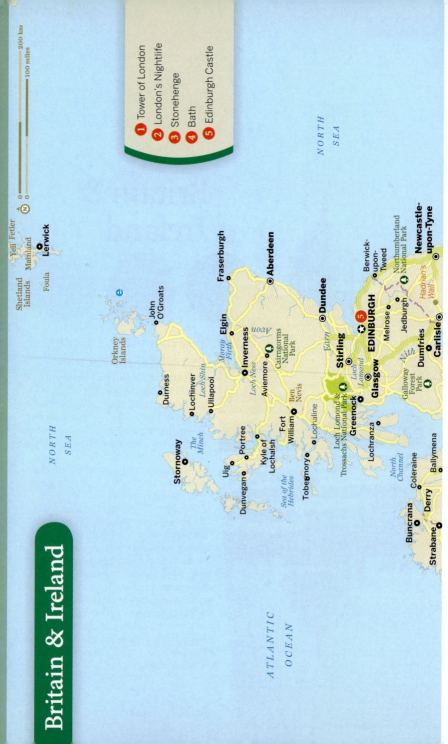

Britain & Ireland

1 Tower of London
2 London's Nightlife
3 Stonehenge
4 Bath
5 Edinburgh Castle

100 miles
200 km

ATLANTIC OCEAN

NORTH SEA

NORTH SEA

Shetland Islands
Yell Fetlar
Mainland
Foula
Lerwick

Orkney Islands
Durness
John O'Groats
Lochinver
Loch Shin
Ullapool

Stornoway
The Minch
Portree
Kyle of Lochalsh
Uig
Dunvegan
Sea of the Hebrides
Tobermory
Lochaline

Fraserburgh
Aberdeen

Elgin
Moray Firth
Inverness
Loch Ness
Aviemore
Cairngorms National Park
Avon
Dundee

Fort William
Ben Nevis
Earn
Stirling
EDINBURGH 5
Melrose
Berwick-upon-Tweed

Loch Lomond & Trossachs National Park
Loch Lomond
Greenock
Glasgow
Jedburgh
Northumberland National Park
Hadrian's Wall

Lochranza
Dumfries
Nith
Carlisle
Newcastle-upon-Tyne

North Channel
Coleraine
Galloway Forest Park

Buncrana
Derry
Strabane
Ballymena

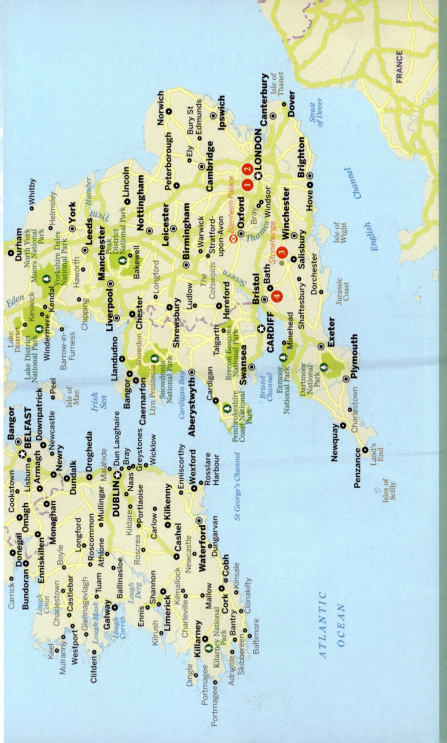

Britain & Ireland Highlights

Tower of London

One of London's world-famous landmarks, the Tower (p68) wraps up almost 1000 years of history within its Thameside turrets and battlements. Famously, it's home to the Crown Jewels, that glittering collection of jewels, sceptres, orbs and crowns used during the coronation of British monarchs. Look out for the Tower's famous flock of ravens and its red-coated Yeoman Warders (or Beefeaters, as they're generally known).

1

MICHAEL ENGLAND/LONELY PLANET ©

London's Nightlife

2

Ever since the days of Shakespeare, London has been renowned for its nightlife (p89). In the Bard's era, most of the action was south of the Thames, but these days you'll find theatres, clubs, cinemas and bars spread across the capital. Catch a musical in the West End, watch a concert at the Royal Albert Hall, experience alfresco Shakespeare at the Globe Theatre, or just settle in for a pint at a landmark pub.

DIVERSE IMAGES/GETTY IMAGES ©

Stonehenge

3

You've seen it a million times in photographs, magazines and TV documentaries, but nothing quite prepares you for your first sight of the real Stonehenge (p104). Built by ancient Britons in several stages between 3000 BC and 1600 BC, it's an unforgettable structure. To see the circle at its best, book an after-hours guided tour, which will enable you to dodge the crowds.

4

Bath

Say what you like about the Romans, but one thing's for sure – they certainly knew how to build a hot tub. The natural geothermal springs of Bath (p106) have been attracting visitors for more than two thousand years, but this city has so much more to offer than a soothing soak: great restaurants, top-notch shopping and some of the finest Georgian architecture in all of England. Royal Crescent (p106)

5

Edinburgh Castle

Dominating the skyline of Edinburgh from practically every angle, the city's magnificent clifftop fortress (p135) is a sight to behold. It's played a key role in Scotland's history since the 11th century, and with its crenellated battlements, massive walls and brooding watchtowers, it's every inch the image of a classic Scottish castle. Don't miss the view from the Argyle Battery, and try and be around to hear the One O'Clock Gun.

Britain & Ireland's Best...

Beauty Spots

○ **Lake District** (p132) Admire the landscape that inspired Wordsworth, Coleridge and Co.

○ **Snowdonia** (p135) Climb the highest mountain in Wales.

○ **Giant's Causeway** (p165) Explore Northern Ireland's great geological oddity.

○ **Scottish Highlands** (p151) Great glens, glassy lochs and snowy mountains.

○ **Ring of Kerry** (p161) Home to some of Ireland's most stunning views.

Houses & Palaces

○ **Hampton Court Palace** (p82) This glorious Tudor structure is just a quick trip from the British capital.

○ **Castle Howard** (p121) Quite possibly the finest stately home in northern England.

○ **Buckingham Palace** (p64) Pomp and ceremony galore at the Queen's London residence.

○ **Palace of Westminster** (p64) The home of British politics, otherwise known as the Houses of Parliament.

○ **Holyroodhouse** (p138) The Queen's official Scottish crash-pad.

Castles

○ **Windsor Castle** (p96) Castles don't come much more regal than this royal weekend getaway.

○ **Leeds Castle** (p97) Despite the name, this classic castle is an easy trip from London.

○ **Warwick Castle** (p97) Is this England's finest fortress? You decide.

○ **Edinburgh Castle** (p135) Gaze out from the battlements across Scotland's capital city.

○ **Conwy Castle** (p135) A majestic medieval castle overlooking the Welsh coastline.

Need to Know

Literary Locations

o **Brontë Parsonage Museum** (p118) Emily and Charlotte Brontë and their family lived here from 1820 to 1861.

o **James Joyce Museum** (p158) Lots of literary memorabilia relating to Ireland's greatest novelist.

o **Charles Dickens Museum** (p67) Charles Dickens' only surviving London residence.

o **Hill Top** (p132) Join the crowds at Beatrix Potter's Lake District cottage.

o **Oxford Bar, Edinburgh** (p143) Drink in the pub favoured by Inspector Rebus.

ADVANCE PLANNING

o **As early as possible** Arrange train tickets and car hire. Buying at least a month in advance secures the cheapest deals.

o **One month before** Book hotels and make restaurant reservations, especially in popular cities such as London, Manchester and Bath.

o **One week before** Book guided tours and confirm prices and opening hours.

RESOURCES

o **Visit Britain** (www.visitbritain.co.uk) The UK's main tourism site covers everything from accommodation to outdoor activities.

o **National Rail Enquiries** (www.nationalrail.co.uk) Check out timetables and book train tickets.

o **Traveline** (www.traveline.org.uk) Journey planning for public transport throughout the British Isles.

o **Discover Ireland** (www.discoverireland.com) Comprehensive info on the Emerald Isle, from places to stay to things to do.

GETTING AROUND

o **Air** Budget flights connect most major British and Irish cities, including London, Manchester, Edinburgh, Glasgow and Dublin.

o **Car** The best option for exploring rural areas, although remember to factor in petrol and parking costs. Road distances in Britain are in miles; Ireland uses kilometres.

o **Train** The best option for intercity travel. There are frequent connections between major towns.

o **Bus** Long-distance coaches and local buses are cheap but slow. Coverage can be patchy outside major towns.

BE FOREWARNED

o **Crowds** Top sights get extremely crowded, especially in summer and on holiday weekends.

o **Bank holidays** Most sights are closed and traffic on main roads can be a nightmare.

o **Nightlife** City centres can be extremely rowdy after dark on weekends.

o **Weather** Notoriously unpredictable, so be prepared. Umbrellas and raincoats essential.

Left: Snowdonia National Park (p135), Wales;
Above: Houses of Parliament (p64), London
(LEFT) MARK GREENWOOD LANDSCAPES/GETTY IMAGES ®;
(ABOVE) JANE SWEENEY/GETTY IMAGES ©

Britain & Ireland Itineraries

It might be great by name, but Britain is surprisingly small by nature. The country's compact geography makes it easy to get around the sights; travelling by train allows you to drink in the scenery and dodge the traffic.

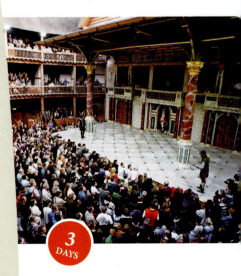

3 DAYS

THE BIG SMOKE & BEYOND
London to Blenheim Palace

World-class museums, historic castles, cutting-edge restaurants: ❶**London** (p60) is a sightseeing overload, and you could devote your whole holiday to exploring the capital. In one day, you might just about fit in visits to Trafalgar Sq, Westminster, St Paul's Cathedral and the Tower of London, before a lightning-fast detour to the Turbine Hall in Tate Modern, and finishing with an unforgettable performance at Shakespeare's Globe Theatre.

Day two is more leisurely. Hop on a scenic boat along the River Thames to spend a morning at Britain's foremost botanical gardens, ❷**Kew Gardens** (p79). In the afternoon, catch the boat downriver to visit Henry VIII's ostentatious abode at ❸**Hampton Court** (p82).

On day three, take an early train to ❹**Oxford** (p111). Spend the morning wandering the quads and admiring the dreaming spires before catching a bus to ❺**Blenheim Palace** (p113), not just one of England's finest stately homes, but also the birthplace of Winston Churchill.

Top Left: Shakespeare's Globe (p67), London, England;
Top Right: Oxford (p111), England
(TOP LEFT) ANDREA PISTOLESI/GETTY IMAGES ©; (TOP RIGHT) SEAN CAFFREY/GETTY IMAGES ©

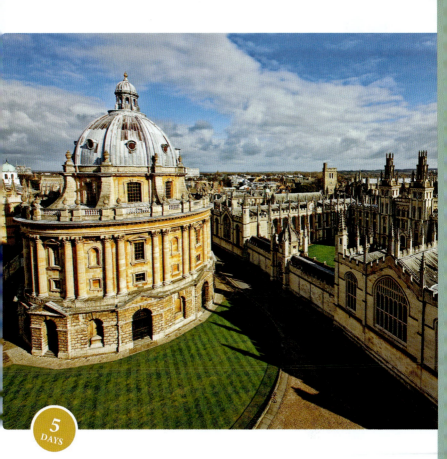

5 DAYS

NORTHERN EXPOSURE
Oxford to Dublin

From ❶**Oxford** (p111), it's an easy train trip west to the gorgeous Georgian city of ❷**Bath** (p102), founded as a spa town by the Romans 2000 years ago and still one of England's most desirable addresses. Devote the day to exploring the Roman Baths, soaking in the Thermae Bath Spa and walking along the city's grandest streets, Royal Crescent and the Circus.

From Bath, it's on to Shakespeare's birthplace at ❸**Stratford-upon-Avon** (p113). The town is packed with sights linked with the Bard, but don't miss the chance to catch his plays in action courtesy of the Royal Shakespeare Company.

On day three, travel northwest to the Viking city of ❹**York** (p118), with its medieval streets and landmark Minster. Next comes a day in Scotland's capital, ❺**Edinburgh** (p135), a city renowned for its arts, architecture and history, as well as a brace of stately castles.

Finish your trip with a flight across the Irish Sea to ❻**Dublin** (p151), a lively river city that's awash with literary heritage, not to mention a cracking pub culture. If you've always wanted to taste an authentic pint of Guinness, this is definitely the place to do it.

Discover Britain & Ireland

At a Glance

○ **London** (p60) The big smoke has big thrills to match.

○ **Northern England** (p118) From revitalised cities to wild hills.

○ **Wales** (p131) Celtic nation with its own language and culture.

○ **Scotland** (p135) Lochs, mountains, castles and glens galore.

○ **Ireland** (p150) From coast to countryside, the Emerald Isle enchants.

LONDON

POP 7.51 MILLION

One of the world's greatest cities, London has enough history, vitality and cultural drive to keep you occupied for weeks. This cosmopolitan capital is at the forefront of international trends in music, fashion and the arts, riding a wave of 21st-century British confidence, breathing new life into established neighbourhoods like Westminster and Knightsbridge, and reinventing areas like Clerkenwell and Southwark that were formerly off the tourist track. And fresh from its stint as host of the Queen's Golden Jubilee celebrations and the 2012 Olympics, London's riding the crest of a creative wave – there's never been a better time to visit.

History

London first came into being as a Celtic village near a ford across the River Thames, but the city only really took off after the Roman invasion in AD 43.

London grew prosperous and increased in global importance throughout the medieval period, surviving devastating challenges like the 1665 Plague and 1666 Great Fire. By the early 1700s Georgian London had become one of Europe's largest and richest cities, but it was during the Victorian era that London really hit its stride, fuelled by vast mercantile wealth and an empire that covered over a quarter of the earth's surface.

In 2000 London got its first elected Mayor (as opposed to the Lord Mayor of London, a largely ceremonial role), and went on to successfully host both the

Trafalgar Square
IMAGE SOURCE/GETTY IMAGES ©

Queen's Golden Jubilee in 2002 and the Olympics in 2012.

◎ Sights

West End

If anywhere is the beating heart of London, it's the West End – a strident mix of culture and consumerism.

Trafalgar Square   Square
(Map p74; WC2; ⊖ Charing Cross) Trafalgar Square is the public heart of London. The square is one of the world's grandest public places, with Admiral Nelson surveying his fleet from the 43.5m-high **Nelson's Column** (Map p74) at its heart, erected in 1843 to commemorate his 1805 victory over Napoleon off Spain's Cape Trafalgar.

National Gallery   Gallery
(Map p74; www.nationalgallery.org.uk; Trafalgar Sq, WC2; ⊙ 10am-6pm Sat-Thu, to 9pm Fri; ⊖ Charing Cross) **FREE** Gazing grandly over Trafalgar Square through its Corinthian columns, the National Gallery is the nation's most important repository of art. Highlights include Turner's *The Fighting Temeraire,* Botticelli's *Venus and Mars* and van Gogh's *Sunflowers.*

National Portrait Gallery   Gallery
(Map p74; www.npg.org.uk; St Martin's Pl, WC2; ⊙ 10am-6pm Sat-Wed, to 9pm Thu & Fri; ⊖ Charing Cross, Leicester Sq) **FREE** The fascinating National Portrait Gallery is like stepping into a picture book of English history. An audiovisual guide (£3) will lead you through the gallery's most famous pictures.

Piccadilly Circus   Square
(Map p74; ⊖ Piccadilly Circus) Despite the crowds and traffic, Piccadilly Circus has become a postcard for the city, buzzing with the liveliness that makes it exciting to be in London. At the centre of the circus is the famous aluminium statue, Anteros, twin brother of Eros, dedicated to the philanthropist and child-labour abolitionist Lord Shaftesbury.

Covent Garden Piazza   Square
(Map p74; www.coventgardenlondonuk.com/-/covent-garden-piazza; ⊖ Covent Garden) London's first planned square, Covent Garden Piazza now hosts bands of tourists shopping in quaint old arcades and ringing street entertainers and buskers.

Westminster & Pimlico

Westminster has been the centre of political power for a millennium, and the area's many landmarks combine to form an awesome display of strength, gravitas and historical import.

Westminster Abbey   Church
(Map p74; ☎ 020-7222 5152; www.westminster-abbey.org; 20 Dean's Yard, SW1; adult/child £18/8, verger tours £3; ⊙ 9.30am-4.30pm Mon, Tue, Thu & Fri, to 7pm Wed, to 2.30pm Sat; ⊖ Westminster) Westminster Abbey has never been a cathedral (the seat of a bishop). It's what is called a 'royal peculiar' and is administered directly by the Crown. Every monarch since William the Conqueror has been crowned here, with the exception of a couple of unlucky Eds who were murdered (Edward V) or abdicated (Edward VIII) before the magic moment. Look out for the strangely ordinary-looking **Coronation Chair**.

Apart from the royal graves, keep an eye out for the many famous commoners interred here, especially in **Poets' Corner**, where you'll find the resting places of Chaucer, Dickens, Hardy, Tennyson, Dr Johnson and Kipling as well as memorials to some other greats (Shakespeare, Austen, Brontë etc).

Verger-led tours are held several times a day (except Sundays) and are limited to 25 people per tour; call ahead to secure your place.

Westminster Cathedral   Church
(Map p74; www.westminstercathedral.org.uk; Victoria St, SW1; tower adult/child £5/2.50; ⊙ 7am-7pm; ⊖ Victoria) With its distinctive candy-striped red-brick and white-stone tower features, John Francis Bentley's 19th-century cathedral, the mother church of Roman Catholicism in England

61

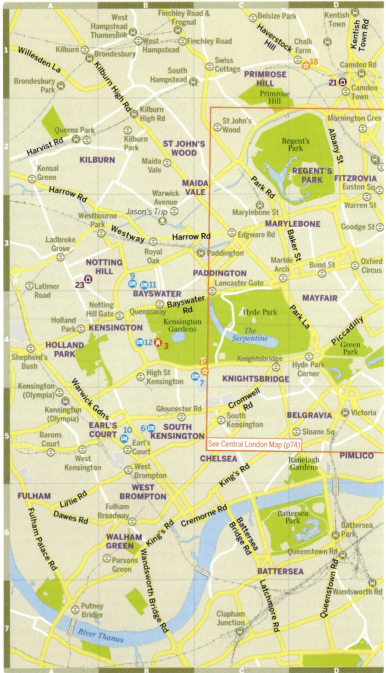

See Central London Map (p74)

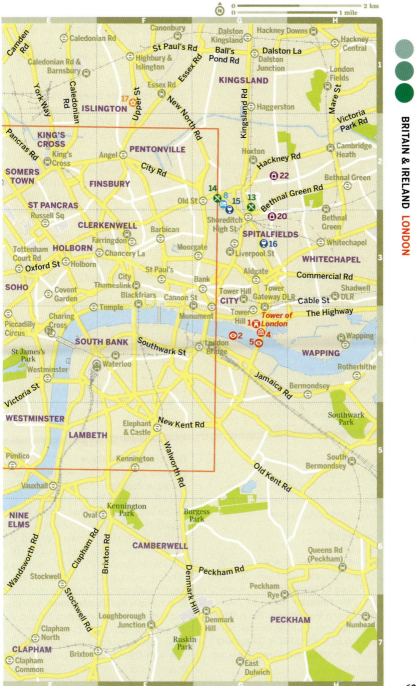

0   2 km
0   1 mile

N

Camden Rd

Caledonian Rd

Caledonian Rd & Barnsbury

York Way

Canonbury

St Paul's Rd

Highbury & Islington

Essex Rd

Essex Rd

Upper St

New North Rd

Dalston Kingsland

Dalston La

Ball's Pond Rd

Dalston Junction

Hackney Downs

Hackney Central

London Fields

Mare St

Victoria Park Rd

Cambridge Heath

1

Pancras Rd

Caledonian Rd

ISLINGTON

17

KING'S CROSS

King's Cross

Angel

PENTONVILLE

City Rd

KINGSLAND

Kingsland Rd

Haggerston

Hoxton

Hackney Rd

22

Bethnal Green

2

SOMERS TOWN

ST PANCRAS

Russell Sq

FINSBURY

CLERKENWELL

Farringdon

Barbican

14

8

Old St

15

13

Shoreditch High St

Bethnal Green Rd

20

Bethnal Green

HOLBORN

Tottenham Court Rd

Oxford St

Chancery La

Holborn

Moorgate

SPITALFIELDS

16

Whitechapel

3

SOHO

Covent Garden

City Thameslink

St Paul's

Bank

Liverpool St

Aldgate

WHITECHAPEL

Commercial Rd

Temple

Blackfriars

Cannon St

Monument

Tower Hill

CITY

Tower Gateway DLR

Tower Hill

Tower of London

1

Cable St

The Highway

Shadwell DLR

Piccadilly Circus

Charing Cross

St James's Park

Westminster

SOUTH BANK

Waterloo

Southwark St

London Bridge

2

5

4

Wapping

WAPPING

Rotherhithe

4

Victoria St

WESTMINSTER

LAMBETH

Elephant & Castle

New Kent Rd

Jamaica Rd

Bermondsey

Southwark Park

Pimlico

Kennington

Walworth Rd

Old Kent Rd

South Bermondsey

5

Vauxhall

NINE ELMS

Oval

Kennington Park

Burgess Park

CAMBERWELL

Queens Rd (Peckham)

6

Wandsworth Rd

Clapham Rd

Brixton Rd

Stockwell

Stockwell Rd

Denmark Hill

Peckham Rd

Peckham Rye

Loughborough Junction

Denmark Hill

Ruskin Park

PECKHAM

Nunhead

7

Clapham North

CLAPHAM

Clapham Common

Brixton

East Dulwich

63

Greater London

◉ Don't Miss Sights
1 Tower of London...................................G4

◉ Sights
2 HMS Belfast...G4
3 Kensington Palace..............................B4
4 Tower Bridge.......................................G4
5 Tower Bridge Exhibition.....................G4

🛏 Sleeping
6 Base2stay...B5
7 Gore...C4
8 Hoxton Hotel......................................G2
9 New Linden Hotel...............................B3
10 Twenty Nevern Square.....................B5
11 Vancouver Studios...........................B3
12 Vicarage Hotel..................................B4

✖ Eating
13 Albion..G2
14 Princess of Shoreditch.....................G2

🍷 Drinking & Nightlife
15 Book Club..G2
16 Ten Bells..G3

✦ Entertainment
17 Almeida..F1
18 Roundhouse.......................................D1
19 Royal Albert Hall..............................C4

🛍 Shopping
20 Brick Lane Market.............................G3
21 Camden Market.................................D1
22 Columbia Road Flower Market.........G2
23 Portobello Road Market....................A3

and Wales, is a splendid example of neo-Byzantine architecture.

The views from the 83m-tall **bell tower** – thankfully, accessible by lift – are unsurprisingly impressive.

Houses of Parliament   Historic Building
(Map p74; www.parliament.uk; Parliament Sq, SW1; ⊖Westminster) FREE Officially called the **Palace of Westminster**, the oldest part is **Westminster Hall** (1097), which is one of only a few sections that survived a catastrophic fire in 1834. Its roof, added between 1394 and 1401, is the earliest known example of a medieval hammer-beam roof.

The palace's most famous feature is its clock tower, aka **Big Ben** (Map p74). Ben is actually the 13-ton bell, named after Benjamin Hall, who was commissioner of works when the tower was completed in 1858.

When parliament is in recess there are guided **75-minute tours** (📞0844 847 1672; www.ticketmaster.co.uk/housesofparliament; tours adult/child £15/6) of both chambers and other historic areas.

Tate Britain   Gallery
(Map p74; www.tate.org.uk; Millbank, SW1; ⏰10am-6pm daily, 6-10pm some Fri; ⊖Pimlico) FREE The more elderly and venerable of the two Tate siblings, this riverside edifice celebrates paintings from 1500 to the present, with works from Blake, Hogarth, Gainsborough, Barbara Hepworth, Whistler, Constable and Turner, whose light-infused visions dominate the **Clore Gallery**.

Churchill War Rooms   Museum
(Map p74; www.iwm.org.uk/visits/churchill-war-rooms; Clive Steps, King Charles St, SW1; adult/child £17/free; ⏰9.30am-6pm; ⊖Westminster) Winston Churchill coordinated the Allied resistance against Nazi Germany on a Bakelite telephone from this underground military HQ during WWII.

St James's & Mayfair

Buckingham Palace   Palace
(Map p74; 📞020-7766 7300; www.royalcollec tion.org.uk; Buckingham Palace Rd, SW1; adult/child £19/10.85; ⏰9.30am-7pm late Jul-Aug, to 6.30pm Sep; ⊖St James's Park, Victoria, Green Park) Built in 1703 for the Duke of Buckingham, Buckingham Palace replaced St James's Palace as the monarch's official London residence in 1837. To know if she's at home, check whether the yellow, red and blue standard is flying. The two-hour tour includes the **Throne Room**, with his-and-hers pink chairs initialled 'ER' and 'P'. Access is by timed tickets with admission every 15 minutes (audioguide included).

A Royal Day Out is a combined ticket including the State Rooms, Queen's

Gallery and Royal Mews (adult/child £31.95/18.20).

At 11.30am daily from May to July (on alternate days, weather permitting, for the rest of the year), the old guard (Foot Guards of the Household Regiment) comes off duty to be replaced by the new guard on the forecourt of Buckingham Palace.

St James's Park & Green Park   Park

With its manicured flowerbeds and ornamental lake, St James's Park is a wonderful place to stroll and take in the views of Westminster, Buckingham Palace and St James's Palace.

Tate-a-tate

To get between London's Tate galleries in style, the **Tate Boat** (Map p74; www.tate.org.uk/visit/tate-boat; adult/child £5/2.80; ⊙10am-6pm) will whisk you from one to the other, stopping en route at the London Eye (p67). Services run from 10.10am to 5.28pm daily at 40-minute intervals. A River Roamer hop-on hop-off ticket (purchased on board) costs £12, single tickets £5.

The City

For centuries, the City (note the capital C) *was* London. Its boundaries have changed little from the Roman walls built in this area two millennia ago, and today it's London's central business district (also known as the 'square mile').

Tower Bridge   Bridge

(Map p62; ⊖Tower Hill) London was still a thriving port in 1894 when Tower Bridge was built. A lift leads up from the northern tower to the overpriced **Tower Bridge Exhibition** (Map p62; www.towerbridge.org.uk; adult/child £8/3.40; ⊙10am-6pm Apr-Sep, 9.30am-5.30pm Oct-Mar; ⊖Tower Hill), where the story of its building is recounted within the upper walkway.

Dr Johnson's House   Museum

(Map p74; www.drjohnsonshouse.org; 17 Gough Sq, EC4; adult/child £4.50/1.50, audioguide £2; ⊙11am-5.30pm Mon-Sat May-Sep, to 5pm Mon-Sat Oct-Apr; ⊕; ⊖Chancery Lane) The Georgian house where Samuel Johnson and his assistants compiled the first English dictionary (between 1748 and 1759) is full of prints and portraits of friends and intimates, including the good doctor's Jamaican servant to whom he bequeathed this grand residence.

Buckingham Palace
DAVID WALL PHOTO/GETTY IMAGES ©

MAREMAGNUM/GETTY IMAGES ©

Don't Miss
St Paul's Cathedral

Dominating the City with one of the world's largest church domes (around 65,000 tonnes worth), St Paul's Cathedral was designed by Christopher Wren after the Great Fire and built between 1675 and 1710.

Inside, some 30m above the main paved area, is the first of three domes (actually a dome inside a cone inside a dome) supported by eight huge columns. The walkway around its base, 257 steps up a staircase on the western side of the southern transept, is called the **Whispering Gallery**, because if you talk close to the wall, your words will carry to the opposite side 32m away. A further 119 steps brings you to the **Stone Gallery**, 152 iron steps above which is the **Golden Gallery** at the very top, rewarded with unforgettable views of London.

Free guided tours leave the tour desk four times daily at 10.45am, 11.15am, 1.30pm and 2pm (90 minutes). Evensong takes place at 5pm (3.15pm on Sunday).

NEED TO KNOW

Map p74; www.stpauls.co.uk; St Paul's Churchyard, EC4; adult/child £15/6; ⏰8.30am-4.30pm Mon-Sat, last entry 4pm; ⊖St Paul's

Monument   Tower

(Map p74; www.themonument.info; Fish Street Hill, EC3; adult/child £3/1; ⏰9.30am-5.30pm; ⊖Monument) Designed by Wren to commemorate the Great Fire, the towering Monument is 60.6m high, the exact distance from its base to the bakery on Pudding Lane where the blaze began. Corkscrew your way up the 311 tight spiral steps (claustrophobes beware) for some of London's best wraparound views and twist down again to collect a certificate commemorating your climb.

Clerkenwell & Holborn

In these now fashionable streets it's hard to find an echo of the notorious 'rookeries' of the 19th century, where families lived in probably the worst conditions in the city's long history, as documented so vividly in the novels of Charles Dickens.

Charles Dickens Museum   Museum
(Map p74; www.dickensmuseum.com; 48 Doughty St, WC1; adult/child £6/3; ◷10am-5pm Mon-Sat, 11am-5pm Sun; ◉Russell Sq) Dickens' sole surviving London residence is where his work really flourished – *The Pickwick Papers*, *Nicholas Nickleby* and *Oliver Twist* were all written here.

Sir John Soane's Museum   Museum
(Map p74; www.soane.org; 13 Lincoln's Inn Fields, WC2; ◷10am-5pm Tue-Sat, 6-9pm 1st Tue of month; ◉Holborn) FREE This little museum is one of the most atmospheric and fascinating sights in London. The building is housed in the beautiful home of architect Sir John Soane (1753–1837), and it's full of his fascinating possessions and personal effects.

South Bank

Londoners once crossed the river to the area controlled by the licentious Bishops of Southwark for all manner of bawdy frolicking frowned upon in the City. It's a much more seemly area now, but the frisson of theatre and entertainment remains.

Tate Modern   Museum
(Map p74; www.tate.org.uk; Queen's Walk, SE1; ◷10am-6pm Sun-Thu, to 10pm Fri & Sat; ◉Southwark) FREE One of London's most popular attractions, this outstanding modern and contemporary art gallery is housed in the creatively revamped **Bankside Power Station** south of the Millennium Bridge. A spellbinding synthesis of funky modern art and capacious industrial brick design, the eye-catching result is one of London's must-see sights.

The multimedia guides (£3.50) are worthwhile and there are free 45-minute

guided tours of the collection's highlights (Level 3 at 11am and noon; Level 5 at 2pm and 3pm). Note the late-night opening hours on Friday and Saturday.

Shakespeare's Globe   Historic Building
(Map p74; www.shakespearesglobe.com; 21 New Globe Walk, SE1; adult/child £13.50/8; ◷9am-5.30pm; ◉London Bridge) The original Globe – known as the 'Wooden O' after its circular shape and roofless centre – was erected in 1599, but burned down within two hours during a performance in 1613 (a stage cannon ignited the thatched roof). Its present-day incarnation is the vision of American actor and director Sam Wanamaker, who sadly died before the opening night in 1997. Admission includes the **exhibition hall** and **guided tour** of the theatre (departing every 15 to 30 minutes), faithfully reconstructed from oak beams, handmade bricks, lime plaster and thatch.

From April to October plays are performed, and while Shakespeare and his contemporaries dominate, modern plays are also staged (see the website for upcoming performances). As in Elizabethan times, seatless 'groundlings' can watch in all-weather conditions (£5; seats are £15 to £39) for the best views.

London Eye   Viewpoint
(Map p74; ☎0871 7813000; www.londoneye. com; adult/child £19.20/12.30; ◷10am-8pm; ◉Waterloo) This 135m-tall, slow-moving Ferris-wheel-like attraction is the tallest in the western hemisphere. Passengers ride in enclosed egg-shaped pods; the wheel takes 30 minutes to rotate completely, offering 25-mile views on clear days. Save money and shorten queues by buying tickets online, or cough up an extra £10 to show off your fast-track swagger.

Imperial War Museum   Museum
(Map p74; www.iwm.org.uk; Lambeth Rd, SE1; ◷10am-6pm; ◉Lambeth North) FREE Fronted by a pair of intimidating 15in naval guns that could lob a 1938lb shell over 16 miles, this riveting museum is housed in what was once Bethlehem Royal Hospital, known as Bedlam. There's not just

⭐

Don't Miss
Tower of London

The Tower of London is one of London's great historic landmarks, and one of the city's four World Heritage sites (joining Westminster Abbey, Kew Gardens and Maritime Greenwich). It was founded in the 1070s by William the Conqueror, and has since served as a royal residence, treasury, mint, arsenal, prison and execution venue.

Map p62

☎ 0844 4827777

www.hrp.org.uk/toweroflondon

Tower Hill, EC3

adult/child £21.45/10.75, audioguide £4/3

🕘 9am-5.30pm Tue-Sat, from 10am Sun & Mon, to 4.30pm Nov-Feb

🚇 Tower Hill

The White Tower & Bloody Tower

The most striking building is the central White Tower, with its Romanesque architecture and four turrets. Today it houses a collection from the Royal Armouries, including Henry VIII's commodious suit of armour. On the 2nd floor is St John's Chapel, dating from 1080 and therefore the oldest church in London.

On the far side of the White Tower rises the Bloody Tower, where the 12-year-old Edward V and his little brother were held 'for their own safety' and later murdered, probably by their uncle, the future Richard III. Sir Walter Raleigh wrote his *History of the World* while doing a 13-year stretch here.

The Waterloo Barracks

The Waterloo Barracks contains the famous Crown Jewels, including the platinum crown of the late Queen Mother, set with the 105-carat Koh-i-Noor (Mountain of Light) diamond and the Imperial State Crown.

On the green in front of the Chapel Royal of St Peter ad Vincula stood Henry VIII's scaffold, where seven people, including Anne Boleyn and her cousin Catherine Howard (Henry's second and fifth wives) were beheaded.

Tower Tours

To get your bearings, take the hugely entertaining free guided tour with any of the Beefeaters (Yeoman Warders). Hour-long tours leave every 30 minutes from the bridge near the main entrance; the last tour is an hour before closing. Book online for cheaper rates for the Tower.

Local Knowledge

Tower of London

RECOMMENDATIONS FROM ALAN KINGSHOTT, CHIEF YEOMAN WARDER AT THE TOWER OF LONDON

1 A BEEFEATER TOUR
To understand the Tower and its history, a guided tour with one of the Yeoman Warders is essential. Very few people realise that the Tower is actually our home as well; all the Warders live inside the outer walls. The Tower is rather like a miniature village – visitors are often surprised to see our washing hanging out beside the castle walls!

2 THE CROWN JEWELS
Visitors often think the Crown Jewels are the Queen's personal jewellery collection. They're not, of course; the Crown Jewels are actually the ceremonial regalia used during the Coronation. The highlights are the Sceptre and the Imperial State Crown, which contains the celebrated diamond known as the Star of Africa. People are often surprised to hear that the Crown Jewels aren't insured (as they could never be replaced).

3 THE WHITE TOWER
The White Tower is the original royal palace of the Tower of London, but it hasn't been used as a royal residence since 1603. It's the most iconic building here. Inside you can see exhibits from the Royal Armouries, including a suit of armour belonging to Henry VIII.

4 THE RAVENS
A Tower legend states that if its resident ravens ever left, the monarchy would topple – a royal decree states that we must keep a minimum of six ravens at any time. We currently have nine ravens, looked after by the Ravenmaster and his two assistants.

5 CEREMONY OF THE KEYS
We hold three daily ceremonies: the 9am Official Opening, the Ceremony of the Word (when the day's password is issued) and the 10pm Ceremony of the Keys, when the gates are locked after the castle has closed. Visitors are welcome to attend the last, but must apply directly to the Tower in writing.

Tower of London

Tackling the Tower

Although it's usually less busy in the late afternoon, don't leave your assault on the Tower until too late in the day. You could easily spend hours here and not see it all. Start by getting your bearings with the hour-long Yeoman Warder (Beefeater) tours; they are included in the cost of admission, entertaining and the only way to access the **Chapel Royal of St Peter ad Vincula** ❶, which is where they finish up.

When you leave the chapel, the **Tower Green Scaffold Site** ❷ is directly in front. The building immediately to your left is Waterloo Barracks, where the **Crown Jewels** ❸ are housed. These are the absolute highlight of a Tower visit, so keep an eye on the entrance and pick a time to visit when it looks relatively quiet. Once inside, take things at your own pace. Slow-moving travelators shunt you past the dozen or so crowns that are the treasury's centrepiece, but feel free to double-back for a second or even third pass – particularly if you ended up on the rear travelator the first time around. Allow plenty of time for the **White Tower** ❹, the core of the whole complex, starting with the exhibition of royal armour. As you continue onto the 2nd floor, keep an eye out for **St John's Chapel** ❺. The famous **ravens** ❻ can be seen in the courtyard around the White Tower. Head next through the towers that formed the **Medieval Palace** ❼, then take the **East Wall Walk** ❽ to get a feel for the castle's mighty battlements. Spend the rest of your time poking around the many, many other fascinating nooks and crannies of the Tower complex.

BEAT THE QUEUES

Buy your fast-track ticket in advance online or at the City of London Information Centre in St Paul's Churchyard.

Palacepalooza An annual Historic Royal Palaces membership allows you to jump the queues and visit the Tower (and four other London palaces) as often as you like.

MIKE BOOTH/ALAMY ©

Chapel Royal of St Peter ad Vincula

This chapel serves as the resting place for the royals and other members of the aristocracy who were executed on the small green out front. Several other historical figures are buried here too, including Thomas More.

Dry Moat

Tower Green Scaffold Site

Seven people, including three queens (Anne Boleyn, Catherine Howard and Jane Grey), lost their heads here during Tudor times, saving the monarch the embarrassment of public executions on Tower Hill. The site now features a sculpture by Brian Catling.

Beauchamp Tower

Main Entrance

Middle Tower

Byward Tower

Bell Tower

White Tower

Much of the White Tower is taken up with an exhibition on 500 years of royal armour. Look for the virtually cuboid suit made to match Henry VIII's bloated body, complete with an oversized armoured pouch to protect, ahem, the crown jewels.

PAWEL LIBERA IMAGES/ALAMY ©

St John's Chapel

Kept as plain and unadorned as it would have been in Norman times, the White Tower's 1st-floor chapel is the oldest surviving church in London, dating from 1080.

Crown Jewels

When they're not being worn for ceremonies of state, Her Majesty's bling is kept here. Among the 23,578 gems, look out for the 530-carat Cullinan I diamond at the top of the Sovereign's Sceptre with cross, the largest part of what was then the largest diamond ever found.

TOM HANLEY/ALAMY ©

Bowyer Tower

Martin Tower

① ② ③ ④ ⑤ ⑥ ⑦ ⑧

Queen's House

Bloody Tower

Constable Tower

Broad Arrow Tower

Traitors' Gate & St Thomas's Tower

Wakefield & St Thomas's Towers

Salt Tower

New Armouries

River Thames

Medieval Palace

This part of the Tower complex was begun around 1220 and was home to England's medieval monarchs. Look for the recreations of the bedchamber of Edward I (1272–1307) in St Thomas's Tower and the throne room of his father, Henry III (1216–72) in the Wakefield Tower.

ENIGMA/ALAMY ©

Ravens

This stretch of green is where the Tower's half-dozen ravens are kept, fed on raw meat and blood-soaked bird biscuits. According to legend, if the birds were to leave the Tower, the kingdom would fall.

East Wall Walk

Follow the inner ramparts, starting from the 13th-century Salt Tower, passing through the Broad Arrow and Constable Towers, and ending at the Martin Tower, where the Crown Jewels were stored till the mid-19th century.

Lawrence of Arabia's 1000cc motorbike here, but a German V-2 rocket, a Sherman tank, a lifelike replica of Little Boy (the atom bomb dropped on Hiroshima), a P-51 Mustang, a Focke-Wulf Fw 190 and other classic fighter planes dangling from the ceiling, plus a recreated WWI trench, WWII bomb shelter, and a Holocaust exhibition.

Shard   Notable Building
(Map p74; www.the-shard.com; 32 London Bridge St, SE1; adult/child £29.95/23.95; ⊙9am-10pm; ⊖London Bridge) Puncturing the skies above London, the dramatic splinterlike form of The Shard – the tallest building in Western Europe – has rapidly become an icon. Approaching completion at the time of writing, the tower will boast the rooms-with-a-view, five-star Shangri-La Hotel, restaurants and a 360-degree viewing gallery in the clouds, accessible via high-speed lifts.

HMS Belfast   Ship
(Map p62; hmsbelfast.iwm.org.uk; Queen's Walk, SE1; adult/child £14.50/free; ⊙10am-5pm; 👪;

⊖London Bridge) This large, light cruiser served in WWII, helping sink the German battleship *Scharnhorst* and shelling the Normandy coast on D-Day. Explore the nine decks and see the engine room, gun decks, galley, chapel, punishment cells, canteen and dental surgery. An audio-guide is available.

London Dungeon   Historic Building
(Map p74; www.thedungeons.com/london; County Hall, Westminster Bridge Rd, SE1; adult/child £24.60/19.20; ⊙10am-5pm, extended hrs holidays; ⊖Westminster or Waterloo) Older kids tend to love the London Dungeon, as the terrifying queues during school holidays and weekends testify. It's all spooky music, ghostly boat rides, macabre hangman's drop-rides, fake blood and actors dressed up as torturers and gory criminals (including Jack the Ripper and Sweeney Todd).

Sea Life   Aquarium
(Map p74; ☎0871 663 1678; www.sealife.co.uk/london; County Hall, SE1; adult/child £18/13;

Left: Tower Bridge (p65) and *Timepiece* by Wendy Taylor; **Below:** London Eye

🕐10am-6pm; 🚇Waterloo)
One of the largest aquariums in Europe, Sea Life has all sorts of aquatic creatures organised into different zones (coral cave, rainforest, River Thames), culminating with the shark walkway.

Chelsea, Kensington & Knightsbridge

It's called the Royal Borough of Kensington and Chelsea, and residents are certainly paid royally, earning the highest incomes in the UK (shops and restaurants will presume you do too).

Natural History Museum   Museum
(Map p74; www.nhm.ac.uk; Cromwell Rd, SW7; 🕐10am-5.50pm; 🚇South Kensington) FREE
This ornate building itself is one of London's finest and a work of art. A sure-fire hit with kids of all ages, this splendid museum is crammed with fascinating discoveries, starting with the giant **Diplodocus** skeleton that greets you in the main hall. In the **dinosaur gallery**, the fleshless fossils are brought to robotic life with the roaring 4m-high animatronic **Tyrannosaurus Rex**. The **Darwin Centre** houses a team of biologists and a staggering 20-million-plus species of animal and plant specimens.

Victoria & Albert Museum   Museum
(V&A; Map p74; www.vam.ac.uk; Cromwell Rd, SW7; 🕐10am-5.45pm Sat-Thu, to 10pm Fri; 🚇South Kensington) FREE Part of Albert's legacy to Londoners in the wake of the Great Exhibition of 1851, the museum is a bit like the nation's attic, spread generously through nearly 150 galleries. Highlights of the world's greatest collection of decorative arts include the **Ardabil Carpet** (Room 42, Level 1), the sumptuous **China Collection** and **Japan Gallery** (Rooms 44 and 47e, Level 1), **Tipu's Tiger** (Room 41, Level 1), the astonishing **Cast Courts** (Room 46a, Level 1), the **Raphael**

73

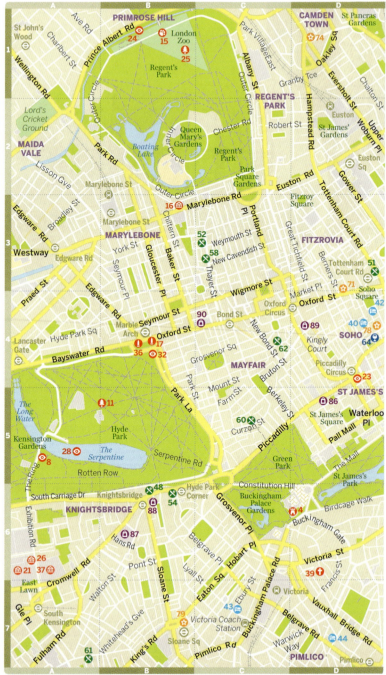

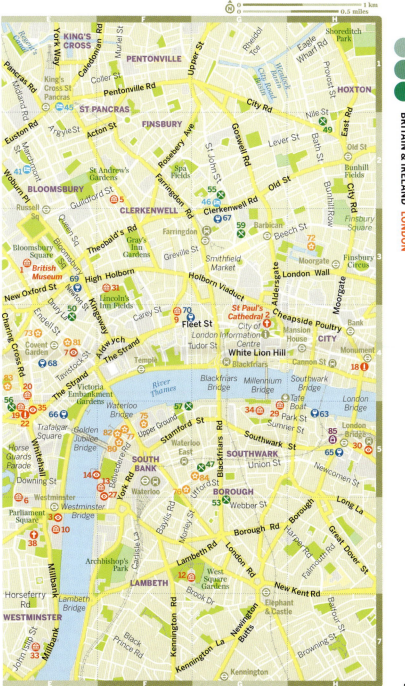

York Way

Regent's Canal

Pancras Rd

Midland Rd

Pancras Rd

Euston Rd

Marchmont St

Woburn Pl

BLOOMSBURY

41

Russell Sq

Bloomsbury Square

Bloomsbury Sq

1

British Museum

New Oxford St

Charing Cross Rd

Drury La

50

73

Covent Garden

7

68

81

83

20

56

19

35

66

22

Whitehall

Trafalgar Square

Golden Jubilee Bridge

82

77

89

Horse Guards Parade

Downing St

6

Westminster

3

Parliament Square

10

38

Millbank

Horseferry Rd

Lambeth Bridge

WESTMINSTER

John Islip St

33

Millbank

KING'S CROSS

Caledonian Rd

Muriel St

Coller St

King's Cross St Pancras

45

ST PANCRAS

Argyle St

Acton St

St Andrew's Gardens

Guildford St

Queen Sq

Bloomsbury Sq

Theobald's Rd

Gray's Inn Gardens

Greville St

5

CLERKENWELL

Farringdon

Newton St

Kingsway

High Holborn

31

Lincoln's Inn Fields

Carey St

70

9

Fleet St

Tudor St

Temple

The Strand

Aldwych

Tavistock St

The Strand

Victoria Embankment Gardens

Waterloo Bridge

Upper Ground

Stamford St

57

75

Belvedere Rd

York Rd

SOUTH BANK

Waterloo East

Waterloo

14

13

27

76

Baylis Rd

Morley St

Carlisle La

LAMBETH

Brook Dr

Archbishop's Park

Black Prince Rd

Kennington Rd

Lambeth Rd

12

West Square Gardens

PENTONVILLE

Upper St

Pentonville Rd

City Rd

FINSBURY

Rosebery Ave

Spa Fields

St John St

Goswell Rd

Farringdon Rd

55

46

67

Clerkenwell Rd

Holborn Viaduct

Smithfield Market

Lever St

Old St

Bath St

59

Beech St

Barbican

London Wall

Aldersgate

72

Moorgate

Moorgate

London Wall

Finsbury Circus

St Paul's Cathedral 2

City of London Information Centre

White Lion Hill

Blackfriars

Blackfriars Bridge

River Thames

Millennium Bridge

Southwark Bridge

Cheapside Poultry

Bank

Mansion House

CITY

Monument

18

Cannon St

34

29

Park St

Sumner St

Tate Boat

Southwark St

47

84

Ufford St

BOROUGH

53

Webber St

Union St

63

65

85

30

London Bridge

Newcomen St

Long La

Borough

Borough Rd

Harper Rd

Great Dover St

Falmouth Rd

London Rd

New Kent Rd

Elephant & Castle

Kennington La

Newington Butts

Browning St

Balfour St

Kennington

Rheidol Tce

Eagle Wharf Rd

Shoreditch Park

Provost St

City Road Basin

Wenlock Basin

HOXTON

Nile St

49

Old St

Bunhill Fields

Bunhill Row

City Rd

East Rd

Finsbury Square

Westminster Bridge

Southwark

Central London

⊙ Don't Miss Sights
1	British Museum	E3
2	St Paul's Cathedral	G4

⊙ Sights
3	Big Ben	E6
4	Buckingham Palace	D6
5	Charles Dickens Museum	F2
6	Churchill War Rooms	E6
7	Covent Garden Piazza	E4
8	Diana, Princess of Wales Memorial Fountain	A5
9	Dr Johnson's House	F4
10	Houses of Parliament	E6
11	Hyde Park	B5
12	Imperial War Museum	F6
13	London Dungeon	F5
14	London Eye	E5
15	London Zoo	B1
16	Madame Tussauds	B3
17	Marble Arch	B4
18	Monument	H4
19	National Gallery	E5
20	National Portrait Gallery	E4
21	Natural History Museum	A6
22	Nelson's Column	E5
23	Piccadilly Circus	D4
24	Regent's Canal	B1
25	Regent's Park	B1
26	Science Museum	A6
27	Sea Life	F5
28	Serpentine Lake	A5
29	Shakespeare's Globe	G5
30	Shard	H5
31	Sir John Soane's Museum	F3
32	Speakers' Corner	B4
33	Tate Britain	E7
34	Tate Modern	G5
35	Trafalgar Square	E5
36	Tyburn Tree	B4
37	Victoria & Albert Museum	A6
38	Westminster Abbey	E6
39	Westminster Cathedral	D6

⊜ Sleeping
40	Dean Street Townhouse	D4
41	Harlingford Hotel	E2
42	Hazlitt's	D4
43	Lime Tree Hotel	C7
44	Luna Simone Hotel	D7
45	Rough Luxe	E1
46	Zetter Hotel & Townhouse	G2

⊗ Eating
47	Anchor & Hope	G5
	Arbutus	(see 42)
48	Dinner by Heston Blumenthal	B6
49	Fifteen	H2
50	Great Queen Street	E4
51	Hakkasan	D3
52	La Fromagerie	C3
53	Laughing Gravy	G6
54	Marcus Wareing at the Berkeley	B6
55	Modern Pantry	G2
56	National Dining Rooms	E5
57	Oxo Tower Restaurant & Brasserie	F5
58	Providores & Tapa Room	C3
59	St John	G3
60	Tamarind	C5
61	Tom's Kitchen	A7
62	Wild Honey	C4

⊙ Drinking & Nightlife
63	Anchor	H5
64	French House	D4
65	George Inn	H5
66	Gordon's Wine Bar	E5
67	Jerusalem Tavern	G3
68	Lamb & Flag	E4
69	Princess Louise	E3
70	Ye Olde Cheshire Cheese	F4

✪ Entertainment
71	100 Club	D3
72	Barbican	H3
73	Donmar Warehouse	E4
74	KOKO	D1
75	National Theatre	F5
76	Old Vic	F5
	Purcell Room	(see 77)
77	Queen Elizabeth Hall	F5
78	Ronnie Scott's	D4
79	Royal Court Theatre	B7
80	Royal Festival Hall	F5
81	Royal Opera House	E4
82	Southbank Centre	F5
83	Tkts	E4
84	Young Vic	G5

⊙ Shopping
85	Borough Market	H5
86	Fortnum & Mason	D5
87	Harrods	B6
88	Harvey Nichols	B6
89	Liberty	D4
90	Selfridges	C4

Cartoons (Rooms 48a, Level 1), the hefty **Great Bed of Ware** (Room 57, Level 2) and the stunning **Jewellery Gallery** (Rooms 91–93, Level 3).

Science Museum Museum

(Map p74; www.sciencemuseum.org.uk; Exhibition Rd, SW7; ⏱10am-6pm; 🚇South Kensington) **FREE** With seven floors of interactive and educational exhibits, this scientifically spellbinding museum will mesmerise even the most precocious of young Einsteins. Highlights include the Energy Hall on the ground floor, the riveting Flight Gallery on the 3rd floor and the flight simulator. There's also a 450-seat Imax cinema.

Hyde Park Park

(Map p74; ⏱5.30am-midnight; 🚇Marble Arch, Hyde Park Corner or Queensway) At 145 hectares, Hyde Park is central London's largest open space.

There's boating on the **Serpentine** (Map p74; Kensington Gardens, W8; 🚇Knightsbridge or South Kensington) for the energetic, while **Speakers' Corner** (Map p74; Park Lane; 🚇Marble Arch) is for oratorical acrobats. Nearby **Marble Arch** (Map p74; 🚇Marble Arch) was designed by John Nash in 1828 as the entrance to Buckingham Palace. It was moved here in 1851. The infamous **Tyburn Tree** (Map p74; W1; 🚇Marble Arch), a three-legged gallows, once stood nearby. It is estimated that up to 50,000 people were executed here between 1196 and 1783.

A soothing structure, the **Diana, Princess of Wales, Memorial Fountain** (Map p74; Kensington Gardens, W2; 🚇Knightsbridge) was unveiled in mid-2004, instigating an inevitable debate over matters of taste and gravitas.

Diana, Princess of Wales, Memorial Fountain, Hyde Park
PHILIP GAME/GETTY IMAGES ©

Kensington Palace Palace

(Map p62; www.hrp.org.uk/kensingtonpalace; Kensington Gardens, W8; adult/child £14.50/free; ⏱10am-6pm; 🚇High St Kensington) Kensington Palace (1605) became the favourite royal residence under the joint reign of William and Mary and remained so until George III became king and moved across the park to Buckingham Palace. It still has private apartments where various members of the royal extended family live. The building underwent magnificent restoration work totalling £12 million and was reopened in early 2012.

Marylebone

Regent's Park Park

(Map p74; www.royalparks.org.uk; ⏱5am-dusk; 🚇Regent's Park, Baker St) A former royal hunting ground, Regent's Park was designed by John Nash early in the 19th century, although what was actually laid out is only a fraction of the celebrated architect's grand plan. Nevertheless, it's one of London's most lovely open spaces – at

FEARGUS COONEY/GETTY IMAGES ©

⭐ Don't Miss
British Museum

The country's largest museum and one of the oldest and finest in the world, this famous museum boasts vast Egyptian, Etruscan, Greek, Roman, European and Middle Eastern galleries, among many others.

Among the must-sees are the **Rosetta Stone**, the key to deciphering Egyptian hieroglyphics, discovered in 1799; the controversial **Parthenon Sculptures**, stripped from the walls of the Parthenon in Athens by Lord Elgin (the British ambassador to the Ottoman Empire), and which Greece wants returned; the stunning **Oxus Treasure** of 7th- to 4th-century BC Persian gold; and the Anglo-Saxon **Sutton Hoo** burial relics.

You'll need multiple visits to savour even the highlights here; happily there are 15 half-hour free 'Eye Opener' tours between 11am and 3.45pm daily, focusing on different parts of the collection. Other tours include the 90-minute highlights tour at 10.30am, 1pm and 3pm daily (adult/child £8/5), and audioguides are available (£4.50).

NEED TO KNOW

Map p74; ☎020-7323 8000; www.britishmuseum.org; Great Russell St, WC1; ◷10am-5.30pm Sat-Thu, to 8.30pm Fri; ⊖Russell Sq, Tottenham Court Rd

once serene and lively, cosmopolitan and local – with football pitches, tennis courts, a boating lake, London Zoo, and **Regent's Canal** (Map p74) along its northern side.

London Zoo   Zoo

(Map p74; www.londonzoo.co.uk; Outer Circle, Regent's Park, NW1; adult/child £25/19; ◷10am-5.30pm Mar-Oct, to 4pm Nov-Feb; ⊖Camden Town) These famous zoological gardens have come a long way since being established in 1828, with massive investment making conservation, education and breeding the name of the game. Highlights include **Penguin Beach**, **Gorilla Kingdom**, **Animal Adventure** (the new children's zoo) and **Butterfly Paradise**.

Madame Tussauds   Museum

(Map p74; ☎ 0870 400 3000; www.madame tussauds.co.uk; Marylebone Rd, NW1; adult/child £30/26; ⊙ 9-10am until 5-7pm (seasonal); ⊖ Baker St) With so much fabulous free stuff to do in London, it's a wonder that people still join lengthy queues to visit pricey Madame Tussauds waxworks, but in a celebrity-obsessed, camera-happy world, the opportunity to pose beside Posh and Becks is not short on appeal.

Tickets are cheaper when ordered online; combined tickets with London Eye and London Dungeon are also available (adult/child £65/48).

Greenwich

An extraordinary cluster of buildings have earned 'Maritime Greenwich' its place on Unesco's World Heritage list. It's also famous for straddling the hemispheres; this is degree zero, the home of Greenwich Mean Time.

Greenwich is easily reached on the DLR train. Or go by boat: **Thames River Services** (www.thamesriverservices.co.uk; adult/child single £12/6, return £15.50/7.75) depart half-hourly from Westminster Pier (one hour, every 40 minutes). **Thames Clippers** (www.thamesclippers.com; adult/child £6.50/3.25) are cheaper.

Old Royal Naval College   Historic Building

(www.oldroyalnavalcollege.org; 2 Cutty Sark Gardens, SE10; ⊙ 10am-5pm; ⓇDLR Cutty Sark) FREE Designed by Wren, the Old Royal Naval College is a magnificent example of classical architecture. Parts are now used by the University of Greenwich and Trinity College of Music, but you can visit the **chapel** and the extraordinary **Painted Hall**, which took artist Sir James Thornhill 19 years to complete. Yeomen-led tours

of the complex leave at 2pm daily, taking in areas not otherwise open to the public (£6, 90 minutes).

National Maritime Museum   Museum

(www.rmg.co.uk/national-maritime-museum; Romney Rd, SE10; ⊙ 10am-5pm; Ⓡ DLR Cutty Sark) FREE With its newly opened Sammy Ofer Wing, the National Maritime Museum houses a splendid collection of nautical paraphernalia recounting Britain's brine-soaked seafaring history.

Emirates Air Line   Cable Car

(www.emiratesairline.co.uk; adult/child single £4.30/2.20, return £8.60/4.40, with Oyster or Travelcard single £3.20/1.60, return £6.40/3.20; ⊙ 7am-9pm Mon-Fri, from 8am Sat, from 9am Sun Apr-Sep, closes 1hr earlier Oct-Mar; Ⓡ DLR Royal Victoria, ⊖ North Greenwich) Destined to become a sight in its own right and capable of ferrying 2400 people per hour across the Thames in either direction, the new Emirates Air Line Cable Car links together the Greenwich Peninsula and the Royal Docks in a five- to 10-minute journey.

O2   Notable Building

(www.theo2.co.uk; Peninsula Sq, SE10; ⊖ North Greenwich) The world's largest dome (365m in diameter) opened on 1 January 2000, at a cost of £789 million, as the Millennium Dome. Renamed the O2, it's now a 20,000-seat sports and entertainment arena. O2 conducts regular guided climbs of the dome's exterior (£22 to £28).

West London

Kew Gardens   Gardens

(www.kew.org.uk; Kew Rd; adult/child £16/free; ⊙ 9.30am-6.30pm Apr-Aug, earlier closing other months; 🛳 Kew Pier, Ⓡ Kew Bridge, ⊖ Kew Gardens) In 1759 botanists began rummaging around the world for specimens they could plant in the 3-hectare plot known as the Royal Botanic Gardens. They never stopped collecting, and the gardens, which have bloomed to 120 hectares, provide the most comprehensive botanical collection on earth (including the world's largest collection of orchids).

The River Thames

A Floating Tour

London's history has always been determined by the Thames. The city was founded as a Roman port nearly 2000 years ago and over the centuries since then many of the capital's landmarks have lined the river's banks. A boat trip is a great way to experience the attractions.

There are piers dotted along both banks at regular intervals where you can hop on and hop off the regular services to visit places of interest.

The best place to board is Westminster Pier, from where boats head downstream, taking you from the City of Westminster, the seat of government, to the original City of London, now the financial district and dominated by a growing band of skyscrapers. Across the river, the once shabby and neglected South Bank now bristles with as many top attractions as its northern counterpart, including the slender Shard.

In our illustration we've concentrated on the top highlights you'll enjoy from a waterborne

MARK DAFFEY / GETTY IMAGES ©

St Paul's Cathedral

Though there's been a church here since AD 604, the current building rose from the ashes of the 1666 Great Fire and is architect Christopher Wren's masterpiece. Famous for surviving the Blitz intact and for the wedding of Charles and Diana, it's looking as good as new after a major clean-up for its 300th anniversary.

Blackfriars

Somerset House

This grand neoclassical palace was once one of many aristocratic houses lining the Thames. The huge arches at river level gave direct access to the Thames until the Embankment was built in the 1860s.

Temple

Blackfriars Pier

Charing Cross

Savoy Pier

Waterloo Bridge

Victoria Embankment Gardens

National Theatre

Blackfriars Bridge

Embankment

Queen Elizabeth Hall

Southbank Centre

OXO Tower

London Eye

Built in 2000 and originally temporary, the Eye instantly became a much-loved landmark. The 30-minute spin takes you 135m above the city from where the views are unsurprisingly amazing.

Waterloo Millennium Pier

Westminster Pier

Houses of Parliament

Rebuilt in neo-Gothic style after the old palace burned down in 1834, the most famous part of the British parliament is the clocktower. Generally known as Big Ben, it's named after Benjamin Hall who oversaw its construction.

Westminster

Westminster Bridge

RICHARD I'ANSON / GETTY IMAGES ©

vessel. These are, from west to east, the **Houses of Parliament** ①, the **London Eye** ②, **Somerset House** ③, **St Paul's Cathedral** ④, **Tate Modern** ⑤, **Shakespeare's Globe** ⑥, the **Tower of London** ⑦ and **Tower Bridge** ⑧.

Apart from covering this central section of the river, boats can also be taken upstream as far as Kew Gardens and Hampton Court Palace, and downstream to Greenwich and the Thames Barrier.

BOAT HOPPING

Thames Clippers hop-on/hop-off services are aimed at commuters but are equally useful for visitors, operating every 15 minutes on a loop from piers at Embankment, Waterloo, Blackfriars, Bankside, London Bridge and the Tower. Other services also go from Westminster. Oyster cardholders get a discount off the boat ticket price.

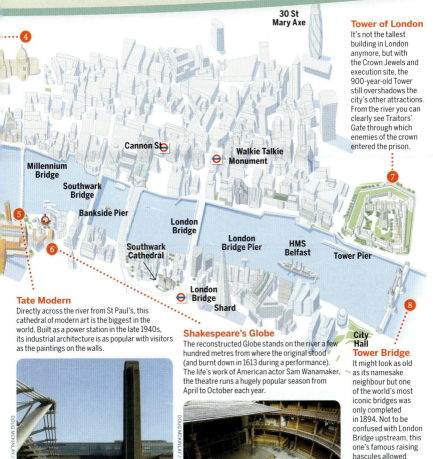

30 St Mary Axe

Cannon St

Walkie Talkie Monument

Millennium Bridge

Southwark Bridge

Bankside Pier

London Bridge

Southwark Cathedral

London Bridge Pier

HMS Belfast

Tower Pier

London Bridge

Shard

Tower of London
It's not the tallest building in London anymore, but with the Crown Jewels and execution site, the 900-year-old Tower still overshadows the city's other attractions. From the river you can clearly see Traitors' Gate through which enemies of the crown entered the prison.

Tate Modern
Directly across the river from St Paul's, this cathedral of modern art is the biggest in the world. Built as a power station in the late 1940s, its industrial architecture is as popular with visitors as the paintings on the walls.

Shakespeare's Globe
The reconstructed Globe stands on the river a few hundred metres from where the original stood (and burnt down in 1613 during a performance). The life's work of American actor Sam Wanamaker, the theatre runs a hugely popular season from April to October each year.

City Hall

Tower Bridge
It might look as old as its namesake neighbour but one of the world's most iconic bridges was only completed in 1894. Not to be confused with London Bridge upstream, this one's famous raising bascules allowed tall ships to dock at the old wharves to the west and are still lifted up to 1000 times a year.

DOUG MCKINLAY / GETTY IMAGES ©

DOUG MCKINLAY / GETTY IMAGES ©

The gardens are easily reached by tube, but you might prefer to take a cruise on a riverboat from the **Westminster Passenger Services Association** (☎020-7930 2062; www.wpsa.co.uk; adult/child return to Kew Gardens £18/9), which runs several daily boats from April to October, departing from Westminster Pier (return adult/child £18/9, 90 minutes).

Hampton Court Palace   Palace
(www.hrp.org.uk/HamptonCourtPalace; adult/child £17.60/8.80; ⏰10am-6pm Apr-Oct, to 4.30pm Nov-Mar; 🚢Hampton Court Palace, 🚉Hampton Court) Built by Cardinal Thomas Wolsey in 1514 but coaxed from him by Henry VIII just before Wolsey (as chancellor) fell from favour, Hampton Court Palace is England's largest and grandest Tudor structure.

Take a themed tour led by costumed historians or, if you're in a rush, visit the highlights: **Henry VIII's State Apartments**, including the Great Hall with its spectacular hammer-beamed roof; the **Tudor Kitchens**, staffed by 'servants'; and the **Wolsey Rooms**. You could easily spend a day exploring the palace and its 24 hectares of riverside gardens, especially if you get lost in the 300-year-old **maze**.

Hampton Court is 13 miles southwest of central London and is easily reached by train from Waterloo. Alternatively, the riverboats that head from Westminster to Kew continue here (return adult/child £22.50/11.25, three hours).

👉 Tours

Big Bus Tours   Bus Tours
(www.bigbustours.com; adult/child/family £29/12/70; ⏰every 20min 8.30am-6pm Apr-Sep, to 5pm Oct & Mar, to 4.30pm Nov-Feb) Informative commentaries in eight languages. The ticket includes a free river cruise with City Cruise and four thematic walking tours (Royal London, Harry Potter film locations, the Beatles, and the Ghosts by Gaslight).

London Walks   Walking Tours
(☎020-7624 3978; www.walks.com; adult £9) Harry Potter tours, ghost walks and the ever popular Jack the Ripper tours.

Hampton Court Palace

Olympic Park

From 2008, a huge, once-contaminated and largely neglected swathe of industrial East London was ambitiously regenerated and transformed into London's **Olympic Park** (http://noordinarypark.co.uk; ⊖Stratford) for the 2012 Games. Complementing its iconic sporting architecture, the Olympic Park was thoughtfully designed with a diverse mix of wetland, woodland, meadow and other wildlife habitats as an environmentally fertile legacy for the future. The twisted, abstract tangle of metal overlooking everything is the ArcelorMittal Orbit, aka the 'Hubble Bubble Pipe', a 115m-high observation tower which opened during the games. Panoramic views of the Olympic Park can also be had from the View Tube on the Greenway, next to the park.

London Mystery Walks   Walking Tours
(☎07957 388280; www.tourguides.org.uk; adult/child £10/9) Tour Jack the Ripper's old haunts at 7pm on Monday, Wednesday and Friday.

Capital Taxi Tours   Taxi Tour
(☎020-8590 3621; www.capitaltaxitours.co.uk; 2hr day tour per taxi £165, 2½hr night tour per taxi £235) Takes up to five people on a variety of tours with Blue Badge, City of London and City of Westminster registered guides/drivers, cheeky Cockney Cabbie option and foreign language availability.

✺ Festivals & Events

University Boat Race   Boat Race
(www.theboatrace.org) A posh-boy grudge match held annually since 1829 between the rowing crews of Oxford and Cambridge Universities (late March).

London Marathon   Running Race
(www.london-marathon.co.uk) Up to half a million spectators watch the whippet-thin champions and bizarrely clad amateurs take to the streets in late April.

Trooping the Colour   Royal Parade
Celebrating the Queen's official birthday (in June), this ceremonial procession of troops, marching along the Mall for their monarch's inspection, is a pageantry overload.

Wimbledon Lawn Tennis Championships   Tennis
(www.wimbledon.com) The world's most splendid tennis event takes place in late June.

Notting Hill Carnival   Street Parade
(www.thenottinghillcarnival.com) Held over two days in August, this is Europe's largest and London's most vibrant outdoor carnival, where the Caribbean community shows the city how to party. Unmissable and truly crazy.

🛏 Sleeping

When it comes to accommodation, London is one of the most expensive places in the world. Public transport is good, so you don't need to be sleeping at Buckingham Palace to be at the heart of things.

West End

Like in Monopoly, land on a Mayfair hotel and you may have to sell your house, or at least remortgage.

Hazlitt's   Historic Hotel £££
(Map p74; ☎020-7434 1771; www.hazlittshotel.com; 6 Frith St, W1; s £222, d/ste from £288/660; ❄ ☎; ⊖Tottenham Court Rd) Staying in this charming Georgian house (1718) is a trip back into a time when four-poster beds and claw-foot baths were the norm for gentlefolk. Each of

the individually decorated 30 rooms is packed with antiques and named after a personage connected with the house.

Dean Street Townhouse
Boutique Hotel **££**

(Map p74; 020-7434 1775; www.deanstreet townhouse.com; 69-71 Dean St, W1; r £180-440; ❄ 🛜; ⊖ Tottenham Court Rd) Afternoon tea in the parlour of the Dean Street Townhouse hardly gets better; it's old-world cosy, with its upholstered furniture and roaring fireplace, and the pastries are divine.

Westminster & Pimlico
Handy for the major sights; these areas have some good-value options.

Lime Tree Hotel
B&B **££**

(Map p74; 020-7730 8191; www.limetreehotel. co.uk; 135-137 Ebury St, SW1; s £99, d £150-175; @ 🛜; ⊖ Victoria) A smartly renovated Georgian townhouse hotel with a beautiful back garden to catch the late-afternoon rays. Contemporary renovations make it the best of the Belgravia crop.

Luna Simone Hotel
B&B **££**

(Map p74; 020-7834 5897; www.lunasimone hotel.com; 47-49 Belgrave Rd, SW1; s £70-75, d £95-120; @; ⊖ Pimlico) Rooms are quite compact but clean and calming at this central, welcoming hotel; the ones at the back are quieter.

Chelsea, Kensington & Knightsbridge
These classy zones offer easy access to the museums and big-name fashion stores. It's all a bit sweetie-darling, along with the prices.

Gore
Hotel **£££**

(Map p62; 020-7584 6601; www.gorehotel. com; 190 Queen's Gate, SW7; r from £205; @ 🛜; ⊖ Gloucester Rd) A short stroll from the Royal Albert Hall, the Gore serves up British grandiosity (antiques, carved four-posters, polished mahogany, a secret bathroom in the Tudor room) in 50 individually furnished, magnificent rooms.

Vicarage Hotel
B&B **££**

(Map p62; 020-7229 4030; www.london vicaragehotel.com; 10 Vicarage Gate, W8; s/d £110/138, without bathroom £65/110; @ 🛜; ⊖ High St Kensington or Notting Hill Gate) On the corner with Palace Gardens Terrace (with its astonishing cherry trees in spring), this place is all about location (between Notting Hill Gate and Kensington High St) and value for money.

Bloomsbury & St Pancras
One step from the West End and crammed with Georgian townhouse conversions, these are more affordable neighbourhoods.

Trooping the Colour (p83), London
ANDREW HOLT/GETTY IMAGES ©

Rough Luxe   Boutique Hotel ££££

(Map p74; 020-7837 5338; www.roughluxe. co.uk; 1 Birkenhead St, WC1H; r £229-289; ✽ ☏; ⊖King's Cross St Pancras) Half rough, half luxury goes the blurb, and the compelling blend of shabby and chic at this Grade-II listed property is a compelling formula.

Harlingford Hotel   Hotel ££

(Map p74; 020-7387 1551; www.harlingford hotel.com; 61-63 Cartwright Gardens, WC1; s/d/tr £88/120/140; ☏; ⊖Russell Sq) This family-run Georgian 43-room hotel sports refreshing, upbeat decor: bright-green mosaic-tiled bathrooms (with trendy sinks), fuchsia bedspreads and colourful paintings in a neighbourhood of stiff competition. It's all stairs and no lift; request a 1st-floor room.

Earl's Court & Fulham

Earl's Court is lively, cosmopolitan and so popular with travelling antipodeans that it's been nicknamed Kangaroo Valley.

Twenty Nevern Square   Hotel ££

(Map p62; 020-7565 9555; www.20nevern square.com; 20 Nevern Sq, SW5; r from £115; ☏; ⊖Earl's Court) An Ottoman theme runs through this Victorian townhouse hotel, where a mix of wooden furniture, luxurious fabrics and natural light helps maximise space – even in the excellent-value cheaper rooms.

Base2stay   Hotel ££

(Map p62; 020-7244 2255; www.base2stay. com; 25 Courtfield Gardens, SW5; s/d from £93/99; ✽ @ ☏; ⊖Earl's Court) ✐ With comfort, smart decor, power showers, flatscreen TVs with internet access, artfully concealed kitchenettes, neat rooms and a sustainable credo, this boutique establishment feels like a four-star hotel, without the wallet-emptying price tag.

Notting Hill, Bayswater & Paddington

Don't be fooled by the movie. Notting Hill and the areas immediately north of Hyde Park are as shabby as they are chic, while scruffy Paddington has lots of cheap hotels, with a major strip along Sussex Gardens, worth checking if you're short on options.

New Linden Hotel   Boutique Hotel ££

(Map p62; 020-7221 4321; www.newlinden. co.uk; Hereford Rd, 59 Leinster Sq, W2; s/d from £79/105; ☏; ⊖Bayswater) Cramming in a fair amount of style for little whack, this terrace house hotel exudes a modern and cool feel. The quiet location, helpful staff and monsoon shower heads in the deluxe rooms make this an excellent proposition.

Vancouver Studios   Apartment ££

(Map p62; 020-7243 1270; www.vancouver studios.co.uk; 30 Prince's Sq, W2; apt £97-350; @ ☏; ⊖Bayswater) It's the addition of kitchenettes and a self-service laundry that differentiate these smart, reasonably priced studios and three bedroom apartment (sleeping one to six people) from a regular Victorian townhouse hotel.

Hoxton, Shoreditch & Spitalfields

It's always had a rough-edged reputation, but London's East End is being speedily gentrified, with some good options close to the nightlife.

Hoxton Hotel   Hotel ££

(Map p62; 020-7550 1000; www.hoxtonhotels. com; 81 Great Eastern St, EC2; d & tw £59-199; @ ☏; ⊖Old St) A revolutionary pricing structure means that while all the rooms are identical, the hotel aims at constantly full occupancy. Book a couple of months ahead (sign up on the website) and you can nab £49 to £69 deals. The reasonably sized rooms all have comfy beds, quality linen and TVs that double as computers.

Zetter Hotel & Townhouse   Boutique Hotel £££

(Map p74; 020-7324 4444; www.thezetter. com; 86-88 Clerkenwell Rd, EC1M; d from £235, studio £300-450; ✽ ☏; ⊖Farringdon) ✐ A slick 21st-century conversion of a Victorian warehouse. The furnishings and

Below: Covent Garden; **Right:** Shakespeare's Globe (p67)
(BELOW) DAVID WALL PHOTO/GETTY IMAGES ©; (RIGHT) PETER PHIPP/GETTY IMAGES ©

facilities are cutting edge. You can even choose the colour of your room's lighting.

🍴 Eating

Dining out in London has become so fashionable that you can hardly open a menu without banging into a celebrity chef, while the range and quality of eating options has increased massively over the last few decades.

West End

Between them, Mayfair, Soho and Covent Garden are the gastronomic heart of London, with stacks of restaurants and cuisines at a wide range of budgets.

National Dining Rooms British ££

(Map p74; ☎020-7747 2525; www.peytonand byrne.co.uk; 1st fl, Sainsbury Wing, National Gallery, Trafalgar Sq, WC2 ; mains £15.50-20.50; ⏱10am-5.30pm Sat-Thu, to 8.30pm Fri; ⊖Charing Cross) It's fitting that this acclaimed restaurant should celebrate British food, being in the National Gallery and overlooking Trafalgar Square. For a much cheaper option with the same views, ambience, quality produce and excellent service, try a salad, pie or tart at the adjoining bakery.

Great Queen Street British ££

(Map p74; ☎020-7242 0622; 32 Great Queen St, WC2; mains £12-16; ⏱noon-2.30pm & 6-10.30pm Mon-Sat, noon-3pm Sun; ⊖Holborn) The claret-coloured walls and mismatched wooden chairs convey cosiness and tie-loosening informality, but the daily changing seasonal menu is still the very best of British, and booking is a must.

Wild Honey Modern European £££

(Map p74; ☎020-7758 9160; www.wild honeyrestaurant.co.uk; 12 St George St, W1; mains £24-30; ⏱noon-2.30pm daily, 6-11pm Mon-Sat, 6-10pm Sun; ⊖Oxford Circus) If you fancy a relatively affordable meal

within the oak-panelled ambience of a top Mayfair restaurant, Wild Honey offers excellent lunch and pre-theatre set menus (respectively, £21.95 and £22.95 for three courses).

Arbutus
Modern European **££**

(Map p74; ☎020-7734 4545; www.arbutus restaurant.co.uk; 63-64 Frith St, W1; mains £18-20; ⏱noon-2.30pm & 5-11pm Mon-Sat, noon-3pm & 5.30-10.30pm Sun; ⊖Tottenham Court Rd) Focusing on seasonal produce, inventive dishes and value-for-money set meals, Anthony Demetre's Michelin-starred brainchild just keeps getting better.

Tamarind
Indian **£££**

(Map p74; ☎020-7629 3561; www.tamarind restaurant.com; 20 Queen St, W1; mains £18.50-24.50; ⏱noon-2.45pm Sun-Fri, 5.30-11pm Mon-Sat, 6-10.30pm Sun; ⊖Green Park) A mix of spicy Moghul classics and new creations have earned this northwest Indian restaurant a Michelin star. The set lunches are a good deal (two/three courses £17/19).

South Bank

For a feed with a local feel, head to Borough Market (p93) or Bermondsey St.

Laughing Gravy
British **££**

(Map p74; ☎020-7998 1707; www.thelaughing gravy.co.uk; 154 Blackfriars Rd, SE1; mains £8.50-17.50; ⏱11am-late Mon-Fri, 5.30pm-late Sat, noon-6pm Sun; ⊖Southwark) Recently steered in a lucrative fresh direction by new owners, this restaurant is a Southwark gem, with a sure-fire menu combining locally sourced food and culinary talent, plus splendid roasts on Sunday and attentive service all round.

Oxo Tower Restaurant & Brasserie
Fusion **£££**

(Map p74; ☎020-7803 3888; www.harvey nichols.com/restaurants/oxo-tower-london; Barge House St, SE1; mains £21.50-35; ⏱restaurant noon-2.30pm & 6-11pm, brasserie noon-11pm; ✒; ⊖Waterloo) The extravagant views are the big drawcard, so skip the restaurant and head for the slightly less extravagantly

87

priced brasserie, or if you're not hungry, the bar.

Anchor & Hope   Pub ££

(Map p74; 36 The Cut, SE1; mains £12-20; ⊙noon-2.30pm Tue-Sat, 6-10.30pm Mon-Sat, from 2pm Sun; ⊖Southwark) The hope is that you'll get a table without waiting hours because you can't book at this quintessential gastropub, except for Sunday lunch at 2pm. The anchor is gutsy, unashamedly carnivorous British food.

Chelsea, Kensington & Knightsbridge

These highbrow neighbourhoods have some of London's very best (and priciest) restaurants.

Dinner by Heston Blumenthal   Modern British £££

(Map p74; ☎020-7201 3833; www.dinnerby heston.com; Mandarin Oriental Hyde Park, 66 Knightsbridge; set lunch £36, mains £26-38; ⊙noon-2.30pm & 6.30-10.30pm; ⊖Knights-bridge) The eagerly awaited opening of sumptuously presented Dinner is a gas-tronomic *tour-de-force,* ushering diners on a tour of British culinary history (with inventive modern inflections).

Tom's Kitchen   Modern European ££

(Map p74; ☎020-7349 0202; www.tomskitchen. co.uk; 27 Cale St; breakfast £4-15, mains £13.90-30; ⊙8-11.30am, noon-2.30pm & 6.30-10.30pm Mon-Fri, 10am-3.30pm & 6-9.30pm Sat & Sun; ⊖South Kensington) Celebrity chef Tom Aikens' restaurant keeps the magic flow-ing through the day, with award-winning breakfasts and pancakes drawing acclaim and crowds to its informal, but engaging, dining setting.

Marcus Wareing at the Berkeley   French £££

(Map p74; ☎020-7235 1200; www.marcus-ware ing.com; Berkeley Hotel, Wilton Pl, SW1; 3-course lunch/dinner £38/80; ⊖Knightsbridge) Wareing runs this one-time Gordon Ramsay restau-rant under his own name, and its reputa-tion for exquisite food and exemplary service has only been enhanced.

Marylebone

Marylebone's charming High St has a huge range of eateries.

Providores & Tapa Room   Fusion £££

(Map p74; ☎020-7935 6175; www.theprovidores. co.uk; 109 Marylebone High St, W1; 2/3/4/5 courses £33/47/57/63; ⊙9am-10.30pm Mon-Fri, 10am-10pm Sat & Sun; ⊖Baker St) New Zealand's most distinctive culinary export since kiwi fruit, chef Peter Gordon works his fusion magic here, matching his crea-tions with NZ wines.

La Fromagerie   Cafe ££

(Map p74; www.lafromagerie.co.uk; 2-6 Moxon St, W1; mains £7-16.50; ⊙8am-7.30pm Mon-Fri, 9am-7pm Sat, 10am-6pm Sun; ⊖Baker St) This deli-cafe has bowls of delectable salads, antipasto, peppers and beans scattered about the long communal table.

Fitzrovia

Tucked away behind busy Tottenham Court Rd, Fitzrovia's Charlotte and Goodge Sts form one of central London's most vibrant eating precincts.

Hakkasan   Chinese £££

(Map p74; ☎020-7927 7000; www.hakkasan.com; 8 Hanway Pl, W1; mains £11-61; ⊙noon-12.30am Mon-Wed, to 1.30am Thu-Sat, to midnight Sun; ⊖Tottenham Court Rd) Michelin-starred Hakkasan – hidden down a lane like all fashionable haunts should be – elegantly pairs fine Chinese dining with stunning design and some persuasive cocktail chemistry.

Clerkenwell & Farringdon

Modern Pantry   Fusion £££

(Map p74; ☎020-7553 9210; www.themodern pantry.co.uk; 47-48 St John's Sq, EC1; mains £15-22; ⊙noon-3pm Mon, noon-3pm & 6-10.30pm Tue-Sat, 11am-4pm Sun; ☎; ⊖Farringdon) This three-floor Georgian townhouse in the heart of Clerkenwell has a cracking fusion menu, which gives almost as much pleasure to read as to eat from. Ingredients are combined sublimely into unusual dishes such as tamarind miso marinated onglet steak or panko and Parmesan crusted veal escalope. Reservations recommended for dinner.

St John   British £££
(Map p74; ☎ 020-7251 0848; www.stjohnrestaurant.com; 26 St John St, EC1; mains £17-23; ⊙noon-3pm & 6-11pm Mon-Sat, 1-3pm Sun; ⊖Farringdon) Whitewashed brick walls, high ceilings and simple wooden furniture keep diners free to concentrate on nose-to-tail offerings such as chitterlings and ox tongue at this modern London classic.

Hoxton, Shoreditch & Spitalfields

Fifteen   Italian £££
(Map p74; ☎ 020-3375 1515; www.fifteen.net; 15 Westland Pl, N1; breakfast £2-8.50, trattoria £6-11, restaurant £11-25; ⊙noon-3pm & 6-10pm; ☎; ⊖Old St) Jamie Oliver's culinary philanthropy started at Fifteen, set up to give unemployed young people a shot at a career. The Italian food is beyond excellent, and, surprisingly, even those on limited budgets can afford a visit.

Albion   British ££
(Map p62; ☎ 020-7729 1051; www.albioncaff.co.uk; 2-4 Boundary St, E2; mains £9-13; ⊙8am-11pm; ☎; ⊖Old St) For those wanting to be taken back to Dear Old Blighty's cuisine but with rather less grease and stodge, this self-consciously retro 'caff' serves up top-quality bangers and mash, steak-and-kidney pies, devilled kidneys and, of course, fish and chips.

Princess of Shoreditch   Pub ££
(Map p62; ☎ 020-7729 9270; www.theprincessofshoreditch.com; 76 Paul St; pub mains £10-18.50; ⊙kitchen noon-3pm & 6.30-10pm Mon-Sat, noon-9pm Sun; ☎; ⊖Old St) Perfect for a drink or a meal, the Princess can get busy thanks to its excellent gastro-pub menu, fine wine list, choice ales and particularly good-looking interior.

🍷 Drinking & Nightlife

As long as there's been a city, Londoners have loved to drink – and, as history shows, often immoderately.

West End

Gordon's Wine Bar   Bar
(Map p74; www.gordonswinebar.com; 47 Villiers St, WC2; ⊙11am-11pm Mon-Sat, noon-10pm Sun; ⊖Embankment) What's not to love about this cavernous, candlelit wine cellar that's practically unchanged for the last 120 years? Get here before the office crowd (generally around 6pm) or forget about getting a table.

Lamb & Flag (p90)
MARK TURNER/GETTY IMAGES ©

TIM E WHITE/ALAMY ©

French House
Bar

(Map p74; www.frenchhousesoho.com; 49 Dean St, W1; ◷noon-11pm Mon-Sat, to 10.30pm Sun; ⊖Leicester Sq) French House is Soho's legendary boho boozer with a history to match: this was the meeting place of the Free French Forces during WWII, and de Gaulle is said to have drunk here often, while Dylan Thomas, Peter O'Toole and Francis Bacon all frequently ended up on the wooden floors.

Princess Louise
Pub

(Map p74; 208 High Holborn, WC1; ◷11.30am-11pm Mon-Fri, noon-11pm Sat, to 10.30 Sun; ⊖Holborn) This late-19th-century Victorian boozer is arguably London's most beautiful pub. Spectacularly decorated with fine tiles, etched mirrors, plasterwork and a gorgeous central horseshoe bar, it gets packed with the after-work crowd.

Lamb & Flag
Pub

(Map p74; www.lambandflagcoventgarden.co.uk; 33 Rose St, WC2; ◷11am-11pm Mon-Sat, noon-10.30pm Sun; ⊖Covent Garden) Everyone's Covent Garden 'find', this historic pub is often as jammed with punters as it is packed with history. Built in 1623 and for-merly called the 'Bucket of Blood', inside it's all brass fittings and creaky wooden floors.

The City

Ye Olde Cheshire Cheese
Pub

(Map p74; Wine Office Court, 145 Fleet St, EC4; ◷11am-11pm Mon-Fri, from noon Sat; ⊖Chancery Lane) Rebuilt six years after the Great Fire, this hoary pub was popular with Dr Johnson, Thackeray, Dickens and the visiting Mark Twain.

South Bank

George Inn
Pub

(Map p74; www.nationaltrust.org.uk/george-inn; 77 Borough High St, SE1; ◷11am-11pm; ⊖London Bridge) This glorious old boozer is London's last surviving galleried coaching inn, dating from 1676 and now a National Trust property.

Anchor
Pub

(Map p74; 34 Park St, SE1; ◷11am-11pm Sun-Wed, to midnight Thu-Sat; ⊖London Bridge) This 18th-century riverside boozer replaced the 1615 original where Samuel Pepys witnessed the Great Fire.

Clerkenwell & Farringdon

Jerusalem Tavern   Pub
(Map p74; www.stpetersbrewery.co.uk; 55 Britton St, EC1; 🕙11am-11pm Mon-Fri; 🛜; 🚇Farringdon) Pick a wood-panelled cubbyhole to park yourself in at this tiny 1720 coffee shop-turned-inn (named after the Priory of St John of Jerusalem) and choose from a selection of St Peter's fantastic beers and ales, brewed in North Suffolk.

Hoxton, Shoreditch & Spitalfields

Book Club   Bar
(Map p62; 📞020-7684 8618; www.wearetbc.com; 100 Leonard St; 🕙8am-midnight Mon-Wed, 8am-2am Thu & Fri, 10am-2am Sat & Sun; 🛜; 🚇Old St) A cerebral/creative vibe animates this fantastic one-time Victorian warehouse in Shoreditch that hosts cultural events and DJ nights to complement the drinking, ping-pong and pool-playing.

Ten Bells   Pub
(Map p62; cnr Commercial & Fournier Sts, E1; 🕙11am-11pm Mon-Sat, noon-10.30pm Sun; 🚇Liverpool St) This landmark Victorian pub, with its large windows and beautiful tiles, is perfect for a pint after a wander round Spitalfields Market. It's famous for being one of Jack the Ripper's pick-up joints, although these days it attracts a rather more salubrious and trendy clientele.

⭐ Entertainment

THEATRE

London is a world capital for theatre and there's a lot more than mammoth musicals to tempt you into the West End. On performance days, you can buy half-price tickets for West End productions (cash only) from the official agency **tkts** (Map p74; www.tkts.co.uk; Leicester Sq, WC2; 🕙10am-7pm Mon-Sat, noon-4pm Sun; 🚇Leicester Sq). For more, see www.official

londontheatre.co.uk or www.theatre monkey.com.

Royal Court Theatre   Theatre
(Map p74; 📞020-7565 5000; www.royalcourt theatre.com; Sloane Sq, SW1; 🚇Sloane Sq) Progressive theatre and champion of new talent.

National Theatre   Theatre
(Map p74; 📞020-7452 3000; www.national theatre.org.uk; South Bank, SE1; 🚇Waterloo) Cheaper tickets for classics and new plays from some of the world's best companies.

Royal Shakespeare Company   Theatre
(RSC; 📞0844 800 1110; www.rsc.org.uk) Productions of the bard's classics and other quality stuff.

Old Vic   Theatre
(Map p74; 📞0844 8717628; www.oldvictheatre. com; The Cut, SE1; 🚇Waterloo) Kevin Spacey continues his run as artistic director (and occasional performer) at this venue, which features classic, highbrow drama.

Donmar Warehouse   Theatre
(Map p74; 📞0844 871 7624; www.donmar warehouse.com; 41 Earlham St, WC2; 🚇Covent Garden) A not-for-profit company that has forged itself a West End reputation.

Almeida   Theatre
(Map p62; 📞020-7359 4404; www.almeida. co.uk; Almeida St, N1; 🚇Highbury & Islington) A plush Islington venue that can be relied on to provide the city with an essential program of imaginative theatre, under its creative artistic director, Michael Attenborough.

Young Vic   Theatre
(Map p74; 📞020-7922 2922; www.youngvic.org; 66 The Cut, SE1; 🚇Waterloo) One of the capital's most respected theatre troupes – bold, brave and talented – the Young Vic stages winning performances.

ROCK, POP & JAZZ

KOKO   Concert Venue
(Map p74; www.koko.uk.com; 1a Camden High St, NW1; 🕙7-11pm Sun-Thu, to 4am Fri & Sat;

⊖Mornington Cres) Occupying the grand Camden Palace theatre, Koko hosts live bands most nights and the regular Club NME (New Musical Express; £5) on Friday.

Ronnie Scott's   Jazz
(Map p74; ☎020-7439 0747; www.ronniescotts. co.uk; 47 Frith St, W1; ⏱6.30pm-3am Mon-Sat, to midnight Sun; ⊖Leicester Sq, Tottenham Court Rd) London's legendary jazz club has been pulling in the hep cats since 1959.

100 Club   Live Music
(Map p74; ☎020-7636 0933; www.the100club. co.uk; 100 Oxford St, W1; admission £8-15; ⊖Oxford Circus, Tottenham Court Rd) Hosting live music for 70 years, this legendary London venue once showcased the Stones and was at the centre of the punk revolution. It now divides its time between jazz, rock and even a little swing.

Roundhouse   Live Music
(Map p62; www.roundhouse.org.uk; Chalk Farm Rd, NW1; ⊖Chalk Farm) Built in 1847 as a railway shed, Camden's Roundhouse has been an iconic concert venue since the 1960s (capacity 3300), hosting the likes of the Rolling Stones, Led Zeppelin and The Clash.

GAY & LESBIAN

The West End, particularly Soho, is the visible centre of gay and lesbian London, with numerous venues clustered around Old Compton St; and many other areas have their own mini-scenes.

The easiest way to find out what's going on is to pick up the free press from a venue (Pink Paper, Boyz, QX). The gay section of *Time Out* is useful, as are www. gaydarnation.com (for men) and www. gingerbeer.co.uk (for women).

CLASSICAL MUSIC, OPERA & DANCE

Royal Albert Hall   Concert Hall
(Map p62; ☎020-7589 8212; www.royalalbert hall.com; Kensington Gore, SW7; ⊖South Kensington) This landmark elliptical Victorian arena – classically based on a Roman amphitheatre – hosts classical concerts and contemporary artists, but is best known as the venue for the annual classical music festival, the Proms.

Royal Albert Hall

Roll Out the Barrow

London has more than 350 markets selling everything from antiques and curios to flowers and fish.

Columbia Road Flower Market (Map p62; Columbia Rd, E2; ⏰8am-3pm Sun; 🚇Old St) The best place for East End barrow boy banter ('We got flowers cheap enough for ya muvver-in-law's grave'). Unmissable.

Borough Market (Map p74; Southwark St; 🚇London Bridge) A farmers' market sometimes called London's Larder.

Camden Market (Map p62; Camden High St, NW1; ⏰10am-6pm; 🚇Camden Town, Chalk Farm) Actually a series of markets spread along Camden High St; the Lock and Stables markets are the place for punk fashion, cheap food, bongs and hippy-dippy stuff.

Portobello Road Market (Map p62; www.portobellomarket.org; Portobello Rd, W10; ⏰8am-6.30pm Mon-Sat, to 1pm Thu; 🚇Notting Hill Gate, Ladbroke Grove) One of London's most famous (and crowded) street markets; new and vintage clothes, antiques and food.

Brick Lane Market (Map p62; www.visitbricklane.org; Brick Lane, E1; ⏰8am-2pm Sun; 🚇Liverpool St) A sprawling East End bazaar featuring everything from fruit to paintings and bric-a-brac.

Barbican   Performing Arts

(Map p74; ☎0845 1216823; www.barbican.org.uk; Silk St, EC2; 🚇Barbican) Home to the London Symphony Orchestra, this famously hulking complex (named after a Roman fortification) has a rich program of film, music, theatre, art and dance including concerts.

Southbank Centre   Concert Hall

(Map p74; ☎020-7960 4200; www.southbankcentre.co.uk; Belvedere Rd, SE1; 🚇Waterloo) Home to the **London Philharmonic Orchestra** (www.lpo.co.uk), **Sinfonietta** (www.londonsinfonietta.org.uk) and the **Philharmonia Orchestra** (www.philharmonia.co.uk), among others, this centre hosts classical, opera, jazz and choral music in three premier venues: the **Royal Festival Hall** (Map p74; ☎020-7960 4242; admission £6-60), the smaller **Queen Elizabeth Hall** (QEH; Map p74) and the **Purcell Room** (Map p74).

Royal Opera House   Opera

(Map p74; ☎020-7304 4000; www.roh.org.uk; Bow St, WC2; tickets £7-175; 🚇Covent Garden) Covent Garden is synonymous with opera thanks to this world-famous venue, which is also the home of the Royal Ballet, Britain's premier classical ballet company. Backstage tours take place three times a day on weekdays and four times on Saturdays (£10.50; book ahead).

🛍 Shopping

Selfridges   Department Store

(Map p74; www.selfridges.com; 400 Oxford St, W1; ⏰9.30am-8pm Mon-Wed, to 9pm Thu-Sat, 11.30am-6.15pm Sun; 🚇Bond St) Famed for its innovative window displays – especially at yuletide – the funkiest of London's one-stop shops bursts with fashion labels, an unparalleled food hall and Europe's largest cosmetics department.

Fortnum & Mason   Department Store

(Map p74; www.fortnumandmason.com; 181 Piccadilly, W1; ⏰10am-8pm Mon-Sat, 11.30am-6pm Sun; 🚇Piccadilly Circus) It's the byword for quality and service from a bygone era, steeped in 300 years of tradition. The old-world basement food hall is where Britain's elite come for their pantry provisions.

Liberty
Department Store

(Map p74; www.liberty.co.uk; Great Marlborough St, W1; ⏱10am-8pm Mon-Sat, noon-6pm Sun; ⊖Oxford Circus) An irresistible blend of contemporary styles and indulgent pampering in a mock-Tudor fantasyland of carved dark wood.

Harrods
Department Store

(Map p74; www.harrods.com; 87 Brompton Rd, SW1; ⏱10am-8m Mon-Sat, 11.30am-6pm Sun; ⊖Knightsbridge) Garish, stylish, kitsch, yet perennially popular department store.

Harvey Nichols
Department Store

(Map p74; www.harveynichols.com; 109-125 Knightsbridge, SW1; ⏱10am-8pm Mon-Sat, 11.30am-6pm Sun; ⊖Knightsbridge) London's temple of high fashion, jewellery and perfume.

🛈 Information

City of London Information Centre (Map p74; www.visitthecity.co.uk; St Paul's Churchyard, EC4; ⏱9.30am-5.30pm Mon-Sat, 10am-4pm Sun; ⊖St Paul's) Tourist information, fast-track tickets to City attractions and guided walks (adult/child £6/4).

🛈 Getting There & Away
Bus & Coach

The London terminus for long-distance buses (called 'coaches' in Britain) is **Victoria Coach Station** (Map p74; 164 Buckingham Palace Rd, SW1; ⊖Victoria).

Train

Most of London's main-line rail terminals are linked by the Circle line on the tube.

Charing Cross Canterbury

Euston Manchester, Liverpool, Carlisle, Glasgow

King's Cross Cambridge, Hull, York, Newcastle, Scotland

Liverpool Street Stansted airport (Express), Cambridge

London Bridge Gatwick airport, Brighton

Paddington Heathrow airport (Express), Oxford, Bath, Bristol, Exeter, Plymouth, Cardiff

St Pancras Gatwick and Luton airports, Brighton, Nottingham, Sheffield, Leicester, Leeds, Paris Eurostar

Victoria Gatwick airport (Express), Brighton, Canterbury

Waterloo Windsor, Winchester, Exeter, Plymouth

🛈 Getting Around
To/From the Airports

Gatwick

Gatwick Express (www.gatwickexpress.com; one way/return £19.90/34.90) trains run to/from Victoria 5am to 11.45pm (one way/return £16/26, 30 minutes, first/last train 3.30am/12.32am).

Heathrow

The cheapest option from Heathrow is to take the underground (tube). The Piccadilly line is accessible from every terminal (£5.30, one hour to central London, departing from Heathrow every five minutes from around 5am to 11.30pm).

Royal Opera House (p93)

London's Your Oyster

The best-value way to get around London is with an **Oyster Card**, a reusable travel card which covers most of the city's public transport system. The card itself costs £5 (refundable when you leave).

London is divided into five travel zones; most sights are in Zones 1 and 2. A weekly/monthly season ticket covering all tube, bus and rail services within these zones currently costs £29/112.

Alternatively, you can load the card with credit, and have fares deducted each time you use a train or bus. Fares are much cheaper compared to standard paper tickets (a Zone 1 tube journey on an Oyster Card is £2.10, compared to £4.50 for a paper ticket). Even better, in any single day your fares will be capped at the Oyster day-pass rate for the zones you've travelled in (Zones 1-2 peak/off-peak £8.40/7).

Oyster Cards can be bought at any London tube or train station, as well as some newsagents, garages and off-licences. Alternatively, you can buy Oyster Cards in advance online from the Transport for London website (http://visitorshop.tfl.gov.uk).

Faster, and much more expensive, is the **Heathrow Express** (www.heathrowexpress.com; one way/return £20/34) train to Paddington station (one way/return £18/34, 15 minutes, every 15 minutes 5.12am to 11.48pm).

A taxi to the centre of London will cost between £50 and £85.

Stansted

The **Stansted Express** (📞 0845 8500150; www.stanstedexpress.com) connects with Liverpool Street station (one way/return £21.50/29.50, 46 minutes, every 15 minutes 6am to 12.30am).

A taxi to/from central London costs about £100.

Bus

Single-journey bus tickets (valid for two hours) cost £2.30 (£1.35 on Oyster, capped at £4.20 per day); a weekly pass is £18.80. At stops with yellow signs, you must buy your ticket from the automatic machine (or use an Oyster) before boarding.

Buses stop on request, so clearly signal the driver with an outstretched arm.

Bicycle

Bikes can be hired from numerous self-service docking stations through London's **Cycle Hire** (www.tfl.gov.uk; free 1st 30min, then 1/2/3/6/24hr £1/6/15/35/50) scheme.

Car

Don't. London was recently rated Western Europe's second most congested city (congratulations Brussels). In addition, you'll pay £8 per day simply to drive into central London from 7am to 6pm on a weekday. If you're hiring a car to continue your trip around Britain, take the tube or train to a major airport and pick it up from there.

Taxi

London's famous black cabs are available for hire when the yellow light above the windscreen is lit. Fares are metered, with flag fall of £2.20 and the additional rate dependent on time of day, distance travelled and taxi speed. A 1-mile trip will cost between £5.20 and £8.40.

Underground & DLR

'The tube', as it's universally known, extends its subterranean tentacles throughout London and into the surrounding counties, with services running every few minutes from roughly 5.30am to 12.30am (from 7am to 11.30pm Sunday).

It helps to know the direction you're travelling in (ie northbound or southbound, eastbound or westbound) as well as the terminus of the line you're travelling on.

Boat

Thames Clippers (www.thamesclippers. com) runs regular commuter services between Embankment, Waterloo, Blackfriars, Bankside, London Bridge, Tower, Canary Wharf, Greenwich, North Greenwich and Woolwich piers (adult/child £5.30/2.65) from 7am to midnight (from 9.30am weekends).

London Waterbus Company (☎020-7482 2660; www.londonwaterbus.com; single/return £7.20/10.30) and **Jason's Trip** (Map p62; www. jasons.co.uk; opposite 42 Blomfield Rd, W9; single/return £8/9) both run canal boat journeys between Camden Lock and Little Venice; see websites for times.

AROUND LONDON

Windsor & Eton

POP 31,000

Dominated by the massive bulk and heavy influence of Windsor Castle, these twin towns have a rather surreal atmosphere, with the morning pomp and ceremony of the changing of the guards in Windsor and the sight of school boys dressed in formal tail coats wandering the streets of Eton.

◉ Sights

Windsor Castle   Windsor Castle
(www.royalcollection.org.uk; adult/child £17.75/10.60, when State Apartments closed £9.70/6.45; ⊙9.45am-5.15pm Mar-Oct, 9.45am-4.15pm Nov-Feb; ◻Bus 701 or 702 from Victoria coach station, ◻Windsor Central or Windsor Riverside) The largest and oldest occupied fortress in the world, Windsor Castle is a majestic vision of battlements and towers used for state occasions and as the Queen's weekend retreat. You can join a free guided tour (every half-hour) or take a multilingual audio tour.

The castle's highlights are undoubtedly the lavish **State Apartments**, including the magnificent St George's Hall: the Waterloo Chamber, with its paintings commemorating the victory over Napoleon; and the King's Dressing Room, with Renaissance masterpieces by van Dyck, Hans Holbein, Rembrandt and Rubens.

While you're here, don't miss a picnic in the groomed grounds of Windsor

Changing of the Guard at Windsor Castle

PAWEL LIBERA/GETTY IMAGES ©

Great Park, and the chance to watch the ceremonial **Changing of the Guard** (⏱11am Mon-Sat Apr-Jul, alternate days Aug-Mar).

Eton College   Notable Building

(www.etoncollege.com; adult/child £.7.50/6.50, extended tour £11; ⏱guided tours 2pm & 3.15pm daily school holidays, Wed, Fri, Sat & Sun term time) Founded in 1440, England's oldest and most prestigious public school, Eton College, has been educating the great and good of English society for over five centuries. Among its famous alumni are 18 prime ministers, as well as the Duke of Wellington, Princes William and Harry, George Orwell, Ian Fleming, Aldous Huxley, Sir Ranulph Fiennes, John Maynard Keynes and Bear Grylls. You may recognise some of the buildings, as *Chariots of Fire*, *The Madness of King George*, *Mrs Brown* and *Shakespeare in Love* are just some of the movies that have been filmed here.

Tickets must be purchased in advance at the tourist office.

ℹ️ Getting There & Away

Trains from Windsor Central station on Thames St go to London Paddington (27 to 43 minutes). Trains from Windsor Riverside station go to London Waterloo (56 minutes).

SOUTHEAST ENGLAND

Canterbury

POP 43,432

With its jaw-dropping cathedral surrounded by medieval cobbled streets, this World Heritage city has been a Christian pilgrimage site for several centuries, and a tourist attraction for almost as long.

🎯 Sights

Canterbury Cathedral   Church

(www.canterbury-cathedral.org; adult/child £8/7, tour adult/child £5/3, audio tour adult/child £3.50/2.50; ⏱9am-5pm Mon-Sat, 12.30-2.30pm

❤️ If You Like...
Castles

Two thousand years of history has left England with a wealth of fascinating castles. Some are little more than crumbling ruins, while others are still impressively intact.

1 DOVER CASTLE
(EH; www.english-heritage.org.uk; adult/child £16.50/9.90; ⏱10am-6pm Apr-Jul & Sep, from 9.30am Aug, to 5pm Oct, 10am-4pm Sat & Sun Nov-Mar; P) Overlooking the coastal town of Dover, this impressive castle was built to guard against raids from nearby France. The robust 12th-century **Great Tower** has walls up to 7m thick, but the biggest draw is the network of secret **wartime tunnels**.

2 LEEDS CASTLE
(www.leeds-castle.com; adult/child £19.75/12.50; ⏱10am-6pm Apr-Sep, to 5pm Oct-Mar) Despite the name, Leeds Castle isn't actually in Leeds – it's 7 miles from Maidstone in Kent. The fortress occupies two islands surrounded by a lake, and is many people's idea of the classic castle.

3 SKIPTON CASTLE
(www.skiptoncastle.co.uk; High St, Skipton; adult/child £6.70/4.10; ⏱10am-6pm Mon-Sat, from noon Sun Mar-Sep, to 4pm Oct-Feb) In the heart of the Yorkshire Dales, Skipton Castle is one of the best-preserved medieval castles in England, and still boasts much of its original structure: battlements, arrowslits and all. It's 44 miles west of York.

4 WARWICK CASTLE
(📞0870 442 2000; www.warwick-castle.co.uk; castle adult/child £19.95/11.95, castle & dungeon £27.45/19.45; ⏱10am-6pm Apr-Sep, to 5pm Oct-Mar; P) Warwick Castle was founded in 1068 by William the Conqueror, and later became the ancestral home of the Earls of Warwick. It's now run by the owners of Madame Tussauds, with lots of kid-centred activities and waxworks populating the turrets and apartments. It's 10 miles northeast of Stratford-upon-Avon.

Sun) A rich repository of more than 1400 years of Christian history, the Church of England's mother ship is an truly extraordinary place with an absorbing history. This ancient structure is packed with monuments commemorating the nation's battles. The spot in the northwest transept where Archbishop Thomas Becket met his grisly end has been drawing pilgrims for more than 800 years and is marked by a flickering candle and striking modern altar.

Sleeping

Abode Canterbury   Boutique Hotel £££
(01227-766266; www.abodehotels.co.uk; 30-33 High St; r from £135; ⊖🛜) The only boutique hotel in town, the 72 rooms at this supercentral option are graded from 'comfortable' to 'fabulous' and, for the most part, live up to their tags.

House of Agnes   Hotel ££
(01227-472185; www.houseofagnes.co.uk; 71 St Dunstan's St; r from £83; @🛜) Situated near the West Gate, this rather wonky 13th-century beamed inn, mentioned in Dickens' *David Copperfield,* has eight themed rooms bearing such names as 'Marrakesh' (Moorish), 'Venice' (inevitable carnival masks), 'Boston' (light and airy) and 'Canterbury' (antiques and heavy fabrics).

Getting There & Away

There are two train stations: Canterbury East for London Victoria and Dover; and Canterbury West for London's Charing Cross and St Pancras stations. Connections:

Dover Priory (£7.50, 25 minutes, every 30 minutes)

London St Pancras (£31.80, one hour, hourly)

London Victoria/Charing Cross (£26.80, 1¾ hours, two to three hourly)

Brighton & Hove

POP 247,817

Brighton is the UK's most colourful and outrageous seaside city. It's also home to the UK's biggest gay community, and has a fantastic cultural and clubbing scene to boot. Brighton rocks all year round, but really comes to life during the summer months.

Sights

Royal Pavilion   Palace
(www.royalpavilion.org.uk; Royal Pavilion Gardens; adult/child £10.50/5.90; 🕑9.30am-5.45pm Apr-Sep, 10am-5.15pm Oct-Mar) The city's must-see attraction is the Royal Pavilion, the glittering party pad and palace of Prince George, who later became the Prince Regent and then King George IV. It's one of the most opulent buildings in England, certainly the finest

Canterbury Cathedral (p97)
HOLGER LEUE/GETTY IMAGES ©

example of early-19th-century Chinoiserie anywhere in Europe, and is an apt symbol of Brighton's reputation for decadence and high living.

Brighton Pier   Amusement Park
(www.brightonpier.co.uk; Madeira Dr) This grand old centenarian pier is the place to experience Brighton's tackier side. There are plenty of stomach-churning fairground rides and dingy amusement arcades to keep you amused, plus candy floss and Brighton rock to chomp on while you're doing so.

The Lanes   Neighbourhood
Brighton's original fishing-village heart is the Lanes, a cobblestone web of 17th-century cottages housing a gentrified cornucopia of independent shops, pubs and one-of-a-kind eateries. The adjacent **North Laine** has a funkier vibe with streets of multicoloured shops, second-hand record stores and vegetarian cafes for local hipsters.

 Festivals & Events

There's always something fun going on in Brighton, but the main events include **Gay Pride** (www.brightonpride.org) in early August and the **Brighton Festival** (☎01273-709709; www.brightonfestival.org) in May, the biggest in Britain after Edinburgh, drawing theatre, dance, music and comedy performers from around the globe.

 Sleeping

Despite a glut of hotels in Brighton, prices are high and you'd be wise to book well ahead for summer weekends and for the Brighton Festival in May. Expect to pay up to a third more at weekends across the board.

Hotel Una   Boutique Hotel ££
(☎01723-820464; www.hotel-una.co.uk; 55-56 Regency Sq; s £55-75, d £115-150; ❄☎) All the 19 rooms here wow guests with their bold-patterned fabrics, supersize leather sofas, in-room free-standing baths and vegan/veggie/carnivorous breakfast in bed.

↱

Detour:
White Cliffs of Dover

Immortalised in song, film and literature, these iconic cliffs are embedded in the national consciousness, a big 'Welcome Home' sign to generations of travellers and soldiers. The cliffs rise to 100m high and extend on either side of Dover, but the best bit is the 6-mile stretch that starts about 2 miles east of town, properly known as the Langdon Cliffs.

The area is managed by the National Trust and there's a small information office, from where you can take the stony path east along the clifftops for a bracing 2-mile walk to the South Foreland Lighthouse.

Neo Hotel   Boutique Hotel ££
(☎01273-711104; www.neohotel.com; 19 Oriental Pl; d from £100; ☎) You won't be surprised to learn that the owner of this gorgeous hotel is an interior stylist; the nine rooms could have dropped straight out of the pages of a design magazine, each finished in rich colours and tactile fabrics, with bold floral and Asian motifs and black-tiled bathrooms.

myhotel   Hotel ££
(☎01273-900300; www.myhotels.com; 17 Jubilee St; r from £89; P@☎) With trend-setting rooms looking like space-age pods, full of curved white walls, floor-to-ceiling observation windows and suspended flat-screen TVs, there's nothing square about this place, daddy-o.

Eating

Terre à Terre   Vegetarian ££
(☎01273-729051; www.terreaterre.co.uk; 71 East St; mains £14; ⏰noon-10.30pm Mon-Fri, 11am-

Below: Brighton Pier (p99); **Right:** Winchester Cathedral
(BELOW) ROGER GAESS/GETTY IMAGES ©: (RIGHT) DIANA JARVIS/GETTY IMAGES ©

11pm Sat, 11am-10pm Sun;) Even staunch meat eaters will come out raving about this legendary vegetarian restaurant.

The Gingerman   Modern European £££

(01273-326688; www.gingermanrestaurant. com; 21a Norfolk Sq; 2/3-course menu £15/18; 12.30-2pm & 7-10pm Tue-Sun) Seafood from Hastings, Sussex beef, Romney Marsh lamb, local sparkling wines and countless other seasonal, local and British treats go into the adroitly flash-fried and slow-cooked dishes at this snug, 32-cover eatery.

JB's American Diner   Bistro £

(31 King's Rd; burgers £7, mains £6.50-12) A hefty slab of authentic Americana teleported to the Brighton seafront, complete with shiny leather booths, 1950s soundtrack and colossal burgers, fries and milkshakes.

English's Oyster Bar   Seafood ££

(www.englishs.co.uk; 29-31 East St; mains £11-25) An almost 70-year-old institution and celebrity haunt, this Brightonian seafood paradise dishes up everything from Essex oysters to locally caught lobster to Dover sole.

Drinking & Nightlife

For up-to-date information on gay Brighton, check out www.gay.brighton.co.uk and www.realbrighton.com, or pick up the free monthly magazine *Gscene* (www. gscene.com) from the tourist office.

Dorset   Pub

(www.thedorset.co.uk; 28 North Rd;) This laid-back Brighton institution throws open its doors and windows in fine weather and spills tables onto the pavement. There's also a decent gastropub menu.

Evening Star   Pub

(www.eveningstarbrighton.co.uk; 55-56 Surrey St;
🕐noon-11pm Sun-Thu, 11.30am-midnight Fri &
Sat) This cosy, unpretentious pub is a beer
drinker's nirvana, with a wonderful selection of award-winning real ales, Belgian
beers, organic lagers and seasonal brews.

ℹ Information

Tourist Office (📞01273-290337; www.
visitbrighton.com; Royal Pavilion Shop;
🕐9.30am-5.30pm) Superbly run office with an
accommodation booking service (£1.50), train
and bus ticketing and a highly recommended
(free) greeter scheme.

ℹ Getting There & Away

All London-bound services pass through Gatwick
airport (£9.50, 30 to 40 minutes, up to five
hourly).

London St Pancras (£15.40, 1¼ hours, half-
hourly)

London Victoria (£16, 50 minutes, three hourly)

Winchester

POP 41,420

Calm, collegiate Winchester is a mellow
must-see for all visitors. It was the capital
of Saxon kings, and its statues and sights
evoke two of England's mightiest myth-
makers: Alfred the Great and King Arthur
(yes, he of the round table).

◎ Sights

Winchester Cathedral   Church

(📞01962-857275; www.winchester-cathedral.
org.uk; adult/child £6/free, incl tower tour £9/
free; 🕐9am-5pm Sat, 12.30-3pm Sun) Winchester Cathedral is one of southern England's most awe-inspiring buildings. The
Cathedral's exterior features a fine Gothic
facade, but it's the inside that steals the
show with one of the longest **medieval
naves** (164m) in Europe, and a fascinating jumble of features from all eras. Jane
Austen, who spent her last weeks at a
nearby house, is buried near the entrance
in the cathedral's northern aisle.

101

Cathedral tours (⏱hourly 10am-3pm Mon-Sat) last one hour. **Tower and roof tours** (tickets £6; ⏱11.30am Sat & 2.15pm Mon, Wed, Fri & Sat Jun-Aug, 11.30am Sat & 2.15pm Wed & Sat Sep-May) venture onto the roof for views as far as the Isle of Wight. For safety reasons these tours are only open to those aged 12 to 70.

Great Hall & Round Table
Historic Building

(Castle Ave; suggested donation adult/child £1/50p; ⏱10am-5pm) `FREE` The cavernous Great Hall is the only part of 11th-century Winchester Castle that Oliver Cromwell spared from destruction. Crowning the wall is what centuries of mythology have dubbed King Arthur's Round Table. It's actually a 700-year-old copy, but is fascinating nonetheless.

Jane Austen's House Museum
Museum

(☎01420-83262; www.jane-austens-house-museum.org.uk; Chawton; adult/child £7/2; ⏱10.30am-4.30pm mid-Feb–Dec) There's more than a touch of period drama at the former home of Jane Austen (1775–1817), where she wrote *Mansfield Park*, *Emma* and *Persuasion*, and revised *Sense and Sensibility*, *Pride and Prejudice* and *Northanger Abbey*. This appealing red-brick house, where the celebrated English novelist lived from 1809 to 1817, is now a museum.

The museum is 18 miles east of Winchester.

🛏 Sleeping

Wykeham Arms
Inn ££

(☎01962-853834; www.fullershotels.com; 75 Kingsgate St; s/d/ste £70/119/150; P 🛜) At 250-odd years old, the Wykeham bursts with history – it used to be a brothel and also put Nelson up for a night. Creaking stairs lead to plush bedrooms with brass bedsteads, jazzy throws, oak dressers and teddy bears.

Dolphin House
B&B ££

(☎01962-853284; www.dolphinhousestudios.co.uk; 3 Compton Rd; s/d £55/70; P 🛜) At this kind of B&B-plus your continental breakfast is delivered to a compact kitchen – perfect for lazy lie-ins. The terrace, complete with cast-iron tables and chairs, overlooks a gently sloping lawn.

🍴 Eating

Black Rat
Modern British ££

(☎01962-844465; www.theblackrat.co.uk; 88 Chesil St; mains £17-20; ⏱dinner daily, lunch Sat & Sun) The decor here is casually countrified, but the food is something else. Accomplished cooking has won it a Michelin star – expect hearty cuts of braised beef cheek, lamb rump and oxtail.

Chesil Rectory
British ££

(☎01962-851555; www.chesilrectory.co.uk; 1 Chesil St; mains £16) Flickering candles and low beams lend this 15th-century restaurant a romantic feel.

ℹ Information

Tourist Office (☎01962-840500; www.visitwinchester.co.uk; High St; ⏱10am-5pm Mon-Sat, plus 11am-4pm Sun May-Sep)

ℹ Getting There & Away

Train

There are fast links to the Midlands. Other train services:

London Waterloo (£30, 1¼ hours, every 30 minutes)

Portsmouth (£10.20, one hour, hourly)

Southampton (£5.80, 20 minutes, every 30 minutes)

SOUTHWEST ENGLAND

Bath

POP 90,144

Britain's littered with beautiful cities, but precious few can hold a candle to Bath. Home to some of the nation's grandest Georgian architecture and stateliest streets – not to mention one of the world's best-preserved Roman bathhouses – this slinky, sophisticated, snooty city has been a tourist draw for nigh-on 2000 years.

Bath

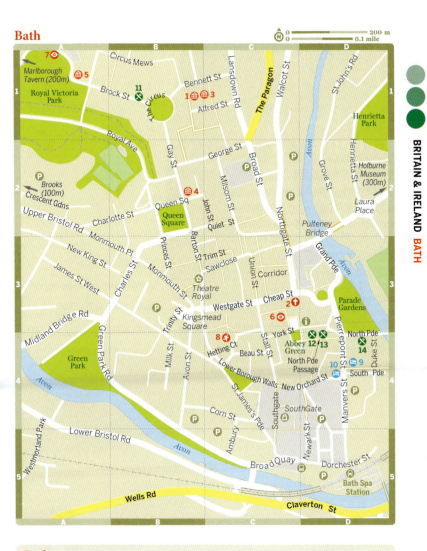

Bath

⊙ Sights

1 Assembly Rooms	B1
2 Bath Abbey	C3
3 Fashion Museum	C1
4 Jane Austen Centre	B2
5 No 1 Royal Crescent	A1
6 Roman Baths	C3
7 Royal Crescent	A1

✪ Activities, Courses & Tours

8 Thermae Bath Spa	C4

🛏 Sleeping

9 Halcyon	D4
10 Henry	D4

✗ Eating

11 Circus	B1
12 Demuth's	D4
13 Sally Lunn's	D4
14 Sotto Sotto	D4

103

Don't Miss
Stonehenge

This compelling ring of monolithic stones has been attracting a steady stream of pilgrims, poets and philosophers for the last 5000 years and is easily Britain's most iconic archaeological site.

☎ 0870-333 1181

www.english-heritage.org.uk

adult/child £6.90/3.50

🕘 9am-7pm

The History

Stonehenge was constructed in several phases, starting around 3000 BC. The inner circle of bluestones were somehow hauled here from the Preseli Mountains in south Wales around 2000 BC, followed 500 years later by more stones which were erected in a circle and crowned by lintels to make the trilithons (two vertical stones topped by a horizontal one). Like many stone circles, the inner horseshoes are aligned to coincide with sunrise at the midsummer solstice, which supports the theory that the site was some kind of astronomical calendar.

Other Sights

Stonehenge forms part of a huge complex of ancient monuments. North of Stonehenge and running roughly east–west is the **Cursus**, an elongated embanked oval; the slightly smaller **Lesser Cursus** is nearby. Theories abound as to what these sites were used for, ranging from ancient sporting arenas to processional avenues for the dead. Two clusters of burial mounds, the **Old and New Kings Barrows**, sit beside ceremonial pathway the Avenue, which originally linked Stonehenge with the River Avon, 2 miles away.

Stone Circle Access

A marked pathway leads around the henge, and although you can't walk freely in the circle itself, it's possible to see the stones fairly close up. An audioguide (in 10 languages) is included in the admission price.

Stone Circle Access Visits (☎01722-343830; www.english-heritage.org.uk; adult/child £14.50/7.50) enable you to wander round the core of the site, getting up-close views of the iconic bluestones and trilithons. Each visit only takes 26 people; to secure a place book at least two months in advance.

Local Knowledge

Stonehenge

RECOMMENDATIONS FROM PAT SHELLEY, SALISBURY & STONEHENGE GUIDED TOURS

1 THE MAIN CIRCLE

Stonehenge covers a large area but the focal point is, of course, the main circle of stones, including the distinctive trilithons. I've been running tours here for a few years and, for me, nowhere sums up the magic and mystery of ancient Britain better than Stonehenge.

2 INSIDE THE CIRCLE

The main stones are fenced off, and you can't get very close – the only way to actually see inside the circle is on a special access tour, which you need to reserve in advance. It's also worth taking the informative audiotour. By early 2014, the site will hopefully also have a brand-new visitor centre which will provide background on the monument's history.

3 THE SLAUGHTER STONE

Look out for the Slaughter Stone, once thought to be a Neolithic altar for human sacrifice. In reality it's a toppled monolith; over the centuries iron ore has mixed with rain in holes in the stone to give the appearance of blood.

4 THE CURSUS AND THE AVENUE

I recommend this short walk to see the route to Stonehenge that Neolithic people would have used. Walk northeast along the bridleway from the car park to reach the Cursus, a long ditchlike earthwork that runs in an east–west line. Turn right to meet the Avenue, an ancient path leading back towards Stonehenge.

5 WOODHENGE AND THE BARROWS

About 2 miles northeast of the stone circle, Woodhenge is an even older site where archaeologists are still discovering new evidence. It was featured on a TV show in the US called *Secrets of Stonehenge*, so many people want to visit. In the area surrounding Woodhenge and Stonehenge, the many hillocks or 'barrows' are ancient burial mounds.

Bath Abbey

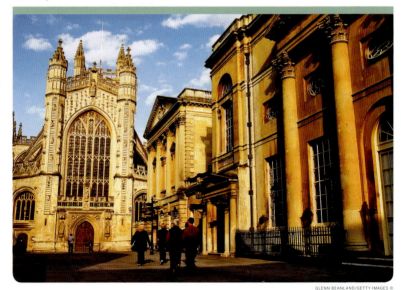

GLENN BEANLAND/GETTY IMAGES ©

◎ Sights

Roman Baths   Historic Site

(www.romanbaths.co.uk; Abbey Churchyard;
adult/child/family £12.75/8.50/36; ⊙9am-
10pm July & Aug, 9am-6pm Mar-Jun, Sep & Oct,
9.30am-5.30pm Nov-Feb) Ever since the
Romans arrived in Bath, life in the city has
revolved around the three geothermal
springs that bubble up near the abbey.
The Romans constructed a glorious
complex of bathhouses above these
thermal waters to take advantage of their
natural temperature, which emerges at a
constant 46°C.

The heart of the complex is the **Great
Bath**, a large lead-lined pool filled with
steaming, geothermally heated water
from the so-called 'Sacred Spring' to a
depth of 1.6m.

One of the most picturesque corners
of the complex is the 12th-century **King's
Bath**, built around the original sacred
spring; 1.5 million litres of hot water still
pour into the pool every day. Beneath
the Pump Room are the remains of the
Temple of Sulis-Minerva; look out for
the famous gilded head of Minerva herself
and the engraved Haruspex stone on
which the statue would originally have
stood.

The Baths get unbelievably busy; you
can usually avoid the worst crowds by
buying tickets online, visiting early on
a midweek morning, and by avoiding
July and August. Admission includes an
audioguide in eight languages, featuring
a special commentary by the bestselling
author Bill Bryson.

Royal Crescent   Street

Bath's grandest street is the Royal Crescent, a semicircular terrace of majestic
townhouses overlooking the green sweep
of Royal Victoria Park. Designed by John
Wood the Younger (1728–82) and built
between 1767 and 1775, the houses were
designed to appear perfectly symmetrical from the outside, but inside no two
houses on the Crescent are quite the
same.

For a glimpse into the splendour and
razzle-dazzle of Georgian life, head for **No
1 Royal Crescent** (http://no1royalcrescent.
org.uk; 1 Royal Cres; adult/child/family
£8.50/3.50/17; ⊙noon-5.30pm Mon, 10.30am-
5.30pm Tue-Sun), which has been restored
using only 18th-century materials.

BRITAIN & IRELAND BATH

Bath Abbey Church

(www.bathabbey.org; requested donation £2.50; ☉9.30am-6pm Mon, 9am-6pm Tue-Sat, 1-2.30pm & 4.30-5.30pm Sun) Looming above the centre of the city, Bath's huge abbey church was built between 1499 and 1616, making it the last great medieval church raised in England.

Holburne Museum Gallery

(www.holburne.org; Great Pulteney St; temporary exhibitions incur fee; ☉10am-5pm) FREE Fresh from a three-year refit, the museum houses an impressive roll call of works by artists including Turner, Stubbs, William Hoare and Thomas Gainsborough, as well as a fine collection of 18th-century majolica and porcelain.

Assembly Rooms Historic Building

(NT; www.nationaltrust.org.uk/bath-assembly-rooms; 19 Bennett St; adult/child £2/free; ☉10.30am-6pm) Opened in 1771, the city's glorious Assembly Rooms were where fashionable Bath socialites once gathered to waltz, play cards and listen to the latest chamber music. You're free to wander around the rooms, as long as they haven't been reserved for a special function; all are lit by their original 18th-century chandeliers.

Fashion Museum Museum

(www.fashionmuseum.co.uk; Assembly Rooms, Bennett St; adult/child £7.75/5.75; ☉10.30am-5pm) In the basement of the Assembly Rooms, this museum contains a wonderful collection of costumes worn from the 16th to late 20th centuries.

Jane Austen Centre Museum

(www.janeausten.co.uk; 40 Gay St; adult/child £7.45/4.25; ☉9.45am-5.30pm) Bath is known to many as a location in Jane Austen's novels, including *Persuasion* and *Northanger Abbey*. Though Austen only lived in Bath for five years from 1801 to 1806, she remained a regular visitor throughout her life. This museum houses a small collection of memorabilia relating to the writer's life in Bath, and costumed guides bring the era to life.

🛏 Sleeping

Halcyon Hotel ££

(☎01225-444100; www.thehalcyon.com; 2/3 South Pde; d £125-145; 🛜) Just what Bath needed – a smart, stylish city-centre hotel that doesn't break the bank. The drawbacks? Rooms are spread out over three floors and there's no lift.

Henry B&B ££

(☎01225-424052; www.thehenry.com; 6 Henry St; d £80-120, f £145-165) This tall, slim townhouse offers a good choice of clean, uncluttered rooms finished in crisp whites and smooth beiges.

Brooks Hotel ££

(☎01225-425543; www.brooksguesthouse.com; 1 & 1a Crescent Gardens; s £59-89, d £80-150, f £120-160; 🛜) On the west side of Bath, this townhouse blends heritage fixtures attractively with snazzy finishes. Parking's problematic.

🍴 Eating

Circus Modern British ££

(☎01225-466020; www.thecircuscafeandrestaurant.co.uk; 34 Brock St; mains lunch £5.50-10,

Thermae Bath Spa

Larking about in the Roman Baths might be off the agenda, but you can still sample the city's curative waters at **Thermae Bath Spa** (☎0844-888 0844; www.thermaebathspa.com; Bath St; ☉9am-9.30pm, last entry 7pm), where the old Cross Bath is now incorporated into an ultramodern shell of local stone and plate glass. The New Royal Bath ticket includes steam rooms, waterfall shower and a choice of bathing venues – including the open-air rooftop pool, where you can swim in the thermal waters with a backdrop of Bath's stunning cityscape.

dinner £11-14; ⏰10am-midnight Mon-Sat) Installed in a converted townhouse between the Circus and Royal Crescent, this is the model of a modern Brit bistro: chef Ali Golden has a taste for hearty dishes such as rabbit pie and roast guinea-fowl. Reserve ahead.

Marlborough Tavern   Pub ££

(📞01225-423731; www.marlborough-tavern. com; 35 Marlborough Buildings; mains £12-17) Bath isn't short on gastropubs, but the Marlborough is still very much top of the class. It's half cosy boozer, half contemporary bistro, with big wooden tables, deep seats, and a crackling fire on winter nights.

Demuth's   Vegetarian ££

(📞01225-446059; www.demuths.co.uk; 2 North Pde Passage; lunch £4.95-11, dinner £14.50-17; 🍴) Even the most committed of carnivores can't fail to fall for this long-established veggie restaurant, which consistently turns out some of the city's most creative food – from cheddar soufflé served with figs, walnut purée and spring greens, to a port-poached pear baked with fennel seeds and sheep's cheese.

Sotto Sotto   Italian ££

(📞01225-330236; www.sottosotto.co.uk; 10a North Pde; pasta £9, mains £13-17; ⏰noon-2.30pm & 5-10.30pm) Authentic Italian food served in a lovely cellar setting complete with barrel-brick roof.

Sally Lunn's   Cafe £

(4 North Pde Passage; lunch mains £5-6, dinner mains from £8) This fabulously frilly tearoom occupies one of Bath's oldest houses, and makes the perfect venue for classic cream tea (served in proper bone china), accompanied by finger sandwiches, dainty cakes and the trademark Sally Lunn's Bun.

ℹ️ Information

Bath Visitor Centre (www.visitbath.co.uk; Abbey Churchyard; ⏰9.30am-5pm Mon-Sat, 10am-4pm Sun) Sells the Bath City Card (£3), which is valid for three weeks and offers discounts at many local shops, restaurants and attractions.

ℹ️ Getting There & Away

Bus

Bath's **bus and coach station** (Dorchester St; ⏰9am-5pm Mon-Sat) is near the train station.

Train

Bath Spa station is at the end of Manvers St. Many services connect through Bristol (£9.90, 20 minutes, two or three per hour), especially to the north of England.

Cardiff Central (£18, one hour, hourly)

Exeter (£27.50, 1¼ hours, hourly)

London Paddington or Waterloo (£39, 1½ hours, half-hourly)

Glastonbury

A long-time bohemian haven and still a favourite hang-out for mystics and counter-cultural types of all descriptions, Glastonbury is best-known for its massive music **festival** (www.glastonburyfestivals.co.uk), held (nearly) every year on Michael Eavis' farm in nearby Pilton.

The town owes much of its spirtual notoriety to nearby **Glastonbury Tor** (NT; www.nationaltrust.org.uk) `FREE`, a grassy hump about a mile from town, topped by the ruins of St Michael's Church. According to local legend, the tor is said to be the mythical Isle of Avalon, King Arthur's last resting place. It's also allegedly one of the world's great spiritual nodes, marking the meeting point of many mystical lines of power known as ley-lines.

There is no train station in Glastonbury, but bus 376/377 runs to Wells (30 minutes, hourly Monday to Saturday, seven on Sunday) and Bristol (1¼ hours), and south to Street (15 minutes).

St Ives

POP 9870

Even if you've seen St Ives many times before, it's still hard not to be dazzled as you gaze across its jumble of slate roofs, church towers and turquoise bays. Once a busy pilchard harbour, St Ives later became the centre of Cornwall's arts scene in the 1920s and 1930s, and the town's cobbled streets are crammed with quirky galleries, cafes and restaurants.

◉ Sights

Tate St Ives   Gallery
(☎01736-796226; www.tate.org.uk/stives; Porthmeor Beach; adult/child £7/4.50, joint ticket with Barbara Hepworth Museum £10/7; ☺10am-5pm Mar-Oct, to 4pm Tue-Sun Nov-Feb) This far-westerly outpost of the Tate focuses mainly on the work of the artists of the so-called 'St Ives School'. Key works by Terry Frost, Patrick Heron, Naum Gabo, Ben Nicholson and Barbara Hepworth are all on show, as well as the naive paintings

Eden Project

If any one thing is emblematic of Cornwall's regeneration, it's the **Eden Project** (☎01726-811911; www.edenproject.com; adult/child £23.50/10.50; ☺10am-6pm Apr-Oct, to 4.30pm Nov-Mar). Ten years ago the site was an exhausted clay pit; a symbol of the county's industrial decline. Now it's home to the largest plant-filled greenhouses on the planet – a monumental education project about the natural world. Tropical, temperate and desert environments have been recreated inside the massive biomes, so a single visit carries you from the steaming rainforests of South America to the dry deserts of northern Africa.

of fisherman-turned-artist Alfred Wallis, who didn't start painting until the ripe old age of 67.

Barbara Hepworth Museum   Museum
(☎01736-796226; Barnoon Hill; adult/child £6/4, joint ticket with Tate St Ives £10/7; ☺10am-5pm Mar-Oct, 10am-4pm Tue-Sun Nov-Feb) Barbara Hepworth (1903–75) was one of the leading abstract sculptors of the 20th century, and a key figure in the St Ives art scene. Her studio on Barnoon Hill has remained almost untouched since her death, and the adjoining garden contains several of her most notable sculptures.

⌂ Sleeping

No 1 St Ives   B&B ££
(☎01736-799047; www.no1stives.co.uk; 1 Fern Glen; d £90-135; `P` `☎`) This renovated granite cottage bills itself as 'shabby chic', but it's nothing of the sort. It's a model of a modern B&B, and full of spoils – filtered water, goose-down duvets, iPod docks and White Company bathstuffs.

ANDREW HOLT/GETTY IMAGES ©

Little Leaf Guest House B&B **££**
(☏01736-795427; www.littleleafguesthouse.
co.uk; Park Ave; r £85-120; ☎) This five-room
B&B is uphill from town. Rooms are sweet
and simple, finished in creamy colours
and pine furniture. Ask for Room 2 or 5 if
you're a sucker for a sea view.

✖ Eating

**Porthminster Beach
Café** Bistro **£££**
(☏01736-795352; www.porthminstercafe.co.uk;
Porthminster Beach; lunch £10.50-16.50, dinner
£10-22; ◷9am-10pm) For a seaside lunch
there's nowhere better than this designer
beach cafe, with its gorgeous suntrap
terrace and Mediterranean-influenced
menu.

Blas Burgerworks Burgers **££**
(☏01736-797-272; www.blasburgerworks.co.uk;
The Warren; burgers £5-10; ◷noon-10pm; ♿)
⚑ Imaginative burger-joint with an eco
friendly, fair-trade, homemade manifesto.

ℹ Information

St Ives Tourist Office (☏01736-796297; www.
stivestic.co.uk; Street-an-Pol; ◷9am-5.30pm
Mon-Fri, 9am-5pm Sat, 10am-4pm Sun) Inside the
Guildhall.

ℹ Getting There & Away

Train

The gorgeous branch line from St Ives is worth
taking just for the coastal views: trains terminate
at St Erth (£3, 14 minutes, half-hourly), where
you can catch connections along the Penzance–
London Paddington main line.

St Michael's Mount

Looming from the waters of Mount's Bay
is the unmistakeable silhouette of **St
Michael's Mount** (NT; ☏01736-710507; www.
stmichaelsmount.co.uk; castle & gardens adult/
child £9.60/4.80; ◷house 10.30am-5.30pm
Sun-Fri late Mar-Oct, gardens Mon-Fri Apr-Jun,
Thu & Fri Jul-Sep), a dreamy abbey set on a
rocky island that's connected to the small
seaside town of Marazion by a cobbled
causeway. There's been a monastery on
the island since at least the 5th century,
but the present abbey was mostly built
during the 12th century by the Benedictine monks of Mont St Michel. It's now
owned by the National Trust.

You can catch a ferry (adult/child £2/1) at high tide from Marazion, about 3 miles from Penzance. At low tide you can walk across on the causeway, just as the monks and pilgrims did centuries ago.

The 513 bus runs three times daily from Penzance.

Land's End

Just nine miles from Penzance, Land's End is the most westerly point of mainland England, where cliffs plunge dramatically into the pounding Atlantic surf. The **Legendary Land's End** (www.landsend-landmark.co.uk; adult/child £10/7; ⊙10am-5pm Mar-Oct) theme park hasn't done much to enhance the view. Take our advice: skip the tacky multimedia shows and opt for an exhilarating clifftop stroll instead.

CENTRAL ENGLAND

Oxford

POP 134,300

Oxford is a privileged place, one of the world's most famous university towns.

The city is a wonderful place to ramble: the oldest of its 39 separate colleges date back almost 750 years, and little has changed inside the hallowed walls since then (with the notable exception of female admissions, which only began in 1878).

 Sights

Much of the centre of Oxford is taken up by graceful university buildings, each one individual in its appearance and academic specialities. Not all are open to the public. Check www.ox.ac.uk/colleges for full details.

Christchurch College   Notable Building
(www.chch.ox.ac.uk; St Aldate's; adult/child £8/6.50; ⊙9am-5pm Mon-Sat, 2-5pm Sun) The largest and grandest of all of Oxford's colleges, Christ Church is also its most

popular. The magnificent buildings, illustrious history and latter-day fame as a location for the Harry Potter films have tourists coming in droves.

Magdalen College   Notable Building
(www.magd.ox.ac.uk; High St; adult/child £5/4; ⊙noon-7pm) Set amid 40 hectares of lawns, woodlands, river walks and deer park, Magdalen (*mawd*-len), founded in 1458, is one of the wealthiest and most beautiful of Oxford's colleges.

Merton College   Notable Building
(www.merton.ox.ac.uk; Merton St; admission £2, guided tour £2; ⊙2-5pm Mon-Fri, 10am-5pm Sat & Sun, guided tour 45min) Founded in 1264, Merton is the oldest college and was the first to adopt collegiate planning, bringing scholars and tutors together into a formal community and providing a planned residence for them.

Bodleian Library   Library
(www.bodley.ox.ac.uk; Broad St; Divinity School adult/child £1/free, audioguide £2.50, library tours £7, 30 min tours £5, extended tour £13; ⊙9am-5pm Mon-Fri, to 4.30pm Sat, 11am-5pm Sun, library tours 10.30am, 11.30am, 1pm & 2pm Mon-Sat, 11.30am, 2pm & 3pm Sun) Oxford's Bodleian Library is one of the oldest public libraries in the world. Most of the

Punting

Punting is a quintessential Oxford experience. A punt is a flat-bottomed boat, propelled (if that's the word) with a pole instead of oars. Punts are available to rent (£13/15 per hour weekdays/weekends, £65 deposit, mid-March to mid-October, 10am to dusk), and hold five people including the punter. The most central location is **Magdalen Bridge Boathouse** (www.oxfordpunting.co.uk; High St; punting max 5 people per hr weekday/weekend £18/20, chauffeured boat max 4 people per 30 mins £25).

rest of the library is closed to visitors, but **library tours** allow access to the medieval Duke Humfrey's library.

Radcliffe Camera — Library

(Radcliffe Sq; extended tours £13) The Radcliffe Camera is the quintessential Oxford landmark and one of the city's most photographed buildings. Tours from the Bodleian Library take place on Wednesdays and Saturdays at 9.15am and most Sundays at 11.15am and 1.15pm, and last about an hour and a half.

Ashmolean Museum — Museum

(www.ashmolean.org; Beaumont St; ⏱10am-6pm Tue-Sun) FREE This is Britain's oldest public museum, and second in repute only to London's British Museum. Its collections, displayed in bright, spacious galleries within one of Britain's best examples of neo-Grecian architecture, span the world and include everything from Egyptian mummies and sarcophagi, Islamic and Chinese art, Japan's 'floating world' and examples of the earliest written languages to rare porcelain, tapestries and silverware, priceless musical instruments and extensive displays of European art (including works by Raphael and Michelangelo).

🛏 Sleeping

Bath Place Hotel — Boutique Hotel ££

(☎01865-791812; www.bathplace.co.uk; 4-5 Bath Pl, Holywell St; s/d from £95/120) Comprising several 17th-century weavers' cottages surrounding a tiny, plant-filled courtyard right in the shadow of New College, this is one of Oxford's more unusual hotels. Inside it's all creaky floors, exposed beams, canopied beds and soothing cream walls.

Ethos Hotel — Boutique Hotel ££

(☎01865-245800; www.ethoshotels.co.uk; 59 Western Rd; d from £125; @ 🛜) Hidden away off Abingdon Rd, this funky new hotel has bright, spacious rooms with bold, patterned wallpaper, enormous beds and marble bathrooms. It's aimed at independent travellers: you get a minikitchen with a microwave, and breakfast is delivered to your room in a basket.

🍴 Eating

Gee's — Modern British ££

(☎01865-553540; www.gees-restaurant.co.uk; 61 Banbury Rd; mains £12-19) Set in a Victorian conservatory, this top-notch restaurant is popular with the visiting parents of university students, thanks to its creative menu of modern British and European dishes. Book ahead.

Door 74 — Modern British ££

(☎01865-203374; www.door74.co.uk; 74 Cowley Rd; mains £10-14; ⏱noon-11pm Tue-Sat, 11am-4pm Sun) This cosy little place woos its fans with a rich mix of British and Mediterranean flavours and friendly service. The menu is limited and the tables tightly packed, but the food is consistently good and weekend brunches (full English breakfast, pancakes) supremely filling.

Atomic Burger — American £

(www.atomicburger.co.uk; 96 Cowley Rd; mains £5.25-11; ⏱10am-10.30pm) Atomic comes with the Fallout Challenge, which involves consuming a triple burger stack complete with fear-inducing ghost chilli hot sauce. Try the inventive Messy Jessie, Dead Elvis, the barbeque ribs and nachos and curly fries, all washed down with mega shakes.

🍷 Drinking & Nightlife

Turf Tavern — Pub

(4-5 Bath Pl; ⏱11am-11pm) Hidden away down a narrow alleyway, this tiny medieval pub is one of the town's best loved and bills itself as 'an education in intoxication' (this is also where president Bill Clinton 'did not inhale').

Bear — Pub

(6 Alfred St) Arguably the oldest pub in Oxford (there's been a pub on this site since 1242).

ℹ Information

Tourist Office (☎252200; www.visitoxfordandoxfordshire.com; 15-16 Broad St; ⏱9.30am-5pm Mon-Sat, 10am-3.30pm Sun, closes 30 mins later in winter)

RELIGIOUS IMAGES/UIG/GETTY IMAGES ©

⭐ Don't Miss
Blenheim Palace

One of the country's greatest stately homes, Blenheim Palace is a monumental baroque fantasy designed by Sir John Vanbrugh and Nicholas Hawksmoor between 1705 and 1722. Now a Unesco World Heritage site, it's home to the 11th Duke of Marlborough. Inside, Blenheim (*blen*-um) is stuffed with statues, tapestries, ostentatious furniture and giant oil paintings in elaborate gilt frames. Highlights include the **Great Hall**, a vast space topped by 20m-high ceilings adorned with images of the 1st duke in battle; the opulent **Saloon**, the most important public room; the three **state rooms** with their plush decor and priceless china cabinets; and the magnificent 55m **Long Library**. You can also visit the **Churchill Exhibition**, dedicated to the life, work and writings of Sir Winston, who was born at Blenheim in 1874. Outside, you can stroll through the lavish gardens.

Blenheim Place is near the town of Woodstock, a few miles northwest of Oxford.

NEED TO KNOW
www.blenheimpalace.com; adult/child £20/10; ⏰10.30am-5.30pm mid-Feb–Oct

ℹ Getting There & Away

Train

There are half-hourly services to London Paddington (£23, one hour) and roughly hourly trains to Birmingham (£16, 1¼ hours). Hourly services also run to Bath (£16, 1¼ hours) and Bristol (£22, one to two hours), but require a change at Didcot Parkway.

Stratford-upon-Avon

POP 22,187

The author of some of the most quoted lines in the English language. William Shakespeare was born in Stratford in 1564 and died here in 1616. The houses linked to his life form the centrepiece of a tourist attraction that verges on a cult of personality.

Detour:
The Cotswolds

A soft rural landscape, filled with glorious honey-coloured villages, old mansions, thatched cottages and atmospheric churches – welcome to the Cotswolds. If you've ever dreamed of falling asleep under English-rose wallpaper or lusted after a cream tea in the mid-afternoon, there's no finer place to fulfil your fantasies. This is prime tourist territory, however, and the most popular villages can be besieged by traffic in summer.

A handy gateway town is **Moreton-in-Marsh**: a bus service runs to/from Cheltenham (seven times daily, one hour, Monday to Saturday) via Stow-on-the-Wold (15 minutes), with two Sunday services from May to September; there are trains roughly every two hours to/from London Paddington (£26.90, one hour 40 minutes) via Oxford (£7.90, 40 minutes).

◎ Sights

Shakespeare Houses   Museum
(☏ 01789-204016; www.shakespeare.org.uk; all 5 properties adult/child £21.50/13.50, 3 houses in town £14/9; ⏰ 9am-5pm Apr-Oct, hours vary Nov-Mar) Five of the most important buildings associated with Shakespeare, all run by the Shakespeare Birthplace Trust, contain museums that form the core of the visitor experience at Stratford. You can buy individual tickets, but it's more cost-effective to buy a combination ticket, either covering the three houses in town, or all five properties.

Holy Trinity Church   Church
(☏ 01789-266316; www.stratford-upon-avon.org; Old Town; church admission free, Shakespeare's grave adult/child £1.50/50p; ⏰ 8.30am-6pm Mon-Sat, 12.30-5pm Sun Apr-Sep, shorter hours Oct-Mar) The final resting place of the Bard is said to be the most visited parish church in England. Inside are handsome 16th- and 17th-century tombs (particularly in the Clopton Chapel), some fabulous carvings on the choir stalls and, of course, the grave of William Shakespeare, with its ominous epitaph: 'cursed be he that moves my bones'.

🛏 Sleeping

**Church Street
Townhouse**   Boutique Hotel £££
(☏ 01789-262222; www.churchstreettownhouse. com; 16 Church St; r £110-180; 📶) The 12 rather decadent rooms at this exquisite boutique hotel are divine and very plush, some with free-standing bath and all with iPod dock, flatscreen TVs and luxurious furnishings. Rooms are pricier at weekends.

White Sails   Guesthouse ££
(☏ 01789-264326; www.white-sails.co.uk; 85 Evesham Rd; r from £95) Plush fabrics, framed prints, brass bedsteads and shabby-chic tables and lamps set the scene at this gorgeous, intimate guesthouse on the edge of the countryside.

✕ Eating & Drinking

Lambs   Modern European ££
(☏ 01789-292554; www.lambsrestaurant.co.uk; 12 Sheep St; mains £10.25-18.75; ⏰ lunch Wed-Sun, dinner daily) Lambs swaps Shakespeare chintz in favour of Venetian blinds and modern elegance, but throws in authentic 16th-century ceiling beams for good measure.

Edward Moon's   Modern British ££
(☏ 01789-267069; www.edwardmoon.com; 9 Chapel St; mains £10-15) Named after a famous travelling chef who cooked up the flavours of home for the British colonial service, this snug and just-refurbished eatery serves delicious, hearty English dishes, many livened up with herbs and spices from the East.

Dirty Duck
Pub

(Waterside) Officially called the 'Black Swan', this enchanting riverside alehouse is a favourite thespian watering hole, boasting a roll-call of former regulars (Olivier, Attenborough etc) that reads like a *Who's Who* of actors.

⭐ Entertainment

Royal Shakespeare Company
Theatre

(RSC; ☎ 0844 800 1110; www.rsc.org.uk; Waterside; tickets £8-38) You just can't come to Stratford without seeing one of the Bard's plays performed by the Royal Shakespeare Company at one of its two main theatres, the Royal Shakespeare Theatre and Swan Theatre on Waterside.

ℹ Information

Tourist Office (☎ 01789-264293; www.shakespeare-country.co.uk; 62 Henley St; 🕐10am-5pm, to 4pm winter)

ℹ Getting There & Away

From Stratford train station, London Midland runs to Birmingham (£6.80, one hour, hourly), Chiltern Railways runs to London Marylebone (£25, 2¼ hours, four daily).

Peak District National Park

Squeezed between the industrial Midlands to the south and the cities of Manchester and Sheffield to the west and east, the surprisingly rural **Peak District** (☎ 01629-816200; www.peakdistrict.gov.uk) is one of the finest areas in England for walking, cycling and other outdoor activities. Don't be misled by the name; there are few peaks, but plenty of wild moors, rolling farmland and deep valleys – plus hardy villages, prehistoric sites and limestone caves. The towns of Buxton to the west or Matlock to the east are good gateways, or you can stay right in the centre at Edale, Bakewell or Castleton.

The park's best-known attraction is **Chatsworth House** (☎ 01246-582204; www.chatsworth.org; house & gardens adult/child £15/9, gardens only £10/6, playground £5, park free; 🕐11am-5.30pm mid-Mar–late Dec, closed late Dec–mid-Mar), locally known as the 'Palace of the Peak'. This vast edifice has been occupied by the earls and dukes of Devonshire for centuries.

Shakespeare's birthplace, Stratford-upon-Avon

King's College Chapel, Cambridge

GRANT FAINT/GETTY IMAGES ©

While the core of the house dates from the 16th century, Chatsworth was altered and enlarged over the centuries. The current building has a Georgian feel, dating back to the last overhaul in 1820. Inside, the lavish apartments and mural-painted staterooms are packed with priceless paintings and period furniture, and outside there are 25 sq miles of grounds and ornamental gardens, some landscaped by Lancelot 'Capability' Brown.

EASTERN ENGLAND

Cambridge

POP 119,100

Drowning in exquisite architecture, steeped in history and tradition, and renowned for its quirky rituals, Cambridge is a university town extraordinaire.

◉ Sights

Cambridge University comprises 31 colleges, though not all are open to the public.

Trinity College Notable Building
(www.trin.cam.ac.uk; Trinity St; adult/child £1.50/1; ⏱10.30am-4.30pm) The largest of Cambridge's colleges, Trinity is entered through an impressive Tudor gateway first created in 1546. The **Great Court** is the largest of its kind in the world; to the right of the entrance is a small tree, planted in the 1950s and reputed to be a descendant of the apple tree made famous by Trinity alumnus Sir Isaac Newton.

King's College Chapel Church
(www.kings.cam.ac.uk/chapel; King's Pde; adult/child £7.50/free, evensong free; ⏱9.45am-4.30pm Mon, from 9.30am Tue-Sun, evensong 5.30pm Mon-Sat, 10.30am & 3.30pm Sun, term time only) Chances are you will already have seen it on a thousand postcards, tea towels and choral CDs before you catch your first glimpse of the grandiose King's College Chapel, but still it inspires awe. The vast 80m-long **fan-vaulted canopy** is the work of John Wastell and is the largest expanse of fan vaulting in the world.

The thickly carved wooden stalls are a stage for the chapel's world-famous **choir**. You can hear them in full voice during the magnificent **evensong**.

The Backs   Park

Behind the grandiose facades, stately courts and manicured lawns of the city's central colleges lies a series of gardens and parklands butting up against the river.

The fanciful **Bridge of Sighs** (built in 1831) at St John's is best observed from the stylish bridge designed by Christopher Wren just to the south. Most curious of all is the flimsy-looking wooden construction joining the two halves of Queen's College, known as the **Mathematical Bridge**, first built in 1749.

Fitzwilliam Museum   Museum

(www.fitzmuseum.cam.ac.uk; Trumpington St; admission by donation, guided tour £5; ⊙10am-5pm Tue-Sat, noon-5pm Sun) Fondly dubbed 'the Fitz' by locals, this colossal neoclassical pile was one of the first public art museums in Britain, built to house the fabulous treasures that the seventh Viscount Fitzwilliam had bequeathed to his old university. You can join a one-hour **guided tour** of the museum on Saturdays at 2.30pm.

🛏 Sleeping

Hotel Felix   Boutique Hotel £££

(☎01223-277977; www.hotelfelix.co.uk; Whitehouse Lane, Huntingdon Rd; s/d from £165/200; P@🖼) This luxurious boutique hotel occupies a lovely grey-brick Victorian villa in landscaped grounds a mile from the city centre. Follow Castle St and then Huntingdon Rd out of the city for about 1.5 miles.

Benson House   B&B ££

(☎01223-311594; www.bensonhouse.co.uk; 24 Huntingdon Rd; d from £90; P🖼) Just a 15-minute walk from the city centre, the rooms at this B&B range from monochrome minimalism to muted classical elegance, and breakfast includes the less usual addition of kippers.

✗ Eating

Oak Bistro   Modern British ££

(☎01223-323361; www.theoakbistro.co.uk; 6 Lensfield Rd; mains £12-20, 2-/3-course set lunch £12/15; ⊙Mon-Sat) This great local favourite serves up simple, classic dishes with modern flair, such as tuna nicoise salad and slow-roasted lamb.

Hakka   Chinese ££

(☎01223-568988; www.hak-ka.co.uk; 24 Milton Rd; mains £7.50-11.50; ⊙closed lunch; 🖼) Chef Daniel's mother has taught him the secrets of Hakka cooking and once you've tasted his signature salt and chilli chicken, you'll be inclined to give her a hug and a kiss.

Chop House   Traditional British ££

(www.cambscuisine.com/cambridge-chop-house; 1 Kings Pde; mains £9.50-24) If you're craving sausage and mash, a sizzling steak, suet pudding, fish pie or potted ham, look no further. Sister restaurant **St John's Chop House** (www.cambscuisine.com/st-johns-chop-house; 21-24 Northampton St) has the same menu and is located near the rear entrance to St John's College.

🍷 Drinking & Nightlife

Eagle   Pub

(Bene't St) Cambridge's most famous pub has loosened the tongues and pickled the grey cells of many an illustrious academic in its day; among them are Nobel Prize–winning scientists Crick and Watson, who discussed their research into DNA here. It's a traditional 17th-century pub with five cluttered, cosy rooms and good pub grub, the back one once popular with WWII airmen, who left their signatures on the ceiling.

Maypole   Pub

(www.maypolefreehouse.co.uk; 20a Portugal Pl) This friendly, popular pub has hit a winning formula: serve a good selection of real ales, throw in some great cocktails, and host a successful beer festival in 2012 (set to become an annual event).

ℹ Information

Tourist Office (☎0871-266 8006; www.visitcambridge.org; Old Library, Wheeler St; ⊙10am-5.30pm Mon-Fri, to 5pm Sat, 11am-3pm Sun) Pick up a guide to the Cambridge colleges

(£4.99) in the gift shop or a leaflet (£1.20) outlining two city walks. Download audio tours from the website or book slots on a plethora of tours.

ℹ️ Getting There & Away

Destinations:

Birmingham New Street (£30, three hours, hourly)

Ely (£4,15 minutes, three hourly)

London King's Cross (£19, 50 minutes to 1¼ hours)

NORTHEAST ENGLAND

Haworth

POP 6100

In the canon of English literature, it seems that only Shakespeare himself is held in higher esteem than the beloved Brontë sisters, judging by the eight million visitors a year who come to this hardy northern town where the classics *Jane Eyre* and *Wuthering Heights* were born.

◎ Sights

Brontë Parsonage Museum   Museum

(www.bronte.info; Church St; adult/child £7/3.60; ⏰10am-5.30pm Apr-Sep, 11am-5pm Oct-Mar) Set in a pretty garden overlooking the church and graveyard, the house where the Brontë family lived from 1820 till 1861 is now a museum. The rooms are meticulously furnished and decorated exactly as they were in the Brontë era, including Charlotte's bedroom, her clothes and her writing paraphernalia.

ℹ️ Information

Tourist Office (☎01535-642329; www.haworth-village.org.uk; 2-4 West Lane; ⏰9am-5.30pm Apr-Sep, to 5pm Oct-Mar)

ℹ️ Getting There & Away

From Leeds, the easiest approach is via Keighley, which is on the Metro rail network. However,

the most interesting way to get from Keighley to Haworth is via the **Keighley & Worth Valley Railway** (www.kwvr.co.uk; adult/child return £10/5, Day Rover £15/7.50).

York

POP 181,100

Nowhere in northern England says 'medieval' quite like York, a city of extraordinary historical wealth that has lost little of its preindustrial lustre. Its spider's web of narrow streets is enclosed by a magnificent circuit of 13th-century walls and the city's rich heritage is woven into virtually every brick and beam.

◎ Sights

If you plan on visiting a lot of sights, you can save yourself some money by using a **York Pass** (www.yorkpass.com; 1/2/3 days adult £34/48/58, child £18/22/26). It grants you free access to more than 70 pay-to-visit sights in Yorkshire, including all the major attractions in York.

York Minster   Church

(www.yorkminster.org; Deangate; adult/child £9/ free, combined ticket incl tower £14/3.50; ⏰9am-5.30pm Mon-Sat Apr-Oct, 9.30am-5.30pm Mon-Sat Nov-Mar, noon-5.30pm Sun year-round) Not content with being Yorkshire's most important historic building, the awe-inspiring York Minster is also the largest medieval cathedral in all of Northern Europe. Seat of the archbishop of York, primate of England, it is second in importance only to Canterbury, home of the primate of *all* England – the separate titles were created to settle a debate over whether York or Canterbury was the true centre of the English church.

Jorvik Viking Centre   Museum

(www.jorvik-viking-centre.co.uk; Coppergate; adult/child £9.25/6.25; ⏰10am-5pm Apr-Oct, to 4pm Nov-Mar) This is a smells-and-all reconstruction of the Viking settlement that was unearthed here during excavations in the late 1970s, brought to you courtesy of a 'time-car' monorail that transports you through 9th-century Jorvik (the Viking name for York).

York

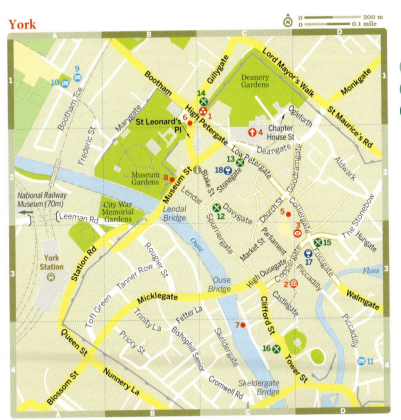

York

◎ Sights
1	City Walls	C1
2	Jorvik Viking Centre	C3
3	Shambles	D3
4	York Minster	C2

✛ Activities, Courses & Tours
5	Ghost Hunt of York	C2
6	York Citysightseeing	B1
7	YorkBoat	C4
8	Yorkwalk	B2

⊟ Sleeping
9	Abbeyfields	A1
10	Elliotts B&B	A1
11	Hotel 53	D4

✕ Eating
12	Bettys	C2
13	Bettys Stonegate	C2
14	Cafe No 8	C1
15	J Baker's Bistro Moderne	D3
16	Olive Tree	C4

⊖ Drinking & Nightlife
17	Blue Bell	D3
18	Ye Olde Starre	C2

City Walls Archaeological Site
(◷ 8am-dusk) **FREE** If the weather's good, don't miss the chance to walk the city walls, which follow the line of the original Roman walls – it gives a whole new perspective on the city. The full circuit is 4.5 miles (allow 1½ to two hours); if you're pushed for time, the short stretch from Bootham Bar to Monk Bar is worth doing for the views of the minster.

National Railway Museum   Museum

(www.nrm.org.uk; Leeman Rd; ⏱10am-6pm) **FREE** York's National Railway Museum – the biggest in the world, with more than 100 locomotives – is so well presented and full of fascinating stuff that it's interesting even to folk whose eyes don't mist over at the thought of a 4-6-2 A1 Pacific class chuffing into a tunnel.

Shambles   Street

(www.yorkshambles.com) The narrow, cobbled lane known as the Shambles, lined with 15th-century Tudor buildings that overhang so much they seem to meet above your head, is the most visited street in Europe. It takes its name from the Saxon word *shamel*, meaning 'slaughterhouse' – in 1862 there were 26 butcher shops on this one street.

👉 Tours

Ghost Hunt of York   Walking Tour

(www.ghosthunt.co.uk; adult/child £5/3; ⏱tours 7.30pm) Award-winning and highly entertaining 75-minute tour laced with authentic ghost stories; the kids will just love this one. Begins at the Shambles, whatever the weather (they never cancel). No need to book.

Yorkwalk   Walking Tour

(www.yorkwalk.co.uk; adult/child £5.50/3.50; ⏱tours 10.30am & 2.15pm Feb-Nov) Offers a series of two-hour themed walks on an ever-growing list of themes, from the classics – Roman York, the snickelways (alleys) and city walls – to specialised walks on chocolates and sweets, women in York, secret York and the inevitable graveyard, coffin and plague tour. Walks depart from Museum Gardens Gate on Museum St; no need to book.

YorkBoat   Boat Tour

(www.yorkboat.co.uk; King's Staith; adult/child £7.50/3.50; ⏱tours 10.30am, noon, 1.30pm & 3pm) Runs one-hour cruises on the River Ouse departing from King's Staith (and Lendal Bridge 10 minutes later).

York Citysightseeing   Bus Tour

(www.city-sightseeing.com; day ticket adult/child £10/4; ⏱9am-5pm) Hop-on/hop-off route with 16 stops, calling at all the main sights.

🛏 Sleeping

Beds are tough to find midsummer, even with the inflated prices of the high season. The tourist office's accommodation booking service charges £4.

Abbeyfields   B&B ££

(📞01904-636471; www.abbeyfields.co.uk; 19 Bootham Tce; s/d from £49/79; 📶) Expect a warm welcome and thoughtfully arranged bedrooms here, with chairs and bedside lamps for comfortable reading.

York Minster (p118), York
STEVE ALLEN/GETTY IMAGES ©

Elliotts B&B
B&B ££

(📞01904-623333; www.elliottshotel.co.uk;
2 Sycamore Pl; s/d from £55/80; P @ 🛜)
A beautifully converted 'gentleman's
residence', Elliotts leans towards the
boutique end of the guesthouse market
with stylish and elegant rooms, and high-
tech touches such as flatscreen TVs and
free wi-fi.

Hotel 53
Hotel ££

(📞01904-559000; www.hotel53.com; 53
Piccadilly; r from £95; P 🛜) Modern and
minimalist, but very central with secure
parking just across the street.

🍴 Eating

J Baker's Bistro
Moderne
Modern British ££

(📞01904-622688; www.jbakers.co.uk; 7 Fossgate; 2-/3-course lunch £20/25, dinner £25/30;
🕐lunch & dinner Tue-Sat) Superstar chef
Jeff Baker left a Michelin star in Leeds to
pursue his own vision of Modern British
cuisine here. The ironic '70s-style decor
matches his gourmet interpretations of
retro classics – try Olde York cheese and
spinach pasties with dried grapes, capers
and aged balsamic vinegar, or a Whitby
crab cocktail with apple 'textures' and
curry-spiced granola.

Cafe No 8
Bistro £

(📞01904-653074; www.cafeno8.co.uk; 8 Gilly-
gate; mains £7-10, 2-course lunch £14; 🕐11am-
10pm Mon-Fri, 10am-10pm Sat & Sun; 🛜🚼) 🌱
A cool little bistro with modern artwork
mimicking the Edwardian stained glass
at the front, No 8 offers a day-long menu
of classic bistro dishes using fresh local
produce, including smoked duck breast
salad, and cassoulet of Yorkshire pork and
chorizo. Booking recommended.

Bettys
Cafe ££

(www.bettys.co.uk; St Helen's Sq; mains £6-13,
afternoon tea £18; 🕐9am-9pm; 🚼) Afternoon
tea, old-school style, with white-aproned
waitresses, linen tablecloths and a
teapot collection ranged along the walls.
Betty's younger sister, **Bettys Stonegate**
(www.bettys.co.uk; 46 Stonegate; mains £6-13;
🕐10am-5.30pm Sun-Fri, 9am-5.30pm Sat; 🚼),

is more demure and less crowded, and
just as good.

Olive Tree
Mediterranean ££

(📞01904-624433; www.theolivetreeyork.co.uk;
10 Tower St; mains £10-17; 🕐lunch & dinner)
Local produce gets a Mediterranean
makeover at this bright and breezy bistro
with a view across the street to Clifford's
Tower.

🍷 Drinking & Nightlife

Blue Bell
Pub

(53 Fossgate) This is what a real English
pub looks like – a tiny, wood-panelled
room with a smouldering fireplace, decor
(and beer and smoke stains) dating from
c 1798, a pile of ancient board games in
the corner, friendly and efficient bar staff,
and Timothy Taylor and Black Sheep ales
on tap.

Ye Olde Starre
Pub

(40 Stonegate) Licensed since 1644, this
is York's oldest pub – a warren of small
rooms and a small beer garden, with a
half-dozen real ales on tap.

ℹ️ Information

York Visitor Centre (📞01904-550099; www.
visityork.org; 1 Museum St; 🕐9am-6pm Mon-Sat,
10am-5pm Sun Apr-Sep, shorter hours Oct-Mar)

ℹ️ Getting There & Away

York is a major railway hub with frequent direct
services to Birmingham (£45, 2¼ hours),
Newcastle (£15, one hour), Leeds (£11, 30
minutes), Londons King's Cross (£80, two hours),
Manchester (£15, 1½ hours) and Scarborough
(£10, 50 minutes). There are also trains to
Cambridge (£60, 2¾ hours), changing at
Peterborough.

Around York
CASTLE HOWARD

Stately homes may be two a penny in England, but you'll have to try hard to find one
as breathtakingly stately as **Castle Howard**
(www.castlehoward.co.uk; adult/child house &
grounds £13/7.50, grounds only £8.50/6;

If You Like...
Cathedrals

Alongside York Minster (p118), Winchester (p101) and Canterbury (p97), Britain is awash with many stunning houses of worship.

1 ELY CATHEDRAL
(www.elycathedral.org; tower tour Mon-Sat £6, Sun £8.50; ⏱7am-6.30pm, evensong 5.30pm Mon-Sat, 4pm Sun, choral service 10.30am Sun) Known as the 'Ship of the Fens', this Romanesque wonder looms from flat fields 17 miles north of Cambridge. Its 12th-century architecture has made it a popular film location: you may recognise it from *Elizabeth: The Golden Age* and *The Other Boleyn Girl*.

2 SALISBURY CATHEDRAL
(☎01722-555120; www.salisburycathedral.org.uk; requested donation adult/child £5/3; ⏱7.15am-6.15pm) An icon of English Gothic, famous for its 123m-high spire (the tallest in England). Needless to say, the views from the top are amazing – if you can handle the 332 vertigo-inducing steps. The 90-minute tours need to be booked in advance. It's about 30 miles east of Winchester.

3 DURHAM CATHEDRAL
(www.durhamcathedral.co.uk; donation requested, guided tours adult/child £4/free; ⏱7.30am-6pm, tours 10.30am, 11am & 2pm Mon-Sat, evensong 5.15pm Mon-Sat, 3.30pm Sun) This exquisite cathedral 18 miles south of Newcastle is the definitive structure of the Anglo-Norman Romanesque style and, since 1986, a Unesco World Heritage site. Look out for the tomb of the Venerable Bede, England's earliest historian.

4 WELLS CATHEDRAL
(www.wellscathedral.org.uk; Cathedral Green; requested donation adult/child £6/3; ⏱7am-7pm) Known for its unique 'scissor arches' (which were added to counter the subsidence of the central tower), this Gothic cathedral utterly dominates England's smallest city. Wells is about 21 miles northeast of Bath.

⏱house 11am-4.30pm Apr-Oct, grounds 10am-5.30pm Mar-Oct & 1st 3 weeks Dec, 10am-4pm Nov-Feb), a work of theatrical grandeur and audacity, and one of the world's most beautiful buildings. It's instantly recognisable from its starring role in the 1980s TV series *Brideshead Revisited* and more recently in the 2008 film of the same name.

Inside, the great house is full of treasures – the breathtaking **Great Hall** with its soaring Corinthian pilasters, Pre-Raphaelite **stained glass** in the chapel, and corridors lined with classical antiquities. Outside, as you wander the grounds (populated by peacocks, naturally), views reveal Vanbrugh's playful **Temple of the Four Winds** and Hawksmoor's stately **mausoleum**, or wider vistas over the surrounding hills.

Castle Howard is 15 miles northeast of York. There are several organised tours from York – check with the tourist office. By public transport, Yorkshire Coastliner bus 840 (40 minutes from York, one daily) links Leeds, York, Castle Howard and Whitby.

Hadrian's Wall

Built in AD 122 to mark the edge of the Roman Empire, this 73-mile coast-to-coast barrier across England remains a major feature on the landscape nearly 2000 years later. Named in honour of the emperor who ordered it built, Hadrian's Wall is one of the Roman Empire's greatest engineering projects, a spectacular testament to ambition and the practical Roman mind. It was built to to protect Roman-occupied Britain from the unruly Pictish tribes to the north, in the area we know now as Scotland. When completed, the mammoth structure ran from the Solway Firth (west of Carlisle) to the mouth of the Tyne (east of Newcastle).

Several of the original forts which once guarded the wall are still in fairly good repair, including the ones at **Chesters**

(EH; ☎01434-681379; Chollerford; adult/child £4.80/2.40; ⊙10am-6pm Apr-Sep) near Chollerford, Vindolanda near Bardon Mill and Housesteads, between Bardon Mill and Haltwhistle.

Most local tourist offices have reams of information on the wall and the **Hadrian's Wall Path** (www.nationaltrail.co.uk/hadrianswall) which runs along almost the entire length of the wall. For general information, see the informative website at www.hadrians-wall.org.

❶ Getting There & Away

The Newcastle–Carlisle train line runs parallel to the wall a mile or two to the south, with stations at Hexham, Haydon Bridge, Bardon Mill, Haltwhistle and Brampton. There are hourly buses between Carlisle and Newcastle, via most of the same towns.

From June to September the hail-and-ride Hadrian's Wall Bus (number AD 122 – geddit?) shuttles between all the major sites, towns and villages along the way.

NORTHWEST ENGLAND

Manchester

POP 394,270

Even accounting for northern bluster, the uncrowned capital of the north is well deserving of the title. And while history and heritage make the city interesting, its distractions of pure pleasure make Manchester fun: you can dine, drink and dance yourself into happy oblivion in the swirl of hedonism that is one of Manchester's most cherished characteristics.

◎ Sights

CITY CENTRE

Museum of Science & Industry   Museum
(MOSI; ☎0161-832 2244; www.msim.org.uk; Liverpool Rd; charges vary for special exhibitions; ⊙10am-5pm) **FREE** If there's anything you want to know about the Industrial (and postindustrial) Revolution and Manchester's key role in it, you'll find the answers among the collection of steam engines and locomotives, factory machinery from the mills, and the excellent exhibition telling the story of Manchester from the sewers up.

People's History Museum   Museum
(☎0161-838 9190; www.phm.org.uk; Left Bank, Bridge St; ⊙10am-5pm) **FREE** The story of Britain's 200-year march to democracy is told in all its pain and pathos at this superb museum, housed in a refurbished Edwardian pumping station.

BRITAIN & IRELAND MANCHESTER

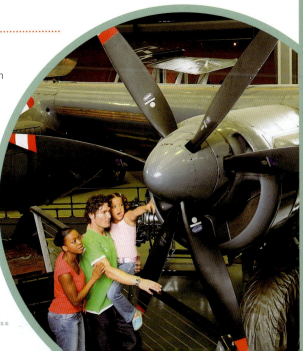

Museum of Science & Industry, Manchester
VISITBRITAIN/PAWEL LIBERA/GETTY IMAGES ©

Hadrian's Wall

Rome's Final Frontier

Of all Britain's Roman ruins, Emperor Hadrian's 2nd-century wall, cutting across northern England from the Irish Sea to the North Sea, is by far the most spectacular; Unesco awarded it world cultural heritage status in 1987.

We've picked out the highlights, one of which is the prime remaining Roman fort on the wall, Housesteads, which we've reconstructed here.

Housesteads' granaries
Nothing like the clever underground ventilation system, which kept vital supplies of grain dry in Northumberland's damp and drizzly climate, would be seen again in these parts for 1500 years.

Milecastle

North Gate

Interval Tower

Birdoswald Roman Fort
Explore the longest intact stretch of the wall, scramble over the remains of a large fort then head indoors to wonder at a full-scale model of the wall at its zenith. Great fun for the kids.

Housesteads Roman Fort
See Illustration Right

Chesters Roman Fort
Built to keep watch over a bridge spanning the River North Tyne, Britain's best-preserved Roman cavalry fort has a terrific bathhouse, essential if you have months of nippy northern winter ahead.

Hexham Abbey
This may be the finest non-Roman sight near Hadrian's Wall, but the 7th-century parts of this magnificent church were built with stone quarried by the Romans for use in their forts.

Housesteads' hospital
Operations performed at the hospital would have been surprisingly effective, even without anaesthetics; religious rituals and prayers to Aesculapius, the Roman god of healing, were possibly less helpful for a hernia or appendicitis.

Housesteads' latrines
Communal toilets were the norm in Roman times and Housesteads' are remarkably well preserved – fortunately no traces remain of the vinegar-soaked sponges that were used instead of toilet paper.

QUICK WALL FACTS & FIGURES
Latin name Vallum Aelium
Length 73.5 miles (80 Roman miles)
Construction date AD 122–128
Manpower for construction
Three legions (around 16,000 men)
Features At least 16 forts, 80 milecastles, 160 turrets
Did you know Hadrian's wasn't the only wall in Britain – the Antonine Wall was built across what is now central Scotland in the AD 140s, but it was abandoned soon after

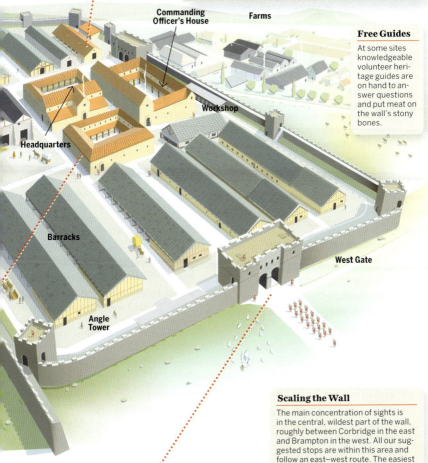

Commanding Officer's House

Farms

Free Guides
At some sites knowledgeable volunteer heritage guides are on hand to answer questions and put meat on the wall's stony bones.

Workshop

Headquarters

Barracks

West Gate

Angle Tower

Scaling the Wall
The main concentration of sights is in the central, wildest part of the wall, roughly between Corbridge in the east and Brampton in the west. All our suggested stops are within this area and follow an east–west route. The easiest way to travel is by car, scooting along the B6318, but special bus AD122 will also get you there. Hiking along the designated Hadrian's Wall Path (84 miles) allows you to appreciate the achievement up close.

Housesteads' gatehouses
Unusually at Housesteads neither of the gates faces the enemy, as was the norm at a Roman fort – builders aligned them east-west. Ruts worn by cart wheels are still visible in the stone.

Angel Of The North

This extraordinary, gigantic statue of a human frame with wings looms over the main A1 highway about 5 miles south of Newcastle. At 20m high, 200 tonnes in weight and with a wingspan wider than a Boeing 767, it's Antony Gormley's best-known sculpture and – thanks to all those passing cars – the most viewed piece of public art in the country.

You can walk right up to the base of the statue, and feel absolutely dwarfed.

National Football Museum   Museum
(📞 0161-605 8200; www.nationalfootball museum.com; Corporation St, Urbis, Cathedral Gardens; ⏰10am-5pm Mon-Sat, 11am-5pm Sun) It's the world's most popular game and Manchester is home to both the world's most popular and the world's richest teams, so it makes sense that a museum dedicated to the global charms of football should find its home here.

Manchester Art Gallery   Gallery
(📞0161-235 8888; www.manchestergalleries. org; Mosley St; ⏰10am-5pm Tue-Sun) FREE A superb collection of British art and a hefty number of European masters are on display at the city's top gallery.

SALFORD QUAYS

It's a cinch to get here from the city centre via Metrolink (£2).

Imperial War Museum North   Museum
(📞0161-836 4000; www.iwm.org.uk/north; Trafford Wharf Rd; ⏰10am-5pm) FREE War museums generally appeal to those with a fascination with military hardware and battle strategy (toy soldiers optional), but Daniel Libeskind's visually stunning Imperial War Museum North takes a radically different approach. The exhibits cover the main conflicts of the 20th century

through a broad selection of displays, but the really effective bit comes every half-hour when the entire exhibition hall goes dark and one of three 15-minute films (*Children and War, The War at Home* or *Weapons of War*) is projected throughout. Take the Metrolink to Harbour City or MediaCityUK.

The Lowry   Arts Centre
(📞0161-876 2020; www.thelowry.com; Pier 8, Salford Quays; ⏰11am-8pm Tue-Fri, 10am-8pm Sat, 11am-6pm Sun & Mon) Looking more like a shiny steel ship than an arts centre, the Lowry is the quays' most notable success. The complex is home to more than 300 paintings and drawings by northern England's favourite artist, LS Lowry (1887–1976), who was born in nearby Stretford.

Old Trafford   Stadium
(📞0870 442 1994; www.manutd.com; Sir Matt Busby Way; ⏰9.30am-5pm) Home of the world's most famous club, the Old Trafford stadium is both a theatre and a temple for its millions of fans worldwide. The **tour** (adult/child £12.50/8.50; ⏰every 10min except match days 9.40am-4.30pm) includes a seat in the stands, a peek at the players' lounge and a walk down the tunnel to the pitchside dugout. The **museum** (adult/child £9/7; ⏰9.30am-5pm) has a comprehensive history of the club.

🛏 Sleeping

Velvet Hotel   Boutique Hotel ££
(📞0161-236 9003; www.velvetmanchester.com; 2 Canal St; r from £99; 📶) Nineteen beautiful bespoke rooms, each oozing style: there's the sleigh bed in Room 24, the double bath of Room 34, and the saucy framed photographs of a stripped-down David Beckham (this is Gay Village, after all!).

Abode   Hotel ££
(📞0161-247 7744; www.abodehotels.co.uk; 107 Piccadilly St; r from £75; @ 📶) Modern British style is the catchphrase at this converted textile factory. The original fittings have been combined successfully with 61 bedrooms divided into four categories of ever-increasing luxury: Comfortable, Desirable, Enviable and Fabulous.

Roomzzz
Apartment ££

(☎ 0161-236 2121; www.roomzzz.co.uk; 36 Princess St; r £59-169; @ ☎) The inelegant name belies the designer digs inside this beautifully restored Grade II building, which features serviced apartments equipped with a kitchen and the latest connectivity gadgetry, including sleek iMac computers and free wi-fi throughout.

✖ Eating

Australasia
Modern Australian ££

(☎ 0161-831 0288; www.australasia.uk.com; 1 The Avenue, Spinningfields; mains £13-30, 2-/3-/4-course lunch £11/15/20) What should you do with the dusty old basement archive of the *Manchester Evening News?* Convert it into the city centre's best new restaurant, of course. The menu combines Pacific Rim cuisine with flavours of Southeast Asia.

Oast House
International ££

(☎ 0161-829 3830; www.theoasthouse.uk.com; Crown Sq, Spinningfields; mains £9-15) An oast house is a 16th-century kiln used to dry out hops as part of the beer-making process, but in Manchester, it means Tim Bacon's exciting new BBQ restaurant.

Sam's Chop House
British £

(☎ 0161-834 3210; www.samschophouse.co.uk; Back Pool Fold, Chapel Walks, off Cross St; mains £6-8) Arguably the city's top gastropub, Sam's is a Victorian classic that serves dishes straight out of a Dickens novel: the highlight is the crispy corned beef hash cake, which is salt-cured for 10 days on the premises. The owners also run **Mr Thomas' Chop House** (52 Cross St; mains £10).

🍷 Drinking & Nightlife

Bluu
Bar

(☎ 0161-839 7740; www.bluu.co.uk; Smithfield Market Buildings, Thomas St; ⏰ noon-midnight Sun-Mon, to 1am Tue-Thu, to 2am Fri & Sat) Bluu is cool, comfortable and comes with a great terrace on which to enjoy a pint and listen to music selected by folks with really good taste.

Britons Protection
Pub

(☎ 0161-236 5895; 50 Great Bridgewater St; mains £8) Whisky – 200 different kinds of it – is the beverage of choice at this liver-threatening, proper English pub that also does Tudor-style meals (boar, venison and the like; mains £8).

Lass O'Gowrie
Pub

(☎ 0161-273 6932; 36 Charles St; meals £6) A Victorian classic, off Princess St, that brews its own beer in the basement.

❶ Information

Tourist Office (www.visitmanchester.com; Piccadilly Plaza, Portland St; guided tours adult/ child £6/5; ⏰ 10am-5.15pm Mon-Sat, 10am-4.30pm Sun) Tours daily.

❶ Getting There & Away

Air

Manchester Airport (☎ 0161-489 3000; www.manchesterairport.co.uk), south of the city, is the largest airport outside London and is served by 13 locations throughout Britain as well as over 50 international destinations.

Train

Manchester Piccadilly is the main station for trains to and from the rest of the country.

Liverpool Lime Street (£11, 45 minutes, half-hourly)

London Euston (£73.20, three hours, seven daily)

Newcastle (£54.20, three hours, six daily)

....

Chester

Marvellous Chester is one of English history's greatest gifts to the contemporary visitor. Its red-sandstone wall, which today gift-wraps a tidy collection of Tudor and Victorian buildings, was built during Roman times, and during the Middle Ages Chester grew into the most important port in the northwest.

◎ Sights

City Walls
Landmark

 A good way to get a sense of Chester's unique character is to walk the

Old Trafford (p126), Manchester

DAVID C TOMLINSON/GETTY IMAGES ©

2-mile circuit along the walls that surround the historic centre.

At **Eastgate**, you can see the most famous **clock** in England after London's Big Ben, built for Queen Victoria's Diamond Jubilee in 1897. At the southeastern corner of the walls are the **wishing steps**, added in 1785; local legend claims that if you can run up and down these uneven steps while holding your breath your wish will come true.

Just inside Southgate is the 1664 **Bear & Billet** (http://bearandbillet.com; Southgate) pub, Chester's oldest timber-framed building and once a tollgate into the city.

Rows   Architecture

Chester's other great draw is the Rows, a series of two-level galleried arcades along the four streets that fan out in each direction from the **Central Cross**. The architecture is a handsome mix of Victorian and Tudor (original and mock) buildings that house a fantastic collection of individually owned shops.

Dewa Roman Experience   Museum

(☎01244-343 407; www.dewaromanexperience.co.uk; Pierpoint Lane; adult/child £4.95/3.25;

⊙9am-5pm Mon-Sat, 10am-5pm Sun) Walk through a reconstructed Roman street to reveal what Roman life was like.

❶ Information

Tourist Office (☎01244-402111; www.visitchester.com; Town Hall, Northgate St; ⊙9am-5.30pm Mon-Sat, 10am-4pm Sun May-Oct, 10am-5pm Mon-Sat Nov-Apr)

❶ Getting There & Away

The train station is about a mile from the city centre via Foregate St and City Rd, or Brook St.

Liverpool (£6.20, 45 minutes, hourly)

London Euston (£73.20, 2½ hours, hourly)

Manchester (£11.30, one hour, hourly)

Liverpool

POP 469,020

A hardscrabble town with a reputation for wit and an obsessive love of football, Liverpool also has an impressive cultural heritage: it has more listed museums than any other outside London, has recently undergone an impressive program of urban regeneration and its collection of museums and galleries is easily among the best in the country. And then, of course, there's the Beatles...

The main attractions are Albert Dock (west of the city centre), and the trendy Ropewalks area (south of Hanover St and west of the two cathedrals).

⊙ Sights

True Beatles fans will also undoubtedly want to visit the National Trust–owned **Mendips**, the home where John lived with his Aunt Mimi from 1945 to 1963, and **20 Forthlin Road**, where Paul grew up. You can only do so by prebooked **tour** (☏0151-427 7231; adult/child £16.80/3.15; ☺10.30am & 11.20am Wed-Sun Easter-Oct), from outside the National Conservation Centre.

CITY CENTRE

World Museum   Museum
(☏0151-478 4399; www.liverpoolmuseums.org.uk/wml; William Brown St; ☺10am-5pm) FREE Natural history, science and technology are the themes of this sprawling museum, whose exhibits range from birds of prey to space exploration. It also includes the country's only free **planetarium**.

Walker Art Gallery   Gallery
(☏0151-478 4199; www.liverpoolmuseums.org.uk/walker; William Brown St; ☺10am-5pm) FREE The city's foremost gallery is the national gallery for northern England, housing an outstanding collection of art from the 14th to the 21st centuries.

St George's Hall   Cultural Centre
(☏0151-707 2391; www.stgeorgesliverpool.co.uk; William Brown St; ☺10am-5pm Tue-Sat, 1-5pm Sun) FREE Arguably Liverpool's most impressive building is the Grade I–listed St George's Hall, a magnificent example of neoclassical architecture that is as imposing today as it was when it was completed in 1854. **Tours** (☏0151-225 6909; per person £3.50; ☺2pm Wed, 11am & 2pm Sat & Sun) of the hall are run in conjunction with the tourist office.

Liverpool Cathedral   Church
(☏0151-709 6271; www.liverpoolcathedral.org.uk; Upper Duke St; visitor centre & tower admission £5; ☺8am-6pm) Liverpool's Anglican cathedral is a building of superlatives. Not only is it Britain's largest church, it's also the world's largest Anglican cathedral, and it's all thanks to Sir Giles Gilbert Scott, who made its construction his life's work.

ALBERT DOCK

Liverpool's biggest tourist attraction is **Albert Dock** (☏0151-708 8854; www.albertdock.com) FREE. This former port and its surrounding buildings is now a Unesco World Heritage site.

International Slavery Museum   Museum
(☏0151-478 4499; www.liverpoolmuseums.org.uk/ism; Albert Dock; ☺10am-5pm) FREE Museums are, by their very nature, like a still of the past, but the extraordinary International Slavery Museum resonates very much in the present. It reveals slavery's unimaginable horrors – including Liverpool's own role in the triangular slave trade – in a clear and uncompromising manner.

Beatles Story   Museum
(☏0151-709 1963; www.beatlesstory.com; Albert Dock; adult/student/child £12.95/9/7, incl Elvis & Us £15.95/12/7; ☺9am-7pm, last admission 5pm) Liverpool's most popular museum won't illuminate any dark, juicy corners in the turbulent history of the world's most famous foursome – there's ne'er a mention of internal discord, drugs or Yoko Ono – but there's plenty of genuine memorabilia to keep a Beatles fan happy. Particularly impressive is the full-size replica Cavern Club (which was actually tiny) and the Abbey Rd studio where the lads recorded their first singles. You can also get a combo ticket for the **Elvis & Us** (☏0151-709 1963; www.elvisandus.com; Mersey Ferries Terminal, Pier Head; admission £6; ☺9am-7pm Apr-Sep, 10am-6pm Oct-Mar) exhibit at the new Beatles Story extension on Pier Head.

Tate Liverpool   Museum
(☏0151-702 7400; www.tate.org.uk/liverpool; Albert Dock; special exhibitions adult/child from

£5/4; ⏱10am-5.50pm Jun-Aug, 10am-5.50pm Tue-Sun Sep-May) FREE Touted as the home of modern art in the north, this gallery features a substantial checklist of 20th-century artists across its four floors, as well as touring exhibitions from the mother ship on London's Bankside.

NORTH OF ALBERT DOCK

The area to the north of Albert Dock is known as **Pier Head**, after a stone pier built in the 1760s. It's home to the city's most famous trio of Edwardian buildings known as the 'Three Graces', dating from the days when Liverpool's star was still ascending.

Museum of Liverpool Museum
(☎0151-478 4545; www.liverpoolmuseums.org.uk; Pier Head; ⏱10am-5pm) FREE Liverpool's storied past is explored within the confines of an eye-catching futuristic building designed in typical Scandinavian verve by Danish firm 3XN.

🧭 Tours

Beatles Fab Four Taxi Tour Guided Tour
(☎0151-601 2111; www.thebeatlesfabfourtaxi tour.co.uk; 2-/3-hour £40/50) Themed tours of the city's mop-top landmarks – there's the three-hour original Lennon tour or the two-hour Epstein express tour.

Magical Mystery Tour Guided Tour
(☎0151-709 3285; www.beatlestour.org; per person £15.95; ⏱2.30pm year-round, plus noon Sat Jul & Aug) Two-hour tour that takes in all Beatles-related landmarks – their birthplaces, childhood homes, schools and places such as Penny Lane and Strawberry Field – before finishing up in the Cavern Club (which isn't the original).

Yellow Duckmarine Tour Water Tour
(☎0151-708 7799; www.theyellowduckmarine.co.uk; adult/child £14.95/9.95; ⏱from 11am) Take to the dock waters in a WWII amphibious vehicle after a quickie tour of the city centre's main points of interest.

🛏 Sleeping

CITY CENTRE

Hotel Indigo Hotel ££
(☎0151-559 0111; www.hotelindigoliverpool.co.uk; 10 Chapel St; r from £65; @ 🛜) It's labelled a boutique hotel, but the 151-room Indigo is just too big and part of a franchise, so the feel is more corporate swish than bespoke boutique.

62 Castle St Boutique Hotel ££
(☎0151-702 7898; www.62castlest.com; 62 Castle St; r from £69; P @ 🛜) This elegant property on (arguably) the city's most handsome street successfully blends the traditional Victorian features of the neo-classical building with a sleek, contemporary style.

Roscoe House Boutique Hotel ££
(☎0151-709 0286; www.hotelliverpool.net; 27 Rodney St; r from £50; 🛜) A handsome Georgian home once owned by Liverpool-born writer and historian William Roscoe (1753–1831) has been given the once-over and is now a chic boutique hotel.

🍴 Eating

The best areas include Ropewalks, along Hardman St and Hope St or along Nelson St in the heart of Chinatown.

Monro Pub ££
(☎0151-707 9933; www.themonro.com; 92 Duke St; 2-course lunch £11.95, dinner mains £14-20; ⏱lunch & dinner) The constantly changing menu of classic British dishes made with ingredients sourced as locally as possible has transformed this handsome old pub into a superb dining experience.

Italian Club Italian £
(☎0151-708 5508; www.theitalianclubliverpool.co.uk; 85 Bold St; mains £6-11; ⏱10am-7pm Mon-Sat) The Crolla family must have been homesick for southern Italy, so they opened this fabulous spot, adorned it with family pictures and began serving the kind of food relatives visiting from the home country would be glad to tuck into.

St George's Hall (p129), Liverpool

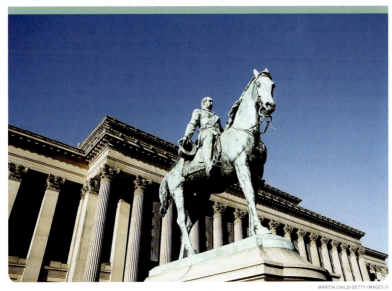

MARTIN CHILD/GETTY IMAGES ©

Noble House
International ££

(☎0151-236 5346; www.thenoblehouse.co.uk; Heywood Bldg, 5 Brunswick St; mains £10-16) The handsome Heywood Building (1799) was once the city's oldest bank – now it's a classy restaurant with a vaguely Manhattanite feel.

🍷 Drinking & Nightlife

Philharmonic
Pub

(36 Hope St; ⏰to 11.30pm) This extraordinary bar, designed by the shipwrights who built the *Lusitania,* is one of the most beautiful bars in all of England. The interior is resplendent with etched and stained glass, wrought iron, mosaics and ceramic tiling – and if you think that's good, just wait until you see inside the marble men's toilets, the only heritage-listed lav in the country.

ℹ️ Information

Most of Liverpool's tourist business is done online, including an **accommodation hotline** (☎0845 601 1125; ⏰9am-5.30pm Mon-Fri, 10am-4pm Sat).

ℹ️ Getting There & Away

Liverpool's main station is Lime St.

Chester (£6.20, 45 minutes)

London Euston (£73.20, 3¼ hours)

Manchester (£11, 45 minutes)

WALES

Lying to the west of England, the nation of Wales is a separate country within the state of Great Britain. It's a nation with Celtic roots, its own language and a rich historic legacy. While some areas in the south are undeniably scarred by coal mining and heavy industry, overall Wales boasts a landscape of wild mountains, rolling hills, rich farmland and some of the most beautiful beaches in all of Britain.

Cardiff

POP 324,800

The capital of Wales since only 1955, Cardiff has embraced its new role with vigour, emerging as one of Britain's leading urban centres in the 21st century.

Lake District National Park

A dramatic landscape of high peaks, dizzying ridges and huge lakes gouged by the march of ice age glaciers, the Lake District in Cumbria is a beautiful corner of Britain. Not surprisingly, the awe-inspiring geography here shaped the literary persona of some of Britain's best-known poets, including William Wordsworth.

Often called simply the Lakes, the national park and surrounding area attract around 15 million visitors annually. But if you avoid summer weekends, and especially if you do a bit of hiking, it's easy enough to miss the crush.

Among the area's many attractions are Beatrix Potter's cottage at **Hill Top** (NT; ☎015394-36269; www.nationaltrust.org.uk/hill-top; adult/child £8/4; ☺10am-5pm Sat-Thu mid-Feb–Oct, shorter hours outside summer) near Hawkshead, where she wrote some of her most famous tales, and William Wordsworth's former home at **Dove Cottage** (☎015394-35544; www.wordsworth.org.uk; adult/child £7.50/4.50; ☺9.30am-5.30pm), near Grasmere.

Windermere is the only town in the national park accessible by train. It's on the branch line to Kendal (£4.20, 15 minutes) and on to Oxenholme (£4.90, 20 minutes), which has frequent connections north and south:

Edinburgh £55, 2½ hours

London Euston £92.10, 3¼ hours

Manchester Piccadilly £32.40, 1½ to two hours via Lancaster (£12.60, 45 minutes)

Caught between an ancient fort and an ultramodern waterfront, this compact city seems to have surprised even itself with how interesting it has become.

◉ Sights

CENTRAL CARDIFF

Cardiff Castle   Castle
(www.cardiffcastle.com; Castle St; adult/child £11/8.50, incl guided tour £14/11; ☺9am-5pm) The grafting of Victorian mock-Gothic extravagance onto Cardiff's most important historical relics makes Cardiff Castle the city's leading attraction. The most conventional castle-y bits are the 12th-century motte-and-bailey **Norman keep** at its centre and the 13th-century **Black Tower**, which forms the entrance gate.

National Museum Cardiff   Museum
(www.museumwales.ac.uk; Gorsedd Gardens Rd; ☺10am-5pm Tue-Sun) FREE Set around the green lawns and colourful flowerbeds of **Alexandra Gardens** is the Civic Centre,

an early-20th-century complex of neo-Baroque buildings in gleaming white Portland stone. They include the **City Hall**, police headquarters, law courts, crown offices, Cardiff University and this excellent **museum**, one of Britain's best, covering natural history, archaeology and art.

Millennium Stadium   Stadium
(☎029-2082 2228; www.millenniumstadium. com; Westgate St; tours adult/child £8.50/5) Attendance at international rugby and football matches has increased dramatically since this 72,500-seat, three-tiered stadium with sliding roof was completed in time to host the 1999 Rugby World Cup. The entrance for guided tours is at Gate 3 on Westgate St.

CARDIFF BAY

The redeveloped waterfront of Cardiff Bay is about 2 miles from the city centre, lined with bars, restaurants and shops, and a collection of stunning buildings.

Doctor Who Experience   Exhibition

(0844 801 2279; www.doctorwhoexperience. com; Porth Teigr; adult/child £15/11; 10am-5pm Wed-Mon, daily school holidays, last admission 3.30pm) Capitalising on Timelord tourism, this permanent exhibition has opened in the Red Dragon Centre, with props and costumes from both shows displayed alongside video clips from the episodes they feature in. Fans can pick up a locations guide (30p) from the nerdalicious shop.

Wales Millennium Centre   Arts Centre

(029-2063 6464; www.wmc.org.uk; Bute Pl; tour adult/child £5.50/4.50; tours 11am & 2.30pm) FREE Designed by Welsh architect Jonathan Adams, this landmark building opened in 2004 as Wales' premier arts complex, housing the Welsh National Opera, National Dance Company, National Orchestra, Academi (Welsh National Literature Promotion Agency), HiJinx Theatre and Ty Cerdd (Music Centre of Wales).

Senedd (National Assembly Building)   Notable Building

(0845 010 5500; www.assemblywales.org; 9.30am-4.30pm Mon-Fri, 10.30am-4.30pm Sat & Sun) FREE Designed by Lord Richard Rogers (the architect behind London's Lloyd's Building and Paris' Pompidou Centre), the Senedd houses Wales' National Assembly.

🛏 Sleeping

Parc Hotel   Hotel ££

(0871 376 9011; www. thistle.com/theparchotel; Park Pl; s/d from £74/79; @ 🛜) A smart contemporary hotel located right at the heart of the main shopping area, with tasteful rooms, good facilities and helpful staff.

Jolyons Boutique Hotel   Hotel ££

(029-2048 8775; www.jolyons.co.uk; 5 Bute Cres; s/d from £76/82; 🛜) A touch of Georgian elegance in the heart of Cardiff Bay. Jolyon's has six individually designed rooms combining antique furniture with contemporary colours and crisp cotton sheets.

🍴 Eating

Riverside Market   Market £

(www.riversidemarket.org.uk; Fitzhamon Embankment; 10am-2pm Sun; 🍴) What it lacks in size it makes up for in sheer yumminess. This riverside market has stalls heaving with cooked meals, cakes, cheese, organic meat, charcuterie, apple juice and real ale.

Goat Major   Pub £

(www.sabrain.com/goatmajor; 33 High St; pies £7.50; food noon-6pm Mon-Sat, noon-4pm Sun) A solidly traditional pub with armchairs, a fireplace and lip-smacking Brains Dark real ale on tap.

Cardiff Castle, Wales
NICOLAS MCCOMBER/GETTY IMAGES ©

JAMES OSMOND/GETTY IMAGES ©

BRITAIN & IRELAND CAERPHILLY

Woods Bar & Brasserie
Modern Welsh ££

(☎ 029-2049 2400; www.knifeandforkfood. co.uk; Stuart St; mains £9-17, 2-/3-course menu £17/20; ⏱ noon-2pm & 5.30-11pm Mon-Sat, noon-3pm Sun) The historic Pilotage Building has been given a modern makeover – zany wallpaper, exposed stone walls and a floor-to-ceiling glass extension – to accommodate Cardiff Bay's best restaurant.

ℹ Information

Cardiff Tourist Office (☎ 029-2087 3573; www.visitcardiff.com; Old Library, The Hayes; internet per 30 min £1; ⏱ 9.30am-5.30pm Mon-Sat, 10am-4pm Sun)

ℹ Getting There & Away

Arriva Trains Wales (www.arrivatrainswales. co.uk) operates all train services in Wales. Direct services from Cardiff include:

London Paddington (£39, 2¼ hours)

Swansea (£7.70, 50 minutes)

Caerphilly

The town of Caerphilly – now almost a suburb of Cardiff – is synonymous with a hard, slightly crumbly white cheese that originated in the surrounding area. However, the main attraction is **Caerphilly Castle** (Cadw; ☎ 029-2088 3143; www.cadw.wales.gov. uk; adult/child £4.75/3.60; ⏱ 9.30am-5pm Mar-Oct, 10am-4pm Nov-Feb), one of the earliest castles to use lakes, bridges and a series of concentric fortifications for defence.

Hay-on-Wye

This pretty little town on the banks of the River Wye, just inside the Welsh border, has become famous as one of Wales' literary landmarks. First came the explosion in secondhand bookshops, a charge led by local maverick Richard Booth, who opened his eponymous bookshop in the 1960s and went on to proclaim himself the King of Hay. Then came the town's famous literary knees-up, the **Hay Festival** (☎ 01497-822629; www.hayfestival.com) – dubbed 'the Woodstock of the mind' by Bill Clinton – which was established in

1988 and now attracts bookworms from all over the world, not to mention a host of heavyweight authors.

The 10-day festival is held in late May, when accommodation is almost impossible to find unless you've booked in advance.

Snowdonia National Park

Snowdonia National Park (Parc Cenedlaethol Eryri; www.eryri-npa.gov.uk) was founded in 1951 (making it Wales' first national park), primarily to keep the area from being loved to death. This is, after all, Wales' best known and most heavily used slice of nature, with the busiest part around Snowdon (1085m) itself. Around 350,000 people climb, walk or take the train to the summit each year, and all those sturdy shoes make trail maintenance a never-ending task for park staff.

On a clear day the views stretch to Ireland and the Isle of Man over Snowdon's fine jagged ridges, which drop away in great swoops to sheltered *cwms* (valleys) and deep lakes. At the top is the striking **Hafod Eryri** visitor centre, opened in 2009 by Prince Charles.

Six paths of varying length and difficulty lead to the summit, all taking around six hours return, or you can cheat and catch the **Snowdon Mountain Railway** (☎0844 493 8120; www.snowdonrailway.co.uk; return diesel adult/child £27/18, steam £35/25; ☾9am-5pm mid-Mar–Oct), opened in 1896 and still the UK's only public rack-and-pinion railway.

However you get to the summit, take warm, waterproof clothing, wear sturdy footwear and check the weather forecast before setting out.

ℹ Information

National Park Information Centre (☎01690-710426; www.eryri-npa.gov.uk; Royal Oak Stables; ☾9.30am-4.30pm)

Tourist Office & National Park Information Centre (☎01766-890615; www.eryri-npa.gov.uk; Canolfan Hebog; ☾9.30am-5.30pm daily Easter-Oct, to 4.30pm Fri-Sun Nov-Easter)

Conwy Castle

On the north coast of Wales, the historic town of Conwy is utterly dominated by the Unesco-designated cultural treasure of **Conwy Castle** (Cadw; adult/child £4.80/4.30; ☾9.30am-6pm Jul & Aug, 9.30am-5pm Mar-Jun, Sep & Oct, 10am-4pm Mon-Sat, 11am-4pm Sun Nov-Feb), the most stunning of all Edward I's Welsh fortresses. Built between 1277 and 1307 on a rocky outcrop, it has commanding views across the estuary and Snowdonia National Park. The 1200m-long **town wall** was built with the castle to guard Conwy's residents at night.

SOUTHERN SCOTLAND

Edinburgh

POP 440,000

Edinburgh is a city that begs to be explored. From the vaults and *wynds* (narrow lanes) that riddle the Old Town to the urban villages of Stockbridge and Cramond, it's filled with quirky come-hither nooks that tempt you to walk just a little bit further. And every corner turned reveals sudden views and unexpected vistas – green sunlit hills, a glimpse of rust-red crags, a blue flash of distant sea.

◉ Sights

Edinburgh's city centre is divided into two parts – Old Town and New Town – split by Princess Street Gardens.

OLD TOWN

Edinburgh Castle Castle
(www.edinburghcastle.gov.uk; adult/child incl audioguide £16/9.60; ☾9.30am-6pm Apr-Sep, to 5pm Oct-Mar, last admission 45 min before closing; ◻23, 27, 41 or 42) Edinburgh Castle has played a pivotal role in Scottish history, both as a royal residence – King Malcolm Canmore (r 1058–93) and Queen Margaret first made their home here in the 11th century – and as a military stronghold.

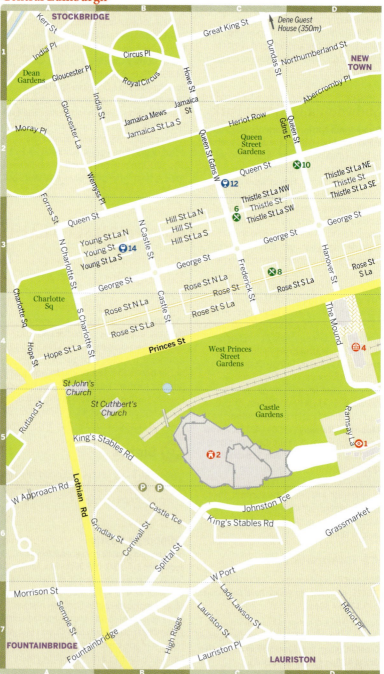

STOCKBRIDGE

Kerr St

India Pl

Dean Gardens

Gloucester Pl

Circus Pl

Royal Circus

Great King St

Dundas St

Northumberland St

Dene Guest House (350m)

NEW TOWN

Gloucester La

India St

Moray Pl

Jamaica St

Jamaica Mews

Jamaica St La S

Heriot Row

Abercromby Pl

Queen St Gdns E

Queen St

Queen Street Gardens

Queen St ⊗10

Forres St

Wemyss Pl

Queen St

N Castle St

Hill St La N

Hill St

Hill St La S

⊕12

Thistle St La NE

Thistle St

Thistle St La SE

Thistle St La NW

Thistle St

Thistle St La SW

6 ⊗

George St

Rose St S La

Young St La N

Young St ⊕14

Young St La S

George St

George St

Frederick St

⊗8

Hanover St

Rose St S La

N Charlotte St

S Charlotte St

Charlotte Sq

George St

Rose St N La

Rose St S La

Castle St

Rose St N La

Rose St

Rose St S La

Rose St S La

The Mound

Charlotte Sq

Hope St

Hope St La

Princes St

West Princes Street Gardens

🏛4

St John's Church

St Cuthbert's Church

Castle Gardens

Ramsay La

Rutland St

King's Stables Rd

⊗2

◉1

W Approach Rd

Lothian Rd

Grindlay St

Cornwall St

Castle Tce

Spittal St

🅿🅿

Johnston Tce

King's Stables Rd

Grassmarket

Morrison St

Semple St

Fountainbridge

High Riggs

W Port

Lady Lawson St

Lauriston St

Lauriston Pl

Heriot Pl

FOUNTAINBRIDGE

LAURISTON

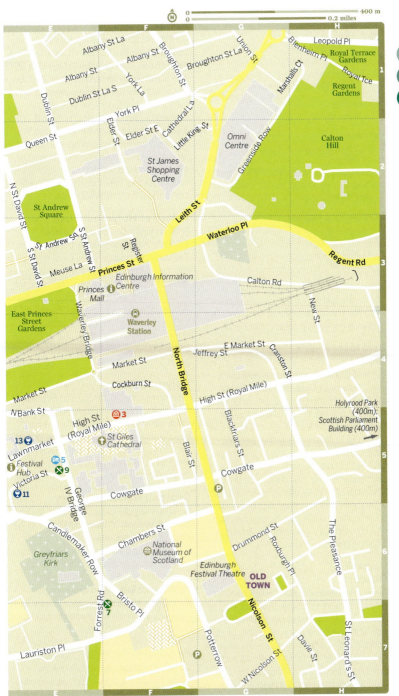

0   400 m
0   0.2 miles

N

Leopold Pl
Royal Terrace
Gardens
Royal Tce
Regent
Gardens
Blenheim Pl
Union St
Albany St La
Albany St
Broughton St La
Marshalls Ct
Greenside Row
Albany St
Broughton St
York La
Dublin St La S
York Pl
Cathedral La
Little King St
Omni
Centre
Calton
Hill
Dublin St
Elder St
Elder St E
St James
Shopping
Centre
N St David St
Queen St
St Andrew
Square
St Andrew Sq
S St Andrew Sq
S St David St
St David St
Register St
Leith St
Meuse La
Waterloo Pl
Princes St
Regent Rd
Edinburgh Information
Centre
Calton Rd
New St
Princes
Mall
East Princes
Street
Gardens
Waverley Bridge
Waverley
Station
Market St
Jeffrey St
E Market St
Cranston St
Market St
Cockburn St
North Bridge
High St (Royal Mile)
N Bank St
High St
(Royal Mile)
3
St Giles
Cathedral
Blackfriars St
Holyrood Park
(400m);
Scottish Parliament
Building (400m)
13
5
9
Festival
Hub
Victoria St
Lawnmarket
George IV Bridge
Blair St
Cowgate
11
Cowgate
Candlemaker Row
Chambers St
National
Museum of
Scotland
Drummond St
Roxburgh Pl
The Pleasance
Greyfriars
Kirk
Edinburgh
Festival Theatre
**OLD
TOWN**
Forrest Rd
Bristo Pl
7
Nicolson St
Potterrow
St Leonard's St
Lauriston Pl
W Nicolson St
Davie St

Central Edinburgh

⊙ Sights
1 Camera Obscura.................................D5
2 Edinburgh Castle C5
3 Real Mary King's Close......................F5
4 Scottish National Gallery...................D4

🛏 Sleeping
5 Hotel Missoni....................................E5

✕ Eating
6 Café Marlayne C3
7 Mums..F7
8 Mussel Inn...C3
9 Ondine..E5
10 The Dogs...D2

🍷 Drinking & Nightlife
11 Bow Bar...E5
12 Bramble...C2
13 Jolly Judge......................................E5
14 Oxford Bar B3

The castle last saw military action in 1745; from then until the 1920s it served as the British army's main base in Scotland.

Real Mary King's Close   Historic Building

(☎ 0845 070 6244; www.realmarykingsclose. com; 2 Warriston's Close, High St; adult/child £12.95/7.45; ⊙ 10am-9pm Apr-Oct, to 11pm Aug, 10am-5pm Sun-Thu, to 9pm Fri & Sat Nov-Mar) Part of the Royal Exchange was built over the sealed-off remains of Mary King's Close, and the lower levels of this medieval Old Town alley have survived almost unchanged in the foundations of the City Chambers for 250 years. Costumed characters give tours through a 16th-century townhouse and the plague-stricken home of a 17th-century gravedigger. Advance booking recommended.

Camera Obscura   Exhibition

(www.camera-obscura.co.uk; Castlehill; adult/ child £11.95/8.95; ⊙ 9.30am-9pm Jul & Aug, 9.30am-7pm Apr-Jun & Sep-Oct, 10am-6pm Nov-Mar; 🚌 2) Edinburgh's camera obscura is a curious 19th-century device – in constant use since 1853 – that uses lenses and mirrors to throw a live image of the city onto a large horizontal screen.

Scottish Parliament Building   Notable Building

(☎ 0131-348 5200; www.scottish.parliament.uk; ⊙ 9am-6.30pm Tue-Thu, 10am-5.30pm Mon, Fri & Sat in session, 10am-6pm Mon-Sat in recess) FREE The Scottish parliament building, built on the site of a former brewery close to the Palace of Holyroodhouse, was officially opened by HM the Queen in October 2005. You can take a free, one-hour guided tour (advance booking recommended) that includes a visit to the Debating Chamber, a committee room, the Garden Lobby and, when possible, the office of an MSP (Member of the Scottish Parliament).

Palace of Holyroodhouse   Palace

(www.royalcollection.org.uk; adult/child £11/6.65; ⊙ 9.30am-6pm Apr-Oct, to 4.30pm Nov-Mar) This palace is the royal family's official residence in Scotland, but is more famous as the 16th-century home of the ill-fated Mary, Queen of Scots. The palace is closed to the public when the royal family is visiting and during state functions (usually in mid-May, and mid-June to early July; check the website for exact dates).

Holyrood Park   Park

The former hunting ground of Scottish monarchs, the park covers 263 hectares of varied landscape, including crags, moorland and a loch. The highest point is the 251m summit of **Arthur's Seat** (Holyrood Park), the deeply eroded remnant of a long-extinct volcano.

Scottish National Gallery   Gallery

(www.nationalgalleries.org; The Mound; fee for special exhibitions; ⊙ 10am-5pm Fri-Wed, to 7pm Thu) FREE Designed by William Playfair, this imposing classical building with its Ionic porticoes dates from the 1850s.

The gallery houses an important collection of **European art** from the Renaissance to post-Impressionism, with works by Verrocchio (Leonardo da Vinci's teacher), Tintoretto, Titian, Holbein, Rubens, Van Dyck, Vermeer, El Greco, Poussin, Rembrandt, Gainsborough, Turner, Constable, Monet, Pissarro, Gauguin and Cézanne. Each January the gallery exhibits its collection of **Turner**

watercolours, bequeathed by Henry Vaughan in 1900.

Royal Yacht Britannia   Ship
(www.royalyachtbritannia.co.uk; Ocean Terminal; adult/child £12/7.50; ☺9.30am-6pm Jul-Sep, to 5.30pm Apr-Jun & Oct, 10am-5pm Nov-Mar, last admission 90 min before closing) One of Scotland's biggest tourist attractions is the former Royal Yacht *Britannia*. She was the British royal family's floating home during their foreign travels from the time of her launch in 1953 until her decommissioning in 1997, and is now moored permanently in front of Ocean Terminal.

Britannia was joined in 2010 by the 1930s racing yacht *Bloodhound,* which was owned by the Queen in the 1960s.

The Majestic Tour bus runs from Waverley Bridge to *Britannia* during opening times. Alternatively, take Lothian Bus 11, 22 or 35 to Ocean Terminal.

 Tours

BUS TOURS
City Sightseeing   Bus Tour
(www.edinburghtour.com; adult/child £12/5) Bright-red, open-top buses depart every 20 minutes from Waverley Bridge.

Majestic Tour   Bus Tour
(www.edinburghtour.com; adult/child £13/6) Runs every 30 minutes (every 20 minutes in July and August) from Waverley Bridge to the Royal Yacht *Britannia* at Ocean Terminal via the New Town, Royal Botanic Garden and Newhaven, returning via Leith Walk, Holyrood and the Royal Mile.

WALKING TOURS
City of the Dead Tours   Walking Tour
(www.cityofthedeadtours.com; adult/concession £10/8) The 'City of the Dead' tour of Greyfriars Kirkyard is probably the scariest of Edinburgh's 'ghost' tours. Not suitable for young children.

Edinburgh Literary Pub Tour   Walking Tour
(www.edinburghliterarypubtour.co.uk; adult/student £14/10) An enlightening two-hour trawl through Edinburgh's literary history – and its associated *howffs* (pubs) – in the entertaining company of Messrs Clart and McBrain. One of the city's best walking tours.

Rebus Tours   Walking Tour
(www.rebustours.com; adult/student £10/9) Tours of the 'hidden Edinburgh'

Festival City

Edinburgh boasts a frenzy of festivals, especially in August. See www.edinburghfestivals.co.uk for more.

Edinburgh Festival Fringe (☎0131-226 0026; www.edfringe.com; 180 High St) The biggest festival of the performing arts anywhere in the world, held over 3½ weeks in August, the last two weeks overlapping with the first two weeks of the Edinburgh International Festival.

Edinburgh International Festival (☎0131-473 2099; www.eif.co.uk) Three weeks of inspirational music, opera, theatre and dance in August. Tickets can be purchased at the **Hub** (☎01131-473 2000; www.thehub-edinburgh.com; Castlehill; ☺ticket centre 10am-5pm Mon-Sat).

Edinburgh Military Tattoo (☎0131-225 1188; www.edintattoo.co.uk; Tattoo Office, 32 Market St) A spectacular display of military marching bands, massed pipes and drums, acrobats, cheerleaders and motorcycle display teams, all played out in front of the magnificent backdrop of the floodlit castle during the first three weeks of August.

Royal Mile

A Grand Day Out

Planning your own procession along the Royal Mile involves some tough decisions – it would be impossible to see everything in a single day, so it's wise to decide in advance what you don't want to miss and shape your visit around that. Remember to leave time for lunch, for exploring the Mile's countless side

alleys and, during festival time, for enjoying the street theatre that is bound to be happening in High St.

The most pleasant way to reach the Castle Esplanade at the start of the Royal Mile is to hike up the zigzag path from the footbridge behind the Ross Bandstand in Princes Street Gardens (in springtime you'll be knee-deep in daffodils). Starting at **Edinburgh Castle** ❶ means that the rest of your walk is downhill. For a superb view up and down the length of the Mile, climb the **Camera Obscura's Outlook Tower** ❷ before visiting **Gladstone's Land** ❸ and **St Giles Cathedral** ❹. If history's your

LONELY PLANET/GETTY IMAGES ©

Edinburgh Castle
If you're pushed for time, visit the Great Hall, the Honours of Scotland and the Prisons of War exhibit. Head for the Half Moon Battery for a photo looking down the length of the Royal Mile.

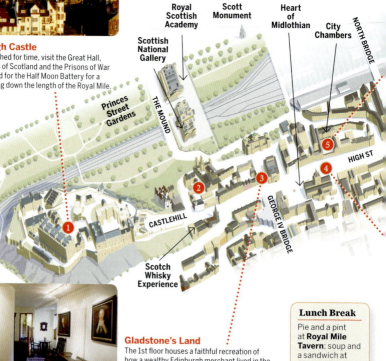

Royal Scottish Academy

Scott Monument

Heart of Midlothian

City Chambers

NORTH BRIDGE

Scottish National Gallery

Princes Street Gardens

THE MOUND

HIGH ST

❺

❹

❸

❷

GEORGE IV BRIDGE

CASTLEHILL

❶

Scotch Whisky Experience

KARL BLACKWELL/GETTY IMAGES ©

Gladstone's Land
The 1st floor houses a faithful recreation of how a wealthy Edinburgh merchant lived in the 17th century. Check out the beautiful Painted Bedchamber, with its ornately decorated walls and wooden ceilings.

Lunch Break
Pie and a pint at **Royal Mile Tavern**; soup and a sandwich at **Always Sunday**; bistro nosh at **Café Marlayne**.

thing, you'll want to add **Real Mary King's Close** ❺, **John Knox House** ❻ and the **Museum of Edinburgh** ❼ to your must-see list.

At the foot of the mile, choose between modern and ancient seats of power – the **Scottish Parliament** ❽ or the **Palace of Holyroodhouse** ❾. Round off the day with an evening ascent of Arthur's Seat or, slightly less strenuously, Calton Hill. Both make great sunset viewpoints.

TAKING YOUR TIME

Minimum time needed for each attraction:

Edinburgh Castle: two hours

Gladstone's Land: 45 minutes

St Giles Cathedral: 30 minutes

Real Mary King's Close: one hour (tour)

Scottish Parliament: one hour (tour)

Palace of Holyroodhouse: one hour

Real Mary King's Close
The guided tour is heavy on ghost stories, but a highlight is standing in an original 17th-century room with tufts of horsehair poking from the crumbling plaster, and breathing in the ancient scent of stone, dust and history.

Canongate Kirk

CANONGATE

❻

ST MARY'S ST

SOUTH BRIDGE

Tron Kirk

❼

❽

❾

Our Dynamic Earth

Scottish Parliament
Don't have time for the guided tour? Pick up a 'Discover the Scottish Parliament Building' leaflet from reception and take a self-guided tour of the exterior, then hike up to Salisbury Crags for a great view of the complex.

Palace of Holyroodhouse
Find the secret staircase joining Mary, Queen of Scots' bedchamber with that of her husband, Lord Darnley, who restrained the queen while his henchmen stabbed to death her secretary (and possible lover), David Rizzio.

St Giles Cathedral
Look out for the Burne-Jones stained-glass window (1873) at the west end, showing the crossing of the River Jordan, and the bronze memorial to Robert Louis Stevenson in the Moray Aisle.

DANITA DELIMONT/GETTY IMAGES ©

RICK LEW/GETTY IMAGES © ARCHITECT: ENRIC MIRALLES

RIEGER BERTRAND/GETTY IMAGES ©

frequented by novelist Ian Rankin's fictional detective, John Rebus. Not recommended for children under 10.

Sleeping

OLD TOWN

Hotel Missoni Boutique Hotel **£££**
(📞0131-220 6666; www.hotelmissoni.com; 1 George IV Bridge; r £90-225; 📶) The Italian fashion house has established a style icon in the heart of the medieval Old Town with this bold statement of a hotel – modernistic architecture, black-and-white decor with well-judged splashes of colour, impeccably mannered staff and, most importantly, very comfortable bedrooms.

NEW TOWN & AROUND

B+B Edinburgh Hotel **££**
(📞0131-225 5084; www.bb-edinburgh.com; 3 Rothesay Tce; s/d £99/140; 📶) Built in 1883 as a grand home for the proprietor of the *Scotsman* newspaper, this Victorian extravaganza of carved oak, parquet floors, stained glass and elaborate fireplaces

was given a designer makeover in 2011 to create a striking contemporary hotel.

Dene Guest House B&B **££**
(📞0131-556 2700; www.deneguesthouse.com; 7 Eyre Pl; per person £25-50) The Dene is a friendly and informal place, set in a charming Georgian townhouse, with a welcoming owner and spacious bedrooms.

Eating

OLD TOWN

Ondine Seafood **£££**
(📞226 1888; www.ondinerestaurant.co.uk; 2 George IV Bridge; mains £15-28; 🕐lunch & dinner Mon-Sat; 🚌2, 23, 27, 41, 42 or 45) Ondine is one of Edinburgh's finest seafood restaurants, with a menu based on sustainably sourced fish. The two-course lunch (noon to 2.30pm) and pretheatre (5pm to 6.30pm) menu costs £17.

Mums Cafe **£**
(www.monstermashcafe.co.uk; 4a Forrest Rd; mains £6-9; 🕐9am-10pm Mon-Sat, 10am-10pm Sun; 🚌2, 23, 27, 41, 42 or 45) 🍴 This nostalgia-fuelled cafe serves up classic British comfort food that wouldn't look out of place on a 1950s menu – bacon and eggs, bangers and mash, shepherd's pie, fish and chips.

NEW TOWN

The Dogs British **££**
(📞220 1208; www.thedogsonline.co.uk; 110 Hanover St; mains £9-13; 🕐noon-4pm & 5-10pm; 🚌23 or 27) 🍴 One of the coolest tables in town, this bistro-style place uses cheaper cuts of meat and less-well-known, more-sustainable species of fish to create hearty, no-nonsense dishes such as lamb sweetbreads on toast, baked coley with

Palace of Holyroodhouse (p138), Edinburgh
TRAVEL INK/GETTY IMAGES ©

skirlie (fried oatmeal and onion), and devilled liver with bacon and onions.

Mussel Inn
Seafood ££

(www.mussel-inn.com; 61-65 Rose St; mains £9-23; ⊙noon-10pm; 🚼) 🅿 Owned by west-coast shellfish farmers, the Mussel Inn provides a direct outlet for fresh Scottish seafood.

Café Marlayne
French ££

(🕿226 2230; www.cafemarlayne.com; 76 Thistle St; mains £12-15; ⊙noon-10pm; 🚍24, 29 or 42) All weathered wood and candlelit tables, Café Marlayne is a cosy nook offering French farmhouse cooking – *brandade de morue* (salt cod) with green salad, slow-roast rack of lamb, *boudin noir* (black pudding) with scallops and sautéed potato – at very reasonable prices.

🍷 Drinking & Nightlife

OLD TOWN

Bow Bar
Pub

(80 West Bow; 🚍2, 23, 27, 41, 42 or 45) One of the city's best traditional-style pubs (it's not as old as it looks), serving a range of excellent real ales and a vast selection of malt whiskies, the Bow Bar often has standing-room only on Friday and Saturday evenings.

Jolly Judge
Pub

(www.jollyjudge.co.uk; 7a James Ct; 🛜; 🚍2, 23, 27, 41, 42 or 45) A snug little *howff* tucked away down a close, the Judge exudes a cosy, 17th-century atmosphere (low, timber-beamed painted ceilings) and has the added attraction of a cheering open fire in cold weather.

NEW TOWN

Oxford Bar
Pub

(www.oxfordbar.co.uk; 8 Young St; 🚍19, 36, 37, 41 or 47) The Oxford is that rarest of things: a real pub for real people, with no 'theme', no music, no frills and no pretensions. 'The Ox' has been immortalised by Ian Rankin, author of the Inspector Rebus novels, whose fictional detective is a regular here.

Detour:
Rosslyn Chapel

The success of Dan Brown's novel *The Da Vinci Code* and the subsequent Hollywood film has seen a flood of visitors descend on Scotland's most beautiful and enigmatic church: **Rosslyn Chapel** (Collegiate Church of St Matthew; www.rosslynchapel.org.uk; adult/child £9/free; ⊙9.30am-5pm Mon-Sat, noon-4.45pm Sun). As well as flowers, vines, angels and biblical figures, the carved stones include many examples of the pagan 'Green Man'; other figures are associated with Freemasonry and the Knights Templar. The symbolism of these images has led some researchers to conclude that Rosslyn might be a secret Templar repository, concealing anything from the Holy Grail or the head of John the Baptist to the body of Christ himself.

The chapel is in Roslin, 7 miles south of Edinburgh's centre.

Bramble
Cocktail Bar

(www.bramblebar.co.uk; 16a Queen St; 🚍23 or 27) One of those places that easily earns the sobriquet 'best-kept secret', Bramble is an unmarked cellar bar where a maze of stone and brick hideaways conceals what is arguably the city's best cocktail bar.

ℹ️ Information

Edinburgh Information Centre (🕿0131-473 3868; www.edinburgh.org; Princes Mall, 3 Princes St; ⊙9am-9pm Mon-Sat, 10am-8pm Sun Jul & Aug, 9am-7pm Mon-Sat, 10am-7pm Sun May-Jun & Sep, 9am-5pm Mon-Wed, to 6pm Thu-Sun Oct-Apr)

Rosslyn Chapel

Deciphering Rosslyn

Rosslyn Chapel is a small building, but the density of decoration inside can be overwhelming. It's well worth buying the official guidebook by the Earl of Rosslyn first; find a bench in the gardens and have a skim through before going into the chapel – the background information will make your visit all the more interesting. The book also offers a useful self-guided tour of the chapel, and explains the legend of the Master Mason and the Apprentice.

Entrance is through the **north door** ❶. Take a pew and sit for a while to allow your eyes to adjust to the dim interior; then look up at the ceiling vault, decorated with engraved roses, lilies and stars (can you spot the sun and the moon?). Walk left along the north aisle to reach the Lady Chapel, separated from the rest of the church by the **Mason's Pillar** ❷ and the **Apprentice Pillar** ❸. Here you'll find carvings of **Lucifer** ❹, the Fallen Angel, and the **Green Man** ❺. Nearby are **carvings** ❻ that appear to resemble Indian corn (maize). Finally, go to the western end and look up at the wall – in the left corner is the head of the **Apprentice** ❼; to the right is the (rather worn) head of the **Master Mason** ❽.

ROSSLYN CHAPEL & THE DA VINCI CODE

Dan Brown was referencing Rosslyn Chapel's alleged links to the Knights Templar and the Freemasons – unusual symbols found among the carvings, and the fact that a descendant of its founder, William St Clair, was a Grand Master Mason – when he chose it as the setting for his novel's denouement. Rosslyn is indeed a coded work, written in stone, but its meaning depends on your point of view. See *The Rosslyn Hoax?* by Robert LD Cooper (www.rosslynhoax.com) for an alternative interpretation of the chapel's symbolism.

SANDRO VANNINI/CORBIS ©

Explore Some More

After visiting the chapel, head downhill to see the spectacularly sited ruins of Roslin Castle, then take a walk along leafy Roslin Glen.

Lucifer, the Fallen Angel

At head height, to the left of the second window from the left, is an upside-down angel bound with rope, a symbol often associated with Freemasonry. The arch above is decorated with the Dance of Death.

The Apprentice

High in the corner, beneath an empty statue niche, is the head of the murdered Apprentice, with a deep wound in his forehead above the right eye. Legend says the Apprentice was murdered in a jealous rage by the Master Mason. The worn head on the side wall to the left of the Apprentice is that of his mother.

North Door

The Master Mason ❽

Baptistery

Practical Tips

Buy your tickets in advance through the chapel's website (except in August, when no bookings are taken). No photography is allowed inside the chapel.

Green Man

On a boss at the base of the arch between the second and third windows from the left is the finest example of more than a hundred 'green man' carvings in the chapel, pagan symbols of spring, fertility and rebirth.

Green Man
①
②
Mason's Pillar
③
④
⑤
Lady Chapel
⑥
⑦

North Aisle
Altar
Choir
South Aisle
Sacristy

The Apprentice Pillar

This is perhaps the chapel's most beautiful carving. Four vines spiral up the pillar, issuing from the mouths of eight dragons at its base. At the top is Isaac, son of Abraham, lying bound upon the altar.

Indian Corn

The frieze around the second window on the south wall is said to represent Indian corn (maize), but it predates Columbus' discovery of the New World in 1492. Other carvings seem to resemble aloe vera.

Getting There & Away

Air

Edinburgh Airport (📞0131-333 1000; www.edinburghairport.com), 8 miles west of the city, has numerous flights to other parts of Scotland and the UK, Ireland and mainland Europe.

Train

The main terminus in Edinburgh is Waverley train station, located in the heart of the city.

First ScotRail (📞08457 55 00 33; www.scotrail.co.uk) operates a regular shuttle service between Edinburgh and Glasgow (£12.90, 50 minutes, every 15 minutes), and frequent daily services to all Scottish cities, including Aberdeen (£45, 2½ hours), Dundee (£23, 1¼ hours) and Inverness (£40, 3½ hours).

CENTRAL SCOTLAND

Loch Lomond

The 'bonnie banks' and 'bonnie braes' of Loch Lomond have long been Glasgow's rural retreat, and today the loch's popularity shows no sign of decreasing. The region's importance was recognised when it

became the heart of **Loch Lomond & the Trossachs National Park** (www.lochlomond-trossachs.org) – Scotland's first national park, created in 2002.

The main centre for boat trips is Balloch, where **Sweeney's Cruises** (📞01389-752376; www.sweeneyscruises.com; **Balloch Rd, Balloch**) offers a range of trips including a one-hour cruise to Inchmurrin and back (adult/child £8.50/5, departs hourly).

Stirling

POP 32,673

With an utterly impregnable position atop a mighty wooded crag (the plug of an extinct volcano), Stirling's beautifully preserved Old Town is a treasure-trove of noble buildings and cobbled streets winding up to the ramparts of its dominant castle, which offer views for miles around.

Sights

Stirling Castle   Castle
(HS; www.historic-scotland.gov.uk; adult/child £13/6.50; ⏱9.30am-6pm Apr-Sep, to 5pm Oct-Mar) This impressive fortress has played

Three Sisters, Glen Coe

MARTIN MCCARTHY/GETTY IMAGES ©

a pivotal role in Scotland's fortunes down the centuries, and it's every bit as dramatic as Edinburgh Castle. The current castle dates from the late 14th to the 16th century, when it was a residence of the Stuart monarchs.

National Wallace Monument — Monument

(www.nationalwallacemonument.com; adult/child £8.25/5.25; ⏱10am-5pm Apr-Jun, Sep & Oct, to 6pm Jul & Aug, 10.30am-4pm Nov-Mar) Towering over Scotland's narrow waist, this nationalist memorial is so Victorian Gothic it deserves circling bats and ravens. It commemorates the bid for Scottish independence depicted in the film *Braveheart*.

Buses 62 and 63 run from Murray Pl in Stirling to the tourist office, otherwise it's a half-hour walk from central Stirling.

ⓘ Information

Tourist Office (☎01786-475019; stirling@visitscotland.com; 41 Dumbarton Rd; ⏱10am-5pm Mon-Sat, plus Sun Jun–mid-Sep)

ⓘ Getting There & Away

Train

First ScotRail (www.scotrail.co.uk) has services to/from a number of destinations, including the following:

Edinburgh (£7.70, 55 minutes, twice hourly Monday to Saturday, hourly Sunday)

Glasgow (£8, 40 minutes, twice hourly Monday to Saturday, hourly Sunday)

NORTHERN & WESTERN SCOTLAND

Loch Ness

Deep, dark and narrow, Loch Ness stretches for 23 miles between Inverness and Fort Augustus. Its bitterly cold waters have been extensively explored in search of the elusive Loch Ness monster, but most visitors see her only in cardboard cut-out form at the monster exhibitions.

The village of **Drumnadrochit** is a hotbed of beastie fever, with two monster exhibitions battling it out for the tourist dollar.

The **Loch Ness Exhibition Centre** (☎01456-450573; www.lochness.com; adult/child £6.95/4.95; ⏱9am-6pm Jul & Aug, to 5.30pm Jun, 9.30am-5pm Easter-May & Sep-Oct, 10am-3.30pm Nov-Easter) is the better of the two Nessie-themed attractions, with a scientific approach that allows you to weigh the evidence for yourself.

Glen Coe

Scotland's most famous glen is also one of the grandest and, in bad weather, the grimmest. The southern side is dominated by three massive, brooding spurs, known as the **Three Sisters**, while the northern side is enclosed by the continuous steep wall of the knife-edged **Aonach Eagach** ridge.

Glencoe was written into the history books in 1692 when the resident MacDonalds were murdered by Campbell soldiers in what became known as the Glencoe Massacre.

🛏 Sleeping & Eating

Clachaig Inn — Hotel ££

(☎01855-811252; www.clachaig.com; s/d from £70/92; 🅿🛜) The Clachaig has long been a favourite haunt of hill walkers and climbers. As well as comfortable en suite accommodation, there's a smart, wood-panelled lounge-bar with lots of sofas and armchairs, mountaineering photos, and climbing magazines to leaf through. Climbers usually head for the lively **Boots Bar**. It's 2 miles southeast of Glencoe village.

ⓘ Getting There & Away

Scottish Citylink (☎0871 266 3333; www.citylink.co.uk) buses run between Fort William and Glencoe (£7.50, 30 minutes, eight daily) and from Glencoe to Glasgow (£20, 2½ hours, eight daily). Buses stop at Glencoe village, Glencoe Visitor Centre and Glencoe Mountain Resort.

Stagecoach (www.stagecoachbus.com) bus 44 links Glencoe village with Fort William (35 minutes, hourly Monday to Saturday, three on Sunday) and Kinlochleven (25 minutes).

Stirling Castle

Planning Your Attack

Stirling's a sizeable fortress, but not so huge that you'll have to decide what to leave out – there's time to see it all. Unless you've got a working knowledge of Scottish monarchs, head to the **Castle Exhibition** ❶ first: it'll help you sort one James from another. That done, take on the sights at leisure. First, stop and look around you from the **ramparts** ❷; the views high over this flat valley, a key strategic point in Scotland's history, are magnificent.

Next, head through to the back of the castle to the **Tapestry Studio** ❸, which is open for shorter hours; seeing these skilful weavers at work is a highlight. Track back towards the citadel's heart, stopping for a quick tour through the **Great Kitchens** ❹; looking at all that fake food might make you seriously hungry, though. Then enter the main courtyard. Around you are the principal castle buildings. During summer there are events (such as Renaissance dancing) in the **Great Hall** ❺ – get details at the entrance. **The Museum of the Argyll & Sutherland Highlanders** ❻ is a treasure trove if you're interested in regimental history, but missable if you're not. Leave the best for last – crowds thin in the afternoon – and enter the sumptuous **Royal Palace** ❼.

The Way Up & Down

If you have time, take the atmospheric Back Walk, a peaceful, shady stroll around the Old Town's fortifications and up to the castle's imposing crag-top position. Afterwards, wander down through the Old Town to admire its facades.

TOP TIPS

Admission Entrance is free for Historic Scotland members. If you'll be visiting several Scottish castles and ruins, a membership will save you plenty.

Vital Statistics First constructed: before AD1110. Number of sieges: at least 9. Last besieger: Bonnie Prince Charlie (unsuccessful). Cost of refurbishing the Royal Palace: £12 million.

DAVID ROBERTSON/ALAMY ©

Museum of the Argyll & Sutherland Highlanders
The history of one of Scotland's legendary regiments – now subsumed into the Royal Regiment of Scotland – is on display here, featuring memorabilia, weapons and uniforms.

Prince's Tower

Guard Room Sq (shop & tickets)

Forework

Robert the Bruce statue

Entrance

Castle Exhibition
A great overview of the Stewart dynasty here will get your facts straight, and also offers the latest archaeological titbits from the ongoing excavations under the citadel. Analysis of skeletons has revealed surprising amounts of biographical data.

Royal Palace
The impressive new highlight of a visit to the castle is this recreation of the royal lodgings originally built by James V. The finely worked ceiling, ornate furniture and sumptuous unicorn tapestries dazzle.

Great Hall & Chapel Royal

Creations of James IV and VI, respectively, these elegant spaces around the central courtyard have been faithfully restored. The vast Great Hall, with its imposing beamed roof, was the largest medieval hall in Scotland.

King's Old Building

Nether Bailey

⑥

③

⑦

⑤

④

Grand Battery

②

Tapestry Studio (until late 2013)

An exquisite series of tapestries depicting a unicorn hunt, full of themes with Christian undertones, is being painstakingly reproduced here: each tapestry takes four years to make. It's fascinating to watch the weavers at work.

Great Kitchens

Dive into this original display that brings home the massive enterprise of organising, preparing and cooking a feast fit for a Renaissance king. Your stomach may rumble at the lifelike haunches of meat, loaves of bread, fowl and fishes.

Ramparts

Perched on the walls you can appreciate the utter dominance of the castle's position atop this lofty volcanic crag. The view includes the site of Robert the Bruce's victory at Bannockburn and the monument to William Wallace.

Detour:
Orkney Islands

Just 6 miles off the northern coast of Scotland, this archipelago is renowned for its dramatic coastal scenery – from soaring cliffs to sandy beaches – abundant bird life, Viking heritage and a plethora of prehistoric sites. There are about 70 islands in all (16 inhabited); the largest goes by the imaginative name of Mainland, with Kirkwall the capital and Stromness the major port.

Stenness, a short bus ride from Kirkwall or Stromness, is the most accessible spot for exploring prehistoric Orkney, including **Skara Brae**, a 5000-year-old village, the **Standing Stones of Stenness** and **Barnhouse Neolithic Village**. Particularly recommended is **Maes Howe** (HS; ☎01856-761606; www.historic-scotland.gov.uk; adult/child £5.50/3.30; ⊙tours hourly 10am-4pm), an ancient – and atmospheric – Stone Age tomb.

There's a good selection of low-priced B&Bs and hostels across the Orkneys – especially on Mainland – and plenty of cafes, restaurants and pubs. **Flybe/Loganair** (☎0871 700 0535; www.flybe.com) flies daily from Kirkwall to Aberdeen, Edinburgh, Glasgow, Inverness and Sumburgh (Shetland). **NorthLink Ferries** (☎0845 6000 449; www.northlinkferries.co.uk) run to/from Aberdeen, while **John O'Groats Ferries** (☎01955-611353; www.jogferry.co.uk) operates a passenger shuttle to/from John O'Groats.

Isle of Skye

POP 9900

The Isle of Skye is the biggest of Scotland's islands, a 50-mile-long smorgasbord of velvet moors, jagged mountains, sparkling lochs and towering sea cliffs. It takes its name from the old Norse *sky-a*, meaning 'cloud island', a Viking reference to the often mist-enshrouded Cuillin Hills. The stunning scenery is the main attraction, but there are plenty of cosy pubs to retire to when the mist closes in.

The Isle of Skye became permanently tethered to the Scottish mainland when the Skye Bridge opened in 1995, but a number of ferries still serve the island.

CalMac (www.calmac.co.uk; per person/car £4.35/22.60) operates the Mallaig to Armadale ferry. It's very popular in July and August, so book ahead if you're travelling by car.

Skye Ferry (www.skyeferry.co.uk; car with up to four passengers £14) runs a tiny vessel (six cars only) on the short Glenelg to Kylerhea crossing.

John O'Groats & Around

Best known as the endpoint of the epic 874-mile trek from Land's End in Cornwall, **John O'Groats** is really nothing more than a car park surrounded by tourist shops, and offers little to the visitor beyond a means to get across to Orkney.

Two miles east, **Duncansby Head** provides a more solemn end-of-Britain moment with a small lighthouse and 60m cliffs sheltering nesting fulmars.

The most northerly point on the British mainland is actually at **Dunnet Head**, 8 miles east of Thurso, which offers inspiring views of the Orkney Islands, flopping seals and nesting seabirds below, and a lighthouse built by Robert Louis Stevenson's granddad.

IRELAND

From shamrocks and shillelaghs to leprechauns and lovable rogues, there's a plethora of platitudes to wade through before you reach the real Ireland. But it's well worth looking beyond the tourist tat, for the Emerald Isle is one of Europe's gems, a scenic extravaganza of lakes, mountains, sea and sky.

Dublin

01 / POP 1.1 MILLION

Form is temporary, but class is permanent: the good times may have gone, but Dublin still knows how to have a good time. From its music, art and literature to the legendary nightlife that has inspired those same musicians, artists and writers, Dublin has always known how to have fun and does it with deadly seriousness, as you'll soon find out.

◉ Sights

Dublin is neatly divided by the River Liffey into the more affluent 'south side' and the less prosperous 'north side'. Immediately south of the river is the bustling Temple Bar district, Trinity College and, just below it, the lovely St Stephen's Green.

Trinity College & Book of Kells   Museum

(www.bookofkells.ie; College Green; admission free to college grounds, Old Library adult/child €9/free, walking tours per person €10; ⏰9.30am-5pm Mon-Sat year-round, 9.30am-4.30pm Sun May-Sep, noon-4.30pm Sun Oct-Apr) Ireland's premier university was founded by Queen Elizabeth I in 1592. Student-guided **walking tours** (twice per hour 10.15am-3.40pm Mon-Sat & 10.15am-3pm Sun mid-May–Sep) depart from inside the main gate on College St. The tour is an especially good deal since it includes admission to the **Old Library** to see the **Book of Kells**, an elaborately illuminated gospel created by monks on the Scottish isle of Iona around AD 800, and the spectacular **Long Room**, an early-18th-century library lined with marble busts of writers and philosophers.

National Museum of Ireland – Archaeology   Museum

(www.museum.ie; Kildare St; ⏰10am-5pm Tue-Sat, 2-5pm Sun) **FREE** Among the highlights of the National Museum's archaeology and history branch are its superb collection of **prehistoric gold objects**; the exquisite 12th-century **Ardagh Chalice**, the world's finest example of Celtic art; and ancient objects recovered from Ireland's bogs, including remarkably well-preserved human bodies.

O'Connell St   Historic Area

(⏰24hr; 🚌all city centre) Dublin's grandest avenue is dominated by the needle-like **Monument of Light** (O'Connell St), better known as 'The Spire', which rises from the spot once occupied by a statue of Admiral Nelson – which disappeared in explosive fashion, thanks to the Irish Republican Army (IRA) in 1966. Soaring 120m into the sky, it is, apparently, the world's tallest sculpture.

Nearby is the 1815 **General Post Office** (www.anpost.ie; O'Connell St; ⏰8am-

Climbing Ben Nevis

Looming over Fort William is Ben Nevis (1344m). As the highest peak in the British Isles, it attracts thousands of people who would not normally go anywhere near the summit of a Scottish mountain. Even if you're climbing 'the Ben' on a fine summer's day, an ascent should not be undertaken lightly. You will need proper walking boots (the path is rough and stony, and there may be wet snowfields on the summit), warm clothing, waterproofs, a map and compass, and plenty of food and water. And don't forget to check the weather forecast (see www.bennevisweather.co.uk). In thick cloud, visibility at the summit can be 10m or less; in such conditions, the only safe way off the mountain requires careful use of a map and compass to avoid walking over 700m cliffs.

Dublin

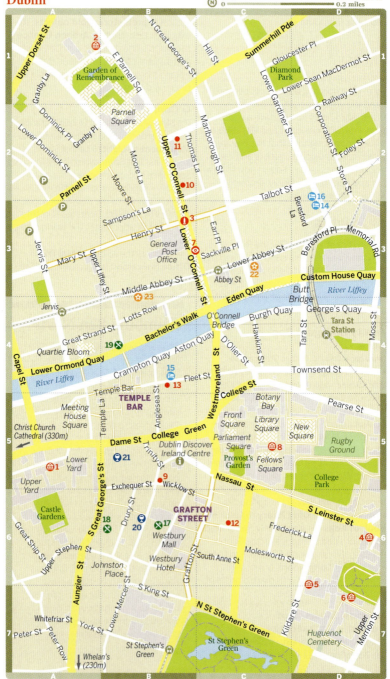

Dublin

⊙ Sights
1 Dublin Castle A5
2 Dublin Writers Museum A1
3 Monument of Light B3
4 National Gallery D6
5 National Museum of Ireland –
   Archaeology D6
6 Natural History Museum D7
7 O'Connell St B3
8 Trinity College & Book of Kells C5

✪ Activities, Courses & Tours
9 1916 Rebellion Walking Tour B5
10 City Sightseeing B2
11 Dublin Bus B2
12 Dublin Literary Pub Crawl C6
13 Dublin Musical Pub Crawl B4

⊜ Sleeping
14 Anchor Guesthouse D3
15 Morgan Hotel B4
16 Townhouse Hotel D2

✗ Eating
   Chapter One ....(see 2)
17 Coppinger Row B6
18 L'Gueuleton B6
19 Winding Stair B4

⊖ Drinking & Nightlife
20 Grogan's Castle Lounge B6
21 Stag's Head B5

✪ Entertainment
22 Abbey Theatre C3
23 Twisted Pepper B4

8pm Mon-Sat; 🖳all city centre, 🚊Abbey), an important landmark of the 1916 Easter Rising, when the Irish Volunteers used it as a base for attacks against the British army.

Guinness Storehouse   Brewery, Museum
(www.guinness-storehouse.com; St James's Gate, South Market St; adult/student/child €16.50/10.50/6.50, Conoisseur Experience €25, discounts apply for online bookings; ⊙9.30am-5pm Sep-Jun, 9.30am-7pm Jul & Aug; 🖳21a, 51b, 78, 78a or 123 from Fleet St, 🚊St James's) The Guinness Storehouse sits in the malty fug of the mighty Guinness Brewery southwest of the city centre. The building is shaped like a pint of Ireland's favourite drink, with a bar in the 'head', and the best part of the tour is getting the finest-tasting Guinness of your life for free at the end. It has wheelchair access. Take bus 123 from O'Connell St or Dame St.

Kilmainham Gaol   Museum
(www.heritageireland.com; Inchicore Rd; adult/child €6/2; ⊙9.30am-6pm Apr-Sep, 9.30am-5.30pm Mon-Sat, 10am-6pm Sun Oct-Mar) The threatening, grey Kilmainham Gaol, 2km west of the city centre, played a key role in Ireland's struggle for independence and was the site of mass executions following the 1916 Easter Rising. Buses 69

or 79 from Aston Quay and 13 or 40 from O'Connell St can all take you here.

National Gallery   Museum
(www.nationalgallery.ie; West Merrion Sq; ⊙9.30am-5.30pm Mon-Wed, Fri & Sat, 9.30am-8.30pm Thu, noon-5.30pm Sun; 🖳7 & 44 from city centre) A magnificent Caravaggio and a breathtaking collection of works by Jack B Yeats – William Butler's younger brother – are the main reasons to visit here. The Millennium wing has a small collection of contemporary Irish works. Free guided tours are held at 3pm on Saturday, and 2pm, 3pm and 4pm on Sunday.

Christ Church Cathedral   Church
(Church of the Holy Trinity; www.cccdub.ie; Christ Church Pl; adult/child €6/2; ⊙9.45am-5pm Mon-Sat & 12.30-2.30pm Sun year-round, longer hrs Jun-Aug; 🖳50, 50A or 56A from Aston Quay, 54 or 54A from Burgh Quay) Christ Church is the mother of all of Dublin's cathedrals, a simple wooden structure until 1169, when the present church was built.

Natural History Museum   Museum
(www.museum.ie; Merrion St; ⊙10am-5pm Tue-Sat, 2-5pm Sun; 🖳7 & 44 from the city centre) FREE Dusty, weird and utterly compelling, this window into Victorian times has barely changed since Scottish explorer Dr David Livingstone opened it in 1857. The

153

creaky-floored interior is crammed with stuffed animals, skeletons, fossils and other specimens from around the world, ranging from West African apes to pickled insects in jars.

Dublin Writers Museum   Museum

(www.writersmuseum.com; 18 North Parnell Sq; adult/child €7.50/4.70; ⊙10am-5pm Mon-Sat, 11am-5pm Sun; 🚌3, 10, 11, 11A, 13, 16, 16A, 19, 19A or 22 from city centre) Celebrates the city's role as a literary centre, with displays on Joyce, Swift, Yeats, Wilde, Beckett and others.

Dublin Castle   Historic Building

(🕿01-677 7129; www.dublincastle.ie; Dame St; adult/child €4.50/2; ⊙10am-4.45pm Mon-Sat, noon-4.45pm Sun; 🚌50, 54, 56a, 77 or 77a) The centre of British power in Ireland, dating back to the 13th century; more higgledy-piggledy palace than castle.

Old Jameson Distillery   Museum

(www.jamesonwhiskey.com; Bow St; adult/child €14/7.70; ⊙9am-6pm Mon-Sat, 10am-6pm Sun; 🚌25, 66, 67 or 90 from city centre, 🚋Smith-field) Guided tours (three or four daily) cover the entire whiskey-distilling process; tastings follow.

👉 Tours

BUS

City Sightseeing   Bus Tour

(www.citysightseeingdublin.ie; 14 Upper O'Connell St; adult/child €18/free; ⊙every 8-15 min 9am-6pm) City Sightseeing's time-tested hop-on, hop-off open-top tours; tickets valid for two days.

Dublin Bus   Bus Tour

(www.dublinsightseeing.ie; Cathal Brugha St; adult/child €18/free; ⊙every 10-15 min 9am-5.30pm, every 30 min 5.30-6.30pm) Hop-on hop-off; tickets valid for two days.

WALKING

Each tour lasts two to three hours and costs around €12. Book through Dublin Tourism, at hostels or by calling direct.

Dublin Literary Pub Crawl   Walking Tour

(🕿01-670 5602; www.dublinpubcrawl.com; 9 Duke St; adult/student €12/10; ⊙7.30pm Apr-Oct, 7.30pm Thu-Sun Nov-Mar) Led by actors performing pieces from Irish literature; begins at the Duke pub.

1916 Rebellion Walking Tour   Walking Tour

(🕿086 858 3847; www.1916rising.com; 23 Wicklow St; per person €12; ⊙11.30am Mon-Sat, 1pm Sun Mar-Oct) Visits key sites of the rebellion; departs from the International Bar.

Dublin Musical Pub Crawl   Walking Tour

(🕿01-478 0193; www.discoverdublin.ie; Oliver St John Gogarty's, 58-59 Fleet St; adult/student €12/10; ⊙7.30pm daily Apr-Oct, 7.30pm Thu-Sat Nov-Mar) Irish traditional music explained and demonstrated by two expert musicians in various Temple Bar pubs.

🛏 Sleeping

Dublin is *always* bustling, so call ahead or book online, especially on weekends. Don't forget that Dublin Tourism Centres can find and book accommodation for €5, plus a 10% deposit for the first night's stay.

NORTH OF THE LIFFEY

Townhouse Hotel   Inn €€€

(🕿01-878 8808; www.townhouseofdublin.com; 47-48 Lower Gardiner St; s/d/tr €140/199/219; 🚌36 or 36A, 🚋Connolly) Elegant but unpretentious, the Georgian Townhouse has beautiful, individually designed bedrooms named after plays by the famous 19th-century playwrights who once lived here (Dion Boucicault and Lafcadio Hearn), and a Japanese garden out back.

Anchor Guesthouse   B&B €€

(🕿01-878 6913; www.anchorhousedublin.com; 49 Lower Gardiner St; r weekday/weekend from €71/143; P; 🚌all city centre, 🚋Connolly) This lovely Georgian guesthouse, with its delicious wholesome breakfasts and an elegance you won't find in many of the other B&Bs along this stretch, comes highly recommended.

SOUTH OF THE LIFFEY

Number 31 — Guesthouse €€€

(📞 01-676 5011; www.number31.ie; 31 Leeson Close; s/d/tr incl breakfast €180/260/300; 🅿 🛜 ; 🖳 all cross-city) The former dwelling of modernist architect Sam Stephenson (1933–2006) still feels like a 1960s designer pad with sunken sitting room, leather sofas, mirrored bar and floor-to-ceiling windows.

Morgan Hotel — Boutique Hotel €€

(📞 01-643 7000; www.themorgan.com; 10 Fleet St; r from €100; @ 🛜 ; 🖳 all city centre) Falling somewhere between *Alice in Wonderland* and a cocaine-and-hooker-fuelled rock 'n' roll fantasy, the ubercool Morgan sports a sexy colour scheme of white floors and walls with dark blue and pink lighting that extends into the bar, the rooms and even the cigar patio.

 Eating

NORTH OF THE LIFFEY

Chapter One — Modern Irish €€€

(📞 01-873 2266; www.chapteronerestaurant.com; 18 North Parnell Sq; 2-course lunch €29, 4-course dinner €65; 🕐 12.30-2pm Tue-Fri, 6-11pm Tue-Sat; 🖳 3, 10, 11, 13, 16, 19 or 22 from city centre) One of the best restaurants in Dublin, this venerable old trooper in the vaulted basement of the Dublin Writers Museum sets its ambitions no further than modern Irish cuisine, which it has realised so brilliantly that those Michelin lads saw fit to throw one of their sought-after stars its way.

Winding Stair
Modern Irish €€€

(📞 01-873 7320; winding-stair.com; 40 Lower Ormond Quay; mains €23-27; 🕐 noon-5pm & 5.30-10.30pm; 🖳 all city centre) This rustic dining room squeezed above a bookshop serves superb Irish grub, from Irish charcuterie with wheaten bread, to locally caught hake with celeriac mash, followed by sticky pear and ginger steam pud. Hugely popular, so book ahead.

SOUTH OF THE LIFFEY

L'Gueuleton — French €€

(www.lgueuleton.com; 1 Fade St; mains €19-26; 🕐 12.30-4pm & 6-10pm Mon-Sat, 1-4pm & 6-9pm Sun) Dubliners just can't get enough of this restaurant's take on French rustic cuisine, which ranges from regulars such as slow-roast pork belly with dauphinoise potatoes, to specials such as braised venison with orange, juniper and roast root vegetables. No reservations – queue for a table, or leave your mobile number and they'll text when a table's ready.

Coppinger Row — Mediterranean €€

(www.coppingerrow.com; Coppinger Row; mains €18-25; 🕐 noon-5.30pm & 6-11pm Mon-Sat, 12.30-4pm & 6-9pm Sun) The chefs here add a Mediterranean touch to the best of Irish

Library at Trinity College (p151), Dublin
IIC/AXIOM/GETTY IMAGES ©

BRITAIN & IRELAND DUBLIN

produce, which can be enjoyed as main courses or afternoon bar bites.

🍷 Drinking & Nightlife

Temple Bar, Dublin's 'party district', is almost always packed with raucous stag (bachelor) and hen (bachelorette) parties, scantily clad girls, and loud guys from Ohio wearing Guinness T-shirts. If that's not your style, there's plenty to enjoy beyond Temple Bar.

Stag's Head   Pub
(1 Dame Ct) Built in 1770, and remodelled in 1895, the Stag's Head is possibly the best traditional pub in Dublin (and therefore the world). You may find yourself philosophising in the ecclesiastical atmosphere, as James Joyce once did.

Grogan's Castle Lounge   Pub
(15 South William St) A city-centre institution, Grogan's has long been a favourite haunt of Dublin's writers and painters, as well as others from the bohemian, alternative set.

Dice Bar   Bar
(☎01-674 6710; 79 Queen St; 🚌25, 25A, 66, 67 from city centre, 🚇Museum) Co-owned by singer Huey from the band Fun Lovin' Criminals, the Dice Bar looks like something you'd find on New York's Lower East Side.

★ Entertainment

For events, reviews and club listings, pick up a copy of the fortnightly music review **Hot Press** (www.hotpress.com), or for free cultural events, check out the weekly e-zine **Dublin Event Guide** (www.dublineventguide.com).

CLUBS & LIVE MUSIC
Twisted Pepper   Nightclub
(☎01-873 4800; www.bodytonicmusic.com/thetwistedpepper; 54 Middle Abbey St; ⏰bar 4pm-late, cafe 11am-6pm; 🚇all city centre, 🚇Abbey) Dublin's coolest new venue comes in four parts: the basement is where you can hear some of the best DJs in town, the stage is for live acts, the mezzanine is a secluded bar area above the stage and the cafe serves Irish breakfast all day.

Whelan's   Live Music
(☎01-478 0766; www.whelanslive.com; 25 Wexford St) A Dublin institution, providing a showcase for Irish singer-songwriters and other lo-fi performers.

THEATRE & CLASSICAL MUSIC
Abbey Theatre   Theatre
(☎01-878 7222; www.abbeytheatre.ie; Lower Abbey St; 🚇all city centre, 🚇Abbey) The famous Abbey is Ireland's national theatre, putting on new Irish works as well as revivals of Irish classics.

National Concert Hall   Live Music
(☎01-417 0000; www.nch.ie; Earlsfort Tce) Just south of the city centre, Ireland's premier orchestral hall hosts a variety of concerts year-round, including a series of lunchtime concerts from 1.05pm to 2pm on Tuesday from June to August.

ℹ Information
Tourist Information
Dublin Discover Ireland Centre (www.visitdublin.com; St Andrew's Church, 2 Suffolk St; ⏰9am-5.30pm Mon-Sat, 10.30am-3pm Sun) Offers tourist information for all of Ireland, as well as accommodation bookings, car hire, maps, and tickets for tours, concerts and more. Ask about the **Dublin Pass** (www.dublinpass.ie), which allows you entrance into more than 30 of Dublin's attractions, as well as some tours and other special offers.

Northern Ireland Tourist Board (NITB; www.discovernorthernireland.com) Has a desk in the Dublin Tourism Centre; same hours.

ℹ Getting There & Away
Air
Dublin airport (☎01-814 1111; www.dublinairport.com), about 13km north of the city centre, is Ireland's major international gateway, with direct flights from Europe, North America and Asia.

Boat
There are direct ferries from Holyhead in Wales to Dublin Port, 3km northeast of the city centre, and to Dun Laoghaire, 13km southeast. Boats also

sail direct to Dublin Port from Liverpool and from Douglas, on the Isle of Man.

Train

Connolly station North of the Liffey; trains to Belfast, Derry, Sligo, other points north and Wexford.

Heuston station South of the Liffey and west of the city centre; trains for Cork, Galway, Killarney, Limerick, and most other points to the south and west.

Regular one-way fares from Dublin:

Belfast €35, 2¼ hours, up to eight daily

Cork €60, 2¾ hours, hourly

Galway €34, 2¾ hours, nine daily

Iarnród Éireann Travel Centre (☎1850-366 222; www.irishrail.ie; Connolly Station, Amiens St; ◷9am-5pm Mon-Fri, to 1pm Sat) For general train information.

ℹ Getting Around

To & From the Airport

A taxi to the city centre should cost around €20 to €25. Some Dublin airport taxi drivers can be unscrupulous, so make sure the meter is on and mention up front that you'll need a meter receipt.

Aircoach (www.aircoach.ie; one-way/return €7/12) Serves various destinations in the city; departs every 10 to 20 minutes from 5am to midnight, hourly through the night (35 to 55 minutes, depending on traffic).

Airlink Express Coach (☎01-873 4222; www.dublinbus.ie; adult/ child €6/3) Bus 747 runs every 10 to 20 minutes from 6am to midnight to Upper O'Connell St (35 minutes) and the central bus station (Busáras; 45 minutes).

Car

Traffic in Dublin is a nightmare and parking is an expensive headache. Better to leave your vehicle at the Red Cow Park & Ride just off Exit 9 on the M50

ring road, and take the **Luas tram** into the city centre (€4.20 return, 30 minutes).

Public Transport

Various public transport passes are available; one day's unlimited bus travel costs €6.50 (including Airlink); bus and tram costs €7.80; and bus and DART costs €11.75.

Bus

Dublin Bus (www.dublinbus.ie) local buses cost from €1.40 to €2.65 for a single journey. You must pay the exact fare when boarding; drivers don't give change.

Train

Dublin Area Rapid Transport (DART; ☎01-836 6222; www.irishrail.ie) provides quick rail access as far north as Howth and south to Bray; Pearse station is handy for central Dublin.

Tram

Luas (www.luas.ie) runs on two (unconnected) lines; the green line runs from the eastern side of St Stephen's Green southeast to Sandyford, and the red line runs from Tallaght to Connolly station, with stops at Heuston station, the National Museum and

Dublin Castle (p154), Dublin
DAVID CORDNER/GETTY IMAGES ©

Busáras. Single fares range from €1.60 to €2.90 depending on how many zones you travel through.

Taxi

Taxis in Dublin are expensive; flag fall costs €4.10, plus €1.03 per kilometre. For taxi service, call **National Radio Cabs** (01-677 2222; www. radiocabs.ie).

Around Dublin
DUN LAOGHAIRE

01 / POP 114,200

Dun Laoghaire (dun-*leary*), 13km south of central Dublin, is a seaside resort and busy harbour with ferry connections to Britain.

At Sandycove, south of the harbour, is the Martello Tower, where James Joyce's epic novel *Ulysses* opens. It now houses the **James Joyce Museum** (01-280 9265; www.visitdublin.com; Joyce Tower, Sandycove; 10am-4pm) FREE. If you fancy a cold saltwater dip, the nearby **Forty Foot Pool** (also mentioned in *Ulysses*) is the place.

Take the Dublin Area Rapid Transport (DART) rail service (€4.70 return, 25 minutes, every 10 to 20 minutes) from Dublin to Dun Laoghaire, then bus 59 to Sandycove Rd, or walk (1km).

Dun Laoghaire harbour

MALAHIDE CASTLE

01

Despite the vicissitudes of Irish history, the Talbot family managed to keep **Malahide Castle** (01-846 2184; www.malahidecastle andgardens.ie; Malahide; adult/child €12/6; 9.30am-5.30pm, last tour of castle 4.30pm) from 1185 through to 1973. The castle is the usual hotchpotch of additions and renovations; the oldest part is a three-storey 12th-century tower house. The facade is flanked by circular towers that were tacked on in 1765. The interior is packed with furniture and paintings, and Puck, the family ghost, is still in residence.

Malahide is 13km northeast of Dublin; take the DART rail service from Dublin Connolly to Malahide station (€4.70, return, 22 minutes, every 10 to 20 minutes).

The Southwest
CORK

021 / POP 120,000

There's a reason the locals call Cork (Corcaigh) 'Ireland's Real Capital' or 'The People's Republic of Cork'; something

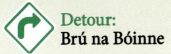

Detour:
Brú na Bóinne

A thousand years older than Stonehenge, the extensive Neolithic necropolis known as Brú na Bóinne (Boyne Palace) is one of the most extraordinary prehistoric sites in Europe. Its tombs date from about 3200 BC, predating the great pyramids of Egypt by six centuries. The complex, including the Newgrange and Knowth passage tombs, can only be visited on a guided walk from the **Brú na Bóinne Visitor Centre** (☎041-988 0300; www.heritageireland.ie; Donore; adult/child visitor centre €3/2, visitor centre & Newgrange €6/3, visitor centre & Knowth €5/3, visitor centre, Newgrange & Knowth €11/6; ☺9am-5pm Nov-Jan, 9.30am-5.30 Feb-Apr, 9am-6.30pm May, 9am-7pm Jun-Sep, 9.30am-5.30pm Oct). At 8.20am during the winter solstice, the rising sun's rays shine directly down Newgrange's long passage and illuminate the chamber for a magical 17 minutes.

The site is 50km north of Dublin, signposted off the M1.

Guided day tours from Dublin by **Mary Gibbons** (☎086 355 1355; www.newgrangetours.com; tour per adult/student €35/30) are excellent.

---

special is going on here. The city has long been dismissive of Dublin, and with a burgeoning arts, music and restaurant scene, it has a cultural reputation to rival the capital's.

Sights

Cork City Gaol — Museum
(☎021-430 5022; www.corkcitygaol.com; Convent Ave, Sunday's Well; adult/child €8/4.50; ☺9.30am-5pm Apr-Oct, 10am-4pm Nov-Mar) Closed down in 1923, this vast 19th-century prison is now a terrific museum about a terrifying subject. Restored cells, mannequins representing prisoners and guards, and a detailed audioguide bring home the horrors of Victorian prison life.

St Fin Barre's Cathedral — Cathedral
(☎021-496 3387; www.cathedral.cork.anglican.org; Bishop St; adult/child €5/3; ☺9.30am-5.30pm Mon-Sat & 12.30-5pm Sun Apr-Oct, closed 12.45-2pm & Sun Nov-Mar) Just south of the city centre sits Cork's Protestant cathedral. Built in 1879, this beautiful Gothic Revival structure has a multitude of notable features, including a Golden Angel who sits on the eastern side of the cathedral, and whose job it is to blow her horn at the onset of the Apocalypse.

English Market — Market
(www.englishmarket.ie; Princes St; ☺9am-5.30pm Mon-Sat) It could just as easily be called the Victorian Market for its ornate vaulted ceilings and columns, but the English Market is a true gem, no matter what you name it. Scores of vendors sell some of the very best meat, fish, cheese and takeaway food in the region. On decent days, take your lunch to nearby Bishop Lucey Park, a popular al fresco eating spot.

Sleeping

Garnish House — B&B €€
(☎021-427 5111; www.garnish.ie; Western Rd; s/d from €75/89; P 🛜) With charming rooms (think flowers and fresh fruit), gourmet breakfasts and hosts who are eager to please, Garnish House is possibly the perfect B&B.

River Lee Hotel — Hotel €€
(☎021-425 2700; www.doylecollection.com; Western Rd; r from €125; P ❄ 🛜 ☒) This modern riverside hotel brings a touch of affordable luxury to the city centre.

Crawford House — B&B €€
(☎021-427 9000; www.crawfordhouse.ie; Western Rd; d €60-90; P @) A top-notch B&B,

159

Crawford House has spacious rooms with king-size beds, gracious furnishings and spa baths. The standard is that of a contemporary hotel, the atmosphere that of a family home.

🍴 Eating

Market Lane   Irish, International €€
(📞021-427 4710; www.marketlane.ie; 5 Oliver Plunkett St; mains €11-25.50; 🕐noon-late Mon-Sat, 1-9pm Sun; 🛜👶) It's always hopping at this bright corner bistro with a walk-in policy (no reservations for fewer than six diners, sip a drink at the bar till a table is free). The menu is broad and hearty, changing to reflect what's fresh at the English Market: how about braised ox cheek stew, or smoked haddock with bacon and cabbage?

Farmgate Café   Cafe, Bistro €€
(www.farmgate.ie; English Market, Princes St; dishes €4.50-15; 🕐8.30am-5pm Mon-Sat) An unmissable experience at the heart of the English Market, the Farmgate is perched on a balcony overlooking the market below, the source of all that fresh local produce on your plate.

Cafe Paradiso   Vegetarian €€
(📞021-427 7939; www.cafeparadiso.ie; 16 Lancaster Quay; lunch mains €13-14, 2-/3-course dinner €33/40; 🕐noon-2.30pm Fri & Sat, 5.30-10pm Tue-Sat year-round, plus 5.50-10pm Mon Jun--late Aug) 🍃 Arguably the best vegetarian restaurant in Ireland, the inventive dishes on offer here will seduce even the most committed carnivore. The pre-theatre menu (5.30pm to 7pm Tuesday to Saturday) offers two/three courses for €23/29.

🍷 Drinking & Nightlife

Cork's pub scene is cracking, easily rivalling Dublin's. Locally brewed Murphy's is the stout of choice here, not Guinness. Check www.corkgigs.com for pubs with live music.

Franciscan Well Brewery   Pub
(www.franciscanwellbrewery.com; 14 North Mall; 🕐3-11.30pm Mon-Thu, 3pm-12.30am Fri-Sat, 3-11pm Sun; 🛜) The copper vats gleaming behind the bar give the game away: the Franciscan Well brews its own beer. The best place to enjoy it is in the enormous beer garden at the back.

Mutton Lane Inn   Pub
(Mutton Lane) With Victorian wallpaper, rock 'n' roll posters, and a covered outdoor area for drinking and smoking, Cork's oldest pub is the type of place that you'll wish you had in your home town.

Long Valley   Pub
(10 Winthrop St) This Cork institution has been going strong more or less since the mid-19th century.

ℹ️ Information

Cork City Tourist Office (📞021-425 5100; www.corkcity.ie; Grand Pde; 🕐9am-6pm Mon-Sat, 10am-5pm Sun Jul & Aug, 9.15am-5pm Mon-Sat Sep-Jun)

ℹ️ Getting There & Away

Air
Cork airport (ORT; 📞021-431 3131; www.cork-airport.com) is 8km south of the city on the N27. Direct flights to Newcastle, Edinburgh, London, Manchester, Amsterdam, Barcelona, Munich, Paris, Warsaw and Rome.

Boat
Brittany Ferries (📞021-427 7801; www.brittanyferries.ie; 42 Grand Pde) has regular sailings from Cork to Roscoff (France). The ferry terminal is at Ringaskiddy, about 15 minutes by car southeast of the city centre along the N28.

Train
Cork's **Kent train station** (📞021-450 4777) is across the river.

Dublin €60, 2¾ hours, hourly

Galway €83, five to six hours, seven daily (two or three changes needed)

Killarney €28, 1½ to two hours, nine daily

AROUND CORK

Rock of Cashel

The **Rock of Cashel** (www.heritageireland.com; adult/child €6/2; 🕐9am-5.30pm mid-Mar–mid-Oct, to 7pm Mid-Jun–Aug, to 4.30pm mid-Oct–

mid-Mar) is one of Ireland's most spectacular archaeological sites. A prominent green hill, banded with limestone outcrops, it rises from a grassy plain on the outskirts of Cashel town and bristles with ancient fortifications. For more than 1000 years it was a symbol of power, and the seat of kings and churchmen who ruled over the region. Sturdy walls circle an enclosure that contains a complete **round tower**, a roofless **abbey** and the finest 12th-century **Romanesque chapel** in Ireland.

Bus Éireann (www.buseireann.ie) runs eight buses daily between Cashel and Cork (€14, 1½ hours).

Blarney

☎ 021 / POP 2150

Lying just northwest of Cork, the village of Blarney (An Bhlarna) receives a *gazillion* visitors a year, for one sole reason: **Blarney Castle** (☎ 021-438 5252; www.blarney castle.ie; adult/child €12/5; ⊙ 9am-7pm Mon-Sat, 9am-6pm Sun Jun-Aug, 9am-6.30pm Mon-Sat, 9am-6pm Sun May & Sep, 9am-6pm Mon-Sat, 9am-5pm Sun Oct-Apr). They come to kiss the castle's legendary **Blarney Stone** and get the 'gift of the gab' (Queen Elizabeth I, exasperated with Lord Blarney's ability to talk endlessly without agreeing to her demands, invented the term 'to talk Blarney' back in the 16th century). The stone is up on the battlements, and bending over backwards to kiss it requires a head for heights, although there's someone there to hold you in position. It also helps if you're not germophobic – there's a greasy mark where millions of lips have been before. (The Blarney stain? Sorry.)

Bus 215 runs from Cork bus station to Blarney (€6.50 return, 30 minutes, every 30 minutes).

RING OF KERRY

This 179km circuit of the Iveragh Peninsula pops up on every self-respecting tourist itinerary, and for good reason. The road winds past pristine beaches, medieval ruins, mountains and loughs (lakes), and the island-dotted Atlantic. Even locals stop their cars to gawk at the rugged coastline – particularly between Waterville and Caherdaniel in the southwest of the peninsula, where the beauty dial is turned up to 11.

Although it can be 'done' in a day by car or bus, or three days by bicycle, the more time you take, the more you'll enjoy it. Tour

Blarney Castle

LAURA CIAPPONI/GETTY IMAGES ©

buses travel the Ring in an anticlockwise direction. Getting stuck behind one is tedious, so driving in the opposite direction is preferred. Alternatively, you can detour from the main road – the **Ballaghbeama Pass** cuts across the peninsula's central highlands, and has spectacular views and little traffic.

The shorter **Ring of Skellig**, at the end of the peninsula, has fine views of the Skellig Rocks and its narrow roads are free of tourist coaches.

🛈 Getting Around

Bus Éireann runs a once-daily Ring of Kerry bus service (No 280) from late June to late August. Buses leave Killarney at 11.30am and stop at Killorglin, Glenbeigh, Caherciveen, Waterville, Caherdaniel and Molls Gap, arriving back at Killarney at 4.45pm (€19).

DINGLE PENINSULA

☏066

Remote and beautiful, the Dingle Peninsula ends in the Irish mainland's most westerly point. This is a Gaeltacht area –

if you're driving, don't bother looking for road signs that say 'Dingle'; they all say 'An Daingean', the Irish equivalent.

The peninsula's capital (population 1800) is a special place whose charms have long drawn runaways from across the world, making the port town a surprisingly creative and cosmopolitan place. There are loads of cafes, bookshops and art and craft galleries, and a friendly dolphin called Fungie who has lived in the bay for 25 years.

🏃 Activities

Fungie the Dolphin   Boat Trip
(☏066-915 2626; www.dingledolphin.com; The Pier; adult/child €16/8) The Dingle Boatmen's Association operates one-hour boat trips to visit Fungie the dolphin (free if Fungie doesn't show, but he usually does). There are also two-hour trips where you can swim with him (€25 per person, wetsuit hire €25 extra). Booking advisable.

Dingle Bay Charters   Cruises
(☏066-915 1344; www.dinglebaycharters.com) Offers two-hour cruises from the marina to the Blasket Islands (adult/child €25/10) and one-hour trips around the bay (€10/5).

🛈 Information

Tourist Office (☏066-915 1188; www.dingle-peninsula.ie; The Pier; ⏱9.15am-5pm Mon-Sat) At Dingle Town pier.

The West Coast
CLIFFS OF MOHER

About 8km south of Doolin are the towering 200m-high Cliffs of Moher, one of Ireland's most famous natural features. In summer the cliffs are overrun with day trippers, so consider

Cliffs of Moher
ROBERT RIDDELL/GETTY IMAGES ©

staying in Doolin and hiking or biking along The Burren's quiet country lanes, where the views are superb and crowds are never a problem. Either way, be careful along these sheer cliffs, especially in wet or windy weather.

The landscaped **Cliffs of Moher Visitor Centre** (www.cliffsofmoher.ie; adult/child €6/free; ⏱8.30am-7.30pm Jun-Aug, 9am-6pm Mar-May, Sep & Oct, 9am-5pm Nov-Feb) has exhibitions about the cliffs and the environment called the 'Atlantic Edge'.

GALWAY
☎091 / POP 72,400

Arty and bohemian, Galway (Gaillimh) is legendary around the world for its entertainment scene. Cafes spill out onto cobblestone streets filled with a frenzy of fiddles, banjos, guitars and bodhráns, and jugglers, painters, puppeteers and magicians in outlandish masks enchant passers-by.

 Sights

Hall of the Red Earl
Archaeological Site

(www.galwaycivictrust.ie; Druid Lane; ⏱9.30am-4.45pm Mon-Fri, 10am-1pm Sat) FREE Back in the 13th century when the de Burgo family ran the show in Galway, Richard – the Red Earl – had a large hall built as a seat of power. After the 14 tribes took over, the hall fell into ruin and was lost. Lost that is until 1997 when expansion of the city's Custom House uncovered its foundations. Artefacts and a plethora of fascinating displays give a sense of Galway life some 900 years ago.

Galway City Museum
Museum

(www.galwaycitymuseum.ie; Spanish Pde; ⏱10am-5pm Tue-Sat) FREE Little remains of Galway's old city walls apart from the **Spanish Arch**, which is right beside the river. The nearby museum has exhibits on the city's history from 1800 to 1950, including an iconic Galway Hooker fishing boat, a collection of currachs (boats made from animal hides) and a much-loved statue of Galway-born writer and hell-raiser Pádraic O'Conaire (1883–1928).

Festivals & Events

Galway Arts Festival
Arts

(www.galwayartsfestival.ie; ⏱mid-Jul) Held in July, this is the main event on Galway's calendar

Galway Oyster Festival
Food, Drink

(www.galwayoysterfest.com) Going strong for more than 50 years now, this festival draws thousands of visitors in late September.

 Sleeping

St Martins B&B
B&B €€

(☎091-568 286; www.stmartins.ie; 2 Nun's Island Rd; s/d from €50/80; @ 📶) St Martin's is in a great location, with back-window views overlooking the William O'Brien Bridge and a simple garden on the banks of the Corrib.

House Hotel
Hotel €€€

(☎091-538 900; www.thehousehotel.ie; Spanish Pde; r €100-220; P 📶) It's a design odyssey at this boutique hotel. The 40 rooms are plush, with beds having elaborately padded headboards (so you don't bonk your, er, well...) and a range of colour schemes.

Eating

Griffin's
Cafe, Bakery €

(www.griffinsbakery.com; Shop St; mains €4-8; ⏱8am-6pm Mon-Sat) A local institution since 1876.

Ard Bia at Nimmo's
Modern Irish €€

(www.ardbia.com; Spanish Arch; lunch mains €5-10, dinner mains €19-24; ⏱cafe 10am-3.30pm, restaurant 6-10pm, wine bar 6-11pm, all Mon-Sat) This cottage-style restaurant serves some of the finest food in the west of Ireland, from scallops to roast Irish lamb.

Drinking & Entertainment

Most of Galway's pubs see musicians performing a few nights a week, whether playing informally or as headline acts, and many even have live music every night of the week.

Good spots to hear traditional music sessions include **Monroe's Tavern** (www.monroes.ie; Upper Dominick St), which has Irish dancing on Tuesday, **Taaffe's Bar** (19 Shop St), **Taylor's Bar** (Upper Dominick St) and **Crane Bar** (www.thecranebar.com; 2 Sea Rd).

Tig Cóilí   Pub
(Mainguard St) Two ceilidh (live-music sessions) a day draw the crowds to this authentic fire-engine-red pub, just off High St.

ℹ Information

Tourist Office (www.discoverireland.ie; Forster St; ⊙9am-5.45pm daily Easter-Sep, closed Sun Oct-Easter)

ℹ Getting There & Around

Trains run to and from Dublin (€33.50, three hours, five daily).

CONNEMARA
🖉 095

With its shimmering black lakes, pale mountains, lonely valleys and more than the occasional rainbow, Connemara in the northwestern corner of County Galway is one of the most gorgeous corners of Ireland. This is one of the most important Gaeltacht areas in the country; the lack of English signposting can be confusing at times.

The most scenic routes through Connemara are Oughterard–Recess (via the N59), Recess–Kylemore Abbey (via the R344) and the Leenane–Louisburgh route (via the R335). From Galway, **Lally Tours** (🖉091-562 905; www.lallytours.com; buses Galway Coach Station, ticket office Forster St; tours adult/child from €20/12) and **O'Neachtain Tours** (www.irelandscenictours.ie) run day-long bus trips through Connemara for around €25 per person.

SURVIVAL GUIDE

ℹ Directory A–Z
Accommodation

Britain

Accommodation in the big cities inevitably tends to be more expensive, with London in a class all of its own.

○ Rates tend to drop in low season (October to April), and rocket during high season (July to September).

  ○ Breakfast is usually included at most B&Bs and hotels, but may be an extra at many hostels and top-end hotels.

    ○ Rates are often quoted per person, rather than per room, and include a private bathroom unless otherwise stated.

      ○ Smoking is banned in all hotels, B&Bs and other accommodation.

        ○ Accommodation can be difficult to find during holidays (especially around Easter and New Year) and major events (such as the Edinburgh Fringe Festival).

Giant's Causeway, Northern Ireland
SLOW IMAGES/GETTY IMAGES ©

Giant's Causeway

This spectacular rock formation – Northern Ireland's only Unesco World Heritage site – is one of Ireland's most impressive and atmospheric landscape features. When you first see it you'll understand why the ancients thought it wasn't a natural feature – the vast expanse of regular, closely packed, hexagonal stone columns looks for all the world like the handiwork of giants.

The more prosaic explanation is that the columns are simply contraction cracks caused by a cooling lava flow some 60 million years ago. The phenomenon is explained in the **Giant's Causeway Visitor Experience** (☎2073 1855; www.giantscausewaycentre.com; adult/child £8.50/4.25; ☼9am-9pm Jul & Aug, to 7pm Apr-Jun & Sep, to 6pm Feb-Mar & Oct, to 7pm Nov-Jan), a spectacular new eco-friendly building half-hidden in a hillside above the sea.

From the centre it's an easy 10- to 15-minute walk downhill to the causeway itself, but a more interesting approach is to follow the clifftop path northeast for 2km to the **Chimney Tops** headland, then descend the **Shepherd's Steps** to the Causeway.

Eight miles to the east of the causeway, the 20m-long **Carrick-a-Rede rope bridge** (☎028-2076 9839; nationaltrust.org.uk/carrick-a-rede; adult/child £5.60/3.10; ☼10am-7pm Jun-Aug, to 6pm Mar-May, Sep & Oct, 10.30am-3.30pm Nov & Dec) that connects Carrick-a-Rede Island to the mainland, swaying some 30m above the pounding waves, is a classic test of nerve. Note that the bridge is closed in high winds.

Price ranges

Our reviews refer to double rooms with a private bathroom, except in hostels or where otherwise specified.

£ less than £60 (less than £90 in London)

££ £50 to £130 (£90 to £180 in London)

£££ more than £130 (more than £180 in London

Ireland

Booking ahead is recommended in peak season (roughly April to October).

Fáilte Ireland (Irish Tourist Board; www.discoverireland.ie) Will book accommodation for a 10% room deposit and a fee of €5.

Northern Ireland Tourist Board (NITB; www.discovernorthernireland.com) Books accommodation at no cost but with a 10% deposit upfront.

Gulliver (www.gulliver.ie) Online booking service for both the Republic and Northern Ireland; deposit of 10% and a €5 fee is payable.

Price Ranges

Prices are listed at high-season rates (low-season rates can be 15% to 20% less), based on two people sharing a double, and include a private bathroom unless otherwise stated.

In the Republic of Ireland:

€ less than €60

€€ €60 to €150

€€€ more than €150

In Northern Ireland:

£ less than £40

££ £40 to £100

£££ more than £100

Business Hours

Britain

Banks 9.30am to 4pm or 5pm Monday to Friday, 9.30am to 1pm Saturday.

Museums Smaller museums may close Monday and/or Tuesday, and close on weekdays in the low season.

Post offices 9am to 5pm Monday to Friday, 9am to 12.30pm Saturday (main branches to 5pm).

Pubs 11am to 11pm Sunday to Thursday, sometimes to midnight or 1am Friday & Saturday; some pubs close between 3pm & 6pm; bars open to midnight or later.

Restaurants Lunch noon to 3pm, dinner 6pm to 11pm; some restaurants close on Sunday evenings or all day Monday; cafes open 7am to 6pm; teashops open for lunch until 5pm, later in summer.

Shops 9am to 5pm Monday to Saturday (to 5.30pm or 6pm in cities), 10am to 4pm Sunday; in smaller towns or country areas, shops may close for lunch from 1pm to 2pm & on Wednesday or Thursday afternoon.

Ireland

Banks 10am to 4pm Monday to Friday, to 5pm Thursday

Post offices 9am to 5.30pm Monday to Friday & 9am to 12.30pm Saturday in Northern Ireland; 9am to 6pm Monday to Friday & 9am to 1pm Saturday in the Republic. Smaller offices may close at lunchtime and one day per week.

Pubs 11.30am to 11pm Monday to Saturday & 12.30 to 10pm Sunday in Northern Ireland, with late licences open until 1am Monday to Saturday & midnight Sunday; 10.30am to 11.30pm

Monday to Thursday, 10.30am to 12.30am Friday & Saturday, noon to 11pm Sunday in the Republic. All pubs close Christmas Day and Good Friday.

Restaurants noon to 10.30pm, many close once a week.

Shops 9am to 5.30pm or 6pm Monday to Saturday (to 8pm Thursday and sometimes Friday), noon to 6pm Sunday (in bigger towns); rural shops may close at lunchtime and one day per week.

Food
Britain
The prices we quote for eateries are for a main meal unless otherwise indicated.

£ less than £9

££ £9 to £18

£££ more than £18

Ireland
In the Republic of Ireland:

€ less than €10

€€ €10 to €20

€€€ more than €20

In Northern Ireland
£ less than £10
££ £10 to £20
£££ more than £20

Gay & Lesbian Travellers
Britain
Most major cities – especially London, Brighton, Manchester and Glasgow – have gay and lesbian scenes. Useful resources:

Diva (www.divamag.co.uk)

Gay Times (www.gaytimes.co.uk)

Pink Paper (www.pinkpaper.com)

Ireland
Only Dublin and, to a lesser extent, Belfast, Cork, Galway and Limerick have open gay and lesbian communities.

Gay Community News (www.gcn.ie) Free monthly mag available at bars and cafes.

Language
Britain
The dominant language of Britain is English. In Wales about 600,000 people (20% of the population) speak Welsh as a first language, while in Scotland, Gaelic – another Celtic language – is spoken by about 80,000 people, mainly in the Highlands and Islands.

Ireland
While Irish Gaelic is the official language of the Republic of Ireland, it is spoken only in a few rural areas (known as Gaeltacht) mainly in Cork, Donegal, Galway and Kerry. English is the everyday language in the Republic and in Northern Ireland.

Money
Scotland issues its own currency (including a £1 note), interchangeable with the money used in the rest of the UK.

Britain
ATMs Often called 'cash machines'; are easy to find in cities and even small towns.

Changing Money Most banks and some post offices offer currency exchange services. Check rates at bureaux de change; they may claim 'no commission' but often rates are poor.

Credit & Debit Cards Smaller businesses, such as pubs or B&Bs, prefer debit cards (or charge a fee for credit cards), and some take cash or cheque only. Nearly all credit and debit cards use a 'Chip and PIN' system (instead of signing).

Currency The currency of Britain is the pound sterling (£). Paper money ('notes') comes in £5, £10, £20 and £50 denominations, although some shops don't accept £50 notes because fakes circulate.

Heritage Organisations

Many of the UK's castles and stately homes, as well as large areas of countryside, are owned by national heritage organisations. If you're a member, you get free admission, free parking, information handbooks and so on. You can join at the first site you visit; if you join an English heritage organisation, it covers you for Wales and Scotland, and vice versa. We have included the relevant acronym (NT, NTS, EH etc) in the information for listed properties.

Annual membership with **English Heritage** (EH; www.english-heritage.org.uk) costs £47. An Overseas Visitors Pass allows free entry to most sites for seven/14 days for £23/27. In Wales and Scotland the equivalent organisations are **Cadw** (www.cadw.wales.gov.uk) and **Historic Scotland** (HS; www.historic-scotland.gov.uk).

National Trust (NT; www.nationaltrust.org.uk) annual membership costs £53 (with discounts for under-26s). The **National Trust for Scotland** (NTS; www.nts.org.uk) is similar.

Holiday Seasons

Roads get busy and hotel prices go up during school holidays.

Easter Holiday Week before and week after Easter.

Summer Holiday Third week of July to first week of September.

Christmas Holiday Mid-December to first week of January.

There are also three week-long 'half-term' school holidays – usually late February (or early March), late May and late October. These vary between Scotland, England and Wales.

Tipping For restaurants, cafés, taxi drivers and pub meals 10% is fine; if you order drinks and food at the bar, there's no need to tip.

Ireland

The Irish Republic uses the euro (€), while Northern Ireland uses the British pound sterling (£). Banks offer the best exchange rates; exchange bureaux, open longer, have worse rates and higher commissions.

In Northern Ireland several banks issue their own Northern Irish pound notes, which are equivalent to sterling but not readily accepted in mainland Britain.

Fancy hotels and restaurants usually add a 10% or 15% service charge onto bills. Simpler places usually don't add a service charge; if you decide to tip, just round up the bill (or add 10% at most). Taxi drivers do not have to be tipped, but if you do, 10% is more than generous.

Public Holidays
Britain

New Year's Day 1 January

Easter March/April (Good Friday to Easter Monday inclusive)

May Day First Monday in May

Spring Bank Holiday Last Monday in May

Summer Bank Holiday Last Monday in August

Christmas Day 25 December

Boxing Day 26 December

Ireland

New Year's Day 1 January

St Patrick's Day 17 March

Easter (Good Friday to Easter Monday inclusive) March/April

May Holiday First Monday in May

Christmas Day 25 December

St Stephen's Day (Boxing Day) 26 December

Only Northern Ireland:

Spring Bank Holiday Last Monday in May

Orangemen's Day 12 July (following Monday if 12th is at weekend)

August Bank Holiday Last Monday in August

Only Ireland:

June Holiday First Monday in June

August Holiday First Monday in August

October Holiday Last Monday in October

Telephone
Britain

Phones from most other countries operate in England, but attract roaming charges. Local SIM cards cost from £10; SIM and basic handset around £30.

You'll mainly see two types of public payphones in Britain: one takes money (and doesn't give change), while the other uses prepaid phonecards and credit cards. The minimum call price is 50p.

- ☎ 0500 or ☎ 0800 – free calls
- ☎ 0845 – calls at the local rate, wherever you're dialling from within the UK
- ☎ 087 – calls at the national rate
- ☎ 089 or ☎ 09 – premium rate
- ☎ 07 – mobile phones, more expensive than calling a landline

To call outside the UK, dial ☎ 00, then the country code (1 for USA, 61 for Australia etc), the area code (you usually drop the initial zero) and the number.
- operator ☎ 100
- international operator ☎ 155 – also for reverse-charge (collect) calls

For directory enquiries, a host of agencies compete for your business and charge from 10p to 40p; numbers include ☎ 118 192, ☎ 118 118, ☎ 118 500 and ☎ 118 811.

Ireland

Local telephone calls from a public phone in the Republic cost a minimum of €0.50 for three minutes; in Northern Ireland a local call costs a minimum of £0.30. Some payphones in Northern Ireland accept euro coins. Prepaid phonecards by Eircom or private operators, available in newsagencies and post offices, work from all payphones and dispense with the need for coins.

To call Northern Ireland from the Republic, do not use ☎0044 as for the rest of the UK. Instead, dial ☎048 and then the local number. To dial the Republic from Northern Ireland, however, use the full international code ☎00-353, then the local number.

The mobile (cell-) phone network in Ireland runs on the GSM 900/1800 system compatible with the rest of Europe and Australia, but not the USA. Mobile numbers in the Republic begin with ☎085, ☎086 or ☎087.

Tourist Information

Britain

All British cities and towns, and some villages, have a tourist information centre (TIC) with helpful staff, books and maps, free leaflets and loads of advice on things to see or do. They can also assist with booking accommodation.

Ireland

The Irish tourist board, **Fáilte Ireland** (www.discoverireland.ie), and the **Northern Ireland Tourist Board** (NITB; ☎head office 028-9023 1221; www.discovernorthernireland.com) operate separately. Every town big enough to have half-a-dozen pubs will have a tourist office, although smaller ones may close in winter. Most will find you a place to stay for a fee of €5.

Tourism Ireland (www.tourismireland.com) handles tourist information for both tourist boards overseas.

Visas

Britain

European Economic Area (EEA) nationals don't need a visa to visit (or work in) Britain. Citizens of Australia, Canada, New Zealand, South Africa and the USA can visit for up to six months (three months for some nationalities), but are prohibited from working. For more info see www.ukvisas.gov.uk or www.ukba.homeoffice.gov.uk.

Ireland

Citizens of the EU, Australia, Canada, New Zealand and the US don't need a visa to visit either the Republic or Northern Ireland. EU nationals are allowed to stay indefinitely, while other visitors can usually remain for three to six months.

Temple Bar district (p156), Dublin

JON ARNOLD/GETTY IMAGES ©

169

ℹ️ Getting There & Away

Air

Britain

You can easily fly to Britain from just about anywhere in the world. In recent years regional airports around Britain have massively increased their choice – especially on budget ('no-frills') airlines to/from mainland Europe.

London is served by five airports; Heathrow and Gatwick are the busiest.

Ireland

There are nonstop flights from Britain, Continental Europe and North America to Dublin, Shannon and Belfast International, and nonstop connections from Britain and Europe to Cork.

Land

Train

Eurostar (www.eurostar.com) has high-speed passenger services that shuttle at least 10 times daily between London and Paris (2½ hours) or Brussels (two hours) via the Channel Tunnel. The normal single fare between London and Paris/Brussels is around £150, but if you buy in advance, deals drop to around £90 return or less.

Drivers use the **Eurotunnel** (www.eurotunnel.com) at Folkestone in England or Calais in France:

you drive onto a train, get carried through the tunnel and drive off at the other end. The trains run four times an hour from 6am to 10pm, then hourly. Loading and unloading takes an hour; the journey takes 35 minutes. The one-way cost for a car and passengers is around £90 to £150 depending on the time of day (less busy times are cheaper); promotional fares bring it nearer to £50.

Sea

Britain

The main ferry routes between Britain and mainland Europe include Dover to Calais or Boulogne (France), Harwich to Hook of Holland (Netherlands), Hull to Zeebrugge (Belgium) or Rotterdam (Netherlands), Rosyth to Zeebrugge, Portsmouth to Santander or Bilbao (Spain), and Newcastle to Bergen (Norway) or Gothenberg (Sweden). Routes to/from Ireland include Holyhead to Dun Laoghaire.

Broker sites covering all routes and options include www.ferrybooker.com and www.directferries.co.uk.

Ireland

There's a wide range of ferry services from Britain and France to Ireland. One-way fares for an adult foot passenger can be as little as £25, but can exceed £75 in summer. For a car plus driver and

Pier Head (p130), Liverpool, England

DAVID BANK/GETTY IMAGES ©

up to four adult passengers, prices can cost from £150 to £300.

DirectFerries (www.directferries.co.uk) lists all the available ferry routes and operators.

❶ Getting Around

When travelling long-distance by train or bus/coach in Britain, it's important to realise that there's no such thing as a standard fare. Book long in advance and travel on Tuesday mid-morning, for example, and it's cheap. Buy your ticket on the spot late Friday afternoon, and it'll be a lot more expensive.

Air
Britain

Britain's domestic air companies include **British Airways** (BA; www.britishairways.com), **EasyJet** (EZY; www.easyjet.com) and **Ryanair** (FR; www.ryanair.com). On most shorter routes (eg London to Newcastle, or Manchester to Bristol), it's often faster to take the train once airport downtime is factored in.

Ireland

There are flights within Ireland from Dublin to Derry and Donegal airports, and from Galway to the Aran Islands. Most domestic flights take 30 to 50 minutes.

Bus
Britain

National Express (www.nationalexpress.com) is England's main coach operator. North of the border, **Scottish Citylink** (☎ 08705 505050; www.citylink.co.uk) is the leading coach company.

Ireland

The Republic of Ireland's national bus line, **Bus Éireann** (☎ 01-836 6111; www.buseireann.ie), operates services all over the Republic and into Northern Ireland. Most intercity buses in Northern Ireland are operated by **Ulsterbus** (☎ 028-9066 6600; www.ulsterbus.co.uk).

Car & Motorcycle
Britain

Most overseas driving licences are valid in Britain for up to 12 months from the date of entry.

Rental

Compared to many countries (especially the USA), car rental is expensive in Britain; you'll pay from around £120 per week for the smallest model, or

Traveline

Traveline (☎ 0871 200 2233; www.traveline.org.uk) is a very useful information service covering bus, coach, taxi and train services nationwide.

£250 per week for a medium-sized car (including insurance and unlimited mileage). All of the major players including Avis, Hertz and Budget operate here.

Using a rental-broker site such as **UK Car Hire** (www.ukcarhire.net) or **Auto Europe** (www.auto-europe.co.uk) can also help find bargains.

It's illegal to drive a car or motorbike in Britain without (at least) third-party insurance. This will be included with all rental cars.

Road Rules

The main ones to remember:
- Always drive on the left
- Give way to your right at junctions and roundabouts
- Always use the left-hand lane on motorways and dual-carriageways, unless overtaking (passing)
- Wear seat belts in cars and crash helmets on motorcycles
- Don't drink and drive; the maximum blood-alcohol level allowed is 80mg/100mL
- Yellow lines (single or double) along the edge of the road indicate parking restrictions, red lines mean no stopping whatsoever
- Speed limits are 30mph in built-up areas, 60mph on main roads, and 70mph on motorways and most dual carriageways

Ireland
Hire

Car hire in Ireland is expensive, so you're better off booking a package deal from home. Extra fees may apply if you cross the North–South border. Automatic cars are more expensive.

People aged under 21 years cannot hire a car; for most hire companies you must be at least 23 and have had a valid driving licence for one year. Some companies will not hire to those aged over 70 or 75. Your own local licence is usually sufficient to hire a car for up to three months.

In the Republic typical weekly high-season hire rates – with insurance, Value-Added Tax (VAT), unlimited distance and collision-damage waiver – cost from €170 for a small car. **Nova Car Hire** (www.novacarhire.com) acts as an agent for Alamo, Budget, European and National, and offers greatly discounted rates.

Road Rules

Driving is on the left-hand side and you should only overtake (pass) to the right of the vehicle ahead of you. The driver and passengers must wear safety belts, and children under 12 years of age cannot sit in the front. Motorcyclists and passengers must wear helmets; headlights should be dipped.

Speed limits are posted in miles per hour in Northern Ireland and kilometres per hour in the Republic: 110km/h (70mph) on motorways, 100km/h (60mph) on main roads and 50km/h (30mph) or as signposted in towns. Ireland's blood-alcohol limit is 0.08% and strictly enforced.

Car parks and other specified areas in Ireland are regulated by 'pay and display' tickets or disc parking. Available from most newsagencies, discs are good for one hour. Double yellow lines by the roadside mean no parking at any time, while single yellow lines indicate restrictions (which will be signposted).

Train

Britain

Around 20 companies operate train services in Britain, including **First Great Western** (www.firstgreatwestern.co.uk), which runs from London to Bristol; **Crosscountry** (☎ 0844 811 0124; www.crosscountrytrains.co.uk), which runs services all the way from Glasgow to Penzance; and **Virgin Trains** (www.virgintrains.co.uk), which runs the 'west coast' route from London to Birmingham and Glasgow.

National Rail Enquiries (☎ 08457 48 49 50; www.nationalrail.co.uk) provides booking and timetable information for Britain's entire rail network.

Rail travel has two classes: 1st and standard. Travelling 1st class costs around 50% more than standard. At weekends some train operators offer 'upgrades' for an extra £10 to £15 on top of your standard-class fare.

Costs & Reservations

For longer journeys, on-the-spot fares are always available, but tickets are much cheaper if bought in advance. You can also save if you travel 'off-peak' (ie the days and times that aren't busy).

If you buy online, you can have the ticket posted (UK addresses only), or collect it from station machines on the day of travel.

Bow Bar (p143), Edinburgh

KARL BLACKWELL/GETTY IMAGES ©

There are three main fare types:

Anytime Buy anytime, travel anytime – usually the most expensive option.

Off-peak Buy anytime, travel off-peak.

Advance Buy in advance, travel only on specific trains (usually the cheapest option).

Train Passes

For country-wide travel, BritRail (www.britrail.com) passes are available for visitors from overseas. They must be bought in your country of origin (not in Britain) from a specialist travel agency. They're available in three different versions (England only; all Britain; UK and Ireland) and for periods from four to 30 days. Eurail cards are not accepted in Britain, and InterRail cards are only valid if bought in another mainland European country.

Ireland

The Republic of Ireland's railway system, Iarnród Éireann (Irish Rail; ✆1850-366 222; www.irishrail.ie), has routes radiating out from Dublin, but there is no direct north–south route along the west coast.

Northern Ireland Railways (NIR; ✆028-9089 9411; www.nirailways.co.uk; Belfast Central Station) has four lines from Belfast, one of which links up with the Republic's rail system.

Train Passes

Travel passes for trains in Ireland include:

Eurail Pass Valid for train travel in the Republic of Ireland but not in Northern Ireland, 50% discount on Irish Ferries crossings to France.

InterRail Pass Discount of 50% on train travel within Ireland and on Irish Ferries and Stena Line services.

Britrail Pass Has an option to add on Ireland for an extra fee. The pass also covers ferry transit.

Irish Explorer Rail For train-only travel (five days' travel out of 15) for €160 within the Republic only.

France

Nowhere provokes passion quite like La Belle France. Love it or loathe it, everyone has their own opinion about this Gallic Goliath. Snooty, sexy, superior, chic, infuriating, arrogant, officious and inspired in equal measures, the French have long lived according to their own idiosyncratic rules, and if the rest of the world doesn't always see eye to eye with them, well, *tant pis* (too bad) – that's the price you pay for being a culinary trendsetter, artistic pioneer and cultural icon.

France is a deeply traditional place: castles, chateaux and ancient churches litter the landscape while centuries-old principles of rich food, fine wine and *joie de vivre* underpin everyday life. Yet it is also a country that has one of Western Europe's most multicultural make-ups, not to mention a well-deserved reputation for artistic experimentation and architectural invention. Enjoy.

Carcassone (p260)

France Highlights

Eiffel Tower

Spiking into the skyline above the City of Lights, the Eiffel Tower (p189) is quite simply one of the world's most unmistakable sights. Built from cast-iron beams and millions of rivets in the late 19th century, it has managed to transcend its industrial components to become nothing short of a work of art. Climb to the top or catch the lifts, and watch the French capital unfold beneath you. It's the Parisian experience par excellence.

Versailles

The French monarchs may have lost their heads during the Revolution, but you can still get a glimpse of their pomp and power at the amazing Château de Versailles (p218). It began life as a hunting lodge for Louis XIV, but was expanded by his successors into a showpiece of extravagant art and architecture, from the famous Hall of Mirrors to the fountain-filled grounds. You'll feel royal for a day.

SAMI SARKIS/GETTY IMAGES ©

Chambord

3

Versailles isn't the only chateau to explore in France. The Loire Valley is lined with scores more lavish castles, mostly built between the 16th and 18th centuries as country estates for the French aristocracy. Chambord (p240) is perhaps the finest of all. This vast Renaissance retreat built for François I is distinguished by a maze of cupolas, turrets, hallways and state rooms, as well as a famous staircase rumoured to have been designed by Leonardo da Vinci.

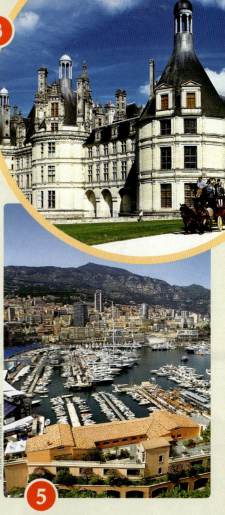

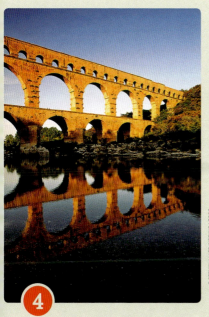

4

Pont du Gard

Two thousand years ago, France (then known as Gaul) was one of the most important provinces of the Roman Empire, and the country is littered with Roman remains. None, however, are as impressive as the Pont du Gard (p265) – an amazing three-tiered aqueduct near Avignon, which was designed to carry 20,000 cubic metres of water per day along the 50km of canals that stretched between Uzès and Nîmes.

5

Côte d'Azur

If there's one place that lives up to its name, it's the Côte d'Azur (French Riviera; p272). Sprinkled with glittering bays, super-exclusive beaches and sunbaked Mediterranean towns, it's been one of Europe's favourite retreats for as long as anyone cares to remember. Nice is essential, but for glitzy Mediterranean glamour you can't beat the pint-sized principality of Monaco, where millionaires step off their yachts straight into Monte Carlo's casino. Monaco (p282)

France's Best...

Iconic Buildings

o **Eiffel Tower** (p189) Admire the view from the top of the 'metal asparagus'.

o **Cathédrale de Notre Dame de Paris** (p190) Gothic gargoyles, gigantic bells and knockout views over Paris.

o **Chartres Cathedral** (p216) Marvel at some of France's finest stained glass.

o **Mont St-Michel** (p226) The island abbey graces a million postcards.

o **Centre Pompidou** (p195) Ponder the merits of the world's first inside-out building.

Artistic Sights

o **Musée d'Orsay** (p185) See France's national collection of Impressionist and post-Impressionist art.

o **Aix-en-Provence** (p271) Follow in the footsteps of Van Gogh and Cézanne.

o **Giverny** (p271) Wander among the lily ponds in Monet's beloved gardens.

o **Louvre-Lens** (p236) Visit this stunning new centre for contemporary art.

o **Vézère Valley** (p257) Home to the world's most important prehistoric paintings.

Historic Locations

o **D-Day Beaches** (p224) Europe's liberation began on Normandy's beaches.

o **Place de la Bastille** (p198) The place where the Revolution originated is now Paris' busiest roundabout.

o **Alignements de Carnac** (p230) Over 3000 menhirs make up the world's largest prehistoric monument.

o **Bayeux** (p222) William the Conqueror's invasion of England is recounted in the massive Bayeux Tapestry.

o **Nîmes** (p261) Wander beneath the arches of the largest Roman amphitheatre in France.

Need to Know

Places to Shop

- **Parisian marchés aux puces** (p213) Paris' fascinating flea markets are a paradise for bargain hunters.

- **Sarlat-la-Canéda** (p253) Sarlat's covered and outdoor markets groan with goodies gathered from across the Dordogne.

- **Markets in Nice** (p272) The chaotic food and flower markets in Nice's historic quarter take over most of cours Saleya.

- **Le Panier, Marseille** (p264) Shoppers have been congregating on this lively quarter of Marseille since the days of ancient Greece.

Left: Cathédrale de Notre Dame de Paris (p190); **Above:** Monet's garden, Giverny (p271)
(LEFT) CHRISTOPHER GROENHOUT/GETTY IMAGES ©;
(ABOVE) DIANA MAYFIELD/GETTY IMAGES ©

ADVANCE PLANNING

- **Two months ahead** Book hotels for Paris, Provence, the Côte d'Azur and Corsica.

- **Two weeks ahead** Plan your train travel on the SNCF website.

- **When you arrive** Pick up a Paris Museum Pass or a Paris Visite Pass for discounts on sights and transport.

RESOURCES

- **France Guide** (www.franceguide.com) Detailed advice from the government tourist office.

- **SNCF** (www.sncf-voyages.com) Plan all train travel and buy tickets online.

- **Météo France** (www.meteo.fr) Get the latest weather forecasts.

- **Paris Convention & Visitors Bureau** (www.parisinfo.com) Paris' tourist site is loaded with useful tips.

GETTING AROUND

- **Air** France's main international airports are Paris' Roissy Charles de Gaulle and Orly; regional airports serve other French cities.

- **Bus** Handy for rural areas; otherwise you're better off with trains.

- **Car** The country's roads are excellent, but tolls operate on most autoroutes.

- **Sea** Cross-channel ferries service Roscoff, St-Malo, Cherbourg and Calais. Nice and Marseille have ferry services to Corsica and Italy.

- **Train** Fast TGVs serve most French cities, while rural areas are served by slower TERs. The Eurostar links Paris' Gare du Nord and London's St Pancras.

BE FOREWARNED

- **Dog poo** Watch where you step, especially in Paris.

- **Closing times** Shops, sights and museums generally shut on Sunday and Monday, and most places close for lunch between noon and 2pm.

- **Manners** It's polite to say *bonjour* (hello) and *au revoir* (goodbye) when entering and leaving shops.

- **Public transport** Remember to stamp your ticket in a *composteur* (validating machine) to avoid being fined.

France Itineraries

France is fascinating enough to fill a lifetime of visits; with these itineraries we've captured the best of both north and south.

3 DAYS

NORTHERN SIGHTS
Paris to Bayeux

Every French adventure has to begin in ❶ **Paris** (p184). You could fill a month here and still not see every sight, so with just a day you'll have to focus on the essentials: a morning at the Louvre, an afternoon at Notre-Dame Cathedral, and a twilight trip up the Eiffel Tower.

On day two take a day trip by either train or car to ❷ **Versailles** (p218), Louis XIV's monumental pleasure palace. Prebook your tickets online to avoid the queues, and take a guided tour to see the secret parts of the palace. You should have time to squeeze in a jaunt across to ❸ **Chartres Cathedral** (p216), famous for its stained glass.

On day three, travel northwest to ❹ **Bayeux** (p222), where you can spend the morning admiring the enormous Bayeux Tapestry before travelling to the ❺ **D-Day Beaches** (p224). Don't miss the moving American Cemetery above Omaha Beach, which you'll recognise from the opening of *Saving Private Ryan*. Unsurprisingly, the beach is still known to veterans as Bloody Omaha.

With a bit of extra time, you could extend the trip with visits to the abbey of ❻ **Mont St-Michel** (p226) and the walled city of ❼ **St-Malo** (p225).

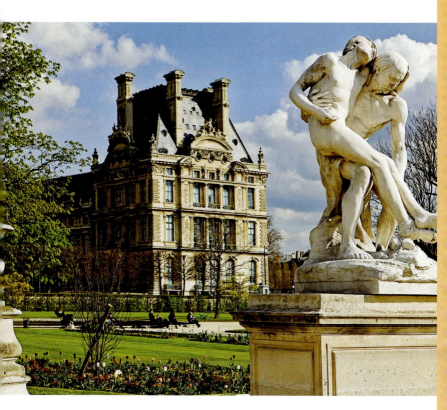

 5 DAYS

THE SULTRY SOUTH
Nîmes to Monaco

France's sun-drenchd south is the perfect place for a road trip. This week-long itinerary begins in ❶ **Nîmes** (p261), once one of the great centres of Roman Gaul, where you can still see the remains of the amphitheatre and Roman walls. Around nearby ❷ **Avignon** (p269), are two of France's most amazing structures: the mighty medieval bridge of Pont St-Bénézet and the breathtaking Roman aqueduct known as the Pont du Gard.

After a couple of days in the Provencal countryside, head for the coast. Multicultural ❸ **Marseille** (p263) comes as something of a shock: it's noisy and chaotic, but if you want to taste authentic *bouillabaisse,* this

is the place to do it. When the din gets too much, beat a retreat to ❹ **Aix-en-Provence** (p271), where Cézanne set up his easel over a century ago; you can visit his atmospheric studio, which has hardly changed since the artist's death in 1906.

Finish up in the quintessential city of the Côte d'Azur, ❺ **Nice** (p272), where you can while away a few days bronzing yourself on the beach, exploring the Old Town's alleyways or tackling the hairpin curves of the *corniches* (coastal roads) en route to the millionaires' playground, ❻ **Monaco** (p282).

Musée du Louvre (p194), Paris
PAUL D. VAN HOY II/GETTY IMAGES ©

Discover France

At a Glance

- **Paris** (p184) The unforgettable, unmissable city of lights.

- **The Loire Valley** (p237) Home to France's grandest chateaux.

- **The Atlantic Coast** (p255) World-class wines and white sandy beaches.

- **Provence** (p263) France at its most photogenic: hilltop towns, bustling markets, Roman ruins.

- **Côte d'Azur** (p272) The dazzling coastline that has inspired artists for centuries.

Sculptures inside Musée Rodin
BRUCE YUANYUE BI/GETTY IMAGES ©

PARIS

POP 2.2 MILLION

What can be said about the sexy, sophisticated City of Lights that hasn't already been said a thousand times before? Quite simply, this is one of the world's great metropolises – a trendsetter, market leader and cultural capital for over a thousand years and still going strong. This is the place that gave the world the can-can and the cinematograph, a city that reinvented itself during the Renaissance, bopped to the beat of the jazz age and positively glittered during the belle époque (literally, 'beautiful era').

As you might expect, Paris is strewn with historic architecture, glorious galleries and cultural treasures galore. But the modern-day city is much more than just a museum piece: it's a heady hodgepodge of cultures and ideas – a place to stroll the boulevards, shop till you drop, flop riverside, or simply do as the Parisians do and watch the world buzz by from a streetside cafe. Savour every moment.

 Sights

Left Bank

Musée du Quai Branly · Museum

(Map p186; www.quaibranly.fr; 37 quai Branly, 7e; adult/child €8.50/free; ⊙11am-7pm Tue, Wed & Sun, 11am-9pm Thu-Sat; Ⓜ Alma-Marceau or RER Pont de l'Alma) No other museum in Paris provides such inspiration to those who appreciate the beauty of traditional craftsmanship. Divided into four main sections, the museum showcases an impressive array of masks, carvings, weapons, jewellery and more, all displayed in a refreshingly unique interior without rooms or high walls. Don't miss the views from the 5th-floor restaurant Les Ombres.

Musée d'Orsay — Museum

(Map p186; www.musee-orsay.fr; 62 rue de Lille, 7e; adult/18-25yr/under 18yr €9/6.50/free; ⏰9.30am-6pm Tue, Wed & Fri-Sun, to 9.45pm Thu; Ⓜ Assemblée Nationale or RER Musée d'Orsay) The home of France's national collection from the impressionist, postimpressionist and art nouveau movements spanning from the 1840s and 1914 is the glorious former Gare d'Orsay railway station – itself an art nouveau showpiece. Highlights include Manet's *On The Beach* and *Woman With Fans*; Monet's gardens at Giverny; Cézanne's card players and still lifes; Renoir's *Ball at the Moulin de la Galette* and *Girls at the Piano*; Degas' ballerinas; Toulouse-Lautrec's cabaret dancers; and Van Gogh's self-portraits, *Bedroom in Arles* and *Starry Night*.

Save time by prepurchasing tickets online or at **Kiosque du Musée d'Orsay** (⏰9am-5pm Tue-Fri school holidays, Tue only rest of year), in front of the museum, and head to entrance C. Admission drops to €6.50 after 4.30pm (after 6pm on Thursday).

Jardin du Luxembourg — Park

(Map p200; numerous entrances; ⏰hrs vary; Ⓜ St-Sulpice, Rennes or Notre Dame des Champs, or RER Luxembourg) The voyeur's spot to peek on Parisians, this 23-hectare park is where Parisians of all ages flock to jog, practise t'ai chi, gossip with friends, read, romance, play tennis, stroll through terraced gardens and orchards heavy with apples, or chase 1920s sailboats around the octagonal **Grand Bassin**.

Musée Rodin — Garden, Museum

(Map p186; www.musee-rodin.fr; 79 rue de Varenne, 7e; adult/under 25yr permanent exhibition €7/5, garden €1/free; ⏰10am-5.45pm Tue-Sun; Ⓜ Varenne) One of the most relaxing spots in the city with a garden bespeckled with sculptures, this lovely art museum inside 18th-century Hôtel Biron displays vital bronze and marble sculptures by sculptor, painter, sketcher, engraver and collector Auguste Rodin. Highlights include that perennial crowd-pleaser *The Thinker*,

and the sublime, the incomparable, that romance-hewn-in-marble called *The Kiss*. Buy tickets online to avoid queuing.

Les Catacombes — Cemetery

(Map p186; www.catacombes.paris.fr; 1 av Colonel Henri Roi-Tanguy, 14e; adult/13-26yr/under 13yr €8/4/free; ⏰10am-5pm Tue-Sun; Ⓜ Denfert Rochereau) Created in 1810, the Catacombes takes visitors along 2km of subterranean passages with a mind-boggling amount of bones and skulls of millions of Parisians neatly packed along each and every wall. During WWII these tunnels were used as a headquarters by the Resistance; thrill-seeking *cataphiles* are often caught (and fined) roaming the tunnels at night.

Renting an audioguide greatly enhances the impossibly spooky experience.

Musée des Égouts de Paris — Museum

(Map p186; place de la Résistance, 7e; adult/child €4.20/3.40; ⏰11am-5pm Sat-Wed May-Sep, 11am-4pm Sat-Wed Oct-Dec & Feb-Apr; Ⓜ Alma Marceau or RER Pont de l'Alma) Raw sewage flows beneath your feet as you walk through 480m of odoriferous tunnels in this working sewer museum. Enter via a rectangular maintenance hole topped with a kiosk across the street from 93 quai d'Orsay, 7e.

Panthéon — Mausoleum

(Map p200; www.monum.fr; place du Panthéon; adult/under 18yr €8.50/free; ⏰10am-6.30pm Apr-Sep, to 6pm Oct-Mar; Ⓜ Maubert-Mutualité, Cardinal Lemoine or RER Luxembourg) A superb example of 18th-century neoclassicism, this domed landmark was commissioned by Louis XV around 1750 as an abbey but due to financial and structural problems it wasn't completed until 1789. Two years later, the Constituent Assembly turned it into a secular mausoleum – now the eternal home of some of France's greatest thinkers including Voltaire, Jean-Jacques Rousseau, Louis Braille, Émile Zola and Jean Moulin.

Hôtel des Invalides — Monument, Museum

(Map p186; www.invalides.org; 129 rue de Grenelle, 7e; adult/child €9/free; ⏰10am-6pm Mon &

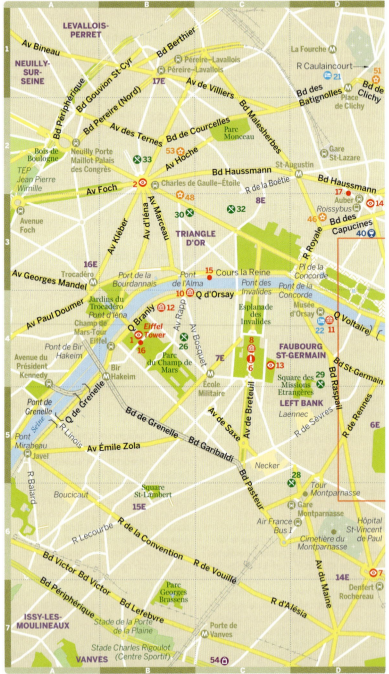

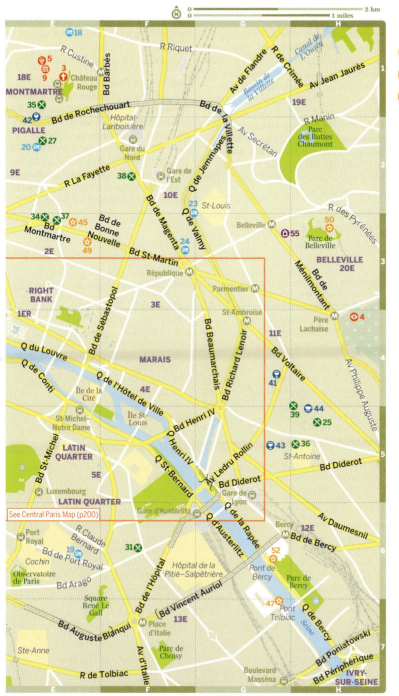

0 — 2 km
0 — 1 miles

R Custine

R Riquet

Canal de L'Ourcq

18
5
3
9
Château Rouge
Bd Barbès
Av de Flandre
R de Crimée
Av Jean Jaurès

18E
MONTMARTRE

Bassin de la Villette

19E

R Manin
Parc des Buttes Chaumont

35
42
PIGALLE
Bd de Rochechouart
Hôpital Lariboisière
Bd de la Villette
Av Secrétan

20 27

9E
R La Fayette
38
Gare du Nord
Gare de l'Est
Q de Jemmapes

10E

23 St-Louis

R des Pyrénées

34 37
45
Bd Montmartre
Bd de Bonne Nouvelle
Bd de Magenta
Q de Valmy
Belleville
55
50
Parc de Belleville

2E
49
Bd St-Martin
24

BELLEVILLE
20E

République

RIGHT BANK
Parmentier
Bd de Ménilmontant

1ER
3E
St-Ambroise
Père Lachaise
4

Q du Louvre
Bd de Sébastopol
11E

Q de Conti
Île de la Cité
Q de l'Hôtel de Ville
MARAIS
4E
Bd Beaumarchais
Bd Richard Lenoir
Bd Voltaire
41

St-Michel–Notre Dame
Île St-Louis
Q Bd Henri IV
39 44
25

LATIN QUARTER
Q Henri IV
Av Ledru Rollin
43 36
St-Antoine
Bd Diderot

Bd St-Michel
5E
Q St-Bernard
Bd Diderot

Luxembourg
LATIN QUARTER
Gare de Lyon

See Central Paris Map (p200)
Gare d'Austerlitz
Q de la Rapée
Av Daumesnil

Port Royal
R Claude Bernard
31
Q d'Austerlitz
Bercy
12E
Bd de Bercy

Cochin
19
Bd de Port Royal
Hôpital de la Pitié–Salpêtrière
Pont de Bercy
52
Parc de Bercy

Observatoire de Paris
Bd Arago

Square René Le Gall
Bd de l'Hôpital
Bd Vincent Auriol
47
Pont Tolbiac
Q de Bercy

Bd Auguste Blanqui
Place d'Italie
13E

Ste-Anne
Av d'Italie
Parc de Choisy
Bd Poniatowski
Bd Périphérique
IVRY-SUR-SEINE

R de Tolbiac
Boulevard Masséna

Wed-Sun, 10am-9pm Tue, to 5pm Oct-Mar, closed 1st Mon of month; M Invalides) Hôtel des Invalides was built in the 1670s by Louis XIV to provide housing for 4000 *invalides* (disabled war veterans). On 14 July 1789, a mob forced its way into the building and, after fierce fighting, seized 32,000 rifles before heading on to the prison at Bastille and the start of the French Revolution.

North of the main courtyard is the **Musée de l'Armée** (Army Museum; Map p186; www.invalides.org; 129 rue de Grenelle, 7e; ⏱10am-6pm Mon & Wed-Sat, to 9pm Tue), home to the nation's largest collection on French military history.

South are **Église St-Louis des Invalides** and **Église du Dôme** which contains the tomb of Napoléon 1er, comprising six coffins fitting into one another like a Russian *matryoshka* doll.

Jardin des Plantes   Botanic Garden

(Map p200; www.jardindesplantes.net; 57 rue Cuvier, 5e; adult/child €6/4; ⏱7.30am-7.45pm Apr-mid-Oct, 8.30am-5.30pm mid-Oct-Mar; M Gare d'Austerlitz, Censier Daubenton or Jussieu) Paris' 24-hectare botanical gardens were created in 1626 as a medicinal herb garden for Louis XIII. On its southern fringe is the Musée National d'Histoire Naturelle, France's natural-history museum.

Greater Paris

⦿ Don't Miss Sights
1 Eiffel Tower... B4

⦿ Sights
2 Arc de Triomphe................................... B2
3 Basilique du Sacré-Cœur E1
4 Cimetière du Père Lachaise H4
5 Clos Montmartre................................... E1
6 Hôtel des Invalides C4
7 Les Catacombes.................................... D6
8 Musée de l'Armée.................................. C4
9 Musée de Montmartre E1
10 Musée des Égouts de Paris B4
11 Musée d'Orsay....................................... D4
12 Musée du Quai Branly B4
13 Musée Rodin... C4
14 Palais Garnier.. D3

⊕ Activities, Courses & Tours
15 Bateaux-Mouches.................................. C3
16 Fat Tire Bike Tours B4
17 L'Open Tour.. D2

🛏 Sleeping
18 Au Sourire de Montmartre E1
19 Five Hotel E6
20 Hôtel Amour.. E2
21 Hôtel Eldorado....................................... D1
22 Le Bellechasse D4
23 Le Citizen Hotel..................................... F2
24 République Hôtel F3

✖ Eating
Arnaud Delmontel.........................(see 27)
25 Bistrot Paul Bert H5
26 Café Constant B4
27 Cul de Poule.. E2

28 La Cabane à Huîtres............................. D6
29 La Pâtisserie des Rêves.......................D4
30 Ladurée B3
31 L'Agrume F6
32 Le Boudoir C3
33 Le Hide... B2
34 Le J'Go E3
35 Le Miroir.. E1
36 Le Siffleur de Ballons H5
37 Le Zinc des Cavistes E3
Les Cocottes ....(see 26)
38 Marché Couvert St-Quentin................. F2
39 Septime H4

🍷 Drinking & Nightlife
40 Harry's New York Bar D3
41 La Fée Verte G4
42 La Fourmi E1
43 Le Baron Rouge G5
44 Le Pure Café.. H5

🎭 Entertainment
45 Au Limonaire E3
46 Kiosque Théâtre Madeleine.................D3
47 Le Batofar.. G7
48 Le Lido de Paris B3
49 Le Rex Club E3
50 Le Vieux Belleville H3
51 Moulin Rouge D1
52 Palais Omnisports de Paris-
Bercy... G6
53 Salle Pleyel.. B2

🛍 Shopping
54 Marché aux Puces de la Porte
de Vanves... C7
55 Marché Belleville G3

NEALE CLARK/GETTY IMAGES ©

⭐ **Don't Miss**
Eiffel Tower

Named after its designer, Gustave Eiffel, this Paris icon was built for the 1889 Exposition Universelle (World Fair), marking the centenary of the French Revolution. At the time it faced massive opposition from Paris' artistic and literary elite, and the 'metal asparagus', as some Parisians snidely called it, was almost torn down in 1909 – spared because it proved an ideal platform for the transmitting antennas needed for the newfangled science of radiotelegraphy.

Today, the three levels are open to the public (entrance to the 1st level is included in all admission tickets), though the top level will close in heavy wind. Take the lifts (in the east, west and north pillars) or the stairs in the south pillar up to the 2nd platform. Highly recommended is the online booking system that allows you to buy your tickets in advance, thus avoiding the monumental queues at the ticket office. Print out your ticket or have it on a smart-phone screen that can be read by the scanner at the entrance.

NEED TO KNOW

Map p186; 📞 01 44 11 23 23; www.tour-eiffel.fr; lift to 3rd fl adult/12-24yr/4-12yr €14/12.50/9.50, lift to 2nd fl €8.50/7/4, stairs to 2nd fl €5/3.50/3; 🕓 lifts & stairs 9am-midnight mid-Jun–Aug, lifts 9.30am-11pm, stairs 9.30am-6pm Sep–mid-Jun; Ⓜ Bir Hakeim or RER Champ de Mars-Tour Eiffel

---

Église St-Germain des Prés Church
(Map p200; www.eglise-sgp.org; 3 place St-Germain des Prés, 6e; 🕓 8am-7pm Mon-Sat, 9am-8pm Sun; Ⓜ St-Germain des Prés) Paris' oldest standing church, the Romanesque St Germanus of the Fields, was built in the 11th century on the site of a 6th-century abbey and was the dominant place of worship in Paris until the arrival of Notre Dame.

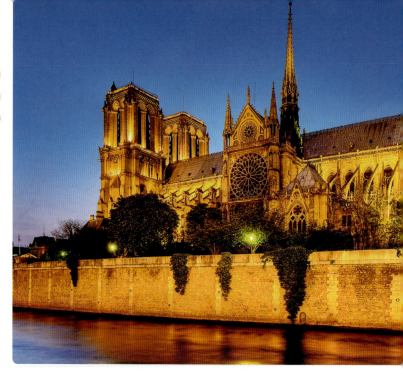

Église St-Sulpice
Church

(Map p200; www.paroisse-saint-sulpice-paris.org; place St-Sulpice, 6e; ⊙7.30am-7.30pm; Ⓜ St-Sulpice) Lined inside with 21 side chapels, this striking twin-towered church took six architects 150 years to build. What draws most people is not its Italianate facade with two rows of superimposed columns, Counter-Reformation-influenced neoclassical decor or even the frescoes by Delecroix, but its setting for a murderous scene in Dan Brown's *The Da Vinci Code*.

The Islands

Paris' twin set of islands could not be more different. **Île de la Cité** is bigger, full of sights and very touristy (few people live here). The seven decorated arches of Paris' oldest bridge, **Pont Neuf**, have linked Île de la Cité with both banks of the River Seine since 1607. Smaller **Île St-Louis** is residential and quieter, with just enough boutiques and restaurants – and

a legendary ice-cream maker – to attract visitors.

Cathédrale de Notre Dame de Paris
Cathedral

(Map p200; www.cathedraledeparis.com; 6 place du Parvis Notre Dame, 4e; ⊙7.45am-7pm; Ⓜ Cité) FREE This is the heart of Paris: distances from Paris to every part of metropolitan France are measured from **place du Parvis Notre Dame**, the square in front of this French Gothic masterpiece. The most visited unticketed site in Paris with upwards of 14 million visitors a year, Notre-Dame is famed for its three spectacular **rose windows** and forest of ornate **flying buttresses**, best viewed from square Jean XXIII, the little park behind the cathedral. Built on a site occupied by earlier churches, it was begun in 1163 according to the design of Bishop Maurice de Sully and largely completed by the early 14th century. Eugène Emmanuel Viollet-le-Duc carried out extensive renovations between 1845 and 1864.

Left: Cathédrale de Notre Dame de Paris;
Below: Cruise boat on the River Seine

The entrance to its famous towers, the **Tours de Notre Dame** (Notre Dame Towers; rue du Cloître Notre Dame, 4e; adult/18-25yr/under 18yr €8.50/5.50/free; ⏲10am-6.30pm daily Apr-Jun & Sep, 10am-6.30pm Mon-Fri, 10am-11pm Sat & Sun Jul & Aug, 10.30am-5.30pm daily Oct-Mar), is from the **North Tower**. Climb 422 spiralling steps and find yourself face-to-face with the cathedral's most frightening gargoyles, the 13-tonne bell **Emmanuel** (all of the cathedral's bells are named) and, last but not least, a spectacular view of Paris.

Ste-Chapelle   Chapel

(Map p200; 4 bd du Palais, 1er; adult/under 18yr €8.50/free; ⏲9.30am-5pm Nov-Feb, to 6pm Mar-Oct; Ⓜ Cité) Built in just under three years (compared with nearly 200 for Notre Dame), this gemlike Holy Chapel – the most exquisite of Paris' Gothic monuments – was consecrated in 1248 within the walls of the city's **Palais de Justice** (Law Courts).

A combined adult ticket with the Conciergerie costs €12.50.

Conciergerie   Monument

(Map p200; www.monuments-nationaux.fr; 2 bd du Palais, Île de la Cité, 1er; adult/under 18yr €8.50/free; 1st Sun of month Nov-Mar free; ⏲9.30am-6pm; Ⓜ Cité) Built as a royal palace in the 14th century, this was the main prison during the Reign of Terror (1793–94), used to incarcerate alleged enemies of the Revolution before they were brought before the Revolutionary Tribunal, next door in the Palais de Justice. Queen Marie-Antoinette was among the almost 2800 prisoners held here before being sent in tumbrels to the guillotine. The 14th-century **Salle des Gens d'Armes** (Cavalrymen's Hall), a fine example of Rayonnant Gothic style, is Europe's largest surviving medieval hall.

A joint ticket with Ste-Chapelle costs €12.50.

Notre Dame

Timeline

1160 Maurice de Sully becomes bishop of Paris. Mission: to grace growing Paris with a lofty new cathedral.

1182–90 The **choir with double ambulatory** ❶ is finished and work starts on the nave and side chapels.

1200–50 The **west facade** ❷, with rose window, three portals and two soaring towers, goes up. Everyone is stunned.

1345 Some 180 years after the foundation stone was laid, the Cathédrale de Notre Dame is complete. It is dedicated to *Notre Dame* (Our Lady), the Virgin Mary.

1789 Revolutionaries smash the original **Gallery of Kings** ❸, pillage the cathedral and melt all its bells except the great bell Emmanuel. The cathedral becomes a Temple of Reason, then a warehouse.

1831 Victor Hugo's novel *The Hunchback of Notre Dame* inspires new interest in the half-ruined Gothic cathedral.

1845–50 Architect Viollet-le-Duc undertakes its restoration. Twenty-eight new kings are sculpted for the west facade. The heavily decorated **portals** ❹ and **spire** ❺ are reconstructed. The neo-Gothic **treasury** ❻ is built.

1860 The area in front of Notre Dame is cleared to create the *parvis*, an alfresco classroom where Parisians can learn a catechism illustrated on sculpted stone portals.

1935 A rooster bearing part of the relics of the Crown of Thorns, St Denis and St Geneviève is put on top of the cathedral spire to protect those who pray inside.

1991 The architectural masterpiece of Notre Dame and its Seine-side riverbanks become a Unesco World Heritage Site.

2013 Notre Dame celebrates 850 years since construction began with a bevy of new bells and restoration works.

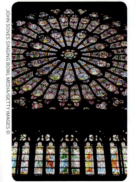

Virgin & Child
Spot all 37 artworks representing the Virgin Mary. Pilgrims have revered the pearly-cream sculpture of her in the sanctuary since the 14th century. Light a devotional candle and write some words to the *Livre de Vie* (Book of Life).

North Rose Window
See prophets, judges, kings and priests venerate Mary in vivid blue and violet glass, one of three beautiful rose blooms (1225–70), each almost 10m in diameter.

Flying Buttresses

Choir Screen
No part of the cathedral weaves biblical tales more evocatively than these ornate wooden panels, carved in the 14th century after the Black Death killed half the country's population. The faintly gaudy colours were restored in the 1960s.

5

Spire

Treasury
This was the cash reserve of French kings, who ordered chalices, crucifixes, baptism fonts and other sacred gems to be melted down in the Mint during times of financial strife – war, famine and so on.

6

Great Bell
Navigate an elf-sized door and 22 wooden steps to reach the bell Emmanuel: its peal is so pure thanks to the precious gems and jewels Parisian women threw into the pot when it was recast from copper and bronze in 1631.

Chimera Gallery
Scale the north tower for a Paris panorama admired by birds, dragons, grimacing gargoyles and grotesque chimera. Nod to celebrity chimera Stryga, who has wings, horns, a human body and sticking-out tongue. This bestial lot warns off demons.

North Tower

South Tower

Great Gallery

West Rose Window

2

3

4

Transept

North Tower Staircase

The 'Mays'
On 1 May 1630, city goldsmiths offered a 3m-high painting to the cathedral – a tradition they continued every 1 May until 1707 when their bankrupt guild folded. View 13 of these huge artworks in the side chapels.

Three Portals
Play I spy (Greed, Cowardice et al) beneath these sculpted doorways, which illustrate the seasons, life and the 12 vices and virtues alongside the Bible.

Portal of the Virgin

Exit

Portal of the Last Judgement

Portal of St-Anne

Entrance

Parvis Notre Dame

Museum Tips

● If you're visiting more than two or three museums and monuments, buy a **Paris Museum Pass** (www.parismuseumpass.fr; 2/4/6 days €39/54/69), valid for entry to some 38 venues including the Louvre, Centre Pompidou, Musée d'Orsay, Musée Rodin and Château de Versailles. Best up, pass-holders bypass *looong* ticket queues at major attractions. Buy it online, at participating museums, tourist desks at airports, Fnac outlets and major metro stations.

● Most Paris museums are closed on Mondays, but some, including the Louvre and Centre Pompidou, are closed on Tuesdays instead.

● The following are free the first Sunday of the month from November to March: Arc de Triomphe, Conciergerie, Panthéon, Ste-Chapelle and the Tours de Notre Dame.

Right Bank

Musée du Louvre   Museum

(Map p200; ☎01 40 20 53 17; www.louvre.fr; rue de Rivoli & quai des Tuileries, 1er; permanent/ temporary collection €11/12, both €15, under 18yr free; ◷9am-6pm Mon, Thu, Sat & Sun, to 9.45pm Wed & Fri; Ⓜ Palais Royal–Musée du Louvre) The vast Palais du Louvre was constructed as a fortress by Philippe-Auguste in the early 13th century and rebuilt in the mid-16th century as a royal residence. The Revolutionary Convention turned it into a national museum in 1793. Its raison d'être: to present Western art from the Middle Ages to about 1848 (at which point the Musée d'Orsay takes over), as well as works from ancient civilisations that formed the starting point for Western art. Late 2012 saw the opening of the new Islamic art galleries in the restored **Cour Visconti**, topped with an elegant, shimmering gold 'flying carpet' roof designed by Italian architects Mario Bellini and Rudy Ricciotti.

With some 35,000 paintings and objets d'art on display today, the sheer size and richness of the Louvre can be overwhelming; the south side facing the Seine is 700m long and it's said it would take nine months just to glance at every work. For many, the star attraction is Leonardo da Vinci's *La Joconde*, better known as the Mona Lisa (Room 6, 1st floor, Denon Wing).

To best navigate the collection, opt for a self-guided **thematic trail** (1½ to three hours; download trail brochures in advance from the website) or a self-paced **multimedia guide** (€5). More-formal, English-language **guided tours** depart from the Hall Napoléon, which also has free English-language maps.

The main entrance and ticket windows are covered by the 21m-high **Grande Pyramide**, a glass pyramid designed by the Chinese-born American architect IM Pei. Avoid the queues outside the pyramid or at the Porte des Lions entrance by entering the Louvre complex via the underground shopping centre **Carrousel du Louvre**, at 99 rue de Rivoli. Buy your tickets in advance – and enter the museum with little or no queue – from the ticket machines inside the latter, by phoning ☎08 92 68 46 94 or ☎01 41 57 32 28, or from *billeteries* (ticket offices) inside Fnac or Virgin Megastores.

Arc de Triomphe   Landmark

(Map p186; www.monuments-nationaux.fr; place Charles de Gaulle; adult/18-25yr €9.50/6; ◷10am-10.30pm Oct-Mar, to 11pm Apr-Sep; Ⓜ Charles de Gaulle–Étoile) If anything rivals the Eiffel Tower as the symbol of Paris, it's this magnificent 1836 monument to

Napoléon's 1805 victory at Austerlitz. From the viewing platform on top of the arch (50m up via 284 steps; it's well worth the climb) you can see the dozen avenues that radiate out from the arch.

Beneath the arch at ground level lies the **Tomb of the Unknown Soldier**, honouring the 1.3 million French soldiers who lost their lives in WWI; an eternal flame is rekindled daily at 6.30pm.

Centre Pompidou   Museum

(Map p200; ☏ 01 44 78 12 33; www.centrepom pidou.fr; place Georges Pompidou, 1er; museum, exhibitions & panorama adult/child €13/free; ⏱ 11am-9pm Wed-Mon; Ⓜ Rambuteau) Paris' premier cultural centre – designed inside out with utilitarian features such as plumbing, pipes, air vents and electrical cables forming part of the external façade to free up the interior space for exhibitions and events – has amazed visitors since it was inaugurated in 1977. Temporary exhibitions fill the ground floor **Forum du Centre Pompidou** and 6th-floor galleries, while the 4th and 5th floors host the **Musée National d'Art Moderne**, France's national collection of art dating from 1905 onward which includes works by the surrealists and cubists, as well as pop art and contemporary works.

West of the centre, **Place Georges Pompidou** and the nearby pedestrian streets attract buskers, musicians, jugglers and mime artists. South of the centre on **place Igor Stravinsky** are fanciful mechanical fountains of skeletons, hearts, treble clefs and a big pair of ruby-red lips, created by Jean Tinguely and Niki de Saint Phalle.

Basilique du Sacré-Cœur   Basilica

(Map p186; www.sacre-coeur-montmartre.com; place du Parvis du Sacré-Cœur; Basilica dome admission €5, cash only; ⏱ 6am-10.30pm, dome 9am-7pm Apr-Sep, to 5.30pm Oct-Mar; Ⓜ Anvers) Crowning the **Butte de Montmartre** (Montmartre Hill), Sacred Heart Basilica was begun in 1876 but not consecrated until 1919. Some 234 spiralling steps lead to its dome, which affords one of Paris' most spectacular panoramas – up to 30km on a clear day. The chapel-lined crypt, visited in conjunction with the dome, is huge.

Palais Garnier   Opera House

(Map p186; ☏ 08 25 05 44 05; www.operadeparis. fr; cnr rues Scribe and Auber; unguided tour adult/10-25yr/under 10yr €9/6/free, guided tour adult/10-25yr/under 10yr €13.50/9.50/6.50; ⏱ 10am-4.30pm; Ⓜ Opéra) Designed in 1860 by Charles Garnier – then an unknown 35-year-old architect – the opera house was part of Baron Haussmann's massive urban renovation project.

The opera is open for visits during the day; highlights include the opulent **Grand Staircase,** the **library-museum** (1st floor), where you'll find old show posters, costumes and original music scores, and

Arc de Triomphe
BRENT WINEBRENNER/GETTY IMAGES ©

The Louvre

A Half-Day Tour

Successfully visiting the Louvre is a fine art. Its complex labyrinth of galleries and staircases spiralling three wings and four floors renders discovery a snakes-and-ladders experience. Initiate yourself with this three-hour itinerary – a playful mix of *Mona Lisa* obvious and up-to-the-minute unexpected.

Arriving by the stunning main entrance, pick up colour-coded floor plans at the lower-ground-floor **information desk** ❶ beneath IM Pei's glass pyramid, ride the escalator up to the Sully Wing and swap passport for multimedia guide (there are limited descriptions in the galleries) at the wing entrance.

The Louvre is as much about spectacular architecture as masterly art. To appreciate this zip up and down Sully's Escalier Henri II to admire **Venus de Milo** ❷, then up parallel Escalier Henri IV to the palatial displays in **Cour Khorsabad** ❸. Cross room 1 to find the escalator up to the 1st floor and staircase-as-art **L'Esprit d'Escalier** ❹. Next traverse 25 consecutive galleries (thank you, floor plan!) to flip conventional contemplation on its head with Cy Twombly's **The Ceiling** ❺ and the hypnotic **Winged Victory of Samothrace sculpture** ❻ – just two rooms away – which brazenly insists on being admired from all angles. End with the impossibly famous **The Raft of Medusa** ❼, **Mona Lisa** ❽ and **Virgin & Child** ❾.

TOP TIPS

Floor Plans Don't even consider entering the Louvre's maze of galleries without a *Plan/Information Louvre* brochure, free from the information desk in the Hall Napoléon

Crowd dodgers The Denon Wing is always packed; visit on late nights Wednesday or Friday or trade Denon in for the notably quieter Richelieu Wing

2nd floor Not for first-timers: save its more specialist works for subsequent visits

---

Mission Mona Lisa

If you just want to venerate the Louvre's most famous lady, use the Porte des Lions entrance (closed Tuesday and Friday), from where it's a five-minute walk. Go up one flight of stairs and through rooms 26, 14 and 13 to the Grande Galerie and adjoining room 6.

L'Esprit d'Escalier
Escalier Lefuel, Richelieu
Discover the 'Spirit of the Staircase' through François Morellet's contemporary stained glass, which casts new light on old stone. **DETOUR »** Napoleon III's gorgeous gilt apartments.

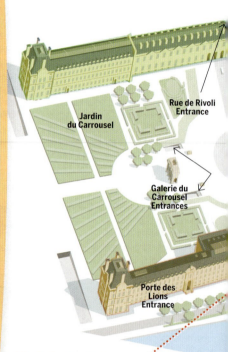

Rue de Rivoli Entrance

Jardin du Carrousel

Galerie du Carrousel Entrances

Porte des Lions Entrance

The Raft of the Medusa
Room 77, 1st Floor, Denon
Decipher the politics behind French romanticism in Théodore Géricault's *Raft of the Medusa*.

TERRY SMITH IMAGES/ALAMY ©

Cour Khorsabad
Ground Floor, Richelieu
Time travel with a pair of winged human-headed bulls to view some of the world's oldest Mesopotamian art. **DETOUR»** Night-lit statues in Cour Puget.

Venus de Milo
Room 16, Ground Floor, Sully
No one knows who sculpted this seductively realistic goddess from Greek antiquity. Naked to the hips, she is a Hellenistic masterpiece.

The Ceiling
Room 32, 1st Floor, Sully
Admire the blue shock of Cy Twombly's 400-sq-metre contemporary ceiling fresco – the Louvre's latest, daring commission. **DETOUR»** *The Braque Ceiling*, room 33.

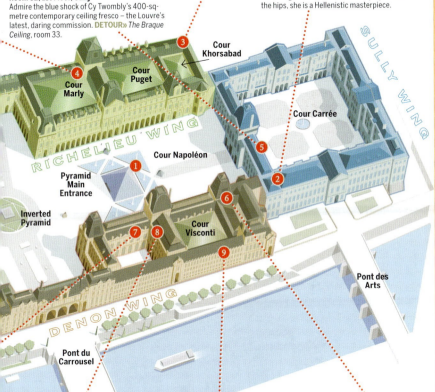

Cour Khorsabad

❸

❹ Cour Marly

Cour Puget

SULLY WING

Cour Carrée

RICHELIEU WING

Cour Napoléon

❶

Pyramid Main Entrance

Inverted Pyramid

❺

❷

❻

Cour Visconti

❼ ❽

❾

Pont des Arts

DENON WING

Pont du Carrousel

Virgin & Child
Room 5, Grande Galerie, 1st Floor, Denon
In the spirit of artistic devotion save the Louvre's most famous gallery for last: a feast of Virgin-and-child paintings by Raphael, Domenico Ghirlandaio, Giovanni Bellini and Francesco Botticini.

Mona Lisa
Room 6, 1st Floor, Denon
No smile is as enigmatic or bewitching as hers. Da Vinci's diminutive *La Joconde* hangs opposite the largest painting in the Louvre – sumptuous, fellow Italian Renaissance artwork *The Wedding at Cana*.

Winged Victory of Samothrace
Escalier Daru, 1st Floor, Sully
Draw breath at the aggressive dynamism of this headless, handless Hellenistic goddess. **DETOUR»** The razzle-dazzle of the Apollo Gallery's crown jewels.

the horseshoe-shaped **auditorium** (2nd floor), with its extravagant gilded interior and red velvet seats. Or reserve a spot on an English-language guided tour.

Musée Picasso   Museum

(Map p200; 📞01 42 71 25 21; www.musee-picasso.fr; 5 rue de Thorigny; Ⓜ St-Paul or Chemin Vert) One of Paris' most beloved art collections opened its doors again after massive renovation works in summer 2013. Housed in the stunning, mid-17th-century Hôtel Salé, the Musée Picasso woos art lovers with more than 3500 drawings, engravings, paintings, ceramic works and sculptures by the *grand maître* (great master) Pablo Picasso (1881–1973).

Place des Vosges   Square

(Map p200; place des Vosges, 4e; Ⓜ St-Paul or Bastille) Paris' oldest square, place des Vosges is a strikingly elegant ensemble of 36 symmetrical houses with ground-floor arcades, steep slate roofs and large dormer windows arranged around a large and leafy square.

Between 1832 and 1848 writer Victor Hugo lived in an apartment on the 3rd floor of the square's **Hôtel de Rohan-Guéménée**, now the museum **Maison de Victor Hugo** (Map p200; www.musee-hugo.paris.fr; 🕐10am-6pm Tue-Sun; Ⓜ St-Paul or Bastille) FREE devoted to his life and times.

Place de la Bastille   Square

(Map p200; Ⓜ Bastille) The Bastille, a 14th-century fortress built to protect the city gates, is the most famous Parisian monument that no longer exists. Transformed into a dreaded state prison under Cardinal Richelieu, it was demolished shortly after a mob stormed it on 14 July 1789. First impressions of today's busy traffic circle can be underwhelming. The bronze column topped with the gilded Spirit of Liberty commemorates victims of later revolutions in 1830 and 1848.

Cimetière du Père Lachaise   Cemetery

(Map p186; 📞01 43 70 70 33; www.pere-lachaise.com; 16 rue du Repos & bd de Ménilmontant, 20e; 🕐8am-6pm Mon-Fri, from 8.30am Sat, from 9am Sun; Ⓜ Père Lachaise or Philippe Auguste) FREE The world's most visited cemetery opened its one-way doors in 1804. Among the 800,000 people buried here are the

Palais Garnier (p195)

composer Chopin; the playwright Molière; the poet Apollinaire; writers Balzac, Proust, Gertrude Stein and Colette; the actors Simone Signoret, Sarah Bernhardt and Yves Montand; the painters Pissarro, Seurat, Modigliani and Delacroix; the *chanteuse* Édith Piaf; the dancer Isadora Duncan; and even those immortal 12th-century lovers, Abélard and Héloïse, whose remains were disinterred and reburied here together in 1817 beneath a neo-Gothic tombstone. Particularly visited graves are those of Oscar Wilde (division 89) and 1960s rock star Jim Morrison (division 6).

Canal St-Martin   Canal
(**M** République, Jaurès or Jacques Bonsergent) The shaded towpaths of the tranquil, 4.5km-long Canal St-Martin are a wonderful place for a romantic stroll or a bike ride past nine locks, metal bridges and ordinary Parisian neighbourhoods. The canal's banks have undergone a real urban renaissance, and the southern stretch in particular is an ideal spot for cafe lounging, quayside summer picnics and late-night drinks.

Parts of the waterway – which was built between 1806 and 1825 in order to link the Seine with the 108km-long **Canal de l'Ourcq** – are actually higher than the surrounding land. Take a **canal boat cruise** to savour the real flavour.

Musée de
Montmartre   History Museum
(Map p186; www.museedemontmartre.fr; 12 rue Cortot, 18e; adult/18-25yr/10-17yr €8/6/4; ☺10am-6pm; **M** Lamarck–Caulaincourt) No address better captures the *quartier*'s rebellious, bohemian and artsy past than Musée de Montmartre, one-time home to painters Renoir, Utrillo and Raoul Dufy. The 17th-century manor house– museum displays paintings, lithographs and documents; hosts art exhibitions by contemporary artists currently living in Montmartre; and sells bottles of wine in its excellent bookshop, produced from grapes grown in the *quartier*'s very own vineyard, **Clos Montmartre** (Map p186; 18 rue des Saules, 18e).

👉 Tours

Bateaux-Mouches   Boat Tour
(Map p186; 📞 01 42 25 96 10; www.bateaux-mouches.com; Port de la Conférence, 8e; adult/4-12yr €11/5.50; ☺Apr-Dec; **M** Alma Marceau) River cruises (70 minutes) with commentary in French and English; set sail from the Right Bank, just east of Pont de l'Alma.

L'Open Tour   Bus Tour
(Map p186; www.pariscityrama.com; 2-day passes adult/child €32/15) Hop-on, hop-off bus tours aboard an open-deck bus.

Paris Walks   Walking Tour
(www.paris-walks.com; adult/child €12/8) Highly rated by Lonely Planet readers, this long-established company runs thematic tours (fashion, chocolate, the French Revolution).

Fat Tire Bike Tours   Cycling
(Map p186; 📞 01 56 58 10 54; www.fattirebike tours.com) City bike tours, day and night, plus trips further afield to Versailles, Monet's garden in Giverny and the Normandy beaches.

🛏 Sleeping

The Paris Convention & Visitors Bureau can find you a place to stay (no booking fee, but you need a credit card), though queues can be long in high season; it also has information on bed-and-breakfast accommodation.

Be it a night, a week or longer, apartment rental is increasingly the modish way to stay in Paris. **Haven in Paris** (www.haveninparis.com) is recommended – it has luxury apartments from €575 per week.

Louvre & Les Halles
Hôtel Crayon   Boutique Hotel €€
(Map p200; 📞 01 42 36 54 19; www.hotelcrayon. com; 25 rue du Bouloi, 1er; s €129-249, d €149-299; ❋ 🛜; **M** Les Halles or Sentier) Line drawings by French artist Julie Gauthron bedeck walls and doors at this creative

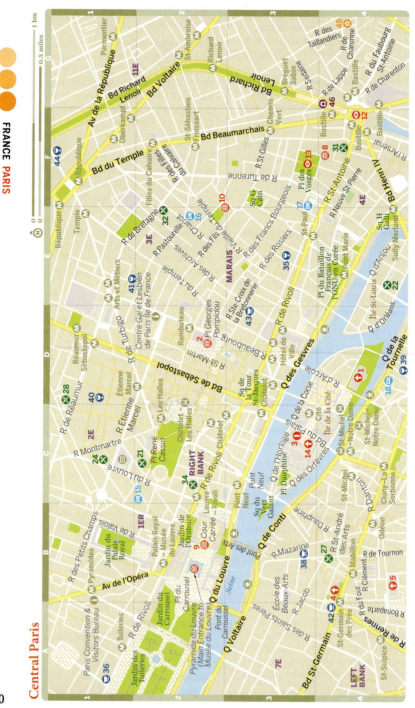

Central Paris

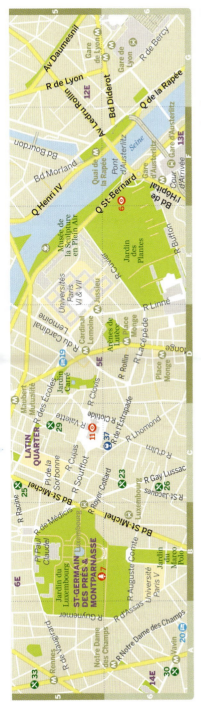

boutique hotel. The pencil *(le crayon)* is the theme, with rooms sporting a different shade of each floor's chosen colour – we love the coloured-glass shower doors and the books on the bedside table guests can swap and take home.

Marais & Bastille

Buzzing nightlife, hip shopping and an inexhaustible range of eating options ensure the popularity of this trendy, right-bank neighbourhood. Nearby Bastille has fewer tourists, allowing you to better glimpse the daily grind of the 'real' Paris.

Hôtel Jeanne d'Arc   Hotel €€
(Map p200; ☎01 48 87 62 11; www.hoteljeanne darc.com; 3 rue de Jarente, 4e; s €65, d €81-96, tr €149, q €164; ☎; MSt-Paul) Book well in advance at this gorgeous address to snag one of its cosy, excellent-value rooms. Games to play, a painted rocking chair for tots in the bijou lounge, knick knacks everywhere and the most extraordinary mirror in the breakfast room create a real 'family home' air to this 35-room house.

Hôtel du Petit
Moulin   Boutique Hotel €€€
(Map p200; ☎01 42 74 10 10; www.hoteldu petitmoulin.com; 29-31 rue du Poitou, 3e; d €190-350; MFilles du Calvaire) This 17-room hotel, a bakery at the time of Henri IV, was designed by Christian Lacroix. Pick from medieval and rococo Marais (rooms sporting exposed beams and dressed in toile de Jouy wallpaper), to more modern surrounds with contemporary murals and heart-shaped mirrors just this side of kitsch.

Latin Quarter

Midrange hotels in this good-value Left Bank neighbourhood are particularly popular with visiting academics, making rooms hardest to find during conferences (March to June and October).

Five Hotel   Design Hotel €€€
(Map p186; ☎01 43 31 74 21; www.thefivehotel-paris.com; 3 rue Flatters, 5e; d €202-342; ❄☎;

Central Paris

⊙ Sights

1	Cathédrale de Notre Dame de Paris	D4
2	Centre Pompidou	D2
3	Conciergerie	C3
4	Église St-Germain des Prés	B4
5	Église St-Sulpice	B4
6	Jardin des Plantes	F6
7	Jardin du Luxembourg	B5
8	Maison de Victor Hugo	F4
9	Musée du Louvre	B2
10	Musée Picasso	E2
11	Panthéon	C5
12	Place de la Bastille	F4
13	Place des Vosges	F3
14	Ste-Chapelle	C3

🛏 Sleeping

15	Hôtel Crayon	C2
16	Hôtel du Petit Moulin	E2
17	Hôtel Jeanne d'Arc	F3
18	Hôtel les Degrés de Notre Dame	D4
19	Hôtel Minerve	D5
20	L'Apostrophe	A6

✗ Eating

21	Beef Club	C2
22	Berthillon	E4
23	Bistrot Les Papilles	C6
24	Blend	C1
25	Bouillon Racine	C5
26	Boulangerie Bruno Solques	C6
27	Cosi	B4
28	Frenchie	D1
29	Le Coupe-Chou	C5
30	Le Dôme	A6
31	Le Nôtre	F4
32	Marché aux Enfants Rouges	E2
33	Marché Raspail	A5
34	Spring	C2

🍷 Drinking & Nightlife

35	3w Kafé	E3
36	Angelina	A1
37	Café de la Nouvelle Mairie	C6
38	Café La Palette	B3
39	Curio Parlor Cocktail Club	D4
40	Experimental Cocktail Club	D1
41	Le Tango	E1
42	Les Deux Magots	A4
43	Open Café	D3
44	Scream Club	F1

🎭 Entertainment

45	La Scène Bastille	G4

🛍 Shopping

46	Marché Bastille	G4

Ⓜ Les Gobelins) Choose from one of five perfumes to fragrance your room at this contemporary romantic sanctum. Its private apartment, One by The Five, has a phenomenal 'suspended' bed.

Hôtel Minerve   Hotel €€

(Map p200; ☎ 01 43 26 26 04; www.parishotel minerve.com; 13 rue des Écoles, 5e; s €99, d €129-165, tr €165; ❄ @ 🛜; Ⓜ Cardinal Lemoine) Oriental carpets, antique books, frescoes of French monuments and reproduction 18th-century wallpaper make this family-run hotel a charming place to stay. Some rooms have small balconies with views of Notre Dame; two have tiny romantic courtyards.

Hôtel les Degrés de Notre Dame   Hotel €€

(Map p200; ☎ 01 55 42 88 88; www.lesdegres hotel.com; 10 rue des Grands Degrés, 5e; d incl breakfast €115-170; 🛜; Ⓜ Maubert-Mutualité) Wonderfully old-school, with a winding timber staircase (no lift), and charming staff, the value is unbeatable at this hotel a block from the Seine.

St-Germain, Odéon & Luxembourg

Staying in chic St-Germain des Prés (6e) is a delight. But beware – budget places just don't exist in this part of the Left Bank.

L'Apostrophe   Design Hotel €€€

(Map p200; ☎ 01 56 54 31 31; www.apostrophe-hotel.com; 3 rue de Chevreuse, 6e; d €150-350; ❄ @ 🛜; Ⓜ Vavin) A street work-of-art with stencilled façade, this hotel's 16 rooms pay homage to the written word. Graffiti tags cover one wall of room U (for 'urbain') which has a ceiling shaped like a skateboard ramp. Room P (for 'Paris parody') sits in clouds overlooking Paris' rooftops.

Le Bellechasse   Design Hotel €€
(Map p186; ☎ 01 45 50 22 31; www.lebellechasse. com; 8 rue de Bellechasse, 7e; d from €161; ❄ 🗟; Ⓜ Solférino) Fashion designer Christian Lacroix's entrancing room themes make you feel like you've stepped into a larger-than-life oil painting. Mod cons include iPod docks and 200 TV channels.

Gare du Nord, Gare de l'Est & République

The areas around the Gare du Nord and Gare de l'Est are far from the prettiest parts of Paris, but decent-value hotels are a dime a dozen.

Le Citizen Hotel   Boutique Hotel €€€
(Map p186; ☎ 01 83 62 55 50; www.lecitizenhotel. com; 96 quai de Jemmapes, 10e; d €177-275, q €450; 🗟; Ⓜ Gare de l'Est, Jacques Bonsergent) A team of forward-thinking creative types put their heads together for this one, and the result is 12 alluring rooms equipped with iPads, filtered water and warm minimalist design.

République Hôtel   Hotel €€
(Map p186; ☎ 01 42 39 19 03; www. republiquehotel.com; 31 rue Albert Thomas, 10e; s €82, d €95-120, tr €120, q €169; 🗟; Ⓜ République) This hip spot is heavy on pop art – local street artists did some of the paintings here. Regardless of the garden gnomes in the breakfast room, you won't be able to fault the inexpensive rates and fantastic location off place République.

Montmartre & Pigalle

What a charmer Montmartre is, with its varied accommodation scene embracing everything from boutique to bohemian, hostel to *hôtel particulier*.

Hôtel Amour   Boutique Hotel €€
(Map p186; ☎ 01 48 78 31 80; www.hotelamour paris.fr; 8 rue Navarin, 9e; s €105, d €155-215; 🗟; Ⓜ St-Georges or Pigalle) The inimitable black-clad Amour (formerly a love hotel by the hour) features original design and artwork – you won't find a more original place to lay your head in Paris at these prices.

Au Sourire de Montmartre   B&B €€
(Map p186; ☎ 06 64 64 72 86; www.sourire-de-montmartre.com; rue du Mont Cenis, 18e; r €125-170, apt per week €600; Ⓜ Jules Joffrin) This charming B&B on the backside of Montmartre has four rooms and a studio, each decorated with French antiques or Moroccan motifs. The surrounding neighbourhood is delightful, though slightly out of the way.

Buskers in the Latin Quarter
KEVIN CLOGSTOUN/GETTY IMAGES ©

Top Five Patisseries

Ladurée (Map p186; www.laduree.fr; 75 av des Champs-Élysées, 8e; pastries from €1.50; ⏰7.30am-11pm; Ⓜ George V) Paris' most historic and decadent; inventor of the *macaron*.

Le Nôtre (Map p200; www.lenotre.fr; 10 rue St-Antoine, 4e; Ⓜ Bastille) Delectable pastries and chocolate; 10-odd outlets around town.

La Pâtisserie des Rêves (Map p186; www.lapatisseriedesreves.com; 93 rue du Bac, 7e; ⏰10am-8.30pm Tue-Sat, 8.30am-2pm Sun; Ⓜ Rue du Bac) Extraordinary cakes and tarts showcased beneath glass at the chic 'art' gallery of big-name *pâtissier* Philippe Conticini.

Boulangerie Bruno Solques (Map p200; 243 rue St-Jacques, 5e; ⏰6.30am-8pm Mon-Fri; 🚹; Ⓜ Place Monge or RER Luxembourg) Paris' most inventive *pâtissier*, Bruno Solques, excels at oddly shaped flat tarts and fruit-filled brioches.

Arnaud Delmontel (Map p186; 39 rue des Martyrs, 9e; ⏰7am-8.30pm Wed-Mon; Ⓜ Pigalle) Award-winning baguettes, gorgeous cakes, pastries to die for.

Hôtel Eldorado   Hotel €
(Map p186; 📞01 45 22 35 21; www.eldoradohotel.fr; 18 rue des Dames, 17e; s €39-65, d €58-85, tr €75-93; 🛜; Ⓜ Place de Clichy) This bohemian place is one of Paris' greatest finds: a welcoming, reasonably well-run place with 23 colourful rooms and a private back garden. Cheaper-category singles have washbasin only.

 Eating

Louvre & Les Halles

Beef Club   Steak €€
(Map p200; 📞09 54 37 13 65; www.eccbeefclub.com; 58 rue Jean-Jacques Rousseau, 1er; mains €20-45; ⏰dinner daily; Ⓜ Les Halles) No steak house is more chic or hipper than this. Packed out ever since it threw its first T-bone on the grill in 2012, this beefy address is all about steak, prepared to sweet perfection by legendary Paris butcher Yves-Marie Le Bourdonnec.

Frenchie   Bistro €€
(Map p200; 📞01 40 39 96 19; www.frenchie-restaurant.com; 5-6 rue du Nil, 2e; menu €34, €38 & €45; ⏰dinner Mon-Fri; Ⓜ Sentier) This bijou bistro with wooden tables and old stone walls is always packed and for good reason: excellent-value dishes are modern, market-driven (the menu changes daily with a choice of two dishes by course) and prepared with just the right dose of unpretentious creative flair by French chef Gregory Marchand. Reserve for one of two sittings (7pm or 9.30pm) two months in advance, arrive at 7pm and pray for a cancellation or – failing that – share tapas-style small plates with friends across the street at no-reservations **Frenchie Bar à Vin**.

Spring   Modern French €€
(Map p200; 📞01 45 96 05 72; www.springparis.fr; 6 rue Bailleul, 1er; lunch/dinner menu €44/76; ⏰lunch & dinner Wed-Fri, dinner Tue & Sat; Ⓜ Palais Royal–Musée du Louvre) One of the Right Bank's 'talk-of-the-town' addresses, with an American in the kitchen and stunning food. It has no printed menu, meaning hungry gourmets put their appetites in the hands of the chef and allow multilingual waiting staff to reveal what's cooking as each course is served. Advance reservations essential.

Blend   Burgers
(Map p200; www.blendhamburger.com; 44 rue d'Argout, 2e; burgers €10, lunch menu €15 & €17; ⏰lunch & dinner Mon-Sat; Ⓜ Sentier) A burger

cannot simply be a burger in gourmet Paris, where burger buffs dissolve into raptures of ecstacy over gourmet burgers at Blend.

Marais & Bastille

The Marais is one of Paris' premier dining neighbourhoods; book ahead for weekend dining.

Septime   Modern French €€€

(Map p186; ☎01 43 67 38 29; 80 rue de Charonne, 11e; lunch/5-course menu €26/55; ☺lunch Tue-Fri, dinner Mon-Fri; Ⓜ Charonne) Reading the menu won't get you far given it more resembles a shopping list than menu. But have no fear: alchemists in the kitchen produce truly beautiful creations, and the blue-smocked waitstaff go out of their way to ensure the culinary surprises are all pleasant ones.

Le Siffleur de Ballons   Wine Bar €

(Map p186; www.lesiffleurdeballons.com; 34 rue de Citeaux, 12e; lunch menu €14, mains €7-15; ☺10.30am-3pm & 5.30-10pm Tue-Sat; Ⓜ Faidherbe Chaligny) With Tom Waits on the stereo and a few cactuses atop the

register, this contemporary wine bar clearly has a dash of California in its soul. The wines are French, natural, and paired to perfection with simple but delicious offerings: tartines, soups, lentil salad with truffle oil, cheeses and Iberian *charcuterie* plates. Look out for the weekly tastings with winemakers.

Bistrot Paul Bert   Bistro €€

(Map p186; ☎01 43 72 24 01; 18 rue Paul Bert, 11e; 3-course lunch/dinner menu €18/36; ☺lunch & dinner Tue-Sat; Ⓜ Faidherbe-Chaligny) An address that stars on every 'best Paris bistro' list, Paul Bert serves perfectly executed classic dishes in a timeless setting.

Latin Quarter

Rue Mouffetard is famed for its food market and food shops; while its side streets, especially pedestrianised rue du Pot au Fer, cook up fine budget dining.

L'Agrume   Neobistro €€

(Map p186; ☎01 43 31 86 48; 15 rue des Fossés St-Marcel, 5e; 2-/3-course lunch menu €19/24, mains €26-39; ☺lunch & dinner Tue-Sat;

Berthillon ice cream shop (p207)

M Censier Daubenton) Snagging a table at 'Citrus Fruit' is tough, but the reward is watching chefs work with seasonal products in the open kitchen while you dine. You have a choice of table, bar stool or *comptoir* (counter). Lunching is magnificent value, while dinner is a no-choice *dégustation* (tasting) melody.

Bistrot Les Papilles   Bistro €€
(Map p200; 📞 01 43 25 20 79; www.lespapilles paris.com; 30 rue Gay Lussac, 5e; lunch/dinner menu from €22/31; 🕐 10.30am-midnight Mon-Sat; M Raspail or RER Luxembourg) This hybrid bistro, wine cellar and *épicerie* (grocery) serves market-driven fare at simply dressed tables wedged beneath bottle-lined walls. Each weekday cooks up a different *marmite du marché* (market casserole).

Le Coupe-Chou   French €€
(Map p200; 📞 01 46 33 68 69; www.lecoupechou. com; 9 & 11 rue de Lanneau, 5e; 2-/3-course lunch menu €27, mains €18-25; 🕐 Mon-Sat; M Maubert-Mutualité) This maze of candlelit rooms inside a vine-clad 17th-century townhouse is overwhelmingly romantic. Ceilings are beamed, furnishings are antique, and background classical music mingles with the intimate chatter of diners. As in the days when Marlene Dietrich et al dined here, advance reservations are essential.

St-Germain, Odéon & Luxembourg

Bouillon Racine   Brasserie €€
(Map p200; 📞 01 44 32 15 60; www.bouillonra-cine.com; 3 rue Racine, 6e; lunch menu €14.50, menu €30-41; 🕐 noon-11pm; M Cluny–La Sorbonne) This heritage-listed 1906 art nouveau 'soup kitchen', with mirrored walls, floral motifs and ceramic tiling, was built in 1906 to feed market workers. Superbly executed dishes inspired by age-old recipes include stuffed, spit-roasted suckling pig, pork shank in Rodenbach red beer, and scallops and shrimp with lobster coulis.

Café Constant   Neobistro €€
(Map p186; www.cafeconstant.com; 139 rue Ste-Dominique, 7e; 2-/3-course menu €16/23; 🕐 lunch & dinner Tue-Sun; M École Militaire or RER Port de l'Alma) Take a former Michelin-star chef and a simple corner cafe and what do you get? This jam-packed address with original mo-

Cheese for sale, Rue Mouffetard street market, Latin Quarter

saic floor, wooden tables and huge queues every meal time. **Les Cocottes** (Map p186; www.leviolondingres.com; 135 rue Ste-Dominique, 7e; 2-/3-course lunch menu €9/15; mains €14-28; ◷lunch & dinner Mon-Sat; Ⓜ École Militaire or RER Port de l'Alma), a couple of doors down, is another Constant hit.

Cosi
Sandwiches €

(Map p200; 54 rue de Seine, 6e; sandwich menu €10-15; ◷noon-11pm; 📶; Ⓜ Odéon) This might just be Paris' most imaginative sandwich maker, with sandwich names like Stonker, Tom Dooley and Naked Willi chalked on the blackboard. Classical music plays in the background and homemade foccacia bread is still warm from the oven.

Montparnasse

La Cabane à Huîtres
Seafood €

(Map p186; ☎ 01 45 49 47 27; 4 rue Antoine Bourdelle, 14e; dozen oysters €14.50, menu €19.50; ◷lunch & dinner Wed-Sat; Ⓜ Montparnasse Bienvenüe) Wonderfully rustic, this wooden-styled *cabane* (cabin) with just nine tables is the pride and joy of fifth-generation oyster farmer Françis Dubourg, who splits his week between the capital and his oyster farm in Arcachon on the Atlantic Coast. The fixed menu includes a dozen oysters, foie gras, *magret de canard fumé* (smoked duck breast) or smoked salmon and scrumptious desserts.

Le Dôme
Brasserie €€

(Map p200; ☎ 01 43 35 25 81; 108 bd du Montparnasse, 14e; mains €37-49, seafood platters €54; ◷lunch & dinner; Ⓜ Vavin) A 1930s art deco extravaganza, Le Dôme is a monumental place for a meal service of the formal white-tablecloth and bow-tied waiter variety. It's one of the swishest places around for shellfish platters piled high with fresh oysters, king prawns, crab claws and so on.

Étoile & Champs-Élysées

Le Boudoir
French €€

(Map p186; ☎ 01 43 59 25 29; www.boudoirparis.fr; 25 rue du Colisée, 8e; lunch menu €25,

The Gourmet Glacier

Berthillon (Map p200; 31 rue St-Louis en l'Île, 4e; ice cream from €2; ◷10am-8pm Wed-Sun; Ⓜ Pont Marie) on Île St-Louis is the place to head to for Paris' finest ice cream. There are 70 flavours to choose from, ranging from fruity cassis to chocolate, coffee, *marrons glacés* (candied chestnuts), *Agenaise* (Armagnac and prunes), *noisette* (hazelnut) and *nougat au miel* (honey nougat). One scoop just won't be enough…

mains €25-29; ◷lunch Mon-Fri, dinner Tue-Sat; Ⓜ St-Philippe du Roule or Franklin D Roosevelt) Spread across two floors, the quirky salons here are works of art. Expect classy bistro fare prepared by chef Arnaud Nicolas, a recipient of France's top culinary honour.

Le Hide
French €€

(Map p186; ☎ 01 45 74 15 81; www.lehide.fr; 10 rue du Général Lanrezac, 17e; menu from €24; ◷lunch Mon-Fri, dinner Mon-Sat; Ⓜ Charles de Gaulle–Étoile) This tiny neighbourhood bistro serves scrumptious traditional French fare: snails, baked shoulder of lamb with pumpkin purée or monkfish in lemon butter. Unsurprisingly, this place fills up faster than you can scamper down the steps at the nearby Arc de Triomphe. Reserve well in advance.

Opéra & Grands Boulevards

Le J'Go
Regional Cuisine €€

(Map p186; ☎ 01 40 22 09 09; www.lejgo.com; 4 rue Drouot, 9e; lunch/dinner menu €16/35; ◷Mon-Sat; Ⓜ Richelieu Drouot) This contemporary Toulouse-style bistro magics you away to southwestern France. Its bright yellow walls are decorated with bull-fighting posters and the flavourful regional cooking is based around the rotisserie –

not to mention other Gascogne standards like cassoulet and foie gras.

Le Zinc des Cavistes   Bar, Cafe €

(Map p186; ☎01 47 70 88 64; 5 rue du Faubourg Montmartre, 9e; lunch menu €16, mains €11-19; ⏰8am-10.30pm; Ⓜ Grands Boulevards) Don't tell the masses standing dutifully in the Chartier queue that there's a much better restaurant right next door – your formerly friendly waiter will probably run off screaming. A local favourite, Le Zinc des Cavistes is as good for a full-blown meal (duck confit, salads) as it is for sampling new vintages.

Montmartre & Pigalle

Neo-bistros, wine bars and world cuisine all feature in this area – pick and choose carefully to avoid tourist traps.

Cul de Poule   Modern French €€

(Map p186; ☎01 53 16 13 07; 53 rue des Martyrs, 9e; lunch 2-/3-course menu €15/18, dinner €23/28; ⏰closed lunch Sun; Ⓜ Pigalle) With plastic orange cafeteria seats outside, you probably wouldn't wander into the Cul de Poule by accident. But the light-hearted spirit (yes, there is a mounted chicken's derrière on the wall) is deceiving; this is one of the best and most affordable kitchens in the Pigalle neighbourhood, with excellent neo-bistro fare that emphasises quality ingredients from the French countryside.

Le Miroir   Bistro €€

(Map p186; ☎01 46 06 50 73; 94 rue des Martyrs, 18e; lunch menu €18, dinner menu €25-40; ⏰lunch Tue-Sun, dinner Tue-Sat; Ⓜ Abbesses) This unassuming modern bistro is smack in the middle of the Montmartre tourist trail, yet it remains a local favourite. There are lots of delightful pâtés and rillettes to start off with – guinea hen with dates, duck with mushrooms, haddock and lemon – followed by well-prepared standards like stuffed veal shoulder.

🍷 Drinking & Nightlife

The line between bars, cafes and bistros is blurred at best. Sitting at a table costs more than standing at the counter, more on a fancy square than a backstreet, more in the 8e than in the 18e. After 10pm many cafes charge a pricier *tarif de nuit* (night rate).

Louvre & Les Halles

Angelina   Teahouse

(Map p200; 226 rue de Rivoli, 1er; ⏰daily; Ⓜ Tuileries) This beautiful, high-ceilinged tearoom has exquisite furnishings, mirrored walls, fabulous fluffy cakes and the best, most wonderfully sickening 'African' hot chocolate (€7.20), served with a pot of whipped cream and a carafe of water.

Les Deux Magots (p210)
BRUNO DE HOGUES/GETTY IMAGES ©

Top Five Food Markets

Marché Bastille (Map p200; bd Richard Lenoir; ⏰7am-2.30pm Thu & Sun; Ⓜ Bastille or Richard Lenoir) Paris' best outdoor food market.

Marché aux Enfants Rouges (Map p200; 39 rue de Bretagne, 3e; ⏰8.30am-1pm & 4-7.30pm Tue-Fri, 4-8pm Sat, 8.30am-2pm Sun; Ⓜ Filles du Calvaire) The city's oldest food market, in the Marais, with food stalls and communal tables to lunch at.

Marché Belleville (Belleville Market; Map p186; blvd de Belleville, btwn rue Jean-Pierre Timbaud & rue du Faubourg du Temple, 11e & 20e; ⏰7am-2.30pm Tue & Fri; Ⓜ Belleville or Couronnes) Fascinating entry into the large, vibrant communities of the eastern neighbourhoods, home to artists, students and immigrants from Africa, Asia and the Middle East.

Marché Couvert St-Quentin (Map p186; 85 bis bd de Magenta, 10e) Iron-and-glass covered market built in 1866; lots of gourmet and upmarket food stalls.

Marché Raspail (Map p200; bd Raspail btwn rue de Rennes & rue du Cherche Midi, 6e; ⏰regular market 7am-2.30pm Tue & Fri, organic market 9am-3pm Sun; Ⓜ Rennes) Much-loved by foodies, particularly on Sunday for its organic produce.

Experimental Cocktail Club   Cocktail Bar

(Map p200; www.experimentalcocktailclub.com; 37 rue St-Saveur, 2e; ⏰daily; Ⓜ Réaumur-Sebastopol) Called ECC by trendies, this fabulous speakeasy with grey facade and old-beamed ceiling is effortlessly hip.

Marais & Bastille

Le Baron Rouge   Wine Bar

(Map p186; 1 rue Théophile Roussel, 12e; ⏰10am-2pm & 5-10pm Mon-Fri, 10am-10pm Sat, 10am-4pm Sun; Ⓜ Ledru-Rollin) Just about the ultimate Parisian wine-bar experience, this place has a dozen barrels of the stuff stacked up against the bottle-lined walls.

Le Pure Café   Cafe

(Map p186; 14 rue Jean Macé, 11e; ⏰daily; Ⓜ Charonne) A classic Parisian haunt, this rustic, cherry-red corner cafe was featured in the art-house film *Before Sunset* but it's still a refreshingly unpretentious spot for a drink or well-crafted fare like veal with chestnut purée.

La Fée Verte   Bar

(Map p186; 108 rue de la Roquette, 11e; dishes €10-16; ⏰daily; 📶; Ⓜ Voltaire) Yes, the 'Green Fairy' specialises in absinthe (served traditionally with spoons and sugar cubes), but this old-fashioned neighbourhood cafe and bar also serves terrific food, including Green Fairy cheeseburgers.

Latin Quarter

Café de la Nouvelle Mairie   Wine Bar

(Map p200; 19 rue des Fossés St-Jacques, 5e; ⏰9am-8pm Mon-Fri; Ⓜ Cardinal-Lemoine) Shh-hh...just around the corner from the Pan-théon but hidden on a small, fountained square, this wine bar is a neighbourhood secret, serving blackboard-chalked wines by the glass or bottle.

Curio Parlor Cocktail Club   Cocktail Bar

(Map p200; www.curioparlor.com; 16 rue des Bernardins, 5e; ⏰7pm-2am Mon-Thu, to 4am Fri-Sun; Ⓜ Maubert-Mutualité) Run by the same switched-on team as the Experimental

Below: Croissants for sale;
Right: View of Paris and the River Seine from the Eiffel Tower (p189)

(BELOW) DAMIEN POLEGATO/GETTY IMAGES ©; (RIGHT) ROBERT BREMEC/GETTY IMAGES ©

CROISSANT
1.00€

Cocktail Club, this hybrid bar-club looks to the interwar *années folles* (crazy years) of 1920s Paris, London and New York for inspiration.

St-Germain, Odéon & Luxembourg

Les Deux Magots   Cafe
(Map p200; www.lesdeuxmagots.fr; 170 bd St-Germain, 6e; ☺7.30am-1am; Ⓜ St-Germain des Prés) If ever there were a cafe that summed up St-Germain des Prés' early-20th-century literary scene, it's this former hangout of anyone who was anyone. You will spend *beaucoup* to sip a coffee in a wicker chair on the terrace shaded by dark-green awnings and geraniums spilling from window boxes, but it's an undeniable piece of Parisian history.

Café La Palette   Cafe
(Map p200; www.cafelapaletteparis.com; 43 rue de Seine, 6e; ☺6.30am-2am Mon-Sat; Ⓜ Mabillon) In the heart of gallery land, this *fin-de-siècle* cafe and erstwhile stomping ground of Paul Cézanne and Georges Braque attracts a grown-up set of fashion people and local art dealers. Its summer terrace is beautiful.

Opéra & Grands Boulevards

Harry's New York Bar   Cocktail Bar
(Map p186; www.harrysbar.fr; 5 rue Daunou, 2e; ☺daily; Ⓜ Opéra) One of the most popular American-style bars in the prewar years, Harry's once welcomed writers like F Scott Fitzgerald and Ernest Hemingway, who no doubt sampled the bar's unique cocktail and creation: the Bloody Mary. The Cuban mahogany interior dates from the mid-19th century and was brought over from a Manhattan bar in 1911.

Montmartre & Pigalle

La Fourmi   Bar, Cafe

(Map p186; 74 rue des Martyrs, 18e; 8am-
1am Mon-Thu, to 3am Fri & Sat, 10am-1am Sun;
Pigalle) A Pigalle institution, La Fourmi
hits the mark with its high ceilings, long
zinc bar and unpretentious vibe.

⭐ Entertainment

To find out what's on, buy *Pariscope*
(€0.40) or *Officiel des Spectacles* (www.
offi.fr, in French) at Parisian news kiosks.
Billeteries (ticket offices) in **Fnac** (www.
fnacspectacles.com) and **Virgin Megastores**
(place Raoul Dautry, Gare Montparnasse;
7am-8.30pm Mon-Thu, to 9pm Fri, 8am-8pm
Sat; Montparnasse Bienvenüe) sell tickets.

If you go on the day of a performance,
you can snag a half-price ticket (plus
€3 commission) for ballet, theatre,
opera and other performances at the
discount-ticket outlet **Kiosque Théâtre
Madeleine** (Map p186; opposite 15 place de la
Madeleine, 8e; 12.30-8pm Tue-Sat, to 4pm
Sun; Madeleine).

CABARET

Whirling lines of feather boa-clad, high-
kicking dancers at grand-scale cabarets
like the can-can creator, the Moulin
Rouge, are a quintessential fixture on
Paris' entertainment scene – for everyone
but Parisians.

Tickets to these spectacles start from
around €90 (from €130 with lunch, from
€150 with dinner), and usually include
a half-bottle of champagne. Advance
reservations are essential.

Moulin Rouge   Cabaret

(Map p186; 01 53 09 82 82; www.moulinrouge.
fr; 82 bd de Clichy, 18e; Blanche) Immortalised in the posters of Toulouse-Lautrec,
the Moulin Rouge twinkles beneath a
1925 replica of its original red windmill.
Yes, it's rife with bus-tour crowds.

Le Lido de Paris — Cabaret

(Map p186; 01 40 76 56 10; www.lido.fr; 116bis av des Champs-Élysées, 8e; George V) Founded at the close of WWII, this gets top marks for its sets and the lavish costumes of its 70 artists, including the famed Bluebell Girls and now the Lido Boy Dancers.

LIVE MUSIC

Palais Omnisports de Paris-Bercy (Map p186; www.bercy.fr; 8 bd de Bercy, 12e; Bercy); **Le Zénith** (08 90 71 02 07, 01 55 80 09 38; www.le-zenith.com; 211 av Jean Jaurès, 19e; Porte de Pantin) and **Stade de France** (08 92 39 01 00; www.stadefrance.com; rue Francis de Pressensé, ZAC du Cornillon Nord, St-Denis La Plaine; St-Denis-Porte de Paris) are Paris' big-name venues.

Salle Pleyel — Classical

(Map p186; 01 42 56 13 13; www.sallepleyel. fr; 252 rue du Faubourg St-Honoré, 8e; box office noon-7pm Mon-Sat, to 8pm on day of performance; Ternes) This highly regarded hall dating from the 1920s hosts many of Paris' finest classical-music recitals and concerts, including those by the celebrated **Orchestre de Paris** (www. orchestredeparis.com).

Le Vieux Belleville — Live Music

(Map p186; www.le-vieux-belleville.com; 12 rue des Envierges, 20e; Pyrénées) This old-fashioned bistro and *musette* at the top of Parc de Belleville is an atmospheric venue for performances of *chansons* featuring accordions and an organ grinder.

Au Limonaire — Live Music

(Map p186; 01 45 23 33 33; http://limonaire. free.fr; 18 cité Bergère, 9e; 7pm-midnight; Grands Boulevards) This little wine bar is one of the best places to listen to traditional French *chansons* and local singer-songwriters. Entry is free, the wine is good and dinner is served (*plat du jour* €7). Reserve if you plan to dine.

CLUBBING

La Scène Bastille — Nightclub

(Map p200; www.scenebastille.com; 2bis rue des Taillandiers, 11e; Thu-Sun; Bastille or Ledru-Rollin) The 'Bastille Scene' puts on a mixed bag of concerts but focuses on electro, funk and hip hop.

Le Batofar — Nightclub

(Map p186; www.batofar.org; opp 11 quai François Mauriac, 13e; 9pm-midnight Mon & Tue, to 4am or later Wed-Sun; Quai de la Gare or Bibliothèque) This much-loved, red-metal tugboat with rooftop bar and restaurant is known for its edgy, experimental music policy and live performances, mostly electro-oriented but also incorporating hip-hop, new wave, rock, punk or jazz.

Le Rex Club — Nightclub

(Map p186; www.rexclub.com; 5 bd Poissonnière, 2e; Wed-Sat; Bonne Nouvelle) Attached to the art deco Grand Rex cinema, this is Paris' premier house and techno venue where some of the world's hottest DJs strut their stuff on a 70-speaker, multidiffusion sound system.

GAY & LESBIAN PARIS

The Marais (4e), especially the areas around the intersection of rue Ste-Croix de la Bretonnerie and rue des Archives, and eastwards to rue Vieille du Temple, has been Paris' main centre of gay nightlife for some three decades.

The single best source of info on gay and lesbian Paris is the **Centre Gai et Lesbien de Paris** (CGL; Map p200; 01 43 57 21 47; www.centrelgbtparis.org; 61-63 rue Beaubourg, 3e; 6-8pm Mon, 3.30-8pm Tue-Thu, 1-8pm Fri & Sat; Rambuteau or Arts et Métiers), with a large library and happening bar.

Our top choices include:

Open Café (Map p200; www.opencafe.fr; 17 rue des Archives, 4e; daily; Hôtel de Ville) This wide, white-seated pavement terrace in the Marais is prime talent-watching.

Scream Club (Map p200; www.scream-paris. com; 18 rue du Faubourg du Temple, 11e; daily; Belleville or Goncourt) Saturday night's the night at 'Paris' biggest gay party'.

3w Kafé (Map p200; 8 rue des , 4e; Tue-Sat; St-Paul) For women.

Le Tango (Map p200; www.boite-a-frissons.fr; 13 rue au Maire, 3e; Fri-Sun; Arts et Métiers)

Historic 1930s dance hosting legendary gay tea dances.

🔒 Shopping

Key areas to mooch with no particular purchase in mind are the maze of backstreet lanes in the Marais (3e and 4e), around St-Germain des Prés (6e), and parts of Montmartre and Pigalle (9e and 18e). There are also some particularly noteworthy flea markets:

Marché aux Puces de Montreuil
Market

(av du Professeur André Lemière, 20e; ⏰8am-7.30pm Sat-Mon; Ⓜ Porte de Montreuil) Particularly known for its secondhand clothing, designer seconds, engravings, jewellery, linen, crockery and old furniture.

Marché aux Puces de St-Ouen
Market

(www.marcheauxpuces-saintouen.com; rue des Rosiers, av Michelet, rue Voltaire, rue Paul Bert & rue Jean-Henri Fabre; ⏰9am-6pm Sat, 10am-6pm Sun, 11am-5pm Mon; Ⓜ Porte de Clignancourt) Around since the late 19th century, and said to be Europe's largest flea market.

Marché aux Puces de la Porte de Vanves
Market

(Map p186; http://pucesdevanves.typepad.com; av Georges Lafenestre & av Marc Sangnier, 14e; ⏰from 7am Sat & Sun; Ⓜ Porte de Vanves) One of the smallest and, some say, friendliest of Paris' flea markets.

ℹ️ Information

Dangers & Annoyances

Metro stations best avoided late at night include: Châtelet-Les Halles and its corridors; Château Rouge in Montmartre; Gare du Nord; Strasbourg St-Denis; Réaumur Sébastopol; and Montparnasse Bienvenüe.

Pickpocketing and thefts from handbags and packs is a problem wherever there are crowds (especially of tourists).

Tourist Information

Paris Convention & Visitors Bureau (Office de Tourisme et de Congrès de Paris; Map p200; ☎08 92 68 30 00; www.parisinfo.com; 25-27 rue des Pyramides, 1er; ⏰9am-7pm Jun-Oct, shorter hrs rest of year; Ⓜ Pyramides) Main tourist office with several branches around the city.

ℹ️ Getting There & Away

Air

Aéroport Roissy Charles de Gaulle (CDG; ☎01 70 36 39 50; www.aeroportsdeparis.fr) Three terminals, 30km northeast of Paris in the suburb of Roissy.

Aéroport d'Orly (ORY; ☎01 70 36 39 50; www.aeroportsdeparis.fr) Aéroport d'Orly is the older, smaller of Paris' two major airports, 19km south of the city.

Moulin Rouge® (p211), Montmartre
BRUCE YUANYUE BI/GETTY IMAGES ©

Aéroport Beauvais (BVA; ☎08 92 68 20 66; www.aeroportbeauvais.com) Used by charter companies and budget airlines, 75km north of Paris.

Bus

Gare Routiére Internationale de Paris-Galliéni (☎08 92 89 90 91; 28 av du Général de Gaulle; MGalliéni)

Train

Paris has six major train stations.

Gare d'Austerlitz (blvd de l'Hôpital, 13e; MGare d'Austerlitz) Trains to/from Spain and Portugal, the Loire Valley and southwestern France.

Gare de l'Est (blvd de Strasbourg, 10e; MGare de l'Est) Trains to/from Luxembourg, parts of Switzerland (Basel, Lucerne, Zurich), southern Germany (Frankfurt, Munich) and points further east; regular services to eastern France (Champagne, Alsace and Lorraine).

Gare de Lyon (blvd Diderot, 12e; MGare de Lyon) Trains to/from parts of Switzerland (Bern, Geneva, Lausanne), Italy and points beyond; domestic services to areas southeast of Paris, including Dijon, Lyon, Provence, the Côte d'Azur and the Alps.

Gare Montparnasse (av du Maine & blvd de Vaugirard, 15e; MMontparnasse Bienvenüe) Trains to/from Brittany and places en route from Paris (eg Chartres, Angers, Nantes); also to Tours, Nantes, Bordeaux and other destinations in southwestern France.

Gare du Nord (rue de Dunkerque, 10e; MGare du Nord) Terminus of high-speed Thalys trains to/from Amsterdam, Brussels, Cologne and Geneva and Eurostar to London; domestic services to Paris' northern suburbs and northern France.

Gare St-Lazare (rue St-Lazare & rue d'Amsterdam, 8e; MSt-Lazare) Trains to Normandy.

ⓘ Getting Around

To/From the Airports

Getting into town is straightforward and inexpensive thanks to a fleet of public-transport options. Bus drivers sell tickets. Children aged four to 11 years pay half-price on most services.

Aéroport Roissy Charles de Gaulle

RER B (☎32 46; www.ratp.fr; adult €9.10; ☺5am-11pm) Departs every 10 to 15 minutes, serving Gare du Nord, Châtelet-Les Halles and St-Michel-Notre Dame stations in the city centre. Journey time approximately 35 minutes.

Gare du Nord train station, Paris

Air France Bus 2 (☎08 92 35 08 20; http://
videocdn.airfrance.com/cars-airfrance; adult €15;
🕐6am-11pm) To/from the Arc de Triomphe and
Porte Maillot metro station (35 to 50 minutes).

Air France Bus 4 (☎08 92 35 08 20; http://
videocdn.airfrance.com/cars-airfrance; adult
€16.50; 🕐 from Roissy Charles de Gaulle 6am-
10pm, from Paris 6am-9.30pm) Shuttles every
30 minutes to/from Gare de Lyon and Gare
Montparnasse (50 to 55 minutes).

RATP Bus 350 (☎32 46; www.ratp.fr; adult
€5.10 or 3 metro tickets; 🕐5.30am-11pm) Every
30 minutes to/from Gare de l'Est and Gare du
Nord (both one hour).

Roissybus (Map p186; ☎32 46; www.ratp.fr;
adult €10; 🕐5.30am-11pm) Every 30 minutes
to/from Opéra, 9e (45 minutes).

Aéroport d'Orly

Air France Bus 1 (Map p186; ☎08 92 35 08 20;
http://videocdn.airfrance.com/cars-airfrance;
adult €11.50; 🕐 from Orly 5am-10.20pm, from
Invalides 6am-11.20pm) Shuttle bus to/from
Gare Montparnasse (35 minutes), Invalides in
the 7e, and the Arc de Triomphe.

Orlybus (☎32 46; www.ratp.fr; adult €6.90;
🕐 from Orly 6am-11.20pm, from Paris 5.35am-
11.05pm) RATP bus every 15 to 20 minutes to/
from metro Denfert Rochereau (30 minutes)
in the 14e.

Orlyval (☎32 46; www.ratp.fr; adult €10.75;
🕐6am-11pm) Orlyval automatic metro from
Orly to Antony station, then RER B to Gare du
Nord, Châtalet-Les Halles and St-Michel-Notre
Dame RER stations in the city centre.

Between Orly & Charles de Gaulle

Air France Shuttle Bus 3 (www.cars-airfrance.
com; adult €20; 🕐6am-10.30pm) Every 30
minutes; journey time 30 to 45 minutes.

Aéroport Paris-Beauvais

Navette Officielle (Official Shuttle Bus; ☎08 92
68 20 64, airport 08 92 68 20 66; adult €15) Links
Beauvais airport with metro station Porte de
Maillot; journey time 1¼ hours.

Bicycle

Vélib' (www.velib.paris.fr; day/week subscription
€1/5, bike hire per 1st/2nd/additional 30 min
free/€2/4) With this self-service bike scheme

pick up a bike from one roadside Vélib' station
and drop it off at another. To get a bike, first
purchase a one-/seven-day subscription
(€1.70/8) online or at any bike terminal (by
credit card with a microchip).

Boat

Batobus (www.batobus.com; 1-/2-/5-day pass
€15/18/21; 🕐10am-9.30pm Apr-Aug, to 7pm rest
of year) Fleet of glassed-in trimarans dock at
eight piers along the Seine; buy tickets at each
stop or at tourist offices and jump on and off as
you like.

Public Transport

Paris' public transit system is operated by the
RATP (www.ratp.fr). The same RATP tickets
are valid on the metro, RER, buses, trams and
Montmartre funicular. A single ticket is €1.70 while
a *carnet* of 10 costs €12.70.

One ticket covers travel between any two metro
stations (no return journeys) for 1½ hours; you
can transfer between buses and between buses
and trams, but not from metro to bus or vice
versa.

Keep your ticket until you exit the station;
ticket inspectors can fine you if you can't produce
a valid ticket.

Bus

Buses run from 5.30am to 8.30pm Monday to
Saturday, with certain evening lines continuing
until midnight or 12.30am, when hourly **Noctilien**
(www.noctilien.fr) night buses kick in.

Metro & RER

Paris' underground network consists of the 14-line
metro and the RER, a network of suburban train
lines. Each metro train is known by the name of its
terminus. The last metro train on each line begins
sometime between 12.35am and 1.15am (2.15am
Friday and Saturday), before starting up again
around 5.30am.

Tourist Passes

The **Mobilis Card** allows unlimited travel for one
day in two to five zones (€6.40 to €14.20) on the
metro, the RER, buses, trams and the Montmartre
funicular; while the **Paris Visite** pass allows
unlimited travel (including to/from airports) plus
discounted entry to museums and activities and
costs €9.75/15.85/21.60/31.15 for one to three
zones for one/two/three/five days.

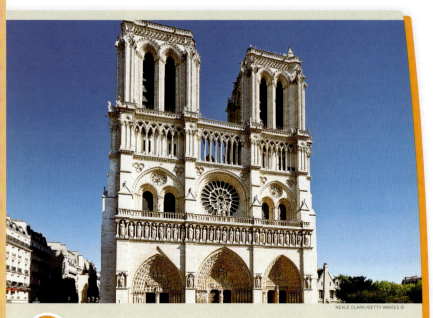

NEALE CLARK/GETTY IMAGES ©

⭐ Don't Miss
Cathédrale Notre Dame

The magnificent 13th-century cathedral of Chartres, crowned by two very different spires – one Gothic, the other Romanesque – rises from rich farmland 88km southwest of Paris and dominates the town. With its astonishing blue stained glass and other treasures, France's best-preserved medieval basilica is a must-see.

The cathedral's west, north and south entrances have superbly ornamented triple portals, but the west entrance, known as the **Portail Royal**, is the only one that predates a devastating fire in 1194. Carved from 1145 to 1155, its superb statues represent the glory of Christ in the centre, and the Nativity and the Ascension. The structure's other main Romanesque feature is the 105m-high **Clocher Vieux** (Old Bell Tower; also called the Tour Sud or 'South Tower'); it's the tallest Romanesque steeple still standing. Superb views of three-tiered flying buttresses and the 19th-century copper roof, turned green by verdigris, reward the 350-step hike up the 112m-high **Clocher Neuf** (New Bell Tower or North Tower; adult/child €7/free; ⊙9.30am-12.30pm & 2-6pm Mon-Sat, 2-6pm Sun May-Aug, 9.30am-12.30pm & 2-5pm Mon-Sat, 2-5pm Sun Sep-Apr).

Inside, 172 **stained-glass windows**, mainly from the 13th century, form one of the most important ensembles of medieval stained glass in the world. The three most exquisite – renowned for the depth and intensity of their tones, famously known as 'Chartres blue' – are above the west entrance and below the rose window.

Frequent SNCF trains link Paris' Gare Montparnasse (€14.40, 55 to 70 minutes) with Chartres via Versailles-Chantiers (€12.10, 45 minutes to one hour).

NEED TO KNOW
www.diocese-chartres.com; place de la Cathédrale; ⊙8.30am-7.30pm daily, to 10pm Tue, Fri & Sun Jun-Aug

Taxi

The flag fall is €2.40, plus €0.96 per kilometre within the city limits from 10am to 5pm Monday to Saturday (Tarif A; white light on meter), and €1.21 per kilometre from 5pm to 10am, all day Sunday, and public holidays (Tarif B; orange light on meter).

Alpha Taxis (☎01 45 85 85 85; www.alphataxis. com)

Taxis Bleus (☎01 49 36 10 10; www.taxis-bleus. com)

AROUND PARIS

Bordered by five rivers – the Epte, Aisne, Eure, Yonne and Marne – the area around Paris looks rather like a giant island, and indeed is known as Île de France. Centuries ago this was where French kings retreated to extravagant chateaux in Versailles and Fontainebleau. These days such royal castles have been joined by a kingdom of an altogether different kind.

Disneyland Resort Paris

In 1992, Mickey Mouse, Snow White and chums set up shop on reclaimed sugar-beet fields 32km east of Paris at a cost of €4.6 billion. Though not quite as over-the-top as its American cousin, France's Disneyland packs in the crowds nonetheless.

The main **Disneyland Park** (☉10am-8pm Mon-Fri, 9am-8pm Sat & Sun Sep-May, 9am-11pm Jun-Aug, hours can vary) comprises five *pays* (lands), including the 1900s idealised **Main St USA**, a recreation of the American Wild West in **Frontierland** with the legendary Big Thunder Mountain ride, futuristic **Discoveryland**, and the exotic-themed **Adventureland**, where you'll find the Pirates of the Caribbean and the spiralling 360-degrees roller coaster, Indiana Jones and the Temple of Peril. Pinocchio, Snow White and other fairy-tale characters come to life in the candy-coated heart of the park, **Fantasyland**.

Adjacent **Walt Disney Studios Park** (☉9am-7pm late Jun-early Sep, 10am-7pm Mon-Fri & 9am-7pm Sat & Sun early Sep-late Jun) has a sound stage, backlot and animation studios illustrating how films, TV programs and cartoons are produced.

Standard admission fees at **Disneyland Resort Paris** (☎hotel booking 01 60 30 60 30, restaurant reservations 01 60 30 40 50; www.disneylandparis.com; one-day admission adult/child €59/53; ☉hours vary; Ⓜ Marne-la-Vallée/Chessy) include admission to either Disneyland Park or Walt Disney, but there's always a multitude of different passes, special offers and accommodation/transport packages on offer.

Marne-la-Vallée/Chessy, Disneyland's RER station, is served by line A4; trains run every 15 minutes or so from central Paris (€7.10, 35 to 40 minutes).

NORMANDY

Famous for cows, cider and Camembert, this largely rural region (www.normandie-tourisme.fr) is one of France's most traditional – and most visited thanks to world-renowned sights such as the Bayeux Tapestry, historic D-Day beaches, Monet's garden at Giverny and spectacular Mont St-Michel.

Rouen

POP 119,927

With its elegant spires, beautifully restored medieval quarter and soaring Gothic cathedral, the ancient city of Rouen is a Normandy highlight. Devastated several times during the Middle Ages by fire and plague, the city was later badly damaged by WWII bombing raids, but has been meticulously rebuilt over the last six decades.

◎ Sights

Église Jeanne d'Arc   Church

(place du Vieux Marché; ☉10am-noon & 2-6pm Apr-Oct) The old city's main thoroughfare, rue du Gros Horloge, runs from the cathedral west to **place du Vieux Marché**. Dedicated in 1979, the thrillingly bizarre Église Jeanne d'Arc, with its fish-scale exterior,

Don't Miss
Versailles

Louis XIV transformed his father's hunting lodge into the monumental Château de Versailles in the mid-17th century, and it remains France's most famous, grandest palace. Versailles, 28km southwest of Paris, was the seat for the royal court from 1682 to 1789 when revolutionaries massacred the palace guard and dragged Louis XVI and Marie Antoinette back to Paris to be guillotined.

📞 01 30 83 78 00

www.chateauversailles.fr

admission passport (estate-wide access) €18, with musical events €25, palace €15

🕐 8am-6pm Tue-Sat, 9am-6pm Sun Apr-Oct, 8.30am-5.30pm Tue-Sat, 9am-5.30pm Sun Nov-Mar

Highlights

Created by architect Louis Le Vau, painter and interior designer Charles Le Brun, and landscape artist André Le Nôtre, the chateau was designed as the last word in luxury. Among the most dazzling features are the **Galerie des Glaces** (Hall of Mirrors), a 75m-long ballroom lined with 17 huge mirrors, and the 17th-century **Bassin de Neptune** (Neptune's Fountain).

Versailles Tours

You can access off-limits areas of the chateau with a **guided tour** (📞01 30 83 77 88; tours €16; 🕐English-language tours 9.30am & 2pm Tue-Sun) of the Private Apartments of Louis XV and Louis XVI and the Opera House or Royal Chapel. They can be prebooked online. If you're short on time, consider renting an **electric car** (📞01 39 66 97 66; per hr €30), **bike** (📞01 39 66 97 66; per hr €6.50) or **boat** (📞01 39 66 97 66; per hr €15) to get around the vast estate.

Dodging the Crowds

Pre-purchase your tickets on the chateau's website, or arrive as early as you can to avoid the midday queues. Steer clear of Tuesday and Sunday (which are the busiest days), and Monday (when the chateau is closed).

Local Knowledge

Versailles

RECOMMENDATIONS FROM SYLVAIN POSTOLLE, OFFICIAL GUIDE

1 KING'S PRIVATE APARTMENT

This is the most fascinating part of the palace as it shows the king as a man and very much reflects his daily life in the 18th century. Of the 10 or so rooms, the most famous is his bedroom where he not only slept but also held ceremonies. Up to 150 courtiers and people would watch him have supper here each evening!

2 KING LOUIS XIV'S LIBRARY

This is a lovely room – full of books, a place where you can really imagine the king coming to read for hours and hours. Louis XVI loved geography and his copy of *The Travels of James Cook* – in English – is still here.

3 HERCULES SALON

I love one particular perspective inside the palace: from the Hercules Salon you can see all the rooms comprising the King's State Apartment, and to the right, through the gallery leading to the opera house. The salon served as a passageway for the king to go from his state apartment to the chapel to celebrate daily Mass.

4 ROYAL CHAPEL

This is an exquisite example of the work of a very important architect of the time, Jules Hardouin-Mansart (1646–1708). The paintings are also stunning: they evoke the idea that the French king was chosen by God and was his lieutenant on earth. The chapel is where the future king Louis XVI wed Marie Antoinette in 1770.

5 ENCELADE GROVE

Versailles' gardens are extraordinary but my favourite spot has to be this grove, typical of the gardens created for Louis XIV by André Le Nôtre. A gallery of trellises surround a pool with a statue of Enceladus, chief of the Titans who was punished for his pride by the gods from Mount Olympus. The fountains are impressive.

Versailles

A Day in Court

Visiting Versailles – even just the State Apartments – may seem overwhelming at first, but think of it as a house where people ate, drank, worked, slept and conspired and you'll be on the right path.

Some two decades into his long reign, Louis XIV began turning his father's hunting lodge into a palace large enough to house his entire court (to keep closer tabs on the 6000-strong army of courtiers). Sparing no expense, the Sun King employed the greatest artists and craftspeople of the day and by 1682 he'd created the most extravagant dormitory in history.

The royal schedule was as accurate and predictable as a Swiss watch. By following this itinerary of rooms you can recreate the king's day, starting with the **King's Bedchamber** ❶ and the **Queen's Bedchamber** ❷, where the royal couple was roused at about the same time. The royal procession then leads through the **Hall of Mirrors** ❸ to the **Royal Chapel** ❹ for morning Mass and returns to the **Council Chamber** ❺ for late-morning meetings with ministers. After lunch the king might ride or hunt or visit the **King's Library** ❻. Later he could join courtesans for an 'apartment evening' starting from the **Hercules Drawing Room** ❼ or play billiards in the Diana **Drawing Room** ❽ before supping at 10pm.

VERSAILLES BY NUMBERS

Rooms 700 (11 hectares of roof)
Windows 2153
Staircases 67
Gardens and parks 800 hectares
Trees 200,000
Fountains 50 (with 620 nozzles)
Paintings 6300 (measuring 11km laid end to end)
Statues and sculptures 2100
Objets d'art and furnishings 5000
Visitors 5.3 million per year

CHRISTOPHE LEHENAFF/GETTY IMAGES ©

Queen's Bedchamber
Chambre de la Reine
The queen's life was on constant public display and even the births of her children were watched by crowds of spectators in her own bedchamber. **DETOUR »** The Guardroom, with a dozen armed men at the ready.

> **Lunch Break**
>
> Diner-style food at Sister's Café, crêpes at Le Phare St-Louis or picnic in the park.

Guardroom

South Wing

King's Library
Bibliothèque du Roi
The last resident, bibliophile Louis XVI, loved geography and his copy of *The Travels of James Cook* (in English, which he read fluently) is still on the shelf here.

DEA/G. DAGLI ORTI/GETTY IMAGES ©

> **Savvy Sightseeing**
>
> Avoid Versailles on Monday (closed), Tuesday (Paris' museums close, so visitors flock here) and Sunday, the busiest day. Also, book tickets online so you don't have to queue.

Hall of Mirrors
Galerie des Glaces
The solid-silver candelabra and furnishings in this extravagant hall, devoted to Louis XIV's successes in war, were melted down in 1689 to pay for yet another conflict. **DETOUR»** The antithetical Peace Drawing Room, adjacent.

King's Bedchamber
Chambre du Roi
The king's daily life was anything but private and even his *lever* (rising) at 8am and *coucher* (retiring) at 11.30pm would be witnessed by up to 150 sycophantic courtiers.

Council Chamber
Cabinet du Conseil
This chamber, with carved medallions evoking the king's work, is where the monarch met his various ministers (state, finance, religion etc) depending on the days of the week.

Peace Drawing Room

Hall of Mirrors

Marble Courtyard

Apollo Drawing Room

Entrance

Entrance

North Wing

To Royal Opera

Diana Drawing Room
Salon de Diane
With walls and ceiling covered in frescos devoted to the mythical huntress, this room contained a large billiard table reserved for Louis XIV, a keen player.

Royal Chapel
Chapelle Royale
This two-storey chapel (with gallery for the royals and important courtiers, and the ground floor for the B-list) was dedicated to St Louis, patron of French monarchs. **DETOUR»** The sumptuous Royal Opera.

Hercules Drawing Room
Salon d'Hercule
This salon, with its stunning ceiling fresco of the strong man, gave way to the State Apartments, which were open to courtiers three nights a week. **DETOUR»** Apollo Drawing Room, used for formal audiences and as a throne room.

marks the spot where 19-year-old Joan of Arc was burned at the stake in 1431.

Cathédrale Notre Dame Cathedral
(place de la Cathédrale; ⊙2-6pm Mon, 7.30am-7pm Tue-Sat, 8am-6pm Sun) Rouen's stunning Gothic cathedral, with its polished, brilliant-white facade, is the famous subject of a series of paintings by Monet.

Musée des Beaux-Arts Museum
(✆02 35 71 28 40; www.rouen-musees.com; esplanade Marcel Duchamp; adult/child €5/free; ⊙10am-6pm Wed-Mon) Housed in a grand structure erected in 1870, Rouen's fine-arts museum features canvases by Caravaggio, Rubens, Modigliani, Pissarro, Renoir, Sisley (lots) and (of course) several works by Monet.

🛏 Sleeping

Hôtel de Bourgtheroulde Hotel €€€
(✆02 35 14 50 50; www.hotelsparouen.com; 15 place de la Pucelle; r €240-380; P❄🤶🛏) This stunning conversion of an old private mansion brings a dash of glamour and luxury to Rouen's hotel scene. Rooms are large, gorgeously designed and feature beautiful bathrooms.

Hôtel de la Cathédrale Hotel €
(✆02 35 71 57 95; www.hotel-de-la-cathedrale.fr; 12 rue St-Romain; s €66-86, d €76-104, q €143; @🤶) Hiding behind a 17th-century half-timbered facade, this atmospheric hotel has 27 stylishly refitted rooms, mostly overlooking a quiet plant-filled courtyard.

🍴 Eating

Les Nymphéas French €€
(✆02 35 89 26 69; www.lesnympheas-rouen.com; 7-9 rue de la Pie; mains €29-37, menu €34-52; ⊙lunch & dinner Tue-Sat) Its formal table settings arrayed under 16th-century beams, this fine restaurant serves cuisine based on fresh ingredients. Even the cheaper lunch menu (€34) is exquisite.

Minute et Mijoté Bistro €
(58 rue de Fontenelle; mains €20, menu €13-30; ⊙lunch & dinner Mon-Sat) This smart bistro

is one of our favourite finds in Rouen. The trademark here is freshness and great value for money, hence its fast-growing reputation.

ℹ Information

Tourist office (✆02 32 08 32 40; www.rouentourisme.com; 25 place de la Cathédrale; ⊙9am-7pm Mon-Sat, 9.30am-12.30pm & 2-6pm Sun & holidays)

ℹ Getting There & Away

Train
Direct services from Rouen train station, just north of the city centre.

Caen from €24.90, 1½ hours, eight to 10 daily

Paris St-Lazare €21.90, 1¼ hours, at least hourly

Bayeux
POP 14,350

Bayeux has become famous throughout the English-speaking world thanks to a 68m-long piece of painstakingly embroidered cloth: the 11th-century Bayeux Tapestry, whose 58 scenes vividly tell the story of the Norman invasion of England in 1066. The town is also one of the few in Normandy to have survived WWII practically unscathed, with a centre crammed with 13th- to 18th-century buildings, wooden-framed Norman-style houses, and a spectacular Norman Gothic cathedral.

🎯 Sights

Bayeux Tapestry Tapestry
(✆02 31 51 25 50; www.tapisserie-bayeux.fr; rue de Nesmond; adult/child incl audioguide €7.80/3.80; ⊙9am-6.30pm mid-Mar–mid-Nov, to 7pm May-Aug, 9.30am-12.30pm & 2-6pm mid-Nov–mid-Mar) The world's most celebrated embroidery recounts the conquest of England from an unashamedly Norman perspective. Fifty-eight scenes fill the central canvas, and religious allegories and illustrations of everyday 11th-century life fill the borders. The final showdown at the Battle of Hastings is depicted in

graphic fashion, complete with severed limbs and decapitated heads (along the bottom of scene 52); Halley's Comet, which blazed across the sky in 1066, appears in scene 32. Scholars believe the 68.3m-long tapestry was commissioned by Bishop Odo of Bayeux, William the Conquerer's half-brother, for the opening of Bayeux' cathedral in 1077.

Musée Mémorial de la Bataille de Normandie   Museum

(Battle of Normandy Memorial Museum; bd Fabien Ware; adult/child €7/3.80; ⊙9.30am-6.30pm May-Sep, 10am-12.30pm & 2-6pm Oct-Apr) Using well-chosen photos, personal accounts, dioramas and wartime objects, this first-rate museum offers an excellent introduction to WWII in Normandy.

 Sleeping

Les Logis du Rempart   B&B €

(📞02 31 92 50 40; www.lecornu.fr; 4 rue Bourbesneur; d €60-80, q €130; 🛜) This *maison de famille* shelters three rooms oozing old-fashioned cosiness and the hosts run a tasting shop downstairs – the perfect place to stock up on top-quality, homemade Calvados and cider.

Villa Lara   Boutique Hotel €€€

(📞02 31 92 00 55; www.hotel-villalara.com; 6 place de Québec; d €180-280, ste €290-450; P ❄ 🛜) Luxury and sophistication are the hallmarks of this 28-room boutique hotel which opened in 2012. Clean lines, trendy colour schemes, top-quality fabrics and minimalist motifs distinguish the rooms, while other facilities include a bistro and a gym.

 Eating

La Rapière   Regional Cuisine €€

(📞02 31 21 05 45; 53 rue St-Jean; menu €15-33.50; ⊙lunch & dinner Fri-Tue) Housed in a late-1400s mansion composed of stone walls and big wooden beams, this atmospheric restaurant specialises in Normandy staples such as terrines, duck and veal with Camembert.

La Reine Mathilde   Patisserie €

(47 rue St-Martin; cakes from €2.50; ⊙8.30am-7.30pm Tue-Sun) A sumptuous, c 1900-style patisserie and *salon de thé* (tearoom)

Cathédrale Notre Dame, Rouen

that's ideal if you've got a hankering for something sweet.

ℹ️ Information

Tourist Office (☎ 02 31 51 28 28; www.bessin-normandie.com; pont St-Jean; 🕐9.30am-12.30pm & 2-6pm)

ℹ️ Getting There & Away

Trains link Bayeux with Caen (€6.20, 20 minutes, hourly), from where there are connections to Paris' Gare St-Lazare (€33.30, two hours) and Rouen (€24.90, 1½ hours).

D-Day Beaches

The D-Day landings, code-named 'Operation Overlord', were the largest military operation in history. Early on 6 June 1944, Allied troops stormed ashore along 80km of beaches north of Bayeux, code-named (from west to east) Utah, Omaha, Gold, Juno and Sword. The landings on D-Day – called 'Jour J' in French – were followed by the Battle of Normandy, which ultimately led to the liberation of Europe from Nazi occupation. Memorial museums in Caen and Bayeux provide a comprehensive overview, and there are many small D-Day museums dotted along the coast. For context, see www.normandiememoire.com and www.6juin1944.com.

The most brutal fighting on D-Day took place 15km northwest of Bayeux along the stretch of coastline now known as **Omaha Beach**, today a glorious stretch of fine golden sand partly lined with sand dunes and summer homes. **Circuit de la Plage d'Omaha**, trail-marked with a yellow stripe, is a self-guided tour along the beach, surveyed from a bluff above by the huge **Normandy American Cemetery & Memorial** (www.abmc.gov; Colleville-sur-Mer; 🕐9am-5pm). Featured in the opening scenes of Steven Spielberg's *Saving Private Ryan,* this is the largest American cemetery in Europe.

Caen's hi-tech, hugely impressive **Mémorial – Un Musée pour la Paix** (Memorial – A Museum for Peace; ☎ 02 31 06 06 45; www.memorial-caen.fr; esplanade Général Eisenhower; adult/child €18.80/16.30; 🕐9am-6.30pm, closed Jan & Mon mid-Nov–mid-Dec) uses sound, lighting, film, animation and lots of exhibits to graphically explore and evoke the events of WWII, D-Day landings and the ensuing Cold War. Tickets remain

WWII memorial at Omaha Beach, Normandy

valid for 24 hours. The museum also runs D-Day beach tours.

Tours

An organised minibus tour is an excellent way to get a sense of the D-Day beaches and their place in history. Bayeux tourist office (p224) handles reservations.

Mémorial   Minibus Tours
(www.memorial-caen.fr; adult/child €77/61) Excellent year-round minibus tours (four to five hours). Rates include entry to Mémorial. Book online.

Normandy Sightseeing
Tours   D-Day Tour
(☏ 02 31 51 70 52; www.normandywebguide.com) From May to October (and on request the rest of the year), this experienced outfit offers morning (adult/child €45/25) tours of various beaches and cemeteries. These can be combined into an all-day excursion (€90/50).

Getting There & Away

Bus Verts (www.busverts.fr) Bus 70 (two or three daily Monday to Saturday, more in summer) goes northwest from Bayeux to Colleville-sur-Mer and Omaha Beach (€2.30, 35 minutes).

BRITTANY

Brittany is for explorers. Its wild, dramatic coastline, medieval towns, thick forests and the eeriest stone circles this side of Stonehenge make a trip here well worth the detour from the beaten track.

St-Malo

POP 48,800

The mast-filled port of fortified St-Malo is inextricably tied up with the deep briny blue: the town became a key harbour during the 17th and 18th centuries, functioning as a base for merchant ships and government-sanctioned privateers, and these days it's a busy cross-Channel ferry port and summertime getaway.

Sights

Walking on top of the city's sturdy 17th-century ramparts (1.8km) affords fine views of the old walled city known as **Intra-Muros** ('within the walls') or Ville Close – access the ramparts from any of the city gates.

Cathédrale St-Vincent   Cathedral
(place Jean de Châtillon; ⊙9.30am-6pm) The city's centrepiece was constructed between the 12th and 18th centuries. The battle to liberate St-Malo destroyed around 80% of the old city during August 1944, and damage to the cathedral was particularly severe.

Fort National   Ruin
(www.fortnational.com; adult/child €5/3; ⊙Easter, school holidays & Jun–mid-Sep) From the city ramparts, spot the remains of St-Malo's former prison and the rocky islet of **Île du Grand Bé**, where the great St-Malo-born 18th-century writer Chateaubriand is buried. Walk at low tide, but check the tide times with the tourist office.

Musée du Château   Museum
(☏02 99 40 71 57; adult/child €6/3; ⊙10am-noon & 2-6pm Apr-Sep, Tue-Sun Oct-Mar) Within **Château de St-Malo**, built by the dukes of Brittany in the 15th and 16th centuries, this museum looks at the life and history of the city.

Grand Aquarium   Aquarium
(☏02 99 21 19 00; www.aquarium-st-malo. com; av Général Patton; adult/child €16/11.50; ⊙9.30am-10pm mid-Jul–mid-Aug, 9.30am-8pm early Jul & late Aug; ⛟; ☐C1) Kids will adore the submarine ride and exhibits on local marine life at this excellent aquarium, about 4km south of the city centre.

Sleeping

Hôtel Quic en
Groigne   Boutique Hotel €€
(☏02 99 20 22 20; www.quic-en-groigne.com; 8 rue d'Estrées; s €64-72, d €79-102; ⊙closed mid-Nov–Feb; P🛜) This exceptional hotel

225

BERTHOLD TRENKEL/GETTY IMAGES ©

⭐ Don't Miss
Mont St-Michel

On a rocky island opposite the coastal town of Pontorson, connected to the mainland by a narrow causeway, the sky-scraping turrets of the **Abbaye du Mont St-Michel** (☎ 02 33 89 80 00; www.monuments-nationaux.fr; adult/child incl guided tour €9/free; ⊙ 9am-7pm, last entry 1hr before closing) provide one of France's iconic sights. The surrounding bay is notorious for its fast-rising tides: at low tide the Mont is surrounded by bare sand for miles around; at high tide, just six hours later, the bay, causeway and nearby car parks can be submerged.

From the **tourist office** (☎ 02 33 60 14 30; www.ot-montsaintmichel.com; ⊙ 9am-12.30pm & 2-6.30pm Mon-Sat, 9am-noon & 2-6pm Sun, no midday closure Jul & Aug), at the base of the mount, a cobbled street winds up to the **Église Abbatiale** (Abbey Church), incorporating elements of both Norman and Gothic architecture. Other notable sights include the arched **cloître** (cloister), the barrel-roofed **réfectoire** (dining hall), and the Gothic **Salle des Hôtes** (Guest Hall), dating from 1213. English-language tours run hourly in summer, twice daily (11am and 3pm) in winter. In July and August, Monday to Saturday, there are illuminated *nocturnes* (night-time visits) with music from 7pm to 10pm.

Check the *horaire des marées* (tide table) at the tourist office. When the tide is out, you can walk all the way around Mont St-Michel, a distance of about 1km. Stray too far from the Mont and you risk getting stuck in wet sand – from which Norman soldiers are depicted being rescued in one scene of the Bayeux Tapestry – or being overtaken by the incoming tide, providing your next of kin with a great cocktail-party story.

There are two to three daily trains to Pontorson from Bayeux (€22.30, 1¾ hr) and Cherbourg (€28.10, three hours).

has 15 rooms that are the epitome of clean, simple style, and many a hotel twice the price should be envious of this place.

Hôtel San Pedro   Hotel €
(☏02 99 40 88 57; www.sanpedro-hotel.com; 1 rue Ste-Anne; s €58-60, d €69-79; P 🛜) Tucked at the back of the old city, the San Pedro has cool, crisp, neutral-toned decor with subtle splashes of colour, friendly service and superb sea views.

✗ Eating & Drinking

Le Bistro de Jean   Bistro €
(☏02 99 40 98 68; 6 rue de la Corne-de-Cerf; mains €15-19, menu from €12; ⊘closed lunch Wed & Sat, all day Sun) Want to know where the locals choose to eat inside the walls? Peer through the windows of this lively and authentic bistro and you'll get your answer.

Le Chalut   Seafood €€
(☏02 99 56 71 58; 8 rue de la Corne-du-Cerf; menu €26-70; ⊘Wed-Sun) This unremarkable-looking establishment is, in fact, St-Malo's most celebrated restaurant. Its kitchen overflows with the best the Breton coastline has to offer – buttered turbot, line-caught sea bass and scallops in champagne sauce.

La Cafe du Coin d'en Bas de la Rue du Bout de la Ville d'en Face du Port... La Java   Cafe
(☏02 99 56 41 90; www.lajavacafe.com; 3 rue Sante-Barbe) Think part-museum, part-toyshop and the work of art of an ever-so-slightly-twisted mind. And the drinks? Ah, well they're actually quite sane – a hundred different kinds of coffee and a quality beer range.

❶ Information

Tourist office (☏€0.15 per min 08 25 13 52 00; www.saint-malo-tourisme.com; esplanade St-Vincent; ⊘9am-7.30pm Mon-Sat, 10am-6pm Sun) Just outside the walls.

❶ Getting There & Away

TGV train services include to/from Rennes (€13.60, one hour) and Paris' Gare Montparnasse (€52 to €64, three hours, up to 10 daily).

....

Cancale

No day trip from St-Malo is tastier than one to **Cancale** (www.cancale-tourisme.fr), an idyllic Breton fishing port 14km east, that's famed for its offshore *parcs à huîtres* (oyster beds).

Learn all about oyster farming at the **Ferme Marine** (☏02 99 89 69 99; www.ferme-marine.com; corniche de l'Aurore; adult/child €7/3.70; ⊘guided tours in French 11am, 3pm & 5pm Jul-Aug, in English 2pm, in German 4pm) and shop for oysters fresh from their beds at the **Marché aux Huîtres** (12 oysters from €3.50, lunch platters €20; ⊘9am-6pm), the local oyster market atmospherically clustered around the Pointe des Crolles lighthouse.

Le Coquillage (☏02 99 89 64 76; www.maisons-de-bricourt.com; 1 rue Duguesclin; menu €27-135; ⊘Mar-Dec), the sumptuous, Michelin-starred kitchen of superchef Olivier Roellinger, is housed in the gobsmackingly impressive Château Richeux, 4km south of Cancale. Crown the culinary experience with lunch or dinner here.

CHAMPAGNE

Known in Roman times as Campania, meaning 'plain', the agricultural region of Champagne is synonymous these days with its world-famous bubbly. This multimillion-dollar industry is strictly protected under French law, ensuring that only grapes grown in designated Champagne vineyards can truly lay claim to the hallowed title. The town of Épernay, 30km south of the regional capital of Reims, is the best place to head for *dégustation* (tasting), and a self-drive **Champagne Route** wends its way through the region's most celebrated vineyards.

Mont St-Michel

Timeline

708 Inspired by a vision from **St Michael** ❶, Bishop Aubert is compelled to 'build here and build high'.

966 Richard I, Duke of Normandy, gives the Mont to the Benedictines. The three levels of the **abbey** ❷ reflect their monastic hierarchy.

1017 Development of the abbey begins. Pilgrims arrive to honour the cult of St Michael. They walk barefoot across the mudflats and up the **Grande Rue** ❸ to be received in the almonry (now the bookshop).

1203 The monastery is burnt by the troops of Philip Augustus, who later donates money for its restoration and the Gothic 'miracle', **La Merveille** ❹, is constructed.

1434 The Mont's **ramparts** ❺ and fortifications ensure it withstands the English assault during the Hundred Years War. It is the only place in northern France not to fall.

1789 After the Revolution, Monasticism is abolished and the Mont is turned into a prison. During this period the **treadmill** ❻ is built to lift up supplies.

1878 The **causeway** ❼ is created. It allows modern-day pilgrims to visit without hip-high boots, but it cuts off the flow of water and the bay silts up.

1979 The Mont is declared a Unesco World Heritage Site.

2012 The car park is set up on the mainland. The Mont is only accessed on foot or by shuttle bus.

TOP TIPS

Bring a packed lunch from Pontorson to avoid the poor lunch selection on the Mont

Leave the car – it's a pleasant walk from Beauvoir, with spectacular views

Pay attention to the tides – they are dangerous

Take the excellent audioguide – it tells some great stories

JOHN ELK III/GETTY IMAGES ©

Îlot de Tombelaine
Occupied by the English during the Hundred Years War, this islet is now a bird reserve. From April to July it teems with exceptional birdlife.

Treadmill
The giant treadmill was powered hamsterlike by half a dozen prisoners, who, marching two abreast, raised stone and supplies up the Mont.

The West Terrace

Chapelle St-Aubert

Tour Gabriel

❺

Les Fanils

Ramparts
The Mont was also a military garrison surrounded by machicolated and turreted walls, dating from the 13th to 15th centuries. The single entrance, Porte de l'Avancée, ensured its security in the Hundred Years War. Tip: Tour du Nord (North Tower) has the best views.

ROCCO FASANO/GETTY IMAGES ©

Abbey

The abbey's three levels reflect the monastic order: monks lived isolated in church and cloister, the abbot entertained noble guests at the middle level, and lowly pilgrims were received in the basement. Tip: night visits run in July and August.

St Michael Statue & Bell Tower

A golden statue of the winged St Michael looks ready to leap heavenward from the bell tower. He is the patron of the Mont, having inspired St Aubert's original devotional chapel.

The Gardens

1

2

4

6

La Merveille

The highlights of La Merveille are the vast refectory hall lit through embrasured windows, the Knights Hall with its elegant ribbed vaulting, and the cloister (above), which is one of the purest examples of 13th-century architecture to survive here.

Église St-Pierre

Cemetery

3

Toilets

Tour de l'Arcade

Tour du Roi

Tourist Office

Porte de l'Avancée (Entrance)

Grande Rue

The main thoroughfare of the small village below the abbey, Grande Rue has its charm despite its rampant commercialism. Don't miss the famous Mère Poulard shop here, for souvenir cookies.

Causeway

In 2014 the causeway will be replaced by a new bridge, which will allow the water to circulate and will return the Mont to an island. Tip: join a barefoot walking tour and see the Mont as pilgrims would.

7

Best Views

The view from the Jardin des Plantes in nearby Avranches is unique, as are the panoramas from Pointe du Grouin du Sud near the village of St-Léonard.

Detour:
The Morbihan Megaliths

Pre-dating Stonehenge by about a hundred years, **Carnac** comprises the world's greatest concentration of megalithic sites. There are more than 3000 of these upright stones scattered across the countryside between **Carnac-Ville** and **Locmariaquer** village, most of which were erected between 5000 BC and 3500 BC. No one's quite sure what purpose these sites served, although theories abound. A sacred site? Phallic fertility cult? Or maybe a celestial calendar? Even more mysterious is the question of their construction – no one really has the foggiest idea how the builders hacked and hauled these vast granite blocks several millennia before the wheel arrived in Brittany, let alone mechanical diggers.

Because of severe erosion, the sites are usually fenced off to allow vegetation to regrow. **Guided tours** (€6) run in French year-round and in English from early July to late August. Sign up at the **Maison des Mégalithes** (📞 02 97 52 29 81; rte des Alignements; tour adult/child €6/free; ⏱10am-8pm Jul & Aug, to 5.15pm Sep-Apr, to 7pm May & Jun).

Reims

POP 184,984

Over the course of a millennium (816 to 1825), some 34 sovereigns – among them two dozen kings – began their reigns in Reims' famed cathedral. Meticulously reconstructed after WWI and again following WWII, the city – whose name is pronounced something like 'rance' and is often anglicised as Rheims – is endowed with handsome pedestrian zones, well-tended parks, lively nightlife and a state-of-the-art tramway.

◉ Sights

Cathédrale Notre Dame   Cathedral

(www.cathedrale-reims.culture.fr; place du Cardinal Luçon; tower adult/child €7.50/free, incl Palais du Tau €11/free; ⏱7.30am-7.30pm, tower tours hourly 10am-5pm Tue-Sat, 2-5pm Sun Apr-Sep) The single most famous event to take place at this Gothic edifice, begun in 1211 and completed 100 years later, was the coronation of Charles VII, with Joan of Arc at his side, on 17 July 1429.

The finest stained-glass windows are the western facade's 12-petalled **great rose window**, its cobalt-blue neighbour below, and the **rose window** in the north transept (to the left as you walk from the entrance to the high altar), above the Flamboyant Gothic **organ case** (15th and 18th centuries). There are **windows by Chagall** (1974; a sign explains each panel) in the central axial chapel (directly behind the high altar) and, two chapels to the left, you'll find a **statue of Joan of Arc** in full body armour (1901).

End by climbing 250 steps up the **cathedral tower** on a one-hour tour. Book at Palais du Tau.

Palais du Tau   Museum

(http://palais-tau.monuments-nationaux.fr; 2 place du Cardinal Luçon; adult/child €7.50/free, incl cathedral tower €11/free; ⏱9.30am-6.30pm Tue-Sun) A Unesco World Heritage site, this former archbishop's residence, constructed in 1690, was where French princes stayed before their coronations – and where they hosted sumptuous banquets afterwards.

Basilique St-Rémi   Basilica

(place du Chanoine Ladame; ⏱8am-nightfall, to 7pm summer) This 121m-long former Benedictine abbey church, a Unesco World Heritage site, mixes Romanesque elements from the mid-11th century (worn but stunning nave and transept) with early Gothic features from the latter half of the 12th century (choir).

Tours

The **Reims City Card** (€16), available at the tourist office, entitles you to a Champagne house visit (including tasting) and two audioguide tours of your choice.

Mumm   Champagne House

(☎ 03 26 49 59 70; www.mumm.com; 34 rue du Champ de Mars; tours €11; ⏰ tours 9am-11am & 2-5pm daily, closed Sun Nov-Feb) The only *maison* in central Reims was founded in 1827 and is now the world's third-largest producer (almost eight million bottles a year).

Taittinger   Champagne Cellar

(☎ 03 26 85 84 33; www.taittinger.com; 9 place St-Niçaise; tours €16; ⏰ tours 9.30-11.50am & 2pm-4.20pm, closed Sat & Sun Dec–mid-Mar) Parts of the cellars here occupy 4th-century Roman stone quarries; other bits were excavated by 13th-century Benedictine monks. Situated 1.5km southeast of Reims centre; take the Citadine 1 or 2 bus to the St-Niçaise or Salines stops.

🛏 Sleeping

Les Telliers   B&B €€

(☎ 09 53 79 80 74; http://telliers.fr; 18 rue des Telliers ; s €76, d €87-110, tr €123, q €142; 🛜) Enticingly positioned down a quiet alley near the cathedral, this bijou B&B extends one of Reims' warmest *bienvenues*. The high-ceilinged rooms are big on art-deco character, and are handsomely decorated with ornamental fireplaces, polished oak floors and the odd antique.

Hôtel de la Paix   Hotel €€€

(☎ 03 26 40 04 08; www.bestwestern-lapaix-reims.com; 9 rue Buirette; d €170-220; ❄ @ 🛜 🏊) Outclassing most of Reims' midrange options, this contemporary, Best Western–affiliated hotel is the place to mellow in a pool, Jacuzzi, hammam or Zen-like courtyard garden.

🍴 Eating

Le Foch   Gastronomic €€€

(☎ 03 26 47 48 22; www.lefoch.com; 37 bd Foch; lunch menu €31, dinner menu €48-80; ⏰ lunch Tue-Fri & Sun, dinner Tue-Sat) Michelin-starred Le Foch serves up cuisine as beautiful as it is delicious. Specialities like scallops with Jerusalem artichokes, pistachios and truffle emulsion are expertly paired with wines and presented with panache.

Brasserie Le
Boulingrin   Brasserie €€

(☎ 03 26 40 96 22; www.boulingrin.fr; 48 rue de Mars; menu €18.50-29; ⏰ lunch & dinner Mon-Sat) A genuine, old-time brasserie – the decor and zinc bar date back to 1925 –

Basilique St-Rémi, Reims
MICHAEL WEBER/ALAMY ©

Below: Toasting with red wine in Lorraine (p234);
Right: A vineyard in the Alsace region (p234)

(BELOW) HOLGER LEUE/GETTY IMAGES ©; (RIGHT) GÁCRARD LABRIET/GETTY IMAGES ©

world's most celebrated Champagne houses.

whose ambience and cuisine make it an enduring favourite.

❶ Information

Tourist office (☎per minute €0.34 08 92 70 13 51; www.reims-tourisme.com; 2 rue Guillaume de Machault; ⏰9am-7pm Mon-Sat, 10am-6pm Sun & holidays)

❶ Getting There & Away

Direct trains link Reims with Épernay (€6.50, 21 to 50 minutes, seven to 18 daily) and Paris' Gare de l'Est (€26 to €34, 12 to 17 daily), half of which are speedy TGVs (45 minutes).

Épernay

POP 25,000

Prosperous Épernay, 25km south of Reims, is the self-proclaimed *capitale du champagne* and home to many of the

◉ Sights

Many of Épernay's *maisons de champagne* (Champagne houses) are based along the handsome and eminently strollable **av de Champagne**. Cellar tours end with a tasting and a visit to the factory-outlet bubbly shop.

Comtesse Lafond Champagne House
(☎03 86 39 18 33; www.deladoucette.net; 79 av de Champagne; 3-glass tasting €9, incl cellar tour €14; ⏰10am-noon & 2-5.30pm) The whimsically turreted Comtesse Lafond is the most intimate and charming of the av de Champagne *maisons*. Tastings of three Champagnes take place in the elegant salon or in manicured gardens overlooking vine-streaked hills.

Moët & Chandon Champagne House
(☎03 26 51 20 20; www.moet.com; 20 av de Champagne; adult incl 1/2 glasses €16.50/23,

10-18yr €9.50; ⊙tours 9.30am-11.30am &
2-4.30pm, closed Sat & Sun mid-Nov–mid-Mar)
Flying the Moët, French, European and
Russian flags, this prestigious *maison*
offers frequent one-hour tours that are
among the region's most impressive.
At the shop pick up a 15L bottle of Brut
Impérial for €1500; a standard bottle
costs €31.

Mercier Champagne House
(📞03 26 51 22 22; www.champagnemercier.
fr; 68-70 av de Champagne; adult incl 1/2/3
glasses €11/16/19, 12-17yr €5.50; ⊙tours 9.30-
11.30am & 2-4.30pm, closed mid-Dec–mid-Feb)
Everything here is flashy, including the
160,000L barrel that took two decades
to build (for the Universal Exposition of
1889), the lift that transports you 30m
underground, and the laser-guided touring train.

De Castellane Champagne House
(📞03 26 51 19 11; www.castellane.com; 64 av
de Champagne; adult incl 1 glass €10, under
12yr free; ⊙tours 10am-noon & 2-6pm, closed

Christmas–mid-Mar) The 45-minute tours,
in French and English, take in a museum
dedicated to elucidating the *méthode
champenoise* and its diverse technolo-
gies. The reward for climbing the 237
steps up the 66m-high tower (built 1905)
is a fine panoramic view.

🛏 Sleeping

Le Clos Raymi Historic Hotel €€
(📞03 26 51 00 58; www.closraymi-hotel.com; 3
rue Joseph de Venoge; s €115, d €155-175; 📶)
Staying here is like being a personal
guest of Monsieur Chandon of Champagne fame, who occupied this luxurious
townhouse over a century ago. The seven
romantic rooms have giant beds, high
ceilings and parquet floors.

La Villa St-Pierre Hotel €
(📞03 26 54 40 80; www.villasaintpierre.fr; 14
av Paul Chandon; d €51-61; 📶) In an early-
20th-century mansion, this homey place,
with 11 simple rooms, retains some of the
charm of yesteryear.

233

✖ Eating & Drinking

La Grillade Gourmande   Regional Cuisine €€

(☎ 03 26 55 44 22; www.lagrilladegourmande.
com; 16 rue de Reims; menu €19-55; ⊙lunch &
dinner Tue-Sat) This chic, red-walled bistro
is an inviting spot to try char-grilled
meats and dishes rich in texture and
flavour, such as crayfish pan-fried in
Champagne and lamb cooked until melt-
ingly tender in rosemary and honey.

C. Comme   Champagne Bar

(8 rue Gambetta; light meals €7.50-12, 6-glass
Champagne tasting €33; ⊙10am-8.30pm Sun-
Wed, 10am-11pm Thu, 10am-midnight Fri & Sat)
The downstairs cellar has a stash of 300
different varieties of Champagne; sample
them (from €5.50 a glass) in the softly lit
bar-bistro upstairs. Accompany your tipple with a tasting plate of regional cheese,
charcuterie and rillettes (pork pâté).

❶ Information

Tourist office (☎03 26 53 33 00; www.
ot-epernay.fr; 7 av de Champagne; ⊙9.30am-
12.30pm & 1.30-7pm Mon-Sat, 11am-4pm Sun

& holidays) Has excellent English brochures
and maps on cellar visits, walking and cycling
options and car touring, and rents out a GPS
unit (€7 per day) with self-guided vineyard
driving tours in French, English and Dutch.

❶ Getting There & Away

Direct trains link Reims (€6.20, 20 to 36 minutes,
11 to 18 daily) and Paris' Gare de l'Est (€21, 1¼
hours, five to 10 daily).

ALSACE & LORRAINE

Alsace is a one-off cultural hybrid. With
its Germanic dialect and French sense of
fashion, love of foie gras and choucroute
(sauerkraut), fine wine and beer, this distinctive region often leaves you wonder-
ing quite where you are.

No matter whether you're planning
to get behind the wheel for a morning or
pedal leisurely through the vineyards for
a week, the picture-book **Route des Vins
d'Alsace** (Alsace Wine Route) is a must.
Swinging 170km from Marlenheim to
Thann, the road is like a 'greatest hits' of
Alsace, with its pastoral views, welcoming
caves (cellars) and half-timbered villages.

Petite France district, Strasbourg

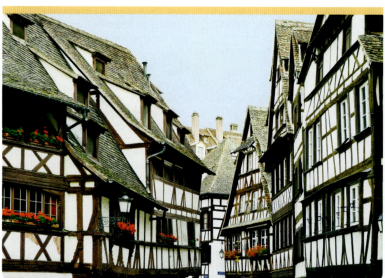

Go to www.alsace-route-des-vins.com to start planning.

Strasbourg

POP 276,136

Strasbourg is the perfect overture to all that is idiosyncratic about Alsace – walking a fine tightrope between France and Germany and between a medieval past and a progressive future, it pulls off its act in inimitable Alsatian style.

Tear your gaze away from that mesmerising Gothic cathedral for just a minute and you'll be roaming the old town's twisting alleys lined with crooked half-timbered houses à la Grimm; feasting in cosy *winstubs* (Alsatian taverns) by the canalside in Petite France; and marvelling at how a city that does Christmas markets and gingerbread so well can also be home to the glittering EU Quarter and France's second-largest student population.

Sights

The **Strasbourg Pass** (adult/child €14/7), a coupon book valid for three consecutive days, includes a visit to one museum, access to the cathedral platform, half a day's bicycle rental and a boat tour, plus hefty discounts on other tours.

Admission to all of Strasbourg's museums (www.musees-strasbourg.org), and to the cathedral's platform, is free on the first Sunday of the month.

Grande Île   Historic Quarter

(⬛Langstross) History seeps through the twisting lanes and cafe-rimmed plazas of Grande Île, Strasbourg's Unesco World Heritage–listed old town, made for aimless ambling. The lantern-lit alleys are most atmospheric at night, while the half-timbered houses and flowery canals of **Petite France** on the Grande Île's southwestern corner are fairy tale pretty.

Cathédrale Notre-Dame   Cathedral

(place de la Cathédrale; astronomical clock adult/child €2/1.50, platform adult/child €5/2.50; ⊙7am-7pm, astronomical clock tickets sold from 11.45am, platform 9am-7.15pm; ⬛Langstross) At once immense and intricate, Strasbourg's centrepiece red-sandstone Gothic cathedral is a riot of filigree stonework and flying buttresses, leering gargoyles and lacy spires. The west facade was completed in 1284, but the 142m spire was not in place until 1439.

A spiral staircase twists up to the 66m-high **platform** above the facade, from which the tower and its Gothic openwork spire soar another 76m.

Musée d'Art Moderne et Contemporain   Art Museum

(MAMCO; www.mamco.ch; Rue des Vieux Grenadiers 10; adult/child Sfr8/free; ⊙noon-6pm Tue-Fri, from 11am Sat & Sun; ⬛Musée d'Art Moderne) This striking glass-and-steel cube showcases an outstanding collection of fine art, graphic art and photography. Kandinsky, Picasso, Magritte and Monet canvases hang out alongside curvaceous works by Strasbourg-born abstract artist Hans Jean Arp.

Palais Rohan   Historic Residence

(2 place du Château; adult/child €6/free; ⊙noon-6pm Mon & Wed-Fri, 10am-6pm Sat & Sun; ⬛Langstross) Hailed a 'Versailles in miniature', this opulent 18th-century residence was built for the city's princely bishops. The basement **Musée Archéologique** spans the Palaeolithic period to AD 800. The ground floor **Musée des Arts Décoratifs** evokes the lavish lifestyle of 18th-century nobility, and the 1st-floor **Musée des Beaux-Arts'** showcases 14th- to 19th-century art.

Cave des Hospices de Strasbourg   Winery

(www.vins-des-hospices-de-strasbourg.fr; 1 place de l'Hôpital; ⊙8.30am-noon & 1.30-5.30pm Mon-Fri, 9am-12.30pm Sat; ⬛Porte de l'Hôpital) **FREE** Founded in 1395, this brick-vaulted wine cellar nestled deep in the bowels of Strasbourg's hospital has first-rate Alsatian wines.

Tours

Batorama   Boat Tour

(www.batorama.fr; rue de Rohan; adult/child €9.20/4.80; ⊙tours half-hourly 9.30am-7pm,

Louvre-Lens

After years of anticipation, Europe's most ballyhooed new art museum has opened its doors. The innovative **Louvre-Lens** (www.louvrelens.fr; 6 rue Charles Lecocq, Lens; Galerie du Temps & Pavillon de Verre free through 2013; ☾10am-6pm Wed-Mon) showcases hundreds of treasures from Paris' venerable Musée du Louvre in a purpose-built, state-of-the-art new exhibition space in the former coal mining town of Lens.

There is no permanent collection moreover; rather, the central 120m-long exhibition space, **Galerie du Temps**, displays a limited but significant, ever-rotating collection of 200+ pieces from the original Louvre.

Lens, 18km north of Arras and 40km southwest of Lille, is accessible by TGV trains from Paris' Gare du Nord (€28 to €46, 65 to 70 minutes) and regional trains from Lille (€7.60, 40 minutes) and Arras (€4.20, 15 minutes).

hourly 8-10pm; 🚊Langstross) Scenic 70-minute boat trips along the storybook canals of Petite France.

 Sleeping

Cour du Corbeau
Boutique Hotel €€€

(📞03 90 00 26 26; www.cour-corbeau.com; 6-8 rue des Couples; r €190-330; ❄@🛜; 🚊Porte de l'Hôpital) A 16th-century inn lovingly converted into a boutique hotel, Cour du Corbeau wins you over with its half-timbered charm and location steps from the river.

Hôtel Régent Petite France
Design Hotel €€

(📞03 88 76 43 43; www.regent-hotels.com; 5 rue des Moulins; r €159-460; ❄@🛜; 🚊Alt Winmärik) Ice factory turned Strasbourg's hottest design hotel, this waterfront pile is quaint on the outside, ubercool inside. Work your relaxed look in the sauna, chic restaurant and champagne bar with dreamy River Ill views.

Eating

Le Gavroche
Mediterranean €€

(📞03 88 36 82 89; www.restaurant-gavroche. com; 4 rue Klein; menu €38; ☾Mon-Fri; ♿; 🚊Porte de l'Hôpital) Bistro food is given a pinch of creativity and southern sunshine at intimate, softly lit Le Gavroche. Mains

like veal in a mint crust with crispy polenta and coriander-infused artichoke tagine are followed by zingy desserts like lime tart with lemon-thyme sorbet.

Le Stras'
International €

(📞03 88 35 34 46; 9 rue des Dentelles; mains €19-24; ☾Tue-Sat; 🚊Langstross) The chef puts an innovative spin on seasonal ingredients at this beamed, gallery-style bistro in Petite France – a terrific choice for an intimate dinner.

Bistrot et Chocolat
Cafe €

(www.bistrotetchocolat.net; 8 rue de la Râpe; snacks €5-8, brunch €10-26; ☾11am-7pm Tue-Fri, 10am-7pm Sat & Sun; ♿♿; 🚊Langstross) 🌿 This boho-flavoured bistro is hailed for its solid and liquid organic chocolate (ginger is superb). The terrace is a local hangout for light bites; also good for weekend brunches and children's cooking classes.

ℹ Information

Tourist office (📞03 88 52 28 28; www. otstrasbourg.fr; 17 place de la Cathédrale; ☾9am-7pm)

ℹ Getting There & Away

Air

Strasbourg's international **airport** (www. strasbourg.aeroport.fr) is 17km southwest of the city centre (towards Molsheim).

Train

European cities with direct services include Basel SNCF (Bâle; €22, 1¼ hours, 25 daily), Brussels-Nord (€74, 5¼ hours, three daily), Karlsruhe (€25, 40 minutes, 16 daily) and Stuttgart (€47, 1¼ hours, four daily). Within France:

Paris Gare de l'Est €71, 2¼ hours, 19 daily

Lyon €71, 4½ hours, 14 daily

Marseille €161, 6¾ hours, 16 daily

Metz €24.50, two hours, 20 daily

Nancy €24, 1½ hours, 25 daily

Nancy

Delightful Nancy has a refined air found nowhere else in Lorraine. With its resplendent central square, fine museums, medieval Old Town, formal gardens and shop windows sparkling with crystal, the former capital of the dukes of Lorraine catapults visitors back to the opulence of the 18th century (when much of the city centre was built).

◉ Sights

Place Stanislas   City Square

Nancy's crowning glory is this neoclassical square, one of France's grandest public spaces and a Unesco World Heritage site. Your gaze will be drawn to an opulent ensemble of pale-stone buildings, gilded wrought-iron gateways and rococo fountains.

Musée des Beaux-Arts

Art Museum

(http://mban.nancy.fr; 3 place Stanislas; adult/child €6/free; ⊙10am-6pm Wed-Mon) Art nouveau glass creations by celebrated French glass maker Daum and a rich selection of paintings from the

14th to 21st centuries are among the star exhibits at this outstanding museum. Caravaggio, Rubens, Picasso and Monet masterpieces hang alongside works by Lorraine-born artists, such as Claude Lorrain's dreamlike baroque landscapes and the pared-down aesthetic of Nancy-born architect and designer Jean Prouvé (1901–1984)

THE LOIRE VALLEY

One step removed from the French capital, the Loire was historically the place where princes, dukes and notable nobles established their country getaways, and the countryside is littered with some of the most extravagant architecture outside Versailles.

April to August, Blois tourist office and TLC offer a twice-daily shuttle (€6) from Blois to the chateaux at Chambord, Cheverny and Beauregard.

Many private companies offer a choice of well-organised itineraries, taking in various combinations of Azay-le-Rideau,

Place Stanislas, Nancy
HIROSHI HIGUCHI/GETTY IMAGES ©

If You Like...
French Chateaux

For architecture aficionados, touring the Loire is a neverending pleasure. Start with Chambord and Cheverny, then seek out these other sumptuous chateaux.

1 CHÂTEAU DE CHENONCEAU
(☎ 02 47 23 90 07; www.chenonceau.com; adult/child €11/8.50, with audioguide €15/12; ⏰9am-7pm Apr-Sep, reduced hours rest of year) This turreted chateau is one of the loveliest in the Loire, with its graceful arches, riverside gardens and delicate towers. Don't miss the yew-tree labyrinth and the 60m-long Grande Gallerie. It's 20km south of Amboise.

2 CHÂTEAU D'AZAY-LE-RIDEAU
(☎ 02 47 45 42 04; azay-le-rideau.monuments-nationaux.fr/en; adult/child €8.50/free; ⏰9.30am-6pm Apr-Sep, to 7pm Jul & Aug, 10am-5.15pm Oct-Mar) Built in the 1500s, this romantic chateau is surrounded by a glassy moat that throws back reflections of its turreted facade. It's particularly well known for its loggia staircase and night-time summer spectacles. It's 26km southwest of Tours.

3 CHÂTEAU DE VILLANDRY
(☎ 02 47 50 02 09; www.chateauvillandry.com; chateau & gardens adult/child €9.50/5.50, gardens only €6.50/4; ⏰9am-6pm Apr-Oct, earlier rest of year, closed mid-Nov–Dec) The gardens at this chateau are almost more impressive than the architecture. From a medieval kitchen garden to an ornamental garden depicting aspects of love (fickle, passionate, tender and tragic), it's a must-see for hardcore horticulturalists. It's 18km west of Tours.

4 CHÂTEAU DE CHAUMONT-SUR-LOIRE
(www.domaine-chaumont.fr; adult/child €10/6, with gardens €15.50/11; ⏰10am-6.30pm Apr-Sep, to 5pm or 6pm Oct-Mar) The classic medieval chateau, complete with cylindrical corner turrets, a sturdy drawbridge and sumptuous écuries (stables), built in 1877. It's 17km southwest of Blois.

Villandry, Cheverny, Chambord and Chenonceau (plus wine-tasting tours). Half-day trips cost between €20 and €35; full-day trips range from €45 to €52. Entry to the chateaux isn't included, although you'll likely get a discount on tickets. Reserve via the tourist offices in Tours or Amboise, from where most tours depart.

Blois
POP 40,057

Blois' historic chateau was the feudal seat of the powerful counts of Blois, and its grand halls, spiral staircases and sweeping courtyards provide a whistlestop tour through the key periods of French architecture. Sadly for chocoholics, the town's historic chocolate factory, Poulain, is off-limits to visitors.

Sights

Château Royal de Blois   Chateau
(www.chateaudeblois.fr; place du Château; adult/child €9.50/4; ⏰9am-6.30pm Apr-Sep, reduced hours rest of year) Blois' Royal Chateau makes an excellent introduction to the chateaux of the Loire Valley, with elements of Gothic (13th century); Flamboyant Gothic (1498–1503), early Renaissance (1515–24) and classical (1630s) architecture in its four grand wings.

Maison de la Magie   Museum
(www.maisondelamagie.fr; 1 place du Château; adult/child €8/5; ⏰10am-12.30pm & 2-6.30pm Apr-Aug, 2-6.30pm Sep) Opposite Blois chateau is the former home of watchmaker, inventor and conjurer Jean Eugène Robert-Houdin (1805–71), after whom the great American magician Harry Houdini is named. Dragons emerge roaring from the windows on the hour, and the museum hosts magic shows and optical trickery.

ℹ Getting There & Away

The train station is 600m uphill from the chateau, on av Jean Laigret.

Amboise €6.60, 20 minutes, 10 daily

Paris Gares d'Austerlitz and **Montparnasse** from €26.70, 1½ to two hours, 26 daily

Tours €10.20, 40 minutes, 13 daily

Around Blois

CHÂTEAU DE CHEVERNY

Thought by many to be the most perfectly proportioned chateau of all, **Cheverny** (📞02 54 79 96 29; www.chateau-cheverny.fr; adult/child €8.70/5.70; ⏱9.15am-6.45pm Jul & Aug, 9.15am-6.15pm Apr-Jun & Sep, 9.45am-5.30pm Oct, 9.45am-5pm Nov-Mar) represents the zenith of French classical architecture, the perfect blend of symmetry, geometry and aesthetic order. It has hardly been altered since its construction between 1625 and 1634. Inside is a formal dining room, bridal chamber and children's playroom (complete with Napoléon III–era toys), as well as a guards' room full of pikestaffs, claymores and suits of armour.

Near the chateau's gateway, the kennels house pedigreed French pointer/English foxhound hunting dogs still used by the owners of Cheverny; feeding time is the **Soupe des Chiens** (⏱5pm Apr-Sep, 3pm Oct-Mar).

Behind the chateau is the 18th-century **Orangerie**, where many priceless art works (including the *Mona Lisa*) were stashed during WWII. Hérgé used the castle as a model for Moulinsart (Marlinspike) Hall, the ancestral home of Tintin's sidekick, Captain Haddock. **Les Secrets de Moulinsart (combined ticket with chateau adult/child €13.20/9.10)** explores the Tintin connections.

Cheverny is 16km southeast of Blois and 17km southwest of Chambord.

Amboise

POP 12,860

The childhood home of Charles VIII and final resting place of Leonardo da Vinci, elegant Amboise, 23km northeast of Tours, is pleasantly perched along the southern bank of the Loire and overlooked by its fortified chateau.

Château de Cheverny, Loire Valley

TRAVEL INK/GETTY IMAGES ©

JOHN BANAGAN/GETTY IMAGES ©

⭐ Don't Miss
Château de Chambord

For full-blown chateau splendour, you can't top Chambord, constructed from 1519 by François I as a lavish base for hunting game in the Sologne forests, but eventually used for just 42 days during the king's 32-year reign (1515–47).

The chateau's most famous feature is its **double-helix staircase**, attributed by some to Leonardo da Vinci, who lived in Amboise (34km southwest) from 1516 until his death three years later. The Italianate **rooftop terrace**, surrounded by cupolas, domes, chimneys and slate roofs, was where the royal court assembled to watch military exercises and hunting parties returning at the end of the day.

Several times daily there are 1½-hour **guided tours** (€4) in English, and during school holidays **costumed tours** entertain kids.

Chambord is 16km east of Blois, 45km southwest of Orléans and 17km northeast of Cheverny.

NEED TO KNOW

📞 02 54 50 40 00; www.chambord.org; adult/child €11/free, parking €4; 🕐 9am-6pm Apr-Sep, 10am-5pm Oct-Mar

🎯 Sights

Château Royal d'Amboise   Castle
(www.chateau-amboise.com; place Michel Debré; adult/child €10.20/7, with audioguide €14.20/10; 🕐 9am-6pm Apr-Oct, earlier closing Nov-Mar)

Sprawling across a rocky escarpment above town, this castle served as a weekend getaway from the official royal seat at nearby Blois. Charles VIII (r 1483–98), born and bred here, was responsible for the chateau's Italianate remodelling in 1492.

Le Clos Lucé
Historic Building

(www.vinci-closluce.com; 2 rue du Clos Lucé; adult/child €13.50/8.50; ⊙9am-7pm Feb-Oct, 10am-6pm Nov-Jan; ♿) Leonardo da Vinci took up residence at this grand manor house in 1516 on the invitation of François I, who was greatly enamoured of the Italian Renaissance. Already 64 by the time he arrived, da Vinci spent his time sketching, tinkering and dreaming up new contraptions, scale models of which are now abundantly displayed throughout the home and its expansive gardens.

Pagode de Chanteloup
Historic Site

(www.pagode-chanteloup.com; adult/child €8.90/6.90; ⊙10am-7pm May-Sep, reduced hrs Oct-Apr) Two kilometres south of Amboise, this curiosity was built between 1775 and 1778 when the odd blend of classical French architecture and Chinese motifs were all the rage. Clamber to the top for glorious views. In summer, picnic hampers (€6.50 to €26) are sold, you can rent rowing boats, and play free outdoor games.

Sleeping

Le Clos d'Amboise
Historic Hotel €€€

(☎02 47 30 10 20; www.leclosamboise.com; 27 rue Rabelais; r €110-180, ste €210-310; ❄ �🛈 ⛳) Backed by a grassy lawn with 200-year-old trees and heated pool, this posh pad is country living in the heart of town.

Villa Mary
B&B €€

(☎02 47 23 03 31; www.villa-mary.fr; 14 rue de la Concorde; d €90-120, apt per week €1180) Sandwiched between the river and chateau, this spacious 18th-century townhouse includes four lovingly restored, old-fashioned rooms plus a 200-square-metre top-floor apartment. The owner, a former economics professor and inveterate world traveller with a passion for history, lives onsite.

✖ Eating

La Fourchette
French €

(☎06 11 78 16 98; 9 rue Malebranche; lunch/dinner menu €15/24; ⊙lunch Tue-Sat, dinner Fri & Sat) Tucked into a back alley behind the tourist office, this is Amboise's favourite address for straightforward home cooking.

Chez Bruno
Regional Cuisine €

(☎02 47 57 73 49; place Michel Debré; menu from €15; ⊙lunch & dinner Tue-Sat) Uncork a host of local vintages in a coolly contemporary setting, accompanied by honest, inexpensive regional cooking. If you're after Loire Valley wine tips, this is the place.

Bigot
Patisserie €

(www.bigot-amboise.com; place du Château; ⊙noon-7.30pm Mon, 9am-7.30pm Tue-Fri, 8.30am-7.30pm Sat & Sun) Since 1913 this cake and chocolate shop has been whipping up some of the Loire's creamiest cakes and gooiest treats.

ℹ Information

Tourist office (☎02 47 57 09 28; www.amboise-valdeloire.com; ⊙9.30am-6pm Mon-Sat, 10am-1pm & 2-5pm Sun) In a riverside building opposite 7 quai du Général de Gaulle.

ℹ Getting There & Around

From the **train station** (bd Gambetta), 1.5km north of the chateau on the opposite side of the Loire, local trains run at least hourly to **Tours** (€5.20, 20 minutes) and **Blois** (€6.60, 20 minutes). Four daily express trains also serve **Paris Gare d'Austerlitz** (€30.10, 1¾ hours).

BURGUNDY & THE RHÔNE VALLEY

If there's one place in France where you're really going to find out what makes the nation tick, it's Burgundy. Two of the country's enduring passions – food and wine – come together in this gorgeously rural region, and if you're a sucker for hearty food and the fruits of the vine, you'll be in seventh heaven.

Beaune

POP 22,720

Beaune (pronounced 'bone'), 44km south of Dijon, is the unofficial capital of the Côte d'Or. This thriving town's raison d'être and the source of its *joie de vivre* is wine: making it, tasting it, selling it, but most of all, drinking it. Consequently, Beaune is one of the best places in all of France for wine tasting.

Sights & Activities

Hôtel-Dieu des Hospices de Beaune   Historic Building
(www.hospices-de-beaune.com; rue de l'Hôtel-Dieu; adult/child €7/3; ⊙9am-5.30pm) Built in 1443, this magnificent Gothic hospital (until 1971) is famously topped by stunning turrets and pitched rooftops covered in multicoloured tiles. Interior highlights include the barrel-vaulted **Grande Salle** (look for the dragons and peasant heads up on the roof beams); an 18th-century **pharmacy** lined with flasks once filled with elixirs and powders; and the multi-panelled masterpiece **Polyptych of the Last Judgement** by 15th-century Flemish painter Rogier van der Weyden, depicting Judgment Day in glorious technicolour.

Cellar Visits   Wine Tasting
Millions of bottles of wine age to perfection in cool dark cellars beneath Beaune's buildings, streets and ramparts. Tasting opportunities abound and dozens of cellars can be visited by guided tour. Our favourites include the candlelit cellars of the former Église des Cordeliers, **Marché aux Vins** (www.marcheauxvins.com; 2 rue Nicolas Rolin; admission €10; ⊙9.30-11.30am & 2-5.30pm, no midday closure Jul & Aug), where 15 wines can be sampled; and **Cellier de la Vieille Grange** (www.bourgogne-cellier. com; 27 bd Georges Clemenceau; ⊙9am-noon & 2-7pm Wed-Sat, by appointment Sun-Tue), where locals flock to buy Burgundy wines *en vrac* (in bulk; bring your own jerrycan or buy a vinibag) for as little as €4.25 per litre for quality AOC wines. Tasting is done direct from barrels using a pipette. **Patriarche Père et Fils** (www.patriarche.com; 5 rue du Collège; audioguide tour €13; ⊙9.30-11.30am & 2-5.30pm), lined with about five million bottles of wine, has Burgundy's largest cellars.

Burgundy Vineyards

Burgundy's most renowned vintages come from the **Côte d'Or** (Golden Hillside), a range of hills made of limestone, flint and clay that runs south from Dijon for about 60km. The northern section, the **Côte de Nuits**, stretches from Marsannay-la-Côte south to Corgoloin and produces reds known for their robust, full-bodied character. The southern section, the **Côte de Beaune**, lies between Ladoix-Serrigny and Santenay and produces great reds and whites.

Tourist offices provide brochures: *The Burgundy Wine Road* is an excellent free booklet published by the Burgundy Tourist Board (www.bourgogne-tourisme.com) and *Roadmap to the Wines of Burgundy* is a useful map. There's also the **Route des Grands Crus** (www.road-of-the-fine-burgundy-wines.com), a signposted road route of some of the most celebrated Côte de Nuits vineyards. Mandatory tasting stops for oenophiles after nirvana include 16th-century **Château du Clos de Vougeot** (✆03 80 62 86 09; www.closdevougeot.fr; Vougeot; adult/child €4/3.10; ⊙9am-5.30pm), excellent guided tours, and **L'Imaginariim** (✆03 80 62 61 40; www.imaginarium-bourgogne.com; av du Jura, Nuits-St-Georges; adult/child €8/5; ⊙2-7pm Mon, 10am-7pm Tue-Sun), with an entertaining wine museum in Nuits-St-Georges.

Wine & Voyages (✆03 80 61 15 15; www.wineandvoyages.com; tours from €53) and **Alter & Go** (✆06 23 37 92 04; www.alterandgo.fr; tours from €70), with an emphasis on history and winemaking methods, run minibus tours in English; reserve online or at the Dijon tourist office.

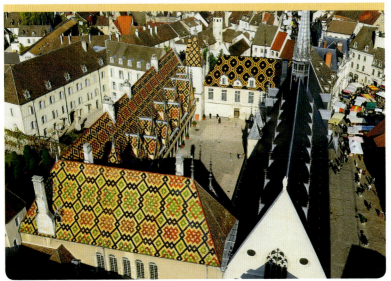

CHICUREL ARNAUD/HEMIS.FR/GETTY IMAGES ©

Sleeping

Hôtel des Remparts   Historic Hotel €€

(03 80 24 94 94; www.hotel-remparts-beaune.
com; 48 rue Thiers; d €80-160; P ❄ 🛜) Set
around two delightful courtyards, this 17th-
century townhouse has red-tiled or parquet floors and simple antique furniture.
Some rooms come with exposed beams
and a fireplace. Friendly staff rent bikes.

Abbaye de Maizières   Historic Hotel €€

(03 80 24 74 64; www.beaune-abbaye-
maizieres.com; 19 rue Maizières; d €118-190;
❄ @) This is a character-laden establishment inside a 12th-century abbey with
modern rooms and contemporary furnishings. Rooms on the top floor offer views
over Beaune's famed multicolour tile roofs.

Eating

Loiseau des Vignes   Gastronomic €€€

(03 80 24 12 06; www.bernard-loiseau.com; 31
rue Maufoux; lunch menu €20-28, dinner menu
€59-95; Tue-Sat) For that extra special

meal, this culinary shrine is the place to go.
Expect stunning concoctions ranging from
caramelised pigeon to *quenelles de sandre*
(dumplings made from pike fish). And even
the most budget-conscious can indulge –
lunch menus are a bargain. In summer, the
verdant garden is a plus.

Le Comptoir des Tontons   Regional Cuisine €€

(03 80 24 19 64; www.lecomptoirdestontons.
com; 22 rue du Faubourg Madeleine; menu €25-
36; Tue-Sat) Stylishly decorated in a hip
bistro style, this local treasure entices
with the passionate Burgundian cooking of chef Pepita. Most ingredients are
organic and locally sourced.

ℹ Information

Tourist office (03 80 26 21 30; www.beaune-
tourisme.fr; 6 bd Perpreuil; 9am-7pm Mon-Sat,
9am-6pm Sun)

ℹ Getting There & Away

Train

Dijon €7.30, 25 minutes, 40 daily

Nuits-St-Georges from €4.50, 10 minutes, 40
daily

FRANCE BEAUNE

243

Paris Gare de Lyon from €41, 2¼ hours by TGV (non-TGV 3½ hours), 20 daily, two direct TGVs daily

Lyon-Part Dieu from €30, 1¾ hours, 16 daily

Lyon

POP 487,980

Gourmets, eat your heart out: Lyon is *the* gastronomic capital of France, with a lavish table of piggy-driven dishes and delicacies to savour. The city has been a commercial, industrial and banking pow- erhouse for the past 500 years, and is still France's second-largest conurbation, with outstanding art museums, a dynamic nightlife, green parks and a Unesco-listed Old Town.

Sights

The **Lyon City Card** (www.lyon-france. com; 1/2/3 days adult €21/31/41, child €12.50/17.50/22.50) covers admission to every Lyon museum and the roof of Basilique Notre Dame de Fourvière, as well as guided city tours, a river excursion

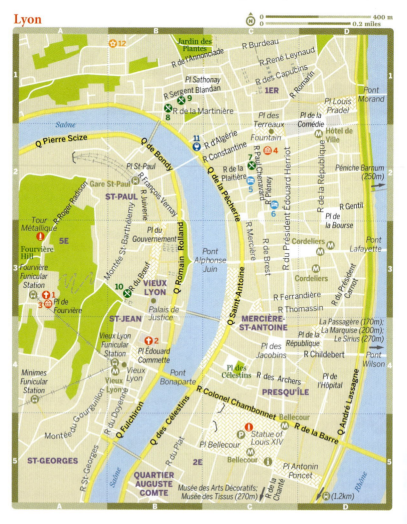

Lyon

0   400 m
0   0.2 miles

(April to October) and discounts on other selected attractions.

The card also includes unlimited travel on buses, trams, the funicular and metro. Buy it online (www.en.lyon-france.com/Lyon-City-Card), from the tourist office, or at some hotels.

VIEUX LYON

Old Lyon, with its cobblestone streets and medieval and Renaissance houses below Fourvière hill, is divided into three quarters: St-Paul at the northern end, St-Jean in the middle and St-Georges in the south. Lovely old buildings languish on **rue du Bœuf**, **rue St-Jean** and **rue des Trois Maries**.

The partly Romanesque **Cathédrale St-Jean** (place St-Jean, 5e; ⏱8am-noon & 2-7pm; MVieux Lyon), seat of Lyon's 133rd bishop, was built from the late 11th to the early 16th centuries. Its **astronomical clock** chimes at noon, 2pm, 3pm and 4pm.

FOURVIÈRE

Over two millennia ago, the Romans built the city of Lugdunum on the slopes of Fourvière. Today, Lyon's 'hill of prayer' – topped by a basilica and the **Tour Métallique**, an Eiffel Tower–like structure built in 1893 and used as a TV transmitter – affords spectacular views of the city and its two rivers. Footpaths wind uphill, but the funicular is the least taxing way up.

Crowning Fourvière hill is the **Basilique Notre Dame de Fourvière** (www.fourviere.org; place de Fourvière, 5e; ⏱8am-7pm; 🚠Fourvière funicular station), an iconic, 27m-high basilica, a superb example of exaggerated 19th-century ecclesiastical architecture.

Around the corner, treasures from its interior enjoy pride of place in the **Musée d'Art Religieux** (8 place de Fourvière, 5e; adult/child €6/free; ⏱10am-12.30pm & 2-5.30pm; 🚠Fourvière funicular station).

PRESQU'ÎLE

The centrepiece of **place des Terreaux** is a 19th-century fountain sculpted by Frédéric-Auguste Bartholdi, creator of the Statue of Liberty. The **Musée des Beaux-Arts** (www.mba-lyon.fr; 20 place des Terreaux, 1er; adult/child incl audioguide €7/free; ⏱10am-6pm Wed, Thu & Sat-Mon, 10.30am-6pm Fri; MHôtel de Ville) showcases France's finest collection of sculptures and paintings outside Paris.

Lyonnais silks are showcased at the **Musée des Tissus** (www.musee-des-tissus.com; 34 rue de la Charité, 2e; adult/child €10/7.50, after 4pm €8/5.50; ⏱10am-5.30pm Tue-Sun; MAmpère). Next door, the **Musée des Arts Décoratifs** (34 Rue de la Charité, 2e; free with Musée des Tissus ticket; ⏱10am-noon & 2-5.30pm Tue-Sun) displays 18th-century furniture, tapestries, wallpaper, ceramics and silver.

Laid out in the 17th century, **place Bellecour** – one of Europe's largest public squares – is pierced by an equestrian **statue of Louis XIV**. South of here, past **Gare de Perrache**, lies the once-downtrodden industrial area of **Lyon Confluence** (www.lyon-confluence.fr), where the Rhône and Saône meet. Trendy restaurants now line its quays, and the ambitious **Musée des Confluences** (www.museedesconfluences.fr; 28 Boulevard des Belges, 6e), a science-and-humanities museum inside a futuristic steel-and-glass transparent crystal, will open here in 2014.

Lyon

⊙ **Sights**

1 Basilique Notre Dame de
    Fourvière A3
2 Cathédrale St-Jean...........................B4
3 Musée d'Art Religieux A3
4 Musée des Beaux-Arts......................C2

🛏 **Sleeping**

5 Hôtel de Paris...................................C2
6 Hôtel Le Boulevardier.......................C2

✖ **Eating**

7 Café des Fédérations C2
8 Le Bistrot du Potager B1
9 Le Bouchon des Filles........................B1
10 Les Adrets..B3

⊙ **Drinking & Nightlife**

11 Le Voxx..B2
    Le Wine Bar d'à Côté...................(see 6)

✪ **Entertainment**

12 Le Club Théâtre.................................B1

North of place Bellecour, the charmful hilltop quarter of **Croix Rousse** is famed for its lush outdoor food market and silk-weaving tradition, illustrated by the **Maison des Canuts** (www.maisondescanuts. com; 10-12 rue d'Ivry, 4e; adult/child €6.50/3.50; ⊙10am-6pm Mon-Sat, guided tours 11am & 3.30pm; Ⓜ Croix Rousse).

RIVE GAUCHE

Parc de la Tête d'Or   Park
(www.loisirs-parcdelatetedor.com; blvd des Belges, 6e; ⊙6am-11pm Apr-Sep, to 9pm Oct-Mar; 🚌41, 47, Ⓜ Masséna) France's largest urban park, landscaped in the 1860s, is graced by a lake (rent a rowing boat), botanic garden, rose garden, zoo, puppet theatre and tip-top **Musée d'Art Contemporain** (www.mac-lyon.com; 81 quai Charles de Gaulle, 6e; adult/child €8/free; ⊙11am-6pm Wed-Fri, 10am-7pm Sat & Sun).

Buses 41 and 47 link the park with metro Part-Dieu.

Musée Lumière   Museum
(www.institut-lumiere.org; 25 rue du Premier Film, 8e; adult/child €6.50/5.50; ⊙10am-6.30pm Tue-Sun; Ⓜ Monplaisir-Lumière) Cinema's glorious beginnings are showcased at the art nouveau home of Antoine Lumière, who moved to Lyon with sons Auguste and Louis in 1870. The brothers shot the first reels of the world's first motion picture, *La Sortie des Usines Lumières* (Exit of the Lumières Factories) here in the grounds of one of their father's photographic factories on 19 March 1895. The former factory is the Hangar du Premier Film cinema today.

Centre d'Histoire de la Résistance et de la Déportation   Museum
(www.chrd.lyon.fr; 14 av Berthelot, 7e; adult/child €4/free; ⊙9am-5.30pm Wed-Sun; Ⓜ Perrache or Jean Macé) The WWII headquarters of Gestapo commander Klaus Barbie

evokes Lyon's role as the 'Capital of the Resistance' through moving multimedia exhibits.

⚙ Festivals & Events

Fête des Lumières Winter Festival
(Festival of Lights; www.lumieres.lyon.fr) Over several days around the Feast of the Immaculate Conception (8 December), sound-and-light shows are projected onto key buildings, while locals illuminate window sills with candles.

🛌 Sleeping

Péniche Barnum B&B €€
(📞 06 63 64 37 39; www.peniche-barnum.com; 3 quai du Général Sarrail, 6e; d €120-150; ❄ 🛜; Ⓜ Foch) Moored on the Rhône, Lyon's most unique B&B is this navy-and-timber barge with two smart en suite guestrooms, a book-filled lounge, and shaded deck terrace. Organic breakfasts €10.

Hôtel Le Boulevardier Hotel €
(📞 04 78 28 48 22; www.leboulevardier.fr; 5 rue de la Fromagerie, 1er; s €47-56, d €49-59; 🛜; Ⓜ Hôtel de Ville, Cordeliers) Quirky touches like old skis and tennis racquets adorn the hallways at this bargain 11-room hotel. It's up a steep spiral staircase above a cool little bistro and jazz club of the same name, which doubles as reception.

Hôtel de Paris Hotel €€
(📞 04 78 28 00 95; www.hoteldeparis-lyon.com; 16 rue de la Platière, 1er; s €52-92, d €64-135; ❄ @ 🛜; Ⓜ Hôtel de Ville) This newly remodelLed hotel in a 19th-century bourgeois building features bright decor and themed rooms with artsy designs. Some have a funky, retro '70s feel.

🍴 Eating

Pick up a round of impossibly runny St Marcellin from legendary cheesemonger **Mère Richard**, or a knobbly Jésus de Lyon from pork butcher **Collette Sibilia** at Lyon's famed indoor market

Les Halles de Lyon (halledelyon.free.fr; 102 cours Lafayette, 3e; ⏲8am-7pm Tue-Sat, to 1pm Sun; Ⓜ Part-Dieu). Or simply sit down and enjoy a lunch of local produce, lip-smacking *coquillages* (shellfish) at one of its stalls.

Les Adrets Regional Cuisine €€

(☎04 78 38 24 30; 30 rue du Boeuf, 5e; lunch menu €15.50, dinner menu €23-45; ⏲lunch & dinner Mon-Fri; Ⓜ Vieux Lyon) This atmospheric spot serves some of Vieux Lyon's best food any time of day. The mix is half classic *bouchon* fare, half alternative choices like Parma ham and truffle risotto, or duck breast with roasted pears.

Le Bouchon des Filles Regional Cuisine €€

(☎04 78 30 40 44; 20 rue Sergent Blandan, 1er; menu €25; ⏲dinner daily, lunch Sun; Ⓜ Hôtel de Ville) This contemporary ode to Lyon's legendary culinary *mères* (mothers) is run by an enterprising crew of young women with deep roots in the local *bouchon* scene. The light and fluffy *quenelles* (Lyonnaise dumplings) are among the best you'll find in Lyon, and the rustic atmosphere is warm and welcoming.

Le Bistrot du Potager Tapas €

(☎04 78 29 61 59; www.lebistrotdupotager.com; 3 rue de la Martinière, 1er; tapas €5-12; ⏲lunch & dinner Tue-Sat; Ⓜ Hôtel de Ville) An offshoot of the renowned Potager des Halles restaurant next door, throngs of happy diners linger here over glasses of wine and Provençal duck carpaccio, grilled vegetables with pistou, stuffed artichokes, octopus salad, Tunisian-style chickpeas and platters of cheeses and *charcuterie*.

Café des Fédérations Bouchon €€

(☎04 78 28 26 00; www.lesfedeslyon.com; 8-10 rue Major Martin, 1er; lunch/dinner menu from €19/25; ⏲lunch & dinner Mon-Sat; Ⓜ Hôtel de Ville) From the vast array of appetisers – lentils in mustardy sauce, slices of *rosette de Lyon* sausage. pickles, beets and more – clear through to a classic *baba au rhum* for dessert, this is *bouchon* dining at its finest.

🍷 Drinking & Nightlife

Cafe terraces on place des Terreaux buzz with all-hours drinkers, as do the British, Irish and other-styled pubs on nearby rue Ste-Catherine, 1er, and rue Lainerie and rue St-Jean, 5e, in Vieux Lyon.

Floating bars with DJs and live bands rock until around 3am aboard the string of *péniches* (river barges) moored along the Rhône's left bank. Scout out the section of quai Victor Augagneur between Pont Lafayette (metro Cordeliers or Guichard) and Pont de la Guillotière (metro Guillotière).

Our favourites: laid-back **La Passagère** (21 quai Victor Augagneur, 3e; ⏲daily; Ⓜ Place Guichard - Bourse du Travail); party-hard **Le Sirius** (www.

Mer de Glace train (p250), Chamonix
A DEMOTES/GETTY IMAGES ©

lesirius.com; 4 quai Victor Augagneur, 3e; ⊙daily; 📶; Ⓜ Place Guichard – Bourse du Travail); and electro-oriented **La Marquise** (www.marquise.net; 20 quai Victor Augagneur, 3e; ⊙Tue-Sun; Ⓜ Place Guichard – Bourse du Travail).

Le Wine Bar d'à Côté   Wine Bar
(www.cave-vin-lyon.com; 7 rue Pleney, 1er; ⊙Mon-Sat; Ⓜ Cordeliers) Hidden in a tiny alleyway, this cultured wine bar feels like a rustic English gentlemen's club with leather sofa seating and a library.

Le Voxx   Bar
(1 rue d'Algérie, 1er; ⊙10am-3am; Ⓜ Hôtel de Ville) Minimalist but lively riverside bar packed with a real mix of people, from students to city slickers.

Ninkasi Gerland   Live Music
(www.ninkasi.fr; 267 rue Marcel Mérieux, 7e; ⊙10am-late; Ⓜ Stade de Gerland) Spilling over with a fun, frenetic crowd, this microbrewery dishes up DJs, bands and film projections amid a backdrop of fish-and-chips, build-your-own burgers and other un-French food.

Le Club Théâtre   Performing Arts
(www.thearte.fr; 4 impasse Flesselles, 1er; annual membership fee €2; Ⓜ Croix Rousse) Hip and unique, this hybrid bar-nightclub-cultural centre sits inside Croix Rousse's old neighbourhood wash-house, with the central wash basin doubling as stage and dance floor.

ⓘ Information

Tourist office (📞 04 72 77 69 69; www.lyon-france.com; place Bellecour, 2e; ⊙9am-6pm; Ⓜ Bellecour)

ⓘ Getting There & Away

Air
Lyon-St-Exupéry Airport (www.lyon.aeroport.fr), 25km east of the city, serves 120 direct destinations across Europe and beyond, including many budget carriers.

Train
Lyon has two main-line train stations: **Gare de la Part-Dieu** (Ⓜ Part-Dieu), 1.5km east of the Rhône, and **Gare de Perrache** (Ⓜ Perrache).

Destinations by direct TGV include:

Dijon from €29, two hours, at least seven daily

Marseille from €45, 1¾ hours, every 30 to 60 minutes

Paris Gare de Lyon from €69, two hours, every 30 to 60 minutes

Paris Charles de Gaulle Airport from €69, two hours, at least 11 daily

Strasbourg €88, 3¾ hours, five daily

ⓘ Getting Around

Tramway **Rhonexpress** (www.rhonexpress.net) links the airport with Part-Dieu train station in under 30 minutes. A single ticket costs €14.

Buses, trams, a four-line metro and two funiculars linking Vieux Lyon to Fourvière are run by **TCL** (www.tcl.fr). Public transport runs from around 5am to midnight. Tickets cost €1.60 while a *carnet* of 10 is €13.70; bring coins as machines don't accept notes (or some international credit cards). Time-stamp tickets on all forms of public transport or risk a fine.

Bikes are available from 200-odd bike stations thanks to **vélo'v** (www.velov.grandlyon.com; first 30 min free, first/subsequent hr €1/2).

THE FRENCH ALPS & JURA

Whether it's paragliding among the peaks, hiking the trails or hurtling down a mountainside strapped to a pair of glorified toothpicks, the French Alps is the undisputed centre of adventure sports in France. Under Mont Blanc's 4810m of raw wilderness lies the country's most spectacular outdoor playground, and if the seasonal crowds get too much, you can always take refuge in the little-visited Jura, a region of dark wooded hills and granite plateaux stretching for 360km along the French–Swiss border.

Chamonix
POP 9378 / ELEV 1037M

With the pearly white peaks of the Mont Blanc massif as sensational backdrop, being an icon comes naturally to Chamonix. First 'discovered' by Brits William

Windham and Richard Pococke in 1741, this is the mecca of mountaineering. Its knife-edge peaks, plunging slopes and massive glaciers have enthralled generations of adventurers and thrill-seekers ever since. Its après-ski scene is equally pumping.

◎ Sights

Mer de Glace   Glacier

France's largest glacier, the glistening 200m-deep Mer de Glace (Sea of Ice) snakes 7km through mighty rock spires and turrets. The glacier moves up to 90m a year, and has become a popular attraction thanks to the rack-and-pinion railway line opened in 1908. The quaint red mountain train trundles up from **Gare du Montenvers** (35 place de la Mer de Glace; adult/child/family €26/22/79; ⏱10am-4.30pm) in Chamonix to Montenvers (1913m), from where a cable car takes you down to the glacier and cave. Besides covering the 20-minute journey, the cable car and the ice cave, your ticket gets you entry into the crystal-laced **Galerie des Cristaux** and the new **Glaciorium**, spotlighting the birth, life and future of glaciers.

Wrap up warm to experience the **Grotte de la Mer de Glace** (⏱late Dec-May & mid-Jun–Sep) ice cave, where frozen tunnels and ice sculptures change colour like mood rings.

⚡ Activities

Get the Mont Blanc lowdown on hiking, skiing and a zillion and one other adrenelin-pumping pursuits at the **Maison de la Montagne** (190 place de l'Église; ⏱8.30am-noon & 3-7pm), opposite the tourist office.

These guide companies have got it. So go on and create your own adventure:

Compagnie des Guides de Chamonix (☎04 50 53 00 88; www.chamonix-guides.com; 190 place de l'Église) The crème de la crème of mountain guides, founded in 1821. Guides for skiing, mountaineering, ice climbing, hiking, mountain biking and every other Alpine pastime.

Association Internationale des Guides du Mont Blanc (☎04 50 53 27 05; www.guides-du-montblanc.com; 85 rue des Moulins) Extreme skiing, mountaineering, glacier trekking, ice and rock climbing, and paragliding.

Aventure en Tête (☎04 50 54 05 11; www.aventureentete.com; 420 rte du Chapeau, Le Lavancher) Ski touring and ski-alpinism expeditions; free-ride and off-piste courses; mountaineering and climbing in summer.

Chamonix Experience (☎09 77 48 58 69; www.chamex.com; 49 place Edmond Desailloud) Courses in off-piste skiing, avalanche awareness, ice climbing and ski touring; in summer, rock and Alpine climbing.

🛏 Sleeping

Auberge du Manoir   Hotel €€

(☎04 50 53 10 77; http://aubergedumanoir.com; 8 rte du Bouchet; s €109-122, d €126-176, q €178; 📶) This beautifully converted farmhouse ticks all the perfect alpine chalet boxes: pristine mountain views, pine-panelled rooms, outdoor hot tub, and a bar with open fire.

Hotel L'Oustalet   Hotel €€

(☎04 50 55 54 99; www.hotel-oustalet.com; 330 rue du Lyret; d/q €148/190; 📶🏊) You'll pray for snow at this alpine chalet near Aiguille du Midi cable car, just so you can curl up by the fire with a *chocolat chaud* (hot chocolate) and unwind in the sauna and whirlpool. The rooms, including family ones, are snugly decorated in solid pine and open onto balconies with Mont Blanc views.

Hôtel Faucigny   Boutique Hotel €€

(☎04 50 53 01 17; www.hotelfaucigny-chamonix.com; 118 place de l'Église; s/d/q €90/120/170; 📶) This bijou hotel is a slice of minimalist alpine cool, with its charcoal-white rooms and slate-walled spa. Your hosts bend over backwards to please: free bike rental and afternoon tea, summer terrace with Mont Blanc views, open fire in winter, whirlpool and sauna.

JOHN ELK/GETTY IMAGES ©

⭐ Don't Miss
Aiguille du Midi

A jagged needle of rock rearing above glaciers, snowfields and rocky crags, 8km from the hump of Mont Blanc, the Aiguille du Midi (3842m) is one of Chamonix' most distinctive landmarks. If you can handle the height, the 360-degree views of the French, Swiss and Italian Alps from the summit are (quite literally) breathtaking.

Year-round, the vertiginous **Téléphérique de l'Aiguille de Midi** (place de l'Aiguille du Midi; adult/child return to Aiguille du Midi €46/39, Plan de l'Aiguille €26/22; ⏰8.30am-4.30pm) cable car links Chamonix with the Aiguille du Midi. Halfway, Plan de l'Aiguille (2317m) is a terrific place to start hikes or paraglide. In summer you will need to obtain a boarding card (marked with the number of your departing *and* returning cable car) in addition to a ticket. Ensure that you bring warm clothes as even in summer the temperature rarely rises above -10°C at the top.

From the Aiguille du Midi, between late June and early September, you can continue for a further 30 minutes of mind-blowing scenery – think suspended glaciers and spurs, seracs and shimmering ice fields – in the smaller bubbles of the **Télécabine Panoramic Mont Blanc** (adult/child return from Chamonix €70/59; ⏰8.30am-3.30pm) to Pointe Helbronner (3466m) on the French-Italian border. From here another cable car descends to the Italian ski resort of Courmayeur.

🍴 Eating

Les Vieilles Luges   French €€

(📞06 84 42 37 00; www.lesvieillesluges.com; Les Houches; menu €20-35; ⏰lunch daily, dinner by reservation) This childhood dream of a 250-year-old farmhouse can only be reached by slipping on skis or taking a scenic 20-minute hike from Maison Neuve chairlift. Under low wood beams, Julie and Claude spoil you with their home cooking washed down with *vin chaud* (mulled wine) warmed over a wood fire. Magic.

251

La Petite Kitchen   International €€

(80 place du Poilu; 2-course lunch menu €12.50, mains €18-28; ⏱lunch & dinner Wed-Mon) The Little Kitchen is just that: a handful of tables for the lucky few who get to indulge in its locally sourced feel-good food – filling English breakfasts, steaks with homemade *frites* (hot chips) and the stickiest of toffee puddings.

Le Bistrot   Gastronomic €€€

(☎04 50 53 57 64; www.lebistrotchamonix. com; 151 av de l'Aiguille du Midi; lunch menu €17-28, dinner menu €50-85; ⏱lunch & dinner daily; 🏨) Michelin-starred chef Mickey experiments with textures and seasonal flavours to create taste sensations like pan-seared Arctic char with chestnuts, and divine warm chocolate macaron with raspberry and red pepper coulis.

Le GouThé   Teahouse €

(95 rue des Moulins; snacks €3-10; ⏱9am-7pm; 🥄) Welcome to the sweetest of tea rooms: hot chocolates, macarons, *galettes* (buckwheat crêpes) and crumbly homemade tarts.

ⓘ Information

Tourist office (☎04 50 53 00 24; www. chamonix.com; 85 place du Triangle de l'Amitié; ⏱8.30am-7pm)

ⓘ Getting There & Away

Bus

From **Chamonix bus station** (www.sat-montblanc.com; place de la Gare), next to the train station, five daily buses run to/from Geneva airport (one way/return €33/55, 1½ to two hours) and Courmayeur (one way/return €13/20, 45 minutes). Advanced booking only.

Train

The Mont Blanc Express narrow-gauge train trundles from St-Gervais-Le Fayet station, 23km west of Chamonix, to Martigny in Switzerland, stopping en route in Les Houches, Chamonix and Argentière. There are nine to 12 return trips daily between Chamonix and St-Gervais (€10, 45 minutes).

From St-Gervais-Le Fayet, there are trains to most major French cities.

Annecy

POP 52,161 / ELEV 447M

Lac d'Annecy is one of the world's purest lakes, receiving only rainwater, spring water and mountain streams. Swimming in its sapphire depths, surrounded by snowy mountains, is a real Alpine highlight. Strolling the geranium-strewn streets of the historic Vieille Ville (Old Town) is not half bad either.

◎ Sights

Vieille Ville & Lakefront   Historic Quarter

It's a pleasure simply to wander aimlessly around Annecy's medieval old town, a photogenic jumble of narrow streets, turquoise canals and colonnaded passageways. Continue down to the tree-fringed lakefront and the flowery **Jardins de l'Europe**, linked to the popular picnic spot **Champ de Mars** by the poetic iron arch of the **Pont des Amours** (Lovers' Bridge).

🛏 Sleeping

Hôtel Alexandra   Hotel €€

(☎04 50 52 84 33; www.hotelannecy-alexandra. fr; 19 rue Vaugelas; s/d/tr/q €55/75/95/110; 🛜) Nice surprise: Annecy's most charming hotel is also one of its most affordable. The welcome is five-star, rooms are fresh and spotless – the best have balconies and canal views – and breakfast (€8) is a generous spread.

Splendid Hôtel   Boutique Hotel €€

(☎04 50 45 20 00; www.hotel-annecy-lac.fr; 4 quai Eustache Chappuis; s/d €109/121; ❄🛜) 'Splendid' sums up the lakefront position of this hotel, with breezy views from its boutique-chic, parquet-floor rooms.

Eating

L'Esquisse   Regional Cuisine €€

(☎04 50 44 80 59; www.esquisse-annecy.fr; 21 rue Royale; lunch menu €19-22, dinner menu €29-60; ⏱lunch & dinner Mon-Tue & Thu-Sat) A talented husband-and-wife team run the show at this intimate bistro, with just six tables that fill predictably quickly. Carefully composed menus sing with natural, integral flavours, from wild mushrooms to spider crab.

La Ciboulette — Gastronomic €€€

(☎04 50 45 74 57; www.laciboulette-annecy.com; 10 rue Vaugelas, cour du Pré Carré; menu €35-63; ☺lunch & dinner Tue-Sat) Such class! Crisp white linen and gold-kissed walls set the scene at this Michelin-starred place, where chef Georges Paccard cooks fresh seasonal specialities. Reservations are essential.

L'Étage — Savoyard €€

(☎04 50 51 03 28; 13 rue du Pâquier; menu €22-34; ☺lunch & dinner) Cheese, glorious cheese... *Fromage* is given pride of place in spot-on fondues and *raclette* (melting cheese, boiled potatoes, *charcuterie* and baby gherkins), with mellow music and cheerful staff as backdrop.

ℹ Information

Tourist office (☎04 50 45 00 33; www.lac-annecy.com; Centre Bonlieu, 1 rue Jean Jaurès; ☺9am-6.30pm Mon-Sat, 10am-1pm Sun)

ℹ Getting There & Away

From Annecy's train station (place de la Gare), there are frequent trains to Lyon (€24.70, two hours) and Paris' Gare de Lyon (€76, four hours).

THE DORDOGNE

If it's French heart and soul you're after, look no further. Tucked in the country's southwestern corner, the Dordogne fuses history, culture and culinary sophistication in one unforgettably scenic package. The region is best known for its sturdy *bastides* (fortified towns), clifftop chateaux and spectacular prehistoric cave paintings, neighboured to the southwest by the Mediterranean-tinged region of the Lot, with its endless vintage vineyards.

Sarlat-La-Canéda

POP 9943

A gorgeous tangle of honey-coloured buildings, alleyways and secret squares make up this unmissable Dordogne village – a natural if touristy launchpad into the Vézère Valley.

Vieille Ville, Annecy

PATRICE COPPEE/GETTY IMAGES ©

Detour:
The Jura

The dark wooded hills, rolling dairy country and limestone plateaux of the Jura Mountains, stretching in an arc for 360km along the Franco-Swiss border from the Rhine to the Rhône, comprise one of the least explored pockets in France. Rural, deeply traditional and *un petit peu* eccentric, the Jura is the place if you're seeking serenity, authentic farmstays and a taste of mountain life.

The Jura – from a Gaulish word meaning 'forest' – is France's premier cross-country skiing area. The range is dotted with ski stations, and every year the region hosts the **Transjurassienne**, one of the world's toughest cross-country skiing events.

Part of the fun of Sarlat is getting lost in its twisting alleyways and backstreets. **Rue Jean-Jacques Rousseau** or **rue Landry** are good starting points, but for the grandest buildings and *hôtels particuliers,* explore **rue des Consuls**. Whichever street you take, sooner or later you'll hit the **Cathédrale St-Sacerdos** (place du Peyrou), a real mix of architectural styles and periods: the belfry and western facade are the oldest parts.

Nearby, the former **Église Ste-Marie** (place de la Liberté) houses Sarlat's mouth-watering **Marché Couvert** (covered market) and a state-of-the-art **panoramic lift** (elevator), designed by French architect Jean Nouvel, in its bell tower.

Three gold-hued, bronze-sculpted geese on **place du Marché aux Oies** ('geese market' square) attest to the enduring economic and gastronomic role of these birds in the Dordogne. Both the covered market and Sarlat's chaotic **Saturday-morning market** (place de la Liberté & rue de la République) – a full-blown French market experience 'must' – sell a smorgasbord of goose-based goodies.

🛌 Sleeping

Villa des Consuls B&B €€
(☎ 05 53 31 90 05; www.villaconsuls.fr; 3 rue Jean-Jacques Rousseau; d €82-103, apt €124-184; @ 🛜) Despite its Renaissance exterior, the enormous rooms here are modern through and through, with shiny wood floors, sofas and original roof trusses.

La Maison des Peyrat Hotel €€
(☎ 05 53 59 00 32; www.maisondespeyrat.com; Le Lac de la Plane; r €56-103) This beautiful 17th-century house with lovingly tended gardens sits on a hill about 1.5km from town. Its 11 generously sized rooms are fairly plain, but ooze country charisma.

🍴 Eating

Le Grand Bleu Gastronomic €€€
(☎ 05 53 29 82 14; www.legrandbleu.eu; 43 av de la Gare; menu €36-65; ⏱ lunch Thu-Sun, dinner Tue-Sat) For a proper supper, this Michelin-starred restaurant is the choice – think creative cuisine that makes maximum use of luxury produce: truffles, lobster, turbot and St-Jacques scallops. Cooking courses as well.

Le Bistrot Regional Cuisine €€
(☎ 05 53 28 28 40; place du Peyrou; menu €18.50-28.50; ⏱ Mon-Sat) This dinky diner is the best of the bunch on cafe-clad place du Peyrou. Gingham cloths and tiny tables create a cosy bistro feel, and the menu's heavy on Sarlat classics – especially walnuts, *magret de canard* (duck breast) and *pommes sarlardaises* (potatoes cooked in duck fat).

ℹ️ Information

Tourist office (☎ 05 53 31 45 45; www.sarlat-tourisme.com; rue Tourny; ⏱ 9am-7pm Mon-Sat, 10am-1pm & 2-6pm Sun Jul & Aug, shorter hrs Sep-Jun)

Getting There & Away

The **train station** (ave de la Gare), 1.3km south of the old city, serves Périgueux (change at Le Buisson; €14.80, 1¾ hours, three daily) and Les Eyzies (change at Le Buisson; €9.80, 50 minutes to 2½ hours, three daily).

Les Eyzies-de-Tayac-Sireuil

POP 860

A hot base for touring the extraordinary cave collection of the **Vézère Valley** (see p257), this village is essentially a clutch of touristy shops strung along a central street. Its **Musée National de Préhistoire** (☎05 53 06 45 45; www.musee-prehistoire-eyzies.fr; 1 rue du Musée; adult/child €5/3, 1st Sun of month free; ⌚9.30am-6pm Wed-Mon), rife with amazing prehistoric finds, makes a great introduction to the area.

About 250m north of the museum is the Cro-Magnon shelter of **Abri Pataud** (☎05 53 06 92 46; pataud@mnhn.fr; 20 rue du Moyen Âge; adult/child €5/3; ⌚10am-noon & 2-6pm Sun-Thu), with an ibex carving dating from about 19,000 BC. Admission includes a guided tour (some in English).

Train services link Les Eyzies with Sarlat-la-Canéda.

THE ATLANTIC COAST

With quiet country roads winding through vine-striped hills and wild stretches of coastal sands interspersed with misty islands, the Atlantic coast is where France gets back to nature.

If you're a surf nut or a beach bum, then the sandy bays around Biarritz will be right up your alley, while oenophiles can sample the fruits of the vine in the high temple of French winemaking, Bordeaux. Towards the Pyrenees you'll find the Basque Country, which in many ways is closer to the culture of northern Spain than France.

Bordeaux

POP 240,500

The new millennium was a turning point for the city long nicknamed La Belle au Bois Dormant (Sleeping Beauty), when the mayor, ex-Prime Minister Alain Juppé, roused Bordeaux, pedestrianising its boulevards, restoring its neoclassical architecture, and implementing a hi-tech public-transport system. Today the city is a Unesco World Heritage site and, with its merry student population and 2.5 million-odd annual tourists, scarcely sleeps at all.

◎ Sights

Cathédrale St-André   Cathedral
This Unesco World Heritage site is almost overshadowed by the gargoyled, 50m-high Gothic belfry, **Tour Pey-Berland**

Sarlat-La-Canéda (p253)
RUTH TOMLINSON/GETTY IMAGES ©

(adult/child €5.50/free; ⏱10am-1.15pm & 2-6pm Jun-Sep, shorter hrs rest of year). Erected between 1440 and 1466, its spire was topped off in 1863 with the statue of Notre Dame de l'Aquitaine (Our Lady of Aquitaine). Scaling the tower's 231 narrow steps rewards you with a spectacular panorama of Bordeaux city.

Museums & Galleries   Museums

Gallo-Roman statues and relics dating back 25,000 years are among the highlights at the impressive **Musée d'Aquitaine** (20 cours Pasteur), while an 1824 warehouse for French colonial produce (coffee, cocoa, peanuts, vanilla and the like) is the dramatic backdrop for cutting-edge modern art at the **CAPC Musée d'Art Contemporain** (rue Ferrére, Entrepôt 7; ⏱11am-6pm Tue & Thu-Sun, to 8pm Wed).

The evolution of Occidental art from the Renaissance to the mid-20th century fills the **Musée des Beaux-Arts** (20 cours d'Albret; ⏱11am-6pm mid-Jul–mid-Aug) inside the 1770s-built Hôtel de Ville.

Faience pottery, porcelain, gold, iron, glasswork and furniture are displayed at the **Musée des Arts Décoratifs** (39 rue Bouffard; ⏱2-6pm Wed-Mon).

🛏 Sleeping

Ecolodge des Chartrons   B&B €€

(☎05 56 81 49 13; www.ecolodgedeschartrons.com; 23 rue Raze; s €96-118, d €98-134; 🛜🅿) Hidden in a side street in Bordeaux' Chartrons wine merchant district, this *chambre d'hôte* is blazing a trail for ecofriendly sleeping with its solar-powered hot-water system, energy-efficient gas heating and hemp-based soundproofing. Each of the five rooms has a bathroom built from natural materials such as basalt. Organic breakfasts are served at a long timber table.

Les Chambres au Coeur de Bordeaux   B&B €€

(☎05 56 52 43 58; www.aucoeurdebordeaux.fr; 28 rue Boulan; s/d from €85/95; 🛜) This swish B&B has five charming rooms that are a very Bordeaux-appropriate mix of old and new; free *apéro* each evening at 7pm.

La Maison Bord'eaux   Boutique Hotel €€

(☎05 56 44 00 45; www.lamaisonbord-eaux.com; 113 rue du Docteur Albert Barraud; s/d from €145/165; 🅿❄🛜) You'd expect to find a

Cathédrale St-André (p255), Bordeaux

SILVIA OTTE/GETTY IMAGES ©

Prehistoric Paintings

Fantastic prehistoric **caves** with some of the world's finest **cave art** is what makes the Vézère Valley so very special. Most of the caves are closed in winter, and get very busy in summer. Visitor numbers are strictly limited, so you'll need to reserve well ahead.

Of the valley's 175 known sites, the most famous include **Grotte de Font de Gaume** (📞05 53 06 86 00; http://eyzies.monuments-nationaux.fr/; adult/child €7.50/free; 🕙9.30am-5.30pm Sun-Fri mid-May–mid-Sep, 9.30am-12.30pm & 2-5.30pm Sun-Fri mid-Sep–mid-May), 1km northeast of Les Eyzies. About 14,000 years ago, prehistoric artists created the gallery of over 230 figures, including bison, reindeer, horses, mammoths, bears and wolves, of which 25 are on permanent display.

About 7km east of Les Eyzies, **Abri du Cap Blanc** (📞05 53 06 86 00; adult/child €7.50/free; 🕙10am-6pm Sun-Fri mid-May–mid-Sep, 10am-noon & 2-6pm Sun-Fri mid-Sep–mid-May) showcases an unusual sculpture gallery of horses, bison and deer.

Then there is **Grotte de Rouffignac** (📞05 53 05 41 71; www.grottederouffignac.fr; adult/child €6.50/4.20; 🕙9-11.30am & 2-6pm Jul & Aug, 10-11.30am & 2-5pm Sep-Jun), sometimes known as the 'Cave of 100 Mammoths' because of its painted mammoths. Access to the caves, hidden in woodland 15km north of Les Eyzies, is aboard a trundling electric train.

Star of the show goes hands down to **Grotte de Lascaux** (Lascaux II; 📞05 53 51 95 03; www.semitour.com; adult/child €8.80/6; 🕙9.30am-6pm), 2km southeast of Montignac, featuring an astonishing menagerie including oxen, deer, horses, reindeer and mammoth, as well as an amazing 5.5m bull, the largest cave drawing ever found. The original cave was closed to the public in 1963 to prevent damage to the paintings, but the most famous sections have been meticulously recreated in a second cave nearby – a massive undertaking that required some 20 artists and took 11 years.

sumptuous 18th-century chateau with conifer-flanked courtyard and stable in the countryside, but this stunning *maison d'hôte* is right in the middle of the city.

🍴 Eating

Le Cheverus Café   Bistro €
(📞05 56 48 29 73; 81-83 rue du Loup; menu from €11.40; 🕙Mon-Sat) This neighbourhood bistro is friendly, cosy and chaotically busy (be prepared to wait for a table at lunchtime). The food dares to veer slightly away from the bistro standards of steak and chips, and lunch *menus,* which, including wine, are an all-out bargain.

La Tupina   Regional Cuisine €€
(📞05 56 91 56 37; www.latupina.com; 6 rue Porte de la Monnaie; menu €18-65, mains €27-45) Filled with the aroma of soup simmering inside an old *tupina* ('kettle' in Basque) over an open fire, this white-tableclothed place is feted far and wide for its seasonal southwestern French specialities. Find it a 10-minute walk upriver from the city centre, on a small side street. Any local can point you in the right direction.

La Boîte à Huîtres   Oysters €€
(📞05 56 81 64 97; 36 cours du Chapeau Rouge; lunch menu €19, 6 oysters from €10) This rickety, wood-panelled place is the best place in Bordeaux to munch fresh Arcachon oysters. Traditionally they're served with sausage but you can have them in a number of different forms, including with foie gras.

On the Wine Trail

Thirsty? The 1000-sq-km wine-growing area around the city of Bordeaux is, along with Burgundy, France's most important producer of top-quality wines. Whet your palate with Bordeaux tourist office's introduction wine-and-cheese courses (€24).

Serious students of the grape can enrol in a two-hour (€25) or two- to three-day course (€335 to €600) at the **École du Vin** (Wine School; ☎ 05 56 00 22 66; www. bordeaux.com) inside the **Maison du Vin de Bordeaux** (3 cours du 30 Juillet).

Bordeaux has over 5000 estates where grapes are grown, picked and turned into wine. Smaller chateaux often accept walk-in visitors, but at many places, especially better-known ones, you have to reserve in advance. If you have your own wheels, one of the easiest to visit is **Château Lanessan** (☎ 05 56 58 94 80; www.lanessan.com; Cussac-Fort-Medoc).

Favourite vine-framed villages brimming with charm and tasting/buying opportunities include medieval **St-Émilion** (www.saint-emilion-tourisme.com), port town **Pauillac** (www.pauillac-medoc.com) and **Listrac-Médoc**. In **Arsac-en-Médoc**, Philippe Raoux's vast glass-and-steel wine centre, **La Winery** (☎ 05 56 39 04 90; www.lawinery.fr; Rond-point des Vendangeurs, D1), stuns with concerts and contemporary art exhibitions alongside tastings to determine your *signe œnologique* ('wine sign'; booking required).

Many chateaux close during October's *vendange* (grape harvest).

ℹ️ Information

Main tourist office (☎ 05 56 00 66 00; www. bordeaux-tourisme.com; 12 cours du 30 Juillet; ⏰ 9am-7.30pm Mon-Sat, 9.30am-6.30pm Sun)

ℹ️ Getting There & Away

Air

Bordeaux airport (p288) is in Mérignac, 10km west of the city centre, with domestic and some international services.

Train

From Gare St-Jean, 3km from the centre:

Paris Gare Montparnasse €73, three hours, at least 16 daily

Toulouse from €35.30, 2¼ hours

Biarritz

POP 26,067

Edge your way south along the coast towards Spain and you arrive in stylish Biarritz, just as ritzy as its name suggests. The resort took off in the mid-19th century (Napoléon III had a rather soft spot for the place) and it still shimmers with architectural treasures from the belle époque and art deco eras.

◎ Sights

Biarritz' raison d'être is its fashionable beaches, particularly central **Grande Plage** and **Plage Miramar**, lined end to end with sunbathing bodies on hot summer days. Stripy 1920s-style beach tents can be hired for €9.50 per day. North of Pointe St-Martin, the adrenaline-pumping surfing beaches of **Anglet** (the final 't' is pronounced) continue northwards for more than 4km. Take bus 10 or 13 from the bottom of av Verdun (just near av Édouard VII).

Cité de l'Océan Museum
(☎ 05 59 22 75 40; www.citedelocean.com; 1 Av de la Plage; adult/child €10.50/7; ⏰ 10am-10pm) Inside an eye-catching, wave-shaped

building south of town, this museum will teach you everything about the ocean and, in between, get you to ride to the depths of the ocean in a submarine and watch giant squid and sperm whales do battle. A combined ticket with the Musée de la Mer costs €17.50/13 per adult/child.

🛏 Sleeping

Hôtel Mirano   Boutique Hotel €€

(📞 05 59 23 11 63; www.hotelmirano.fr; 11 av Pasteur; d €68-130; P 📶) Squiggly purple, orange and black wallpaper and oversize orange perspex light fittings are some of the rad '70s touches at this retro boutique hotel, a 10-minute stroll from the town centre.

Hôtel de Silhouette   Designer Hotel €€€

(📞 05 59 24 93 82; www.hotel-silhouette-biarritz.com; 30 rue Gambetta; d from €220; ❄ 📶) This fabulous new addition to the Biarritz hotel scene has designer rooms with big-city attitude that would feel quite at home in an upmarket Manhattan apartment. In order to remind you that the country-side is close at hand there are a couple of 'sheep' in the garden and frequently changing outdoor art and sculpture exhibitions.

✗ Eating

Casa Juan Pedro   Seafood €

(📞 05 59 24 00 86; Port des Pêcheurs; mains €7-10) Down by the old port, this cute fishing-shack cooks up tuna, sardines and squid with plenty of friendly banter.

Le Crabe-Tambour   Seafood €€

(📞 05 59 23 24 53; 49 rue d'Espagne; menu €13-18) Named after the famous 1977 film of the same name (the owner was the cook for the film set), this local hangout serves great seafood for a price that is hard to fault.

🍷 Drinking & Nightlife

Ventilo Caffé   Bar

(rue du Port Vieux; ⏱ closed Tue Oct-Easter) Dressed up like a boudoir, this fun and funky place continues its domination of the Biarritz bar scene.

Sunbathers in Biarritz

Detour:
Dune du Pilat

This colossal sand dune (sometimes referred to as the Dune de Pyla because of its location in the resort town of Pyla-sur-Mer), 65km west of Bordeaux, stretches from the mouth of the Bassin d'Arcachon southwards for almost 3km. Already the largest in Europe, it's spreading eastwards at 4.5m a year – it has swallowed trees, a road junction and even a hotel.

The view from the top – approximately 114m above sea level – is magnificent. To the west you can see the sandy shoals at the mouth of the Bassin d'Arcachon, including the **Banc d'Arguin bird reserve** and Cap Ferret. Dense dark-green pine forests stretch from the base of the dune eastwards almost as far as the eye can see.

Take care swimming in this area: powerful currents swirl out to sea from the deceptively tranquil *baïnes* (little bays).

Although an easy day trip from Bordeaux, the area around the dune is an enjoyable place to kick back for a while. Most people choose to camp in one of the swag of seasonal campgrounds. Lists and information on all of these (and more bricks-and-mortar-based accommodation) can be found at www.bassin-arcachon.com.

Arena Café Bar   Bar
(Plage du Port Vieux; ⏰9am-2am Apr-Sep, 10am-2am Wed-Sun Oct-Mar) Tucked into a tiny cove, this beachfront hang-out combines a style-conscious restaurant with a fashionista bar with DJs and sunset views.

ⓘ Getting There & Away

Air
Biarritz-Anglet-Bayonne Airport (www.biarritz.aeroport.fr), 3km southeast of Biarritz, is served by several low-cost carriers.

Train
Biarritz-La Négresse train station, 3km south of town, is linked to the centre by bus A1.

LANGUEDOC-ROUSSILLON

Languedoc-Roussillon comes in three distinct flavours: Bas-Languedoc (Lower Languedoc), land of bullfighting, rugby and robust red wines, where the region's major sights are found; sunbaked Nîmes with its fine Roman amphitheatre; and

fairy-tale Carcassonne, crowned with a ring of witch-hat turrets.

Inland, Haut Languedoc (Upper Languedoc) is a mountainous, sparsely populated terrain made for lovers of the great outdoors; while to the south sits Roussillon, snug against the rugged Pyrenees and frontier to Spanish Catalonia. Meanwhile, Languedoc's traditional centre, Toulouse, was shaved off when regional boundaries were redrawn almost half a century ago, but we've chosen to include it in this section.

Carcassonne

Perched on a rocky hilltop and bristling with zig-zag battlements, stout walls and spiky turrets, the fortified city of Carcassonne looks like something out of a children's storybook from afar. It's most people's perfect idea of a medieval castle, and it's undoubtedly an impressive spectacle – not to mention one of the Languedoc's biggest tourist draws.

Unfortunately, the medieval magic's more than a tad tarnished by an annual influx of over four million visitors and it can be a tourist hell in high summer.

The old city, **La Cité**, is dramatically illuminated at night and enclosed by two rampart walls punctuated by 52 stone towers, Europe's largest city fortifications. Successive generations of Gauls, Romans, Visigoths, Moors, Franks and Cathars reinforced the walls, but only the lower sections are original; the rest, including the turrets, were stuck on by the 19th-century architect Viollet-le-Duc.

A drawbridge leads to the old gate of **Porte Narbonnaise** and rue Cros Mayrevieille en route to place Château and the 12th-century **Château Comtal** (adult/child €8.50/free; ⏱10am-6.30pm Apr-Sep). South is **Basilique St-Nazaire** (⏱9-11.45am & 1.45-5pm or 5.30pm), illuminated by delicate medieval rose windows.

Carcassonne is on the main rail line to/from Toulouse (€14, 50 minutes).

Nîmes

POP 146,500

This buzzy city boasts some of France's best-preserved classical buildings, including a famous Roman amphitheatre, although the city is most famous for its sartorial export, *serge de Nîmes* – better known to cowboys, clubbers and couturiers as denim.

◎ Sights

A **Pass Nîmes Romaine** (adult/child €10/7.70), valid for three days, covers all three sights; buy one at the first place you visit.

Les Arènes
Roman Site

(www.arenes-nimes.com; place des Arènes; adult/child €7.90/6; ⏱9am-8pm Jul & Aug, earlier closing at other times) Nîmes' twin-tiered amphitheatre, the

best preserved in the Roman Empire, was built around AD 100 to stage gladiatorial contests and public executions – watched by an audience of 24,000 spectators. Public events of a less gory nature are held here today (although bullfights are still a regular fixture).

Maison Carrée
Roman Sites

(place de la Maison Carrée; adult/child €4.60/3.80; ⏱10am-8pm Jul & Aug, earlier closing at other times) This gleaming limestone temple built around AD 5 to honour Emperor Augustus' two adopted sons is not actually square, despite its name, which means 'Square House' – to the Romans, 'square' simply meant a building with right angles.

Carré d'Art
Museum

(www.carreartmusee.com; place de la Maison Carrée; permanent collection free, exhibitions adult/child €5/3.70; ⏱10am-6pm Tue-Sun) The striking glass-and-steel art museum facing the Maison Carrée was designed by British architect Sir Norman Foster. The rooftop restaurant makes a lovely lunch spot.

Château Comtal, Carcassonne
GLENN BEANLAND/GETTY IMAGES ©

Below: Lavender field, Provence;
Right: Les Arènes amphitheatre (p261), Nîmes

🛏 Sleeping

Le Cheval Blanc   Hotel €€

(☎ 04 66 76 05 22; www.lechevalblanc-nimes.
com; 1 place des Arènes; d €115, f €180-210;
📶) A prime position overlooking Les
Arènes and a spare, stripped-back style
make this the swishest place to stay in
central Nîmes. Bare wood, plaster and
stone define the design, and there are
several split-level apartments with galley
kitchens. The building itself began life as
a textile factory, but it feels deliciously
modern now.

Hôtel Amphithéâtre   Hotel €

(☎ 04 66 67 28 51; www.hoteldelamphitheatre.
com; 4 rue des Arènes; s/d €65/85) Tucked
away along a narrow backstreet, this tall
townhouse hotel run by an ex-pat Cor-
nishman and his wife has chic and stylish
rooms; some have balconies overlooking
place du Marché.

🍴 Eating

Look out for *cassoulet* (pork, sausage
and white bean stew, sometimes served
with duck), aïoli and *rouille* (a spicy chilli
mayonnaise).

L'Imprévu   Modern French €€

(☎ 04 66 38 99 59; www.l-imprevu.com; 6 place
d'Assas; mains €19.50-27.50; ⏰ lunch & dinner)
The simple, amber-stoned facade of this
fine-dining French bistro looks homey,
but the interior is light and contemporary,
with swirly modern art, an open-plan
kitchen and interior courtyard. There's a
posh mix of *terre-et-mer* (surf-and-turf)
dishes, mainly served à la carte.

**Le Marché sur
la Table**   Modern French €€

(☎ 04 66 67 22 50; 10 rue Littré; mains €18-22;
⏰ Wed-Sun) Husband-and-wife team
Éric and Caroline Vidal focus on organic
ingredients picked up from the market.
The interior feels homespun and there's a
quiet courtyard for alfresco dining.

ℹ️ Information

Tourist office (📞04 66 58 38 00; www.ot-nimes.fr; 6 rue Auguste; ⊙8.30am-8pm Mon-Fri, 9am-7pm Sat, 10am-6pm Sun Jul & Aug, shorter hrs rest of year)

ℹ️ Getting There & Away

More than 12 TGVs daily run to/from Paris Gare de Lyon (€52 to €99.70, three hours). Local destinations include:

Arles €8 to €14, 30 minutes

Avignon €9, 30 minutes

Montpellier €9.20, 30 minutes

PROVENCE

Provence conjures up images of rolling lavender fields, blue skies, gorgeous villages, wonderful food and superb wine. It certainly delivers on all those fronts, but it's not just worth visiting for its good looks – dig a little deeper and you'll also discover the multicultural metropolis of Marseille, the artistic haven of Aix-en-Provence and the old Roman city of Arles.

Marseille

POP 858,902

There was a time when Marseille was the butt of French jokes. No more. The *cité phocéenne* has made an unprecedented comeback, undergoing a vast makeover. Marseillais will tell you that the city's rough-and-tumble edginess is part of its charm and that, for all its flaws, it is a very endearing place. They're right: Marseille grows on you with its unique history, souklike markets, millennia-old port and spectacular *corniches* (coastal roads) – all good reasons indeed why Marseille was chosen European Capital of Culture in 2013.

The recent opening of several high-profile museums and galleries have added to the city's newfound swagger. The flagship MuCEM (Musée des Civilisations de l'Europe et de la Méditerranée) explores the various cultures that have flourished along the Mediterranean over the past two thousand years, while the flashy new Villa Méditerranée documents the region's present and future, with everything from film screenings to live discussions. Meanwhile, modern art takes centre stage at the MAMO and FRAC galleries.

◎ Sights

Buy a cent-saving **Marseille City Pass** (one-/two-day €22/29) at the tourist office. It covers admission to 15 museums, a city tour, unlimited public-transport travel, boat trips and so on.

Vieux Port   Historic Quarter
(Ⓜ Vieux Port) Ships have docked for more than 26 centuries at Marseile's colourful Old Port.

Guarding the harbour are **Bas Fort St-Nicolas** and **Fort St-Jean**, founded in the 13th century by the Knights Hospitaller of St John of Jerusalem. The 40,000 sq m, state-of-the-art museum **Musée des Civilisations de l'Europe et de la Méditerranée** (MuCEM; Museum of European & Mediterranean Civilisations; ☎ 04 96 13 80 90; www.mucem.org; ◔ 1-7pm Wed, Thu & Sat) FREE opened in 2013.

Basilique Notre Dame de la Garde   Church
(Montée de la Bonne Mère; ◔ 7am-8pm Apr-Sep, to 7pm Oct-Mar) Everywhere you go in Marseille, you can see the opulent, domed 19th-century Romano-Byzantine basilica, privy to dazzling 360-degree panoramas of the city's sea of terracotta roofs below.

The church's bell tower is crowned by a 9.7m-tall gilded statue of the Virgin Mary on a 12m-high pedestal. Walk or take bus 60 from the Vieux Port.

Château d'If   Island, Castle
(www.if.monuments-nationaux.fr; adult/child €5/free; ◔ 9.30am-6.30pm May-Sep, to 4.45pm Tue-Sun Oct-Apr) Immortalised in Alexandre Dumas' 1844 novel *Le Comte de Monte Cristo* (The Count of Monte Cristo), this 16th-century fortress-turned-prison sits on an island 3.5km west of the Vieux Port.

Political prisoners were incarcerated here, along with hundreds of Protestants, the Revolutionary hero Mirabeau, and the Communards of 1871.

Frioul If Express (www.frioul-if-express.com; 1 quai des Belges) boats leave for Château d'If from the Vieux Port. Over 15 daily departures in summer, fewer in winter (€10 return, 20 minutes).

Le Panier   Historic Neighbourhood
(Ⓜ Vieux Port) From the Vieux Port, hike north up to this fantastic history-woven quarter, dubbed Marseille's Montmartre as much for its sloping streets as its artsy ambience. In Greek Massilia it was the site of the *agora* (marketplace), hence its name, which means 'the basket'. During WWII the quarter was dynamited and afterwards rebuilt. Today it's a mishmash of lanes hiding artisan shops, *ateliers* (workshops) and terraced houses strung with drying washing.

La Friche La Belle de Mai   Cultural Centre
(☎ 04 95 04 95 04; www.lafriche.org; 41 rue Jobin; 🚌 49 stop Jobin) This former sugar-refining plant and subsequent tobacco factory is now host to artists' workshops, cinema studios, radio stations, multi-media displays, al fresco installation art, skateboard camps and electro/world-music parties – enter the gregarious 'voice' of contemporary Marseille. Check its program online, view art in the **Galerie de la Friche Belle de Mai** (◔ 3-7pm Tue-Sat) FREE and dine in its stylishly industrial **Les Grandes Tables de la Friche** (☎ 04 95 04 95 85; www.lesgrandestables.com; 12 rue François Simon; mains €10; ◔ 8.30am-8pm Mon-Fri).

🛏 Sleeping

Casa Honoré   B&B €€€
(☎ 04 96 11 01 62; www.casahonore.com; 123 rue Sainte; d incl breakfast €150-200; ❄ 🛜 ⌕; Ⓜ Vieux Port) Los Angeles meets Marseille at this four-room *maison d'hôte*, built around a central courtyard with lap pool shaded by banana trees. One complaint: some bathrooms are partitioned by curtains, not doors.

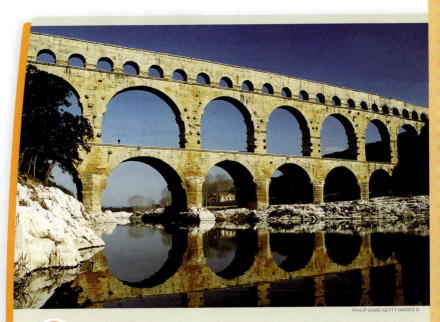

PHILIP GAME/GETTY IMAGES ©

⭐ Don't Miss
Pont du Gard

Southern France has some fine Roman sites, but for audacious engineering, nothing can top Unesco World Heritage site Pont du Gard, 21km northeast of Nîmes. This three-tiered aqueduct was once part of a 50km-long system of water channels, built around 19 BC to transport water from Uzès to Nîmes. The scale is huge: 50m high, 275m long and graced with 35 precision-built arches, the bridge was sturdy enough to carry up to 20,000 cu metres of water per day. Each block was carved by hand and transported here from nearby quarries – no mean feat, considering the largest blocks weight more than 5 tonnes.

There are large car parks on both banks of the river, about 400m walk from the bridge. Parking costs a flat-rate €5.

Crowds can be a real problem in high summer; early evening is usually a great time to visit, especially since parking is free after 7pm and the bridge is stunningly lit after dark.

NEED TO KNOW

📞 04 66 37 50 99; www.pontdugard.fr; car & up to 5 passengers €18, after 8pm €10, cyclists & walkers free; 🕓 visitors centre & museum 9am-7pm Jun-Sep, 9am-6pm Mar-May & Sep, 9am-5pm Oct-Feb, parking lots 9am-1am

---

Le Ryad Boutique Hotel **€€**
(📞 04 91 47 74 54; www.leryad.fr; 16 rue Sénac de Meilhan; s €80-105, d €95-125, family €170; 🛜; Ⓜ Noailles, 🚊 Canebière Garibaldi) Le Ryad draws sumptuous influence from Morocco. Beautiful bathrooms, garden-view rooms and great service make up for the sometimes-sketchy neighbourhood. Book the top-floor room (Mogador) for its rooftop terrace.

Vieux Port

An Itinerary

Bold and busy and open-armed to the sea, Marseille is France's oldest city. Standing on the quai des Belges it's hard to get a sense of the extent of the old port, a kilometre long on either side, running down to the great bastions of St-Jean and St-Nicolas, which once had their guns trained on the rebellious population rather than out to sea. Immerse yourself in the city's history with this full-day itinerary.

Go early to experience the **fish market** ❶, where you'll swap tall tales with the gregarious vendors. Hungry? Grab a balcony seat at La Caravelle, where views of the Basilique Notre Dame de la Garde accompany your morning coffee. Afterwards, take a **boat trip** ❷ to Château d'If, made famous by the Dumas novel *The Count of Monte Cristo*. Alternatively, stay landside and explore the apricot-coloured alleys of **Le Panier** ❸, browsing the exhibits at the **Centre de la Vieille Charité** ❹.

In the afternoon, hop on the free cross-port ferry to the port's south side and wander into the **Abbaye St-Victor** ❺ to see the bones of martyrs enshrined in gold. You can then catch the sunset from the stone benches in the **Jardin du Pharo** ❻. As the warm southern evening sets in, join the throngs on cours Honoré d'Estienne d'Orves, where you can drink pastis beneath a giant statue of a lion devouring a man – the **Milo de Croton** ❼.

CAPITAL OF CULTURE 2013

The largest urban renewal project in Europe, the Euroméditerranée project aims to rehabilitate the commercial Joliette docks along the same lines as London's Docklands. The city's green-and-white striped Cathédrale de la Major, for years abandoned in an area of urban wasteland, will form its centrepiece.

GLENN BEANLAND/GETTY IMAGES ©

Le Panier
The site of the Greek town of Massilia, Le Panier woos walkers with its sloping streets. Grand Rue follows the ancient road and opens out into place de Lenche, the location of the Greek market. It is still the place to shop for artisanal products.

Cathédrale de la Major

❹

Fort St-Jean

Centre de la Vieille Charité
Before the 18th century, beggar hunters rounded up the poor for imprisonment. The Vieille Charité almshouse, which opened in 1749, improved their lot by acting as a workhouse. It's now an exhibition space and only the barred windows recall its original use.

Jardin & Palais du Pharo

❻

Jardin du Pharo
Built by Napoléon for the Empress Eugénie, the Pharo Palace was designed with its 'feet in the water'. Today it is a private centre, but the gardens with their magnificent view are open all day.

Fish Market

Marseille's small fish market still sets up each morning to hawk the daily catch. Take a lesson in local seafood, spotting sea squirts, scorpion fish, sea urchins and conger eels. Get there before 9am if you're buying.

Milo de Croton

Subversive local artist Pierre Puget carved the savage *Milo de Croton* for Louis XIV. The statue, whose original is in the Louvre, is a meditation on man's pride and shows the Greek Olympian being devoured by a lion, his Olympic cup cast down.

Frioul If Express

Catch the Frioul If Express to Château d'If, France's equivalent to Alcatraz. Prisoners were housed according to class: the poorest at the bottom in windowless dungeons, the wealthiest in paid-for private cells, with windows and a fireplace.

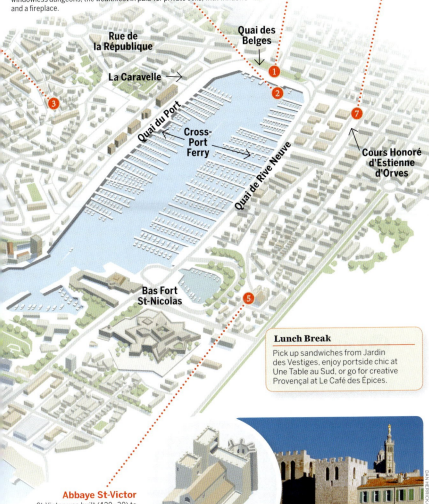

Rue de la République

La Caravelle →

Quai des Belges

Quai du Port

Cross-Port Ferry

Quai de Rive Neuve

Cours Honoré d'Estienne d'Orves

Bas Fort St-Nicolas

Lunch Break

Pick up sandwiches from Jardin des Vestiges, enjoy portside chic at Une Table au Sud, or go for creative Provençal at Le Café des Épices.

Abbaye St-Victor

St-Victor was built (420–30) to house the remains of tortured Christian martyrs. On Candlemas (2 February) the black Madonna is brought up from the crypt and the archbishop blesses the city and the sea.

Les Calanques

Marseille abuts the wild and spectacular Les Calanques, a protected 20km stretch of high, rocky promontories rising from the bright turquoise sea. Sheer cliffs are occasionally interrupted by idyllic beach-fringed coves, many only possible to reach with kayak. They've been protected since 1975 and became a national park in 2012.

Marseille's tourist office leads guided hikes in Les Calanques and has information on walking trails (shut July and August due to forest-fire risk). For great views from out at sea hop aboard a boat trip to the wine-producing port of **Cassis**, 30km east along the coast, with **Croisières Marseille Calanques.** (www.croisieres-marseille-calanques.com; 74 quai du Port).

Mama Shelter   Design Hotel €€
(01 43 48 48 48; www.mamashelter.com; 64 rue de la Loubière; d €99-139, q €159, ste €209; ❄ 🛜; Ⓜ Notre Dame du Monte–Cours Julien) The brainchild of Serge Trigano, son of Gilbert (Club Med creator), this affordable-chic new kid on the block sports design by Philippe Starck.

 Eating

The Vieux Port overflows with restaurants, but choose carefully. Head to Cours Julien and its surrounding streets for world cuisine.

The small but enthralling **fish market** (quai des Belges; ⏱8am-1pm; Ⓜ Vieux Port) is a daily fixture at the Vieux Port. **Cours Julien** hosts a Wednesday-morning organic fruit and vegetable market and **Prado Market** (av du Prado; ⏱8am-1pm; Ⓜ Castellane or Périer) is the place to go for anything and everything other than food.

Le Café des Épices   Modern French €€
(04 91 91 22 69; www.cafedesepices.com; 4 rue du Lacydon; 3-course lunch/dinner menu €25/40; ⏱lunch Tue-Sat, dinner Thu-Fri; 👬; Ⓜ Vieux Port) One of Marseille's best young chefs, Arnaud de Grammont, infuses his cooking with a panoply of flavours...think squid ink spaghetti with sesame and perfectly cooked scallops, or tender roasted potatoes with hints of coriander and citrus, topped by the catch of the day.

La Cantinetta   Italian €
(04 91 48 10 48; 24 cours Julien; mains €9-19; ⏱lunch & dinner Tue-Sat; Ⓜ Notre Dame du Mont–Cours Julien) The top table at cours Julien serves perfectly al dente housemade pasta, paper-thin prosciutto, marinated vegetables, *bresaola* (air-dried beef) and risotto.

Le Comptoir Dugommier   Bistro €
(04 91 62 21 21; www.comptoirdugommier.fr; 14 bd Dugommier; mains €11-12, 3-course menu with drink €20; ⏱7.30am-3.30pm Mon-Wed, 7.30am-1am Thu & Fri; Ⓜ Noailles, 🚋 Canebière Garibaldi) Tin molding, wooden floors and vintage signs make a homey escape from the busy street outside. The place gets packed for its downhome French fare.

La Part des Anges   Bistro €
(33 rue Sainte; mains €15; ⏱lunch Mon-Sat, dinner daily) No address buzzes with Marseille's hip, buoyant crowd more than this fabulous all-rounder wine bistro, named after the amount of alcohol that evaporates through a barrel during wine or whisky fermentation: the angels' share.

🍷 Drinking & Nightlife

La Caravelle   Bar
(34 quai du Port; ⏱7am-2am; Ⓜ Vieux Port) Look up or miss this upstairs hideaway with tiny but treasured portside terrace. Fridays hear live jazz 9pm to midnight.

Les Buvards   Wine Bar
(04 91 90 69 98 ; 34 Grand Rue; ⏱10am-1am; Ⓜ Vieux Port, 🚋 Sadi Carnot) Grand selection of natural wines and munchies.

ℹ️ Information

Dangers & Annoyances

Petty crimes and muggings are common. Avoid the Belsunce area (southwest of the train station, bounded by La Canebière, cours Belsunce and rue d'Aix, rue Bernard du Bois and blvd d'Athènes) at night. Walking La Canebiére is annoying, but generally not dangerous; expect to encounter kids peddling hash.

Tourist information

Tourist office (📞04 91 13 89 00; www. marseille-tourisme.com; 4 La Canebière; ⏰9am-7pm Mon-Sat, 10am-5pm Sun; Ⓜ Vieux Port)

ℹ️ Getting There & Away

Air

Aéroport Marseille-Provence (p288), 25km northwest in Marignane, has numerous budget flights to various European destinations. **Shuttle buses** (📞 Marseille 04 91 50 59 34, airport 04 42 14 31 27; www.lepilote.com) link it with Marseille train station (€8; 25 minutes, every 20 minutes).

Boat

The **passenger ferry terminal** (www.marseille-port.fr; Ⓜ Joliette) is 250m south of Place de la Joliette (1er). **SNCM** (📞08 91 70 18 01; www. sncm.fr; 61 bd des Dames; Ⓜ Joliette) boats sail to Corsica, Sardinia and North Africa.

Train

From Marseille's Gare St-Charles, trains including TGVs go all over France and Europe.

Avignon €24, 35 minutes

Lyon €50, 1¾ hours

Nice €35, 2½ hours

Paris Gare de Lyon €103, three hours

ℹ️ Getting Around

Marseille has two metro lines, two tram lines and an extensive bus network, all run by **RTM** (📞04 91 91 92 10; www.rtm.fr; 6 rue des Fabres; ⏰8.30am-6pm Mon-Fri, 9am-12.30pm & 2-5.30pm Sat; Ⓜ Vieux Port), where you can obtain information and transport tickets (€1.50).

Avignon

POP 92,454

Hooped by 4.3km of superbly preserved stone ramparts, this graceful city is the belle of Provence's ball. Famed for its annual performing arts festival and fabled bridge, Avignon is an ideal spot from

View of Basilique Notre Dame de la Garde from Vieux Port (p264), Marseille

which to step out into the surrounding region. Wrapping around the city, Avignon's defensive ramparts were built between 1359 and 1370, and are punctuated by a series of sturdy *portes* (gates).

◎ Sights

Discount card, *Avignon Passion*, yields discounts of 10% to 50% on city museums, tours and monuments (pay full price at the first site, then discounts at each susbsequent site). The pass covers five people and is valid for 15 days. Available from the tourist office and tourist sites.

Palais des Papes   Palace
(Papal Palace; www.palais-des-papes.com; place du Palais; adult/child €6/3; ⏱9am-8pm Jul, 9am-9pm Aug, shorter hrs Sep-Jun) This Unesco World Heritage site, the world's largest Gothic palace, was built when Pope Clement V abandoned Rome in 1309 to settle in Avignon, it was the seat of papal power for 70-odd years. Today, it takes imagination to picture the former luxury of these vast, bare rooms, but

PDA-style audio-video guides show 2- and 3D imagery of the once sumptuous furnishings.

Pont St-Bénézet   Bridge
(adult/child €4.50/3.50; ⏱9am-8pm Jul, 9am-9pm Aug, shorter hrs Sep-Jun) This fabled bridge, immortalised in the French nursery rhyme 'Sur le Pont d'Avignon', was completed in 1185 and rebuilt several times before all but four of its spans were washed away in the mid-1600s.

Musée Calvet   Gallery
(☎04 90 86 33 84; 65 rue Joseph Vernet; adult/child €6/3; ⏱10am-1pm & 2-6pm Wed-Mon) The elegant Hôtel de Villeneuve-Martignan (1741–54) provides a fitting backdrop for Avignon's fine-arts museum.

Musée Angladon   Gallery
(www.angladon.com; 5 rue Laboureur; adult/child €6/4; ⏱1-6pm Tue-Sun Apr-Nov, 1-6pm Wed-Sun Jan-Mar) This tiny museum harbours impressionist treasures, including Van Gogh's *Railway Wagons*, a handful of early Picasso sketches and artworks by Cézanne, Sisley, Manet and Degas.

✺ Festivals & Events

Hundreds of artists take to the stage and streets during the world-famous **Festival d'Avignon** (www.festival-avignon.com; ⏱Jul) and fringe **Festival Off** (www.avignonleoff.com; ⏱Jul), held early July to early August.

🛏 Sleeping

Le Limas   B&B €€
(☎04 90 14 67 19; www.le-limas-avignon.com; 51 rue du Limas; d/tr incl breakfast from €120/200; ❄@) This chic B&B in an 18th-century townhouse is like something out of *Vogue Living*. Breakfast on the

Portraits of popes inside Palais des Papes, Avignon
MANIN RICHARD/GETTY IMAGES ©

sun-drenched terrace is a treat, as is bubbly owner Marion.

Hôtel Boquier   Hotel €
(📞04 90 82 34 43; www.hotel-boquier.com; 6 rue du Portail Boquier; d €50-70; ❄️📶) The owners' infectious enthusiasm informs this upbeat, colourful, small central hotel; try for themed rooms Morocco or Lavender. Excellent value.

Eating

Cuisine du
Dimanche   Provençal €€
(📞04 90 82 99 10; www.lacuisinedudimanche. com; 31 rue Bonneterie; mains €15-25; ⏰daily Jun-Sep, Tue-Sat Oct-May) Spitfire chef Marie shops every morning at Les Halles to find the freshest ingredients for her earthy flavour-packed cooking. The menu changes daily, but specialities include scallops and simple roast chicken with pan gravy.

L'Epice and Love   French €
(📞04 90 82 45 96; 30 rue des Lices; mains €11-12; ⏰dinner Mon-Sat) Tables are cheek by jowl at this tiny bohemian restaurant with nothing fancy, just straightforward bistro fare, stews, roasts and other reliably good, homestyle French dishes. Cash only.

ℹ️ Information

Main tourist office (41 cours Jean Jaurès; ⏰ 9am-6pm Mon-Fri, 9am-5pm Sat, 10am-noon Sun Nov-Mar, 9am-6pm Mon-Sat, 10am-5pm Sun Apr-Oct)

ℹ️ Getting There & Away

Avignon has two stations. **Gare Avignon TGV**, 4km southwest in Courtine; and **Gare Avignon Centre** (42 bd St-Roch), with multiple daily services to/from: Arles (€6.50, 20 minutes), Nîmes (€8.50, 30 minutes), Marseille Airport (Vitrolles Station, €16, one to 1½ hours).

Some TGVs to/from Paris (€75, 3½ hours) stop at Gare Avignon Centre, but TGVs to/from Marseille (€29, 35 minutes) and Nice (€52.50, 3¼ hours) only use Gare TGV.

❤️ If You Like…
Artistic
Landmarks

From marvellous art museums to inspirational Impressionists, France is littered with fascinating artistic sights.

1 VAN GOGH TRAIL
(📞tel, info 04 90 18 41 20; www.arlestourism. com; esplanade Charles de Gaulle) If Arles' winding streets seem familiar, it's hardly surprising – Vincent van Gogh lived here for many years, and the town often featured in his canvases. You can follow in Vincent's footsteps on the Van Gogh Trail, marked out by footpath plaques. Frequent trains run from Nîmes, Marseille and Avignon.

2 MAISON ET JARDINS DE CLAUDE MONET
(📞02 32 51 28 21; www.fondation-monet.com; adult/child €9/5; ⏰9.30am-5.30pm Apr-Oct) Monet's former home in the village of Giverny is now the Maison et Jardins de Claude Monet, where you can wander around his house and gardens, complete with lily pond and Japanese bridge. Giverny is 66km southeast of Rouen; you can catch a train, or a combo train-and-bus from Paris' Gare St-Lazare.

3 CÉZANNE SIGHTS
The town of Aix-en-Provence is famous for its connections with local-born Paul Cézanne. You can visit the artist's **studio**, the family's country manor **Le Jas de Bouffan** and a **cabin** the artist rented in 1895. Trains run to Marseille, 12 minutes away.

4 CENTRE POMPIDOU-METZ MUSEUM
(www.centrepompidou-metz.fr; 1 parvis des Droits de l'Homme; adult/child €7/free; ⏰11am-6pm Mon, Wed & Sun, 11am-8pm Thu, Fri & Sat) This architecturally innovative new museum is the satellite branch of Paris' Centre Pompidou, and has become a must-not-miss destination for modern art. It's just outside Metz, 58km north of Nancy.

Around Avignon

CARPENTRAS MARKET

Don't miss **Carpentras**, 25km northeast of Avignon, on a Friday morning when its streets and squares spill over with hundreds of market stalls laden with breads, honeys, cheeses, olives, fruit and a rainbow of *berlingots* (the local striped, pillow-shaped hard-boiled sweet). Late November to March, pungent black-truffle stalls murmur with hushed-tones transactions.

LES BAUX DE PROVENCE

At the heart of the Alpilles, spectacularly perched above picture-perfect rolling hills of vineyards, olive groves and orchards, is the hilltop village of Les Baux de Provence. Van Gogh painted it and if you stroll around the deep dungeons, up crumbling towers and around the maze-like ruins of **Château des Baux** (www.chateau-baux-provence.com; adult/child €7.60/5.70; ⊙9am-6pm Sep-Jun, 9am-8pm Jul & Aug) you'll see why. Lunch afterwards at legendary **L'Oustau de Baumanière** (🕿04 90 54 33 07; www.oustaudebaumaniere.com; menu €95-150; 🔗).

VAISON-LA-ROMAINE

This traditional market town 17km north of Avignon still has a thriving Tuesday-morning market, a delightful cobbled medieval quarter and a rich Roman legacy.

The **Gallo-Roman ruins** (adult/child €8/3.50; ⊙closed Jan-early Feb) of Vasio Vocontiorum, the city that flourished here between the 6th and 2nd centuries BC, fill two central Vaison sites. Two neighbourhoods of this once-opulent city, Puymin (with the still-functioning 6000-seat Théâtre Antique) and La Villasse, lie on either side of the tourist office and l'avénue du Général-de-Gaulle. To make sense of the remains (and gather your audioguide), head for the archaeological museum, which revives Vaison's Roman past with incredible swag – superb mosaics, carved masks, and statues that include a 3rd-century silver bust and marble renderings of Hadrian and wife Sabina.

THE FRENCH RIVIERA & MONACO

With its glistening seas, idyllic beaches and fabulous weather, the French Riviera (Côte d'Azur in French) screams exclusivity, extravagance and excess. It has been a favourite getaway for the European jet set since Victorian times and there is nowhere more chichi or glam in France than St-Tropez, Cannes and super-rich, sovereign Monaco.

Nice

POP 344,460

Riviera queen Nice is what good living is all about – shimmering shores, the very best of Mediterranean food, a unique historical heritage, free museums, a charming Old Town, exceptional art and Alpine wilderness within an hour's drive. To get stuck-in straight away, make a beeline upon arrival for Promenade des Anglais, Nice's curvaceous palm-lined seafront that follows its busy pebble beach for 6km from the city centre to the airport.

◎ Sights

Vieux Nice   Historic Quarter
Ditch the map and get lost in this mellow-hued rabbit warren of 18th-century passages, alleyways, historic churches and hidden squares. **Cours Saleya**, running parallel to the seafront, remains a joyous, thriving market square with one of France's most vibrant **food and flower markets** (⊙food markets 6am-1.30pm Tue-Sun). Rue de la Boucherie and rue Pairolièreare are excellent for food shopping, a daily fish market fills place St François, and baroque aficionados wil fall head over heels in love with architectural gems such as **Cathédrale Ste-Réparate** and the exuberant **Chapelle de la Miséricorde**.

MAMAC   Museum
(Musée d'Art Moderne et d'Art Contemporain; www.mamac-nice.org; promenade des Arts; ⊙10am-6pm Tue-Sun) This ode to contemporary art houses some fantastic avant-garde art from the 1960s to the

GARDEL BERTRAND/HEMIS.FR/GETTY IMAGES ©

present, including iconic pop art from Roy Lichtenstein and Andy Warhol's 1965 *Campbell's Soup Can*. An awesome panorama of Vieux Nice unfolds from its rooftop garden-gallery.

Musée Matisse   Gallery

(www.musee-matisse-nice.org; 164 av des Arènes de Cimiez; ⌚10am-6pm Wed-Mon) FREE About 2km north in the leafy quarter of Cimiez, this museum houses a fascinating assortment of works by Matisse. Its permanent collection is displayed in a red-ochre 17th-century Genoese villa overlooking an olive-tree-studded park. Temporary exhibitions are hosted in the futuristic basement building. The artist is buried in the **Monastère de Cimiez** cemetery, across the park from the museum.

Musée National Marc Chagall   Gallery

(www.musee-chagall.fr; 4 av Dr Ménard; adult/ child €7.50/5.50; ⌚10am-5pm Wed-Mon Oct-Jun, to 6pm Jul-Sep) Discover the largest public collection of works by Belarusian painter Marc Chagall (1887–1985) in this small museum, a 20-minute walk from the centre (signposted from av de l'Olivetto).

Beaches   Beaches

Nice's beaches are all pebbly; sensitive behinds can opt for a comfy mattress at a private beach (€15 to €20 per day). Out of the free public sections of beach, **Plage Publique des Ponchettes**, opposite Vieux Nice, is the most popular.

⚓ Tours

Nice Guided Walking Tours   Walking Tour

The **Centre du Patrimoine** (75 Quai des Etats-Unis; ⌚8.30am-1pm & 2-5pm Mon-Thu, to 3.45pm Fri) runs a two-hour Vieux Nice Baroque tour (Tuesday afternoon), as well as themed tours, including art deco, neoclassical and belle époque Nice. The tourist office (p278) runs a 2½-hour Vieux Nice tour in English (adult/child €12/6) at 9.30am on Saturday.

Trans Côte d'Azur   Boat Tour

(www.trans-cote-azur.com; quai Lunel; ⌚Apr-Oct) Trans Côte d'Azur runs one-hour trips along the Baie des Anges and the Rade de Villefranche (adult/child €16/10) from April to October. From mid-June to mid-September it also runs regular excursions to Île Ste-Marguerite (€35/25,

273

FRANCE NICE

Nice

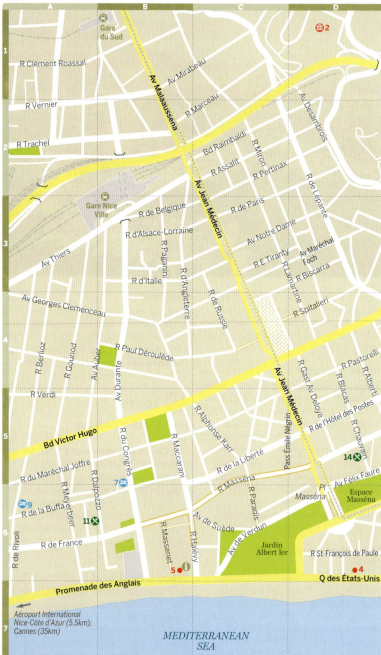

Gare
du Sud

🏛 2

R Clément Roassal

Av Mirabeau

Av Malaussena

R Vernier

R Marceau

R Trachel

Bd Raimbaldi

R Miron

Av Desambrois

R Assalit

R Pertinax

R de Lépante

Av Jean Médecin

R de Paris

Gare Nice
Ville

R de Belgique

Av Notre Dame

R d'Alsace-Lorraine

R E Tiranty

Av Maréchal
Foch

R Paganini

R de Russie

R Lamartine

R Biscarra

Av Thiers

R d'Angleterre

R Spitalieri

R d'Italie

Av Georges Clemenceau

R Paul Déroulède

R Gast Av Deloye

R Pastorelli

R Berlioz

R Gounod

Av Auber

Av Durante

R Blacas

R Alberti

R Verdi

R de l'Hôtel des Postes

R Chauvain

Av Jean Médecin

Pass Émile Négrin

Bd Victor Hugo

R du Congrès

R Alphonse Karr

R Maccarani

14 🍴

R de la Liberté

R du Maréchal Joffre

R Dalpozzo

7 🛏

R Masséna

Av Félix Faure

R Meyerbeer

R Paradis

Pl
Masséna

Espace
Masséna

9 💶

R de la Buffa

11 🍴

Av de Suède

Av de Verdun

R de Rivoli

R de France

R Massenet

R Halévy

Jardin
Albert Ier

R St-François de Paule

5 ● ℹ

● 4

Q des États-Unis

Promenade des Anglais

Aéroport International
Nice-Côte d'Azur (5.5km);
Cannes (35km)

*MEDITERRANEAN
SEA*

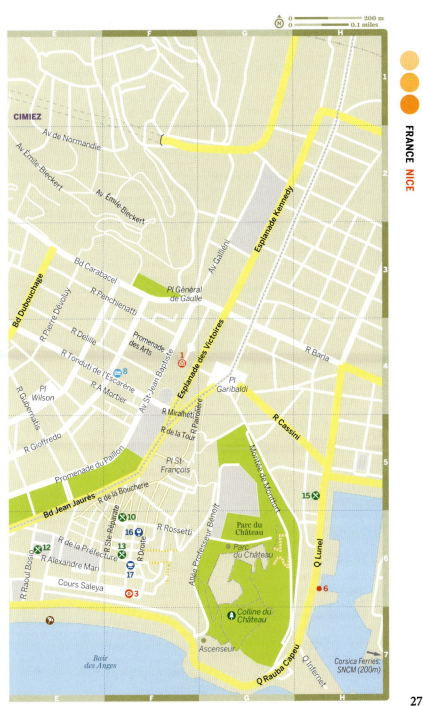

CIMIEZ

Av de Normandie

Av Émile-Bieckert

Av Émile-Bieckert

Bd Dubouchage

Bd Carabacel

R Penchienatti

R Pierre Dévoluy

R Delille

Promenade
des Arts

R Tonduti de l'Escarène

Av St-Jean Baptiste

Pl Général
de Gaulle

Av Galliéni

Esplanade Kennedy

Esplanade des Victoires

R Barla

1

8

R A Mortier

Pl
Wilson

R Gubernatis

R Gioffredo

R Miralhéti

R Paroilière

Pl
Garibaldi

R Cassini

R de la Tour

Promenade du Paillon

Pl St-
François

Montée de Montfort

Bd Jean Jaurès

R de la Boucherie

X 10

Parc du
Château

15 X

R Ste-Réparate

16

R Rossetti

R de la Préfecture

13

R Droite

Allée Professeur Bénoit

Parc
du Château

Q Lunel

X 12

R Raoul Bosio

R Alexandre Mari

17

Cours Saleya

3

6

Colline du
Château

Ascenseur

Baie
des Anges

Q Rauba Capeu

Q Internet

Corsica Ferries;
SNCM (200m)

0   200 m
0   0.1 miles

N

Nice

⦿ Sights
1 MAMAC F4
2 Musée National Marc Chagall D1
3 Vieux Nice F6

⊕ Activities, Courses & Tours
4 Centre du Patrimoine Walking
   Tours D6
5 Nice Guided Walking Tours B6
6 Trans Côte d'Azur H6

Sleeping
7 Nice Garden Hôtel B5
8 Nice Pebbles F4
9 Villa Rivoli A6

⊗ Eating
10 Fenocchio F6
11 La Cave de l'Origine A6
12 La Merenda E6
13 Le Bistrot d'Antoine F6
14 Luna Rossa D5
15 Zucca Magica H5

⊖ Drinking & Nightlife
16 L'Abat-Jour F6
17 Les Distilleries Idéales F6

crossing one hour), St-Tropez (€58/44, crossing 2½ hours) and Monaco (€34/25, crossing 45 minutes). Reservations are essential.

🎊 Festivals & Events

Carnaval de Nice   Carnival
(www.nicecarnaval.com) Held each year around Mardi Gras (Shrove Tuesday) since 1294 – highlights include the *batailles de fleurs* (battles of flowers), and the ceremonial burning of the carnival king on promenade des Anglais, followed by a fireworks display.

Nice Jazz Festival   Music Festival
(www.nicejazzfestival.fr) France's original jazz festival has taken on a life of its own in its new promenade location, with fringe concerts popping up all around the venue, from Vieux Nice to Massena and the shopping streets around Rue de France.

🛏 Sleeping

Nice Garden Hôtel   Boutique Hotel €€
(☎ 04 93 87 35 63; www.nicegardenhotel.com; 11 rue du Congrès; s/d €75/100; ❄ 🛜) Heavy iron gates hide this gem. Nine rooms are a subtle blend of old and new, and overlook a delightful garden with orange tree. Amazingly, all this charm and peacefulness is just two blocks from the promenade.

Nice Pebbles   Self-Contained €€
(☎ 04 97 20 27 30; www.nicepebbles.com; 23 rue Gioffredo; 1-/3-bedroom apt from €105/320; 🛜 ▨) The concept is simple: the quality of a four-star boutique hotel in holiday flats.

  Apartments (one to three bedrooms) are equipped with flat-screen TV, kitchen, linen bedding and, in some cases, wi-fi, swimming pool, balcony etc and come with a useful starter pack (no need to rush to the supermarket). Nightly rates significantly cheaper during low season.

Villa Rivoli   Boutique Hotel €€
(☎ 04 93 88 80 25; www.villa-rivoli.com; 10 rue de Rivoli; s/d/q from 85/99/210; ❄ 🛜) Built in 1890, this stately villa feels like your own *pied-à-terre* in the heart of Nice. Take breakfast in the garden's sun-dappled shade, or in the grand belle époque salon.

🍴 Eating

Niçois nibbles include *socca* (a thin layer of chickpea flour and olive oil batter), *salade niçoise* and *farcis* (stuffed vegetables). Restaurants in Vieux Nice are a mixed bag, so choose carefully.

Le Bistrot d'Antoine   Modern French €€
(☎ 04 93 85 29 57; 27 rue de la Préfecture; mains €13-18; ⊙lunch & dinner Tue-Sat) This brasserie is full every night (booking essential), yet the 'bistro chic' cuisine never wavers, the staff are cool as cucumbers, the atmosphere is reliably jovial and the prices incredibly good value.

Luna Rossa
Italian €€

(📞 04 93 85 55 66; www.lelunarossa.com; 3 rue Chauvain; mains €15-25; 🕐 Tue-Fri, dinner Sat) Luna Rossa is like your dream Mediterranean dinner come true: fresh pasta, exquisitely cooked seafood, sun-kissed vegetables and divine meats.

Fenocchio
Ice Cream €

(2 place Rossetti; ice cream from €2; 🕐 9am-midnight Feb-Oct) Eschew predictable favourites and indulge in a new taste sensation: black olive, tomato-basil, avocado, rosemary, or lavender.

La Cave de l'Origine
Modern French €€

(📞 04 83 50 09 60; 3 rue Dalpozzo; mains €15-22; 🕐 lunch & dinner Tue-Sat) This sleek new wine bar–restaurant has as much substance as style: great selection of wines by the glass, many local, and fantastic advice about what to pair with your food (well-executed, modern French fare with a touch of fusion).

La Merenda
Niçois €€

(4 rue Raoul Bosio; mains €12-15; 🕐 Mon-Fri) Simple, solid Niçois cuisine by former Michelin-starred chef Dominique Le Stanc draws the crowds to this pocket-sized bistro. No credit cards.

Zucca Magica
Vegetarian €€

(📞 04 93 56 25 27; www.lazuccamagica.com; 4bis quai Papacino; menu €30; 🕐 Tue-Sat; 🍴) The Magic Pumpkin serves a fixed five-course menu, dictated simply by the market and the chef's fancy. Seating is amid a fabulous collection of pumpkins and fairy lights.

🍷 Drinking & Nightlife

Les Distilleries Idéales
Cafe

(24 rue de la Préfecture; 🕐 9am-12.30am) Whether you're after an espresso on your way to the cours Saleya market or an *apéritif* (complete with cheese and *charcuterie* platters, €5.20) before trying out one of Nice's fabulous restaurants, Les Distilleries is one of the most atmospheric bars in town.

L'Abat-Jour
Bar

(25 rue Benoît Bunico) With its vintage furniture, rotating art exhibitions and alternative music, l'Abat-Jour is all the rage with Nice's young and trendy crowd. The basement has live music or DJ sessions.

Nice's main beach (p273)

The Corniches

Some of the Riviera's most spectacular scenery stretches east between Nice and Monaco. A trio of *corniches* (coastal roads) hugs the cliffs between the two seaside cities, each higher up the hill than the last. The middle *corniche* ends in Monaco; the upper and lower continue to Menton near the French–Italian border.

ℹ Information

Tourist office (☎ 08 92 70 74 07; www. nicetourisme.com; 5 promenade des Anglais; ⏰ 9am-6pm Mon-Sat)

ℹ Getting There & Away

Air

Nice-Côte d'Azur airport is 6km west of Nice, by the sea. A taxi to Nice centre costs around €25.

Buses 98 and 99 link the airport terminal with Nice Gare Routière and Nice train station (€4, 35 minutes, every 20 minutes). Bus 110 (€18, hourly) links the airport with Monaco (40 minutes).

Boat

Nice is the main port for ferries to Corsica. **SNCM** (www.sncm.fr; quai du Commerce, ferry terminal) and **Corsica Ferries** (www.corsicaferries.com; quai Lunel) are the two main companies.

Train

From **Gare Nice Ville** (av Thiers), 1.2km north of the beach, there are frequent services to Cannes (€6.40, 40 minutes) and Monaco (€3.60, 20 minutes).

....

Cannes

POP 74,445

Most have heard of Cannes and its celebrity film festival. The latter only lasts for two weeks in May, but the buzz and glitz linger all year thanks to regular visits from celebrities who come here to indulge in designer shopping, beaches and the palace hotels of the Riviera's glammest seafront, blvd de la Croisette.

◎ Sights & Activities

La Croisette   Architecture
The multi-starred hotels and couture shops that line the famous bd de la Croisette (aka La Croisette) may be the preserve of the rich and famous, but anyone can enjoy the palm-shaded promenade and take in the atmosphere. In fact, it's a favourite amongst Cannois (natives of Cannes), particularly at night when it's lit with bright colours.

Climb the red carpet, walk down the auditorium, tread the stage and learn about cinema's most glamorous event and its numerous anecdotes on a **Palais des Festivals guided tour** (adult/child €3/ free; ⏰ 1½ hr); tickets can only be booked in person at the tourist office.

Le Suquet   Historic Quarter
Cannes' historic quarter, pre-dating the glitz and glam of the town's festival days, retains a quaint village feel with its steep, meandering alleyways.

Îles de Lérins   Islands
Although just 20 minutes away by boat, these tranquil islands feel far from the madding crowd. **Île Ste-Marguerite**, where the mysterious Man in the Iron Mask was incarcerated during the late 17th century, is known for its bone-white beaches, eucalyptus groves and small marine museum. Tiny **Île St-Honorat** has been a monastery since the 5th century. Boats leave Cannes from quai des Îles on the western side of the harbour.

Beaches   Beaches
Cannes is blessed with sandy beaches although much of bd de la Croisette is taken up by private beaches (open to all). This arrangement leaves only a small strip of free sand near the Palais des Festivals for the bathing hoi polloi; the much bigger **Plage du Midi** (bd Jean Hibert) and **Plage de la Bocca**, west from Vieux Port, are also free.

🛏 Sleeping

Hôtel Le Canberra
Boutique Hotel €€€

(☎04 97 06 95 00; www.hotel-cannes-canberra.com; 120 rue d'Antibes; d from €255; ❄@🛜⛹) This boutique stunner, just a couple of blocks back from La Croisette, is the epitome of Cannes glamour: designer grey rooms with splashes of candy pink, sexy black-marble bathrooms with coloured lighting, heated pool (April to October) in a bamboo-filled garden, intimate atmosphere (there are just 35 rooms) and impeccable service.

Hôtel 7e Art
Boutique Hotel €

(☎04 93 68 66 66; www.7arthotel.com; 23 rue Maréchal Joffre; s €68, d €60-98; ❄🛜) Hôtel 7e Art has put boutique style within reach of budgeters. The snappy design of putty-coloured walls, padded headboards and pop art, and perks like iPod docks in every room, far exceed what you'd expect at this price.

Hôtel Le Mistral
Boutique Hotel €€

(☎04 93 39 91 46; www.mistral-hotel.com; 13 rue des Belges; d from €89; ❄🛜) This small bou-tique hotel wins the *palme d'or* for best value in town: rooms are decked out in flattering red and plum tones, bathrooms feature lovely designer fittings, there are seaviews from the top floor and the hotel is a mere 50m from La Croisette.

🍴 Eating

Sea Sens
Fusion €€€

(☎04 63 36 05 06; www.five-hotel-cannes.com; Five Hotel & Spa, 1 rue Notre Dame; 2-/3-course lunch menu €29/39, mains €26-55; 🛜🍴) Run by the brilliant Pourcel brothers, Cannes' latest food sensation serves divine food blending French gastronomy and Asian elegance, with panoramic views of Le Suquet and Cannes' rooftops on the side. Come here for lunch to make the best of the great-value menus.

Mantel
Modern European €€

(☎04 93 39 13 10; www.restaurantmantel.com; 22 rue St-Antoine; menu €25-38; 🕑lunch Fri-Mon, dinner Mon & Tue, Thu-Sun) Discover why Noël Mantel is the hotshot of the Cannois gastronomic scene at his refined old-town restaurant. Best of all, you get not one but two desserts from pastry-chef wonder

Carnaval de Nice (p276), Nice

HUGHES HERVÁC/HEMIS.FR/GETTY IMAGES ©

Detour:
Grasse

Mosey some 20km northwest of Cannes to inhale the sweet smell of lavender, jasmine, mimosa and orange-blossom fields. In **Grasse**, one of France's leading perfume producers, dozens of perfumeries create essences to sell to factories (for aromatically enhanced foodstuffs and soaps) as well as to prestigious couture houses – the highly trained noses of local perfume-makers can identify 3000 scents in a single whiff.

Learn about three millennia of perfume-making at the **Musée International de la Parfumerie** (MIP; www.museesdegrasse.com; 2 bd du Jeu de Ballon; adult/child €3/free; ⏱11am-6pm Wed-Mon; 👫) and watch the process first-hand during a guided tour at **Fragonard** (www.fragonard.com; 20 bd Fragonard; ⏱9am-6pm Feb-Oct, 9am-12.30pm & 2-6pm Nov-Jan) perfumery, the easiest to reach by foot.

Christian Gonthier, who bakes the bread, and prepares the sweets served with coffee.

ℹ️ Information

Tourist office (☎04 92 99 84 22; www.cannes.travel; Palais des Festivals, bd de la Croisette; ⏱9am-7pm)

ℹ️ Getting There & Away
Train
From Cannes train station there are at least hourly services to/from:

Antibes €2.70, 12 minutes

Monaco €8.70, one hour

Marseille €28.40, two hours

Nice €6.40, 40 minutes

St-Tropez
POP 4986

In the soft autumn or winter light, it's hard to believe the pretty terracotta fishing village of St-Tropez is a stop on the Riviera celebrity circuit. It seems far removed from its glitzy siblings further up the coast, but come spring or summer, it's a different world: the population increases tenfold, prices triple and fun-seekers pile in to party till dawn, strut around the luxury-yacht-packed Vieux Port and enjoy the creature comforts of exclusive A-listers' beaches in the Baie de Pampelonne.

🎯 Sights

Musée de l'Annonciade   Museum
(place Grammont; adult/child €6/4; ⏱10am-noon & 2-6pm Wed-Mon Oct & Dec-May, 10am-noon & 3-7pm Wed-Mon Jun-Sep) Pointillist Paul Signac bought a house in St-Tropez in 1892 and introduced others to the area. The museum's collection includes his *St-Tropez, Le Quai* (1899) and *St-Tropez, Coucher de Soleil au Bois de Pins* (1896), which hangs juxtaposed with a window-view of contemporary St-Tropez.

Plage de Pampelonne   Beach
The golden sands of **Plage de Tahiti**, 4km southeast of town, morph into the 5km-long, celebrity-studded **Plage de Pampelonne**, which sports a line-up of exclusive beach restaurants and clubs in summer. The bus to Ramatuelle stops at various points along a road, 1km inland from the beach.

Citadelle de St-Tropez   Historic Site
(admission €2.50; ⏱10am-6.30pm) Built in 1602 to defend the coast against Spain, the citadel dominates the hillside overlooking St-Tropez to the east. The views (and peacocks!) are fantastic.

🛏️ Sleeping

Hôtel Lou Cagnard   Pension €€
(☎04 94 97 04 24; www.hotel-lou-cagnard.com; 18 av Paul Roussel; d €75-156; ⏱Jan-Oct; ❄️📶) Book well ahead for this great-value courtyard charmer, shaded by lemon

and fig trees. This pretty Provençal house with lavender shutters has its very own jasmine-scented garden, strung with fairy lights at night. The cheapest rooms have private washbasin and standup-bathtub but share a toilet, 15 of the 19 rooms have air-con.

Pastis   Hotel €€€

(04 98 12 56 50; www.pastis-st-tropez.com; 61 av du Général Leclerc; d from €200; ✻ ☀) This stunning townhouse-turned-hotel is the brainchild of an English couple besotted with Provence and passionate about modern art. You'll die for the pop-art-inspired interior, and long for a swim in the emerald-green pool.

✗ Eating

One of southern France's busiest and best, St-Tropez's **place des Lices market** (◷ mornings Tue & Sat) is a highlight of local life, with colourful stalls groaning under the weight of plump fruit and veg, mounds of olives, local cheeses, chestnut purée and fragrant herbs. Afterwards meander to the port and duck beneath the stone arch to the bijou **fish market** (◷ mornings Tue-Sun, daily summer), hidden between stone walls on place aux Herbes.

Auberge de l'Oumède   Provençal €€€

(04 94 44 11 11; www.aubergede-loumede.com; Chemin de l'Oumède; mains €39-59, d from €225; ◷ dinner Tue-Sat May–mid-Sep, dinner daily Jul & Aug; ✻ ☏) Epicureans come from far and wide to sample Jean-Pierre Frezia's Provençal cuisine served in a sea of vineyards. Dining at this isolated *bastide* down a single-lane track is indeed a rare treat. It has seven

rooms and a pool – handy should you really not want to leave.

Auberge des Maures   Provençal €€

(04 94 97 01 50; 4 rue du Docteur Boutin; mains €31-39; ◷ dinner) The town's oldest restaurant remains the locals' choice for always-good, copious portions of earthy Provençal cooking, like *daube* (a Provençal beef stew) or tapenade-stuffed lamb shoulder. Book a table (essential) on the leafy courtyard.

ℹ Information

Tourist office (04 94 97 45 21; www.ot-saint-tropez.com; quai Jean Jaurès; ◷ 9.30am-8pm Jul & Aug, 9.30am-12.30pm & 2-7pm Apr-Jun & Sep–mid-Oct, 9.30am-12.30pm & 2-6pm mid-Oct–Mar)

ℹ Getting There & Away

From the **bus station** (04 94 56 25 74; av du Général de Gaulle), buses run by **VarLib** (www.varlib.fr) serve Ramatuelle (€2, 35 minutes) and St-Raphaël train station (€2, 1¼ hours) via Grimaud, Port Grimaud and Fréjus. There are four daily buses to Toulon-Hyères airport (€15, 1½ hours).

Le Suquet disctict (p278), Cannes
MOIRENC CAMILLE/HEMIS.FR/GETTY IMAGES ©

Monaco

📱377 / POP 32,350

Your first glimpse of this pocket-sized principality will probably make your heart sink: after all the gorgeous medieval hilltop villages, glittering beaches and secluded peninsulas of the surrounding area, Monaco's concrete high-rises and astronomic prices come as a shock.

But Monaco is beguiling. The world's second-smallest state (a smidgen bigger than the Vatican), it is as famous for its tax-haven status as for its glittering casino, sports scene (Formula One, world-famous circus festival and tennis open) and a royal family on a par with British royals for best gossip fodder.

In terms of practicalities, Monaco is a sovereign state but has no border control. It has its own flag (red and white), national holiday (19 November) and telephone country code (377), but the official language is French and the country uses the euro even though it is not part of the European Union.

Most visit Monaco as a day trip from Nice, a 20-minute train ride away.

◎ Sights

Casino de Monte Carlo Casino
(www.casinomontecarlo.com; place du Casino; ⏱European Rooms from noon Sat & Sun, from 2pm Mon-Fri) Living out your James Bond fantasies just doesn't get any better than at Monte Carlo's monumental, richly decorated showpiece, the 1910-built casino. The jacket-and-tie dress code kicks in after 8pm. Minimum entry age for both rooms is 18; bring photo ID.

Musée Océanographique de Monaco Aquarium
(www.oceano.org; av St-Martin; adult/child €13/6.50; ⏱9.30am-7pm) Stuck dramatically to the edge of a cliff since 1910, the world-renowned Musée Océanographique de Monaco, founded by Prince Albert I (1848–1922), is a stunner. Its centrepiece is its **aquarium**, with a 6m-deep **lagoon** where sharks and marine predators are separated from colourful tropical fish by a coral reef.

Le Rocher Historic Quarter
Monaco Ville, also called Le Rocher, thrusts skywards on a pistol-shaped rock. Built as

Casino de Monte Carlo, Monaco

HANS-PETER MERTEN/GETTY IMAGES ©

Corsica

The rugged island of Corsica (Corse in French) is officially a part of France, but remains fiercely proud of its own culture, history and language. It's one of the Mediterranean's most dramatic islands, with a bevy of beautiful beaches, glitzy ports and a mountainous, maquis-covered interior to explore, as well as a wild, independent spirit all of its own.

The island has long had a love-hate relationship with the mother mainland – you'll see plenty of anti-French slogans and 'Corsicanised' road signs – but that doesn't seem to deter the millions of French tourists who descend on the island every summer. Prices skyrocket and accommodation is at a premium during the peak season between July and August, so you're much better off saving your visit for spring and autumn.

Regular flights and ferries cross from Marseille and Nice to Corsica's main towns, Ajaccio and Bastia. For ferry schedules, see SNCM (www.sncm.fr). Air France (www.airfrance.com) has the most frequent flights, but other budget carriers including Easyjet also serve the island.

a fortress in the 13th century, the **palace** is now the private residence of the Grimaldis. It is protected by the Carabiniers du Prince; **changing of the guard** takes place daily at 11.55am.

For a glimpse into royal life, you can tour the state apartments inside the **Palais du Prince** (www.palais.mc; adult/child €8/3.50; ☉10am-6pm Apr-Sep) with an audioguide; rooms are what you would expect of any aristocratic abode – lavish furnishings and expensive 18th- and 19th-century art.

Cathédrale de Monaco   Cathedral
(4 rue Colonel) An adoring crowd continually shuffles past Prince Rainier's and Princess Grace's graves, located inside the cathedral choir of the 1875 Romanesque-Byzantine Cathédrale de Monaco.

🎊 Festivals & Events

Formula One Grand Prix   Sports
(Automobile Club de Monaco; www.formula1 monaco.com; ☉late May) One of Formula One's most iconic races. If you're dead keen, you can walk the 3.2km circuit; the tourist office has maps.

🍴 Eating & Drinking

La Montgolfière   Fusion €€
(☎97 98 61 59; www.lamontgolfiere.mc; 16 rue Basse; mains €21-30; ☉lunch & dinner Mon, Tue, Thu, Fri & Sun, dinner Sat) This tiny fusion wonder is an unlikely find amid the touristy jumble of Monaco's historic quarter. Henri and Fabienne Geraci had a great idea to breathe new life into the Rocher. They have spent a lot of time in Malaysia, and Henri's fusion cuisine is outstanding, as is Fabienne's welcome in the pocket-sized dining room.

Zelo's   Fusion €€
(☎99 99 25 50; 10 av Princesse Grace, Grimaldi Forum; mains €25-30; ☉dinner) With enormous chandeliers, intensely blue walls, a ceiling fitted with hundreds of star-like lights and uninterrupted sea views, it's hard to say which makes more of an impression, the setting or the food (modern dishes such as a trio of Carpaccio – sea bass, king crab and salmon). The restaurant also has a huge terrace for magical summer dining.

Café Llorca   Modern French €€
(☎99 99 29 29; www.cafellorca.mc; 10 av Princesse Grace, Grimaldi Forum; mains €15-26;

Monte Carlo Casino

Timeline

1863 Charles III inaugurates the first Casino on the Plateau des Spélugues. **The atrium** is a room with a wooden platform from which an orchestra 'enlivens' the gambling.

1864 Hôtel de Paris opens and the area becomes known as the 'Golden Square'.

1865 Construction of **Salon Europe** ❷. Cathedral-like, it is lined with onyx columns and lit by eight Bohemian crystal chandeliers weighing 150kg each.

1868 The steam train arrives in Monaco and **Café de Paris** ❸ is completed.

1878–79 Gambling moves to Hôtel de Paris while Charles Garnier is charged with building a new casino with a miniature replica of the Paris Opera House, **Salle Garnier** ❹.

1890 The advent of electricity casts a glow on architect Jules Touzet's newly added **gaming rooms** ❺ for high rollers.

1903 Inspired by female gamblers, Henri Schmit decorates **Salle Blanche** ❻ with caryatids and the painting *Les Grâces Florentines*.

1904 Smoking is banned in the gaming rooms and **Salon Rose** ❼, a new smoking room, is added.

1910 **Salle Médecin** ❽, immense and grand, hosts the high-spending Private Circle.

1966 Celebrations mark 100 years of uninterrupted gambling despite two world wars.

TOP TIPS

Bring photo ID

Jackets are required in the private gaming rooms, and after 8pm

The cashier will exchange any currency

In the main room, the minimum bet is €5, the maximum €2000

In the Salons Privés, the minimum bet is €10, with no maximum

Salle Blanche

Transformed into a superb bar-lounge in 2012, the Salle Blanche opens onto an outdoor gaming terrace, a must on balmy evenings. The caryatids on the ceiling were modelled on fashionable courtesans like La Belle Otero, who placed her first bet here aged 18.

Salon Rose

Smoking was banned in the gaming rooms after a fraud involving a croupier letting his ash fall on the floor. The gaze of Gallelli's famous cigarillo-smoking nudes are said to follow you around the room, now a restaurant.

Hôtel de Paris

Notice the horse's shiny leg (and testicles) on the lobby's statue of Louis XIV on horseback. Legend has it that rubbing them brings good luck in the casino.

Hôtel de Paris

Salle Garnier

Taking eight months to build and two years to restore (2004–06), the opera's original statuary is rehabilitated using original moulds saved by the creator's grandson. Individual air-con and heating vents are installed beneath each of the 525 seats.

Atrium

The casino's 'lobby', so to speak, is paved in marble and lined with 28 Ionic columns, which support a balustraded gallery canopied with an engraved glass ceiling.

BONNEMAISON JOACHIM ®

Salon Europe

The oldest part of the casino, where they continue to play *trente-et-quarante* and European roulette, which have been played here since 1863. Tip: the bull's-eye windows around the room originally served as security observation points.

COTE D'AZUR/ALAMY ®

Café de Paris

With the arrival of Diaghilev as director of the Monte Carlo Opera in 1911, Café de Paris becomes the go-to address for artists and gamblers. It retains the same high-glamour ambience today. Tip: snag a seat on the terrace and people-watch.

Jardins et Terrasses du Casino

3

Place du Casino

1

2

5

4

7

8

6

Salles Touzet

This vast partitioned hall, 21m by 24m, is decorated in the most lavish style: oak, Tonkin mahogany and oriental jasper panelling are offset by vast canvases, Marseille bronzes, Italian mosaics, sculptural reliefs and stained-glass windows.

Terraces, gardens & walkways

Hexagrace mosaic

Fairmont Monte Carlo

Best Views

Wander behind the casino through manicured gardens and gaze across Victor Vasarely's vibrant op-art mosaic, *Hexagrace*, to views of the harbour and the sea.

Salle Médecin

Also known as Salle Empire because of its extravagant Empire-style decor, Monégasque architect François Médecin's gaming room was originally intended for the casino's biggest gamblers. Part of it still remains hidden from prying eyes as a Super Privé room.

lunch) This new restaurant is Michelin-starred-chef Alain Llorca's version of a traditional cafe: the menu is classic French fare (pork loin with sautéed potatoes; *daube*, a local beef stew) but elevated to new heights in taste and presentation. In summer, tables are set out on the terrace overlooking the sea.

Brasserie de Monaco Microbrewery
(www.brasseriedemonaco.com; 36 rte de la Piscine; 11am-1pm Sun-Thu, 11am-3am Fri & Sat) Tourists and locals rub shoulders at Monaco's only microbrewery, which crafts rich organic ales and lager, and serves tasty (if pricey) antipasti plates. Happy hour is 5pm to 8pm.

ℹ Information

Telephone

Calls between Monaco and France are international calls. Dial 📞00 followed by Monaco's country code (📞377) when calling Monaco from France or elsewhere abroad. To phone France from Monaco, dial 📞00 and France's country code (📞33).

Tourist information

Tourist office (www.visitmonaco.com; 2a blvd des Moulins; 9am-7pm Mon-Sat, 11am-1pm Sun)

ℹ Getting There & Away

Monaco's **train station** (av Prince Pierre) has frequent trains to Nice (€3.60, 20 minutes), and east to Menton (€2, 10 minutes) and beyond into Italy.

SURVIVAL GUIDE

ℹ Directory A–Z

Accommodation

France has accommodation to suit every taste, pocket and mood.

- Budget covers everything from bare-bones hostels to simple family-run places; midrange means a few extra creature comforts such as satellite TV, air-conditioning and free wi-fi; while top-end places stretch from luxury five-star chains with the mod cons and swimming pools to boutique-chic chalets in the Alps.

- Many tourist offices make room reservations, often for a fee of €5, but many only do so if you stop by in person.

- French hotels almost never include breakfast in their advertised nightly rates.

Price Ranges

Our reviews refer to the cost of a double room with private bathroom, except in hostels or where otherwise specified. Quoted rates are for high season, which is July and August in southern France (Provence and the French Riviera, Languedoc-Roussilon, Corsica) and December to March in the French Alps.

€ less than €80 (€110 in Paris)

€€ €80 to €180 (€110 to €200 in Paris)

€€€ more than €180 (€200 in Paris)

Aerial view of Paris (p184)

Standard Opening Hours

BUSINESS	OPENING HOURS
Bank	9am-noon & 2-5pm Mon-Fri or Tue-Sat
Bar	7pm-1am Mon-Sat
Cafe	7am or 8am-10pm or 11pm Mon-Sat
Nightclub	10pm-3am, 4am or 5am Thu-Sat
Post office	8.30am or 9am-5pm or 6pm Mon-Fri, 8am-noon Sat
Restaurant	lunch noon-2.30pm (or 3pm in Paris), dinner 7-11pm (until 10pm to midnight in Paris) six days a week
Shop	9am or 10am-7pm Mon-Sat (often with lunch break noon-1.30pm)
Supermarket	8.30am-7pm Mon-Sat, 8.30am-12.30pm Sun

Business Hours

○ French business hours are regulated by a maze of government regulations, including the 35-hour working week.

○ The midday break is uncommon in Paris but, in general, gets longer the further south you go.

○ French law requires most businesses to close Sunday; exceptions include grocery stores, boulangeries, florists and businesses catering to the tourist trade.

○ In many places shops close on Monday.

○ Restaurants generally close one or two days of the week.

○ Most (but not all) national museums are closed on Tuesday, while most local museums are closed on Monday, though in summer some open daily. Some museums close for lunch.

Food

Price ranges refer to a two-course meal:

€ less than €20

€€ €20 to €40

€€€ more than €40

Gay & Lesbian Travellers

Gay mayors (including Paris' very own Bertrand Delanoë), artists and film directors, camper-than-camp fashion designers...the rainbow flag flies high in France, one of Europe's most liberal countries when it comes to homosexuality.

○ Major gay and lesbian organisations are based in Paris.

○ Bordeaux, Lille, Lyon, Toulouse and many other towns have active communities.

○ Attitudes towards homosexuality tend to be more conservative in the countryside and villages.

Money

Credit and debit cards are accepted almost everywhere in France.

○ Some places (eg 24hr petrol stations and some autoroute toll machines) only take credit cards with chips and PINs.

○ In Paris and major cities, bureaux de change (exchange bureaux) are fast, easy, open longer hours and offer competitive exchange rates.

Public Holidays

New Year's Day (Jour de l'An) 1 January

Easter Sunday & Monday (Pâques & lundi de Pâques) March or April

May Day (Fête du Travail) 1 May – traditional parades.

Victoire 1945 8 May – commemorates the Allied victory in Europe that ended WWII.

Ascension Thursday (Ascension) May – celebrated on the 40th day after Easter.

Pentecost/Whit Sunday & Whit Monday (Pentecôte & lundi de Pentecôte) Mid-May to mid-June – celebrated on the seventh Sunday after Easter.

Bastille Day/National Day (Fête Nationale) 14 July – the national holiday.

Assumption Day (Assomption) 15 August

All Saints' Day (Toussaint) 1 November

Remembrance Day (L'onze novembre) 11 November – marks the WWI armistice.

Christmas (Noël) 25 December

Telephone
Mobile Phones

French mobile phones numbers begin with 06 or 07.

- France uses GSM 900/1800, compatible with the rest of Europe and Australia but not with the North American GSM 1900 or the totally different system in Japan (though some North Americans have tri-band phones that work here).

- It's usually cheaper to buy your own French SIM card (€20 to €30) sold at ubiquitous outlets run by France's three mobile phone companies, **Bouygues** (www.bouyguestelecom.fr), France Telecom's **Orange** (www.orange.com) and **SFR** (www.sfr.com).

- Recharge cards are sold at *tabacs* (tobacconists) and newsagents; domestic prepaid calls cost about €0.50 per minute.

Phone Codes

Calling France from abroad Dial your country's international access code, ☎33 (France's country code), and the 10-digit local number *without* the initial 0.

Calling internationally from France Dial ☎00 (the international access code), the country code, area code (without the initial zero if there is one) and local number.

Directory inquiries For France Telecom's *service des renseignements* (directory inquiries), dial ☎11 87 12 or use the online service for free www.118712.fr.

International directory inquiries For numbers outside France, dial ☎11 87 00.

Emergency number ☎112, can be dialled from public phones without a phonecard.

Toilets

- Public toilets, signposted WC or *toilettes,* are not always plentiful in France.

- Love them (sci-fi geek) or loathe them (claustrophobe), France has its fair share of 24hr self-cleaning toilets, €0.50 in Paris and free elsewhere.

- Some older cafes and restaurants still have the hole-in-the-floor squat toilets.

- The French are blasé about unisex toilets; save your blushes when tiptoeing past the urinals to reach the loo.

Visas

- EU nationals and citizens of Iceland, Norway and Switzerland need only a passport or national identity card to enter France and stay in the country, even for stays of over 90 days.

- Citizens of Australia, the USA, Canada Israel, Hong Kong, Japan, Malaysia, New Zealand, Singapore, South, Korea and many Latin American countries do not need visas to visit France as tourists for up to 90 days.

- Other people wishing to come to France as tourists have to apply for a **Schengen Visa**.

ⓘ Getting There & Away
Entering the Country

Entering France from other parts of the EU should be a breeze – no border checkpoints or customs thanks to Schengen Agreements signed by all of France's neighbours except the UK, the Channel Islands and Andorra.

Major Airports

Aéroport de Bordeaux (www.bordeaux.aeroport.fr)

Aéroport Lyon-Saint Exupéry (www.lyonaeroports.com)

Aéroport Marseille-Provence (www.marseille.aeroport.fr)

Aéroport Nice Côte d'Azur (http://societe.nice.aeroport.fr)

Paris Charles de Gaulle (CDG; www.aeroportsdeparis.fr)

Paris Orly (ORY; www.aeroportsdeparis.fr)

Land
Car & Motorcycle

A right-hand-drive vehicle brought to France from the UK or Ireland must have deflectors affixed to the headlights to avoid dazzling oncoming traffic.

Departing from the UK, **Eurotunnel Le Shuttle** (www.eurotunnel.com) trains whisk bicycles, motorcycles, cars and coaches in 35 minutes from Folkestone through the Channel Tunnel to Coquelles, 5km southwest of Calais. The earlier you book, the less you pay. Fares for a car, including up to nine passengers, start at UK£30.

RICHARD I'ANSON/GETTY IMAGES ©

Train

Rail services – including a dwindling number of overnight services to/from Spain, Italy and Germany – link France with virtually every country in Europe. Book tickets and get train information from **Rail Europe** (www.raileurope.com). In France ticketing is handled by **SNCF** (📞 from abroad +33 8 92 35 35 35, in France 36 35; www.sncf.com); internet bookings are possible but they won't post tickets outside France.

High-speed train travel between France and the UK, Belgium, the Netherlands, Germany and Austria is covered by **Railteam** (www.railteam.co.uk) and **TGV-Europe** (www.tgv-europe.com). **Eurostar** (📞 in France 08 92 35 35 39, in UK 08432 186 186; www.eurostar.com) runs from London St Pancras station to Paris Gare du Nord in 2¼ hours, with easy onward connections available to destinations all over France. Ski trains connecting England with the French Alps run weekends mid-December to mid-April.

Sea

Regular ferries travel to France from Italy, the UK, Channel Islands and Ireland. Several ferry companies ply the waters between Corsica and Italy.

🛈 Getting Around

Air

Air France (www.airfrance.com) and its subsidiaries **Brit Air** (www.britair.fr) and **Régional** (📞 36 54; www.regional.com) control the lion's share of France's long-protected domestic airline industry.

Budget carriers offering flights within France include **EasyJet** (www.easyjet.com), **Airlinair** (www.airlinair.com), **Twin Jet** (www.twinjet.net) and **Air Corsica** (www.aircorsica.com).

Bus

You're nearly always better off travelling by train in France if possible, as the SNCF domestic railway system is heavily subsidised by the government and is much more reliable than local bus companies. Nevertheless, buses are widely used for short-distance travel within *départements*, especially in rural areas with relatively few train lines (eg Brittany and Normandy).

Bicycle

Most French cities and towns have at least one bike shop that rents out mountain bikes (VTT; around €15 a day), road bikes (VTCs) and cheaper city bikes. You have to leave ID and/or a deposit (often a credit-card slip) that you forfeit if the bike is damaged or stolen. A growing number of cities have automatic bike rental systems.

Car & Motorcycle

Bringing Your Own Vehicle

All foreign motor vehicles entering France must display a sticker or licence plate identifying its country of registration. If you're bringing a right-hand-drive vehicle remember to fix deflectors on your headlights to avoid dazzling oncoming traffic.

Driving Licence & Documents

All drivers must carry a national ID card or passport; a valid driving licence (*permis de conduire;* most foreign licences can be used in France for up to a year); car-ownership papers, known as a *carte grise* (grey card); and proof of third party (liability) insurance.

Fuel & Tolls

Essence (petrol), also known as *carburant* (fuel), costs around €1.45/L for 95 unleaded (Sans Plomb 95 or SP95, usually available from a green pump), and €1.30 for diesel (*diesel, gazole* or *gasoil,* usually available from a yellow pump).

Many French motorways (*autoroutes*) are fitted with toll (*péage*) stations that charge a fee based on the distance you've travelled; factor in these costs when driving.

Hire

To hire a car you'll usually need to be over 21 and in possession of a valid driving licence and a credit card. Auto transmissions are *very* rare in France; you'll need to order one well in advance.

Insurance

Unlimited third-party liability insurance is mandatory in France. Third-party liability insurance is provided by car-rental companies, but collision-damage waivers (CDW) vary between companies. When comparing rates check the *franchise* (excess). Your credit card may cover CDW if you use it to pay for the car rental.

Road Rules

Cars drive on the right in France. Speed limits on French roads are as follows:

- 50km/h in built-up areas
- 90km/h (80km/h if it's raining) on N and D highways
- 110km/h (100km/h if it's raining) on dual carriageways
- 130km/h (110km/h if it's raining) on *autoroutes*

Child-seat rules:

- Children under 10 are not permitted to ride in the front seat (unless the back is already occupied by other children under 10).
- A child under 13kg must travel in a backward-facing child seat (permitted in the front seat only for babies under 9kg and if the airbag is deactivated).
- Up to age 10 and/or a minimum height of 140cm, children must use a size-appropriate type of front-facing child seat or booster.

Other key rules of the road:

- Blood-alcohol limit is 0.05% (0.5g per litre of blood) – the equivalent of two glasses of wine for a 75kg adult. Police often conduct random breathalyser tests and penalties can be severe, including imprisonment.
- Mobile phones may be used only if they are equipped with a hands-free kit or speakerphone.

Bir Hakeim metro station, Paris
JULIAN ELLIOTT ETHEREAL LIGHT/GETTY IMAGES ©

- All passengers must wear seatbelts.
- All vehicles must carry a reflective safety jacket (stored inside the car, not the trunk/ boot), a reflective triangle, and a portable, single-use breathalyser kit. The fine for not carrying any of these items is €90.
- Riders of any type of two-wheeled vehicle with a motor (except motor-assisted bicycles) must wear a helmet.
- North American drivers, remember: turning right on a red light is illegal.

Train

France's superb rail network is operated by the state-owned **SNCF** (www.sncf.com); many rural towns not on the SNCF train network are served by SNCF buses.

The flagship trains on French railways are the superfast TGVs, which reach speeds in excess of 200mph and can whisk you from Paris to the Côte d'Azur in as little as three hours.

Many non-high-speed lines are also served by TGV trains; otherwise you'll find yourself aboard a non-TGV train, referred to as a *corail* or TER *(train express régional)*.

- 1st-class travel, where available, costs 20% to 30% extra.
- The further in advance you reserve, the lower the fares.
- Children under four travel for free (€8.50 to any destination if they need a seat).
- Children aged four to 11 travel for half price.

Discount Tickets

Prem's The SNCF's most heavily discounted, use-or-lose tickets, sold online, by phone and at ticket windows/machines a maximum of 90 days and minimum 14 days before you travel.

Bons Plans A grab-bag of cheap options for different routes/dates, advertised online under the tab '*Dernière Minute*' (Last Minute).

iDTGV Cheap tickets on advance-purchase TGV travel between about 30 cities; only sold at www.idtgv.com.

Discount Cards

Reductions of 25% to 60% are available with several discount cards (valid for one year):

Carte 12-25 (www.12-25-sncf.com; €50) For travellers aged 12 to 25 years.

Priority to the Right

Under the *priorité à droite* (priority to the right) rule, any car entering an intersection from a road on your right has the right of way, unless the intersection is marked '*vous n'avez pas la priorité*' (you do not have right of way) or '*cédez le passage*' (give way).

Carte Enfant Plus (www.enfantplus-sncf.com; €71) For one to four adults travelling with a child aged four to 11 years.

Carte Escapades (www.escapades-sncf.com; €76) Discounts on return journeys of at least 200km that include a Saturday night away or only involve travel on a Saturday or Sunday; for 26- to 59-year-olds.

Carte Sénior (www.senior-sncf.com; €57) Over 60 years.

Tickets

Buying online at the various SNCF websites can reward with you some great reductions on fares, but be warned – these are generally intended for domestic travellers, and if you're buying abroad be aware of the pitfalls. Many tickets can't be posted outside France, and if you buy with a non-French credit card, you might not be able to use it in the automated ticket collection machines at many French stations.

Before boarding any train, you must validate (*composter*) your ticket by time-stamping it in a *composteur*, one of those yellow posts located on the way to the platform. If you forget (or don't have a ticket for some other reason), find a conductor on the train before they find you – or risk an unwelcome fine.

Rail Passes

The **InterRail One Country Pass** (www.interrailnet.com; 3/4/6/8 days €205/226/288/319, 12-25yr €139/149/190/211), valid in France, entitles residents of Europe who do not live in France to unlimited travel on SNCF trains for three to eight days over a month.

Spain

Feisty, fiery and full of life – that pretty much sums up Spain in a nutshell. This sunbaked corner of southern Europe knows all about the good things in life, and certainly isn't shy about wearing its emotions on its sleeve.

It's an intoxicating place that seems to march to its own beguiling beat. Whether it's exploring the shady lanes of Barcelona's Barri Gòtic, watching some authentic flamenco in a Seville *tablao* (flamenco venue) or trying delicious tapas on Madrid's backstreets, Spain offers a wealth of enticing experiences that seem to seep into your soul, and will stay with you long after you've left for home. From the sexy cities of Madrid and Barcelona to the Moorish-influenced towns of Granada, Cádiz and Seville and the hilltop *pueblos blancos* (white villages), there are many different aspects to Spain, each providing a new perspective on this fascinating country. Dance till dawn, hike the hills, bask on a beach or savour a siesta – they're all part of the essential Spanish experience. Enjoy every moment.

Palau de la Música Catalana (p331), Barcelona
NEIL SETCHFIELD/GETTY IMAGES ©

FRANCE

Nîmes
Avignon
Montpellier
Toulouse

Golfe de Beauduc

Irún
San
Sebastián
Pamplona
Jaca
Calahorra
Huesca
Parque Nacional
de Órdesa y
Monte Perdido
ANDORRA
LA VELLA
Perpignan
Figueres
Girona
Fornells
Riu Ter
Vallée
d'Ossau
Río Arga
Río Gállego
Río Cinca
Riu Segre
Zaragoza
Lleida
Barcelona ❶
Tarragona
Río Ebro
Teruel
Amposta
Peñíscola
Costa del
Azahar
Castellón de la Plana
(Castelló de la Plana)
Cuenca
❺
Río Túria
Valencia
Sagunto
Barcelona-Ibiza
Barcelona-Palma de Mallorca
Palma de
Mallorca
Palma de Mallorca-Maó
VALENCIA
Alginet
Valencia-Palma de Mallorca
Valencia-Ibiza
Denia-Palma de Mallorca
Ibiza-Palma de Mallorca
Río Cábriel
Albacete
Almansa
Denia
Denia-Ibiza
Ibiza
Benidorm
Elche
Alicante
Cieza
Río Segura
Murcia
Cartagena
Mojácar

ALGERIA

❶ La Sagrada Família
❷ Museo del Prado
❸ Alhambra
❹ Flamenco in Madrid
❺ Cuenca

200 km
120 miles

Tarn
Garonne
Adour
Étang
de Berre

Spain Highlights

La Sagrada Família

Halfway between an architectural experiment and a monumental artwork, this fantastical cathedral (p332) in the centre of Barcelona has been under construction since 1882, and is still thought to be several decades away from completion. It's the work of the visionary architect Antoni Gaudí, whose playful buildings can be seen along many of Barcelona's boulevards, as well as the lovely Parc Güell.

Museo del Prado

Housed in a glorious 18th-century palace (enhanced by a modern extension) in the heart of old Madrid, the Museo del Prado (p302) is Spain's foremost art museum and houses the nation's top artistic treasures. Around 7000 pieces are on show: Rubens, Rembrandt and Van Dyck are all represented, but it's the Spanish boys, Goya and El Greco, who inevitably take the prize.

Alhambra

3

This fabulous Moorish palace (p372) in Granada is one of Spain's architectural marvels. It was built for the Muslim rulers of Granada between the 13th and 15th centuries, although parts of the structure date back to the 11th century. Seeing the medieval Palacio Nazaríes (Nasrid Palace) illuminated at twilight is an image that will linger. Palacio Nazaríes (p372)

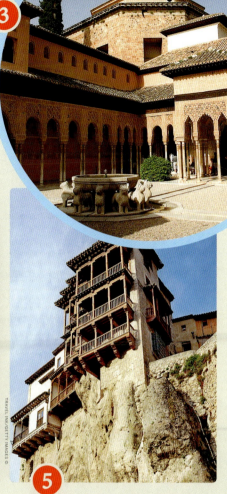

4

Flamenco

Nothing sums up the Spanish spirit better than flamenco (p318). This ancient dance form has been a cornerstone of Spanish culture for centuries, and is still going strong – although you'll have to choose carefully if you want to see the real thing. The best places to see authentic flamenco are Madrid and Seville, where you can watch some of the country's top performers strut their fiery stuff. Flamenco dancer at Casa Patas (p318), Madrid

5

Cuenca

Spain has plenty of clifftop villages, but few of them can hold a candle to the *casas colgadas* (hanging houses) of Cuenca (p327). These balconied houses seem to have been carved straight from the cliff face, and perch precariously above the deep ravine of Río Huécar – a true marvel of medieval engineering. Unsurprisingly, the village has been named a Unesco World Heritage site.

Spain's Best...

Festivals

● **Semana Santa** (p365)
This holy week is a highlight of the pre-Easter calendar.

● **Sanfermines** (p355) See the brave (and the barmy) run with the bulls during Pamplona's hair-raising street race.

● **Carnaval Cádiz** (p376) Spain's wildest carnival kicks off on the streets of Cádiz in February.

● **Feria de Abril** (p365) Seville's six-day street party in April is packed with Andalucian passion.

Sacred Sites

● **Montserrat** (p349) Make a pilgrimage to this otherworldly mountain monastery near Barcelona.

● **Santiago de Compostela** (p325) Join the pilgrims on the last leg of the Camino de Santiago.

● **The Mezquita** (p367) Córdoba's Moorish mosque-cum-cathedral is almost as impressive as the Alhambra.

● **Toledo Cathedral** (p324) Considered to be the heart of Catholic Spain.

● **Burgos Cathedral** (p325) Pay your respects at the tomb of Spain's national hero, El Cid.

Spanish Experiences

● **Markets** (p327) Drink in the sights, sounds and smells of Barcelona's Boqueria market.

● **Flamenco** (p367) Experience traditional flamenco in an Andalucían *tablao*.

● **Zarzuela** (p317) Catch this Spanish blend of dance, music and theatre.

● **Café life** (p315) Drink till dawn with the locals: there's always tomorrow for a siesta.

● **Football** (p347) Watch the soccer superstars in action at Barcelona's Camp Nou.

Culinary Specialities

○ **Tapas** (p313) Join the locals over Spanish snacks in Madrid's lively tapas bars.

○ **Pintxos** (p351) Try this Basque version of tapas in San Sebastián.

○ **Chocolate and churros** (p316) Savour this sweet pick-me-up at Madrid's Chocolatería de San Ginés.

○ **Cochinillo asado** (p313) Madrid or Segovia are both great places to try roast suckling pig.

○ **Basque cooking** (p353) Bilbao is a great place to experience Basque cuisine.

ADVANCE PLANNING

○ **Three months before** Book hotels and transport tickets, especially during festival season.

○ **One month before** Arrange theatre, opera and flamenco tickets, and book tables at top restaurants.

○ **One week before** Beat the queues at the Alhambra by buying your ticket online for a €1 supplement.

RESOURCES

○ **Turespaña** (www.spain.info, www.tourspain.es) The national tourism site.

○ **Renfe** (www.renfe.es) Plan your train travel.

○ **Fiestas.net** (www.fiestas.net) Handy online guide to fiestas and festivals.

○ **Tour Spain** (www.tourspain.org) Useful resource for culture and food, with links to hotels and transport.

GETTING AROUND

○ **Bus** Spain's bus network is extensive but chaotic. ALSA (www.alsa.es) is one of the largest companies.

○ **Car** Traffic and parking can be a nightmare around the big cities, so it's more convenient to hire cars from airport kiosks. Major motorways are called *autopistas;* tolls are compulsory on many routes.

○ **Sea** Frequent ferries connect Spain with the UK, Italy, Morocco and Algeria. Major ports are in Santander, Bilbao and Barcelona.

○ **Train** Spain's railways are run by Renfe (www.renfe.es). High-speed AVE trains link Madrid, Barcelona and major towns in between, and travel across the Pyrenees into France.

BE FOREWARNED

○ **Public holidays** Most of Spain goes on holiday during August and Semana Santa (the week before Easter Sunday).

○ **Smoking** 'Officially' banned in most public places, but many Spanish people don't seem to take much notice.

○ **Scams** Watch out for pickpocketing and bag snatching, and be wary of common scams.

Left: Ladies in flamenco dresses at Feria de Abril; **Above:** *Pintxos* in San Sebastián

Spain Itineraries

Spain is famous for its laid-back approach to life –
this is, after all, the land that invented the siesta – so
take things slowly if you want to make the most of the
sights.

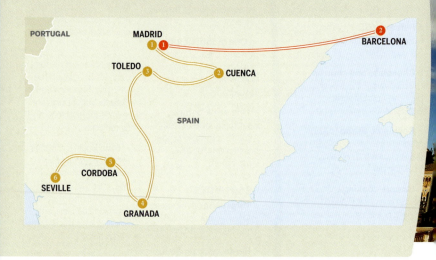

CITY SIGHTS
Madrid to Barcelona
3 DAYS

This trip gives you a taste of both of Spain's must-see cities. Start out in ❶ **Madrid** (p302), with incredible art at the Museo del Prado, the Museo Thyssen-Bornemisza and the Caixa Forum, followed by a spot of people-watching on the Plaza Mayor and an after-dark visit to the *tabernas* (taverns) and tapas bars of La Latina, Chueca and Los Austrias. Book yourself a spot at a *tablao* for some late-night flamenco.

On day two, spend the morning at the Palacio Real, the monarch's Madrid residence, then visit one of the city's markets and take a picnic to Parque del Buen Retiro. In the late afternoon, it's on to ❷ **Barcelona** (p327); thanks to the high-speed AVE trains, the trip now takes under three hours, leaving you plenty of time to check in before delving into the bars and bistros of the Barri Gòtic.

Day three's for sightseeing. Top of the list is La Sagrada Família, Gaudí's fantasy cathedral. Spend the afternoon at the Museu Picasso, have an early evening mooch around the shops and boutiques of El Raval and La Ribera, before finishing up with sophisticated Spanish food in the restaurants of L'Eixample.

5
DAYS

THE SOUTH
Madrid to Seville

This adventure heads into Spain's sultry, sun-drenched south, a region that's full of flamboyant passion. Start in **❶ Madrid** (p302), and make a detour southwest to see the marvellous 'hanging houses' of **❷ Cuenca** (p327), a Unesco site. On day two you can either backtrack to the capital or head west to the elegant city of **❸ Toledo** (p324), renowned for its cathedral.

Next comes **❹ Granada** (p371), where you can visit one of the great monuments of Spain's Moorish past, the mighty Alhambra, built as a palace and fortress for the region's rulers during the 14th century, and impressively preserved.

There's another Moorish structure in nearby **❺ Córdoba** (p367): the stunning Mezquita, a unique combination of Muslim and Christian cultures.

Finish off your trip in sexy **❻ Seville** (p359), the archetypal Andalucian city. This is the spiritual home of flamenco, and its lively bars and *tablaos* are probably the best places in Spain to experience this ancient art form. In summer, bars spring up along both sides of the river, and the action doesn't really get going till midnight – so it's best just to forget your watch and join the party.

Seville (p359)
WALTER BIBIKOW/GETTY IMAGES ©

Discover Spain

At a Glance

o **Madrid** (p302) Spain's sophisticated capital never seems to sleep.

o **Castilla y León** (p321) The heartland of traditional Spain.

o **Catalonia** (p327) Historic region that's home to Spain's most exciting city, Barcelona.

o **Basque Country** (p350) A country within a country, governed by its own language and culture.

o **Andalucía** (p359) The spiritual home of flamenco, full of fiery passion.

MADRID

POP 3.26 MILLION

No city on earth is more alive than Madrid, a beguiling place whose sheer energy carries a simple message: *madrileños* know how to live. Explore the old streets of the centre, relax in the plazas, soak up the culture in Madrid's excellent art museums, and spend at least one night exploring the city's legendary nightlife scene.

Sights

Get under the city's skin by walking its streets, sipping coffee and beer in its plazas and relaxing in its parks. Madrid de los Austrias, the maze of mostly 15th- and 16th-century streets that surround Plaza Mayor, is the city's oldest district. Tapas-crazy La Latina, alternative Chueca, bar-riddled Huertas and Malasaña, and chic Salamanca are other districts that reward pedestrian exploration.

Museo del Prado   Museum

(Map p306; www.museodelprado.es; Paseo del Prado; adult/child €12/ free, admission free 6-8pm Mon-Sat & 5-7pm Sun, audioguides €3.50; ⊙10am-8pm Mon-Sat, to 7pm Sun; M Banco de España) Spain's premier art museum, the Prado is a seemingly endless parade of priceless works from Spain and beyond. The 1785 neoclassical Palacio de Villanueva opened as a museum in 1819.

The collection is roughly divided into eight major collections: Spanish paintings (1100–1850), Flemish paintings (1430–1700), Italian paintings (1300–1800), French paintings (1600–1800), German paintings (1450–1800), sculptures, decorative arts, and drawings and prints. There is generous

Plaza Mayor, Madrid
PETER BARRITT/GETTY IMAGES ©

coverage of Spanish greats including Goya, Velázquez and El Greco. In addition to these Spanish masterpieces, don't miss El Jardín de las Delicias (The Garden of Earthly Delights; Room 56A), a three-panelled painting by Hieronymus Bosch of the creation of man, the pleasures of the world, and hell, or the works by Peter Paul Rubens, Pieter Bruegel, Rembrandt, Anton Van Dyck, Dürer, Rafael, Tiziano (Titian), Tintoretto, Sorolla, Gainsborough, Fra Angelico and Tiepolo.

From the 1st floor of the Palacio de Villanueva, passageways lead to the Edificio Jerónimos, the Prado's modern extension. The main hall contains information counters, a bookshop and a cafe. Rooms A and B (and Room C on the first floor) host temporary exhibitions.

Museo Thyssen-Bornemisza   Museum

(Map p310; 902 760 511; www.museothyssen. org; Paseo del Prado 8; adult/child €9/free; 10am-7pm Tue-Sun; M Banco de España) Opposite Museo del Prado, the Museo Thyssen-Bornemisza is an outstanding collection of international masterpieces. Begin your visit on the 2nd floor, where you'll start with medieval art, and make your way down to modern works on the ground level, passing paintings by Titian, El Greco, Rubens, Rembrandt, Anton van Dyck, Canaletto, Cézanne, Monet, Sisley, Renoir, Pissarro, Degas, Constable, Van Gogh, Miró, Modigliani, Matisse, Picasso, Gris, Pollock, Dalí, Kandinsky, Toulouse-Lautrec, Lichtenstein and many others on the way.

Centro de Arte Reina Sofía   Museum

(Map p306; 91 774 10 00; www.museoreina sofia.es; Calle de Santa Isabel 52; adult/conces-sion €6/free, admission free Sun, 7-9pm Mon-Fri & 2.30-9pm Sat; 10am-9pm Mon-Sat, to 2.30pm Sun; M Atocha) If modern art is your thing, the Reina Sofía is your museum. A stunning collection of mainly Spanish modern art, the Centro de Arte Reina Sofía is home to Picasso's *Guernica* – his protest against the German bombing of the Basque town

of Guernica during the Spanish Civil War in 1937 – in addition to important works by surrealist Salvador Dalí and abstract paintings by the Catalan artist Joan Miró.

Caixa Forum   Museum, Architecture

(Map p310; www.fundacio.lacaixa.es; Paseo del Prado 36; 10am-8pm; M Atocha) FREE The Caixa Forum, opened in 2008, seems to hover above the ground. On one wall is the *jardín colgante* (hanging garden), a lush vertical wall of greenery almost four storeys high. Inside are four floors used to hold top quality art and multimedia exhibitions.

Palacio Real   Palace

(Map p310; 91 454 88 00; www.patrimonio nacional.es; Calle de Bailén; adult/concession €10/5, guide/audioguide/pamphlet €7/4/1, EU citizens free 5-8pm Wed & Thu; 10am-8pm Apr-Sep, to 6pm Oct-Mar; M Ópera) Dating from 1755 and still used for important events of pomp and state, Madrid's opulent royal palace has 2800-plus rooms, of which 50 are open to the public.

Look out in particular for the **Salón de Gasparini**, with its exquisite stucco ceiling and walls resplendent with embroidered silks, the 215 clocks of the royal clock collection and the five Stradivarius violins, used occasionally for concerts and balls. Poke your head into the **Farmacia Real** (Royal Pharmacy) and the **Armería Real** (Royal Armoury).

Plaza Mayor   Square

(Map p310; Plaza Mayor; M Sol) Ringed with cafes and restaurants and packed with people day and night, the 17th-century arcaded Plaza Mayor is an elegant and bustling square. First designed by Juan de Herrera in 1560 at the request of Phillip II, and completed by Juan Gómez de Mora in 1619, the plaza hosted bullfights watched by 50,000 spectators (until 1878), while the *autos-da-fé* (the ritual condemnation of heretics) of the Spanish Inquisition also took place here. Fire largely destroyed the square in 1790 but it was rebuilt and became an important market and hub of city life.

Museo del Prado

Plan of Attack

Begin on the 1st floor with **Las Meninas** ❶ by Velázquez. Although alone worth the entry price, it's a fine introduction to the 17th-century golden age of Spanish art; nearby are more of Velázquez' royal paintings and works by Zurbarán and Murillo. While on the 1st floor, seek out Goya's **La Maja Vestida and La Maja Desnuda** ❷ with more of Goya's early works in neighbouring rooms. Downstairs at the southern end of the Prado, Goya's anger is evident in the searing **El Dos de Mayo** and **El Tres de Mayo** ❸, and the torment of Goya's later years finds expression in the adjacent rooms with his **Pinturas Negras** ❹, or Black Paintings. Also on the lower floor, Hieronymus Bosch's weird and wonderful **Garden of Earthly Delights** ❺ is one of the Prado's signature masterpieces. Returning to the 1st floor, El Greco's **Adoration of the Shepherds** ❻ is an extraordinary work, as is Peter Paul Rubens' **Las Tres Gracias** ❼, which forms the centrepiece of the Prado's gathering of Flemish masters. (This painting may have been moved to the 2nd floor.) A detour to the 2nd floor takes in some lesser-known Goyas, but finish in the **Edificio Jerónimos** ❽ with a visit to the cloisters and the outstanding bookshop.

Also Visit:

Nearby are Museo Thyssen-Bornemisza and Centro de Arte Reina Sofía. They form an extraordinary trio of galleries.

Las Tres Gracias (Rubens)
A late Rubens masterpiece, *The Three Graces* is a classical and masterly expression of Rubens' preoccupation with sensuality, here portraying Aglaia, Euphrosyne and Thalia, the daughters of Zeus.

PETER BARRITT/ALAMY ©

Goya Entrance (up)

Goya Entrance

Edificio Jerónimos
Opened in 2007, this state-of-the-art extension has rotating exhibitions of Prado masterpieces held in storage for decades for lack of wall space, and stunning 2nd-floor granite cloisters that date back to 1672.

Adoration of the Shepherds (El Greco)
There's an ecstatic quality to this intense painting. El Greco's distorted rendering of bodily forms came to characterise much of his later work.

Las Meninas (Velázquez)

This masterpiece depicts Velázquez and the Infanta Margarita, with the king and queen whose images appear, according to some experts, in mirrors behind Velázquez.

La Maja Vestida & La Maja Desnuda (Goya)

These enigmatic works scandalised early-19th-century Madrid society, fuelling the rumour mill as to the woman's identity and drawing the ire of the Spanish Inquisition. (La Maja Vestida pictured above.)

Edificio Villanueva

El Dos de Mayo & El Tres de Mayo (Goya)

Few paintings evoke a city's sense of self quite like Goya's portrayal of Madrid's valiant but ultimately unsuccessful uprising against French rule in 1808. (El Tres de Mayo pictured here.)

①

②

Jerónimos Entrance

Murillo Entrance

③

④

⑤

Velázquez Entrance

Las Pinturas Negras (Goya)

Las Pinturas Negras are Goya's darkest works. *Saturno Devorando a Su Hijo* evokes a writhing mass of tortured humanity, while *La Romería de San Isidro* and *El Akelarre* are profoundly unsettling.

The Garden of Earthly Delights (Bosch)

A fantastical painting in triptych form, this overwhelming work depicts the Garden of Eden and what the Prado describes as 'the lugubrious precincts of Hell' in exquisitely bizarre detail.

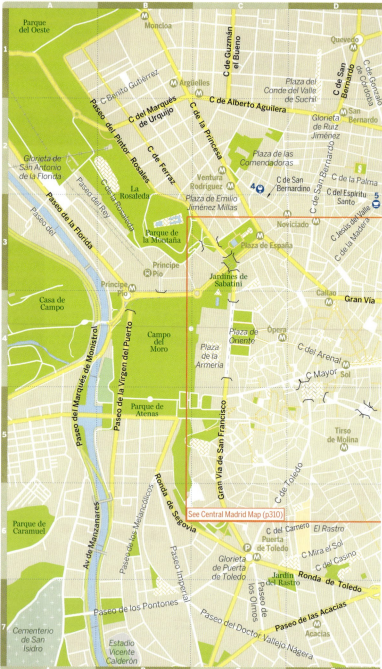

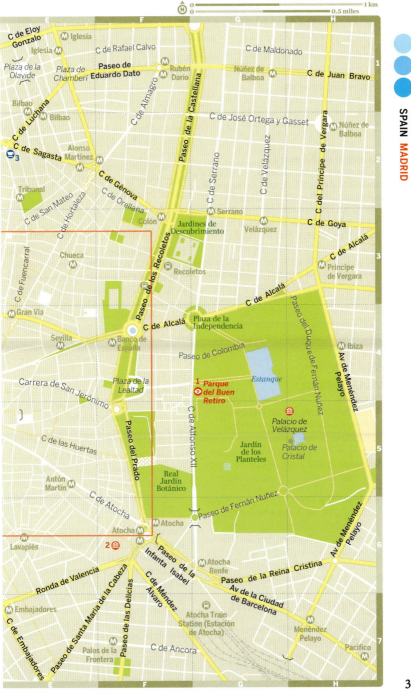

0   1 km
0   0.5 miles

C de Eloy Gonzalo
Iglesia
Iglesia
C de Rafael Calvo
C de Maldonado
Plaza de la Olavide
Plaza de Chamberí
Paseo de Eduardo Dato
Rubén Darío
Núñez de Balboa
C de Juan Bravo
C de Almagro
Paseo de la Castellana
C de José Ortega y Gasset
Bilbao
Bilbao
C de Luchana
C de Sagasta
Alonso Martínez
C de Génova
C de Orellana
C de Serrano
C de Velázquez
C del Príncipe de Vergara
Núñez de Balboa
3
Tribunal
C de San Mateo
C de Hortaleza
Colón
Serrano
Velázquez
C de Goya
C de Fuencarral
Chueca
Jardines de Descubrimiento
Recoletos
Paseo de los Recoletos
C de Alcalá
Príncipe de Vergara
Gran Vía
Sevilla
Banco de España
C de Alcalá
Plaza de la Independencia
C de Alcalá
Paseo del Duque de Fernán Núñez
Ibiza
Carrera de San Jerónimo
Plaza de la Lealtad
Paseo de Colombia
Estanque
Av de Menéndez Pelayo
1 Parque del Buen Retiro
C de las Huertas
Paseo del Prado
Palacio de Velázquez
Antón Martín
C de Atocha
Real Jardín Botánico
C de Alfonso XII
Jardín de los Planteles
Palacio de Cristal
Atocha
Paseo de Fernán Núñez
Lavapiés
2
Atocha
Paseo de la Infanta Isabel
Atocha Renfe
Paseo de la Reina Cristina
Ronda de Valencia
C de Méndez Álvaro
C de la Cabeza
Santa María de la Cabeza
Paseo de las Delicias
Av de la Ciudad de Barcelona
Embajadores
C de Embajadores
Paseo de Santa María de la Cabeza
Palos de la Frontera
C de Ancora
Atocha Train Station (Estación de Atocha)
Menéndez Pelayo
Pacífico

Greater Madrid

⊙ Don't Miss Sights
1 Parque del Buen Retiro........................G4

⊙ Sights
2 Centro de Arte Reina Sofía.................F6

⊖ Drinking & Nightlife
3 Café Comercial....................................E2
4 El Jardín Secreto................................C2
5 Lolina Vintage Café............................D3

Catedral de Nuestra Señora de la Almudena · Cathedral

(Map p310; ☎ 91 542 22 00; www.museocatedral. archimadrid.es; Calle de Bailén; cathedral & crypt by donation, museum adult/child €6/4; ⊙ 9am-8.30pm Mon-Sat, for Mass Sun, museum 10am-2.30pm Mon-Sat; Ⓜ Ópera) Although the exterior of Madrid's cathedral sits in harmony with the adjacent Palacio Real, Madrid's cathedral is cavernous and largely charmless within; its colourful, modern ceilings do little to make up for the lack of old-world gravitas that so distinguishes great cathedrals. It's possible to climb to the cathedral's summit, with fine views.

⊕ Tours

Visitas Guiadas Oficiales · Guided Tour

(Official Guided Tours; ☎ 902 221424; www. esmadrid.com/guidedtours; Plaza Mayor 27; adult/child €3.90/free; Ⓜ Sol) Twenty highly recommended guided tours conducted in Spanish and English. Organised by the Centro de Turismo de Madrid (p320).

Madrid City Tour · Bus Tour

(☎ 902 024758; http://www.esmadrid.com/en/ tourist-bus; 1-day ticket adult €21, child free-€9; ⊙ 9am-10pm Mar-Oct, 10am-6pm Nov-Feb) Hop-on, hop-off, open-topped buses that run every 10 to 20 minutes along two routes: Historical Madrid and Modern Madrid.

✸ Festivals & Events

Fiesta de San Isidro · Cultural Festival

(www.esmadrid.com/sanisidro) Around 15 May, Madrid's patron saint is honoured with a week of nonstop processions, parties, bullfights and free concerts.

Suma Flamenca · Flamenco Festival

(www.madrid.org/sumaflamenca) A soul-filled flamenco festival that draws some of the biggest names in the genre in June.

🛏 Sleeping

Where you decide to stay will play an important role in your experience of Madrid. Los Austrias, Sol and Centro put you in the heart of the busy downtown area, while La Latina (the best *barrio* – neighbourhood – for tapas), Lavapiés and Huertas (good for nightlife) are ideal for those who love Madrid nights and don't want to stagger too far to get back to their hotel.

Los Austrias, Sol & Centro

Hotel Meninas · Boutique Hotel €€

(Map p310; ☎ 91 541 28 05; www.hotelmeninas. com; Calle de Campomanes 7; s/d from €99/119; ✳ 🛜; Ⓜ Ópera) Inside a refurbished 19th-century mansion, the Meninas combines old-world comfort with modern, minimalist style. The colour scheme is blacks, whites and greys, with dark-wood floors and splashes of fuchsia and lime-green.

Posada del Dragón · Boutique Hotel €€

(Map p310; ☎ 91 119 14 24; www.posadadel dragon.com; Calle de la Cava Baja 14 ; r from €91; ✳ 🛜; Ⓜ La Latina) This restored 19th-century inn sits on one of our favourite streets in Madrid and rooms either look out over the street or over the pretty internal patio. Bold, brassy colour schemes and designer everything dominates the rooms.

Hostal Madrid · Hostal, Apartment €

(Map p310; ☎ 91 522 00 60; www.hostal-madrid. info; Calle de Esparteros 6; s €35-55, d €45-75, d apt per night €55-150, per month €1200-2500; ✳ 🛜; Ⓜ Sol) The 24 rooms at this well-run *hostal* have been wonderfully renovated with exposed brickwork, brand-new bathrooms and a look that puts many three-star hotels to shame. It also has terrific apartments (www.apartamentos mayorcentro.com).

KRZYSZTOF DYDYNSKI/GETTY IMAGES ©

Don't Miss
Parque del Buen Retiro

The splendid gardens of El Retiro are littered with marble monuments, landscaped lawns, the occasional elegant building and abundant greenery. It's quiet and contemplative during the week, but comes to life on weekends.

The focal point for so much of El Retiro's life is the artificial **estanque** (lake), which is watched over by the massive ornamental structure of the **Monument to Alfonso XII** on the east side of the lake, complete with marble lions. Hidden among the trees south of the lake, the late-19th-century **Palacio de Cristal**, a magnificent metal and glass structure that is arguably El Retiro's most beautiful architectural monument, is now used for temporary exhibitions.

At the southern end of the park, near **La Rosaleda** (Rose Garden) with its more-than-4000 roses, is a statue of **El Ángel Caído** (the Fallen Angel, aka Lucifer), one of the few statues to the devil anywhere in the world. It sits 666m above sea level...

In the northeastern corner of the park is the ruined **Ermita de San Isidro**, a small country chapel noteworthy as one of the few, albeit modest, examples of Romanesque architecture in Madrid.

NEED TO KNOW
Map p306; ⏰6am-midnight May-Sep, to 11pm Oct-Apr; Ⓜ Retiro, Príncipe de Vergara, Ibiza or Atocha

---

Hotel Plaza Mayor   Hotel €€
(Map p310; ☎91 360 06 06; www.h-plazamayor.com; Calle de Atocha 2; s/d from €55/85; ❄ 🛜; Ⓜ Sol, Tirso de Molina) Stylish decor, charming original elements of a 150-year-old

building and helpful staff are selling points here. The attic rooms have great views.

Hotel de Las Letras   Hotel €€
(Map p310; ☎91 523 79 80; www.hoteldelasletras.com; Gran Vía 11; d from €100; ❄ 🛜; Ⓜ Gran

Central Madrid

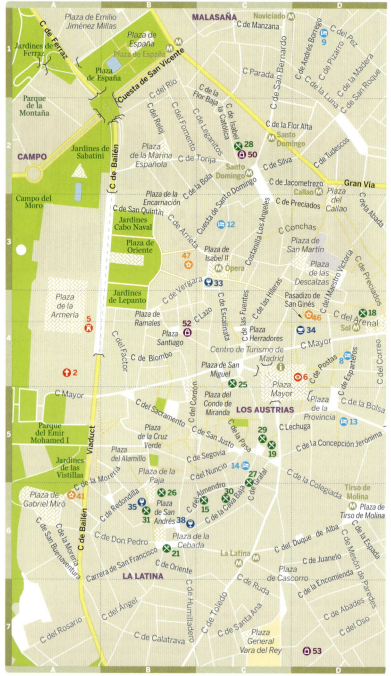

310

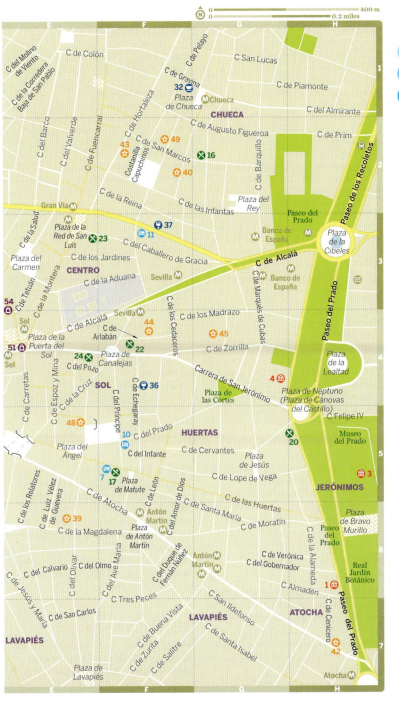

C del Molino de Viento
C de Colón
C de Pelayo
C San Lucas
C de la Corredera Baja de San Pablo
C de Gravina
C de Piamonte
32
Plaza de Chueca
Chueca
CHUECA
C del Almirante
C del Barco
C de Hortaleza
C de Augusto Figueroa
C de Prim
C del Valverde
C de Fuencarral
43
C de San Marcos
49
16
C de Barquillo
40
C de la Reina
Plaza del Rey
C de las Infantas
Gran Vía
Paseo de los Recoletos
Plaza de la Red de San Luis
23
11
37
C del Caballero de Gracia
Paseo del Prado
Plaza de la Cibeles
C de la Salud
Banco de España
C del Carmen
CENTRO
C de los Jardines
C de Alcalá
C de la Aduana
Sevilla
Banco de España
Paseo del Prado
C de Tetuán
Sol
C de la Montera
Sevilla
C de Alcalá
C de los Madrazo
C de Marqués de Cubas
54
51
Plaza de la Puerta del Sol
C de Arlabán
44
45
C de Zorrilla
Sol
24
22
Plaza de Canalejas
Plaza de la Lealtad
Sol
C del Pozo
36
Carrera de San Jerónimo
C de Carretas
C de Espoz y Mina
SOL
4
Plaza de Neptuno (Plaza de Cánovas del Castillo)
C de la Cruz
C del Príncipe
C del Echegaray
Plaza de las Cortes
C Felipe IV
48
Museo del Prado
10
C del Prado
HUERTAS
C del Infante
C de Cervantes
20
Plaza del Ángel
Plaza de Jesús
7
17
Plaza de Matute
C de León
C de Lope de Vega
JERÓNIMOS
C de los Relatores
C de Luis Vélez de Guevara
C de Atocha
C de Amor de Dios
C de Santa María
C de las Huertas
3
C de Moratín
Plaza de Bravo Murillo
39
Anton Martín
Plaza de Antón Martín
Paseo del Prado
C de la Magdalena
C de la Alameda
Real Jardín Botánico
C del Calvario
C del Olivar
C del Olmo
C del Ave María
C del Duque de Fernán Núñez
Antón Martín
C de Verónica
C del Gobernador
C de Jesús y María
C de San Carlos
C Tres Peces
C San Ildefonso
C Almadén
1
Paseo del Prado
LAVAPIÉS
LAVAPIÉS
C de Buena Vista
C de Santa Isabel
ATOCHA
C de Cenicero
42
Plaza de Lavapiés
C de Zurita
C de Salitre
Atocha

0   400 m
0   0.2 miles

311

Central Madrid

◉ Sights
1 Caixa Forum H6
2 Catedral de Nuestra Señora de la
   Almudena A4
3 Museo del Prado H5
4 Museo Thyssen-Bornemisza G4
5 Palacio Real A4
6 Plaza Mayor D4

🛏 Sleeping
7 Chic & Basic Colors F5
8 Hostal Madrid D4
9 Hotel Abalú D1
10 Hotel Alicia F5
11 Hotel de Las Letras F3
12 Hotel Meninas C3
13 Hotel Plaza Mayor D5
14 Posada del Dragón C5

✖ Eating
15 Almendro 13 .... C6
16 Bazaar G2
17 Casa Alberto F5
18 Casa Labra D4
19 Casa Revuelta C5
20 Estado Puro H5
21 Juana La Loca B6
22 La Finca de Susana F4
23 La Gloria de Montera E3
24 Lhardy E4
25 Mercado de San Miguel C4
26 Naïa Restaurante B6
27 Posada de la Villa C5
28 Restaurante Sandó C2

29 Restaurante Sobrino de
   Botín C5
30 Txacolina C6
31 Viva La Vida B6

🍷 Drinking & Nightlife
32 Café Acuarela F1
33 Café del Real C3
34 Chocolatería de San Ginés D4
35 Delic B6
36 La Venencia F4
37 Museo Chicote F3
38 Taberna Tempranillo B6

✪ Entertainment
39 Casa Patas E6
40 Club 54 Studio F2
41 Corral de la Morería A6
42 Kapital H7
   Liquid Madrid .... (see 40)
43 Mamá Inés F2
44 Stella F4
45 Teatro de la Zarzuela G4
46 Teatro Joy Eslava D4
47 Teatro Real B3
48 Villa Rosa E5
49 Why Not? F2

🛍 Shopping
50 Antigua Casa Talavera C2
51 Casa de Diego E4
52 El Flamenco Vive B4
53 El Rastro D7
54 Real Madrid Store E3

Vía) Hotel de las Letras started the rooftop hotel-bar trend in Madrid. The bar's wonderful, but the whole hotel is excellent with individually styled rooms, each with literary quotes scribbled on the walls.

Huertas & Atocha

Hotel Alicia   Boutique Hotel €€

(Map p310; ☎91 389 60 95; www.room-matehoteles.com; Calle del Prado 2; d €100-175, ste from €200; ✳🛜; Ⓜ Sol, Sevilla or Antón Martín) With beautiful, spacious rooms, Alicia overlooks Plaza de Santa Ana. It has an ultra-modern look and the downstairs bar is oh-so-cool.

Chic & Basic Colors   Hotel €

(Map p310; ☎91 429 69 35; www.chicandbasic.com; 2nd fl, Calle de las Huertas 14; r €50-75; ✳🛜🏊; Ⓜ Antón Martín) The rooms here are white in a minimalist style with free internet, flat-screen TVs, dark hardwood floors with a bright colour scheme superimposed on top, with every room a different shade. It's all very comfortable, contemporary and casual.

Malasaña & Chueca

Hotel Abalú   Boutique Hotel €€

(Map p310; ☎91 531 47 44; www.hotelabalu.com; Calle del Pez 19; d/apt from €84/110; ✳🛜;

M Noviciado) Malasaña's very own boutique hotel is an oasis of style amid the *barrio*'s timeworn feel. Suitably located on cool Calle del Pez, each room here has its own design, from retro chintz to Zen, baroque and pure white, and most aesthetics in between. You're close to Gran Vía, but away from the tourist scrum.

🍴 Eating

It's possible to find just about any kind of cuisine and eatery in Madrid, from traditional to trendy fusion.

From the chaotic tapas bars of La Latina to countless neighbourhood favourites, you'll have no trouble tracking down specialities like *cochinillo asado* (roast suckling pig) or *cocido madrileño* (a hearty stew made of chickpeas and various meats).

. . . .

Los Austrias, Sol & Centro

Mercado de San Miguel   Tapas €
(Map p310; www.mercadodesanmiguel.es; Plaza de San Miguel; tapas from €1; ⏰10am-midnight Sun-Wed, to 2am Thu-Sat; M Sol) One of Madrid's oldest and most beautiful markets, the Mercado de San Miguel has undergone a stunning major renovation and bills itself as a 'culinary cultural centre'. You can order tapas at most of the counter-bars.

Restaurante Sobrino de Botín   Castilian €€€
(Map p310; 📞91 366 42 17; www.botin.es; Calle de los Cuchilleros 17; mains €18.50-28; M La Latina or Sol) It's not every day that you can eat in the oldest restaurant in the world (1725), which also appears in many novels about Madrid, most notably Hemingway's *The*

Sun Also Rises. The secret of its staying power is fine *cochinillo* (suckling pig) and *cordero asado* (roast lamb) cooked in wood-fired ovens. Eating in the vaulted cellar is a treat.

Restaurante Sandó   Contemporary Spanish €€€
(Map p310; 📞91 547 99 11; www.restaurante-sando.es; Calle de Isabel la Católica 2; mains €18-26, menú degustación €49; ⏰lunch & dinner Tue-Sat, lunch Sun; M Santo Domingo) Juan Mari Arzak, one of Spain's most famous chefs, and his increasingly celebrated daughter Elena, have finally set up shop in Madrid. Bringing Basque innovation to bear upon local tradition, their cooking is assured with dishes such as bites of beef with fresh garlic and pineapple.

La Gloria de Montera   Spanish €
(Map p310; www.lagloriademontera.com; Calle del Caballero de Gracia 10; mains €7-10; M Gran Vía) Minimalist style, tasty Mediterranean dishes and great prices mean that you'll probably have to wait in line (no reservations taken) to eat here.

Monument to Alfonso XII in Parque del Buen Retiro (p309), Madrid
SERGIO PITAMITZ/GETTY IMAGES ©

La Latina & Lavapiés

Naïa Restaurante · Fusion €€
(Map p310; 91 366 27 83; Plaza de la Paja 3; mains €12-19; lunch & dinner Tue-Sun; La Latina) On the lovely Plaza de la Paja, Naïa has a real buzz about it, with modern Spanish cuisine, a chill-out lounge downstairs and a cooking laboratory overseen by Carlos López Reyes.

Viva La Vida · Vegetarian €
(Map p310; www.vivalavida.com.es; Costanilla de San Andrés 16; buffet 500g plus drink €10; noon-midnight Mon-Wed, 11am-2am Thu-Sun; ; La Latina) This organic food shop has as its centrepiece an appealing vegetarian buffet with hot and cold food that's always filled with flavour. It's a great place at any time of the day, especially outside normal Spanish eating hours.

Posada de la Villa · Madrileño €€€
(Map p310; 91 366 18 80; www.posadadela villa.com; Calle de la Cava Baja 9; mains €20-28; lunch & dinner Mon-Sat, lunch Sun, closed Aug; La Latina) This wonderfully restored 17th-century *posada* (inn) is something of a local landmark. The atmosphere is formal, the decoration sombre and traditional, and the cuisine decidedly local.

Huertas & Atocha

Casa Alberto · Spanish, Tapas €€
(Map p310; 91 429 93 56; www.casaalberto.es; Calle de las Huertas 18; mains €16-20; lunch & dinner Tue-Sat, lunch Sun; Antón Martín) One of the most atmospheric old *tabernas* (taverns) of Madrid, Casa Alberto has been around since 1827. The secret to its staying power is vermouth on tap, excellent tapas at the bar and fine sit-down meals; Casa Alberto's *rabo de toro* (bull's tail) is famous among aficionados.

Lhardy · Madrileño €€€
(Map p310; 91 521 33 85; www.lhardy.com; Carrera de San Jerónimo 8; mains €18.50-39; lunch & dinner Mon-Sat, lunch Sun, closed Aug; Sol, Sevilla) This Madrid landmark (since 1839) is an elegant treasure-trove

A Tapas Tour of Madrid

Madrid's home of tapas is La Latina, especially along Calle de la Cava Baja and the surrounding streets. **Almendro 13** (Map p310; 91 365 42 52; Calle del Almendro 13; mains €7-15; 12.30-4pm & 7.30pm-midnight Sun-Thu, 12.30-5pm & 8pm-1am Fri & Sat; La Latina) is famous for quality rather than frilly elaborations, with cured meats, cheeses, tortillas and *huevos rotos* (literally, 'broken eggs') the house specialities. Down on Calle de la Cava Baja, **Txacolina** (Map p310; 91 366 48 77; Calle de la Cava Baja 26; tapas from €3; dinner Mon & Wed-Fri, lunch & dinner Sat, lunch Sun; La Latina) does some of the biggest *pintxos* (Basque tapas) you'll find. Not far away, **Juana La Loca** (Map p310; 91 364 05 25; Plaza de la Puerta de Moros 4; tapas from €4, mains €8-19; lunch & dinner Tue-Sun, dinner Mon; La Latina) does a magnificent *tortilla de patatas* (potato and onion omelette).

In the centre, for *bacalao* (cod) the historic **Casa Labra** (Map p310; 91 532 14 05; www.casalabra.es; Calle de Tetuán 11; tapas from €1; 9.30am-3.30pm & 5.30-11pm; Sol) and **Casa Revuelta** (Map p310; 91 366 33 32; Calle de Latoneros 3; tapas from €2.60; 10.30am-4pm & 7-11pm Tue-Sat, 10.30am-4pm Sun, closed Aug; Sol, La Latina) have no peers.

Nearby, along the Paseo del Prado, there's supercool **Estado Puro** (Map p310; 91 330 24 00; www.tapasenestadopuro.com; Plaza de Cánovas del Castillo 4; tapas €5-12.50; 11am-1am Tue-Sat, to 4pm Sun; Banco de España, Atocha) with gourmet tapas inspired by Catalonia's world-famous (but now closed) El Bulli restaurant.

Mercado de San Miguel (p313), Madrid

MATTES RENĀC/GETTY IMAGES ©

of takeaway gourmet tapas. Upstairs is the upscale preserve of house specialities. It's expensive, but the quality and service are unimpeachable.

La Finca de Susana   Spanish €€
(Map p310; www.lafinca-restaurant.com; Calle de Arlabán 4; mains €7-12; M Sevilla) It's difficult to find a better combination of price, quality cooking and classy atmosphere anywhere in the centre. The softly lit dining area is bathed in greenery and the sometimes innovative, sometimes traditional food draws a hip, young crowd. No reservations taken.

Malasaña & Chueca

Bazaar   Contemporary Spanish €
(Map p310; www.restaurantbazaar.com; Calle de la Libertad 21; mains €6.50-10; ⊙lunch & dinner; M Chueca) Bazaar's popularity among the well-heeled and often-famous shows no sign of abating. Its pristine white interior design with theatre lighting may draw a crowd that looks like it stepped out of the pages of *Hola!* magazine, but the food is extremely well priced and innovative. It doesn't take reservations so be prepared to wait whether you're famous or not.

🍷 Drinking & Nightlife

The essence of Madrid lives in its streets and plazas, and bar-hopping is a pastime enjoyed by young and old alike. If you're after the more traditional, with tiled walls and flamenco tunes, head to Huertas. For gay-friendly drinking holes, Chueca is the place. Malasaña caters to a grungy, funky crowd, while La Latina has friendly bars that guarantee atmosphere most nights of the week.

The bulk of Madrid bars open to 2am Sunday to Thursday, and to 3am or 3.30am Friday and Saturday.

Los Austrias & Centro

Museo Chicote   Cocktail Bar
(Map p310; www.museo-chicote.com; Gran Vía 12; ⊙6pm-3am Mon-Thu, to 4am Fri & Sat; M Gran Vía) The founder of this Madrid landmark is said to have invented more than a hundred cocktails, which the likes of Hemingway, Ava Gardner, Grace Kelly, Sophia Loren and Frank Sinatra all enjoyed at one time or another.

315

Hot Chocolate & Churros

Join the sugar-searching throngs who end the night at **Chocolatería de San Ginés** (Map p310; Pasadizo de San Ginés 5; ⏰9.30am-7am; Ⓜ Sol), a legendary bar, famous for its freshly fried *churros* (fried sticks of dough) and syrupy hot chocolate.

Café del Real   Bar, Cafe
(Map p310; Plaza de Isabel II 2; ⏰9am-1am Mon-Thu, to 3am Fri & Sat; Ⓜ Ópera) A cafe and cocktail bar in equal parts, this intimate little place serves up creative coffees and a few cocktails to the soundtrack of chill-out music.

La Latina & Lavapiés

Delic   Bar, Cafe
(Map p310; www.delic.es; Costanilla de San Andrés 14; ⏰11am-2am Fri-Sun & Tue-Thu, 7pm-2am Mon; Ⓜ La Latina) We could go on for hours about this long-standing cafe-bar, but we'll reduce it to this most basic element: nursing an exceptionally good mojito (€8) or three on a warm summer's evening at Delic's outdoor tables on one of Madrid's prettiest plazas is one of life's great pleasures.

Taberna Tempranillo   Wine Bar
(Map p310; Calle de la Cava Baja 38; ⏰1-3.30pm & 8pm-midnight Tue-Sun, 8pm-midnight Mon; Ⓜ La Latina) You could come here for the tapas, but we recommend Taberna Tempranillo primarily for its wines, of which it has a selection that puts many Spanish bars to shame, and many are sold by the glass.

Huertas & Atocha

La Venencia   Bar
(Map p310; Calle de Echegaray 7; ⏰1-3.30pm & 7.30pm-1.30am; Ⓜ Sol, Sevilla) La Venencia is a *barrio* classic, with fine sherry from San-lúcar and manzanilla from Jeréz poured straight from the dusty barrel, accompanied by a small selection of tapas with an Andalucian bent.

Malasaña & Chueca

Café Comercial   Cafe
(Map p306; Glorieta de Bilbao 7; ⏰7.30am-midnight Mon-Thu, 7.30am-2am Fri, 8.30am-2am Sat, 9am-midnight Sun; Ⓜ Bilbao) This glorious old Madrid cafe proudly fights a rearguard action against progress with heavy leather seats, abundant marble and old-style waiters.

El Jardín Secreto   Bar, Cafe
(Map p306; Calle del Conde Duque 2; ⏰5.30pm-12.30am Sun-Thu, 6.30pm-2.30am Fri & Sat; Ⓜ Plaza de España) 'The Secret Garden' is all about intimacy and romance in a *barrio* that's one of Madrid's best-kept secrets.

Lolina Vintage Café   Cafe
(Map p306; www.lolinacafe.com; Calle del Espíritu Santo 9; ⏰9am-2.30am Mon-Fri, 10am-2.30am Sat, 11am-2.30am Sun; Ⓜ Tribunal) Lolina Vintage Café seems to have captured the essence of the *barrio* in one small space. With a studied retro look (comfy old-style chairs and sofas, gilded mirrors and 1970s-era wallpaper), it confirms that the new Malasaña is not unlike the old.

⭐ Entertainment

The **Guía del Ocio** (www.guiadelocio.com) is the city's classic weekly listings magazine.

GAY & LESBIAN

The heartbeat of gay Madrid is the inner-city *barrio* of Chueca, where Madrid didn't just come out of the closet, but ripped the doors off in the process.

A good place to get the low-down is the laid-back **Mamá Inés** (Map p310; www.mamaines.com; Calle de Hortaleza 22; ⏰10am-2pm Sun-Thu, to 3am Fri & Sat; Ⓜ Gran Vía or Chueca). **Café Acuarela** (Map p310; www.cafeacuarela.es; Calle de Gravina 10; ⏰11am-2am Sun-Thu, to 3am Fri & Sat; Ⓜ Chueca) is another dimly lit centrepiece of gay Madrid.

Two of the most popular Chueca nightspots are **Club 54 Studio** (Map p310;

www.studio54madrid.com; Calle de Barbieri 7; ⏰ 11.30am-3.30am Wed-Sat; Ⓜ Chueca), modelled on the famous New York club Studio 54, and **Liquid Madrid** (Map p310; www.liquid.es; Calle de Barbieri 7; ⏰ 9pm-3am Mon-Thu, to 3.30am Fri & Sat; Ⓜ Chueca). **Why Not?** (Map p310; www.whynotmadrid.com; Calle de San Bartolomé 7; admission €10; ⏰ 10.30pm-6am; Ⓜ Chueca) is the sort of place where nothing's left to the imagination.

NIGHTCLUBS

Don't expect dance clubs or *discotecas* (nightclubs) to get going until after 1am at the earliest. Standard entry fee is €12, which usually includes the first drink, although megaclubs and swankier places charge a few euros more.

Teatro Joy Eslava   Club

(Map p310; Joy Madrid; ☎ 91 366 37 33; www.joy-eslava.com; Calle del Arenal 11; admission €12-15; ⏰ 11.30pm-6am; Ⓜ Sol) The only things guaranteed at this grand old Madrid dance club (housed in a 19th-century theatre) are a crowd and the fact that it will be open; the club claims to have opened every single day for the past 30 years.

Kapital   Club

(Map p310; ☎ 91 420 29 06; www.grupo-kapital.com; Calle de Atocha 125; admission from €12; ⏰ 5.30-10.30pm & midnight-6am Fri & Sat, midnight-6am Thu & Sun; Ⓜ Atocha) One of the most famous megaclubs in Madrid, this massive seven-storey nightclub has something for everyone: from cocktail bars and dance music to karaoke, salsa, hip hop and more chilled spaces for R&B and soul, as well as an area devoted to 'Made in Spain' music.

Stella   Club

(Map p310; ☎ 91 531 63 78; www.web-mondo.com; Calle de Arlabán 7; admission €12; ⏰ 12.30am-6am Thu-Sat; Ⓜ Sevilla) One of Madrid's enduring success stories, Stella is one of the city's best nightclubs. If you arrive here after 3am, there simply won't be room and those inside have no intention of leaving until dawn.

THEATRE

Teatro de la Zarzuela   Theatre

(Map p310; ☎ 91 524 54 00; http://teatrodelazarzuela.mcu.es; Calle de Jovellanos 4; tickets €5-42; ⏰ box office noon-6pm Mon-Fri, 3-6pm Sat & Sun;

Café Comercial, Madrid

LONELY PLANET/GETTY IMAGES ©

317

CORRAL DE LA MORERIA

Ⓜ Banco de España, Sevilla) This theatre, built in 1856, is the premier place to see *zarzuela*, the uniquely Spanish combination of theatre and music.

Teatro Real   Opera

(Map p310; ☎902 24 48 48; www.teatro-real. com; Plaza de Oriente; ⓂÓpera) After spending €100 million-plus on a long rebuilding project, the Teatro Real is the city's grandest stage for elaborate operas, ballets and classical music. You'll pay as little as €6 for distant seats and as much as €125 for the best seats in the house.

FLAMENCO

Corral de la Morería   Flamenco

(Map p310; ☎91 365 84 46; www.corraldela moreria.com; Calle de la Morería 17; admission incl drink €42-45, meals from €43; ☺8.30pm-2.30am, shows 9.30pm & 11.30pm Sun-Fri, 7pm, 10pm & midnight Sat; ⓂÓpera) This is one of the most prestigious flamenco stages in Madrid, with 50 years' experience as a

leading flamenco venue with top performers most nights.

Casa Patas   Flamenco

(Map p310; ☎91 369 04 96; www.casapatas. com; Calle de Cañizares 10; admission €32; ☺shows 10.30pm Mon-Thu, 9pm & midnight Fri & Sat; ⓂAntón Martín, Tirso de Molina) One of the top flamenco stages in Madrid, this *tablao* (flamenco venue) always offers flawless quality that serves as a good introduction to the art.

Villa Rosa   Flamenco

(Map p310; ☎91 521 36 89; www.villa-rosa.es; Plaza de Santa Ana 15; admission €17; ☺shows 8.30pm & 10.45pm Sun-Thu, 8.30pm, 10.45pm & 12.15am Fri & Sat, 11pm-6am Mon-Sat; ⓂSol) The extraordinary tiled facade appeared in the Pedro Almodóvar film *Tacones Lejanos* (High Heels; 1991). It's been going strong since 1914 and has seen many manifestations – it has recently returned to its flamenco roots with well-priced shows and meals that won't break the bank.

Left: Flamenco dancers, Corral de la Morería, Madrid;
Below: Teatro Real, Madrid

SPORT

Estadio Santiago Bernabéu

Football

(📞 91 398 43 00, 902 301709; www.realmadrid. com; Calle Concha Espina 1; 🕐 10am-7.30pm Mon-Sat, 10.30am-6.30pm Sun, except match days; Ⓜ Santiago Bernabéu) El Estadio Santiago Bernabéu is one of the world's great football arenas; watching a game here is akin to a pilgrimage for sports fans and doing so alongside 80,000 passionate *Madridistas* (Real Madrid supporters) will send chills down your spine. Those who can't come to a game can at least stop by for a **tour** (📞 91 398 43 00, 902 291709; www.realmadrid.com; Avenida de Concha Espina 1; tour adult/child €19/13; 🕐 10am-7pm Mon-Sat, 10.30am-6.30pm Sun, except match days; Ⓜ Santiago Bernabéu), a peek at the trophies or to buy Real Madrid memorabilia in the **club shop** (Gate 57, Estadio Santiago Bernabéu, Avenida de Concha Espina 1; 🕐 10am-8.30pm; Ⓜ Santiago Bernabéu). There is another **branch** (Map p310; Tienda Real Madrid; 📞 521 79 50; Calle del Carmen 3; 🕐 10am-8.45pm Mon-Sat, 10am-6.45pm Sun; Ⓜ Sol) in the centre of town.

🔒 Shopping

The key to shopping Madrid-style is knowing where to look. Salamanca is the home of upmarket fashions, with chic boutiques lining up to showcase the best that Spanish and international designers have to offer. Some of it spills over into Chueca, but Malasaña is Salamanca's true alter ego, home to fashion as funky as it is offbeat and ideal for that studied underground look that will fit right in with Madrid's hedonistic after-dark crowd. Central Madrid – Sol, Huertas or La Latina – offers plenty of individual surprises.

El Rastro

Market

(Map p310; Calle de la Ribera de Curtidores; 🕐 8am-3pm Sun; Ⓜ La Latina, Puerta de Toledo, Tirso de Molina) A Sunday morning at El

Rastro, Europe's largest flea market, is a Madrid institution. A word of warning: pickpockets love El Rastro as much as everyone else.

Antigua Casa Talavera   Ceramics
(Map p310; Calle de Isabel la Católica 2; ⏱10am-1.30pm & 5-8pm Mon-Fri, 10am-1.30pm Sat; Ⓜ Santo Domingo) The extraordinary tiled facade of this wonderful old shop conceals an Aladdin's cave of ceramics from all over Spain.

El Flamenco Vive   Flamenco
(Map p310; www.elflamencovive.es; Calle Conde de Lemos 7; ⏱10.30am-2pm & 5-9pm Mon-Sat; Ⓜ Ópera) This temple to flamenco has it all, from guitars and songbooks to well-priced CDs, polka-dotted dancing costumes, shoes, colourful plastic jewellery and literature about flamenco.

Casa de Diego   Accessories
(Map p310; www.casadediego.com; Plaza de la Puerta del Sol 12; ⏱9.30am-8pm Mon-Sat; Ⓜ Sol) This classic shop has been around since 1858, making, selling and repairing Spanish fans, shawls, umbrellas and canes.

ⓘ Information

Dangers & Annoyances
Madrid is a generally safe city although, as in most European cities, you should be wary of pickpockets in the city centre, on the metro and around major tourist sights.

Prostitution along Calle de la Montera means that you need to exercise extra caution along this street.

Discount Cards
The Madrid Card (☎91 360 47 72; www.madridcard.com; 1/2/3 days adult €39/49/59, child 6-12 yr €20/28/34) includes free entry to more than 40 museums in and around Madrid and discounts on public transport.

Left Luggage
At Madrid's Barajas airport, there are three *consignas* (left-luggage offices; ⏱24hr). In either, you pay €4.95 for the first 24-hour period (or fraction thereof). Thereafter, it costs €4.33/5.56 per day per small/large bag. Similar services operate for similar prices at Atocha and Chamartín train stations (open 7am to 11pm).

Tourist Information
Centro de Turismo de Madrid (☎91 588 16 36; www.esmadrid.com; Plaza Mayor 27; ⏱9.30am-

El Rastro flea market (p319), Madrid

8.30pm; **M** Sol) Excellent city tourist office with a smaller office underneath Plaza de Colón and information points at Plaza de la Cibeles, Plaza de Callao, outside the Centro de Arte Reina Sofía and at the T4 terminal at Barajas airport.

ℹ Getting There & Away

Air

Madrid's international Barajas airport (MAD), 15km northeast of the city, is Europe's fourth- or fifth-busiest airport (depending on the year), with flights coming in from all over Europe and beyond.

Car & Motorcycle

The city is surrounded by two main ring roads, the outermost M-40 and the inner M-30; there are also two additional partial ring roads, the M-45 and the more-distant M-50.

Train

Madrid is served by two main train stations. The bigger of the two is **Puerta de Atocha** (**M** Atocha Renfe), at the southern end of the city centre. **Chamartín train station** (**M** Chamartín) lies in the north of the city. The bulk of trains for Spanish destinations depart from Atocha, especially those going south. International services arrive at and leave from Chamartín. For bookings, contact **Renfe** (☎ 902 240 202; www.renfe.es) at either station.

High-speed Tren de Alta Velocidad Española (AVE) services connect Madrid with Seville (via Córdoba), Valladolid (via Segovia), Toledo, Valencia, Málaga and Barcelona (via Zaragoza and Tarragona).

ℹ Getting Around

To/From the Airport

Bus

The **Exprés Aeropuerto** (Airport Express; www.emtmadrid.es; €5; ⊙24hr; 🛜) bus runs between Puerta de Atocha train station and the airport. Buses run every 13 to 23 minutes from 6am to 11.30pm, and every 35 minutes throughout the rest of the night. The trip takes 40 minutes. From 11.55pm until 5.35am, departures are from the Plaza de Cibeles, not the train station.

The excellent, privately run **AeroCITY** (☎ 91 747 75 70; www.aerocity.com; per person from €20, express service from €35 per minibus) operates a door-to-door service from the airport.

Metro

Line 8 of the metro (entrances in T2 and T4) runs to the Nuevos Ministerios transport interchange, which connects with lines 10 and 6. It operates from 6.05am to 2am. A one-way ticket to/from the airport costs €4.50. The journey from the airport to Nuevos Ministerios takes around 15 minutes, around 25 minutes from T4.

Taxi

A taxi to the city centre will cost you around €25 in total (up to €35 from T4), depending on traffic and where you're going; in addition to what the meter reads, you pay a €5.50 airport supplement.

Public Transport

Madrid's **metro** (www.metromadrid.es) is extensive and well maintained. A single ride costs €1.50 and a 10-ride ticket is €12.20. The metro is quick, clean, relatively safe and runs from 6.05am until 2am.

The bus system is also good; contact **EMT** (www.emtmadrid.es) for more information. Twenty-six night-bus *búhos* (owls) operate from midnight to 6am, with all routes originating in Plaza de la Cibeles.

Taxi

You can pick up a taxi at ranks throughout town or simply flag one down. Flag fall is €2.15 from 6am to 10pm daily, €2.20 from 10pm to 6am Sunday to Friday and €3.10 from 10pm Saturday to 6am Sunday. Several supplementary charges, usually posted inside the taxi, apply; these include €5.50 to/from the airport and €2.95 from taxi ranks at train and bus stations.

Radio-Teléfono Taxi (☎ 91 547 82 00; www.radiotelefono-taxi.com)

Tele-Taxi (☎ 91 371 21 31; www.tele-taxi.es)

CASTILLA Y LEÓN

Spain's Castilian heartland, Castilla y León is scattered with hilltop towns sporting magnificent Gothic cathedrals, monumental city walls and mouth-watering restaurants.

Salamanca

POP 153,470

Whether floodlit by night or bathed in midday sun, Salamanca is a dream

If You Like...
Spanish Architecture

From Córdoba's Mezquita (p367) to the hanging houses of Cuenca (p327), the Spanish certainly have a taste for eye-catching architecture.

1 AVILA'S MURALLAS
(adult/child €4/2.50; ⏱10am-8pm Tue-Sun) Ávila's splendid 12th-century walls rank among the world's best-preserved medieval defensive perimeters. Raised to a height of 12m between the 11th and 12th centuries, the walls stretch for 2.5km atop the remains of earlier Roman and Muslim battlements. Two sections of the walls can be climbed. The regional tourist office runs free guided tours. More than 30 trains run daily to Madrid and Salamanca.

2 SEGOVIA'S ALCÁZAR
(www.alcazardesegovia.com; Plaza de la Reina Victoria Eugenia; adult/child €4/3, tower €2, EU citizens free 3rd Tue of month; ⏱10am-7pm Apr-Sep) Supposedly the inspiration for Sleeping Beauty's castle in Walt Disney's film, Segovia's Alcázar definitely has fairytale dimensions. The 13th-century structure burned down in 1862 and was later rebuilt: it now houses a collection of armour and military gear, and the views across town are stunning. Regular trains run from Madrid to Segovia's train station.

3 RONDA
Ronda is the most dramatically sited of Andalucía's *pueblos blancos* (white villages). Look out for the amazing 18th-century Puente Nuevo (New Bridge) to the old town, and the Plaza de Toros, considered the national home of bullfighting. Trains and buses run to/from Algeciras, Granada, Córdoba and Málaga.

destination. This is a city of rare architectural splendour, awash with golden sandstone overlaid with Latin inscriptions in ochre, and with an extraordinary virtuosity of plateresque and Renaissance styles.

⊙ Sights

Plaza Mayor   Square
Built between 1729 and 1755, Salamanca's exceptional grand square is widely considered to be Spain's most beautiful central plaza. The square is particularly memorable at night when illuminated (until midnight) to magical effect.

Catedral Nueva & Catedral Vieja   Churches
(www.catedralsalamanca.org) Curiously, Salamanca is home to two cathedrals: the newer and larger cathedral was built beside the old Romanesque one instead of on top of it, as was the norm. The **Catedral Nueva** (Plaza de Anaya; ⏱9am-8pm) FREE, completed in 1733, is a late-Gothic masterpiece that took 220 years to build. Its magnificent Renaissance doorways stand out. For fine views over Salamanca, head to the southwestern corner of the cathedral facade and the **Puerta de la Torre** (Jeronimus; Plaza de Juan XXIII; admission €3.75; ⏱10am-7.15pm), from where stairs lead up through the tower.

The largely Romanesque **Catedral Vieja** (Plaza de Anaya; admission €4.75; ⏱10am-7.30pm) is a 12th-century temple with a stunning 15th-century altarpiece, which has 53 panels depicting scenes from the life of Christ and Mary, topped by a representation of the Final Judgement. The entrance is inside the Catedral Nueva.

Universidad Civil   Historic Building
(Calle de los Libreros; adult/child €4/2, Mon morning free; ⏱9.30am-1.30pm & 4-6.30pm Mon-Fri, 10am-1.30pm Sun) Founded initially as the Estudio Generál in 1218, Salamanca's university came into being in 1254 and reached the peak of its renown in the 15th and 16th centuries. You can visit the old classrooms and the oldest university library in Europe.

The university's facade is an ornate mass of sculptures and carvings, and hidden among this 16th-century plateresque creation is a tiny stone frog. Legend says that those who find the frog will have good luck in studies, life and love. It's sitting on a skull on the pillar that runs up the right-hand side of the facade.

Casa de las Conchas · Historical Building

(Calle de la Compañía 2; ☺9am-9pm Mon-Fri, 10am-2pm & 4-7pm Sat & Sun) FREE This glorious building has been a city symbol since it was built in the 15th century.

Sleeping

Microtel Placentinos · Boutique Hotel €€

(☎923 28 15 31; www.microtelplacentinos.com; Calle de Placentinos 9; s/d incl breakfast Sun-Thu €56/72, Fri & Sat €86/99; ❄🐱) One of Salamanca's most charming boutique hotels, Microtel Placentinos is tucked away on a quiet street and has rooms with exposed stone walls and wooden beams.

Hostal Concejo · Hostal €

(☎923 21 47 37; www.hconcejo.com; Plaza de la Libertad 1; s/d €45/60; P❄🐱) A cut above the average hostal, the stylish Concejo has polished-wood floors, tasteful furnishings, light-filled rooms and a superb central location. Try and snag one of the corner rooms (like number 104) with its traditional glassed-in balcony.

Eating

La Cocina de Toño · Tapas €€

(www.lacocinadetoño.es; Calle Gran Vía 20; menú del día €17, tapas €1.30-3.80, mains €6.90-23; ☺lunch & dinner Tue-Sat, lunch Sun) We're yet to hear a bad word about this place and its loyal following owes everything to its creative *pinchos* (tapas) and half-servings of exotic dishes. The restaurant serves more

traditional fare as befits the decor, but the bar is one of Salamanca's gastronomic stars.

Mesón Cervantes · Castilian €€

(www.mesoncervantes.com; Plaza Mayor 15; menú del día €13.50, mains €10-22; ☺10am-midnight) Although there are outdoor tables on the plaza, the dark wooden beams and atmospheric buzz of the Spanish crowd on the 1st floor should be experienced at least once; if you snaffle a window table in the evening, you've hit the jackpot. The food's a mix of *platos combinados,* salads and *raciones*.

El Pecado · Modern Spanish €€

(☎923 26 65 58; www.elpecadorestaurante. es; Plaza de Poeta Iglesias 12; menú del día €15, mains €15-33) A trendy place that regularly attracts Spanish celebrities (eg Pedro Almodóvar and Ferran Adrià), El Pecado (The Sin) has an intimate dining room and a quirky, creative menu; it's a reasonably priced place to sample high-quality, innovative Spanish cooking.

Catedral Nueva, Salamanca
CAMILO MARANCHÓN/GETTY IMAGES ©

ℹ Information

Municipal tourist office (☏ 923 21 83 42; www.turismodesalamanca.com; Plaza Mayor 14; ⏱ 9am-2pm & 4.30-8pm Mon-Fri, 10am-8pm Sat, 10am-2pm Sun)

Regional tourist office (☏ 923 26 85 71; www. turismocastillayleon.com; Casa de las Conchas, Rúa Mayor; ⏱ 9am-8pm)

ℹ Getting There & Away

Up to eight trains depart daily for Madrid's Chamartín station (€19.85, 2½ hours) via Ávila (€10.05, one hour). The train station is about 1km beyond Plaza de España.

CASTILLA-LA MANCHA

Known as the stomping ground of Don Quijote and Sancho Panza, Castilla-La Mancha conjures up images of lonely windmills, medieval castles and bleak, treeless plains. The characters of Miguel de Cevantes provide the literary context, but the richly historic cities of Toledo and Cuenca are the most compelling reasons to visit.

Toledo

POP 83,110

Toledo is Spain's equivalent of a downsized Rome. Commanding a hill rising above the Tajo River, it's crammed with monuments that attest to the waves of conquerors and communities – Roman, Visigoth, Jewish, Muslim and Christian – who have called the city home during its turbulent history. It's one of the country's major tourist attractions.

◎ Sights

Catedral   Cathedral

(Plaza del Ayuntamiento; adult/child €7/free; ⏱ 10.30am-6.30pm Mon-Sat, 2-6.30pm Sun) Toledo's cathedral dominates the skyline, reflecting the city's historical significance as the heart of Catholic Spain. Within its hefty stone walls there are stained-glass windows, tombs of kings and art in the sacristy by the likes of El Greco, Zurbarán, Crespi, Titian, Rubens and Velázquez.

Alcázar   Fortress, Museum

(Museo del Ejército; Calle Alféreces Provisionales; adult/child €5/free; ⏱ 10am-9pm Thu-Tue Jun-Sep, to 7pm Oct-May) At the highest point in the city looms the foreboding Alcázar. Abd ar-Rahman III raised an *al-qasr* (fortress) here in the 10th century, which was thereafter altered by the Christians. The Alcázar was heavily damaged during the siege of the garrison by loyalist militias at the start of the Civil War in 1936. Rebuilt under Franco, the Alcázar has recently been reopened as an absolutely enormous military museum, with strict staff barking orders adding to the martial experience. The usual displays of uniforms and medals are here, but the best part is the exhaustive historical

Toledo
KEN WELSH/DESIGN PICS/GETTY IMAGES ©

section, with an in-depth overview of the nation's history in Spanish and English.

Sinagoga del Tránsito — Synagogue

(http://museosefardi.mcu.es; Calle Samuel Leví; adult/child €3/1.50, with Museo del Greco €5; ⏱9.30am-8pm Tue-Sat Apr-Sep, to 6.30pm Oct-Mar, 10am-3pm Sun) Toledo's former *judería* (Jewish quarter) was once home to 11 synagogues. The bulk of Toledo's Jews were expelled in 1492. This magnificent synagogue was built in 1355 by special permission of Pedro I (construction of synagogues was prohibited in Christian Spain). The synagogue now houses the **Museo Sefardi**.

Monasterio San Juan de los Reyes — Monastery

(Calle San Juan de los Reyes 2; admission €2.50; ⏱10am-6.45pm) This early 17th-century Franciscan monastery and church of San Juan de los Reyes is notable for its delightful cloisters.

Iglesia de Santo Tomé — Church

(www.santotome.org; Plaza del Conde; admission €2.50; ⏱10am-6pm mid-Oct–mid-Mar, to 7pm mid-Mar–mid-Oct) This otherwise modest church contains El Greco's masterpiece, *El Entierro del Conde de Orgaz* (The Burial of the Count of Orgaz).

Mezquita del Cristo de la Luz — Mosque

(Calle Cristo de la Luz; admission €2.50; ⏱10am-2pm & 3.30-6.45pm Mon-Fri, 10am-6.45pm Sat & Sun) On the northern slopes of town you'll find this modest, yet beautiful mosque where architectural traces of Toledo's medieval Muslim conquerors are still in evidence. Built around AD 1000, it suffered the usual fate of being converted to a church (hence the religious frescoes), but the original vaulting and arches survived.

🛏 Sleeping

Accommodation is often full, especially from Easter to September. Many visitors choose to come on a day trip from Madrid.

❤ If You Like…
Spanish Cathedrals

The soaring spires of La Sagrada Família (p332) are a must-see, but they're just the most recent in a long line of amazing ecclesiastical edifices.

1 CATEDRAL DE SANTIAGO DE COMPOSTELA

(www.catedraldesantiago.es; Praza do Obradoiro; ⏱7am-9pm) The cathedral in Santiago de Compostela has been a magnet for pilgrims for over 1000 years. It's a mix of Romanesque, baroque and Gothic; the bulk of the building was built between 1075 and 1211. For a bird's-eye view, don't miss the **cathedral rooftop tour** (📞981 55 29 85; www.catedraldesantiago.es; per person €10; ⏱10am-2pm & 4-8pm).

2 LEÓN CATEDRAL

(www.catedraldeleon.org; adult/concession/child €5/4/free; ⏱8.30am-1.30pm & 4-8pm Mon-Sat, 8.30am-2.30pm & 5-8pm Sun) León's 13th-century cathedral, with its soaring towers, flying buttresses and breathtaking interior, is the city's heart. It's notable for its medieval stained glass: there are 128 windows in all, covering an area of 1800 sq metres. Trains run to Burgos, Madrid and Barcelona.

3 GIRONA CATEDRAL

(www.catedraldegirona.org; Plaça de la Catedral; museum adult/child €5/1.20, Sun free; ⏱10am-8pm) Girona's baroque cathedral has Europe's widest Gothic nave (23m) and a beautiful 12th-century Romanesque cloister. Girona is 103km northeast of Barcelona and well served by trains.

4 BURGOS CATEDRAL

(Plaza del Rey Fernando; adult/child €5/2.50; ⏱9.30am-6.30pm) Burgos' Unesco-listed cathedral is a French-Gothic creation dating from the 13th century. It's notable as the last resting place of the Spanish hero El Cid, whose elaborate tomb can be seen beneath the cathedral's star-vaulted dome. The city is well connected by train and bus to Madrid, León and Bilbao.

Casa de Cisneros   Boutique Hotel €€
(☎ 925 22 88 28; www.hostal-casa-de-cisneros.com; Calle Cardenal Cisneros; s/d incl breakfast €55/75; ❄ 🛜) Right by Toledo's cathedral, this lovely 16th-century house was once the home of the cardinal and Grand Inquisitor Cisneros (often known as Ximénes). It's a superb choice, with cosy, seductive rooms with original wooden beams and walls and voguish bathrooms.

La Posada de Manolo   Boutique Hotel €€
(☎ 925 28 22 50; www.laposadademanolo.com; Calle de Sixto Ramón Parro 8; s/d incl breakfast €46/76; ❄ 🛜) This memorable hotel has themed each floor with furnishings and decor reflecting one of the three cultures of Toledo: Christian, Islamic and Jewish. There are stunning views of the old town and cathedral from the terrace.

🍴 Eating

Alfileritos 24   Modern Spanish €€€
(www.alfileritos24.com; Calle de los Alfileritos 24; mains €15-21, bar food €6-11; ⏰ 9.30am-midnight, to 1am Fri & Sat) The 14th-century surroundings of columns, beams and barrel-vault ceilings are snazzily coupled with modern artwork and bright dining rooms in an atrium space spread over four floors. The menu demonstrates an innovative flourish in the kitchen. The ground-floor bar offers good-value tapas and cheaper fare designed for sharing.

La Abadía   Tapas €
(www.abadiatoledo.com; Plaza de San Nicolás 3; raciones €4-15) In a former 16th-century palace, arches, niches and subtle lighting are spread over a warren of brick-and-stone-clad rooms. The menu includes lightweight dishes and tapas portions – perfect for small appetites.

ℹ Information

Main tourist office (☎ 925 25 40 30; www.toledo-turismo.com; Plaza del Ayuntamiento; ⏰10am-6pm)

Provincial tourist office (www.diputoledo.es; Subida de la Granja; ⏰10am-5pm Mon-Sat, to 3pm Sun)

ℹ Getting There & Away
The high-speed AVE service runs every hour or so to Madrid (€10.60, 30 minutes).

Mercat de la Boqueria, Barcelona

CATALONIA

Home to stylish Barcelona, ancient Tarragona, romantic Girona, and countless alluring destinations along the coast, in the Pyrenees and in the rural interior, Catalonia (Catalunya in Catalan, Cataluña in Castilian) is a treasure box waiting to be opened.

Barcelona

POP 1.62 MILLION

Barcelona is one of Europe's coolest cities. Despite two millennia of history, it's a forward-thinking place, always on the cutting edge of art, design and cuisine. Whether you explore its medieval palaces and plazas, admire the modernista masterpieces, shop for designer fashions along its bustling boulevards, sample its exciting nightlife or just soak up the sun on the beaches, you'll find it hard not to fall in love with this vibrant city.

 Sights

LA RAMBLA

La Rambla is Spain's most talked-about boulevard. It certainly packs a lot of colour into a short walk, with flower stands, historic buildings, a sensory-rich produce market, overpriced beers and tourist tat, and a ceaselessly changing parade of people from all corners of the globe.

Mercat de la Boqueria   Market
(Map p342; 93 412 13 15; www.boqueria.info; La Rambla 91; ⏰8am-8.30pm Mon-Sat; MLiceu) One of the greatest sound, smell and colour sensations in Europe is Barcelona's most central produce market, the Mercat de la Boqueria. It spills over with all the rich and varied colour of plentiful fruit and vegetable stands, seemingly limitless varieties of sea critters, sausages, cheeses, meat (including the finest Jabugo ham) and sweets. Note also its Modernista-influenced design.

Plaça Reial   Square
(Map p342; MLiceu) One of the most photogenic squares in Barcelona, the Plaça Reial is a delightful retreat from

---

Detour:
Cuenca

A World Heritage site, Cuenca is one of Spain's most memorable small cities, its old centre a stage set of evocative medieval buildings. Most emblematic are the 14th-century *casas colgadas*, the hanging houses that jut out precariously over the steep defile of Río Huécar. Inside one of the houses is the **Museo de Arte Abstracto Español** (Museum of Abstract Art; www.march.es/arte/cuenca; adult/child €3/free; ⏰11am-2pm & 4-6pm Tue-Fri, 11am-2pm & 4-8pm Sat, 11am-2.30pm Sun). Cuenca is also famous for its Semana Santa (Holy Week) processions; stop by the **Museo de la Semana Santa** (www.msscuenca.org; Calle Andrés de Cabrera 13; adult/child €3/free; ⏰11am-2pm & 4.30-7.30pm Thu-Sat, 11am-2pm Sun; 👪) to see why.

There's a **tourist office** (http://turismo.cuenca.es; Calle Alfonso VIII 2; ⏰9am-9pm Mon-Sat, to 2.30pm Sun), and Cuenca is most easily reached along the Madrid–Valencia rail line.

---

the traffic and pedestrian mobs on the nearby Rambla. Numerous eateries, bars and nightspots lie beneath the arcades of 19th-century neoclassical buildings, with a buzz of activity at all hours.

The lamp posts by the central fountain are Antoni Gaudí's first known works in the city.

Mirador de Colom   Viewpoint
(Map p342; 93 302 52 24; Plaça del Portal de la Pau; lift adult/child €4/3; ⏰8.30am-8.30pm; MDrassanes) High above the swirl of traffic on the roundabout below, Columbus keeps permanent watch, pointing vaguely out to the Mediterranean. Built for the Universal Exhibition in 1888, the monument allows you to zip up 60m in the lift

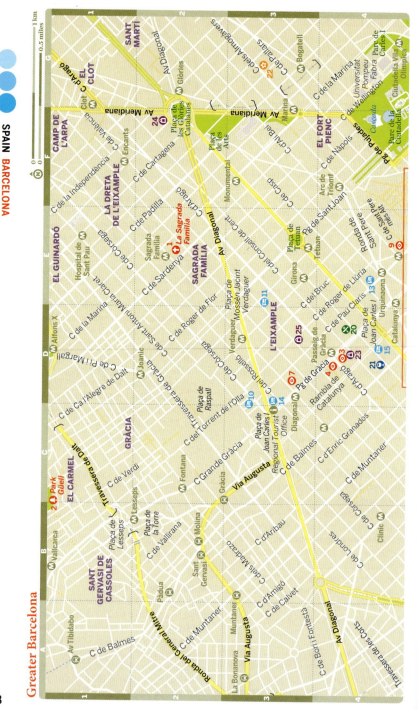

Greater Barcelona

1 km
0.5 miles

SANT MARTÍ

EL CLOT

CAMP DE L'ARPA

Clot C d'Aragó

Av Meridiana

Av Diagonal

Glòries

C de Cartagena

C de València

Encants

LA DRETA DE L'EIXAMPLE

EL GUINARDÓ

C de la Independència

C de Padilla

C de Còrsega

Hospital de Sant Pau

Sagrada Família

C de Sardenya

1 La Sagrada Família

SAGRADA FAMÍLIA

C d'Aragó

Av Diagonal

C de Roger de Flor

C del Consell de Cent

Plaça de les Glòries Catalanes

Plaça de les Arts

C d'Ali Bei

Av Meridiana

Marina

EL FORT PIENC

C de la Marina

C de Napols

Pg de Pujades

Arc de Triomf

Ronda de Sant Pere

Parc de la Ciutadella

Parc de Carles I

Ciutadella Vila Olímpica

Universitat Pompeu Fabra

C de Wellington

C de la Marina

Cascada

24

22

9

13

11

25

20

23

3

21

15

7

4

10

14

2 Park Güell

Tettuan

Plaça de Tetuan

Girona

C del Bruc

C de Roger de Llúria

C de Pau Claris

Plaça de Joan Carles I

Urquinaona

Catalunya

Passeig de Gràcia

Pg de Sant Joan

Casp

Monumental

Plaça de Mossèn Jacint Verdaguer

Verdaguer

C de Còrsega

C de Rosselló

L'EIXAMPLE

Pg de Gràcia

Rambla de Catalunya

C d'Aragó

Diagonal

C de Balmes

C d'Enric Granados

C de Muntaner

Clínic

C de Còrsega

C de Londres

Av Diagonal

Regional Tourist Office

Plaça de Joan Carles I

Via Augusta

Diagonal

Alfons X

C de la Marina

Joanic

C de Sant Antoni Maria Claret

C de Pi i Margall

GRÀCIA

EL CARMEL

Travessera de Dalt

C de Cal'Alegre de Dalt

Travessera de Gràcia

Plaça de Raspall

C del Torrent de l'Olla

Plaça del Sol

C de Verdi

C Grande Gràcia

Fontana

M Gràcia

Lesseps

Plaça de Lesseps

Vallcarca

SANT GERVASI DE CASSOLES

Plaça de la Torre

C de Vallirana

Molina

Sant Gervasi

Pàdua

C dels Madrazo

C d'Amigó

C d'Aribau

Via Augusta

Muntaner

La Bonanova

Av Tibidabo

C de Balmes

C de Muntaner

Ronda del General Mitre

C de Calvet

C de Borí i Fontestà

Travessera de les Corts

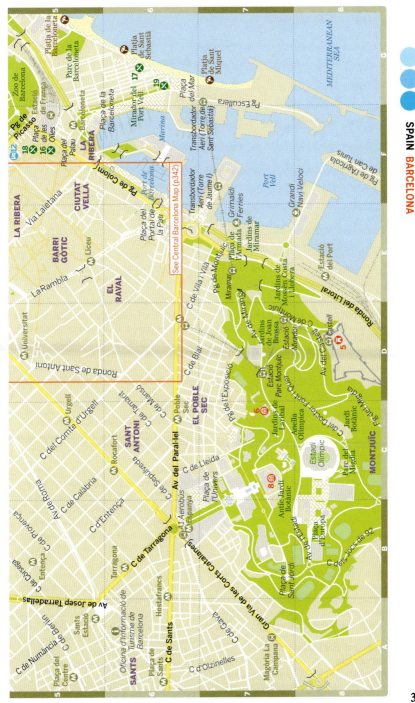

Platja de la
Barceloneta

Parc de la
Barceloneta

Zoo de
Barcelona

Estació
de França

17 ❌
19 ❌

Platja de
Sant
Sebastià

Platja
de Sant
Miquel

MEDITERRANEAN
SEA

Pg de
Picasso

18
16 ❌

Plaça
de les
Olles

Plaça
del
Palau

LA
BARCELONETA

Plaça de la
Barceloneta

Mirador del
Port Vell

Plaça
del Mar

Pg d'Escullera

Marina

LA
RIBERA

Pg de Colom

Port de
Barcelona

Transbordador
Aeri (Torre de
Sant Sebastià)

LA RIBERA

Via Laietana

CIUTAT
VELLA

Liceu

Plaça del
Portal de
la Pau

Transbordador
Aeri (Torre
de Jaume I)

Port
Vell

Pg de l'Agrícola
Pg de Can Tunis

BARRI
GÒTIC

See Central Barcelona Map (p342)

Grimaldi
Ferries

Jardins de
Miramar

Grandi
Navi Veloci

Estació
del Port

La Rambla

EL
RAVAL

Plaça de
l'Armada

Jardins de
Mossèn Costa
i Llobera

Universitat

Ronda de Sant Antoni

Pg de Montjuïc

C de Vila i Vila

Miramar

Av de Miramar

Jardins de
Joan
Brossa

Estació
Mirador

C de Montjuïc

Estació
del Port

Ronda del Litoral

C del Comte d'Urgell

Rocafort

SANT
ANTONI

C de Tamarit

C de Blai

Poble
Sec

EL POBLE
SEC

Pg de l'Exposició

5

Castell

C del Castell

Av del Castell

Pg de la Mare

C de Calàbria

C d'Entença

C de sepúlveda

Av del Paral·lel

C de Manso

Estació
Parc Montjuïc

Jardins de
Laribal

6

Anella
Olímpica

C del Doctor Font i Quer

Jardí
Botànic

MONTJUÏC

C de Lleida

Plaça de
l'Univers

Estadi
Olímpic

Parc del
Migdia

Av de Roma

C de Corsega

Entença

Tarragona

Al Aerobús
Espanya

Antic Jardí
Botànic

8

Plaça
d'Europa

C de Provença

C de Tarragona

Hostafrancs

Gran Via de les Corts Catalanes

Plaça de
Sant Jordi

Av del Estadi

C dels Jocs de 92

Oficina d'Informació de
Turisme de
Barcelona

Av de Josep Tarradellas

Sants
Estació

Plaça del
Centre

SANTS

C de Numància

C de Berlín

Plaça
de Sants

Sants

C de Sants

C de Gavà

C d'Olzinelles

Magòria La
Campana

Greater Barcelona

⊚ **Don't Miss Sights**
1 La Sagrada Família E2
2 Park Güell C1

⊚ **Sights**
3 Casa Amatller D4
4 Casa Batlló D4
5 Castell de Montjuïc D8
6 Fundació Joan Miró C7
7 La Pedrera D3
8 Museu Nacional d'Art de
   Catalunya C7
9 Palau de la Música Catalana E4

🛌 **Sleeping**
10 Aparteasy D3
11 Barcelona On Line E3
12 Chic & Basic F5
13 Hostal Goya E4
14 Hotel Omm D3

15 Hotel Praktik D4

🍴 **Eating**
16 Cal Pep F5
17 Can Majó G6
18 Casa Delfín F5
19 Suquet De L'Almirall G6
20 Tapaç 24 .... D4

🍷 **Drinking & Nightlife**
21 Monvínic D4

★ **Entertainment**
   Palau de la Música Catalana .... (see 9)
22 Razzmatazz G3

🛍 **Shopping**
23 Antonio Miró D4
24 Els Encants Vells .... on F2
25 Joan Murrià D3

for bird's-eye views back up La Rambla and across the ports of Barcelona.

BARRI GÒTIC

You could easily spend several days or even a week exploring the Barri Gòtic, Barcelona's oldest quarter, without leaving the medieval streets.

La Catedral   Church
(Map p342; ☎ 93 342 82 60; www.website.es/catedralbcn; Plaça de la Seu; special visit €5, choir admission €2.20; ☺8am-12.45pm & 5.15-8pm Mon-Sat, special visit 1-5pm Mon-Sat, 2-5pm Sun & holidays; MJaume I) FREE Barcelona's Gothic Catedral was built atop the ruins of an 11th-century Romanesque church. Highlights include the cool cloister, the crypt tomb of martyr Santa Eulàlia (one of Barcelona's two patron saints), the choir stalls, the lift to the rooftop and the modest art collection in the **Sala Capitular** (Map p342; Chapter House; admission €2; ☺10am-12.15pm & 5.15-7pm Mon-Sat, 10am-12.45pm & 5.15-7pm Sun). You only pay the individual prices if you visit outside the special visiting hours.

Museu d'Història de
Barcelona   Museum
(Map p342; ☎ 93 256 21 00; www.museuhistoria.bcn.cat; Plaça del Rei; adult/child €7/free; from

4pm 1st Sat of month and from 3pm Sun free; ☺10am-7pm Tue-Sat, 10am-8pm Sun; MJaume I) Not far from the Barcelona Catedral is pretty Plaça del Rei and the fascinating Museu d'Història de Barcelona, where you can visit a 4000-sq-metre excavated site of Roman Barcelona under the plaza.

EL RAVAL

To the west of La Rambla is El Raval district, a once-seedy, now-funky area overflowing with cool bars and shops.

MACBA   Museum
(Map p342; Museu d'Art Contemporani de Barcelona; ☎ 93 412 08 10; www.macba.cat; Plaça dels Àngels 1; adult/concession €7.50/6; ☺11am-8pm Mon & Wed, to midnight Thu-Fri, 10am-8pm Sat, 10am-3pm Sun & holidays; MUniversitat) Designed by Richard Meier and opened in 1995, Macba (Museu d'Art Contemporani de Barcelona) has become the city's foremost contemporary art centre, with captivating exhibitions for the serious art lover. The permanent collection is on the ground floor and dedicates itself to Spanish and Catalan art from the second half of the 20th century, with works by Antoni Tàpies, Joan Brossa and Miquel Barceló, among others, though international art-

ists, such as Paul Klee, Bruce Nauman and John Cage are also represented.

LA RIBERA

In medieval days, La Ribera was a stone's throw from the Mediterranean and the heart of Barcelona's foreign trade, with homes belonging to numerous wealthy merchants. Now it's a trendy district full of boutiques, restaurants and bars.

Església de Santa Maria del Mar   Church
(Map p342; ☎93 319 05 16; Plaça de Santa Maria del Mar; ⊙9am-1.30pm & 4.30-8pm; Ⓜ Jaume I) At the southwest end of Passeig del Born stands Barcelona's finest Catalan Gothic church, Santa Maria del Mar (Our Lady of the Sea). Built in the 14th century with record-breaking alacrity for the time (it took just 54 years), the church is remarkable for its architectural harmony and simplicity.

Palau de la Música Catalana   Architecture
(Map p328; ☎902 475 485; www.palaumusica. org; Carrer de Sant Francesc de Paula 2; adult/ child/student & EU senior €15/free/€7.50; ⊙50 min tours every 30 minutes 10am-6pm Easter week & Aug, 10am-3.30pm Sep-Jul; Ⓜ Urquinaona) The opulent Palau de la Música Catalana is one of the city's most delightful modernista works. Designed by Lluís Domènech i Montaner in 1905, it hosts concerts regularly. It is well worth joining the guided tours to get a look inside if you don't make a concert.

Mercat de Santa Caterina   Market
(Map p342; ☎93 319 17 40; www.mercatsantacaterina. net; Avinguda de Francesc Cambó 16; ⊙7.30am-2pm Mon, to 3.30pm Tue, Wed & Sat, to 8.30pm Thu & Fri; Ⓜ Jaume I) With its loop- ily pastel-coloured wavy roof, Mercat de Santa Caterina is a temple to

fine foods designed by the adventurous Catalan architect Enric Miralles.

L'EIXAMPLE

Modernisme, the Catalan version of art nouveau, transformed Barcelona's cityscape in the early 20th century. Most modernista works were built in L'Eixample, the grid-plan district that was developed from the 1870s on.

La Pedrera   Architecture
(Map p328; Casa Milà; ☎902 400 973; www. lapedrera.com; Carrer de Provença 261-265; adult/ student/child €15/13.50/7.50; ⊙9am-8pm Mar-Oct, to 6.30pm Nov-Feb; Ⓜ Diagonal) This undulating beast is another madcap Gaudí masterpiece, built in 1905–10 as a com- bined apartment and office block. Formally called Casa Milà, after the businessman who commissioned it, the building is better known as La Pedrera (the Quarry) because of its uneven grey stone facade, which ripples around the corner of Carrer de Provença.

The Fundació Caixa Catalunya has opened the top-floor apartment, attic

La Pedrera, Barcelona

Don't Miss
La Sagrada Família

If you have time for only one sight-seeing outing in Barcelona, this should be it. La Sagrada Família inspires awe by its sheer verticality and, in the manner of the medieval cathedrals it emulates, it's still under construction after more than 100 years. When completed, the highest tower will be more than half as high again as those that stand today.

Map p328

☎ 93 207 30 31

www.sagradafamilia.org

Carrer de Mallorca 401

adult/child under 10yr/senior & student €13/free/11

🕙 9am-8pm Apr-Sep, to 6pm Oct-Mar

Ⓜ Sagrada Família

History

The Temple Expiatori de la Sagrada Família (Expiatory Temple of the Holy Family) was Antoni Gaudí's all-consuming obsession. Given the commission by a conservative society that wished to build a temple as atonement for the city's sins of modernity, Gaudí saw its completion as his holy mission. Many scholars believe it's his masterpiece, and so it should be, considering he worked on it for 43 years.

Design

Gaudí devised a temple 95m long and 60m wide, able to seat 13,000 people, with a central tower 170m high above the transept (representing Christ) and another 17 towers of 100m or more. It's a slender structure devoted to geometric perfection and sacred symbolism. It's also a work in progress, spanning the generations but never losing Gaudí's breathtaking originality and architectural synthesis of natural forms. Some of the many highlights include the apse, Nativity Facade, Passion Facade, Glory Facade and the Museu Gaudí.

The Present Day

Unfinished though it may be, La Sagrada Família still attracts around 2.8 million visitors a year and is the most visited monument in Spain. The most important recent tourist was Pope Benedict XVI, who consecrated the church in a huge ceremony in November 2010.

La Sagrada Família

RECOMMENDATIONS FROM JORDI FAULÍ, DEPUTY ARCHITECTURAL DIRECTOR FOR LA SAGRADA FAMÍLIA

1 PASSION FACADE
Among the Fachada de la Pasión's stand-out features are the angled columns, dramatic scenes from Jesus' last hours, an extraordinary rendering of the Last Supper and a bronze door that reads like a sculpted book. But the most surprising view is from inside the door on the extreme right.

2 MAIN NAVE
The majestic Nave Principal showcases Gaudí's use of tree motifs for columns to support the domes: he described this space as a forest. But it's the skylights that give the nave its luminous quality, even more so since the scaffolding has been removed and light floods onto the apse and main altar from the skylight 75m above the floor.

3 SIDE NAVE & NATIVITY TRANSEPT
Although beautiful in its own right with windows that project light into the interior, this is the perfect place to view the sculpted treelike columns and get an overall perspective of the main nave. Turn around and you're confronted with the inside of the Nativity Facade, an alternative view that most visitors miss; the stained-glass windows are superb.

4 NATIVITY FACADE
The Fachada del Nacimiento is Gaudí's grand hymn to Creation. Begin by viewing it front-on from a distance, then draw close enough (but to one side) to make out the details of its sculpted figures. The complement to the finely wrought detail is the majesty of the four parabolic towers that reach for the sky and are topped by Venetian stained glass.

5 THE MODEL OF COLÒNIA GÜELL
Of the many original models used by Gaudí on display in the Museu Gaudí, the most interesting is the church at Colònia Güell. From the side you can, thanks to the ingenious use of rope and cloth, visualise the harmony and beauty of the interior.

La Sagrada Família

A Timeline

1882 Francesc del Villar is commissioned to construct a neo-Gothic church.

1883 Antoni Gaudí takes over as chief architect, and plans a far more ambitious church to hold 13,000 faithful.

1926 Death of Gaudí; work continues under Domènec Sugrañes. Much of the **apse ①** and **Nativity Facade ②** is completed.

1930 Bell towers ③ of the Nativity Facade completed.

1936 Construction is interrupted by Spanish Civil War; anarchists destroy Gaudí's plans.

1939-40 Architect Francesc de Paula Quintana i Vidal restores the crypt and meticulously reassembles many of Gaudí's lost models, some of which can be seen in the **museum ④**.

1976 Completion of **Passion Facade ⑤**.

1986-2006 Sculptor Josep Subirachs adds sculptural details to the Passion Facade including the panels telling the story of Christ's last days, amid much criticism for employing a style far removed from what was thought typical of Gaudí.

2000 Central nave vault ⑥ completed.

2010 Church completely roofed over; Pope Benedict XVI consecrates the church; work begins on a high-speed rail tunnel that will pass beneath the church's **Glory Facade ⑦**.

2020-40 Projected completion date.

TOP TIPS

Light The best light through the stained-glass windows of the Passion Facade bursts through into the heart of the church in the late afternoon.

Time Visit at opening time on weekdays to avoid the worst of the crowds.

Views Head up the Nativity Facade bell towers for the views, as long queues generally await at the Passion Facade towers.

KRZYSZTOF DYDYNSKI/GETTY IMAGES ©

Spiral staircase

Nativity Facade
Gaudí used plaster casts of local people and even of the occasional corpse from the local morgue as models for the portraits in the Nativity scene.

Central nave vault

Apse
Built just after the crypt in mostly neo-Gothic style, it is capped by pinnacles that show a hint of the genius that Gaudí would later deploy in the rest of the church.

MICHELLE CHAPLOW/ALAMY ©

Bell towers
The towers (eight completed) of the three facades represent the 12 Apostles. Lifts whisk visitors up one tower of the Nativity and Passion Facades (the latter gets longer queues) for fine views.

Passion Facade

See the story of Christ's last days from Last Supper to burial in an S-shaped sequence from bottom to top of the facade. Check out the cryptogram in which the numbers always add up to 33, Christ's age at his death.

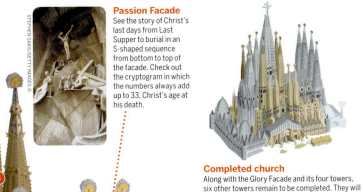
STEPHEN SAKS/GETTY IMAGES ©

Completed church

Along with the Glory Facade and its four towers, six other towers remain to be completed. They will represent the four Evangelists, the Virgin Mary and, soaring above them all over the transept, a 170m colossus symbolising Christ.

3

2

6

5

Crypt

The first completed part of the church, the crypt is in largely neo-Gothic style and lies under the transept. Gaudí's burial place here can be seen from the Museu Gaudí.

7

4

Escoles de Gaudí

Museu Gaudí

Jammed with old photos, drawings and restored plaster models that bring Gaudí's ambitions to life, the museum also houses an extraordinarily complex plumb-line device he used to calculate his constructions.

DIANA BIER/ALAMY ©

Glory Facade

This will be the most fanciful facade of all, with a narthex boasting 16 hyperboloid lanterns topped by cones that will look something like an organ made of melting ice cream.

and roof, together called the Espai Gaudí (Gaudí Space), to visitors.

Casa Batlló Architecture

(Map p328; ☎93 216 03 06; www.casabatllo.es; Passeig de Gràcia 43; adult/child under 7yr/ €18.15/free; ⏰9am-8pm; Ⓜ Passeig de Gràcia) One of the strangest residential buildings in Europe, this is Gaudí at his hallucinogenic best. The facade, sprinkled with bits of blue, mauve and green tiles and studded with wave-shaped window frames and balconies, rises to an uneven blue-tiled roof with a solitary tower.

Casa Amatller Architecture

(Map p328; ☎93 487 72 17; www.amatller.org; Passeig de Gràcia 41; ⏰10am-8pm Mon-Sat, to 3pm Sun, guided tour in English noon Fri, in Catalan & Spanish noon Wed; Ⓜ Passeig de Gràcia) FREE One of Puig i Cadafalch's most striking bits of Modernista fantasy, Casa Amatller combines Gothic window frames with a stepped gable borrowed from Dutch urban architecture.

MONTJUÏC

Southwest of the city centre and with views out to sea and over the city, Montjuïc serves as a Central Park of sorts and is a great place for a jog or stroll.

Museu Nacional d'Art de Catalunya Museum

(Map p328; MNAC; ☎93 622 03 76; www.mnac.es; Mirador del Palau Nacional; adult/senior & child under 15yr €10/free, 1st Sun of month free; ⏰10am-7pm Tue-Sat, to 2.30pm Sun & holidays, library 10am-6pm Mon-Fri, to 2.30pm Sat; Ⓜ Espanya) From across the city, the bombastic neobaroque silhouette of the Palau Nacional can be seen on the slopes of Montjuïc. Built for the 1929 World Exhibition and restored in 2005, it houses a vast collection of mostly Catalan art spanning the early Middle Ages to the early 20th century.

Fundació Joan Miró Museum

(Map p328; www.bcn.fjmiro.es; Plaça de Neptu; adult/senior & child €10/7; ⏰10am-8pm Tue, Wed, Fri & Sat, to 9.30pm Thu, to 2.30pm Sun & holidays; 🚌50, 55, 193, 🚋Paral·lel) Joan Miró, the city's best-known 20th-century artistic progeny, bequeathed this art foundation to his hometown in 1971. Its light-filled buildings are crammed with seminal works, from Miró's earliest timid sketches to paintings from his last years.

Castell de Montjuïc Fortress, Gardens

(Map p328; ⏰9am-9pm Tue-Sun Apr-Sep, to 7pm Tue-Sun Oct-Mar; 🚌193, Telefèric de Montjuïc Castell de Montjuïc) FREE The forbidding Castell (castle or fort) de Montjuïc dominates the southeastern heights of Montjuïc and enjoys commanding views over the Mediterranean.

Tours

Barcelona Walking Tours Walking

(Map p342; ☎93 285 38 34; www.barcelonaturisme.com; Plaça de Catalunya 17-S; Ⓜ Catalunya) The Oficina d'Informació de Turisme de Barcelona organises guided walking tours. One explores the **Barri Gòtic** (adult/child €14/5; ⏰in English 9.30am daily, in Spanish & Catalan 11.30am Sat); another follows in the footsteps of **Picasso** (adult/child €20/7; ⏰in English 3pm Tue, Thu & Sun) and winds up at the Museu Picasso, entry to which is included in the price; and a third takes in the main jewels of **modernisme** (adult/child €14/5; ⏰in English 4pm Fri & Sat Oct-May, 6pm Fri & Sat Jun-Sep). Also offered is a **gourmet tour** (adult/child €20/7; ⏰in English 10am Fri & Sat, in Spanish & Catalan 10.30am Sat) of traditional purveyors of fine foodstuffs across the old city. All tours last two hours and start at the tourist office. All tours are also available in both English and Spanish at 6pm from June to September.

Bus Turístic Bus

(☎93 285 38 32; www.barcelonaturisme.com; day ticket adult/child €24/14; ⏰9am-8pm) This hop-on, hop-off service covers three circuits (44 stops) linking virtually all the major tourist sights. Tourist offices, TMB transport authority offices and many hotels have leaflets explaining the system.

Festivals & Events

The **Festes de la Mercè** (www.bcn.cat/merce), held around 24 September, is the city's biggest party, with four days of concerts,

TRAVEL PICTURES/ALAMY ©

⭐ Don't Miss
Museu Picasso

The setting alone, in five contiguous medieval stone mansions, makes the Museu Picasso unique (and worth the probable queues). The pretty courtyards, galleries and staircases preserved in the first three of these buildings are as delightful as the collection inside.

While the collection concentrates on the artist's formative years – sometimes disappointing for those hoping for a feast of his better-known later works (they had better head for Paris) – there is enough material from subsequent periods to give you a thorough impression of the man's versatility and genius.

NEED TO KNOW

Map p342; 📞 93 256 30 00; www.museupicasso.bcn.es; Carrer de Montcada 15-23; adult/senior & child under 16yr/student €11/free/6, temporary exhibitions adult/senior & child under 16yr/student €6/free/2.90, 3-8pm Sun & 1st Sun of month free; ⏰ 10am-8pm Tue-Sun & holidays; Ⓜ Jaume I

dancing, *castellers* (human castle-builders), fireworks and *correfocs* – a parade of firework-spitting dragons and devils.

The evening before the **Dia de Sant Joan** (24 June) is a colourful midsummer celebration with bonfires and fireworks. The beaches are crowded with revellers to the wee hours.

🛏 Sleeping

There's no shortage of hotels in Barcelona. Those looking for cheaper accommodation close to the action should check out the Barri Gòtic and El Raval. Some good lower-end *pensiones* are scattered about L'Eixample, as well as a broad range of midrange and top-end places, most in easy striking distance of the old town.

Montjuïc

A Day Itinerary

Possibly the site of ancient pre-Roman settlements, Montjuïc today is a hilltop green lung looking over city and sea. Interspersed across varied gardens are major art collections, a fortress, Olympic Stadium and more. A solid one-day itinerary can take in the key spots.

Alight at Espanya metro stop and make for **CaixaForum** 1 , always host to three or four free top-class exhibitions. The **Pavelló Mies van der Rohe** 2 across the road is an intriguing look at 1920s futurist housing by one of the 20th century's greatest architects. Uphill, the Romanesque art collection in the **Museu Nacional d'Art de Catalunya** 3 should not be missed. The restaurant here makes a pleasant lunch stop. Escalators lead further up the hill towards the **Estadi Olímpic** 4 , scene of the 1992 Olympic Games. The road leads east to the **Fundació Joan Miró** 5 , a shrine to the surrealist artist's creativity. Relax in the **Jardins de Mossèn Cinto Verdaguer** 6 , the prettiest on the hill, before taking the cable car to the **Castell de Montjuïc** 7 . If you pick the right day, you can round off by contemplating the gorgeously kitsch **La Font Màgica** 8 sound and light show.

TOP TIPS

Moving views Take the Transbordador Aeri from La Barceloneta for a bird's eye approach to Montjuïc. Or use the Teléferic de Montjuïc cable car to the Castell for more aerial views.

Summer fun The Castell de Montjuïc is the scene for outdoor summer cinema and concerts (see http://salamontjuic.org).

Beautiful bloomers Bursting with colour and serenity, the Jardins de Mossèn Cinto Verdaguer are exquisitely laid out with bulbs, especially tulips, and aquatic flowers.

CaixaForum
This former factory and barracks designed by Josep Puig i Cadafalch is an outstanding work of Modernista architecture; like a Lego fantasy in brick.

Piscines Bernat Picornell

Olympic Needle

Poble Espanyol
Amid the rich variety of traditional Spanish architecture created in replica for the 1929 Barcelona World Exhibition, browse the art on show in the Fundació Fran Daurel.

Pavelló Mies van der Rohe
Admire the inventiveness of the great German architect Ludwig Mies van der Rohe in this recreation of his avant garde German pavillion for the 1929 World Exhibition.

La Font Màgica
Take a summer evening to behold the Magic Fountain come to life in a unique 15-minute sound and light performance, when the water glows like a cauldron of colour.

8

Museu Nacional d'Art de Catalunya
Make a beeline for the Romanesque art selection and the 12th-century polychrome image of Christ in majesty, which was recovered from the apse of a country chapel in northwest Catalonia.

3

Museu Etnològic

Teatre Grec

5

6

Museu Olímpic i de l'Esport

4

Estadi Olímpic

Jardí Botànic

7

Jardins de Mossèn Cinto Verdaguer

Castell de Montjuïc
Enjoy the sweeping views of the sea and city from atop this 17th-century fortress, once a political prison and long a symbol of oppression.

Fundació Joan Miró
Take in some of Joan Miró's giant canvases, and discover little-known works from his early years in the Sala Joan Prats and Sala Pilar Juncosa.

Museu d'Arqueologia de Catalunya
Seek out the Roman mosaic depicting the Three Graces, one of the most beautiful items in this museum, which was dedicated to the ancient past of Catalonia and neighbouring parts of Spain.

Casa Batlló (p336), Barcelona

SERGIO PITAMITZ/GETTY IMAGES ©

Numerous private apartment-rental companies operate in Barcelona. These can often be a better deal than staying in a hotel. Start your search at **Aparteasy** (Map p328; ☎93 451 67 66; www.aparteasy. com; Carrer de Santa Tecla 3; Ⓜ Diagnoal), **Barcelona On Line** (Map p328; ☎902 887017, 93 343 79 93; www.barcelona-on-line.es; Carrer de València 352) and **Rent a Flat in Barcelona** (☎93 342 73 00; www.rentaflatinbarcelona.com; Ronda del Guinardó 2).

LA RAMBLA & BARRI GÒTIC

Hotel Neri   Design Hotel €€€
(Map p342; ☎93 304 06 55; www.hotelneri.com; Carrer de Sant Sever 5; d from €270; ✳@🛜; Ⓜ Liceu) This tranquil hotel occupies a beautifully adapted, centuries-old building backing on Plaça de Sant Felip Neri. The sandstone walls and timber furnishings lend a sense of history, while the rooms feature cutting-edge technology, including plasma-screen TVs and infrared lights in the stone-clad designer bathrooms.

EL RAVAL

Casa Camper   Design Hotel €€€
(Map p342; ☎93 342 62 80; www.casacamper. com; Carrer d'Elisabets 11; s/d €240/270; ➡✳@; Ⓜ Liceu) The massive foyer looks like a contemporary-art museum, but the rooms are the real surprise. Decorated in red, black and white, each room has a sleeping and bathroom area, where you can put on your Camper slippers, enjoy the Vinçon furniture and contemplate the hanging gardens outside your window. Across the corridor is a separate, private sitting room with balcony, TV and hammock.

Whotells   Apartment €€
(Map p342; ☎93 443 08 34; www.whotells. com; Carrer de Joaquín Costa 28; apt from €180; ✳@🛜; Ⓜ Universitat) These comfortable home-away-from-home apartments, decked out with Muji furniture, can sleep four to six people.

Hotel San Agustín   Hotel €€
(Map p342; ☎93 318 16 58; www.hotelsa.com; Plaça de Sant Agustí 3; r from €80-180; ✳@🛜; Ⓜ Liceu) This former 18th-century monastery opened as a hotel in 1840, making it the city's oldest. The location is perfect – a quick stroll off La Rambla on a curious square. Rooms sparkle, and are mostly spacious and light-filled.

LA RIBERA & LA BARCELONETA

Hotel Banys
Orientals   Boutique Hotel €€
(Map p342; ☎ 93 268 84 60; www.hotelbanys
orientals.com; Carrer de l'Argenteria 37; s/d
€88/105, ste €130; ❄ @; Ⓜ Jaume I) Book
well ahead to get into this magnetically
popular designer haunt. Cool blues and
aquamarines combine with dark-hued
floors to lend this clean-lined, boutique hotel a quiet charm. All rooms, on the small
side, look onto the street or back lanes.

Chic & Basic   Design Hotel €€
(Map p328; ☎ 93 295 46 52; www.chicandbasic.
com; Carrer de la Princesa 50; s €96, d €132-192;
❄ @; Ⓜ Jaume I) This is a very cool hotel
indeed, with its 31 spotlessly white rooms
and fairy-light curtains that change colour, adding an entirely new atmosphere
to the space. The ceilings are high and the
beds enormous.

L'EIXAMPLE

Hotel Praktik   Boutique Hotel €€
(Map p328; ☎ 93 343 66 90; www.hotelpraktik
rambla.com; Rambla de Catalunya 27; r from
€80-170; ❄ @ 🛜; Ⓜ Passeig de Gràcia) This
modernista gem hides a gorgeous little
boutique experience. While the high ceilings and the bulk of the original tile floors
have been maintained, the 43 rooms have
daring ceramic touches, spot lighting and
contemporary art.

Hotel Omm   Design Hotel €€€
(Map p328; ☎ 93 445 40 00; www.hotelomm.
es; Carrer de Rosselló 265; d from €360;
P ❄ @ 🛜; Ⓜ Diagonal) Design meets
plain zany here, where the balconies look
like strips of skin peeled back from the
shiny hotel surface. The idea would no
doubt have appealed to Dalí. In the foyer,
a sprawling, minimalist and popular bar
opens before you. Light, clear tones dominate in the ultramodern rooms, of which
there are several categories.

Hostal Goya   Hostal €€
(Map p328; ☎ 93 302 25 65; www.hostalgoya.
com; Carrer de Pau Claris 74; s €70, d €96-113;
❄; Ⓜ Passeig de Gràcia, Urquinaona) The
Goya is a modestly priced gem on the

chichi side of L'Eixample. Rooms have
a light colour scheme that varies from
room to room. In the bathrooms, the
original mosaic floors have largely been
retained, combined with contemporary
design features.

🍴 Eating

Barcelona is foodie heaven. The city has
firmly established itself as one of Europe's gourmet capitals, and innovative,
cutting-edge restaurants abound. Some
of the most creative chefs are one-time
students of world-renowned chef Ferran
Adrià, whose influence on the city's
cuisine is strong.

Although Barcelona has a reputation
as a hot spot of 'new Spanish cuisine',
you'll still find local eateries serving up
time-honoured local grub, from squid-ink
fideuà (a satisfying paella-like noodle
dish) to pigs' trotters, rabbit and snails,
and *butifarra* (a tasty local sausage).

LA RAMBLA & BARRI GÒTIC

Skip the overpriced traps along La Rambla and get into the winding lanes of the
Barri Gòtic.

Pla   Fusion €€
(Map p342; ☎ 93 412 65 52; www.elpla.cat; Carrer de la Bellafila 5; mains €18-24; 🕐 dinner; 🍴;
Ⓜ Jaume I) One of Gòtic's long-standing
favourites, Pla is a stylish, romantically
lit medieval den (with a huge stone arch)
where the cooks churn out such temptations as oxtail braised in red wine, seared
tuna with roasted aubergine, and 'Thai-
style' monkfish with prawns, lemongrass
and apple foam. It has a tasting menu for
€36 Sunday to Thursday.

La Vinateria del Call   Spanish €€
(Map p342; ☎ 93 302 60 92; www.lavinateriadel
call.com; Carrer de Sant Domènec del Call 9; small
plates €7-11; 🕐 dinner; Ⓜ Jaume I) In a magical setting in the former Jewish quarter,
this tiny jewelbox of a restaurant serves
up tasty Iberian dishes, including Galician
octopus, cider-cooked chorizo and the
Catalan *escalivada* (roasted peppers,
aubergine and onions) with anchovies.

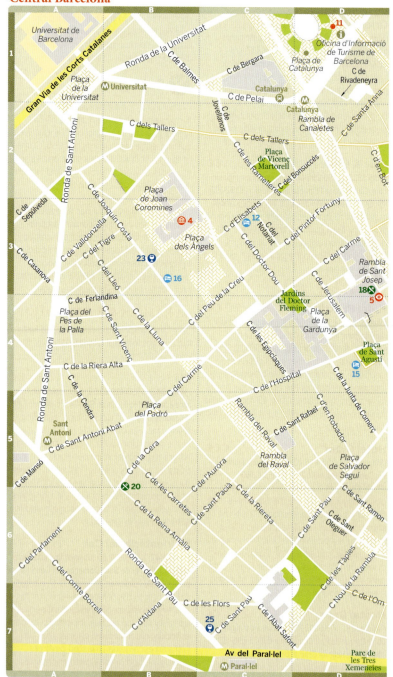

SPAIN BARCELONA

Universitat de Barcelona

Gran Via de les Corts Catalanes

Ronda de la Universitat

C de Balmes

C de Bergara

Plaça de Catalunya

11

Oficina d'Informació de Turisme de Barcelona

C de Rivadeneyra

Plaça de la Universitat

Universitat

C dels Tallers

C de Jovellanos

C de Pelai

Catalunya

Catalunya

Rambla de Canaletes

C de Santa Anna

Ronda de Sant Antoni

C dels Tallers

C dels Tallers

Plaça de Vicenç Martorell

C de les Ramelleres

C del Bonsuccés

C d'en Bot

C de Sepúlveda

C de Joaquín Costa

Plaça de Joan Coromines

4

C d'Elisabets

12

C del Notariat

C del Pintor Fortuny

C de Casanova

C de Valldonzella

C del Tigre

Plaça dels Àngels

23

C del Doctor Dou

C del Carme

Rambla de Sant Josep

18

5

C del Lleó

16

C de Ferlandina

C del Peu de la Creu

Jardins del Doctor Fleming

C de Jerusalem

Plaça del Pes de la Palla

C de Sant Vicenç

C de la Lluna

Plaça de la Gardunya

Plaça de Sant Agustí

15

Ronda de Sant Antoni

C de la Riera Alta

C del Carme

C de les Egipcíaques

C de la Cendra

C de l'Hospital

C de la Junta de Comerç

Plaça del Padró

Rambla del Raval

C de Sant Rafael

C d'en Robador

Sant Antoni

C de Sant Antoni Abat

C de la Cera

C de l'Aurora

Rambla del Raval

Plaça de Salvador Seguí

C de Mansó

20

C de les Carretes

C de Sant Pacià

C de la Rierata

C de Sant Pau

C de Sant Ramon

C de la Reina Amàlia

C de Sant Oleguer

C del Parlament

Ronda de Sant Pau

C del Comte Borrell

C de les Tàpies

C Nou de la Rambla

C de l'Om

C d'Aldana

C de les Flors

C de Sant Pau

C de l'Abat Safont

25

Av del Paral·lel

Paral·lel

Parc de les Tres Xemeneies

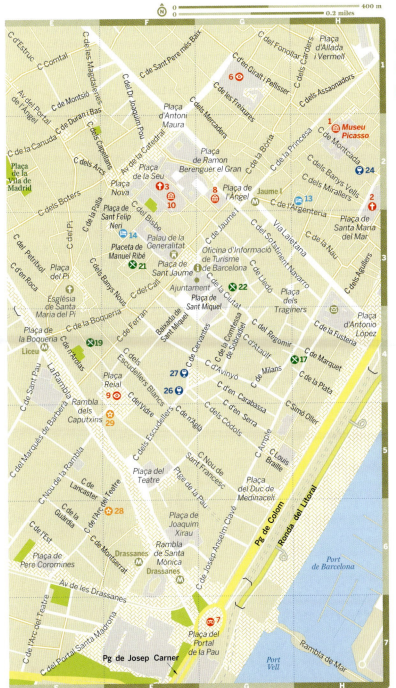

N

0   400 m
0   0.2 miles

C d'Estruc
C Comtal
C de les Magdalenes
C de Montsió
Av del Portal de l'Angel
C de la Canuda
C de Duran i Bas
C dels Capellans
C dels Arcs
Plaça de la Vila de Madrid
C dels Boters
C de la Palla
C del DR Joaquim Pou
C de Sant Pere més Baix
C de Sant Pere més Baix
Plaça d'Antoni Maura
C dels Mercaders
C de les Freixures
C d'en Giralt i Pellisser
6
C del Fonollar
C dels Carders
Plaça d'Allada i Vermell
C dels Assaonadors
1 Museu Picasso
C de Montcada
C de la Bòria
C de la Princesa
C dels Banys Vells
C dels Mirallers
24
Plaça de Ramon Berenguer el Gran
Av de la Catedral
Plaça de la Seu
3
10
8
Plaça de l'Àngel
Jaume I
13
C de l'Argenteria
C de la Nau
2
Plaça de Santa Maria del Mar
Plaça Nova
C del Bisbe
Plaça de Sant Felip Neri
14
Palau de la Generalitat
Placeta de Manuel Ribé
21
Plaça de Sant Jaume
Oficina d'Informació de Turisme de Barcelona
C de Jaume I
C del Sotstinent Navarro
Via Laietana
C de Lledó
C dels Agullers
C del Pi
C del Petritxol
C d'en Roca
Plaça del Pi
C dels Banys Nous
Església de Santa Maria del Pi
C del Call
Plaça de Sant Jaume
Ajuntament
Plaça de Sant Miquel
22
C de la Ciutat
Plaça dels Traginers
Plaça d'Antonio López
C de la Fusteria
Plaça de la Boqueria
C de la Boqueria
19
Liceu
C de n'Arolas
C de Sant Pau
La Rambla
C de Ferran
Baixada de Sant Miquel
C de Cervantes
C de la Comtessa de Sobradiel
C d'Ataülf
C del Regomir
17
C de Marquet
C de la Plata
C dels Escudellers Blancs
27
26
C d'Avinyó
C de Milans
Plaça Reial
9
Rambla dels Caputxins
29
C de Vidre
C dels Escudellers
C de n'Aglà
C d'en Carabassa
C d'en Serra
C dels Còdols
C Simó Oller
C Ample
C Louis Braille
C del Marqués de Barberà
C Nou de la Rambla
C de Lancaster
C de l'Arc del Teatre
Plaça del Teatre
C Nou de Sant Francesc
Ptge de la Pau
Plaça del Duc de Medinaceli
Pg de Colom
Ronda del Litoral
C de la Guàrdia
C de l'Est
C de Montserrat
28
Plaça de Joaquim Xirau
Plaça de Pere Cominas
Av de les Drassanes
Drassanes
Rambla de Santa Mònica
Drassanes
C de Josep Anselm Clavé
Port de Barcelona
C de l'Arc del Teatre
C del Portal Santa Madrona
Pg de Josep Carner
7
Plaça del Portal de la Pau
Port Vell
Rambla de Mar

Can Culleretes
Catalan €€

(Map p342; 93 317 30 22; www.culleretes.com; Carrer Quintana 5; mains €8-14; lunch & dinner Tue-Sat, lunch Sun; Liceu) Founded in 1786, Barcelona's oldest restaurant is still going strong, with tourists and locals flocking to enjoy its rambling interior, old-fashioned tile-filled decor, and enormous helpings of traditional Catalan food. The multicourse lunch specials are good value.

Agut
Catalan €€

(Map p342; www.restaurantagut.com; Carrer d'en Gignàs 16; mains €16-25; lunch & dinner Tue-Sat, lunch Sun; Jaume I) Deep in the Gothic labyrinth lies this classic eatery. A series of cosy dining areas is connected by broad arches while, high up, the walls are tightly lined by artworks. There's art in what the kitchen serves up too, from the oak-grilled meat to a succulent variety of seafood offerings.

EL RAVAL

Bar Pinotxo
Tapas €€

(Map p342; www.pinotxobar.com; Mercat de la Boqueria; meals €20; 6am-5pm Mon-Sat Sep-Jul; Liceu) Bar Pinotxo is arguably Barcelona's best tapas bar. It sits among the half-dozen or so informal eateries within Mercat de la Boqueria (p327), and the popular owner, Juanito, might serve up chickpeas with a sweet sauce of pine nuts and raisins, soft baby squid with cannellini beans, or a quivering cube of caramel sweet pork belly.

Can Lluís
Catalan €€€

(Map p342; Carrer de la Cera 49; meals €30-35; Mon-Sat Sep-Jul; Sant Antoni) Three generations have kept this spick and span old-time classic in business since 1929. Beneath the olive-green beams in the back dining room you can see the spot where an anarchist's bomb went off in 1946, killing the then owner. Expect fresh fish and seafood.

LA RIBERA & WATERFRONT

La Barceloneta is the place to go for seafood; Passeig Joan de Borbó is lined with eateries but locals head for the back lanes.

Cal Pep
Tapas €€

(Map p328; 93 310 79 61; www.calpep.com; Plaça de les Olles 8; mains €8-18; lunch Tue-Sat, dinner Mon-Fri Sep-Jul; Barceloneta) It's getting a foot in the door here that's the problem. Elbow your way to the bar for some of the tastiest gourmet seafood tapas in town. Pep recommends *cloïsses amb pernil*

Central Barcelona

Don't Miss Sights
1 Museu Picasso H2

Sights
2 Església de Santa Maria del Mar........... H2
3 La Catedral F2
4 MACBA... B3
5 Mercat de la Boqueria D4
6 Mercat de Santa Caterina.................... G1
7 Mirador de Colom................................. G7
8 Museu d'Història de Barcelona............ G2
9 Plaça Reial F4
10 Sala Capitular.. F2

Activities, Courses & Tours
11 Barcelona Walking Tours......................D1

Sleeping
12 Casa Camper..C3
13 Hotel Banys Orientals H2
14 Hotel Neri...F3

15 Hotel San Agustín...................................D4
16 Whotells...B3

Eating
17 Agut..H4
18 Bar Pinotxo..D3
19 Can Culleretes E4
20 Can Lluís...B5
21 La Vinateria dell Call............................... F3
22 Pla...G3

Drinking & Nightlife
23 33|45...B3
24 El Xampanyet..H2
25 La Confitería..C7
26 Marula Cafè... F4
27 Oviso F4

Entertainment
28 Moog...F6
29 Sala Tarantos...F5

HIROSHI HIGUCHI/GETTY IMAGES ©

Don't Miss
Park Güell

North of Gràcia and about 4km from Plaça de Catalunya, Park Güell is where Gaudí turned his hand to landscape gardening. It's a strange, enchanting place where his passion for natural forms really took flight – to the point where the artificial almost seems more natural than the natural.

Park Güell originated in 1900, when Count Eusebi Güell bought a tree-covered hillside (then outside Barcelona) and hired Gaudí to create a miniature city of houses for the wealthy in landscaped grounds. The project was a commercial flop and was abandoned in 1914 – but not before Gaudí had created 3km of roads and walks, steps, a plaza and two gatehouses in his inimitable manner. In 1922 the city bought the estate for use as a public park.

NEED TO KNOW

Map p328; ☎93 413 24 00; Carrer d'Olot 7; ☉10am-9pm Jun-Sep, 10am-8pm Apr, May & Oct, 10am-7pm Mar & Nov, 10am-6pm Dec-Feb; ☐24, ⓜLesseps or Vallcarca

---

(clams and ham) or the *trifàsic* (combo of calamari, whitebait and prawns).

Casa Delfín   Spanish €
(Map p328; Passeig del Born 36; mains €4-12; ☉noon-1am; ⓜBarceloneta) One of Barcelona's culinary delights, Casa Delfín is everything you dream of when you think of Catalan (and Mediterranean) cooking. Start with the tangy and sweet *calçots* (a cross

between a leek and an onion; February and March only) or salt-strewn *padron* peppers, moving on to grilled sardines specked with parsley, then tackle the meaty monkfish roasted in white wine and garlic.

Can Majó   Seafood €€
(Map p328; ☎93 221 54 55; www.canmajo.es; Carrer del Almirall Aixada 23; mains €18-24; ☉lunch & dinner Tue-Sat, lunch Sun; ☐45, 57,

345

59, 64 or 157, **M**Barceloneta) Virtually on the beach (with tables outside in summer), Can Majó has a long and steady reputation for fine seafood, particularly its rice dishes and bountiful *suquets* (fish stews).

Suquet De L'Almirall — Seafood €€

(Map p328; ☎ 93 221 62 33; www.suquetdel almirall.com; Passeig de Joan de Borbó 65; meals €45-50; ☺ lunch & dinner Tue-Sat, lunch Sun; ☒17, 39, 57 or 64, **M**Barceloneta) A family business run by an alumnus of Ferran Adrià's El Bulli, the order of the day is top-class seafood with the occasional unexpected twist. The house specialty is *suquet*.

L'EIXAMPLE & GRÀCIA

Tapaç 24 — Tapas €€

(Map p328; www.carlesabellan.com; Carrer de la Diputació 269; mains €10-20; ☺9am-midnight Mon-Sat; **M**Passeig de Gràcia) Carles Abellán runs this basement tapas haven known for its gourmet versions of old faves. Specials include the *bikini* (toasted ham and cheese sandwich – here the ham is cured and the truffle makes all the difference) and a thick black *arròs negre de sípia* (squid-ink black rice).

🍷 Drinking & Nightlife

Barcelona abounds with day-time cafes, laid-back lounges and lively night-time bars. Closing time is generally 2am from Sunday to Thursday, and 3am Friday and Saturday.

BARRI GÒTIC

Oviso — Bar

(Map p342; Carrer d'Arai 5; ☺10am-2am; **M**Liceu) Oviso is a popular, budget-friendly restaurant with outdoor tables on the plaza, but shows its true bohemian colours by night, with a wildly mixed crowd, a rock-and-roll vibe and a two-room fin-de-siecle interior plastered with curious murals.

Marula Cafè — Bar

(Map p342; www.marulacafe.com; Carrer dels Escudellers 49; ☺11pm-5am; **M**Liceu) A fantastic funk find in the heart of the Barri Gòtic, Marula will transport you to the 1970s and the best in funk and soul.

EL RAVAL

La Confitería — Bar

(Map p342; Carrer de Sant Pau 128; ☺11am-2am; **M**Paral·lel) This is a trip into the 19th century. Until the 1980s it was a confectioner's shop and, although the original cabinets are now lined with booze, the look of the place has barely changed in its conversion into a laid-back bar.

33|45 — Bar

(Map p342; Carrer Joaquín Costa 4; ☺10am-1:30am Mon-Thu, to 3am Fri & Sat, to midnight Sun; **M**Universitat) A supertrendy cocktail bar on the nightlife-laden Joaquín Costa street, this place has excellent mojitos – even pink, strawberry ones! – and a fashionable crowd.

LA RIBERA

El Xampanyet — Wine Bar

(Map p342; Carrer de Montcada 22; ☺noon-4pm & 7-11pm Tue-Sat, noon-4pm Sun; **M**Jaume I) Nothing has changed for decades in this, one of the city's best-known *cava* (Catalan version of champagne) bars. Plant yourself at the bar or seek out a table against the decoratively tiled walls for a glass or three of *cava* and an assortment of tapas.

L'EIXAMPLE & GRÀCIA

Monvínic — Wine Bar

(Map p328; ☎ 932 72 61 87; www.monvinic. com; Carrer de la Diputació 249 ; ☺wine bar 1.30-11.30pm, restaurant 1.30-3.30pm & 8.30-10.30pm; **M**Passeig de Gracia) Proclaimed as 'possibly the best wine bar in the world' by the *Wall Street Journal,* and apparently considered unmissable by El Bulli's former sommelier, Monvínic is an ode, a rhapsody even, to wine loving. The interactive wine list sits on the bar for you to browse on a digital tablet similar to an iPad and boasts more than 3000 varieties.

⭐ Entertainment

To keep up with what's on, pick up a copy of the weekly listings magazine, *Guía del Ocio* (€1) from news stands.

NIKO GUIDO/GETTY IMAGES ©

NIGHTCLUBS

Barcelona clubs are spread a little more thinly than bars across the city. They tend to open from around midnight until 6am. Entry can cost from nothing to €20 (one drink usually included).

Elephant   Club

(☎ 93 334 02 58; www.elephantbcn.com; Passeig dels Til·lers 1; ⏰ 11.30pm-4am Thu, to 5am Fri & Sat ; Ⓜ Palau Reial) Getting in here is like being invited to a private fantasy party in Beverly Hills. A big tentlike dance space is the main game here, but smooth customers slink their way around a series of garden bars in summer too.

Moog   Club

(Map p342; www.masimas.com/moog; Carrer de l'Arc del Teatre 3; admission €10; ⏰ midnight-5am; Ⓜ Drassanes) This fun and minuscule club is a standing favourite with the downtown crowd. In the main dance area, DJs dish out house, techno and electro, while upstairs you can groove to a nice blend of indie and occasional classic-pop throwbacks.

Razzmatazz   Club

(Map p328; ☎ 93 320 82 00; www.salarazz matazz.com; Carrer de Pamplona 88; admission €15-30; ⏰ midnight-3.30am Thu, to 5.30am Fri & Sat; Ⓜ Marina, Bogatell) Bands from far and wide occasionally create scenes of near hysteria in this, one of the city's classic live-music and clubbing venues.

LIVE MUSIC

Palau de la Música
Catalana   Classical

(Map p328; ☎ 902 442882; www.palaumusica. org; Carrer de Sant Francesc de Paula 2; ⏰ box office 10am-9pm Mon-Sat; Ⓜ Urquinaona) A feast for the eyes, this modernista confection is also the city's traditional venue for classical and choral music.

Sala Tarantos   Flamenco

(Map p342; ☎ 93 319 17 89; www.masimas. net; Plaça Reial 17; admission from €7; ⏰ shows 8.30pm, 9.30pm & 10.30pm; Ⓜ Liceu) Since 1963, this basement locale has been the stage for up-and-coming flamenco groups performing in Barcelona.

SPORT

FC Barcelona (Barça for aficionados) has one of the best stadiums in Europe – the 99,000-capacity **Camp Nou** (☎ 93 496 36 00; www.fcbarcelona.com; Carrer d'Aristides Maillol; adult/child €23/17; ⏰ 10am-8pm Mon-Sat, to 2.30pm Sun; **M**Palau Reial) in the west of the city. Tickets for national-league games are available at the stadium, by phone or online. For the latter two options, non-members must book 15 days before the match.

🔒 Shopping

Most mainstream fashion stores are along a shopping 'axis' that runs from Plaça de Catalunya along Passeig de Gràcia, then left (west) along Avinguda Diagonal.

The El Born area in La Ribera is awash with tiny boutiques, especially those purveying young, fun fashion. There are plenty of shops scattered throughout the Barri Gòtic (stroll Carrer d'Avinyò and Carrer de Portaferrissa). For secondhand stuff, head for El Raval, especially Carrer de la Riera Baixa.

Joan Murrià   Food
(Map p328; 📞93 215 57 89; www.murria.cat; Carrer de Roger de Llúria 85; **M**Passeig de Gràcia) Note the century-old modernista shop-front advertisements featured at this culinary temple. For a century the gluttonous have trembled here at this altar of speciality food goods from around Catalonia and beyond.

Els Encants Vells   Market
(Map p328; Fira de Bellcaire; 📞93 246 30 30; www.encantsbcn.com; Plaça de les Glòries Catalanes; ⏰7am-6pm Mon, Wed, Fri & Sat; **M**Glòries) The 'Old Charms' flea market is the biggest of its kind in Barcelona. It's all here, from antique furniture through to secondhand clothes. A lot of it is junk, but occasionally you'll stumble across a *ganga* (bargain). The most interesting time to be here is from 7am to 9am on Monday, Wednesday and Friday, when the public auctions take place.

Antonio Miró   Fashion
(Map p328; 📞93 487 06 70; www.antoniomiro. es; Carrer del Consell de Cent 349; ⏰10am-8pm Mon-Sat; **M**Passeig de Gràcia) Antonio Miró is one of Barcelona's haute couture kings. The entrance to the airy store, with dark hardwood floor, seems more like a hip hotel reception.

ℹ️ Information

Dangers & Annoyances
Purse snatching and pickpocketing are major problems, especially around Plaça de Catalunya, La Rambla and Plaça Reial.

Tourist Information
Oficina d'Informació de Turisme de Barcelona has a main branch (📞93 285 38 34; www.barcelonaturisme. com; underground at Plaça de Catalunya 17-S; ⏰8.30am-8.30pm; **M**Catalunya) and several others at **Aeroport del Prat** (terminals 1, 2B & 2A; ⏰9am-9pm), **Estació Sants** (⏰8am-8pm; 🚆Estació Sants) and **Town hall** (Plaça Sant Jaume; 📞93 285 38 32; Carrer de la Ciutat 2;

Detour:
Monestir de Montserrat

The monks who built the Monestir de Montserrat (Monastery of the Serrated Mountain), 50km northwest of Barcelona, chose a spectacular spot. The Benedictine **monastery** (www.abadiamontserrat.net; ⊙9am-6pm) sits on the side of a 1236m-high mountain of weird, bulbous peaks. The monastery was founded in 1025 and pilgrims still come from all over Christendom to kiss the Black Virgin (La Moreneta), the 12th-century wooden sculpture of the Virgin Mary.

If you're around the basilica at the right time, you'll catch a brief performance by the **Montserrat Boys' Choir** (www.escolania.cat; ⊙performances 1pm Mon-Fri, noon Sun, late Aug–late Jun).

You can explore the mountain above the monastery on a web of paths leading to some of the peaks and to 13 empty and rather dilapidated hermitages. Running every 20 minutes, the **Funicular de Sant Joan** (one way/return €5.05/8; ⊙every 20 min 10am-6.50pm, closed Jan & Feb) will carry you up the first 250m from the monastery.

Montserrat is an easy day trip from Barcelona. The R5 line trains operated by FGC run from Plaça d'Espanya station in Barcelona to Monistrol de Montserrat up to 18 times daily, starting at 5.16am. They connect with the rack-and-pinion train, or **cremallera** (☏902 312020; www.cremalleramontserrat.com; one way/return €6/9), which takes 17 minutes to make the upwards journey.

⊙8.30am-8.30pm Mon-Fri, 9am-7pm Sat, 9am-2pm Sun & holidays; Ⓜ Jaume I).

Regional Tourist Office (www.gencat.net/probert; Passeig de Gràcia 107; ⊙10am-7pm Mon-Sat, to 2.30pm Sun; Ⓜ Diagonal)

❶ Getting There & Away

Air

Barcelona's airport, **El Prat de Llobregat** (☏902 404704; www.aena.es), is 12km southwest of the city centre.

Boat

Regular passenger and vehicular ferries to/from the Balearic Islands, operated by **Acciona Trasmediterránea** (☏902 454645; www.trasmediterranea.es; Ⓜ Drassanes), dock along both sides of the Moll de Barcelona wharf in Port Vell.

The Grimaldi group's **Grandi Navi Veloci** (☏in Italy 010 209 4591; www1.gnv.it; Ⓜ Drassanes) runs high-speed, thrice-weekly luxury ferries between Barcelona and Genoa, while **Grimaldi Ferries** (☏902 531333, in Italy 081 496444; www.grimaldi-lines.com; Ⓜ Drassanes) operates similar services to Civitavecchia (near Rome),

Livorno (Tuscany) and Porto Torres (northwest Sardinia).

Train

Virtually all trains travelling to and from destinations within Spain stop at **Estació Sants** (Plaça dels Països Catalans; Ⓜ Estació Sants). High-speed trains to Madrid via Lleida and Zaragoza take as little as two hours and 40 minutes; prices vary wildly. Other trains run to Valencia (€36 to €45, three to 4½ hours, 15 daily) and Burgos (from €66, six to seven hours, four daily).

There are also international connections with French cities from the same station.

❶ Getting Around

To/From the Airport

The **A1 Aerobús** (☏93 415 60 20; one way €5.65) runs from Terminal 1 to Plaça de Catalunya from 6.05am to 1.05am, taking 30 to 40 minutes. A2 Aerobús does the same run from Terminal 2, from 6am to 12.30am. Buy tickets on the bus.

Renfe's R2 Nord train line runs between the airport and Passeig de Gràcia (via Estació Sants) in central Barcelona (about 35 minutes). Tickets cost €3.60, unless you have a T-10 multitrip public-transport ticket.

A taxi to/from the centre, about a half-hour ride depending on traffic, costs around €25 to €30.

Public Transport

Barcelona's metro system spreads its tentacles around the city in such a way that most places of interest are within a 10-minute walk of a station. Buses and suburban trains are needed only for a few destinations. A single metro, bus or suburban train ride costs €2, but a T-1 ticket, valid for 10 rides, costs €9.25.

Taxi

Barcelona's black-and-yellow taxis are plentiful and reasonably priced. The flag fall is €2.05. If you can't find a street taxi, call ☎ 93 303 30 33.

BASQUE COUNTRY

The Basques, whose language is believed to be among the world's oldest, claim two of Spain's most interesting cities – San Sebastián and Bilbao – as their own.

San Sebastián

POP 185,500

Stylish San Sebastián (Donostia in Basque) has the air of an upscale resort, complete with an idyllic location on the shell-shaped Bahía de la Concha. The natural setting – crystalline waters, a flawless beach, green hills on all sides – is captivating. But this is one of Spain's true culinary capitals, with more Michelin stars (14) per capita here than anywhere else on earth.

Sights

Beaches & Isla de Santa Clara   Beach

Fulfilling almost every idea of how a perfect city beach should be formed, **Playa de la Concha** and its westerly extension, **Playa de Ondarreta**, are easily among the best city beaches in Europe. The **Isla de Santa Clara**, about 700m from the beach, is accessible by **glass-bottom boats** (to the island €3.80, tour the bay €6) that

run every half-hour from June to September from the fishing port. Less popular, but just as showy, **Playa de Gros** (Playa de la Zurriola), east of Río Urumea, is the city's main surf beach.

Museo Chillida Leku   Museum, Park

(www.museochillidaleku.com; adult/child €8.50/free; ⏰10.30am-8pm Mon-Sat, to 3pm Sun Jul & Aug, shorter hr rest of year) This open-air museum is the most engaging one in rural Basque Country. Amid the beech, oak and magnolia trees, you'll find 40 sculptures of granite and iron created by the renowned Basque sculptor Eduardo Chillida. Many more of Chillida's works appear inside the renovated 16th-century farmhouse.

To get here, take the G2 bus (€1.35) for Hernani from Calle de Okendo in San Sebastián and get off at Zabalaga.

Aquarium   Aquarium

(www.aquariumss.com; Paseo del Muelle 34; adult/4-12yr €12/6; ⏰10am-8pm Mon-Fri, to 9pm Sat & Sun Apr-Jun & Sep, shorter hr rest of year) In San Sebastián's excellent aquarium, huge sharks bear down on you, and you'll be tripped out by fancy fluoro jellyfish. The highlights of a visit are the cinema-screen-sized deep-ocean and coral-reef exhibits and the long tunnel, around which swim monsters of the deep.

Monte Igueldo   Viewpoint

The views from the summit of Monte Igueldo, just west of town, will make you feel like a circling hawk staring over the vast panorama of the Bahía de la Concha and the surrounding coastline and mountains. The best way to get there is via the old-world **funicular railway** (return adult/child €2.80/2.10; ⏰10am-10pm).

Sleeping

Pensión Bellas Artes   Boutique Hotel €€

(☎943 47 49 05; www.pension-bellasartes.com; Calle de Urbieta 64; s €69-89, d €89-109; 🛜) To call this magnificent place a mere *pensión* is to do it something a disservice. Its rooms (some with glassed-in balconies), with their exposed stone walls and excel-

Playa de la Concha, San Sebastián

WALTER BIBIKOW/GETTY IMAGES ©

lent bathrooms, should be the envy of many a more-expensive hotel.

Pensión Amaiur Ostatua Boutique Hotel **€**
(☎943 42 96 54; www.pensionamaiur.com; Calle de 31 de Agosto 44; s €45, d €54-65; @📶) This old town classic has always been one of the city's stand out accommodation options. At the time of research it was closed for major renovations that promise to make it even better than before.

Eating

San Sebastián is paradise for food lovers. Considered the birthplace of *nueva cocina española* (Spanish nouvelle cuisine), this area is home to some of the country's top chefs. Yet not all the good food is pricey. Head to the Parte Vieja for San Sebastián's *pintxos,* Basque-style tapas.

Pintxo etiquette is simple. Ask for a plate and point out what *pintxos* (often tasty mounds of food on little slices of baguette) you want. Keep the toothpicks and go back for as many as you'd like. Accompany with *txakoli,* a cloudy white wine poured like cider to create a little fizz. When you're ready to pay, hand over the plate with all the toothpicks and tell bar staff how many drinks you've had. Expect to pay €2.50 to €3.50 for a *pintxo* and *txakoli*.

La Cuchara de San Telmo Contemporary Basque **€€**
(www.lacucharadesantelmo.com; Calle de 31 de Agosto 28) This unfussy, hidden-away (and hard to find) bar offers miniature *nueva cocina vasca* from a supremely creative kitchen. Chefs Alex Montiel and Iñaki Gulin conjure up delights and a percentage of profits goes to the Fundación Vicente Ferrer charity.

Arzak Contemporary Basque **€€€**
(☎943 27 84 65; www.arzak.info; Avenida Alcalde Jose Elosegui 273; meals €175; 🕐closed Sun-Mon & Nov & late Jun) With three shining Michelin stars, acclaimed chef Juan Mari Arzak takes some beating when it comes to *nueva cocina vasca* and his restaurant is, not surprisingly, considered one of the best places to eat in Spain. Reservations, well in advance, are obligatory. The restaurant is about 1.5km east of San Sebastián.

If You Like...
Spanish Art

After exploring the Prado (p302) in Madrid and the Guggenheim (p354) in Bilbao, you might feel inspired to seek out some of Spain's other artistic landmarks.

1 TEATRE-MUSEU DALÍ
(www.salvador-dali.org; Plaça de Gala i Salvador Dalí 5; admission incl Dalí Joies & Museu de l'Empordá adult/child €12/free; ☺9am-8pm Jul-Sep, 9.30am-6pm Mar-Jun & Oct, shorter hrs rest of year) A short train ride north of Girona, Figueres is home to the zany Teatre-Museu Dalí, housed in a 19th-century theatre converted by Salvador Dalí (who was born here). As you'd expect, it's full of surprises and illusions, and contains a substantial portion of Dalí's life's work.

2 MUSEO PICASSO MÁLAGA
(☎902 44 33 77; www.museopicassomalaga. org; Calle San Agustín 8; permanent/temporary collection €6/4.50, combined ticket €8; ☺10am-8pm Tue-Thu & Sun, to 9pm Fri & Sat) Pablo Picasso was born in Málaga in 1881, so it seems appropriate that the town should own a world-class Picasso collection. The museum's paintings, drawings, engravings, sculptures and ceramics span almost every phase of the artist's colourful career. Trains run to Madrid, Córdoba and Seville.

3 MUSEO DE BELLAS ARTES
(www.museobellasartesvalencia.gva.es; Calle San Pío V 9; ☺10am-7pm Tue-Sun, 11am-5pm Mon) Valencia's Museo de Bellas Artes ranks among Spain's best fine arts museums. Highlights include the Roman *Mosaic of the Nine Muses* and works by El Greco, Goya, Velázquez, Murillo and Ribalta. The town also has an excellent modern art museum, the Instituto Valenciano de Arte Moderno (IVAM).

4 MUSEO OTEIZA
(www.museooteiza.org; Calle de la Cuesta 7, Alzuza; adult €4, free Fri; ☺11am-7pm Tue-Sat, to 3pm Sun) This impressive museum contains almost 3000 pieces by the renowned Navarran sculptor Jorge Oteiza. It's 9km northeast of Pamplona in Alzuza.

Astelena   Basque €€
(Calle de Iñigo 1) The *pintxos* draped across the counter in this bar, tucked into the corner of Plaza de la Constitución, stand out as some of the best in the city. Many of them are a fusion of Basque and Asian inspirations, but the best of all are perhaps the foie-gras-based treats.

La Mejíllonera   Basque €€
(Calle del Puerto 15) If you thought mussels only came with garlic sauce, come here to discover mussels (from €3) by the thousand in all their glorious forms.

ℹ Information

Oficina de Turismo (☎943 48 11 66; www. sansebastianturismo.com; Alameda del Boulevard 8; ☺9.30am-1.30pm & 3.30-7pm Mon-Thu, 10am-7pm Fri & Sat, 10am-2pm Sun)

ℹ Getting There & Away

The main **Renfe train station** (Paseo de Francia) is just across Río Urumea. There are regular services to Madrid (from €54.20, five hours) and Barcelona (from €63.30, eight hours).

Bilbao

POP 351,300

The commercial hub of the Basque Country, Bilbao (Bilbo in Basque) is best known for the magnificent Guggenheim Museum. An architectural masterpiece by Frank Gehry, the museum was the catalyst of a turn-around that saw Bilbao transformed from an industrial port city into a vibrant cultural centre.

◎ Sights

Museo de Bellas Artes Art Gallery
(Fine Arts Museum; www.museobilbao.com; Plaza del Museo 2; adult/child €6/free, admission free Wed; ☺10am-8pm Tue-Sun) A mere five minutes from Museo Guggenheim is Bilbao's Museo de Bellas Artes. There are three main subcollections: classical art, with works by Murillo, Zurbarán, El Greco, Goya and van Dyck; contemporary

art, featuring works by Gauguin, Francis Bacon and Anthony Caro; and Basque art, with the works of the great sculptors Jorge de Oteiza and Eduardo Chillida, and also strong paintings by the likes of Ignacio Zuloaga and Juan de Echevarria.

Casco Viejo
Old Town

The compact Casco Viejo, Bilbao's atmospheric old quarter, is full of charming streets, boisterous bars, and plenty of quirky and independent shops. At the heart of the Casco are Bilbao's original 'seven streets', Las Siete Calles, which date from the 1400s. The 14th-century Gothic **Catedral de Santiago** (Plaza de Santiago; ⏰10am-1pm & 4-7pm Tue-Sat, 10.30am-1.30pm Sun) has a splendid Renaissance portico and a pretty little cloister.

Euskal Museoa
Museum

(Museo Vasco; Plaza Miguel Unamuno 4; adult/child €3/free, admission free Thu; ⏰11am-5pm Tue-Sat, to 2pm Sun) This is probably the most complete museum of Basque culture and history in all the Basque regions.

🛏 Sleeping

Pensión Iturrienea Ostatua
Boutique Hotel €€

(📞944 16 15 00; www.iturrieneaostatua.com; Calle de Santa María 14; r €50-70; 🛜) Easily the most eccentric hotel in Bilbao, it's part farmyard, part old-fashioned toyshop, and a work of art in its own right. The nine rooms here are so full of character that there'll be barely enough room for your own! There's a lovely breakfast area and, with baby beds and chairs and lots of toys, it's family friendly.

Hostal Begoña
Boutique Hotel €

(📞944 23 01 34; www.hostalbegona.com; Calle de

la Amistad 2; s/d from €50/55; @🛜) Begoña speaks for itself with colourful rooms decorated with modern artworks, all with funky tiled bathrooms and wrought-iron beds. It's probably the best hotel in the city in which to meet other travellers. There's a car park nearby.

Gran Hotel Domine
Design Hotel €€€

(📞944 25 33 00; www.granhoteldominebilbao.com; Alameda Mazarredo 61; r from €132; P❄@🐾) Designer chic all the way, from the Javier Mariscal interiors to the Phillipe Starck and Arne Jacobsen fittings – and that's just in the toilets. This stellar showpiece of the Silken chain has views of the Guggenheim from some of its pricier rooms, a giant column of rounded beach stones reaching for the heavens and a water feature filled with plates and glasses.

🍴 Eating

Rio-Oja
Basque €

(📞944 15 08 71; Calle de Perro 4; mains €8-11) An institution that shouldn't be missed.

Catedral de Santiago, Bilbao
CHRIS MELLOR/GETTY IMAGES ©

KIMBERLEY COOLE/GETTY IMAGES © ARCHITECT: FRANK GEHRY

Don't Miss
Museo Guggenheim

Opened in 1997, Bilbao's Museo Guggenheim lifted modern architecture and Bilbao into the 21st century – with sensation. Some might say, probably quite rightly, that structure overwhelms function here and that the Guggenheim is more famous for its architecture than its content. But Canadian architect Frank Gehry's inspired use of flowing canopies, cliffs, promontories, ship shapes, towers and flying fins is irresistible. The interior of the Guggenheim is purposefully vast. The cathedral-like atrium is more than 45m high. Light pours in through the glass cliffs. Permanent exhibits fill the ground floor and include such wonders as mazes of metal and phrases of light reaching for the skies. For most people, though, it is the temporary exhibitions that are the main attraction (check the Guggenheim's website for a full program of upcoming exhibitions).

NEED TO KNOW

www.guggenheim-bilbao.es; Avenida Abandoibarra 2; adult/child €13/free; ☺10am-8pm, closed Mon Sep-Jun

It specialises in light Basque seafood and heavy inland fare, but to most foreigners the snails, sheep brains or squid floating in pools of its own ink are the makings of a culinary adventure story they'll be recounting for years.

Nerua   Basque €€€
(☎944 00 04 30; www.nerua.com; tasting menu €80; ☺closed Mon & Jan–mid-Feb) The Guggenheim's modernist, chic restaurant, Nerua, is under the direction of super chef Josean Martínez Alija. Needless to say, the *nueva cocina vasca* is breathtaking – even the olives come from

1000-year-old olive trees! Reservations are essential.

ℹ️ Information

Tourist office (www.bilbao.net/bilbaoturismo; Plaza del Ensanche 11; ⏱9am-2pm & 4-7.30pm Mon-Fri) Other branches at the Teatro Arriaga, Museo Guggenheim and airport.

ℹ️ Getting There & Away

Air

Bilbao's **airport** (BIO; ☎902 404704; www.aena. es), with domestic and a handful of international flights, is near Sondika, 12km northeast of the city. The airport bus Bizkaibus A3247 (€1.30, 30 minutes) runs to/from Termibus (bus station), where there is a tram stop and a metro station.

Train

Two Renfe trains runs daily to Madrid (from €50.50, six hours) and Barcelona (€64.80, six hours) from the Abando train station. Slow **FEVE** (www.feve.es) trains run from Concordia station, heading west into Cantabria and Asturias.

NAVARRA

Navarra, historically and culturally linked to the Basque Country, is known for its fine wines and for the Sanfermines festival in Pamplona.

Pamplona

POP 195,800

Immortalised by Ernest Hemingway in *The Sun Also Rises,* the pre-Pyrenean city of Pamplona (Iruña in Basque) is home of the wild Sanfermines (aka Encierro or Running of the Bulls) festival, but is also an extremely walkable city that's managed to mix the charm of old plazas and buildings with modern shops and a lively nightlife.

🎯 Sights

Cathedral   Church

(Calle Dormitalería; guided tours adult/child €4.40/2.60; ⏱10am-7pm Mon-Fri, to 2pm Sat mid-Jul–mid-Sep) Pamplona's main cathedral stands on a rise just inside the city

ramparts amid a dark thicket of narrow streets. It's a late-medieval Gothic gem spoiled only by its rather dull neoclassical facade, an 18th-century appendage. The real joys are the vast interior and the Gothic cloister, where there is marvellous delicacy in the stonework.

Ciudadela & Parks   Fortress, Park

(Avenida del Ejército) The walls and bulwarks of the grand fortified citadel, the star-shaped Ciudadela, lurk amid the verdant grass and trees in what is now a charming park, the portal to three more parks that unfold to the north and lend Pamplona a beautiful green escape.

Museo de Navarra   Museum

(www.cfnavarra.es/cultura/museo; Calle Cuesta de Santo Domingo 47; adult €2, free Sat afternoon & Sun; ⏱9.30am-2pm & 5-7pm Tue-Sat, 11am-2pm Sun) Housed in a former medieval hospital, this superb museum has an eclectic collection of archaeological finds (including a number of fantastic Roman mosaics unearthed mainly in southern Navarra), as well as a selection of art including Goya's *Marqués de San Adrián.*

Surviving Sanfermines

The Sanfermines festival is held from 6 to 14 July, when Pamplona is overrun with thrill-seekers, curious onlookers and, yes, bulls. The Encierro (Running of the Bulls) begins at 8am daily, when bulls are let loose from the Coralillos Santo Domingo. The 825m race lasts just three minutes, and rarely ends well for the bull. The safest place to watch the Encierro is on TV. If that's too tame for you, try to sweet-talk your way onto a balcony or book a room in a hotel with views. The anti-bullfighting event, the Running of the Nudes, takes place two days earlier.

Detour:
Picos de Europa

These jagged mountains straddling Asturias, Cantabria and northeast Castilla y León amount to some of the finest walking country in Spain.

They comprise three limestone massifs (whose highest peak rises 2648m). The 647-sq-km **Parque Nacional de los Picos de Europa** (www.picosdeeuropa.com) covers all three massifs and is Spain's second-biggest national park.

There are numerous places to stay and eat all over the mountains. Getting here and around by bus can be slow going but the Picos are accessible from Santander and Oviedo (the latter is easier) by bus.

🛏 Sleeping

Accommodation is hard to come by during Sanfermines – book months in advance.

Palacio Guendulain   Historic Hotel €€
(☎948 22 55 22; www.palacioguendulain.com; Calle Zapatería 53; d incl breakfast from €134; 🅿❄🛜) To call this stunning hotel, inside the converted former home of the Viceroy of New Granada, sumptuous is an understatement. The rooms contain *Princess and the pea*–soft beds, enormous showers and regal armchairs.

Hotel Puerta del Camino   Boutique Hotel €€
(☎948 22 66 88; www.hotelpuertadelcamino.com; Calle Dos de Mayo 4; s/d from €89/95; 🅿❄🛜) A very stylish hotel inside a converted convent beside the northern gates to the old city. The functional rooms have clean, modern lines and it's positioned in one of the prettier, and quieter, parts of town. Some rooms have Pyrenean views.

🍴 Eating & Drinking

Baserri   Basque €
(☎948 22 20 21; Calle de San Nicolás 32; menú del día €14) This place has won enough *pintxo* awards that we could fill this entire book listing them. As you'd expect from such a certificate-studded bar, the *pintxos* and full meals are superb.

Casa Otaño   Basque €€
(☎948 22 50 95; Calle de San Nicolás 5; mains €15-18) A little pricier than many on this street but worth the extra. Great dishes range from the locally caught trout to heavenly duck dishes. The *menú del día* is good value.

Café Iruña   Historic Cafe
(www.cafeiruna.com; Plaza del Castillo 44) Opened on the eve of Sanfermines in 1888, Café Iruña's dominant position, powerful sense of history and frilly belle-époque decor make this by far the most famous and popular watering hole in the city.

ℹ Information

Tourist office (www.turismo.navarra.es; Calle de Esclava 1; ⏱9am-8pm Mon-Sat, to 2pm Sun)

ℹ Getting There & Away

Pamplona's train station is linked to the city centre by bus 9 from Paseo de Sarasate every 15 minutes. Trains run to/from Madrid (€57.90, three hours, four daily) and San Sebastián (from €21.20, two hours, two daily).

VALENCIA & MURCIA

A warm climate, an abundance of seaside resorts and interesting cities make this area of Spain a popular destination.

Valencia

POP 815,000

Valencia, where paella first simmered over a wood fire, is a vibrant, friendly, slightly chaotic place. It has two outstanding fine-arts museums, an accessible old quarter, Europe's newest cultural and scientific complex, and one of Spain's most exciting nightlife scenes.

◎ Sights

Ciudad de las Artes y las Ciencias
Science Centre

(City of Arts & Sciences; ☎902 100031; www. cac.es; combined ticket adult/child €31.50/24) The aesthetically stunning City of Arts & Sciences occupies a massive 350,000-sq-metre swath of the old Turia riverbed. It's mostly the work of local architect Santiago Calatrava, designer of, among many other exciting creations around the world, the transport terminal for the new World Trade Center site in New York.

Barrio del Carmen
Historic Area

You'll see Valencia's best face by simply wandering around the Barrio del Carmen. Valencia's Romanesque-Gothic-baroque-Renaissance **catedral** (Plaza de la Virgen; adult/child incl audioguide €4.50/3; ☉10am-4.45pm or 5.45pm Mon-Sat, 2-4.45pm Sun) is a compendium of centuries of architectural history and home to the **Capilla del Santo Cáliz**, a chapel said to contain the Holy Grail (the chalice Christ supposedly used in the last supper). Climb the 207 stairs of the **Miguelete bell tower** (adult/child €2/1; ☉10am-7pm or 7.30pm) for sweeping city views.

Plaza del Mercado
Historic Plaza

Valencia's Modernista covered market, the **Mercado Central** (www. mercadocentralvalencia. es; ☉7.30am-3pm Mon-Sat) recently scrubbed and glowing as new, was constructed in

1928. With over 900 stalls, it's a swirl of smells, movement and colour. **La Lonja** (adult/child €2/1; ☉10am-7pm Tue-Sat, to 3pm Sun) is a splendid late-15th-century building, a Unesco World Heritage site and was originally Valencia's silk and commodity exchange.

Instituto Valenciano de Arte Moderno (IVAM)
Art

(www.ivam.es; Calle Guillem de Castro 118; adult/child €2/1; ☉10am-8pm Tue-Sun) IVAM ('ee-bam') hosts excellent temporary exhibitions and houses an impressive permanent collection of 20th-century Spanish art.

🛏 Sleeping

Ad Hoc
Hotel €€

(☎96 391 91 40; www.adhochoteles.com; Calle Boix 4; s €65-101, d €76-125; ❄ 🛜) Friendly, welcoming Ad Hoc offers comfort and charm deep within the old quarter and also runs a splendid small **restaurant** (Monday to Friday and lunch Saturday).

Sanfermines festival (p355), Pamplona
MATTHEW MICAH WRIGHT/GETTY IMAGES ©

Valencia

SPAIN VALENCIA

0   200 m
0   0.1 miles

Jardines del Turia

C de Blanquerías

Jardines del Turia

Puente de Serranos

Pont de Fusta

C de Salvador Giner

C de Liria

C Na Jordana

2

BARRIO DEL CARMEN

C del Dr Chiarri

C Ripalda

C de San Ramón

Plaza del Carmen

C de Santo Tomás

Plaza de los Fueros (dels Furs)

C de Roteros

Plaza de los Fueros

C de Conde de Trénor

Puente de la Trinidad

C de San Pio V

6

C Alboraya

Jardines del Turia

C Pintor López

C Franciscanos

C Navellos

C de los Trinitarios

8

C de Almudín

Plaza de Mosén Sorell

C Alta (Dalt)

C Baja (Baix)

C Landerer

C de la Mare Vella

C de Serranos

C Dr Beltrán Bigorra

C del Pintor Zariñena

Plaza del Tossal

C de Quart

C del Moro Zeit

C de Caballeros

C de Calatrava

Plaza del Horno de San Nicolás

CENTRO HISTÓRIO NORTH

10

Plaza de la Virgen

5

10

Plaza del Arzobispo

Plaza de Nápoles y Sicilia

C de Avellanas

C Milagro

C del Gobernador Viejo

C Murillo

C Cardà

C de la Lonja

3

Plaza del Mercado

Plaza del Dr Collado

Turismo Valencia (VLC) Tourist Office

Plaza de la Reina

C del Mar

C de Valeriola

Plaza Don Juan de Villarrasa

C Carniceros

C Balmes

4

C Marias

C Trench

Plaza Redonda

C del Marqués de dos Aguas

C de la Paz

C de las Comedias

C Editor Manueal Aguilar

C Pie de la Cruz

7

9

San Martín

C Abadia

C Guillem Sorolla

CENTRO HISTÓRICO SOUTH

C Linterna

Av María Cristina

C de Moratín

C Embajador Vich

Plaza del Patriarca

C del Poeta Querol

C de Salvá

C del Hospital

Av Barón de Cárcer

C de Garrigues

C d'En Sanz

C de Padilla

C de San Vicente Mártir

Av del Marques de Sotelo

Av María Cristina

C Barcelonina

C de Barcas

C Correos

C del Pintor Sorolla

C Juan de Austria

C de Pascual y Genís

C de Perez Bayer

C Roger de Lauria

Gran Via Ramón y Cajal

C de Guillem de Castro

C de Quevedo

C de Jesús

C de San Vicente Mártir

Plaza San Agustín

C San Pablo

Plaza del Ayuntamiento

C Convento Santa Clara

C de Colón

C de Pizarro

C de Xàtiva

Xàtiva

C de Troya

C Pelayo

C Bailén

Turismo Valencia (VLC) Tourist Office

Plaza de Toros

C de Russafa

C de Cirilo Amorós

Plaza de España

Estación del Norte

Valencia

◎ Sights
1 Catedral..C3
2 Instituto Valenciano de Arte
    Moderno (IVAM) A1
3 La Lonja..B4
4 Mercado Central................................B4
5 Miguelete Bell Tower.........................C3
6 Museo de Bellas Artes D1
7 Plaza del Mercado B4

🛏 Sleeping
8 Ad Hoc...D2
9 Petit Palace Bristol C4

✴ Eating
10 Delicat C2

Petit Palace Bristol   Boutique Hotel €€
(☎96 394 51 00; www.hthoteles.com; Calle Abadía San Martín 3; r €60-130; ✳@🖤) Hip and minimalist, this boutique hotel, a comprehensively made-over 19th-century mansion, retains the best of its past and does a particularly scrumptious buffet breakfast.

✴ Eating

La Pepica   Seafood €€
(☎96 371 03 66; www.lapepica.com; Paseo de Neptuno 6-8; meals around €25; ☺lunch & dinner Mon-Sat, lunch Sun) More expensive than its many beach-side competitors, La Pepica, run by the same family for more than a century, is renowned for its rice dishes and seafood.

Delicat   Tapas, Fusion €
(☎96 392 33 57; seudelicat@hotmail.es; Calle Conde Almodóvar 4; mains €4-11, menus €12; ☺Tue-Sun) This particularly friendly, intimate option (there are only nine tables, plus the terrace in summer), offers an unbeatable five-course menu for lunch and a range of innovative tapas anytime.

A Tu Gusto   Mediterranean €€
(☎96 322 70 26; www.atugusto.com; cnr Avenida Instituto Obrero & Calle Escritor Rafael Ferreres; mains €14-20, menus €10-36; ☺lunch & dinner Wed-Sat, lunch Sun & Tue) At this strictly contemporary place, the decor is sleek, all pistachio and pitch black but for the gleaming white bar. Salvador Furió, the powerhouse in the kitchen, has worked with some of Spain's finest chefs.

❶ Information

Turismo Valencia (VLC) Tourist Office (☎96 315 39 31; www.turisvalencia.es; Plaza de la Reina 19; ☺9am-7pm Mon-Sat, 10am-2pm Sun) Has several other branches around town, including the train station and airport arrivals area.

❶ Getting There & Away

Air
Valencia's **Aeropuerto de Manises** (☎96 159 85 00) is 10km west of the city centre along the A3, towards Madrid. It's served by metro lines 3 and 5.

Train
From Valencia's Estación del Norte, major destinations include the following:

Alicante €17-29, 1¾ hours, 10 daily

Barcelona €40-44, 3-3½ hours, at least 12 daily

Madrid €63-80, 1¾ hours, up to 15 daily

ANDALUCÍA

Images of Andalucía are so potent, so quintessentially Spanish that it's sometimes difficult not to feel a sense of déjà vu. It's almost as if you've already been there in your dreams: a solemn Easter parade, an ebullient spring festival, exotic nights in the Alhambra.

Seville

POP 703,000

A sexy, gutsy and gorgeous city, Seville is home to two of Spain's most colourful festivals, fascinating and distinctive *barrios* (neighbourhoods) and a local population that lives life to the fullest. A fiery place (as you'll soon see in its packed and noisy tapas bars), it is also hot climate-wise – avoid July and August!

SPAIN SEVILLE

Seville

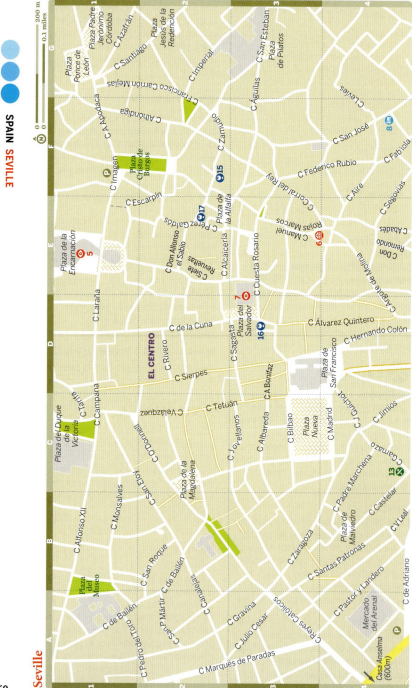

200 m
0.1 miles

EL CENTRO

Plaza Padre Jerónimo Córdoba
Plaza Ponce de León
Plaza Jesús de la Redención
Plaza de Pilatos
Plaza de la Encarnación 5
Plaza Cristo de Burgus
Plaza de la Alfalfa
Plaza del Salvador 7
Plaza del Duque de la Victoria
Plaza de la Magdalena
Plaza del Museo
Plaza de San Francisco
Plaza Nueva
Plaza de Malviedro
Mercado del Arenal

C Azafrán
C Santiago
Plaza de San Esteban
C San Esteban
C Francisco Carrión Mejías
C Alhóndiga
C Imperial
C Águilas
C Levies
C A Apodaca
C Imagen
C Escarpín
C Zamudio
C San José
C Federico Rubio
C Fabiola
C Aire
C Segovias
C Abades
C Don Remondo
C Corral del Rey
C Manuel Rojas Marcos 9
C Pérez Galdós
C Don Alfonso el Sabio
C Siete Revueltas
C Alcaicería
C Cuesta Rosario
C Argote de Molina
C Laraña
C de la Cuna
C Sagasta
C Álvarez Quintero
C Hernando Colón
C Rivero
C Sierpes
C A Bonifaz
C Tetuán
C Velázquez
C Campana
C Tarifa
C O Donnell
C San Eloy
C Jovellanos
C Albareda
C Bilbao
C Madrid
C Gurdini
C Jimios
C Monsalves
C Alfonso XII
C Pedro del Toro
C de Bailén
C San Roque
C P Mártir
C de Bailén
C Canalejas
C Gravina
C Julio César
C Reyes Católicos
C Zaragoza
C Santas Patronas
C Padre Marchena
C Gamazo
C Castelar
C V Leal
C Pastor y Landero
C Adriano
C Marqués de Paradas
Casa Anselma (600m)

15
17
16
13

Seville

⊙ Sights
1 Alcázar E6
2 Archivo de Indias D6
3 Barrio de Santa Cruz......................F5
4 Cathedral & Giralda D5
5 Metropol Parasol E1
6 Museo del Baile Flamenco.................E3
7 Plaza del Salvador D3

🛏 Sleeping
8 Hotel Amadeus F4
9 Hotel Casa 1800................................E5
10 Un Patio en Santa Cruz.....................G5

✗ Eating
11 Bodega Santa Cruz............................E5
12 Catalina G5
13 Mesón Cinco Jotas C4
14 Vinería San Telmo G5

⊕ Drinking & Nightlife
15 El Garlochi..F2
16 La Antigua Bodeguita........................D3
17 La Rebótica..E2

⊕ Entertainment
18 Casa de la Memoria de Al-
   Andalus F5

⊙ Sights

Cathedral & Giralda   Church
(www.catedraldesevilla.es; adult/child €8/
free; ⊙11am-5.30pm Mon-Sat, 2.30-6.30pm
Sun Sep-Jun, 9.30am-4.30pm Mon-Sat, 2.30-
6.30pm Sun Jul & Aug) After Seville fell to
the Christians in 1248 its main mosque
was used as a church until 1401 when
it was knocked down to make way for
what would become one of the world's
largest cathedrals and an icon of Gothic
architecture. Over 90m high, the perfectly
proportioned and exquisitely decorated
La Giralda was the minaret of the
mosque that stood on the site before the
cathedral. The views from the summit are
exceptional.

Alcázar   Castle
(adult/child €7.50/free; ⊙9.30am-7pm Apr-
Sep, to 6pm Oct-Mar) Seville's Alcázar, a
royal residence for many centuries, was
founded in 913 as a Muslim fortress. The
Catholic Monarchs, Fernando and Isabel,

Seville Cathedral

What To Look For

'We're going to construct a church so large future generations will think we were mad,' declared the inspired architects of Seville in 1402 at the beginning of one of the most grandiose building projects in medieval history. Just over a century later their madness was triumphantly confirmed.

To avoid getting lost, orient yourself by the main highlights. Directly inside the southern (main) entrance is the grand **mausoleum of Christopher Columbus** ❶. Turn right here and head into the south-eastern corner to uncover some major art treasures: a Goya in the Sacristía de los Cálices, a Zurbarán in the **Sacristía Mayor** ❷, and Murillo's shining Immaculada in the Sala Capitular. Skirt the cathedral's eastern wall taking a look inside the **Capilla Real** ❸ with its important royal tombs. By now it's impossible to avoid the lure of **Capilla Mayor** ❹ with its fantastical altarpiece. Hidden over in the northwest corner is the **Capilla de San Antonio** ❺ with a legendary Murillo. That huge doorway almost in front of you is rarely opened **Puerta de la Asunción** ❻. Make for the **Giralda** ❼ next, stealing admiring looks at the high, vaulted ceiling on the way. After looking down on the cathedral's immense footprint, descend and depart via the **Patio de los Naranjos** ❽.

TOP TIPS

Queue-dodge Reserve tickets online at www.servicaixa.com for an extra €1 up to six weeks in advance.

Pace yourself Don't visit the Alcazar and Cathedral on the same day. There is far too much to take in.

Viewpoints Take time to admire the cathedral from the outside. It's particularly stunning at night from the Plaza Virgen de los Reyes, and from across the river in Triana.

Capilla Mayor
Behold! The cathedral's main focal point contains its greatest treasure, a magnificent gold-plated altarpiece depicting various scenes in the life of Christ. It constitutes the life's work of one man, Flemish artist Pieter Dancart.

Patio de los Naranjos
Inhale the perfume of 60 Sevillan orange trees in a cool patio bordered by fortress-like walls – a surviving remnant of the original 12th-century mosque. Exit is gained via the horseshoe-shaped Puerta del Perdón.

Puerta del Perdón

Iglesia del Sagrario

Puerta del Bautismo

Puerta de la Asunción
Located on the western side of the cathedral and also known as the Puerta Mayor, these huge, rarely opened doors are pushed back during Semana Santa to allow solemn processions of Catholic *hermanadades* (brotherhoods) to pass through.

Giraldillo

Giralda

Ascend, not by stairs, but by a long continuous ramp, to the top of this 11th-century minaret topped by a Gothic-baroque belfry. Standing 104m tall it has long been the defining symbol of Seville.

7

Sacristía Mayor

Art lovers will love this large domed room containing some of the city's greatest paintings, including Zurbarán's *Santa Teresa* and Pedro de Campaña's *Descendimiento*. It also guards the city key captured in 1248.

Capilla Real

Keep a respectful silence in this atmospheric chapel dedicated to the Virgen de los Reyes. In a silver urn lie the hallowed remains of the city's Christian conqueror Ferdinand III and his son, Alfonso the Wise.

3

4

2

1

Main Entrance

Capilla de San Antonio

One of 80 interior chapels, you'll need to hunt down this little gem notable for housing Murillo's 1666 painting, *The Vision of St Anthony*. The work was pillaged by thieves in 1874 but later restored.

Tomb of Columbus

Buried in Valladolid in 1506, the remains of Christopher Columbus were moved four times before they arrived in Seville in 1898 encased in an elaborately carved catafalque. Or were they? A longstanding debate rages about whether these are actually Columbus' remains or if, in a postdeath mix-up, he still resides in the Dominican Republic.

Below: Barrio de Santa Cruz, Seville;
Right: Semana Santa festival, Seville
(BELOW) DIANA MAYFIELD/GETTY IMAGES ©; (RIGHT) IAN CUMMING/GETTY IMAGES ©

set up court here in the 1480s as they prepared for the conquest of Granada. Later rulers created the Alcázar's lovely gardens. The highlights include exquisitely adorned patios and the showpiece **Palacio de Don Pedro**.

Archivo de Indias   Museum

(Calle Santo Tomás; ☺10am-4pm Mon-Sat, to 2pm Sun & holidays) `FREE` On the western side of Plaza del Triunfo, the Archivo de Indias is the main archive of Spain's American empire, with 80 million pages of documents dating from 1492 through to the end of the empire in the 19th century: a most effective statement of Spain's power and influence during its Golden Age.

Barrio de Santa Cruz   Historic District

Seville's medieval *judería* (Jewish quarter), east of the cathedral and Alcázar, is today a tangle of atmospheric, winding streets and lovely plant-decked plazas perfumed with orange blossom. Among its most characteristic plazas is **Plaza de Santa Cruz**, which gives the *barrio* its name. **Plaza de Doña Elvira** is another romantic perch, especially in the evening.

Metropol Parasol   Landmark

(www.metropolsevilla.com; Plaza de la Encarnación) The opinion-dividing Metropol Parasol which opened in March 2011 in the Plaza de la Encarnación claims to be the largest wooden building in the world. Its undulating honeycombed roof is held up by giant five mushroom-like pillars.

Museo del Baile Flamenco   Museum

(www.museoflamenco.com; Calle Manuel Rojas Marcos 3; adult/child €10/6; ☺9.30am-7pm) The brainchild of Sevillana flamenco dancer, Cristina Hoyos, this museum is spread over three floors of an 18th-century palace, although at €10 a pop

it's a little overpriced. Exhibits include sketches, paintings, photos of erstwhile (and contemporary) flamenco greats, plus a collection of dresses and shawls.

⭐ Festivals & Events

The first of Seville's two great festivals is **Semana Santa** (www.semana-santa.org), the week leading up to Easter Sunday. Throughout the week, thousands of members of religious brotherhoods parade in penitents' garb with tall, pointed *capirotes* (hoods) accompanying sacred images through the city, while huge crowds look on.

The **Feria de Abril**, a week in late April, is a welcome release after this solemnity: the festivities involve six days of music, dancing, horse riding and traditional dress, plus daily bullfights.

The city also stages Spain's largest flamenco festival, the month-long **Bienal de Flamenco** (www.labienal.com). It's held in September in even-numbered years.

🛏 Sleeping

Hotel Casa 1800   Luxury Hotel €€€
(☎ 954 56 18 00; www.hotelcasa1800sevilla.com; Calle Rodrigo Caro 6; d €145-198; ✳@🛜) Straight in at number one as Seville's favourite hotel is this newly revived Santa Cruz jewel. Highlights include a sweet afternoon tea buffet, plus a quartet of penthouse garden suites with Giralda views.

Un Patio en Santa Cruz   Hotel €€
(☎ 954 53 94 13; www.patiosantacruz.com; Calle Doncellas 15; s €65-85, d €65-125; ✳🛜) Feeling more like an art gallery than a hotel, this place has starched white walls coated in loud works of art, and strange sculptures and preserved plants. The rooms are immensely comfortable, staff are friendly, and there's a cool rooftop terrace with mosaic Moroccan tables.

Hotel Amadeus   Hotel €€
(☎ 954 50 14 43; www.hotelamadeussevilla.com; Calle Farnesio 6; s/d €85/95; P✳🛜) Just

365

Detour:
Altamira

The country's finest prehistoric art, in the Cueva de Altamira, 2km southwest of Santillana del Mar, is off-limits to all but the scientific community. Since 2002, however, the **Museo Altamira** (museodealtamira. mcu.es; adult/child, EU senior or student €3/free, admission free Sun & from 2.30pm Sat; ⊙9.30am-8pm Tue-Sat, to 3pm Sun & holidays; **P**) has allowed all comers to view the inspired, 14,500-year-old depictions of bison, horses and other beasts (or rather, their replicas) in this full-size, dazzling re-creation of the cave's most interesting chamber, the Sala de Polícromos (Polychrome Hall).

The nearest town is Santillana del Mar, about 35km west of Santander.

when you thought you could never find hotels with pianos in the rooms anymore, along came Hotel Amadeus, run by an engaging musical family in the old Judería, where several of the astutely decorated rooms come complete with soundproofed walls and upright pianos ensuring you don't miss out on your daily practice.

Eating

Vinería San Telmo   Tapas, Fusion €€
(☏954 41 06 00; www.vineriasantelmo.com; Paseo Catalina de Ribera 4; tapas €3.50, media raciones €10) San Telmo invented the rasco-cielo (skyscraper) tapa, an 'Empire State' of tomatoes, aubergine, goat's cheese and smoked salmon.

Catalina   Tapas €€
(Paseo Catalina de Ribera 4; raciones €10) If your view of tapas is 'glorified bar snacks'; then your ideas could be blown out of the water here with a creative mix of just

about every ingredient known to Iberian cooking.

Bodega Santa Cruz   Tapas €
(Calle Mateos Gago; tapas €2) Forever crowded and with a mountain of paper on the floor, this place is usually standing room only, with tapas and drinks enjoyed alfresco as you dodge the marching army of tourists squeezing through Santa Cruz's narrow streets.

Mesón Cinco Jotas   Tapas €€
(www.mesoncincojotas.com; Calle Castelar 1; tapas €3.80, media raciones €10) In the world of jamón-making, if you are awarded 'Cinco Jotas' (Five Js) for your jamón, it's like getting an Oscar. The owner of this place, Sánchez Romero Carvajal, is the biggest producer of Jabugo ham, and has a great selection on offer.

Drinking & Nightlife

Plaza del Salvador is brimful of drinkers from mid-evening to 1am. Grab a drink from **La Antigua Bodeguita** (☏954 56 18 33) and sit on the steps of the Parroquia del Salvador.

El Garlochi   Bar
(Calle Boteros 4) Dedicated entirely to the iconography, smells and sounds of Semana Santa, the ubercamp El Garlochi is a true marvel. Taste the rather revolting sounding cocktails Sangre de Cristo (Blood of Christ) or Agua de Sevilla, both heavily laced with vodka, whisky and grenadine, and pray they open more bars like this.

La Rebótica   Bar
(Calle Pérez Galdós 11) Two's a crowd in the cramped, sinuous Rebótica, the place to come for cheap shots and 1980s flashbacks accompanied by an appropriately retro soundtrack.

Bulebar Café   Bar, Cafe
(☏954 90 19 54; Alameda de Hércules 83; ⊙4pm-late) This place gets pretty caliente (hot) at night but is pleasantly chilled in the early evening, with friendly staff.

⭐ Entertainment

Seville is arguably Spain's flamenco capital and you're most likely to catch a spontaneous atmosphere (of unpredictable quality) in one of the bars staging regular nights of flamenco with no admission fee.

Casa de la Memoria de Al-Andalus   Flamenco

(☏954 56 06 70; www.casadelamemoria.es; Calle Ximénez de Enciso 28; tickets €15; ⏰9pm) This flamenco *tablao* in Santa Cruz is without doubt the most intimate and authentic nightly flamenco show outside the Museo del Baile Flamenco (p364), offering a wide variety of *palos* (flamenco styles) in a courtyard of shifting shadows and overhanging plants. Reserve tickets a day or so in advance.

Casa Anselma   Flamenco

(Calle Pagés del Corro 49; ⏰midnight-late Mon-Sat) Casa Anselma (beware: there's no sign, just a doorway embellished with *azulejos* tiles) is the antithesis of a tourist flamenco *tablao,* with cheek-to-jowl crowds, thick cigarette smoke, zero amplification and spontaneous outbreaks of dexterous dancing. Pure magic.

ℹ Information

Seville Tourism (www.turismo.sevilla.org)

ℹ Getting There & Away

The modern, efficient **Estación de Santa Justa** (☏902 43 23 43; Avenida Kansas City) is 1.5km northeast of the city centre. There's also a city-centre **Renfe ticket office** (Calle Zaragoza 29).

Twenty or more superfast AVE trains, reaching speeds of 280km/h, whiz daily to/

from Madrid (€83.80, 2½ hours). Other services include Cádiz (€13.25, 1¾ hours, 13 daily), Córdoba (€17 to €33.20, 40 minutes to 1½ hours, 21 or more daily), Granada (€24.80, three hours, four daily) and Málaga (€38.70, two hours, 11 daily).

Córdoba

POP 328,000

Córdoba was once one of the most enlightened Islamic cities on earth, and enough remains to place it in the contemporary top three Andalucian draws. The centrepiece is the gigantic and exquisitely rendered Mezquita. Surrounding it is an intricate web of winding streets, geranium-sprouting flower boxes and cool intimate patios that are at their most beguiling in late spring.

◎ Sights & Activities

Mezquita   Great Mosque

(Mosque; ☏957 47 05 12; www.mezquitadecordoba.org; Calle Cardenal Herrero; adult/child €8/4, 8.30-10am Mon-Sat free; ⏰10am-7pm Mon-Sat,

Mezquita, Córdoba
MICHELE FALZONE/GETTY IMAGES ©

Mezquita

Timeline

AD 600 Foundation of the Christian Visigothic church of St Vincent on the site of the present Mezquita.

AD 785 Salvaging Visigoth and Roman ruins, Emir Abd ar-Rahman I converts the Mezquita into a mosque.

AD 822-5 Mosque enlarged in reign of Abd ar-Rahman II.

AD 912-961 A new minaret is ordered by Abd ar-Rahman III.

AD 961-6 Mosque enlarged by Al-Hakam II who also enriches the **mihrab** ❶.

AD 987 Mosque enlarged for the last time by Al-Mansur Ibn Abi Aamir. With the addition of the Patio de los **Naranjos** ❷, the building reaches its current dimensions.

1236 Mosque reconverted into a Christian church after Córdoba is recaptured by Ferdinand III of Castile.

1271 Instead of destroying the mosque, the overawed Christians elect to modify it. Alfonso X orders the construction of the **Capilla de Villaviciosa** ❸ and **Capilla Real** ❹.

1300s Original minaret is replaced by the baroque **Torre del Alminar** ❺.

1520s A Renaissance-style cathedral nave is added by Charles V. 'I have destroyed something unique to the world,' he laments on seeing the finished work.

2004 Spanish Muslims petition to be able to worship in the Mezquita again. The Vatican doesn't consent.

Capilla de Villaviciosa

Sift through the building's numerous chapels till you find this gem, an early Christian modification added in 1277 which fused existing Moorish features with Gothic arches and pillars. It served as the Capilla Mayor until the 1520s.

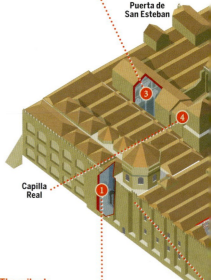

Puerta de San Esteban

Capilla Real

The mihrab

Everything leads to the mosque's greatest treasure – a scallop-shell-shaped prayer niche facing Mecca that was added in the 10th century. Cast your eyes over the gold mosaic cubes crafted by imported Byzantium sculptors.

The cathedral choir

Few ignore the impressive *coro* (choir): a late-Christian addition dating from the 1750s. Once you've admired the skilfully carved mahogany choir stalls depicting scenes from the Bible, look up at the impressive baroque ceiling.

⑤

Torre del Alminar

This is the Mezquita's cheapest sight because you don't have to pay to see it. Rising 93m and viewable from much of the city, the baroque-style bell tower was built over the mosque's original minaret.

The Mezquita arches

No, you're not hallucinating. The Mezquita's most defining characteristic is its unique terracotta-and-white striped arches that support 856 pillars salvaged from Roman and Visigoth ruins. Glimpsed through the dull light they're at once spooky and striking.

Puerta del Perdón

②

Patio de los Naranjos

Abandon architectural preconceptions all ye who enter here. The ablutions area of the former mosque is a shady courtyard embellished with orange trees that acts as the Mezquita's main entry point.

Capilla Mayor

A Christian monument inside an Islamic mosque sounds beautifully ironic, yet here it is: a Gothic church commissioned by Charles V in the 16th century and planted in the middle of the world's third largest mosque.

The maksura

Guiding you towards the mihrab, the maksura is a former royal enclosure where the caliphs and their retinues prayed. Its lavish, elaborate arches were designed to draw the eye of worshippers towards the mihrab and Mecca.

8.30-10am & 2-7pm Sun Mar-Oct, 8.30am-6pm Mon-Sat, 8.30-10am & 2-6pm Sun Nov-Feb) Founded in 785, Córdoba's gigantic mosque is a wonderful architectural hybrid with delicate horseshoe arches making this unlike anywhere else in Spain. The main entrance is the **Puerta del Perdón**, a 14th-century Mudéjar gateway, with the ticket office immediately inside. Also inside the gateway is the aptly named **Patio de los Naranjos** (Courtyard of the Orange Trees). You can see straight ahead to the *mihrab*, the prayer niche in a mosque's *qibla* (the wall indicating the direction of Mecca) that was the focus of prayer. The first 12 transverse aisles inside the entrance, a forest of pillars and arches, comprise the original 8th-century mosque.

Judería   Historic Neighbourhood

The medieval *judería*, extending northwest from the Mezquita almost to Av del Gran Capitán, is today a maze of narrow streets and whitewashed buildings with flowery window boxes. The beautiful little 14th-century **Sinagoga (Calle de los Judíos**

20; admission €0.30; ⏱9.30am-2pm & 3.30-5.30pm Tue-Sat, 9.30am-1.30pm Sun & holidays) is one of only three surviving medieval synagogues in Spain and the only one in Andalucía.

Alcázar de los Reyes Cristianos   Castle

(Castle of the Christian Monarchs; Campo Santo de Los Mártires; admission €4, Fri free; ⏱10am-2pm & 5.30-7.30pm Tue-Sat, 9.30am-2.30pm Sun & holidays) Just southwest of the Mezquita, the Alcázar began as a palace and fort for Alfonso X in the 13th century. From 1490 to 1821 the Inquisition operated from here. Today its gardens are among the most beautiful in Andalucía.

Medina Azahara   Islamic Ruins

(Madinat al-Zahra; adult/EU citizen €1.50/free; ⏱10am-6.30pm Tue-Sat, to 8.30pm May–mid-Sep, to 2pm Sun) Even in the cicada-shrill heat and stillness of a summer afternoon, the Medina Azahara whispers of the power and vision of its founder, Abd ar-Rahman III. The self-proclaimed caliph began the construction of a magnificent new capital 8km west of Córdoba around 936, and took up full residence around 945. It was destroyed in the 11th century and just 10% of the site has been excavated. A taxi from Córdoba costs €37 for the return trip, with one hour to view the site, or you can book a three-hour coach tour for €6.50 to €10 through many Córdoba hotels.

Hammam Baños Árabes   Bathhouse

(☎957 48 47 46; www.hammamspain.com/cordoba; Calle del Corregidor Luis de la Cerda 51; bath/bath & massage €26/33; ⏱2hr sessions 10am, noon, 2pm, 4pm, 6pm, 8pm & 10pm) Follow the lead of the medieval Cordobans and dip your toe in these beautifully renovated

Alcázar de los Reyes Cristianos, Córdoba

Arab baths, where you can enjoy an aromatherapy massage, with tea, hookah and Arabic sweets in the cafe afterwards.

🛏 Sleeping

Hospedería Alma Andalusí   Boutique Hotel €€
(☏957 76 08 88; www.almaandalusi.com; Calle Fernández Ruano 5; s/d €45/100; ❄🕸) The builders of this guesthouse in a quiet section of the *judería* have brilliantly converted an ancient structure into a stylish, modern establishment while keeping the rates down.

Casa de los Azulejos   Hotel €€
(☏957 47 00 00; www.casadelosazulejos.com; Calle Fernando Colón 5; s/d incl breakfast from €85/107; ❄@🕸) Mexican and Andalucian styles converge in this chic hotel, where the patio is all banana trees, ferns and potted palms bathed in sunlight. Colonial-style rooms feature tall antique doors, massive beds, walls in lilac and sky blues, and floors adorned with the beautiful old *azulejos* tiles that give the place its name.

Hotel Mezquita   Hotel €€
(☏957 47 55 85; www.hotelmezquita.com; Plaza Santa Catalina 1; s/d €42/74; ❄) One of the best deals in town, Hotel Mezquita stands right opposite its namesake monument, amid the bric-a-brac of the tourism zone. The 16th-century mansion has large, elegant rooms with marble floors, tall doors and balconies, some affording views of the great mosque.

🍴 Eating & Drinking

Taberna San Miguel El Pisto   Tapas €
(www.casaelpisto.com/en; Plaza San Miguel 1; tapas €3, media raciones €5-10; ⊙closed Sun & Aug) Brimming with local character, El Pisto is one of Córdoba's best *tabernas*, both in terms of atmosphere and food. Traditional tapas and *media-raciones* are done perfectly, and inexpensive Moriles wine is ready in jugs on the bar.

Bodegas Campos   Andalucian €€
(☏957 49 75 00; www.bodegascampos.com; Calle de Lineros 32; tapas €5, mains €13-21) One of Córdoba's most atmospheric and famous wine cellar/restaurants, this sprawling hall features dozens of rooms and patios, with oak barrels signed by local and international celebrities stacked up alongside. The bodega produces its own house Montilla wine.

Bodega Guzmán   Bar
(Calle de los Judíos 7; ⊙noon to 4pm & 8pm-midnight, closed Thu) Close to the Sinagoga, this atmospheric drinking spot bedecked with bullfighting memorabilia is frequented by both locals and tourists. Montilla wine is dispensed from three giant barrels behind the bar: don't leave without trying some *amargoso* (bitter).

ℹ Information

Municipal Tourist Office (Plaza de Judá Levi; ⊙8.30am-2.30pm Mon-Fri)

Regional Tourist Office (Calle de Torrijos 10; ⊙9am-7.30pm Mon-Fri, 9.30am-3pm Sat, Sun & holidays)

ℹ Getting There & Away

From Córdoba's **train station** (☏957 40 02 02; Glorieta de las Tres Culturas), destinations include Seville (€11 to €33, 40 to 90 minutes, 23 or more daily), Madrid (€53 to €68, 1¾ to 6¼ hours, 23 or more daily), Málaga (€22 to €45, one to 2½ hours, nine daily) and Barcelona (€138, 4½ hours, four daily).

Granada

POP 258,000 / ELEV 685M

Granada's eight centuries as a Muslim capital are symbolised in its keynote emblem, the remarkable Alhambra, one of the most graceful architectural achievements in the Muslim world. Islam was never completely expunged here, and today it seems more present than ever in the shops, restaurants, tearooms and the mosque of a growing North African community in and around the maze of the Albayzín.

🎯 Sights

Alhambra   Palace

(📞902 44 12 21; www.alhambra-tickets.es; adult/under 8yr €13/free, Generalife only €6; ⏰8.30am-8pm 16 Mar-31 Oct, to 6pm 1 Nov-14 Mar, night visits 10-11.30pm Tue-Sat Mar-Oct, 8-9.30pm Fri & Sat Nov-Feb) The mighty Alhambra is breathtaking. Much has been written about its fortress, palace, patios and gardens, but nothing can really prepare you for seeing the real thing.

The **Alcazaba**, the Alhambra's fortress, dates from the 11th to the 13th centuries. There are spectacular views from the tops of its towers. The **Palacio Nazaríes** (Nasrid Palace), built for Granada's Muslim rulers in their 13th- to 15th-century heyday, is the centrepiece of the Alhambra. The beauty of its patios and intricacy of its stuccoes and woodwork, epitomised by the **Patio de los Leones** (Patio of the Lions) and **Sala de las Dos Hermanas** (Hall of the Two Sisters), are stunning. The **Generalife** (Palace Gardens) is a great spot to relax and contemplate the complex from a little distance.

Up to 6600 tickets to the Alhambra are available for each day. About one-third of these are sold at the ticket office on the day, but they sell out early and you need to start queuing by 7am to be reasonably sure of getting one. It's highly advisable to book in advance (you pay €1 extra per ticket) through the **Alhambra Advance Booking** (📞for international calls 0034 934 92 37 50, for national calls 902 888001; www.alhambra-tickets.es; ⏰8am-9pm).

Go to **Servicaixa** (www.servicaixa.com) for online bookings in Spanish and English.

For internet or phone bookings you need a Visa card, MasterCard or Eurocard. You receive a reference number, which you must show, along with your passport, national identity card or credit card, at the Alhambra ticket office when you pick up the ticket on the day of your visit.

Albayzín   Historic Neighbourhood

Exploring the narrow, hilly streets of the Albayzín, the old Moorish quarter across the river from the Alhambra, is the perfect complement to the Alhambra. The cobblestone streets are lined with gorgeous *cármenes* (large mansions with walled gardens, from the Arabic *karm* for garden). Head uphill to reach the **Mirador de San Nicolás** – a viewpoint with breathtaking vistas and a relaxed scene.

Capilla Real   Historic Building

(www.capillarealgranada.com; Calle Oficios; admission €3.50; ⏰10.30am-1.30pm & 4-7.30pm Mon-Sat, 11am-1.30pm & 4-7pm Sun Apr-Oct) The **Royal Chapel**, adjoins Granada's cathedral, and is an outstanding Christian building. Catholic Monarchs Isabella and Ferdinand commissioned this elaborate Isabelline-Gothic-style mausoleum.

🛏 Sleeping

Casa Morisca
Hotel   Historic Hotel €€

(📞958 22 11 00; www.hotelcasamorisca.com; Cuesta de la Victoria 9; d €118-148; ❄@📶) This late-15th-century mansion perfectly captures the spirit of the Albayzín. A heavy wooden door shuts out city noise, and rooms are soothing, with lofty ceilings, fluffy white beds and flat-weave rugs over brick floors.

Carmen de la
Alcubilla   Historic Hotel €€

(📞958 21 55 51; www.alcubilladelcaracol.com; Calle del Aire Alta 12; s/d €100/120; ❄@📶) This exquisitely decorated place is located on the slopes of the Alhambra. Rooms are washed in pale pastel colours contrasting with cool cream and antiques. There are fabulous views and a pretty terraced garden.

Parador de
Granada   Historic Hotel €€€

(📞958 22 14 40; www.parador.es; Calle Real de la Alhambra; r €315; P❄@📶) It would be remiss not to mention this hotel, the most luxurious of Spain's *paradors*. If you're looking for romance and history (it's in a converted 15th-century convent in the Alhambra grounds) and money is no object, then book well ahead.

INGRAM PUBLISHING/GETTY IMAGES ©

Hotel Zaguán del Darro
Historic Hotel €€

(☏958 21 57 30; www.hotelzaguan.com; Carrera del Darro 23; s/d €55/70; ❄ @) This place offers excellent value for the Albayzín. The 16th-century house has been tastefully restored, with sparing use of antiques. Its 13 rooms are all different; some look out over the Río Darro.

 Eating

Granada is one of the last bastions of that fantastic practice of free tapas with every drink, and some have an international flavour.

Arrayanes
Moroccan €€

(☏958 22 84 01; www.rest-arrayanes.com; Cuesta Marañas 4; mains €8-15; ⊙from 8pm; ✒) The best Moroccan food in a city that is well known for its Moorish throwbacks? Recline on lavish patterned seating, try the rich, fruity tagine casseroles and make your decision. Note that Restaurante Arrayanes does not serve alcohol.

El Ají
Modern Spanish €€

(Plaza San Miguel Bajo 9; mains €12-20; ✒) Up in the Albayzín, this chic but cosy neighbourhood restaurant is no bigger than a shoebox but serves from breakfast right through to the evening.

Bodegas Castañeda
Bar €

(Calle Almireceros; tapas €2-3, raciónes €6-8) An institution among locals and tourists alike, this buzzing bar doles out hearty portions of food (try a hot or cold *tabla*, or platter; a half order is ample for two) and dispenses drinks from big casks mounted in the walls.

ℹ Information

Provincial tourist office (www.turismodegranada.org; Plaza de Mariana Pineda 10; ⊙9am-10pm Mon-Fri, 10am-7pm Sat)

ℹ Getting There & Away

The **train station** (☏958 24 02 02; Avenida de Andaluces) is 1.5km west of the centre. Trains run to/from Seville (€24, three hours, four daily), Almería (€16.50, 2¼ hours, four daily), Ronda (€15, three hours, three daily), Algeciras (€25, 4½ hours, three daily), Madrid (€68, four to five hours, one or two daily), Valencia (€52.50, 7½ to eight hours, one daily) and Barcelona (€58, 12 hours, one daily).

Alhambra

Timeline

900 The first reference to *al-qala'at al-hamra* (red castle) atop Granada's Sabika Hill.

1237 Founder of the Nasrid dynasty, Muhammad I, moves his court to Granada. Threatened by belligerent Christian armies he builds a new defensive fort, the **Alcazaba** ❶.

1302-09 Designed as a summer palace-cum-country estate for Granada's foppish rulers, the bucolic **Generalife** ❷ is begun by Muhammad III.

1333-54 Yusuf I initiates the construction of the **Palacio Nazaríes** ❸, still considered the highpoint of Islamic culture in Europe.

1350-60 Up goes the **Palacio de Comares** ❹, taking Nasrid lavishness to a whole new level.

1362-91 The second coming of Muhammad V ushers in even greater architectural brilliance exemplified by the construction of the **Patio de los Leones** ❺.

1527 The Christians add the **Palacio de Carlos V** ❻. Inspired Renaissance palace or incongruous crime against the Moorish art? You decide.

1829 The languishing, half-forgotten Alhambra is 'rediscovered' by American writer Washington Irving during a protracted sleep-over.

1954 The Generalife gardens are extended southwards to accommodate an outdoor theatre.

TOP TIPS

Queue-dodger Reserve tickets in advance online at www.alhambra-tickets.es

Money-saver You can visit the general areas of the palace free of charge any time by entering through the Puerta de Justica

Stay over Two fine hotels are encased in the grounds: Parador de Granada (expensive) and Hotel América (more economical)

MICHAEL TAYLOR/GETTY IMAGES ©

Sala de la Barca
Throw your head back in the anteroom to the Comares Palace where the gilded ceiling is shaped like an upturned boat. Destroyed by fire in the 1890s, it has been painstakingly restored.

Mexuar

Patio de Machuca

Palacio de Carlos V
It's easy to miss the stylistic merits of this Renaissance palace added in 1527. Check out the ground floor Museo de la Alhambra with artefacts directly related to the palace's history.

Palacio Nazaríes

Detail

Puerta de Justica

Alcazaba
Find time to explore the towers of the original citadel, the most important of which – the Torre de la Vela – takes you, via a winding staircase, to the Alhambra's best viewpoint.

DAVID TOMLINSON/GETTY IMAGES ©

Patio de Arrayanes

If only you could linger longer beside the rows of myrtle bushes *(arrayanes)* that border this calming rectangular pool. Shaded porticos with seven harmonious arches invite further contemplation.

Torre de Comares

4

Patio de Arrayanes

Palacio de Comares

The neck-ache continues in the largest room in the Comares Palace renowned for its rich geometric ceiling. A negotiating room for the emirs, the Salón de los Embajadores is a masterpiece of Moorish design.

Baños Reales

Washington Irving Apartments

Sala de Dos Hermanas

Focus on the *dos hermanas* – two marble slabs either side of the fountain – before enjoying the intricate cupola embellished with 5000 tiny moulded stalactites. Poetic calligraphy decorates the walls.

Jardín de Lindaraja

5

Palacio del Partal

Jardines del Partal

Sala de los Abencerrajes

Patio de los Leones

Count the 12 lions sculpted from marble, holding up a gurgling fountain. Then pan back and take in the delicate columns and arches built to signify an Islamic vision of paradise.

Generalife

A coda to most people's visits, the 'architect's garden' is no afterthought. While Nasrid in origin, the horticulture is relatively new: the pools and arcades were added in the early 20th century.

Cádiz

POP 125,000

Cádiz, widely considered the oldest continuously inhabited settlement in Europe, is crammed onto the head of a promontory like an overcrowded ocean liner. Columbus sailed from here on his second and fourth voyages, and after his success in the Americas, the town grew into Spain's richest and most cosmopolitan city in the 18th century. The best time to visit is during the February *carnaval* (carnival).

⊙ Sights

Catedral   Church

(Plaza de la Catedral; adult/student €5/3, admission free 7-8pm Tue-Fri & 11am-1pm Sun; ⊙10am-6.30pm Mon-Sat, 1.30-6.30pm Sun) Cádiz' yellow-domed cathedral is an impressively proportioned baroque–neoclassical construction. It fronts a broad, traffic-free plaza where the cathedral's ground-plan is picked out in the paving stones. From a separate entrance on Plaza de la Catedral, climb to the top of the **Torre de Poniente** (Western Tower; adult/child €4/3; ⊙10am-6pm mis-Sep–mid-Jun, to 8pm mid-Jun–mid-Sep) for marvellous views.

Museo de Cádiz   Museum

(Plaza de Mina; admission €1.50; ⊙2.30-8.30pm Tue, 9am-8.30pm Wed-Sat, 9.30am-2.30pm Sun) The Museo de Cádiz, on one of Cádiz' leafiest squares, is outstanding with fine Phoenician and Roman artefacts on the ground floor and fine arts upstairs; in the latter look especially for the 18 superb canvases of saints, angels and monks by Francisco de Zurbarán.

Playa de la Victoria   Beach

This lovely, wide strip of fine Atlantic sand stretches about 4km along the peninsula from its beginning at the Puertas de Tierra. At weekends in summer almost the whole city seems to be out here.

🛏 Sleeping & Eating

Hotel Argantonio   Hotel €€

(☎956 21 16 40; www.hotelargantonio.com; Calle Argantonio 3; s/d incl breakfast €90/107; ✳@🛜) At this small-is-beautiful hotel in Cádiz's old quarter, the stand-out features are the hand-painted doors, beautifully tiled floors that adorn both bedrooms and bathrooms, and the intricate Moorish arch in the lobby.

Hotel Patagonia Sur   Hotel €€

(☎856 17 46 47; www.hotel patagoniasur.es; Calle Cobos 11; d €80-130; ✳@🛜) This sleek gem opened in Cádiz's old town in 2009 and offers clean-lined modernity just steps from the 18th-century cathedral. Bonuses include its sun-filled attic rooms on the 5th floor with cathedral views.

Catedral, Cádiz

El Aljibe

Tapas €€

(www.pablogrosso.com; Calle Plocia 25; tapas €2-3.50, mains €10-15) Refined restaurant upstairs and supercool tapas bar downstairs, El Aljibe on its own is almost reason enough to come to Cádiz. The cuisine developed by *gaditano* chef Pablo Grosso is a delicious combination of the traditional and the adventurous.

Arrocería La Pepa

Spanish €€

(🖉956 26 38 21; www.restaurantelapepa.es; Paseo Maritimo 14; paella per person €12-17) To get a decent paella you have to leave the old town behind and head for a few kilometres southeast along Playa de la Victoria – a pleasant, appetite-inducing ocean-side walk or a quick ride on the No 1 bus.

🛈 Information

Municipal Tourist Office (Paseo de Canalejas; ⏱8.30am-6pm Mon-Fri, 9am-5pm Sat & Sun)

Regional Tourist Office (Avenida Ramón de Carranza; ⏱9am-7.30pm Mon-Fri, 10am-2pm Sat, Sun & holidays)

🛈 Getting There & Away

From the **train station** (🖉902 240202) trains run daily to Seville (€13.50, 1¾ hours) and Madrid (€72.50, 4½ hours). High-speed AVE services to Madrid are due to commence in 2015.

SURVIVAL GUIDE

🛈 Directory A–Z

Accommodation

Budget options include everything from dorm-style youth hostels to family-style *pensiones* and slightly better-heeled *hostales*. At the upper end of this category you'll find rooms with air-conditioning and private bathrooms. Midrange *hostales* and hotels are more comfortable and most offer standard hotel services. Business hotels, trendy boutique hotels and luxury hotels are usually in the top-end category.

Virtually all accommodation prices are subject to IVA *(impuesto sobre el valor añadido),* the Spanish version of value-added tax, which is 10%. This may or may not be included in the quoted price. To check, ask: *Está incluido el IVA?* (Is IVA included?).

Price Ranges

Our reviews refer to double rooms with a private bathroom, except in hostels or where otherwise specified. Quoted rates are for high season, which is generally May to September (though this varies greatly from region to region).

€ less than €65 (less than €75 for Madrid/Barcelona)

€€ €65 to €140 (€75 to €200 for Madrid/Barcelona)

€€€ more than €140 (more than €200 for Madrid/Barcelona)

Business Hours

Banks 8.30am to 2pm Monday to Friday; some also open 4pm to 7pm Thursday and 9am to 1pm Saturday

Central post offices 8.30am to 9.30pm Monday to Friday, 8.30am to 2pm Saturday

Nightclubs midnight or 1am to 5am or 6am

Restaurants lunch 1pm to 4pm, dinner 8.30pm to midnight or later

Shops 10am to 2pm and 4.30pm to 7.30pm or 5pm to 8pm; big supermarkets and department stores generally open from 10am to 10pm Monday to Saturday

Food

Each eating review is accompanied by one of the following symbols (the price relates to a main course):

€ less than €10

€€ €10 to €20

€€€ more than €20

Gay & Lesbian Travellers

Homosexuality is legal in Spain. In 2005 the Socialists gave the country's conservative Catholic foundations a shake with the legalisation of same-sex marriages in Spain.

Lesbians and gay men generally keep a fairly low profile, but are quite open in the cities. Madrid, Barcelona, Sitges, Torremolinos and Ibiza have particularly lively scenes.

Legal Matters

Drugs Cannabis is legal but only for personal use and in very small quantities. Public consumption of any drug is illegal.

Smoking Not permitted in any enclosed public space, including bars, restaurants and nightclubs.

Money

ATMs Many credit and debit cards can be used for withdrawing money from *cajeros automáticos* (automatic teller machines) that display the relevant symbols such as Visa, MasterCard, Cirrus etc.

Cash Most banks will exchange major foreign currencies and offer the best rates. Ask about commissions and take your passport.

Credit & Debit Cards Can be used to pay for most purchases. You'll often be asked to show your passport or some other form of identification, or to type in your pin. The most widely accepted cards are Visa and MasterCard.

Moneychangers Exchange offices, indicated by the word *cambio* (exchange), offer longer opening hours than banks, but worse exchange rates and higher commissions.

Taxes & Refunds In Spain, value-added tax (VAT) is known as IVA (*ee*-ba; *impuesto sobre el valor añadido*). Visitors are entitled to a refund of the 18% IVA on purchases costing more than €90.16 from any shop if they are taking them out of the EU within three months.

Tipping Menu prices include a service charge. Most people leave some small change. Taxi drivers don't have to be tipped but a little rounding up won't go amiss.

Public Holidays

The two main periods when Spaniards go on holiday are Semana Santa (the week leading up to Easter Sunday) and July or August.

There are at least 14 official holidays a year – some observed nationwide, some locally. National holidays:

Año Nuevo (New Year's Day) 1 January

Viernes Santo (Good Friday) March/April

Fiesta del Trabajo (Labour Day) 1 May

La Asunción (Feast of the Assumption) 15 August

Fiesta Nacional de España (National Day) 12 October

La Inmaculada Concepción (Feast of the Immaculate Conception) 8 December

Navidad (Christmas) 25 December

Regional governments set five holidays and local councils two more. Common dates include the following:

Epifanía (Epiphany) or **Día de los Reyes Magos** (Three Kings' Day) 6 January

Alcázar, Segovia (p322)

Día de San José (St Joseph's Day) 19 March

Jueves Santo (Good Thursday) March/April. Not observed in Catalonia and Valencia.

Corpus Christi June. The Thursday after the eighth Sunday after Easter Sunday.

Día de San Juan Bautista (Feast of St John the Baptist) 24 June

Día de Santiago Apóstol (Feast of St James the Apostle) 25 July

Día de Todos los Santos (All Saints Day) 1 November

Día de la Constitución (Constitution Day) 6 December

Safe Travel

Most visitors to Spain never feel remotely threatened, but a sufficient number have unpleasant experiences to warrant an alert. The main thing to be wary of is petty theft (which may of course not seem so petty if your passport, cash, travellers cheques, credit card and camera go missing). Stay alert and you can avoid most thievery techniques. Algeciras, Barcelona, Madrid and Seville are the worst offenders, as are popular beaches in summer (never leave belongings unattended). Common scams include the following:

○ Kids crowding around you asking for directions or help.

○ A person pointing out bird droppings on your shoulder (some substance their friend has sprinkled on you) – as they help clean it off they are probably emptying your pockets.

○ The guys who tell you that you have a flat tyre. While your new friend and you check the tyre, his pal is emptying the car.

○ The classic snatch-and-run. Never leave your purse, bag, wallet, mobile phone etc unattended or alone on a table.

○ An old classic: the ladies offering flowers for good luck. We don't know how they do it, but your pockets always wind up empty.

Telephone

Blue public payphones are common and fairly easy to use. They accept coins, phonecards and, in some cases, credit cards. Phonecards come in €6 and €12 denominations and, like postage stamps, are sold at post offices and tobacconists.

International reverse-charge (collect) calls are simple to make: dial ☎ 900 99 followed by the appropriate code. For example: ☎ 900 99 00 61 for Australia, ☎ 900 99 00 44 for the UK, ☎ 900 99 00 11 (AT&T) for the USA etc.

To speak to an English-speaking Spanish international operator, dial ☎ 1008 (for calls within Europe) or ☎ 1005 (rest of the world).

Mobile Phones

All Spanish mobile phone companies (Telefónica's MoviStar, Orange and Vodafone) offer *prepagado* (prepaid) accounts for mobiles. The SIM card costs from €50, which includes some prepaid phone time.

Mobile phone numbers in Spain start with ☎ 6.

Phone Codes

Telephone codes in Spain are an integral part of the phone number. All numbers are nine digits and you just dial that nine-digit number.

Numbers starting with ☎ 900 are national toll-free numbers, while those starting ☎ 901 to ☎ 905 come with varying costs; most can only be dialled from within Spain. In a similar category are numbers starting with ☎ 800, ☎ 803, ☎ 806 and ☎ 807.

Tourist Information

All cities and many smaller towns have an *oficina de turismo*. Spain's official tourism site is **Turespaña** (www.spain.info).

Visas

Spain is one of 26 member countries of the Schengen Convention and Schengen visa rules apply.

ⓘ Getting There & Away

Air

Flights from all over Europe, including numerous budget airlines, serve main Spanish airports. All of Spain's airports share the user-friendly website and flight information telephone number of **Aena** (☎ 902 404 704; www.aena.es), the national airports authority.

Madrid's Aeropuerto de Barajas is Spain's busiest (and Europe's fifth-busiest) airport.

Land

Spain shares land borders with France, Portugal and Andorra.

In addition to the rail services connecting Spain with France and Portugal, there are direct trains between Zurich and Barcelona (via Bern, Geneva, Perpignan and Girona), and between Milan and Barcelona (via Turin, Perpignan and Girona). For these and other services, visit the website of

Transport from France

CAR & MOTORCYCLE

The main road crossing into Spain from France is the highway that links up with Spain's AP7 tollway, which runs down to Barcelona and follows the Spanish coast south (with a branch, the AP2, going to Madrid via Zaragoza). A series of links cut across the Pyrenees from France and Andorra into Spain, as does a coastal route that runs from Biarritz in France into the Spanish Basque Country.

TRAIN

The main rail lines into Spain cross the Franco–Spanish frontier along the Mediterranean coast and via the Basque Country. Another minor route runs inland across the Pyrenees from Latour-de-Carol to Barcelona.

TGV (high-speed) trains connect Paris Montparnasse with Irún, where you change to a normal train for the Basque Country and on towards Madrid. Up to three TGVs also put you on track to Barcelona (leaving from Paris Gare de Lyon), with a change at Montpellier or Narbonne.

The new high-speed rail link from Paris to Madrid has brought travel times down to an impressive eight hours.

FERRIES TO SPAIN

Ferries run to mainland Spain regularly from the Canary Islands, Italy, North Africa (Algeria, Morocco and the Spanish enclaves of Ceuta and Melilla) and the UK. Most services are run by the Spanish national ferry company, **Acciona Trasmediterránea** (902 454645; www.trasmediterranea.es). You can take vehicles on the following routes.

Renfe (for international trips 902 24 34 02; www.renfe.com), the Spanish national railway company.

Getting Around

Air

Iberia (www.iberia.es) Spain's national airline and its subsidiary, Iberia Regional-Air Nostrum, have an extensive domestic network.

Bicycle

All regional trains have space for carrying bikes, and they're also permitted on most *cercanías* (local area trains around big cities such as Madrid and Barcelona). On long-distance trains there are more restrictions. As a rule, you have to be travelling overnight in a sleeper or couchette to have the (dismantled) bike accepted as normal luggage.

Boat

Regular ferries connect the Spanish mainland with the Balearic Islands.

Bus

Spain's bus network is operated by countless independent companies, and reaches into the most remote towns and villages. Many towns and cities have one main station for arrivals and departures, which usually has an information desk. Tourist offices can also help with information on bus services.

ALSA (902 422242; www.alsa.es) The biggest player, this company has routes all over the country in association with various other companies.

Car & Motorcycle

Spain's roads vary enormously but are generally good. Fastest are the *autopistas;* on some, you have to pay hefty tolls.

Every vehicle should display a nationality plate of its country of registration and you must always carry proof of ownership of a private vehicle. Third-party motor insurance is required throughout Europe. A warning triangle and a reflective jacket (to be used in case of breakdown) are compulsory.

Driving Licences

All EU member states' driving licences are recognised. Other foreign licences should be accompanied by an International Driving Permit (although in practice local licences are usually accepted). These are available from automobile clubs in your country and valid for 12 months.

Hire

To rent a car in Spain you have to have a licence, be aged 21 or over and have a credit or debit card. Rates vary widely: the best deals tend to be in major tourist areas, including airports. Prices are especially competitive in the Balearic Islands. Expect a compact car to cost from €30 and up per day.

Road Rules

Blood-alcohol limit 0.05%

Legal driving age for cars 18

Legal driving age for motorcycles & scooters 16 (80cc and over) or 14 (50cc and under). A licence is required.

Motorcyclists Must use headlights at all times and wear a helmet if riding a bike of 125cc or more.

Side of the road Drive on the right.

Speed limits In built-up areas 50km/h (and in some cases, such as inner-city Barcelona, 30km/h), which increases to 100km/h on major roads and up to 120km/h on *autovías* and *autopistas* (toll-free and tolled dual-lane highways, respectively). Cars towing caravans are restricted to a maximum speed of 80km/h.

Train

Renfe (☏902 240 202; www.renfe.es) is the national railway company. Trains are mostly modern and comfortable, and late arrivals are the exception rather than the rule. The high-speed network is in constant expansion.

Passes are valid for all long-distance Renfe trains; Inter-Rail users pay supplements on Talgo, InterCity and AVE trains.

All long-distance trains have 2nd and 1st classes, known as *turista* and *preferente*, respectively. The latter is 20% to 40% more expensive.

Italy

Italy, the land that has turned its lifestyle into a designer accessory, is one of Europe's great seducers. Ever since the days of the 18th-century Grand Tour, travellers have been falling under its spell, and still today it stirs strong emotions. The rush of seeing the Colosseum for the first time or cruising down Venice's surreal canals are experiences you'll remember for life.

Of course, Italy is not all about ancient ruins, Michelangelo masterpieces and frescoed churches. There's also the food, imitated the world over, and a landscape that boasts beautiful Alpine peaks, stunning coastlines and remote, silent valleys. So if the noise, heat and chaos of the cities start getting to you – as they do many locals – change gear and head out to the country and rural villages for a taste of the sun-kissed slow life.

Trevi Fountain (p405), Rome

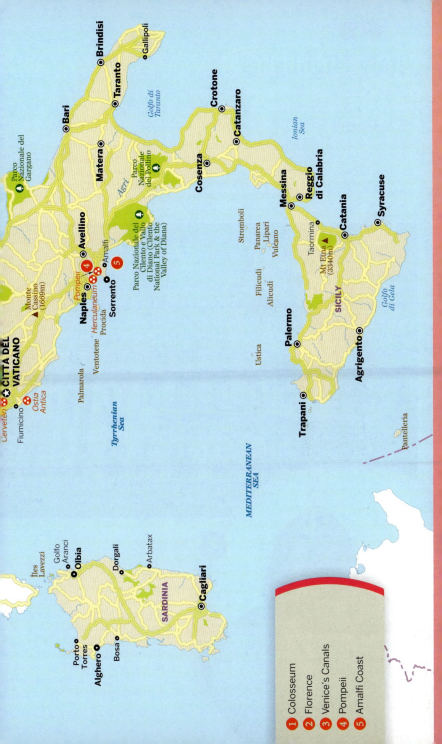

Gallipoli

Brindisi

Taranto

Bari

Golfo di
Taranto

Parco
Nazionale del
Gargano

Matera

Agri

Parco
Nazionale
del Pollino

Crotone

Catanzaro

Ionian
Sea

Cosenza

Avellino

**Reggio
di Calabria**

Messina

Stromboli

Panarea
Lipari
Vulcano

Catania

Syracuse

Taormina

Mt Etna
(3340m)

SICILY

Amalfi

Parco Nazionale del
Cilento e Vallo
di Diano (Cilento
National Park & the
Valley of Diana)

Pompeii

Naples

Herculaneum

Sorrento

Procida

Filicudi
Alicudi

Golfo
di Gela

★ **CITTÀ DEL
VATICANO**

Monte
Cassino
(1669m)

Palermo

Cerveteri

Ostia
Antica

Fiumicino

Palmarola

Ventotene

Ustica

Agrigento

Trapani

Tyrrhenian
Sea

Pantelleria

MEDITERRANEAN
SEA

Îles
Lavezzi

Golfo
Aranci

Olbia

Dorgali

Arbatax

SARDINIA

Cagliari

**Porto
Torres**

Alghero

Bosa

① Colosseum
② Florence
③ Venice's Canals
④ Pompeii
⑤ Amalfi Coast

Italy Highlights

Colosseum

Even before setting foot in this ancient stadium, most visitors are gobsmacked to find the Colosseum (p394) looming before them in all its glory as soon as they leave the metro station. Not only is this Roman arena impressive for its size and endurance, but its well-preserved condition makes for an unparalleled insight into the life of ancient Rome.

Florence

If it's art you're after, look no further than Florence (p446). During the Middle Ages the Medicis transformed this merchant town into the centre of the Italian Renaissance, and it's brimful of artistic treasures. Marvel at the priceless canvases of the Uffizi, admire the architecture of the Duomo or join the queue to glimpse Michelangelo's masterpiece, *David* – just don't expect to have the city to yourself. Florence's Duomo (p446)

MAREMAGNUM/GETTY IMAGES ©

Venice's Canals

3

What else is there to say about Venice (p429)? Quite simply, this is one of the world's unmissable cities, renowned for its glorious architecture, romantic canals, historic churches and stunning museums. Whether you're riding the gondolas, wandering the alleyways or joining the throngs in Piazza San Marco, you'll find it impossible not to fall head over heels for this Italian beauty.

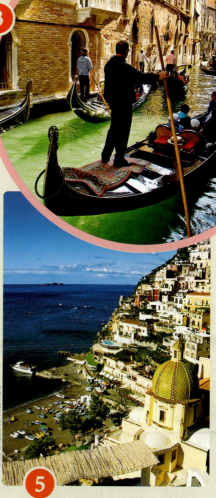

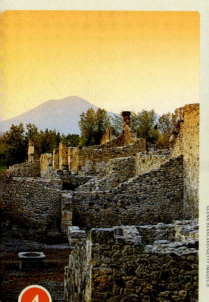

4

Pompeii

You know the story: 2000 years ago, the bustling town of Pompeii (p469) was devastated by a catastrophic eruption from Mt Vesuvius. But nothing can prepare you for the eerie experience of standing in Pompeii itself; the deserted streets and squares and spooky body casts bring a whole new meaning to the term 'ghost town'. It's an unmissable experience, and probably gives you a better insight into the reality of ancient Rome than anywhere else on earth.

5

Amalfi Coast

For a classic Italian road trip, nothing can hold a candle to the Amalfi Coast (p474). Stretching for 50km along the southern Sorrento Peninsula, this glittering coastline is one of the most beautiful spots in the Mediterranean – studded with sparkling beaches, secluded bays and clifftop towns. It's tailor-made for cruising with the top down... just watch out for those hairpin bends. Positano (p475)

Italy's Best...

Artistic Treasures

David (p454)
Michelangelo's masterpiece in the Galleria dell'Accademia in Florence is a celebration of the human form.

Sistine Chapel (p402)
This incredible ceiling fresco needs no introduction.

St Peter's Basilica (p403)
Rome's most impressive architectural landmark.

Ravenna Mosaics (p458)
Amazing mosaics mentioned in Danté's *Divine Comedy*.

Galleria degli Uffizi (p447) Famous Florence gallery crammed with Botticellis, da Vincis and Raphaels.

Roman Remains

Colosseum (p394) See where the gladiators slugged it out.

Roman Forum (p393)
Stand in the heart of the Roman Republic.

Via Appia Antica (p410)
Walk on one of the world's oldest roads.

Villa Adriana (p410)
Take a day trip from Rome to Hadrian's incredible weekend retreat.

Ostia Antica (p410)
Explore the quays of ancient Rome's port.

Festivals

Carnevale (p437) Don your costume for Venice's crazy carnival.

Scoppio del Carro (p455)
Fireworks explode above Florence on Easter Sunday.

Il Palio (p464) Siena's annual horse races are a lively spectacle.

Venice International Film Festival (p437) Italy's most prestigious film festival brings big-name stars to the city.

Natale di Roma (p411)
Rome celebrates its birthday in style.

City Views

○ **Leaning Tower of Pisa** (p461) Where else?

○ **Duomo** (p446) Climb the campanile for the quintessential Florence photo op.

○ **Basilica di San Marco** (p435) See Venice's Piazza San Marco from the basilica's bell tower.

○ **Pincio Hill** (p407) Fantastic outlook over Rome.

○ **Torre del Mangia** (p463) Gaze over Siena's rooftops to the Tuscan countryside beyond.

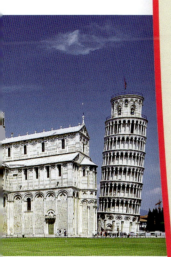

Left: Michelangelo's *David* (p454), Florence; **Above:** Leaning Tower of Pisa (p461), Pisa

Need to Know

ADVANCE PLANNING

○ **As early as possible** Book accommodation in Rome, Venice and Florence.

○ **Two weeks before** Beat the queues by booking online for the Colosseum, the Leaning Tower of Pisa and the Vatican Museums.

○ **When you arrive** Pick up discount cards for Rome, Venice, Florence's museums and the Cinque Terre villages.

RESOURCES

○ **Italia** (www.italia.it) Inspiration, ideas and planning tips.

○ **Trenitalia** (www.ferroviedellostato.it) Plan your train trips.

○ **Agriturismo** (www.agriturismo.com) Find the perfect Italian farm stay.

○ **Turismo Roma** (www.turismoroma.it) Rome Tourist Board's website.

○ **Pierreci** (www.pierreci.it) Online booking for many museums and monuments.

GETTING AROUND

○ **Air** Italy's largest airport is Leonardo da Vinci (aka Fiumicino) in Rome. International flights also serve Milan, Pisa, Venice, Florence and other main cities.

○ **Train** Italy's main rail hubs are Rome, Milan and Venice. High-speed services operate on the main line from Milan to Rome/Naples via Bologna and Florence. Other routes operate local *regionale* or faster InterCity (IC) services.

○ **Sea** Dozens of options to France, Spain and other Mediterranean destinations; main ports are in Rome, Ancona and Genoa.

○ **Bus** Extensive, and often the only option to many rural areas.

○ **Car** Autostradas (motorways) are quick but often charge a toll; regional roads are better for sightseeing.

BE FOREWARNED

○ **Scams** Watch out for pickpockets and moped thieves in Rome, Florence and Venice, and count your change carefully.

○ **Driving** Expect the unexpected – Italians have a notoriously relaxed attitude to road rules.

○ **Prices** Prices for everything skyrocket during peak season and major holidays.

Italy Itineraries

Maybe it's the art, maybe it's the architecture or maybe it's just the atmosphere – but there's something about Italy that seems to get under your skin. Don't be surprised if you're smitten.

ROME TO TIVOLI

Exploring Ancient Rome

3 DAYS

Its empire may have long since sailed into the sunset, but there's still nowhere better to experience Italy at its passionate, pompous, pizza-spinning best than ❶ **Rome** (p392). There are too many sights to squeeze into a couple of days, so you'll need to plan carefully. On day one, you could cover the Colosseum and the Roman Forum, followed by an early evening visit to the Pantheon, the city's best pizza at Baffetto and a late-night wander around vibrant Trastevere. Devote day two to the Vatican, allowing time for St Peter's Basilica, the Vatican Museums and, of course, the jaw-dropping Sistine Chapel.

On day three, take a trip outside the city to see some of the other landmarks of ancient Rome. Spend the morning at the great port of ❷ **Ostia Antica** (p410), where you can still see the ruins of restaurants, shops, houses and even the place where the Romans used to do their laundry. Then head up to Emperor Hadrian's lavish country retreat near ❸ **Tivoli** (p410), the Villa Adriana, one of the best-preserved villas in Italy, and a fine example of the extravagant tastes of Rome's all-powerful emperors.

5 DAYS

LUCCA TO FLORENCE
A Taste of Tuscany

If anywhere encapsulates the Italian character, it's Tuscany. This sunbaked corner of Italy is one of the country's most rewarding regions for culture vultures. **① Lucca** (p465) makes a fine place to start thanks to its hilltop architecture, but even it can't hold a candle to the scenic splendour of **② Parco Nazionale delle Cinque Terre** (p422). Spend a day exploring the national park before braving the crowds at **③ Pisa**'s (p460) punch-drunk tower – book online and get there early or late to dodge the queues.

On day four, swing south via another of Tuscany's heart-meltingly beautiful hilltop towns, **④ San Gimignano** (p466). From

here it's a short drive to **⑤ Siena** (p462), renowned for its medieval buildings and fabulous restaurants. The annual horse race, Il Palio, takes over the town for two hectic days in July and August, but you'll need to book way ahead if you plan to join the party.

Complete your Tuscan trip in **⑥ Florence** (p446), a city that's brimming with artistic and architectural treasures. From landmark buildings such as the Duomo to the priceless artworks housed at the Uffizi and the Galleria dell'Accademia, Florence is a place where it's impossible not to feel inspired.

Florence (p446)

Discover Italy

At a Glance

○ **Rome** (p392) Few cities have more history and chutzpah than the Italian capital.

○ **Northern Italy** (p422) Italy's affluent north: from stately cities to clifftop towns.

○ **Tuscany** (p446) Home to Italy's artistic and cultural highlights.

○ **Southern Italy** (p468) Hot, fiery, chaotic and quintessentially Italian.

ROME

POP 2.76 MILLION

Even in this country of exquisite cities, Rome is special. Pulsating, seductive and utterly disarming, the Italian capital is an epic, monumental metropolis that will steal your heart and haunt your soul. They say a lifetime's not enough *(Roma, non basta una vita)*, but even on a short visit you'll be swept off your feet by its artistic and architectural masterpieces, its operatic piazzas, romantic corners and cobbled lanes.

History

According to legend Rome was founded by Romulus and Remus in 753 BC. Historians debate this, but archaeological evidence has confirmed the existence of a settlement on the Palatine Hill in that period.

The city was originally ruled by a king, but in 509 BC the Roman Republic was founded. Over the next five centuries the Republic flourished, growing to become the dominant force in the Western world. The end came in the 1st century BC when internal rivalries led to the murder of Julius Caesar in 44 BC and the outbreak of civil war between Octavian and Mark Antony. Octavian emerged victorious and was made Rome's first emperor with the title Augustus.

Christianity had been spreading since the 1st century AD, and under Constantine it received official recognition. Pope Gregory I (590–604) did much to strengthen the Church's grip over the city, laying the foundations for its later role as capital of the Catholic Church.

Piazza Navona (p403), Rome
P. EOCHE/GETTY IMAGES ©

Under the Renaissance popes of the 15th and 16th centuries, Rome was given an extensive facelift.

By the 17th century Rome needed rebuilding, and turned to baroque masters Bernini and Borromini. With their exuberant churches, fountains and *palazzi* (palaces), these two bitter rivals changed the face of the city.

◎ Sights

Most of Rome's sights are concentrated in the area between Stazione Termini and the Vatican. Halfway between the two, the Pantheon and Piazza Navona lie at the heart of the *centro storico* (historic centre), while to the southeast, the Colosseum lords it over the city's ancient core.

The **Roma Pass** (www.romapass.it; 3 days €34) provides free admission to two museums or sites (choose from a list of 45), as well as reduced entry to extra sites, unlimited city transport and discounted entry to other exhibitions and events. Valid for three days, it's available online or from tourist information points and participating museums.

Ancient Rome

Palatino   Ruins
(Palatine Hill; Map p404; ☑06 3996 7700; www.
coopculture.it; Via di San Gregorio 30; adult/re-
duced incl Colosseum & Roman Forum €12/7.50;
⊙8.30am-1hr before sunset; MColosseo) Ris-
ing above the Roman Forum, the Palatine Hill is where Romulus supposedly killed his twin Remus and founded the city in 753 BC. Archaeological evidence can't prove the legend, but it has dated human habitation here to the 8th century BC. Later, the Palatine was Rome's most exclusive neighbourhood and the emperor Augustus lived here all his life. After Rome's fall, it fell into disrepair, and in the Middle Ages churches and castles were built over the ruins and wealthy Renaissance families established gardens here.

Most of the area is covered by the ruins of Emperor Domitian's vast complex, which served as the main imperial palace

for 300 years. Divided into the **Domus Flavia** (Imperial Palace; Map p404), **Domus Augustana** (Emperor's Residence; Map p404) and a **stadio** (Stadium; Map p404), it was built in the 1st century AD.

Among the best-preserved buildings on the Palatine Hill is the **Casa di Livia** (Map p404), home of Augustus' wife Livia, and, in front, Augustus' separate residence, the frescoed **Casa di Augusto** (Map p404; ⊙11am-3.30pm Mon, Wed, Sat & Sun; MColosseo).

For grandstand views over the Roman Forum, head to the **Orti Farnesiani** (Map p404) gardens in the north of the complex.

Roman Forum   Ruins
(Foro Romano; Map p404; ☑06 3996 7700; www.
coopculture.it; Largo della Salara Vecchia; adult/
reduced incl Colosseum & Palatino €12/7.50;
⊙8.30am-1hr before sunset; ☐Via dei Fori
Imperiali) Now a collection of fascinating, if rather confusing, ruins, the Roman Forum was ancient Rome's showpiece centre, a grandiose district of temples, basilicas and vibrant public spaces. Originally an Etruscan burial ground, the area was first developed in the 7th century BC, and expanded to become the social, political and commercial heart of the Roman world.

As you enter from Largo della Salara Vecchia, ahead to your left is the **Tempio di Antonino e Faustina** (Map p404), built by the senate in AD 141 and transformed into a church in the 8th century. To your right, the **Basilica Aemilia** (Map p404), built in 179 BC, was 100m long with a two-storey porticoed facade lined with shops. Opposite the basilica, over **Via Sacra** (Map p404), the Forum's main drag, stands the **Tempio di Giulio Cesare** (Map p404), erected by Augustus in 29 BC on the site where Caesar's body had earlier been cremated.

Head right up Via Sacra to reach the **Curia** (Map p404), the original seat of the Roman senate. Nearby, the **Arco di Settimio Severo** (Map p404) was erected in AD 203 to honour Emperor Septimus Severus' victory over the Parthians. Southwest of the arch, eight granite

ⓧ Don't Miss
The Colosseum

Rome's great gladiatorial arena is the most thrilling of its ancient sights. Originally known as the Flavian Amphitheatre, the 50,000-seat Colosseum was started by Emperor Vespasian in AD 72 and finished by his son Titus in AD 80. It's a mighty reminder of the power and pomp of Rome in its heyday.

Map p404

☎ 06 3996 7700

www.coopculture.it

Piazza del Colosseo

adult/reduced incl Roman Forum & Palatine Hill €12/7.50

🕗 8.30am-1hr before sunset

Ⓜ Colosseo

History

The Colosseum would originally have been clad in travertine and covered by a canvas awning held aloft by 240 masts. Inside, tiered seating encircled the sand-covered arena, itself built over underground chambers (known as the hypogeum) where animals were caged and elaborate stage sets prepared. Games involved gladiators fighting wild animals or each other, but, contrary to Hollywood folklore, bouts rarely ended in death.

Tours

The top tier and hypogeum can be visited on guided tours (€6 or €8 for both), which must be booked in advance, either at www.pierreci.it or by calling ☎06 399 67 700. You can also join an official English-language tour – €5 on top of the regular Colosseum ticket price.

Avoiding the Queues

You can avoid the inevitable Colosseum queues by booking your ticket online at www.coopculture.it (plus booking fee of €1.50) or buying the the Roma Pass, which is valid for three days and valid for a host of sites, including the Colosseum. Alternatively, buy your ticket from the Palatine entrance (about 250m away at Via di San Gregorio 30) or the Roman Forum (Largo della Salara Vecchia).

Local Knowledge

The Colosseum

RECOMMENDATIONS FROM VINCENZO MACCARRONE, COLOSSEUM STAFF MEMBER

1 THE ARENA
The arena had a wooden floor covered in sand to prevent combatants from slipping and to soak up blood. Gladiators arrived directly from their training ground via underground passageways, and were hoisted onto the arena by a complicated system of pulleys.

2 THE CAVEA AND THE PODIUM
The *cavea*, for spectator seating, was divided into three tiers: knights sat in the lowest, wealthy citizens in the middle and plebs at the top. The podium – close to the action but protected from the animals on stage by nets made of hemp – was reserved for emperors, senators and VIPs.

3 THE FACADE
The exterior mimics the Teatro di Marcello; the walls were once clad in travertine, with marble statues filling the niches on the 2nd and 3rd floors. On the top level you'll see square holes that held wooden masts supporting the *velarium* (a canvas awning over the arena).

4 TEMPORARY EXHIBITIONS
The 2nd floor hosts some fantastic exhibitions, either about the Colosseum or on the wider history of Rome. Walk past the bookshop to the end of the corridor and look towards the eastern side of the Roman Forum – there's a wonderful view of the Tempio di Venere e Roma (Temple of Venus and Rome), hard to see from the ground.

5 THE PERFECT PHOTO
Towards closing time, the Colosseum is bathed in a beautiful light. For great views of the building, head up Colle Oppio (Oppio Hill) right above the Colosseo metro station, or up Colle Celio (Celio Hill) opposite the Palatine and Colosseum exit.

Roman Forum

In ancient times, a forum was a market place, civic centre and religious complex all rolled into one, and the greatest of all was the Roman Forum (Foro Romano). Situated between the Palatino (Palatine Hill), ancient Rome's most exclusive neighbourhood, and the Campidoglio (Capitoline Hill), it was the city's busy, bustling centre. On any given day it teemed with activity. Senators debated affairs of state in the **Curia** ❶, shoppers thronged the squares and traffic-free streets, crowds gathered under the **Colonna di Foca** ❷ to listen to politicians holding forth from the **Rostrum** ❷. Elsewhere, lawyers worked the courts in basilicas including the **Basilica di Massenzio** ❸, while the Vestal Virgins quietly went about their business in the **Casa delle Vestali** ❹.

Special occasions were also celebrated in the Forum: religious holidays were marked with ceremonies at temples such as the **Tempio di Saturno** ❺ and the **Tempio di Castore e Polluce** ❻, and military victories were honoured with dramatic processions up Via Sacra and the building of monumental arches like the **Arco di Settimio Severo** ❼ and the **Arco di Tito** ❽.

The ruins you see today are impressive but they can be confusing without a clear picture of what the Forum once looked like. This spread shows the Forum in its heyday, complete with temples, civic buildings and towering monuments to heroes of the Roman Empire.

TOP TIPS

Get grandstand views of the Forum from the Palatino and Campidoglio.

Visit first thing in the morning or late afternoon; crowds are worst between 11am and 2pm.

In summer it gets hot in the Forum and there's little shade, so take a hat and plenty of water.

Colonna di Foca & Rostrum

The free-standing, 13.5m-high Column of Phocus is the Forum's youngest monument, dating to AD 608. Behind it, the Rostrum provided a suitably grandiose platform for pontificating public speakers.

Campidoglio (Capitoline Hill)

Admission

Although valid for two days, admission tickets only allow for one entry into the Forum, Colosseum and Palatino.

Tempio di Saturno

Ancient Rome's Fort Knox, the Temple of Saturn was the city treasury. In Caesar's day it housed 13 tonnes of gold, 114 tonnes of silver and 30 million sestertii worth of silver coins.

JONATHAN SMITH/GETTY IMAGES ©

LONELY PLANET/GETTY IMAGES ©

Tempio di Castore e Polluce

Only three columns of the Temple of Castor and Pollux remain. The temple was dedicated to the Heavenly Twins after they supposedly led the Romans to victory over the Etruscans.

Arco di Settimio Severo

One of the Forum's signature monuments, this imposing triumphal arch commemorates the military victories of Septimius Severus. Relief panels depict his campaigns against the Parthians.

Curia

This big barnlike building was the official seat of the Roman Senate. Most of what you see is a reconstruction, but the interior marble floor dates to the 3rd-century reign of Diocletian.

Basilica di Massenzio

Marvel at the scale of this vast 4th-century basilica. In its original form the central hall was divided into enormous naves; now only part of the northern nave survives.

Julius Caesar RIP

Julius Caesar was cremated on the site where the Tempio di Giulio Cesare now stands.

Via Sacra

Tempio di Giulio Cesare

Casa delle Vestali

White statues line the grassy atrium of what was once the luxurious 50-room home of the Vestal Virgins. The virgins played an important role in Roman religion, serving the goddess Vesta.

Arco di Tito

Said to be the inspiration for the Arc de Triomphe in Paris, the well-preserved Arch of Titus was built by the emperor Domitian to honour his elder brother Titus.

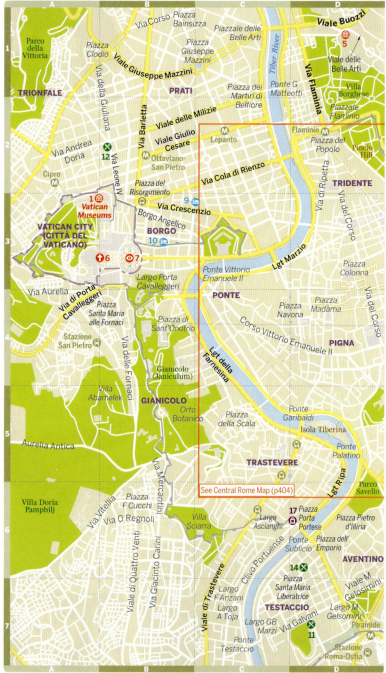

ITALY ROME

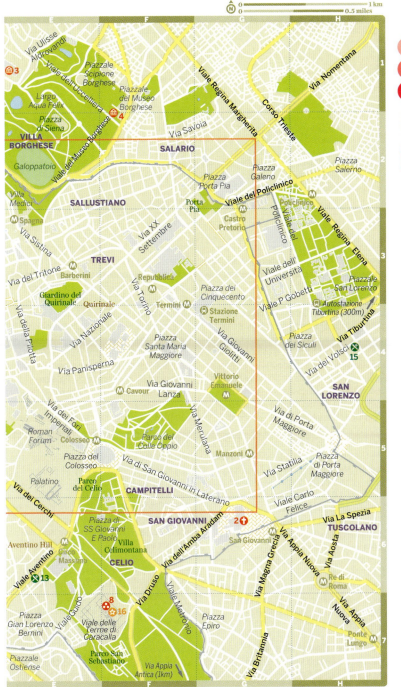

N 0 — 1 km
0 — 0.5 miles

Via Ulisse Aldrovandi

Piazzale Scipione Borghese

Viale dell'Uccelliera

Piazzale del Museo Borghese

Viale Regina Margherita

Corso Trieste

Via Nomentana

3

Largo Aqua Felix

Piazza di Siena

Viale del Museo Borghese

4

Via Savoia

Piazza Salerno

1

VILLA BORGHESE

SALARIO

2

Galoppatoio

Piazza Porta Pia

Piazza Galeno

Viale del Policlinico

Policlinico

Via Nomentana

Villa Medici

SALLUSTIANO

Potta Pia

Viale del Policlinico

Policlinico

Viale del

Viale Regina Elena

Spagna

Castro Pretorio

Piazzale San Lorenzo

2

Via Sistina

Via XX Settembre

Viale dell'Università

Via P Gobetti

Autostazione Tiburtina (300m)

TREVI

Via del Tritone

Barberini

Repubblica

Piazza dei Cinquecento

Viale P Gobetti

Via Tiburtina

3

Giardino del Quirinale

Quirinale

Via Torino

Termini

Via della Pilotta

Via Nazionale

Via Panisperna

Piazza Santa Maria Maggiore

Stazione Termini

Via Giovanni Giolitti

Piazza dei Siculi

Via dei Volsci

15

4

Via Giovanni Lanza

Cavour

Vittorio Emanuele

SAN LORENZO

Via dei Fori Imperiali

Roman Forum

Colosseo

Parco del Colle Oppio

Via Merulana

Manzoni

Via di Porta Maggiore

Via Statilia

Piazza di Porta Maggiore

5

Piazza del Colosseo

Palatino

Parco del Celio

Via di San Giovanni in Laterano

Viale Carlo Felice

Via La Spezia

Via dei Cerchi

CAMPITELLI

SAN GIOVANNI

Via dell'Amba Aradam

2

San Giovanni

Via Magna Grecia

Via Appia Nuova

Via Aosta

TUSCOLANO

6

Aventino Hill

Circo Massimo

Piazza di SS Giovanni E Paolo

Villa Celimontana

Re di Roma

Viale Aventino

13

CELIO

Via Druso

Via Guido

8

16

Viale delle Terme di Caracalla

Viale Metronio

Piazza Epiro

Via Appia Nuova

Ponte Lungo

7

Piazza Gian Lorenzo Bernini

Parco San Sebastiano

Via Appia Antica (1km)

Via Brittannia

Piazzale Ostiense

Greater Rome

◎ Don't Miss Sights
1 Vatican Museums A3

◎ Sights
2 Basilica di San Giovanni in
   Laterano G6
3 Galleria Nazionale d'Arte
   Moderna E1
4 Museo e Galleria Borghese F2
5 Museo Nazionale Etrusco di
   Villa Giulia D1
6 St Peter's Basilica B3
7 St Peter's Square B3
8 Terme di Caracalla F7

⊛ Sleeping
9 Colors Hotel C3
10 Hotel Bramante B3

⊗ Eating
11 Flavio al Velavevodetto D7
12 Hostaria Dino & Tony B2
13 Il Gelato E6
14 Pizzeria Da Remo D6
15 Pommidoro H4

⊛ Entertainment
16 Terme di Caracalla F7

⊕ Shopping
17 Porta Portese Flea Market D6

columns are all that remain of the 5th-century BC **Tempio di Saturno** (Map p404), an important temple that doubled as the state treasury.

To the southeast, the 7th-century **Colonna di Foca** (Column of Phocus; Map p404) stands at the centre of what was once the forum's main square, Piazza del Foro. To your right are the foundations of the **Basilica Giulia** (Map p404), a law court built by Julius Caesar in 55 BC. At the end of the basilica rise three columns, all that's left of the **Tempio di Castore e Polluce** (Map p404), a 489 BC temple dedicated to Castor and Pollux.

Back towards Via Sacra, white statues line the grassy atrium of the **Casa delle Vestali** (Map p404), the once-luxurious home of the Vestal Virgins who kept the sacred flame alight in the adjoining **Tempio di Vesta** (Map p404).

Continuing up Via Sacra, you come to the vast **Basilica di Massenzio** (Map p404), also known as the Basilica di Costantino, and the **Arco di Tito** (Map p404). This squat arch, said to be the inspiration for the Arc de Triomphe in Paris, was built in AD 81 to celebrate victories against Jewish rebels in Jerusalem.

Piazza del Campidoglio   Piazza
(Map p404; ⊡ Piazza Venezia) This elegant Michelangelo-designed piazza sits atop the Capitoline Hill (Campidoglio), the lowest of Rome's seven hills. In ancient times, it was home to the city's two most important temples: one dedicated to Juno Moneta and the other to Jupiter Capitolinus.

You can reach the piazza from the Roman Forum but the most dramatic approach is via the graceful **Cordonata** (Map p404) staircase. At the top, the piazza is flanked by three *palazzi*: **Palazzo Nuovo** (Angelo Mai Library; Map p404) on the left, **Palazzo dei Conservatori** (Map p404) on the right, and **Palazzo Senatorio** (Map p404), seat of Rome's City Hall since 1143. In the centre, the bronze **statue of Marcus Aurelius** (Map p404) is a copy; the original is in the Capitoline Museums.

Capitoline Museums   Museum
(Musei Capitolini; Map p404; ☎ 06 06 08; www.museicapitolini.org; Piazza del Campidoglio 1; adult/reduced €9.50/7.50; ⊙9am-8pm Tue-Sun, last admission 7pm; ⊡ Piazza Venezia) Housed in Palazzo dei Conservatori and Palazzo Nuovo on Piazza del Campidoglio, the Capitoline Museums are the world's oldest public museums, dating to 1471. Their collection of classical art is one of Italy's finest, including masterpieces such as the *Lupa Capitolina* (Capitoline Wolf), a sculpture of Romulus and Remus under a wolf, and the *Galata morente* (Dying Gaul), a moving depic-

tion of a dying Gaul. The rich 2nd-floor **pinacoteca** (picture gallery) contains paintings by the likes of Titian, Tintoretto, Van Dyck, Rubens and Caravaggio.

Il Vittoriano Monument

(Map p404; Piazza Venezia; ⏰9.30am-5.30pm summer, to 4.30pm winter; 🚊Piazza Venezia) **FREE** Love it or loathe it as most locals do, you can't ignore Il Vittoriano (aka the *Altare della Patria;* Altar of the Fatherland), the massive mountain of marble that looms over Piazza Venezia. Begun in 1885 to honour Italy's first king, Vittorio Emanuele II, it incorporates the **Tomb of the Unknown Soldier** and the **Museo Centrale del Risorgimento** (Map p404; Via di San Pietro in Carcere; ⏰9.30am-6.30pm) **FREE**, documenting Italian unification. At the back, a **panoramic lift** (Map p404; adult/reduced €7/3.50; ⏰9.30am-6.30pm Mon-Thu, to 7.30pm Fri-Sun) whisks you up to the top for Rome's best 360-degree views.

Mercati di Traiano Museo dei Fori Imperiali Museum

(Map p404; 📞06 06 08; www.mercatiditraiano.it; Via IV Novembre 94; adult/reduced €9.50/7.50; ⏰9am-7pm Tue-Sun, last admission 6pm; 🚊Via IV Novembre) This striking museum brings to life the **Mercati di Traiano**, emperor Trajan's great 2nd-century market complex. From the main hallway, a lift whisks you up to the **Torre delle Milizie** (Militia Tower), a 13th-century red-brick tower, and the upper levels of the vast three-storey semi-circular construction that once housed hundreds of market traders.

Bocca della Verità Monument

(Map p404; Piazza Bocca della Verità 18; donation €0.50; ⏰9.30am-4.50pm winter, to 5.50pm summer; 🚊Piazza Bocca della Verità) A mask-shaped round marble disc that was once part of an ancient fountain, or possibly an ancient manhole cover, the Mouth of Truth is one of Rome's great curiosities. According to legend, if you put your hand in the carved mouth and tell a lie, it will bite your hand off.

The mouth lives in the portico of the 8th-century **Chiesa di Santa Maria in Cosmedin**, one of Rome's most beautiful medieval churches.

The Vatican

The world's smallest sovereign state – it covers just 0.44 sq km – the Vatican is the modern vestige of the Papal States. This papal empire encompassed Rome and much of central Italy for more than a thousand years until it was forcibly incorporated into the Italian state during unification in 1861. Relations between Italy and the landless papacy remained strained until 1929 when Mussolini and Pope Pius XI signed the Lateran Treaty, formally establishing the Vatican State.

Staircase inside the Vatican Museums (p402), Rome
ROBERT HARDING/GETTY IMAGES ©

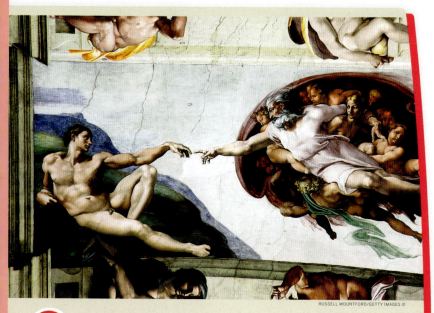

RUSSELL MOUNTFORD/GETTY IMAGES ©

⭐ **Don't Miss**
Vatican Museums

Boasting one of the world's great art collections, the Vatican Museums are housed in the Palazzo Apostolico Vaticano, a vast 5.5-hectare complex comprising two palaces and three internal courtyards. You'll never cover it all in one day – there are about 7km of exhibits – so it pays to be selective.

For spectacular classical statuary, head to the **Museo Pio-Clementino**, home to the peerless *Apollo Belvedere* and the 1st-century *Laocoön*, both in the Cortile Ottagono (Octagonal Courtyard). Further on, beyond the magnificent **Galleria delle Carte Geografiche** (Map Gallery), are the **Stanze di Raffaello** (Raphael Rooms).

From the Raphael Rooms, it's a short walk to the **Sistine Chapel** (Cappella Sistina), the museums' grand finale. The chapel was originally built in 1484, but it was Julius II who commissioned Michelangelo to decorate it in 1508. Over the next four years, the artist painted the entire 800-sq-metre ceiling with episodes from the book of Genesis. He returned 22 years later to paint the *Last Judgment* on the 200-sq-metre west wall. The other walls feature frescos produced by a crack team of Renaissance artists including Botticelli, Domenico Ghirlandaio, Pinturicchio and Luca Signorelli.

To reduce waiting time, book tickets online (http://biglietteriamusei.vatican.va/musei/tickets; plus booking fee of €4), and time your visit: Wednesday mornings are good as everyone is at the Pope's weekly audience at St Peter's; afternoon is better than the morning; avoid Mondays, when many other museums are shut.

NEED TO KNOW

Musei Vaticani; Map p398; ☎06 6988 4676; http://mv.vatican.va; Viale Vaticano; adult/reduced €16/8, admission free last Sun of month; ⊙9am-6pm Mon-Sat, last admission 4pm, 9am-2pm last Sun of month, last admission 12.30pm; Ⓜ Ottaviano-San Pietro

St Peter's Basilica   Basilica

(Map p398; www.vatican.va; St Peter's Square; ⏱7am-7pm Apr-Sep, to 6.30pm Oct-Mar; Ⓜ Ottaviano-San Pietro) FREE In this city of outstanding churches, none can hold a candle to St Peter's Basilica, Italy's biggest, richest and most spectacular church. Standing over St Peter's tomb, the current basilica, the world's second largest, was built atop an earlier 4th-century church by an army of major league architects and artists, including Bramante, who produced the original design in 1506, Raphael, Antonio de Sangallo, Carlo Maderno and Michelangelo, who took over the project in 1507 and designed the soaring 120m-high dome. The entrance to climb the **dome (with/without lift €7/5;** ⏱8am-6pm Apr-Sep, 8am-5pm Oct-Mar) is to the right of the stairs that lead up to the basilica's atrium.

The cavernous 187m-long interior contains numerous treasures, including two of Italy's most celebrated masterpieces: Michelangelo's hauntingly beautiful *Pietà,* the only work to carry his signature; and Bernini's 29m-high **baldachin** over the main altar.

Note that the basilica is one of Rome's busiest attractions, so expect queues in peak periods. Also, dress rules are stringently enforced, so no shorts, miniskirts or sleeveless tops.

St Peter's Square   Piazza

(Piazza San Pietro; Map p398; Ⓜ Ottaviano-San Pietro) The Vatican's central space was designed by baroque artist Gian Lorenzo Bernini and laid out between 1656 and 1667. Seen from above, it resembles a keyhole with two semicircular colonnades, each consisting of four rows of Doric columns, encircling a giant ellipse that straightens out to funnel believers into the basilica. The effect was deliberate – Bernini described the colonnades as representing 'the motherly arms of the church'.

The 25m obelisk in the centre was brought to Rome by Caligula from Heliopolis in Egypt and later used as a turning post for the chariot races in Nero's circus.

Historic Centre

Pantheon   Church

(Map p404; Piazza della Rotonda; ⏱8.30am-7.30pm Mon-Sat, 9am-6pm Sun; 🚌Largo di Torre Argentina) FREE A striking 2000-year-old temple, now church, the Pantheon is the best preserved of ancient Rome's great monuments. In its current form it dates to around AD 120 when the Emperor Hadrian built over Marcus Agrippa's original 27 BC temple (Agrippa's name remains inscribed on the pediment). The **dome**, considered the Romans' greatest architectural achievement, was the largest in the world until the 15th century and is still the largest unreinforced concrete dome ever built. It's a mind-boggling structure whose harmonious appearance is due to a precisely calibrated symmetry – its diameter is exactly equal to the Pantheon's interior height of 43.3m. Light (and rain, which drains away through 22 holes in the floor) enters through the **oculus**, an 8.7m opening that acts as a compression ring, absorbing and redistributing the dome's vast structural forces.

Inside, you'll find the tombs of Raphael and kings Vittorio Emanuele II and Umberto I.

Piazza Navona   Piazza

(Map p404; 🚌Corso del Rinascimento) With its ornate fountains, baroque *palazzi,* pavement cafes and colourful cast of street artists, hawkers, tourists and pigeons, Piazza Navona is Rome's most celebrated square. Built over the ruins of the 1st-century Stadio di Domiziano (Domitian's Stadium), it was paved over in the 15th century and for almost 300 years hosted the city's main market.

Campo de' Fiori   Piazza

(Map p404; 🚌Corso Vittorio Emanuele II) Noisy, colourful 'Il Campo' is a major focus of Roman life: by day it hosts a much-loved market, while at night it morphs into a raucous open-air pub. For centuries this was the site of public executions, and it was here that philosopher monk Giordano Bruno (the hooded figure in Ettore Ferrari's sinister statue) was burned at the stake for heresy in 1600.

Central Rome

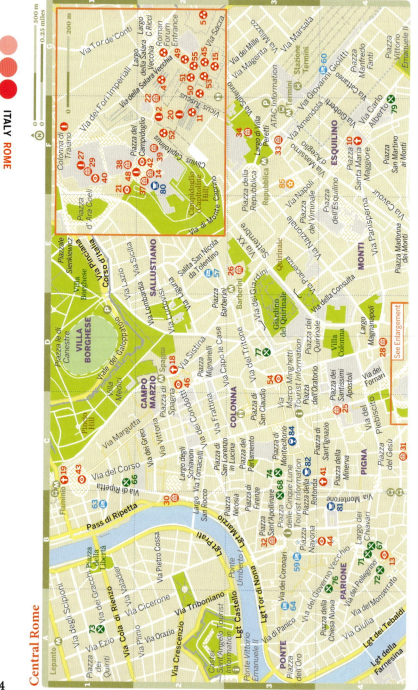

Galleria Doria Pamphilj   Museum

(Map p404; ☎ 06 679 73 23; www.dopart.it; Via del Corso 305; adult/reduced €11/7.50; ⏰9am-7pm, last admission 6pm; 🚌Piazza Venezia) Behind the grimy grey walls of Palazzo Doria Pamphilj is one of Rome's finest private art collections, with works by Raphael, Tintoretto, Brueghel, Titian, Caravaggio and Bernini.

Trevi Fountain   Fountain

(Fontana di Trevi; Map p404; Piazza di Trevi; Ⓜ Barberini) Immortalised by Anita Ekberg's sensual dip in Fellini's *La dolce vita,* the Trevi Fountain is Rome's largest and most famous fountain. The flamboyant ensemble was designed by Nicola Salvi in 1732 and depicts Neptune in a shell-shaped chariot being led by the Tritons and two sea horses representing the moods of the sea. The water comes from the *aqua virgo,* a 1st-century BC underground aqueduct, and the name 'Trevi' refers to the *tre vie* (three roads) that converge at the fountain.

The custom is to throw a coin into the fountain, thus ensuring your return to Rome. On average about €3000 is chucked away daily.

Galleria Nazionale d'Arte Antica: Palazzo Barberini   Gallery

(Map p404; ☎ 06 3 28 10; www.gebart.it; Via delle Quattro Fontane 13; adult/reduced €7/3.50, incl Palazzo Corsini €9/4.50; ⏰8.30am-7pm Tue-Sun; Ⓜ Barberini) A must for anyone who's into Renaissance and baroque art, this sumptuous gallery is housed in Palazzo Barberini, one of Rome's most spectacular *palazzi.* Inside, you'll find works by Raphael, Caravaggio, Guido Reni, Bernini, Filippo Lippi and Holbein, as well as Pietro da Cortona's breathtaking *Trionfo della Divina Provvidenza* (Triumph of Divine Providence).

Spanish Steps   Architecture

(Map p404; Piazza di Spagna; Ⓜ Spagna) Rising above Piazza di Spagna, the Spanish Steps, aka the Scalinata della Trinità dei Monti, have been a magnet for foreigners since the 18th century. The piazza was named after the Spanish embassy to the Holy See, although the staircase, which

Central Rome

⊙ Don't Miss Sights
1 Colosseum...E6

⊙ Sights
2 Arco di Settimio Severo.......................F2
3 Arco di Tito D5
4 Basilica Aemilia..................................G2
5 Basilica di Massenzio G2
6 Basilica di San Clemente F6
7 Basilica di San Pietro in Vincoli.............E5
8 Basilica di Santa Cecilia in
   Trastevere...B6
9 Basilica di Santa Maria in
   Trastevere... A6
10 Basilica di Santa Maria
   Maggiore..F4
11 Basilica Giulia F2
12 Bocca della Verità...............................C6
13 Campo de' Fiori B4
14 Capitoline Museums F2
15 Casa delle Vestali...............................G2
16 Casa di Augusto D6
17 Casa di Livia.......................................D6
18 Chiesa della Trinità dei Monti.............. D2
19 Chiesa di Santa Maria del
   Popolo C1
20 Colonna di Foca.................................F2
21 Cordonata F1
22 Curia...F2
23 Domus Augustana D6
24 Domus Flavia......................................D6
25 Galleria Doria Pamphilj.......................C4
26 Galleria Nazionale d'Arte
   Antica: Palazzo Barberini E3
27 Il Vittoriano F1
28 Mercati di Traiano Museo dei
   Fori Imperiali................................... D4
29 Museo Centrale del
   Risorgimento F1
30 Museo dell'Ara Pacis B2
31 Museo Nazionale Romano:
   Crypta Balbi.....................................C4
32 Museo Nazionale Romano:
   Palazzo Altemps B3
33 Museo Nazionale Romano:
   Palazzo Massimo alle
   Terme...F3
34 Museo Nazionale Romano:
   Terme di Diocleziano.........................F3
35 Orti Farnesiani....................................D6
36 Palatino D6
37 Palazzo dei Conservatori....................F2
38 Palazzo Nuovo F1
39 Palazzo Senatorio...............................F2
40 Panoramic Lift F1
41 Pantheon C4
42 Piazza del Campidoglio F2
43 Piazza del Popolo C1
44 Piazza Navona....................................B4
45 Roman Forum.....................................G2
46 Spanish Steps.....................................D2
47 Stadio...D6
48 Statue of Marcus Aurelius....................F1
49 Tempio di Antonino e Faustina.............G2
50 Tempio di Castore e Polluce.................G2
51 Tempio di Giulio Cesare G2
52 Tempio di Saturno...............................F2
53 Tempio di Vesta..................................G2
54 Trevi Fountain.....................................D3
55 Via Sacra..G2

🛏 Sleeping
56 Arco del Lauro....................................B6
57 Daphne Inn E2
58 Duca d'Alba E5
59 Hotel Raphaël.....................................B3
60 Hotel Reservation Service....................G4
61 Maria-Rosa Guesthouse......................C6
62 Nicolas Inn E5
63 Okapi Rooms B1
64 Relais Palazzo Taverna........................A3
65 Villa Della Fonte B5

✖ Eating
66 Al Gran Sasso.....................................C1
67 Baffetto 2..B4
68 Casa Coppelle.....................................B3
69 Da Lucia..A5
70 Dar Poeta..A5
71 Ditirambo..B4
72 Forno di Campo de' Fiori......................B4
73 Gelarmony...A1
74 Giolitti...C3
75 Hostaria dar Buttero............................B6
76 Pizzeria da Baffetto.............................B4
77 San Crispino..D3
78 Trattoria degli Amici A5
79 Trattoria Monti.....................................F4

🍷 Drinking & Nightlife
80 Caffè Capitolino.................................. F2
81 Caffè Sant'Eustachio B4
82 La Tazza d'Oro....................................C3
83 Open Baladin......................................B5
84 Salotto 42...C3

🎭 Entertainment
85 Teatro dell'Opera di Roma...................F3

ITALY ROME

was built with French money in 1725, leads to the French church, **Chiesa della Trinità dei Monti** (Map p404; Piazza Trinità dei Monti; ⊘6am-8pm Tue-Sun; **M**Spagna).

Piazza del Popolo   Piazza

(Map p404; **M**Flaminio) This elegant landmark square was laid out in 1538 at the point of convergence of three roads – Via di Ripetta, Via del Corso and Via del Babuino – at what was then Rome's northern entrance. Guarding its southern approach are the twin 17th-century churches of **Santa Maria dei Miracoli** and **Santa Maria in Montesanto**, while on the northern flank is the **Porta del Popolo**, created by Bernini in 1655. The 36m-high obelisk in the centre was brought by Augustus from Heliopolis in ancient Egypt.

Chiesa di Santa Maria
del Popolo   Church

(Map p404; Piazza del Popolo; ⊘7.30am-noon & 4-7pm; **M**Flaminio) On the northern side of Piazza del Popolo stands one of Rome's earliest and richest Renaissance churches. Inside, the star attraction is the pair of Caravaggio masterpieces: the *Conversione di San Paolo* (Conversion of St Paul) and the *Crocifisssione di San Pietro* (Crucifixion of St Peter).

Museo dell'Ara Pacis   Museum

(Map p404; ☎06 06 08; http://en.arapacis. it; Lungotevere in Augusta; adult/reduced €8.50/6.50; ⊘9am-7pm Tue-Sun, last admission 6pm; **M**Flaminio) The first modern construction in Rome's historic centre since WWII, Richard Meier's white pavilion houses the **Ara Pacis Augustae** (Altar of Peace), one of the most important works of ancient Roman sculpture. The vast marble altar was completed in 13 BC as a monument to the peace that Augustus established both at home and abroad.

Villa Borghese

Just north of the historic centre, Villa Borghese is Rome's best-known park. The grounds, which were created in the 17th century by Cardinal Scipione Borghese, are accessible from Piazzale Flaminio, Pincio Hill and the top of Via Vittorio Veneto. Bike hire is available at various points, typically costing €5 per hour.

St Peter's Basilica (p403), Rome

IZZET KERIBAR/GETTY IMAGES ©

Museo Nazionale Romano

Spread over four sites, the Museo Nazionale Romano (National Roman Museum) houses one of the world's most important collections of classical art. A combined ticket including each of the sites costs adult/EU child €7/free (plus possible €3 exhibition supplement), and is valid for three days.

Palazzo Massimo alle Terme (Map p404; ☏06 3996 7700; www.coopculture.it; Largo di Villa Peretti 1; adult/reduced €7/3.50; ⏱9am-7.45pm Tue-Sun; Ⓜ Termini) A fabulous museum with amazing frescos and wall paintings.

Terme di Diocleziano (Map p404; ☏06 3996 7700; www.coopculture.it; Viale Enrico de Nicola 78; adult/reduced €7/3.50; ⏱9am-7.30pm Tue-Sun; Ⓜ Termini) Ancient epigraphs and tomb artefacts in the Terme di Diocleziano (Diocletian's Baths), ancient Rome's largest baths complex.

Palazzo Altemps (Map p404; ☏06 399 67 700; http://archeoroma.beniculturali.it/en/museums/national-roman-museum-palazzo-altemps; Piazza Sant'Apollinare 44; adult/reduced €7/3.50; ⏱9am-7.45pm Tue-Sun; 🚌Corso del Rinascimento) Wonderful classical sculpture in an exquisite Renaissance *palazzo*.

Crypta Balbi (Map p404; ☏06 3996 7700; http://archeoroma.beniculturali.it/en/museums/national-roman-museum-crypta-balbi; Via delle Botteghe Oscure 31; adult/reduced €7/3.50; ⏱9am-7.45pm Tue-Sun; 🚌Via delle Botteghe Oscure) Set atop an ancient Roman theatre, the Teatro di Balbus (13 BC).

Museo e Galleria Borghese   Museum

(Map p398; ☏06 3 28 10; www.galleriaborghese.it; Piazzale del Museo Borghese 5; adult/reduced €9/4.50, plus €2 booking fee & possible exhibition supplement; ⏱9am-7pm Tue-Sun, pre-booking necessary; 🚌Via Pinciana) If you only have time, or inclination, for one art gallery in Rome, make it this one. Housing the 'queen of all private art collections', it boasts paintings by Caravaggio, Botticelli and Raphael, as well as some spectacular sculptures by Gian Lorenzo Bernini. There are highlights at every turn, but look out for Bernini's *Ratto di Proserpina* (Rape of Persephone) and *Apollo e Dafne;* Antonio Canova's *Venere vincitrice* (Conquering Venus); and the Caravaggios in room VIII.

Note that you'll need to pre-book your ticket and enter at an allotted time.

Museo Nazionale Etrusco di Villa Giulia   Museum

(Map p398; ☏06 322 65 71; www.villagiulia.beniculturali.it; Piazzale di Villa Giulia; adult/reduced €8/4; ⏱Villa Giulia 8.30am-7.30pm Tue-Sun, Villa Poniatowski 9am-1.45pm Tue-Sat; 🚌Via delle Belle Arti) Italy's finest collection of Etruscan treasures is beautifully housed in Villa Giulia, Pope Julius III's 16th-century pleasure palace.

Galleria Nazionale d'Arte Moderna   Art Gallery

(Map p398; ☏06 3229 8221; www.gnam.beniculturali.it; Viale delle Belle Arti 131, disabled entrance Via Gramsci 71; adult/reduced €8/4; ⏱8.30am-7.30pm Tue-Sun; 🚌Piazza Thorvaldsen) Set in a vast belle-époque palace, this oft-overlooked museum displays works by some of the most important exponents of modern art, including Modigliani, De Chirico, Cezanne, Kandinsky, Klimt, Pollock and Henry Moore.

Trastevere

Trastevere is one of central Rome's most vivacious neighbourhoods, a tightly packed warren of ochre *palazzi,* ivy-clad facades and photogenic lanes. Taking its name from the Latin *trans Tiberium*, meaning over the Tiber, it was originally a working-class district, but has since been gentrified and is today a trendy hang-out full of bars, trattorias and restaurants.

Basilica di Santa Maria in Trastevere
Basilica

(Map p404; Piazza Santa Maria in Trastevere; ⏰7.30am-9pm; 🚌Viale di Trastevere, 🚊Viale di Trastevere) Nestled in a quiet corner of **Piazza Santa Maria in Trastevere**, Trastevere's picturesque focal square, this exquisite basilica is believed to be Rome's oldest church dedicated to the Virgin Mary. Inside, the glittering 12th-century apse mosaics are the main drawcard.

Basilica di Santa Cecilia in Trastevere
Basilica

(Map p404; Piazza di Santa Cecilia; basilica free, fresco & crypt each €2.50; ⏰basilica & crypt 9.30am-2.30pm & 4-7.30pm, fresco 10am-2.30pm Mon-Sat; 🚌Viale di Trastevere, 🚊Viale di Trastevere) The last resting place of St Cecilia, the patron saint of music, this church features a stunning 13th-century fresco by Pietro Cavallini and, below the altar,

a breathtaking sculpture of St Cecilia by Stefano Moderno. Beneath the basilica, you can visit excavations of several Roman houses.

Termini & Esquiline

The largest of Rome's seven hills, the Esquiline (Esquilino) extends from the Colosseum up to Stazione Termini, Rome's main transport hub.

Basilica di San Pietro in Vincoli
Basilica

(Map p404; Piazza di San Pietro in Vincoli 4a; ⏰8am-12.30pm & 3-7pm Apr-Sep, to 6pm Oct-Mar; Ⓜ Cavour) Pilgrims and art lovers flock to this church, just off Via Cavour, for two reasons: to see the chains worn by St Peter before his crucifixion (hence the church's name – St Peter in Chains), and to marvel at Michelangelo's *Moses*, the centrepiece of his unfinished tomb for Pope Julius II.

Basilica di Santa Maria Maggiore
Basilica

(Map p404; Piazza Santa Maria Maggiore; basilica free, museum €3, loggia €2; ⏰7am-7pm,

Pantheon (p403), Rome

JEAN-PIERRE LESCOURRET/GETTY IMAGES ©

If You Like...
Roman Ruins

Beyond the crumbling Colosseum (p394) and the remains of Pompeii (p469), Italy is littered with countless other ruins created during the heyday of the Roman empire.

1 SCAVI ARCHEOLOGICI DI OSTIA ANTICA

(📞06 563 52 830; www.ostiantica.info; adult/reduced/EU child €6.50/3.25/free, plus possible exhibition supplement; ⏰8.30am-6pm Tue-Sun Apr-Oct, to 5pm Mar, to 4pm Nov-Dec & Jan-Feb) An easy day trip from Rome are the ruins of the Scavi Archeologici di Ostia Antica, ancient Rome's main seaport. Among the ruins, you can wander around the Terme di Nettuno (Baths of Neptune), amphitheatre and the Thermopolium, an ancient cafe. Trains run from Rome's Stazione Porta San Paolo.

2 VIA APPIA ANTICA

(Appian Way; 📞06 512 63 14; www.parcoappiaantica.it; bike/electric bike hire per hr €3/6, per day €15/20; ⏰Information Point 9.30am-1pm & 2-5pm Mon-Fri, 9.30am-5pm Sat & Sun, to 5.30pm Aug, to 6.30pm Apr-Oct; 🚌Via Appia Antica) Completed in 190 BC to connect Rome with the southern Adriatic coast, the Appian Way has a dark history – it was here that Spartacus and 6000 of his slave rebels were crucified in 71 BC. It's also where Rome's early Christians buried their dead in underground catacombs such as the **Catacombe di San Sebastiano** (📞06 785 03 50; www.catacombe.org; Via Appia Antica 136; adult/reduced €8/5; ⏰10am-5pm Mon-Sat, closed mid-Nov–mid-Dec). Take bus 660 from Colli Albani metro station (line A) or bus 118 from Piramide (line B).

3 VILLA ADRIANA

(📞06 3996 7900; www.villaadriana.beniculturali.it; adult/reduced €8/4, plus possible exhibition supplement, car park €3; ⏰9am-1hr before sunset) Just outside Tivoli, 30km east of Rome, Emperor Hadrian's sprawling 1st-century summer residence was one of the most sumptuous villas in the Roman Empire. Hadrian designed much of it, taking inspiration from buildings he'd seen around the world. It's a great place to get a sense of the emperor's luxurious lifestyle.

museum & loggia 9.30am-6.30pm; 🚌Piazza Santa Maria Maggiore) One of Rome's four patriarchal basilicas, this hulking church was built in AD 352 on the site of a miraculous snowfall. An architectural hybrid, it has a 14th-century Romanesque belfry (at 75m Rome's highest), an 18th-century baroque facade, a largely baroque interior and a series of glorious 5th-century mosaics.

San Giovanni & Caelian Hill

Basilica di San Giovanni in Laterano   Basilica

(Map p398; Piazza di San Giovanni in Laterano 4; basilica free, cloister €3; ⏰7am-6.30pm, cloister 9am-6pm; Ⓜ San Giovanni) For a thousand years this monumental cathedral was the most important church in Christendom. Founded by Constantine in AD 324, it was the first Christian basilica built in the city and, until the late 14th century, was the pope's main place of worship. It is still Rome's official cathedral and the pope's seat as bishop of Rome.

Basilica di San Clemente   Basilica

(Map p404; www.basilicasanclemente.com; Via di San Giovanni in Laterano; church/excavations free/€5; ⏰9am-12.30pm & 3-6pm Mon-Sat, noon-6pm Sun; Ⓜ Colosseo) Nowhere better illustrates the various stages of Rome's turbulent history than this fascinating, multilayered church. The ground-level, 12th-century basilica sits atop a 4th-century church which, in turn, stands over a 2nd-century temple dedicated to the pagan god Mithras and a 1st-century Roman house.

Terme di Caracalla   Ruins

(Map p398; 📞06 3996 7700; www.coopculture.it; Viale delle Terme di Caracalla 52; adult/reduced €7/4; ⏰9am-1hr before sunset Tue-Sun, 9am-2pm Mon; 🚌Viale delle Terme di Caracalla) Inaugurated in AD 217, the 10-hectare leisure complex could hold up to 1600 people and included richly decorated pools, gymnasiums, libraries, shops and gardens. The ruins are now used to stage summer opera.

✴ Festivals & Events

Easter   Religious
On Good Friday, the pope leads a candlelit procession around the Colosseum. At noon on Easter Sunday he blesses the crowds in St Peter's Square.

Settimana della Cultura   Cultural
(www.beniculturali.it) During Culture Week admission is free to many state-run museums, monuments, galleries and otherwise closed sites. Dates change annually but it's usually in April.

Natale di Roma   Culture
Rome celebrates its birthday on 21 April with music, historical recreations, fireworks and free entry to many museums.

Festa de'Noantri   Culture
Trastevere's annual party, held in the third week of July, involves plenty of food, wine, prayer and dancing.

Festival Internazionale del Film di Roma   Film
(www.romacinemafest.org) Held at the Auditorium Parco della Musica in late October or early November, Rome's film festival rolls out the red carpet for Hollywood hotshots and Italian celebs.

🛏 Sleeping

Rome has plenty of accommodation, but rates are universally high. The best, most atmospheric places to stay are the historic centre, the Prati area near the Vatican and Trastevere.

Always try to book ahead, even if it's just for the first night. But if you arrive without a booking, there's a **hotel reservation service** (Map p404; ☎ 06 699 10 00; booking fee €3; ⏱ 7am-10pm) next to the tourist office at Stazione Termini.

Ancient Rome

Nicolas Inn   B&B €
(Map p404; ☎ 06 9761 8483; www.nicolasinn.com; 1st fl, Via Cavour 295; s €95-160, d €100-180; ❄ 🤶; Ⓜ Cavour) This sunny B&B offers a warm welcome and a convenient location, a stone's throw from the Roman Forum. Run by a friendly couple, it has four big guest rooms, each with homely furnishings, colourful pictures and large en suite bathrooms.

Duca d'Alba   Hotel €€
(Map p404; ☎ 06 48 44 71; www.hotelducadalba.com; Via Leonina 14; r €70-200; ❄ 🤶; Ⓜ Cavour) This refined four-star sits amid the boutiques and wine bars of the hip Monti district. It's a tight squeeze, but the individually decorated guest rooms are sleek and stylish with parquet floors and modern grey-white colour schemes.

Piazza del Popolo (p407), Rome
P. EOCHE/GETTY IMAGES ©

The Vatican

Hotel Bramante   Hotel €€

(Map p398; ☎06 6880 6426; www.hotelbra
mante.com; Vicolo delle Palline 24-25; s €100-160,
d €140-240, tr €170-250, q €175-260; ❄️🛜;
🚇Piazza del Risorgimento) Tucked away in
an alley under the Vatican walls, the Hotel
Bramante exudes country-house charm
with its quietly elegant rooms and cosy
internal courtyard. It's housed in the
16th-century building where architect Domenico Fontana lived before Pope Sixtus
V banished him from Rome.

Colors Hotel   Hotel €

(Map p398; ☎06 687 40 30; www.colorshotel.
com; Via Boezio 31; s €35-90, d €45-125; ❄️🛜;
🚇Via Cola di Rienzo) Popular with young
travellers, this is a bright budget hotel
with smart, vibrantly coloured rooms
spread over three floors (no lift, though).
There are also cheaper rooms with
shared bathrooms and, from June to
August, dorms (€12 to €35 per person)
for guests under 38 years of age.

Historic Centre

Daphne Inn   Boutique Hotel €€

(Map p404; ☎06 8745 0086; www.daphne-
rome.com; Via di San Basilio 55; s €110-180, d
€140-230, without bathroom s €70-130, d €90-
160; ❄️🛜; 🚇Barberini) Daphne is a gem.
Spread over two sites (Daphne Veneto
and Daphne Trevi) near Piazza Barberini,
it offers value for money, exceptional
service and chic modern rooms. The
English-speaking staff go that extra mile,
even lending guests a cell phone during
their stay.

Okapi Rooms   Hotel €

(Map p404; ☎06 3260 9815; www.okapirooms.
it; Via della Penna 57; s €65-80, d €85-120,
tr €110-140, q €120-180; ❄️🛜; 🚇Flaminio)
Occupying a tall townhouse near Piazza
del Popolo, the Okapi is a bargain low-
midrange option. Rooms, spread over six
floors, are small and simple with cream
walls, terracotta-tiled floors and tiny en
suite bathrooms. Several also have small
terraces.

Relais Palazzo Taverna   Boutique Hotel €€

(Map p404; ☎06 2039 8064; www.relaispalazzo
taverna.com; Via dei Gabrielli 92; s €80-150, d
€100-210, tr €120-240; ❄️🛜; 🚇Corso del
Rinascimento) Housed in a 15th-
century *palazzo*, this boutique
hotel is superbly located in the
heart of the historic centre. Its
six rooms cut a stylish dash
with white wood-beamed
ceilings, funky wallpaper
and dark parquet.

Hotel Raphaël   Historic Hotel €€€

(Map p404; ☎06 68 28
31; www.raphaelhotel.
com; Largo Febo 2; d from
€280; ❄️🛜; 🚇Corso
del Rinascimento) An
ivy-clad landmark just
off Piazza Navona, the
Raphaël boasts a serious

Piazza Navona (p403), Rome
MAREMAGNUM/GETTY IMAGES ©

Gelato Galore

To get the best out of Rome's *gelaterie* (ice-cream shops) look for the words *'produzione proprio',* meaning 'own production'. As a rough guide, expect to pay from €1.50 for a *cono* (cone) or *coppa* (tub).

San Crispino (Map p404; 06 679 39 24; Via della Panetteria 42; ice cream from €2.30; noon-12.30am Mon, Wed, Thu & Sun, 11am-1.30am Fri & Sat; MBarberini) Near the Trevi Fountain, it serves natural, seasonal flavours – think *fichi secci* (dried figs) and *miele* (honey) – in tubs only.

Gelarmony (Map p404; Via Marcantonio Colonna 34; ice cream from €1.50; 10am-late; MLepanto) A Sicilian *gelateria* serving 60 flavours and heavenly *cannoli* (pastry tubes filled with ricotta and candied fruit).

Il Gelato (Map p398; Viale Aventino 59; 11am-9pm Tue-Sun, to 10.30pm daily summer; MCirco Massimo) Creative, preservative-free combos from Rome's *gelato* king Claudio Torcè.

Gelateria Giolitti (Map p404; 06 699 12 43; www.giolitti.it; Via degli Uffici del Vicario 40; 7am-1am; Via del Corso) Rome's most famous *gelateria,* near the Pantheon.

art collection – Picasso ceramics and lithographs by Miró – as well as minimalist Richard Meier–designed rooms and a panoramic rooftop restaurant.

Trastevere

Arco del Lauro B&B €€
(Map p404; 9am-2pm 06 9784 0350, mobile 346 2443212; www.arcodellauro.it; Via Arco de' Tolomei 27; s €75-125, d €95-145; ❄@❞; Viale di Trastevere, Viale di Trastevere) This friendly B&B is in a medieval *palazzo* on a narrow cobbled street in Trastevere's quieter eastern half. Its five gleaming doubles sport an understated modern look with white walls, parquet and modern furnishings, while the upstairs quad retains a high wood-beamed ceiling. Book well ahead.

Maria-Rosa Guesthouse B&B €
(Map p404; 338 770 00 67; www.maria-rosa.it; Via dei Vascellari 55; s €53-73, d €66-86, tr €104-124, q €122-142; @❞; Viale di Trastevere, Viale di Trastevere) This delightful B&B on the 3rd floor of a Trastevere townhouse is a home away from home. It's a simple affair with two guest rooms sharing a single bathroom and a small common area, but the sunlight, pot plants and books create a lovely, warm atmosphere. The owner, Sylvie, is a fount of local knowledge and goes out of her way to help. No breakfast.

Villa Della Fonte B&B €€
(Map p404; 06 580 37 97; www.villafonte.com; Via della Fonte dell'Olio 8; s €110-145, d €135-180; ❄❞; Viale di Trastevere, Viale di Trastevere) Near Piazza Santa Maria in Trastevere, this charming B&B occupies an ivy-clad, 17th-century *palazzo*. The five rooms are small but tastefully decorated and there's a sunny garden terrace for alfresco breakfasts.

Eating

Eating out is one of the great joys of visiting Rome and everywhere you go you'll find trattorias, pizzerias, *gelaterie* (ice-cream shops) and restaurants. Traditional Roman cooking holds sway but *cucina creativa* (creative cooking) has taken off in recent years and there are plenty of exciting, contemporary restaurants to try.

The best areas are the historic centre and Trastevere, but there are also excellent choices in San Lorenzo east

413

Inside Terme di Diocleziano (p408), Museo Nazionale Romano, Rome

PAOLO CORDELLI/GETTY IMAGES ©

of Termini and Testaccio. Watch out for overpriced tourist traps around Termini and the Vatican.

Roman specialities include *cacio e pepe* (pasta with pecorino cheese, black pepper and olive oil), *pasta all'amatriciana* (with tomato, pancetta and chilli), *fiori di zucca* (fried courgette flowers) and *carciofi alla romana* (artichokes with garlic, mint and parsley).

The Vatican

Hostaria Dino & Tony   Trattoria €€

(Map p398; 🖉06 397 33 284; Via Leone IV 60; mains €12; ⏱Mon-Sat, closed Aug; MOttaviano-San Pietro) An authentic trattoria in the Vatican area. Kick off with the monumental antipasto before plunging into its signature dish, *rigatoni all' amatriciana*. Finish up with a *granita di caffè* (a crushed ice coffee served with a full inch of whipped cream). No credit cards.

Historic Centre

Casa Coppelle   Modern Italian €€

(Map p404; 🖉06 6889 1707; www.casacoppelle. it; Piazza delle Coppelle 49; meals €35; ⏱lunch & dinner; 🚃Corso del Rinascimento) Exposed brick walls, books, flowers and subdued lighting set the stage for wonderful French-inspired food at this intimate, romantic restaurant. There's a full range of starters and pastas but the real *tour de force* is the steak served with crisp, thinly sliced potato crisps. Book ahead.

Al Gran Sasso   Trattoria €

(Map p404; 🖉06 321 48 83; www.trattoriaalgran sasso.com; Via di Ripetta 32; meals €25; ⏱lunch & dinner Sun-Fri; MFlaminio) The perfect lunchtime spot, this is a classic, died-in-the-wool trattoria. It's a relaxed place with a welcoming vibe, garish murals on the walls (strangely, often a good sign) and tasty country food.

Forno di Campo de' Fiori   Bakery €

(Map p404; Campo de' Fiori 22; pizza slices about €3; ⏱7.30am-2.30pm & 4.45-8pm Mon-Sat; 🚃Corso Vittorio Emanuele II) This is one of Rome's best bakeries, serving bread, panini and delicious straight-from-the-oven *pizza al taglio* (by the slice). Aficionados swear by the *pizza bianca* (white pizza), but the panini and *pizza rossa* (with tomato) are just as good.

Pizzeria da Baffetto   Pizzeria €

(Map p404; ☎06 686 16 17; www.pizzeriabaffetto.it; Via del Governo Vecchio 114; pizzas €6-9; ☺6.30pm-1am; ☐Corso Vittorio Emanuele II) For the full-on Roman pizza experience, get down to this local institution. Meals are raucous, chaotic and fast, but the thin-crust pizzas are spot on and the vibe is fun. To partake, join the queue and wait to be squeezed in wherever there's room. There's also **Baffetto 2 (Map p404; Piazza del Teatro di Pompeo 18; ☺6.30pm-12.30am Mon & Wed-Fri, 12.30-3.30pm & 6.30pm-12.30am Sat & Sun; ☐Corso Vittorio Emanuele II)** near Campo de' Fiori.

Ditirambo   Modern Italian €€

(Map p404; ☎06 687 16 26; www.ristorante ditirambo.it; Piazza della Cancelleria 72; meals €40; ☺closed lunch Mon; ☐Corso Vittorio Emanuele II) This popular new-wave trattoria dishes up a laid-back atmosphere and innovative, organic cooking. The menu changes regularly, but there's always a good choice of vegetarian dishes such as ricotta ravioli with cherry tomatoes and capers. Book ahead.

Trastevere

Trattoria degli Amici   Trattoria €€

(Map p404; ☎06 580 60 33; www.trattoria degliamici.org; Piazza Sant'Egidio 6; mains €15; ☐Viale di Trastevere, ☐Viale di Trastevere) Boasting a prime piazza location, this cheerful trattoria is run by a local charity and staffed by volunteers and people with disabilities who welcome guests with a warmth not always apparent in this touristy neck of the woods. With its outside tables, it's a lovely place to dig into well-prepared Italian classics and enjoy the neighbourhood vibe.

Da Lucia   Trattoria €€

(Map p404; ☎06 580 36 01; Vicolo del Mattinato 2; mains €12.50; ☺Tue-Sun; ☐Viale di Trastevere, ☐Viale di Trastevere) For a real Trastevere experience, search out this terrific neighbourhood trattoria on a hidden cobbled backstreet. It's popular with locals and tourists alike for its authentic Roman soul food, including a fine *spaghetti alla gricia* (with pancetta and cheese). Cash only.

Dar Poeta   Pizzeria €

(Map p404; ☎06 588 05 16; Vicolo del Bologna 46; pizzas from €6; ☺lunch & dinner; ☐Piazza Trilussa) Loud and always busy, this much-loved pizzeria guarantees a bustling, cheery atmosphere and hearty wood-fired pizzas that fall somewhere between wafer-thin Roman pizzas and the softer, doughier Neapolitan version. Expect queues.

Hostaria dar Buttero   Trattoria €€

(Map p404; ☎06 580 05 17; Via della Lungaretta; mains €13; ☺Mon-Sat; ☐Viale di Trastevere, ☐Viale di Trastevere) On Trastevere's quieter eastern side, this is a typical old-school trattoria, attracting a mixed crowd of tourists and Romans. The menu lists all the usual pastas, grilled meats and pizzas (evenings only), but the food is well cooked, the atmosphere is convivial and the prices are right for the area.

Testaccio

Flavio al Velavevodetto   Trattoria €€

(Map p398; ☎06 574 41 94; www.flavioal velavevodetto.it; Via di Monte Testaccio 97-99; meals €30-35; ☺closed Sat lunch & Sun summer; ☐Via Marmorata) This welcoming Testaccio eatery is the sort of place that gives Roman trattorias a good name. Housed in a rustic Pompeian-red villa, complete with intimate covered courtyard and an open-air terrace, it specialises in earthy, no-nonsense Italian food, prepared with skill and served in mountainous portions.

Pizzeria Da Remo   Pizzeria €

(Map p398; ☎06 574 62 70; Piazza Santa Maria Liberatrice 44; pizzas from €5.50; ☺7pm-1am Mon-Sat; ☐Via Marmorata) Remo is one of Rome's most popular pizzerias, its spartan interior always full of noisy young Romans. Tick your order on a sheet of paper slapped down by an overstretched waiter and wait for your huge, sizzling, charred disc. Queues are the norm after 8.30pm.

Below: Different pizza toppings;
Right: St Peter's Square (p403), the Vatican, Rome
(BELOW) SIMON WATSON/GETTY IMAGES ©; (RIGHT) BERNARD JAUBERT/GETTY IMAGES ©

Termini & Esquiline

Trattoria Monti   Ristorante €€
(Map p404; ☏06 446 65 73; Via di San Vito 13a;
meals €45; ◷12.45-2.45pm Tue-Sun, 7.45-11pm
Tue-Sat, closed Aug; Ⓜ Vittorio Emanuele)
Loved by locals and visitors alike, this intimate, arched restaurant – it's a trattoria
in name only – serves top-notch regional
cooking from Le Marche (a hilly region on
Italy's Adriatic coast). Expect exemplary
game stews and pungent truffles, as
well as wonderful fried starters like *olive
ascolane* (fried meat-stuffed olives). Book
for dinner.

Pommidoro   Trattoria €€
(Map p398; ☏06 445 26 92; Piazza dei Sanniti
44; meals €35; ◷Mon-Sat, closed Aug; ☐Via
Tiburtina) Unchanged throughout San
Lorenzo's metamorphosis from working-
class district to bohemian enclave,

century-old Pommidoro is a
much-loved local institution. It
was a favourite of film director Pier
Paolo Pasolini, and contemporary celebs
still stop by, but it's an unpretentious
place with traditional food and magnificent grilled meats.

🍷 Drinking & Nightlife

Rome has plenty of drinking venues,
ranging from neighbourhood hang-outs
to elegant streetside cafes, dressy lounge
bars and Irish-theme pubs.

Caffè Sant'Eustachio   Cafe
(Map p404; Piazza Sant'Eustachio 82; ◷8.30am-
1am Sun-Thu, to 1.30am Fri, to 2am Sat; ☐Corso
del Rinascimento) This small, unassuming
cafe, generally three-deep at the bar, is
famous for its *gran caffè*, said by many
to be the best coffee in town. Created by
beating the first drops of espresso and
several teaspoons of sugar into a frothy
paste, then adding the rest of the coffee,

it's guaranteed to put some zing into your sightseeing.

Open Baladin   Bar
(Map p404; www.openbaladinroma.it; Via degli Specchi 6; ⊙12pm-2am; 🚊Via Arenula) This designer bar is a leading light on Rome's burgeoning beer scene. It's a slick, stylish place with more than 40 beers on tap and up to 100 bottled beers, many produced by Italian artisanal breweries.

La Tazza d'Oro   Cafe
(Map p404; ☎06 679 27 68; Via degli Orfani 84-86; ⊙7am-8pm Mon-Sat, 10.30am-7.30pm Sun; 🚊Via del Corso) A busy, burnished cafe, this is one of Rome's best coffee houses.

Salotto 42   Bar
(Map p404; www.salotto42.it; Piazza di Pietra 42; ⊙10am-2am Tue-Sat, to midnight Sun & Mon; 🚊Via del Corso) On a picturesque piazza facing a 2nd-century Roman temple, this is a hip lounge bar, complete with vintage armchairs, suede sofas and heavy-as-houses designer tomes. Come for the

daily lunch buffet or to hang out with the beautiful people over an aperitif.

Caffè Capitolino   Cafe
(Map p404; Piazzale Caffarelli 4; ⊙9am-7.30pm Tue-Sun; 🚊Piazza Venezia) The stylish rooftop cafe of the Musei Capitolini is a good place for a timeout over a coffee, cool drink or light snack. And you don't need a museum ticket to drink here – it's accessible via an independent entrance on Piazza Caffarelli.

⭐ Entertainment

Rome has a thriving cultural scene, with a year-round calendar of concerts, performances and festivals. In summer, the **Estate Romana** (www.estateromana.comune.roma.it) festival sponsors hundreds of cultural events, many staged in atmospheric parks, piazzas and churches.

Upcoming events are also listed on www.turismoroma.it, www.060608.it and www.auditorium.com.

CLASSICAL MUSIC & OPERA

Auditorium Parco della Musica   Concert Venue

(✆06 8024 1281; www.auditorium.com; Viale Pietro de Coubertin 30; ☐shuttle bus M from Stazione Termini, ☐Viale Tiziano) This Renzo Piano–designed modernist complex is Rome's cultural hub and premier concert venue.

Teatro Olimpico   Theatre

(✆06 326 59 91; www.teatroolimpico.it; Piazza Gentile da Fabriano 17; ☐Piazza Mancini, ☐Piazza Mancini) The Accademia Filarmonica Romana (www.filarmonicaromana.org), one of Rome's major classical music organisations, stages a varied program of classical and chamber music here as well as opera, ballet and contemporary multimedia events.

Teatro dell'Opera di Roma   Opera

(Map p404; ✆06 481 70 03; www.operaroma. it; Piazza Beniamino Gigli; ballet €12-80, opera €17-150; ⏱box office 9am-5pm Mon-Sat, 9am-1.30pm Sun; Ⓜ Repubblica) Rome's premier opera house also stages the city's ballet company. The opera season runs from December to June, with summer performances staged at the **Terme di Caracalla** (Map p398; Viale delle Terme di Caracalla 52; ☐Viale delle Terme di Caracalla).

🅐 Shopping

Rome boasts the usual cast of flagship chain stores and glitzy designer outlets, but what makes shopping here fun is its legion of small, independent shops – historic, family-owned delis, small-label fashion boutiques, artists' studios, neighbourhood markets. For designer clothes head to Via dei Condotti and the area around Piazza di Spagna, while for something more left-field check out the vintage shops and boutiques on Via del Governo Vecchio, around Campo de' Fiori, and in the Monti neighbourhood.

Rome's markets are great places for bargain hunting. The most famous, **Porta Portese** (Map p398; Piazza Porta Portese; ⏱7am-1pm Sun; ☐Viale di Trastevere, ☐Viale

di Trastevere), is held every Sunday morning near Trastevere, and sells everything from antiques to clothes, bikes, bags and furniture.

ℹ Information

Dangers & Annoyances

Rome is not a dangerous city but petty theft can be a problem. Watch out for pickpockets around the big tourist sites, at Stazione Termini and on crowded public transport – the 64 Vatican bus is notorious.

Emergency

Main Police Station (Questura; ✆06 4 68 61; http://questure.poliziadistato.it; Via San Vitale 15; ⏱8.30am-11.30pm Mon-Fri, 3-5pm Tue & Thu)

Medical Services

For problems that don't require hospital treatment call the **Guardia Medica Turistica** (✆06 7730 6650; Via Emilio Morosini 30).

Ospedale Santo Spirito (✆06 6 83 51; Lungotevere in Sassia 1) Near the Vatican; multilingual staff.

Pharmacy (✆06 488 00 19; Piazza Cinquecento 51) There's also a pharmacy in Stazione Termini, next to platform 1, open 7.30am to 10pm.

Policlinico Umberto I (✆06 4 99 71; www. policlinicoumberto1.it; Viale del Policlinico 155) East of Stazione Termini.

Money

Most midrange and top-end hotels accept credit cards, as do most restaurants and large shops. Some cheaper *pensioni,* trattorias and pizzerias only accept cash. Don't rely on credit cards at museums or galleries.

There are money-exchange booths at Stazione Termini and Fiumicino and Ciampino airports.

Tourist Information

For phone enquiries, the Comune di Roma runs a multilingual **tourist information line** (✆060608; www.060608.it; ⏱9am-9pm).

There are tourist information points at **Fiumicino** (Terminal 3, International Arrivals; ⏱8am-7.30pm) and **Ciampino** (International Arrivals, baggage reclaim area; ⏱9am-6.30pm) airports. Also at the following locations across the city, open 9.30am to 7pm (except at Stazione Termini):

Auditorium Parco della Musica (designed by Renzo Piano), Rome

MOCKFORD AND BONETTI/GETTY IMAGES © DESIGNER: RENZO PIANO

Castel Sant'Angelo Tourist Information (Map p404; Piazza Pia; ⏱9.30am-7pm)

Fori Imperiali Tourist Information (Map p404; Via dei Fori Imperiali; ⏱9.30am-7pm; 🖵Via dei Fori Imperiali)

Piazza delle Cinque Lune Tourist Information (Map p404; Piazza delle Cinque Lune; ⏱9.30am-7pm) Near Piazza Navona.

Via Marco Minghetti Tourist Information (Map p404; ⏱9.30am-7pm) Near the Trevi Fountain.

Websites

060608 (www.060608.it) Provides information on sites, shows, transport etc.

Coop Culture (www.coopculture.it) Information and ticketing for Rome's monuments, museums and galleries.

Turismo Roma (www.turismoroma.it) Rome's official tourist website.

Vatican (www.vatican.va) The Vatican's official website.

ℹ Getting There & Away

Air

Rome's main international airport, Leonardo da Vinci (p481), better known as Fiumicino, is on the coast 30km west of the city. The much smaller Ciampino airport (p481), 15km southeast of the city centre, is the hub for low-cost carrier **Ryanair** (☎899 552589; www.ryanair.com).

Boat

Rome's port is at Civitavecchia, about 80km north of Rome.

Ferry bookings can be made at the Termini-based **Agenzia 365** (☎06 474 09 23; www.agenzie365.it; ⏱8am-9pm), at travel agents or online at www.traghettionline.net. You can also buy directly at the port.

Half-hourly trains depart from Roma Termini to Civitavecchia (€5 to €14.50, 40 minutes to one hour). On arrival, it's about 700m to the port (to your right) as you exit the station.

The main ferry companies:

Grimaldi Lines (☎081 49 64 44; www.grimaldi-lines.com) To/from Trapani (Sicily), Porto Torres (Sardinia), Barcelona (Spain) and Tunis (Tunisia).

Tirrenia (☎89 21 23; www.tirrenia.it) To/from Arbatax, Cagliari and Olbia (all Sardinia).

Car & Motorcycle

Driving into central Rome is a challenge, involving traffic restrictions, one-way systems, a shortage of street parking and aggressive drivers.

419

Car Hire

Rental cars are available at the airport and Stazione Termini. As well as international companies:

Maggiore National (www.maggiore.it)

Bici & Baci (☎06 482 84 43; www.bicibaci.com; Via del Viminale 5; ⊙8am-7pm) Near Termini; one of many agencies renting out scooters. Bank on from €19 per day.

Train

Almost all trains arrive at and depart from Stazione Termini.

Train information is available from the Customer Service area on the main concourse to the left of the ticket desks. Alternatively, check www.trenitalia.com, or phone the **Trenitalia Call Centre** (☎89 20 21; ⊙24hr).

Left luggage (1st 5hr €5, 6-12hr per hr €0.70, 13hr & over per hr €0.30; ⊙6am-11pm) is on the lower ground floor under platform 24.

❶ Getting Around

To/From the Airport

Fiumicino

The set taxi fare to the city centre is €48 (valid for up to four people with luggage).

FR1 Train (€8) Connects the airport to Trastevere, Ostiense and Tiburtina stations, but not Termini. Departures from the airport every 15 minutes (hourly on Sunday and public holidays) between 5.58am and 11.28pm; from Ostiense between 5.18am and 10.48pm.

Leonardo Express Train (adult/child under 4 yr €14/free) Runs to/from platform 24 at Stazione Termini. Departures from the airport every 30 minutes between 6.38am and 11.38pm, from Termini between 5.52am and 10.52pm. Journey time is 30 minutes.

Ciampino

The best option is to take one of the regular bus services into the city centre. The set taxi fare is €30.

Cotral Bus (www.cotralspa.it; one way €3.90) Runs 15 daily services to/from Via Giolitti near Stazione Termini. Also buses to/from Anagnina metro station (€1.20) and Ciampino train station (€1.20), where you can get a train to Stazione Termini (€1.30).

SIT Bus (www.sitbusshuttle.com; from airport €4, to airport €6) Regular departures from the airport to Via Marsala outside Stazione Termini between 7.45am and 11.15pm, and from Termini between 4.30am and 9.30pm. Journey time is 45 minutes.

Various flavours of gelato

Detour: Villa d'Este

The town of Tivoli is home to two Unesco-listed sites: Emperor Hadrian's lavish villa (p410) and the equally grand Villa d'Este, a sumptuous Renaissance residence. The villa was originally a Benedictine convent before Lucrezia Borgia's son, Cardinal Ippolito d'Este, transformed it into a pleasure palace in 1550. Later, in the 19th century, the composer Franz Liszt lived and worked here.

More than the villa itself, it's the elaborate gardens and fountains that are the main attraction. Highlights include the **Fountain of the Organ**, an extravagant baroque ensemble that uses water pressure to play music through a concealed organ, and the 130m-long **Avenue of the Hundred Fountains**.

Tivoli is 30km east of Rome and accessible by Cotral bus (€1.30, 50 minutes, every 10 minutes) from Ponte Mammolo metro station. The fastest route by car is on the Rome–L'Aquila autostrada (A24).

Terravision Bus (www.terravision.eu; one way €4) Twice hourly departures to/from Via Marsala outside Stazione Termini. From the airport, services are between 8.15am and 12.15am; from Via Marsala between 4.30am and 9.20pm. Buy tickets at Terracafé in front of the Via Marsala bus stop. Journey time is 40 minutes.

Car & Motorcycle

Most of the historic centre is closed to normal traffic from 6.30am to 6pm Monday to Friday, from 2pm to 6pm Saturday, and from 11pm to 3am Friday to Sunday – see http://muovi.roma.it for details of the capital's limited traffic zones (*zone a traffico limitato;* ZTL).

Parking

Blue lines denote pay-and-display parking spaces with tickets available from meters (coins only) and *tabacchi* (tobacconists). Expect to pay up to €1.20 per hour between 8am and 8pm (11pm in some places). After 8pm (or 11pm) parking is generally free until 8am the next morning. If your car gets towed away, check with the **traffic police** (☎06 676 92 303).

Public Transport

Rome's public transport system includes buses, trams, metro and a suburban train network.

Tickets

Tickets are valid for all forms of transport and come in various forms:

Single (BIT; €1.50) Valid for 100 minutes, during which time you can use as many buses or trams as you like but can only go once on the metro.

Daily (BIG; €6) Unlimited travel until midnight of the day of purchase.

Three-day (BTI; €16.50) Unlimited travel for three days.

Weekly (CIS; €24) Unlimited travel for seven days.

Buy tickets at *tabacchi,* newsstands and from vending machines at main bus stops and metro stations. They must be purchased before you start your journey and validated in the machines on buses, at the entrance gates to the metro or at train stations. Ticketless riders risk an on-the-spot €50 fine.

Children under 10 travel free.

Bus

Buses and trams are run by **ATAC** (☎06 5 70 03; www.atac.roma.it). The main bus station is in front of Stazione Termini on Piazza dei Cinquecento, where there's an **information booth** (Map p404; ⏰7.30am-8pm).

Metro

Rome's two main metro lines, A (orange) and B (blue), cross at Termini, the only point at which you can change from one line to the other.

Take line A for the Trevi Fountain (Barberini), Spanish Steps (Spagna) and Vatican (Ottaviano-San Pietro); line B for the Colosseum (Colosseo).

Trains run between 5.30am and 11.30pm (to 1.30am on Friday and Saturday).

Taxi

Official licensed taxis are white with the symbol of Rome on the doors. Always go with the metered fare, never an arranged price (the set fares to and from the airports are exceptions).

There are major taxi ranks at the airports, Stazione Termini, Largo di Torre Argentina, Piazza della Repubblica and the Colosseum. You can book a taxi by phoning the Comune di Roma's automated taxi line (☎ 06 06 09) or calling a taxi company direct:

La Capitale (☎ 06 49 94)

Radio Taxi (☎ 06 35 70)

Samarcanda (☎ 06 55 51)

NORTHERN ITALY

Italy's well-heeled north is a fascinating area of historical wealth and natural diversity. Bordered by the northern Alps and boasting some of the country's most spectacular coastline, it also encompasses Italy's largest lowland area, the fertile Po valley plain.

Cinque Terre

Liguria's eastern Riviera boasts some of Italy's most dramatic coastline, the highlight of which is the Unesco-listed **Parco Nazionale delle Cinque Terre** (Cinque Terre National Park) just north of La Spezia. Running for 18km, this awesome stretch of plunging cliffs and vine-covered hills is named after its five tiny villages: Riomaggiore, Manarola, Corniglia, Vernazza and Monterosso.

The area's beauty masks its vulnerability; in autumn 2011 heavy rainfall caused severe flooding and mudslides, leaving four people dead. Further problems arose a year later when four Australian tourists were injured by rockfalls on the coast's most popular trail. The villages are now up and running again but several paths remain closed.

It gets very crowded in summer, so try to come in spring or autumn.

◎ Sights & Activities

The Cinque Terre villages are linked by the 9km **Sentiero Azzurro** (Blue Trail; admission with Cinque Terre Card), a magnificent, mildly challenging five-hour trail. At the time of writing, the Sentiero was closed for reconstruction work after the floods in 2011 and rockfalls in 2012. For the latest information check www.parconazionale5terre.it.

🛏 Sleeping & Eating

L'Eremo sul Mare B&B €
(☎ 346 019 58 80; www.eremosulmare.com; d €80-110; ❄) On the Sentiero Azzurro, about a 15-minute steep walk from Vernazza, this charming B&B is set in an idyllic cliffside position. With only three

Riomaggiore village, Cinque Terre
OPIFICIO 42/GETTY IMAGES ©

rooms and stunning sea views, it's a wonderful spot for a romantic escape. Cash only.

Hotel Ca' d'Andrean
Hotel €

(☎0187 92 00 40; www.cadandrean.it; Via Doscovolo 101, Manarola; s €55-75, d €70-105; ❄ 🤝) An excellent family-run hotel offering comfortable rooms and value-for-money in the upper part of Manarola. Rooms are big and cool with tiled floors and unobtrusive furniture; some also have private terraces. Breakfast (€6) is served in the garden. No credit cards.

Dau Cila
Modern Italian €€

(☎0187 76 00 32; www.ristorantedaucila.com; Via San Giacomo 65, Riomaggiore; mains €18; ⏰8am-2am Mar-Oct) Perched within pebble-lobbing distance of Riomaggiore's snug harbour, Dau Cila is a smart restaurant-cum-*enoteca* (wine bar) specialising in excellent local wine and classy seafood such as *paccheri* (large pasta rings) with cuttle fish and red cabbage.

Marina Piccola
Seafood €

(☎0187 76 20 65; www.hotelmarinapiccola.com; Via Lo Scalo 16, Manarola; mains €16, s/d €90/120, half-/full-board per person €90/105; ⏰noon-10:30pm Wed-Mon; ❄ 🤝) Dine on fresh-off-the-boat seafood and house speciality *zuppa di datteri* (date soup) at this popular harbour-side restaurant in Manarola. If you want to stay, the adjoining hotel has small, comfortable rooms.

ℹ Information

The most convenient **information office** (☎0187 92 06 33; ⏰8am-7pm) is at Riomaggiore train station.

ℹ Getting There & Away

Boat

Between July and September, **Golfo Paradiso** (☎0185 77 20 91; www.golfoparadiso.it) operates excursions from Genoa's Porto Antico to Vernazza and Monterosso. These cost €18 one-way, €33 return.

From late March to October, **Consorzio Marittimo Turistico 5 Terre** (☎0187 73 29 87; www.navigazionegolfodeipoeti.it) runs daily

Cinque Terre Card

To walk the Sentiero Azzurro or any other of the Cinque Terre paths, you'll need a Cinque Terre Card. This comes in two forms:

Cinque Terre Card (adult/child 1 day €5/2.50, 2 days €8/4, family card 1/2 days €12.50/20) Available at all park offices.

Cinque Terre Treno Card (adult/child 1 day €10/6, 2 days €19) As for the Cinque Terre Card plus unlimited train travel between La Spezia and the five villages.

ferries between La Spezia and four of the villages (not Corniglia), costing €18 one-way. Return trips are covered by a daily ticket (weekdays/weekends €25/27).

Train

From Genoa Principe (€7.30) and Brignole (€6.60) direct trains run to Riomaggiore (1½ to two hours, 18 daily), stopping at each of the Cinque Terre villages.

Between 4.30am and 11.10pm, one to three trains an hour crawl up the coast from La Spezia to Levanto (€3.30, 30 minutes), stopping at all of the villages en route.

Milan

POP 1.32 MILLION

Few Italian cities polarise opinion like Milan, Italy's financial and fashion capital. Some people love the cosmopolitan, can-do atmosphere, the vibrant cultural scene and the sophisticated shopping; others grumble that the city's dirty, ugly and expensive. Certainly, it lacks the picture-postcard beauty of many Italian towns, but in among the urban hustle are some truly great sights – Leonardo da Vinci's *Last Supper*, the immense Duomo and the world-famous La Scala opera house.

⊙ Sights

Duomo   Cathedral

(www.duomomilano.it; Piazza del Duomo; adult/
reduced Battistero di San Giovanni €4/2, terraces
stairs €7/3.50, terraces lift €12/6, treasury €2;
⊙7am-6.45pm, roof terraces 9am-6pm, baptistry
9.30am-5pm, treasury 9.30am-5pm Mon-Sat;
🚻; Ⓜ Duomo) With a capacity of 40,000
people, this is the world's largest Gothic
cathedral and the third-largest church
in Europe. Commissioned in 1386 to a
florid French-Gothic design and finished
nearly 600 years later, it's a fairytale
ensemble of 3200 statues, 135 spires and
146 stained-glass windows. Climb to the
roof for memorable city views with tickets
bought at the nearby **Duomo Information
Point** (📞02 720 23 375; www.duomomilano.it;
Via dell'Arcivescovado 1; ⊙9am-8.30pm).

Galleria Vittorio
Emanuele II   Shopping Arcade

(Piazza del Duomo; Ⓜ Duomo) Opening onto
Piazza Duomo, the neoclassical Galleria
Vittorio Emanuele is a soaring iron-and-
glass shopping arcade known locally as
il salotto bueno, the city's fine drawing
room. Long-standing Milanese tradition claims you can ward off bad luck by
grinding your heel into the testicles of the
mosaic bull on the floor.

Teatro alla Scala   Opera House

(La Scala; www.teatroallascala.org; Via Filodram-
matici 2) Milan's legendary opera house
hides its sumptuous six-tiered interior
behind a surprisingly severe exterior. You
can peek inside as part of a visit to the
theatre's **Museo Teatrale alla Scala** (La
Scala Museum; 📞02 433 53 521; Largo Ghiring-
helli 1; adult/child €6/4; ⊙9am-12.30pm & 1.30-

Central Milan

⊙ Sights
1 Castello Sforzesco.................................A1
2 Duomo...C3
3 Galleria Vittorio Emanuele II...............C3
4 Musei del Castello...............................A1
5 Museo Teatrale alla Scala...................C2
6 Pinacoteca di Brera............................C1
7 Teatro alla Scala C2

⊕ Activities, Courses & Tours
8 Autostradale...A2

⊗ Eating
9 Peck Delicatessen B3
10 Peck Italian Bar B3

5.30pm) providing there are no performances or rehearsals in progress.

The Last Supper   Mural

(Il Cenacolo Vinciano; ☏ 02 928 00 360; www.cenacolovinciano.net; Piazza Santa Maria delle Grazie 2; adult/reduced/EU child €6.50/3.25/free, plus booking fee €1.50; ⊙ 8.15am-6.45pm Tue-Sun; Ⓜ Cadorna) Milan's most famous tourist attraction – Leonardo da Vinci's mural of *The Last Supper* – is in the Cenacolo Vinciano, the refectory of the **Chiesa di Santa Maria delle Grazie**, west of the city centre. To see it you need to book ahead or take a city tour.

Castello Sforzesco   Castle, Museum

(☏ 02 884 63 700; www.milanocastello.it; Piazza Castello; ⊙ 7am-7pm summer, to 6pm winter; Ⓜ Cairoli) Originally a Visconti fortress, this immense red-brick castle was later home to the Sforza dynasty that ruled Renaissance Milan. Today, it shelters the **Musei del Castello** (www.milanocastello.it; Piazza Castello 3; adult/EU child €3/free; ⊙ 9am-5.30pm Tue-Sun), a series of museums dedicated to art, sculpture, archaeology and music. Entry is free on Friday between 2pm and 5.30pm and on Tuesday, Wednesday, Thursday, Saturday and Sunday between 4.30pm and 5.30pm.

Pinacoteca di Brera   Gallery

(☏ 02 722 63 264; www.brera.beniculturali.it; Via Brera 28; adult/concession/EU child €6/3/free; ⊙ 8.30am-7.15pm Tue-Sun; Ⓜ Lanza) Above the prestigious Brera Academy, this gallery houses Milan's most impressive collection of old masters, including works by Rembrandt, Goya, van Dyck, Titian, Tintoretto and Caravaggio. A highlight is Andrea Mantegna's brutal masterpiece *Cristo morto nel Sepolcro e tre Dolenti* (Lamentation over the Dead Christ).

Tours

Autostradale

(☏ 02 720 01 304; www.autostradale.it; Piazza Castello 1; ⊙ 9.30am Tue-Sun Sep-Jul) runs walking tours (€20) and three-hour multilingual bus tours (€60) that take in the main sights and include entry to *The Last Supper*. Book tickets online or at the Autostradale office.

Sleeping

Milan is a business city, which means hotels are expensive and it can be hard to find a room, particularly when trade fairs are on (which is often). Booking is essential.

Antica Locanda Leonardo   Hotel €€

(☏ 02 480 14 197; www.anticalocandaleonardo.com; Corso Magenta 78; s €80-120, d €90-200; ❄ @ 🛜; Ⓜ Conciliazione) A charming little hotel in a 19th-century *palazzo* near Leonardo's *Last Supper*. Rooms are individually styled but there's a homey feel about the place with period furniture, plush drapes, parquet and pot plants.

Hotel De Albertis   Hotel €€

(☏ 02 738 34 09; www.hoteldealbertis.it; Via De Albertis 7; s €50-100, d €50-160; @ 🛜) Out from the centre in a leafy residential street, this small hotel is a welcoming, family-run affair. There are few frills but rooms are clean and quiet, and breakfast is made with locally sourced organic produce. Take bus 92 from Stazione Centrale or 27 from the Duomo.

⊗ Eating & Drinking

Local specialities include *risotto alla milanese* (saffron-infused risotto cooked in bone-marrow stock) and *cotoletta alla milanese* (breaded veal cutlet).

Piccola Ischia
Pizzeria €

(📞02 204 76 13; Via Morgagni 7; pizzas €3-8; 🕐lunch & dinner Mon, Tue, Thu & Fri, dinner only Sat & Sun) This bustling, boisterous pizzeria brings a touch of Naples to Milan. Everything from the wood-fired pizza to the Campanian potato croquettes and exuberant decor screams of the sunny south. It's hugely popular so book or expect to queue.

Rinomata
Gelateria €

(Ripa di Porta Ticinese; ice creams from €2.50) If dining in Navigli, skip dessert and grab an ice cream from this historic hole-in-the-wall *gelateria*.

Peck Italian Bar
Italian €€

(📞02 869 30 17; www.peck.it; Via Cesare Cantù 3; mains from €16.50; 🕐7.30am-8.30pm Mon-Fri, 9am-8.30pm Sat; ❄; Ⓜ Duomo) Round the corner from the legendary **Peck Delicatessen** (Via Spadari 9), this bar oozes Milanese chic. Black-jacketed waiters serve coffees, wine and a daily dose of pasta to a stylish, sharply dressed crowd.

BQ Navigli
Bar

(Birra Artigianale di Qualità; Via Alzaia Naviglio Grande 44; 🕐6pm-2am) In recent years Italy has been rediscovering the joys of beer and this canal-front bar has a fine selection of local brews ranging from light lagers to dark, hardcore bitters.

🔒 Shopping

For designer clobber head to the so-called Golden Quad, the area around Via della Spiga, Via Sant'Andrea, Via Monte Napoleone and Via Alessandro Manzoni. Street markets are held around the canals, notably on Viale Papiniano on Tuesday mornings and Saturdays.

ℹ Information

There are tourist offices at **Piazza Castello** (📞02 774 04 343; Piazza Castello 1; 🕐9am-6pm Mon-Fri, 9am-1.30pm & 2-6pm Sat, to 5pm Sun) and **Stazione Centrale** (📞02 774 04 318; opposite platform 13, Stazione Centrale; 🕐9am-6pm Mon-Fri, 9am-1.30pm & 2-6pm Sat, to 5pm Sun).

Useful websites include www.visitamilano.it and www.hellomilano.it.

ℹ Getting There & Away

Air
Most international flights fly into Malpensa Airport (p481), about 50km northwest of Milan. Domestic and some European flights use **Linate airport** (LIN; 📞02 7485 2200; www.milanolinate.eu), about 7km east of the city. Low-cost airlines often use **Orio al Serio airport** (BG; 📞035 32 63 23; www.sacbo.it), near Bergamo.

Train
Regular daily trains depart Stazione Centrale for Venice (€36, 2½ hours), Bologna (€40, one hour), Florence (€50, 1¾ hours), Rome (€86, three to 3½ hours) and other Italian and European cities. Note that these prices are for the fast Frecce services.

ℹ Getting Around

To/From the Airport

Malpensa
Malpensa Shuttle (📞02 585 83 185; www.malpensashuttle.it; adult/child €10/5) Buses run to/from Piazza Luigi di Savoia next to Stazione Centrale every 20 minutes between 4.15am and 12.30pm. Buy tickets at Stazione Centrale or the airport. Journey time is 50 minutes.

Malpensa Express (📞02 7249 4494; www.malpensaexpress.it; adult/child €10/5) Trains depart every 30 minutes to Terminal 1 from Stazione Centrale (adult/child €10/5, 45 minutes) and Stazione Nord (adult/child €11/5, 40 minutes).

Linate
ATM (📞800 80 81 81; www.atm.it) Local bus 73 runs from Piazza San Babila every 10 to 15 minutes between 5.30am and 12.30am. Use a regular bus ticket (€1.50).

Starfly (📞02 585 87 237; www.starfly.net; tickets €5) Buses to/from Piazza Luigi di Savoia half-hourly between 5.30am and 10.45pm. Journey time is 30 minutes. Buy tickets at newsstands or on board.

Orio al Serio
Autostradale (📞02 720 01 304; www.autostradale.it; tickets €5) Half-hourly buses to/

TODD KEITH/GETTY IMAGES ©

from Piazza Luigi di Savoia between 4am and 11.30pm. Journey time is one hour.

Orio Shuttle (☎035 33 07 06; www.orioshuttle. com; adult/child €5/3.50, one hour) Runs half-hourly to/from outside Stazione Centrale (one hour) between 3am and 12.15am.

Bus & Metro

Milan's excellent public transport system is run by ATM. Tickets (€1.50) are valid for one underground ride or up to 90 minutes' travel on city buses and trams. A day ticket costs €4.50.

Verona

POP 263,700

Wander Verona's atmospheric streets and you'll understand why Shakespeare set *Romeo and Juliet* here – this is one of Italy's most beautiful and romantic cities. Known as *piccola Roma* (little Rome) for its importance in imperial days, its heyday came in the 13th and 14th centuries when it was ruled by the Della Scala (aka Scaligeri) family, who built *palazzi* and bridges, sponsored Giotto, Dante and Petrarch, oppressed their subjects and feuded with everyone else.

🎯 Sights

The **Verona Card** (www.veronacard.it; 2/5 days €15/20), available from tourist offices, sites and tobacconists, covers city transport and the city's main monuments and churches.

Arena di Verona   Amphitheatre
(www.arena.it; Piazza Brà; adult/reduced/child €6/4.50/free; ⊙1.30am-7.30pm Mon, plus 8.30am-7.30pm Tue-Sun, to 4.30pm on performance days) In the corner of Piazza Brà, the 1st-century pink marble Arena is the third-largest Roman amphitheatre in Italy. And although it can no longer seat 30,000, it still draws sizeable crowds to its summer opera performances.

Casa di Giulietta   Museum
(Juliet's House; ☎045 803 43 03; Via Cappello 23; adult/reduced €6/4.50 or with VeronaCard; ⊙8.30am-7.30pm Tue-Sun, 1.30-7.30pm Mon) Juliet and her lover Romeo were entirely fictional characters but that doesn't stop visitors flocking to this 14th-century *palazzo* to act out their romantic fantasies and add their lovelorn words to the graffiti on the arched gateway.

Piazzas

Piazza

Set over the city's Roman forum, **Piazza delle Erbe** is lined with sumptuous *palazzi* and filled with touristy market stalls. Through the **Arco della Costa**, the quieter **Piazza dei Signori** is flanked by the early Renaissance **Loggia del Consiglio**, aka the Loggia Fra Gioconda, and the **Palazzo del Podestà**, the 14th-century residence of Cangrande I, the most celebrated of the Della Scala rulers. Nearby, the **Arche Scaligere** are the Della Scala family's elaborate Gothic tombs.

Basilica di San Zeno Maggiore

Basilica

(www.chieseverona.it; Piazza San Zeno; adult/child €2.50/free, combined Verona church ticket €6 or VeronaCard; 8.30am-6pm Tue-Sat, 12.30-6pm Sun Mar-Oct, 10am-1pm & 1.30-5pm Tue-Sat, 12.30-5pm Sun Nov-Feb) This masterpiece of Romanesque architecture honours the city's patron saint. Note Mantegna's 1457–59 altarpiece, *Maesta della Vergine* (Majesty of the Virgin), and the 12th-century bronze doors.

🛏 Sleeping

Hotel Aurora

Hotel €€€

(045 59 47 17; www.hotelaurora.biz; Piazza delle Erbe; s €100-160, d €110-240; ❄ 🛜) Gleaming after a recent makeover, this friendly three-star is right in the heart of the action on central Piazza delle Erbe. Rooms, some of which have piazza views, are smart with laminated parquet, polished wood and modern mosaic-tiled bathrooms. Breakfast can be enjoyed on a lovely terrace overlooking the piazza.

Appartamenti L'Ospite

Apartment €€

(045 803 69 94; www.lospite.com; Via XX Settembre 3; apt 1 or 2 people €35-105, apt 2-4 people €40-180; ❄ 🛜) Over the river from the *centro storico*, L'Ospite has six self-contained apartments for up to four people. Simple and bright with fully equipped kitchens, they come with wi-fi and are ideal for families.

🍴 Eating

Al Pompiere

Trattoria €€

(045 803 05 37; www.alpompiere.com; Vicolo Regina d'Ungheria 5; mains €16; Tue-Sat) Near the Casa di Giulietta, this handsome trattoria – think low wooden ceiling, hanging sausages and framed photos – is famed for its vast cheese selection and house-cured *salumi*. Make a meal of the starters with wine by the glass, or fill up on robust meaty mains. Reservations recommended.

Trattoria Al Bersagliere

Trattoria €€

(045 800 48 24; www. trattoriaalbersagliere.it; Via Dietro Pallone 1; mains €11-15; Tue-Sat) With its wood-beamed ceilings and internal courtyard, this much-loved trattoria

Piazza dei Signori, Verona
ALTRENDO TRAVEL/GETTY IMAGES ©

is a lovely place to dine on rustic Veronese cooking such as *pasta e fasoi* (Veneto-style bean soup) and *patissada de Caval con polenta* (stewed horse meat with polenta), a local speciality since the 15th century.

ℹ️ Information

Information, opera tickets and hotel reservations are available at the central **tourist office** (☏ 045 806 86 80; www.tourism.verona.it; Via degli Alpini 9; 🕑9am-7pm Mon-Sat, 10am-4pm Sun) just off Piazza Brà. There's a second **office** (☏ 045 861 91 63; Verona-Villafranca airport; 🕑10am-4pm Mon & Tue, to 5pm Wed-Sat) in the airport arrivals hall.

ℹ️ Getting There & Around

Direct trains connect with Milan (€11.30 to €19, one hour 20 minutes to two hours, three hourly), Venice (€7.40 to €19, 50 minutes to 2¼ hours, half-hourly) and Bologna (€8.90 to €19, 50 minutes to 1½ hours, 20 daily).

Venice

POP 270,900

Venice (Venezia) is a hauntingly beautiful city. At every turn you're assailed by unforgettable images – tiny bridges crossing limpid canals, delivery barges jostling chintzy gondolas, excited tourists posing on Piazza San Marco. Its celebrated sights are legion and its labyrinthine backstreets exude a unique, almost eerie, atmosphere, redolent of dark passions and dangerous secrets. Parts of the Cannaregio, Dorsoduro and Castello *sestieri* (districts) rarely see many tourists, and you can lose yourself for hours in the lanes between the Accademia and train station.

Despite its romantic reputation, the reality of modern Venice is a city besieged by rising tides and up to 20 million visitors a year. This and the sky-high property prices mean that most locals live over the lagoon in Mestre.

Venice's origins date to the 5th and 6th centuries when barbarian invasions forced the Veneto's inhabitants to seek refuge on the lagoon's islands. Initially the city was ruled by the Byzantines

from Ravenna, but in 726 the Venetians went it alone and elected their first doge (duke). Over successive centuries, the Venetian Republic grew into a great merchant power, dominating half the Mediterranean and the trade routes to the Levant – it was from Venice that Marco Polo set out for China in 1271. Decline began in the 16th century and in 1797 the city authorities opened the gates to Napoleon, who, in turn, handed the city over to the Austrians. In 1866, Venice was incorporated into the Kingdom of Italy.

🎯 Sights

Whet your sightseeing appetite by taking *vaporetto* (small passenger ferry) No 1 along the **Grand Canal** lined with rococo, Gothic, Moorish and Renaissance palaces. Alight at Piazza San Marco, Venice's main square.

Piazza San Marco   Piazza
Piazza San Marco beautifully encapsulates the splendour of Venice's past and its tourist-fuelled present. Flanked by the arcaded **Procuratie Vecchie** and **Procuratie Nuove**, it's filled for much of the day with tourists, pigeons and policemen. While you're taking it all in, you might see the bronze *mori* (Moors) strike the bell of the 15th-century **Torre dell'Orologio** (Clock Tower; ☏ 041 4273 0892; www.museiciviciveneziani.it; Piazza San Marco; adult/reduced with Museum Pass €12/7; 🕑tours in English 10am & 11am Mon-Wed, 2pm & 3pm Thu-Sun, in Italian noon & 4pm daily, in French 2pm & 3pm Mon-Wed, 10am & 11am Thu-Sun; 🚤San Marco).

Palazzo Ducale   Museum
(Ducal Palace; ☏ 848 08 20 00; www.palazzoducale.visitmuve.it; Piazzetta San Marco 52; adult/reduced/child incl Museo Correr €16/8/free or with Museum Pass; 🕑8.30am-7pm Apr-Oct, to 5.30pm Nov-Mar; 🚤San Zaccaria) The official residence of the *doges* from the 9th century and the seat of the Republic's government, Palazzo Ducale also housed Venice's prisons. The *doges'* apartments on the 1st floor are suitably lavish, but it's the vast **Sala del Maggiore Consiglio** on the 2nd floor that will really take your breath away. Measuring 53m by 25m, this

Grand Canal

The 3.5km route of *vaporetto* (passenger ferry) No 1, which passes some 50 *palazzi* (mansions), six churches and scene-stealing backdrops featured in four James Bond films, is public transport at its most glamorous.

The Grand Canal starts with controversy: **Ponte di Calatrava** ①, a luminous glass-and-steel bridge that cost triple the original €4 million estimate. Ahead are castle-like **Fondaco dei Turchi** ②, the historic Turkish trading-house that now houses Venice's Museum of Natural History; Renaissance **Palazzo Vendramin** ③, housing the city's casino; and double-arcaded **Ca' Pesaro** ④. Don't miss **Ca' d'Oro** ⑤, a 1430 filigree Gothic marvel.

Points of Venetian pride include the **Pescaria** ⑥, built in 1907 on the site where fishmongers have been slinging lagoon crab for 600 years, and neighbouring **Rialto Market** ⑦ stalls, overflowing with island-grown produce. Cost overruns for 1592 **Ponte di Rialto** ⑧ rival Calatrava's, but its marble splendour stands the test of time.

The next two canal bends could cause architectural whiplash, with Sanmicheli-designed Renaissance **Palazzo Grimani** ⑨ and Mauro Codussi's **Palazzo Corner-Spinelli** ⑩ followed by Giorgio Masari-designed **Palazzo Grassi** ⑪ and Baldassare Longhena's baroque jewel box, **Ca' Rezzonico** ⑫.

Wooden **Ponte dell'Accademia** ⑬ was built in 1930 as a temporary bridge, but the beloved landmark was recently reinforced. Stone lions flank **Peggy Guggenheim Collection** ⑭, where the American heiress collected ideas, lovers and art. You can't miss the dramatic dome of Longhena's **Chiesa di Santa Maria della Salute** ⑮ or **Punta della Dogana** ⑯, Venice's triangular customs warehouse reinvented as a contemporary art showcase. The Grand Canal's grand finale is pink Gothic **Palazzo Ducale** ⑰ and its adjoining **Ponte dei Sospiri (Bridge of Sighs)** ⑱.

LONELY PLANET/GETTY IMAGES ©

Palazzo Grassi
French magnate François Pinault scandalised Paris when he relocated his contemporary art collection here, where there are galleries designed by Gae Aulenti and Tadao Ando.

Ca' Rezzonico
See how Venice lived in baroque splendour at this 18th-century art museum with Tiepolo ceilings, silk-swagged boudoirs and even an in-house pharmacy.

Ponte dell'Accademia

Peggy Guggenheim Collection

Chiesa di Santa Maria delle Salute

Punta della Dogana
Minimalist architect Tadao Ando creatively repurposed abandoned warehouses as galleries, which now host contemporary art installations from François Pinault's collection.

ADAM EASTLAND ITALY/ALAMY ©

DANITA DELIMONT/GETTY IMAGES ©

⭐ Don't Miss
Basilica di San Marco

With its spangled spires, Byzantine domes, luminous mosaics and lavish marble work, Venice's signature church is an unforgettable sight. It was first built to house the corpse of St Mark, but the original chapel was destroyed by fire in 932 and a new basilica was built over it in 1094. For the next 500 years it was a work in progress as successive doges added mosaics and embellishments looted from the East.

Inside, behind the main altar, check out the **Pala d'Oro** (admission €2; ⏱9.45am-5pm Mon-Sat, 2-4.30pm Sun, to 4pm winter), a stunning gold altarpiece decorated with priceless jewels.

Outside in the piazza, the basilica's 99m freestanding **campanile** (Bell Tower; www.basilicasanmarco.it; Piazza San Marco; admission €8; ⏱9am-9pm Jul-Sep, to 7pm Apr-Jun & Oct, 9.30am-3.45pm Nov-Mar; 🚤San Marco) dates from the 10th century, although it collapsed on 14 July 1902 and had to be rebuilt.

NEED TO KNOW
St Mark's Basilica; ☎041 270 83 11; www.basilicasanmarco.it; Piazza San Marco; ⏱9.45am-4.45pm Mon-Sat, 2-4pm Sun & holidays, baggage storage 9.30am-5.30pm; 🚤San Marco

Punta della Dogana €20/15/free; ⏱10am-7pm Wed-Mon; 🚤San Samuele) One of the most impressive buildings on the Grand Canal, the 18th-century Palazzo Grassi provides the dramatic setting for exhibitions and installations by big-name contemporary artists like Jeff Koons and Richard Prince. In 2009, the museum opened a second exhibition space, the **Punta della Dogana** (☎041 271 90 39; www.palazzograssi.it; adult/reduced/child €15/10/free, incl Palazzo Grassi €20/15/free; ⏱10am-7pm Wed-Mon; 🚤Salute).

Venice Discounts

Venice Card (☎041 24 24; www.venicecard.com; adult/junior €39.90/29.90; ☉call centre 8am-7.30pm) Valid for seven days, gives free entry to Palazzo Ducale, 10 civic museums, the 16 churches covered by the Chorus Pass, as well as discounts on exhibitions, concerts and parking. Buy it at tourist offices and HelloVenezia booths.

Venice Card San Marco (☎041 24 24; www.venicecard.com; €24.90) Provides free admission to Palazzo Ducale, three civic museums and three Chorus churches, plus discounts on exhibitions, concerts and parking. Available at tourist offices and HelloVenezia booths.

Museum Pass (Musei Civici Pass; ☎041 240 52 11; www.visitmuve.it; adult/reduced €20/14) Valid for single entry to 10 civic museums, or just the four museums around Piazza San Marco (adult/concession €16/8). Buy it at participating museums or online at www.visitmuve.it or www.veniceconnected.com.

Churches   Church

As in much of Italy, Venice's churches harbour innumerable treasures; unusually, though, you have to pay to get into many of them. The **Chorus Pass** (☎041 275 04 62; www.chorusvenezia.org; adult/reduced/child €10/7/free) gives admission to 16 of the city's most important churches, which otherwise charge adult/reduced €3/1.50.

Scene of the annual Festa del Redentore (Feast of the Redeemer), the **Chiesa del Santissimo Redentore** (Church of the Redeemer; Campo del SS Redentore 194; adult/reduced/child €3/1.50/free or with Chorus Pass; ☉10am-5pm Mon-Sat; 🚤Redentore) was built by Palladio on the island of Giudecca to commemorate the end of the Great Plague in 1577.

At the entrance to the Grand Canal, the 17th-century **Basilica di Santa Maria della Salute** (La Salute; ☎041 241 10 18; www.seminariovenezia.it; Campo della Salute 1b; admission free, sacristy adult/reduced €3/1.50; ☉9am-noon & 3-5.30pm; 🚤Salute) contains works by Tintoretto and Titian. Arguably the greatest of Venetian artists, Titian is buried in the **Basilica di Santa Maria Gloriosa dei Frari** (www.basilicadeifrari.it; Campo dei Frari, San Polo; adult/reduced/child €3/1.50/free or Chorus Pass; ☉9am-6pm Mon-Sat, 1-6pm Sun), near his celebrated *Assunta* (Assumption; 1518).

Islands   Island

The island of **Murano** is the home of Venetian glass. Tour a factory for a behind-the-scenes look at production or visit the **Museo del Vetro** (Glass Museum; ☎041 73 95 86; www.museovetro.visitmuve.it; Fondamenta Giustinian 8; adult/reduced €8/5.50; ☉10am-6pm Apr-Oct, to 5pm Nov-Mar; 🚤Museo) near the Museo *vaporetto* stop. **Burano**, with its cheery pastel-coloured houses, is renowned for its lace. **Torcello**, the republic's original island settlement, was largely abandoned due to malaria and now counts no more than 80 residents. Its not-to-be-missed Byzantine cathedral, the **Basilica di Santa Maria Assunta** (Piazza Torcello; adult/reduced €5/4, incl museum €8/6; ☉10.30am-6pm Mar-Oct, 10am-5pm Nov-Feb; 🚤Torcello), is Venice's oldest.

To get to Murano take *vaporetto* 4.1, 4.2 from San Zaccaria or Fondamente Nove. For Burano take No 12 from Fondamente Nove. Torcello is linked to Burano by *vaporetto* 9.

🏃 Activities

Be prepared to pay through the nose for that quintessential Venetian experience, a **gondola ride**. Official rates start at €80 or €100 from 7pm to 8am – these prices are per gondola (maximum six people). Additional time is charged in 20-minute increments (day/night €40/50). Haggling is unlikely to get you a reduction but you can save money by taking a gondola tour with the tourist office or a reliable tour operator.

Tours

Between April and October, Venice's tourist offices offer a range of tours, including a 35-minute gondola ride (€28 per person), a 40-minute gondola serenade (€40), a 1½-hour city walking tour (€21) and a four-hour trip to Murano, Burano and Torcello (€20).

There are also private outfits running tours, including **TU.RI.VE** (✆041 241 34 22; www.turive.it), which organises itineraries exploring the city's Byzantine heritage (€36) and legends (€20).

Festivals & Events

Carnevale   Carnival
(www.carnevale.venezia.it) Venice's carnival celebrations take over town in the two-week run-up to Ash Wednesday.

Venice Biennale   Art
(www.labiennale.org) An important exhibition of international visual arts. It's held every odd-numbered year from June to November.

Venice International Film Festival   Film
(Mostra del Cinema di Venezia; www.labiennale.org/en/cinema) Italy's top film fest comes to town in late August or early September at the Lido's Palazzo del Cinema.

Regata Storica   Boat Race
(www.regatastoricavenezia.it) Costumed parades precede gondola races

on the Grand Canal; held on the first Sunday in September.

Sleeping

Venice is Italy's most expensive city. It's always advisable to book ahead, especially at weekends, in May and September, and during Carnevale and other holidays.

SAN MARCO

Novecento   Boutique Hotel €€
(✆041 241 37 65; www.novecento.biz; Calle del Dose 2683/84; d €140-300; ❄ 🛜; 🚤Santa Maria del Giglio) Sporting a bohemian-chic oriental look, the Novecento is a real charmer. Its nine individually decorated rooms feature Turkish kilim pillows, Fortuny draperies, carved bedsteads and immaculate designer bathrooms, and its garden is a gorgeous spot for a leisurely breakfast.

PalazzinaG   Boutique Hotel €€€
(✆041 528 46 44; www.palazzinag.com; San Marco 3247; r from €288; ❄ 🛜) Luxury goes hand in hand with a fashionable Philippe

Basilica di Santa Maria della Salute, Venice
OLIVIER LANTZENDÖRFFER/GETTY IMAGES ©

Navigating Venice

Everybody gets lost in Venice. It's impossible not to in a city of 117 islands, 150-odd canals and 400 bridges (only four of which – the Rialto, Accademia, Scalzi and Costituzione – cross the Grand Canal). To make matters worse, Venetian addresses are all but meaningless without detailed walking directions. Instead of a street and civic number, addresses generally consist of no more than the *sestiere* (Venice is divided into six *sestieri* or districts: Cannaregio, Castello, San Marco, Dorsoduro, San Polo and Santa Croce) followed by a long number.

You'll also need to know that in Venice a street is called a *calle, ruga* or *salizada;* beside a canal it's a *fondamenta.* A canal is a *rio,* a filled canal-turned-street a *rio terrà,* and a square a *campo* (Piazza San Marco is Venice's only piazza).

When walking around, the most helpful points of reference are Santa Lucia train station (signposted as *ferrovia*) and Piazzale Roma in the northwest, and Piazza San Marco (St Mark's Square) in the south. The signposted path from the station to Piazza San Marco (Venice's main drag) is a good 40- to 50-minute walk.

Stark design at this Grand Canal boutique hotel. Common areas are lavishly decorated while the light-drenched rooms cleverly use mirrors and white furnishings to maximise space.

DORSODURO

Pensione La Calcina — Hotel €€

(☎ 041 520 64 66; www.lacalcina.com; Fondamenta Zattere ai Gesuati 780, Dorsoduro 780; s €90-170, d €110-310; ❄ 🛜) A historic landmark on the Giudecca canalfront, this centuries-old hotel exudes character. Author John Ruskin stayed here in 1877 (in room 2) and there's an air of quiet gentility about the sunny antique-clad rooms. Out front, the elegant bar/restaurant is a prime spot for a relaxed waterfront meal.

SAN POLO & SANTA CROCE

Oltre il Giardino — Boutique Hotel €€€

(☎ 041 275 00 15; www.oltreilgiardino-venezia.com; Fondamenta Contarini, San Polo 2542; d incl breakfast €180-250; ❄ @; 🚤 San Tomà) Once home to Alma Mahler, the composer's widow, this gorgeous hotel is hidden behind a walled garden full of pomegranate, olive and magnolia trees. Inside, six sharply designed rooms combine mod cons and deftly chosen antiques to stylish effect.

Ca' Angeli — Boutique Hotel €€

(☎ 041 523 24 80; www.caangeli.it; Calle del Traghetto de la Madonnetta 1434, San Polo; d incl breakfast €70-215; ❄ 🛜; 🚤 San Silvestro) 🍃 An elegant choice overlooking the Grand Canal, Ca' Angeli offers tastefully decorated rooms and suites with canal views. Staff are friendly, the organic breakfast is excellent, and wi-fi is free if you book through the hotel's website.

Pensione Guerrato — Inn €€

(☎ 041 528 59 27; www.pensioneguerrato.it; Calle Drio la Scimia 240a, San Polo; d/tr/q incl breakfast €145/165/185; ❄ 🛜; 🚤 Rialto Mercato) Housed in a 13th-century tower near the Rialto market, this hospitable *pensione* has comfortable, good-sized rooms on several floors (no lift) and friendly, helpful owners. Check the website for low-season offers.

CANNAREGIO

Giardino dei Melograni — Guesthouse €€

(☎ 041 822 61 31; www.pardesrimonim.net; Ghetto Nuovo, Cannaregio 2873/c; s €70-100, d €80-160, tr €110-190, q €140-220; ❄ 🛜) Run by Venice's Jewish community, the 'Garden of Pomegranates' is a sparkling new kosher residence. It's wonderfully located on the tranquil Campo Ghetto Nuovo and offers 14 modern white-grey rooms and a courtyard restaurant serving Jewish and Venetian cuisine (€25 for a meal or €30 on Friday night and Saturday lunch).

Hotel Bernardi
Hotel €

(📞 041 522 72 57; www.hotelbernardi.com; SS Apostoli Calle dell'Oca 4366; s €48-72, d €57-90, f €75-130, without bathroom s €25-32, d €45-62; ❄️🛜) Just off Venice's main drag, this excellent budget option has rooms spread over two sites – this, the main hotel, and a nearby annexe. Rooms come in various shapes and sizes but the general look is classic Venetian with chandeliers, wooden beams, rugs and antiques.

🍴 Eating

Venetian specialities include *risi e bisi* (pea soup thickened with rice) and *sarde in saor* (fried sardines marinated in vinegar and onions).

DORSODURO

Ristorante La Bitta
Ristorante €€

(📞 041 523 05 31; Calle Lunga San Barnaba 2753a; meals €30-40; 🕐dinner Mon-Sat; 🚤Ca'

Rezzonico) With its woody bottle-lined interior and attractive internal courtyard, this is a lovely place to enjoy rustic dishes such as *tagliolini con verdure e zenzero* (thin pasta ribbons with vegetables and ginger) and *galletto al peperone* (chicken with peppers). Cash only.

Grom
Gelateria €

(📞041 099 17 51; www.grom.it; Campo San Barnaba 2461; ice cream €2.50-4; 🕐11am-midnight Sun-Thu, to 1am Fri & Sat; 🚼; 🚤Ca' Rezzonico) An ice cream from this Slow Food–rated *galeteria* is the perfect pick-me-up. Seasonal flavours are made with top ingredients from around the world – lemons and almonds from Sicily, chocolate from South America, cinnamon from Sri Lanka. There's a second **Grom (Cannaregio 3844, Ca' d'Oro)** on the main station to San Marco strip near Ca' d'Oro.

SAN POLO & SANTA CROCE

All'Arco
Venetian €

(📞041 520 56 66; Calle dell'Ochialer 436; cicheti €1.50-4; 🕐8am-3.30pm Mon-Sat, plus 6-9pm Apr-Oct, closed Jul & Aug; 🚤Rialto-Mercato) Popular with locals from the nearby Rialto market, this authentic neighbourhood

Piazza San Marco (p429), Venice

ITALY VENICE

osteria serves excellent *cicheti* (typical Venetian bar snacks) and a range of good-quality wine by the glass. Even with copious *prosecco,* hardly any meal here tops €20 or falls short of five stars.

Birraria La Corte   Pizzeria, Ristorante €€
(☎041 275 05 70; www.birrarialacorte.it; Campo San Polo 2168; pizzas €8-13, mains €15) Head to this animated eatery for perfectly cooked pizzas, a buzzing atmosphere and square-side seating on Campo San Polo.

Vecio Fritolin   Venetian €€€
(☎041 522 28 81; www.veciofritolin.it; Calle della Regina 2262, Santa Croce; mains €45-55, tasting menu €55; ⏲noon-2.30pm & 7-10.30pm Wed-Sun, 7-10.30pm Tue; 🚤San Stae) 🌿 Traditionally a *fritolin* was an eatery where diners sat at a communal table and tucked into fried fish. This is the modern equivalent, if considerably smarter and more sophisticated.

Osteria La Zucca   Modern Italian €€
(☎041 524 15 70; www.lazucca.it; Calle del Tintor 1762, Santa Croce; meals €30-45; ⏲12.30-2.30pm & 7-10.30pm Mon-Sat; 🍴; 🚤San Stae) A snug wood-panelled restaurant in an out-of-the-way spot, La Zucca serves a range of innovative Mediterranean dishes. The emphasis is on fresh, seasonal vegetarian dishes, but you can also order classic meat dishes such as duck with green apple or English-style roast beef.

CANNAREGIO

Trattoria da Bepi   Venetian €€
(☎041 528 50 31; Cannaregio 4550; mains €10-20; ⏲Fri-Wed) One of the better eateries on the touristy main drag – actually it's a few metres off it near Santi Apostoli – this is a classic old-school trattoria with a few outside tables and a cheerfully cluttered interior. The food is traditional Venetian with an emphasis on seafood, including an excellent *sarde in saor*.

Anice Stellato   Venetian €€€

(📞 041 72 07 44; Fondamenta della Sensa 3272; mains €18-23; 🕐 noon-2pm & 7.30-11pm Wed-Sun; 🚤 Madonna dell'Orto) 🏷 An inviting trattoria in the little-visited Jewish ghetto that serves huge plates of seafood antipasti, delicious pastas and a super-sized house speciality of fried fish with polenta. Book a table outside by the boats or share a communal table inside.

Fiaschetteria
Toscana   Ristorante €€€

(📞 041 528 52 81; Salizada San Giovanni Grisostomo 5719; mains €22-40, tasting menu €48; 🕐 lunch & dinner Thu-Mon, dinner Wed; 🚤 Ca' d'Oro) This formal, old-fashioned restaurant specialises in classic local cuisine and fresh lagoon seafood, but varies the formula with a few Tuscan triumphs, including delectable Chianina-beef steaks. Tuscan wines feature on the mighty 600-label wine list.

Da Marisa   Trattoria €€

(📞 041 72 02 11; Fondamenta di San Giobbe 652b; lunch set price €15, dinner €35-40; 🕐 lunch daily, dinner Tue & Thu-Sat) Search out this modest family-run trattoria for a taste of authentic Venetian home cooking and sunset views over the lagoon. Expect brusque service and a fixed daily menu, which is mostly meat but sometimes seafood. Reservations recommended. Cash only.

🍷 Drinking & Nightlife

Al Mercà   Wine Bar

(📞 393 992 47 81; Campo Cesare Battisti 213, San Polo; 🕐 9.30am-2.30pm & 6-9pm Mon-Sat; 🚤 Rialto) This hole-in-the-wall bar draws daily crowds for its excellent snacks (meatballs and mini-panini from €1.50) and keenly priced drinks, including top-notch *prosecco* and DOC wines by the glass (from €2).

Cantina Do Spade   Pub

(📞 041 521 05 83; www.cantinadospade.it; Calle delle Do Spade 860, San Polo; 🕐 10am-3pm & 6-10pm; 🚤 Rialto) A warm, woody neighbourhood *osteria* great for a relaxed glass of local wine or a double-malt beer. Keep

441

hunger at bay by snacking on *cicheti* (from €1) such as *sarde fritte* (fried sardines), anchovies and meatballs.

Harry's Bar   Bar

(☎041 528 57 77; Calle Vallaresso 1323; cocktails €12-22; ☺10.30am-11pm; 🚤San Marco) To try a Bellini (white peach pulp and *prosecco*) at the bar that invented them is to follow in prestigious footsteps – Ernest Hemingway, Charlie Chaplin and Orson Welles have all drunk here, and Woody Allen likes to pop in when in town.

Caffè Florian   Cafe

(☎041 520 56 41; www.caffeflorian.com; Piazza San Marco 56/59; drinks €6.50-16; ☺10am-midnight Thu-Tue; 🚤San Marco) With its historic pedigree (it opened in 1720), house orchestra and eye-watering prices (a cappuccino costs €9), Venice's most celebrated cafe is everything you'd expect it be. Byron, Goethe and Rousseau are among the luminaries who have sipped here.

☆ Entertainment

Upcoming events are listed in the free *Shows & Events* guide, available at tourist offices, and at www.veneziadavivere.com. Tickets for most events are sold at **Hello-Venezia ticket outlets** (☎041 24 24; www.hellovenezia.it) in front of the train station, at Piazzale Roma and near key *vaporetto* stops.

Teatro La Fenice   Opera

(☎041 78 65 11; www.teatrolafenice.it; Campo San Fantin 1965; theatre visits adult/reduced €8.50/6, opera tickets from €40; ☺tours 9.30am-6pm) One of Italy's top opera houses, La Fenice hosts a year-round program of opera, ballet and classical music. You can also visit on a guided tour between 9.30am and 6pm most days – check www.festfenice.com for details.

ℹ Information

Emergency

Police Station (☎041 270 55 11; Castello 5053, Fondamenta di San Lorenzo)

Medical Services

Ospedale Civile (☎041 529 41 11; Campo SS Giovanni e Paolo 6777)

Tourist Information

Tourist office (Azienda di Promozione Turistica; ☎041 529 87 11; www.turismovenezia.it) Marco Polo airport (**Marco Polo airport, arrivals hall;** ☺9am-8pm); Piazzale Roma (**Piazzale Roma, ground fl, multistorey car park;** ☺9.30am-2.30pm; 🚤Santa Chiara); Piazza San Marco (**Piazza San Marco 71f;** ☺9am-7pm; 🚤San Marco); Stazione di Santa Lucia (**Stazione di Santa Lucia;** ☺9am-7pm Nov-Mar, 1.30-7pm Apr-Oct; 🚤Ferrovia Santa Lucia); Venice Pavilion (☎041 529 87 11; fax 041 523 03 99; **Venice Pavilion, ex-Palazzina dei Santi, next to the Giardini Ex Reali near St Mark's Square;** ☺9am-6pm)

ℹ Getting There & Away

Air

Most European and domestic flights land at Marco Polo airport (p481), 12km outside Venice. Ryanair flies to **Treviso airport** (TSF; ☎0422 31 51 11; www.trevisoairport.it; Via Noalese 63), about 30km away.

Boat

Venezia Lines (☎041 882 11 01; www.venezialines.com) operates high-speed boats to/from several ports in Croatia between mid-April and early October, including Pola (€69 to €74).

Train

Venice's Stazione di Santa Lucia is directly linked by regional trains to Padua (€3.50, one hour, every 20 minutes) and Verona (€7.40 to €19, 50 minutes to 2¼ hours, half-hourly), and has fast services to/from Bologna, Milan, Rome and Florence. International trains run to/from points in France, Germany, Austria and Switzerland.

ℹ Getting Around

To/From the Airport

To get to/from Marco Polo airport there are several options.

Alilaguna (☎041 240 17 01; www.alilaguna.com; Marco Polo airport) operates three fast-ferry lines (€15/27 one-way/return, approximately half-hourly) – the *Arancio* (Orange) line goes to Piazza San Marco via Rialto and the Grand Canal; the *Blu*

(Blue) line stops off at Murano, the Lido and San Marco; and the *Rosso* (Red) line runs to Murano and the Lido.

There is an **ATVO (Azienda Trasporti Veneto Orientale; ☎ 0421 59 46 71; www.atvo.it)** shuttle bus to/from Piazzale Roma (€6/11 one-way/return, 20 minutes, half-hourly).

Water taxis to/from the train station cost €100 for up to five passengers.

For Treviso airport, there's an ATVO shuttle bus (one-way/return €7/13, 70 minutes, six times daily) to/from Piazzale Roma.

Boat

The city's main mode of public transport is the *vaporetto.* Useful routes include:

1 From Piazzale Roma to the train station and down the Grand Canal to San Marco and the Lido.

2 From San Zaccaria (near San Marco) to the Lido via Giudecca, Piazzale Roma, the train station and Rialto.

4.1 To/from Murano via Fondamente Nove, the train station, Piazzale Roma, Giudecca and San Zaccaria.

9 From Burano to Torcello and vice versa.

Tickets, available from ACTV and HelloVenezia booths at the major *vaporetti* stops, are expensive: €7 for a single trip; €18 for 12 hours; €20 for 24 hours; €25 for 36 hours; €30 for two days; €35 for three days; €50 for seven days.

There are significant discounts for holders of the Rolling Venice Card and all tickets are cheaper if you purchase them online at www. veniceconnected.com.

The poor man's gondola, *traghetti* (€2 per crossing), are used to cross the Grand Canal where there's no nearby bridge.

Bologna

POP 380,200

Boasting a boisterous bonhomie rare in Italy's reserved north, Bologna is one of Italy's great unsung destinations. Its medieval centre, one of Italy's finest, is an eye-catching ensemble of red-brick *palazzi,* Renaissance towers and 40km of arcaded porticos, and there are enough sights to excite without exhausting. A university town since 1088 (Europe's oldest), it is also one of Italy's foremost foodie destinations, home to the eponymous bolognese sauce *(ragù)* as well as *tortellini* (pasta pockets stuffed with meat), lasagne and *mortadella* (aka baloney or Bologna sausage).

Cafe tables and Palazzo Comunale in Piazza Maggiore (p444), Bologna

RUTH EASTHAM & MAX PAOLI/GETTY IMAGES ©

◎ Sights

The city has recently introduced a **Bologna Welcome Card** (€20), available in tourist offices, which gives free entrance to city-run museums, public transport for 24 hours or two tickets for the aiport shuttle bus, and discounts in shops and restaurants.

Piazza Maggiore   Piazza

Pedestrianised Piazza Maggiore is Bologna's showpiece square. Overlooking it are several impressive Renaissance *palazzi* and the Gothic **Basilica di San Petronio** (Piazza Maggiore; ⊙8am-1pm & 3-6pm), the world's fifth-largest church.

To the basilica's west, **Palazzo Comunale** (Bologna's Town Hall) is home to the city's art collection, the **Collezioni Comunali d'Arte** (☎051 20 36 29; Palazzo Comunale; adult/reduced/child €5/3/free; ⊙9am-6.30pm Tue-Fri, 10am-6.30pm Sat & Sun), and the **Museo Morandi** (☎tel, info 051 20 36 29; www.mambo-bologna.org/museomorandi; Palazzo Comunale; adult/reduced €6/4; ⊙11am-6pm Tue-Fri, 11am-8pm Sat & Sun)

dedicated to the work of Giorgio Morandi. At the time of research the Museo Morandi was about to be temporarily transferred to the MAMbo to allow for repair work.

Le Due Torri   Tower

(Torre degli Asinelli admission €3; ⊙Torre degli Asinelli 9am-6pm May-Oct, to 5pm Oct-May) Standing sentinel over Piazza di Porta Ravegnana are Bologna's two leaning towers. You can climb the taller of the two, the 97.6m-high **Torre degli Asinelli**, which was built between 1109 and 1119. The neighbouring 48m-high **Torre Garisenda** is sensibly out of bounds given its drunken 3.2m tilt.

Museo Civico Archeologico   Museum

(Via dell'Archiginnasio 2; adult/reduced/child €5/3/free; ⊙9am-3pm Tue-Fri, 10am-6.30pm Sat & Sun) Impressive in its breadth of historical coverage, this museum displays well-documented Egyptian and Roman artefacts along with one of Italy's best Etruscan collections.

MAMbo   Museum

(Museo d'Arte Moderna di Bologna; www.mambo-bologna-org; Via Don Minzoni 14; adult/reduced/child €6/4/free; ⊙noon-6pm Tue, Wed & Fri, to 10pm Thu, to 8pm Sat & Sun) An excellent modern-art museum in a converted bakery.

🛏 Sleeping

Il Convento dei Fiori di Seta

Boutique Hotel €€€

(☎051 27 20 39; www.silkflowersnunnery.com; Via Orfeo 34; r €140-420, ste €250-520; ❀ ☏) This seductive boutique hotel is a model of sophisticated design. Housed in a 15th-century convent, it features contemporary furniture juxtaposed

Basilica di San Petronio, Bologna
RUSSELL MOUNTFORD/GETTY IMAGES ©

Detour:
The Dolomites

A Unesco Natural Heritage site since 2009, the Dolomites stretch across the northern regions of **Trentino-Alto Adige** and the **Veneto**. Their stabbing sawtooth peaks and vertiginous walls provide thrilling scenery and superb sport.

Ski resorts abound, offering downhill and cross-country skiing as well as snowboarding and other winter sports. Hiking opportunities run the gamut from kid-friendly strolls to hard-core mountain treks. Recommended areas include the **Alpe di Siusi**, a vast plateau above the Val Gardena; the area around Cortina; and the **Pale di San Martino**, a highland plateau accessible by cable car from **San Martino di Castrozza**.

Tourist offices in individual resorts can provide local advice, but for area-wide information contact the offices in **Trento** (✆0461 21 60 00; www.apt.trento.it; Via Manci 2; ☺9am-7pm) and **Bolzano** (✆0471 30 70 00; www.bolzano-bozen.it; Piazza Walther 8; ☺9am-7pm Mon-Fri, 9.30am-6pm Sat). The best online resource is www.dolomiti.org.

Most places are accessible by bus, with services run by **Trentino Trasporti** (✆0461 82 10 00; www.ttesercizio.it) in Trento; **SAD** (✆0471 45 01 11; www.sad.it) in Alto Adige; and **Dolomiti Bus** (✆0437 21 71 11; www.dolomitibus.it) in the Veneto. During winter, most resorts also offer 'ski bus' services.

against exposed brick walls and religious frescos, Mapplethorpe-inspired flower motives and mosaic-tiled bathrooms.

Albergo delle Drapperie   Hotel €
(✆051 22 39 55; www.albergodrapperie.com; Via delle Drapperie 5; s/d €70/85; ❄ 🛜) Bed down in the heart of the atmospheric Quadrilatero district at this welcoming three-star. Rooms, which all differ slightly, are attractive with wood-beamed ceilings, wrought-iron beds and the occasional brick arch. Breakfast costs €5 extra and wi-fi €2. At a second site, the **Residence delle Drapperie** (✆051 22 39 55; www.residencedrapperie.com; Via Galliera 48; apt from €55) has 10 mini-apartments for stays of two nights or more.

 Eating

Osteria de' Poeti   Ristorante €€
(www.osteriadepoeti.com; Via de' Poeti 1b; mains €12; ☺7:30pm-3am Tue-Sat , 12:30-2:30pm Sun) In the wine cellar of a 14th-century *palazzo*, this historic eatery is a bastion of old-style service and classic local cuisine.

Il Saraceno   Ristorante €€
(✆051 23 66 28; www.ristorantesaraceno bologna.com; Via Calcavinazzi 2; pizzas from €5, mains €12-20) Popular with lunching locals, this is a good all-purpose eatery just off central Via Ugo Basso.

Trattoria del Rosso   Trattoria €
(✆051 23 67 30; www.trattoriadelrosso.com; Via A Righi 30; daily menu €10, mains €7.50-10; ☺noon-11pm) The oldest trattoria in town is the perfect place for a cheap lunchtime fill-up. Sit down to filling pastas and honest journeyman's fare, cooked simply and served fast.

🍷 Drinking & Nightlife

Café de Paris   Bar
(Piazza del Francia 1c; ☺7.30am-3am Mon-Sat, 4pm-3am Sun) Modish bar with daily aperitifs between 7.30pm and 9.30pm.

Caffè degli Orefici   Cafe
(Via Orefici 6; ☺Mon-Sat) A modern cafe next to a historic coffee shop.

🛈 Information

🛈 Getting There & Around

Air

European and domestic flights serve **Guglielmo Marconi airport** (☎051 647 96 15; www.bologna-airport.it), 6km northwest of the city. From the airport, an Aerobus shuttle (€6, 30 minutes, every 15 to 30 minutes) connects with the main train station; tickets can be bought on board.

Train

From the central train station on Piazza delle Medaglie d'Oro, fast trains run to Venice (€30, 1½ hours, hourly), Florence (€24 to €36, 40 minutes, half-hourly), Rome (€56 to €81, 2½ hours, half-hourly) and Milan (€32 to €40, one to two hours, hourly).

TUSCANY

Tuscany is one of those places that well and truly lives up to its hype. The fabled landscape of rolling, vine-covered hills dotted with cypress trees and stone villas has long been considered the embodiment of rural chic, and its historically intact cities are home to a significant portfolio of the world's medieval and Renaissance art.

Florence

POP 371,300

Visitors have rhapsodised about the beauty of Florence (Firenze) for centuries, and once here you'll appreciate why. An essential stop on every Italian itinerary, this Renaissance time capsule is busy year-round, but even the enormous and inevitable crowds of tourists fail to diminish its lustre. A list of the city's famous sons reads like a Renaissance who's who – under 'M' alone you'll find Medici, Machiavelli and Michelangelo – and its treasure trove of galleries, museums and churches showcases a magnificent array of Renaissance artworks.

Though it was a rich merchant city by the 12th century, Florence's golden age took a bit longer to arrive, and did so under the auspices of the Medici family. They ruled the city between the 14th and 17th centuries and their visionary patronage of writers, artists and thinkers culminated in the Renaissance.

🎯 Sights

Piazza del Duomo & Around *Church*

(Cattedrale di Santa Maria del Fiore; www.opera duomo.firenze.it; ⊙10am-5pm Mon-Wed & Fri, to 4pm Thu, to 4.45pm Sat, 1.30-4.45pm Sun) **FREE** Photographs don't do justice to the exterior of Florence's Gothic **Duomo** (Cattedrale di Santa Maria del Fiore or St Mary of the Flower; www.operaduomo.firenze.it; Piazza del Duomo; admission dome/crypt/campanile €8/3/6; ⊙10am-5pm Mon-Wed & Fri, to 4pm Thu, to 4.45pm Sat, 1.30-4.45pm Sun; dome 8.30am-6.20pm Mon-Fri, to 5pm Sat; crypt 10am-5pm Mon-Wed & Fri, to 4pm Thu, to 4.45pm Sat; campanile 8.30am-6.50pm). While they reproduce the startling colours of the tiered red, green and white marble facade and the beautiful symmetry of the dome, they fail to give any real sense of its monumental size and its importance as the city's major landmark. Officially known as the Cattedrale di Santa Maria del Fiore, the building's construction began in 1294 but the cathedral itself wasn't consecrated until 1436. Construction of the enormous octagonal **Cupola**, was overseen by Brunelleschi after his design won a public competition in 1420. There's a magnificent view from the top of the cupola, but the climb is steep (463 steps) and also extremely cramped in places, so it's best avoided if you are unfit or claustrophobic.

The cathedral's interior is decorated with frescos by Vasari and Zuccari, and the stained-glass windows are by Donatello, Paolo Uccello and Lorenzo Ghiberti. The facade is a 19th-century replacement of the unfinished original, pulled down in the 16th century.

JUERGEN RICHTER/GETTY IMAGES ©

⭐ Don't Miss
Galleria degli Uffizi

This magnificent gallery safeguards the Medici family's private art collection, which was bequeathed to the city in 1743 on the condition that it never leaves Florence. It occupies the Palazzo degli Uffizi, a handsome structure built between 1560 and 1580 to house government offices.

A major refurbishment and redevelopment of the gallery was under way as this book went to print. The completion date was uncertain, although nine new exhibition rooms opened in mid-2012 and remaining works are progressing.

The gallery is home to the world's greatest collection of Italian Renaissance art. Highlights include Simone Martini's shimmering *Annunciation* (room 3); Piero della Francesca's famous profile portraits of the Duke and Duchess of Urbino (room 7); Botticelli's *Birth of Venus* and *Allegory of Spring* (Primavera; rooms 10 to 14); Leonardo da Vinci's *Annunciation* (room 15); and Michelangelo's *Holy Family* (room 25). Allow at least four hours for your visit.

For a break, head to the gallery's rooftop cafe. Members of the Medici family once congregated here to watch events in the Piazza della Signoria.

NEED TO KNOW
Uffizi Gallery; www.uffizi.firenze.it; Piazzale degli Uffizi 6; adult/reduced €6.50/3.25, incl temporary exhibition €11/5.50; ⊗8.15am-6.05pm Tue-Sun

The design of the 82m **Campanile (bell tower;** ☎055 230 28 85; www.operaduomo.firenze.it; Piazza del Duomo; adult €7; ⊗9am-6pm) was begun by Giotto in 1334 and completed after his death by Andrea Pisano and Francesco Talenti. The views from the top make the 414-step climb worthwhile.

●●●
The Uffizi

Journey into the Renaissance

Navigating the Uffizi's main art collection, chronologically arranged in 45 rooms on one floor, is straightforward; knowing which of the 1500-odd masterpieces to view before gallery fatigue strikes is not. Swap coat and bag (travel light) for floor plan and audioguide on the ground floor, then meet 16th-century Tuscany head-on with a walk up the *palazzo's* magnificent bust-lined staircase (skip the lift – the Uffizi is as much about masterly architecture as art).

Allow four hours for this journey into the High Renaissance. At the top of the staircase, 2nd floor, show your ticket, turn left and pause to admire the full length of the First Corridor sweeping south towards the Arno river. Then duck left into room 2 to witness first steps in Tuscan art – shimmering altarpieces by **Giotto** ❶ et al. Journey through medieval art to room 8 and **Piero della Francesca's** ❷ impossibly famous portrait, then break in the corridor with playful **ceiling art** ❸. Backtrack through room 8 to room 9 and beyond to **Botticelli** ❹ and **da Vinci** ❺. Pause to admire the **Tribuna** ❻, then enjoy the daylight streaming in through the vast windows and panorama of the riverside **Second Corridor** ❼. Lap up soul-stirring views of the Arno, crossed by Ponte Vecchio and its echo of four bridges drifting towards the Apuane Alps on the horizon. Then saunter into the third corridor, pausing between rooms 25 and 34 to ponder the entrance to the enigmatic Vasari Corridor. End on a high with High Renaissance maestro **Michelangelo** ❽.

THE ART ARCHIVE/ALAMY ©

The Ognissanti Madonna
Room 2

Draw breath at the shy blush and curvaceous breast of Giotto's humanised Virgin (*Maestà*; 1310) – so feminine compared with those of Duccio and Cimabue painted just 25 years before.

Portraits of the Duke & Duchess of Urbino
Room 8

Revel in realism's voyage with these uncompromising, warts-and-all portraits (1472–75) by Piero della Francesca. No larger than A3 size, they originally slotted into a portable, hinged frame that folded like a book.

Start of Vasari Corridor (linking the Palazzo Vecchio with the Uffizi and Palazzo Pitti)

Entrance to 2nd Floor Gallery

Palazzo Vecchio

Piazza della Signoria

Grotesque Ceiling Frescoes
First Corridor

Take time to study the make-believe monsters and most unexpected of burlesques (spot the arrow-shooting satyr outside room 15) waltzing across this eastern corridor's fabulous frescoed ceiling (1581).

IMAGE REPRODUCED WITH THE PERMISSION OF MINISTERO PER I BENI E LE ATTIVITÀ CULTURALI

ALINARI ARCHIVES, FLORENCE ©

The Genius of Botticelli
Room 10–14

The miniature form of *The Discovery of the Body of Holofernes* (c 1470) makes Botticelli's early Renaissance masterpiece all the more impressive. Don't miss the artist watching you in *Adoration of the Magi* (1475), left of the exit.

View of the Arno

Indulge in intoxicating city views from this short glassed-in corridor – an architectural masterpiece. Near the top of the hill, spot one of 73 outer towers built to defend Florence and its 15 city gates below.

Second Corridor

Tribuna

⑥

First Corridor

⑤

④

③

②

①

⑦

Arno River

⑧

Tribuna

No room in the Uffizi is so tiny or so exquisite. It was created in 1851 as a 'treasure chest' for Grand Duke Francesco and in the days of the Grand Tour, the Medici Venus here was a tour highlight.

Entrance to Vasari Corridor

Third Corridor

> **Matter of Fact**
>
> The Uffizi collection spans the 13th to 18th centuries, but its 15th- and 16th-century Renaissance works are second to none.

Doni Tondo
Room 35

The creator of *David*, Michelangelo, was essentially a sculptor and no painting expresses this better than *Doni Tondo* (1506–08). Mary's muscular arms against a backdrop of curvaceous nudes are practically 3D in their shapeliness.

Annunciation
Room 15

Admire the exquisite portrayal of the Tuscan landscape in this painting (c 1472), one of few by Leonardo da Vinci to remain in Florence.

> **Value Lunchbox**
>
> Try the Uffizi rooftop cafe or – better value – gourmet *panini* at 'Ino (www .ino-firenze .com; Via dei Georgofili 3-7r).

Florence

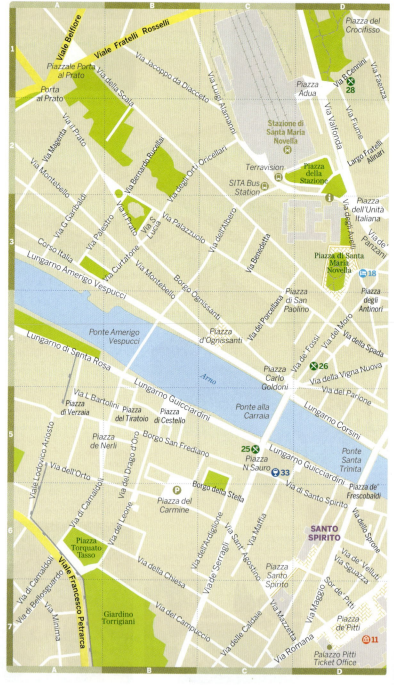

Piazza del Crocifisso

Viale Belfiore

Viale Fratelli Rosselli

Via Jacoppo da Diacceto

Piazzale Porta al Prato

Via della Scala

Porta al Prato

Via B Cennini

Via Faenza

Piazza Adua

28

Via Luigi Alamanni

Via Valfonda

Via Fiume

Via il Prato

Via Magenta

Via Montebello

Via Bernardo Rucellai

Via degli Orti Oricellari

Stazione di Santa Maria Novella

Terravision

SITA Bus Station

Largo Fratelli Alinari

Piazza della Stazione

Via S. Lucia

Via il Prato

Via Palestro

Via Palazzuolo

Via dell'Albero

Piazza dell'Unità Italiana

Via degli Avelli

Via de' Panzani

Corso Italia

Via G Garibaldi

Via Curtatone

Via Montebello

Via Benedetta

Piazza di Santa Maria Novella

18

Lungarno Amerigo Vespucci

Borgo Ognissanti

Via del Porcellana

Piazza di San Paolino

Piazza degli Antinori

Ponte Amerigo Vespucci

Piazza d'Ognissanti

Arno

Piazza Carlo Goldoni

Via de' Fossi

Via del Moro

Via della Spada

26

Lungarno di Santa Rosa

Lungarno Guicciardini

Via della Vigna Nuova

Via del Parione

Via L Bartolini

Piazza di Verzaia

Piazza del Tiratoio

Piazza di Cestello

Ponte alla Carraia

Lungarno Corsini

Viale Lodovico Ariosto

Piazza de Nerli

Borgo San Frediano

25

Lungarno Guicciardini

Ponte Santa Trinita

Via dell'Orto

Via del Drago d'Oro

Piazza N Sauro

33

Via di Santo Spirito

Piazza de' Frescobaldi

Via di Camaldoli

Via del Leone

Borgo della Stella

P

Piazza del Carmine

Via dell'Ardiglione

Via Sant'Agostino

Via Maffia

SANTO SPIRITO

Via dello Sprone

Via de' Velluti

Via Sguazza

Via di Camaldoli

Via di Bellosguardo

Via Minima

Viale Francesco Petrarca

Piazza Torquato Tasso

Via della Chiesa

Via de' Serragli

Via del Campuccio

Giardino Torrigiani

Via delle Caldaie

Piazza Santo Spirito

Via Mazzetta

Via Maggio

Via Sdrucciolo de' Pitti

Via Romana

Piazza de' Pitti

11

Palazzo Pitti Ticket Office

450

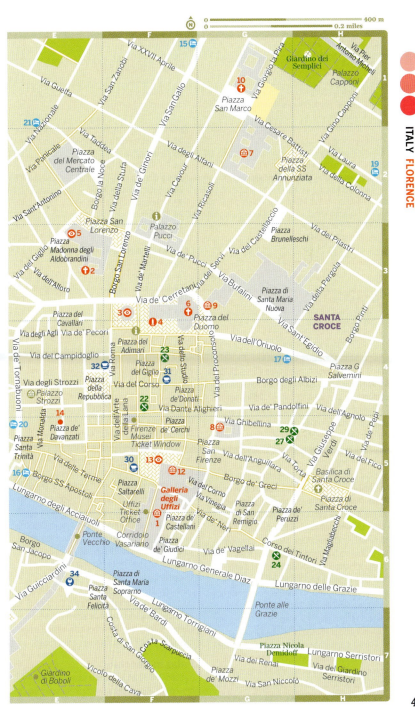

Florence

◉ Don't Miss Sights
1 Galleria degli Uffizi F6

◉ Sights
2 Basilica di San Lorenzo...........................E3
3 Battistero di San Giovanni....................F3
4 Campanile..F4
5 Cappelle Medicee..E3
6 Duomo..F3
7 Galleria dell'Accademia G2
8 Museo del Bargello..................................G5
9 Museo dell'Opera di Santa Maria
   del Fiore..G3
10 Museo di San Marco.................................G1
11 Palazzo Pitti.. D7
12 Palazzo Vecchio..F5
13 Piazza della Signoria F5

◔ Activities, Courses & Tours
14 Art Viva...E5

◔ Sleeping
15 Antica Dimora Johlea................................F1
16 Hotel Cestelli..E5

17 Hotel Dalí...G4
18 Hotel L'O..D3
19 Hotel Morandi alla
   Crocetta..H2
20 Hotel Scoti...E5
21 Sette Angeli Rooms...................................E1

✖ Eating
22 Cantinetta dei Verrazzano F4
23 Coquinarius...F4
24 Del Fagioli..G6
25 La Carraia..C5
26 L'Osteria di Giovanni...............................D4
27 Osteria del Caffè Italiano........................G5
28 Trattoria I Due G..D1
29 Vivoli...H5

◔ Drinking & Nightlife
30 Caffè Rivoire.. F5
31 Chiaroscuro..F4
32 Gilli...F4
33 Il Santino..C5
34 Le Volpi e l'Uva...E6

The Romanesque **Battistero** (Baptistry; Piazza di San Giovanni; admission €5; ⏱11.15am-6.30pm Mon-Sat, 8.30am-1.30pm Sun & 1st Sat of month) is one of the oldest buildings in Florence. Built on the site of a Roman temple between the 5th and 11th centuries, it's famous for its gilded-bronze doors, particularly Lorenzo Ghiberti's *Gate of Paradise*.

Surprisingly overlooked by the crowds, the **Museo dell'Opera di Santa Maria del Fiore** (Cathedral Museum; www.operaduomo. firenze.it; Piazza del Duomo 9; admission €6, combined with campanile €10, with cathedral dome €11; ⏱9am-6.50pm Mon-Fri, 9am-1pm Sat & Sun) safeguards treasures that once adorned the Duomo, Battistero and Campanile and is one of the city's most impressive museums. Its collection includes Ghiberti's *Gate of Paradise* panels (those on the Baptistry doors are copies) and a Pietà by Michelangelo.

Three cumulative tickets are available: €11 for entrance to the Cupola and the Museo dell'Opera di Santa Maria del Fiore; €15 for the Campanile, Battistero and Museo; and €23 for every Duomo

sight (valid four days). All can be purchased at the ticket desk at the Museo.

Piazza della Signoria   Piazza

(Piazza della Signoria) The city's most splendid piazza was created in the 13th century and has been the hub of Florentine political and social life ever since. It is home to the Palazzo Vecchio as well as the Loggia dei Lanzi, an open-air showcase of sculpture from the 14th and 16th centuries – look for Giambologna's *Rape of the Sabine Women* and Agnolo Gaddi's *Seven Virtues*. The loggia is named after the *Lanzichenecchi* (Swiss Guards) who were stationed here during the rule of Cosimo I.

Other statues in the piazza include a copy of Michelangelo's *David* (the original is in the Galleria dell'Accademia) and Cellini's *Perseus,* which shows the Greek hero holding Medusa's severed head.

Palazzo Vecchio   Museum

(☎055 276 82 24; www.palazzovecchio-family-museum.it; Piazza della Signoria; museum adult/

reduced/ €6.50/4.50, tower €6.50, combined ticket €10; ⊙ museum 9am-midnight Fri-Wed, 9am-2pm Thu summer, 9am-7pm Fri-Wed, 9am-2pm Thu winter; tower 9am-9pm Fri-Wed, 9am-2pm Thu summer, 10am-5pm Fri-Wed, 10am-2pm Thu winter) Built between 1298 and 1340 for the Signoria, the highest level of Florentine republican government, this palace became the residence of Cosimo I in the 16th century. It remains the mayor's office today.

The series of lavish apartments created for the Medici is well worth seeing, as is the **Salone dei Cinquecento** (16th-Century Room), created within the original building in the 1490s to accommodate the Consiglio dei Cinquecento (Council of Five Hundred) that ruled Florence at the end of the 15th century.

The best way to visit is on a guided tour. These cost a mere €2 (or €1 per tour if two or more are taken on the same day). Book in advance at the ticket desk, by telephone or by email.

Museo del Bargello   Art Museum
(www.polomuseale.firenze.it; Via del Proconsolo 4; adult/reduced €4/2, incl temporary exhibition €6/3; ⊙ 8.15am-4.20pm Tue-Sun & 1st & 3rd Mon of month, to 2pm winter) Home to Italy's most comprehensive collection of Tuscan Renaissance sculpture, the Bargello features Donatello's two versions of *David* (one in marble and the other in bronze) plus a number of important early works by Michelangelo.

Palazzo Pitti   Museum
(www.polomuseale.firenze.it; Piazza Pitti; ticket one adult/EU 18-25 yr/EU child & senior €8.50/4.25/free, ticket two €7/3.50/free, ticket three €11.50/5.75/free; ⊙ 8.15am-6.50pm Tue-Sun summer, shorter hrs winter) Originally commissioned by the Pitti family, great rivals of the Medici, this vast 15th-century palace was acquired by Cosimo I and Ele-onoradi Toledo in 1549 and became the Medici family residence. It remained the official residence of Florence's rulers until 1919, when the Savoys gave it to the state.

Today it houses four museums, of which the **Galleria Palatina** is the most important. Works by Raphael, Botticelli, Caravaggio, Filippo Lippi, Titian and Rubens adorn its lavishly decorated rooms, culminating in the **Appartamenti Reali** (Royal Apartments), which retain their late-19th-century decoration. Three

Duomo (p446), Florence

Cutting the Queues

Sightseeing in Florence can entail hours spent in queues. Fortunately, there are two ways of saving time – one of which can also save you money.

For €4 extra per museum you can book tickets for the Uffizi and Galleria dell'Accademia (the museums with the longest queues) through **Firenze Musei** (Florence Museums; ☎ 055 29 48 83; www.firenzemusei.it; ⏰ telephone booking line 8.30am-6.30pm Mon-Fri, 8.30am-12.30pm Sat). Book online in advance, or purchase tickets in person before your visit from the ticket desks at the Palazzo Pitti, Museo di San Marco or at the rear of the Chiesa di Orsanmichele.

If you are planning to visit most of the major museums, consider purchasing a **Firenze Card** (www.firenzecard.it; adult €72). These are valid for 72 hours, allow the holder to bypass both advance booking and queues, and also give free entry to one accompanying child under 18 (EU citizens only). Cards can be purchased online, at the tourist information offices opposite Stazione Santa Maria Novella and in Via Cavour, and at the ticket desks at the Palazzo Pitti, Palazzi Vecchio and Galleria degli Uffizi (door 2).

other museums – the **Museo degli Argenti** (Medici Treasury), **Galleria d'Arte Moderna** (Gallery of Modern Art) and **Galleria del Costume** (Costume Gallery) – are located within the palace buildings.

Behind the palace are the **Boboli Gardens** (Giardino di Boboli) and the adjacent **Bardini Gardens** (Giardino di Bardini).

Ticketing can be confusing: ticket one gives entrance to the Galleria Palatina, Appartamenti Reali and Galleria d'Arte Moderna; ticket two gives entrance to the Museo degli Argenti and Galleria del Costume, plus the Boboli and Bardini Gardens; and ticket three gives entrance to all museums and gardens and is valid for three days.

Galleria dell'Accademia   Art Museum
(www.polomuseale.firenze.it; Via Ricasoli 60; adult/reduced €6.50/3.25; ⏰ 8.15am-6.50pm Tue-Sun) Expect a lengthy queue when visiting the home of Michelangelo's *David*. Fortunately, the most famous statue in the world is well worth the wait. Carved from a single block of marble, the nude warrior assumed his pedestal in the Piazza della Signoria in 1504, providing Florentines with a powerful emblem of power, liberty and civic pride. The statue was moved here in 1873.

Adjacent rooms contain paintings by Andrea Orcagna, Taddeo Gaddi, Domenico Ghirlandaio, Filippino Lippi and Sandro Botticelli.

Basilica di San Lorenzo   Church
(Piazza San Lorenzo; admission €4.50, with Biblioteca Medicea Laurenziana €7; ⏰ 10am-5.30pm Mon-Sat, plus 1.30-5pm Sun Mar-Oct) One of the city's finest examples of Renaissance architecture, this basilica was designed by Brunelleschi in the 15th century and includes his austerely beautiful **Sagrestia Vecchia** (Old Sacristy), which features sculptural decoration by Donatello.

Cappelle Medicee   Mausoleum
(☎ 055 294 883; www.polomuseale.firenze.it; Piazza Madonna degli Aldobrandini; adult/reduced €6/3; ⏰ 8.15am-1.20pm, closed 2nd & 4th Sun & 1st, 3rd & 5th Mon of month) Principal burial place of the Medici rulers, this mausoleum is home to the stark but graceful **Sagrestia Nuova** (New Sacristy), Michelangelo's first architectural work and the showcase for three of his most haunting sculptures: *Dawn and Dusk, Night and Day* and *Madonna and Child*.

Museo di San Marco
Church, Museum

(www.polomuseale.firenze.it; Piazza San Marco 1; adult/reduced €4/2; ⏱8.15am-1.50pm Mon-Fri, 8.15am-4.50pm Sat & Sun, closed 1st, 3rd & 5th Sun & 2nd & 4th Mon of month) Housed in a Dominican monastery, this spiritually uplifting museum is a showcase of the work of Fra' Angelico, who decorated the cells with deeply devotional frescos to guide the meditation of his fellow friars. His most famous work, *Annunciation* (c 1450), is at the top of the stairs that lead to the cells.

 Tours

Freya's Florence Tours Walking Tour
(☎349 074 89 07; www.freyasflorence.com; per hr €70) A knowledgeable and enthusiastic Australian-born, Florence-based private tour guide; you'll pay admission fees on top of the guiding fee.

Art Viva Walking Tour
(☎055 264 50 33; www.italy.artviva.com; Via de' Sassetti 1; tours per person from €25) The Artviva outfit offers a range of city tours, all led by English-speaking guides.

🎖 Festivals & Events

Scoppio del Carro Easter
A cart of fireworks is exploded in front of the cathedral at 11am on Easter Sunday – get there at least two hours early to grab a good position.

Maggio Musicale Fiorentino Arts
(www.maggiofiorentino. com) Italy's oldest arts festival is held in the Teatro del Maggio Musicale Fiorentino and stages performances of theatre, classical music, jazz and dance; April to June.

Festa di San Giovanni Midsummer
Florence celebrates its patron saint, John, with a *calcio storico* (historical football) match on Piazza di Santa Croce and fireworks over Piazzale Michelangelo; 24 June.

🛏 Sleeping

Although there are hundreds of hotels in Florence, it's still prudent to book ahead.

DUOMO & PIAZZA DELLA SIGNORIA

Hotel Dalí Hotel €
(☎055 234 07 06; www.hoteldali.com; Via dell'Oriuolo 17; d/tr €85/110, apt from €95, with shared bathroom s/d €40/70; P @ 🛜) This overwhelmingly friendly hotel offers 10 light and airy rooms with double-glazed windows, tea- and coffee-making facilities and ceiling fans; the best overlook the rear garden. Parking is included in the room cost, but breakfast isn't. The owners also offer three nearby self-catering apartments sleeping between two and six.

Michelangelo's *David* in the Galleria dell'Accademia, Florence
ROGER ANTROBUS/GETTY IMAGES ©

Below: Palazzo Vecchio (p452), Florence;
Right: Galleria Palatina in the Palazzo Pitti (p453), Florence

(BELOW) IZZET KERIBAR/GETTY IMAGES ©. (RIGHT) JEAN-PIERRE LESCOURRET/GETTY IMAGES ©

ground floor offers lounges and a popular wine bar.

Hotel Cestelli
Boutique Hotel €

(☎055 21 42 13; www.hotelcestelli.com; Borgo SS Apostoli 25; d €100-115, s/d with shared bathroom €60/80, extra bed €25; ✆closed 4 weeks Jan-Feb, 3 weeks Aug) Run by Florentine photographer Alessio and his Japanese wife Asumi, this eight-room hotel on the 1st floor of a 12th-century *palazzo* is wonderfully located. Though dark, rooms are attractively furnished, clean, quiet and cool. No breakfast.

SANTA MARIA NOVELLA

Hotel L'O
Luxury Hotel €€€

(☎055 27 73 80; www.hotelorologioflorence.com; Piazza di Santa Maria Novella 24; d from €315; P✳@☎) This design-driven hotel has four stars, five floors and 54 well-equipped and extremely comfortable rooms. The magnificent top-floor breakfast area commands views over Piazza Santa Maria Novella, and the elegant

Hotel Scoti
Historic Hotel €

(☎055 29 21 28; www.hotelscoti.com; Via de' Tornabuoni 7; s/d/tr/q €80/125/150/175; ☎) Wedged between Prada and McQueen, this *pensione* on Florence's most famous and glamorous shopping strip is a splendid mix of old-fashioned charm and value for money. Run with smiling aplomb by Australian Doreen and Italian Carmello, it offers 16 clean and comfortable rooms and a magnificent frescoed living room. Breakfast costs €5.

SAN LORENZO

Antica Dimora Johlea
B&B €€

(☎055 463 32 92; www.johanna.it; Via San Gallo 80; s €50-160, d €70-220; ✳@☎) This highly regarded, professionally run operation has two elegant suite apartments and more than a dozen beautifully decorated and well-equipped ensuite B&B rooms housed in five historic residences

in the quiet San Marco and San Lorenzo districts.

Sette Angeli Rooms — B&B €

(☎ 393 949 08 10; www.setteangelirooms.com; Via Nazionale 31; s €45-60, d €85-110, tr €95-135; ❄ 📶) Tucked behind the central market on a mainstream shopping street, Seven Angels is a tantalising mix of great value and recent renovation. Its rooms are perfectly comfortable and guests can pay an extra €10 to use the self-catering kitchen corner.

SAN MARCO

Hotel Morandi alla Crocetta — Boutique Hotel €€

(☎ 055 234 47 47; www.hotelmorandi.it; Via Laura 50; s €70-120, d €100-170, tr €130-210, q €150-250; P ❄ 📶) This medieval convent-turned-hotel away from the madding crowd is a stunner. Rooms have traditional furnishings and an old-fashioned ambience; a couple have handkerchief-sized gardens to laze in and one (No 29) is the frescoed former chapel.

 Eating

Classic Tuscan dishes include *ribollita,* a heavy vegetable soup, and *bistecca alla fiorentina* (Florentine steak served rare). Chianti is the local tipple.

DUOMO & PIAZZA DELLA SIGNORIA

Cantinetta dei Verrazzano — Bakery €

(Via dei Tavolini 18-20; focaccia €2.50-3; ⏰ noon-9pm Mon-Sat, 10am-4.30pm Sun) Together, a *forno* (baker's oven) and *cantinetta* (small cellar) equal a match made in heaven. Head here for a foccacia straight from the oven and a glass of wine from the Verrazzano estate in Chianti.

Coquinarius — Wine Bar

(www.coquinarius.com; Via delle Oche 11r; crostini & carpacci €4; ⏰ noon-10.30pm) Nestled within the shadow of the Duomo, this *enoteca* is extremely popular with tourists – try the justly famous ravioli with cheese and pear. Bookings essential.

457

If You Like...
Historic Towns

From hilltop San Gimignano (p466) to lovely Lucca (p465), every Italian town seems to have its own historical tale to tell.

1 PADUA

Medieval Padua (Padova) sees only a fraction of the visitors who pile into Venice, but it's just as fascinating: Galileo taught astronomy here, Shakespeare set parts of *The Taming of the Shrew* here, and Giotto painted one of Italy's greatest works of art in the city's **Cappella degli Scrovegni**. Padua is 40km west of Venice.

2 RAVENNA

The refined town of Ravenna is famous for its remarkable Early Christian **mosaics**. These Unesco-listed treasures have been impressing visitors ever since the 13th century when Dante described them in his *Divine Comedy* (much of which was written here). Ravenna is 82km west of Bologna.

3 ASSISI

Famous as the birthplace of St Francis, this medieval town is a major pilgrimage destination. Its major sight is the **Basilica di San Francesco**, a treasure trove of Renaissance frescos spread across two churches. Dress modestly: no shorts, miniskirts, low-cut tops. Assisi is 25km east of Perugia.

4 ORVIETO

This spectacularly sited hilltop town has one major drawcard: its extraordinary Gothic-style **Cattedrale** (☎ 0763 34 11 67; www.opsm.it; Piazza Duomo; admission €3; ⏰ 9.30am-7pm Mon-Sat, 1-6.30pm Sun summer, 9.30am-1pm & 2.30-5pm Mon-Sat, 2.30-5.30pm Sun winter), which was begun in 1290 and took three centuries to complete. Its facade is perhaps the most beautiful to grace any Italian church. Orvieto is 80km southwest of Perugia.

5 LECCE

Lecce is a must-see for architecture lovers: among the town's highlights are the **Basilica di Santa Croce** and its elaborately carved facade, and the grand **Piazza del Duomo**, a baroque masterpiece. Lecce is 40km southeast of Brindisi.

SANTA MARIA NOVELLA

L'Osteria di Giovanni   Tuscan €€

(☎ 055 28 48 97; www.osteriadigiovanni.it; Via del Moro 22; meals €35; ⏰ dinner Mon-Fri, lunch & dinner Sat & Sun) The house antipasto is a great way to sample Tuscan specialities such as *crostini* (small toasts with toppings) and *lardo* (pork fat), and both the pasta dishes and the *bistecca alla fiorentina* are sensational.

La Carraia   Gelato

(Piazza Nazario Sauro 25r; ⏰ 9am-11pm summer, to 10pm winter) Look for the ever-present queue next to the Ponte Carraia, and you will find this fantastic *gelateria*.

SAN LORENZO

Trattoria I Due G   Trattoria €€

(☎ 055 21 86 23; www.trattoriai2g.com; Via B Cennini 6r; mains €10-17; ⏰ lunch & dinner Mon-Sat) There isn't a tourist in sight at this old-fashioned trattoria near the train station (well, there wasn't before we published this review). Huge servings of tasty salads, pastas and mains tempt every palate, but the sentimental favourite is undoubtedly the delicious *pollo fritto* (fried chicken).

SANTA CROCE

Trattoria Cibrèo   Trattoria €€

(www.edizioniteatrodelsalecibreofirenze. it; Via dei Macci 122r; meals €30; ⏰ lunch & dinner Tue-Sat, closed Aug) The small casual dining annexe of Florence's most famous (and considerably more expensive) restaurant is a gem. *Primi* include a justly famous fish soup and *secondi* comprise a small main dish matched with a side of seasonal vegetables; everything is exceptionally well priced considering its quality. No reservations and no credit cards.

Del Fagioli   Trattoria €

(☎ 055 24 42 85; Corso Tintori 47r; mains €8.50-10; ⏰ lunch & dinner Mon-Fri, closed Aug) This Slow Food favourite near the Basilica di Santa Croce is the archetypical Tuscan trattoria. It opened in 1966 and has been serving well-priced bean dishes, soups and roasted meats to throngs of appreciative local workers and residents ever since. No credit cards.

Osteria del Caffè Italiano
Tuscan €€€

(☎ 055 28 93 68; www.osteriacaffeitaliano.com; Via dell'Isola delle Stinche 11-13r; meals €45; ☺ lunch & dinner Tue-Sun) This old-fashioned *osteria* occupies the ground floor of a 14th-century *palazzo* and is an excellent spot to try the city's famous *bistecca alla fiorentina* (per kg €60). The adjoining **pizzeria** (pizzas €7 to €8) offers a choice of three pizza types – margherita, napoli and marinara – which are best enjoyed with an icy-cold beer (€6). No credit cards at the pizzeria.

Vivoli
Gelato

(Via dell'Isola delle Stinche 7; tub €2-10; ☺ 7.30am-midnight Tue-Sat & 9am-midnight Sun summer, to 9pm winter) Choose a flavour from the huge choice on offer (the chocolate with orange is a perennial favourite) and scoff it in the pretty piazza opposite; tubs only.

🍷 Drinking & Nightlife

Le Volpi e l'Uva
Wine Bar

(www.levolpieluva.com; Piazza dei Rossi 1; crostini €6.50, cheese/meat platters €8-10; ☺ 11am-9pm Mon-Sat) This intimate *enoteca con degustazione* (wine bar with tasting) offers an impressive list of wines by the glass (€4 to €8).

Caffè Rivoire
Historic Cafe

(Piazza della Signoria 4; ☺ Tue-Sun) Rivoire's terrace has the best view in the city. Settle in for a long *aperitivo* or coffee break – it's worth the high prices.

Gilli
Historic Cafe

(www.gilli.it; Piazza della Repubblica 39r; ☺ Wed-Mon) The city's grandest cafe, Gilli has been serving excellent coffee and delicious cakes since 1733. Claiming a table on the piazza is *molto* expensive – we prefer standing at the spacious Libertystyle bar.

Chiaroscuro
Cafe, Bar

(☎ 055 21 42 47; www.chiaroscuro.it; Via del Corso 36r; ☺ 7.30am-9pm Mon-Sat, noon-9pm Sun, closed 1 week mid-Aug) This casual cafe

Assorted sweets at Gilli cafe, Florence

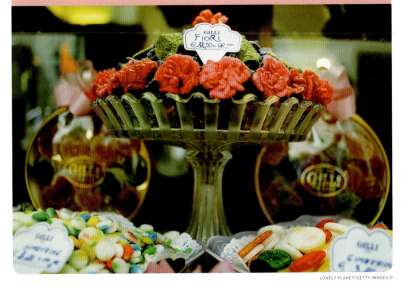

roasts its own beans and serves what may well be the best coffee in Florence. Its *aperitivo* buffet (6pm to 8pm) is justly popular.

Il Santino   Wine Bar

(Via Santo Spirito 34; glass wine & crostini €6.50-8; ⏰10am-10pm) This pocket-sized wine bar is the much-loved sibling of Il Santo Bevitore, one of the city's most fashionable eateries.

ℹ️ Information

Emergency

Police Station (Questura; 📞055 4 97 71; http://questure.poliziadistato.it; Via Zara 2; ⏰24hr)

Tourist Information

Tourist offices (www.firenzeturismo.it) Located at Via Cavour (📞055 29 08 32, 055 29 08 33; www.firenzeturismo.it; Via Cavour 1r; ⏰8.30am-6.30pm Mon-Sat); the airport (📞055 31 58 74; Via del Termine , Airport; ⏰9am-7pm Mon-Sat, 9am-4pm Sun); Piazza della Stazione (📞055 21 22 45; Piazza della Stazione 4; ⏰9am-7pm Mon-Sat, 9am-4pm Sun); and the Bigallo (📞055 28 84 96; www.comune.fi.it; Loggia del Bigallo, Piazza San Giovanni 1; ⏰9am-7pm Mon-Sat, 9am-2pm Sun).

ℹ️ Getting There & Away

Air

The main airport serving Florence is Pisa international airport (p481). There's also the small, city **Florence airport** (www.aeroporto.firenze.it), 5km northwest of Florence.

Car & Motorcycle

Florence is connected by the A1 autostrada to Bologna and Milan in the north and Rome and Naples to the south. The A11 links Florence with Pisa and the coast, and a *superstrada* (expressway) joins the city to Siena.

Train

Florence is well connected by train. There are regular services to/from Pisa (Regionale €7.80, one hour, every 30 minutes), Rome (Freccia Rossa; €29, 90 minutes, hourly), Venice (Freccia Argento; €29 to €45, 2¼ hours, 12 daily) and Milan (Freccia Rossa; €39 to €49, 1¾ hours, hourly).

ℹ️ Getting Around

To/From the Airport

ATAF (📞800 42 45 00; www.ataf.net) runs a shuttle bus (€5, 25 minutes, half-hourly from 5.30am to 11pm) connecting Florence airport with the SITA bus station.

Taxis charge a fixed rate of €20 plus €1 per bag (€23.30 at night) for the trip between Florence airport and the historic centre.

Terravision (www.terravision.eu) runs a bus service between Pisa (Galileo Galilei) airport and the paved bus park in front of Stazione Santa Maria Novella (one way/return €6/10, 70 minutes, 12 daily). In Florence, buy your tickets at the Terravision desk inside Deanna Café, opposite the station.

A limited number of trains run from Pisa airport directly to Florence each day (€7.80, one hour); regular services run to Pisa Centrale from where you can change to a Florence train.

Car & Motorcycle

Note that there is a strict Limited Traffic Zone (ZTL) in the historic centre from 7.30am to 7.30pm Monday to Friday and 7.30am to 6pm on Saturday. Fines are hefty if you enter the centre during these times without a special permit having been organised by your hotel in advance.

The ZTL means that the best option is to leave your car in a car park and use public transport to access the centre. Porta al Prato is a good choice as it's only one tram stop away from Santa Maria Novella. It charges €1 for the first hour, €2 per hour for the second or subsequent hour, or €20 per 24 hours. Buy tickets for the tram (No 1 to/from Villa Costanza; €1.20) from the machines at the tram stop. Details of other car parks are available from **Firenze Parcheggi** (📞055 500 19 94; www.firenzeparcheggi.it).

Pisa

POP 88,300

Most people know Pisa as the home of an architectural project gone terribly wrong, but the Leaning Tower is just one of a number of noteworthy sights in this compact and compelling university city.

🎯 Sights

The Piazza dei Miracoli (p461) is a straightforward 1.5km walk from the bus

LUIS DAVILLA/GETTY IMAGES ©

⭐ Don't Miss
Piazza dei Miracoli

Pisans claim that the Piazza dei Miracoli is among the most beautiful urban spaces in the world. The centrepiece is the **Duomo** (Piazza dei Miracoli; admission free with coupon from ticket office; ⏰10am-8pm Apr-Sep, 10am-7pm Oct, 10am-1pm & 2-5pm Nov-Feb, 10am-6pm Mar) **FREE**, the construction of which began in 1064. But it's to the campanile, better known as the **Leaning Tower** (Torre Pendente; www.opapisa.it; Piazza dei Miracoli; admission incl cathedral €18; ⏰8am-8pm Apr-Sep, 9am-7pm Oct, 10am-5pm Nov-Feb, 9am-6pm Mar), that all eyes are drawn. Construction began in 1173 under the supervision of Bonanno Pisano, but his plans came a cropper almost immediately. Only three of the tower's seven tiers were completed before it started tilting – continuing at a rate of about 1mm per year. By 1990 the lean had reached 5.5 degrees – a tenth of a degree beyond the critical point established by computer models. Stability was finally ensured in 1998 when a combination of biased weighting and soil drilling forced the tower into a safer position. Today it's almost 4.1m off the perpendicular.

Visits to the tower are limited to groups of 40 and children under eight years are not allowed entrance; entry times are staggered and queuing is inevitable. It is wise to book ahead. Tickets to the Leaning Tower and Duomo are sold individually, but for the remaining sights combined tickets are available. These cost €5/6/8/10 for one/two/four/five sights and cover the Duomo, Baptistry, **Camposanto cemetery** (Piazza dei Miracoli; adult/reduced €5/3; ⏰8am-8pm Apr-Sep, 9am-7pm Oct, 10am-5pm Nov-Feb, 9am-6pm Mar), Museo dell'Opera del Duomo and Museo delle Sinópie. To ensure your visit to the tower, book tickets via the website at least 15 days in advance.

NEED TO KNOW

Campo dei Miracoli; www.opapisa.it; ⏰10am-5pm Jan-Feb & Nov-Dec, 9am-6pm Mar, 8am-8pm Apr-Sep, 9am-7pm Oct

and train stations – follow Viale F Crispi north, cross the Ponte Solferino over the Arno and continue straight up Via Roma to Campo dei Miracoli.

🍴 Eating & Drinking

Il Montino   Pizzeria €
(Vicolo del Monte 1; pizza €3 to €6.50; ⏱10.30am-3pm & 5-10pm Mon-Sat) Students and sophisticates alike adore the *cecina* (chickpea pizza) and *spuma* (sweet, non-alcoholic drink) that are the specialities of this local institution. Order to go or claim one of the outdoor tables.

biOsteria 050   Organic €€
(☎050 54 31 06; Via San Francesco 36; meals €20-30; ⏱lunch Mon-Sun, dinner Tue-Sun; ✈) ✿ The chef here uses produce that is strictly local and organic to create his tasty dishes.

Salza   Cafe
(Borgo Stretto 44; ⏱8am-8.30pm summer, shorter hrs Tue-Sun winter) This old-fashioned cafe and cake shop has been tempting Pisans off Borgo Stretto and into sugar-induced indulgence since the 1920s.

Sottobosco   Cafe
(www.sottoboscocafe.it; Piazza San Paolo all'Orto; ⏱10am-midnight Tue-Fri, noon-1am Sat, 7pm-midnight Sun) Enjoy coffee, herbal teas, pastries and light lunches during the day, or head here on Friday, Saturday and Sunday nights for live music (often jazz).

ℹ Information

For city information, check www.pisaunicaterra.it or pop into the tourist office at the airport or in the city centre.

ℹ Getting There & Around

Pisa international airport (p481) is linked to the city centre by train (€1.40, five minutes, 15 daily), or by the **CPT** (www.cpt.pisa.it) LAM Rossa bus (€1.10, 10 minutes, every 10 minutes). Buy bus tickets at the newsstand at the train station or any *tabacchi*.

A taxi between the airport and the city centre costs €15 (€20 at night).

Regular trains run to Lucca (Regionale €3.30, 30 minutes, every 30 to 60 minutes), Florence

(Regionale €7.80, 1¼ hours, every 30 minutes), Rome (Freccia Bianca €19 to €44.50, three hours, five daily) and Genoa (InterCity €9 to €18, 2½ hours, eight daily).

Siena
POP 54,600

Siena is one of Italy's most enchanting medieval towns. Its walled centre, a beautifully preserved warren of dark lanes punctuated with Gothic *palazzi,* has at its centre Piazza del Campo (known as Il Campo), the sloping square that is the venue for the city's famous annual horse race, Il Palio.

According to legend, Siena was founded by the sons of Remus (one of the founders of Rome).

⊙ Sights

There are a number of money-saving passes to Siena's churches and museums on offer:

○ **Siena Itinerari d'Arte** (€17 mid-March to October, €14 November to mid-March, valid seven days) Museo Civico, Complesso Museale Santa Maria della Scala, Museo Opera del Duomo and Battistero.

○ **Musei Comunali Ticket** (€11, valid two days) Museo Civico and Complesso Museale Santa Maria della Scala.

○ **OPA Si Pass** (€8, valid three days) Duomo, Libraria Piccolomini, Battistero, Museo Opera del Duomo and Panoramic Terrace.

All three passes can be purchased at the Duomo ticket office.

Piazza del Campo   Piazza
Il Campo has been Siena's civic and social centre for nearly 600 years. Near the top of the slope is a copy of the **Fonte Gaia** (Happy Fountain), decorated in 1419 by Sienese sculptor Jacopo della Quercia. The recently restored originals are on show in the Complesso Museale Santa Maria della Scala. Down the slope from the fountain is the **Palazzo Comunale** (aka Palazzo Pubblico), a striking example

of Sienese Gothic architecture that is home to the splendid Museo Civico.

Museo Civico
Museum

(www.comune.siena.it; Palazzo Comunale, Il Campo; adult/EU reduced €8/4.50; 10am-6.15pm mid-Mar–Oct, to 5.15pm Nov–mid-Mar) The collection here includes Simone Martini's famous *Maestà* (Virgin Mary in Majesty; 1315–16) and his oft-reproduced fresco (1328–30) of Guidoriccio da Fogliano, a captain of the Sienese army.

Also here is the most important secular painting of the Renaissance, Ambrogio Lorenzetti's fresco cycle known as the *Allegories of Good and Bad Government* (c 1337–40).

The museum is on the 1st floor of the *palazzo;* from the ground floor it is possible to access the **Torre del Mangia** (admission €8; 10am-6.15pm Mar–mid-Oct, to 3.15pm mid-Oct–Feb), a 102m-high bell tower offering great views over the city. A combined ticket to the museum and tower costs €13.

Duomo
Church

(www.operaduomo.siena.it; Piazza del Duomo; admission Mar-Oct €4, Nov-Feb free; 10.30am-7pm Mon-Sat, 1.30-6pm Sun Mar-mid-Aug, 10.30am-7pm Mon-Sat & 9.30am-6pm Sun mid-Aug–Oct, 10.30am-5.30pm Mon-Sat, 1.30-5.30pm Sun Nov-Feb) Siena's cathedral is one of Italy's greatest Gothic churches. Begun in 1196, it was opened in 1215, although work continued on features such as the apse and dome well into the 13th century.

Through a door from the north aisle is the **Libreria Piccolomini** (Piccolomini Library; included in duomo ticket Mar-Oct, €2 Nov-Feb), which is decorated with vivid narrative frescos by Pinturicchio.

Battistero di San Giovanni
Baptistry

(Piazza San Giovanni; admission €4; 10.30am-7pm Mon-Sat & 1.30-6pm Sun Mar-Oct, 10.30am-5.30pm Mon-Sat & 1.30-5.30pm Sun Nov-Feb) While this baptistry's Gothic facade has remained unfinished, the interior is richly decorated with frescos. The centrepiece is a marble font by Jacopo della Quercia, decorated with bronze panels in relief and depicting the life of St John the Baptist. Artists include Lorenzo Ghiberti (*Baptism of Christ* and *St John in Prison*) and Donatello (*Herod's Feast*).

Complesso Museale Santa Maria della Scala
Cultural Building

(www.santamariadellascala.com; Piazza del Duomo 1; adult/reduced/child under 11 yr €6/3.50/free; 10.30am-4pm, to 6.30pm in high season) This former hospital, parts of which date to the 13th century, is directly opposite the Duomo and houses three museums – the Archaeological Museum, Art Museum for Children, and Center of Contemporary Art (SMS Contemporanea) – as well as a variety of historic halls,

Duomo, Siena
RICHARD I'ANSON/GETTY IMAGES ©

chapels and temporary exhibition spaces. Though the atmospheric **Archaeological Museum** housed in the basement tunnels is impressive, the complex's undoubted highlight is the upstairs **Pellegrinaio** (Pilgrim's Hall), with its vivid 15th-century frescos.

✷ Festivals & Events

Siena's great annual event is the **Palio** (🕑 2 Jul & 16 Aug), a pageant culminating in a bareback horse race round Il Campo. The city is divided into 17 *contrade* (districts), of which 10 are chosen annually to compete for the *palio* (silk banner).

🛏 Sleeping

It's always advisable to book in advance, but for August and the Palio, it's essential.

Campo Regio Relais   Boutique Hotel €€€

(☏ 0577 22 20 73; www.camporegio.com; Via della Sapienza 25; s €150-300, d €190-300, ste €250-600; ❉ @ 🛜) Siena's most charming hotel occupies a 16th-century *palazzo* and has only six rooms, all of which are individually decorated and luxuriously equipped. Breakfast is served in the sumptuous lounge or on the terrace, which has a sensational view of the Duomo and Torre del Mangia.

Hotel Alma Domus   Hotel €

(☏ 0577 4 41 77; www.hotelalmadomus.it; Via Camporegio 37; s €40-48, d without view €60-75, d with view €65-85, q €95-125; ❉ @ 🛜) Owned by the Catholic diocese and still home to eight Dominican nuns who act as guardians at the Casa Santuario di Santa Caterina (in the same complex), this convent is now privately operated as a budget hotel. Most of the simple but spotlessly clean rooms have views over the narrow green Fontebranda valley across to the Duomo. There's a 1am curfew.

Antica Residenza Cicogna   B&B €

(☏ 0577 28 56 13; www.anticaresidenzacicogna. it; Via dei Terme 67; s €65-90, d €85-110, ste €120-150; ❉ @ 🛜) Charming host Elisa supervised the recent restoration of this 13th-century building and will happily recount its history (it's been owned by her family for generations). The seven rooms are clean and well maintained, with comfortable beds, painted ceilings and tiled floors.

Lucca

🍴 Eating & Drinking

Among many traditional Sienese dishes are *panzanella* (summer salad of soaked bread, basil, onion and tomatoes), *pappardelle con la lepre* (ribbon pasta with hare) and panforte (a rich cake of almonds, honey and candied fruit).

Enoteca I Terzi Modern Tuscan €€
(☎ 0577 4 43 29; www.enotecaiterzi.it; Via dei Termini 7; meals €35, antipasto plate €9; ⏱ 11am-1am Mon-Sat) Close to the Campo but off the well-beaten tourist trail, this classy, modern *enoteca* is a favourite with bankers from the nearby headquarters of the Monte dei Paschi di Siena bank, who love to linger over their working lunches of handmade pasta, flavoursome risotto and succulent grilled meats.

Morbidi Deli €
(www.morbidi.com; Via Banchi di Sopra 75; ⏱ 9am-8pm Mon-Sat, lunch buffet 12.30-2.30pm) Local gastronomes shop here, as the range of cheese, cured meats and imported delicacies is the best in Siena. If you are self-catering you can join them, but make sure you also investigate the downstairs lunch buffet (€12), which offers fantastic value.

Kopa Kabana Gelateria €
(www.gelateriakopakabana.it; Via dei Rossi 52-55; gelati €1.80-4.30; ⏱ noon-8pm mid-Feb–mid-Nov, later closing in warm weather) Come here for fresh gelato made by self-proclaimed ice-cream master, Fabio (we're pleased to concur). There's a second location at Via San Pietro 20.

Caffè Fiorella Cafe
(www.torrefazionefiorella.it; Via di Città 13; ⏱ 7am-8pm Mon-Sat) Squeeze into this tiny space behind the Campo to enjoy Siena's best coffee. In summer, the coffee granita with a dollop of cream is a wonderful indulgence.

ℹ Information

Tourist Office (☎ 0577 28 05 51; www.terresiena.it; Piazza del Campo 56; ⏱ 9.30am-6.30pm Easter-Sep, 9.30am-5.30pm Mon-Fri, till 12.30pm Sun Oct-Easter)

ℹ Getting There & Away

Siena is not on a main train line, so it's easier to arrive by bus. From the bus station on Piazza Gramsci, SITA buses run to/from Florence (€7.10, 1½ hours, every 30 to 60 minutes) and San Gimignano (€5.50, 1¼ hours, hourly), either direct or via Poggibonsi. A Train SPA bus travels to/from Pisa airport (€14, two hours, one daily) and a **My Tour** (☎ 0577 23 63 30; www.mytours.it; one way/return €30/50, bookings essential) shuttle bus travels to/from Florence airport (bookings essential).

Sena (☎ 861 199 19 00; www.sena.it) operates services to/from Rome (€22, three hours, 11 daily weekdays, fewer on weekends), Milan (€35, 4½ hours, five daily), Perugia (€12, 1½ hours, one daily) and Naples (€30, 6½ hours, one daily).

Lucca
POP 85,000

Lucca is a love-at-first-sight type of place. Hidden behind monumental Renaissance walls, its historic centre is chock-full of handsome churches, excellent restaurants and tempting *pasticcerie*. Founded by the Etruscans, it became a city state in the 12th century and stayed that way for 600 years. Most of its streets and monuments date from this period.

◎ Sights

A two-hour guided walking tour of the historical centre (adult/child under 15 years €10/free) leaves from the Città di Lucca tourist office at 2pm every day between April and September.

Opera buffs should visit in July and August, when the **Puccini Festival** (www.puccinifestival.it) is held in a purpose-built outdoor theatre in the nearby settlement of Torre del Lago.

City Walls Fortification
Lucca's massive *mura* (walls), built around the old city in the 16th and 17th centuries and defended by 126 cannons, remain in almost perfect condition. Twelve metres high and 4km in length, the

465

Detour:
San Gimignano

This tiny hilltop town deep in the Tuscan countryside is a mecca for day-trippers from Florence and Siena. Its nickname is 'The Medieval Manhattan' courtesy of the 11th-century towers that soar above its pristine *centro storico*. Originally 72 were built as monuments to the town's wealth but only 14 remain. The Romanesque cathedral, known as the **Collegiata** (Duomo Collegiata o Basilica di Santa Maria Assunta; Piazza del Duomo; adult/child €3.50/1.50; ⏱10am-7.10pm Mon-Fri, to 5.10pm Sat, 12.30-7.10pm Sun Apr-Oct, shorter hrs rest of year, closed 2nd half Nov & Jan), boasts an interior covered with 14th-century frescos by Bartolo di Fredi, Lippo Memmi and Tadeo di Bartolo. The small **Cappella di Santa Fina** off the south aisle features frescos by Domenico Ghirlandaio.

While in town, be sure to sample the local wine, Vernaccia, while marvelling at the spectacular view from the terrace of the **Museo del Vino** (Wine Museum; museodelvino@sangimignano.com; Parco della Rocca; ⏱11.30am-6.30pm Apr-Oct) FREE, located next to the Rocca (fortress).

Regular buses link San Gimignano with Florence (€6.25, 1¼ hours, 14 daily), travelling via Poggibonsi. There are also services to/from Siena (€5.50, 1¼ hours, hourly).

ramparts are crowned with a tree-lined footpath that looks down on the old town and out towards the Apuane Alps – it's the perfect spot to stroll, cycle, run and get a feel for local Lucchesi life.

Cattedrale di San Martino   Cathedral

(Piazza San Martino; sacristy adult/reduced €3/2, with cathedral museum & Chiesa e Battistero dei SS Giovanni e Reparata €7/5; ⏱7am-6pm summer, to 5pm winter, sacristy 9.30am-4.45pm Mon-Fri, 9.30am-6.45pm Sat, 11.30am-5pm Sun) Lucca's predominantly Romanesque cathedral dates to the start of the 11th century. Its exquisite facade was constructed in the prevailing Lucca-Pisan style and designed to accommodate the pre-existing campanile. Inside, there's a simply fashioned image of a dark-skinned, life-sized Christ on a wooden crucifix, known as the *Volto Santo,* and a magnificent *Last Supper* by Tintoretto. The **sacristy** features Domenico Ghirlandaio's 1479 *Madonna Enthroned with Saints* and a marble memorial carved by Jacopo della Quercia in 1407.

Chiesa e Battistero dei SS Giovanni e Reparata   Church

(Piazza San Giovanni; adult/reduced €4/3, with cathedral museum & sacristy €7/5; ⏱10am-6pm mid-Mar–Oct, 10am-5pm Sat & Sun Nov–mid-March) The 12th-century interior of this deconsecrated church is a hauntingly atmospheric setting for one-hour opera recitals staged by **Puccini e la sua Lucca** (☎340 810 60 42; www.puccinielasualucca.com; adult/reduced €17/13; ⏱7pm daily mid-Mar–Oct, 7pm Fri-Wed Nov–mid-Mar) every evening from mid-March to November. Professional singers present a one-hour program of arias and duets dominated by the music of Puccini. Tickets are available from the church between 10am and 6pm.

🛏 Sleeping

2italia   Apartment €€

(☎392-996 02 71; www.2italia.com; Via della Anfiteatro 74; apt for 2 adults & up to 4 children €190; 🛜) This clutch of family-friendly self-catering apartments overlooks Piazza Anfiteatro, one of the city's major landmarks. Available on a nightly basis (minimum two nights), they sleep up to six, have fully equipped kitchen and washing machine, and come with sheets and towels. The owners also organise cycling tours, cooking courses, wine tastings and olive pickings.

Piccolo Hotel Puccini   Hotel €

(☎0583 5 54 21; www.hotelpuccini.com; Via di Poggio 9; s/d €73/97; ❄ 🛜) Close to the Casa Natale Giacomo Puccini, this well-run, small hotel has rooms with old-fashioned decor, satellite TV and small clean bathrooms. Breakfast costs €3.

✖ Eating

La Pecora Nera   Trattoria €

(☎0583 46 97 38; www.lapecoraneralucca.it; Piazza San Francesco 4; pizzas €5-9, mains €8.50-13; ⏰lunch Sat, dinner Wed-Sun) The Black Sheep is the only Lucchesi restaurant recommended by the Slow Food Movement. It also scores extra brownie points for social responsibility (its profits fund workshops for young people with Down syndrome). The menu features pizzas (dinner only), Tuscan favourites and daily specials.

Taddeucci   Pastries & Cakes

(www.taddeucci.com; Piazza San Michele 34; 300/600/900g loaf €4.50/9/13.50; ⏰8.30am-7.45pm, closed Thu winter) This *pasticceria* is where the traditional Lucchesi treat of *buccellato* was created in 1881. These ring-shaped loaves made with flour, sultanas, sugar and aniseed seeds are the perfect accompaniment to a mid-morning or afternoon espresso.

Da Felice   Pizzeria €

(www.pizzeriadafelice.com; Via Buia 12; focaccias €1-3, pizza slices €1.30; ⏰10am-8.30pm Mon-Sat) This

buzzing local favourite behind Piazza San Michele serves *cecina* and *castagnacci* (chestnut cakes).

ℹ Information

The **Città di Lucca tourist office** (☎0583 58 31 50; www.luccaitinera.it; Piazzale Verdi; ⏰9am-7pm Apr-Oct, to 5pm Nov-Mar) holds luggage (€7.50 per day), offers toilet facilities (€0.50), hires bicycles (€2.50 per hour), operates an internet point (€1 per 30 minutes), sells concert tickets, and supplies free maps and information. In the high season there's another tourist office near **Porta Elisa** (☎0583 355 51 00; www. luccatourist.it; Piazza Napoleone; ⏰10am-1pm & 2-6pm Mon-Sat).

ℹ Getting There & Around

Lucca is on the Florence–Pisa–Viareggio train line. Regional trains run to/from Florence (€7, 1½ hours, every 30 to 90 minutes) and Pisa (€3.30, 30 minutes, every 30 to 60 minutes).

There are plenty of car parks around the walls. Most charge €1.50 per hour between 8am and 6.30pm.

San Gimignano
ROBERT HARDING/GETTY IMAGES ©

SOUTHERN ITALY

Southern Italy is a robust contrast to the genteel north. Its beaches, baroque towns and classical ruins exist alongside ugly urban sprawl and scruffy coastal development (sometimes in the space of a few kilometres) and its residents are a raucous lot who are often wary of interlopers, be they from other countries or the regions north of Rome.

Yet for all its flaws – organised crime, corrupt officialdom, unchecked and outrageous property development – *il mezzogiorno* (the midday sun, as southern Italy is known) is an essential part of every Italian itinerary, offering cheeky charm, culinary masterpieces and architectural treasures galore.

Capri
POP 14,200

The most visited of the islands in the Bay of Naples, Capri deserves more than a quick day trip. Beyond the glamorous veneer of chichi cafes and designer boutiques is an island of rugged seascapes, desolate Roman ruins and a surprisingly unspoiled rural inland.

The island is easily reached from Naples and Sorrento. Hydrofoils and ferries dock at Marina Grande, from where it's a short funicular ride up to Capri, the main town. A further bus ride takes you up to the island's second settlement, Anacapri.

For the best views on the island, take the **seggiovia** (chairlift; one-way/return €7/10; ⏱9am-5pm Mar-Oct, 9am-3pm Nov-Feb) up from Piazza Vittoria to the summit of **Mt Solaro** (589m), Capri's highest point.

⊙ Sights

Grotta Azzurra   Grotto
(Blue Grotto; grotto admission €12.50, return boat trip €13.50; ⏱9am-1hr before sunset) This stunning sea cave illuminated by an other-worldly blue light is Capri's major attraction and is best visited in the morn-

ing. Boats leave from Marina Grande and the return trip costs €24.50 (€12 for the trip plus the entrance fee for the grotto); allow a good hour or so. Alternatively, take a bus from Viale Tommaso de Tommaso in Anacapri (€1.80, 15 minutes) or take a bus to Piazza Vittoria and then follow the pedestrian-only path down Via G Orlandi, Via Pagliaro and Via Grotta Azzura (35 minutes). Note that the grotto is not visitable when seas are rough or tides are high.

Giardini di Augusto   Garden
(Gardens of Augustus; admission €1; ⏱9am-1hr before sunset) Once you've explored Capri Town's picture-perfect streets, head to this garden to enjoy breaktaking views.

Villa Jovis   Ruin
(Jupiter's Villa; ☎081 837 06 86; Via Amaiuri; adult/reduced €2/1; ⏱11am-3pm, closed Tue 1st to 15th of month, closed Sun rest of month) Standing 354m above sea level, this was the largest and most sumptuous of the island's 12 Roman villas and was Tiberius' main Capri residence.

🛏 Sleeping

Hotel Villa Eva   Hotel €€
(☎081 837 15 49; www.villaeva.com; Via La Fabbrica 8, Anacapri; r €100-120; ⏱Mar-Oct; P @ ☎) Hidden among fruit and olive trees, Villa Eva has rooms with lashings of character, a swimming pool and treetop views down to the sea. To get here take a taxi (€30) or the Grotta Azzura bus from Anacapri and ask the driver where to get off.

Capri Palace   Luxury Hotel €€€
(☎081 978 01 11; www.capripalace.com; Via Capodimonte 2b, Anacapri; s/d/ste from €195/295/620; ⏱Apr-Oct; ❄ 🏠 ☎) This ultra-fashionable retreat has a stylish Mediterranean-style decor and is full of contemporary art. Guests rarely leave the hotel grounds, taking full advantage of the huge pool, on-site health spa and top-notch L'Olivo restaurant. There's a three-night minimum stay in high season.

WOJTEK BUSS/GETTY IMAGES ©

Don't Miss
Pompeii & Herculaneum

On 24 August AD 79 Mt Vesuvius erupted, submerging the town of Pompeii in lapilli (burning fragments of pumice stone) and the town of Herculaneum in mud. As a result, both towns were destroyed and over 2000 residents died. The Unesco-listed ruins of both provide remarkable models of working Roman cities, complete with streets, temples, houses, baths, forums, taverns, shops and even a brothel. Exploring both gives a fascinating glimpse into ancient Roman life.

Visitors can choose to visit one site, or can purchase a combination ticket that covers both and is valid for three days.

To visit **Herculaneum** (📞081 732 43 38; www.pompeiisites.org; Corso Resina 6, Ercolano; adult/reduced €11/5.50, combined ticket incl Pompeii €20/10; ⏰8.30am-7.30pm summer, to 5pm winter, last entry 90min before closing; 🚇Circumvesuviana to Ercolano-Scavi), take the Circumvesuviana train from Naples (€2.10, 10 minutes), alight at the Ercolano stop and walk straight down the main street to reach the archaeological site. Highlights of the site include the Sede degli Augustali, the Casa del Salone Nero and the Casa Sannitica.

For **Pompeii** (📞081 857 53 47; www.pompeiisites.org; entrances at Porta Marina & Piazza Anfiteatro; adult/reduced €11/5.50, combined ticket incl Herculaneum €20/10; ⏰8.30am-7.30pm summer, 8.30am-5pm winter, last entry 90min before closing), take the Circumvesuviana to the Pompeii Scavi-Villa dei Misteri stop (€2.10, 35 minutes), located right next to the Porta Marina entrance to the ruins. There really is a huge amount to see here, but you should be sure not to miss the Lupanare (Brothel), the Casa del Menandro, the *anfiteatro* (ampitheatre) and the Villa dei Misteri with its extraordinary frescos.

Tragedy in Pompeii

24 August AD 79

8am Buildings including the **Terme Suburbane** ❶ and the **foro** ❷ are still undergoing repair after an earthquake in AD 63 caused significant damage to the city. Despite violent earth tremors overnight, residents have little idea of the catastrophe that lies ahead.

Midday Peckish locals pour into the **Thermopolium di Vetutius Placidus** ❸. The lustful slip into the **Lupanare** ❹, and gladiators practise for the evening's planned games at the **anfiteatro** ❺. A massive boom heralds the eruption. Shocked onlookers witness a dark cloud of volcanic matter shoot some 14km above the crater.

3pm–5pm Lapilli (burning pumice stone) rains down on Pompeii. Terrified locals begin to flee; others take shelter. Within two hours, the plume is 25km high and the sky has darkened. Roofs collapse under the weight of the debris, burying those inside.

25 August AD 79

Midnight Mudflows bury the town of Herculaneum. Lapilli and ash continue to rain down on Pompeii, bursting through buildings and suffocating those taking refuge within.

4am–8am Ash and gas avalanches hit Herculaneum. Subsequent surges smother Pompeii, killing all remaining residents, including those in the **Orto dei Fuggiaschi** ❻. The volcanic 'blanket' will safeguard frescoed treasures like the **Casa del Menandro** ❼ and **Villa dei Misteri** ❽ for almost two millennia.

TOP TIPS
Visit in the afternoon

Allow three hours

Wear comfortable shoes and a hat

Bring drinking water

Don't use flash photography

Terme Suburbane
The *laconicum* (sauna), *caldarium* (hot bath) and large, heated swimming pool weren't the only sources of heat here; scan the walls of this suburban bathhouse for some of the city's raunchiest frescoes.

Terme Suburbane ❽

Villa di Diomede

Casa de Vettii

Casa del Poeta Tragico

Porta Ercolano

Casa de Fauno

Basilica

Tempio di Apollo

Porta Marina ❶

Terme del Foro

❷

❹

Macellum

Teatro Grande

Quadriportico dei Teatri

Porta di Stabia

Teatro Piccolo

Foro
An ancient Times Square of sorts, the forum sits at the intersection of Pompeii's main streets and was closed to traffic in the 1st century AD. The plinths on the southern edge featured statues of the imperial family.

Villa dei Misteri

Home to the world-famous *Dionysiac Frieze* fresco. Other highlights at this villa include *trompe l'oeil* wall decorations in the *cubiculum* (bedroom) and Egyptian-themed artwork in the *tablinum* (reception).

Lupanare

The prostitutes at this brothel were often slaves of Greek or Asian origin. Mattresses once covered the stone beds and the names engraved in the walls are possibly those of the workers and their clients.

Thermopolium di Vetutius Placidus

The counter at this ancient snack bar once held urns filled with hot food. The *lararium* (household shrine) on the back wall depicts Dionysus (the god of wine) and Mercury (the god of profit and commerce).

Eyewitness Account

Pliny the Younger (AD 61–c 112) gives a gripping, first-hand account of the catastrophe in his letters to Tacitus (AD 56–117).

Porta del Vesuvio

Porta di Nola

Casa della Venere in Conchiglia

Porta di Sarno

3

7

6

Grande Palestra

5

Tempio di Iside

Casa del Menandro

This dwelling most likely belonged to the family of Poppaea Sabina, Nero's second wife. A room to the left of the atrium features Trojan War paintings and a polychrome mosaic of pygmies rowing down the Nile.

Orto dei Fuggiaschi

The Garden of the Fugitives showcases the plaster moulds of 13 locals seeking refuge during Vesuvius' eruption – the largest number of victims found in any one area. The huddled bodies make for a moving scene.

Anfiteatro

Magistrates, local senators and the games' sponsors and organisers enjoyed front-row seating at this veteran amphitheatre, home to gladiatorial battles and the odd riot. The parapet circling the stadium featured paintings of combat, victory celebrations and hunting scenes.

Eating

Be warned that restaurants on Capri are overpriced and underwhelming. Many close between November and Easter.

La Taverna di Pulcinella   Pizzeria €

(☏081 837 64 85; Via Tiberio 7; pizzas from €7; ⊗Apr-Oct) If you can bear being served by waiters in Punchinello (Pulcinella) costumes, you'll be rewarded by what are generally acknowledged to be the best pizzas on Capri.

Salemeria da Aldo   Deli €

(Via Cristoforo Colombo 26, Marina Grande; panini from €3.50) Ignore the restaurant touts and head straight to this honest portside deli, where bespectacled Aldo will make you his legendary *panino alla Caprese* (crusty bread stuffed with silky mozzarella and tomatoes from his own garden).

Lo Sfizietto   Gelateria €

(☏081 837 00 91; Via Longano 6) Located just off La Piazzetta, this *gelateria* uses only organic ingredients with choices that include *cremolate* with 60% fresh fruit and the namesake choice *sfizietto* (caramel with pine nuts).

Pulalli   Wine Bar €€

(☏081 837 41 08; Piazza Umberto I 4, Capri Town; meals €25; ⊗Wed-Mon) Climb the clock-tower steps to the right of Capri Town's tourist office and your reward is this laid-back local hang-out, where fabulous vino meets a discerning selection of cheeses, *salumi* and pastas.

ⓘ Information

Information is available online at www.capritourism.com or from one of the three tourist offices: **Marina Grande** (☏081 837 06 34; www.capritourism.com; Quayside; ⊗9.30am-1.30pm & 3.30-6.45pm Mon-Sat, 9am-3pm Sun), **Capri Town** (☏081 837 06 86; Piazza Umberto 1; ⊗9.30am-1pm & 3.30-6.45pm Mon-Sat, 9am-3pm Sun) and **Anacapri** (☏081 837 15 24; Via G Orlando 59; ⊗9am-3pm Mon-Sat Apr-Sep).

ⓘ Getting There & Around

There are year-round hydrofoils and ferries to Capri from Naples. Timetables and fare details are available online at www.capritourism.com; look under 'Shipping timetable'. Services are regular

Southern coast of Capri (p468)

DAVID C TOMLINSON/GETTY IMAGES ©

and tickets cost €19 to €21 (hydrofoil), €17.80 (fast ferry) and €11.50 (ferry).

There are services to/from Sorrento (hydrofoil €17 to €18, fast ferry €15 to €16.20, 20 minutes, 11 daily) and from Easter to November there are also services to Positano (€15.50, 45 minutes, four daily).

On the island, buses run from Capri Town to/from Marina Grande, Anacapri and Marina Piccola. There are also buses from Marina Grande to Anacapri. Single tickets cost €1.80 on all routes, as does the funicular (€1.80) that links Marina Grande with Capri Town in a four-minute trip.

Taxis between Marina Grande and Capri Town cost €15 (€20 to Anacapri) and can carry up to six people.

A private tour around the island by motorboat (stopping for a swim and at the Grotta Azzurra on the way) costs between €150 and €200 per group; a couple of companies based at Marina Grande offer one-hour public tours (€15).

Sorrento

POP 16,600

A stunning location overlooking the Bay of Naples and Mt Vesuvius makes Sorrento a popular package-holiday destination, despite the fact that it has no decent beach. Its profusion of sweet-smelling citrus trees and laid-back local lifestyle are certainly attractive, and its relative proximity to the Amalfi Coast, Pompeii and Capri make it a good base for those who don't wish to deal with the chaos and cacophony of Naples.

Sights & Activities

You'll probably spend most of your time in the *centro storico,* which is full of narrow streets lined with shops, cafes, churches and restaurants. To the north, the **Villa Comunale Park** (⏱8am-midnight) commands grand views over the sea to Mt Vesuvius.

The two main swimming spots are **Marina Piccola** and **Marina Grande**, although neither is especially appealing. Nicer by far is **Bagni Regina Giovanna**,

If You Like…
Italian Islands

If you've been dazzled by the seaside charms of Capri (p468), you might feel like venturing across the Med to explore some of Italy's other islands.

1 SARDINIA
Just to the south of the French island of Corsica, Sardinia is renowned for its golden beaches and glorious coastline. The island is Italy's favourite summer getaway, and fancy resorts litter the coastline, but inland the island reveals a more rugged side: granite peaks, dizzying valleys and remote villages. It gets very busy in summer, so it's best to visit in spring or autumn. Flights from major Italian cities land in Cagliari and Alghero, while ferries arrive from various Italian ports, including Genoa, Livorno, Piombino, Civitavecchia, Naples and Palermo.

2 SICILY
Dominated by the smoking summit of Mt Etna, the Mediterranean's largest island has always marched to its own tune: geographically, linguistically, politically and gastronomically. From sunbaked plains to sparkling coast, Greek ruins to baroque cities, it's a fascinating island that feels several steps removed from the rest of Italy. Among the must-sees are the chaotic capital Palermo, the ancient port city of Syracuse and the stately city of Taormina. Flights from Italy's main cities land at Palermo and Catania, and ferries cross regularly from Calabria.

3 AEOLIAN ISLANDS
Rising out of the cobalt-blue seas off Sicily's northeastern coast, the Unesco-listed Aeolian Islands (Isole Eolie) have been seducing visitors since Odysseus' time. The seven islands (Lipari, Salina, Vulcano, Stromboli, Alicudi, Filicudi and Panarea) comprise a ridge of ancient volcanoes, many of which are still active: Stromboli still regularly supplies spectacular fire shows, while on Vulcano you can tackle a dip in hot volcanic mud. Ustica Lines runs hydrofoils from the islands to/from Messina (€22.70, 1¾ hours) and Milazzo (€23.70, one hour).

a rocky beach set among the ruins of a Roman villa, 2km west of town.

Sleeping

Casa Astarita   B&B €

(📞081 877 49 06; www.casastarita.com; Corso Italia 67, Sorrento; d €90-120, tr €110-140; ❄ @ 🛜) Housed in a 16th-century building on the town's major *passaggiata* strip, this family-run place offers six quiet rooms combining rustic charm with modern comforts (iPod docks, Apple TV, kettle, fridge). The colourful decor is extremely attractive, and all rooms are freshly painted and immaculately maintained.

🍴 Eating

Aurora Light   Campanian €€

(📞081 877 26 31; www.auroralight.it; Piazza Tasso 3-4; mains €15) Close examination of its seasonally driven menu shows that Aurora Light's enthusiastic young owner enjoys giving traditional Campanian dishes an innovative twist. There are plenty of vegetarian options on offer.

Garden   Campanian €€

(📞081 878 11 95; Corso Italia 50-52; mains €15; ⏰closed Jan-Mar) Enjoy local and Italian wines by the glass accompanied by slices of prosciutto and cheese in the sophisticated downstairs wine bar, or head to the upstairs terrace garden where the menu includes all the mainstay pasta dishes and plenty of seafood.

ℹ Information

The main **tourist office** (📞081 807 40 33; Via Luigi De Maio 35; ⏰8.30am-4.10pm Mon-Sat) is near Piazza San Antonino, but there are also information points at **Marina Piccola** (⏰8am-1pm) and on **Corso Italia** (⏰9am-1pm & 3-10pm) near Piazza Tasso. Note that their opening hours can be erratic, especially in the low season.

ℹ Getting There & Away

Circumvesuviana trains run half-hourly between Sorrento and Naples (€4, 65 minutes) via Pompeii (€2.10, 30 minutes) and Ercolano (€2.10, 45 minutes). A daily ticket covering all stops on the route costs €12 (€6.30 on weekends) and a daily ticket covering stops at Ercolano, Pompeii and Sorrento costs €6.30 (€3.40 on weekends).

There are boat services to Capri (€17 to €18 hydrofoil, €15 to €16.20 fast ferry, 20 minutes, 11 daily) and Naples (return hydrofoil €22, 35 minutes, six daily).

Amalfi Coast

Stretching 50km along the southern side of the Sorrentine Peninsula, the Amalfi Coast (Costiera Amalfitana) is a postcard-perfect vision of shimmering blue water fringed by vertiginous cliffs to which whitewashed villages with terraced lemon groves cling. This Unesco-protected area is

Marina Grande (p468), Capri
SIMEONE HUBER/GETTY IMAGES ©

Detour:
Matera

Set atop two rocky gorges, Matera is one of Italy's most remarkable towns and is certainly the most compelling reason to visit the region of Basilicata. Dotting the ravines are the famous **sassi** (cave dwellings), where up to half the town's population lived until the late 1950s.

Within Matera there are two *sassi* areas: the largely restored **Barisano** and more impoverished and run-down **Caveoso**. Both feature serpentine alleyways and staircases, Byzantine-era cave churches and hidden piazzas. With a map you can explore them on your own, although you might find an audioguide (€8) from **Viaggi Lionetti** (☎0835 33 40 33; www.viaggilionetti.com; Via XX Settembre 9; ☺9am-1pm & 4-8pm Mon-Fri, 9am-1pm Sat) helpful. It and **Ferula Viaggi** (www.ferulaviaggi.it) also offer guided tours.

Inhabited since the Paleolithic age, the *sassi* were brought to public attention with the publication of Carlo Levi's book *Cristo si é fermato a Eboli* (Christ Stopped at Eboli; 1945). His description of children begging for quinine to stave off endemic malaria shamed the authorities into action and about 15,000 people were forcibly relocated in the late 1950s. In 1993 the *sassi* were declared a Unesco World Heritage site.

The **Agenzia di Promozione Territoriale Basilicata** (APT; ☎0835 33 19 83; www.aptbasilicata.it; 1st fl, Via De Viti De Marco 9; ☺9am-1.30pm Mon-Fri, 4-6.30pm Mon & Tue) has a Matera office near the train station that can supply maps and brochures. Online information is available at the APT's website and at www.sassiweb.it.

By train, the **Ferrovie Appulo Lucano** (☎080 572 52 29; www.fal-srl.it) runs services to/from Bari (€4.50, 1¼ hour, 14 daily). Note that these do not run on Sundays.

one of Italy's top tourist destinations, attracting hundreds of thousands of visitors each year (70% of them between June and September).

🛈 Getting There & Away

There are two main entry points to the Amalfi Coast: Sorrento and Salerno. Both can be accessed by train from Naples (Sorrento on the Circumvesuviana and Salerno on Treitalia).

Boat services are generally limited to the period between April and October. **Gescab-Alicost** (☎089 87 14 83; www.alicost.it; Salita Sopramuro 2, Amalfi) operates one daily ferry/hydrofoil from Salerno to Amalfi (€7/9), Positano (€11/13) and Capri (€18.50/20). It also runs daily ferries from Sorrento to Positano (€13) and Amalfi (€14). **TraVelMar** (☎089 87 29 50; www.travelmar.it) and Mètro del Mare also run services over summer; check their websites for details.

By car, take the SS163 coastal road at Vietri sul Mare.

POSITANO

POP 4000

Approaching Positano by boat, you will be greeted by an unforgettable view of colourful, steeply stacked houses clinging to near-vertical green slopes.

The **tourist office** (☎089 87 50 67; Via del Saracino 4; ☺8.30am-7pm Mon-Sat, to 2pm Sun Easter-Oct, 9am-4.30pm Mon-Sat Nov-Easter) can provide information on walking in the densely wooded Lattari Mountains, including details of the spectacular 12km **Sentiero degli Dei** (Path of the Gods) between Positano and Praiano, and the **Via degli Incanti** (Trail of Charms) between Positano and Amalfi.

🛏 Sleeping

Pensione Maria Luisa　　Pension €
(☎089 87 50 23; www.pensionemarialuisa.com; Via Fornillo 42; r €70-85; ☺Mar-Oct; @ 🛜) The best budget choice in town is run by Carlo,

Below: Positano (p475); **Right:** Grotta dello Smeraldo, Amalfi
(BELOW) GIO/GETTY IMAGES ©; (RIGHT) TIPS IMAGES/TIPS ITALIA SRL A SOCIO UNICO/ALAMY ©

a larger-than-life character who will go out of his way to assist and advise. Rooms are attractive and have modern bathrooms; those with private terraces are well worth the extra €10 to €15 for the view of the bay. Breakfast costs an additional €5.

Albergo Miramare   Hotel €€€
(☎089 87 50 02; www.miramarepositano.it; Via Trara Genoino 29; s €150-175, d €195-480; ⊙Apr-Oct; ❄@🛜) Every room at this gorgeous hotel has a terrace with sea view, just one of the features that makes it a dream holiday destination. Rooms are extremely comfortable, sporting all mod cons, and the common areas include a comfortable lounge and breakfast room with spectacular views.

🍴 Eating & Drinking

Next2   Campanian €€
(☎089 812 35 16; www.next2.it; Viale Pasitea 242; meals €40; ⊙6.30-11.30pm) We're not

sure which is the more enticing: Next 2's outside terrace with oversized white parasols and wicker seating, or its menu, which showcases organic ingredients as much as possible and includes interesting takes on classic Neapolitan dishes.

Da Vincenzo   Campanian €€
(☎089 87 51 28; Viale Pasitea 172-178; meals €40; ⊙noon-2.30pm & 6-11pm Wed-Mon, 6.30-11pm Tue) The emphasis at this old-fashioned place is on fish dishes. Listen to the sound of Neapolitan guitarists during the summer months and be sure to try co-owner Marcella's legendary desserts, which are widely considered to be the best in town.

Da Costantino   Trattoria €
(☎089 87 57 38; Via Montepertuso; mains €12, pizzas from €4; ⊙closed Wed) One of the few authentic trattorias in Positano, this place high up the hill serves honest, down-to-earth Italian grub. Expect amazing views, good pastas and pizzas and a selection of fail-safe grilled meats.

La Zagara · Cafe

(☎089 812 28 92; Via dei Mulini 4; panini €5, cakes €3) A terrace draped with foliage and flowers is but one of the attractions of this cafe, bar and *pasticceria,* alongside decadent cakes, live music and plenty of Positano poseur-watching potential.

AMALFI

POP 5400

Amalfi is a popular summer holiday destination for no good reason. The beach is unappealing, there's a surfeit of souvenir shops and crowds can be oppressive. Outside the high season, its tangle of narrow alleyways, whitewashed houses and sun-drenched piazzas make it worthy of a day trip but little more.

Sights

Grotta dello Smeraldo · Cave

(admission €6; ⊙9am-4pm; 🚻) The local version of Capri's famous sea cave can be visited on one-hour boat trips from Amalfi's harbour (€14 return, 9.20am to 3pm daily May to October).

🛏 Sleeping & Eating

Hotel Lidomare · Hotel €€

(☎089 87 13 32; www.lidomare.it; Largo Duchi Piccolomini 9; s/d €50/120; ❄🖧) The spacious rooms at this old-fashioned, family-run favourite have an endearing air of gentility; the best have sea views.

A'Scalinatella Hostel · Hostel €

(☎089 87 14 92; www.hostelscalinatella.com; Piazza Umberto I; dm €20-25, s €35-50, d €70-90) This bare-bones operation, just around the headland in Atrani, has dorms, rooms and apartments scattered across the village. Breakfast is included in the price.

Marina Grande · Seafood €€€

(☎089 87 11 29; www.ristorantemarinagrande. com; Viale Delle Regioni 4; mains €16-26, tasting menu lunch €22, dinner €48; ⊙Tue-Sun Mar-Oct) 🌿 Run by the third generation of the same family and patronised primarily by locals, this classy restaurant fronting the beach serves food made with seasonal ingredients. It's known for its fresh fish dishes.

Dolcería dell' Antíco Portico
Pasticceria €

(☎ 089 87 11 43; Via Supportico Rua 10; cakes from €3) Named for its location under the arches, this celebrated cake shop and small cafe gives a contemporary twist to traditional sweet treats such as *sfogliatella*.

SURVIVAL GUIDE

ℹ Directory A–Z

Accommodation
The bulk of Italy's accommodation is made up of *alberghi* (hotels) and *pensioni* – often housed in converted apartments. Other options are youth hostels, camping grounds, B&Bs, *agriturismi* (farm-stays), mountain *rifugi* (Alpine refuges), monasteries and villa/apartment rentals.

High-season rates apply at Easter, in summer (mid-June to August), and over the Christmas to New Year period.

The north of Italy is generally more expensive than the south.

Many city-centre hotels offer discounts in August to lure clients from the crowded coast. Check hotel websites for last-minute offers.

Most hotels in coastal resorts shut for winter, typically from November to March. The same applies to *agriturismi* and villa rentals in rural areas.

Price Ranges
In this chapter prices quoted are the minimum-maximum for rooms with a private bathroom, and unless otherwise stated include breakfast. The following price indicators apply (for a high-season double room):

€ less than €110

€€ €110 to €200

€€€ more than €200

Hotel Tax
Since early 2011 a number of Italian cities, including Rome, Florence and Venice, have introduced a hotel occupancy tax (*tassa di soggiorno*). This is charged on top of your regular hotel bill and must sometimes be paid in cash. The exact amount, which varies from city to city, depends on your type of accommodation, but as a rough guide expect to pay €1 per night in a one-star hotel or hostel, €2 in a B&B, €2 to €3 in a three-star hotel etc.

Note that prices quoted in this book do not include the tax.

Business Hours

Banks 8.30am to 1.30pm & 3 to 4.30pm Monday to Friday

Bars & Cafes 7.30am to 8pm; many open earlier and some stay open until the small hours; pubs often open noon to 2am

Discos & Clubs 10pm to 4am

Pharmacies 9am to 1pm & 4 to 7.30pm Monday to Friday, to 1pm Saturday; outside of these hours, pharmacies open on a rotation basis – all are required to post a list of places open in the vicinity

Post offices Major offices 8am to to 7pm Monday to Friday, to 1.15pm Saturday; branch offices 8.30am to 2pm Monday to Friday, to 1pm Saturday

Restaurants Noon to 3pm & 7.30 to 11pm or midnight; most restaurants close one day a week

Shops 9am to 1pm & 3.30 to 7.30pm or 4 to 8pm Monday to Saturday; in larger cities many chain stores and supermarkets open from 9am to 7.30pm Monday to Saturday; some also open Sunday morning, typically 9am to 1pm; food shops are generally closed Thursday afternoon; some other shops are closed Monday morning

Many museums, galleries and archaeological sites operate summer and winter opening hours. Typically, winter hours will apply between November and late March or early April.

Food
Throughout this chapter, the following price indicators have been used (prices refer to the cost of a main course):

€ less than €10

€€ €10 to €18

€€€ more than €18

Gay & Lesbian Travellers
Homosexuality is legal in Italy, but same-sex couples have no shared rights to property, social security and inheritance. There is a push to

legalise gay marriage, but this seems unlikely in the near future.

Homosexuality is well tolerated in major cities but overt displays of affection could attract a negative response, particularly in small towns and in the more conservative south.

Italy's main gay and lesbian organisation is **Arcigay** (www.arcigay.it), based in Bologna.

Internet Access

Most hotels, hostels, B&Bs and *pensioni* offer wi-fi, either free or for a daily charge. Access is also available in internet cafes throughout the country, although many have closed in recent years. Charges are typically around €5 per hour. To use internet points in Italy you must present photo ID.

Money

Italy's currency is the euro.

ATMs, known in Italy as *bancomat,* are widespread and will accept cards displaying the appropriate sign. Visa and MasterCard are widely recognised, as are Cirrus and Maestro; American Express is less common. If you don't have a PIN, some, but not all, banks will advance cash over the counter.

Credit cards are widely accepted, although many small trattorias, pizzerias and *pensioni* only take cash. Don't assume museums, galleries and the like accept credit cards.

If your credit/debit card is lost, stolen or swallowed by an ATM, telephone toll-free to block it: **Amex** (☏06 7 22 82 or your national call number); **MasterCard** (☏800 870866); and **Visa** (☏800 819014).

Post

Italy's postal system, **Poste Italiane** (☏80 31 60; www. poste.it), is reasonably reliable.

The standard service is *posta prioritaria*. Registered mail is known as *posta raccomandata,* insured mail as *posta assicurato.*

Francobolli (stamps) are available at post offices and *tabacchi* (tobacconists) – look for a big white 'T' against a blue/black background.

Public Holidays

Most Italians take their annual holiday in August. This means that many businesses and shops close down for at least a part of the month, usually around Ferragosto (15 August). Easter is another busy holiday.

Public holidays:

New Year's Day (Capodanno) 1 January

Epiphany (Epifania) 6 January

Anniversary of the Unification of Italy (Anniversario dell'Unità d'Italia) 17 March

Easter Monday (Pasquetta) March/April

Liberation Day (Giorno delle Liberazione) 25 April

Labour Day (Festa del Lavoro) 1 May

Republic Day (Festa della Repubblica) 2 June

Feast of the Assumption (Ferragosto) 15 August

All Saints' Day (Ognisanti) 1 November

Day of National Unity and the Armed Forces (Giornata dell'Unità Nazionale e delle Forze Armate) 4 November

Feast of the Immaculate Conception (Immacolata Concezione) 8 December

View across the Giudecca canal, Venice (p429)

Train in the hills above Bolzano (p445), the Dolomites

GLENN VAN DER KNIJFF/GETTY IMAGES ©

Christmas Day (Natale) 25 December

Boxing Day (Festa di Santo Stefano) 26 December

Individual towns also have holidays to celebrate their patron saints:

St Mark (Venice) 25 April

St John the Baptist (Florence, Genoa and Turin) 24 June

Sts Peter and Paul (Rome) 29 June

St Rosalia (Palermo) 15 July

St Janarius (Naples) First Sunday in May, 19 September and 16 December

St Ambrose (Milan) 7 December

Safe Travel

- Petty theft is prevalent in Italy. Be on your guard against pickpockets and moped thieves in popular tourist centres such as Rome, Florence and Venice, and especially in Naples.

- Don't take it for granted that cars will stop at red lights.

Telephone

Area codes are an integral part of all Italian phone numbers and must be dialled even when calling locally. The area codes have been listed in telephone numbers throughout this chapter.

- To call Italy from abroad, dial ☎0039 and then the area code, including the first zero.

- To call abroad from Italy, dial ☎00, then the relevant country code followed by the telephone number.

- To make a reverse-charge (collect) international call, dial ☎170. All operators speak English.

- You'll find cut-price call centres in all of the main cities. For international calls, their rates are often cheaper than at payphones.

- Skype is available in many internet cafes and on hostel computers.

Mobile Phones

Italy uses the GSM 900/1800 network, which is compatible with the rest of Europe and Australia, but not with the North American GSM 1900 or the Japanese system (although some GSM 1900/900 phones do work here).

If you have a GSM dual- or tri-band cellular phone that you can unlock (check with your service provider), you can buy a *prepagato* (prepaid) SIM card in Italy.

Companies offering SIM cards include **TIM** (Telecom Italia Mobile; www.tim.it), **Wind** (www.wind.it) and **Vodafone** (www.vodafone.it). You'll need ID to open an account.

Phone Codes

- Italy's country code is 📞39.
- Mobile phone numbers begin with a three-digit prefix starting with a 3.
- Toll-free (free-phone) numbers are known as *numeri verdi* and start with 800. These are not always available if calling from a mobile phone.

Phonecards

To phone from a public payphone you'll need a *scheda telefonica* (telephone card; €3, €5). Buy these at post offices, *tabacchi* and newsstands.

Tourist Information

For pre-trip information, check out the website of the **Ministro del Turismo** (www.italia.it). The ministry also runs a multilingual telephone information service, **Easy Italy** (📞039 039 039; 🕘9am-10pm).

Travellers with Disabilities

Italy is not an easy country for travellers with disabilities. Cobbled streets, blocked pavements and tiny lifts all make life difficult. Rome-based **Consorzio Cooperative Integrate** (COIN; 📞06 712 90 11; www.coinsociale.it) is the best point of reference for travellers with disabilities.

If you're travelling by train, **Trenitalia** (www.trenitalia.com) runs a telephone info line (📞199 30 30 60) with details of assistance available at stations.

Visas

Schengen visa rules apply for entry to Italy.

Non-EU citizens who want to study in Italy must obtain a study visa from their nearest Italian embassy or consulate.

A *permesso di soggiorno* (permit to stay) is required by all non-EU nationals who stay in Italy longer than three months. You must apply within eight days of arriving in Italy. Check the exact documentary requirements on www.poliziadistato.it.

ⓘ Getting There & Away

Air

Italy's main international airports:

Rome Leonardo da Vinci (📞06 6 59 51; www.adr.it/fiumicino) Italy's main airport, also known as Fiumicino.

Milan Malpensa (📞02 23 23 23; www.milanomalpensa1.eu/it)

Rome Ciampino (📞06 6 59 51; www.adr.it/ciampino) Rome's second airport. Hub for Ryanair flights.

Pisa International Airport Galileo Galilei (📞050 84 93 00; www.pisa-airport.com; Piazzale D'Ascanio) Main gateway for Florence and Tuscany.

Venice Marco Polo (VCE; 📞041 260 92 60; www.veniceairport.it)

Land

Border Crossings

Italy borders France, Switzerland, Austria and Slovenia. The main points of entry:

From France The coast road from Nice; the Mont Blanc tunnel from Chamonix.

From Switzerland The Grand St Bernard tunnel; the Simplon tunnel; the Lötschberg Base tunnel.

From Austria The Brenner Pass.

Car & Motorcycle

If traversing the Alps, note that border crossings from the Brenner Pass, Grand St Bernard tunnel, Simplon tunnel and Lötschberg Base tunnel are open year-round. Other mountain passes are often closed in winter and sometimes in spring and autumn. Bring snow chains in your car.

Train

Direct international trains connect with various cities:

Milan To/from Paris, Basel, Lugano, Geneva, Zürich.

Rome To/from Munich.

Venice To/from Paris, Munich, Geneva, Innsbruck.

There are also international trains from Verona, Padua, Bologna and Florence. Get details at www.trenitalia.com.

In the UK, the **Rail Europe Travel Centre** (www.raileurope.co.uk) can provide fare information on journeys to/from Italy, most of which require a change at Paris. Another excellent resource is www.seat61.com. Eurail and Inter-Rail passes are both valid in Italy.

Sea

Dozens of ferry companies connect Italy with other Mediterranean countries. Timetables are seasonal, so always check ahead – you'll find details of routes, companies and online booking at www.traghettiweb.it. See table p483 for more information.

ℹ️ Getting Around

Bicycle

- Tourist offices can generally provide details of designated bike trails and bike hire (at least €10 per day).
- Bikes can be taken on regional and international trains carrying the bike logo, but you'll need to pay a supplement (€3.50 on regional trains, €12 on international trains). Bikes can be carried free if dismantled and stored in a bike bag.
- Bikes generally incur a small supplement on ferries, typically €10 to €15.

Boat

Navi (large ferries) service Sicily and Sardinia; *traghetti* (smaller ferries) and *aliscafi* (hydrofoils) cover the smaller islands. The main embarkation points for Sardinia are Genoa, Piombino, Livorno, Civitavecchia and Naples; for Sicily, it's Naples and Villa San Giovanni in Calabria.

Bus

- Italy boasts an extensive and largely reliable bus network.
- Buses are not necessarily cheaper than trains, but in mountainous areas they are often the only choice.
- In larger cities, companies have ticket offices or operate through agencies but in most villages and small towns tickets are sold in bars or on the bus.
- Reservations are only necessary for high-season long-haul trips.

Car & Motorcycle

- Roads are generally good and there's an excellent system of autostradas (motorways).
- There's a toll to use most autostradas, payable in cash or by credit card at exit barriers.
- Autostradas are indicated by an A with a number (eg A1) on a green background; *strade statali* (main roads) are shown by an S or SS and number (eg SS7) against a blue background.
- Italy's motoring organisation **Automobile Club d'Italia** (ACI; www.aci.it; Via Colombo 261) provides 24-hour roadside assistance – call ☎803 116 from a landline or Italian mobile, ☎800 116 800 from a foreign mobile.
- Cars use unleaded petrol *(benzina senza piombo)* and diesel *(gasolio);* both are expensive but diesel is slightly cheaper.
- All EU driving licences are recognised in Italy. Holders of non-EU licences must get an International Driving Permit (IDP) to accompany their national licence.

Hire

To hire a car you must:

- have a valid driving licence (plus IDP if required)
- have had your licence for at least a year
- be 21 or over. Under-25s will often have to pay a young-driver's supplement on top of the usual rates
- have a credit card

Make sure you understand what is included in the price (unlimited kilometres, tax, insurance, collision damage waiver etc) and what your liabilities are.

Vernazza wharf (p422), Cinque Terre
KRZYSZTOF DYDYNSKI/GETTY IMAGES ©

Main International Ferry Routes

FROM	TO	COMPANY	MIN-MAX FARE (€)	DURATION (HR)
Ancona	Igoumenitsa	Minoan, Superfast	75-111	16
Ancona	Patra	Minoan, Superfast	75-111	15½-22
Ancona	Split	Jadrolinija, SNAV	46-63	4½-11
Bari	Igoumenitsa	Superfast	78-93	8-12
Bari	Patra	Superfast	78-93	16
Bari	Dubrovnik	Jadrolinija	46-63	10-12
Bari	Bar	Montenegro	50-55	9
Brindisi	Igoumenitsa	Endeavor, Agoudimos	48-83	8
Brindisi	Patra	Endeavor	56-94	14
Brindisi	Corfu	Endeavor, Agoudimos	48-83	6½-11½
Brindisi	Kefallonia	Endeavor	56-94	12½
Genoa	Barcelona	GNV, SNAV	95	19½
Genoa	Tunis	GNV, SNAV	99	23½

For the best rental rates, book your car before leaving home. Note also that most cars have manual gear transmission.

In addition to the major rental agencies, local firms often offer competitive deals:

Italy by Car (☎ 334 6481920; www.italybycar.it)

Maggiore (☎ 199 151120; www.maggiore.it)

Insurance

If you're driving your own car, you'll need an international insurance certificate, known as a Carta Verde (Green Card), available from your insurance company.

Road Rules

- Drive on the right, overtake on the left and give way to cars coming from the right.
- It's obligatory to wear seatbelts, to drive with your headlights on when outside built-up areas, and to carry a warning triangle and fluorescent waistcoat in case of breakdown.
- Wearing a helmet is compulsory on all two-wheeled vehicles.
- The blood alcohol limit is 0.05% or zero for drivers who have had their licence for less than three years.

Unless otherwise indicated, speed limits are as follows:

- 130km/h (in rain 110km/h) on autostradas
- 110km/h (in rain 90km/h) on all main, non-urban roads

- 90km/h on secondary, non-urban roads
- 50km/h in built-up areas

Most major Italian cities operate a Limited Traffic Zone in their historic centres. You can enter a ZTL (*Zona a Traffico Limitato*) on a *motorino* (moped/scooter) but not in private or hire cars.

Train

Italy has an extensive rail network. Most services are run by **Trenitalia** (☎ 89 20 21; www.trenitalia.com) but as of April 2012 **Italo Treno** (☎ 06 07 08; www.italotreno.it) high-speed trains also connect Salerno, Naples, Rome, Florence, Bologna, Milan, Turin, Padua and Venice.

- Train prices quoted here are for the most common trains on any given route – that might be a slow Regionale train or a fast Frecciarossa.
- InterCity trains require a supplement, which is incorporated in the ticket price. If you have a standard ticket and board an InterCity you'll have to pay the difference on board.
- Generally, it's cheaper to buy all local train tickets in Italy.
- If your ticket doesn't include a reservation with an assigned seat, you must validate it before boarding by inserting it into one of the machines dotted around stations.
- Children under four travel free; kids between four and 12 are entitled to discounts of between 30% and 50%.

483

The Netherlands & Belgium

They might be next-door neighbours, but Belgium and the Netherlands couldn't be more different in attitude and outlook. On the one side, there's Belgium: best known for its bubbly beer, top-quality chocolate and political position at the heart of the EU. But look beyond these well-worn clichés and you'll discover an eccentric little nation packed with centuries of history, art and architecture, not to mention a longstanding identity crisis between its Flemish and Walloon sides.

On the other side is the Netherlands: liberal, laid-back and flat as a pancake, famous for its brown cafes, spinning windmills and colourful tulip fields. But again, the stereotypes tell only half the story. Look beyond Amsterdam's canals and you'll discover a whole different side to Holland, from buzzing urban centres like Rotterdam, gorgeous medieval towns such as Leiden and Delft, and wide-open spaces such as the stunning national park of Hoge Veluwe.

Woman cycling on frozen river, the Netherlands

485

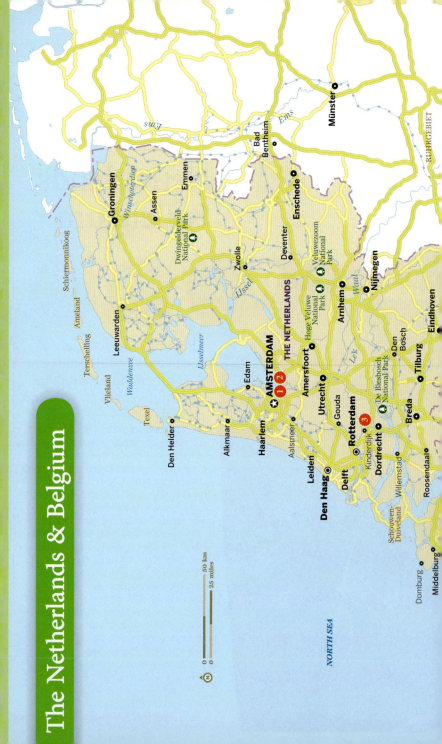

The Netherlands & Belgium

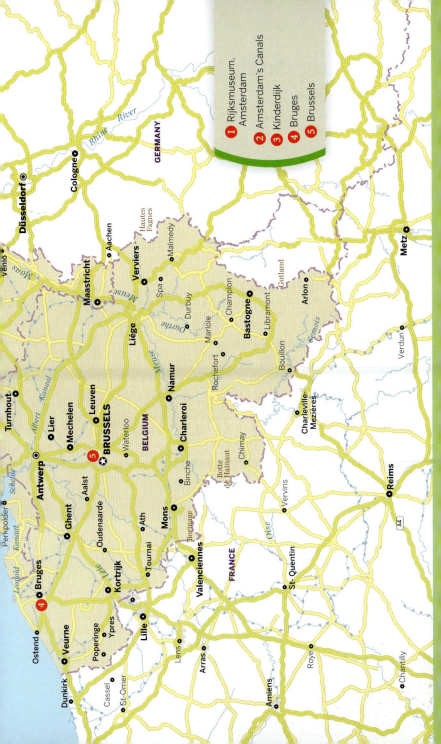

1 Rijksmuseum, Amsterdam
2 Amsterdam's Canals
3 Kinderdijk
4 Bruges
5 Brussels

GERMANY

Rhine River

Düsseldorf ◉

Cologne ●

Venlo ●

Maas

Aachen ●

Hautes Fagnes

Maastricht

Verviers ●

Malmedy ●

Metz ◉

Meuse

Spa ●

Durbuy ●

Champlon ●

Gutland

Liège ●

Ourthe

Marloie ●

Bastogne ●

Libramont ●

Arlon ●

Verdun ●

Turnhout ●

Albert Kanaal

Lier ●

Mechelen ●

Leuven ●

Namur ●

Charleroi ●

Meuse

Rochefort ●

Bouillon

Semois

Charleville-Mézières ●

BRUSSELS ✪ 5

Waterloo ●

BELGIUM

Schelde

Antwerp ◉

Aalst ●

Binche ●

Botte de Hainaut

Chimay ●

Reims ◉

A4

Ghent ●

Oudenaarde ●

Ath ●

Mons ●

Borinage

Vervins ●

Oise

Perkpolder ●

Kanaal

Leie

Kortrijk ●

Tournai ●

Valenciennes ●

FRANCE

St-Quentin ●

Leopold Kanaal

Bruges ● 4

Ypres ●

Lille ●

Lens ●

Royle ●

Ostend ●

Veurne ●

Poperinge ●

Arras ●

Chantilly ●

Dunkirk ●

Cassel ●

St-Omer ●

Amiens ◉

The Netherlands & Belgium Highlights

Rijksmuseum

It's been a long wait, but the Netherlands' national museum (p496) is finally open again to visitors. From priceless Delft pottery to ancient Egyptian artefacts, it's a dazzling affair. But it's the museum's unmatched collection of Dutch art that steals the show, with famous names such as Bosch, Cranach, van Gogh, Vermeer and Rubens all represented, and the biggest draw of all, Rembrandt's masterpiece *Night Watch*.

Amsterdam's Canals

If any European city was tailor-made for a romantic break, it's Amsterdam (p494). The city is criss-crossed by a web of waterways left over from its days as a maritime hub, and they're still a fundamental part of the city's laid-back character. Take a river cruise, hire a houseboat, cycle along the cobbled quays or just sit back in a canalside cafe and watch the world spin by.

Kinderdijk

3

Kinderdijk is perhaps the quintessential Dutch landscape. This Unesco-protected landscape southeast of Rotterdam (p516) boasts some of the Netherlands' oldest dikes and windmills, built during the 18th century to drain agricultural land. Regular boat cruises run from Rotterdam, and bikes are readily available for hire once you arrive.

4

Bruges

With a beautiful medieval centre and charmingly old-world atmosphere, Bruges (p537) is a Belgian treasure. The city's most famous landmark is the huge Belfort (83m; bell tower) overlooking the central marketplace – 366 winding steps lead to the top for one of the best views in Belgium. The only drawback is its popularity – try to visit in the low season if you can.

5

Brussels

With its impressive squares, colonnaded arcades and art nouveau architecture, Brussels (p520) is a city that oozes grace and sophistication. Browse for antiques, taste handmade chocolates and shop till you drop, then sit back and immerse yourself in the city's famous cafe culture on Grand Place.

The Netherlands & Belgium's Best...

Historic Towns

○ **Haarlem** (p508) The Netherlands in a nutshell: canals, cobbles, churches and cosy bars.

○ **Delft** (p512) This pretty Dutch town is famous for its delicate blue-and-white pottery.

○ **Ghent** (p534) Just as beautiful as Bruges, but much less crowded.

○ **Utrecht** (p517) Parts of this canal city date back to the 13th century.

○ **Ypres** (p542) Home to one of Belgium's grandest public squares, the Grote Markt.

Views

○ **The Canal Belt** (p495) Watch narrowboats putter past in Amsterdam's canal quarter.

○ **Belfort, Bruges** (p537) Bruges' iconic bell tower offers knockout views across the city.

○ **Euromast** (p515) This striking 185m-high tower soars above Rotterdam's historic harbour.

○ **Kinderdijk** (p516) The classic Dutch landscape: pancake-flat fields and spinning windmills.

○ **Domtoren** (p518) Climb 465 steps to the top of Utrecht's church tower.

Architectural Landmarks

○ **Oude Kerk** (p495) This 14th-century church is Amsterdam's oldest building.

○ **The Bourse** (p520) Brussels' 19th-century stock exchange is a neoclassical landmark.

○ **Grand Place** (p521) Grand by name and nature: the finest public square in Belgium.

○ **Overblaak** (p514) Piet Blom's controversial cube-shaped apartment block dates from the early 1980s.

○ **Atomium** (p525) A giant molecule built for the 1958 World Fair.

Need to Know

Art Museums

o **Rijksmuseum** (p496) Still the daddy of Dutch art galleries.

o **Van Gogh Museum** (p495) The world's largest collection of Vincent's works.

o **Museum Boijmans van Beuningen** (p514) Admire Dutch old masters, surrealists and pop artists at this Rotterdam landmark.

o **Rembrandthuis** (p501) Rembrandt's former Amsterdam studio is now a museum.

o **SMAK** (p535) Belgium's top contemporary gallery, near Ghent.

ADVANCE PLANNING

o **Two months before** Book accommodation for popular cities, especially Amsterdam, Bruges and Ghent.

o **At least a month before** Book Eurostar tickets for the cheapest deals.

o **When you arrive** Pick up a Museumkaart, which covers entry to 400 Dutch museums.

RESOURCES

o **Netherlands Tourism Board** (www.holland.com) Hotels, sights, restaurants and more.

o **Dutch Railways** (www.ns.nl) Plan your travel on the Dutch train system.

o **Flanders** (www.visitflanders.com) Specific information for the Flanders region.

o **Brussels** (www.brusselsinternational.be and www.otp.be) The latest lowdown on Belgium's capital.

o **Belgian beer tourism** (www.belgianstyle.com) All you need to know about Belgian beer.

GETTING AROUND

o **Air** The Netherlands' main airports are at Schiphol (Amsterdam) and Rotterdam. Most Belgian flights land in Brussels, Antwerp, Charleroi or Liège. All airports have shuttle buses and/or trains to relevant cities.

o **Bus** Regular buses serve major Dutch cities plus Brussels, Antwerp, Ghent and Liège.

o **Car** Rental costs and petrol can be pricey.

o **Train** Both countries have good rail networks; high-speed trains (Thalys in Belgium; Hispeed in the Netherlands) connect several major cities.

BE FOREWARNED

o **Public transport** The prepaid *OV-chipkaart* covers all public transport in the Netherlands.

o **Drugs** In the Netherlands, soft drugs are tolerated, but hard drugs are a serious crime. You can smoke pot *without* tobacco in coffee shops (but not cafes!).

o **Languages** Belgium has three official languages: French, German and Dutch (also called Flemish). Many Dutch people speak excellent English.

Left: Delftware pottery (p512), the Netherlands;
Above: Utrecht region (p517), the Netherlands
(LEFT) DANITA DELIMONT/GETTY IMAGES ©;
(ABOVE) FRANS LEMMENS/GETTY IMAGES ©

491

The Netherlands & Belgium Itineraries

The Netherlands and Belgium both have a lot to offer – great museums, groundbreaking architecture and some of Europe's most interesting cities.

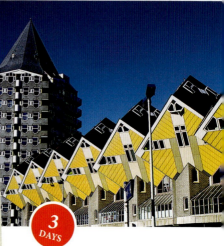

3 DAYS

THE DUTCH ESSENTIALS

Amsterdam to Rotterdam

For an introduction to the Netherlands, you simply can't beat ❶ **Amsterdam** (p494). It won't take you long to fall head over heels for this lovely, laid-back city. On day one head to the Rijksmuseum, Van Gogh Museum and Rembrandtshuis, and spend the evening exploring the Red Light District.

On day two visit Anne Frank's house, where the teenager penned her diary during the Nazi occupation. Spend the afternoon exploring the canals along Prinsengracht and Herengracht and the lovely area around Jordaan. Finish up with the essential Amsterdam experience – a romantic canal cruise.

On your last day, hop on a train to ❷ **Rotterdam** (p513), Holland's funky second city, and home to some of its wackiest architecture. Don't miss the experimental Overblaak Development and the 185m-tall Euromast, but make sure you leave time for the city's arts museum, the Museum Boijmans van Beuningen. Spend the evening dining and drinking in the old harbour area, Delfshaven.

Top Left: Overblaak Development (p514), Rotterdam, the Netherlands; **Top Right:** Grand Place (p521), Brussels, Belgium

(TOP LEFT) VISIONS OF OUR LAND/GETTY IMAGES © ARCHITECT: PIET BLOM;
(TOP RIGHT) MICHAEL FREEMAN/GETTY IMAGES ©

5 DAYS

THE ROAD TO BELGIUM

Delft to Ghent

After the cities, it's time to explore further afield. Two historic towns are within easy reach of Rotterdam – **①Delft** (p512), famous for its decorative china, and **②Leiden** (p510), Rembrandt's home town. Frequent train links make travelling to either town a breeze, so devote a day to each. Then it's on to **③Kinderdijk** (p516), a wonderfully Dutch landscape of antique windmills spinning above pancake-flat polders. The best transport there is the Waterbus from central Rotterdam.

On day four, catch the train south into Belgium and hop off at **④Antwerp** (p530), a fascinating old city whose main claim to fame is as the birthplace of Rubens; you can even visit the artist's original studio.

On day five, catch the train south to **⑤Brussels** (p520), Belgium's elegant capital and one of the EU's most important cities. All roads lead to Grand Place, the magnificent main square, where you can browse for Belgian goodies in the historic Galeries St-Hubert before sampling locally brewed beers in one of the many *belle époque* cafes.

Finish with a visit to gorgeous **⑥Ghent** (p534): with its haphazard streets, old squares and waterfront cafes, it feels a lot like Bruges but without the crowds.

Discover the Netherlands & Belgium

At a Glance

- **Amsterdam** (p494) Edgy and eccentric, lined by canals, this is the Netherlands' must-see city.

- **The Randstad** (p508) Postcard Holland, from windmills and dikes to revitalised harbours.

- **Brussels** (p520) Sip a coffee on Belgium's grandest Grand Place, then shop for the world's finest chocolate.

- **Flanders** (p530) Half-Belgian, half-Flemish, and crammed with history.

Oude Kerk in Amsterdam, the Netherlands
AMANDA HALL/GETTY IMAGES ©

THE NETHERLANDS

Amsterdam

♪ 020 / POP 781,000

If Amsterdam were a staid place it would still be one of Europe's most beautiful and historic cities, right up there with Venice and Paris. But add in the qualities that make it Amsterdam – the funky and mellow bars, brown cafes full of characters, pervasive irreverence, whiffs of pot and an open-air marketplace for sleaze and sex – and you have a literally intoxicating mix.

Wander the 17th-century streets, tour the iconic canals, stop off to enjoy a masterpiece, discover a funky shop and choose from food around the world. Walk or ride a bike around the concentric rings of the centre then explore the historic lanes of the Jordaan district or the Plantage, and bask in the many worlds-within-worlds, where nothing ever seems the same twice.

◎ Sights

CITY CENTRE

The not-overly-impressive **Royal Palace** (Koninklijk Paleis; ♪ 620 40 60; www.paleisamsterdam.nl; Dam; adult/child €7.50/3.75; ◷ 11am-5pm daily Jul & Aug, noon-5pm Tue-Sun Sep-Jun) and the square that puts the 'Dam' in Amsterdam anchor Amsterdam's oldest quarter. This is the busiest part of town for tourists: many leave the train station and head straight for the coffee shops and the Red Light District.

Nieuwe Kerk   Church
(New Church; ♪ 638 69 09; www.nieuwekerk.nl; Dam; adult/child €8/free; ◷ 10am-5pm; 🚊 1/2/5/13/14/17 Raadhuisstraat) The Nieuwe

Kerk is a historical stage for Dutch coronations. The 15th-century late-Gothic basilica is only 'new' in relation to the Oude Kerk. The building is now used for exhibitions and organ concerts.

Oude Kerk   Church

(Old Church; ☎ 625 82 84; www.oudekerk.nl; Oudekerksplein 23; adult/child €8/6; ⏱11am-5pm Mon-Sat, 1-5pm Sun; 🚊4/9/16/24/25 Dam) Amsterdam's oldest building, the 14th-century Oude Kerk, was built to honour the city's patron saint, St Nicholas. Inside there's a dramatic Müller organ, gilded oak vaults and 929 impressive stained-glass windows.

Red Light District   Neighbourhood

The Red Light District retains the power to make your jaw go limp, even if near-naked prostitutes propositioning passers-by from black-lit windows is the oldest Amsterdam cliché. Note that even in the dark heart of the district there are charming shops and cafes where the only thing that vibrates is your mobile phone. Despite the neon-lit sleaze, the district is tightly regulated and reasonably safe for strolling.

Amsterdam Museum   Museum

(☎ 523 18 22; www.amsterdammuseum.nl; Kalverstraat 92; adult/child €10/5; ⏱10am-5pm; 🚊1/2/5 Spui) Housed in the old civic orphanage, the Amsterdams Historisch Museum takes you through all the fascinating twists and turns of Amsterdam's convoluted history.

CANAL BELT

Created in the 17th century as an upscale neighbourhood, the Canal Belt, especially in the west and south, remains Amsterdam's top district. Wandering here amid architectural treasures and their reflections on the narrow waters of the Prinsengracht, Keizersgracht and Herengracht can cause days to vanish quicker than some of Amsterdam's more lurid pursuits. No two buildings are alike, yet they combine in ever-changing, ever-pleasing harmony.

Anne Frank Huis   Museum

(Anne Frank House; ☎ 556 71 05; www.annefrank.org; Prinsengracht 263-267; adult/child €9/4.50; ⏱9am-10pm Jul & Aug, 9am-9pm Sun-Fri, 9am-10pm Sat mid-Mar–Jun & mid-Sep, 9am-7pm Sun-Fri, 9am-9pm Sat mid-Sep–mid-Mar; 🚊13/14/17 Westermarkt) The Anne Frank Huis, where Anne wrote her famous diary, lures almost a million visitors annually with its secret annexe, reconstruction of Anne's melancholy bedroom, and her actual diary, with its sunnily optimistic writing tempered by quiet despair. Look for the photo of Peter Schiff, her 'one true love'. Try going in the early morning or evening when crowds are lightest; book online to avoid long queues.

FOAM   Gallery

(Fotografie Museum Amsterdam; www.foam.org; Keizersgracht 609; adult/child €8.50/free; ⏱10am-6pm Sat-Wed, to 9pm Thu & Fri; 🚊16/24/25 Keizersgracht) Two storeys of changing exhibitions feature world-renowned photographers such as Sir Cecil Beaton, Annie Leibovitz and Henri Cartier-Bresson.

MUSEUMPLEIN

Van Gogh Museum   Museum

(☎ 570 52 00; www.vangoghmuseum.nl; Paulus Potterstraat 7; adult/child €14/free, audioguide €5; ⏱10am-6pm Sat-Thu, to 10pm Fri; 🚊2/3/5/12 Van Baerlestraat) This outstanding museum, recently reopened after a seven-month renovation, houses the world's largest Van Gogh collection. Trace the artist's life from his tentative start through to his Japanese phase, and on to the black cloud that descended over him and his work. There's also works by contemporaries Gauguin, Toulouse-Lautrec, Monet and Bernard.

Stedelijk Museum   Museum

(☎ 573 29 11; www.stedelijk.nl; Museumplein 10; adult/child €15/free; ⏱11am-5pm Tue & Wed, 11am-10pm Thu, 10am-6pm Fri-Sun; 🚊2/3/5/12 Van Baerlestraat) Amsterdam's weighty modern art museum is among the world's best. It struts Matisse cut-outs, Kandinsky abstracts, Picasso drawings, Rodin sculptures and a vivid collection

Don't Miss
Rijksmuseum

Fresh from a 10-year renovation, the Netherlands' foremost museum finally reopened its doors in April 2013, revealing more than 1.5km of refurbished galleries lined with old master paintings, priceless artefacts and historical oddities.

National Museum

📞 674 70 00

www.rijksmuseum.nl

Stadhouderskade 42

adult/child €15/free

🕐 9am-5pm

🚊 2/5 Hobbemastraat

The Building

One of the main attractions of the renovated Rijksmuseum is the building itself. The 19th-century facade has been thoroughly spruced up during its 10-year refit, and and shines once again in crimson-and-cream stone. Of particular note are the wonderful entrance hall, with its mosaic and stained glass, and the new Asian Pavilion, which provides a bold, modern contrast to the museum's classical surroundings. The original architect, Pierre Cuypers, would no doubt be thrilled with the care, attention and expense that's been lavished on his most famous building.

The Old Masters

The Rijksmuseum owns the world's finest collection of paintings from the golden age of Dutch art (7500 in all). Among its priceless canvases are four Vermeers, as well as an array of works by notable names such as Franz Hals and Jan Steen. But it's Rembrandt's iconic *Night Watch* (1642) which takes pride of place: it's the museum's prize painting and is displayed to suitably dramatic effect in its very own gallery.

Other Highlights

The Rijksmuseum isn't just about paintings, though. It also houses one of the world's great collections of Delftware, the delicate blue-and-white pottery that was all the rage in aristocratic Europe during the 17th and 18th centuries. There are also countless curiosities to seek out, from antique dolls' houses to vintage weaponry and insanely detailed model ships. In fact, you could spend every day of your trip here and still only scratch the surface.

Rijksmuseum

RECOMMENDATIONS FROM PIETER ROELOFS, CURATOR OF 17TH CENTURY PAINTING AT THE RIJKSMUSEUM

1 WOMAN IN BLUE READING A LETTER BY JOHANNES VERMEER

Painted around 1660, this is one of four Vermeer paintings in the museum's collection. It shows a woman standing in the corner of a room reading a letter from her lover. It's a classic Vermeer composition, and is remarkable for its intense blues: blue was by far the most expensive colour to use at the time, as it had to be made from lapis lazuli brought to the Netherlands all the way from Afghanistan.

2 THE BATTLE OF WATERLOO BY JAN WILLEM PIENEMAN

Painted in 1824, this huge painting is the largest in the museum's collection, measuring around 8m by 6m. It's full of drama and movement, and features all the key characters from the Battle of Waterloo, including the Duke of Wellington and the wounded Dutch prince, Willem II, lying on a stretcher.

3 THE BEUNING ROOM

This beautiful room illustrates what life was like in Amsterdam in the mid-18th century. It was originally part of a canal house, but the original building was demolished and the entire mahogany room has been reconstructed inside the museum, complete with original stucco and painted decorations.

4 TERRACOTTA BUST OF THE WEEPING MADONNA

This wonderful medieval bust, with its slightly opened mouth, was made by an Italian sculptor who was working in Flanders around 1500. It's so lifelike and full of emotion.

5 THE F.K. 23 BANTAM BIPLANE

This aeroplane was built in 1917 by the Dutch engineer Frederick Koolhoven as a WWI fighter plane. The wooden fuselage was made by hand, including the propeller, which is a work of art in itself. People don't expect to see a full-sized aeroplane inside, so it comes as quite a surprise!

Central Amsterdam

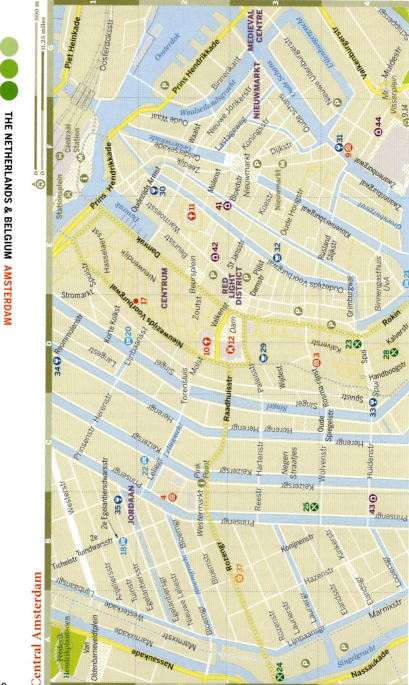

0 500 m
0 0.25 miles

G F E D C B A

Piet Heinkade

Oosterdok

Oosterdokskade

Prins Hendrikkade

Binnenkant

Waalseilandsgracht

Oude Waal

Waalst

Nieuwe Jonkerstr

Lastageweg

Oude schans

Nieuwe Uilenburgerstr

Nieuwe Uilenburgerstr

MEDIEVAL
CENTRE

Valkenburgerstr

Mr. Muldestr
Visserplein

44

9.14

NIEUWMARKT

Koningsstr

Dijkstr

Geldersekade

Gelderskade

Zeedijk

Molenst

Bloedstr

Koestr

Nieuwmarkt

Nieuwe Hoogstr

31

9

Zwanenburgwal

Zwanenburgwal

Groenburgwal

Kloveniersburgwal

Prins Hendrikkade

Oudezijds Armst

30

Warmoesstr

11

41

St Jansstr

32

Oude Hoogstr

Rusland

Slijkstr

21

Oudezijds Voorburgwal

Stationsplein

Centraal
Station

Damrak

Beursstr

42

Damstr

Pijlst

RED
LIGHT
DISTRICT

Binnengasthuis
UvA

Nieuwendijk

Spuistr

Hasselaerst

Nieuwezijds Voorburgwal

CENTRUM

Beursplein

Zoutst

Valkenst

Dam

12

Oudezijds Voorburgwal

Grimburgwal

Rokin

Stromarkt

17

Molst

Paleisstr

29

3

Kalverstr

Kalverstr

23

28

Spui

Handboogstr

Langestr

Korte Kolkst

Lijnbaansst

Singel

20

10

Wijdest

Rosmarijnst

33

Spuistr

Spui

Roomolenstr

34

Torensluis

Raadhuisstr

Paleisstr

Singel

Oude
Spiegelstr

Herengr

Herengr

Herengr

Herengr

Negen
Straatjes

Wolvenstr

Huidenstr

Prinsenstr

Herenstr

Keizersgr

Keizersgr

Keizersgr

Reestr

Hartenstr

Herengr

43

Prinsengr

22

Leliegr

Pink
Point

Westermarkt

4

Westerstr

35

2e Egelantiersdwarsstr

JORDAAN

Bloemgr

Bloemgr

Prinsengr

Rozengr

25

Konijnenstr

Hazenstr

Prinsengr

Tichelstr

2e
Tuindwarsstr

18

Anjelierstr

Tuinstr

Egelantiersstr

Nieuwe Leliestr

Bloemgr

Bloemgr

Rozengr

Laurierstr

Laurierstr

Lijnbaansgr

Elandsstr

Elandsgr

Looiersgr

Marnixstr

Westerstr

37

Tichelstr

Lijnbaansgr

Frederik
Hendrikplantsoen

Van
Oldenbarneveldtplein

Marnixkade

Anjelierstr

Marnixstr

Nieuwe

Singelgracht

Nassaukade

Nassaukade

24

Zeedijk

Koningsstr

Koestr

498

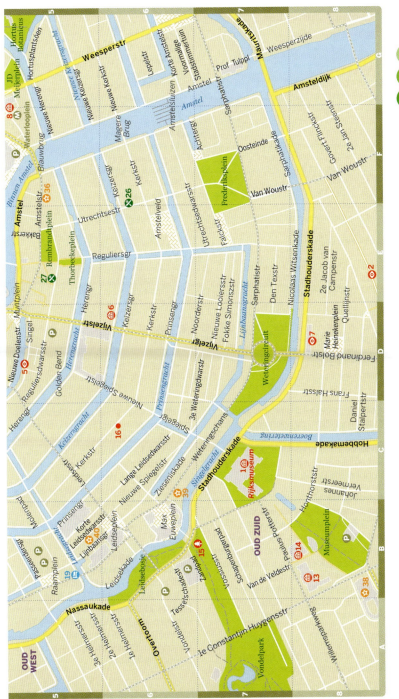

Hortus
Botanicus
JD
Meijerplein
Hortusplantsoen
Weesperstr
Marnixkade
Weesperzijde
Amsteldijk
Lepelstr
Korte Amstelstr
Nieuwe Kerkstr
Amstelsluzen
Voormalige
Nieuwe Kerkstr
Stadstimmertuin
Amstel
Prof Tulpl
Nieuwe Herengr
Nieuwe Keizersgracht
Waterlooplein
Blauwbrug
Magere
Brug
Amstel
Oosteinde
Sarphatistr
Govert Flinckstr
2e Jan Steenstr
Amstelstr
Keizersgr
Kerkstr
Frederiksplein
Van Woustr
Sarphatikade
Van Woustr
Amstelstr
Bakkerstr
Rembrandtplein
Amstelveld
Utrechtsedwarsstr
Utrechtsestr
Falckstr
Sarphatistr
Stadhouderskade
2e Jacob van
Campenstr
Quellijnstr
Regulliersgr
Thorbeckeplein
Herengr
Kerkstr
Prinsengr
Noorderstr
Nieuwe Looiersstr
Fokke Simonszstr
Den Texstr
Nicolaas Witsenkade
Muntplein
Singel
Herengr
Keizersgr
Vijzelstr
Vijzelgr
Lijnbaansgracht
Sarphatistr
Marie
Heinekenplein
Nieuwe Doelenstr
Reguliersdwarsstr
Golden Bend
Herengracht
Nieuwe Spiegelstr
Prinsengracht
3e Weteringdwarsstr
Weteringcircuit
Weteringschans
Ferdinand Bolstr
Frans Halsstr
Daniel
Stalpertstr
Herengr
Keizersgracht
Spiegelgr
Weteringschans
Boerenwetering
Hobbemakade
Leidsestr
Kerkstr
Lange Leidsedwarsstr
Nieuwe Spiegelstr
Ziezeniskade
Spiegelgr
Singelgracht
Stadhouderskade
Rijksmuseum
Johannes
Vermeerstr
Hobbemastr
Prinsengr
Korte
Leidsedwarsstr
Lijnbaansgr
Max
Euweplein
Weteringschans
Museumplein
Pieter
Molenpad
Leidseplein
Leidsekade
Van de Veldestr
OUD ZUID
Passeerdersgr
Raamplein
Leidsebosje
Tesselschadestr
Zandpad
Vossiusstr
Schapenburgerpad
Paulus Potterstr
Nassaukade
Vondelstr
Constantijn Huygensstr
OUD
WEST
3e Helmersstr
2e Helmersstr
1e Helmersstr
Overtoom
Vondelstr
1e Constantijn Huygensstr
Vondelpark
Willemsparkweg

8
M
36
26
5
27
6
16
7
2
1
39
40
15
14
13
38
19

Central Amsterdam

◉ Don't Miss Sights
1 Rijksmuseum............................ C7

◉ Sights
2 Albert Cuypmarkt E8
3 Amsterdam Museum D3
4 Anne Frank Huis.........................B2
5 Bloemenmarkt D5
6 FOAM...D6
7 Heineken Experience..................D8
8 Joods Historisch Museum...........F5
9 Museum het Rembrandthuis F4
10 Nieuwe Kerk D2
11 Oude Kerk E2
12 Royal Palace..............................D3
13 Stedelijk Museum B8
14 Van Gogh Museum B8
15 Vondelpark B7

✪ Activities, Courses & Tours
16 St Nicolaas Boat Club C6
17 Yellow Bike................................D1

🛏 Sleeping
18 All Inn the Family B&B...............B1
19 Backstage Hotel B5
20 Hotel Brouwer D1
21 Hotel de L'Europe E4
22 Toren C2

✕ Eating
23 Gartine D4
24 Moeders.....................................A3
25 Pancakes!..................................B3
26 Tempo Doeloe............................F6
27 Van Dobben...............................E5
28 Vleminckx..................................D4

✪ Drinking & Nightlife
29 Abraxas D3
30 Brouwerij De Prael F2
31 De Sluyswacht F4
32 Greenhouse................................E3
33 Hoppe...C4
34 't Arendsnest.............................D1
35 't Smalle B1

✪ Entertainment
36 Air F5
37 Boom Chicago B3
38 Concertgebouw..........................B8
39 Paradiso.....................................C6
40 Sugar Factory............................B5

🔒 Shopping
41 Absolute Danny..........................E2
42 Condomerie Het Gulden Vlies ...E2
43 De Kaaskamer B4
44 Waterlooplein Flea Market.........F4

of paintings by Dutch homeboys Piet Mondrian, Willem de Kooning, Charlie Toorop and Karel Appel. After a nine-year renovation, the Stedelijk reopened in September 2012 with a huge new wing (dubbed 'the Bathtub').

Vondelpark
Park

(www.vondelpark.nl; Stadhouderskade; ⏱24hr; 🚋2/5 Hobbemastraat) Vondelpark is an English-style park with free concerts, ponds, lawns, thickets, winding footpaths and three outdoor cafes. It was named after the poet and playwright Joost van den Vondel, the 'Dutch Shakespeare', and is popular with joggers, skaters, buskers and lovers.

JORDAAN

Originally a stronghold of the working class, the Jordaan is now one of the most desirable areas to live in Amsterdam. It's a pastiche of modest 17th- and 18th-century merchants' houses, humble workers' homes and a few modern carbuncles, squashed in a grid of tiny lanes peppered with bite-sized cafes and shops. Its intimacy is contagious, and now the average Jordaan dweller is more likely to be a gallery owner than a labourer.

DE PIJP

Heineken Experience
Brewery

(☎523 9435; www.heinekenexperience.com; Stadhouderskade 78; adult/child €18/14; ⏱11am-7.30pm Mon-Thu, 11am-8.30pm Fri-Sun; 🚋16/24/25 Stadhouderskade) The Heineken Experience is the much-gussied-up reincarnation of the brewer's old brewery tour featuring multimedia displays, rides and plenty of gift shops.

NIEUWMARKT & PLANTAGE

Museum het Rembrandthuis   Museum

(Rembrandt House Museum; ☎ 520 04 00; www.rembrandthuis.nl; Jodenbreestraat 4-6; adult/child €10/3; ⏰10am-5pm; 🚊9/14 Waterlooplein) You almost expect to find the master himself at the Museum het Rembrandthuis, the house where Rembrandt van Rijn ran his painting studio, only to lose the lot when profligacy set in, enemies swooped, and bankruptcy came knocking. The museum has scores of etchings and sketches.

Joods Historisch Museum   Museum

(Jewish Historical Museum; ☎ 626 99 45; www. jhm.nl; Nieuwe Amstelstraat 1; adult/child €12/3; ⏰11am-5pm; 🚻; 🚊9/14 Mr Visserplein) A beautifully restored complex of four Ashkenazic synagogues from the 17th and 18th centuries shows the history of Jews in the Netherlands.

Tours

There are bike tours as well as canal boat tours of Amsterdam that let you hop on and hop off.

Van Gogh Museum (p495) in Amsterdam, the Netherlands

St Nicolaas Boat Club   Boat Tour

(www.amsterdamboatclub.com; Kerkstraat 134) By far the best boat tour in the city. The open-air, 10-seat boats can manoeuvre into the narrowest canals. Rides last 60 to 90 minutes. There is no set fee, just a suggested donation of €10. Departure times vary according to numbers; sign up after noon at the bar at Boom Chicago.

🛏 Sleeping

Book ahead for weekends and in summer. Wi-fi is near universal but elevators are not.

All Inn the Family B&B   B&B $$

(☎776 36 36; www.allinnthefamily.nl; 2e Egelantiersdwarsstraat 10; r €95-140; 📶) This new B&B, in a charming old Amsterdam canal house, gets rave reviews for embodying the very qualities of the inimitable Jordaan itself. Spirited hosts who speak five languages, a bountiful organic Dutch breakfast, and a quiet location in the heart of the neighbourhood.

Toren   Boutique Hotel $$

(☎622 60 33; www.toren.nl; Keizersgracht 164; r €130-210, ste from €300; ❄ @ 📶; 🚊13/17

501

Westermarkt) A title-holder for price, room size and personal service, the Toren's communal areas mix 17th-century decadence – gilded mirrors, fireplaces and magnificent chandeliers – with a sensual, decadent flair that screams (or, rather, whispers) Parisian boudoir. Guest rooms are elegantly furnished with modern facilities (including Nespresso coffee machines).

Hotel de L'Europe Luxury Hotel **$$$**
(☎ 531 17 77; www.leurope.nl; Nieuwe Doelenstraat 2-8; r from €340; ❄ @ 🛜 🏊) Oozing Victorian elegance, L'Europe welcomes you with a glam chandelier, a marble lobby, 100 gloriously large rooms (some have terraces and all have handsome marble bathrooms) and smart extras like a shoeshine service and boats for canal cruises.

Hotel Brouwer Hotel **$$**
(☎ 624 63 58; www.hotelbrouwer.nl; Singel 83; r €60-100; @ 🛜) Our favourite hotel in this price range, it has just eight rooms in a house dating back to 1652. Its rooms, named for Dutch painters, are furnished with simplicity, but all have canal views. There's – get this – a tiny lift.

Backstage Hotel Hotel **$$**
(☎ 624 40 44; www.backstagehotel.com; Leidsegracht 114; d with/without bathroom from €125/85; @ 🛜) We wanna rock all night at the Backstage. This seriously fun music-themed hotel is a favourite among musicians jamming at nearby Melkweg and Paradiso, as evidenced by the lobby bar's band-signature-covered piano and pool table.

🍴 Eating

Happy streets for hunting include Utrechtsesraat, Spuistraat and any of the little streets lining and connecting the west canals, such as Berenstraat.

Van Dobben Traditional Dutch **$**
(☎ 624 42 00; www.eetsalonvandobben.nl; Korte Reguliersdwarsstraat 5-9; items €2.75-6.50;

Left: Vondelpark (p500) in Amsterdam, the Netherlands;
Below: Royal Palace (p494) in Amsterdam, the Netherlands
(LEFT) GEORGE TSAFOS/GETTY IMAGES ©; (BELOW) INGOLF POMPE/GETTY IMAGES ©

🕙10am-9pm Mon-Wed, 10am-1am Thu, 10am-2am Fri & Sat, 11.30am-8pm Sun; 🚋4/9/14 Rembrandt-plein) Open since the 1940s, the venerable Van Dobben has white-tile walls and white-coated counter men who specialise in snappy banter. Traditional meaty Dutch fare is its forte: try the *pekelvlees* (something close to corned beef). The *kroketten* (croquettes) are the best in town.

Gartine   Cafe $$

(📞320 41 32; www.gartine.nl; Taksteeg 7; mains €6-12, high tea €12-21; 🕙10am-6pm Wed-Sun; ✈️; 🚋4/9/14/16/24/25 Spui) Gartine makes delectable breakfast pastries, sandwiches and salads from produce grown in its own garden plot. Throw in slow-food credentials and gorgeous antique plates and it's a winner.

Tempo Doeloe   Indonesian $$$

(📞625 67 18; www.tempodoeloerestaurant.nl; Utrechtsestraat 75; mains €23.50-37.50, rijsttafel & set menus €29-49; 🕙6pm-midnight Mon-Sat; ✈️; 🚋4 Keizersgracht) Tempo Doeloe's

setting and service are pleasant and decorous without being overdone. The same applies to the *rijsttafel* (rice table): a ridiculously overblown affair at many places, here it's a fine sampling of the range of flavours found in the country.

Pancakes!   Traditional Dutch $

(www.pancakesamsterdam.com; Berenstraat 38; pancakes €5-13; 🕙10am-7pm; ✈️👶; 🚋13/14/17 Westermarkt) Just as many locals as tourists grace the blue-tile tables at snug little Pancakes!, carving into all the usual options, plus daily creations like ham, chicory and cheese or chicken curry pancakes. The batter is made with flour sourced from a local mill.

Moeders   Traditional Dutch $$

(📞626 79 57; www.moeders.com; Rozengracht 251; mains €15-19.50, 3-course menus €26-30; 🕙5pm-midnight Mon-Fri, noon-midnight Sat & Sun; 👶; 🚋10/13/14/17 Marnixstraat) Mum's the word at 'Mothers'. When this friendly

503

't Smalle cafe in Amsterdam, the Netherlands

INGOLF POMPE/GETTY IMAGES ©

place opened over 20 years ago, staff asked customers to bring their own plates and photos of their mums as donations, and the result is still a delightful hotch-potch. Book ahead.

Vleminckx   Frites $
(Voetboogstraat 31; small/large €2.20/2.70, sauces €0.80; ⊙11am-6pm Tue-Sat, to 7pm Thu, noon-6pm Sun & Mon; 🚋1/2/5 Koningsplein) This hole-in-the-wall takeaway has drawn the hordes for its monumental *frites* since 1887. The standard is smothered in mayonnaise.

🍷 Drinking & Nightlife

A particular Amsterdam joy is discovering your own brown cafe. They are found everywhere, often tucked into the most atmospheric of locations. Many serve food.

Hoppe   Brown Cafe
(www.cafehoppe.nl; Spui 18-20; 🚋1/2/5 Spui) Go on. Do your bit to ensure Hoppe maintains one of the highest beer turnovers in the city. The gritty brown cafe has been filling glasses for more than 300 years.

't Smalle   Brown Cafe
(www.t-smalle.nl; Egelantiersgracht 12; ⊙10am-1am Sun-Thu, 10am-2am Fri & Sat; 🚋13/14/17 Westermarkt) Take your boat and dock right on 't Smalle's pretty stone terrace – there's hardly a more convivial setting in the daytime or a more romantic one at night. It's equally charming inside, dating back to 1786 as a *jenever* (Dutch gin) distillery and tasting house.

De Sluyswacht   Brown Cafe
(www.sluyswacht.nl; Jodenbreestraat 1; ⊙from 11.30am; 🚋9/14 Waterlooplein) Listing like a ship in a high wind, this tiny black building was once a lock-keeper's house on the Oude Schans. Today the canalside terrace is one of the nicest spots we know in town to relax and down a beer.

't Arendsnest   Beer Cafe
(www.arendsnest.nl; Herengracht 90; ⊙2pm-midnight Sun-Thu, 2pm-2am Fri & Sat; 🚋1/2/5/13/17 Nieuwezijds Kolk) This gorgeous, restyled brown cafe, with its glowing copper *jenever* boilers behind the bar, only serves Dutch beer.

Brouwerij De Prael — Beer Cafe

(📞408 44 69; www.deprael.nl; Oudezijds Armsteeg 26; 🕐11am-11pm Tue-Sun; 🚊4/9/16/24/25 Centraal Station) Sample organic beers named after classic Dutch singers in this spacious, wood-panelled tasting room decorated with old radios and album covers.

⭐ Entertainment

Find out what's on in **I Amsterdam** (www.iamsterdam.com/events).

GAY & LESBIAN AMSTERDAM

Gay Amsterdam (www.gayamsterdam.com) Lists hotels, shops, restaurants and clubs, and provides maps.

Pink Point (📞428 10 70; www.pinkpoint.org; Westermarkt; 🕐10am-6pm; 🚊14 Westermarkt) On the Keizersgracht, behind the Westerkerk. Part information kiosk, part souvenir shop, with details on myriad gay and lesbian hangouts, and copies of the candid *Bent Guide*.

COFFEE SHOPS

Cafes have coffee, 'coffee shops' are where one buys pot.

In coffee shops, ask at the bar for the menu of cannibis-related goods on offer, usually packaged in small bags. You can also buy ready-made joints (€3 to €7). Most shops offer rolling papers, pipes or even bongs to use. Alcohol and tobacco products are not permitted in coffee shops.

Don't light up anywhere besides a coffee shop without checking that it's OK to do so.

Abraxas — Coffee Shop

(www.abraxas.tv; Jonge Roelensteeg 12; 🕐from 10am; 📶) Hands down the most beautiful coffee shop in town. Choose from southwest USA, Middle Eastern and other styles of decor, spread over three floors.

Greenhouse — Coffee Shop

(Oudezijds Voorburgwal 191; 🕐from 9am; 📶; 🚊4/9/16/24/25 Dam) One of the most popular coffee shops in town. Smokers love the funky music, multicoloured mo-saics, psychedelic stained-glass windows, and high-quality weed and hash.

NIGHTCLUBS

Sugar Factory — Live Music, Club

(www.sugarfactory.nl; Lijnbaansgracht 238; 🕐6pm-5am; 🚊1/2/5/7/10 Leidseplein) A cool vibe, an excellent location and a varied line-up are the hallmarks here. But this ain't your average club – most nights start with music, cinema, or a dance or spoken-word performance, followed by late-night DJs and dancing.

Air — Club

(📞820 06 70; www.air.nl; Amstelstraat 16; 🕐Thu-Sun; 🚊4/9/14 Rembrandtplein) One of Amsterdam's It clubs, Air has an environmentally friendly design and a unique tiered dance floor.

LIVE MUSIC

Concertgebouw — Classical Music

(📞671 83 45; www.concertgebouw.nl; Concertgebouwplein 2-6; 🕐box office 1-7pm Mon-Fri, 10am-7pm Sat & Sun; 🚊3/5/12/16/24 Museumplein) One of the world's great concert halls, the Concertgebouw has near-perfect acoustics that flatter the already esteemed Royal Concertgebouw Orchestra. Every Wednesday at 12.30pm from September till the end of June, the Concertgebouw holds free half-hour concerts, traditionally of chamber music or public rehearsals of an evening event.

Paradiso — Live Music

(📞622 05 50; www.paradiso.nl; Weteringschans 6; 🕐from 6pm; 🚊7/10 Spiegelgracht) Worship rock 'n' roll in a gorgeous old church where the Beatles once played.

THEATRE

Boom Chicago — Comedy, Club

(📞423 01 01; www.boomchicago.nl; Rozengracht 117, Rosentheater; 🕐box office 4-8.30pm Wed-Fri, 3-11pm Sat; 🚊13/14/17 Marnixstraat/Rozengracht) It's a comedy club, a late night bar, and a nightclub. Add to that the fact you can enjoy Amsterdam's leading English-language improv comedy show over dinner and a few drinks.

🔒 Shopping

MEDIEVAL CENTRE & RED LIGHT DISTRICT

Condomerie Het Gulden Vlies
Specialty Shop

(www.condomerie.nl; Warmoesstraat 141; 🚋4/9/16/24/25 Dam) This is where the well-dressed Johnson shops for variety. Perfectly positioned for the Red Light District, the boutique stocks hundreds of types of condoms.

Absolute Danny
Erotica

(www.absolutedanny.com; Oudezijds Achterburgwal 78; ⏰11am-9pm Mon-Sat, from noon Sun; 🚋4/9/16/24/25 Dam) Named by Dutch *Playboy* as Amsterdam's classiest sex shop, Absolute Danny specialises in fetish clothing, lingerie and leather, along with hard-core videos and dildos just for fun.

JORDAAN & WESTERN CANAL BELT

Several streets along the Western Canals are dotted with surprising little shops: try Reesstraat and Hartenstraat and the blocks south to Runstraat and Huidenstraat.

De Kaaskamer
Food & Drink

(www.kaaskamer.nl; Runstraat 7; ⏰noon-6pm Mon, 9am-6pm Tue-Fri, 9am-5pm Sat, noon-5pm Sun; 🚋1/2/5 Spui) The name means 'cheese room' and it is indeed stacked to the rafters with Dutch and organic varieties, as well as olives, tapenades, salads and other picnic ingredients.

ℹ️ Information

GWK Travelex (📞0900 05 66; www.gwk.nl; Centraal Station; ⏰8am-10pm Mon-Sat, 9am-10pm Sun; 🚉Centraal Station) Exchanges travellers cheques and makes hotel reservations; also at Schiphol airport.

I Amsterdam Card (www.iamsterdam.com; per 24/48/72hr €40/50/60) Available at VVV offices and some hotels. Provides admission to many museums, canal boat trips, and discounts and freebies at shops, attractions and restaurants. Also includes a GVB transit pass.

Tourist office (www.iamsterdam.nl; Stationsplein 10; ⏰9am-7pm Mon-Fri, 10am-6pm Sat & Sun)

Concertgebouw (p505) in Amsterdam, the Netherlands

🛈 Getting There & Away

Air

Most major airlines serve **Schiphol** (AMS; www. schiphol.nl) airport, 18km southwest of the city centre.

Train

Amsterdam's main train station is fabled **Centraal Station** (⏰8am-10pm Mon-Sat, 9am-10pm Sun), with services to the rest of the country and major European cities.

🛈 Getting Around

To/From the Airport

A **taxi** into Amsterdam from Schiphol airport takes 25 to 45 minutes and costs about €45. **Trains** to Centraal Station leave every few minutes, take 15 to 20 minutes, and cost €4/7 per single/return.

Bicycle

Amsterdam is cycling nirvana: flat, beautiful, with dedicated bike paths. About 150,000 bicycles are stolen each year in Amsterdam, so always lock up. Rental agencies include the following:

Bike City (📞626 37 21; www.bikecity.nl; Bloemgracht 68-70; bikes per 4/24hrs from €10/13.50; ⏰9am-6pm) There's no advertising on the bikes, so you can pretend you're a local.

Yellow Bike (📞620 69 40; www.yellowbike. nl; Nieuwezijds Kolk 29; city/countryside tours €19.50/29.50) Choose from city tours or the longer countryside tour through the pretty Waterland district to the north. Also rents bikes.

Boat

Amsterdam's **canal boats** are a popular way to tour the town but most are actually a bit claustrophobic, with steamed-up glass windows surrounding passengers. Look for a boat with an open seating area.

There are also free **ferries** from behind Centraal Station to destinations around the IJ, notably Amsterdam Noord.

Canal Bus (www.canal.nl; day pass adult/child €22/11) Offers a unique hop-on, hop-off service; has 17 docks around the city near the big museums.

Car & Motorcycle

Amsterdam is horrendous for parking, with charges averaging €5 per hour. Your best bet is to ditch the car at an outlying train station and ride in.

Markets

Markets of just about every description are scattered across the city. Amsterdam's largest and busiest market, **Albert Cuypmarkt** (www.albertcuypmarkt.nl; Albert Cuypstraat, btwn Ferdinand Bolstraat & Van Woustraat; ⏰10am-5pm Mon-Sat; 🚋16/24 Albert Cuypstraat) is 100 years old. Food of every description, flowers, souvenirs, clothing, hardware and household goods can be found here.

Bloemenmarkt (Flower Market; Singel, btwn Muntplein & Koningsplein; ⏰9am-5.30pm Mon-Sat, 11am-5.30pm Sun; 🚋1/2/5 Koningsplein) is a touristy 'floating' flower market that's actually on pilings. Still, at the stalls that actually stock flowers (as opposed to plastic clogs), the vibrant colours burst forth.

Waterlooplein Flea Market (www. waterloopleinmarkt.nl; ⏰9am-5pm Mon-Sat) is Amsterdam's most famous flea market: curios, secondhand clothing, music, used footwear, ageing electronic gear, New Age gifts, cheap bicycle parts.

Public Transport

Services – including Amsterdam's iconic **trams** – are run by the local transit authority, GVB. Its highly useful **GVB information office** (www.gvb. nl; Stationsplein 10; ⏰7am-9pm Mon-Fri, 10am-6pm Sat & Sun) is located across the tram tracks from the Centraal Station main entrance. You can avoid the often-long lines by buying day passes at the adjoining VVV office instead.

Public transport in Amsterdam uses the *OV-chipkaart*. Rides cost €2.70 when bought on the tram or bus. Unlimited-ride passes are available for between one to seven days (€7.50 to €31), valid on trams, most buses and the metro are good value.

Night buses take over shortly after midnight, which is when the trams and regular buses stop running.

If You Like...
Dutch Cheeses

If your taste buds have been tickled by the amazing cheese market in Alkmaar (p508), there are a couple more iconic Dutch cheeses you simply have to try.

1 EDAM

This spherical, semi-hard cheese is undoubtedly the best-known Dutch cheese, and is instantly recognisable thanks to its coat of red paraffin wax. You'll see it for sale everywhere. In Edam itself, you can browse vintage tools and a remarkable floating cellar at the **Edams Museum** (www.edamsmuseum.nl; museum Damplein 8, annexe Damplein 1; adult/child €4/free; ☑10am-4.30pm Tue-Sat, 1-4.30pm Sun Apr-Oct), and then head off for a tasting session at **Gestam** (www.gestam.com; Voorhaven 127; ☑10am-4pm Wed & Fri), a warehouse for local cheesemakers.

2 GOUDA

The first mention of the Netherlands' second-most famous *fromage* was allegedly in 1184, making it one of the world's oldest cheeses. Gouda is a hugely attractive little town, with many old buildings and quaint canals, as well as a huge **cheese market** (www.goudakaas.nl; ☑10am-12.30pm Thu late Jun-Aug), held on the main square every Thursday in summer.

Taxi

Amsterdam taxis are expensive, even over short journeys. Try **Taxicentrale Amsterdam** (TCA; ☎777 77 77; www.tcataxi.nl).

Around Amsterdam

ALKMAAR

☑072 / POP 94,000

This picturesque town stages its famous **cheese market** (Waagplein; ☑10am-noon Fri Apr-early Sep) in the historic main square. The market dates from the 17th century. Dealers in officious white smocks insert a hollow rod to extract cheese samples, sniffing and crumbling for fat and moisture content. Then the porters, wearing colourful hats to signify their cheese guild, heft the cheeses on wooden sledges to a large scale. An average 30 tonnes of cheese is on display at the Alkmaar market at any one time.

Arrive early for more than fleeting glimpses. There are four trains per hour from Amsterdam Centraal Station (€7, 30 to 40 minutes).

The Randstad

When people think of the Netherlands outside of Amsterdam, they are often really thinking about the Randstad. One of the most densely populated places on the planet, it stretches from Amsterdam to Rotterdam and features the classically Dutch towns and cities of Den Haag, Utrecht, Haarlem, Leiden, Delft and Gouda. Most people focus their visit to the Netherlands here, enjoying the peerless cycling network that links the towns amid tulip fields.

HAARLEM

☑023 / POP 152,000

Haarlem is the Netherlands in microcosm, with canals, gabled buildings and cobblestone streets. Its historic buildings, grand churches, museums, cosy bars, good restaurants and antique shops draw scores of day trippers – it's only 15 minutes by train from Amsterdam.

Sights

A couple of hour's stroll – with stops for refreshments – will cover Haarlem's tidy centre, which radiates out from the **Grote Markt**, where there are markets on many days.

Town Hall   Historic Building

At the western end of the Grote Markt stands the florid, 14th-century town hall, which sprouted many extensions including a balcony where judgements from the high court were pronounced.

Grote Kerk van St Bavo   Church

(www.bavo.nl; Oude Groenmarkt 23; adult/child €2.50/free; ☑10am-5pm Mon-Sat) This Gothic cathedral with a towering 50m-high steeple contains some fine Renaissance artworks, but the star attraction is its stunning Müller organ – one of the most magnificent in the world, standing 30m high with about 5000 pipes. It was played by Handel and Mozart, the latter when he was just 10.

Frans Hals Museum Gallery
(www.franshalsmuseum.nl; Groot Heiligland 62; adult/child €7.50/free; ⊙11am-5pm Tue-Sat, noon-5pm Sun) A short stroll south of Grote Markt, the Frans Hals Museum is a must for anyone interested in the Dutch Masters.

Corrie ten Boom House Historic Building
(www.corrietenboom.com; Barteljorisstraat 19; ⊙10am-4pm Tue-Sat Apr-Oct, 11am-3pm Tue-Sat Nov-Mar) `FREE` Also known as 'the hiding place', the Corrie Ten Boom House is named for the matriarch of a family that lived in the house during WWII. In 1944 the family was betrayed and sent to concentration camps, where three died. Tours are in English.

🛏 Sleeping

Stempels Hotel $$
(📞512 39 10; www.stempelsinhaarlem. nl; Klokhuisplein 9; r €95-160; @ 🛜) Haarlem's most interesting lodging has 17 spacious rooms (with high ceilings and stark, artful decor) in a gorgeous old printing house on the east side of the Grote Kerk. The on-site cafe may keep you from venturing far; the included breakfast is excellent.

Hotel Carillon Hotel $$
(📞531 05 91; www.hotel carillon.com; Grote Markt 27; s/d from €60/80; 🛜)

Small but tidy white rooms in the shadow of the Grote Kerk are the hallmark here. A couple share bathrooms and cost from €40. Breakfast (included) can be taken in wicker chairs on the sidewalk cafe.

🍴 Eating

Lange Veerstraat has a bounty of cafes, while Schagchelstraat is lined with restaurants. The Saturday morning market on Grote Markt is one of Holland's best; try the fresh *Stroopwafels* (small caramel-filled waffles).

De Haerlemsche Vlaamse Frites $
(Spekstraat 3; frites €2.10) Practically on the doorstep of the Grote Kerk, this *frites* joint, not much bigger than a telephone box, is a local institution. Line up for its crispy, golden fries made from fresh potatoes.

Jacobus Pieck International $$
(www.jacobuspieck.nl; Warmoesstraat 18; mains lunch €6-10, dinner €10-20; ⊙lunch & dinner Tue-Sat) Touches such as freshly squeezed

Grote Kerk van St Bavo in Haarlem, the Netherlands
JOHN ELK/GETTY IMAGES ©

Detour:
Zaanse Schans

People come for an hour and stay for several at this open-air museum on the Zaan river, which is *the* place to see **windmills** operating. It's got a touristy element, but the six operating mills are completely authentic and are operated with enthusiasm and love. Visitors can explore the windmills at their leisure, seeing firsthand the vast moving parts that make these devices a combination of sailing ship and Rube Goldberg. As a bonus, the river-bank setting is lovely.

The site is free; entrance fees to the individual windmills average €3/1.50 per adult/child. At least a couple are open on any given day; hours tend to be 10am to 4pm. There are several cafes and restaurants on-site.

From Amsterdam Centraal Station (€3, 17 minutes, four times hourly) take the train towards Alkmaar and get off at Koog Zaandijk – it's a well-signposted 1km walk to Zaanse Schans.

OJ put this tidy bistro on a higher plane. The menu bursts with fresh dishes, from salads and sandwiches at lunch to more complex pasta and seafood choices at dinner.

ℹ Information

The **tourist office** (☎0900 616 16 00; www. haarlemmarketing.com; Verwulft 11; ☺9.30am-6pm Mon-Fri, 9.30am-5pm Sat, noon-4pm Sun Apr-Sep, closed Sun Oct-Mar) is located in a free-standing glass house in the middle of the main shopping district.

ℹ Getting There & Away

Trains serve Haarlem's stunning art deco station, a 10-minute walk from the centre. Destinations include Amsterdam (€4, 15 minutes, five to eight services per hour), Den Haag (€8, 35 to 40 minutes, four to six per hour) and Rotterdam (€11, 50 minutes, four per hour).

LEIDEN
☎071 / POP 118,700

Leiden is a busy, vibrant town that is another popular day trip from Amsterdam. Claims to fame: it's Rembrandt's birthplace, it's home to the Netherlands' oldest university (and 20,000 students) and it's where America's pilgrims raised money to lease the leaky Mayflower that took them to the New World in 1620.

◎ Sights

The best way to experience Leiden is by strolling the historic centre, especially along the Rapenburg canal.

Follow the huge steeple of **Pieterskerk** (Pieterskerkhof; ☺10am-4pm Mon-Fri, 1.30-4pm Sat & Sun May-Sep, 1.30-4pm daily Oct-Apr), which shines after a grand restoration (a good thing as it's been prone to collapse since it was built in the 14th century). Across the plaza, look for the **Gravensteen**, which dates to the 13th century and once was a prison.

Head east to the 15th-century **St Pancraskerk** (Nieuwstraat), which is surrounded by tiny buildings unchanged since the pilgrims were here in 1620.

Lakenhal   Museum
(www.lakenhal.nl; Oude Singel 28-32; adult/child €7.50/free; ☺10am-5pm Tue-Fri, noon-5pm Sat & Sun) Get your Rembrandt fix at the 17th-century Lakenhal, which houses the Municipal Museum, with an assortment of works by Old Masters, as well as period rooms and temporary exhibits.

Rijksmuseum van
Oudheden   Museum
(National Museum of Antiquities; www.rmo.nl; Rapenburg 28; adult/child €9/free; ☺10am-5pm Tue-Sun) This museum has a world-class

collection of Greek, Roman and Egyptian artefacts, the pride of which is the extraordinary Temple of Taffeh.

De Valk
Museum

(The Falcon; ☎ 071-516 53 53; 2e Binnenvestgracht 1; adult/child €3/2; ⏰ 10am-5pm Tue-Sat, 1-5pm Sun) Leiden's landmark windmill museum, De Valk receives loving care (another restoration commenced in 2012), and many consider it the best example of its kind.

🛏 Sleeping

Hotel Nieuw Minerva
Hotel $$

(☎ 512 63 58; www.hotelleiden.com; Boommarkt 23; s/d from €75/80; @ 🛜) Located in six 16th-century canalside houses, this central hotel has a mix of 40 regular (ie nothing special) and some very fun themed rooms, including a room with a bed in which King Lodewijk Bonaparte (aka Louis Bonaparte) slept.

Hotel de Doelen
Hotel $$

(☎ 512 05 27; www.dedoelen.com; Rapenburg 2; s/d from €85/105; @ 🛜) It has a slightly faded air of classical elegance; some

canalside rooms in this regal building are larger and better appointed than others. There are 128 rooms overall, some on the ground floor.

🍴 Eating & Drinking

De Dames Proeverij
Cafe $$

(www.proeverijdedames.nl; Nieuwe Rijn 37; mains €12-20) Run by two women who have excellent taste, this cafe seems to have just what you want at any time of day. There is an excellent range of coffee drinks as well as dozens of top wines by the glass. Enjoy your sips at the tables out front overlooking the canal.

Café L'Esperance
Brown Cafe

(www.lesperance.nl; Kaiserstraat 1) Long, dark and handsome, all decked out in nostalgic wood panelling *and* overlooking an evocative bend in the canal. Tables abound outside in summer; good meals too.

ℹ Information

The **tourist office** (☎ 516 60 00; www.vvvleiden.nl; Stationsweg 41; ⏰ 8am-6pm Mon-Fri, 10am-4pm Sat, 11am-5pm Sun), across from the train station, has good maps and historic info.

Tulips in Keukenhof Gardens (p512), the Netherlands

Detour:
Keukenhof Gardens

One of the Netherlands' top attractions is near Lisse, between Haarlem and Leiden. **Keukenhof** (www.keukenhof.nl; adult/child €15/7.50, parking €6; ⏰8am-7.30pm mid-Mar–mid-May, last entry 6pm) is the world's largest bulb-flower garden, attracting nearly 800,000 visitors during a season almost as short-lived as the blooms on the millions of multicoloured tulips, daffodils and hyacinths.

Buses 50 and 54 travel from Leiden Centraal Station to Keukenhof (30 minutes, four times per hour). All tickets can be purchased online, which helps avoid huge queues.

❶ Getting There & Away

Buses leave from directly in front of Centraal Station. **Train** destinations, all with six departures per hour, include Amsterdam (€8, 34 minutes), Den Haag (€3.50, 10 minutes) and Schiphol Airport (€6, 15 minutes).

DELFT

📍 015 / POP 98,700

Compact, charming and relaxed, Delft may be the perfect Dutch day trip. Found-ed around 1100, it maintains tangible links to its romantic past despite the pressures of modernisation and tourist hordes. Many of the canalside vistas could be scenes from the *Girl with a Pearl Earring*, the novel about Golden Age painter Johannes Vermeer, which was made into a movie (and partially shot here) in 2003. Delft is also famous for its 'delftware', the distinctive blue-and-white pottery origi-nally duplicated from Chinese porcelain by 17th-century artisans.

◎ Sights

The 14th-century **Nieuwe Kerk** (www.nieuwekerk-delft.nl; Markt; adult/child incl Oude Kerk €3.50/1.50, ; ⏰9am-6pm Apr-Oct, 11am-4pm Nov-Mar, closed Sun) houses the crypt of the Dutch royal family and the mausoleum of Willem the Silent. The fee includes entrance to the **Oude Kerk** (www.oudekerk-delft.nl; Heilige Geestkerkhof 25; adult/child incl Nieuwe Kerk €3.50/1.50). The latter, 800 years old, is a surreal sight: its tower leans 2m from the vertical.

Vermeer Centrum Delft   Museum
(www.vermeerdelft.nl; Voldersgracht 21; adult/child €7/3; ⏰10am-5pm) As the place where Vermeer was born, lived, and worked, Delft is 'Vermeer Central' to many art-history and Old Masters enthusiasts. Along with viewing life-sized images of Vermeer's oeuvre, you can tour a replica of Vermeer's studio, which gives insight into the way the artist approached the use of light and colour in his craft.

De Candelaer   Porcelain Studio
(www.candelaer.nl; Kerkstraat 13; ⏰9am-5.30pm Mon-Fri, to 5pm Sat year-round, 9am-5pm Sun Mar-May) The most central and modest Delftware outfit is de Candelaer, just off the Markt. It has five artists, a few of whom work most days.

🛏 Sleeping

Hotel de Emauspoort   Hotel $$
(📞015-219 02 19; www.emauspoort.nl; Vrouwen-regt 9-11; s/d from €90/100; @ 🛜) Couples, singles, and business travellers alike rave about this sweet, well-priced little hotel near the Markt. Spacious rooms strike a nice balance of old-world antique and totally modern comfort.

Hotel Coen   Hotel $$
(📞214 59 14; www.hotelcoendelft.nl; Coender-straat 47; s/d from €72/90; @ 🛜) Just behind the train station construction site, this family-run hotel has 55 beds in a variety of rooms, from budget singles as thin as your wallet to grander doubles.

✖️ Eating & Drinking

Spijshuis de Dis
Contemporary Dutch $$

(www.spijshuisdedis.com; Beestenmarkt 36; lunch €5-15, dinner €16-25; ⏰noon-2pm & 5-9.30pm Tue-Sun; 🍴🕴) Foodies, romantics and oenophiles flock to this cosily elegant restaurant, where fresh fish and amazing soups served in bread bowls take centre stage.

De Visbanken
Seafood $

(Camaretten 2; snacks from €3; ⏰10am-6pm) People have been selling fish on this spot since 1342. The present vendors line the display cases in the old open-air pavilion with all manner of things fishy.

Locus Publicus
Brown Cafe

(Brabantse Turfmarkt 67) Glowing from within, this beer cafe has more than 200 beers. It's charming and filled with cheery locals who are quaffing their way through the list. Good people watching from the front-terrace tables.

ℹ️ Information

The **tourist office** (VVV; ☎215 40 51; www. delft.nl; Hippolytusbuurt 4; ⏰10am-4pm Sun & Mon, 9am-6pm Tue-Fri, 10am-5pm Sat) has free internet; the thematic walking guides are excellent.

ℹ️ Getting There & Away

The area around the **train station** will be a vast construction site for years to come as the lines are moved underground. Train services include Amsterdam (€12, one hour, two per hour), Den Haag (€3, 12 minutes, four per hour) and Rotterdam (€3.50, 12 minutes, four per hour).

ROTTERDAM
☎010 / POP 616,000

Rotterdam bursts with energy. Vibrant nightlife, a diverse, multi-ethnic community, an intensely interesting maritime tradition and a wealth of top-class museums all make it a must-see part of any visit to Holland, especially if you are passing by on the high-speed trains.

The Netherlands' 'second city', central Rotterdam was bombed flat during WWII and spent the following decades

Statue of Willem the Silent in Nieuwe Kerk, Delft, the Netherlands

MERTEN SNIJDERS/GETTY IMAGES ©

If You Like…
Dutch Art

Amsterdam's Rijksmuseum (p496) and the Van Gogh Museum (p495) attract the most attention, but the Netherlands has some other stellar art institutions.

1 MAURITSHUIS
(www.mauritshuis.nl; Korte Vijverberg 8; adult/child €13.50/free; ⏱11am-5pm Tue-Sun) In the Dutch capital of Den Haag (The Hague), this renowned museum is a fine place for a primer on Dutch and Flemish art. Highlights include Vermeer's *Girl with a Pearl Earring* and several superb Rembrandts, including a self-portrait from the year of his death, *1669*.

2 KRÖLLER-MÜLLER MUSEUM
(☎0318-59 12 41; www.kmm.nl; Houtkampweg 6; park admission plus museum adult/child €8.20/4.10; ⏱10am-5pm Tue-Sun) This superb museum is in the Netherlands' largest national park, Hoge Veluwe. The collection runs from Bruyn the Elder to Picasso, and the Van Gogh collection is world class, including *The Potato Eaters* and *Weavers*. Impressionists include Renoir, Sisley, Monet and Manet, and there's a sculpture garden featuring works by Rodin, Moore and more.

3 GEMEENTEMUSEUM
(Municipal Museum; www.gemeentemuseum.nl; Stadhouderslaan 41; adult/child €13.50/free; ⏱11am-5pm Tue-Sun) Admirers of the De Stijl movement mustn't miss the Gemeentemuseum in Den Haag. Piet Mondrian's unfinished *Victory Boogie Woogie* takes pride of place (as it should: the museum paid €30 million for it), and there are some Picassos and other works by major 20th-century names.

4 BONNEFANTENMUSEUM
(www.bonnefantenmuseum.nl; Ave Cèramique 250; adult/child €9/free; ⏱11am-5pm Tue-Sun) Impressive both artistically and architecturally, this modern museum in Maastricht divides its collection between Old Masters and medieval sculpture on one floor, contemporary art on the next.

rebuilding. You won't find the classic Dutch medieval centre here – it was swept away along with the other rubble and detritus of war. In its place is an architectural aesthetic that's unique in Europe, a progressive, perpetual-motion approach to architecture that's clearly a result of the city's postwar, postmodern, anything-goes philosophy (a fine example of this is the Paul McCarthy statue titled **Santa with Butt Plug** that the city placed in the main shopping district).

⊙ Sights

Rotterdam is split by the vast Nieuwe Maas shipping channel, which is crossed by a series of tunnels and bridges, notably the fabulously postmodern Erasmusbrug. The centre is on the north side of the water and is easily strolled. The historic neighbourhood of Delfshaven is 3km west.

Museum Boijmans van Beuningen   Museum
(www.boijmans.nl; Museumpark 18-20; adult/child €12.50/free, Wed free; ⏱11am-5pm Tue-Sun) Museum Boijmans van Beuningen is among Europe's very finest museums and has a permanent collection taking in Dutch and European art (Bosch, Van Eyck, Rembrandt, Tintoretto, Titian and Bruegel's *Tower of Babel*). The surrealist wing features ephemera, paraphernalia and famous works from Dalí, Duchamp, Magritte, Man Ray and more.

Architecture   Notable Buildings
The **Overblaak Development** (1978–84), designed by Piet Blom, is marked by its pencil-shaped tower and arresting up-ended, cube-shaped apartments. One unit, the **Kijk-Kubus Museum-House** (www.kubuswoning.nl; adult/child €2.50/1.50; ⏱11am-5pm), lets you see what it's like to live at odd angles.
Designed by Ben van Berkel, the 1996 800m-long **Erasmusbrug** bridge is a city icon. Nearby, on the south bank, look for **KPN Telecom headquarters**, built in

2000 and designed by Renzo Piano, who also designed Paris' Pompidou Centre. The building leans at a sharp angle, seemingly resting on a long pole. There's also the 165m-tall **MaasToren** and **De Rotterdam**, which will be the largest building in the country when completed in 2014.

Museum Rotterdam   Museum
(www.hmr.rotterdam.nl; Korte Hoogstraat 31; adult/child €6/free; ⏲11am-5pm Tue-Sun) The city's history is preserved at one of the centre's few surviving 17th-century buildings. Exhibits focus on everyday life through the ages, such as the (purportedly) oldest surviving wooden shoe. It has a branch at the De Dubbelde Palmboom in Delftshaven.

Euromast   Viewpoint
(www.euromast.com; Parkhaven 20; adult/child from €9/6; ⏲10am-11pm) A shimmy up the 185m Euromast offers unparalleled 360-degree views of Rotterdam from the 100m-high observation deck.

Delfshaven   Neighbourhood
One of Rotterdam's best districts for strolling, quaint Delfshaven (it survived the war) was once the official seaport for the city of Delft. A reconstructed 18th-century **windmill** (Voorhaven 210; ⏲1-5pm Wed, 10am-4pm Sat) overlooks the water at Voorhaven 210. One of the area's claims to fame is that it was where the Pilgrims tried leaving for America aboard the leaky *Speedwell*. The **Oude Kerk** (Voorhaven 210; ⏲10am-noon Mon-Sat, 2-4pm Sun) on Voorhaven is where the Pilgrims prayed for the last time before leaving on 22 July 1620.

It is best reached by taking trams 4 and 9 or the Metro.

🛏 Sleeping

Hotel New York   Luxury Hotel $$$
(☎439 05 00; www.hotelnewyork.nl; Koninginnenhoofd 1; r €110-280; @ 🛜) The city's favourite hotel is housed in the former headquarters of the Holland-America passenger-ship line, and has excellent service and facilities. It's noted for its views, cafe and water taxi that takes guests across the Nieuwe Maas to the city centre.

Maritime Hotel Rotterdam   Hotel $$
(☎411 92 60; www.maritimehotel.nl; Willemskade 13; r €50-140; @ 🛜) Popular with shore-leave-seeking seamen and travellers who appreciate the fine value here. The 135 rooms are small and the cheapest share bathrooms, but spend a little extra and you can enjoy the best waterfront views in town.

Hotel Bazar   Hotel $$
(☎206 51 51; www.hotelbazar.nl; Witte de Withstraat 16; r €70-130) Bazar is deservedly popular for its 27 Middle Eastern–,

Erasmusbrug bridge, Rotterdam
GLENN VAN DER KNIJFF/GETTY IMAGES ©

FRANS LEMMENS/GETTY IMAGES ©

⭐ Don't Miss
Kinderdijk

In 1740 a series of windmills were built to drain a polder about 12km southeast of Rotterdam. Today 19 of the Dutch icons survive at Kinderdijk, which is a Unesco monument. You can wander the dikes for over 3km amid the spinning sails and visit inside one of the windmills. It's a good bicycle ride; you can rent bikes once there or travel from Rotterdam (16km); get a map from the tourist office.

A fantastic day trip is by the **Waterbus** (www.waterbus.nl; Willemskade; day pass adult/ child €12.50/9). The fast ferries leave from Rotterdam every 30 minutes and a connection puts you at Kinderdijk, 1km from the first mill. After the visit, continue by ferry to utterly charming Dordrecht and then return to Rotterdam by train.

NEED TO KNOW
www.kinderdijk.nl; admission free

African- and South American–themed rooms. Breakfast is spectacular: Turkish bread, international cheeses, yoghurt, pancakes and coffee.

Eating

Central Rotterdam
Look for myriad eating choices in Veerhaven, Witte de Single, Nieuwe Binnenweg and Oude Haven.

De Ballentent   Cafe $
(www.deballentent.nl; Parkkade 1; meals from €6; 🕘9am-11pm) Rotterdam's best waterfront pub-cafe is also a great spot for a meal. Mussels, schnitzels and more line the menu, but the real speciality here are *bals*, huge homemade meatloafy meatballs.

Z&M   Bistro $$
(🖉436 65 79; www.zenmdelicatessen.nl; Veerhaven 13; lunch mains from €7, dinner mains

from €20; ⏱noon-10pm Tue-Sun) A cosy, chic French/Mediterranean bistro revered for using only organic produce from small farms, a rarity in the factory-farm-laden Netherlands.

Bazar   Middle Eastern **$$**
(Witte de Withstraat 16; mains €7-15) On the ground floor of the creative Hotel Bazar, this vast and popular eatery comes up with creative Middle Eastern fusion fare that compliments the stylised decor. The outside tables are *the* neighbourhood meeting spot day and night.

Delfshaven

Het Eethuisje   Traditional Dutch **$**
(Mathenesserdijk 436; mains €8-10; ⏱4-9pm Mon-Sat) Traditional meaty, filling Dutch food is served from this little storefront near a canal. Utterly tourist free.

Stadsbrouwerij De Pelgrim   Traditional Dutch **$$**
(www.pelgrimbier.nl; Aelbrechtkolk 12; mains €12-22) It's named for the religious folk who passed through on their way to America, and you can take your own voyage through the various beers brewed in the vintage surrounds. Meals range from casual lunches to more ambitious multicourse dinners.

🍷 Drinking & Nightlife

Rotown   Bar
(www.rotown.nl; Nieuwe Binnenweg 17-19) A smooth bar, a dependable live rock venue, an agreeable restaurant, a popular meeting place.

De Witte Aap   Brown Cafe
(Witte de Withstraat 78) Fine corner boozer that's always crowded with locals from this artist-filled 'hood. The front opens right up and a huge awning keeps inclement weather at bay.

ℹ Information

The Rotterdam Welcome Card (adult/child from €10/7) offers discounts for sights, hotels and restaurants and free public transport. Buy it from the tourist office.

Tourist office (VVV; ☎790 01 40; www.rotterdam.info; 📞) The main (city) branch is located in the City Information Centre (Coolsingel 197; ⏱9am-6pm Mon-Fri, to 5pm Sat & Sun), with a good display on architecture since the war and a huge town model. A second location is near the train station in the landmark Groothandelsgebouw (Weena; ⏱9am-5.30pm Mon-Sat, 10am-5pm Sun).

ℹ Getting There & Away

Rotterdam Centraal Station is a new architectural stunner that will be fully open in 2014. Destinations include:

Amsterdam (via Leiden) €14, 65 minutes, five per hour

Amsterdam (high speed) €16-21, 43 minutes, two per hour

Brussels €22-62, 70-76 minutes, one to two per hour

Schiphol €11-14, 25-50 minutes, four to five per hour

Utrecht €10, 40 minutes, four per hour

ℹ Getting Around

Rotterdam's trams, buses and metro are provided by **RET** (www.ret.nl). Most converge in front of CS, where there is an **information booth** (⏱7am-7pm) that also sells tickets. Day passes are sold for varying durations: 1/2/3 days costs €7/10.50/14. A single-ride ticket purchased from a bus driver or tram conductor costs €3.

UTRECHT
☎030 / POP 317,000

Utrecht is one of the Netherlands' oldest cities and boasts a beautiful, vibrant, old-world city centre, ringed by striking 13th-century canal wharves. The wharves, well below street level, are unique to Utrecht. Canalside streets alongside brim with shops, restaurants and cafes.

Initial impressions may be less auspicious. When you step off the train you'll find yourself lost in the maze that is the Hoog Catharijne shopping centre. The Hoog is huge...and it's attached to the station...and it seemingly goes on forever... and ever. It's really a nightmare but a vast construction project (www.nieuwhc.nl) is transforming the entire area.

◉ Sights

Focus your wanderings on the **Domplein** and south along the tree-lined **Oude-gracht**. The tourist office has a good booklet that covers Utrecht's myriad small museums, which feature everything from waste water to old trains.

Domtoren   Historic Building

(Cathedral Tower; www.domtoren.nl; Domplein; adult/child €9/5; ⏱11am-4pm) The Dom-toren is 112m high, with 465 steps and 50 bells. It's a tough haul to the top but well worth the exertion, given that the tower gives unbeatable city views; on a clear day you can see Amsterdam. The guided tour, in Dutch and English, is detailed and gives privileged insight into this beautiful structure.

Finished in the 14th century, the cathedral and its tower are the most striking medieval landmarks in a city that once had 40 cathedrals. Appreciate the craft: it took almost 300 years to complete. In 1674 the North Sea winds reached hurricane force and blew down the cathedral's nave, leaving the tower and transept behind.

Centraal Museum   Museum

(www.centraalmuseum.nl; Nicolaaskerkhof 10; adult/child €9/4; ⏱11am-5pm Tue-Sun) The Centraal Museum has a wide-ranging collection. It displays applied arts dating back to the 17th century, as well as paintings by some of the Utrecht School artists and a bit of De Stijl to boot – including the world's most extensive Gerrit Rietveld collection. Admission here includes Dick Bruna House and Rietveld-Schröderhuis.

Dick Bruna House

One of Utrecht's favourite sons, author and illustrator Dick Bruna is the creator of beloved cartoon rabbit Miffy and she naturally takes pride of place at his **studio** (www.dickbrunahuis.nl; Nicolaaskerkhof 10; ⏱11am-5pm Tue-Sun) across from the museum.

Rietveld-Schröderhuis

This Unesco-recognised landmark **house** (📞reservations 236 23 10; Prins Hendriklaan 50; admission surcharge €3; ⏱11am-5pm Wed-Sun) is just outside the city centre. Built in 1924 by Utrecht architect Gerrit Rietveld, it is a stark example of 'form follows function'. Visits are by mandatory tour, which should be booked in advance at Centraal Museum (see website for details); the museum will give you a map for the pleasant 25-minute stroll to the house or loan you a free bike.

Museum Catharijneconvent   Museum

(www.catharijneconvent.nl; Lange Nieuwegracht 38; adult/child €12/7; ⏱10am-5pm Tue-Fri, 11am-5pm Sat & Sun) The Museum Catharijneconvent has the finest collection of medieval religious art in the Netherlands – virtually the history of Christianity.

Utrecht, the Netherlands

Sleeping

B&B Utrecht
Guesthouse **$**

(06 5043 4884; www.hostelutrecht.nl; Lucas Bolwerk 4; dm/r from €21/60; @ ?) Straddling the border between hostel and hotel, this spotless inn located in an elegant old building has an internal Ikea vibe. Breakfast, lunch and dinner ingredients are free! Internet access (in a computer room with scanners, printers etc) is also free, as is use of a huge range of musical instruments and DVDs.

Mary K Hotel
Hotel **$$**

(230 48 88; www.marykhotel.com; Oudegracht 25; r €120-180; ?) A bevy of Utrecht artists decorated the rooms at this creative new Utrecht hotel in an ideal location. Rooms come in three basic sizes (small, medium and large) but no two are like.

Eating

Blauw
Indonesian **$$$**

(www.restaurantblauw.nl; Springweg 64; set menu from €25; dinner) Blauw is *the* place for stylish Indonesian food in Utrecht. Young and old alike enjoy superb *rijsttafels* (array of spicy dishes served with rice) amid the red decor that mixes vintage art with hip minimalism.

Deeg
Fusion **$$$**

(233 11 04; www.restaurantdeeg.nl; Lange Nieuwstraat 71; set menus from €35; dinner) A charming corner location in the museum quarter is but the first draw at this casual bistro, which has nightly set menus that change regularly. Fresh local produce gets a Mediterranean accent and many items – such as the cheeses – are organic.

Drinking & Nightlife

't Oude Pothuys
Brown Cafe

(Oudegracht 279) Small and dark, this basement pub has nightly music – jam sessions with locals trying their hand at rock and jazz. Enjoy drinks on the canalside pier.

Detour:
Hoge Veluwe National Park

Hoge Veluwe (www.hogeveluwe.nl; adult/child/car €8.20/4.10/6; 8am-10pm Jun & Jul, 9am-6pm Dec-Mar) is the Netherlands' largest national park, featuring a mix of forests and woods, shifting sands and heathery moors, along with red deer, wild boar and mouflon (wild sheep).

It also features the world-class Kröller-Müller Museum (p514), which has a superb collection of works by Van Gogh, as well as other pieces by Picasso, Renoir and Manet.

From Arnhem train station (Utrecht to Arnhem by train: €10, 37 minutes, four per hour), take bus 21 (20 minutes, every 30 minutes) to the Schaarsbergen park entrance (stop: Museum 40 45). Various buses run inside the park to the museum or you can ride one of the famous free white bikes.

Café Ledig Erf
Bar

(Tolsteegbrug 3) This classy pub overlooks a confluence of canals (and other cafes) at the southern tip of town.

Information

The **tourist office** (VVV; 0900 128 87 32; www.utrechtyourway.nl; Domplein 9; noon-5pm Sun & Mon, 10am-5pm Tue-Sat) sells maps and tours of the nearby Domtoren.

Getting There & Away

The **train station**, which is in the process of being replaced, is a major connection point and is Holland's busiest. It is on the line linking Amsterdam to Cologne. Sample fares include Amsterdam (€7, 30 minutes, four per hour),

Maastricht (€24, two hours, two per hour) and Rotterdam (€10, 40 minutes, four per hour).

BELGIUM

Stereotypes of comic books, chips and sublime chocolates are just the start in eccentric little Belgium; its self-deprecating people have quietly spent centuries producing some of Europe's finest art and architecture. Bilingual Brussels is the dynamic yet personable EU capital, but also sports what's arguably the world's most beautiful city square. Flat, Dutch-speaking Flanders has many other alluring medieval cities, all easily linked by regular train hops. In hilly, French-speaking Wallonia, the attractions are contrastingly rural – castle villages, outdoor activities and extensive cave systems.

Brussels

POP 1.12 MILLION

Like the country it represents, Brussels (Bruxelles, Brussel) is a surreal, multilayered place pulling several disparate identities into one enigmatic core. It subtly seduces with great art, tempting chocolate shops and classic cafes. Meanwhile a confusing architectural smorgasbord pits awesome art-nouveau and 17th-century masterpieces against shabby suburbanism and the disappointingly soulless glass-faced anonymity of the EU area. Note that Brussels is officially bilingual, so all names – from streets to train stations – have both Dutch and French versions, but for simplicity we use only the French versions in this chapter.

◎ Sights

The **BrusselsCard** (www.brusselscard.be; 24/48/72hr €24/34/40) allows free visits to over 30 Brussels-area museums, various other discounts, plus unlimited free use of city public transport. You'll need to be a seriously hyperactive museum fan to save much money, but it's fun trying. Remember that most museums close Mondays.

On the first Wednesday afternoon of each month many museums are free.

CENTRAL BRUSSELS

Galeries St-Hubert   Covered Arcade
(www.galeries-saint-hubert.com; off Rue du Marché aux Herbes; M Gare Centrale) Europe's very first shopping arcade opened in 1847 with neoclassical glassed-in arches flanked by marble pilasters. Directly west are two enchantingly colourful lanes of close-packed fish restaurants (Rue/Petit Rue des Bouchers) but beware that (with some exceptions) many of those are notorious tourist traps.

Bourse   Stock Exchange
(Place de la Bourse) You can't enter Belgium's 1873 stock exchange building but its grandiose neoclassical facade is brilliantly festooned with friezes, reclining nudes, lunging horses and a multitude of allegorical figures. Some of the work was by Rodin when he was a young apprentice sculptor.

Manneken Pis   Monument
(Cnr Rue de l'Étuve & Rue du Chêne; M Gare Centrale) This tiny fountain-statue of a little boy cheerfully taking a leak is a perversely perfect national symbol for surreal Belgium. More often than not the tiny statue's nakedness is largely hidden beneath a costume relevant to an anniversary, national day or local event: his ever-growing wardrobe is partly displayed at the **Maison du Roi** (Musée de la Ville de Bruxelles; Grand Place).

Musées Royaux des Beaux-Arts   Art Museum
(☑ 02-508 32 11; www.fine-arts-museum.be; Rue de la Régence 3; adult/student/BrusselsCard €8/5/free, €13 combined with Magritte Museum; ☉10am-5pm Tue-Sun; M Gare Centrale, Parc) Belgium's national gallery has a superb collection ranging from 15th-century Flemish Primitives via the fleshy religious works of Rubens to a top quality selection of 20th-century works. Highlights include Rogier Van der Weyden's *Pietà* with its hallucinatory dawn sky, Hans Memling's refined portraits and the world-famous

ALAN COPSON/GETTY IMAGES ©

★ Don't Miss
Grand Place

Brussels' incomparable central square tops any itinerary. Its splendidly spired Gothic **Hôtel de Ville** was the only building to escape bombardment by the French in 1695, quite ironic considering that it was their main target. Today the pedestrianised square's splendour is due largely to its intact collection of **guildhalls**, rebuilt by merchant guilds after 1695 and fancifully adorned with gilded statues. If you're using a BrusselsCard don't miss your free beer at the two-room **Brewery Museum** (www.beerparadise.be; Grand Place 10; adult/BrusselsCard €6/free; ⊙10am-5pm daily Easter-Nov, noon-5pm Sat & Sun Dec-Easter; Ⓜ Gare Centrale).

NEED TO KNOW
Ⓜ Gare Centrale

Fall of Icarus, long attributed to Bruegel, though possibly a copy.

Musée Magritte   Art Museum
(www.musee-magritte-museum.be; Place Royale; adult/under 26yr/BrusselsCard €8/2/free; ⊙10am-5pm Tue-Sun; Ⓜ Gare Centrale, Parc) Opened in 2009, this beautifully presented museum traces the stylistic development of Belgium's foremost surrealist artist René Magritte, from colourful Braque-style cubism in 1920 through a Dalí-esque phase and a late-1940s period

of Kandinsky-like brushwork. Regular screenings of a 52-minute documentary provide insights into Magritte's unconventionally conventional life. Discounted entrance fees apply if you also visit the Musées Royaux des Beaux-Arts next door.

Place Royale   Neighbourhood
(Ⓜ Gare Centrale, Parc) Dominating this neoclassical square is a bold equestrian **statue of Godefroid de Bouillon**, the Belgian crusader knight who very briefly became the first European ruler of Jerusalem in

521

Central Brussels

THE NETHERLANDS & BELGIUM BRUSSELS

522

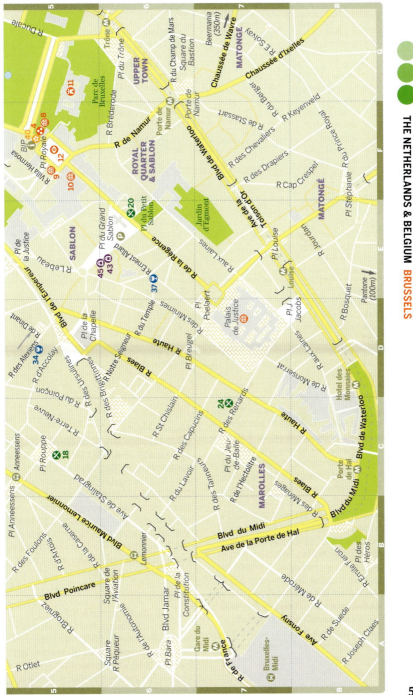

R Ducale

Trône

Pl du Trône

UPPER TOWN

R du Champ de Mars

Square du Bastion

Beermania (350m)

Chaussée de Wavre

MATONGÉ

Chaussée d'Ixelles

R E Solvay

R du Berger

R Keyenveld

Parc de Bruxelles

11

R Bréderode

Porte de Namur

R de Stassart

R des Chevaliers

Pl Royale

R de Namur

Porte de Namur

Blvd de Waterloo

R des Drapiers

R Cap Crespel

MATONGÉ

Pl Stéphanie

BIP

R Villa Hermosa

10
4
8
12
9
10

ROYAL QUARTER & SABLON

R Bréderode

Ave de la Toison d'Or

Jardin d'Egmont

Pl Louise

R Jourdan

SABLON

Pl de la Justice

R Lebeau

Pl du Grand Sablon

20

Pl du Petit Sablon

R aux Laines

Pl Louise

Louise

Pantone (100m)

R Bosquet

R Ernest Allard

R de la Régence

45
43

37

Pl Poelaert

Pl J Jacobs

R aux Laines

Blvd de l'Empereur

R de Dinant

Pl de la Chapelle

R du Temple

R des Minimes

Palais de Justice

Hôtel des Monnaies

Blvd de Waterloo

R des Alexiens

34

R d'Accolay

R des Brig

R Notre Seigneur

R Haute

Pl Breughel

R de Montserrat

R aux Laines

Blvd du Midi

R de Dinant

R du Poinçon

R des Ursulines

R Blaes

24

R des Renards

R Haute

Porte de Hal

R Terre-Neuve

Pl du Jeu-de-Balle

R des Tanneurs

R du Lavoir

R de l'Hectolitre

MAROLLES

Blvd du Midi

Anneessens

Pl Rouppe

18

Ave de Stalingrad

R des Capucins

R St Chislain

Pl des Ménages

Blvd de Waterloo

Pl Anneessens

Anneessens

Blvd Maurice Lemonnier

Lemonnier

Pl de la Constitution

Blvd du Midi

Ave de la Porte de Hal

Pl des Héros

R Emile Féron

R de la Caserne

R d'Artois

R des Foulons

Blvd Poincare

Square de l'Aviation

Blvd Jamar

R de l'Autonomie

R de Suede

R de Mérode

R Brogniez

Square R Péqueur

Pl Bara

Gare du Midi

Bruxelles-Midi

Ave Fonsny

R Joseph Claes

R Otlet

R de France

Central Brussels

◎ Don't Miss Sights
1 Grand Place D3

◎ Sights
2 Bourse D3
3 Brewery Museum.................................... D4
4 Coudenberg.. F5
5 Galeries St-Hubert................................. E3
6 Maison du Roi.. D3
7 Manneken Pis.. D4
8 Musée BELvue... F5
9 Musée Magritte....................................... F5
10 Musées Royaux des Beaux-Arts............F5
11 Palais Royal G5
12 Place Royale F5

🛏 Sleeping
13 Chambres d'Hôtes du Vaudeville E3
14 Hôtel Le Dixseptième E4
15 Hôtel Noga C1
16 Maison Noble..C1

✕ Eating
17 Belga Queen Brussels E2
18 Comme Chez Soi C5
19 Fin de Siècle.. C3
20 L'Ecailler du Palais Royal E6
21 L'Ogenblik E3
22 Mer du Nord... C2
23 Mokafé..E3

24 Restobières..C7
25 Sea Grill... E2

🍷 Drinking & Nightlife
26 À la Bécasse...D3
27 À la Mort Subite......................................E3
28 A l'Image de Nostre-Dame.....................D3
29 Au Bon Vieux Temps...............................D3
30 Café des Halles.......................................C3
31 Chaloupe d'Or... E3
32 Délirium Café E3
33 Falstaff...D3
34 La Fleur en Papier Doré D5
35 Le Cercle des Voyageurs.......................D4
36 Le Cirio...D3
37 Le Perroquet E6
38 Le Roy d'Espagne...................................D3
39 Moeder Lambic Fontainas C4

★ Entertainment
40 Arsène50 .... F5

🛍 Shopping
41 Corné Port Royal E4
42 Délices et Caprices................................E3
43 Leonidas E6
44 Neuhaus...E3
45 Pierre Marcolini E6
46 Stijl...C2

1099. Around the corner, the 19th-century **Palais Royal** (🗗02-551 20 20; www.monarchy. be; Place des Palais; admission free; 🕙10.30am-4.30pm Tue-Sun late Jul-early Sep; Ⓜ Parc) is Belgium's slightly less-inspired cousin to Buckingham Palace. It's the Belgian king's office, but the royals no longer live here.

If you've bought a BrusselsCard, peep into **Musée BELvue** (🗗07-022 04 92; www.belvue.be; Place des Palais 7; adult/concession €5/4; 🕙10am-5pm Tue-Fri, to 6pm Sat & Sun; Ⓜ Parc), which introduces Belgian history through a fascinating overload of documents, images and videos. Then descend into the attached **Coudenberg** (www.coudenberg.com; adult/under 26yr/BrusselsCard €5/3/free, with Musée BELvue €8/4/free), the subterranean archaeological site of Charles Quint's 16th-century palace complex. You'll emerge eventually near MIM.

IXELLES

Musée Horta   Museum
(🗗02-543 04 90; www.hortamuseum.be; Rue Américaine 25; adult/child €7/3.50; 🕙2-5.30pm Tue-Sun; Ⓜ Horta, 🚊91, 92) Behind a typically austere exterior, the former home (built 1898–1901) of superstar architect Victor Horta has an outstanding art nouveau interior. Floor mosaics, glittering stained glass and ceramic brick walls are all memorable but the structural triumph is the stairway, which becomes more exuberant as you ascend.

HEYSEL

A 15-minute metro ride to Brussels' northern edge brings you to an area of trade fairs, the national stadium and curious **Mini Europe** (www.minieurope.com; adult/child €14/10.50, with Atomium €23.25/15.25; 🕙10am-5pm Apr-Jun & Sep-Dec, 9.30am-8pm

Jul-Aug; Ⓜ Heysel), featuring walk-through re-creations of the continent's top tourist sights at 1:25 scale.

Atomium   Monument, Museum

(www.atomium.be; Sq de l'Atomium; adult/BrusselsCard €11/9; ◷ 10am-7pm May-Sep, to 6pm Oct-Apr; Ⓟ; Ⓜ Heysel, 🚌 51) This space-age leftover from the 1958 World Fair consists of nine house-sized metallic balls linked by steel tube-columns containing escalators and lifts. Like an alien schoolchild's chemistry set, this represents an iron crystal lattice enlarged 165 billion times. It's an unforgettable sight and the top sphere offers wide views but inside exhibits aren't enormously compelling.

🛏 Sleeping

With much of Brussels' accommodation scene aimed squarely at Eurocrats and business travellers, many business hotels drop their rates dramatically at weekends and in summer.

Beware that several otherwise decent hotels around Rogier and Bruxelles-Nord lie uncomfortably close to a seedy red-light district. Nicer Ste-Catherine area is central but calm, St-Gilles offers a more 'local' experience.

Brussels has a reasonable network of B&Bs, many bookable through Bed & Brussels (www.bnb-brussels.be) and Airbnb (www.airbnb.com).

Hôtel Le Dixseptième
Boutique Hotel **$$$**

(🕿 02-502 57 44; www.ledixseptieme.be; Rue de la Madeleine 25; s/d/ste from €180/200/270, weekend from €100/100/200; ❄ 🛜) A hushed magnificence greets you in this alluring boutique hotel, partly occupying the former 17th-century

residence of the Spanish ambassador. Spacious executive suites come with four-poster beds; some of the less expensive rooms are a big step down in opulence.

Maison Noble   B&B **$$**

(🕿 02-219 23 39; www.maison-noble.eu; Rue du Marcq 10; from €129; ❄ @ 🛜) This splendidly refined four-room guesthouse includes a neoRenaissance piano room where, once in a while, recitals feature up-and-coming concert pianists. Hotel-standard rooms have rainforest showers, fine linens, and framed Breugel prints over the beds. The target market is married gay couples but it's very much hetero-friendly.

Chambres d'Hôtes du Vaudeville   B&B **$$**

(🕿 0471 47 38 37; www.chambresdhotesduvaudeville.be; Galerie de la Reine 11; d from €115; 🛜) This classy B&B has an incredible location right within the gorgeous (if reverberant) Galeries St-Hubert. Delectable decor styles include African, modernist and 'Madame Loulou' (with 1920s nude

Galeries St-Hubert (p520) in Brussels, Belgium
VISIONS OF OUR LAND/GETTY IMAGES ©

THE NETHERLANDS & BELGIUM **BRUSSELS**

Le Cirio cafe in the Bourse area of Brussels, Belgium

MARTIN MOOS/GETTY IMAGES ©

sketches). Larger front rooms have claw-foot bathtubs and *galerie* views, but can be noisy with clatter that continues all night. Get keys via the art deco influenced Café du Vaudeville, where breakfast is included.

Pantone   Hotel $$

(☎02-541 48 98; pantonehotel.com; Place Loix 1; r €99-129) Modern, stylishly functional and surprisingly affordable the Pantone greets you with an eye-popping array of colours, from the turquoise pushbike at reception to the moulded plastic chairs to the lime green bedrooms – all with refreshing swathes of white too.

Hôtel Noga   Family Hotel $$

(☎02-218 67 63; www.nogahotel.com; Rue du Béguinage 38; weekday/weekend from s €95/70, d €110/85; ❄@☎) This very welcoming family hotel established in 1958 uses model yachts to give the lobby and piano room a certain nautical feel. Sepia photos of Belgian royalty, along with historic bellows, top hats and assorted random kitsch, lead up to variously decorated rooms that are neat and clean without particular luxury. Wi-fi is free for the first hour.

🍴 Eating

CENTRAL BRUSSELS

Several interesting options are dotted along Rue de Flandre, with reliable seafood restaurants around nearby Place Ste-Catherine and Marché aux Poissons. Restaurants reviewed here focus on value for money, but with formal attire, advance bookings and a plutonium credit card, central gourmet options include **Comme Chez Soi** (www.commechezsoi.be; Place Rouppe 23), **Sea Grill** (☎02-212 08 00; www.seagrill. be; Radisson SAS Royal Hotel Brussels, Rue du Fossé aux Loups 47; ⏰noon-2pm & 7-10pm, closed mid-July–mid-Aug; Ⓜ De Brouckère) and **L'Ecailler du Palais Royal** (www.lecailler dupalaisroyal.be). Beware of unscrupulous 'deals' at the very attractive tourist-trap seafood restaurants of Rue/Petit Rue des Bouchers.

L'Ogenblik   French $$$

(☎02-511 61 51; www.ogenblik.be; Galerie des Princes 1; mains €23-28, lunch €11; ⏰noon-2.30pm & 7pm-midnight) This archetypal bistro–restaurant is more convivially casual than most top-notch Brussels restaurants, with its lace curtains, resident cat and marble-topped tables. But the classic French dishes and fish specialities show a deft culinary expertise, and the saucy humour of the waiters adds to the fun of a special dining experience.

Fin de Siècle   Belgian $

(Rue des Chartreux 9; mains €11.25-20; ⏰bar 4.30pm-1am, kitchen 6pm-12.30am) From *carbonade* (beer-based hot-pot) and chicken in cherry beer to mezzes and tandoori dishes, the food selection is as eclectic as the decor in this low-lit cult place. Tables are rough, music constant, ceilings purple and prices still converted to the nearest centime from Belgian Francs. To quote the barman 'there's no phone, no bookings, no sign on the door… we do everything to put people off but they still keep coming'. Queues are common.

Belga Queen Brussels   Belgian $$

(☎02-217 21 87; www.belgaqueen.be; Rue du Fossé aux Loups 32; mains €16-25, weekday lunch €16; ⏰noon-2.30pm & 7pm-midnight) Belgian cuisine is given a chic, modern twist within a magnificent if reverberant 19th-century bank building. Classical stained-glass ceilings and marble columns are hidden behind an indecently hip oyster counter and bar (open noon till late) offering wide-ranging beers and cocktails. In the former bank vaults beneath, there's a cigar lounge that morphs into a nightclub after 10pm Wednesday to Saturday.

Mer du Nord   Takeaway Seafood $

(www.vishandelnoordzee.be; Rue Ste-Catherine 1; ⏰8am-6pm Tue-Sun; Ⓜ Ste-Catherine) Well-reputed fishmonger's window catering to a queue of stand-and-snack lunch-grabbers around bare metal outdoor tables.

Mokafé   Waffles $

(☎02-511 78 70; Galerie du Roi; waffles from €3; ⏰7.30am-11.30pm; Ⓜ De Brouckère) Locals get their waffles in this old-fashioned cafe under the glass arch of the Galeries-St Hubert. It's a little timeworn inside but wicker chairs in the beautiful arcade provide you with a *m'as-tu-vu* view of passing shoppers.

MARROLES & SABLON

The Sablon has many interesting, relatively upmarket eateries. Dotted along Rue Haute are several more idiosyncratic choices.

Bourse Area Cafes

Many of Brussels' most iconic cafes are within stumbling distance of the Bourse. Don't miss century-old **Falstaff** (www.lefalstaff.be/; Rue Henri Maus 17; ⏰10am-1am; 🚇Bourse) with its festival of stained glass ceilings, or **Le Cirio** (Rue de la Bourse 18; ⏰10am-midnight), a sumptuous yet affordable 1866 marvel full of polished brasswork serving great-value pub meals. Three more classics are hidden up shoulder-wide alleys: the medieval yet unpretentious **A l'Image de Nostre-Dame** (off Rue du Marché aux Herbes 5; ⏰noon-midnight Mon-Fri, 3pm-1am Sat, 4-10.30pm Sun); the 1695 Rubenseque **Au Bon Vieux Temps** (Impasse Saint Michel; ⏰11am-midnight), which sometimes stocks ultra-rare Westvletteren beers (€10!); and lambic specialist **À la Bécasse** (www.alabecasse.com; Rue de Tabora 11; ⏰11am-midnight, to 1am Fri & Sat; Ⓜ Gare Centrale), with its vaguely Puritanical rows of wooden tables.

If those classics seem a little staid for your taste, head a block west of the Bourse to Place Saint-Géry where a whole series of characterful but youthfully fashion-conscious cafes surround the **Café des Halles** (www.cafedeshalles.be), an 1881 market hall that's now part bar, part exhibition hall and hosts a free weekend nightclub in its cellars. Great options for sipping a quiet coffee by day or being buffeted by music at night.

Le Perroquet   Bar

(Rue Watteeu 31; light meals €6.50-11; ⏰noon-1am; Ⓜ Porte de Namur) One of Brussels' most perfectly preserved art nouveau cafes, the Perroquet retains its stained glass, marble tables and timber panelling yet is comparatively inexpensive for a drink or an imaginatively filled pitta snack.

Restobières   Belgian $$

(☎02-502 72 51; www.restobieres.eu; Rue des Renards 9; mains €12-22, menus €18-38; ⏰noon-3pm daily, 6.30pm-11pm Wed-Sun) Beer-based twists on typical Belgian meals served in a delightful if slightly cramped restaurant. The walls are plastered with bottles, grinders and countless antique souvenir biscuit tins featuring Belgian royalty.

🍷 Drinking & Nightlife

Cafe culture is one of Brussels' greatest attractions. On the Grand Place itself, 300-year-old gems, like **Le Roy d'Espagne** (www.roydespagne.be/; Grand Place 1) and **Chaloupe d'Or** (Grand Place 24) are magnificent but predictably pricey. Some-

what cheaper classics lie around the Bourse, with livelier pubs ranged around Place St-Géry and further south around fashion-conscious Flagey.

Moeder Lambic Fontainas Beer Hall

(www.moederlambic.eu; Place Fontainas 8; ⏰11am-1am Mon-Thu & Sun, to 2am Fri & Sat; 🚇Annessens, Bourse) Dozens of artisanal draft beers served in a contemporary rather than old world setting with a mood that's upbeat and set to music.

Délirium Café   Pub

(www.deliriumcafe.be; Impasse de la Fidélité 4A; ⏰10am-4am Mon-Sat, to 2am Sun) The main bar has barrel tables, beer-tray ceilings and over 2000 world beers. The tap house has 25 more on draft. And now there's an associated rum garden and Floris Bar (from 8pm) serving hundreds of *jenevers* (dutch gin), vodkas and absinthes. No wonder it's lively. Live music after 10pm.

À la Mort Subite   Classic Cafe

(☎02-513 13 18; www.alamortsubite.com; Rue Montagne aux Herbes Potagères 7; ⏰11am-1am Mon-Sat, noon-midnight Sun; Ⓜ Gare Centrale) An absolute classic – unchanged since

Handmade chocolates, Belgium

Buying Belgian Chocolates

Mouth-watering Belgian chocolate is some of the world's best as it always uses 100% pure cocoa butter and involves lengthy 'conching' (stirring) to create a silky smooth texture. Within any specialist chocolatiershop, archetypal pralines (filled, bite-size chocolates) and creamy manons cost the same whether you select piece-by-piece or take a pre-mixed ballotin selection pack. But prices vary radically between brands. Although maligned by Belgian choco snobs, ubiquitous **Leonidas** (www.leonidas.com; per kg €24.30) has a price-quality ratio that's hard to beat. You'll pay around double at **Corné Port Royal** (www.corneportroyal. be), **Galler** (www.galler.com), **Chocolate Line** (www.thechocolateline.be) and **Neuhaus** (☎02-512 63 59; www.neuhaus.be; Galerie de la Reine 25; per kg €52; ☺10am-8pm Mon-Sat, 10am-7pm Sun; Ⓜ Gare Centrale), creator of Belgium's original pralines. Or three times at exclusive **Pierre Marcolini** (☎02-512 43 14; www.marcolini.be; Rue des Minimes 1; per kg €70; ☺10am-7pm Sun-Thu, to 6pm Fri & Sat; Ⓜ Porte de Namur), famed for using rare chocolate beans, experimental flavours and fashion-conscious black-box packaging.

1928, with lined-up wooden tables, arched mirror-panels and entertainingly brusque service.

Le Cercle des Voyageurs Brasserie
(☎02-514 39 49; www.lecercledesvoyageurs. com; Rue des Grands Carmes 18; mains €9-12; ☺8am-11pm Wed-Mon; ☎; Ⓜ Annessens, Bourse) Invite Phileas Fogg for coffee to this delightful bistro featuring globes, an antique-map ceiling and a travel library. The global brasserie food is pretty good, and there's free live music, piano jazz Tuesdays, experimental music Thursdays.

La Fleur en Papier Doré Brown Cafe
(www.goudblommekeinpapier.be; Rue des Alex-iens 53; ☺11am-midnight Tue-Sat, to 7pm Sun) Once popular with Magritte and his sur-realist pals, this tiny cafe has its nicotine-stained walls covered with writings, art and scribbles, some reputedly traded for free drinks.

🔒 Shopping

Tourist-oriented shops selling chocolate, beer, lace and Atomium baubles stretch between the Grand Place and Manneken Pis. For better **chocolate shops** in calm-er, grander settings, peruse the resplend-ent **Galeries St-Hubert** or the upmarket Sablon area. In the Marolles, Rue Haute and Rue Blaes are full of quirky **interior design shops** while Place du Jeu-de-Balle has a daily **flea market** (☺6am-2pm). Rue Antoine Dansaert has most of Brussels' **high-fashion boutiques**, with **Stijl** (www. stijl.be; Rue Antoine Dansaert 74) hosting many cutting-edge collections.

Supermarkets sell a range of **Belgian beers** relatively cheaply. For wider selections and the relevant glasses, try **Beermania** (www.beermania.be; Chaussée de Wavre 174; ☺11am-9pm Mon-Sat) or the very personal little **Délices et Caprices** (www.the-belgian-beer-tasting-shop.be; Rue des Bouchers 68; ☺2-8pm Thu-Mon).

ℹ️ Information

Tourist Information

Visit Brussels (☎02-513 89 40; visitbrussels. be; Hôtel de Ville; ☺9am-6pm; Ⓜ Bourse) Stacks of city-specific information. A second branch (☎02-548 04 58; www.biponline.be; Rue Royale 2-4; ☺10am-6pm) at 2 Rue Royale is much less crowded and its Arsène50 (☎02-512 57 45; www.arsene50.be; Rue Royale 2; ☺12.30-5.30pm Tue-Sat) ticketing desk provides discounts for cultural events.

ℹ Getting There & Away

Train

Eurostar, TGV and Thalys high-speed trains stop only at Bruxelles-Midi (Brussel-Zuid). Jump on any local service for the four-minute hop to conveniently central Bruxelles-Central. All domestic trains, plus some Amsterdam services, stop there anyway. Consult www.belgianrail.be for timetable information.

ℹ Getting Around

To/From the Airports

Brussels Airport

Taxi Fares start around €35. Very bad idea in rush hour traffic.

Train Four per hour (5.30am to 11.50pm), €7.60. Takes 20 minutes to Bruxelles-Central, 24 minutes to Bruxelles-Midi.

Charleroi ('Brussels-South') Airport

Bus Direct services operated by L'Elan (www. voyages-lelan.be) run to/from a stop behind Bruxelles-Midi station roughly every half hour (single/return €13/22); last services to/from the airport are 8.30pm/11.45pm. Should take around an hour but allow far more at rush-hour.

Train The nearest mainline train station, Charleroi-Sud, is linked to Charleroi Airport by TEC bus A (€3, 18 minutes) twice hourly on weekdays, hourly at weekends. A combined bus-and-rail ticket never costs more than €12 to anywhere in Belgium if pre-purchased. Brussels–Charleroi-Sud trains take around 50 minutes.

Public Transport

Costs

Tickets valid for one hour are sold at metro stations, STIB/MIVB kiosks, newsagents and on buses and trams. Single-/five-/10-journey STIB/MIVB tickets cost €1.80/7.50/12 including transfers. Unlimited one-/two-/three-day passes cost €6/10/13. Airport buses are excluded. Tickets must be machine-validated before travel or you could face a €55 fine.

Information

For fare/route information go to: www.stib.be.

Operating hours

Services operate 6am to midnight daily. Limited 'Noctis' buses (€3) run from midnight to 3am Friday and Saturday.

Taxi

Taxis (www.autolux.be) cost €2.40 flag fall plus €1.35 per kilometre in Brussels, €2.70 per kilometre beyond city limits. There are taxis ranks at Bruxelles-Midi and Madeleine, or pre-book on ☎02-268 00 00 or ☎02-349 49 49. Flagging down cabs London-style doesn't work.

Flanders

ANTWERP

POP 511,700

Cosmopolitan, confident and full of contrasts, Antwerp (Antwerpen in Dutch, Anvers in French) was one of northern Europe's foremost cities in the 17th century when

Onze-Lieve-Vrouwekathedraal in Antwerp, Belgium
KRZYSZTOF DYDYNSKI/GETTY IMAGES ©

it also was home to Pieter Paul Rubens, diplomat, philosopher and northern Europe's greatest baroque artist. Today it once again revels in fame and fortune-attracting art lovers and mode moguls, club queens and diamond dealers.

Sights

City Centre

Website www.antwerpforfree.be lists a daily calendar of free concerts and events. Most major city-run museums are free on the last Wednesday of each month. At other times a 48-hour Antwerp Card (€28) will save you money if you visit four of the city's splendid museums.

Brabo Fountain · Statue
(Grote Markt) As with every great Flemish city, Antwerp's medieval heart is a classic **Grote Markt** (Market Sq). It's flanked on two sides by very photogenic **guild-halls** and dominated by an impressive Italo-Flemish Renaissance-style **stad-huis** (town hall), completed in 1565. The central feature is a voluptuous, baroque fountain depicting the Roman hero Brabo who, having slain the giant that terrorised the city, cut off his forearm and flung it into the air. This unlikely Hand Werpen (hand throwing) is popularly cited as the source of the settlement's name Antwerpen.

Onze-Lieve-Vrouwekathedraal · Cathedral
(www.dekathedraal.be; Handschoenmarkt; adult/concession €5/3; ⏰10am-5pm Mon-Fri, to 3pm Sat, to 4pm Sun) Belgium's finest Gothic cathedral was 169 years in the making (1352–1521). Wherever you wander in Antwerp, its gracious, 123m-high spire has a habit of popping unexpectedly into view and rarely fails to jolt a gasp of awe. Guided tours at 11am.

Museum Plantin-Moretus · Historic Building
(www.museumplantinmoretus.be; Vrijdag Markt 22; adult/child €8/1; ⏰10am-5pm Tue-Sun) Once home to the world's first indus-trial printing works, this impressive medieval courtyard mansion has been a museum since 1876. Highlights include the preserved 1640 library, the historic bookshop, a roomful of antique printing presses and the priceless collection of manuscripts, paintings and tapestries.

Rubenshuis · Museum
(www.rubenshuis.be; Wapper 9-11; adult/child €8/1, audioguide €2; ⏰10am-5pm Tue-Sun) Re-stored and furnished along original lines, the 1611 building was built as a home and studio by celebrated painter Pieter Paul Rubens. The splendid art collection includes 10 Rubens canvases, including one where Eve appears to glance lustfully at Adam's fig-leaf (guide-ref 50).

Station Area

Antwerpen-Centraal train station is an attraction in itself and the famous **Antwerp zoo** (www.zooantwerpen.be) is just outside.

Diamond Quarter · Neighbourhood
(www.awdc.be) An astounding 80% of the world's uncut diamonds are traded in Antwerp. Though now Indian dominated, historically the diamond business was mainly the domain of Orthodox Jews, whose black coats, broad-rimmed hats and long hair-curls remain a distinctive sight here.

🛏 Sleeping

Hotel Julien · Boutique Hotel $$$
(☎03-229 06 00; www.hotel-julien.com; Korte Nieuwstraat 24; r €195-295; ❄ @ 🛜) This very discreet boutique mansion-hotel exudes an exquisitely tasteful understated elegance. Rooms feature underfloor heating, Moroccan plaster, DVD players and fresh orchids. A swish new wellness centre hides in the subterranean caverns and the rooftop view is a well kept secret.

Hotel Les Nuits · Designer Hotel $$$
(☎03-225 02 04; www.hotellesnuits.be; Lange Gasthuisstraat 12; d/ste from €149/179; 🛜) Black-on-black corridors that are fash-ionable fantasies more than Halloween howlers lead to 24 designer-modernist rooms, each with its own special touches,

supercomfy bed and rainforest shower. Breakfast (€16) is taken in the casually suave restaurant where you check in; there's no reception.

Matelote Hotel   Boutique Hotel $$

(☎03-201 88 00; www.hotel-matelote.be; Haarstraat 11; r €90-190; ✳@✆) In a 16th-century building on a pedestrianised old-city backstreet, the Matelote has 10 contemporary styled rooms in five different types, some rather small, others with original beams and pebble-floored bathrooms. Air conditioning in upper rooms.

Hotel O   Hotel $$

(☎03-500 89 50; www.hotelhotelo.com; Handschoenmarkt 3; r €89-129) In an unbeatable location staring right at the cathedral frontage, the O has an intriguing little foyer of 1950s radios and big low-wattage lamp-bulbs. All-black interior decor is relieved in midsized rooms by giant Ru-bens prints spilling over onto the ceilings. Some rooms are very small.

🍴 Eating

De Groote Witte Arend   Belgian $$

(☎03-233 50 33; www.degrootewittearend.be; Reyndersstraat 18; mains €13-22; ⏰10.30am-midnight, kitchen 11.30am-3pm & 5-10pm; ✆) Retaining the Tuscan stone arcade of a 15th to 17th century convent building, this relaxed central gem combines the joys of a good beer bar with the satisfaction of well-cooked, sensibly priced Flemish home cuisine.

Het Vermoeide Model   Belgian $$

(☎03-233 52 61; www.hetvermoeidemodel.be; Lijnwaadmarkt 2; mains €16.50-25, set menu €26; ⏰4-10pm Tue-Sun) This very atmospheric, if somewhat touristy, medieval house-restaurant has rooms full of exposed brickwork, and there's live piano music on some winter weekends. But the 'secret' surprise is a steep, creaky

staircase leading up to a little roof terrace for which reservations are essential in summer. The menu includes steaks, ribs, *waterzooi* and seasonal mussels in calvados.

't Brantyser — European $

(☎ 03-233 18 33; www.brantyser.be; Hendrik Conscienceplein 7; snacks €6-12.50, mains €16.50-26.50; ⏰ 11.15am-10pm) The cosy, double-level Brantyser gets the antique clutter effect just right while its enviable terrace surveys one of old Antwerp's most appealing pedestrian squares. Other restaurants nearby might be more refined, but the food here is tasty and portions are generous.

Kathedraalcafe — Belgian $$

(www.kathedraalcafe.be; Torfbrug 10; mains €14-24.50, sandwiches €8.50; ⏰ noon-11pm) This ivy-clad medieval masterpiece has an astounding interior decked with angels, saints, pulpits and several deliciously sacrilegious visual jokes.

🍷 Drinking & Nightlife

To sound like a local, stride into a pub and ask for a *bolleke*. Don't worry, that means a 'little bowl' (ie glass) of De Koninck, the city's favourite ale. Cheap places to try it include classic cafes **Oud Arsenaal** (Pijpelincxstraat 4; ⏰ 10am-10pm Wed-Fri, 7.30am-7.30pm Sat & Sun), **De Kat** (Wolstraat 22) and the livelier **Pelikaan** (www.facebook.com/cafepelikaan; Melkmarkt 14; ⏰ 8.30am-3am).

Den Engel — Pub

(www.cafedenengel.be; Grote Markt 5; ⏰ 9am-2am) Historic guildhall pub with cathedral views from the terrace.

De Vagant — Pub

(www.devagant.be; Reyndersstraat 25; ⏰ noon-late) More than 200 *jenever* (€2.20 to €7.50) are served in this bare-boards local cafe or sold by the bottle across the road from its *slijterij* (bottle-shop), which resembles an old-style pharmacy.

Bierhuis Kulminator

(Vleminckveld 32; ⏰4pm-midnight Tue-Sat, 8pm-midnight Mon) Classic beer-pub boasting 700 mostly Belgian brews, including notably rare 'vintage' bottles laid down to mature for several years like fine wine.

ℹ Information

Tourism Antwerp (☎03-232 01 03; www. visitantwerpen.be; Grote Markt 13; ⏰9am-5.45pm Mon-Sat, to 4.45pm Sun & holidays) is a central tourist office with a branch on level zero of Antwerpen-Centraal train station.

ℹ Getting There & Away

Train

Located 1.5km east of the historic centre, **Antwerpen-Centraal Station** (🚇Diamant) is a veritable cathedral of a building, considered by many to be among the world's most handsome stations. Destinations include:

Amsterdam €34.50/77, 135/74 minutes, one per hour

Bruges €14.25, 75 minutes, two per hour

Brussels €6.90, 35 to 49 minutes, five per hour

Ghent-Dampoort €9, 46 minutes, three per hour

Leuven €6.90, 42 to 63 minutes, four per hour

Lier €2.70, 17 minutes, five per hour

Mechelen-Nekkerspoel €3.70, 15 minutes, two per hour

Paris €106, 138 minutes, seven daily

ℹ Getting Around

Franklin Rooseveltplaats and Koningin Astridplein are hubs for the integrated network of **De Lijn** (www.delijn.be) buses and trams (some running underground metro-style).

GHENT

POP 248,200

Known as Gent in Dutch and Gand in French, Ghent is Flanders' unsung historic city. Like a grittier Bruges without the crush of tourists, it sports photogenic canals, medieval towers, great cafes and some of Belgium's most inspired museums.

◉ Sights

City Centre

The main sights are strolling distance from Korenmarkt, the westernmost of three interlinked squares that form the heart of Ghent's historic core.

The good value **Museumpass** (www. visitgent.be; 3-day ticket €20) provides three days' free entrance to a number of sights and attractions (except for boat tours),and all city transport. It's sold at museums, De Lijn booths and the tourist office.

St-Baafskathedraal

(www.users.skynet.be/sintbaafskathedraal-gent; St-Baafsplein; ⏰8.30am-6pm Apr-Oct, to 5pm Nov-Mar) A €0.20 leaflet guides you round the cathedral's numerous art treasures, including a big original Rubens opposite the stairway that leads down into the partly muralled crypts. But most visitors come to see just one magnificent work – the Van Eyck's 1432 'Flemish Primitive' altarpiece, **The Adoration of the Mystic Lamb** (Het Lam Gods; http://vaneyck.kikirpa.be; St- Baafskathedraal; adult/child €4/1.50, audio guide €1; ⏰9.30am-4.45pm Mon-Sat, 1-4.30pm Sun, closes 4pm Nov-Mar) kept in a specially temperature-controlled, half-darkened chapel near the west entrance. Some panels have been temporarily removed to MSK for restoration.

Belfort

(Botermarkt; adult/concession €5/3.75; ⏰10am-5.30pm) Ghent's soaring Unesco-listed 14th-century belfry is topped by a large dragon. That's a weathervane not a fire breather and it's become something of a city mascot. You'll meet two previous dragon incarnations on the climb to the top (mostly by lift) but other than some bell making exhibits the real attraction is the view. Enter through the **Lakenhalle**, Ghent's cloth hall that was left half-built in 1445 and only completed in 1903.

Gravensteen

(St-Veerleplein; adult/child €8/4; ⏰10am-6pm Apr-Oct, 9am-5pm Nov-Mar) The Counts of

Flanders' quintessential 12th-century stone castle comes complete with moat, turrets and arrow slits. If you just wish to photograph the castle's exterior there's a great **viewpoint** on St-Widostraat.

Grasbrug   Viewpoint
To admire Ghent's towers and gables at their most photogenic, stand just west of the little Grasbrug bridge at dusk. Canal boat trips depart from either end of the Grasbrug and nearby Vleeshuisbrug bridges.

Patershol   Neighbourhood
(www.patershol.be) Dotted with half-hidden restaurants, enchanting Patershol is a web of twisting cobbled lanes with old-world houses that were once home to leather tradespeople and to the Carmelite Fathers (Paters), hence the name.

Out of the Centre

SMAK   Gallery
(www.smak.be; Citadelpark; adult/child €6/free, 10am-1pm Sun free; ☺10am-6pm Tue-Sun; ☒5) Ghent's highly regarded Museum of Contemporary Art features regularly changing exhibitions of provocative, cutting-edge installations.

🛏 Sleeping

Websites www.gent-accommodations.be and www.bedandbreakfast-gent.be help you judge availability in the city's numerous appealing B&Bs.

Chambres d'Hôtes Verhaegen
Boutique B&B **$$$**
(☎09-265 07 60; www.hotelverhaegen.be; Oude Houtlei 110; d €195-265; ☺reception 2-6pm) This sumptuous 1770s urban palace retains original sections of 18th-century Chinese wallpaper, a dining room with romantic Austrian-

era murals, dazzling salon and neatly manicured parterre garden. The five exclusive guest rooms combine well-placed modernist and retro touches. Breakfast costs €18.

Hotel Harmony   Boutique Hotel **$$$**
(☎09-324 26 80; www.hotel-harmony.be; Kraanlei 37; s €139-209, d €154-229; ☎☒) Luxuriously heaped pillows, fine linens, Miro-esque art and swish modern colours lie beneath the 18th-century beams of this old-meets-new beauty. Each of the 25 rooms has a coffee maker and even the smallest is amply sized, but shapes and views vary. Check Facebook for promotional deals.

Atlas B&B   B&B **$$**
(☎09-233 49 91; www.atlasbenb.be; Rabotstraat 40; s €57-72, d €73-93; P@☎) This fine 1863 townhouse has gorgeous belle-époque, art deco and art nouveau touches in a lounge featuring maps, globes and an honesty bar. Four very distinctive guest rooms are themed by continent.

Gravensteen castle in Ghent, Belgium
HIROSHI HIGUCHI/GETTY IMAGES ©

LOUISE HEUSINKVELD/GETTY IMAGES ©

Eating

House of Eliott
Lobster $$$

(☎09-225 21 28; www.thehouseofeliott.be; J Breydelstraat 36; mains €25-45, menus €46-59; ⏰noon-2pm & 6-11pm Thu-Mon, closed Sep) Oozing pseudo-1920s charm, this gently camp, canalside gem is full of flapper mannequins and sepia photos inspired by an old British TV series. Its little balcony terrace perches just above the canal waters. Gastronomically, lobster dominates.

Brasserie Pakhuis
European, Oysters $$

(☎09-223 55 55; www.pakhuis.be; Schuurkenstraat 4; mains €17-29, weekday lunch €13.50, menus €27-43; ⏰lunch & dinner Mon-Sat, bar 11am-1am) This hip, if mildly ostentatious, modern brasserie-bar-restaurant is set in a magnificently restored former textile warehouse. It retains the original century-old wrought ironwork and an incredible roof. It's well worth popping inside, even if you only stop for a drink.

Amadeus
Ribs $

(☎09-225 13 85; www.amadeusspareribrestau rant.be; Plotersgracht 8/10; mains €13.75-19; ⏰6.30-11pm) All-you-can-eat spare ribs at

four Ghent addresses, all within ancient buildings that are full of atmosphere, bustle and cheerful conversation.

't Oud Clooster
Tavern $

(☎09-233 78 02; Zwartezustersstraat 5; mains €9-17; ⏰6pm-late Mon-Sat, kitchen till midnight) Mostly candlelit at night, this atmospheric double level 'pratcafe' is built into sections of what was long ago a nunnery, hence the sprinkling of religious statues and cherub lamp-holders. Well-priced cafe food is presented with unexpected style.

🍷 Drinking & Nightlife

Hotsy Totsy
Jazz Bar

(www.hotsytotsy.be; Hoogstraat 1; ⏰6pm-1am Mon-Fri, 8pm-2am Sat & Sun) A 1930s vamp pouts above the zinc of this classic artist's cafe with silver-floral wallpaper, black-and-white film photos and free live jazz at 9pm most Thursdays (October to April).

Het Waterhuis aan de Bierkant
Beer Pub

(www.waterhuisaandebierkant.be; Groentenmarkt 12; ⏰11am-1am) Sharing an enticing waterfront terrace with atmospherically austere *jenever* bar **'t Dreupelkot** (⊘4pm-late), this photogenic classic beer-pub has an interior draped in dried hops and three exclusive house beers amid the wide selection.

Rococo — Bar
(Corduwaniersstraat 5; ⊘from 10pm) Lit only by candles, this classic late night cafe-bar with carved wooden ceilings is an ideal place for cosy midnight conversations.

ⓘ Information

Ghent tourist office (☑09-266 56 60; www.visitgent.be; Oude Vismijn, St-Veerleplein 5; ⊘9.30am-6.30pm mid-Mar–mid-Oct, to 4.30pm winter) Very helpful for free maps and accommodation bookings.

ⓘ Getting There & Away

Train
Gent-Dampoort, 1km west of the old city, is the handiest station with useful trains to Antwerp (€8.50, fast/slow 42/64 minutes, three per hour), Bruges (€6.20, 36 minutes, hourly) and Kortrijk (€6.60, 35 minutes, hourly).

The main station, **Gent-St-Pieters** (2.5km south of centre), has more choice, including Brussels (€9, 36 minutes, twice hourly), Bruges (fast/slow 24/42 minutes, five per hour), Kortrijk (€6.60, fast/slow 26/33 minutes) and Ostend (€9, fast/slow 38/55 minutes).

ⓘ Getting Around
Driving a car in Ghent is purgatory. Park it and walk or ride.

Bicycle
Bicycles can be hired from:

Biker (Steendam 16; per half-/full day €6.50/9; ⊘9am-12.30pm & 1.30-6pm Tue-Sat)

Max Mobiel (www.max-mobiel.be; Vokselslaan 27; per day/week/month €9/25/30) Two minutes' walk south of Gent-St-Pieters station. Branch kiosk at Gent-Dampoort station.

Bus & Tram
One-hour/all-day tickets cost €1.20/5 if purchased ahead of time from ticket machines or De Lijn offices beside **Gent-St-Pieters** (⊘7am-1.30pm & 2-7pm Mon-Fri) or in the centre. Handy tram 1 runs from Gent-St-Pieters to and through the centre passing walkably close to most major sites.

BRUGES
POP 117,000

Cobblestone lanes, dreamy canals, soaring spires and whitewashed old almshouses combine to make central Bruges (Brugge in Dutch) one of Europe's most picture-perfect historic cities. The only problem is that everyone knows.

◎ Sights

A **Bruges City Card** (www.bruggecitycard.be; 48/72 hours €35/€40) gives entry to all the main city museums, plus private attractions including Choco-Story and De Halve Maan brewery. You'll also score a canal boat ride and discounts on bicycle rental, concerts, films and theatre.

Groeningemuseum — Art Gallery
(www.brugge.be; Dijver 12; adult/concession €8/6; ⊘9.30am-5pm Tue-Sun) Bruges' most celebrated art gallery packs 11 rooms with an astonishingly rich collection. Superb Flemish Primitive works including Jan van Eyck's radiant, if rather odd, masterpiece *Madonna with Canon George Van der Paele* (1436) are the main drawcard but later artistic genres also get a look in.

Markt — Square
The heart of ancient Bruges, the old market square is lined with pavement cafes beneath step-gabled facades. The scene is dominated by the **Belfort** (Belfry; adult/child €8/5; ⊘9.30am-5pm, last tickets 4.15pm), Belgium's most famous belfry – its iconic octagonal tower is arguably better appreciated from afar than by climbing 366 claustrophobic steps to the top.

Burg — Square
Bruges' 1420 **Stadhuis** (City Hall; Burg 12) is smothered in statuettes and contains a breathtaking **Gotische Zaal** (Gothic Hall; Burg; adult/concession €4/3; ⊘9.30am-5pm), featuring dazzling polychromatic ceilings, hanging vaults and historicist murals. Tickets include entry to part of the early

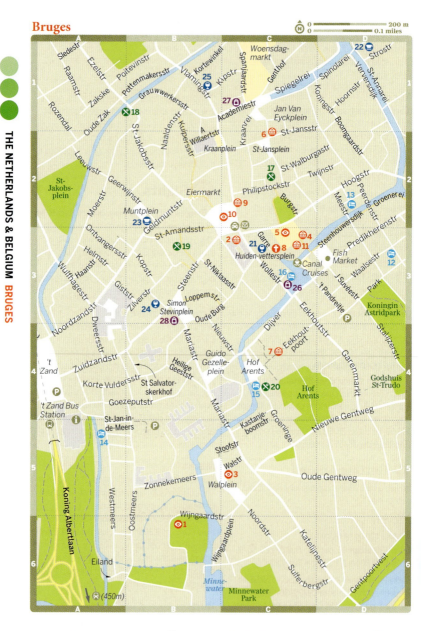

baroque **Brugse Vrije** (Burg 11a; 9.30am-noon & 1.30-4.30pm) next door. With its gilt highlights and golden statuettes, this palace was once the administrative centre for a large autonomous territory ruled from Bruges between 1121 and 1794.

Heilig-Bloedbasiliek   Church

(Basilica of the Holy Blood; Burg 5; 9.30-11.50am & 2-5.50pm Apr-Sep, 10-11.50am & 2-3.50pm Thu-Tue, 10-11.50am Wed Oct-Mar) The Stadhuis's western end morphs into the strangely invisible Heilig-Bloedbasiliek.

Bruges

⊙ Sights

1	Begijnhof	B6
2	Belfort	C3
3	Brouwerij De Halve Maan	C5
4	Brugse Vrije	C3
5	Burg	C3
6	Choco-Story	C2
	Gotische Zaal	(see 11)
7	Groeningemuseum	C4
8	Heilig-Bloedbasiliek	C3
9	Historium	C2
10	Markt	C2
11	Stadhuis	C3

⊕ Sleeping

12	B&B Dieltiens	D3
13	B&B Huyze Hertsberge	D2
14	Baert B&B	A5
15	Guesthouse Nuit Blanche	C4
16	Relais Bourgondisch Cruyce	C3

⊗ Eating

17	Cambrinus	C2
18	De Bottelier	A1
19	De Stove	B3
20	Den Gouden Harynck	C4

⊖ Drinking & Nightlife

21	De Garre	C3
22	Herberg Vlissinghe	D1
23	Merveilleux Tearoom	B2
24	't Brugs Beertje	B3
25	't Poatersgat	B1

⊕ Shopping

26	2-Be	C3
27	Bacchus Cornelius	C1
28	Chocolate Line	B3

The basilica takes its name from a phial supposedly containing a few drops of Christ's blood that was brought here after the 12th-century Crusades.

Historium   Museum

(www.historium.be; Markt 1; adult/child €11/5.50; ⊙10am-9pm) Taking visitors back to 1435, this immersive multimedia experience was due to open as we went to press. Claiming to be more medieval movie than museum, the museum features a fictional love story to provide narrative structure, and you can nose around Van Eyck's studio.

Begijnhof   Begijnhof

(⊙6.30am-6.30pm) FREE Bruges' delightful *begijnhof* originally dates from the 13th century. Although the last *begijn* has long since passed away, today residents of the pretty, whitewashed garden complex include a convent of Benedictine nuns. Despite the hoards of summer tourists, the *begijnhof* remains a remarkably tranquil haven. In spring a carpet of daffodils adds to the quaintness of the scene. Outside the *begijnhof*'s 1776 gateway bridge lies a tempting, if predictably tourist-priced, array of terraced restaurants, lace shops and waffle peddlers.

Choco-Story   Museum

(www.choco-story.be; Wijnzakstraat 2, on Sint-Jansplein; adult/child €7/4; ⊙10am-5pm) This highly absorbing chocolate museum traces the cocoa bean back to its role as an Aztec currency, shows videos on cocoa production and provides samples of pralines that are made as you watch (last demonstration 4.45pm).

Brouwerij De Halve Maan   Brewery

(☎050 33 26 97; www.halvemaan.be; Walplein 26; ⊙10.30am-6pm, closed 2 weeks mid-Jan) Founded in 1856, this is the last family *brouwerij* (brewhouse) in central Bruges. Multilingual **guided visits** (tours €6.50; ⊙11am-4pm Apr-Sep, 11am & 3pm Oct-Mar), lasting 45 minutes, depart each hour and include a tasting. Alternatively simply sip one of its excellent *Brugse Zot* beers in the appealing brewery cafe.

⊕ Sleeping

Although there are well over 250 hotels and B&Bs, accommodation can still prove oppressively overbooked from Easter to September, over Christmas and, especially, at weekends, when two-night minimum stays are commonly required.

Guesthouse Nuit Blanche   B&B $$$

(☎0494 40 04 47; www.bruges-bb.com; Groeninge 2; d €175-195) Step into a Van Eyck painting where original Gothic fireplaces and period furniture cunningly hide an array of modern fittngs. The historic house once hosted Churchill as well as Belgian royalty. Room rates cover the bottle of bubbly in your minibar. Drink it in the fabulous canalside garden or on 'Lovers' Bridge' to which the guesthouse has a unique private entrance.

B&B Huyze Hertsberge   B&B $$$

(☏050 33 35 42; www.bruges-bedandbreakfast. be; Hertsbergestraat 8; r €150-165) Very spacious and oozing with good taste, this late-17th-century house has a gorgeous period salon decked with antiques and sepia photos of the charming owner's great-great-grandparents (who first moved in here in 1901). The four guest rooms are comfortably grand, each with at least partial views of the tranquil little canalside garden.

Relais Bourgondisch Cruyce   Boutique Hotel $$$

(☏050 33 79 26; www.relaisbourgondischcruyce. be; Wollestraat 41-47; d €185-375) This luxurious little boutique hotel occupies a unique part-timbered medieval house graced with art, antiques, Persian carpets and fresh orchids. Relax in the canalside

lounge while tourists cruise past on barge tours. Most rooms are somewhat small but full of designer fittings, including top-quality Vispring beds, Ralph Lauren fabrics and (in some) Philippe Starck bathrooms.

B&B Dieltiens   B&B $$

(☏050 33 42 94; www.bedandbreakfastbruges. be; Waalsestraat 40; s €60-80, d €70-90) Old and new art fills this lovingly restored classical mansion, which remains an appealingly real home run by charming musician hosts. Superbly central yet quiet.

Baert B&B   B&B $$

(☏050 33 05 30; www.bedandbreakfastbrugge. be; Westmeers 28; s/d €75/85) In a 1613 former stable this is one of very few places in Bruges that you'll get a private canalside terrace – adorably flower-decked, though not on the loveliest canal section. Floral rooms have bathrooms across the landing; bathrobes are provided. A big breakfast spread is served in a glass verandah, and extras include a welcome drink and a pack of chocolates.

🍴 Eating

Touristy terraces crowd the Markt and line pedestrianised St-Amandsstraat where there are many cheaper eateries. Along eclectic Langestraat (the eastward extension of Hoog-straat), you'll find everything from kebabs to Michelin stars.

De Stove   Gastronomic $$

(☏050 33 78 35; www. restaurantdestove.be; Kleine St-Amandsstraat 4; mains €19-33, menu without/with wine €48/64; ⏲noon-1.30pm Sat & Sun, 7-9pm Fri-Tue) Despite perennial rave reviews, this calm, one-room family restaurant remains friendly,

Old bottling machine at Brouwerij De Halve Maan (p539) in Bruges, Belgium
MARTIN MOOS/GETTY IMAGES ©

reliable and inventive, without a hint of tourist-twee-ness. The monthly changing menu often favours fresh fish. Almost everything is homemade, from the bread to the ice cream.

Den Gouden Harynck
Gastronomic **$$$**

(☎050 33 76 37; www.dengoudenharynck.be; Groeninge 25; mains €38-45, set lunch menu €39, 4-/5-course menu €75/89; ⏱lunch & dinner Tue-Sat) Behind an ivy-clad facade, this uncluttered Michelin-starred restaurant garners consistent praise and won't hurt the purse quite as severely as certain better-known competitors. A lovely location: both central and secluded.

In 't Nieuwe Museum
Brown Cafe **$$**

(☎050 33 12 12; Hooistraat 42; mains €16-22; ⏱noon-2pm & 6-10pm Thu-Tue, closed lunch Sat) This family-owned local favourite is so-called because of the museum-like collection of brewery plaques and money boxes. It serves great value lunches (€7 to €12.50) and dinners of succulent meat cooked at a 17th-century open fireplace along with vegie burgers, eel dishes and creamy *vispannetje* (fish casserole). To find it follow Hoogstraat/Langestraat west past the famous **de Karmeliet**, then turn right and walk one block down Ganzenstraat.

De Bottelier
Mediterranean **$$**

(☎050 33 18 60; www.debottelier.com; St-Jakobsstraat 63; pasta/veg dishes from €9/13.50, mains from €16; ⏱lunch & dinner Tue-Fri, dinner Sat) Decorated with hats and old clocks, this adorable little restaurant sits above a wine shop overlooking a delightful handkerchief of canalside garden. Local diners predominate, reservations recommended.

Cambrinus
Beer Pub **$$**

(☎050 33 23 28; www.cambrinus.eu; Philipstockstraat 19; ⏱11am-11pm Sun-Thu, to late Fri & Sat) This 17th-century sculpture-adorned brasserie/pub is a tourist favourite for traditional Belgian and Italian inspired snacks as well as good-value menus that help soak up the hundreds of varieties of beer.

🍺 Drinking & Nightlife

't Brugs Beertje
Beer Pub

(www.brugsbeertje.be; Kemelstraat 5; ⏱4pm-1am Thu-Tue) Legendary for its hundreds of Belgian brews, this cosy brown cafe is one of those perfect beer bars with smoke-yellowed walls, enamel signs, hop-sprig ceilings and knowledgeable staff to help you choose from a book full of brews.

Herberg Vlissinghe
Historic Cafe

(☎050 34 37 37; www.cafevlissinghe.be; Blekerstraat 2; ⏱11am-10pm Wed-Sat, to 7pm Sun) First opened in 1515, this is where, according to local legend, Rubens once painted an imitation coin on the table then did a runner. The interior is gorgeously preserved.

De Garre
Beer Pub

(☎050 34 10 29; www.degarre.be; Garre 1; ⏱noon-midnight) This hidden two-floor *estaminet* (tavern) stocks dozens of fine Belgian brews, including remarkable Struise Pannepot (€3.50) but don't miss the pub's fabulous 11% Garre house beer, which comes with a thick floral head in a glass that's almost a brandy balloon.

't Poatersgat
Pub

(www.poatersgat.com; Vlaamingstraat 82; ⏱5pm-late) Look carefully for the concealed 'Monk's hole' in the wall and follow the staircase down into this cross-vaulted cellar glowing with ethereal white lights and flickering candles.

Merveilleux Tearoom
Tearoom

(☎050 61 02 09; www.merveilleux.eu; Muntpoort 8; high tea €10, mains €15-22; ⏱10am-6pm) Elegant marble-floored tearoom on a cobbled passage near the Markt.

🔒 Shopping

't Apostelientje
Lace

(www.apostelientje.be; Balstraat 11; ⏱1-5pm Tue, 9.30am-12.15pm & 1.15-5pm Wed-Sat, 10am-1pm Sun) Bruges overflows with lace vendors, but this sweet little 'museum shop' is authentic and well off the normal tourist trail.

Damme

Historic, quaint but often tourist-jammed, the inland port-village of **Damme** (www.toerismedamme.be) makes a popular summer excursion by canal **paddle steamer** (adult/child one-way €7.50/5.50, return €10/8; ⊙10am-5pm Easter–mid-Oct), departing every two hours from Bruges' Noorweegse Kaai (bus 4 from Markt). Consider cycling instead: it's only 5km and, by continuing 2km further along the idyllic canal, you'll escape from the worst of the visitor overload. If you're still energetic, consider then heading 10km northwest via Dudzele and **Hof Ter Doest** (www.terdoest.be) to sweet little **Lissewege** (www.lissewege.be), an artists village from which hourly trains return to Bruges.

Quasimodo (📞050 37 04 70; www.quasimodo.be; adult/under-26yr €62.50/52.50) visits most of these by minibus on its **Triple Treat tours** (under/over 26yr €45/55; ⊙9am Mon, Wed & Fri Feb–mid-Dec), adding castles at **Loppem** and **Tillegem** and fascinating **WWII coastal defences** near Ostend. The same company's **Flanders Fields tours** (under/over 26yr €45/55; ⊙9am Tue-Sun Apr-Oct) visit Ypres Salient.

Chocolate Line — Chocolate
(www.thechocolateline.be; Simon Stevinplein 19; per kg €50; ⊙10am-6pm) 'Shock-o-latier' Dominique Persoone is famous for using wildly experimental flavours and creating novel new products, from chocolate body paint to nasal choco-shots.

2-Be — Food, Drink
(www.2-be.biz; Wollestraat 53; ⊙10am-7pm) Vast range of Belgian products, from beers to biscuits.

Bacchus Cornelius — Beer
(www.bacchuscornelius.com; Academiestraat 17; ⊙1-6.30pm) Around 450 beers, plus flavoured *jenevers* and liqueurs to take home.

ℹ Information

The **tourist office** (📞050 44 46 46; www.brugge.be; 't Zand 34; ⊙10am-6pm Mon-Sun) is situated at street level of the Concertgebouw with a branch at the train station. Standard city maps cost €0.50, comprehensive guide pamphlets €2. Excellent *Use-It* guide-maps (www.use-it.be) are free if you ask for one.

ℹ Getting There & Away

Bruges' train station is about 1.5km south of the Markt, a lovely walk via the Begijnhof. It offers the following services:

Antwerp (€14.25, 75 minutes) Twice hourly.

Brussels (€14, one hour) Twice hourly.

Ghent (€6.20, fast/slow 24/42 minutes) Five hourly, two continue to more central Gent-Dampoort.

Ypres (Ieper in Dutch) Take a train to Roeselare (€4.50, fast/slow 22/33 minutes), then bus 94 or 95: both buses pass key WWI sites en route.

ℹ Getting Around

Boat
A classic way to see and 'feel' Bruges from new angles, **Canal Tours** (adult/child €7.60/3.40; ⊙10am-6pm Mar–mid-Nov) are a must for many visitors. Boats depart roughly every 20 minutes from various jetties, taking 30 minutes.

Horse-Drawn Carriage
Up to five people per carriage (€39) on a well-trodden, 35-minute route from the Markt.

YPRES

Especially when viewed from the south-east, the Grote Markt of Ypres (Ieper in Dutch, pronounced 'eepr' in French and English) is one of the most breathtaking market squares in Flanders. It's all the more astonishing once you discover that virtually all of its convincingly 'medieval' buildings are in fact 20th-century copies. The originals had been brutally bombarded into oblivion between 1914 and 1918 when the historic city failed to capitulate to German WWI advances. WWI battles in the surrounding poppy fields, known as the Ypres Salient, killed hundreds of thousands of soldiers. A century later, countless lovingly tended cemeteries remain, along with numerous widely spread WWI-based museums and trench remnants. Together they present a thoroughly moving introduction to the horrors and futility of war.

 Sights

Central Ypres

Grote Markt   Square

The brilliantly rebuilt **Lakenhallen**, a vast Gothic edifice originally serving as the 13th-century cloth market, dominates this very photogenic central square. It sports a 70m-high belfry, reminiscent of London's Big Ben, and hosts the gripping museum **In Flanders Fields** (www.inflandersfields.be; Lakenhalle, Grote Markt 34; adult/child €8/1; ⊙10am-6pm Apr–mid-Nov, 10am-5pm Tue-Sun mid-Nov–Mar), a highly rec-

ommended multimedia WWI experience honouring ordinary people's experiences of wartime horrors. The ticket allows free entry to three other minor city museums.

Ypres Salient

Many Salient sites are awkward to reach without a car or tour bus. But the following are all within 600m of Ypres–Roeselare bus routes 94 and 95 (once or twice hourly on weekdays, five daily on weekends), so could be visited en route to or from Bruges.

Memorial Museum
Passchendaele 1917   Museum

(www.passchendaele.be; leperstraat 5; admission €5; ⊙10am-6pm Feb-Nov; 🚌94) In central **Zonnebeke village** (www.zonnebeke.be), a lake-fronted Normandy chalet-style mansion (built 1922) now hosts an impressive WWI museum charting local battle progressions with plenty of multilingual commentaries. The big attraction here is descending into its multiroom 'trench experience' with low-lit wooden-clad subterranean bunk rooms and a soundtrack to add wartime atmosphere. Entirely indoors, explanations are much more helpful here than in 'real' trenches elsewhere.

Lakenhallen in Grote Markt, Ypres, Belgium

DENNIS K. JOHNSON/GETTY IMAGES ©

Tyne Cot   Cemetery
(🕐24hr, visitor centre 9am-6pm Feb-Nov; 🚌94) **FREE** With 11,956 graves, this is the world's biggest British Commonwealth war cemetery, and a huge semicircular wall commemorates another 34,857 lost-in-action soldiers whose names wouldn't fit on Ypres' Menin Gate. The name Tyne Cot was coined by Northumberland Fusiliers who fancied that German bunkers on the hillside here looked like Tyneside cottages. Three such dumpy concrete bunkers still sit amid the graves here. Bus 94 stops 600m away.

Deutscher Soldatenfriedhof   Cemetery
FREE The area's main German WWI cemetery is smaller than Tyne Cot but arguably more memorable, amid oak trees and trios of squat, mossy crosses. Some 44,000 corpses were grouped together here, up to 10 per granite grave slab and four eerie silhouette statues survey the site. Entering takes you through a black concrete 'tunnel' that clanks and hisses with distant war sounds, while four short video-montages commemorate the trag-edy of war. It's beyond the northern edge of Langemark on bus route 95.

Tours

There are dozens more WWI sites to seek out. Two bookshops towards Menin Gate sell a range of useful guidebooks and specialist publications and each offer twice-daily, half-day guided minibus tours of selected war sites (advance booking suggested):

Over the Top   Bookshop, Tours
(📞0472 34 87 47; www.overthetoptours.be; Meensestraat 41; 🕐9am-12.30pm, 1.30-5.30pm & 7.30-8.30pm)

British Grenadier   Bookshop, Tours
(📞057 21 46 57; www.salienttours.be; Meensestraat 5; 🕐9.30am-1pm, 2-6pm & 7.30-8.30pm)

ℹ️ Getting There & Around
Train
Services run hourly to Ghent (€11, one hour) and Brussels (€16.75, 1¾ hours) via Kortrijk (€5, 30 minutes), where you could change for Bruges or Antwerp.

Decorated bicycle in Amsterdam, the Netherlands

Detour:
Moselle Valley, Luxembourg

Welcome to wine country. Smothering the Moselle River's steeply rising banks are the neatly clipped vineyards that produce Luxembourg's balanced rieslings, fruity rivaners and excellent crémants (sparkling *méthode traditionelle* wines). The region's various wine towns aren't architecturally memorable but **Ahn** and hillside **Wellenstein** are gently picturesque villages, while bigger **Remich** offers one-hour summer **river cruises** (www.navitours.lu; adult/child/dog €7/4/1). About 1.5km north of Remich's bus terminal (bus 175 from Luxembourg City), **St-Martin** (☏23 69 97 74; www.cavesstmartin.lu; 53 Route de Stadtbredimus; tour with one taster €4.75, free with Luxembourg Card [LC]; ☺10am, 1.30pm & 3pm Tue-Sun Apr-Oct) has wine *caves* that really are caves – cool, damp tunnels hewn deep into the rock face. To join its hour-long **tours** (€3.50; ☺11am, 1pm & 3pm Tue-Sun Apr-Oct) it's worth reserving. In contrast, bookings are unnecessary if you continue to the grand **Caves Bernard-Massard** (☏75 05 45 1; www.bernard-massard.lu; 8 Rue du Pont; tour adult/child/LC from €4/2.50/free; ☺9.30am-6pm Apr-Oct) in central **Grevenmacher** where frequent 20-minute **winery tours** (adult/child from €4/2.50) are multilingual, spiced with humour and culminate in a genteel sampling cafe. The Enner der Bréck bus stop outside is on bus routes 130 (to Rue Heine in Luxembourg City) and 450 to Remich.

Bicycles from **Rentabike Miselerland** (www.visitmoselle.lu/rentabike-miselerland; per day €7, LC free) can be picked up at Remich bus station and returned at Grevenmacker's Butterfly Garden (amongst various other points) allowing visits en route to Ehnen's **wine museum** (☏76 00 26; 115 Route du Vin; adult/child/LC €3.50/1.50/free; ☺9.30-11.30am & 2-5pm Tue-Sun Apr-Oct) and winery **Poll-Fabaire** (☏76 82 11; www.pollfabaire.lu; 115 Route du Vin; tours €4; ☺tours 1pm-5.30pm, tasting room 10.30am-8pm May-Oct, 10.30am-6pm Nov-Apr).

SURVIVAL GUIDE

❶ Directory A–Z

Accommodation

The Netherlands

Always book accommodation ahead, especially during high season; note that many visitors choose to stay in Amsterdam even if travelling elsewhere. Many Dutch hotels have steep, perilous stairs but no lifts, although most top-end and some midrange hotels are exceptions.

Prices quoted here include private bathrooms unless otherwise stated and are high-season rates. Breakfast is not included unless specified.

€ less than €80

€€ €80 to €160

€€€ more than €160

Belgium

Tourist offices are superb sources of accommodation assistance, usually free.

B&Bs Rooms rented in local homes (*gastenkamers/chambres d'hôtes*) can be cheap and cheerful but some offer standards equivalent to a boutique hotel (up to €160 double). Discounts of around €10 per room are common if you stay at least a second night.

Holiday houses (*gîtes*) Are easily rented in Wallonia (www.gitesdewallonie.be), but minimum stays apply and there's a hefty 'cleaning fee' on top of quoted rates.

Short term apartments Bookable through sites including www.airbnb.com and www.wimdu.com.

Hostels Typically charge around €20 to €26 for dormitory beds, somewhat less in Bruges. HI hostels (*jeugdherbergen* in Dutch, *auberges de* *jeunesse* in French) affiliated with **Hostelling International** (www.youthhostels.be), charge €3 less for members, and some take off €2 for under-26-year-olds. Prices usually include sheets and a basic breakfast. Always read the conditions.

Our sleeping reviews refer to double rooms with a private bathroom, except in hostels or where otherwise specified.

€ less than €60; expect shared bathrooms and only basic facilities.

€€ €60 to €140; good B&B or relatively functional hotel.

€€€ more than €140; note that top-end business establishments in Brussels often cut prices radically at weekends and in summer.

Business Hours
The Netherlands
Opening hours given in the text are for high season. Many tourism-based businesses reduce their hours off season.

Banks 9am to 3.30pm Monday to Friday

Brasseries 11am to midnight

Clubs 11pm to 6am Friday to Sunday

Pubs & cafes till 1am or later

Restaurants 11.30am to 2.30pm and 6.30 to 10.30pm

Shops 10am to 6pm Monday to Saturday, some close for lunch. Limited opening Sunday in Belgium.

Supermarkets 9am to 8pm Monday to Saturday, some open Sundays.

Belgium
Banks & government offices 9.30am to 4pm Monday to Friday

Bars & cafes 11am to 1am

Clubs Mostly 10pm to 4am

Museums Most closed Monday

Post offices 9am to 6pm Monday to Friday

Restaurants 10am to 10pm or 11am to 10pm, with a 3 to 6pm break

Shops Noon to 6pm Monday, 9am to 6pm Tuesday to Saturday (also Sunday in large cities), to 9pm Thursday; supermarkets to 8pm

Food
The Netherlands
Price ranges for average main courses are as follows:

€ less than €15

€€ €15 to €25

€€€ more than €25

Belgium
The following price categories are for the cost of a main course.

€ less than €12

€€ €12 to €25

€€€ more than €25

Legal Matters
Drugs are actually illegal in the Netherlands. Possession of soft drugs up to 5g is tolerated but larger amounts can get you jailed. Hard drugs are treated as a serious crime.

Rembrandtplein in Amsterdam (p494), the Netherlands
TRAVEL INK/GETTY IMAGES ©

Smoking is banned in all public places, including most bars (except for tiny family-run pubs). In a uniquely Dutch solution, you can still smoke pot in coffee shops as long as there's no tobacco mixed in.

Money
The Netherlands

Credit Cards All major international credit cards are recognised in the Netherlands, and you will find most hotels, restaurants and sights will accept them (although not the Dutch railway).

ATMs Can be found outside banks and at train stations.

Tipping Not essential as restaurants, hotels, bars etc all include a service charge.

Belgium

Banks usually offer better exchange rates than **exchange bureaux** (*wisselkantoren* in Dutch, *bureaux de change* in French), though often only for their banking clients.

ATMs Widespread, but often hidden within bank buildings.

Tipping Not expected in restaurants or cabs: service and VAT are always included.

Public Holidays
The Netherlands

Nieuwjaarsdag New Year's Day

Goede Vrijdag Good Friday

Eerste Paasdag Easter Sunday

Tweede Paasdag Easter Monday

Koningsdag (King's Day) 30 April

Bevrijdingsdag (Liberation Day) 5 May

Hemelvaartsdag Ascension Day

Eerste Pinksterdag Whit Sunday (Pentecost)

Tweede Pinksterdag Whit Monday

Eerste Kerstdag (Christmas Day) 25 December

Tweede Kerstdag (Boxing Day) 26 December

Belgium

School holidays are July and August, one week in early November; two weeks at Christmas; one week around Carnival; two weeks at Easter; one week in May (Ascension).

Public holidays are as follows:

New Year's Day 1 January

Easter Monday March/April

Labour Day 1 May

Ascension Day Fortieth day after Easter

Whit Monday Seventh Monday after Easter

Flemish Community Festival 11 July (Flanders only)

National Day 21 July

Assumption 15 August

Francophone Community Festival 27 September (Wallonia only)

All Saints' Day 1 November

Armistice Day 11 November

German-Speaking Community Festival 15 November (eastern cantons only)

Christmas Day 25 December

Telephone
The Netherlands

Most public phones will accept credit cards as well as various phonecards.

Country code 31

Collect call (gesprek) domestic 0800 01 01; international 0800 04 10

International access code 00

International directory inquiries 0900 84 18

National directory inquiries 1888

Operator assistance 0800 04 10

Belgium

Dial full numbers: there's no optional area code.

International operator 1324

Directory Enquiries www.whitepages.be

Visas

Schengen visa rules apply. Embassies are listed at www.diplomatie.belgium.be/en and www.mae.lu.

🛈 Getting There & Away
Air
Belgium

Antwerp airport (ANR; www.antwerpairport.be) is tiny with just a few flights to the UK on **CityJet** (WX; www.cityjet.com).

Below: Bloemenmarkt (p507) in Amsterdam, the Netherlands;
Right: Singel canal in Amsterdam's Jordaan district (p500), the Netherlands
(BELOW) RICHARD I'ANSON/GETTY IMAGES ©; (RIGHT) RICHARD I'ANSON/GETTY IMAGES ©

Brussels airport (BRU; www.brusselsairport.
be) is Belgium's main long-haul gateway.
Domestic airline **Brussels Airlines** (SN; www.
brusselsairlines.com) flies from here to numerous
European and African destinations. Brussels is
also a European hub for Chinese airline **Hainan
Airlines** (HU; www.global.hnair.com), Gulf-based
Etihad (EY; www.etihadairways.com) and **Qatar
Airways** (QR; www.qatarairways.com), and Indian
airline **Jet Airways** (QJ; www.jetairways.com),
with useful connections to North America and
throughout Asia.

Budget airlines **Ryanair** (www.ryanair.com),
JetAirFly (www.jetairfly.com) and **WizzAir**
(www.wizzair.com) use the misleadingly named
Brussels-South Charleroi Airport (CRL; ☎07
125 12 11; www.charleroi-airport.com), which is
actually 55km south of Brussels, 6km north of the
ragged, post-industrial city of Charleroi.

The Netherlands

Huge **Schiphol Airport** (AMS; www.schiphol.nl)
is the Netherlands' main international airport.

Rotterdam Airport (RTM;
www.rotterdamthehagueairport.
nl) and **Eindhoven Airport** (EIN; www.
eindhovenairport.nl) are small.

Train

The Netherlands

The Netherlands has good train links to Germany,
Belgium and France. All Eurail, Inter-Rail, Europass
and Flexipass tickets are valid on the Dutch
national train service, **Nederlandse Spoorwegen**
(Netherlands Railway | NS; www.ns.nl). Many
international services, including those on the
high-speed line to Belgium, are operated under
the **Hispeed** (www.nshispeed.nl) and **Fyra** (www.
fyra.com) brands. In addition, **Thalys** (www.thalys.
com) fast trains serve Brussels (where you can
connect to Eurostar) and Paris.

Finally open (years late and far over budget),
the high-speed line from Amsterdam (via Schipol
and Rotterdam) speeds travel times to Antwerp
(70 minutes), Brussels (two hours) and Paris (3¼
hours).

German ICE high-speed trains run six times a
day between Amsterdam and Cologne (2½ hours)

via Utrecht. Many continue on to Frankfurt (four hours) via Frankfurt Airport.

Belgium

For comprehensive timetables and international bookings, see www.belgianrail.be or www.cfl.lu.

International high-speed trains have compulsory pre-booking requirements and charge radically different prices according to availability, so advance booking can save a packet.

Thalys (www.thalys.com) operates on the following routes:

Brussels Midi–Liege–Aachen–Cologne 2¾ hours, five daily

Brussels Midi–Paris–Nord 82 minutes, 12 daily

Brussels Midi–Antwerp–Rotterdam– Schiphol–Amsterdam 109 minutes

Fyra (www.fyra.com) runs trains from both Brussels Midi and Brussels Central to Amsterdam (€25 to €54, two hours) 10 times daily via Antwerp, Rotterdam and Schipol.

Eurostar (www.eurostar.com) runs Brussels Midi–Lille–London St Pancras (two hours) up to 10 times daily.

ICE (www.db.de) runs Brussels Midi–Liège– Aachen–Frankfurt (3¼ hours, three daily) via Cologne (2¼ hours) and Frankfurt airport (three hours).

TGV (www.sncf.com) runs Bruxelles Midi–Paris CDG Airport-Marne-la-Vallée (for Eurodisney, 1¾ hours) continuing to various southern French cities. TGVs from Brussels don't stop in central Paris, but those from Luxembourg reach Paris–Est in 2¼ hours.

Sea

The Netherlands

There are several companies operating car/ passenger ferries between the Netherlands and the UK:

DFDS Seaways (www.dfds.co.uk) Sails between Newcastle and IJmuiden (15 hours), which is close to Amsterdam.

P&O Ferries (www.poferries.com) Operates an overnight ferry every evening (11 hours) between Hull and Europoort (near Rotterdam).

Stena Line (www.stenaline.co.uk) Sails between Harwich and Hoek van Holland (3¾ to 6¼ hours).

549

Belgium

Most UK-bound motorists drive a couple of hours west to Calais in France. However there are two direct options from Belgium:

Zeebrugge–Hull P&O (www.poferries.com) has a 14-hour overnight service that costs from UK£106 one-way for pedestrians. A very useful connecting bus to/from Bruges train station (£6.75) can be pre-booked through P&O.

Ostend–Ramsgate TransEuropa Ferries (www.transeuropaferries.com) charges €59/60 one-way for cars/motorbikes, but from just €30 for a 72-hour return. Crossing takes 4½ hours, three times daily. No pedestrians are carried.

Getting Around

Bicycle

The Netherlands

The Netherlands has more than 20,000km of dedicated bike paths *(fietspaden)*, which makes it the most bike-friendly place on the planet. You can criss-cross the country on the motorways of cycling: the LF routes. Standing for *landelijke fietsroutes* (long-distance routes), but virtually always simply called LF, there are more than 25 routes comprising close to 7000km.

Independent rental shops are available in abundance. Many day trippers avail themselves of the train-station bicycle shops, called **Rijwiel shops** (www.ov-fiets.nl), which are found in more than 100 stations. Operating long hours (6am to midnight is common), the shops hire out bikes from €3 to €12 per day, with discounts by the week. You'll have to show an ID and leave a deposit (usually €25 to €100).

You may bring your bicycle onto any train as long as there is room; a day pass is required for bicycles *(dagkaart fiets;* €6).

Belgium

Cycling is a great way to get around in flat Flanders, less so in chaotic Brussels or undulating Wallonia. The Belgian countryside is riddled with cycling routes and most tourist offices sell helpful regional cycling maps.

In Belgium it costs €5 one-way (or €8 all day) on top of the rail fare to take bikes on the train. A few busy city-centre train stations don't allow bicycle transportation.

Bike hire is available in or near most major train stations. Short hop hire schemes are available in Brussels, Antwerp and Namur.

Car & Motorcycle

The Netherlands

○ You'll need the vehicle's registration papers, third-party insurance and an international driver's permit in addition to your domestic licence.

○ Traffic travels on the right and the minimum driving age is 18 for vehicles and 16 for motorcycles. Seat belts are required and children under 12 must ride in the back if there's room.

○ Speed limits are 50km/h in built-up areas, 80km/h in the country, 100km/h on major through-roads, and 120km/h on freeways (sometimes 100km/h, clearly indicated).

○ Outside Amsterdam, car-hire companies can be in inconvenient locations if

Delfshaven neighbourhood (p515) of Rotterdam, the Netherlands
LUKE PRICE PHOTOGRAPHY/GETTY IMAGES ©

you're arriving by train. You must be at least 23 years of age to hire a car in the Netherlands.

Belgium

- Speed limits are 50km/h in most towns (30km/h near schools), 70km/h to 90km/h on inter-town roads, and 120km/h on motorways in Belgium.
- The maximum legal blood alcohol limit is 0.05%.
- Car hire is available at airports and major train stations, but is usually cheaper from city centre offices.
- A driving licence from your home country will usually suffice for foreign drivers.
- Priorité à droite – as in France, give way to the right (see p291).

Train

The Netherlands

The train network is run by NS (www.ns.nl). Several ticket types are available:

Enkele reis One-way; you can break your journey along the direct route.

Dagretour Day return; 10% to 15% cheaper than two one-way tickets.

Weekendretour Weekend return; costs the same as a normal return and is valid from 7pm Friday to 4am Monday.

Dagkaart Day pass; allows unlimited train travel throughout the country. Only good value if you're planning to spend the day on the train.

Keep in mind that:

- Only some ticket machines accept cash, and those are coins-only, so you need a pocketful of change.
- Ticket windows do not accept credit or ATM cards, although they will accept paper euros. Lines are often quite long and there is a surcharge for the often-unavoidable need to use a ticket window.
- Discounted tickets for Hispeed and Fyra trains sold on the web require a Dutch credit card. The cheap fares can't be bought at ticket windows.

Belgium

NMBS/SNCB (Belgian Railways; ☏ 02 528 28 28; www.b-rail.be) trains are completely non-smoking. Special fare categories:

Children After 9am, kids under 12 travel for free if accompanied by an adult.

Seniors People over 65 pay only €5 for a return 2nd-class trip anywhere in Belgium (some exclusions apply).

B-Excursions Good-value one-day excursion fares including return rail ticket plus selected entry fees.

Go Pass/Rail Pass Ten one-way 2nd-class trips to anywhere in Belgium (except frontier points) cost €50/76 for people under/over 26 years.

Weekend Return Tickets Valid from 7pm Friday to Sunday night, for just 20% more than a single.

Germany

Forget what you think you know about Germany. While some of the stereotypes have a grain of truth to them, this is a country that never fails to turn up surprises. From the edgy city of Berlin to revitalised Dresden and hedonistic Hamburg, Germany is a country that likes nothing better than to confound clichés.

Yes, the Germans are efficient and industrious. But they also like nothing more than a good party, as Munich's annual beerfest and Berlin's underground bars will testify. You'll certainly find plenty of half-timbered villages and historic *Schlösser* (castles) dotted around, but you'll also discover vine-clad valleys, wild mountains, vast forests and shimmering lakes, not to mention some of Europe's most beautiful riverside scenery. And while the ghosts of the past certainly still cast a shadow here, Germany is a country with an eye firmly on the future, with a host of experimental art galleries and groundbreaking buildings to admire.

Savour the contradictions – Germany's at the heart of Europe in more ways than one.

Reichstag (p563), Berlin
RAIMUND KOCH/GETTY IMAGES ©

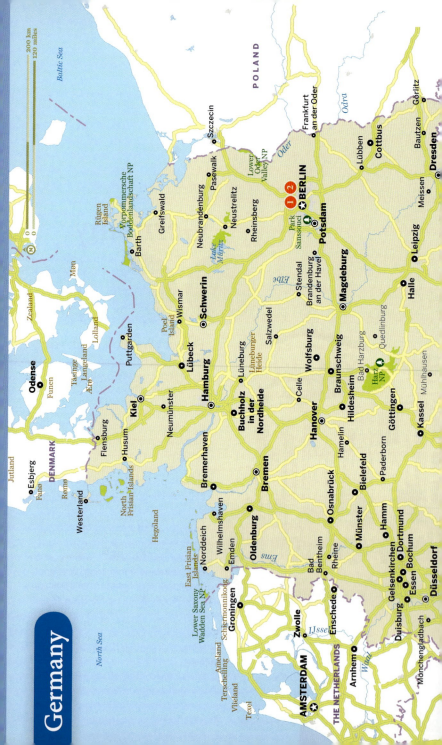

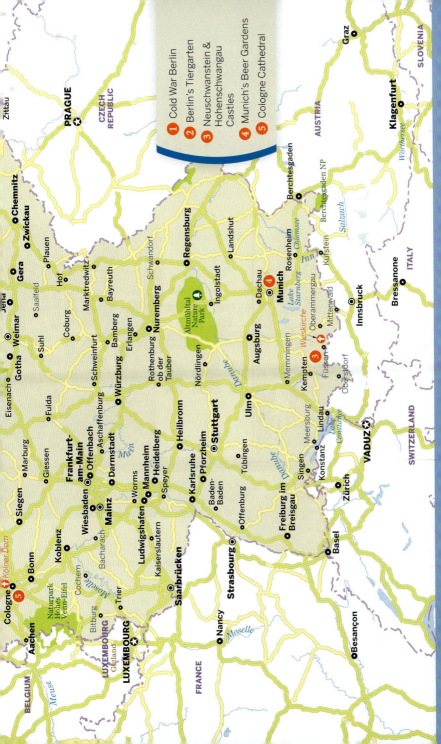

1 Cold War Berlin
2 Berlin's Tiergarten
3 Neuschwanstein & Hohenschwangau Castles
4 Munich's Beer Gardens
5 Cologne Cathedral

SLOVENIA

Zittau

PRAGUE

CZECH REPUBLIC

AUSTRIA

Graz

Klagenfurt

Wörthersee

Berchtesgaden

Berchtesgaden NP

Salzach

Chemnitz

Zwickau

Plauen

Gera

Jena

Weimar

Gotha

Eisenach

Saalfeld

Hof

Marktredwitz

Coburg

Bayreuth

Suhl

Bamberg

Erlangen

Schweinfurt

Fulda

Regensburg

Landshut

Schwandorf

Nuremberg

Altmühltal Nature Park

Ingolstadt

Dachau

Rosenheim

Chiemsee

Inn

Kufstein

ITALY

Bressanone

Munich 4

Starnberg

Lake Starnberg

Mittenwald

Oberammergau

Innsbruck

Würzburg

Rothenburg ob der Tauber

Nördlingen

Augsburg

Wieskirche

Kempten 3 Füssen

Oberstdorf

Marburg

Giessen

Aschaffenburg

Offenbach

Darmstadt

Frankfurt am-Main

Main

Heilbronn

Stuttgart

Ulm

Danube

Memmingen

Lindau

Meersburg

Lake Constance

VADUZ

SWITZERLAND

Siegen

Wiesbaden

Mainz

Worms

Mannheim

Heidelberg

Speyer

Ludwigshafen

Karlsruhe

Pforzheim

Baden-Baden

Tübingen

Offenburg

Freiburg im Breisgau

Danube

Singen

Konstanz

Zürich

Basel

Koblenz

Bonn

Bacharach

Cochem

Mosel

Kaiserslautern

Saarbrücken

Strasbourg

Besançon

Kölner Dom

Cologne 5

Naturpark Hohes Venn-Eifel

Aachen

Bitburg

Trier

 Gtland

LUXEMBOURG

LUXEMBOURG

Nancy

Moselle

FRANCE

BELGIUM

Meuse

Germany Highlights

Cold War Berlin

It's hard to believe nowadays, but two decades ago Berlin (p562) was still one of the most infamous symbols of the Cold War. For 28 years, between 1961 and 1989, the Berlin Wall divided the city in two, separating the democratic West from the communist-controlled East. Berlin has moved on since reunification, but the shadow of the Cold War still lingers in some places. Checkpoint Charlie (p563)

1

2 ### Berlin's Tiergarten

Most cities have green spaces, but not many have a park as breathtakingly beautiful as Berlin's Tiergarten (p572). This oasis of calm in the heart of the city is traversed by a tangle of paths, cycleways and wooded trails, and on sunny days it seems like half of Berlin heads for the park and lets it all hang out. Literally.

Neuschwanstein & Hohenschwangau Castles

3

These towering castles (p602) could have fallen from the pages of an old European fairy tale, but they both date from the 18th century. Their history is inextricably bound with King Ludwig II, whose twin obsessions – Wagnerian operas and swans – have left an indelible mark on the castles' decor. If you have time to visit only a couple of castles, make sure it's these. Schloss Neuschwanstein

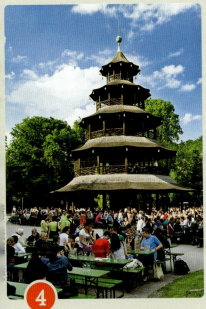

4

Munich's Beer Gardens

Germany is one of Europe's great beer-guzzling nations, but the sheer variety of brews on offer can be bewildering. Regardless of whether you're a first-time tippler or a hardened hophead, there's nowhere better to get to grips with Germany's favourite drink than Munich's many beer gardens (p596) – and if you can time your visit to coincide with the annual outdoor booze-up known as Oktoberfest, all the better. Chinesischer Turm beer garden (p596)

5

Cologne Cathedral

Travelling around Europe can bring on a bad case of cathedral fatigue, but even if you've seen a hundred churches, you still can't fail to be wowed by Cologne's gargantuan cathedral, Kölner Dom (p616). Blackened with age and festooned with gargoyles, flying buttresses and luminous stained glass, it's quite simply one of the world's most dramatic structures. Unmissable.

Germany's Best...

Cold War & WWII Sites

○ **Checkpoint Charlie** (p563) This infamous checkpoint between East and West Berlin was once a symbol of divided Germany.

○ **Dokumentation Obersalzberg** (p598) This fascinating museum near Berchtesgarden explores the area's links with the Nazi regime.

○ **Buchenwald** (p588) Pay your respects at this chilling concentration camp.

○ **Eagle's Nest** (p598) Survey the scene from Hitler's mountain-top retreat.

Relaxation Spots

○ **Park Sanssouci** (p583) Explore the stately palaces and gardens of this landscaped Potsdam park.

○ **Tiergarten** (p572) Kick back with the locals in Berlin's idyllic city park.

○ **Baden-Baden** (p609) Lose your inhibitions and bathe like a German – in the nude.

○ **Lake Constance** (p608) Catch a boat across Germany's loveliest lake.

○ **The Rhine** (p609) Take a soothing cruise along this great river.

Historic Buildings

○ **Reichstag** (p563) This landmark Berlin building was built to house the German parliament.

○ **Cologne Cathedral** (p616) Germany's most celebrated church: a masterpiece of Gothic grandeur.

○ **Residenz, Munich** (p593) Bavarian rulers occupied this vast palace for over six centuries.

○ **Wieskirche** (p599) The rococo splendour of this 18th-century church has earned it a place on Unesco's World Heritage list.

Places for a Drink

o **Beer gardens, Munich** (p596) There's nowhere better to sink a few German brews than Munich's Englischer Garten.

o **Bars of East Berlin** (p578) Drink and dance till dawn in Berlin's hippest quarters.

o **Bars, Hamburg** (p621) You'll find drinking dens aplenty in downtown Hamburg.

o **Moselle Valley** (p611) Take a tipple in Germany's wine-making heartland.

Need to Know

ADVANCE PLANNING

o **As early as possible** In summer book accommodation early, especially in popular spots such as the Black Forest, Moselle and Rhine Valleys and Bavarian Alps.

o **One month before** Arrange hotel accommodation and car hire.

o **Two weeks before** Book city tours in Berlin, Munich and other cities, and plan train journeys using Deutsche Bahn (www.bahn.de).

RESOURCES

o **German National Tourist Office** (www.germany-tourism.de) The official site for the German National Tourist Board.

o **Facts about Germany** (www.tatsachen-ueber-deutschland.de) Full of fascinating facts about the German nation.

o **Online German Course** (www.deutsch-lernen.com) Brush up your Deutsch before you go.

GETTING AROUND

o **Air** Germany is well served by major airlines, but budget carriers often use small regional airports. Frankfurt and Munich are the main hubs.

o **Car** Germany's road system is fast and efficient; autobahns (motorways) are fastest, but regional roads are much more pleasant. Traffic can be a problem on summer weekends and around holidays.

o **Train** Germany's rail system, operated by Deutsche Bahn, is one of the best in Europe. Trains are frequent, fast and very comfortable.

o **Bus** Buses are much less comfortable and efficient than trains, but are often the only option for rural towns and villages.

BE FOREWARNED

o **Autobahns** Unless otherwise indicated, there is no official speed limit on German motorways.

o **Accommodation** Can be hard to come by in peak seasons such as Oktoberfest and the Christmas markets.

Left: Statues in Park Sanssouci (p583), Potsdam; **Above:** Lake Constance (p608)

Germany Itineraries

From sophisticated cities to snowy mountains, Germany offers a smorgasbord of contrasting experiences. It's a place where old and new worlds collide; the real trick is finding enough time to see it all in one trip.

3 DAYS

BERLIN & BEYOND
Berlin to Dresden

Those in the know rate **① Berlin** (p562) as Europe's most exciting city. Since reunification the city has rediscovered its sense of self, and is home to a host of fascinating museums, art galleries and historic sites – and that's before you even get started on the nightlife. In a couple of days you can tick off the major sights: day one covers the Brandenburg Gate, the Reichstag, the Holocaust Memorial and the Tiergarten. Set aside day two for East Berlin, Alexanderplatz, Checkpoint Charlie, and the DDR and Stasi Museums. After dark you'll really start to see what makes Berlin tick – Kreuzberg and Prenzlauer Berg are both excellent areas to experience the Berlin underground.

On day three, travel south on one of Germany's efficient high-speed trains to **② Dresden** (p582), a city effectively wiped off the map during WWII. Thankfully, the city's baroque centre has been rebuilt in elegant style along with its landmark cathedral, the Frauenkirche. For something more up to date, cross the River Elbe to explore the Neustadt's latest bars and restaurants.

Top Left: Frauenkirche (p582), Dresden;
Top Right: Schloss Nymphenburg (p605), Munich
(TOP LEFT) H & D ZIELSKE/GETTY IMAGES ©; (TOP RIGHT) ROBIN SMITH/GETTY IMAGES ©

5
DAYS

A BAVARIAN ADVENTURE

Munich to Bamberg

From Dresden, it's a two-hour train trip to the Bavarian capital, ❶**Munich** (p589), an excellent base from which to launch forays around the wider Bavarian region. You'll need at least a day to do the city justice: key sights include the Residenz and the royal retreat of Schloss Nymphenburg, but for many people Munich's main highlights are its beer halls and beer gardens, which really come alive during the city's annual booze-up, Oktoberfest.

On day two, it's a couple of hours by train or car to the ❷**Bavarian Alps** (p597), which brood on the border with Austria and provide some of Germany's finest hiking and climbing. The mountains were a favourite haunt of the Nazi elite in the years before WWII, and you should set aside time to visit the Führer's infamous mountaintop retreat, the Eagle's Nest, as well as the former Nazi HQ at Obersalzberg, which now houses a superb history museum.

On day three, head east to ❸**Füssen** (p602), where you can tour two of Germany's most picturesque castles, Neuschwanstein and Hohenshwangau. Füssen also marks the start of one of Germany's most scenic drives, the Romantic Road, which links together a string of picturesque German towns including ❹**Nuremberg** (p605) and ❺**Bamberg** (p610).

Discover Germany

At a Glance

○ **Berlin** (p562) Germany's most historic and happening city.

○ **Dresden & Saxony** (p582) From lovingly restored cities to classic German countryside.

○ **Bavaria** (p589) Storybook scenery: mountains, villages, castles, churches and more.

○ **The Rhine & Moselle** (p609) Cruise along these grand rivers and taste the local wines.

BERLIN

030 / POP 3.5 MILLION

There's just no escaping history in Berlin. You might be distracted by the trendy, edgy, gentrified streets, by the bars bleeding a laid-back cool factor, by the galleries sprouting talent and pushing the envelope, but make no mistake – reminders of the German capital's past assault you while modernity sits around the corner. Norman Foster's Reichstag dome, Peter Eisenman's Holocaust Memorial and the iconic Brandenburg Gate are all contained within a few neighbouring blocks. Potsdamer Platz and its shiny Sony Center hosts Berlin's star-studded film festival each year, on the very site where only 25 years ago you could climb up a viewing platform in the West and peer over the Berlin Wall for a glimpse behind the Iron Curtain. Renowned for its diversity and its tolerance, its alternative culture and its night-owl stamina, the best thing about Berlin is the way it reinvents itself and isn't shackled by its mind-numbing history.

◎ Sights

Key sights like the Reichstag, Brandenburger Tor, Checkpoint Charlie and Museumsinsel cluster in the historic city centre – Mitte – which is also home to a maze-like hipster quarter around Hackescher Markt. North of here, residential Prenzlauer Berg has a lively cafe and restaurant scene, while to the south loom the contemporary high-rises of Potsdamer Platz. Further south, gritty but cool Kreuzberg is party central, as is student-flavoured Friedrichshain east across the Spree River and home to the East Side Gallery stretch of the Berlin Wall. Western

Brandenburg Gate, Berlin
MARK DAFFEY/GETTY IMAGES ©

Berlin's hub is Charlottenburg, with great shopping and a famous royal palace.

Reichstag & Unter den Linden

Reichstag   Historic Building
(Map p574; www.bundestag.de; Platz der Republik 1; ☺lift ride 8am-midnight, last entry 11pm; 🚌100 Ⓢ Bundestag Ⓡ Hauptbahnhof) One of Berlin's most iconic buildings, the Reichstag has been burned, bombed, rebuilt, buttressed by the Berlin Wall, wrapped in fabric and eventually turned into the modern home of Germany's parliament, the Bundestag.

The grand old structure was designed by Paul Wallot in 1894 and given a total post-reunification makeover by Norman Foster. The famous architect preserved only its historical shell while adding the glistening glass dome, which can be reached by lift (reservations mandatory). At the top, pick up a free auto-activated audioguide and learn about the building, city landmarks and the workings of the parliament while following the ramp spiralling up and around the dome's mirror-clad central funnel.

Brandenburger Tor & Pariser Platz   Historic Site
(Map p574; Ⓢ Brandenburger Tor Ⓡ Brandenburger Tor) A symbol of division during the Cold War, the landmark Brandenburg Gate now epitomises German reunification. Its architect Carl Gotthard Langhans found inspiration in Athen's Acropolis for this elegant triumphal arch, completed in 1791 as the royal city gate. It is crowned by the Quadriga sculpture of the winged goddess of victory piloting a chariot drawn by four horses.

Holocaust Memorial   Memorial
(Map p574; 🕿 2639 4336; www.stiftung-denkmal.de; Cora-Berliner-Strasse 1; audioguide €3; ☺field 24hr, information centre 10am-8pm Tue-Sun, last entry 7.15pm Apr-Sep, 6.15pm Oct-Mar; Ⓢ Brandenburger Tor Ⓡ Brandenburger Tor) FREE The football field–sized Memorial to the Murdered European Jews is Germany's central memorial to the Nazi-planned

genocide and is colloquially known as the Holocaust Memorial. American architect Peter Eisenman created a maze of 2711 sarcophagi-like concrete columns rising in sombre silence from undulating ground.

Hitler's Bunker   Historic Site
(Map p574; cnr In den Ministergärten & Gertrud-Kolmar-Strasse; ☺24hr; Ⓢ Brandenburger Tor Ⓡ Brandenburger Tor) Berlin was burning and Soviet tanks advancing relentlessly when Adolf Hitler committed suicide on 30 April 1945 alongside Eva Braun, his long-time female companion, hours after their marriage. Today, a parking lot covers the site, revealing its dark history only via an information panel with a diagram of the vast bunker network and information on its construction and post-WWII history.

Unter den Linden   Street
(Map p574; 🚌100, 200 Ⓢ Brandenburger Tor Ⓡ Brandenburger Tor) This chic boulevard stretches 1.5km from the Brandenburger Tor to the giant treasure chest of the Museumsinsel, past a phalanx of grand old structures built under various Prussian kings and reflecting the one-time grandeur of the royal family.

Deutsches Historisches Museum   Museum
(Map p574; 🕿 203 040; www.dhm.de; Unter den Linden 2; adult/concession €8/4; ☺10am-6pm; 🚌100, 200 Ⓡ Alexanderplatz, Hackescher Markt) This engaging museum zeroes in on two millennia of German history in all its gore and glory; not in a nutshell but on two floors of a Prussian-era armoury. Check out the Nazi globe, the pain-wrecked faces of dying warrior sculptures in the courtyard, and the temporary exhibits in the boldly modern **annex** designed by IM Pei.

Checkpoint Charlie   Historic Site
(Map p564; cnr Zimmerstrasse & Friedrichstrasse; ☺24hr; Ⓢ Kochstrasse, Stadtmitte) Checkpoint Charlie was the principal gateway for foreigners and diplomats between the two Berlins from 1961 to 1990. Unfortunately, this potent symbol of the Cold War has become a tacky tourist trap, although a free **open-air exhibit** that illustrates milestones in Cold War history

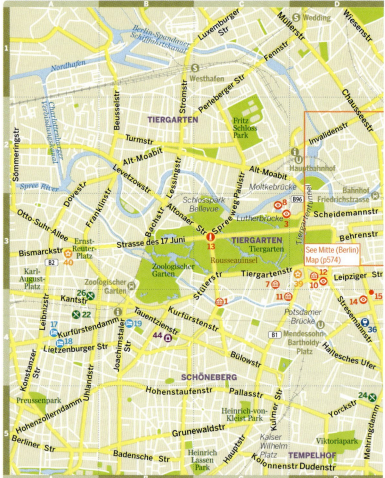

is one redeeming aspect. New since September 2012 is Yadegar Asisi's **Berlin Wall Panorama** (Map p564; www.asisi.de; cnr Friedrichstrasse & Zimmerstrasse; adult/concession €10/8.50; ⏰10am-6pm; S Kochstrasse). An official Cold War Museum is in the planning stages and may open by 2015.

Nearby, the privately run **Mauermuseum** (Haus am Checkpoint Charlie; Map p564; ☎253 7250; www.mauermuseum. de; Friedrichstrasse 43-45; adult/concession €12.50/9.50; ⏰9am-10pm; 🚼; S Kochstrasse, Stadtmitte) is especially strong when it

comes to documenting spectacular escape attempts (through tunnels, in hot-air balloons and even using a one-man submarine).

Tränenpalast   Museum
(Map p574; ☎4677 7790; www.hdg.de; Reich-stagsufer 17; ⏰9am-7pm Tue-Fri, 10am-6pm Sat & Sun; S Friedrichstrasse 🚌100) East Berliners had to bid adieu to family visiting from West Germany in this glass-and-steel border crossing pavilion – hence its moniker 'Palace of Tears'. Photographs, historical

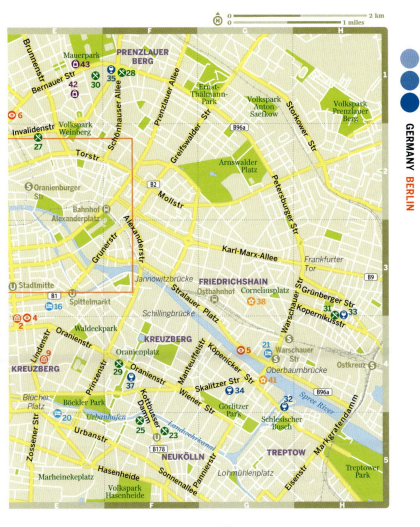

footage and the original claustrophobic passport control booths help illustrate the social impact the division had on the daily lives of Germans on both sides of the border.

Museumsinsel & Scheunenviertel

Museumsinsel   Museum

(📞2090 5577; www.smb.museum; day pass for all museums adult/concession €14/7; 🚌100, 200 🚇Hackescher Markt, Friedrichstrasse) Spread across five grand museums built between 1830 and 1930, the complex takes up the entire northern half of the little Spree Island where Berlin's settlement began in the 13th century and has been a Unesco World Heritage site since 1999.

The **Pergamonmuseum** (Map p574; 📞266 424 242; www.smb.museum; Am Kupfergraben 5; adult/concession €8/4; ⏰10am-6pm Fri-Wed, to 9pm Thu; 🚌100 🚇Hackescher Markt, Friedrichstrasse) is the island's top draw with monumental architecture from

Berlin

⊙ Sights
1 Bauhaus Archiv..C4
2 Berlin Wall Panorama.............................E4
3 Carillon...C3
4 Checkpoint Charlie...................................E4
5 East Side Gallery.......................................G4
6 Gedenkstätte Berliner Mauer..................E1
7 Gemäldegalerie...C3
8 Haus der Kulturen der Welt....................C3
9 Jüdisches Museum....................................E4
   Mauermuseum......................................(see 2)
10 Museum für Film und Fernsehen..........D3
11 Neue Nationalgalerie...............................C4
12 Panoramapunkt..D3
13 Siegessäule...C3
14 Topographie des Terrors.........................D4

⊕ Activities, Courses & Tours
15 Trabi Safari..D4

🛌 Sleeping
16 Adina Apartment Hotel Berlin
   Checkpoint Charlie...............................E3
17 Hotel Askanischer Hof.............................A4
18 Hotel Bogota..A4
19 Hotel Concorde Berlin.............................B4
20 Hotel Johann...E5
21 Michelberger Hotel...................................G4

✖ Eating
22 Ali Baba...A4

23 Cafe Jacques..F5
24 Curry 36..D5
25 Defne...F5
26 Dicke Wirtin..A4
27 Katz Orange...E2
28 Konnopke's Imbiss....................................F1
29 Max und Moritz...F4
30 Oderquelle...E1
31 Spätzle & Knödel.......................................H3

🍷 Drinking & Nightlife
32 Freischwimmer..G4
33 Hops & Barley..H3
34 Madame Claude..G4
35 Prater...F1
36 Solar..D4
37 Würgeengel...F4

☆ Entertainment
38 Berghain/Panorama Bar...........................G3
39 Berliner Philharmonie..............................D3
   Lab.oratory...(see 38)
40 Staatsoper unter den Linden @
   Schillertheater.......................................A3
41 Watergate...G4

🛍 Shopping
42 Flohmarkt am Arkonaplatz......................E1
43 Flohmarkt am Mauerpark.......................E1
44 KaDeWe..B4

ancient worlds, including the namesake Pergamon Altar and the stunning Babylonian Ishtar Gate.

The **Altes Museum** (Old Museum; Map p574; ☎ 266 424 242; www.smb.museum; Am Lustgarten; adult/concession €8/4; ⏰ 10am-6pm Fri-Wed, to 8pm Thu; 🚌 100, 200 🚊 Friedrichstrasse) was the first repository to open on the island, in 1830, and presents Greek, Etruscan and Roman antiquities. Note the *Praying Boy* bronze sculpture, Roman silver vessels and portraits of Caesar and Cleopatra.

The show-stopper of the Egyptian collection at the **Neues Museum** (New Museum; Map p574; ☎ 266 424 242; www.smb.museum; adult/concession €10/5; ⏰ 10am-6pm Sun-Wed, to 8pm Thu-Sat; 🚌 100, 200 🚊 Hackescher Markt) is the 3300-year-old bust of Queen Nefertiti; the equally

enthralling Museum of Pre- and Early History has treasure from Troy.

The **Alte Nationalgalerie** (Old National Gallery; Map p574; ☎ 266 424 242; www.smb.museum; Bodestrasse 1-3; adult/concession €8/4; ⏰ 10am-6pm Fri-Wed, to 10pm Thu; 🚌 100, 200 🚊 Hackescher Markt) trains its focus on 19th-century European art.

Berliner Dom   Church
(Berlin Cathedral; Map p574; ☎ 2026 9110; www.berlinerdom.de; Am Lustgarten; adult/concession €7/4; ⏰ 9am-8pm Mon-Sat, noon-8pm Sun Apr-Sep, to 7pm Oct-Mar; 🚌 100, 200 🚊 Hackescher Markt) Pompous yet majestic, the Italian Renaissance-style former royal court church (1905) does triple duty as house of worship, museum and concert hall. Inside it's gilt to the hilt and outfitted with a lavish marble-and-onyx altar, a 7269-pipe Sauer organ and elaborate royal

sarcophagi. Climb up the 267 steps to the gallery for glorious city views.

DDR Museum   Museum

(GDR Museum; Map p574; 📞847 123 731; www.ddr-museum.de; Karl-Liebknecht-Strasse 1; adult/concession €6/4; ⏱10am-8pm Sun-Fri, to 10pm Sat; 🚻; 🚌100, 200 🚉Hackescher Markt) The touchy-feely GDR Museum does a delightful job at pulling back the Iron Curtain on an extinct society. You'll learn that in East Germany, kids were put through collective potty training, engineers earned little more than farmers and everyone, it seems, went on nudist holidays. The more sinister sides of GDR life are also addressed, including the chronic supply shortages and Stasi surveillance.

Humboldt-Box   Museum

(Map p574; 📞0180-503 0707; www.humboldt-box.com; Schlossplatz; adult/concession €4/2.50; ⏱10am-8pm Apr-Oct, to 6pm Nov-Mar; 🚌100, 200 🚉Alexanderplatz, Hackescher Markt) This oddly shaped structure offers a sneak preview of the planned reconstruction of the Berlin City Palace, to be known as Humboldtforum, on Schlossplatz, opposite the Museumsinsel museums.

Fernsehturm   Landmark

(Map p574; www.tv-turm.de; Panoramastrasse 1a; adult/child €12/7.50, VIP tickets €19.50/11.50; ⏱9am-midnight Mar-Oct, from 10am Nov-Feb;

Ⓢ Alexanderplatz 🚉Alexanderplatz) Germany's tallest structure, the needle-like TV Tower is as iconic to Berlin as the Eiffel Tower is to Paris and has been soaring 368m high (including the antenna) since 1969. Come early to beat the queue for the lift to the panorama platform at 203m.

Gedenkstätte
Berliner Mauer   Memorial

(Map p564; 📞467 986 666; www.berliner-mauer-gedenkstaette.de; Bernauer Strasse btwn Gartenstrasse & Brunnenstrasse; ⏱9.30am-7pm Apr-Oct, to 6pm Nov-Mar, open-air exhibit 24hr; 🚉Nordbahnhof) FREE The central memorial site of German division incorporates a stretch of original Berlin Wall along with vestiges of the border installations, escape tunnels, a chapel and a monument. Multimedia stations, 'archaeological windows' and markers sprinkled throughout the memorial provide detailed background.

Potsdamer Platz & Tiergarten

Berlin newest quarter, Potsdamer Platz, was forged in the 1990s from ground once bisected by the Berlin Wall. It's a showcase of contemporary architecture by such illustrious architects as Renzo

---

Discount Cards

Berlin Museum Pass (www.visitberlin.de; adult/concession €19/9.50) Buys admission to the permanent exhibits of about 60 museums for three consecutive days, including top draws like the Pergamonmuseum. Sold at tourist offices and participating museums.

Berlin Welcome Card (www.visitberlin.de; 48- /72hr €17.90/23.90, 48hr incl Potsdam & up to 3 children under 15yr €19.90, 72hr incl Museum Island €34) Unlimited public transport and up to 50% discount to 200 sights, attractions and tours for periods of two, three or five days. It's also sold at tourist offices, U-Bahn and S-Bahn ticket vending machines and many hotels.

CityTourCard (www.citytourcard.com; 48hr/72hr/5 days €16.90/22.90/29.90) Similar to the Berlin Welcome Card, but a bit cheaper and with fewer discounts.

Piano and Helmut Jahn whose flashy Sony Center – anchored by a plaza canopied by a tentlike glass roof – is the most eye-catching complex.

Museum für Film und Fernsehen   Museum

(Map p564; ☎ 300 9030; www.deutsche-kinemathek.de; Potsdamer Strasse 2; adult/concession €6/4.50; ⊙ 10am-6pm Tue, Wed & Fri-Sun, to 8pm Thu; ☐ 200 S Potsdamer Platz, ☒ Potsdamer Platz) Every February, celluloid celebs sashay down the red carpet at Potsdamer Platz venues during the Berlin International Film Festival. Germany's film history, meanwhile, gets the star treatment year-round in this engaging museum.

Panoramapunkt   Viewpoint

(Map p564; ☎ 2593 7080; www.panoramapunkt.de; Potsdamer Platz 1; adult/concession €5.50/4; ⊙ 10am-8pm, last ride 7.30pm, reduced hours in winter; ☐ M41, 200 S Potsdamer Platz ☒ Potsdamer Platz) A super-speedy lift yo-yos up and down the red-brick Kollhoff

Building on Potsdamer Platz for fabulous 360-degree views from a lofty 100m.

Neue Nationalgalerie   Gallery

(Map p564; ☎ 266 2951; www.neue-national-galerie.de; Potsdamer Strasse 50; adult/concession €10/5; ⊙ 10am-6pm Tue, Wed & Fri, to 10pm Thu, 11am-6pm Sat & Sun; S Potzdamer Platz ☒ Potsdamer Platz) The New National Gallery is a glass and steel temple designed in 1968 by Ludwig Mies van der Rohe. It presents changing exhibits of paintings and sculpture created by 20th-century European artists before 1960. Look for works by Picasso, Miró and Klee, along with German expressionists like Otto Dix, George Grosz and Ernst Ludwig Kirchner.

Gemäldegalerie   Gallery

(Map p564; ☎ 266 424 242; www.smb.museum/gg; Matthäikirchplatz 8; adult/concession €8/4; ⊙ 10am-6pm Tue, Wed & Fri-Sun, to 10pm Thu; ☐ M29, M41, 200 S Potsdamer Platz ☒ Potsdamer Platz) The principal Kulturforum museum boasts one of the world's finest and most comprehensive collections of

Left: Glass cupola on top of the Reichstag (p563), Berlin;
Below: Jüdisches Museum (p570), Berlin

(LEFT) SYLVAIN SONNET/GETTY IMAGES ©; (BELOW) PAOLO CORDELLI/GETTY IMAGES ©

European art from the 13th to the 18th centuries. Wear comfy shoes when exploring the 72 galleries: a walk past masterpieces by Rembrandt, Dürer, Vermeer, Gainsborough and many more Old Masters covers almost 2km.

Bauhaus Archiv   Museum

(Map p564; ☏ 254 0020; www.bauhaus.de; Klingelhöferstrasse 14; adult/concession Sat-Mon €7/4, Wed-Fri €6/3; ☉10am-5pm Wed-Mon; S Nollendorfplatz) Changing exhibits using study notes, workshop pieces, photographs, blueprints, models and other objects and documents, illustrate the theories of this influential 20th-century design movement. Bauhaus founder Walter Gropius himself drafted the blueprints for the distinctive white shed-roofed building.

Topographie des Terrors   Memorial

(Topography of Terror; Map p564; ☏ 2548 6703; www.topographie.de; Niederkirchner Strasse 8; ☉10am-8pm May-Sep, to dusk Oct-Apr; ♿;

S Potsdamer Platz ⓡ Potsdamer Platz) FREE In the same spot where once stood the most feared institutions of Nazi Germany (including the Gestapo headquarters and the SS central command), this compelling exhibit dissects the anatomy of the Nazi state. A short stretch of the Berlin Wall runs along Niederkirchner Strasse.

Kreuzberg & Friedrichshain

Kreuzberg gets its street cred from being delightfully edgy, wacky and bipolar. While the western half around Bergmannstrasse has an upmarket, genteel air, eastern Kreuzberg (around Kottbusser Tor and still nicknamed SO36 after its old postal code) is a multicultural mosaic of tousled students, aspiring creatives, shisha-smoking immigrants and international life artists.

East Side Gallery · Historic Site

(Map p564; www.eastsidegallery-berlin.de; Mühlenstrasse btwn Oberbaumbrücke & Ostbahnhof; ☺24hr; Ⓢ Warschauer Strasse Ⓡ Ostbahnhof, Warschauer Strasse FREE) At 1.3km, the East Side Gallery is not only the longest surviving stretch of Berlin Wall, it is also the world's largest open-air mural collection. In 1989, dozens of international artists translated the era's global euphoria and optimism into more than 100 paintings that are a mix of political statements, drug-induced musings and truly artistic visions. It was restored in 2009.

Jüdisches Museum · Museum

(Jewish Museum; Map p564; ☎ 2599 3300; www.jmberlin.de; Lindenstrasse 9-14; adult/concession €5/2.50; ☺10am-10pm Mon, to 8pm Tue-Sun, last admission 1 hour before closing; Ⓢ Hallesches Tor, Kochstrasse) This engaging museum offers a chronicle of the trials and triumphs in 2000 years of Jewish history in Germany but it's Daniel Libeskind's landmark building that steals the show. A 3D metaphor for the tortured history of the Jewish people, its zigzag outline symbolises a broken Star of David.

Stasimuseum · Museum

(☎ 553 6854; www.stasimuseum.de; Haus 1, Ruschestrasse 103; adult/concession €5/4; ☺11am-6pm Mon-Fri, noon-6pm Sat & Sun; Ⓢ Magdalenenstrasse) The former headquarters of East Germany's much-feared Ministry of State Security is now the Stasi Museum. Marvel at cunningly low-tech surveillance devices (hidden in watering cans, neckties, even rocks), a claustrophobic prisoner transport van and the obsessively neat offices of Stasi chief Erich Mielke.

Stasi Prison · Memorial Site

(Gedenkstätte Hohenschönhausen; ☎ 9860 8230; www.stiftung-hsh.de; Genslerstrasse 66; tour adult/concession €5/2.50; ☺tours hourly 11am-3pm Mon-Fri, 10am-4pm Sat & Sun, English tour 2.30pm daily; ☐M5 to Freienwalder Strasse) Victims of Stasi persecution often ended up in this grim prison. Tours (some in English, call ahead) reveal the full extent of the terror and cruelty perpetrated upon thousands of suspected regime opponents, many utterly innocent. Take tram M5 from Alexanderplatz to Freienwalder Strasse, then walk 10 minutes along Freienwalder Strasse.

Charlottenburg

The glittering heart of West Berlin during the Cold War, Charlottenburg has been eclipsed by historic Mitte and other eastern districts since reunification, but is now trying hard to stage a comeback with major construction and redevelopment around Zoo station. Its main artery is the 3.5km-long Kurfürstendamm (Ku'damm for short), Berlin's busiest shopping strip.

Schloss Charlottenburg, Berlin
WESTEND61/GETTY IMAGES ©

Schloss Charlottenburg   Palace

(320 911; www.spsg.de; Spandauer Damm 20-24; day pass adult/concession €15/11; 145, 309 Richard-Wagner-Platz, Sophie-Charlotte-Platz) The grandest Prussian palace to survive in Berlin consists of the main building and three smaller structures scattered about the sprawling park. Each building charges separate admission; the day pass (Tageskarte) is good for one-day admission to every open building.

Charlottenburg palace started out as the summer residence of Sophie Charlotte, wife of King Friedrich I. The couple's baroque living quarters in the palace's oldest section, the **Altes Schloss** (320 911; www.spsg.de; Spandauer Damm; adult/concession €12/8; 10am-6pm Tue-Sun Apr-Oct, to 5pm Tue-Sun Nov-Mar; 145, 309 Richard-Wagner-Platz, Sophie-Charlotte-Platz), are an extravaganza in stucco, brocade and overall opulence, although the private chambers of Frederick the Great in the **Neuer Flügel** (New Wing; 320 911; www.spsg.de; Spandauer Damm 20-24; adult/concession incl audioguide €6/5; 10am-6pm Wed-Mon Apr-Oct, to 5pm Wed-Mon Nov-Mar; M45, 309 Richard-Wagner-Platz, Sophie-Charlotte-Platz) – designed in flamboyant rococo style – are even more impressive.

Other buildings dotted around the park house 19th-century paintings (**Neuer Pavillon**), fancy porcelain (**Belvedere**) and dead royals (**Mausoleum**).

Tours

Most of these English-language walking tours don't require reservations – just show up at one of the meeting points.

Berlin Walks   Walking Tour
(301 9194; www.berlinwalks.de; adult €12-15, concession €9-12) Get under the skin of Berlin's history and what makes the city tick today with the local expert guides of Berlin's longest-running English-language walking tour company.

New Berlin Tours   Walking Tour
(www.newberlintours.com; adult €12-15, concession €10-15) Energetic and entertaining English-language walking tours by the

1 **BERLINER MAUER**
For an introduction to Berlin's divided history, don't miss this open-air memorial on Bernauer Strasse, one of the city's most infamous Cold War streets. It's the only place in Berlin where the so-called death strip between the two walls still exists, and you can see two exhibitions documenting the wall's 28-year history. The memorial is opposite the Nordbahnhof station, where there's another exhibition on the 'ghost stations' that were closed after the wall was built in 1961.

2 **CHECKPOINT CHARLIE**
This free exhibition on Zimmerstrasse opened in 2011 next to Checkpoint Charlie and documents the practices of East Germany's secret police, the Stasi – the biggest spy organisation of the Cold War. The exhibition explores the techniques the Stasi used to keep people under surveillance, and the web of spies they used to hunt down the 'enemies' of the East German state.

3 **DDR MUSEUM**
This brilliant museum on Alexanderplatz allows you to experience daily life in East Berlin. It's really hands-on and explores what it was like to live behind the Iron Curtain: you can sit in an old Trabi car, see a communist concrete-slab apartment and even experience East Berlin's nudist beaches! There's a great restaurant next door, which sells classic East German dishes, too.

4 **BORNHOLMER STRASSE CHECKPOINT**
Don't miss the chance to stand on one of the most important locations of the 20th century – the first checkpoint forced open by protesters on 9 November 1989. The exhibition gives an hour-by-hour explanation of the last days of the wall's existence, and the amazing events behind its fall.

MARK DAFFEY/GETTY IMAGES ©

⭐ Don't Miss
Berlin's Tiergarten

Lolling about in the grass on a sunny afternoon is the quintessential Berlin pastime. Germans adore the outdoors and flock to urban green spaces whenever the weather is fine. They also dislike tan lines, so don't be surprised if you stumble upon locals sunbathing in the nude.

The Tiergarten is criss-crossed by a series of major roads and anchored by the Brandenburg Gate and the Reichstag on its northwestern edge. It's a tangle of curved walking and cycling paths, tiny ponds, open fields and thick woods. You'll probably get lost, but there are dozens of maps scattered about to help you find your way.

From the Reichstag, the Tiergarten's **carillon** (Map p564; John-Foster-Dulles-Allee; 🚌100 or 200) and the **Haus der Kulturen der Welt** (House of World Cultures; Map p564; 📞397 870; www.hkw.de; John-Foster-Dulles-Allee 10; admission varies; 🕐exhibits 11am-7pm Wed-Mon; 🚌100, Ⓢ Bundestag) are clearly visible. The latter was the US contribution to the 1957 International Building Exposition and it's easy to see why locals call it the 'pregnant oyster'.

Further west, the wings of the **Siegessäule** (Victory Column; Map p564; Grosser Stern; 🚌100, 200) were the *Wings of Desire* in that famous Wim Wenders film. This golden angel was built to commemorate Prussian military victories in the 19th century.

---

pioneers of the donation-based 'free tour' and the pub crawl.

Fat Tire Bike Tours Bicycle Tour
(Map p574; 📞2404 7991; www.fattirebiketours. com/berlin; Panoramastrasse 1a; adult/conces-

sion €24/22; Ⓢ Alexanderplatz 🚃 Alexander- platz) Offers a huge range of tours, from standard city tours to themed tours along the former course of the Berlin Wall and/or a Cold War tour, historical tours and more.

Trabi Safari
Driving Tour

(Map p564; 2759 2273; www.trabi-safari.
de; Zimmerstrasse 97; per person €30-90, Wall
Ride €79-89, prices depending on group size;
underground rail Kochstrasse) Catch the *Good
Bye, Lenin!* vibe on tours of Berlin's classic
sights or the 'Wild East' with you driving or
riding in convoy of a 'Trabi', East Germany's
(now) cult car with live commentary (in
English by prior arrangement) piped into
your vehicle. Bring your driver's licence.

Sleeping

Mitte & Prenzlauer Berg

Circus Hotel
Hotel €€

(Map p574; 2000 3939; www.circus-berlin.
de; Rosenthaler Strasse 1; d €80-110; @
S Rosenthaler Platz) At our favourite budget
boutique hotel, none of the mod rooms
are alike but all feature upbeat colours,
thoughtful design details, sleek oak floors
and quality beds. Unexpected perks include a well-stocked library and free iPod,
netbook and DVD player rentals. Fabulous
breakfast buffet to boot.

Hotel Honigmond
Hotel €€

(Map p574; 284 4550; www.honigmond-berlin.
de; Tieckstrasse 12; d €145-235; P @
S Oranienburger Tor) This delightful hotel
scores a perfect 10 on our 'charmometer',
not for being particularly lavish but for
its homey yet elegant ambience. The
nicest rooms flaunt such historic features
as ornate stucco ceilings, frescoes and
parquet floors.

Adina Apartment
Hotel Berlin
Checkpoint Charlie
Apartment €€

(Map p564; 200 7670; www.adina.eu; Krau-
senstrasse 35-36; d €110-160, 1-bedroom apt
from €140; P @ S Stadtmitte, Spit-
telmarkt) Adina's contemporary and roomy
one- and two-bedroom apartments with
full kitchens are tailor-made for cost-
conscious families, anyone in need of
elbow room, and self-caterers (a supermarket is a minute away). Kitchenless
rooms also available. See the website

about other Berlin Adina properties.
Optional breakfast is €15.

Hotel Adlon
Kempinski
Luxury Hotel €€€

(Map p574; 226 10; www.kempinski.com;
Pariser Platz, Unter den Linden 77; r from
€250; @ S Brandenburger Tor
Brandenburger Tor) Opposite Brandenburger Tor, the Adlon has been Berlin's
most high-profile defender of the grand
tradition since 1907. The striking lobby is
a mere overture to the full symphony of
luxury awaiting in spacious, amenity-laden
rooms and suites where the decor is old-
fashioned in a regal sort of way. A ritzy day
spa, gourmet restaurants and the swank
Felix nightclub add 21st-century spice.

Kreuzberg & Friedrichshain

Michelberger Hotel
Hotel €€

(Map p564; 2977 8590; www.michelbergerho-
tel.com; Warschauer Strasse 39; d €80-180;
S Warschauer Strasse Warschauer Strasse)
The pinnacle of creative crash pads,
Michelberger perfectly encapsulates
Berlin's offbeat DIY spirit. Rooms don't
hide their factory pedigree but are comfortable and come in sizes suitable for
lovebirds, families or rock bands. Great
for the young and forever young.

Hotel Johann
Hotel €€

(Map p564; 225 0740; www.hotel-johann-ber-
lin.de; Johanniterstrasse 8; d €95-120; P @
S Prinzenstrasse, Hallesches Tor) This 33-
room hotel consistently tops the popularity charts, thanks to its eager-to-please
service and rooms pairing minimalist
designer style with historic flourishes.
Nice garden and within strolling distance
of the Jüdisches Museum.

Charlottenburg
Hotel Askanischer Hof
Hotel €€

(Map p564; 881 8033; www.askanischer-hof.
de; Kurfürstendamm 53; d €120-180; S Ade-
nauerplatz) If you're after character and
vintage flair, you'll find heaps of both at

Mitte (Berlin)

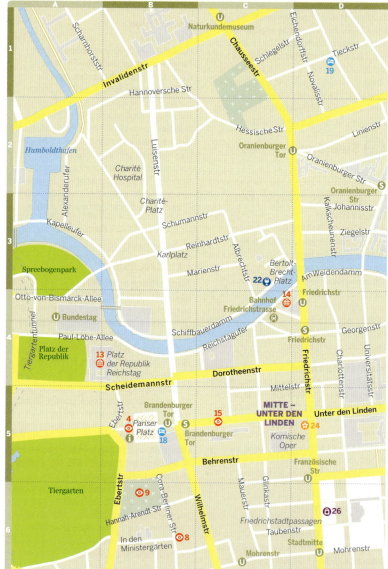

this 17-room jewel with a Roaring Twenties pedigree. No two rooms are alike but all are filled with antiques, lace curtains, frilly chandeliers and time-worn oriental rugs; often used for fashion shoots.

Hotel Bogota Hotel €€
(Map p564; ☏ 881 5001; www.bogota.de; Schlüterstrasse 45; d €90-150, without bathroom €64-77; ☎; ⓈUhlandstrasse) Bogota has charmed travellers with charisma and vintage flair since 1964. Helmut Newton

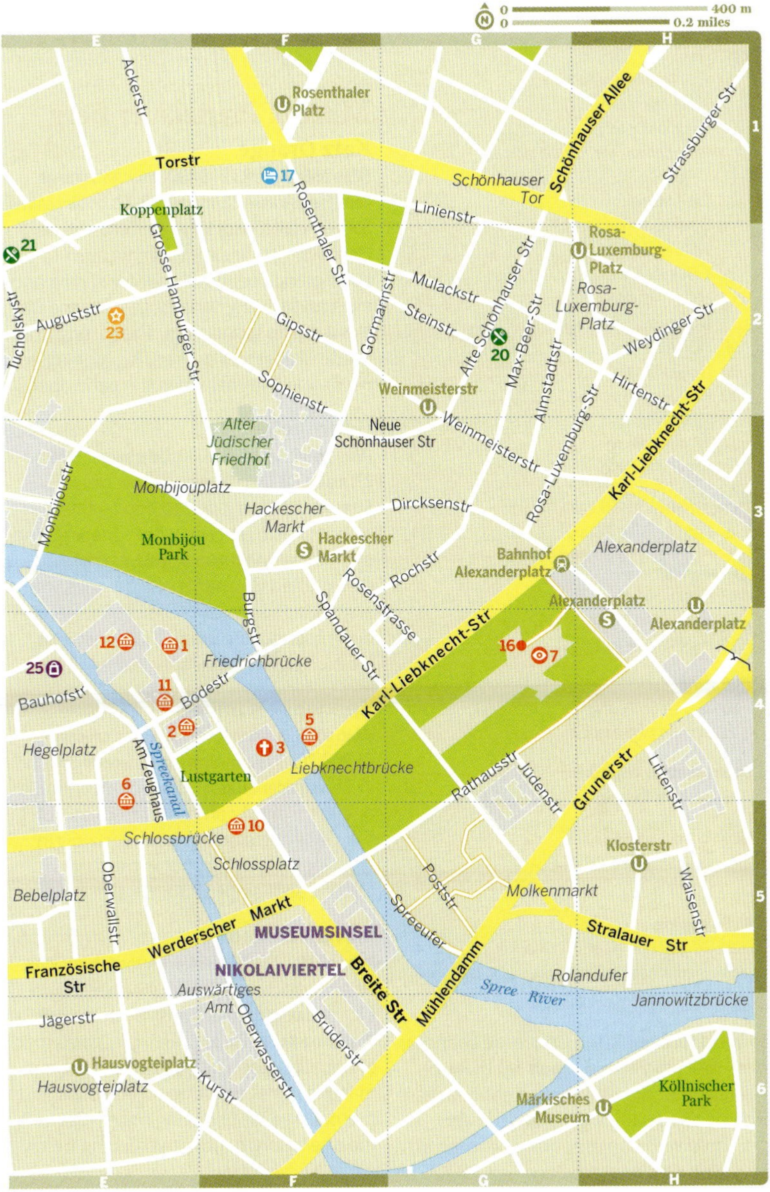

Map Labels (Map p564)

0   400 m
0   0.2 miles

Schönhauser Allee

Strassburger Str

Rosenthaler Platz

Torstr

Koppenplatz

21

Linienstr

Schönhauser Tor

17

Rosenthaler Str

Grosse Hamburger Str

Tucholskystr

Augustr

23

Gipsstr

Sophienstr

Gormannstr

Steinstr

Mulackstr

Alte Schönhauser Str

Max-Beer-Str

Rosa-Luxemburg-Platz

Rosa-Luxemburg-Platz

Almstadtstr

Weydinger Str

Hirtenstr

20

Weinmeisterstr

Neue Schönhauser Str

Weinmeisterstr

Rosa-Luxemburg-Str

Karl-Liebknecht-Str

Monbijoustr

Alter Jüdischer Friedhof

Monbijouplatz

Hackescher Markt

Dircksenstr

Monbijou Park

Hackescher Markt

Rochstr

Rosenstrasse

Bahnhof Alexanderplatz

Alexanderplatz

Alexanderplatz

Alexanderplatz

Burgstr

Spandauer Str

25

12

1

Friedrichbrücke

11

Bodestr

2

5

3

6

Lustgarten

Liebknechtbrücke

10

Schlossbrücke

Schlossplatz

Karl-Liebknecht-Str

16

7

Rathausstr

Jüdenstr

Grunerstr

Littenstr

Klosterstr

Bauhofstr

Hegelplatz

Am Zeughaus

Spreekanal

Bebelplatz

Oberwallstr

Werderscher Markt

MUSEUMSINSEL

NIKOLAIVIERTEL

Schlossplatz

Poststr

Spreeufer

Molkenmarkt

Stralauer Str

Waisenstr

Französische Str

Auswärtiges Amt

Breite Str

Mühlendamm

Rolandufer

Spree River

Jannowitzbrücke

Jägerstr

Oberwasserstr

Brüderstr

Hausvogteiplatz

Hausvogteiplatz

Kurstr

Märkisches Museum

Köllnischer Park

---

studied with fashion photographer Yva here in the 1930s and to this day the retro landmark hosts glam-mag photo shoots. Room sizes and amenities vary greatly, so ask to see a few before settling in.

Hotel Concorde Berlin   Hotel €€€
(Map p564; ☏ 800 9990; www.concorde-hotels. com/concordeberlin; Augsburger Strasse 41; d €150-300; P ❄ @ 🛜; S Kurfürstendamm) Designed by German architect Jan Klei-hues, from the curved limestone facade

575

Mitte (Berlin)

⊙ Sights
1 Alte Nationalgalerie E4
2 Altes Museum E4
3 Berliner Dom F4
4 Brandenburger Tor & Pariser
   Platz B5
5 DDR Museum F4
6 Deutsches Historisches
   Museum E4
7 Fernsehturm.. G4
8 Hitler's Bunker B6
9 Holocaust Memorial B6
10 Humboldt-Box... F5
11 Neues Museum E4
12 Pergamonmuseum.................................. E4
13 Reichstag A4
14 Tränenpalast C4
15 Unter den Linden C5

✪ Activities, Courses & Tours
16 Fat Tire Bike Tours G4

🛏 Sleeping
17 Circus Hotel...F1
18 Hotel Adlon Kempinski........................... B5
19 Hotel Honigmond................................... D1

✖ Eating
20 Monsieur Vuong...................................... G2
21 Schwarzwaldstuben E2

🍷 Drinking & Nightlife
22 Berliner Republik C3

✪ Entertainment
23 Clärchens Ballhaus................................ E2
24 Cookies..D5

🛍 Shopping
25 Berlin Art & Nostalgia Market E4
26 Friedrichstadtpassagen.......................D6

to the door knobs, the Concorde channels New York efficiency, French lightness of being and Berlin-style unpretentiousness. Rooms and suites are supersized and accented with contemporary German art. Free wi-fi. Optional breakfast is €28.

✖ Eating

If you crave traditional German comfort food, you'll certainly find plenty of places in Berlin to indulge in pork knuckles, smoked pork chops and calves liver. Meat eaters should not leave the city without trying Berlin's famous *currywurst*.

Mitte & Prenzlauer Berg

Katz Orange   International €€€
(Map p564; ☎ 983 208 430; www.katzorange. com; Bergstrasse 22; mains €13-22; ⊙ dinner Tue-Sat year-round, lunch May-Sep; Ⓢ Rosenthaler Platz) With its gourmet organic farm-to-table menu, feel-good country styling and swift and smiling servers, the 'Orange Cat' hits a gastro grand slam. The setting in a castle-like former brewery is stunning, especially in summer when the patio opens.

Oderquelle   German €€
(Map p564; ☎ 4400 8080; Oderberger Strasse 27; mains €8-16; ⊙ dinner; Ⓢ Eberswalder Strasse) It's always fun to pop by this woodsy resto and see what's inspired the chef today. Most likely, it'll be a delicious well-crafted German meal, perhaps with a slight Mediterranean nuance. The generously topped and crispy *Flammekuche* (French pizza) are a reliable standby.

Konnopke's Imbiss   German €
(Map p564; Schönhauser Allee 44a; sausages €1.30-1.70; ⊙ 10am-8pm Mon-Fri, noon-8pm Sat; Ⓢ Eberswalder Strasse) Brave the inevitable queue for great *currywurst* from one of the city's cult sausage kitchens, now in shiny new glass digs but in the same historic spot since 1930.

Monsieur Vuong   Asian €€
(Map p574; ☎ 9929 6924; www.monsieurvuong. de; Alte Schönhauser Strasse 46; mains around €8; ⊙ noon-midnight; Ⓢ Weinmeisterstrasse, Rosa-Luxemburg-Platz) At Berlin's 'godfather' of upbeat Indochina nosh-stops, the mini-menu features flavour-packed soups and two or three oft-changing mains. Come in the afternoon to avoid the feeding frenzy.

Schwarzwaldstuben   German €€
(Map p574; ☎ 2809 8084; Tucholskystrasse 48; mains €7-14; Ⓡ Oranienburger Strasse) In the mood for a Hansel and Gretel moment? Then join the other 'lost kids' in this send-up of the Black Forest complete with plastic pines and baseball-capped

Bambi heads. We can't get enough of the '*geschmelzte Maultaschen*' (sautéed ravioli-like pasta), the giant schnitzel and the Rothaus Tannenzäpfle beer.

Kreuzberg & Friedrichshain

Cafe Jacques   International €€
(Map p564; ☎ 694 1048; Maybachufer 8; mains €12-20; ☺ dinner; Ⓢ Schönleinstrasse) A favourite with off-duty chefs and local foodies, Jacques infallibly charms with flattering candlelight, warm decor and fantastic wine. It's the perfect date spot but, quite frankly, you only have to be in love with good food to appreciate the French- and North African-inspired blackboard menu. Reservations essential.

Max und Moritz   German €€
(Map p564; ☎ 6951 5911; www.maxundmoritzberlin.de; Oranienstrasse 162; mains €9-15; ☺ dinner; Ⓢ Moritzplatz) This ode-to-old-school brew-pub has lured hungry diners and drinkers with sudsy home brews and granny-style Berlin fare since 1902. A menu favourite is the *Kutschergulasch* (goulash cooked with beer).

Defne   Turkish €€
(Map p564; ☎ 8179 7111; www.defne-restaurant.de; Planufer 92c; mains €7.50-16; ☺ dinner; Ⓢ Kottbusser Tor, Schönleinstrasse) If you thought Turkish cuisine stopped at the doner kebab, canal-side Defne will teach you otherwise. The appetizer platter alone elicits intense food cravings (fabulous walnut-chilli paste!), but inventive mains such as *ali nacik* (sliced lamb with pureed eggplant and yoghurt) also warrant repeat visits.

Gedenkstätte Berliner Mauer (p567), Berlin
DAVID PEEVERS/GETTY IMAGES ©

Curry 36   German €
(Map p564; www.curry36.de; Mehringdamm 36; snacks €2-6; ☺ 9am-4pm Mon-Sat, to 3pm Sun; Ⓢ Mehringdamm) Day after day, night after night, a motley crowd of tattooed scenesters, office jockeys, noisy school kids and savvy tourists wait their turn at this top-ranked *currywurst* purveyor that's been frying 'em up since 1981.

Spätzle & Knödel   German €€
(Map p564; ☎ 2757 1151; Wühlischstrasse 20; mains €8-15; ☺ dinner; Ⓢ Samariterstrasse) This elbows-on-the-table gastropub is a great place to get your southern German comfort food fix with waist-expanding portions of roast pork, goulash and of course the eponymous *Spätzle* (German mac 'n cheese) and *Knödel* (dumplings).

Charlottenburg

Ali Baba   Italian €
(Map p564; ☎ 881 1350; www.alibaba-berlin.de; Bleibtreustrasse 45; dishes €3-9; ☺ 11am-2am Sun-Thu, to 3am Fri & Sat; Ⓡ Savignyplatz)

GERMANY BERLIN

Everybody feels like family at this been-here-forever port of call where the thin-crust pizza is delicious, the pasta piping hot and nothing costs more than €9.

Dicke Wirtin   German €€

(Map p564; ☎312 4952; www.dicke-wirtin.de; Carmerstrasse 9; mains €6-15; ☻noon-1am or later; ☒Savignyplatz) Old Berlin charm oozes from every nook and cranny of this longserving pub which pours eight draught beers (including the superb Kloster Andechs) and nearly three dozen homemade schnapps varieties. Hearty local fare like roast pork, fried liver or breaded schnitzel keep brains balanced.

🍷 Drinking & Nightlife

Madame Claude   Pub

(Map p564; Lübbener Strasse 19; ☻from 7pm; ⑤Schlesisches Tor) Gravity is literally upended at Kreuzberg's David Lynch-ian booze burrow where the furniture dangles from the ceiling and the moulding's on the floor. Doesn't fill up until around 11pm.

Hops & Barley   Pub

(Map p564; ☎2936 7534; Wühlischstrasse 40; ⑤Warschauer Strasse, ☒Warschauer Strasse) Conversation flows as freely as the unfiltered pilsner, malty *dunkel* (dark), fruity *weizen* (wheat) and potent cider produced right at this congenial Friedrichshain microbrewery inside a former butchers shop.

Würgeengel   Bar

(Map p564; www.wuergeengel.de; Dresdener Strasse 122; ☻from 7pm; ⑤Kottbusser Tor) For a swish night out, point the compass to this '50s-style Kreuzberg cocktail cave complete with glass ceiling, chandeliers and shiny black tables. Smoking allowed.

Prater   Beer Garden

(Map p564; ☎448 5688; www.pratergarten.de; Kastanienallee 7-9; ☻from noon Apr-Sep in good weather; ⑤Eberswalder Strasse) In Prenzlauer Berg, Berlin's oldest beer garden (since 1837) has kept much of its traditional charm and is a fantastic place to hang and guzzle a cold one beneath the ancient chestnut trees (self-service). In foul

weather or winter, the adjacent woodsy restaurant is a fine place to sample classic local fare (mains €8 to €19).

Berliner Republik   Pub

(Map p574; www.die-berliner-republik.de; Schiffbauerdamm 8; ☻10am-6am; ⑤Friedrichstrasse ☒Friedrichstrasse) Just as in a mini–stock exchange, the cost of drinks fluctuates with demand at this raucous riverside pub near Friedrichstrasse.

Solar   Bar

(Map p564; ☎0163-765-2700; www.solar-berlin.de; Stresemannstrasse 76; ☻6pm-2am Sun-Thu, to 4am Fri & Sat; ☒Anhalter Bahnhof) Views of Potsdamer Platz and surrounds are truly impressive from this chic 17th-floor sky lounge above a posh restaurant (mains €18 to €29). Great for sunset drinks.

Freischwimmer   Beer Garden

(Map p564; ☎6107 4309; www.freischwimmer-berlin.de; Vor dem Schlesischen Tor 2a; mains €7-15; ☻from 4pm Tue-Fri, from 10am Sat & Sun; ⑤Schlesisches Tor) In summertime, few places are more idyllic than this rustic ex-boathouse turned all-day, canal-side chill zone.

⭐ Entertainment

With no curfew, this is a notoriously late city, where bars stay packed from dusk to dawn and beyond and some clubs don't hit their stride until 6am.

NIGHTCLUBS

Berghain/Panorama Bar   Club

(Map p564; www.berghain.de; Wriezener Bahnhof; ☻midnight Fri-Mon morning; ☒Ostbahnhof) Still the holy grail of techno-electro clubs. Only world-class spinmasters heat up this hedonistic bass junkie hellhole inside a labyrinthine ex-power plant.

Watergate   Club

(Map p564; ☎6128 0394; www.water-gate.de; Falckensteinstrasse 49a; ☻from 11pm Fri & Sat; ⑤Schlesisches Tor) Top DJs keep electro-hungry hipsters hot and sweaty till way past sunrise at this high-octane riverside club with two floors, panoramic windows and a floating terrace overlooking the

Oberbaumbrücke bridge. Long queues, tight door on weekends.

Cookies
Club

(Map p574; www.cookies.ch; cnr Friedrichstrasse & Unter den Linden; ⊙from midnight Tue, Thu & Sat; S Französische Strasse) This indoor playground complete with wicked little theme rooms (a mirror cabinet, a 'wedding' chapel) is still an essential after-dark player in Berlin.

Clärchens Ballhaus
Club

(Map p574; ☑ 282 9295; www.ballhaus.de; Auguststrasse 24; ⊙restaurant 12.30-11.30pm, dancing nightly; ☒M1 ☒Oranienburger Strasse) Yesteryear is now at this late, great 19th-century dance hall where groovers and grannies hoof it across the parquet without even a touch of irony. There's different sounds nightly – salsa to swing, tango to disco – and a live band on Saturday.

MUSIC & OPERA

Berliner Philharmonie
Classical Music

(Map p564; ☑2548 8999; www.berliner-philharmoniker.de; Herbert-von-Karajan-Strasse 1; ☒200 S Potsdamer Platz ☒Potsdamer Platz)

Berliner Philharmonie, Berlin

This landmark concert hall has supreme acoustics and, thanks to Hans Scharoun's clever terraced vineyard design, not a bad seat in the house. It's the home base of the world-famous Berliner Philharmoniker, currently led by Sir Simon Rattle.

Staatsoper unter den Linden @ Schillertheater
Opera

(Map p564; ☑information 203 540, tickets 2035 4555; www.staatsoper-berlin.de; Bismarckstrasse 110; S Ernst-Reuter-Platz) Point your highbrow compass towards the Daniel Barenboim–led Staatsoper, Berlin's top opera company.

GAY & LESBIAN BERLIN

Berlin's legendary liberalism has spawned one of the world's biggest and most diverse GLBT playgrounds. The closest that Berlin comes to a 'gay village' is Schöneberg (Motzstrasse and Fuggerstrasse especially, get off at U-Bahn station Nollendorfplatz), where the rainbow flag has proudly flown since the 1920s. There's still plenty of (old-school) partying going on here.

Current hipster central is Kreuzberg, which teems with party pens along

Restaurant at the KaDeWe department store, Berlin

JOHN FREEMAN/GETTY IMAGES ©

Mehringdamm and Oranienstrasse. Across the river, Friedrichshain has such key clubs as Berghain and the hardcore **Lab.oratory** (Map p564; www.lab-oratory.de; Am Wriezener Bahnhof; ⏱Thu-Mon; ⑤Ostbahnhof).

🔒 Shopping

For high street shopping, head to Berlin's main shopping boulevard Kurfürstendamm and its extension Tauentzienstrasse, which are chock-a-bloc with the usual-suspect high-street chains. You'll find more of the same in malls such as Alexa near Alexanderplatz and Potsdamer Platz Arkaden at Potsdamer Platz.

Flea market–hopping is a popular local pastime on the weekend, particularly Sundays. The **Berlin Art & Nostalgia Market** (Map p574; Georgenstrasse, Mitte; ⏱8am-5pm Sat & Sun; underground rail S-Bahn Friedrichstrasse) is heavy on collectables, books, ethnic crafts and GDR memorabilia; the **Flohmarkt am Mauerpark** (Map p564; www.mauerparkmarkt. de; Bernauer Strasse 63-64; ⏱10am-5pm Sun; ⑤Eberwalder Strasse) is known for its vintage wear and young-designer retro fashions; and the **Flohmarkt am Arkonaplatz** (Map p564; www.

mauerparkmarkt.de; Arkonaplatz; ⏱10am-4pm Sun; ⑤Bernauer Strasse) is the best spot to hit if you're looking for retro 1960s and 1970s furniture and accessories.

KaDeWe   Department Store

(Map p564; www.kadewe.de; Tauentzienstrasse 21-24; ⏱10am-8pm Mon-Thu, to 9pm Fri, 9.30am-8pm Sat; ⑤Wittenbergplatz) This venerable department store has an assortment so vast that a pirate-style campaign is the best way to plunder its bounty. Don't miss the legendary 6th-floor gourmet food hall.

Friedrichstadtpassagen
Shopping Centre

(Map p574; Friedrichstrasse btwn Französische Strasse & Mohrenstrasse; ⏱10am-8pm Mon-Sat; ⑤Französische Strasse, Stadtmitte) Even if you're not part of the Gucci and Prada brigade, the wow factor of this trio of indoor shopping arcades (called *Quartiere*) is undeniable.

ℹ Information

Berlin Tourismus (📞2500 2333; http:// visit berlin.de; ⏱call centre 9am-7pm Mon-Fri, 10am-5pm Sat, 10am-2pm Sun) Berlin's tourist board operates three walk-in offices and a call centre with multilingual staff who field general questions and can make hotel and ticket bookings.

Hauptbahnhof (Map p564; Europaplatz, ground fl, north entrance; ⏰8am-10pm; Ⓢ Hauptbahnhof Ⓡ Hauptbahnhof) Extended hours April to October.

Brandenburger Tor (Map p574; Brandenburger Tor, Pariser Platz; ⏰9.30am-7pm daily; Ⓢ Brandenburger Tor Ⓡ Brandenburger Tor)

Kurfürstendamm (Map p564; Neues Kranzler Eck, Kurfürstendamm 22; ⏰9.30am-8pm Mon-Sat, to 6pm Sun; Ⓢ Kurfürstendamm) Extended hours April to October.

ⓘ Getting There & Away

Air

Berlin's brand-new airport, Berlin Brandenburg airport has been taking shape next to Schönefeld airport, about 24km southeast of the city centre, since 2006. In the meantime, most major international airlines, as well as many discount carriers, including Ryanair, easyJet, Air Berlin and Germanwings, continue to fly into Berlin's two other airports.

Tegel airport (TXL; ☏01805 000 186; www.berlin-airport.de) About 8km northwest of the city centre.

Schönefeld airport (SXF; ☏0180 5000 186; www.berlin-airport.de) About 22km southeast.

Train

Berlin is well connected by train to other German cities, as well as to popular European destinations, including Prague, Warsaw and Amsterdam. All long-distance trains converge at the **Hauptbahnhof** (www.berlin-hauptbahnhof.de; Europaplatz, Washingtonplatz; Ⓢ Hauptbahnhof Ⓡ Hauptbahnhof).

The left-luggage office (€5 per piece per 24 hours) is behind the ReiseBank currency exchange on the first upper level, opposite the Reisezentrum.

ⓘ Getting Around

To/From the Airport

Tegel

The TXL bus connects Tegel with Alexanderplatz (40 minutes) every 10 minutes. For

Kurfürstendamm and Zoo Station, take bus X9 (20 minutes). Tegel is not directly served by the U-Bahn, but both bus 109 and X9 stop at Jakob-Kaiser-Platz (U7), the station closest to the airport. Each of these trips costs €2.40. Taxi rides cost about €20 to Zoologischer Garten and €23 to Alexanderplatz and should take between 30 and 45 minutes.

Schönefeld

Airport-Express trains make the 30-minute trip to central Berlin twice hourly. Note: these are regular regional trains, identified as RE7 and RB14 in timetables. The S-Bahn S9 runs every 20 minutes and is slower but useful if you're headed to Friedrichshain or Prenzlauer Berg. For the Messe (trade-fair grounds), take the S45 to Südkreuz and change to the S41. Trains stop about 400m from the airport terminals. Free shuttle buses run every 10 minutes; walking takes about five minutes. You need a transport ticket covering zones ABC (€3.10). Taxi rides average €40 and take 35 minutes to an hour.

Car & Motorcycle

Garage parking is expensive (about €2 per hour) and vehicles entering the environmental zone (within the S-Bahn rail ring) must display a special sticker (*Umweltplakette;* €5 to €15). Order it online at www.berlin.de/sen/umwelt/luftqualitaet/de/luftreinhalteplan/doku_umweltzone.shtml. The fine for getting caught without the sticker is €40. Rental cars automatically have this sticker.

Public Transport

One type of ticket is valid on all public transport, including the U-Bahn, buses, trams and ferries run by **BVG** (☏194 49; www.bvg.de), as well as the S-Bahn and regional RE, SE and RB trains operated by **Deutsche Bahn** (www.bahn.de).

Buy tickets from vending machines (English instructions available) in U-Bahn or S-Bahn stations and aboard trams, from bus drivers and at station offices and news kiosks sporting the yellow BVG logo.

Stamp all tickets, except those bought from bus drivers, before boarding or risk a €40 on-the-spot fine if caught without a validated ticket.

Services operate from 4am until just after midnight on weekdays, with half-hourly *Nachtbus* (night bus) services in between. At weekends, the U-Bahn and S-Bahn run all night long (except the U4 and U55).

Public Transport Tickets

Three tariff zones exist – A, B and C. Unless venturing to Potsdam or Schönefeld airport, you'll only need an AB ticket.

TICKET	AB (€)	BC (€)	ABC (€)
Single	2.40	2.80	3.10
Day pass	6.50	6.80	7
Group day pass (up to 5 people)	15.50	15.80	16
7-day pass	28	28.90	34.60

Taxi

You can order a **taxi** (☏ 20 20 20, 44 33 11) by phone, flag one down or pick one up at a rank. Flag fall is €3.20, then it's €1.65 per kilometre up to 7km and €1.28 for each kilometre after that. Up to four passengers travel for the price of one. Tip about 10%.

DRESDEN & SAXONY

Dresden

☏0351 / POP 512,000

Proof that there is life after death, Dresden has become one of Germany's most popular attractions, and for good reason. Restorations have returned the city to the glory days when it was famous throughout Europe as 'Florence on the Elbe', owing to the efforts of Italian artists, musicians, actors and master craftsmen who flocked to the court of Augustus the Strong, bestowing countless masterpieces upon the city.

The devastating bombing raids in 1945 levelled most of these treasures. But Dresden is a survivor and many of the most important landmarks have since been rebuilt, including the elegant Frauenkirche.

⊙ Sights

The Elbe River splits Dresden in a rough V-shape, with the **Neustadt** (new city) to the north and the **Altstadt** (old city) to the south.

The Dresden-Card, sold at the tourist offices, provides free public transportation as well as sweeping sightseeing discounts. Various schemes are available, including a one-day version (single/family €10/12.50), a two-day version (€25/46) and a three-day regional version (€48/68).

Frauenkirche   Church

(www.frauenkirche-dresden.de; Neumarkt; audioguide €2.50; ⊙usually 10am-noon & 1-6pm) **FREE** The domed Frauenkirche – one of Dresden's most beloved symbols – has literally risen from the city's ashes. The original graced its skyline for two centuries before collapsing two days after the devastating February 1945 bombing. The East Germans left the rubble as a war memorial, but after reunification a grassroots movement helped raise the funds to rebuild the landmark.

The altar, reassembled from nearly 2000 fragments, is especially striking. You can also climb the **dome (Neumarkt; adult/concession €8/5; ⊙10am-6pm Mon-Sat, 12.30-6pm Sun Mar-Oct, to 4pm Nov-Feb)** for sweeping city views.

Residenzschloss   Palace

(☏4914 2000; www.skd.museum; Schlossplatz; adult/concession €10/7.50; ⊙10am-6pm Wed-Mon) Dresden's fortress-like Renaissance city palace was home to the Saxon rulers from 1485 to 1918 and now shelters four precious collections, including the unmissable **Grünes Gewölbe** (Green Vault), a real-life Aladdin's Cave spilling over with precious objects wrought from gold, ivory, silver, diamonds and jewels.

Another important collection in the palace is the **Kupferstich-Kabinett**, which counts around half a million prints and drawings by 20,000 artists (including Dürer, Rembrandt and Michelangelo) in its possession.

Tickets to the Residenzschloss are good for all these collections except for the **Historisches Grünes Gewölbe** (☏4914 2000; www.skd.museum; Residenzschloss, enter via Sophienstrasse or Kleiner Schlosshof; adult/under 16 incl audioguide €10/free; ⊙10am-7pm Wed-Mon). Admission

DANITA DELIMONT/GETTY IMAGES ©

⭐ **Don't Miss**
Park Sanssouci

Featuring ornate palaces and manicured parks, the Prussian royal seat of Potsdam is the most popular day trip from Berlin. Park Sanssouci is the heart of Potsdam and what everyone comes to see. Its most celebrated palace is **Schloss Sanssouci** (www. spsg.de; adult/concession incl audioguide Apr-Oct €12/8, Nov-Mar €8/5 ; ⊙10am-6pm Tue-Sun Apr-Oct, to 5pm Nov-Mar; 🚌695, 606), a rococo extravaganza built by Frederick the Great in the 18th century. Admission is by timed ticket only, so come early. Standouts include the whimsically decorated Concert Hall, the Library and the elegant Marble Room.

At the far western end of the park, the vast, domed **Neues Palais** (New Palace; 📞969 4200; Am Neuen Palais; adult/concession €6/5; ⊙10am-6pm Wed-Mon Apr-Oct, to 5pm Nov-Mar; 🚌695 or 605 to Neues Palais, 🚉to Potsdam, Park Sanssouci Bahnhof) was built for representational purposes and only used as a residence by the last German Kaiser, Wilhelm II, until 1918.

Among the park's many other pearls, the **Chinesisches Haus** (Am Grünen Gitter; admission €2; ⊙10am-6pm Tue-Sun May-Oct; 🚌605 to Schloss Charlottenhof, 606 or 695 to Schloss Sanssouci 🚉91 to Schloss Charlottenhof) is a standout. It's a circular pavilion of gilded columns, palm trees and figures of Chinese musicians and animals that houses a porcelain collection.

The local tourist office runs the 3½-hour **Potsdam Sanssouci Tour** (tours with/ without Sanssouci Palace €27/16; ⊙Tue-Sun Apr-Oct), which checks off the highlights and guarantees admission to Schloss Sanssouci. Tours are in English and German and leave at 11.10am from the tourist office at the Hauptbahnhof.

Regional trains leaving from Berlin-Hauptbahnhof and Zoologischer Garten take about half an hour to reach Potsdam Hauptbahnhof; some continue on to Potsdam-Charlottenhof and Potsdam-Sanssouci, which are actually closer to Park Sanssouci. You need a ticket covering zones A, B and C (€3) for either service.

here is by timed ticket only and you're strongly advised to order advance tickets online or by phone since only 40% are sold at the palace box office for same-day admission.

Zwinger
Museum

(☎ 4914 2000; www.skd.museum; Theaterplatz 1; adult/concession €10/7.50; ⏱10am-6pm Tue-Sun) A ravishing baroque complex, the sprawling Zwinger was primarily a royal party palace and now houses numerous precious collections. The most important is the **Gemäldegalerie Alte Meister**, which features a roll call of Old Masters including Botticelli, Titian, Rubens, Vermeer and Dürer.

Albertinum
Gallery

(www.skd.museum; enter from Brühlsche Terrasse or Georg-Treu-Platz 2; adult/concession €8/6; ⏱10am-6pm; P) After massive renovations following severe 2002 flood damage, the Renaissance-era former arsenal is now the stunning home of the **Galerie Neue Meister** (New Masters Gallery), an ark of paintings by leading artistic lights since the Romantic period – Caspar David Friedrich to Claude Monet and Gerhard Richter – in gorgeous rooms orbiting a light-filled central courtyard.

Militärhistorisches Museum Dresden
Museum

(☎ 823 2803; www.mhmbw.de; Olbrichtplatz 2; adult/concession €5/3; ⏱10am-6pm Tue-Sun, to 9pm Mon; 🚊7 or 8 to Stauffenbergallee) Even devout pacifists will be awed by this engaging museum that reopened in 2011 in a 19th-century arsenal bisected by a bold glass-and-steel wedge designed by Daniel Libeskind. Standouts among the countless intriguing objects are a 1975 Soyuz landing capsule, a V2 rocket and personal items of concentration camp victims.

Tours

Sächsische Dampfschiffahrt   River Tour
(www.saechsische-dampfschiffahrt.de; adult/child from €16/8) Ninety-minute Elbe paddle-wheel steamer tours leave from the Terrassenufer docks several times daily in summer along with service to Meissen and the villages of Saxon Switzerland.

Grosse Stadtrundfahrt   Bus Tour
(☎899 5650; www.stadtrundfahrt.com; day pass adult/concession €20/18; ⊙9.30am-5pm) This narrated hop-on, hop-off tour stops at 22 sights and also includes short walking tours of the Zwinger, Fürstenzug and Frauenkirche.

🛏 Sleeping

Hotel Martha Dresden   Hotel €€
(☎817 60; www.hotel-martha-hospiz.de; Nieritzstrasse 11; d €113-120; 🛜) Fifty rooms with big windows, wooden floors and Biedermeier-inspired furnishings combine with an attractive winter garden and friendly staff into a pleasant place to hang your hat. The rustic restaurant serves local food and wine.

Radisson Blu Gewandhaus Hotel   Hotel €€
(☎494 90; www.radissonblu.com/gewand-haushotel-dresden; Ringstrasse 1; d from €133; P✲@🛜⊛) Public areas in this restored and converted 18th-century trading house are stunning and the Biedermeier-style rooms have marble-fitted bathrooms with whirlpool tubs. Tops for class and personal service.

Hotel Taschenbergpalais Kempinski   Hotel €€€
(☎491 20; www.kempinski-dresden.de; Taschen-berg 3; r €170-230; ✲@🛜⊛) Luxury is taken very seriously indeed at Dresden's grandest hotel. Checking in here buys views over the Zwinger from rakishly

handsome rooms that beautifully bridge the traditional and the contemporary. In winter, the courtyard turns into an ice rink.

🍴 Eating

The Neustadt has oodles of cafes and restaurants, many found along Königstrasse and the streets north of Albertplatz. Restaurants in the Altstadt are mostly tourist-geared.

La Casina Rosa
Italian €€

(📞 801 4848; www.la-casina-rosa.de; Alaunstrasse 93; pizza & pasta €6.50-9.50; 🕐 lunch Tue-Sat, dinner Mon-Sat) Everybody feels like family at this neighbourhood-adored trattoria with its warren of cosy rooms (plus idyllic summer garden) and feisty pasta and pizza, plus seasonally inspired specials. Reservations are key.

Raskolnikoff
Cafe, Bar €€

(📞 804 5706; www.raskolnikoff.de; Böhmische Strasse 34; mains €5-13; 🕐 9am-2am) An artist squat in GDR times, Raskolnikoff still brims with artsy-bohemian flair. The menu is sorted by compass direction (borscht to fish soup and steak) and in summer, the sweet little beer garden beckons. The beer itself comes from the Neustadt-based Schwingheuer brewery and is a steal at €2.40 per half litre.

Cafe Alte Meister
International €€

(📞 481 0426; www.altemeister.net; Theaterplatz 1a; mains €7-15; 🕐 10am-1am) If you've worked up an appetite from museumhopping, retreat to this elegant filling station between the Zwinger and the Semperoper for a smoked-trout sandwich, light salad, luscious cake or energyrestoring steak.

Grand Café
Cakes, Saxon €€

(📞 496 2444; www.coselpalais-dresden.de; An der Frauenkirche 12; mains €10-15; 🕐 10ammidnight) The cakes and imaginative mains are good, but frankly, they almost play second fiddle to the gold-trimmed baroque setting of the Coselpalais.

ℹ️ Information

Tourist office – Hauptbahnhof (Hauptbahnhof; 🕐 9am-7pm)

Tourist office Frauenkirche (Schlossstrasse 23; 🕐 10am-7pm Mon-Fri, 10am-6pm Sat, 10am-3pm Sun, reduced hours Jan-Mar)

ℹ️ Getting There & Around

Dresden airport is about 9km north of the city centre. The S2 train links the airport with the city centre several times hourly (€2). Taxis are about €20.

By train, Dresden is linked to such major cities as Leipzig (€30, 70 minutes) and Berlin-Hauptbahnhof (€38, two hours) as well as to Meissen (€5.60, 40 minutes) by the local S1.

Buses and trams are run by **Dresdner Verkehrsbetriebe** (DVB; 📞 857 1011). Fares within

Schloss Schwerin (p605)
WITOLD SKRYPCZAK/GETTY IMAGES ©

Detour:
Meissen

Straddling the Elbe around 25km upstream from Dresden, Meissen is the cradle of European porcelain manufacturing and still hitches its tourism appeal to the world-famous china first cooked up in its imposing 1710 castle.

There's no 'quiet time' to arrive at the popular and unmissable **porcelain museum** (📞 468 208; www.meissen.com; Talstrasse 9; adult/child €9/4.50; ⏰ 9am-6pm May-Oct, 9am-5pm Nov-Apr) where you can witness the astonishing artistry and craftsmanship that makes Meissen porcelain unique. It's next to the porcelain factory, about 1km south of the Altstadt. Visits start with a 30-minute tour (with English audioguide) of the **Schauwerkstätten**, where you can observe live demonstrations of vase throwing, plate painting, figure moulding and the glazing process.

Half-hourly S1 trains run from Dresden's Hauptbahnhof and Neustadt train stations (€5.80, 40 minutes). For the Erlebniswelt, get off at Meissen-Triebischtal.

Steam boats operated by **Sächsische Dampfschiffahrt** (📞 0331-452 139; www.saechsische-dampfschiffahrt.de; one-way/return €14/19.50; ⏰ May-Sep) depart from the Terrassenufer in Dresden.

town cost €2, a day pass €5. Buy tickets from vending machines at stops or aboard trams. Trams 3, 7, 8 and 9 provide good links between the Hauptbahnhof, Altstadt and Neustadt.

WEIMAR & THURINGIA

Weimar

📞 03643 / POP 65,500

Neither a monumental town nor a medieval one, Weimar appeals to those whose tastes run to cultural and intellectual pleasures. Over the centuries, it has been home to an entire pantheon of intellectual and creative giants, including Goethe, Schiller, Cranach, Bach, Herder, Liszt and Nietzsche.

In the 20th century, Weimar won international name recognition as the place where the constitution of the Weimar Republic was drafted after WWI, though there are few reminders of this historical moment. Around the same time, Walter Gropius and other progressive architects founded the seminal Bauhaus design movement in

town. The ghostly ruins of the nearby Buchenwald concentration camp, on the other hand, provide haunting evidence of the Nazi terror.

◉ Sights

Goethe Haus & Nationalmuseum   Museum
(Frauenplan 1; combined ticket Goethe Haus & museum adult/concession €10.50/8.50, permanent museum exhibition only adult/concession €6.50/5.50; ⏰ 9am-6pm Tue-Fri & Sun, to 7pm Sat) No other individual is as closely associated with Weimar as Johann Wolfgang von Goethe, who lived in this town from 1775 until his death in 1832, the last 50 years in what is now the **Goethe Haus**. His study and the bedroom where he died are both preserved in their original state. To get the most from your visit, use the audioguide (free). Visitors numbers are limited and tickets timed.

Schiller Haus   Museum
(Schillerstrasse 12; adult/concession €5/4; ⏰ 9am-6pm Tue-Fri & Sun, to 7pm Sat) Dramatist (and Goethe friend) Friedrich von Schiller lived in Weimar from 1799 until his

early death in 1805. Study up on the man, his family and life before plunging on to the private quarters, including the study with his deathbed and the desk where he wrote *Wilhelm Tell* and other famous works.

Park an der Ilm
Park

This sprawling park, just east of the Altstadt, is as inspiring and romantic now as it was in Goethe's time. **Goethes Gartenhaus** (Goethe's Garden House; Park an der Ilm; adult/concession €4.50/3.50; ⏰10am-6pm Wed-Mon), where the writer lived from 1776 to 1782, is a highlight. A few decades later, the composer Franz Liszt resided – and wrote the *Faust Symphony* – in what is now the **Liszt-Haus** (Liszt House; Marienstrasse 17; adult/concession 16 €4/3; ⏰10am-6pm Tue-Sun Apr-Sep, to 4pm Sat & Sun Oct-Mar).

Bauhaus Museum
Museum

(www.das-bauhaus-kommt.de; Theaterplatz; adult/concession €4.50/3.50; ⏰10am-6pm) Considering that Weimar is the birthplace of the influential Bauhaus school, this museum is a rather modest affair. Plans are to move to newer, larger premises, so check the situation again from 2013.

🛏 Sleeping

Hotel Amalienhof
Hotel €€

(☎5490; www.amalienhof-weimar.de; Amalienstrasse 2; s €67-75, d €97-105, ste €115-130; P🛜) The charms of this hotel are manifold: classy antique furnishings, richly styled rooms that point to history without burying you in it, and a late breakfast buffet for those who take their holidays seriously.

Hotel Elephant Weimar
Luxury Hotel €€€

(☎8020; www.luxurycollection.com/elephant; Markt 19; r €109-221, ste €291; P@🛜) The moment you enter this charmer's elegant art deco lobby, you sense that it's luxury all the way to the top. For over 300 years, this classic has wooed statesmen, artists, scholars and the merely rich with first-class service and amenities.

✖ Eating

Jo Hanns
German €€

(☎493 617; Scherfgasse 1; mains €11.50-17.50; ⏰11am-midnight) The food is satisfying but it's the 130 local wines that give Jo Hanns a leg up on the competition. No matter

Buchenwald

The Buchenwald concentration camp **museum and memorial** (☎03643-4300; www.buchenwald.de; Ettersberg; ⏰buildings & exhibits 10am-6pm Tue-Sun Apr-Oct, to 4pm Tue-Sun Nov-Mar, grounds open until sunset) FREE are 10km northwest of Weimar. Between 1937 and 1945, more than one-fifth of the 250,000 people incarcerated here died, among them such prominent German communists and social democrats as Ernst Thälmann and Rudolf Breitscheid. After 1943, prisoners were exploited in the production of weapons. Shortly before the end of the war, some 28,000 prisoners were sent on death marches. After the war, the Soviet victors established Special Camp No 2, in which 7000 so-called anticommunists and ex-Nazis were literally worked to death.

Pamphlets and books in English are sold at the bookshop, where you can also rent an excellent multilanguage audioguide (€3 or €5 with images).

From Weimar, take bus 6 (direction Buchenwald) from Goetheplatz. By car, head north on Ettersburger Strasse from Weimar train station and turn left onto Blutstrasse.

HANS-PETER MERTEN/GETTY IMAGES ©

whether you order the classic steak, roast lamb or scallops and shrimp with mint-lime spaghetti, there's a bottle to suit.

ACC
German €

(www.acc-cafe.de; Burgplatz 1; dishes €5-10; ⏰11-1am; 📶) Goethe's first pad upon arriving in Weimar is now an alt-vibe, artsy hang-out, where the food and wine are organic whenever possible and the upstairs gallery delivers a primer on the local art scene.

Residenz-Café
International €€

(Grüner Markt 4; mains €5-18; ⏰8am-1am; 📶) Everyone should find something to their taste at the 'Resi', one of Weimar's enduring favourites, no matter if it's time for breakfast, lunch, cake or dinner.

❶ Information

Tourist office (📞7450; www.weimar.de; Markt 10; ⏰9.30am-7pm Mon-Sat, to 3pm Sun)

❶ Getting There & Away

Weimar's Hauptbahnhof is a 20-minute walk from the centre. Frequent connections include Erfurt (€8, 15 minutes), Eisenach (€14.40, one hour),

Leipzig (€22, 1¼ hours), Dresden (€43, 2½ hours) and Berlin-Hauptbahnhof (€54, 2¼ hours).

BAVARIA

From the cloud-shredding Alps to the fertile Danube plain, Bavaria is a place that keeps its clichéd promises. Story-book castles bequeathed by an oddball king poke through dark forest, cowbells tinkle in flower-filled meadows, the thwack of palm on lederhosen accompanies the clump of frothy stein on timber benches, and medieval walled towns go about their time-warped business.

Munich

📞089 / POP 1.38 MILLION

Munich is a flourishing success story that revels in its own contradictions. It's the natural habitat of wellheeled power dressers and lederhosen-clad thigh-slappers, Mediterranean-style street cafes and olde-worlde beer halls, high-brow art and high-tech industry. If you're looking for Alpine clichés, they're all here, but the Bavarian capital also has plenty of unexpected cards down its Dirndl.

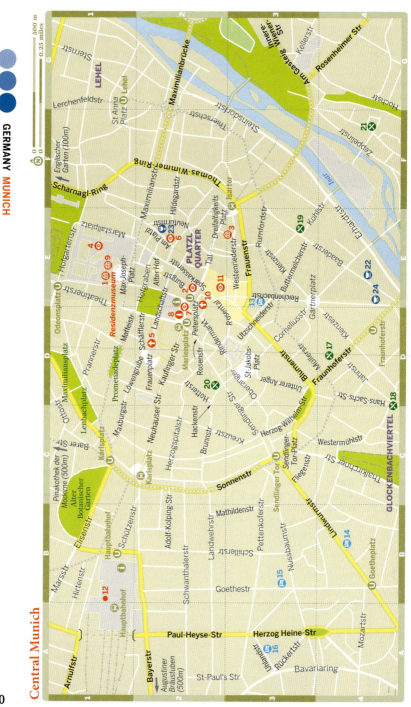

Central Munich

Central Munich

◎ **Don't Miss Sights**
 1 Residenzmuseum...................................E1

◎ **Sights**
 2 Altes Rathaus...E2
 3 Bier & Oktoberfestmuseum.................E3
 4 Cuvilliés-Theater..................................E1
 5 Frauenkirche...D2
   Glockenspiel.................................(see 7)
 6 Hofbräuhaus..E2
 7 Marienplatz...D2
 8 Neues Rathaus Tower..........................D2
 9 Schatzkammer der Residenz...............E1
   Spielzeugmuseum.........................(see 2)
10 St Peterskirche.....................................E2
11 Viktualienmarkt....................................E2

◎ **Activities, Courses & Tours**
12 Radius Tours..B1

◎ **Sleeping**
13 Hotel am Viktualienmarkt...................E3
14 Hotel Cocoon..B4
15 Hotel Mariandl......................................B3
16 Hotel Uhland...A3

◎ **Eating**
17 Fraunhofer...D4
18 Götterspeise..D4
19 Königsquelle..E3
20 Prinz Myshkin..D2
21 Wirtshaus in der Au..............................F4

◎ **Drinking & Nightlife**
22 Baader Café..E4
23 Hofbräuhaus..E2
24 Trachtenvogl...E4

◎ Sights

ALTSTADT

Marienplatz   Square
(Ⓢ Marienplatz) The heart and soul of the Altstadt, Marienplatz is a popular gathering spot and packs a lot of personality into its relatively small frame.

The square is dominated by the heavily ornamented neo-Gothic **Neues Rathaus** (New Town Hall) whose highlight is the endearing **Glockenspiel** (carillon) whose 43 bells and 32 figures perform two actual historic events. For pinpointing Munich's landmarks without losing your breath, catch the lift up the 85m-tall **tower** (Neues Rathaus; adult/child €2/€1; ⏱9am-7pm Mon-Fri, 10am-7pm Sat & Sun).

Altes Rathaus   Historic Building
(Old Town Hall; Marienplatz; Ⓢ Marienplatz Ⓡ Marienplatz) The eastern side of Marienplatz is dominated by the Altes Rathaus (Old Town Hall). On 9 November 1938 Joseph Goebbels gave a hate-filled speech here that launched the nationwide *Kristallnacht* pogroms. Today it houses the adorable **Spielzeugmuseum** (Toy Museum; www.toymuseum.de; Marienplatz 15; adult/child €4/1; ⏱10am-5.30pm) with its huge collection of rare and precious toys from Europe and the US.

St Peterskirche   Church
(Church of St Peter; Rindermarkt 1; church admission free, tower adult/child €1.50/1; ⏱tower 9am-5.30pm Mon-Fri, from 10am Sat & Sun; Ⓢ Marienplatz Ⓡ Marienplatz) Some 306 steps divide you from the best view of central Munich from the 92m tower of St Peterskirche, Munich's oldest church (1150).

Viktualienmarkt   Market
(⏱Mon-Fri & Sat morning; Ⓢ Marienplatz Ⓡ Marienplatz) Viktualienmarkt is a feast of flavours and one of Germany's finest gourmet markets where many of the stalls have been run by generations of the same family.

Hofbräuhaus   Beer Hall
(www.hofbraeuhaus.de; Am Platzl 9 ; Ⓢ Marienplatz, Ⓡ Marienplatz) **FREE** Even teetotalling cliche-haters will at some point gravitate, out of simple curiosity, to the Hofbräuhaus, the world's most celebrated beer hall.

Frauenkirche   Church
(Church of Our Lady; Frauenplatz 1; tower €2; ⏱7am-7pm Sat-Wed, to 8.30pm Thu, to 6pm Fri) This 15th-century church is Munich's spiritual heart. No other building in the central city may stand taller than the 99m of its onion-domed twin towers. From April to October, you can enjoy panoramic city views from the **south tower**.

Bier & Oktoberfestmuseum   Museum

(Beer & Oktoberfest Museum; www.bier-und-okto-berfestmuseum.de; Sterneckerstrasse 2; adult/concession €4/2.50; ⏰1-5pm Tue-Sat; 🚇Isartor 🚉Isartor) If you can't be in town for the real thing, head to this popular museum to learn all about Bavarian suds and the world's most famous booze-up.

MAXVORSTADT, SCHWABING & ENGLISCHER GARTEN

Alte Pinakothek   Art Museum

(www.pinakothek.de; Barer Strasse 27; adult/child €7/5, Sun €1, audioguide €4.50; ⏰10am-8pm Tue, to 6pm Wed-Sun; 🚇Pinakotheken 🚉Pina-kotheken) Munich's main repository of Old European Masters is crammed with all the major players that decorated canvases between the 14th and 18th centuries.

The collection is world famous for its exceptional quality and depth, especially when it comes to German masters such as Lucas Cranach the Elder and Albrecht Dürer. Rubens fans also have reason to rejoice thanks, in part, to the 6m-high *Last Judgment* in its custom-designed hall. The Italians are represented by Botticelli, Rafael, Titian and many others, while the Spaniards field such heavy hitters as El Greco, Murillo and Velázquez.

Neue Pinakothek   Art Museum

(www.pinakothek.de; Barer Strasse 29; adult/child €7/5, Sun €1; ⏰10am-6pm Thu-Mon, to 8pm Wed; 🚇Pinakotheken 🚉Pinakotheken) Picking up where the Alte Pinakothek leaves off, the Neue Pinakothek harbours a well-respected collection of 19th- and early 20-century paintings and sculpture, from rococo to Jugendstil (art nouveau).

All the main household names get wall space here, including crowd-pleasing French impressionists such as Monet, Cézanne, Degas and Van Gogh. Memorable canvases also include the brooding landscapes of German Romantic painter Caspar David Friedrich and those of local artists Carl Spitzweg and Franz Lenbach.

Pinakothek der Moderne   Art Museum

(www.pinakothek.de; Barer Strasse 40; adult/child €10/7, Sun €1; ⏰10am-6pm Tue, Wed & Fri-Sun, 10am-8pm Thu; 🚇Pinakotheken 🚉Pinako-theken) This vast modern art museum has a spectacular four-storey interior centred on an eye-like dome that spreads soft natural light throughout white galleries.

The museum unites four significant collections under a single roof, most notably the **State Gallery of Modern Art**, which showcases exemplary modern classics by Picasso, Klee, Dalí, Kandinsky and more recent big shots like Andy Warhol, Cy Twombly and Joseph Beuys.

Englischer Garten   Park

(🚇Universität) The sprawling English Garden is among Europe's biggest city parks – bigger than even London's Hyde Park and New York's Central Park – and a favourite playground for locals and visitors alike.

🏃 Tours

Radius Tours   Guided Tour

(📞543 487 7720; www.radiustours.com; opposite track 32, Hauptbahnhof; ⏰8.30am-6pm Apr-Oct, to 2pm Nov-Mar) Entertaining and informative English-language tours include the two-hour pay-what-you-like **Priceless Munich Walk** (⏰10am daily); the fascinating 2½-hour **Hitler & The Third Reich Tour** (adult/student €12/10; ⏰3pm Apr–mid-Oct, 11.30am Fri-Tue mid-Oct–Mar); and the three-hour **Prost! Beer & Food tour** (adult/student €29/27; ⏰6pm selected days). The company also runs popular excursions to Neuschwanstein, Salzburg and Dachau as well as a range of other themed tours.

✹ Festivals & Events

Hordes come to Munich for **Oktoberfest** (www.oktoberfest.de), running the 15 days before the first Sunday in October. The action takes place at the Theresienwiese grounds, about a 10-minute walk southwest of the Hauptbahnhof. While there is

ALTRENDO TRAVEL/GETTY IMAGES ©

⭐ Don't Miss
Residenz

The Residenz is a suitably grand palace that reflects the splendour and power of the Bavarian rulers who lived here from 1385 to 1918. Taking up half the compound is the treasure-packed **Residenzmuseum** (☎ 290 671; www.residenz-muenchen.de; adult/child €7/ free, combination ticket for the museum, Schatzkammer and Cuvilliés-Theater €13/free; ⏱ 9am-6pm Apr–mid-Oct, 10am-5pm mid-Oct–Mar). Start at the **Grottenhof** (Grotto Court), home of the wonderful **Perseusbrunnen** (Perseus Fountain), with its namesake holding the dripping head of Medusa. Next door is the famous **Antiquarium**, a barrel-vaulted hall smothered in frescoes and built to house the Wittelsbach's enormous antique collection. It's widely regarded as the finest Renaissance interior north of the Alps.

Upstairs are the **Kurfürstenzimmer** (Electors Rooms), with some stunning Italian portraits and a passage lined with two dozen views of Italy. Also up here are François Cuvilliés' **Reiche Zimmer** (Rich Rooms), a six-room extravaganza of exuberant rococo. More rococo magic awaits in the **Ahnengallery** (Ancestors Gallery), a chronological roll call of 121 portraits of Bavarian rulers. The superb rococo **Steinzimmer** (Stone Rooms) are awash in intricately patterned and coloured marble.

The Residenzmuseum entrance also leads to the **Schatzkammer der Residenz** (Residence Treasury; adult/concession/under 18yr with parents €7/6/free; ⏱ 9am-6pm Apr–mid-Oct, 10am-5pm mid-Oct–Mar), a veritable banker's bonus worth of jewel-encrusted bling of yesteryear, from golden toothpicks to finely crafted swords, miniatures in ivory to gold entombed cosmetics trunks.

Another highlight is the **Cuvilliés-Theater** (adult/child €3.50/free; ⏱ 2-6pm Mon-Sat, from 9am Sun Apr-Jul & mid-Sep–mid-Oct, 9am-6pm daily Aug–mid-Sep, shorter hours mid-Oct– Mar), named for its architect and one of Europe's finest rococo theatres.

no entrance fee, those €9 1L steins of beer (called *Mass*) add up fast. Although its origins are in the marriage celebrations of Crown Prince Ludwig in 1810, there's nothing regal about this beery bacchanalia now: expect mobs, expect to meet new and drunken friends, expect decorum to vanish as night sets in and you'll have a blast.

🛏 Sleeping

Munich has no shortage of places to stay – except during Oktoberfest or some busy summer periods, when the wise (meaning those with a room) will have booked.

Hotel Cocoon   Design Hotel €€
(☎5999 3907; www.hotel-cocoon.de; Lindwurmstrasse 35; s/d €79/99; Ⓢ Sendlinger Tor Ⓜ Sendlinger Tor) If retro-design is your thing, you just struck gold. Things kick off in the reception with its faux '70s veneer and suspended '60s ball chairs, and continue in the rooms, all identical and decorated in cool retro oranges and greens.

Hotel am Viktualienmarkt   Hotel €€
(☎231 1090; www.hotel-am-viktualienmarkt. de; Utzschneiderstrasse 14; d €50-120; 🛜; Ⓢ Marienplatz Ⓜ Marienplatz) Owners Elke and her daughter Stephanie run this good-value property with panache and a sunny attitude. The best of the up-to-date 26 rooms have wooden floors and framed poster art. All this, plus the city centre location, makes it a superb deal.

La Maison   Design Hotel €€
(☎3303 5550; www.hotel-la-maison.com; Occamstrasse 24; s/d from €109/119; 🅿 ➖ ❄ @; Ⓢ Münchner Freiheit) Discerningly retro, this sassy number flaunts heated oak floors, jet-black basins and starkly contrasting design throughout. Cool bar on ground level.

Hotel Mariandl   Hotel €€
(☎552 9100; www.mariandl.com; Goethestrasse 51; s €65-115, d €70-165; Ⓢ Sendlinger Tor Ⓜ Sendlinger Tor) If you like your history

laced with quirkiness, you'll find both aplenty in this rambling neo-Gothic mansion where rooms ooze *Jugendstil* flair with hand-selected antiques and ornamented ceilings. Breakfast is served until 4pm in the Vienna-style downstairs cafe, which also has live jazz or classical music nightly.

Hotel Uhland   Hotel €€
(☎543 350; www.hotel-uhland.de; Uhlandstrasse 1; s/d from €69/87; 🅿 🛜; Ⓢ Theresienwiese) The Uhland is an enduring favourite with regulars who expect their hotel to feel like a home away from home. Three generations of family members are constantly finding ways to improve their guests' experience, be it with wi-fi, bathroom phones, ice cubes, bike rentals or mix-your-own organic breakfast muesli.

✖ Eating

Fraunhofer   Bavarian €€
(Fraunhoferstrasse 9; mains €7-17.50; ⏱4pm-1am; ✎; Ⓜ Müllerstrasse) With its screechy parquet floors, stuccoed ceilings, wood panelling and virtually no trace that the last century even happened, this characterful brewpub is one of the city centre's best places to explore the region with a fork.

Prinz Myshkin   Vegetarian €€
(☎265 596; www.prinzmyshkin.com; Hackenstrasse 2; mains €10-17; ⏱11am-12.30am; ✎; Ⓢ Marienplatz Ⓜ Marienplatz) Munich's premier meat-free dining spot fills out an open-plan, but strangely intimate vaulted dining space in a former brewery with health-conscious eaters.

Wirtshaus in der Au   Bavarian €€
(☎448 1400; Lilienstrasse 51; mains €8-19; ⏱5pm-midnight Mon-Fri, from 10am Sat & Sun; Ⓜ Deutsches Museum) Though this traditional Bavarian restaurant has a solid 21st-century vibe, it's that time-honoured staple the dumpling that's been declared top speciality here. When spring springs, the beer garden fills.

Königsquelle   Alpine €€

(☎220 071; Baaderplatz 2; mains €9-18;
🕐dinner; 🚇Isartor, 🚌Isartor) This Munich
institution is well loved for its attentive
service, expertly prepared food, and dark,
well-stocked hardwood bar (great selection of malt whiskeys). The handwritten,
Alpine-inflected menu hopscotches from
schnitzel to linguine and goat's cheese to
cannelloni.

Tantris   Fine Dining €€€

(☎361 9590; www.tantris.de; Johann-Fichte-
Strasse 7; menu from €75; 🕐lunch & dinner Tue-
Sat; 🅂Dietlindenstrasse) Tantris means 'the
search for perfection' and here, at one
of Germany's most famous restaurants,
they're not far off it. The interior design is
full-bodied '70s – all postbox reds, truffle
blacks and illuminated yellows – the
food gourmet sublimity and the service
sometimes as unintrusive as it is efficient.
Great wine cellar to boot.

Götterspeise   Cafe €

(Jahnstrasse 30; snacks from €3; 🕐8am-7pm
Mon-Fri, 9am-6pm Sat; 🚇Müllerstrasse) The
name of this place translates as 'food
of the gods' and the edible in question

is that most sinful of treats, chocolate.
This comes in many forms, both liquid
and solid, but there are also teas, coffees
and cakes and we love the little smokers'
perches outside for puffing chocoholics.

🍷 Drinking & Nightlife

Alter Simpl   Pub

(Türkenstrasse 57; 🕐11am-3am Mon-Fri, 11am-
4am Sat & Sun; 🚇Schellingstrasse) Thomas
Mann and Hermann Hesse used to knock
'em back at this well-scuffed and wood-
panelled thirst parlour.

Baader Café   Cafe

(Baaderstrasse 47; 🕐9.30am-1am; 🚇Fraunhof-
erstrasse) This literary think-and-drink
institution lures all sorts, from short skirts
to tweed jackets who linger over daytime
coffees and night-hour cocktails. Popular
Sunday brunch.

Trachtenvogl   Cafe, Lounge

(Reichenbachstrasse 47; 🕐10am-1am Sun-Thu,
to 2am Fri & Sat; 🚇Fraunhoferstrasse) At night
you'll have to shoehorn your way into this
buzzy lair favoured by a chatty, boozy
crowd of scenesters, artists and students.

Beer tent at Oktoberfest (p592)

Beer Halls & Beer Gardens

Beer drinking is not just an integral part of Munich's entertainment scene, it's a reason to visit. Beer halls can be vast boozy affairs seating thousands, or much more modest neighbourhood hang-outs. The same goes for beer gardens. What's common is a certain camaraderie among strangers, huge 1L glasses of beer and lots of pretzels and sausages. In beer gardens you are usually allowed to bring your own picnic as long as you sit at tables without tablecloths and order something to drink.

Here are our top choices:

Augustiner Bräustuben (Landsberger Strasse 19; 🕑10am-midnight; 🚋Holzapfelstrasse) At this authentic beer hall inside the actual Augustiner brewery, the Bavarian grub here is superb, especially the *Schweinshaxe* (pork knuckles). It's about 700m west of the Hauptbahnhof.

Hofbräuhaus (Am Platzl 9; 🕑9am-11.30pm; Ⓢ Marienplatz, 🚋Kammerspiele 🚇Marienplatz) The ultimate cliché of Munich beer halls where tourists arrive by the busload but no one seems to mind.

Hirschgarten (Hirschgartenallee 1; 🕑11am-11pm; 🚋Kriemhildenstrasse 🚇Laim) The Everest of Munich beer gardens can accommodate up to 8000 Augustiner lovers, but still manages to feel airy and uncluttered. It's in a lovely spot in a former royal hunting preserve a short walk south of Schloss Nymphenburg.

Chinesischer Turm (Chinese Tower; 🖉383 8730; Englischer Garten 3; 🕑10am-11pm; 🚇Chinesischer Turm 🚋Tivolistrasse) This one's hard to ignore because of its English Garden location and pedigree as Munich's oldest beer garden (open since 1791).

ℹ Information

Tourist office (🖉2339 6500; www.muenchen. de) There are two branches: Hauptbahnhof (Bahnhofplatz 2; 🕑9am-8pm Mon-Sat, 10am-6pm Sun) and Marienplatz (Marienplatz 8, Neues Rathaus; 🕑10am-7pm Mon-Fri, to 5pm Sat, to 2pm Sun).

City Tour Card (www.citytourcard-muenchen. com; 1/3 days €9.90/19.90) Includes public transport in the *Innenraum* (zones 1 to 4, marked white on transport maps) and discounts of between 10% and 50% for more than 50 attractions, tours, eateries and theatres. Available at some hotels, tourist offices, and U-Bahn, S-Bahn and DB vending machines.

ℹ Getting There & Away

Air

Munich airport (MUC; www.munich-airport.de), aka Flughafen Franz-Josef Strauss, is second in importance only to Frankfurt's. It's linked to the Hauptbahnhof every 20 minutes by S-Bahn (S1 and S8, €10, 40 minutes) and by the Lufthansa Airport Bus (€10.50, 45 minutes, between 5am and 8pm). Budget between €50 and €70 for a taxi ride.

Note that Ryanair flies into Memmingen's **Allgäu airport** (www.allgaeu-airport.de), 125km to the west. Seven buses daily shuttle between here and the Hauptbahnhof (€13, 1¾ hours).

Car & Motorcycle

Munich has autobahns radiating in all directions. Take the A9 to Nuremberg, the A8 to Salzburg, the A95 to Garmisch-Partenkirchen and the A8 to Ulm or Stuttgart.

Train

All services leave from the Hauptbahnhof, where **Euraide** (www.euraide.de; Desk 1, Reisezentrum, Hauptbahnhof; 🕑10am-7pm Mon-Fri Aug-Apr) is a friendly English-speaking agency that sells train tickets, makes reservations and can create personalised rail tours of Germany and beyond.

Useful connections from Munich include:

Baden-Baden (€81, five hours, hourly) Change in Mannheim.

Berlin (€121, six hours, every two hours)

Cologne (€134, 4½ hours, hourly)

Frankfurt (€95, 3¼ hours, hourly)

Nuremberg (€52, 1¼ hours, twice hourly)

Prague (€66, five hours 50 minutes, two daily)

Vienna (€85.80, 4½ hours, every two hours)

Würzburg (€67, two hours, twice hourly)

❶ Getting Around

Public Transport

Munich's efficient public transport system is run by **MVV** (www.mvv-muenchen.de) and is composed of buses, trams, the U-Bahn and the S-Bahn.

Short rides (*Kurzstrecke*; four bus or tram stops or two U-Bahn or S-Bahn stops) cost €1.20, longer trips cost €2.50. Children aged six to 14 pay a flat €1.20. Day passes are €5.60 for individuals and €10.20 for up to five people travelling together.

Bus drivers sell single tickets and day passes, but tickets for the U-/S-Bahn and other passes must be purchased from station vending machines.

Taxi

Taxis (☎216 10) are expensive and not much more convenient than public transport.

BAVARIAN ALPS

Stretching west from Germany's remote southeastern corner to the Allgäu region near Lake Constance, the Bavarian Alps (Bayerische Alpen) form a stunningly beautiful natural divide along the Austrian border.

The region is pocked with cute villages, sprightly spas and plenty of possibilities for skiing, snowboarding, hiking, canoeing and paragliding. The ski season lasts from about late December until April.

Berchtesgaden

☎08652 / POP 7600

Steeped in myth and legend, the Berchtesgadener Land is almost preternaturally beautiful. Framed by six formidable mountain ranges and home to Germany's second-highest mountain, the Watzmann (2713m), its dreamy, fir-lined valleys are filled with gurgling streams and peaceful Alpine villages.

Much of the terrain is protected as the Nationalpark Berchtesgaden, which embraces the pristine Königssee, one of Germany's most photogenic lakes. Yet, Berchtesgaden's history is also indelibly entwined with the Nazi period, as chronicled at the disturbing Dokumentation Obersalzberg. The Eagle's Nest, a mountaintop lodge built for Hitler, is now a major tourist attraction.

Königssee (p598), Berchtesgaden
FLORIAN WERNER/GETTY IMAGES ©

Sights

Königssee
Lake

Crossing the serenely picturesque, emerald-green Königssee makes for some unforgettable memories. Contained by steep mountain walls some 5km south of Berchtesgaden, it's Germany's highest lake (603m), with drinkable waters shimmering into fjordlike depths. Bus 841 makes the trip out here from the Berchtesgaden Hauptbahnhof roughly every hour.

Escape the hubbub of the bustling lakeside tourist village by taking an electric **boat tour** (www.seenschifffahrt. de; return adult/child €13.30/6.70) to **St Bartholomä**, a quaint onion-domed chapel on the western shore. At some point, the boat will stop while the captain plays a horn towards the Echo Wall – the sound will bounce seven times.

Dokumentation Obersalzberg
Museum

(www.obersalzberg.de; Salzbergstrasse 41, Obersalzberg; adult/child €3/free; ⏰9am-5pm daily Apr-Oct, 10am-3pm Tue-Sun Nov-Mar) In 1933 the quiet mountain retreat of **Obersalzberg** (3km from the town of Berchtesgaden) became the southern headquarters of Hitler's government, a dark period that's given the full historical treatment at the Dokumentation Obersalzberg. Half-hourly bus 838 runs here from Berchtesgaden Hauptbahnhof.

Eagle's Nest
Historic Site

(☎2969; www.kehlsteinhaus.de; ⏰mid-May–Oct) Berchtesgaden's most sinister draw is Mt Kehlstein (as the Eagle's Nest is known in German), a sheer-sided peak at Obersalzberg where Martin Bormann, a key henchman of Hitler's, engaged 3000 workers to build a diplomatic meeting-house for the Führer's 50th birthday. As the Allies never regarded the site worth bombing, it survived WWII untouched and today houses a restaurant that donates profits to charity.

To get there, drive or take half-hourly bus 838 from the Hauptbahnhof to the

Hotel Intercontinental. From here the road is closed to private traffic and you must take a special **bus** (adult/child €15.50/9) up the mountain (35 minutes). The final 124m stretch to the summit is aboard a snazzy brass-clad lift (elevator).

You can also experience the sinister legacy of the Obersalzberg area, including the Eagle's Nest and the underground bunker system, on a four-hour guided English-language tour run by **Eagle's Nest Tours** (☎649 71; www.eagles-nest-tours. com; Königsseer Strasse 2; adult/child €50/35; ⏰1.15pm mid-May–Oct). Reservations are advised.

Salzbergwerk
Historic Site

(www.salzzeitreise.de; Bergwerkstrasse 83; adult/child €15.50/9.50; ⏰9am-5pm May-Oct, 11am-3pm Nov-Apr) Once a major producer of 'white gold', Berchtesgaden has thrown open its salt mines for fun-filled 90-minute tours. Kids especially love donning miners' garb and whooshing down a wooden slide into the depth of the mine. Down below, highlights include mysteriously glowing salt grottoes and the crossing of a 100m-long subterranean salt lake on a wooden raft.

🛏 Sleeping & Eating

Hotel Bavaria
Hotel €€

(☎660 11; www.hotelbavaria.net; Sunklergässchen 11; r €50-130; 🅿) In the same family for over a century, this well-run hotel offers a romantic vision of Alpine life with rooms bedecked in frilly curtains, canopied beds, heart-shaped mirrors and knotty wood galore. Five of the pricier rooms have their own whirlpools. Gourmet breakfasts include sparkling wine.

Holzkäfer
Cafe, Bar €

(☎600 90; Buchenhöhe 40; dishes €4-9; ⏰11am-1am Wed-Mon) This funky log cabin in the Obersalzberg hills is a great spot for a night out with fun-loving locals. Cluttered with antlers, carvings and backwoods oddities, it's known for its tender pork roasts, dark beer and Franconian wines.

RAINER DITTRICH/GETTY IMAGES ©

★ Don't Miss
Wieskirche

Known as 'Wies' for short, the Wieskirche is one of Bavaria's best-known baroque churches and a Unesco-listed heritage site. About a million visitors a year flock to see this stuccoed wonder by the artist brothers Dominikus and Johann Baptist Zimmermann.

In 1730, a farmer in Steingaden, about 30km northeast of Füssen, claims to have witnessed the miracle of his Christ statue shedding tears. Pilgrims poured into the town in such numbers over the next decade that the local abbot commissioned a new church to house the weepy work. Inside the almost circular structure, eight snow-white pillars are topped by gold capital stones and swirling decorations. The unsupported dome must have seemed like God's work in the mid-17th century, its surface adorned with a pastel ceiling fresco celebrating Christ's resurrection.

From Füssen, regional RVO bus 73 (www.rvo-bus.de) makes the journey up to six times daily. The Europabus also stops here long enough in both directions to have a brief look round then get back on. By car, take the B17 northeast and turn right (east) at Steingaden.

NEED TO KNOW
☎ 08862-932 930; www.wieskirche.de; ⏲ 8am-5pm

❶ Information

The **tourist office** (www.berchtesgaden.de; Königsseer Strasse 2; ⏲ 8.30am-6pm Mon-Fri, to 5pm Sat, 9am-3pm Sun Apr–mid-Oct, reduced hours mid-Oct–Mar) is just across the river from the train station.

❶ Getting There & Away

Travelling from Munich by train involves a change at Freilassing (€30.90, three hours, five daily). The best option between Berchtesgaden and Salzburg is **RVO bus 840** (www.rvo-bus.de) (45 minutes) which links both towns' train stations twice hourly.

Below: Augsburg's town hall; **Right:** Eagle's Nest (p598), Berchtesgaden
(BELOW) JOHN FREEMAN/GETTY IMAGES ©; (RIGHT) SCOTT KEMPER/ALAMY ©

Berchtesgaden is south of the Munich–Salzburg A8 autobahn.

Romantic Road

From the vineyards of Würzburg to the foot of the Alps, the almost 400km-long Romantic Road (Romantische Strasse) draws two million visitors every year, making it by far the most popular of Germany's holiday routes. It passes through more than two dozen cities and towns, including Rothenburg ob der Tauber, Dinkelsbühl and Augsburg. Expect tourist coaches and kitsch galore, but also a fair wedge of *Gemütlichkeit* and genuine hospitality.

ℹ️ Getting There & Around

The ideal way to travel is by car, though Deutsche Touring's **Europabus** (☎0719-126 268, 0171-653 234; www.touring-travel.eu) is an alternative. From April to October the special coach runs daily in each direction between Frankfurt and Füssen (for Neuschwanstein); the entire journey takes around 12 hours. There's no charge for breaking the journey and continuing the next day.

AUGSBURG

☎0821 / POP 264,700

The largest city on the Romantic Road, Augsburg is also one of Germany's oldest, founded over 2000 years ago by the step-children of Roman emperor Augustus. Today it's a lively provincial city, criss-crossed by little streams and imbued with an appealing ambience and vitality.

◎ Sights

Look for the very impressive onion-shaped towers on the 17th-century **Rathaus** and the adjacent **Perlachturm**, a former guard tower. North of here is the 10th-century **Dom Maria Heimsuchung** (Hoher Weg; ⏰7am-6pm), which has more 'modern' additions, such as the 14th-

century doors showing scenes from the Old Testament.

The Fuggers – a 16th-century banking family – left their mark everywhere. They have lavish tombs inside **St Anna Kirche** (Im Annahof 2, off Annastrasse; ⏰10am-12.30pm & 3-6pm Tue-Sat, 10am-12.30pm & 3-4pm Sun), a place also known for being a Martin Luther bolt-hole. The 16th-century **Fuggerei** (www.fugger.de; Jakober Strasse; adult/concession €4/3; ⏰8am-8pm Apr-Sep, 9am-6pm Oct-Mar) was built with banking riches to house the poor, which, remarkably, it still does. The excellent **museum** (Mittlere Gasse 14; free with Fuggerei admission) shows how they lived.

🛏 Sleeping & Eating

Hotel am Rathaus   Hotel €€
(📞346 490; www.hotel-am-rathaus-augsburg.de; Am Hinteren Perlachberg 1; s €79-98, d €98-125; 📶) Just steps from Rathausplatz and Maximilianstrasse, this super-central boutique hotel hires out 31 rooms with freshly neutral decor and a sunny little breakfast room.

Bauerntanz   German €€
(Bauerntanzgässchen 1; mains €7-16; ⏰11am-11.30pm) Belly-satisfying helpings of creative Swabian and Bavarian food (*spätzle*, veal medallions and more *spätzle*) are plated up by friendly staff at this prim Alpine tavern with lace curtains, hefty timber interior and chequered fabrics.

ℹ Getting There & Away

Trains between Munich and Augsburg are frequent (€12 to €20, 40 minutes); it's on the main line to Frankfurt. The Romantic Road bus stops at the train station and the Rathaus.

ROTHENBURG OB DER TAUBER
📞09861 / POP 11,000

In the Middle Ages, Rothenburg's town fathers built strong walls to protect the town from siege; today they are the reason the town is under siege from tourists. The most stereotypical of all German walled towns, Rothenburg can't help

Neuschwanstein & Hohenschwangau Castles

In the foothills of the Alps, the town of Füssen itself is often overlooked by the mobs swarming to Schloss Neuschwanstein and Hohenschwangau, the two fantasy castles associated with King Ludwig II.

Schloss Neuschwanstein (📞930 830; www.hohenschwangau.de; adult/concession €12/11, with Hohenschwangau €23/21; 🕐8am-5pm Apr-Sep, 9am-3pm Oct-Mar) Appearing through the mountaintops like a misty mirage is the world's most famous castle, and the model for Disney's citadel, fairy-tale Schloss Neuschwanstein.

Ludwig foresaw his showpiece palace as a giant stage on which to recreate the world of Germanic mythology in the operatic works of Richard Wagner. At its centre is the lavish **Sängersaal** (Minstrels' Hall), created to feed the king's obsession with Wagner and medieval knights.

Other completed sections include Ludwig's *Tristan and Isolde*–themed **bedroom**, dominated by a huge Gothic-style bed crowned with intricately carved cathedral-like spires; a gaudy artificial grotto (another allusion to *Tannhäuser*); and the Byzantine **Thronsaal** (Throne Room) with an incredible mosaic floor containing over two million stones.

Schloss Hohenschwangau (📞930 830; www.hohenschwangau.de; adult/concession €12/11, with Neuschwanstein €23/21; 🕐8am-5.30pm Apr-Sep, 9am-3.30pm Oct-Mar) Ludwig spent his formative years at the sun-yellow Schloss Hohenschwangau. Far less showy than Neuschwanstein, Hohenschwangau has a distinctly lived-in feel and every piece of furniture is original. Some rooms have frescos from German history and legend (including the story of the Swan Knight, *Lohengrin*).

Both Neuschwanstein and Hohenschwangau must be seen on guided tours (in German or English), which last about 35 minutes each. Timed tickets are only available from the Ticket Centre at the foot of the castles. In summer, come as early as 8am to ensure you get in that day.

Trains from/to Munich (€24, two hours) run every two hours. RVO buses 78 and 73 serve the castles from Füssen Bahnhof (€4 return).

---

being so cute. Granted 'free imperial city' status in 1274, it's a confection of twisting cobbled lanes and pretty architecture enclosed by towered stone walls. Swarmed during the day, the underlying charm oozes out after the last bus leaves.

🎯 Sights

Jakobskirche   Church
(Klingengasse 1; adult/child €2/0.50; 🕐9am-5pm) Rothenburg's most famous church sports wonderful stained-glass windows, but its real pièce de résistance is the **Heilig Blut Altar** (Sacred Blood Altar) carved with dizzying intricacy by medieval master Tilmann Riemenschneider.

Rathaus   Historic Building
(Marktplatz; Rathausturm adult/concession €2/0.50; 🕐tower 9.30am-12.30pm & 1-5pm daily Apr-Oct, noon-3pm daily Dec, shorter hours Sat & Sun Nov & Jan-Mar) The highlight of Rothenburg's Renaissance town hall is the widescreen views of the city and surrounds from the tower's viewing platform (220 steps).

🛏 Sleeping & Eating

Burg-Hotel   Hotel €€
(📞948 90; www.burghotel.eu; Klostergasse 1-3; s €100-135, d €100-170; P ❀ 🛜) Each of the 15 elegantly furnished guest rooms at this boutique hotel built into the town

walls has its own private sitting area. The lower floors shelter a decadent spa while phenomenal valley views unfurl from the breakfast room and stone terrace.

Altfränkische Weinstube   Hotel €
(📞6404; www.altfraenkische-weinstube-rothenburg.de; Klosterhof 7; r €59-89; 📶) In a quiet side street, this characterful inn has six atmosphere-laden rooms, most with four-poster or canopied beds. The restaurant (dinner only) serves up sound regional fare.

Zur Höll   German €€
(📞4229; Burggasse 8; mains €6.50-18; ⊙dinner) This medieval wine tavern, with an appreciation for slow food, is in the town's oldest original building, dating back to the year 900. There's a small regional menu and some excellent wines from nearby Würzburg.

ⓘ Getting There & Away

There are hourly trains to/from Steinach, a transfer point for service to Würzburg (€12.20, 1¼ hours). The Europabus pauses here for 35 minutes.

WÜRZBURG
📞0931 / POP 133,500

Tucked in among river valleys lined with vineyards, Würzburg beguiles even before you reach the city centre and is renowned for its art, architecture and delicate wines. For centuries the resident prince-bishops wielded enormous power and wealth, and the city grew in opulence under their rule. Its crowning glory is the Residenz, one of the finest baroque structures in Germany and a Unesco World Heritage site.

◎ Sights

Residenz   Palace
(www.residenz-wuerzburg.de; Balthasar-Neumann-Promenade; adult/child €7.50/6.50; ⊙9am-6pm Apr-Oct, 10am-4.30pm Nov-Mar) The Unesco-listed Residenz is one of Germany's most important and beautiful baroque palaces. Its undisputed highlight is the **Grand Staircase** designed by Balthasar Neumann, a single set of steps that splits and zigzags up to the 1st floor and is lidded by a humongous Tiepolo fresco (667 sq metres).

Schloss Neuschwanstein, Füssen

REINHARD DIRSCHERL/GETTY IMAGES ©

Visits are by guided tour only and also take in the **Weisser Saal** (White Hall) with its ice-white stucco, the **Kaisersaal** (Imperial Hall) canopied by yet another impressive fresco by Tiepolo and the gilded stucco **Spiegelkabinett** (Mirror Hall). German-language groups leave half-hourly; English tours leave at 11pm and 3pm year-round and, additionally, at 4.30pm April to October.

Festung Marienberg   Fortress

Panoramic views over the city's red rooftops and vine-covered hills extend from Marienberg Fortress. It has presided over Würzburg since the city's prince-bishops commenced its construction in 1201; they governed from here until 1719.

The fortress is a 30-minute walk up the hill from the Alte Mainbrücke via the **Tellsteige trail**, which is part of the 4km-long **Weinwanderweg** (wine hiking trail) through the vineyards around Marienberg.

🛏 Sleeping & Eating

Hotel Rebstock   Hotel €€

(☎309 30; www.rebstock.com; Neubaustrasse 7; s/d from €101/120; ❄@🖤) Don't be misled

by the Best Western sign out front: Würzburg's top digs, in a squarely renovated rococo townhouse, has 70 unique, stylishly finished rooms, impeccable service and an Altstadt location.

Bürgerspital Weinstube   Wine Restaurant €€

(☎352 880; Theaterstrasse 19; mains €7-23; 🕑lunch & dinner) The cosy nooks of this labyrinthine medieval place are among Würzburg's most popular eating and drinking spots. Choose from a broad selection of Franconian wines and wonderful regional dishes, including *Mostsuppe*, a tasty wine soup.

Alte Mainmühle   Franconian €€

(☎167 77; Mainkai 1; mains €7-21; 🕑10am-midnight) Accessed straight from the old bridge, tourists and locals alike cram onto the double-decker terrace suspended above the Main River to savour modern twists on old Franconian favourites.

ℹ Getting There & Away

Train connections from Würzburg:

Bamberg (€19, one hour, twice hourly)

Frankfurt (€33, one hour, hourly)

Nuremberg (€19.20 to €27, one hour, twice hourly)

Rothenburg ob der Tauber (€12.20, one hour, hourly) Change in Steinach.

Nuremberg

🌐 0911 / POP 503,000

Nuremberg (Nürnberg) woos visitors with its wonderfully restored medieval Altstadt, its grand castle and, in December, its magical *Christkindlmarkt* (Christmas market).

Nuremberg played a major role during the Nazi years. It was here that the fanatical party rallies were held, the boycott of Jewish businesses began and the infamous Nuremberg Laws outlawing Jewish citizenship were enacted. After WWII the city was chosen as the site of the War Crimes Tribunal, now known as the Nuremberg Trials.

⊙ Sights

Hauptmarkt   Square

This bustling square in the heart of the Altstadt is the site of daily markets as well as the famous *Christkindles-markt*. At the eastern end is the ornate Gothic **Pfarrkirche Unsere Liebe Frau** (Hauptmarkt 14), also known as the Frauenkirche. Daily at noon crowds crane their necks to witness the clock's figure enact a spectacle called *Männleinlaufen*. Rising from the square like a Gothic spire is the gargoyle-adorned, 19m-tall **Schöner Brunnen** (Beautiful Fountain). Touch the seamless golden ring in the ornate wrought-iron gate for good luck.

Kaiserburg   Castle

(www.schloesser.bayern.de; adult/child incl museum €7/6; ⊙ 9am-6pm Apr-Sep, 10am-4pm Oct-Mar) Construction of Nuremberg's landmark, the immensely proportioned Kaiserburg, began in the 12th century and dragged on for about 400 years. The complex, for centuries the receptacle of the Holy Roman Empire's treasures, consists of three parts: the Kaiserburg

♥ If You Like… German Castles

The twin castles of Neuschwanstein (p602) and Hohenschwangau (p602) are undoubtedly the most famous *Schlösser* (castles) in Germany, but they're certainly not the only ones to explore.

1 SCHLOSS NYMPHENBURG
(www.schloss-nymphenburg.de; adult/child €6/5; ⊙ 9am-6pm Apr-mid-Oct, 10am-4pm mid-Oct-Mar; 🚋 Schloss Nymphenburg) Just 5km from Munich's Altstadt, this lavish palace was begun in 1664 as a villa for Electress Adelaide of Savoy, and later extended to create the royal family's summer residence. Take tram 17 from the Hauptbahnhof.

2 SCHLOSS SCHWERIN
(🖀 525 2920; www.schloss-schwerin.de; adult/child €4/2.50; ⊙ 10am-6pm mid-Apr-mid-Oct, 10am-5pm Tue-Sun mid-Oct-mid-Apr) Gothic turrets, onion domes and Ottoman architecture are among the mishmash of styles that make up Schwerin's *Schloss*. See the collection of Meissen porcelain, and fine stained glass in the **Schlosskirche**. Train links include Hamburg and Berlin.

3 SCHLOSS HEIDELBERG
(www.schloss-heidelberg.de; adult/child incl Bergbahn €5/3, audioguide €4; ⊙ 24hr, ticket required 8am-5.30pm) Rising above the Altstadt like a picture-book pop-up, Heidelberg's ruined *Schloss* has seen the lot, from marauding invaders to lightning strikes. The 19th-century **Bergbahn** (Funicular Railway; www.bergbahn-heidelberg.de; ⊙ every 10min 9am-about 5pm) creeps up the hill to the castle from the Kornmarkt station. There are hourly trains to/from Frankfurt and Stuttgart.

4 WARTBURG
(www.wartburg-eisenach.de; tour adult/concession €9/5, museum & Luther study only €5/4; ⊙ tours 8.30am-5pm, in English 1.30pm) When it comes to medieval castles, the Wartburg is the mother lode. Parts of the building date back to the 11th century, but its fame is due to the Protestant reformer Martin Luther, who went into hiding here in 1521 after being excommunicated. Regional trains run to Erfurt.

and Stadtburg (the Emperor's Palace and City Fortress) and the Burggrafenburg (Count's Residence), which was largely destroyed in 1420.

Enjoy panoramic city views from atop the **Sinwellturm** (Sinwell Tower; 113 steps) or peer into the amazing 48m-deep **Tiefer Brunnen** (Deep Well).

Memorium Nuremberg Trials   Historic Building
(☏3217 9372; www.memorium-nuremberg.de; Bärenschanzstrasse 72; adult/concession €5/3; ☺10am-6pm Wed-Mon) Nazis were tried in 1945 to 1946 for crimes against peace and humanity in Schwurgerichtssaal 600 (Court Room 600) of what is still Nuremberg's regional courthouse.

In addition to viewing the courtroom (if not in use), a new exhibition provides comprehensive background on the trials. The courthouse is about 2km from the Altstadt centre. To get here, take the U1 towards Bärenschanze and get off at 'Sielstrasse'.

Reichsparteitagsgelände
Historic Site
(Luitpoldhain) If you've ever wondered where the infamous black-and-white im-

Christmas Markets

Beginning in late November every year, central squares across Germany are transformed into Christmas markets or *Christkindlmärkte* (also known as *Weihnachtsmärkte*). Folks stamp about between the wooden stalls, perusing seasonal trinkets (from hand-carved ornaments to plastic angels) while warming themselves with *Glühwein* (mulled, spiced red wine) and grilled sausages. Locals love 'em and, not surprisingly, the markets are popular with tourists, so bundle up and carouse for hours. Markets in Nuremberg, Dresden, Cologne and Munich are especially famous.

ages of ecstatic Nazi supporters hailing their Führer were filmed, it was here in Nuremberg. Much of the outsize grounds was destroyed during Allied bombing raids, but 4 sq km remain, enough to get a sense of the megalomania behind it.

Take tram 9 from the Hauptbahnhof to 'Doku-Zentrum'.

Germanisches Nationalmuseum   Museum
(www.gnm.de; Kartäusergasse 1; adult/child €6/4; ☺10am-6pm Tue & Thu-Sun, to 9pm Wed) Spanning prehistory to the early 20th century, the German National Museum is the country's most important museum of German culture. It features paintings and sculptures, an archaeological collection, arms and armour, musical and scientific instruments and toys.

🛏 Sleeping

Nuremberg hosts many a trade show through the year (including a huge toy fair in February). During these times – and Christmas market weekends – rates soar like a model rocket.

Hotel Elch   Hotel €€
(☏249 2980; www.hotel-elch.com; Irrerstrasse 9; s/d from €75/95; ☎) This 14th-century, half-timbered house is a snug and romantic 12-room gem. Rooms 2 and 7 have half-timbered walls and ceilings, but modern touches include contemporary art, glazed terracotta bathrooms and rainbow-glass chandeliers. Note the multicoloured elk heads throughout (the hotel's name means 'Elk').

Art & Business Hotel   Hotel €€
(☏232 10; www.art-business-hotel.com; Gleissbühlstrasse 15; s/d €89/115; ☎) You don't have to be an artist or a business person to stay at this up-to-the-minute place near the Hauptbahnhof. From the trendy bar to slate bathrooms, design here is bold, but not overpoweringly so.

Hotel Deutscher Kaiser   Hotel €€
(☏242 660; www.deutscher-kaiser-hotel.de; Königstrasse 55; s/d from €89/108; @☎)

Christmas market in Hauptmarkt square (p605), Nuremberg

RICHARD NEBESKY/GETTY IMAGES ©

Super-central and with posh design and service, this treat of a historic hotel has been in the same family for over a century. Climb the castle-like granite stairs to find rooms of understated simplicity, flaunting oversize beds, Italian porcelain, silk lampshades and period furniture. Renovation work is ongoing.

🍴 Eating

Don't leave Nuremberg without trying its famous *Nürnberger Bratwürste*. Order 'em by the half dozen with *Meerrettich* (horseradish) on the side.

Bratwursthäusle   German €€

(http://die-nuernberger-bratwurst.de; Rathausplatz 2; meals €6-14; ⊙closed Sun) Seared over a flaming beech-wood grill, the little links sold at this rustic inn arguably set the standards for grilled sausages across the land. You can dine in the timbered restaurant or on the terrace with views of the Hauptmarkt.

Goldenes Posthorn   Franconian €€

(☎225 153; Glöckleinsgasse 2, cnr Sebalder Platz; mains €6-19; ⊙11am-11pm; 🔊) Push

open the heavy copper door to find a real culinary treat that has been serving the folk of Nuremberg since 1498. The miniature local sausages are big here, but there's plenty else on the menu including many an obscure country dish and some vegie options.

Hütt'n   German €€

(Bergstrasse 20; mains €5.50-15; ⊙4pm-midnight Mon-Fri, 11am-12.30am Sat, 11am-10.30pm Sun) This local haunt perpetually overflows with admirers of *Krustenschäufele* (roast pork with crackling, dumplings and sauerkraut salad) and the finest *Bratwurst* put to work in various dishes, though menus change daily (Friday is fish day). Also try a tankard of the Franconian *Landbier*.

ℹ️ Information

Tourist office (www.tourismus.nuernberg. de) Two branches: Künstlerhaus (☎233 60; Königstrasse 93; ⊙9am-7pm Mon-Sat, 10am-4pm Sun) and Hauptmarkt (Hauptmarkt 18; ⊙9am-6pm Mon-Sat, 10am-4pm Sun May-Oct)

607

ℹ️ Getting There & Around

Nuremberg airport (NUE; www.airport-nuernberg.de), 5km north of the centre, is served by regional and international carriers, including Lufthansa, Air Berlin and Air France. U-Bahn 2 runs every few minutes from the Hauptbahnhof to the airport (€2.40, 12 minutes). A taxi costs about €16.

Rail connections from Nuremberg include:

Berlin (€93, five hours, at least hourly)

Frankfurt (€51, two hours, at least hourly)

Munich (€52, one hour, twice hourly)

Vienna (€94.20, five hours, every two hours)

STUTTGART & THE BLACK FOREST

Germany's southwest is taken up by Baden-Württemberg, a prosperous, modern state created in 1951 out of three smaller regions: Baden, Württemberg and Hohenzollern (thank goodness the names stopped at two!). With the exception of cuckoo clocks in the Black Forest, it runs a distant second in the cliché race to Bavaria. But that's really all the better, as it leaves more for you to discover on your own.

Black Forest

The Black Forest (Schwarzwald) gets its name from its dark canopy of evergreens, which evoke mystery and allure in many. Although some parts heave with visitors, a 20-minute walk from even the most crowded spots will put you in quiet countryside interspersed with hulking traditional farmhouses and patrolled by amiable dairy cows. It's not nature wild and remote, but bucolic and picturesque. And, yes, there are many, many places to buy cuckoo clocks (you pay at least €150 for a good one).

ℹ️ Getting Around

With a car you'll find a visit especially rewarding, as you can explore the rolling hills and deep valleys at will. One of the main tourist roads is the scenic **Schwarzwald-Hochstrasse** (B500), which runs from Baden-Baden to Freudenstadt and from Triberg to Waldshut.

An hourly train line links Freudenstadt with Offenburg via Alpirsbach, Schiltach and other villages. From Hausach, trains run roughly hourly southeast to Triberg and Constance.

Lake Constance

Straddling Germany, Austria and Switzerland, Lake Constance is Central Europe's third largest lake. Formed by the Rhine Glacier during the last ice age and fed and drained by that same sprightly river today, this whopper of a lake measures 63km long, 14km wide and up to 250m deep. Historic towns line its vineyard-dappled periphery, which can be explored by boat or bicycle or on foot.

Cows grazing in the Black Forest region
HEINZ WOHNER/GETTY IMAGES ©

Detour:
Baden-Baden

'So nice that you have to name it twice', enthused Bill Clinton about Baden-Baden, whose air of old-world luxury and curative waters have attracted royals, the rich and celebrities over the years – Bismarck, Queen Victoria and Victoria Beckham included.

This grand dame of German spa towns is as timeless as it is enduring. Baden-Baden's thermal baths (which put the 'Baden' [bathe] in Baden-Baden) are the main reason for a visit. The sumptuous 19th-century **Friedrichsbad** (☎ 275 920; www.roemisch-irisches-bad.de; Römerplatz 1; 3hr ticket €23, incl soap-and-brush massage €33; ☺ 9am-10pm, last admission 7pm) is the most historic spa, but you'll have to abandon your modesty (and your clothes) to indulge. Alternatively, you can keep your bathing suit on at the glass-fronted **Caracalla Therme** (www.caracalla.de; Römerplatz 11; 2/3/4hr €14/17/20; ☺ 8am-10pm, last admission 8pm) as you dip into the indoor and outdoor pools, grottos and surge channels.

Post-pamper, you can also head to the grand Kurhaus and its gilded **casino** (www.kurhaus-baden-baden.de; Kaiserallee 1; guided tour €5; ☺ guided tour 9.30am-11.30am daily). Gents must wear a jacket and tie (rentable for €8 and €3 respectively) – but there's no need to dress up for the 25-minute guided tour.

Baden-Baden is close to the A5 (Frankfurt–Basel autobahn) and is the northern starting point of the zigzagging Schwarzwald-Hochstrasse, which follows the B500. Trains run to Freiburg (€19.20 to €28, 45 to 90 minutes) and Karlsruhe (€10 to €15, 15 to 30 minutes).

The three-day card **Bodensee Erlebniskarte** (adult/child €72/36, not incl ferries €40/21), available at local tourist and ferry offices from early April to mid-October, is good for unlimited travel on almost all boats and mountain cableways on and around Lake Constance (including its Austrian and Swiss shores) as well as free entry to around 180 tourist attractions and museums.

ⓘ Getting There & Around

The most enjoyable, albeit slowest, way to get around is by ferry. Konstanz is the main hub, but Meersburg and Friedrichshafen also have plentiful ferry options. The most useful lines, run by **German BSB** (www.bsb-online.com) and **Austrian ÖBB** (www.bodenseeschifffahrt.at), link Constance with Meersburg (€5.30, 30 minutes), Friedrichshafen (€11.70, 1¾ hours), Lindau (€15.40, three hours) and Bregenz (€16.40, 3½ hours); children aged six to 15 years pay half-price. The websites list timetables.

Euregio Bodensee (www.euregiokarte.com), which groups all Lake Constance-area public transport, publishes a free *Fahrplan* with schedules for all train, bus and ferry services.

THE RHINE VALLEY

A trip along the mighty Rhine is a highlight for most travellers, as it should be. The section between Koblenz and Mainz is Unesco-protected and also called Romantic Rhine for good reason. This is Germany's landscape at its most dramatic – forested hillsides alternate with craggy cliffs and nearly-vertical terraced vineyards.

Spring and autumn are the best times to visit as it's overrun in summer and goes into hibernation in winter.

Although Koblenz and Mainz are the best starting points, the Rhine Valley is also easily accessible from Frankfurt on a very long day trip. Note that there are only car ferries (no bridges) along this stretch of river.

If You Like…
Pretty German Towns

If you've been smitten by the *aldstadts* (old towns) of Rothenburg (p601) and Nuremberg (p605), you definitely won't want to miss these historic treasures.

1 HAMELIN
Renowned for its fairy-tale connections with the Pied Piper, the quaint town of Hamelin is one of the prettiest in Lower Saxony. The best way to explore it is along the Pied Piper Trail, which is marked, of course, by white rats on the pavement. Trains run from Hanover.

2 LÜNEBURG
Packed with off-kilter buildings and houses with 'beer-belly' facades, it's as if charming Lüneburg has drunk too much of the Pilsener lager it used to brew. In fact the town's wonky buildings are the result of subsidence caused by the salt mines below town. It's an easy day trip from Hamburg.

3 SCHILTACH
A contender for the prettiest town in the Black Forest, Schiltach is a chocolate-box collection of half-timbered buildings leaning at angles along the hillside lanes. Centred on a trickling fountain, the sloping, triangular Marktplatz is Schiltach at its picture-book best. Trains run from Freudenstadt.

4 BAMBERG
Off the major tourist routes, Bamberg is revered for its beautiful 17th- and 18th-century merchants' houses, palaces and churches. A canal and fast-flowing river spanned by bridges run through the town, which even has its own local style of beer. No wonder it's a World Heritage site. Rail connections include Berlin, Munich and Nuremberg.

ℹ️ Getting There & Around

The **Köln-Düsseldorfer Line** (KD; ☎0221-2088 318; www.k-d.com) runs numerous services daily between Koblenz and Mainz (as well as the less-interesting stretch between Cologne and Koblenz) with boats stopping at riverside towns along the way.

Villages on the Rhine's left bank (eg Bingen, Bacharach, Oberwesel and Boppard) are served hourly by local trains on the Koblenz–Mainz run. Right-bank villages such as Rüdesheim, Assmannshausen, Kaub, St Goarshausen and Braubach are linked hourly to Koblenz' Hauptbahnhof and Wiesbaden by the RheingauLinie, operated by Vias.

St Goar & St Goarshausen
☎06741 / POP 3100

These twin towns face each other across the Rhine. On the left bank, St Goar is lorded over by **Burg Rheinfels** (www.st-goar.de; adult/child €4/2; ⏰9am-6pm mid-Mar–early Nov, 11am-5pm Sat & Sun in good weather early Nov–mid-Mar), one of the most impressive castles on the river. Its labyrinthine ruins reflect the greed and ambition of the local count who built the behemoth in 1245 to levy tolls on passing ships.

Across the river, just south of St Goarshausen, is the most fabled spot along the Romantic Rhine, the **Loreley Rock**. This vertical slab of slate owes its fame to a mythical maiden whose siren songs are said to have lured sailors to their death in the river's treacherous currents. Learn more at the multimedia **Loreley Besucherzentrum** (☎599 093; www.loreley-besucherzentrum. de; adult/student €2.50/1.50; ⏰10am-6pm Apr-Oct, 10am-5pm Mar, 11am-4pm Sat & Sun Nov-Feb) (visitors' centre). The outcrop can be reached by car, by shuttle bus from Goarshausen's Marktplatz (€2.65, hourly 10am to 5pm) and via the 400-step Treppenweg stairway, which begins about 2km upriver from St Goarshausen at the base of the breakwater.

St Goar's **Jugendherberge** (☎388; www. djh.de; Bismarckweg 17; dm/s/d €18/30/50) is right below the castle, which also houses the upmarket **Romantik Hotel Schloss Rheinfels** (☎06741-8020; www.schloss-rheinfels.de; d €115-265, cheaper in winter; @🛜♨️) and its three restaurants.

Bacharach

📞06743 / POP 2250

One of the prettiest of the Rhine villages, Bacharach conceals its considerable charms behind a 14th-century wall (you can stroll on top along most of it). Beyond the thick arched gateways awaits a beautiful medieval old town graced with half-timbered mansions such as the **Altes Haus**, the **Posthof** and the off-kilter **Alte Münze** along Oberstrasse. All house places to eat, drink and be merry.

Right on the medieval ramparts, the **Rhein Hotel** (📞1243; www.rhein-hotel-bacharach.de; Langstrasse 50; s €39-65, d €78-130; ❄🛜) has 14 well-lit, soundproofed rooms with original artwork.

Mainz

📞06131 / POP 199,000

An easy day trip from Frankfurt, Mainz has an attractive old town anchored by its massive **Dom** (Marktplatz; ⊙9am-6.30pm Mon-Fri, 9am-4pm Sat, 12.45-6.30pm Sun & holidays, shorter hours Nov-Feb), which has a blend of Romanesque, Gothic and baroque architecture.

Sampling local wines in a half-timbered Altstadt tavern is as much a part of any Mainz visit as viewing the ethereal Marc Chagall–designed windows in **St-Stephan-Kirche** (Kleine Weissgasse 12; ⊙10am-4.30pm) or the first printed Bible in the **Gutenberg Museum** (www.gutenberg-museum.de; Liebfrauenplatz 5; adult/child €5/3; ⊙9am-5pm Tue-Sat, 11am-5pm Sun), which honours local boy and moveable-type inventor Johannes Gutenberg.

In a 15th-century Carmelite nunnery near the cathedral, **Hotel Hof Ehrenfels** (📞971 2340; www.hof-ehrenfels.de; Grebenstrasse 5-7; s/d/tr €80/100/120, €10 less Fri-Sun) has Dom views that are hard to beat. For wine and sustenance, sit beneath the soaring Gothic vaults of a medieval hospital at **Heiliggeist** (www.heiliggeist-mainz.de; Mailandsgasse 11; mains €9.80-19.80; ⊙4pm-1am Mon-Fri, 9am-1am or 2am Sat, Sun & holidays).

MOSELLE VALLEY

Like a vine right before harvest, the Moselle hangs heavy with visitor fruit. It's one of the country's most scenic regions,

Lake Constance (p608)

GLENN VAN DER KNIJFF/GETTY IMAGES ©

Porta Nigra, Trier

HANS GEORG EIBEN/GETTY IMAGES ©

GERMANY KOBLENZ

with constant views rewarding the intrepid hikers who brave the hilly trails. Unlike the Romantic Rhine, it's spanned by plenty of bridges. The region is busiest in May, on summer weekends and during the wine harvest (mid-September to mid-October).

ⓘ Getting There & Around

The most scenic part of the Moselle Valley runs 195km from Trier to Koblenz; it's most practical to begin your Moselle Valley trip from either town. Driving is the easiest way to explore this area. If you're coming from Koblenz, the B49 and then, after Bullay, the B53 follow the river all the way to Trier, crossing it several times.

Trains linking Koblenz with Trier (€19.20, 1½ to two hours, at least hourly) stop at river villages only as far as Bullay. From there, hourly shuttle trains head upriver to Traben-Trarbach.

Koblenz

🕿0261 / POP 106,000

Koblenz sits at the confluence of the Rhine and Moselle Rivers, a point known as **Deutsches Eck** (German 'Corner') and dominated by a bombastic 19th-century statue of Kaiser Wilhelm I on horseback. On the right Rhine bank high above the

Deutsches Eck – and reached by an 850m-long **Seilbahn** (aerial cable car; www.seilbahn-koblenz.de; adult/6-14yr return €8/4, incl fortress €11.20/5.60, bicycle one-way €3; ◷10am-6pm or 7pm Apr-Oct, to 5pm Nov-Mar) – **Festung Ehrenbreitstein** (www.diefestunge-hrenbreitstein.de; adult/child €6/3; ◷10am-6pm Apr-Oct, to 5pm Nov-Mar) is one of Europe's mightiest fortresses. Views are great and there's a regional museum inside.

Several boat companies dock on the Rhine, south of the Deutsches Eck. Koblenz has two train stations, the main Hauptbahnhof on the Rhine's left bank about 1km south of the city centre, and Koblenz-Ehrenbreitstein on the right bank (right below the fortress).

Burg Eltz

South of Koblenz, at the head of the beautiful Eltz Valley, **Burg Eltz** (www.burg-eltz.de; adult/child €8/5.50; ◷9.30am-5.30pm Apr-Oct) is not to be missed. Towering over the surrounding hills, this superb medieval castle has frescoes, paintings, furniture and ornately decorated rooms.

By car, you can reach Burg Eltz via the village of Münstermaifeld; the castle is 800m from the car park (shuttle bus €1.50). Trains link Koblenz and Moselkern (also reachable by boat), where a 35-minute trail to the castle begins at the Ringelsteiner Mühle car park.

Beilstein

On the right bank of the Moselle about 50km upriver from Koblenz, Beilstein is a pint-sized village right out of the world of fairy tales. Little more than a cluster of houses surrounded by steep vineyards, its historic highlights include the **Mark-tplatz** and **Burg Metternich**, a hilltop castle reached via a staircase.

The **Zehnthauskeller** (Marktplatz; ⊙11am-evening Tue-Sun) houses a romantically dark, vaulted wine tavern owned by the same family that also runs two local **hotels** (⌕1850; www.hotel-lipmann.de).

Traben-Trarbach

Full of fanciful art nouveau villas, the double town of Traben-Trarbach provides respite from the 'romantic half-timbered town' circuit. Pick up a map of the town at the **tourist office** (⌕839 80; www.traben-trarbach.de; Am Bahnhof 5, Traben; ⊙10am-5pm Mon-Fri May-Aug, to 6pm Sep & Oct, to 4pm Nov-Apr, 11am-3pm Sat May-Oct; ☎). The ruined medieval **Grevenburg** castle sits high in the craggy hills above Trarbach and is reached via a steep footpath, the Spon-heimer Weg, that begins a block north of the bridge.

Weingut Caspari (⌕5778; www.weingut-caspari.de; Weiherstrasse 18, Trarbach; mains €6.50-16.90) is a rustic, old-time wine restaurant serving hearty local specialities; it's six short blocks inland from the bridge.

Bernkastel-Kues

The twin town of Bernkastel-Kues is at the heart of the middle Moselle region. On the right bank, Bernkastel has a charming

Markt, a romantic ensemble of half-timbered houses with beautifully deco-rated gables. On Karlstrasse, the alley to the right as you face the Rathaus, the tiny **Spitzhäuschen** resembles a giant bird's house, its narrow base topped by a much larger, precariously leaning, upper floor.

Get your heart pumping by hoofing it from the Spitzhäuschen up to **Burg Landshut**, a ruined 13th-century castle – framed by vineyards and forests – on a bluff above town; allow 30 minutes. You'll be rewarded with glorious valley views and a cold drink at the **beer garden** (⊙10am-6pm mid-Feb–Nov).

Trier

⌕0651 / POP 105,250

Founded by the Romans around 16 BC as Augusta Treverorum, Trier became the capital of Roman Gaul in the 3rd century and the residence of Constantine the Great in the 4th century. To this day, you'll find more – and better preserved – Roman ruins here than anywhere else north of the Alps.

◉ Sights

Porta Nigra   Roman Gate
(adult/student €3/2.10, incl Stadtmuseum Simeonstift €7.20/5.80; ⊙9am-6pm Apr-Sep, to 5pm Mar & Oct, to 4pm Nov-Feb) Trier's chief landmark, the brooding 2nd-century city gate is held together by nothing but grav-ity and iron rods.

Amphitheater   Roman Site
(Olewiger Strasse; adult/child €3/2.10; ⊙9am-6pm Apr-Sep, to 5pm Mar & Oct, to 4pm Nov-Feb) This classic outdoor space once held 20,000 spectators during gladiator tournaments and animal fights – or when Constantine the Great crowned his bat-tlefield victories by feeding his enemies to voracious animals.

Kaiserthermen   Roman Site
(Imperial Baths; Palastgarten; adult/student €3/2.10) This vast thermal bathing com-plex was created by Constantine.

Karl Marx Haus   Historic Site

(www.fes.de/karl-marx-haus; Brückenstrasse 10; adult/child €3/2; ⊙10am-6pm daily Apr-Oct, 2-5pm Tue-Sun Nov-Mar) The suitably modest birthplace of the author of *Das Kapital* is fast becoming a major pilgrimage stop for the growing numbers of mainland Chinese tourists to Europe.

🛏 Sleeping

Hotel Römischer Kaiser   Hotel €€

(☎977 00; www.friedrich-hotels.de; Porta-Nigra-Platz 6; s/d from €73.50/111; 🛜) Built in 1894, this hotel – convenient to the train station and the old centre – offers 43 bright, comfortable rooms with solid wood furnishings, parquet floors and spacious bathrooms.

Becker's Hotel   Boutique Hotel €€

(☎938 080; www.beckers-trier.de; Olewiger Strasse 206; d €110-220; 🅿❄@🛜) This classy establishment pairs 31 supremely tasteful rooms – some ultramodern, others rustically traditional – with stellar dining. It's 3km southeast of the centre in the quiet wine district of Olewig, across the creek from the old monastery church. Served by buses 6, 16 and 81.

🍴 Eating

Zum Domstein   Roman €€

(www.domstein.de; Hauptmarkt 5; mains €8.90-18.50, Roman dinner €17-35) A German-style bistro where you can either dine like an ancient Roman or feast on more conventional German and international fare.

Kartoffel Kiste   Potatoes €€

(www.kiste-trier.de; Fahrstrasse 13-14; mains €7.20-17; ⊙11am-midnight; 🖐) A local favourite, this place specialises in baked, breaded, gratineed, soupified and sauce-engulfed potatoes, as well as schnitzel and steaks.

ℹ Getting There & Away

Trier has at least hourly train connections to Koblenz (€20.80, 1½ to two hours) and frequent service to Luxembourg (same-day return €10.80, 50 minutes, at least hourly), with onward connections to Paris.

NORTH RHINE-WESTPHALIA

North Rhine-Westphalia harbours within its boundaries flat, windswept expanses and forested hills high enough to hold onto snow during winter. Villages sweetly lost in time contrast with frenzied metropolises habitually on fast-forward. And through it all carves the muscular Rhine, fed by tributaries such as the Ruhr that gave an entire region its name.

....

Cologne

☎0221 / POP 1 MILLION

Cologne (Köln) offers lots of attractions, led by its famous cathedral whose filigree twin spires dominate the skyline. The city's museum landscape is especially strong when it comes to art but also has something in store for fans of chocolate, sports and Roman history.

◎ Sights

Römisch-Germanisches Museum   Museum

(Roman Germanic Museum; ☎2212 2304; www.museenkoeln.de; Roncalliplatz 4; adult/child €8/4; ⊙10am-5pm Tue-Sun) Sculptures and ruins displayed outside are merely the overture to a full symphony of Roman artefacts found along the Rhine. Highlights include the giant **Poblicius tomb** (AD 30–40), the magnificent 3rd-century **Dionysus mosaic** and astonishingly well-preserved glass items.

Museum Ludwig   Museum

(☎2212 6165; www.museenkoeln.de; Bischofsgartenstrasse 1; adult/child €10/7; ⊙10am-6pm Tue-Sun) This grand art museum gets extra big kudos for its collections of 1960s pop art (Warhol's *Brillo Boxes* are a highlight), German expressionism and Russian avant-garde painting, as well as photography.

Kolumba   Museum

(☎933 1930; www.kolumba.de; Kolumbastrasse 4; adult/child €5/free; ⊙noon-5pm Wed-Mon, to 7pm Thu) Art, history, architecture and spirituality form a harmonious tapestry in this spectacular collection of religious treasures.

Wallraf-Richartz-Museum & Fondation Corboud Museum

(☎2212 1119; www.museenkoeln.de; Obenmarspforten; adult/child €9/6; ⏰10am-6pm Tue-Sun, to 9pm Thu) A famous collection of paintings from the 13th to the 19th centuries, this museum occupies a postmodern cube designed by the late OM Ungers.

Chocolate Museum Museum

(Schokoladen Museum; ☎931 8880; www.schokoladenmuseum.de; Am Schokoladenmuseum 1a; adult/concession €8.50/6; ⏰10am-6pm Tue-Fri, 11am-7pm Sat & Sun) At this high-tech temple to the art of chocolate-making, exhibits on the origin of the 'elixir of the gods', as the Aztecs called it, and the cocoa-growing process are followed by a live-production factory tour and a stop at a chocolate fountain for a sample.

Tours

KD River Cruises Boat Tour

(☎258 3011; www.k-d.com; Frankenwerft 35; tour €10; ⏰10.30am-5pm) One of several companies offering one-hour spins taking in the splendid Altstadt panorama; other options include sunset cruises.

Sleeping

Hotel Hopper et cetera Hotel €€

(☎924 400; www.hopper.de; Brüsseler Strasse 26; s €95-120, d €135-180; P @ Wi-Fi) A waxen monk welcomes you to this former monastery whose 49 rooms sport eucalyptus floors, cherry furniture and marble baths, along with such Zeitgeist-compatible touches as iPod docks.

Hotel Cristall Hotel €€

(☎163 00; www.hotelcristall.de; Ursulaplatz 9-11; s €70-180, d €90-250; ❄ @ Wi-Fi) This stylish boutique hotel makes excellent use of colour, customised furniture and light accents. Some rooms are rather compact; light sleepers should not get a street-facing one.

Lint Hotel Hotel €€

(☎920 550; www.lint-hotel.de; Lintgasse 7; s €60-90, d €90-130; Wi-Fi) The 18 rooms of this cute, contemporary and eco-conscious (solar-panelled roof) hotel in the heart of the Altstadt are comfortable and sport hardwood floors.

Eating

Alcazar Pub €

(Bismarckstrasse 39; snacks €4-9, mains €10-16; ✎) This is the kind of place that never goes out of fashion, thanks to its winning combination of freshly prepared international dishes, unpretentious ambience and chirpy service. No food service in the afternoon.

Chocolate Museum, Cologne

GUIDO SCHIEFER/ALAMY ©

DAN HERRICK/GETTY IMAGES ©

⭐ Don't Miss
Kölner Dom

As easy as it is to get church fatigue in Germany, the huge Kölner Dom is one you shouldn't miss. Blackened with age, this gargoyle-festooned Gothic cathedral has a footprint of 12,470 sq metres, with twin spires soaring to 157m. Although its ground stone was laid in 1248, stop-start construction meant it wasn't finished until 1880, as a symbol of Prussia's drive for unification. Just over 60 years later it escaped WWII's heavy bombing largely intact.

Sunshine filtering softly through stained-glass windows and the weak glow of candles are the only illumination in the moody, high-ceilinged interior. Behind the altar lies the cathedral's most precious reliquary, the **Shrine of the Three Magi** (c 1150–1210), which reputedly contains the bones of the Three Wise Men.

To see the shrine properly, you need to take a guided tour. For fine views, embark on the seriously strenuous climb of 509 steps of the Dom's south tower, passing the 24-tonne **Peter Bell**, the world's largest working clanger.

NEED TO KNOW

Cologne Cathedral; ☎ 1794 0200; www.koelner-dom.de; ⊙ 6am-10pm May-Oct, to 7.30pm Nov-Apr, south tower 9am-6pm May-Sep, to 5pm Mar-Apr & Oct, to 4pm Nov-Feb

Salon Schmitz Modern European €
(Aachener Strasse 28; snacks €4-8) No matter whether you prefer sidling up to the long bar or grabbing an ultra-comfy sofa in the retro lounge, Schmitz is a perfect pit stop for relaxed chats over coffee, cocktails or

its house-brand Kölsch beer. If hunger strikes, pop next door to the affiliated deli in a former butcher's shop.

Bei Oma Kleinmann German €€
(www.beiomakleinmann.de; Zülpicher Strasse 9; mains €12; ⊙ 5pm-1am Tue-Sun, kitchen to

11pm) Named for its long-time owner, who was still cooking almost to her last day at age 95 in 2009, this cosy trad restaurant has timeless dishes, including 14 kinds of schnitzel.

Feynsinn
International €€

(📞240 9210; www.cafe-feynsinn.de; Rathenau-platz 7; mains €7-18) At this well-respected restaurant organic ingredients are woven into sharp-flavoured dishes. The owners raise their own meat. Get a table over-looking the park for a meal or just a drink.

Engelbät
European €

(📞246 914; www.engelbaet.de; Engelbert-strasse 7; crepes €3-9; ⏰11am-1am) This cosy restaurant-pub is famous for its habit-forming crepes, which come as sweet, meat or vegetarian.

🍷 Drinking & Nightlife

As in Munich, beer in Cologne reigns su-preme. Local breweries turn out a variety called *Kölsch,* which is relatively light and served in skinny 200mL glasses.

Früh am Dom
Beer Hall

(📞258 0394; www.frueh.de; Am Hof 12-14; mains €5-12) This warren of a beer hall near the Dom epitomises Cologne earthiness. Sit inside amid loads of knick-knacks or on the flower-filled terrace next to a fountain. It's also known for great breakfasts.

Päffgen
Beer Hall

(www.paeffgen-koelsch.de; Friesenstrasse 64-66) Busy, loud and boisterous, Päffgen has been pouring *Kölsch* since 1883 and hasn't lost a step since. In summer you can enjoy the refreshing brew and local specialities beneath starry skies in the beer garden.

ℹ️ Information

Tourist office (📞2213 0400; www.koelntourismus.de; Unter Fettenhennen 19; ⏰9am-8pm Mon-Sat, 10am-5pm Sun)

ℹ️ Getting There & Away

Air
About 18km southeast of the city centre, **Köln Bonn airport** (CGN; 📞02203-404 001; www.

airport-cgn.de) has direct flights to 130 cities and is served by numerous airlines, with destinations across Europe. The S13 train connects the airport and the Hauptbahnhof every 20 minutes (€2.80, 15 minutes). Taxis charge about €30.

Train
Cologne's Hauptbahnhof sits just a Frisbee toss away from the Dom. Services are fast and frequent in all directions. A sampling: Berlin (€113, 4¼ hours), Frankfurt (€67, 1¼ hours) and Munich (€134, 4½ hours). In addition there are fast trains to Brussels (for connecting to the Eurostar for London or Paris).

ℹ️ Getting Around

Cologne's comprehensive mix of buses, trams, and U-Bahn and S-Bahn trains is operated by **VRS** (📞01803-504 030; www.vrsinfo.de) in cooperation with Bonn's system. Short trips (up to four stops) cost €1.80, longer ones €2.60. Day passes are €7.50 for one person and €11.10 for up to five people travelling together. Buy your tickets from the orange ticket machines at stations and aboard trams; be sure to validate them.

HAMBURG

📞040 / POP 1.8 MILLION

'The gateway to the world' might be a bold claim, but Germany's second-largest city and biggest port has never been shy. Hamburg has engaged in business with the world ever since it joined the Hanseatic League trading bloc back in the Middle Ages, and this 'harbourpolis' is now the nation's premier media hub and among its wealthiest cities.

Hamburg's maritime spirit infuses the entire city, from architecture to menus to the cry of gulls, you always know you're near the water. The city has given rise to vibrant neighbourhoods awash with multicultural eateries, as well as the gloriously seedy Reeperbahn red-light district.

🎯 Sights

Old Town
Historic Area

Hamburg's medieval **Rathaus** (📞4283 120 10; tours adult/child €3/0.50; ⏰English-language tours hourly 10.15am-3.15pm Mon-Thu,

Below: HafenCity development, Hamburg; **Right:** Hamburg at night
(BELOW) ARNE THAYSEN/GETTY IMAGES ©; (RIGHT) BEATE ZOELLNER/GETTY IMAGES ©

to 1.15pm Fri, to 5.15pm Sat, to 4.15pm Sun; **S** Rathausmarkt or Jungfernstieg) is one of Europe's most opulent. North of here, you can wander through the **Alsterarkaden**, the Renaissance-style arcades sheltering shops and cafes alongside a canal or 'fleet'.

The 1920s, brown-brick **Chile Haus** (cnr Burchardstrasse & Johanniswall; **S** Mönckebergstrasse/Messberg) is shaped like an ocean liner, with remarkable curved walls meeting in the shape of a ship's bow and staggered balconies that look like decks.

Speicherstadt & Harbour   Historic Area

The seven-storey redbrick warehouses lining the **Speicherstadt** archipelago are a well-recognised Hamburg symbol, stretching to Baumwall in the world's largest continuous warehouse complex. It's best appreciated by simply wandering through its streets or taking a boat up its canals.

The Speicherstadt merges into Europe's biggest inner-city urban development, the **HafenCity**.

Reeperbahn   Neighbourhood

(**S** Reeperbahn) No discussion of Hamburg is complete without mentioning St Pauli, home of the Reeperbahn, Europe's biggest red-light district. Sex shops, peep shows, dim bars and strip clubs line the streets, which generally start getting crowded with the masses after 8pm or 9pm.

Fischmarkt   Market

(⊙ 5-10am Sun; 🚆 Reeperbahn) Every Sunday between 5am and 10am, curious tourists join locals of every age and walk of life at the famous Fischmarkt in St Pauli. The market has been running since 1703, and its undisputed stars are the boisterous *Marktschreier* (market criers) who hawk their wares at full volume.

Internationales Maritimes Museum · Museum

(📞 3009 3300; www.internationales-maritimes-museum.de; Koreastrasse 1; adult/concession €12/8.50; 🕑 10am-6pm Tue, Wed & Fri-Sun, 10am-8pm Thu; [S] Messberg) Hamburg's maritime past – and future – is fully explored in this excellent private museum which sprawls over 10 floors of a rehabbed brick shipping warehouse. The vast collection includes 26,000 model ships.

Hamburger Kunsthalle · Museum

(📞 428 131 200; www.hamburger-kunsthalle.de; Glockengiesserwall; adult/concession €8.50/5; 🕑 10am-6pm Tue, Wed & Fri-Sun, to 9pm Thu; underground rail Hauptbahnhof) Consists of two buildings, the old one housing Old Masters and 19th-century art, and a white concrete cube – the Galerie der Gegenwart – showcasing contemporary German artists, including Georg Baselitz and Gerhard Richter, alongside international stars such as David Hockney and Jeff Koons.

Mahnmal St-Nikolai · Memorial

(Memorial St Nicholas; www.mahnmal-st-nikolai.de; Willy-Brandt-Strasse 60; adult/child €4/2; 🕑 10am-5pm; [S] Rödingsmarkt) Destroyed in WWII, this memorial now houses an unflinching exhibit on the horrors of war focussing on three events in World War II: the German bombing of Coventry in 1940, the German destruction of Warsaw and Operation Gomorrha, the combined British and American bombing of Hamburg over three days and nights in 1943 that killed 35,000 and incinerated much of the centre. Great views from the 76.3m-high viewing platform inside the surviving spire.

🛏 Sleeping

Hotel Wedina · Hotel €€

(📞 280 8900; www.wedina.de; Gurlittstrasse 23; s €70-195, d €120-225; @ 🛜; [S] Hauptbahnhof) You might find a novel instead of a chocolate on your pillow at this literary hotel which has bedded Margaret Atwood, Jonathan Franzen and JK Rowling,

619

The History of the Hamburger

A classic *Calvin and Hobbes* comic strip once asked if hamburgers were made out of people from Hamburg. And while Hamburg's citizens are, of course, known as Hamburgers, it was the city's role as an international port that gave rise to its most famous namesake.

The origins of the ubiquitous fast food date back to the 12th century. The Tartars (Mongolian and Turkish warriors) wedged pieces of beef between their saddles and the horses' backs, softening the meat as they rode until it was tender enough to be eaten raw. By the 17th century, Hamburg ships brought 'steak tartare' back to Germany, which visiting seafarers then referred to as 'steak in the Hamburg style'. These patties of salted minced beef – usually slightly smoked and mixed with breadcrumbs and onions – were highly durable, making them ideal for long sea voyages.

Hamburg emigrants to America continued making the patties, which they served in bread. As for who in America officially launched the burger remains a fanatical culinary debate.

among others. The 59 rooms spread over four colourful buildings with a choice of traditional or mod-urban decor.

Fritz Hotel Boutique Hotel €€
(☎8222 2830; www.fritzhotel.com; Schanzenstrasse 101-103; s/d from €65/95; 🛜; Ⓢ Sternschanze) This stylish town-house hotel is as cool as a cucumber and has only 17 rooms total. If you want a room with a balcony, be prepared for some street noise, otherwise get one in back.

Hotel SIDE Hotel €€€
(☎309 990; www.side-hamburg.de; Drehbahn 49; r €120-300; Ⓟ 🍽 ❄ @ 🛜 ✕; Ⓢ Gänsemarkt) This Matteo Thun–designed stunner is built around a prism-shaped central atrium and has suites featuring vividly coloured free-standing bathtubs. The 8th-floor chill-out lounge, strewn with 1950s-style saucers-from-outer-space sofas, opens to a panoramic sun deck.

Hotel Hafen Hotel €€
(☎311 1370; www.hotel-hafen-hamburg.de; Seewartenstrasse 9; r €70-200; @ 🛜; Ⓢ Landungsbrücken) Location, location, location. For superb views, score a harbour-facing room at this behemoth of a hotel on a small hill overlooking the port action.

Eating

Oberhafenkantine German €€
(www.oberhafenkantine-hamburg.de; Stockmeyerstrasse 39; mains €7-16; 🚃 Steinstrasse) Serving traditional local fare since 1925, this is where you can order a 'Hamburger' and get the real thing: a patty made with various seasonings and onions.

Fleetschlösschen International €€
(Brooktorkai 17; snacks €7-10; 🕗 8am-8pm Mon-Fri, 11am-6pm Sat & Sun; Ⓢ Messberg) One of the cutest cafes you ever saw, this former customs post overlooks a Speicherstadt canal and has brilliant outdoor seating areas.

Café Paris French €€
(www.cafeparis.net; Rathausstrasse 4; mains €10-20; 🕘 9am-11.30pm Mon-Fri, from 10am Sat & Sun; Ⓢ Rathaus) Within a spectacularly tiled 1882 butchers' hall and adjoining art deco salon, this elegant yet relaxed brasserie serves classical French cafe fare and a killer breakfast for two.

Deichgraf German €€€
(☎364 208; www.deichgraf-hamburg.de; Deichstrasse 23; mains €18-29; 🕛 lunch Mon-Sat,

dinner Sat; S Rödingsmarkt) In a prime setting, with the water on one side and long street-side tables on the other, Deichgraf excels in Hamburg specialties cooked to a high standard. Much of the food is sourced regionally.

 Drinking & Nightlife

Bar M & V   Bar
(www.mvbar.de; Lange Reihe 22; ☒Hauptbahnhof) The drinks menu is like a designer catalogue at this grand old St Georg bar that's had a beautiful restoration. Settle into one of the wooden booths, smell the freesias and enjoy.

Amphore   Cafe
(www.cafe-amphore.de; Hafenstrasse 140; ☒Reeperbahn) Beguiling in its trad beauty, non-fussy Amphore has terrace views out to the Elbe and pavement tables for neighbourhood gawking. An excellent St Pauli spot for a drink.

⭐ Entertainment

Grosse Freiheit
36/Kaiserkeller   Live Music
(☎3177 7811; Grosse Freiheit 36; ☒Reeperbahn) The Beatles once played in the basement Kaiserkeller at this now-mainstream venue mounting pop and rock concerts. It's the best reason today to detour up the Grosse Freiheit.

ℹ Information

Hamburg Tourismus
(☎3005 1200; www.
hamburg-tourismus.
de) There are branches
in Hauptbahnhof
(Kirchenallee exit; ⊙8am-
9pm Mon-Sat, 10am-6pm
Sun) and Landungsbrücken
(btwn piers 4 & 5; ⊙8am-
6pm Apr-Oct, 10am-6pm
Nov-Mar; underground rail
Landungsbrücken).

Hamburger Kunsthalle (p619)
DAVID PEEVERS/GETTY IMAGES ©

ℹ Getting There & Away

Air
Hamburg's airport (HAM; www.flughafen-hamburg.de) has frequent flights to domestic and European cities. The S1 S-Bahn travels to the city centre in 24 minutes (€2.85).

Bus
The Zentral Omnibus Busbahnhof (Central Bus Station; ☎247 576; www.zob-hamburg.de; Adenauerallee 78; ⊙ticket counters 5am-10pm Mon-Tue, Thu, Sat & Sun, to midnight Wed & Fri) is southeast of the Hauptbahnhof. Eurolines (www.eurolines.com) has buses to such eastern European destinations as Prague (€59).

Car & Motorcycle
The major A1 and A7 autobahns cross south of the Elbe River.

Train
Hamburg has four mainline train stations: the Hauptbahnhof, Dammtor, Altona and Harburg. Direct ICE trains depart frequently for Berlin-Hauptbahnhof (€68, 2¼ hours), Cologne (€79, four hours), Munich (€127, six hours), Frankfurt (€106, three hours) and Copenhagen (€78.80, five hours).

Warehouses and canal in the Speicherstadt (p618), Hamburg

GUY VANDERELST/GETTY IMAGES ©

Getting Around

HVV (☎194 49; www.hvv.de) operates buses, ferries, and U-Bahn and S-Bahn trains. The city is divided into zones. **Ring A** covers the city centre, inner suburbs and airport. Single tickets are €2.85, day passes €6.95.

SURVIVAL GUIDE

Directory A-Z

Accommodation

Germany has all types of places to unpack your suitcase, from hostels, camping grounds and family hotels to chains, business hotels and luxury resorts. Reservations are a good idea, especially if you're travelling in the busy summer season.

Unless noted, the following price ranges refer to a double room with private bathroom and breakfast in high season.

€ less than €80

€€ €80 to €150

€€€ more than €150

Business Hours

Banks 9am to 4pm Monday to Friday, extended hours usually on Tueday or Thursday

Bars 6pm to 1am

Cafes 8am to 8pm

Clubs 10pm to 4am

Post offices 9am to 6pm Monday to Friday, some Saturday mornings

Restaurants 11am to 10pm (varies widely, food service often stops at 9pm in rural areas)

Major stores & supermarkets 9.30am to 8pm Monday to Saturday (shorter hours in suburbs and rural areas, possible lunchtime break)

Discount Cards

Tourist offices in many cities sell 'Welcome Cards' entitling visitors to free or reduced admission on museums, sights and tours, plus unlimited local public transportation for the period of their validity (usually 24 or 48 hours).

Food

The following price categories are for the cost of a main course.

€ less than €8

€€ €8 to €15

€€€ more than €15

Gay & Lesbian Travellers

○ Germany is a magnet for *schwule* (gay) and *lesbische* (lesbian) travellers, with the rainbow flag flying especially proudly in Berlin and

Cologne, and with sizeable communities in Hamburg, Frankfurt and Munich.

- Attitudes towards homosexuality tend to be more conservative in the countryside, among older people and in the eastern states.

Legal Matters

- By law you must carry some form of photo identification, such as your passport, national identity card or driving licence.
- There is no universal nationwide smoking law, with regulations left to each of the 16 German states. It's best to ask first before lighting up.

Money

- Cash is king in Germany, so always carry some with you and plan to pay in cash almost everywhere.
- The easiest and quickest way to obtain cash is by using your debit (bank) card at an ATM (Geldautomat) linked to international networks such as Cirrus, Plus, Star and Maestro.
- Credit cards are becoming more widely accepted, but it's best not to assume that you'll be able to use one – enquire first.
- Change currency in foreign-exchange offices (Wechselstuben) at airports and train stations, particularly those of the Reisebank.

Tipping

Restaurant bills always include a service charge (Bedienung) but most people add 5% or 10% unless the service was truly abhorrent.

Hotel porters €1 to €1.50 per bag

Room cleaners €1 per night per person

Bartenders 5%

Taxi drivers around 10%

Public Holidays

Germany observes eight religious and three secular holidays nationwide. States with predominantly Catholic populations, such as Bavaria and Baden-Württemberg, also celebrate Epiphany (6 January), Corpus Christi (10 days after Pentecost), Assumption Day (15 August) and All Saints' Day (1 November).

The following are gesetzliche Feiertage (public holidays):

Neujahrstag (New Year's Day) 1 January

Ostern (Easter) Good Friday, Easter Sunday and Easter Monday

Christi Himmelfahrt (Ascension Day) Forty days after Easter

Maifeiertag/Tag der Arbeit (Labour Day) 1 May

Pfingsten (Whit/Pentecost Sunday & Monday) Fifty days after Easter.

Tag der Deutschen Einheit (Day of German Unity) 3 October

Weihnachtstag (Christmas Day) 25 December

Zweiter Weihnachtstag (Boxing Day) 26 December

Telephone

German phone numbers consist of an area code followed by the local number, which can be between three and nine digits long.

Country code ☑ 49

International access code ☑ 00

Directory inquiries ☑ 11837 for an English-speaking operator (charged at €1.99 per minute)

Travellers with Disabilities

Deutsche Bahn Mobility Service Centre (☑ ext 9 for English 0180-599 6633512; www.bahn.com; ☺ 24hr) Train access information and route planning assistance. The website has useful information in English (search for 'barrier-free travel').

German National Tourism Office (www.germany.travel) Your first port of call, with inspirational information in English.

Visas

- EU nationals only need their passport or national identity card to enter, stay and work in Germany, even for stays over six months.
- Citizens of Australia, Canada, Israel, Japan, New Zealand, Poland, Switzerland and the US need only a valid passport but no visa if entering Germany as tourists for up to three months within a six-month period. Passports must be valid for another three months beyond the intended departure date.
- Nationals from other countries need a Schengen Visa.

ℹ️ Getting There & Away

If you're arriving from any of the 24 other Schengen countries, such as the Netherlands, Austria or the Czech Republic, you no longer have to show your passport or go through customs in Germany, no matter which nationality you are.

Air

Budget carriers, **Lufthansa** (www.lufthansa.com) and international airlines serve numerous German airports from across Europe and the rest of the world. Frankfurt and Munich are the hubs, but there are also sizeable airports in Berlin, Hamburg, Cologne/Bonn and Stuttgart, and smaller ones in Bremen, Dresden, Hanover, Leipzig, Münster-Osnabrück and Nuremberg.

Practically every other national carrier from around the world serves Germany, along with budget carriers **Air Berlin** (www.airberlin.com), **easyJet** (EZY; ☎0900-1100 161; www.easyjet. com), **Flybe** (BE; www.flybe.com), **airBaltic** (BT; www.airbaltic.com), **Ryanair** (FR; ☎0900-116 0500; www.ryanair.com) and **Germanwings** (www.germanwings.com).

Note that Ryanair usually flies to remote airports, which are often little more than recycled military airstrips. Frankfurt-Hahn, for instance, is actually near the Moselle River, about 125km west of Frankfurt proper.

Land

Car & Motorcycle

When bringing your own vehicle to Germany, you need a valid driving licence, your car registration certificate and proof of insurance. Foreign cars must display a nationality sticker unless they have official European plates. You also need to carry a warning (hazard) triangle and a first-aid kit.

Train

In Germany ticketing is handled by **Deutsche Bahn** (www.bahn.com). Seat reservations are essential during the peak summer season and around major holidays.

Germany is also linked by overnight train to many European cities; routes include Amsterdam to Munich, Zurich to Berlin and Paris to Hamburg.

Sea

Germany's main ferry ports are Kiel, Lübeck and Travemünde in Schleswig-Holstein, and Rostock and Sassnitz in Mecklenburg-Western Pomerania.

🛈 Getting Around

Air

There are lots of domestic flights, many with budget carriers such as Air Berlin and Germanwings, as well as Lufthansa. Unless you're flying from one end of the country to the other, planes are only marginally quicker than trains once you factor in check-in and transit times.

Bus

- In some rural areas buses may be your only option for getting around without your own vehicle.

- In cities, buses generally converge at the *Busbahnhof* or *Zentraler Omnibus Bahnhof* (ZOB; central bus station), which is often near the Hauptbahnhof (central train station).

- For long-distance travel between German cities, the main operators are **Deutsche Touring** (☎069-790 3501; www.touring.de) and **Berlin Linien Bus** (www. berlinlinienbus.de).

Sony Centre at Potsdamer Platz (p567), Berlin

Car & Motorcycle

- Germany's pride and joy is its 11,000km network of autobahns (motorways). Every 40km to 60km, you'll find elaborate service areas with petrol stations, toilet facilities and restaurants; many are open 24 hours.

- Autobahns are supplemented by an extensive network of Bundesstrassen (secondary 'B' roads, highways) and smaller Landstrassen (country roads, 'L'). No tolls are charged on any public roads.

- Cars are impractical in urban areas. Leaving your car in a central *Parkhaus* (car park) can cost €20 per day or more.

Hire

- To hire your own wheels, you'll need to be at least 25 years old and possess a valid driving licence and a major credit card. Some companies lease to drivers between the ages of 21 and 24 for an additional charge.

- For insurance reasons, driving into an Eastern European country, such as the Czech Republic or Poland, is usually a no-no.

- All the main companies maintain branches at airports, major train stations and towns.

- Rental cars with automatic transmission are rare in Germany and will usually need to be ordered well in advance.

Road Rules

Road rules are easy to understand, and standard international signs are in use. You drive on the right, and cars are right-hand drive. Right of way is usually signed, with major roads given priority, but at unmarked intersections traffic coming from the right always has right of way.

The blood-alcohol limit for drivers is 0.05%. Obey the road rules carefully: the German police are very efficient and issue heavy on-the-spot fines. Germany also has one of the highest concentrations of speed cameras in Europe.

Speed limits:

Towns & cities On bigger roads 50km/h, on residential streets 30km/h (or as posted).

Open road/country 100km/h

Autobahn Unlimited but many exceptions as posted.

Public Transport

- Public transport is excellent within big cities and small towns and may include buses, trams (Strassenbahn), S-Bahn (light rail) and U-Bahn (underground/subway trains).

- Tickets cover all forms of transit, and fares are determined by zones or time travelled, sometimes both. Multiticket strips and day passes are generally available, offering better value than single-ride tickets.

- Tickets must be bought from vending machines at the stations or stops. Only buses and some trams let you buy tickets from the driver.

- Normally, tickets must be stamped upon boarding in order to be valid. Inspections are random but fines (usually €40) are levied if you're caught without a valid ticket.

Train

- Operated almost entirely by Deutsche Bahn (p624), the German train system is the finest in Europe and is generally the best way to get around the country.

- It's rarely worth buying a 1st-class ticket on German trains; 2nd class is quite comfortable.

- Most train stations have coin-operated lockers costing from €1 to €4 per 24-hour period. Larger stations have staffed left-luggage offices *(Gepäckaufbewahrung)*.

- Seat reservations (€4) for long-distance travel is highly recommended, especially if you're travelling on a Friday or Sunday afternoon, during holiday periods or in summer. Reservations can be made online and at ticket counters as late as 10 minutes before departure.

Tickets

- Tickets may be bought online at www.bahn.de, using a credit card, at no surcharge. However, you will need to present a printout of your ticket, as well as the credit card used to buy it, to the conductor.

- Many train stations have a *Reisezentrum* (travel centre), where staff sell tickets (for a small fee) and can help you plan an itinerary (ask for an English-speaking agent).

- Smaller stations may only have a few ticket windows and the smallest ones aren't staffed at all. In this case, you must buy tickets from multilingual vending machines.

- Only conductors on long-distance trains sell tickets on board, at a surcharge; major credit cards are usually accepted. Not having a ticket carries a stiff penalty.

German Rail Pass

If your permanent residence is outside Europe, you qualify for the German Rail Pass. Tickets are sold through www.bahn.com, through agents in your home country and on www.raileurope.com.

Austria, Switzerland & the Czech Republic

If it's mountain scenery that inspires you, then Austria and Switzerland will seem like seventh heaven. This is a corner of Europe where Mother Nature has done her work on a grand scale: icy peaks, sheer cliffs and silver glaciers stand out against the open sky, providing the perfect mountain playground for skiers and snowboarders. While winter sports are the main attraction, there are plenty more reasons to visit: from the grand cities of Vienna and Salzburg to the sparkling waters of Lake Geneva.

Out to the east, the Czech Republic has emerged from behind the Iron Curtain to become one of Europe's most captivating places to travel. The charming city of Prague is packed with incredible architecture and historic sights, and further afield you could spend your time exploring the splendid castles of Konopiště and Karlštejn, hiking through the rolling Moravian countryside or sampling the world-class beer for which the Czech Republic is rightly renowned.

North face of the Eiger mountain, Grindelwald
GRANT DIXON/GETTY IMAGES ©

627

Fountain outside St Nicholas Church, Prague (p703)

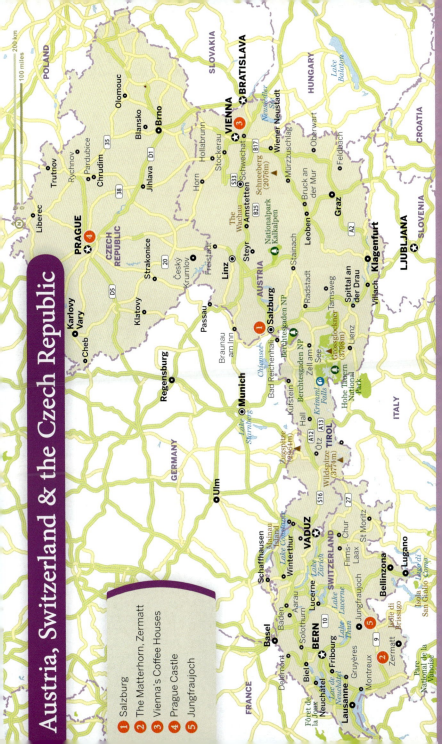

Austria, Switzerland & the Czech Republic

1 Salzburg
2 The Matterhorn, Zermatt
3 Vienna's Coffee Houses
4 Prague Castle
5 Jungfraujoch

Austria, Switzerland & the Czech Republic Highlights

Salzburg

Salzburg (p656) has a lot more to offer than just Mozart and *The Sound of Music*. There's one of Austria's most atmospheric Altstadts to explore, for a start. Then there are boat trips down the Danube, a wealth of baroque architecture to admire and a fantastic funicular ride up to the clifftop fortress of Festung Hohensalzburg, offering unforgettable views across Salzburg's higgledy-piggledy rooftops.

The Matterhorn, Zermatt

No mountain packs the same wow factor as the Matterhorn (p681). This sheer fang of ice, snow and rock stands in dramatic isolation above the town of Zermatt, and has been an irresistible draw for aspiring mountaineers since the sport began in the 19th century. You could just admire the view from the bottom, but those with a head for heights should catch Europe's highest cable car up to the cloud-top viewing platform at 3883m.

Vienna's Coffee Houses

There's one pastime the Viennese know how to do better than almost anyone else, and that's drink coffee (preferably accompanied by a thick slice of cake). The city's coffee houses (p649) have been the favourite haunts of intellectuals, impoverished artists and cultural types for centuries, and they're still by far the best places to take the city's pulse. Interior of Café Sperl

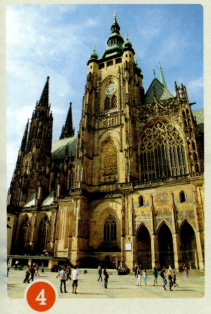

Prague Castle

Prague is littered with historical monuments, but in terms of sheer scale and ambition, Prague Castle (p701) definitely takes top prize. Overlooking the Vltava River, this mighty fortress covers a vast area of Prague's historic centre, and contains the city's largest house of worship, St Vitus Cathedral, within its crenellated walls. You'll need a whole day to do it justice, and don't miss a guided tour.
St Vitus Cathedral

Jungfraujoch

You'll be king of the mountain at Europe's highest train station, Jungfraujoch (p688). At 3471m, this icy wonderland of glaciers inspires scores of people to make the journey, so it's a good idea to start early. Whatever you do, save the trip for a clear day – the ride's not worth the price of the ticket if all you see up there are clouds, so check the weather forecast before you set out.

Austria, Switzerland &
the Czech Republic's Best...

Palaces & Chateaux

○ **Hofburg** (p643) The might of the Austrian monarchy is summed up by this monumental Viennese palace.

○ **Český Krumlov** (p718) The second-most famous Czech castle outside Prague.

○ **Konopiště Chateau** (p713) Archduke Franz Ferdinand's country estate.

○ **Schloss Schönbrunn** (p637) The Habsburg dynasty's summer palace is a Unesco-listed treasure.

○ **Schloss Hellbrunn** (p665) A palace renowned for its watery wonders.

Old Towns

○ **Malá Strana** (p703) This rabbit warren of medieval streets is the place to lose yourself in Prague.

○ **Salzburg** (p656) Winding alleyways, cobbled streets and photo ops aplenty.

○ **Vienna** (p636) Re-enact some of those famous scenes from *The Third Man*.

○ **Bern** (p682) Switzerland's dynamic capital conceals a much older heart.

○ **Olomouc** (p716) This ancient Czech town is well off the tourist radar.

Epicurean Experiences

○ **Swiss chocolate** (p672) Shop for something sweet and sinful in Geneva.

○ **Coffee and cake** (p649) Practically an art form in the cafes of Vienna and Salzburg.

○ **Beisls** (p647) These cosy Austrian beer dens are full of atmosphere: Vienna has some of the best.

○ **Fondue** (p680) This cheesy indulgence is a Swiss speciality, especially in mountain towns like Zermatt.

○ **Pilsner Urquell Brewery** (p715) Take a tipple at the Czech Republic's best-known beer factory.

Lofty Views

● **Gornergrat** (p680) Catch the cable car in Zermatt and behold the mighty Matterhorn.

● **Schilthorn** (p688) Enjoy one of the most dramatic mountain panoramas in the Swiss Alps.

● **Bergisel** (p667) Hold your nerve at the top of this gravity-defying ski jump in Innsbruck.

● **Grindelwald** (p687) Gaze over Grindelwald's sparkling glacier.

Need to Know

ADVANCE PLANNING

● **Two months before** Reserve as early as possible in the Alps during the ski season.

● **One month before** Book hotels for summer travel in Prague, Vienna, Salzburg, Geneva and other big-ticket cities.

● **Two weeks before** Reserve tickets for the Staatsoper and the Spanish Riding School in Vienna.

RESOURCES

● **Österreich Werbung** (www.austria.info) Austria's national tourism authority.

● **Prague Information Service** (www.praguewelcome.cz) Official Prague info.

● **Czech Tourism** (www.czechtourism.com) Czech-wide travel planning from the state tourism body.

● **Switzerland Tourism** (www.myswitzerland.com) The full Swiss lowdown: accommodation, activities and more.

GETTING AROUND

● **Boat** Ferry services and cruise boats ply many Austrian and Swiss lakes.

● **Bus** Postbuses supplement regional train lines in Austria and Switzerland, and serve many smaller Czech towns and villages.

● **Car** Driving is best for rural areas, and pricey parking and incomprehensible one-way systems make Prague, Vienna, Salzburg and Zürich a no-no. *Vignettes* (motorway taxes) are charged on Austrian autobahns, and many tunnels incur a toll.

● **Train** Train services in all three countries are fast, frequent and efficient, although Switzerland really shines.

BE FOREWARNED

● **Czech manners** It's customary to say *dobrý den* (good day) when entering a shop, cafe or quiet bar, and *na shledanou* (goodbye) when leaving.

● **Mountain passes** Many road passes in Austria and Switzerland are closed in winter due to snowfall.

● **Scams** Prague pickpockets work the crowds at the Astronomical Clock, Prague Castle and Charles Bridge. Book a reputable taxi firm to avoid unscrupulous drivers.

Austria, Switzerland & the Czech Republic Itineraries

Take in the baroque beauty of Austria's top cities, then head for the stirring scenery of the Alps.

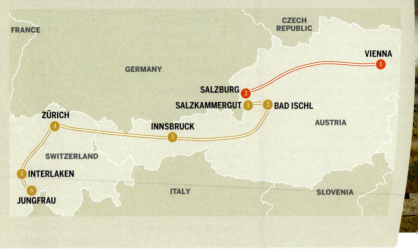

3 DAYS

BAROQUE BEAUTY
Vienna to Salzburg

Three days will give you just enough time to explore Austria's two must-see cities. Start with two days in the capital, ❶ **Vienna** (p636), a city that's been synonymous with culture and refinement since the days of the Habsburg empire. You'll need a full day to explore the incredible Hofburg and Schloss Schönbrunn palaces, which illustrate the immense wealth and political power this ancient dynasty wielded before being deposed in 1918 following the end of WWI.

On day two, take in more baroque splendour at the Schloss Belvedere and centuries of history in the MuseumsQuartier, then venture into the world of contemporary art at the wonderfully weird KunstHausWien. Leave a few hours aside for discovering the city's wonderful cafes – nowhere does coffee and cake quite like Vienna.

On day three, catch the train to ❷ **Salzburg** (p656), another Austrian city that's awash with impressive baroque architecture, especially around the Altstadt. Salzburg is most famous as the birthplace of Mozart, but for many people it's the chance to tour the locations from *The Sound of Music* that is the real draw. Don't miss the creaky cable car up to the Festung Hohensalzburg, a clifftop castle offering unparalleled vistas over the whole of Salzburg.

INTO THE ALPS

Salzkammergut to Jungfrau

5 DAYS

From Salzburg, you're within reach of breathtaking mountain scenery. Spend at least a day exploring the attractions of **❶Salzkammergut** (p664), including the old salt mines and the ice caves, before detouring via **❷Bad Ischl** (p664) to visit Franz Ferdinand's opulent summer residence. On day three, catch a train west to **❸Innsbruck** (p666), the capital of the Tirol region and a thriving centre for outdoor sports. The Nordkettenbahnen whisks you via a funicular and two cable cars from the town centre to the tip of Hafelekar peak (2334m) in just 25 minutes.

From here, the mighty Alps unfold all the way into Switzerland and France. Fast and frequent trains run west from Innsbruck to **❹Zürich** (p689), a squeaky-clean city with a surprisingly lively heart, but the real scenery starts further south at **❺Interlaken** (p687), where you can paraglide, ice-climb or zorb the days away beneath the shadow of the Eiger, Mönch and Jungfrau peaks. Further south lies the **❻Jungfrau** (p688) region, where some of Europe's largest glaciers snake their way among the snow-dusted peaks.

Jungfrau peak, Bernese Oberland (p688)
GLENN VAN DER KNIJFF/GETTY IMAGES ©

635

Discover Austria, Switzerland & the Czech Republic

At a Glance

● **Austria** (p636) Awash with imperial grandeur and sparkling lakes, not to mention numerous Mozart connections.

● **Switzerland** (p672) Famously efficient, this squeaky-clean nation is dominated by Europe's highest peaks.

● **Czech Republic** (p696) Baroque architecture, dramatic castles, world-class beer, and a fascinating post-communist past.

AUSTRIA

For such a small country, Austria has made it big. This is, after all, the land where Mozart was born, Strauss taught the world to waltz and Julie Andrews grabbed the spotlight with her twirling entrance in *The Sound of Music*. This is where the Habsburgs built their 600-year empire, and where past glories still shine in the resplendent baroque palaces and chandelier-lit coffee houses of Vienna, Innsbruck and Salzburg. This is a perfectionist of a country and whatever it does – mountains, classical music, new media, castles, cake, you name it – it does exceedingly well.

Vienna

🎵01 / POP 1.72 MILLION

Few cities in the world waltz so effortlessly between the present and the past like Vienna. Its splendid historical face is easily recognised: grand imperial palaces and bombastic baroque interiors, revered opera houses and magnificent squares.

But Vienna is also one of Europe's most dynamic urban spaces. A stone's throw from Hofburg (the Imperial Palace), the MuseumsQuartier houses some of the world's most provocative contemporary art behind a striking basalt facade. In the Innere Stadt, up-to-the-minute design stores sidle up to old-world confectioners, and Austro-Asian fusion restaurants stand alongside traditional *Beisl* (small taverns).

Throw in the mass of green space within the confines of the city limits and the 'blue' Danube cutting a path east of the historical centre, and this is a capital that is distinctly Austrian.

Stephansdom, Vienna
YADID LEVY/GETTY IMAGES ©

636

🎯 Sights

If you're planning on doing a lot of sightseeing, consider purchasing the **Wien-Karte** (Vienna Card; €19.90) for 72 hours of unlimited travel plus discounts at selected museums, attractions, cafes and shops. It's available from hotels and ticket offices.

Vienna's stately buildings and beautifully tended parks are made for the aimless ambler. Some former homes of the great composers, including those of Mozart and Beethoven, are open to the public; ask at the tourist office.

Many sights and attractions open slightly later in July and August, and close earlier from November to March.

Stephansdom   Church
(St Stephan's Cathedral; www.stephanskirche.at; 01, Stephansplatz; ⏱6am-10pm Mon-Sat, 7am-10pm Sun, main nave & Domschatz audio tours 9-11.30am & 1-5.30pm Mon-Sat, 1-5.30pm Sun; Ⓜ Stephansplatz) Rising high and mighty above Vienna with its dazzling mosaic tiled roof is Stephansdom, or Steffl (little Stephen) as the Viennese call it. The cathedral was built on the site of a 12th-century church but its most distinctive features are Gothic. Only limited areas can be visited without a ticket. Taking centre stage inside is the magnificent Gothic **stone pulpit**, fashioned in 1515 by Anton Pilgram.

Dominating the cathedral is the skeletal, 136.7m-high **Südturm** (adult/child €3.50/1; ⏱9am-5.30pm). Negotiating 343 steps brings you to a cramped viewing platform for a stunning panorama of Vienna. You can also explore the cathedral's **Katakomben** (tours adult/child €5/2.50; ⏱10-11.30am & 1.30-4.30pm Mon-Sat, 1.30-4.30pm Sun), housing the remains of plague victims in a bone house and urns containing some of the organs of Habsburg rulers – gripping stuff.

Albertina   Gallery
(www.albertina.at; 01, Albertinaplatz 3; adult/child €11/free; ⏱10am-6pm Thu-Tue, to 9pm Wed; Ⓜ Karlsplatz, Stephansplatz, ᭡ D, 1, 2, 71 Kärntner Ring/Oper) Among its enormous

collection (1.5 million prints and 50,000 drawings) are 70 Rembrandts, 145 Dürers (including the famous *Hare*) and 43 Raphaels, as well as works by da Vinci, Michelangelo, Rubens, Cézanne, Picasso, Klimt and Kokoschka.

Schloss Schönbrunn   Palace
(www.schoenbrunn.at; 13, Schönbrunner Schlossstrasse 47; Imperial Tour with audio guide adult/child €11.50/8.50, Grand Tour adult/child €14.50/9.50, gardens admission free; ⏱8.30am-5.30pm, gardens 6am-dusk, maze 9am-6pm) The Habsburgs' overwhelmingly opulent summer palace is now a Unesco World Heritage site. Of the palace's 1441 rooms, 40 are open to the public; the Imperial Tour takes you into 26 of these. Because of the popularity of the palace, tickets are stamped with a departure time and there may be a time lag, so buy your ticket straight away and then explore the gardens.

Fountains dance in the French-style formal **gardens**. The gardens harbour the world's oldest zoo, the **Tiergarten** (www.zoovienna.at; adult/child €15/7; ⏱9am-6.30pm), founded in 1752; a 630m-long hedge **maze**; and the **Gloriette** (adult/child €3/2.20; ⏱9am-btwn 4pm & 7pm, closed early Nov-late Mar), whose roof offers a wonderful view over the palace grounds and beyond.

Kaisergruft   Church
(Imperial Burial Vault; www.kaisergruft.at; 01, Neuer Markt; adult/child €5/2; ⏱10am-6pm; Ⓜ Stephansplatz, Karlsplatz, ᭡ D, 1, 2, 71 Kärntner Ring/Oper) Beneath the Kapuzinerkirche (Church of the Capuchin Friars), the high-peaked Kaisergruft is the final resting place of most of the Habsburg elite.

Kunsthistorisches Museum   Museum
(Museum of Fine Arts; www.khm.at; 01, Maria-Theresien-Platz; adult/under 19yr €14/free; ⏱10am-6pm Tue-Sun, to 9pm Thu; Ⓜ Museumsquartier, Volkstheater) When it comes to classical works of art, nothing comes close to the Kunsthistorisches Museum. It houses a huge range of art amassed by the Habsburgs and includes works by Rubens, Van Dyck, Holbein and Caravaggio.

637

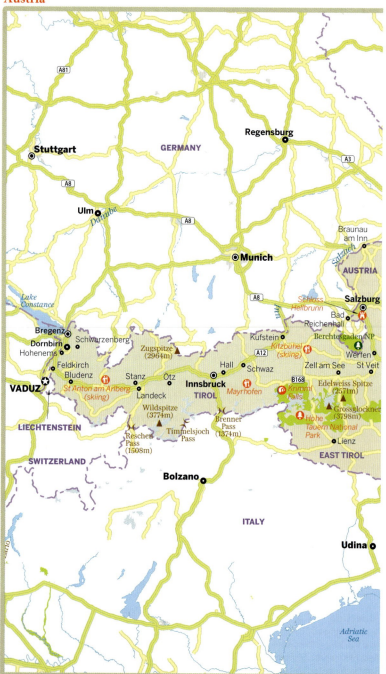

0 ——————— 100 km
0 ——————— 50 miles

CZECH REPUBLIC

20

Brno

Drosendorf

Retz

Horn

Hollabrunn

R43

SLOVAKIA

Passau

Danube

Freistadt

UPPER AUSTRIA

Krems an der Donau

Dürnstein

Stockerau

D2

Linz

Traun

A8

Ansfelden

Melk

Tulln

St Pölten

A1

Wels

THE SALZKAMMERGUT

Amstetten

Perchtoldsdorf

VIENNA

BRATISLAVA

Schwechat

Mödling

Steyr

Baden bei Wien

Bad Vöslau

Neusiedl am See

A1

Gmunden

Wiener Neustadt

A3

Eisenstadt

M1

Attersee

St Gilgen

Ebensee

Nationalpark Kalkalpen

Schneeberg (2076m)

Bad Ischl

Hoher Nock (1963m)

Mariazell

AUSTRIA

Neunkirchen

Bad Aussee

Admont

Eisenerz

Gloggnitz

Mürzzuschlag

Neusiedler See

Stainach

B320

Kapfenberg

S6

Oberpullendorf

Haus

Leoben

Bruck an der Mur

BURGENLAND

Radstadt

A9

STYRIA

Oberwart

Tamsweg

Unzmarkt-Frauenburg

Judenburg

Bad Blumau

HUNGARY

Murau

Köflach

Graz

Rennweg

CARINTHIA

Voitsberg

Güssing

Spittal an der Drau

St Veit an der Glan

Wolfsberg

A9

Feldbach

Feldkirchen

St Andrä

Ehrenhausen

Bad Radkersberg

Villach

Wörthersee

Völkermarkt

Klagenfurt

Drava

A2

E57

LJUBLJANA

Sava

E59

Drava

SLOVENIA

ZAGREB

CROATIA

Kupa

Sava

639

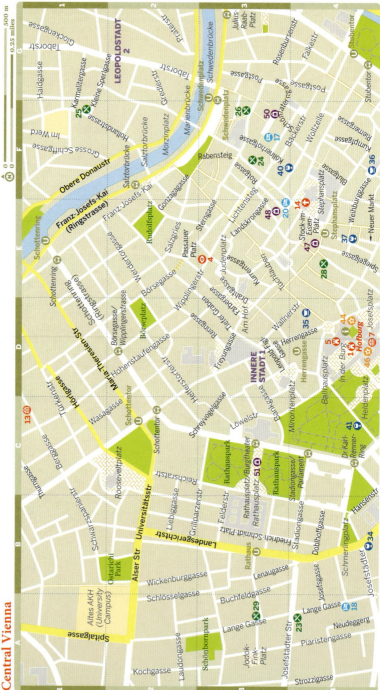

Central Vienna

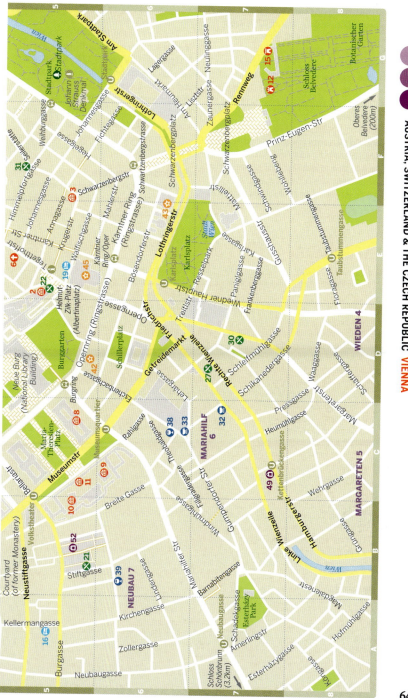

641

MuseumsQuartier
Museum

(Museum Quarter; www.mqw.at; 07, Museumsplatz; combined ticket €25; ⏱info & ticket centre 10am-7pm; Ⓜ Museumsquartier, Volkstheater) Small books have been written on this popular site, so only a taste can be given here. Spanning 60,000 sq metres, it's one of the world's most ambitious cultural spaces.

The highpoint is undoubtedly the **Leopold Museum** (www.leopoldmuseum.org; 07, Museumsplatz 1; adult/child €12/7; ⏱10am-6pm Wed-Mon, to 9pm Thu; Ⓜ Museumsquartier, Volkstheater), which showcases the world's largest collection of Egon Schiele paintings, alongside some fine works by Austrian artists like Klimt, Kokoschka and Albin Egger-Lienz.

The dark basalt **MUMOK** (Museum of Modern Art; www.mumok.at; 07, Museumsplatz 1; adult/child €10/free; ⏱2-7pm Mon, 10am-7pm Tue-Sun, to 9pm Thu, free guided tours 1pm Fri, 2pm & 4pm Sat & Sun, 7pm Thu; Ⓜ Museumsquartier, Volkstheater, 🚌49 Volkstheater) is alive with Vienna's premier collection of 20th-century art, centred on fluxus, nouveau realism, pop art and photo-realism.

Schloss Belvedere
Palace, Gallery

(www.belvedere.at; combined ticket adult/child €16/free; Ⓜ Taubstummengasse, Südtiroler Platz, 🚌D, 71 Schwarzenbergplatz) Belvedere is a

Central Vienna

◉ Don't Miss Sights
1 Hofburg D4

◉ Sights
2 Albertina E5
3 Haus der Musik F5
4 Holocaust-Denkmal E3
5 Kaiserappartements D4
6 Kaisergruft E5
7 Kaiserliche Schatzkammer D4
8 Kunsthistorisches Museum C5
9 Leopold Museum C6
10 MUMOK B5
11 MuseumsQuartier C5
12 Schloss Belvedere G7
13 Sigmund Freud Museum C1
14 Stephansdom E4
15 Unteres Belvedere G7

⬡ Sleeping
16 Altstadt A5
17 Hotel Kärntnerhof F3
18 Hotel Rathaus Wein & Design A4
19 Hotel Sacher E5
20 Pension Sacher E3

✕ Eating
21 Amerlingbeisl B5
22 Bitzinger Würstelstand am
   Albertinaplatz E5
23 Cupcakes Wien A4
24 Eis Griessler F3
25 Fett+Zucker F1
   Figlmüller .... (see 40)

26 Griechenbeisl F3
27 Naschmarkt D7
28 Reinthaler's Beisl E4
29 Schnattl A3
30 Süssi D7
31 Tian F5

⊙ Drinking & Nightlife
32 Café Drechsler C7
   Café Sacher .... (see 19)
33 Café Sperl C6
34 Dachboden B4
35 Demel D4
36 Kleines Café F4
37 Loos American Bar E4
38 Phil C6
39 Siebensternbräu B6
40 Vis-à-vis F3
41 Volksgarten Pavillon C4

✪ Entertainment
42 Burg Kino D5
43 Musikverein E6
44 Spanische Hofreitschule D4
45 Staatsoper E5
46 Vienna Boys' Choir Tickets D4

⊕ Shopping
47 Altmann & Kühne E4
48 Art Up E3
49 Flohmarkt C7
50 Heiligenkreuzerhof F3
51 Rathausplatz C3
52 Spittelberg B5

⭐ Don't Miss
Hofburg

Nothing symbolises the culture and heritage of Austria more than its Hofburg, home base of the Habsburgs for six centuries, from the first emperor (Rudolf I in 1273) to the last (Karl I in 1918). The Hofburg owes its size and architectural diversity to plain old one-upmanship; the oldest section is the 13th-century **Schweizerhof** (Swiss Courtyard).

The **Kaiserappartements** (Imperial Apartments; www.hofburg-wien.at; 01, Michaelerplatz; adult/child €10.50/6.50, with guided tour €13/7.50; ⊙ 9am-5.30pm; M Herrengasse), once occupied by Franz Josef I and Empress Elisabeth, are extraordinary for their chandelier-lit opulence. Included in the entry price, the **Sisi Museum** is devoted to the life of Austria's beauty-obsessed Empress Elisabeth, nicknamed 'Sisi'. Highlights include a reconstruction of her luxurious coach and the dress she wore on the eve of her wedding. A ticket to the Kaiserappartements also includes entry to the **Silberkammer** (Silver Chamber), showcasing fine silverware and porcelain.

Among several other points of interest within the Hofburg you'll find the Burgkapelle (Royal Chapel), where the Vienna Boys' Choir performs (p652); the Spanische Hofreitschule (p652) (Spanish Riding School); and the **Schatzkammer** (Imperial Treasury; www.kaiserliche-schatzkammer.at; 01, Schweizerhof; adult/under 19yr €12/free; ⊙ 9am-5.30pm Wed-Mon; M Herrengasse), which holds all manner of wonders including the 10th-century Imperial Crown, a 2860-carat Columbian emerald and even a thorn from Christ's crown.

NEED TO KNOW

Imperial Palace; www.hofburg-wien.at; 01, Michaelerkuppel; 🚌 1A, 2A Michaelerplatz, M Herrengasse, 🚊 D, 1, 2, 71, 46, 49 Burgring

masterpiece of total art and one of the world's finest baroque palaces, designed by Johann Lukas von Hildebrandt (1668–1745).

The first of the palace's two main buildings is the **Oberes Belvedere** (Upper Belvedere; 03, Prinz-Eugen-Strasse 27; adult/child €11/free; ⊙10am-6pm). Pride and joy of the gallery is Gustav Klimt's rich gold *The Kiss* (1908), which perfectly embodies Viennese art nouveau, accompanied by other late-19th- to early-20th-century Austrian works. The second is the grandiose **Unteres Belvedere** (Lower Belvedere; 03, Rennweg 6; adult/child €11/free; ⊙10am-6pm Thu-Tue, to 9pm Wed; 🚌D), which contains a baroque museum. The buildings sit at opposite ends of a manicured garden.

KunstHausWien Museum

(Art House Vienna; www.kunsthauswien.com; 03, Untere Weissgerberstrasse 13; adult/child €10/5; ⊙10am-7pm; Ⓜ1, O Radetzkyplatz) Like something out of a toy shop, this gallery was designed by eccentric Viennese artist

and architect Friedensreich Hundertwasser (1928–2000), whose love of uneven floors, colourful mosaic ceramics, irregular corners and rooftop greenery shines through.

Down the road there's a block of residential flats by Hundertwasser, the **Hundertwasserhaus** (03, cnr Löwengasse & Kegelgasse; 🚋1 Hetzgasse). It's not possible to see inside, but you can visit the **Kalke Village** (www.kalke-village.at; Kegelgasse 37-39, 03; ⊙9am-6pm; 🚋1 Hetzgasse) FREE , also the handiwork of Hundertwasser, created from an old Michelin factory, in typical fashion with a distinct absence of straight lines.

Trams 1 and O to Radetzkyplatz stop close by.

Prater Park

(www.wiener-prater.at; Ⓜ Praterstern) This large park encompasses grassy meadows, woodlands, an amusement park known as the **Würstelprater** and one of the city's icons, the **Riesenrad** (www.wienerriesenrad.com; 02, Prater 90; adult/child €9/4; ⊙9am-

Left: Fountain outside the Kunsthistorisches Museum (p637);
Below: Ferris wheel at Prater amusement park
(LEFT) RICHARD NEBESKY/GETTY IMAGES ©; (BELOW) ANDY CHRISTIANI/GETTY IMAGES ©

11.45pm, shorter hours in winter; metor Praterstern). Built in 1897, this 65m-high Ferris wheel takes about 20 minutes to rotate its 430-tonne weight, offering far-reaching views of Vienna. It achieved celluloid fame in *The Third Man*. Take U1 to Praterstern.

Haus der Musik   Museum
(☎ 513 4850; www.hdm.at; 01, Seilerstätte 30; adult/child €12/5.50, with Mozarthaus Vienna €17/7; ☺ 10am-10pm; Ⓜ Karlsplatz, 🚋 D, 1, 2 Kärntner Ring/Oper) Delving into the physics of sounds and paying tribute to Austria's great composers, this interactive museum is a fascinating journey through music. Most fun of all is the room where you can virtually conduct the Vienna Philharmonic.

Holocaust-Denkmal   Memorial
(01, Judenplatz; Ⓜ Stephansplatz) This is Austria's first Holocaust memorial, the 'Nameless Library'. The squat, boxlike structure pays homage to the 65,000 Austrian Jews who were killed during the Holocaust.

Sigmund Freud Museum   House Museum
(www.freud-museum.at; 09, Berggasse 19; adult/child €8/3.50; ☺ 9am-6pm; Ⓜ Schottentor, Schottenring, 🚋 D Schlickgasse) Former house of the famous psychologist, now housing a small museum featuring some of his personal belongings. The museum is 600m north of Schottentor.

🔶 Tours

Vienna Tour Guides   Walking Tour
(www.wienguide.at; adult/child €14/7) Conducts 60 different guided walking tours, some of which are in English, from art nouveau architecture to Jewish traditions and the ever-popular *Third Man* Tour.

✸ Festivals & Events

Opernball   Ball
(01, Staatsoper) Of the 300 or so balls held in January and February, the Opernball (Opera Ball) is the ultimate.

Viennale Film Festival   Film Festival
(☏ 526 59 47; www.viennale.at) The country's biggest and best film festival, featuring fringe and independent films from around the world in October.

Christkindlmärkte   Christmas Market
(www.christkindlmarkt.at) Vienna's much-loved Christmas market season runs from mid-November to Christmas Eve.

🛏 Sleeping

Hotel Rathaus
Wein & Design   Boutique Hotel €€
(☏ 400 11 22; www.hotel-rathaus-wien.at; 08, Lange Gasse 13; s/d/tr €150/210/240; ❄ @ 📶; Ⓜ Rathaus, Volkstheater) Each stylish room in this boutique hotel is dedicated to an Austrian winemaker and the chandelier-lit wine bar zooms in on a different winery

every month. The open-plan, minimalist-chic rooms reveal a razor-sharp eye for design, especially the opalescent ones with hybrid beds and bathtubs.

Pension Sacher   Pension €€
(☏ 533 32 38; www.pension-sacher.at; 01, Rothenturmstrasse 1; apt €90-136; ❄ 📶) Filled with chintzy knick-knacks, florals and solid wood furnishings, these super-central, spacious apartments are lovingly kept by the Sacher family of chocolate cake fame.

Boutiquehotel
Stadthalle   Hotel €€
(☏ 982 42 72; www.hotelstadthalle.at; 15, Hackengasse 20; s €78-138, d €118-198; 📶; Ⓜ Schweglerstrasse) 🖉 Welcome to Vienna's most sustainable hotel, which makes the most of solar power, rainwater collection and LED lighting, and has a roof fragrantly planted with lavender. An organic breakfast is served in the leafy garden in summer. Arrive by bike or train for a 10% discount. The hotel is 650m northwest of Westbahnhof.

Schloss Schönbrunn (p637)

FUSE/GETTY IMAGES ©

Altstadt
Pension €€

(☎ 522 66 66; www.altstadt.at; 07, Kirchengasse
41; s €125-175, d €145-215, ste €195-350; @ ☎;
Ⓜ Volkstheater) One of Vienna's finest pen-
sions, Altstadt has charming, individually
decorated rooms, with high ceilings,
plenty of space and a cosy lounge with
free afternoon tea and cakes. Staff are
genuinely affable and artworks are from
the owner's personal collection.

Hotel Sacher
Luxury Hotel €€€

(☎ 514 560; www.sacher.com; 01, Philharmonikerstrasse 4; r €480-1350, ste €1600-2900;
❄ @ ☎; Ⓜ Karlsplatz, 🚋 D, 1, 2, 71 Kärntner
Ring/Oper) Walking into the Sacher is like
turning back the clock a hundred years.
All of the lavishly decorated rooms boast
baroque furnishings and 19th-century oil
paintings, and the top-floor spa pampers
with chocolate treatments.

Hotel Kärntnerhof
Hotel €€

(☎ 512 19 23; www.karntnerhof.com; 01, Grashof-
gasse 4; s €99-129, d €135-195, tr €199-235, ste
€279-299; @ ☎; Ⓜ Stephansplatz) Tucked
away from the bustle, this treasure
oozes old Vienna charm, from the period
paintings to the wood- and frosted-glass-
panelled lift to the roof terrace. Rooms
mix a few plain pieces with antiques,
chandeliers and elegant curtains.

Altwienerhof
Hotel €€

(☎ 892 60 00; www.altwienerhof.at; 15, Herk-
lotzgasse 6; s €50-65, d €89-99, q €125; @;
Ⓜ Gumpendorfer Strasse) This pseudo-plush
family-run hotel, just outside the Gürtel
ring, offers ridiculously romantic abodes –
think miniature chandeliers, antique
pieces, floral bedding and lace tablecloths.
The hotel is a minute's walk west of U6
station Gumpendorfer Strasse.

Eating

Vienna has thousands of restaurants covering all budgets and styles of cuisine, but
dining doesn't stop there. *Kaffeehäuser*
(coffee houses), *Beisl* (small taverns) and
Heurigen (wine taverns) are just as fine
for a good meal. *Würstel Stande* (sausage
stands) are conveniently located on street
corners and squares.

Sweetness & Light

Indulge your sweet tooth at these
three Viennese favourites.

Cupcakes Wien (www.cupcakes-wien.at;
08, Josefstädter Strasse 17; cupcake €3.90;
⏰ 10am-7.30pm Mon-Fri, to 6pm Sat; 🚼;
Ⓜ Rathaus) A pretty pink wonderland
of cupcakes, with mascarpone
toppings in flavours like lime,
peanut and mint.

Süssi (☎ 943 13 24; www.suessi.at;
04, Operngasse 30; desserts €3.50-6,
afternoon tea €17; ⏰ 11am-9pm Tue-Sat,
1-9pm Sun; Ⓜ Karlsplatz) This tiny and
fabulously OTT French tea room
serves Mariage Frères brews with
delectable nut tarts, cream cakes
and macaroons.

Fett+Zucker (www.fettundzucker.at; 02,
Hollandstrasse 16; cakes & snacks €2.50-6;
⏰ 1-9pm Wed-Fri, 11am-9pm Sat & Sun; 🍴;
Ⓜ Taborstrasse, 🚋 2 Karmeliterplatz) As
the name suggests, the cheesecakes,
strudels and brownies at this retro
cafe don't skimp on the fat and sugar.

Foodies gravitate towards the
sprawling **Naschmarkt** (06, Linke & Rechte
Wienzeile; ⏰ 6am-7.30pm Mon-Fri, to 6pm Sat;
Ⓜ Karlsplatz, Kettenbrückengasse), the place
to *nasch* (snack) in Vienna.

Mill
Austrian €€

(☎ 966 40 73; www.mill32.at; 06, Millergasse 32;
mains €8-17.50; ⏰ 11.30am-3pm & 5pm-midnight
Mon-Fri, 11am-4pm Sun; Ⓜ Westbahnhof) This
art-slung bistro, with a hidden courtyard
for summer days, still feels like a local secret. Scarlet brick walls and wood floors
create a warm backdrop for spot-on seasonal food such as chanterelle cannelloni
and Styrian chicken salad drizzled with
pumpkin-seed oil. The two-course lunch
is a snip at €6.90. Mill is 400m south of
the U3 Westbahnhof station on Mariahilfer Strasse.

Tian
Vegetarian €€

(☎ 890 4665; www.tian-vienna.com; 01, Himmelpfortgasse 23; 3-course lunch €12.50-16, 3-6-course evening menu €39-69, mains €18; ⊙ noon-4pm & 6pm-midnight Mon-Fri, from 9am Sat; ⊿; Ⓜ Stephansplatz, ⊡ 2 Weihburggasse) ⊿ Vaulted charm meets urban attitude at this sleek lounge-style restaurant which takes vegetarian cuisine to delicious heights. Lunch menus offer the best value; you can also enjoy a drink at the cocktail bar.

Schnattl
International €€€

(☎ 405 34 00; www.schnattl.com; 08, Lange Gasse 40; mains €21-26, 3-course menus €33-38; ⊙ 6pm-midnight Mon-Fri; ⊿; Ⓜ Rathaus, ⊡ 2 Rathaus, Josefstädter Strasse) Wilhelm Schnattl gives flight to culinary fantasy at this wood-panelled bistro, centred on an inner courtyard and attracting a food-loving crowd of artists and actors.

Reinthaler's Beisl
Austrian €

(☎ 513 12 49; 01, Dorotheergasse 2-4; mains €9-13) This warm, woody *Beisl* has got everything going for it: a cracking location

just off Graben, a buzzy pavement terrace and a menu championing Viennese home cooking from brothy goulash with dumplings to perfectly crisp schnitzel.

Bitzinger Würstelstand am Albertinaplatz
Sausage Stand €

(01, Albertinaplatz; sausages €3.70-4.10; ⊙ 9.30am-5am, drinks from 8am; Ⓜ Karlsplatz, Stephansplatz, ⊡ Kärntner Ring/Oper) Located behind the Staatsoper, this is one of Vienna's best sausage stands.

Amerlingbeisl
Austrian €

(☎ 526 16 60; www.amerlingbeisl.at; 07, Stiftgasse 8; mains €7-14; ⊙ 9am-2am; ⊿; Ⓜ Volkstheater, ⊡ 49 Stiftgasse) The cobbled inner courtyard of this Spittelberg *Beisl*, with tables set up under the trees, is a summer evening magnet. The chef cooks Austro-Italian, hitting the mark with homemade pasta and dishes like pike perch with saffron noodles.

Figlmüller
Bistro Pub €€

(☎ 512 61 77; www.figlmueller.at; 01, Wollzeile 5; mains €13-23; ⊙ 11am-10.30pm, kitchen closes 9.30pm; 📶; Ⓜ Stephansplatz) This famous *Beisl* has been sizzling up some of the biggest (and best) schnitzels in town since 1905. Sure, the rural decor is contrived, but it doesn't get more Viennese than this.

Eis Griessler
Ice Cream €

(01, Rotenturmstrasse 14; scoop €1.30; ⊙ 10.30am-11pm) Organic milk and fresh fruit go into dreamily smooth ice creams like Alpine caramel and Wachau apricot at this hole-in-the-wall parlour.

Griechenbeisl
Bistro Pub €€

(☎ 533 19 77; www.griechenbeisl.at; 01, Fleischmarkt 11; mains €11.60-25; ⊙ 11am-1am; Ⓜ Schwedenplatz, ⊡ 1, 2 Schwedenplatz) This is Vienna's oldest

Cakes at Demel
GREG ELMS/GETTY IMAGES ©

Coffee House Culture

Vienna's legendary *Kaffeehäuser* (coffee houses) are wonderful places for people-watching, daydreaming and catching up on gossip or world news. Most serve light meals alongside mouth-watering cakes and tortes. Expect to pay around €8 for a coffee with a slice of cake. These are just five of our favourites.

Café Sperl (www.cafesperl.at; 06, Gumpendorfer Strasse 11; �
7am-11pm Mon-Sat, 11am-8pm Sun; 📶; 🅼Museumsquartier, Kettenbrückengasse) Gorgeous Jugendstil fittings, grand dimensions, cosy booths and an unhurried air. The must-try is *Sperl Torte* – an almond and chocolate cream dream.

Kleines Café (01, Franziskanerplatz 3; �
10am-2am Mon-Sat, 1pm-2am Sun; 🅼Stubentor, 🚋2 Weihburggasse) Tiny bohemian cafe with wonderful summer seating on Franziskanerplatz.

Café Sacher (01, Philharmonikerstrasse 4; �
8am-midnight) This opulent coffee house is celebrated for its *Sacher Torte* (€4.90), a rich chocolate cake with apricot jam once favoured by Emperor Franz Josef.

Demel (www.demel.at; 01, Kohlmarkt 14; �
9am-7pm; 🚌1A, 2A Michaelerplatz, 🅼Herrengasse, Stephansplatz) An elegant, regal cafe near the Hofburg. Demel's speciality is the *Anna Torte,* a chocolate and nougat calorie-bomb.

Café Drechsler (www.cafedrechsler.at; Linke Wienzeile 22; �
open 23hr, closed 2-3am; 📶; 🅼Kettenbrückengasse) Sir Terence Conran revamped this stylish yet distinctly Viennese cafe. Its goulash is legendary, as are the DJ tunes that keep the vibe hip and upbeat.

Beisl (dating from 1447), once frequented by the likes of Beethoven, Schubert and Brahms. The vaulted, wood-panelled rooms are a cosy setting for classic Viennese dishes.

🍷 Drinking & Nightlife

Phil   Bar, Cafe
(www.phil.info; 06, Gumpendorfer Strasse 10-12; �
5pm-1am Mon, 9am-1am Tue-Sun; 🅼Museumsquartier, Kettenbrückengasse) A retro bar, book and record store, Phil attracts a bohemian crowd happy to squat on kitsch furniture your grandma used to own. Staff are super-friendly and the vibe is as relaxed as can be.

Volksgarten Pavillon   Bar
(www.volksgarten-pavillon.at; 01, Burgring 1; �
11am-2am Apr–mid-Sep; 📶; 🅼Volkstheater, 🚋D, 1, 2, 71 Dr-Karl-Renner-Ring) A lovely 1950s-style pavilion with views of Heldenplatz and an ever-popular garden.

Dachboden   Bar
(http://25hours-hotels.com; 07, 25hours Hotel, Lerchenfelder Strasse 1-3; �
2pm-1am Tue-Sat, to 10pm Sun; 📶; 🅼Volkstheater) The terrace with knockout views of Vienna is the big deal, but even in winter this arty attic bar is wonderfully relaxed, with low cushion seating and the occasional DJ night.

Vis-à-vis   Wine Bar
(📞512 93 50; www.weibel.at; 01, Wollzeile 5; �
4.30pm-10.30pm Tue-Sat; 🅼Stephansplatz) Hidden down a narrow, atmospheric passage is this wee wine bar. It may only seat close to 10 but it makes up for it with over 350 wines on offer (with a strong emphasis on Austrian faves) and great antipasti.

Loos American Bar   Cocktail Bar
(www.loosbar.at; 01, Kärntner Durchgang 10; �
noon-5am Thu-Sat, to 4am Sun-Wed; 🅼Stephansplatz) Designed by Adolf Loos in 1908, this tiny box decked head-to-toe

in onyx is *the* spot for a classic cocktail in the Innere Stadt, expertly whipped up by talented mixologists.

Siebensternbräu — Microbrewery
(www.7stern.at; 07, Siebensterngasse 19; ⊙11am-midnight; Ⓜ Neubaugasse) **FREE**
Large brewery with all the main varieties, plus hemp beer, chilli beer and smoky beer. The hidden back garden is sublime in summer.

⭐ Entertainment

Vienna is, and probably will be till the end of time, the European capital of opera and classical music.

Box offices are generally open from Monday to Saturday.

Staatsoper — Opera
(☎514 44 7880; www.wiener-staatsoper.at; 01, Opernring 2; Ⓜ Karlsplatz, 🚋 D 1, 2 Kärntner Ring/Oper) Performances at Vienna's premier opera and classical music venue are lavish, formal affairs, where people dress up. Standing-room tickets (€3 to €4) are sold 80 minutes before performances begin.

Musikverein — Concert Venue
(☎505 81 90; www.musikverein.at; 01, Bösendorferstrasse 12; Ⓜ Karlsplatz) The opulent Musikverein, home to the Vienna Philharmonic Orchestra, is celebrated for its acoustics. Standing-room tickets in the main hall cost €5 to €6.

Pratersauna — Club
(www.pratersauna.tv; 02, Waldsteingartenstrasse 135; ⊙club 9pm-6am Wed-Sun, pool 1-9pm Fri & Sat Jun-Sep; Ⓜ Messe-Prater) Pool, cafe, bistro and club converge in a former sauna – these days, you'll sweat it up on the dance floor any given night, with DJs playing mostly techno and electro. Take U2 to Messe-Prater and walk south 600m.

Volksoper — Concert Venue
(People's Opera; ☎514 44 3670; www.volksoper.at; 09, Währinger Strasse 78; Ⓜ Währinger Strasse) Vienna's second opera house features operettas, dance and musicals. Standing tickets go for as little as €2 to €6.

Burg Kino — Cinema
(☎587 84 06; www.burgkino.at; 01, Opernring 19; Ⓜ Museumsquartier, 🚋 D, 1, 2 Burgring) English films; has regular screenings of *The Third Man*.

🔒 Shopping

Vienna's atmospheric **Flohmarkt** (Flea Market; 05, Kettenbrückengasse; ⊙dawn-4pm Sat; Ⓢ U4 Kettenbrückengasse) shouldn't be missed, with goods piled up in apparent chaos on the walkway. Come prepared to haggle.

From mid-November, *Christkindlmärkte* (Christmas markets) bring festive sparkle to Vienna, their stalls laden with gifts, *glühwein* (mulled wine) and *Maroni* (roasted chestnuts). Some of the best include the pretty but touristy **Rathausplatz market** (🚋1, 2), the traditional **Spittelberg market** (🚋48A, Ⓢ U2, U3 Volkstheater, 🚋49) in Spittelberg's cobbled streets, where you can pick up quality crafts, and the authentic, oft-forgotten **Heiligenkreuzerhof market** (01; Ⓜ Schwedenplatz, 🚋2 Stubentor).

Blühendes Konfekt — Confectionery
(www.bluehendes-konfekt.com; 06, Schmalzhofgasse 19; ⊙10am-6.30pm Wed-Fri; Ⓜ Zieglergasse, Westbahnhof) Violets, forest strawberries and cherry blossom, wild mint and oregano – Michael Diewald makes the most of the seasons and what grows in his garden to create one-of-a-kind candied bouquets and confectionery. The shop is 350m southwest of U3 Zieglergasse station on Mariahilfer Strasse.

Art Up — Fashion, Accessories
(www.artup.at; 01, Bauernmarkt 8; ⊙11am-6.30pm Mon-Fri, to 5pm Sat; Ⓜ Stephansplatz) Take the temperature of Vienna's contemporary design scene at Art Up, showcasing the latest designs of around 80 Austrian creatives.

Altmann & Kühne — Food
(www.altmann-kuehne.at; 01, Graben 30; ⊙9am-6.30pm Mon-Fri, 10am-5pm Sat; Ⓜ Stephans-

platz) Altmann & Kühne has been producing and beautifully packaging handmade bonbons for over 100 years. Stop by for a box of its famous *Liliputkonfekt* (miniature pralines).

ℹ Information

Tourist Info Wien (☎245 55; www.wien. info; 01, Albertinaplatz; ⏱9am-7pm; 📶; Ⓜ Stephansplatz, 🚋D, 1, 2, 71 Kärntner Ring/ Oper) Vienna's main tourist office, with a ticket agency, hotel booking service, free maps and every brochure you could ever wish for.

ℹ Getting There & Away

Boat

Heading west, a series of boats ply the Danube between Krems and Melk, with a handful of services originating in Vienna. Two respectable operators include DDSG Blue Danube and **Brandner** (☎07433-25 90 21; www.brandner. at; Ufer 50, Wallsee), the latter located in Wallsee. Both run trips from April through October that start at around €15 one way.

Train

Vienna is one of central Europe's main rail hubs. **Österreichische Bundesbahn** (ÖBB; www.oebb. at; Austrian Federal Railway) is the main operator. Sample destinations include Budapest (2½ to three hours, €37.40), Munich (four to five hours, €88), Paris (11½ to 15 hours, €88), Prague (4½ hours, €64.40) and Venice (seven to 11 hours, €63 to €99).

Vienna's shiny new **Hauptbahnhof** (Vienna Central Station; www.hauptbahnhof-wien.at; 🚌13A, 69A, Ⓜ U1, 🚋D, 0, 18) partially reopened in December 2012, with an eastern section set up to serve some trains to/from the east, including Bratislava. The rail project is a massive €987 million undertaking and operations are expected to fully resume in 2015, with the main station receiving international trains. Currently, most long-distance trains are being rerouted among the rest of Vienna's train stations, including the recently revamped Westbahnhof.

ℹ Getting Around

To/From the Airport

It is 19km from the city centre to **Vienna International Airport** (VIE; www.viennaairport. com) in Schwechat. The **City Airport Train** (CAT; www.cityairporttrain.com; return adult/child €19/ free; ⏱departs airport 5.36am-11.06pm) runs every 30 minutes and takes 16 minutes between the airport and Wien Mitte; book online for a €2

Schloss Belvedere (p642)

MANCHAN/GETTY IMAGES ©

Imperial Entertainment

Founded over five centuries ago by Maximilian I as the imperial choir, the world-famous **Vienna Boys' Choir** (Wiener Sängerknaben; www.wienersaengerknaben.at) is the original boy band. These cherubic angels in sailor suits still hold a fond place in Austrian hearts. **Tickets** (📞 533 99 27; www.hofburgkapelle.at; 01, Schweizerhof; Sunday performances in Burgkapelle €5-29) for their Sunday performances at 9.15am (September to June) in the Burgkapelle (Royal Chapel) in the Hofburg should be booked around six weeks in advance. The group also performs regularly in the Musikverein.

Another throwback to the Habsburg glory days is the **Spanische Hofreitschule** (Spanish Riding School; 📞 533 90 31; www.srs.at; 01, Michaelerplatz 1; 🕐 performances 11am Sat & Sun mid-Feb–Jun & late Aug-Dec). White Lipizzaner stallions gracefully perform equine ballet to classical music, while chandeliers shimmer from above and the audience cranes to see from pillared balconies. Tickets, costing between €23 and €158, are ordered through the website, but be warned that performances usually sell out months in advance. Unclaimed tickets are sold about two hours before performances. **Morning Training** (adult/child/family €14/7/28; 🕐 10am-noon Tue-Fri Feb-Jun & mid-Aug–Dec) same-day tickets are available at the **visitor centre** (🕐 9am-4pm Tue-Sun) on Michaelerplatz.

---

discount. The S-Bahn (S7) does the same journey (single €4), but in 25 minutes.

Taxis cost about €35. **C&K Airport Service** (📞 444 44; www.cundk.at) charges €32 one way for shared vans.

Bicycle

Cycling is an excellent way to get around and explore the city – over 800km of cycle tracks criss-cross the capital.

Vienna's city bike scheme is called **Vienna City Bike** (www.citybikewien.at; 1st hour free, 2nd/3rd hr €1/2, per hour thereafter €4), with more than 60 bicycle stands across the city. A credit card is required to rent bikes – just swipe your card in the machine and follow the instructions (in a number of languages).

Car & Motorcycle

Due to a system of one-way streets and expensive parking, you're better off using the excellent public transport system.

Fiakers

More of a tourist novelty than anything else, a *Fiaker* is a traditional-style horse-drawn carriage. Expect to pay a cool €80/105 for a 40-/60-minute ride from Stephansplatz, Albertinaplatz or Heldenplatz.

Public Transport

Vienna's unified public transport network encompasses trains, trams, buses, and underground (U-Bahn) and suburban (S-Bahn) trains. Tickets are cheaper to buy from ticket machines in U-Bahn stations and in *Tabak* (tobacconist) shops, where singles cost €2. On board, they cost €2.20.

A 24-hour ticket costs €6.70, a 48-hour ticket €11.70 and a 72-hour ticket €14.50. Weekly tickets (valid Monday to Sunday) cost €15; the Vienna Card (€19.90) includes travel on public transport for up to three days. The Strip Ticket (*Streifenkarte*) costs €8 and gives you four single tickets.

Taxi

Taxis are metered for city journeys and cost €2.60 flag fall during the day and €2.70 at night, plus a small per kilometre fee.

The Danube Valley

The stretch of Danube between Krems and Melk, known locally as the Wachau, is arguably the loveliest along the entire length of the mighty river. Both banks are dotted with ruined castles and medieval towns, and lined with terraced vineyards.

Further upstream is the industrial city of Linz, Austria's avant garde art and new technology trailblazer.

KREMS AN DER DONAU

☎02732 / POP 24,110

Sitting on the northern bank of the Danube against a backdrop of terraced vineyards, Krems marks the beginning of the Wachau. It has an attractive cobbled centre, a small university, some good restaurants and the gallery-dotted Kunstmeile (Art Mile).

⦿ Sights

Kunsthalle   Gallery
(www.kunsthalle.at; Franz-Zeller-Platz 3; admission €10; ⊙10am-6pm) The flagship of Krems' **Kunstmeile** (www.kunstmeile-krems.at), an eclectic collection of galleries and museums, the Kunsthalle has a program of small but excellent changing exhibitions.

🛏 Sleeping & Eating

▓▓ el Krems   Hotel €€
▓▓ww.arte-hotel.at; Dr-Karl-Dorrek-▓▓; s €85-105, d €128-162; P 🛜) This comfortable new art hotel close to the university has large, well-styled rooms in bright colours and with open-plan bathrooms.

Hotel Unter den
▓den   Hotel €€
▓82 115; www.udl.at; ▓illerstrasse 5; s €50, d ▓4-98) This big, yellow, family-run hotel has knowledgeable and helpful owners, bright comfortable rooms and a convenient location in Krems itself.

Mörwald
Kloster Und
Austrian €€€
(☎70 493; www.moerwald.at; Undstrasse 6; mains €35-39, 5-course menu €75, 3-course lunch €29; ⊙lunch & dinner Tue-Sat) Run by celebrity chef and winemaker Toni Mörwald, this is one of the Wachau's best restaurants. Delicacies from roast pigeon breast to fish dishes with French touches are married with top wines. There's a lovely garden.

ℹ Getting There & Away

Frequent daily trains connect Krems with Vienna's Franz-Josefs-Bahnhof (€15.20, one hour) and Melk (€11.90, 1¼ hours).

The South

Austria's two main southern states, Styria (Steiermark) and Carinthia (Kärnten), often feel worlds apart from the rest of the country, both in climate and attitude. Styria is a blissful amalgamation of genteel architecture, rolling green hills, vine-covered slopes and soaring mountains. Its capital, Graz, is one of Austria's most attractive cities.

Danube River, Wachau Valley
DANITA DELIMONT/GETTY IMAGES ©

Detour: Melk

Rising like a vision on a hill overlooking the town, **Stift Melk** (Benedictine Abbey of Melk; ☎5550; www.stiftmelk.at; Abt Berthold Dietmayr Strasse 1; adult/child €9.50/5, with guided tour €11.50/7; ⊙9am-5.30pm May-Sep, tours at 11am & 2pm only Oct-Apr) is Austria's most famous abbey. It has been home to Benedictine monks since the 11th century, though it owes its current good looks to 18th-century mastermind Jakob Prandtauer.

The interior of the twin-spired monastery church is baroque gone barmy, with endless prancing angels and gold twirls. Other highlights include the **Bibliothek** (Library) and the **Marmorsaal** (Marble Hall); the trompe l'oeil on the ceiling (by Paul Troger) gives the illusion of greater height. Eleven of the imperial rooms, where dignitaries (including Napoleon) stayed, now house a **museum**.

From around November to March, the monastery can only be visited by guided tour (11am and 2pm daily). Always phone ahead to ensure you get an English-language tour.

Boats leave from the canal by Pionierstrasse, 400m north of the abbey. There are hourly trains to Vienna (€17.10, 1¼ hours).

GRAZ

☎0316 / POP 265,400

Austria's second-largest city is probably its most relaxed and, after Vienna, its liveliest for after-hours pursuits. It's an attractive place with bristling green parkland, red rooftops and a small, fast-flowing river gushing through its centre.

◎ Sights

Admission to all of the major museums with a 24-hour ticket costs €11/4 for adults/children.

Neue Galerie Graz Joanneumsviertel
Gallery

(www.museum-joanneum.at; Joanneumsviertel; adult/child €8/3; ⊙10am-5pm Tue-Sun; 🚋1, 3, 4, 5, 6, 7 Hauptplatz) The crowning glory of this Styria-wide ensemble of museums and palaces is the new **Joanneumsviertel** (www.joanneumsviertel.at; Kalchberggasse ; ⊙visitor centre 10am-5pm) cultural quarter, gathered around squares and courtyards and seamlessly bringing together baroque and contemporary architecture. Besides the state library and multimedia collections, the complex is home to the **Neue Galerie Graz** (Joanneumsviertel, Kalchberggasse ; adult/child €8/3; ⊙10am-5pm Tue-Sun), with an outstanding collection of 19th- and 20th-century art, placing the emphasis o[n Aus]trian masters from Klimt to Otto[...]

Kunsthaus Graz

(www.kunsthausgraz.at; Lendkai 1; adult/child €8/3; ⊙10am-5pm Tue-Sun; 🚋1, 3, 6, 7 Südtiroler Platz) Designed by British architects Peter Cook and Colin Fournier, this world-class contemporary art space looks something like a space-age sea slug.

Schloss Eggenberg
Palac[e]

(Eggenberger Allee 90; adult/child €8/3; ⊙pa[l]ace tours 10am-4pm Tue-Sun Palm Sunday-Oct; 🚋1 Schloss Eggenberg) A blend of Gothic, Renaissance and baroque styles, this beautiful Unesco World Heritage palace can be reached by tram 1 from Hauptplatz. Admission includes a guided tour (on the hour except at 1pm), taking in 24 *Prunkräume* (staterooms), which are based around astronomy, the zodiac and classical or religious mythology.

Murinsel
Bridge

(🚋4, 5 Schlossplatz/Murinsel, 🚋1, 3, 6, 7 Südtiroler Platz) FREE This artificial island-cum-bridge in the Mur River is an open seashell of glass, concrete and steel by New York artist Vito Acconci.

Schlossberg   Viewpoint
(Glass Lift 1hr ticket €1.90; ⛴4, 5 Schlossplatz/Murinsel [for lift]) FREE The wooded slopes ███████ ossberg (473m) can be reached on █████ funicular **Schlossbergbahn** ██████ 1hr ticket adult/child €2/1) ████nz-Josef-Kai, or by **Glass Lift** from ████hlossbergplatz. The townsfolk paid Napoleon a ransom of 2987 florins and 11 farthings to spare the tower during the 1809 invasion.

Landeszeughaus   Museum
(www.museum-joanneum.at; Herrengasse 16; adult/child €8/3; ⏱10am-5pm Mon & Wed-Sun; ⛴1, 3, 4, 5, 6, 7 Hauptplatz) A must-see for fans of armour and weapons, housing an astounding array of 30,000 gleaming exhibits.

🛏 Sleeping

Hotel zum Dom   Hotel €€
(☎82 48 00; www.domhotel.co.at; Bürgergasse 14; s €84, d €129-179, ste €199; P ❄ 🛜; 📶30 Palais Trauttmansdorff/Urania, ⛴1, 3, 4, 5, 6, 7

Murinsel, Graz

Hauptplatz) Hotel zum Dom's individually furnished rooms come with power showers or whirlpools, and one suite even has a terrace whirlpool.

Hotel Daniel   Hotel €
(☎711 080; www.hoteldaniel.com; Europaplatz 1; r €59-79, breakfast per person €11 ; P ❄ @ 🛜; 📶1, 3, 6, 7 Hauptbahnhof) Perched at the top of Annenstrasse, the Daniel is an exclusive design hotel. All rooms are tastefully furnished in minimalist designs.

Augarten Hotel   Hotel €€
(☎20 800; www.augartenhotel.at; Schönaugasse 53; s €89-169, d €114-194, penthouse ste s €204-280, d € 229-305; P ❄ 🛜 ♒; 📶4, 5 Finanzamt) The arty Augarten is decorated with the owner's private collection. All rooms are bright and modern, and the pool and sauna round off an excellent option.

Eating

With leafy salads dressed in delicious pumpkin-seed oil, fish specialities and *Pfand'l* (pan-grilled) dishes, Styrian cuisine is Austrian cooking at its light and healthy best.

FRANZ MARC FREI/GETTY IMAGES ©

Below: Mozart Monument, Mozartplatz, Salzburg;
Right: Residenzplatz, Salzburg
(BELOW) DENNIS K. JOHNSON/GETTY IMAGES ©; (RIGHT) WESTEND61/GETTY IMAGES ©

Der Steirer   Beisl €€

(703 654; www.dersteirer.at; Belgiergasse 1;
mains €10-19.50, tapas €2, lunch menu €7.90;
11am-midnight; ; 1, 3, 6, 7 Südtiroler
Platz) This Styrian neo-*Beisl* and wine bar
has a small but excellent selection of local
dishes and a large choice of wines. The
goulash with fried polenta is easily one of
the best in the country.

Magnolia   Austrian €€€

(823 835; www.restaurant-magnolia.at/;
Schöngaugasse 53; 3-5-course evening menu
€62-82, 2-/3-course lunch menu €16/30;
lunch & dinner Mon-Fri; 4, 5, 13 Finanzamt)
Alongside Augarten Hotel, with outdoor
seating, this stylish restaurant with a
seasonal menu and Austro-international
cuisine is highly rated.

Landhauskeller   Austrian €€

(83 02 76; Schmiedgasse 9; mains €10.50-
28.50; 11.30am-midnight Mon-Sat; 1, 3 ,4, 5,
6, 7 Hauptplatz) What started as a spit-and-
sawdust pub in the 16th
century evolved into an atmospheric, medieval-style restaurant
serving specialities like its four different
sorts of *Tafelspitz* (prime broiled beef).

ℹ Information

Graz Tourismus (80 75; www.graztourismus.
at; Herrengasse 16; 10am-6pm; ; 1, 3, 4,
5, 6, 7 Hauptplatz)

ℹ Getting There & Away

Trains to Vienna (€37, 2½ hours) depart hourly,
and six daily go to Salzburg (€48.60, four hours).

Salzburg

0662 / POP 149,600

The joke 'If it's baroque, don't f
perfect maxim for Salzburg; the tranquil
Old Town burrowed below steep hills
looks much as it did when Mozart lived
here 250 years ago. Second only to Vienna in numbers of visitors, this compact

stars from late July to late August. Book on its website before January, or ask the **Festspiele Ticket Office** (☏80 45-500; info@salzburgfestival.at; Herbert-von-Karajan-Platz 11; ⊘9.30am-1pm & 2-5pm Mon-Sat) about cancellations during the festival.

🛏 Sleeping

Haus Ballwein   Guesthouse €
(☏82 40 29; www.haus-ballwein.at; Moosstrasse 69a; s €35-45, d €58-68, apt €100-115; Ⓟ 🛜)
Country or city? Why not both at this farmhouse guesthouse, a 10-minute trundle from the Altstadt on bus 21. With its bright, pine-filled rooms, mountain views, free bike hire and garden patrolled by duck duo, Rosalee and Clementine, this place is big on charm.

Arte Vida   Guesthouse €€
(☏87 31 85; www.artevida.at; Dreifaltigkeitsgasse 9; s €55-140, d €80-152; 🛜) Arte Vida has the boho-chic feel of a Marrakesh *riad*, with its lantern-lit salon, communal kitchen and individually designed rooms done out in rich colours and fabrics.

Hotel Am Dom   Boutique Hotel €€€
(☏84 27 65; www.hotelamdom.at; Goldgasse 17; s €90-160, d €130-280; ❄ 🛜) Antique meets boutique at this Altstadt hotel, where the original vaults and beams of the 800-year-old building contrast with razor-sharp design features.

Hotel & Villa Auersperg   Boutique Hotel €€
(☏88 94 40; www.auersperg.at; Auerspergstrasse 61; s €129-155, d €165-205, ste 235-310; Ⓟ @ 🛜) This charismatic villa-hotel hybrid fuses late-19th-century flair with contemporary design. Relax by the lily pond in the garden or in the rooftop wellness area with mountain views.

Haus Wartenberg   Guesthouse €€
(☏84 84 00; www.hauswartenberg.com; Riedenburgerstrasse 2; d €128; Ⓟ @ 🛜) Set in vine-strewn gardens, this 17th-century chalet guesthouse is a 10-minute stroll west of the Altstadt. Country-style rooms done out in chunky pinewood and florals are in keeping with the character of the place.

1 SCHLOSS MIRABELL
Fans of *The Sound of Music* absolutely mustn't miss the gardens of Schloss Mirabell. Several key scenes were filmed here, most famously the sequences on the steps and around the fountain during 'Do-Re-Mi'. The rest of the park is gorgeous to explore, too – look out for the little gnome garden!

2 SCHLOSS HELLBRUNN
Another must-see for musical aficionados, where you can see the gazebo under which Liesl and Rolf sang 'Sixteen Going on Seventeen'. The grounds are also home to the famous Wasserspiele fountains and the oldest-known outdoor theatre in Austria.

3 MÜNCHSBERG
This rocky hill high above the city has one of the best views over Salzburg, which you can see in the film when Julie Andrews emerges from the monastery. At the top is the Museum der Moderne, which has a great restaurant, the M32, with a panoramic window over the city. Very romantic!

4 HOHENSALZBURG
Salzburg's castle is touristy, but catching the funicular to the top is just one of those experiences everyone should do. Nearby there's a trail to Nunnberg Abbey, which features in the film during scenes between Maria and the Reverend Mother.

5 KAPUZINERBERG
It's a bit off the beaten track, about 30 minutes' walk from the centre, but the Kapuzinerberg is a lovely, little-known area of Salzburg. There's an old monastery, the Franziskischloessl, with a sweet cloister and a guesthouse. It feels really hidden, and it's a great place for an evening beer.

Wolf Dietrich — Historic Hotel €€

(📞 87 12 75; www.salzburg-hotel.at; Wolf-Dietrich-Strasse 7; s €90-130, d €152-222, ste €197-277; 🅿️ 🛜 ♨️) For old-fashioned elegance you can't beat this central hotel, where rooms are dressed in polished wood furnishings and floral fabrics. In contrast, the spa and pool are ultramodern. Organic produce is served at breakfast.

🍴 Eating

Self-caterers can find picnic fixings at the **Grüner Markt** (Green Market; Universitätsplatz; ⏱️Mon-Sat).

Magazin — Modern European €€€

(📞 84 15 84; www.magazin.co.at; Augustinergasse 13a; mains €25-31, tasting menus €57-79, cookery classes €130-150; ⏱️Mon-Sat) Gathered around a courtyard below Mönchsberg's sheer rock wall, Magazin shelters a deli, wine store, cookery school and restaurant. Chef Richard Brunnauer's menus, fizzing with seasonal flavours like scallops with vine-ripened peaches and venison medallions in porcini sauce, are matched with wines from the 850-bottle cellar.

No Tourist Trapp

Did you know that there were 10 (not seven) von Trapp children? Or that Rupert was the eldest (so long Liesl) and the captain a gentle-natured man? For the truth behind the Hollywood legend, stay at **Villa Trapp** (📞 630 860; www.villa-trapp.com; Traunstrasse 34; d €109-500) in Aigen district, 3km southeast of the Altstadt. Marianne and Christopher have transformed the von Trapp's elegant 19th-century villa into a beautiful guesthouse, brimming with family heirlooms and snapshots. The villa sits in Salzburg's biggest private park.

Bärenwirt — Austrian €€

(📞 42 24 04; www.baerenwirt-salzburg.at; Müllner Hauptstrasse 8; mains €9-18; ⏱️11am-11pm) Sizzling and stirring since 1663, Bärenwirt combines a woody, hunting-lodge-style interior with a river-facing terrace. Go for hearty *Bierbraten* (beer roast) with dumplings, locally caught trout or organic wild boar bratwurst.

Alter Fuchs — Austrian €€

(📞 88 20 22; Linzer Gasse 47-49; mains €10-17; ⏱️noon-midnight Mon-Sat; 🧒 ♿) This old fox prides itself on serving up old-fashioned Austrian fare, such as schnitzels fried to golden perfection. Foxes clad in bandanas guard the bar in the vaulted interior and there's a courtyard for good-weather dining.

Riedenburg — Modern European €€€

(📞 83 08 15; www.riedenburg.at; Neutorstrasse 31; lunch €18, mains €26-35; ⏱️Tue-Sat) At this romantic Michelin-starred pick, creative Austrian signatures such as venison and guinea fowl crêpes with wild herbs are expertly matched with top wines. Take bus 1, 4 or 5 to Moosstrasse.

M32 — Fusion €€

(📞 84 10 00; www.m32.at; Mönchsberg 32; 3-course lunch €27, 5-course dinner €68-70, mains €14-23; ⏱️9am-1am Tue-Sun; 🧒 ♿) Bold colours and a forest of stag antlers reveal architect Matteo Thun's imprint at Museum der Moderne's glass-walled restaurant. The seasonal food and views are fantastic.

IceZeit — Ice Cream €

(Chiemseegasse 1; scoop €1.20; ⏱️11am-8pm) Grab a cone at Salzburg's best ice-cream parlour.

🍷 Drinking & Nightlife

Augustiner Bräustübl — Brewery

(www.augustinerbier.at; Augustinergasse 4-6; ⏱️3-11pm Mon-Fri, 2.30-11pm Sat & Sun) Who says monks can't enjoy themselves? Since 1621, this cheery monastery-run brewery has been serving potent home brews in the vaulted hall and beneath the chestnut trees in the 1000-seat beer garden.

Mozart's Birthplace (Mozarts Geburtshaus, p659), Salzburg

MICHAEL ZEGERS/GETTY IMAGES ©

Unikum Sky · Cafe

(Unipark Nonntal; ⏱10am-7pm Mon-Fri, 9.30am-6pm Sat) For knockout fortress views, drinks and inexpensive snacks, head up to this sun-kissed terrace atop the new Unipark Nonntal campus.

Café Tomaselli · Cafe

(www.tomaselli.at; Alter Markt 9; ⏱7am-9pm Mon-Sat, 8am-9pm Sun) If you like your service with a dollop of Viennese grumpiness and strudel with a dollop of cream, this grand, wood-panelled coffee house in the city centre is just the ticket.

⭐ Entertainment

Some of the high-brow venues include the **Schlosskonzerte** (☎84 85 86; www.salzburger-schlosskonzerte.at; Theatergasse 2; ⏱8pm), in Schloss Mirabell's sublime baroque Marble Hall, and the **Mozarteum** (☎889 40; www.mozarteum.at; Schwarzstrasse 26-28). Marionettes bring *The Sound of Music* and Mozart's operas magically to life at **Salzburger Marionettentheater** (☎87 24 06; www.marionetten.at; Schwarzstrasse 24; ⏱May-Sep, Christmas, Easter; 👪).

ℹ Information

Tourist office (☎889 87-330; www.salzburg.info; Mozartplatz 5; ⏱9am-6pm or 6.30pm, closed Sun Sep-Mar) Has plenty of information about the city and its immediate surrounds; there's a ticket booking agency in the same building. For information on the rest of the province, visit the Salzburgerland Tourismus (www.salzburgerland.com) website.

ℹ Getting There & Away

Air

Salzburg airport (www.salzburg-airport.com) has regular scheduled flights to destinations all over Austria and Europe.

Car & Motorcycle

Three motorways converge on Salzburg to form a loop around the city: the A1/E60 from Linz, Vienna and the east; the A8/E52 from Munich and the west; and the A10/E55 from Villach and the south.

Train

Fast trains leave hourly for Vienna (€49.90, three hours) via Linz (€23.70, 1¼ hours). There is a two-hourly express service to Klagenfurt (€38.70, three hours). The quickest way to Innsbruck (€41.30, two hours) is by the 'corridor' train through Germany via Kufstein; trains depart at least every two hours. There are trains every hour or so to Munich (€34, 1¾ hours).

ⓘ Getting Around

To/From the Airport

Salzburg airport (www.salzburg-airport.com) is located 5.5km west of the city centre. Bus 2 goes there from the Hauptbahnhof (€2.30, 19 minutes). A taxi costs about €20.

Bicycle

Top Bike (www.topbike.at; Staatsbrücke; ◷10am-5pm) rents bikes for around €15 per day (half-price for kids). The Salzburg Card yields a 20% discount.

Car & Motorcycle

Parking places are limited and much of the Altstadt is pedestrian-only, so it's easier to leave your car at one of three park-and-ride points to the west, north and south of the city. The largest car park in the centre is the Altstadt Garage under Mönchsberg (€14 per day).

Fiaker

A *Fiaker* (horse-drawn carriage) for up to four people costs €40 for 25 minutes. The drivers line up on Residenzplatz.

Salzkammergut

A wonderland of glassy blue lakes and tall craggy peaks, Austria's Lake District is a long-time favourite holiday destination. The peaceful lakes attract visitors in droves from Salzburg and beyond, with limitless opportunities for boating, fishing, swimming or just lazing on the shore.

BAD ISCHL

☏06132 / POP 14,000

During the last century of the Habsburg reign, Bad Ischl became the favourite summertime retreat for the imperial family and its entourage. Today the town and many of its dignified buildings still have a stately aura, and a perhaps surprisingly high proportion of the local women still go about their daily business in *Dirndl* (Austria's traditional full pleated skirt).

◎ Sights & Activities

Kaiservilla   Palace

(www.kaiservilla.com; Jainzen 38; adult/child €13/7.50, grounds only €4.50/3.50; ◷9.30am-4.45pm, closed Thu-Tue Jan-Mar, closed Nov) This Italianate building was Franz Josef's summer residence and shows that he loved huntin', shootin' and fishin' – it's decorated with an obscene number of animal trophies. It can be visited only by guided tour, during which you'll pick up little gems, like the fact that it was here that the Kaiser signed the letter declaring war on Serbia, which led to WWI.

Salzkammergut Therme   Spa

(www.eurothermen.at; Voglhuberstrasse 10; adult/child 4-hr ticket €15.50/11.50; ◷9am-midnight) If you'd like to follow in Princess Sophie's footprints, take the thermal waters at this effervescent spa.

🛏 Sleeping & Eating

Hotel Garni Sonnhof   Hotel €€

(☏230 78; www.sonnhof.at; Bahnhofstrasse 4; s €65-95, d €90-150; P⑀) Nestled in a leafy glade of maple trees next to the station, this hotel has cosy, traditional decor, a beautiful garden, chickens that deliver breakfast eggs, and a sunny conservatory.

Goldenes Schiff   Hotel €€

(☏242 41; www.goldenes-schiff.at; Adalbert-Stifter-Kai 3; s €87-117, d €136-184, apt €184-198, junior ste €184-198; ◷restaurant closed Tue; P@⑀) The best rooms at this comfortable hotel pick have large windows overlooking the river. There's also a spa area and an excellent restaurant (mains €14 to €21) serving regional cuisine from game to Wolfgangsee fish.

Grand Café & Restaurant
Zauner Esplanade   Austrian €€

(Hasner Allee 2; mains €11.50-19.90; ◷10am-10pm) This offshoot of Café Zauner, the famous pastry shop at Pfarrgasse 7, serves Austrian staples, some using organic local meats, in a pleasant location beside the river.

KEN GILLHAM/GETTY IMAGES ©

⭐ Don't Miss
Schloss Hellbrunn

A prince-archbishop with a wicked sense of humour, Markus Sittikus built Italianate Schloss Hellbrunn as a 17th-century summer palace and an escape from his Residenz functions.

The ingenious trick fountains and water-powered figures are the big draw. When the tour guides set them off, expect to get wet! Admission includes entry to the baroque palace. The rest of the sculpture-dotted gardens are free to visit. Look out for *The Sound of Music* pavilion of 'Sixteen Going on Seventeen' fame.

Bus 25 runs to Hellbrunn, 4.5km south of Salzburg, every 20 minutes from Rudolfskai in the Altstadt.

NEED TO KNOW
www.hellbrunn.at; Fürstenweg 37; adult/concession/family €9.50/6.50/24; ⏰9am-5.30pm, to 9pm Jul & Aug; 🚼

ℹ Getting There & Around

Car & Motorcycle
Most major roads in the Salzkammergut go to or near Bad Ischl; Hwy 158 from Salzburg and the north–south Hwy 145 intersect just north of the town centre.

Train
Hourly trains to Hallstatt (€3.80, 25 minutes) go via Steeg/Hallstätter See, at the northern end of the lake, and continue on the eastern side via Hallstatt station to Obertraun (€5.70, 30 minutes). A boat from Hallstatt station (€2.40) takes you to the township.

HALLSTATT

With pastel-hued homes, swans and towering mountains on either side of a glassy green lake, Hallstatt looks like some kind of greeting card for tranquillity.

Boats chug lazily across the water from the train station to the village itself, which clings precariously to a tiny bit of land between mountain and shore.

◉ Sights

Salzbergwerk   Salt Mine
(funicular return plus tour adult/child/family €26/13/54, tour only €19/9.50/40; ⏰9.30am-4.30pm, closed late Oct–late Apr) The region's major cultural attraction is situated high above Hallstatt on Salzberg (Salt Mountain). In 1734 the fully preserved body of a prehistoric miner was found and today he is known as the 'Man in Salt'. The standard tour revolves around his fate, with visitors travelling down an underground railway and miners' slides (a photo is taken of you while sliding) to an illuminated subterranean salt lake.

The mine can be reached on foot or with the funicular.

❶ Getting There & Away

About a dozen trains daily connect Hallstatt and Bad Ischl (€3.80, 22 minutes) and Hallstatt with Bad Aussee (€3.80, 15 minutes).

Tirol

With converging mountain ranges behind lofty pastures and tranquil meadows, Tirol (also Tyrol) captures a quintessential Alpine panoramic view. Occupying a central position is Innsbruck, the region's jewel, while in the northeast and southwest are superb ski resorts.

INNSBRUCK
☏ 0512 / POP 121,400

Tirol's capital is a sight to behold. The mountains are so close that within 25 minutes it's possible to travel from the heart of the city to over 2000m above sea level. Summer and winter outdoor activities abound, and it's understandable why some visitors only take a peek at Innsbruck proper before heading for the hills.

◉ Sights

The **Innsbruck Card** gives one visit to Innsbruck's main sights and attractions, a return journey on seven cable cars, unlimited use of public transport includ-

Innsbruck

JEREMY VOISEY/GETTY IMAGES ©

ing the Sightseer bus, and five-hour bike rental. It's available at the tourist office and costs €31/39/45 for 24/48/72 hours (half-price for children).

Goldenes Dachl & Museum   Museum

(Golden Roof; Herzog-Friedrich-Strasse 15; adult/child €4/2; ⏱10am-5pm, closed Mon Oct-Apr) Innsbruck's golden wonder is this Gothic oriel, built for Emperor Maximilian I in 1500 and glittering with 2657 fire-gilt copper tiles. An audioguide whizzes you through the history in the museum; look for the grotesque tournament helmets designed to resemble the Turks of the rival Ottoman Empire.

Hofkirche   Church

(www.tiroler-landesmuseum.at; Universitätstrasse; adult/child €5/4, combined Volkskunstmuseum ticket adult/child €10/6; ⏱9am-5pm Mon-Sat, 12.30-5pm Sun) The 16th-century Hofkirche is one of Europe's finest royal court churches. Top billing goes to the empty **sarcophagus** of Emperor Maximilian I (1459–1519), a masterpiece of German Renaissance sculpture, guarded by 28 giant bronze figures including Dürer's legendary King Arthur.

Volkskunstmuseum   Museum

(Folk Art Museum; www.tiroler-landesmuseum.at; Universitätstrasse; combined Hofkirche ticket adult/child €10/6; ⏱9am-5pm) Next door to the Hofkirche, the Volkskunstmuseum houses Tyrolean folk art from handcarved sleighs and Christmas cribs to carnival masks and cow bells.

Hofburg   Palace

(Imperial Palace; www.hofburg-innsbruck.at; Rennweg 1; adult/child €8/free, Hofgarten admission free; ⏱palace 9am-5pm, garden 6am-dusk) Empress Maria Theresia gave this Habsburg palace a total baroque makeover in the 16th century. The highlight of the state apartments is the Riesensaal (Giant's Hall), lavishly adorned with frescos and paintings of Maria Theresia and her 16 children, including Marie Antoinette.

♥ **If You Like…**
Austria's Natural Wonders

From glittering lakes to snowy mountains, Austria is blessed with glorious scenery.

1 EISRIESENWELT

(www.eisriesenwelt.at; adult/concession/child €9/8/4.50, with cable car €20/18/10; ⏱9am-3.30pm May-Oct) Hovering more than 1000m above Werfen, the Eisriesenwelt are the world's largest accessible ice caves. They're a once-seen, never-forgotten experience: the 1¼-hour tour takes you through twinkling chambers where lamps pick out otherworldly ice sculptures. Dress for subzero temperatures. Werfen is 45km south of Salzburg on the A10/E55 motorway. Trains run frequently to Salzburg; regular minibuses run to the caves in summer.

2 KRIMML FALLS

(www.wasserfaelle-krimml.at; adult/child €2.50/0.50, free Dec-Apr; ⏱ticket office 8am-6pm mid-Apr–late Oct) The thunderous, three-tier Krimml Falls is Europe's highest waterfall at 380m, and one of Austria's most unforgettable sights. Krimml is on Hwy 168 (which becomes Hwy 165). Buses run year-round from Krimml to Zell am See (€9.90, 1¼ hours, hourly), with frequent onward train connections to Salzburg (€21.50, 1½ hours) .

3 DACHSTEIN EISHÖHLE

(www.dachstein-salzkammergut.com; tour adult/child €13.50/8; ⏱core tour 9.20am-4pm May-late Oct) Near Obertraun, this fabulous cave complex extends into the mountain for almost 80km in places. The ice itself is around 500 years old, but is increasing in thickness each year; the 'ice mountain' is 8m high – that's twice as high now as it was when the caves were first explored in 1910.

Bergisel   Ski Jump

(www.bergisel.info; adult/child €9/4; ⏱9am-6pm) Rising above Innsbruck like a celestial staircase, this glass-and-steel ski jump was designed by much-lauded Iraqi architect Zaha Hadid.

Detour:
Wolfgangsee

Wolfgangsee is a hugely popular place to spend the summer swimming, boating, walking or simply lazing by its soothing waters.

Coming from Salzburg, the first town you come across is **St Gilgen**. It's a fine point from which to explore the surrounding region, and its **tourist office** (📞 06227-23 48; www.wolfgangsee.at; Mondsee Bundesstrasse 1a; ⏰ 9am-7pm Mon-Fri, 9am-6pm Sat, 10am-5pm Sun) can help with accommodation and activities. **St Wolfgang**, towards the southern end of Wolfgangsee, is squeezed between the northern shoreline of the lake and the towering peak of Schafberg (1783m). Its **tourist office** (📞 80 03; www.wolfgangsee.at; Au 140; ⏰ 9am-7pm Mon-Fri, 9am-6pm Sat, 10am-5pm Sun) has plenty of information for travellers.

In the heart of the village you'll find the 14th-century **Pilgrimage Church** (donation €1; ⏰ 9am-6pm), a highly ornate example that still attracts pilgrims. Reaching the top of **Schafberg** is an easy exercise – from May to October, a cogwheel railway climbs to its summit in 40 minutes (one way/return €20.40/29.80).

A ferry operates May to October between Strobl and St Gilgen (one way €9, 75 minutes), stopping at points en route. Boats run from St Wolfgang to St Gilgen almost hourly during the day (one way €6.80, 50 minutes); the free *Eintauchen & Aufsteigen* timetable from local tourist offices gives exact times.

A Postbus service from St Wolfgang via Strobl to St Gilgen (€4.20, 30 minutes) is frequent out of season, but tails off somewhat in summer when the ships run. For Salzburg you need to connect in Strobl (€2.20, 12 minutes).

It's 455 steps or a two-minute funicular ride to the 50m-high **viewing platform**. Here, the panorama of the Nordkette range, Inn Valley and Innsbruck is breathtaking, though the cemetery at the bottom has undoubtedly made a few ski jumping pros quiver in their boots.

Tram 1 trundles from central Innsbruck to Bergisel.

Schloss Ambras   Castle
(www.khm.at/ambras; Schlossstrasse 20; adult/child €10/free; ⏰ 10am-5pm) Archduke Ferdinand II transformed Schloss Ambras from a fortress into a Renaissance palace in 1564. A visit takes in the ever-so-grand banquet hall, shining armour (look out for the 2.6m suit created for giant Bartlmä Bon) and room upon room of Habsburg portraits, with Titian, Velázquez and Van Dyck originals. It's free to stroll or picnic in the expansive **gardens**.

Schloss Ambras is 4.5km southeast of the centre. Take bus 4134 from the Hauptbahnhof for discounted entry and a free return journey. The Sightseer bus also stops here.

Alpenzoo   Zoo
(www.alpenzoo.at; Weiherburggasse 37; adult/child €8/4; ⏰ 9am-6pm) Home to Alpine wildlife like golden eagles, chamois and ibex. To get there, walk up the hill from Rennweg or take bus W from Marktplatz.

Stadtturm   Tower
(Herzog-Friedrich-Strasse 21, City Tower; adult/child €3/1.50; ⏰ 10am-8pm) Climb this tower's 148 steps for 360-degree views of the city's rooftops, spires and surrounding mountains.

🏃 Activities

Nordkettenbahnen   Funicular
(www.nordkette.com; one way/return to Hungerburg €4/6.80, Seegrube €14.60/23.40, Hafelekar €16.20/27; ⏰ Hungerburgbahn 7am-

7.15pm Mon-Fri, 8am-7.15pm Sat, Seegrubenbahn 8.30am-5.30pm, Hafelekarbahn 9am-5pm) Zaha Hadid's space-age funicular runs every 15 minutes, whizzing you from the Congress Centre to the slopes in no time. Patrolled by inquisitive Alpine sheep, the 2334m summit of **Hafelekar** affords tremendous views over Innsbruck to the snow-capped giants of the Austrian Alps, including 3798m Grossglockner.

Olympia SkiWorld Innsbruck — Skiing

Innsbruck is the gateway to this massive ski arena, covering nine surrounding resorts and 300km of slopes to test all abilities. The most central place to pound powder is the **Nordkette/Seegrube**, accessed by the Nordkettenbahnen. A three-/seven-day OlympiaWorld Ski Pass covering all areas costs €117/218; ski buses are free to anyone with a Club Innsbruck Card.

Sleeping

Hotel Weisses Kreuz — Historic Hotel €€

(594 79; www.weisseskreuz.at; Herzog-Friedrich-Strasse 31; s €38-78, d €78-142; P @) Beneath the Altstadt's arcades, this atmospheric 500-year-old pile has played host to famous guests including a 13-year-old Mozart. With its wood-panelled parlours and twisting staircase, the hotel oozes history with every creaking beam. Rooms are supremely comfortable, staff charming and breakfast is a lavish spread.

Goldener Adler — Historic Hotel €€

(571 111; www.goldeneradler.com; Herzog-Friedrich-Strasse 6; s €85-125, d €126-240; P) Since opening in 1390, the grand Goldener Adler has welcomed kings, queens and Salzburg's two biggest exports: Mozart and Mrs von Trapp. Rooms are elegant with gold drapes and squeaky-clean marble bathrooms.

Mondschein — Hotel €€

(227 84; www.mondschein.at; Mariahilfstrasse 6; s €87-105, d €105-180; P @) As the name suggests, the moon lights the way to this riverside hotel. Done up in midnight blue and cream tones, rooms are light, spacious and classically elegant. Most have Altstadt views and the best sport Swarovski–crystal studded bathrooms.

Eating

Chez Nico — Vegetarian €€

(0650-451 06 24; www.chez-nico.at; Maria-Theresien-Strasse 49; lunch €12.50, 6-course menu €51; lunch & dinner Tue-Fri, dinner Sat;) Take a creative Parisian chef with an artistic eye and a passion for herbs, *et voilà,* you get Chez Nico. Nicolas Curtil (Nico) cooks seasonal vegetarian delights like porcini-sage ravioli and

Wolfgangsee

baked figs with rose sorbet at this intimate bistro.

Lichtblick — Fusion €€€
(📞 566 550; www.restaurant-lichtblick.at; Rathaus Galerien; lunch €9.50-13, set menus €40-50; ⏰10am-1am Mon-Sat) On the 7th floor of the Rathaus Galerien, this glass-walled restaurant has knockout views over Innsbruck to the mountains beyond.

Cafe Munding — Cafe €
(www.munding.at; Kiebachgasse 16; cake €2-4; ⏰8am-8pm) Scrumptious fruit tortes, cheesecakes, chocolate cake and home-roasted coffee.

Fischerhäusl — Austrian €€
(📞 583 535; www.fischerhaeusl.com; Herrengasse 8; mains €9-21; ⏰10.30am-1am Mon-Sat) The lemon-fronted Fischerhäusl has stood in this hidden spot between Domplatz and the Hofburg since 1758. On the menu is Tyrolean grub such as *Kaspressknödelsuppe*, cheesy dumplings swimming in broth, and *Gröstl*, a potato, bacon and onion fry-up. The terrace fills quickly on warm days.

🍷 Drinking & Nightlife

Moustache — Bar
(www.cafe-moustache.at; Herzog-Otto-Strasse 8; ⏰11am-2am Tue-Sun) You too can try your hand at playing Spot-the-Moustache (Einstein, Charlie Chaplin and others), the preferred pastime at this retro newcomer. It has a terrace overlooking pretty Domplatz, as well as Club Aftershave in the basement.

360° — Bar
(Rathaus Galerien; ⏰10am-1am Mon-Sat) There's no better place to see Innsbruck start to twinkle. Grab a cushion and drink in 360-degree views of the city and Alps from the balcony skirting the circular bar.

Theresienbräu — Pub
(Maria-Theresien-Strasse 53; ⏰11am-1am Mon-Wed, to 2am Thu-Sat, noon-9pm Sun) A lively microbrewery with a big beer garden for quaffing a cold one.

ℹ️ Information

Innsbruck Information (📞 535 60; www.innsbruck.info; Burggraben 3; ⏰9am-6pm) Main tourist office with truckloads of info on the city

Grossglockner Road

Detour:
Hohe Tauern National Park

If you thought Mother Nature pulled out all the stops in the Austrian Alps, Hohe Tauern National Park was her magnum opus. Straddling Tirol, Salzburg and Carinthia, this national park is the largest in the Alps; a 1786-sq-km wilderness of 3000m peaks, Alpine meadows and waterfalls. At its heart lies **Grossglockner** (3798m), Austria's highest mountain, which towers over the 8km-long **Pasterze Glacier**, best seen from the outlook at **Kaiser-Franz-Josefs-Höhe** (2369m).

The 48km **Grossglockner Road** (www.grossglockner.at; Hwy 107; car/motorcycle €32/22; ☺ May–early Nov) from Bruck in Salzburgerland to Heiligenblut in Carinthia is one of Europe's greatest Alpine drives. A feat of 1930s engineering, the road swings giddily around 36 switchbacks, passing jewel-coloured lakes, forested slopes and wondrous glaciers.

If you have wheels, you'll have more flexibility, although the road is open only between May and early November, and you must pay tolls.

The major village on the Grossglockner Road is **Heiligenblut**, dominated by mountain peaks and the needle-thin spire of its 15th-century pilgrimage church. Here you'll find a **tourist office** (☏ 04824-27 00; www.heiligenblut.at; Hof 4; ☺ 9am–6pm), which can advise on guided ranger hikes, mountain hiking and skiing. The village also has a campsite, a few restaurants and a spick-and-span **Jugendherberge** (☏ 22 59; www.oejhv.or.at; Hof 36; dm/s/d €20.50/28.50/49; P @).

Bus 5002 runs frequently between Lienz and Heiligenblut on weekdays (€15.80, one hour), less frequently at weekends. From late June to mid-September, three buses run from Monday to Friday and Sunday, plus one on Saturday between Heiligenblut and Kaiser-Franz-Josefs-Höhe (€7.90, 30 minutes). Check the timetables with the tourist office in Lienz before setting off.

and surrounds, including skiing and walking. Sells ski passes, public-transport tickets and city maps (€1); will book accommodation (€3 commission) and has an attached ticketing service.

🛈 Getting There & Away

Air

Innsbruck airport (INN; ☏ 0512-22 525; www.innsbruck-airport.com), 4km to the west of the city centre, caters to national and international flights, handled mostly by Austrian Airlines, BA, easyJet and Welcome Air.

Car & Motorcycle

The A12 and the parallel Hwy 171 are the main roads heading west and east. The B177, to the west of Innsbruck, continues north to Munich (Germany). The A13 is a toll road (€8) running south through the Brenner Pass to Italy and crossing the 192m Europabrücke, spanning the Sill River. Toll-free Hwy 182 follows the same route, passing under the bridge.

Train

Fast trains depart at least every two hours for Bregenz (€34.40, 2½ hours), Salzburg (€41.30, two hours), Kitzbühel (€19.20, 1½ hours) and Munich (€39.60, two hours). There are several daily services to Lienz (€19.20 to €35.20, 3¼ to 4½ hours).

🛈 Getting Around

To/From the Airport The airport is 4km west of the centre and served by bus F. Buses depart every 15 or 20 minutes from Maria-Theresien-Strasse (€1.90); taxis charge about €10 for the same trip.

Car & Bicycle Street parking is very limited in the city centre. Parking garages (eg under the

Altstadt) cost around €17 per day. At the same address as **Inntour** (☎214 466; www.inntour. com; Leopoldstrasse 4; ⏰9am-6.30pm Mon-Fri, to 5pm Sat) Die Börse rents city, mountain, electric and children's bikes for €18/25/25/13 per day respectively.

Public Transport Single tickets on buses and trams cost €1.90 (from the driver; valid upon issue). A 24-hour ticket is €4.30.

AROUND INNSBRUCK

Just 9km east of Innsbruck is the town of Hall in Tirol. The labyrinth of pretty cobbled streets at its medieval heart pays testament to the massive wealth it accumulated from silver mines over the centuries. You can learn more about this legacy at **Burg Hasegg** (Burg Hasegg 6; adult/child €8/6; ⏰10am-5pm Tue-Sun), a 14th-century castle that had a 300-year career as a mint for silver *Thalers* (coins, the root of the modern word 'dollar').

Another 9km east along the valley in Wattens is **Swarovski Kristallwelten** (Swarovski Crystal Worlds; http://kristallwelten. swarovski.com; Kristallweltenstrasse 1; adult/ child €11/free; ⏰9am-6.30pm), one of Austria's most-visited attractions. A crystal winterscape by Alexander McQueen, a kaleidoscopic crystal dome and a striking Terence Conran–designed shop are part of the fabulously glittering experience.

From Innsbruck, trains run frequently to Hall in Tirol (€2, eight minutes) and Fritzens-Wattens (€3.60, 16 minutes), 3km north of Swarovski Kristallwelten.

SWITZERLAND

Geneva

POP 192,400

Slick and cosmopolitan, Geneva (Genève in French, Genf in German) is a rare breed of city. It's one of Europe's priciest. Its people chatter in every language under the sun (184 nationalities comprise 45% of the city's population) and it's constantly thought of as the Swiss capital – which it isn't. This business-like city strung around the sparkling shores of Europe's largest alpine lake is, in fact, only Switzerland's second-largest city.

Yet the whole world is here: the UN, International Red Cross, International Labour Organization, World Health Organization – 200-odd governmental and nongovernmental international organisations fill the city's plush hotels with big-name guests, feast on an incredulous choice of cuisine and help prop up the overload of banks, jewellers and chocolate shops for which Geneva is known. Strolling manicured city parks, lake sailing and skiing next door in the Alps are weekend pursuits.

Jet d'Eau, Geneva
ALLAN BAXTER/GETTY IMAGES ©

Sights

Lake Geneva   Lake

Begin your exploration of Europe's largest alpine lake by having a coffee on **Île Rousseau**, where a statue honours the celebrated freethinker. Cross to the southern side of the lake and walk west to the **Horloge Fleurie** (Flower Clock; Quai du Général-Guisan) in the Jardin Anglais. Geneva's most photographed clock, crafted from 6500 flowers, can be oddly disappointing after all the hype.

Far more rewarding is the iconic 140m-tall **Jet d'Eau** (Lake Geneva, Jetée des Eaux-Vives; ⏱9.30am-11.15pm Mar-Oct) FREE on the lake's southern shore. When the fountain climaxes there are seven tonnes of water in the air, shooting up to create its sky-high plume, kissed by a rainbow on sunny days.

Old Town   Historic Area

The main street of the Vieille Ville (Old Town), Grand-Rue, shelters the **Espace Rousseau** (☎022 310 10 28; www.espace-rousseau.ch; Grand-Rue 40; adult/child Sfr5/3; ⏱11am-5.30pm Tue-Sun) at No 40, where the 18th-century philosopher was born. It's Geneva's best area for walking; the Place du Bourg-de-Four is timeless and ringed by good cafes.

Nearby, the part-Romanesque, part-Gothic **Cathédrale de St-Pierre** (St Peter's Cathedral; Cour St-Pierre; ⏱9.30am-6.30pm Mon-Sat, noon-6.30pm Sun Jun-Sep, 10am-5.50pm Mon-Sat, noon-5.30pm Sun Oct-May) FREE is where Protestant John Calvin preached from 1536 to 1564. Revel in the flamboyant **Chapel of the Maccabees**.

Palais des Nations   Landmark

(☎022 907 48 96; www.unog.ch; Av de la Paix 14; adult/child Sfr12/7; ⏱10am-noon & 2-4pm Mon-Fri Sep-Mar, 10am-noon & 2-4pm daily Apr-Jun, 10am-5pm daily Jul & Aug) The art deco Palais des Nations is the European arm of the UN and the home of 3000 international civil servants. You can see where decisions about world affairs are made on the hour-long tour. An ID or passport is obligatory for admission. Tram 15 stops here.

International Red Cross & Red Crescent Museum   Museum

(Musée Internationale de la Croix Rouge et du Croissant-Rouge; ☎022 748 95 25; www.micr.org; Av de la Paix 17) Closed at the time of research, the museum was set to reopen in 2013 after a massive rethink. Visitors engage with displays along three themes: 'Defending Human Dignity', 'Restoring Family Links' and 'Reducing Natural Risks'. All highlight recent atrocities perpetuated by humanity set against the noble goals of the Red Cross & Red Crescent. Take bus 8 to the Appia stop.

Musée d'Art et d'Histoire   Museum

(☎022 418 26 00; www.ville-ge.ch/mah; Rue Charles Galland 2; adult/child Sfr3/free; ⏱11am-6pm Tue-Sun) Konrad Witz' *La pêche miraculeuse* (c 1440–44), portraying Christ walking on water on Lake Geneva, is a highlight of the art and history museum.

Patek Phillipe Museum   Museum

(☎022 807 09 10; www.patekmuseum.com; Rue des Vieux Grenadiers 7; adult/child Sfr10/free; ⏱2-6pm Tue-Fri, 10am-6pm Sat) A treasure trove of precision art, this museum displays exquisite timepieces from the 16th century to the present.

Parks   Park

Geneva has loads of parkland, much of it lakefront. Flowers, art installations and soul-stirring views of Mont Blanc on clear days make the northern lakeshore promenade a pleasure to walk. Pass hip **Bains des Pâquis** (☎022 732 29 74; www.bains-des-paquis.ch; Quai du Mont-Blanc 30; ⏱9am-8pm mid-Apr–mid-Sep), where Genevans have frolicked in the sun since 1872, then continue north to **Parc de la Perle du Lac** (Quai du Mont-Blanc) and the peacock-studded lawns of the **Jardin Botanique** (⏱8am-7.30pm Apr-Oct, 9.30am-5pm Nov-Mar) FREE.

South of the Old Town, 4.5m-tall figures of Bèze, Calvin, Farel and Knox – in their nightgowns ready for bed – loom large in **Parc des Bastions**.

Switzerland

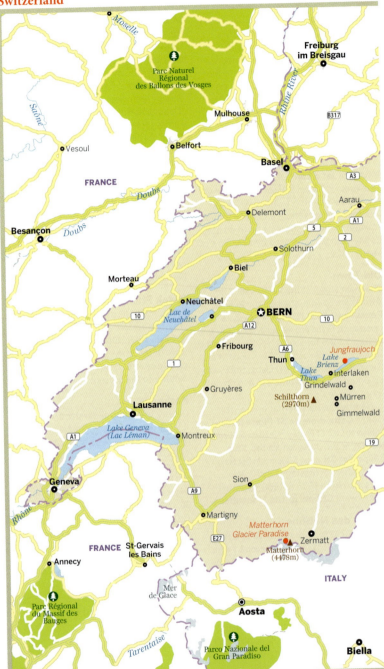

Moselle

Parc Naturel
Régional
des Ballons des Vosges

Freiburg
im Breisgau

Mulhouse

Rhine River

B317

Saône

Vesoul

Belfort

Basel

A3

FRANCE

Aarau

Doubs

Delemont

A1

Besançon

Doubs

5

2

Solothurn

Morteau

Biel

Neuchâtel

BERN

10

Lac de
Neuchâtel

A12

10

Fribourg

A6

Jungfraujoch

Thun

Lake
Brienz

1

Lake
Thun

Interlaken

Gruyères

Grindelwald

Schilthorn
(2970m)

Mürren

Lausanne

Gimmelwald

Lake Geneva
(Lac Léman)

A1

Montreux

19

Sion

Geneva

A9

Rhône

Martigny

Matterhorn
Glacier Paradise

E27

Zermatt

FRANCE

St-Gervais
les Bains

Matterhorn
(4478m)

ITALY

Annecy

Mer
de Glace

Parc Régional
du Massif des
Bauges

Aosta

Tarentaise

Parco Nazionale del
Gran Paradiso

Biella

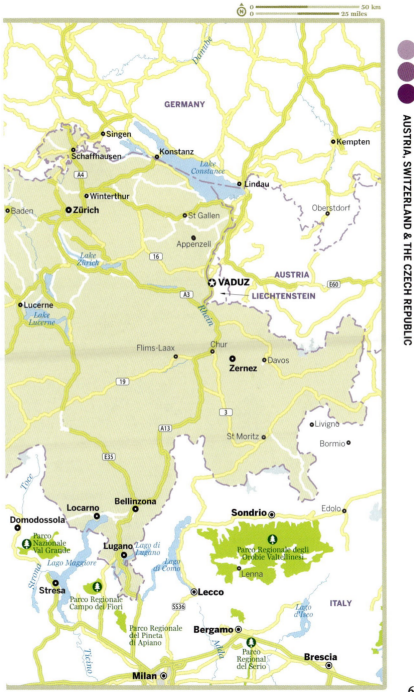

0 — 50 km
0 — 25 miles

GERMANY

Singen
Schaffhausen
Konstanz
Lake Constance
Lindau
Kempten

A4

Winterthur
St Gallen
Oberstdorf
Baden
Zürich
Appenzell

Lake Zürich

16

AUSTRIA
VADUZ
E60
LIECHTENSTEIN

Lucerne
Lake Lucerne

Flims-Laax
Chur
Zernez
Davos

Rhein

19

3

A13

St Moritz
Livigno
Bormio

E35

Toce

Locarno
Bellinzona
Sondrio
Edolo

Domodossola
Parco Nazionale Val Grande
Lugano
Lago di Lugano
Parco Regionale degli Orobie Valtellinesi
Lago di Como
Lenna

Lago Maggiore

Strona

Stresa
Parco Regionale Campo dei Fiori
Lecco
Lago d'Iseo

SS36

ITALY

Parco Regionale del Pineta di Apiano

Ticino

Bergamo
Parco Regional del Serio

Brescia

Adda

Milan

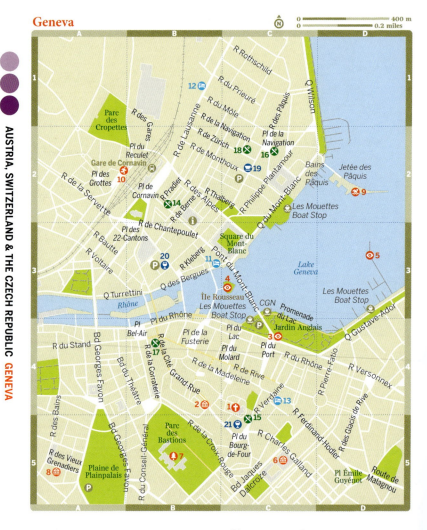

0 — 400 m
0 — 0.2 miles

CERN
Laboratory

(☎022 767 84 84; www.cern.ch; ⊗tours 10.30am Mon-Sat) See why electrons and positrons are shot down a 27km circular tube (the Large Hadron Collider, the world's biggest machine) and how the resulting collisions create new forms of matter at the European Organisation for Nuclear Research (CERN). The laboratory for research into particle physics is funded by 20 nations and can be visited on free tours (book at least one month in advance). Otherwise, enjoy **Microcosm**

(☎022 767 84 84; ⊗8.30am-5.30pm Mon-Fri, 9am-5pm Sat) FREE, the on-site multimedia and interactive visitors centre. CERN is 8km west of Geneva; take tram 14.

🎇 Festivals & Events

August's two-week **Fêtes de Genève** (www. fetes-de-geneve.ch) ushers in parades, open-air concerts, lakeside merry-go-rounds and fireworks. On 11 December, the **Escalade** celebrates the foiling of an invasion by the Duke of Savoy in 1602 with

Geneva

◎ Sights
1	Cathédrale de St-Pierre	C4
2	Espace Rousseau	B4
3	Horloge Fleurie	C4
4	Île Rousseau	C3
5	Jet d'Eau	D3
6	Musée d'Art et d'Histoire	C5
7	Parc des Bastions	B5
8	Patek Phillipe Museum	A5

✪ Activities, Courses & Tours
9	Bains des Pâquis	D2
10	Genève Roule	A2

🛏 Sleeping
11	Four Seasons Hôtel des Bergues	B3
12	Hôtel Auteuil	B1
13	Hôtel Bel'Esperance	C4

✖ Eating
14	Café de Paris	B2
15	Chez Ma Cousine	C5
16	Edelweiss	C2
17	Gilles Desplanches	B4
18	Les 5 Portes	C2

◉ Drinking & Nightlife
19	Café des Arts	C2
20	La Bretelle	B3
21	La Clémence	C5

a costumed parade, the smashing and eating of chocolate cauldrons, and a day of running races around the Old Town.

🛏 Sleeping

When checking in, ask for your free public transport ticket covering unlimited bus travel for the duration of your hotel stay.

Hôtel Bel'Esperance   Hotel €€

(☎022 818 37 37; www.hotel-bel-esperance.ch; Rue de la Vallée 1; s/d from Sfr105/160; @ 📶) This two-star hotel is a two-second flit to the Old Town and offers extraordinary value for a pricey city like Geneva. Rooms are quiet and cared for, and those on the 1st floor share a kitchen. Ride the lift to the 5th floor to flop in a chair on its wonderful flower-filled rooftop terrace.

Four Seasons Hôtel des Bergues   Luxury Hotel €€€

(☎022 908 70 00; www.fourseasons.com/geneva; Quai des Bergues 33; r from Sfr625; ❋@📶) Geneva's oldest hotel continues to live up to its magnificent heritage. Chandelier-lit moulded ceilings, grandiose flower arrangements, original oil paintings in heavy gold frames and diamonds glittering behind glass is what this lakeside neoclassical gem from 1834 is all about.

La Cour des Augustins   Hotel €€

(☎022 322 21 00; www.lacourdesaugustins.com; Rue Jean-Violette 15; s/d from Sfr190/250; P❋@📶) 'Boutique gallery design hotel' is how this slick, contemporary space in Carouge markets itself. Disguised by a 19th-century facade, its crisp white interior screams cutting edge.

Hôtel Auteuil   Hotel €€€

(☎022 544 22 22; www.manotel.com; Rue de Lausanne 33; r from Sfr320; P⇦❋@📶) The star of this crisp, design-driven hotel near the station is its enviable collection of black-and-white photos of 1950s film stars in Geneva.

 Eating

If it's local and traditional you're after, dip into a cheese fondue or platter of pan-fried *filets de perche* (perch fillets). But beware: not all those cooked up are fresh from the lake. Many come frozen from Eastern Europe, so it's imperative to pick the right place to sample this simple Lake Geneva speciality.

Eateries crowd Place du Bourg-de-Four, Geneva's oldest square, in the lovely Old Town.

Les 5 Portes   Bistro €

(☎022 731 84 38; Rue de Zürich 5; mains Sfr16-24; ⏱11am-11pm) The Five Doors is a fashionable Pâquis port of call that embraces every mood and moment. It has a rich, retro bistro feel yet works fine for just a glass of wine. The menu changes nightly and reflects what's fresh. Service is excellent and there is a long – and reasonable – wine list. Tables outside are good for a stylish pause.

Three Languages

Located in the corner of Europe where Germany, France and Italy meet, Switzerland is a linguistic melting pot with three official federal languages: German (spoken by 64% of the population), French (19%) and Italian (8%). Swiss 'German' speakers write standard or 'high' German, but speak their own language: Schwyzertütsch has no official written form and is mostly unintelligible to outsiders.

A fourth language, Romansch, is spoken by less than 1% of the population, mainly in the canton of Graubünden. Derived from Latin, it's a linguistic relic that has survived in the isolation of mountain valleys. Romansch was recognised as a national language by referendum in 1938 and given federal protection in 1996.

English-speakers will have few problems being understood in the German-speaking parts. However, it is simple courtesy to greet people with the Swiss-German *grüezi* and to enquire *Sprechen Sie Englisch?* (Do you speak English?) before launching into English. In French Switzerland you shouldn't have too many problems either; in Italian-speaking Switzerland, people are more monolingual but you'll still encounter plenty of English-speakers.

Edelweiss
Fondue €€

(022 544 51 51; Place de la Navigation 2; mains from Sfr35; 6-10pm Mon-Sat) This chalet-style restaurant in the namesake hotel is a key address among Genevans for traditional cheese fondue.

Café de Paris
French €€

(www.cafe-de-paris.ch; rue du Mont-Blanc 26; mains Sfr42; 11am-11pm) A memorable dining experience since 1930. Everyone goes for the same thing here: green salad, beef steak with a killer herb-and-butter sauce, and as many *frites* (fries) as you can handle.

Chez Ma Cousine
Chicken €

(022 310 96 96; www.chezmacousine.ch; 11am-10pm) *'On y mange du poulet'* (we eat chicken) is the tagline of this institution near the cathedral, which appeals for one good reason – generously handsome and homely portions of chicken, potatoes and salad at a price that can't possibly break the bank.

Gilles Desplanches
Cafe €

(022 810 30 28; www.gillesdesplanches.com; Rue de la Confédération 2; mains Sfr12-20; 7am-7pm Mon-Wed & Fri, 7am-8pm Thu, 8am-7pm Sat, 10am-6pm Sun) One for serious Swiss chocolate fanatics. With its shocking-pink facade and exquisitely crafted cakes and chocolates alongside imaginative savoury tarts, this is one address that bursts at the seams at lunchtime. Good sandwiches, quiches, salads and more.

🍷 Drinking & Nightlife

La Clémence
Bar

(022 312 24 98; www.laclemence.ch; Place du Bourg-de-Four 20; 7am-1am Mon-Thu & Sun, to 2am Fri & Sat) Indulge in a glass of local wine or an artisanal beer at this venerable cafe-bar located on Geneva's loveliest square.

Café des Arts
Cafe

(022 321 58 85; Rue des Pâquis 15; 11am-2am Mon-Fri, 8am-2am Sat & Sun) As much a place to drink as a daytime cafe, this Pâquis hang-out lures a local crowd with its Parisian-style terrace and artsy interior.

Le Cheval Blanc
Bar

(022 343 61 61; www.lechevalblanc.ch; Place de l'Octroi 15; 11.30am-1am or 2am Tue-Sat,

10.30am-1am Sun) The White Horse is a real Carouge favourite. Quaff cocktails and eat tapas – some of Geneva's best – at the pink neon-lit bar upstairs, then head downstairs to its club and concert space, Le Box.

La Bretelle   Bar
(☏ 022 732 75 96; Rue des Étuves 17; ⊙6pm-2am) Little has changed since the 1970s, when this legendary bar opened. Live accordion accompanies French chansons most nights.

🔒 Shopping

Designer shopping is wedged between Rue du Rhône and Rue de Rive; the latter has lots of chain stores. Grand-Rue in the Old Town and Carouge boast artsy boutiques.

ℹ Information

Tourist office (☏ 022 909 70 00; www.geneve-tourisme.ch; Rue du Mont-Blanc 18; ⊙9am-6pm Mon-Sat, 10am-4pm Sun) The Geneva Pass (from Sfr25) offers free admissions and discounts.

ℹ Getting There & Away

Air
Aéroport International de Genève (p724), 5km from town, has connections to major European cities and many others worldwide.

Boat
CGN (Compagnie Générale de Navigation; ☏ 084 881 18 48; www.cgn.ch) operates a web of scenic steamer services from its Jardin Anglais jetty to other villages on Lake Geneva. Many only sail May to September, including those to/from Lausanne (Sfr43, 3½ hours). Eurail and Swiss Pass holders are valid on CGN boats or there is a one-day CGN boat pass (Sfr56).

Train
Trains run to major Swiss towns including at least every 30 minutes to/from Lausanne (Sfr22, 33 to 48 minutes), Bern (Sfr49, 1¾ hours) and Zürich (Sfr84, 2¾ hours).

International daily rail connections from Geneva include Paris by TGV (3¼ hours) and Milan (four hours).

ℹ Getting Around

To/From the Airport
Getting from the airport is easy with regular trains into Gare de Cornavin (Sfr3, eight minutes). Slower bus 10 (Sfr3) does the same 5km trip. A metered taxi costs from Sfr30 to Sfr50.

Bicycle
Pick up a bike at **Genève Roule** (☏ 022 740 13 43; www.geneveroule.ch; Place de Montbrillant 17; ⊙8am-6pm Mon-Sat) or its seasonal Jetée des Pâquis pick-up point for Sfr12/20 per day/weekend. May to October, borrow a bike (with advertisements on it) for free.

Public Transport
Buses, trams, trains and boats service the city, and ticket dispensers are found at all stops.

Cathédrale de St-Pierre (p673)

Most services are operated by **TPG** (www.tpg.ch; ⏲7am-7pm Mon-Fri, 7am-6pm Sat). Typical tickets cost Sfr3.50 (one hour); a day pass is Sfr8 when purchased after 9am. The same tickets are also valid on the yellow shuttle boats known as Les Mouettes (the seagulls) that criss-cross the lake every 10 minutes between 7.30am and 6pm.

Valais

This is Matterhorn country, an intoxicating land that seduces the toughest of critics with its endless panoramic vistas and breathtaking views. Switzerland's 10 highest mountains – all over 4000m – rise to the sky here, while snow fiends ski and board in one of Europe's top resorts, Zermatt. When snows melt and valleys turn lush green, hiking opportunities are boundless.

The main train line from Lake Geneva to Brig runs along the Rhône River at the base of the beautiful valley.

ZERMATT

POP 5850

Since the mid-19th century, Zermatt has starred among Switzerland's glitziest resorts. Today it attracts intrepid mountaineers and hikers, skiers who cruise at a snail's pace, spellbound by the scenery, and style-conscious darlings flashing designer togs in the lounge bars. But all are smitten with the **Matterhorn** (4478m), the Alps' most famous peak and an unfathomable monolith synonymous with Switzerland that you simply can't quite stop looking at.

🎯 Sights

Gornergratbahn   Railway
(www.gornergrat.ch; Bahnhofplatz 7; adult/child from Sfr40/20; ⏲2-3 departures hourly 7am-6pm May & mid-Oct–Nov, 7am-10pm Jun-Sep, every 20min 7am-5.15pm Dec-Apr) This splendid cogwheel railway – Europe's highest – climbs through picture-postcard scenery to Gornergrat (3089m). Tickets allow you to get on and off en route; Matterhorn views abound.

Matterhorn Museum   Museum
(📞027 967 41 00; www.matterhornmuseum.ch; Kirchplatz; adult/child Sfr10/5; ⏲11am-6pm Dec-Oct) This crystalline, state-of-the-art museum provides a fascinating insight into Valaisian village life, mountaineering, the dawn of tourism in Zermatt and the lives the Matterhorn has claimed.

🤸 Activities

Zermatt is **skiing** heaven, with mostly long, scenic red runs, plus a smattering of blues for ski virgins and knuckle-whitening blacks for experts. The main skiing areas in winter are **Rothorn**, **Stockhorn** and **Klein Matterhorn**, 350km of ski runs in all with a link from Klein Matterhorn to the Italian resort of Cervinia and a freestyle park with half-pipe for snowboarders. A day pass covering all ski lifts in Zermatt (excluding Cervinia) costs Sfr67/57/34 per adult/student/child (Sfr75/64/38 including Cervinia).

Summer skiing (20km of runs, May to mid-October) and boarding (gravity park at Plateau Rosa on the Theodul glacier) are the most extensive in Europe.

Alpin Center   Skiing, Hiking
(📞027 966 24 60; www.alpincenter-zermatt.ch; Bahnhofstrasse 58; ⏲9am-noon & 3-7pm mid-Nov–Apr & Jul-Sep) This activities centre houses the ski school and mountain guides office.

🛏 Sleeping

Hotel Bahnhof   Hotel €€
(📞027 967 24 06; www.hotelbahnhof.com; Bahnhofstrasse; dm Sfr40-60, r Sfr80-220; 🛜) Opposite the train station, these five-star budget digs have proper beds and spotless bathrooms that are a godsend after scaling or schussing down mountains all day. Rooms for four are fabulous for families. There's a kitchen for preparing your own breakfast.

Berggasthaus Trift   Guesthouse €
(📞079 408 70 20; www.zermatt.net/trift; dm/d with half-board from Sfr66/156; ⏲Jul-Sep) Run by Hugo (a whizz on the alpenhorn) and

CARO/ALAMY ©

⭐ Don't Miss
Matterhorn Glacier Paradise

Views from Zermatt's cable cars and gondolas are all pretty remarkable, but the Matterhorn Glacier Paradise is the icing on the cake. Ride Europe's highest-altitude cable car up to 3883m and gawp at a top-of-the-beanstalk panorama of 14 glaciers and 38 mountain peaks over 4000m from the **Panoramic Platform**. Don't miss the **Glacier Palace**, an ice palace complete with glittering ice sculptures, a glacier crevasse to walk through and – one for the kids – an ice slide to swoosh down.

NEED TO KNOW
www.matterhornparadise.ch; adult/child from Sfr72/40; ⊘7am-4.20pm Jul & Aug, 8.30am-3.35pm mid-Oct–Dec, 8.30am-4.20pm rest of year

Fabienne at the foot of the Triftgletscher. A stiff two-hour hike from Zermatt, it has simple rooms, mesmerising views of its glacial 4000m surrounds and a great terrace to kick back on over home-cured beef and oven-warm apple tart. Call in advance to ensure a bed.

Eating

Whymper Stube   Swiss €€
(☎027 967 22 96; www.whymper-stube.ch; Bahnhofstrasse 80; mains Sfr22-44) An advance

reservation is essential at this legendary address, known for its excellent raclette and fondues, both cheese and meat.

Bayard Metzgerei   Swiss €
(☎027 967 22 66; Bahnhofstrasse 9; sausages from Sfr6; ⊘noon-6.30pm Jul-Sep, 4-6.30pm Dec-Mar) Join the line in the street for a sausage (pork, veal or beef) and chunk of bread to down with a beer on the hop – or at a bar stool with the sparrows in the alley by this butcher's shop.

Below: Skier, Stockhorn (p680);
Right: Gornergratbahn (p680), Matterhorn
(BELOW) BERNARD VAN DIERENDONCK/GETTY IMAGES ©; (RIGHT) BUENA VISTA IMAGES/GETTY IMAGES ©

(Sfr235/134, 7½ hours) and St
Moritz (Sfr198/113, eight hours).

ℹ Information

The **tourist office** (☎ 027 966 81 00; www.
zermatt.ch; Bahnhofplatz 5; ⊙ 8.30am-6pm mid-
Jun–Sep, 8.30am-noon & 1-6pm Mon-Fri, 8.30am-
6pm Sat, 9.30am-noon & 4-6pm Sun rest of year)
has all the bumph.

ℹ Getting There & Around

Car

Zermatt is car-free. Motorists have to park in
Täsch (www.matterhornterminal.ch; Sfr14.50/
day), load luggage onto a trolley (Sfr5) and
ride the Zermatt Shuttle (adult/child Sfr8/4, 12
minutes, every 20 minutes from 6am to 9.40pm)
train the last 5km to Zermatt.

Train

Like a glacier faced with climate change, you'll
have a hard time avoiding the hype for the **Glacier
Express** (www.glacierexpress.ch), the train that
links Zermatt with the eastern towns and resorts of
Chur (1st/2nd class Sfr254/145, 5¾ hours), Davos

Bern

POP 125,700

One of the planet's most underrated
capitals, Bern is a fabulous find. With the
genteel old soul of a Renaissance man
and the heart of a high-flying 21st-century
gal, the riverside city is both medieval and
modern. The 15th-century Old Town is
gorgeous enough to sweep you off your
feet and make you forget the century (it's
definitely worthy of its 1983 Unesco World
Heritage site status).

◎ Sights

Old Town   Historic Area
Bern's flag-bedecked medieval centre is
an attraction in its own right, with 6km of
covered arcades and cellar shops/bars
descending from the streets.

Bern's **Zytglogge** (clock tower)
is a focal point; crowds congregate

around to watch its figures twirl rather somnolently at four minutes before the hour, after which the actual chimes begin. Equally enchanting are the 11 decorative **fountains** (1545) depicting historical and folkloric characters.

Inside the 15th-century Gothic **Münster** (Cathedral; www.bernermuenster.ch; tower adult/child Sfr5/2; ☉10am-5pm Tue-Sat, 11.30am-5pm Sun Easter-Nov, noon-4pm Tue-Fri, to 5pm Sat, 11.30am-4pm Sun rest of year, tower closes 30min earlier), a 344-step hike up the lofty spire – Switzerland's tallest – is worth the climb.

Paul Klee Centre Museum

(☎031 359 01 01; www.zpk.org; Monument im Fruchtland 3; adult/child Sfr20/7; ☉10am-5pm Tue-Sun) The architecturally bold Paul Klee Centre is an eye-catching 150m-long building filled with modern art, with a huge emphasis on its namesake. Renzo Piano's curvaceous building swoops up and down like waves to create a trio of 'hills' that blend into the landscape east of town.

Take bus 12 from Bubenbergplatz to Zentrum Paul Klee (Sfr4.20, 15 minutes).

By car the museum is right next to the Bern-Ostring exit off the A6.

Einstein Museum Museum

(☎031 312 00 91; www.einstein-bern.ch; Kramgasse 49; adult/student Sfr6/4.50; ☉10am-5pm Feb-Dec) The world's most famous scientist developed his special theory of relativity in Bern in 1905. Find out more at the small museum inside the humble apartment where Einstein lived with his young family between 1903 and 1905 while working in the Bern patent office.

Houses of Parliament Historic Site

(Bundeshäuser; ☎031 332 85 22; www.parliament.ch; Bundesplatz; ☉hourly tours 9am-4pm Mon-Sat) FREE The 1902 home of the Swiss Federal Assembly is impressively ornate, with statues of the nation's founding fathers and a stained-glass dome adorned with cantonal emblems. Tours are offered when parliament is in recess; otherwise watch from the public gallery. Bring your passport to get in.

Bärengraben
Bear Park

(www.baerenpark-bern.ch; ⏱9.30am-5pm)
After decades of living in a cramped
concrete pit (and lots of protests from
animal-rights advocates), Bern's iconic
bears got a new spacious 6000-sq-metre
open-air riverside park dotted with trees
and terraces in 2009, in which a number
of bears roam (although they still have access to the old pit). The bear park is at the
eastern end of the Nydeggbrücke.

Kunstmuseum
Museum

(☎031 328 09 44; www.kunstmuseumbern.
ch; Hodlerstrasse 8-12; adult/child Sfr7/free;
⏱10am-9pm Tue, to 5pm Wed-Sun) The
permanent collection at the workmanlike
Museum of Fine Arts includes works by
Italian artists such as Fra Angelico and
Swiss artists such as Ferdinand Hodler,
alongside Picasso and Dalí pieces.

🛏 Sleeping

Hotel Landhaus
Hotel €

(☎031 331 41 66; www.albertfrida.ch; Altenberg-
strasse 4; dm from Sfr33, r from Sfr160, without
bathroom from Sfr120; P🞀@🞀) Backed by
the grassy slope of a city park and fronted
by the river and Old Town spires, this
historic hotel oozes character. Its soulful
ground-floor restaurant, a tad Bohemian,
draws a staunchly local crowd.

Hotel National
Hotel €

(☎031 381 19 88; www.nationalbern.ch;
Hirschengraben 24; s/d Sfr100/150, without
bathroom from Sfr65/130 ; @🞀) A quaint,
endearing hotel, the National charms with
its wrought-iron lift and Persian rugs over
wooden floors. All 58 rooms are unique.
Breakfast at the in-house restaurant is
included.

Hotel Belle Epoque
Hotel €€

(☎031 311 43 36; www.belle-epoque.ch;
Gerechtigkeitsgasse 18; s/d from Sfr170/240;
🞀@🞀) A romantic Old Town hotel with
opulent art nouveau furnishings, the belle
epoque's design ethos sees TVs tucked
away into steamer-trunk-style cupboards
so as not to spoil the look. It's a small
operation, with a popular cafe.

🍴 Eating

Lötschberg AOC
Swiss €€

(☎031 311 34 55; www.loetschberg-aoc.ch;
Zeughausgasse 16; mains Sfr14-30; ⏱9am-
11pm) Take an all-Swiss wine and beer list,
add cheese specialities from the Valais
(including fondue and raclette, of course),
toss in some salads, decorate the cheerful yellow walls with circular, wooden
wine racks and you have one of the most
dynamic Swiss restaurants in the country.
Book for dinner.

Altes Tramdepot
Swiss €

(☎031 368 14 15; www.altestramdepot.ch; Am
Bärengraben; mains Sfr16-20; ⏱11am-12.30am)
Even locals recommend this cavernous
microbrewery by the bear pits. Swiss
specialities snuggle up to wok-cooked
stir-fries, pasta and international dishes
on its bistro-styled menu.

Kornhauskeller
Modern European
€€€

(☎031 327 72 72; Kornhausplatz 18; mains
Sfr25-50; ⏱noon-11pm Mon-Sat, from 5pm Sun)
Fine dining takes place beneath vaulted
frescoed arches at Bern's surprisingly
ornate former granary, now a stunning
cellar restaurant serving Mediterranean
cuisine. In its neighbouring cafe, punters
lunch in the sun on the busy pavement
terrace. The buzzy bar is open late.

ℹ Information

Bern Tourismus (☎031 328 12 12; www.
berninfo.com; Bahnhoftplatz; ⏱9am-8.30pm
Jun-Sep, to 6.30pm Mon-Sat, 10am-5pm Sun Oct-
May) Street-level floor of the train station. City
tours, free hotel bookings, internet access (per
hour Sfr12). There is a second **office** (☎031 328
12 12; Bärengraben; ⏱9am-6pm Jun-Sep, 10am-
4pm Mar-May & Oct, 11am-4pm Nov-Feb) in the
Altes Tram depot by the bear pits.

ℹ Getting There & Around

Frequent trains connect to most Swiss towns,
including Geneva (Sfr49, 1¾ hours), Basel (Sfr39,
one hour) and Zürich (Sfr49, one hour).

Handmade Swiss chocolates, Bern

BRUCE YUANYUE BI/GETTY IMAGES ©

Central Switzerland & Bernese Oberland

The Bernese Oberland should come with a health warning – caution: may cause trembling in the north face of Eiger, uncontrollable bouts of euphoria at the foot of Jungfrau and 007 delusions at Schilthorn. Up at Europe's highest train station, Jungfraujoch, husky yapping mingles with a cacophony of 'oohs' and 'ahhs'. Just paces away, the serpentine Aletsch Glacier flicks out its tongue and you're surrounded by 4000m turrets and frosty stillness.

LUCERNE

POP 76,200

Recipe for a gorgeous Swiss city: take a cobalt lake ringed by mountains of myth, add a medieval Old Town and sprinkle with covered bridges, sunny plazas, candy-coloured houses and waterfront promenades. Lucerne is bright, beautiful and has been Little Miss Popular since the likes of Goethe, Queen Victoria and Wagner savoured her views in the 19th century.

◉ Sights

Your first port of call should be the medieval Old Town, with its ancient rampart walls and towers. **Kapellbrücke** (Chapel Bridge), dating from 1333, is Lucerne's best-known landmark. It's famous for its distinctive water tower and the spectacular 1993 fire that nearly destroyed it. Though it has been rebuilt, fire damage is still obvious on the 17th-century pictorial panels under the roof. In contrast are the spooky and dark *Dance of Death* panels under the roofline of **Spreuerbrücke** (Spreuer Bridge, 1408).

Museum Sammlung Rosengart
Museum

(☎041 220 16 60; www.rosengart.ch; Pilatusstrasse 10; adult/student Sfr18/16; ☉10am-6pm Apr-Oct, 11am-5pm Nov-Mar) Lucerne's blockbuster cultural attraction is the Rosengart Collection, occupying a graceful neoclassical pile. It displays the outstanding stash of Angela Rosengart, a Swiss art dealer and close friend of Picasso. Alongside works by the great Spanish master are paintings and sketches by Cézanne, Kandinsky, Miró (including the stunning 1925 *Dancer II*), Matisse and Monet.

The basement has over 100 works of Paul Klee, which show the full range of his prodigious talents.

Lion Monument   Monument

(Löwendenkmal; Denkmalstrasse) Lukas Ahorn's sculpture of a dying lion commemorates Swiss soldiers who died defending King Louis XVI during the French Revolution. Mark Twain once called it the 'saddest and most moving piece of rock in the world'.

Verkehrshaus   Museum

(☎041 370 44 44; www.verkehrshaus.ch; Lidostrasse 5; adult/child Sfr30/15; ⊙10am-6pm Apr-Oct, to 5pm Nov-Mar) Planes, trains and automobiles are the name of the game in the huge, family oriented Transport Museum, east of the city centre, which is devoted to Switzerland's proud transport history.

🛏 Sleeping

Palace Luzern   Hotel €€€

(☎041 416 16 16; www.palace-luzern.ch; Haldenstrasse 10; r from Sfr400) This luxury belle époque hotel on the lakefront is a favourite with those looking for trad splendour. Inside it's all gleaming marble, chandeliers and turn-of-the-century grandeur. Go for a room with a view across the lake to the Alps beyond. Look for online deals for the smaller rooms in the eaves.

The Hotel   Hotel €€€

(☎041 226 86 86; www.the-hotel.ch; Sempacherstrasse 14; ste from Sfr430; ❄@🛜) This shamelessly hip hotel, bearing the imprint of architect Jean Nouvel, is all streamlined chic, with refined suites featuring stills from movie classics on the ceilings.

🍴 Eating & Drinking

There is an excellent **market** (⊙8am-3pm **Sat)** that runs along both sides of the Reuss.

Wirtshaus Galliker   Swiss €€

(☎041 240 10 01; Schützenstrasse 1; mains Sfr22-50; ⊙11.30am-2pm & 5-10pm Tue-Sat, closed Jul–mid-Aug) This old-style tavern has been passionately run by the Galliker family over four generations since 1856. Motherly waiters dish up Lucerne soul food (rösti, *chögalipaschtetli* and the like) that is batten-the-hatches filling. Book ahead for dinner.

Restaurant Schiff   Swiss €€

(☎041 418 52 52; Unter den Egg 8; mains Sfr20-45) Under the waterfront arcades and lit by tea lights at night, this restaurant has bags of charm. Try fish from Lake Lucerne and some of the city's most celebrated *chögalipaschtetli*.

Heini   Cafe €

(☎041 412 20 20; www.heini.ch; Falkenplatz; snacks from Sfr5) The original outlet for this lavish local chain of bakery-cafes is by the Lion Monument,

Kapellbrücke (Chapel Bridge; p685), Lucerne
IZZET KERIBAR/GETTY IMAGES ©

but we prefer this modern version on a key square in the Old Town.

Rathaus Bräuerei Brewery
(☎041 410 52 57; www.rathausbrauerei.ch; Unter den Egg 2; mains from Sfr15; ⊙8am-midnight) Sip house-brewed beer (try the bock) under the vaulted arches of this buzzy tavern, or nab a pavement table and watch the river flow.

❶ Information

Lucerne Card (24/48/72hr Sfr19/27/33) Offers 50% discount on museum admissions, unlimited use of public transport and other reductions.

Luzern Tourism (☎041 227 17 17; www.luzern.com; Zentralstrasse 5; ⊙8.30am-7pm Mon-Sat, 9am-5pm Sun May-Oct, 8.30am-5.30pm Mon-Fri, 9am-5pm Sat & Sun Nov-Apr) Accessed from platform 3 of the train station.

❶ Getting There & Around

Frequent trains serve Bern (Sfr37, one hour), Geneva (Sfr76, 2¾ hours), Lugano (Sfr58, 2½ hours) and Zürich (Sfr24, one hour).

Trains also connect Lucerne and Interlaken East on the stunning GoldenPass Line via Meiringen (Sfr31, two hours).

SGV (www.lakelucerne.ch) operates boats (sometimes paddle-steamers) on Lake Lucerne daily.

INTERLAKEN

POP 5300

Once Interlaken made the Victorians swoon with its dreamy mountain vistas, viewed from the chandelier-lit confines of its grand hotels. Today it makes dare-devils scream with its adrenalin-loaded adventures.

 Activities

Tempted to hurl yourself off a bridge, down a cliff or along a raging river? You're in the right place. Switzerland is the world's second-biggest adventure-sports centre and Interlaken is its busiest hub.

If You Like…
Mountain Scenery

There are three classic day trips to Alpine peaks from Lucerne. The summits offer a variety of walks and activities, but it's the jaw-dropping views that steal the show – so save these trips for a clear day.

1 MT PILATUS
(www.pilatus.com) Rearing above Lucerne, Mt Pilatus is 2132m high, and from May to October features as part of a classic 'golden round-trip'. Board the lake steamer from Lucerne to Alpnachstad, then rise with the world's steepest cog railway to Mt Pilatus. From the summit, cable cars bring you down to Kriens via Fräkmüntegg and Krienseregg, where bus 1 takes you back to Lucerne. The return trip costs Sfr91.

2 MT RIGI
(www.rigi.ch) The Jungfrau peaks dominate the horizon from 1797m-high Mt Rigi. Two rival railways carry passengers to the top. One runs from Arth-Goldau (one way/return Sfr40/64), the other from Vitznau (one way/return Sfr45/72).

3 MT TITLIS
(www.titlis.ch) Central Switzerland's tallest mountain, Mt Titlis is reached on a breathtaking four-stage journey; the final link is on a revolving cable car. At Titlis station (3020m) the oohs and aahs come when you step out onto the terrace, where the panorama of glacier-capped peaks stretches to Eiger, Mönch and Jungfrau in the Bernese Oberland. The return trip to Titlis (45 minutes each way) costs Sfr90 from Engelberg. Engelberg is at the end of a train line, about an hour from Lucerne (Sfr17). If on a day trip, check the Lucerne tourist office's Mt Titlis excursion tickets.

Almost every heart-stopping pursuit you can think of is offered here. You can white-water raft on the Lütschine, Simme and Saane Rivers, go canyoning in the Saxetet, Grimsel or Chli Schliere gorges, and canyon jump at the Gletscherschlucht near Grindelwald. If that doesn't grab you, there's paragliding,

BUENA VISTA IMAGES/GETTY IMAGES ©

Don't Miss
Jungfraujoch

If the Bernese Oberland is Switzerland's Alpine heart, the Jungfrau region is where yours will skip a beat. Presided over by glacier-encrusted monoliths Eiger, Mönch and Jungfrau (Ogre, Monk and Virgin), the scenery stirs the soul and strains the neck muscles. Come summer, hundreds of kilometres of walking trails allow you to capture the landscape from many angles, but it never looks less than astonishing.

It's also where you'll find one of Switzerland's top tourist attractions: the world's highest train station, Jungfraujoch (3471m). The icy wilderness of swirling glaciers and 4000m turrets that unfolds is truly enchanting. Clear good weather is essential for the trip; check www.jungfrau.ch or call ☎ 033 828 79 31, and don't forget warm clothing, sunglasses and sunscreen.

From Interlaken Ost, the journey time is 2½ hours each way (return Sfr191; discounts with rail passes). The last train back is at 5.50pm in summer, 4.40pm in winter.

There's an equally impressive panorama available from the 2970m Schilthorn, which featured as Blofeld's HQ in *On Her Majesty's Secret Service*. On a clear day, you can see over 200 peaks, from Titlis to Mont Blanc.

From Interlaken East a combined ticket to the summit costs Sfr125.

glacier bungee jumping, skydiving, ice climbing, hydrospeeding and, phew, much more.

Sample prices are around Sfr110 for rafting or canyoning, Sfr130 for bungee or canyon jumping, Sfr160 for tandem paragliding, Sfr180 for ice climbing, Sfr225 for hang-gliding, and Sfr430 for sky-diving. A half-day mountain-bike tour will set you back around Sfr25.

The major operators able to arrange most sports from May to September include the following. Advance bookings are essential.

Alpinraft (☎ 033 823 41 00; www.alpinraft.ch; Hauptstrasse 7)

Outdoor Interlaken (☎ 033 826 77 19; www.outdoor-interlaken.ch; Hauptstrasse 15)

Swissraft (☎ 033 821 66 55; www.swissraft-activity.ch; Obere Jungfraustrasse 72)

 Sleeping

Hotel Rugenpark   B&B €
(☎ 033 822 36 61; www.rugenpark.ch; Rugenparkstrasse 19; s/d from Sfr87/130, without bathroom from Sfr62/105; ⊗closed Nov–mid-Dec; P⊕@) Chris and Ursula have worked magic to transform this place into a sweet B&B. Rooms are humble, but the place is spotless and has been enlivened with colourful butterflies, beads and travel trinkets. Quiz your knowledgeable hosts for help and local tips.

Victoria-Jungfrau Grand Hotel & Spa   Hotel €€€
(☎ 033 828 28 28; www.victoria-jungfrau.ch; Höheweg 41; s/d from Sfr560/680; P⊕@ 🛜🏊) The reverent hush and impeccable service evoke an era when only royalty and the seriously wealthy travelled. It's a perfect melding of well-preserved Victorian features and modern luxury.

Hôtel du Lac   Hotel €€
(☎ 033 822 29 22; www.dulac-interlaken.ch; Höheweg 225; s/d Sfr160/280) Smiley old-fashioned service and a riverfront location near Interlaken Ost make this 19th-century hotel a solid choice. It has been in the same family for generations.

 Eating

Benacus   Swiss €€
(☎ 033 821 20 20; www.benacus.ch; Stadthausplatz; mains Sfr20-33; ⊗closed Sun) Supercool Benacus is a breath of urban air with its glass walls, slick wine-red sofas, lounge music and street-facing terrace. The German TV show *Funky Kitchen Club* is filmed here. The menu stars creative, seasonal flavours.

Schuh   Cafe €€
(☎ 033 822 94 41; www.schuh-interlaken.ch; Höheweg 56; meals from Sfr20; ⊗9am-11.30pm) A Viennese-style coffee house famous for its pastries, pralines and park-facing terrace. The menu covers all the bases, from rösti to Asian accents. The chocolate-making show (Sfr15) is touristy but fun, it runs at 5pm most days in the high season.

Goldener Anker   International €€
(☎ 033 822 16 72; www.anker.ch; Marktgasse 57; mains Sfr18-42; ⊗dinner; 🎵) This beamed restaurant covers a lot of bases with its menu, which runs from Switzerland to Asia with a brief stop in Mexico.

ℹ️ **Information**

Tourist office (☎ 033 826 53 00; www.interlakentourism.ch; Höheweg 37; ⊗8am-7pm Mon-Fri, to 5pm Sat, 10am-noon & 5-7pm Sun Jul & Aug, 8am-noon & 1.30-6pm Mon-Fri, 9am-noon Sat rest of year)

ℹ️ **Getting There & Away**

The only way south for vehicles without a detour around the mountains is the car-carrying train from Kandersteg, south of Spiez.

There are two train stations. Interlaken West is slightly closer to the centre and is a stop for trains to Bern (Sfr27, one hour). Interlaken East is the rail hub for all lines, including the scenic ones up into the Jungfrau region and the lovely GoldenPass Line to Lucerne (Sfr31, two hours).

Zürich
POP 376,000

Zürich is an enigma. A savvy financial centre with possibly the densest public transport system in the world, it also has a gritty, post-industrial edge that always surprises. The nation's largest city has an evocative Old Town and lovely lakeside location.

⊙ **Sights**

Old Town   Historic Area
Explore the cobbled streets of the pedestrian Old Town lining both sides of the river.

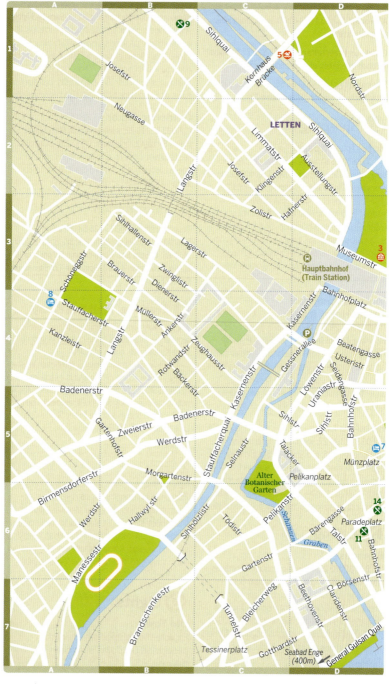

Sihlquai

Josefstr

Neugasse

Langstr

Sihlhallenstr

Lagerstr

Brauerstr

Schöneggstr

Zwinglistr

Dienerstr

Müllerstr

Ankerstr

Stauffacherstr

Kanzleistr

Langstr

Rotwandstr

Bäckerstr

Zeughausstr

Badenerstr

Gartenhofstr

Zweierstr

Werdstr

Badenerstr

Birmensdorferstr

Werdstr

Hallwylstr

Morgartenstr

Manessestr

Brandschenkestr

Tunnelstr

Bleicherweg

Tessinerplatz

Gotthardstr

Sihlquai

Kornhaus Brücke

5

LETTEN

Limmatstr

Josefstr

Klingenstr

Zolistr

Sihlquai

Ausstellungstr

Hafnerstr

Museumstr

3

Hauptbahnhof (Train Station)

Bahnhofplatz

Kasernenstr

Kasernenstr

Gessnerallee

Stauffacherquai

Selnaustr

Werdstr

Alter Botanischer Garten

Pelikanstr

Pelikanstr

Schanzen

Graben

Tödlstr

Sihlhölzlistr

Gartenstr

Löwenstr

Uraniastr

Sihlstr

Sihlstr

Talacker

Beatengasse

Usteristr

Seidengasse

Bahnhofstr

Münzplatz

7

Pelikanplatz

Bärengasse

Talstr

11

Paradeplatz

14

Bahnhofstr

Beethovenstr

Claridenstr

Börsenstr

General Gulsan Quai

Seebad Enge (400m)

Nordstr

9

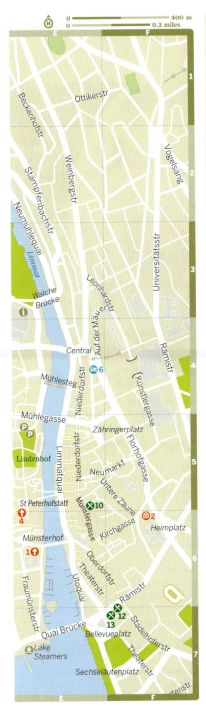

Zürich

Sights
1 Fraumünster...E6
2 Kunsthaus..F6
3 Schweizerisches
    Landesmuseum.............................D3
4 St Peterskirche..................................E6

Activities, Courses & Tours
5 Letten...C1

Sleeping
6 Hotel du Thèâtre...............................E4
7 Hotel Widder......................................D5
8 Pension für Dich...............................A4

Eating
9 Alpenrose..B1
10 Café Schober....................................E5
11 Café Sprüngli...................................D6
12 Kronenhalle......................................F7
13 Sternen Grill.....................................F7
14 Zeughauskeller................................D6

The bank vaults beneath **Bahnhofstrasse**, the city's most elegant street, are said to be crammed with gold and silver. Indulge in affluent Züricher-watching and ogle at the luxury shops selling watches, clocks, chocolates, furs, porcelain and fashion labels galore.

Walk up to the **Lindenhof**, a large shady square that perches above the Old Town, for views down over the city and Limmat River. As you walk, see how many of the city's 1221 fountains you can spot – each with a spout of drinkable glacier-fed water.

On Sundays all of Zürich strolls around its namesake lake. On a clear day you'll glimpse the Alps in the distance.

Fraumünster   Church
(www.fraumuenster.ch; Münsterplatz; ⏱9am-6pm Apr-Oct, 10am-4pm Nov-Mar) The 13th-century cathedral is renowned for its distinctive stained-glass windows, designed by the Russian-Jewish master Marc Chagall (1887–1985).

St Peterskirche   Church
(St Peter's Church; St Peterhofstatt; ⏱8am-6pm Mon-Fri, to 4pm Sat, 11am-5pm Sun) From any position in the city, it's impossible to

overlook the 13th-century tower of St Peterskirche. Its prominent clock face, 8.7m in diameter, is Europe's largest.

Kunsthaus
Museum

(☎044 253 84 84; www.kunsthaus.ch; Heimplatz 1; adult/child Sfr15/free, Wed free; ⏰10am-8pm Wed-Fri, to 6pm Tue, Sat & Sun) Zürich's Fine Arts Museum boasts a rich collection of Alberto Giacometti stick-figure sculptures, Monets, Van Goghs, Rodin sculptures and other 19th- and 20th-century art.

Schweizerisches Landesmuseum
Museum

(Swiss National Museum; www.musee-suisse. ch; Museumstrasse 2; adult/child Sfr10/free; ⏰10am-5pm Tue-Sun, to 7pm Thu) Inside a purpose-built cross between a mansion and a castle sprawls an eclectic and imaginatively presented tour through Swiss history.

🏃 Activities

Swimming Areas
Swimming

(admission Sfr6; ⏰9am-7pm May & Sep, to 8pm Jun-Aug) From mid-May to mid-September, outdoor swimming areas – think a rectangular wooden pier partly covered by a pavilion – open around the lake and up the Limmat River. Many offer massages, yoga and saunas, as well as snacks and rollicking bars. Our favourites include **Seebad Enge** (☎044 201 38 89; www. seebadenge.ch; Mythenquai 95; admission Sfr7), a trendy bar that opens until midnight in fine weather (it's about 700m southwest of Bürkliplatz); and **Letten** (☎044 362 92 00; Lettensteg 10) FREE, a hipster hang-out where people swim, barbecue, play volleyball or just drink and loll on the grass and concrete.

🎇 Festivals & Events

Sechseläuten (www.sechselaeuten.ch) is a spring festival on the third Monday

of April that features guild members parading down the streets in historical costume. In one of Europe's more spectacular – and odd – traditions, a fireworks-filled 'snowman' (the *Böögg*) is ignited atop a huge pyre on Bellevueplatz to celebrate the end of winter. The entire country watches the spectacle on live TV and how long it takes for the snowman's head to explode is said to determine whether summer will be warm and sunny or wet and dreary (six minutes is *very* good).

 Sleeping

Hotel du Thèâtre   Hotel €€

(☎ 044-2672670; www.hotel-du-theatre.ch; Seilergraben 69; s/d from Sfr155/205; ❄ ☎) Located in the lively Niederdorf and within walking distance to the train station, this boutique hotel is decorated with designer furniture and old film stills (an ode to the hotel's past – in the 1950s it was a combined theatre and hotel).

Pension für Dich   Pension €

(☎ 044 317 91 60; www.fuerdich.ch; Stauffacherstrasse 141; s/d without bathroom from Sfr100/110; ➔ ☎) These simple but fabulous apartments have been converted into comfy rooms – think retro furnishings meets Ikea. A number of rooms have balconies.

Hotel Widder   Hotel €€€

(☎ 044 224 25 26; www.widderhotel.ch; Rennweg 7; d from Sfr500; P ❄ @ ☎) A stylish hotel in the equally grand Augustiner district, the Widder is a pleasing fusion of modernity and traditional charm. Rooms and public areas across the eight town houses here boast art and designer furniture.

Eating

Alpenrose   Swiss €€

(☎ 044 271 39 19; Fabrikstrasse 12; mains Sfr24-42; ⏰ noon-11pm Wed-Sun) With its timber-clad walls, 'No Polka Dancing' warning

693

Detour:
St Gallen's Treasure

St Gallen's 16th-century **Stiftsbibliothek** (abbey library; ☎ 071 227 34 16; www.stiftsbibliothek.ch; Klosterhof 6d; adult/child Sfr10/7; ⏱ 10am-5pm Mon-Sat, to 4pm Sun, closed late Nov) is one of the world's oldest and the finest example of rococo architecture. Along with the rest of the monastery complex surrounding it, the library forms a Unesco World Heritage site.

Filled with priceless books and manuscripts painstakingly handwritten by monks during the Middle Ages, it's a dimly lit confection of ceiling frescos, stucco, cherubs and parquetry. Only 30,000 of the total 150,000 volumes are in the library at any one time, and only a handful in display cases, arranged into special exhibitions. If there's a tour guide in the library at the time, you might see the monks' filing system, hidden in the wall panels.

There are regular trains from St Gallen to Bregenz in Austria (Sfr19, 35 minutes) and Zürich (Sfr29, 65 minutes via Winterthur).

---

and fine cuisine from regions all over the country, the Alpenrose makes for an inspired meal out. You could try risotto from Ticino or *Pizokel* (aka Bizochel, a kind of long and especially savoury noodle) from Graubünden or fresh perch fillets. Book.

Zeughauskeller
Swiss €€

(☎ 044 211 26 90; www.zeughauskeller.ch; Bahnhofstrasse 28a; mains Sfr18-35; ⏱ 11.30am-11pm; 🍴) The menu at this huge, atmospheric beer hall – set inside a former armoury – offers 20 different kinds of sausages as well as numerous other Swiss specialities of a carnivorous and vegetarian variety. It's a local institution; expect queues during the week between noon and 2pm.

Café Schober
Cafe €

(www.conditorei-cafe-schober.ch; Napfgasse 4; snacks from Sfr10; ⏱ 8am-7pm) Steady yourself for the best hot chocolate you've ever had at this grand cafe. On entry you'll see lavish displays of sweets, treats and other enticing edible baubles.

Kronenhalle
Brasserie €€€

(☎ 044 251 66 69; Rämistrasse 4; mains Sfr32-87; ⏱ noon-11pm) A haunt of city movers and shakers in suits, the Crown Hall is a brasserie-style establishment with an old-world feel, white tablecloths and lots of dark wood. Impeccably mannered waiters move discreetly below Chagall, Miró, Matisse and Picasso originals.

Café Sprüngli
Swiss €

(☎ 044 224 47 31; www.spruengli.ch; Bahnhofstrasse 21; mains Sfr9-15; ⏱ 8am-5pm) Indulge in cakes, chocolate and coffee at this epicentre of sweet Switzerland, in business since 1836. You can have a light lunch too but whatever you do, don't fail to check out the chocolate shop heaven around the corner on Paradeplatz.

Sternen Grill
Swiss €

(Theatrestrasse 22; snacks from Sfr7; ⏱ 11.30am-midnight) This is the city's most famous – and busiest – sausage stand; just follow the crowds streaming in. The classic *Kalbsbratwurst mit Gold Bürli* (veal sausage with bread roll) costs Sfr7. There are a few vegetarian options too.

🔒 Shopping

For high fashion, head for Bahnhofstrasse and surrounding streets. Across the river, funkier boutiques are dotted about the lanes of Niederdorf. For grunge, preloved gear and some none-too-serious fun young stuff, have a stroll along Langstrasse in Kreis 4.

ℹ Information

Zürich Tourism (☎ 044 215 40 00, hotel reservations 044 215 40 40; www.zuerich.com; train station; ⏰ 8am-8.30pm Mon-Sat, 8.30am-6.30pm Sun) Offers excellent walking tours (Sfr25) most mornings at 11am.

ZürichCard (adult/child 24hr Sfr20/14, 72hr Sfr40/28) Excellent value discount card available from the tourist office and airport train station. Provides free public transport, free museum admission and more.

ℹ Getting There & Away

Air

Zürich airport (ZRH; ☎ 043 816 22 11; www.zurich-airport.com), 10km north of the centre, is Switzerland's main airport.

Train

Zürich has service to all neighbouring countries. Destinations include Milan (4¼ hours), Munich (four hours), Paris (four hours) and Vienna (eight hours).

There are regular direct departures to most major Swiss towns, such as Basel (Sfr32, one hour), Bern (Sfr49, one hour), Geneva (Sfr84, 2¾ hours), Lucerne (Sfr24, one hour) and Lugano (Sfr62, 2¾ hours).

ℹ Getting Around

To/From the Airport

Up to nine trains an hour run each direction between the airport and the main train station (Sfr7, nine to 13 minutes). Most continue on to cities such as Lucerne and Geneva.

Bicycle

City bikes (www.zuerirollt.ch) can be picked up at **Velogate** (train station; ⏰ 8am-9.30pm) for free day use; if you keep it overnight it costs Sfr10.

Boat

Lake steamers (☎ 044 487 13 33; www.zsg.ch) run between April and October. They leave from Bürkliplatz. A small circular tour (kleine Rundfahrt) takes 1½ hours (adult/child Sfr8.20/4.10) and departs every 30 minutes between 11am and 7.30pm. There are longer tours as well.

Public Transport

The comprehensive, unified bus, tram and S-Bahn **public transit system** (ZVV; www.zvv.ch) includes boats plying the Limmat River. Short trips under five stops are Sfr2.40, typical trips are Sfr4.20. A 24-hour pass for the city centre is Sfr8.40.

Bahnhofstrasse, Zürich

CZECH REPUBLIC

Two decades after the fall of the Berlin Wall, the Czech Republic has flourished into one of Europe's most fascinating – and popular – corners. With its Renaissance squares, grand castles and lively bars, the charms of Prague are well-known – but it's worth exploring beyond the capital too, with attractions including the audacious hilltop chateau of Český Krumlov, the original Pilsner brewery in Plzeň and a host of rural towns to discover.

Prague

POP 1.22 MILLION

Since the fall of communism in 1989 and the opening of Central and Eastern Europe, Prague has evolved into one of Europe's most popular travel destinations. The city offers an intact medieval core that transports you back 500 years in time.

Prague nestles on the Vltava River, separating Hradčany (the Castle district) and Malá Strana (Lesser Quarter) on the west bank, from Staré Město (Old Town) and Nové Město (New Town) on the east. Prague Castle overlooks Malá Strana, while the twin Gothic spires of Týn Church dominate Old Town Sq (Staroměstské nám). The broad avenue of Wenceslas Sq (Václavské nám) stretches southeast from Staré Město towards the National Museum and the main train station.

◎ Sights

HRADČANY

St Vitus Cathedral   Church

(Katedrála Sv Víta; Map p702; ☎257 531 622; www.katedralasvatehovita.cz; III nádvoří, Pražský hrad; admission incl in Prague Castle ticket; ⊙9am-6pm Mon-Sat & noon-5pm Sun Apr-Oct, 9am-4pm Mon-Sat & noon-4pm Sun Nov-Mar; Ⓜ Malostranská, ⬚22) Prague's principal cathedral anchors the castle grounds and is visible from around the city. Though it looks ancient, it was only completed in 1929. Its many treasures include **art nouveau stained glass** by Alfons Mucha.

The spectacular, baroque silver **tomb of St John of Nepomuk**, toward the back, contains two tonnes of silver in all. The biggest and most beautiful of the cathedral's numerous side chapels is the **Chapel of St Wenceslas**. Its walls are adorned with gilded panels containing polished slabs of semiprecious stones.

Old Royal Palace   Palace

(Starý královský Palác; Map p702; admission with Prague Castle tour ticket; ⊙9am-6pm Apr-Oct, to 4pm Nov-Mar) The Old Royal Palace is one of the oldest parts of the castle, dating from 1135. At its heart is the grand **Vladislav Hall** (Map p702) and the **Bohemian Chancellery** (Map p702), scene of the famous Defenestration of Prague.

Basilica of St George   Church

(Bazilika Sv Jiří; Map p702; Jiřské náměstí; admission with Prague Castle tour ticket; ⊙9am-6pm Apr-Oct, to 4pm Nov-Mar) The striking, brick-red, early-baroque facade that dominates St George Sq (Jiřské náměstí) conceals the Czech Republic's best-preserved Romanesque church, the Basilica of St George, established in the 10th century by Vratislav I. Next to the basilica is the **Convent of St George** (Klášter Sv Jiří; Map p702; ☎257 531 644; www.ngprague.cz; Jiřské náměstí 33; adult/concession 150/80Kč; ⊙10am-6pm Tue-Sun), the current home of the National Gallery's Museum of 19th-Century Czech Art.

Lobkowicz Palace   Museum

(Lobkovický Palác; Map p702; ☎233 312 925; www.lobkowicz.cz; Jiřská 3; adult/concession/family 275/200/690Kč; ⊙10.30am-6pm) This 16th-century palace houses a private museum known as the 'Princely Collections', which includes priceless paintings, furniture and musical memorabilia.

Šternberg Palace   Gallery

(Šternberský palác; Map p702; ☎233 090 570; www.ngprague.cz; Hradčanské náměstí 15; adult/child 150/80Kč; ⊙10am-6pm Tue-Sun; ⬚22) The baroque Šternberg Palace is home to the National Gallery's collection of 14th- to 18th-century European art, including works by Goya and Rembrandt. Fans of medieval altarpieces will be in heaven;

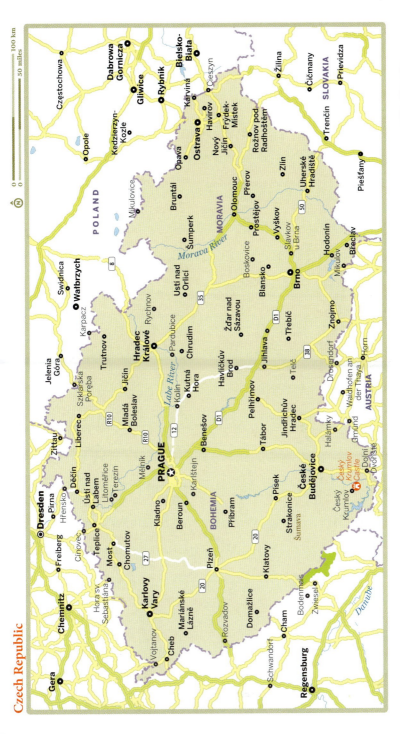

Czech Republic

100 km
50 miles

POLAND

SLOVAKIA

MORAVIA

BOHEMIA

AUSTRIA

Częstochowa
Dąbrowa Górnicza
Gliwice
Rybnik
Bielsko-Biała
Kędzierzyn-Koźle
Opole
Karviná
Cieszyn
Havířov
Ostrava
Opava
Frýdek-Místek
Nový Jičín
Rožnov pod Radhoštěm
Žilina
Čičmany
Prievidza
Trenčín
Piešťany
Zlín
Uherské Hradiště
Mikulovice
Bruntál
Olomouc
Přerov
Prostějov
Vyškov
Slavkov u Brna
Hodonín
Břeclav
Mikulov
Šumperk
Morava River
Boskovice
Blansko
Brno
Znojmo
Dresden
Swidnica
Wałbrzych
Jelenia Góra
Karpacz
Szklárska Poręba
Zittau
Liberec
Trutnov
Rychnov
Ústí nad Orlicí
Hradec Králové
Pardubice
Chrudim
Žďár nad Sázavou
Jihlava
Třebíč
Drosendorf
Waidhofen an der Thaya
Horn
Gmünd
Dolní Dvořiště
Telč
Dačice
Havlíčkův Brod
Kolín
Kutná Hora
Pelhřimov
Mladá Boleslav
Jičín
Mělník
PRAGUE
Kladno
Beroun
Karlštejn
Benešov
Tábor
Jindřichův Hradec
Halámky
Písek
České Budějovice
Český Krumlov Castle
Český Krumlov
Šumava
Příbram
Strakonice
Klatovy
Domažlice
Plzeň
Rozvadov
Cham
Bodenmais
Zwiesel
Schwandorf
Regensburg
Mariánské Lázně
Karlovy Vary
Cheb
Vojtanov
Hora sv. Šebestiána
Chomutov
Most
Teplice
Cínovec
Freiberg
Chemnitz
Gera
Zwickau
Pirna
Hřensko
Děčín
Ústí nad Labem
Litoměřice
Terezín

Danube

Labe River

8
35
50
D1
38
R10
12
20
27

697

Central Prague

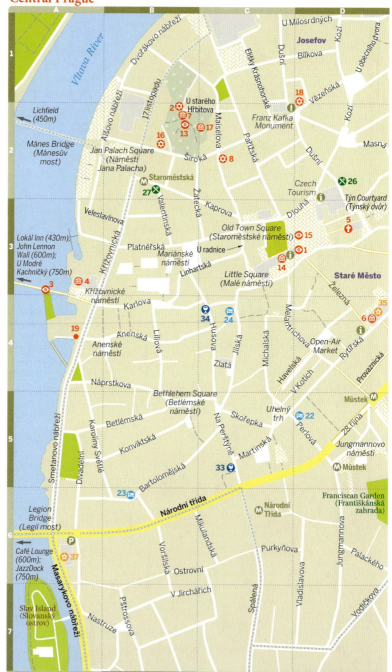

Vltava River

Lichfield
(450m)

Mánes Bridge
(Mánesův
most)

Dvořákovo nábřeží

17.listopadu

Alšovo nábřeží

U Milosrdných

Josefov

Eliška Krásnohorské

Dušní

Bílkova

Kozí

U obecního dvora

Vězeňská

Kozí

2
U starého
Hřbitova
7
17
13
16

Maiselova

18

Franz Kafka
Monument

Masná

Jan Palach Square
(Náměstí
Jana Palacha)

Široká

Pařížská

Dušní

8

Staroměstská
27

Valentinská

Žatecká

Kaprova

Czech
Tourism

Dlouhá

26

Týn Courtyard
(Týnský dvůr)

5

Veleslavínova

Křížovnická

Platnéřská

Mariánské
náměstí

Old Town Square
(Staroměstské náměstí)

15

Lokál Inn (430m);
John Lennon
Wall (600m);
U Modré
Kachničký (750m)

4

3

Linhartská

U radnice

14

1

Little Square
(Malé náměstí)

Staré Město

Železná

35

6

Křížovnické
náměstí

Karlova

19

Anenská

Anenské
náměstí

Liliová

Husova

Jilská

Michalská

Melantrichova

Havelská

V Kotcích

Open-Air
Market

Rytířská

Provaznická

34

24

Zlatá

Můstek

Náprstkova

Bethlehem Square
(Betlémské
náměstí)

Skořepka

Uhelný
trh

22

Perlová

28. října

Jungmannovo
náměstí

Betlémská

Karoliny Světlé

Konviktská

Na Perštýně

Martinská

33

Můstek

Divadelní

Smetanovo nábřeží

Bartolomějská

23

Národní třída

Franciscan Garden
(Františkánská
zahrada)

Legion
Bridge
(Legií most)

P

Masarykovo nábřeží

37

Café Lounge
(600m);
JazzDock
(750m)

Mikulandská

Voršilská

Ostrovní

Národní
Třída

Purkyňova

Jungmannova

Palackého

Slav Island
(Slovanský
ostrov)

Nástruže

Pštrossova

V Jirchářích

Spálená

Vladislavova

Vodičkova

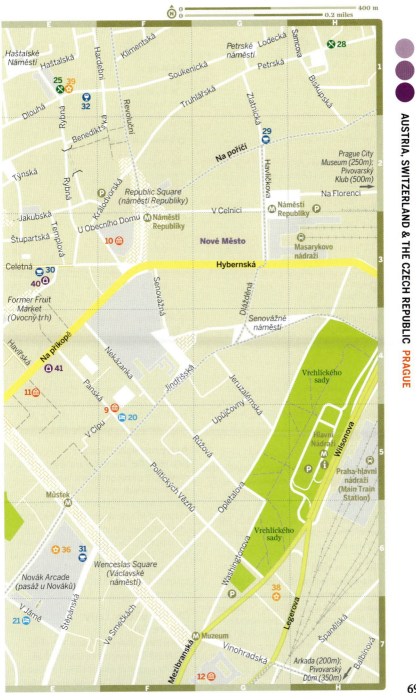

0
400 m
0
0.2 miles

Haštalské
Náměstí
Haštalská
Klimentská
Petrské
náměstí
Lodecká
Samcova
28
Dlouhá
Hardebni
Rybná
Revoluční
Soukenická
Truhlářská
Zlatnická
Petrská
Biskupská
25
39
32
Benediktská
Rybná
Týnská
Na poříčí
29
Havlíčkova
Prague City
Museum (250m);
Pivovarský
Klub (500m)
Jakubská
Templová
Kralodvorská
Republic Square
(náměstí Republiky)
V Celnici
Náměstí
Republiky
Na Florenci
Štupartská
U Obecního Domu
Náměstí
Republiky
Nové Město
Masarykovo
nádraží
10
Celetná
30
40
Hybernská
Former Fruit
Market
(Ovocný trh)
Senovážná
Dlážděná
Senovážné
náměstí
Havířská
Na příkopě
Nekázanka
Jindřišská
Jeruzalémská
Vrchlického
sady
Wilsonova
41
11
Panská
V Cípu
9
20
Upůjčovny
Růžová
Politických Vězňů
Opletalova
Hlavní
Nádraží
Praha-hlavní
nádraží
(Main Train
Station)
Můstek
36
31
Vrchlického
sady
Novák Arcade
(pasáž u Nováků)
Wenceslas Square
(Václavské
náměstí)
Washingtonova
Legerova
38
21
V Jámě
Štěpánská
Ve Smečkách
Mezibranská
Muzeum
Vinohradská
Španělská
Balbínova
Arkada (200m);
Pivovarský
Dům (350m)
12

Central Prague

⊙ Sights
1 Astronomical Clock D3
2 Ceremonial Hall B2
3 Charles Bridge A3
4 Charles Bridge Museum A3
5 Church of Our Lady Before
   Týn D3
6 Estates Theatre D4
7 Klaus Synagogue B2
8 Maisel Synagogue C2
9 Mucha Museum F5
10 Municipal House F3
11 Museum of Communism E4
12 National Museum G7
13 Old Jewish Cemetery B2
14 Old Town Hall C3
15 Old Town Square D3
16 Pinkas Synagogue B2
17 Prague Jewish Museum C2
18 Spanish Synagogue D1

✪ Activities, Courses & Tours
19 Wittmann Tours A4

🛏 Sleeping
20 Fusion Hotel F5
21 Icon Hotel E7
22 Perla Hotel D5

23 Residence Karolina B6
24 Savic Hotel C4

✖ Eating
25 Lokál E1
26 Maitrea D2
27 Mistral Café B2
28 Sansho H1

🍷 Drinking & Nightlife
29 Café Imperial G2
30 Grand Cafe Orient E3
31 Kávovarna E6
32 Prague Beer Museum E1
33 U Medvídků C5
34 U Zlatého Tygra C4

🎭 Entertainment
35 Estates Theatre D4
36 Lucerna Music Bar E6
37 National Theatre A6
38 Prague State Opera G6
39 Roxy E1

🛍 Shopping
40 Kubista E3
41 Moser E4

there are also several Rubens, some Rembrandts and Breughels, and a large collection of Bohemian miniatures.

STARÉ MĚSTO

One of Europe's most beautiful urban spaces, the **Old Town Square** (Staroměstské náměstí; Map p698; Ⓜ Staroměstská), usually shortened in Czech to *Staromák*, has been Prague's principal public square since the 10th century, and was its main marketplace until the beginning of the 20th century.

Old Town Hall   Historic Building
(Staroměstská radnice; Map p698; ☎ 12444; www.prazskeveze.cz; Staroměstské náměstí 1; guided tour adult/child 105/85Kč; ⊙ 11am-6pm Mon, 9am-6pm Tue-Sun; Ⓜ Staroměstská) Prague's Old Town Hall, founded in 1338, is a hotchpotch of medieval buildings acquired over centuries, presided over by a tall Gothic tower with its splendid Astronomical Clock. As well as housing the

main tourist information office (p712), the town hall has several historic attractions, and hosts art exhibitions on the ground floor. The tower view is the best in town.

Astronomical Clock   Historic Site
(Map p698; Old Town Hall, Staroměstské náměstí; ⊙ chimes on the hour 9am-9pm; Ⓜ Staroměstská) Ironically, if you wish to tell the time in Old Town Sq, it's easier to look at the clock above this, because this 1490 mechanical marvel is tricky to decipher. The clock's creator, Master Hanuš, was allegedly blinded so he could not duplicate the clock elsewhere. Stop by on the hour for a little medieval marionette show.

Church of Our Lady Before Týn   Church
(Kostel Panny Marie před Týnem; Map p698; ☎ 222 318 186; www.tyn.cz; Staroměstské náměstí; suggested donation 25Kč; ⊙ 10am-1pm & 3-5pm Tue-Sat, 10.30am-noon Sun Mar-Oct;

CHRISTIAN KOBER/GETTY IMAGES ©

⭐ Don't Miss
Prague Castle

Immense Prague Castle is the city's most popular sight. It has always been the seat of Czech rulers as well as the official residence of the head of state. The main attractions of the castle complex include the Old Royal Palace, Basilica of St George, **Golden Lane** (Zlatá ulička; Map p702; admission with Prague Castle tour ticket; ⏱ 9am-6pm Apr-Oct, to 4pm Nov-Mar), and St Vitus Cathedral, among many others.

Entry to the castle grounds is free, but to visit the sights, including St Vitus Cathedral, requires a combined-entry ticket. Several options are available, depending on how much time you have. Two main options are available: full-price and reduced-price tickets. The latter include admission to most major sights and will satisfy the demands of most visitors.

NEED TO KNOW

Pražský hrad; Map p702; ☎ 224 372 423; www.hrad.cz; Hradčanské náměstí; grounds free, sights adult/concession full 350/175Kc, reduced 250/125Kc; ⏱ grounds 5am-midnight Apr-Oct, 6am-11pm Nov-Mar; gardens 10am-6pm Apr & Oct, to 7pm May & Sep, to 9pm Jul & Aug, closed Nov-Mar; historic buildings 9am-6pm Apr-Oct, to 4pm Nov-Mar; Ⓜ Malostranská, 🚋 22

Ⓜ Staroměstská) Its distinctive twin Gothic spires make the Týn Church an unmistakable Old Town landmark. Like something out of a 15th-century – and probably slightly cruel – fairy tale, they loom over Old Town Sq, decorated with a golden image of the Virgin Mary made in the 1620s from the melted-down Hussite chalice that previously adorned the church.

Prague Jewish Museum   Museum
(Židovské muzeum Praha; Map p698; ☎ 222 317 191; www.jewishmuseum.cz; Reservation Centre, U starého hřbitova 3a; ordinary ticket adult/child 300/200Kč, combined ticket including

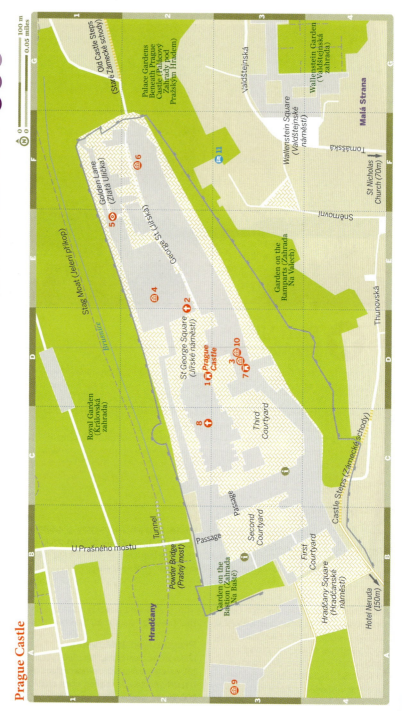

Prague Castle

Hradčany

N
0   100 m
0   0.05 miles

Old Castle Steps (Staré Zámecké schody)

Palace Gardens Beneath Prague Castle (Palácový Zahrady pod Pražským Hradem)

Valdštejnská

Wallenstein Garden (Valdštejnská zahrada)

Malá Strana

Wallenstein Square (Valdštejnské náměstí)

St Nicholas Church (70m)

Tomášská

Stag Moat (Jelení příkop)

Golden Lane (Zlatá Ulička)

George St (Jiřská)

🏛 6

5 ◎

Garden on the Ramparts (Zahrada Na Valech)

Sněmovní

Thunovská

Royal Garden (Královská zahrada)

Brusnice

🏛 4

⊕ 2

St George Square (Jiřské náměstí)

Prague Castle

1 🏰

3 🏛 10
7 🏰

Third Courtyard

8 ⊕

ℹ

Castle Steps (Zámecké schody)

Tunnel

U Prašného mostu

Passage

Passage

Second Courtyard

Powder Bridge (Prašný most)

Garden on the Bastion (Zahrada Na Baště)

ℹ

First Courtyard

Hradčany Square (Hradčanské náměstí)

Hotel Neruda (150m)

Hradčany

🏛 9

Prague Castle

⊙ Don't Miss Sights
1 Prague Castle...D2

⊙ Sights
2 Basilica of St George...........................E2
3 Bohemian Chancellery.......................D3
4 Convent of St George........................E2
5 Golden Lane...E1
6 Lobkowicz Palace...............................F2
7 Old Royal Palace.................................D3
8 St Vitus Cathedral...............................C2
9 Šternberg Palace.................................A3
10 Vladislav Hall......................................D3

🛏 Sleeping
11 Golden Well Hotel...............................F3

entry to Old-New Synagogue 480/320Kč;
⊙9am-6pm Sun-Fri Apr-Oct, to 4.30pm Nov-Mar;
M Staroměstská) This museum consists
of six Jewish monuments: the **Maisel
Synagogue** (Maiselova synagóga; Map p698;
Maiselova 10; ⊙9am-6pm Sun-Fri Apr-Oct,
to 4.30pm Nov-Mar; M Staroměstská); the
Pinkas Synagogue (Pinkasova synagóga;
Map p698; www.jewishmuseum.cz; Široká 3;
⊙9am-6pm Sun-Fri Apr-Oct, to 4.30pm Nov-Mar;
M Staroměstská); the **Spanish Synagogue**
(Španělská synagóga; Map p698; www.jewishmu-
seum.cz; Vězeňská 1; ⊙9am-6pm Sun-Fri Apr-
Oct, to 4.30pm Nov-Mar; M Staroměstská); the
Klaus Synagogue (Klauzová synagóga; Map
p698; www.jewishmuseum.cz; U starého hřbitova
1; ⊙9am-6pm Sun-Fri Apr-Oct, to 4.30pm Nov-
Mar; 🚊17, 18); the **Ceremonial Hall** (Obřadní
síň; Map p698; ⊙9am-6pm Sun-Fri Apr-Oct, to
4.30pm Nov-Mar; 🚊17); and the **Old Jewish
Cemetery** (Starý židovský hřbitov; Map p698;
www.jewishmuseum.cz; Pinkas Synagogue, Široká
3; M Staroměstská). The monuments are
clustered together in **Josefov**, a small
corner of the Old Town that was home to
Prague's Jews for some 800 years before
an urban renewal project at the start of
the 20th century and the Nazi occupation
during WWII brought this all to an end.

The monuments cannot be visited
separately but require a combined
entry ticket which is good for all of the
sights and available at ticket windows
throughout Josefov.

Municipal House — Historic Building

(Obecní dům; Map p698; 📞222 002 101; www.
obecnidum.cz; náměstí Republiky 5; guided tour
adult/child 290/240Kč; ⊙public areas 7.30am-
11pm, information centre 10am-8pm; M Náměstí
Republiky) Restored in the 1990s, Prague's
most exuberant and sensual building is
a labour of love, every detail of its design
and decoration carefully considered,
every painting loaded with symbolism.
The restaurant and cafe flanking the
entrance are like walk-in museums of art
nouveau design; upstairs are half a dozen
sumptuously decorated halls that you can
visit by guided tour.

MALÁ STRANA

Across the river from the Old Town are
the baroque backstreets of Malá Strana
(Little Quarter), built in the 17th and 18th
centuries by victorious Catholic clerics
and nobles on the foundations of their
Protestant predecessors' Renaissance
palaces.

Charles Bridge — Bridge

(Karlův most; Map p698; Malostranské náměstí;
🚊17, 18 to Karlovy lázně) Strolling across the
14th-century Charles Bridge is everybody's favourite Prague activity. In 1357
Charles IV commissioned Peter Parler
(the architect of St Vitus Cathedral) to
replace the 12th-century Judith Bridge,
which had been washed away by floods
in 1342. The new bridge was completed in
1390, and took Charles' name only in the
19th century.

St Nicholas Church — Church

(Kostel sv Mikuláše; 📞257 534 215; Malostranské
náměstí 38; adult/child 70/35Kč; ⊙9am-5pm
Mar-Oct, to 4pm Nov-Feb; 🚊12, 20, 22) Malá
Strana is dominated by the huge green
cupola of St Nicholas Church, one of
Central Europe's finest baroque buildings.
Don't confuse it with the other Church of
St Nicholas, on Old Town Sq. It was begun
by famed German baroque architect
Kristof Dientzenhofer; his son Kilian
continued the work and Anselmo Lurago
finished the job in 1755.

AUSTRIA, SWITZERLAND & THE CZECH REPUBLIC PRAGUE

John Lennon Wall
Historic Site

(Velkopřevorské náměstí; 🚋12, 20, 22) After his murder in New York on 8 December 1980, John Lennon became a pacifist hero for young Czechs. An image of Lennon was painted on a wall in a secluded square opposite the French Embassy (there is a niche on the wall that looks like a tombstone), along with political graffiti and Beatles lyrics.

Vrtbov Garden
Gardens

(Vrtbovská zahrada; 📞257 531 480; www. vrtbovska.cz; Karmelitská 25; adult/concession 60/50Kč; ⊙10am-6pm Apr-Oct; 🚋12, 20, 22) This 'secret garden', hidden along an alley at the corner of Tržiště and Karmelitská, was built in 1720 for the Earl of Vrtba, the senior chancellor of Prague Castle. It's a formal baroque garden, climbing steeply up the hillside to a terrace graced with baroque statues of Roman mythological figures by Matthias Braun.

NOVÉ MĚSTO & VYŠEHRAD

Nové Město surrounds the Old Town on all sides and was originally laid out in the 14th century. Its main public area is Wenceslas Sq.

National Museum
Museum

(Národní muzeum; Map p698; 📞224 497 111; www.nm.cz; Václavské náměstí 68; ⊙closed until 2015; Ⓜ Muzeum) Looming above Wenceslas Sq is the neo-Renaissance bulk of the National Museum, designed in the 1880s by Josef Schulz as an architectural symbol of the Czech National Revival. The museum mainly displays rocks, fossils and stuffed animals but was closed during our research for renovation and not expected to reopen until 2015.

Mucha Museum
Gallery

(Muchovo muzeum; Map p698; 📞221 451 333; www.mucha.cz; Panská 7; adult/child 180/120Kč; ⊙10am-6pm; Ⓜ Můstek) This fascinating (and busy) museum features the sensuous art nouveau posters, paintings and decorative panels of Alfons Mucha (1860–1939), as well as many sketches, photographs and other memorabilia.

Prague City Museum
Museum

(Muzeum hlavního města Prahy; 📞224 816 773; www.muzeumprahy.cz; Na Poříčí 52, Karlín; adult/child 120/50Kč; ⊙9am-6pm Tue-Sun; Ⓜ Florenc) This excellent museum, opened in 1898, is devoted to the history of Prague from prehistoric times to the 20th century. Among the many intriguing exhibits are the Astronomical Clock's original 1866 calendar wheel with Josef Mánes' beautiful painted panels representing the months – that's January at the top, toasting his toes by the fire.

Museum of Communism
Museum

(Muzeum Komunismu; Map p698; 📞224 212 966; www. muzeumkomunismu.cz; Na Příkopě 10; adult/concession/ child under 10 yr 190/150Kč/

Astronomical Clock (p700) on the Old Town Hall
JONATHAN SMITH/GETTY IMAGES ©

free; ⏱9am-9pm; Ⓜ Můstek) It's difficult to think of a more ironic site for a museum of communism – an 18th-century aristocrat's palace, between a casino and a McDonald's. Put together by an American expat and his Czech partner, the museum tells the story of Czechoslovakia's years behind the Iron Curtain in photos, words and a fascinating collection of...well, stuff.

Charles Bridge Museum Museum
(Muzeum Karlova Mostu; Map p698; ☎776 776 779; www.charlesbridgemuseum.com; Křížovnické náměstí 3; adult/concession 150/70Kč; ⏱10am-8pm May-Sep, to 6pm Oct-Apr; 🚋17, 18) Founded in the 13th century, the Order of the Knights of the Cross with the Red Star were the guardians of Judith Bridge (and its successor Charles Bridge), with their 'mother house' at the Church of St Francis Seraphinus on Křížovnické náměstí. This museum, housed in the order's headquarters, covers the history of Prague's most famous landmark.

Tours

Amazing Walks of Prague Walking Tour
(☎777 069 685; www.amazingwalks.com; per person 300-500Kč) Guide Roman Bílý is especially strong on WWII, the communist era and the Jewish Quarter.

Prague Walks Walking Tour
(☎222 322 309; www.praguewalks.com; per person 220-990Kč) Runs interesting walking tours with themes such as Prague architecture, Žižkov pubs and the Velvet Revolution. Meet at the Astronomical Clock, or you can arrange to be met at your hotel.

Wittmann Tours Guided Tour
(Map p698; ☎222 252 472; www.wittmann-tours.com; Novotného lávka 5; per person 880Kč; ⏱Josefov tours 10.30am & 2pm Sun-Fri mid-Mar–Dec; 🚋17, 18) Offers a three-hour walking tour of Josefov, and seven-hour day trips to Terezín (1250Kč per person), daily May to October, four times a week April, November and December.

Prague's Architecture

RECOMMENDATIONS FROM MARTINA ŠVAJCROVÁ, PRAGUE INFORMATION SERVICE

1 PRAGUE CASTLE
For a millennium, Prague Castle has been a symbol of the Czech state. It was built in the 9th century for the princes and kings of Bohemia, but since 1918 it has served as the official seat of the Czech president. It's a mix of architectural styles – ecclesiastical, residential, military, regal – and comprises one of the largest ancient castles in the world.

2 CHARLES BRIDGE & BRIDGE TOWERS
Prague's oldest and most iconic structure is Charles Bridge, begun by King Charles IV in 1357 and completed in 1402. The bridge's ends are fortified by towers – the smallest one is a relic of the 12th-century Judita's Bridge, the first stone bridge ever built in Prague. The bridge is also decorated by 30 saints, added between 1683 and 1928.

3 OLD TOWN HALL & THE ASTRONOMICAL CLOCK
Prague's town hall was established in 1338 to house the Old Town authorities. The oldest part of the complex includes a beautiful tower, an oriel chapel and an astronomical clock, where the 12 apostles appear every hour between 9am and 9pm. The eastern wing was destroyed during the Prague uprising in 1945, and has never been rebuilt.

4 VYŠEHRAD
For astonishing views, this clifftop castle is one of the best-kept secrets in Prague. It began as a fort built around the 10th century, and briefly served as a residence for Czech royalty. Its notable buildings include the precious Romanesque rotunda of St Martin and the Gothic church of St Peter and Paul. Don't miss the Vyšehrad cemetery, where many Czech personalities have been buried since 1869.

✱ Festivals & Events

Prague Spring   Classical Music
(www.festival.cz) In May, the Czech Republic's biggest annual cultural event, and one of Europe's most important festivals of classical music.

Prague Fringe Festival   Arts
(www.praguefringe.com) Eclectic action in late May and early June.

Christmas Market Seasonal Festival
1 to 24 December in Old Town Sq.

🛏 Sleeping

For better value stay outside of the Old Town (Staré Město) and take advantage of Prague's excellent public transport network.

HRADČANY & MALÁ STRANA

Golden Well Hotel   Hotel €€€
(Map p702; ☎257 011 213; www.goldenwell.cz; U Zlaté Studně 4; d/ste from 6250/12,500Kč; P ⊕ ❄ @ 🛜; M Malostranská) The Golden Well is one of Malá Strana's hidden secrets, tucked away at the end of a cobbled cul-de-sac – a Renaissance house that once belonged to Emperor Rudolf II, perched on the southern slope of the castle hill. The rooms are quiet and spacious, with polished wood floors, reproduction period furniture, and blue-and-white bathrooms with underfloor heating.

Lokál Inn   Inn €€
(☎257 014 800; www.lokalinn.cz; Míšeňská 12; d/ste from 3475/4475Kč; ⊕ 🛜; 🚋12, 20, 22) Polished parquet floors and painted wooden ceilings abound in this 18th-century house designed by Prague's premier baroque architect, Kilian Dientzenhofer. The eight rooms and four suites are elegant and uncluttered, and the rustic, stone-vaulted cellars house a deservedly popular pub and restaurant run by the same folk as Lokál (p708).

Hotel Neruda   Boutique Hotel €€
(☎257 535 557; www.hotelneruda.cz; Nerudova 44; r from 2225Kč; ⊕ ❄ 🛜; 🚋12, 20, 22) Set in a tastefully renovated Gothic house dating from 1348, the Neruda has decor that is chic and minimalist in neutral tones enlivened by the odd splash of colour, with a lovely glass-roofed atrium and a sunny roof terrace. The bedrooms

Old Town Square (p700), Prague

share the modern, minimalist decor and are mostly reasonably sized.

STARÉ MĚSTO

Residence Karolina   Apartments €€
(Map p698; ☎ 224 990 900; www.residence-karolina.com; Karoliny Světlé 4; 2-/4-person apt 3175/5475Kč; ➔ @ 🛜; 🚋 6, 9, 19, 21, 22) We're going to have to invent a new category of accommodation – boutique apartments – to cover this array of 20 beautifully furnished flats. Offering one- or two-bedroom options, all apartments have spacious seating areas with comfy sofas and flat-screen TVs, sleek modern kitchens and dining areas.

Savic Hotel   Hotel €€€
(Map p698; ☎ 224 248 555; www.savic.eu; Jilská 7; r from 4125Kč; ❄ @ 🛜; Ⓜ Můstek) From the complimentary glass of wine when you arrive to the comfy king-size beds, the Savic certainly knows how to make you feel welcome. Housed in the former monastery of St Giles, the hotel is bursting with character and full of delightful period details including old stone fireplaces, beautiful painted timber ceilings and fragments of frescoes.

Perla Hotel   Boutique Hotel €€
(Map p698; ☎ 221 667 707; www.perlahotel.cz; Perlová 1; s/d from 1975/2225Kč; ➔ 🛜; Ⓜ Můstek) The 'Pearl' on Pearl St is typical of the slinky, appealing designer hotels that have sprung up all over central Prague. Here the designer has picked a – surprise, surprise – pearl motif that extends from the giant pearls that form the reception desk to the silky, lustrous bedspreads and huge screen prints on the bedroom walls.

NOVÉ MĚSTO

Fusion Hotel   Boutique Hotel, Hostel €€
(Map p698; ☎ 226 222 800; www.fusionhotels.com; Panská 9; dm/d/tr 400/2000/2600Kč; @ 🛜; 🚋 3, 9, 14, 24) Billing itself as an 'affordable design hotel', Fusion certainly has style in abundance. From the revolving bar and the funky sofas that litter the public areas, to the individually decorated bedrooms that resemble miniature modern-art galleries – all white walls and black trim with tiny splashes of colour – the place exudes 'cool'.

Icon Hotel   Boutique Hotel €€€
(Map p698; ☎ 221 634 100; www.iconhotel.eu; V Jámě 6; r from 3000Kč; ❄ @ 🛜; 🚋 3, 9, 14, 24) Staff clothes by Diesel, computers by Apple, beds by Hästens – pretty much everything in this gorgeous boutique hotel has a designer stamp on it.

VINOHRADY & ŽIŽKOV

Arkada   Boutique Hotel €€
(☎ 242 429 111; www.arkadahotel.cz; Balbínová 8, Vinohrady; s/d from 1750/2250Kč; Ⓟ ➔ @ 🛜; Ⓜ Muzeum, 🚋 11) This relatively new hotel in Vinohrady comes highly recommended for offering a great combination of style, comfort and location. The rooms are well appointed, with a retro-1930s feel that fits the style of the building.

✖ Eating

Eating in Prague's tourist areas is pricey, but cheaper eats are available just a block or two away.

HRADČANY & MALÁ STRANA

Café Lounge   Cafe €€
(☎ 257 404 020; www.cafe-lounge.cz; Plaská 8; mains 100-300Kč; ⏰ 7.30am-10pm Mon-Fri, 9am-1pm Sat, 9am-5pm Sun; 🛜; 🚋 6, 9, 12, 20, 22) Cosy and welcoming, Café Lounge sports an art deco atmosphere, superb coffee, exquisite pastries and an extensive wine list.

Lichfield   International €€
(☎ 266 112 284; www.theaugustine.com; Letenská 12; mains 270-460Kč; ⏰ 11am-11pm; 🛜; 🚋 12, 20, 22) Named after society photographer Lord Lichfield, whose images of celebrities adorn the walls, this stylish yet relaxed restaurant is worth seeking out (it's hidden away in the Augustine Hotel). The menu ranges from down-to-earth but delicious dishes such as ox cheeks braised in the restaurant's own St Thomas beer, to top-end favourites such as grilled lobster and caviar.

U Modré Kachničky   Czech €€€

(☎ 257 320 308; www.umodrekachnicky.cz; Nebovidská 6; mains 450-600Kč; ⏱noon-4pm & 6.30pm-midnight; ☒12, 20, 22) A plush 1930s-style hunting lodge hidden away on a quiet side street, 'At the Blue Duckling' is a pleasantly old-fashioned place with quiet, candlelit nooks perfect for a romantic dinner. The menu is heavy on traditional Bohemian duck and game dishes, such as roast duck with *slivovice* (plum brandy), plum sauce and potato pancakes.

STARÉ MĚSTO

Mistral Café   Bistro €

(Map p698; ☎ 222 317 737; www.mistralcafe. cz; Valentinská 11; mains 130-250Kč; ⏱9am-11pm Mon-Fri, 10am-11pm Sat & Sun; 🛜; Ⓜ Staroměstská) Is this the coolest bistro in the Old Town? Pale stone, bleached birchwood and potted shrubs make for a clean, crisp, modern look, and the clientele of local students and office workers clearly appreciate the competitively priced, well-prepared food. Fish and chips in crumpled brown paper with lemon and black-pepper mayo – yum!

Maitrea   Vegetarian €

(Map p698; ☎ 221 711 631; www.restaurace-maitrea.cz; Týnská ulička 6; mains 130-160Kč; ⏱11.30am-11.30pm Mon-Fri, noon-11.30pm Sat & Sun; 🖊; Ⓜ Staroměstská) Maitrea (a Buddhist term meaning 'the future Buddha') is a beautifully designed space full of flowing curves and organic shapes, from the sensuous polished-oak furniture and fittings to the blossom-like lampshades. The menu is inventive and wholly vegetarian, with dishes such as red bean chilli tortillas, beetroot cakes with sauerkraut and polenta, and pasta with smoked tofu, spinach and parmesan.

Lokál   Czech €

(Map p698; ☎ 222 316 265; lokal-dlouha.ambi. cz; Dlouhá 33; mains 100-200Kč; ⏱11am-1am Mon-Fri, noon-1am Sat, noon-10pm Sun; ☒5, 8, 14) Who'd have thought it possible? A classic Czech beer hall (albeit with slick modern decor); excellent *tankové pivo* (tanked Pilsner Urquell); a daily-changing menu of traditional Bohemian dishes; smiling, efficient, friendly service; and a no-smoking area!

NOVÉ MĚSTO & VINOHRADY

Sansho   Asian, Fusion €€

(Map p698; ☎ 222 317 425; www.sansho.cz; Petrská 25; mains 120-300Kč, 6-course dinner 750Kč; ⏱11.30am-10.30pm Tue-Thu, to 11.30pm Fri, 6-11.30pm Sat; ☒3, 8, 24) Friendly and informal best describes the atmosphere at this ground-breaking restaurant where British chef Paul Day champions Czech farmers by sourcing all his meat and vegetables locally. There's no menu – the waiter will explain what dishes are available, depending on market produce – typical dishes include salmon sashimi, pork belly with Asian spices, and 12-hour beef rendang.

Kofein   Spanish €

(☎ 273 132 145; www.ikofein.cz; Nitranská 9, Vinohrady; tapas plates 55-75Kč; ⏱11am-midnight Mon-Fri, 5pm-midnight Sat & Sun; 🛜🖊; Ⓜ Jiřího z Poděbrad, ☒11) One of the hottest restaurants in town is this Spanish-style tapas place not far from the Jiřího z Poděbrad metro station. Descend into a lively space to see a red-faced chef minding the busy grill.

Mozaika   International €€

(☎ 224 253 011; www.restaurantmozaika.cz; Nitranská 13, Vinohrady; mains 180-450Kč; 🛜; Ⓜ Jiřího z Poděbrad) One of the most dependably good restaurants in the neighbourhood. The theme is an updated French bistro, with beef tournedos and *boeuf bourguignon* sharing the spotlight with international entrees such as stir-fries and barbecue pork ribs. Advance booking essential.

🍷 Drinking & Nightlife

Czech beers are among the world's best. The most famous brands are Budvar, Plzeňský Prazdroj (Pilsner Urquell) and Prague's own Staropramen. Independent microbreweries and regional Czech beers are also becoming more popular in Prague.

BARS & PUBS

Prague Beer Museum   Pub

(Map p698; ☎ 732 330 912; www.praguebeer-museum.com; Dlouhá 46; ⏰ noon-3am; 🚊 5, 8, 14) Although the name seems aimed at the tourist market, this lively and always heaving pub is very popular with Praguers. There are no fewer than 31 beers on tap (plus an extensive beer menu with tasting notes to guide you).

Pivovarský Klub   Beer Hall

(☎ 222 315 777; www.gastroinfo.cz/pivoklub; Křižíkova 17, Karlín; ⏰ 11am-11.30pm; Ⓜ Florenc) This bar is to beer what the Bodleian Library is to books – wall-to-wall shelves lined with myriad varieties of bottled beer from all over the world, and six guest beers on tap.

Letná Beer Garden   Beer Garden

(Letenský zámeček; ☎ 233 378 208; www. letenskyzamecek.cz; Letenské sady 341, Bubeneč; ⏰ 11am-11pm summer only; 🚊 1, 8, 15, 25, 26 to Letenské náměstí) No accounting of watering holes would be complete without a nod toward the city's best beer garden, situated at the eastern end of Letna park.

Pivovarský Dům   Brewery

(☎ 296 216 666; www.gastroinfo.cz/pivodum; cnr Ječná & Lipová; ⏰ 11am-11pm; 🚊 4, 6, 10, 16, 22) While the tourists flock to U Fleků, locals gather here to sample the classic Czech lager (40Kč per 0.5L) that is produced on the premises, as well as wheat beer and a range of flavoured beers (including coffee, banana and cherry, 40Kč per 0.3L).

U Vystřeleného oka   Pub

(☎ 222 540 465; www. uvoka.cz; U Božích Bojovníků 3, Žižkov; ⏰ 4.30pm-1am Mon-Sat; 🚊 133, 207) You've got to love a pub that has vinyl pads on the wall above the gents' urinals to rest your forehead on. 'The Shot-Out Eye' – the name pays homage to the one-eyed Hussite hero atop the hill behind the pub – is a bohemian (with a small 'b') hostelry with a raucous Friday-night atmosphere where the cheap Pilsner Urquell pulls in a typically heterogeneous Žižkov crowd.

U Medvídků   Beer Hall

(At the Little Bear; Map p698; ☎ 224 211 916; www.umedvidku.cz; Na Perštýně 7; ⏰ beer hall 11.30am-11pm, museum noon-10pm; 📶; Ⓜ Můstek) The most micro of Prague's microbreweries, with a capacity of only 250L, U Medvídků started producing its own beer only in 2005, though its beer hall has been around for years. What it lacks in size, it makes up for in strength – the dark lager produced here is the strongest in the country, with an alcohol content of 11.8%.

U Zlatého Tygra   Pub

(Map p698; ☎ 222 221 111; www.uzlatehotygra. cz; Husova 17; ⏰ 3-11pm; Ⓜ Staroměstská) The

Charles Bridge (p703), Prague
FRANK CHMURA/GETTY IMAGES ©

Christmas Market (p706), Old Town Square, Prague

FRANK CHMURA/GETTY IMAGES ©

'Golden Tiger' is one of the few Old Town drinking holes that has hung onto its soul, considering its location. It was novelist Bohumil Hrabal's favourite hostelry – there are photos of him on the walls – and the place that Václav Havel took Bill Clinton in 1994 to show him a real Czech pub.

CAFES

Kávovarna   Cafe
(Map p698; ☎ 296 236 233; Štěpánská 61, Pasáž Lucerna; ⊙ 8am-midnight; Ⓜ Můstek) This retro-styled place has bentwood chairs and curved wooden benches in the smoky, dimly lit front room (there's a nonsmoking room beyond the bar), with exhibitions of arty black-and-white photography on the walls. The coffee is good and reasonably priced, and there's delicious Kout na Šumavě beer on tap at a very reasonable 37Kč per half litre.

Café Imperial   Cafe
(Map p698; ☎ 246 011 440; www.cafeimperial.cz; Na Poříčí 15; ⊙ 7am-11pm; Ⓜ Náměstí Republiky) First opened in 1914, and given a complete facelift in 2007, the Imperial is a tour de force of art nouveau tiling – the walls and ceiling are covered in original ceramic tiles, mosaics, sculptured panels and bas-reliefs. The coffee is good, there are cocktails in the evening, and the Czech lunch and dinner offerings are first rate.

Grand Cafe Orient   Cafe
(Map p698; Ovocný trh 19, Nové Město; Ⓜ Náměstí Republiky) Prague's only Cubist café, the Orient was designed by Josef Gočár and is Cubist down to the smallest detail, including the lampshades and coat-hooks. It was restored and reopened in 2005, having been closed since 1920.

⭐ Entertainment

PERFORMING ARTS

National Theatre   Opera, Ballet
(Národní divadlo; Map p698; ☎ 224 901 377; www.narodni-divadlo.cz; Národní třída 2; tickets 30-1000Kč; ⊙ box offices 10am-6pm; 🚊 6, 9, 18, 21, 22) The much-loved National Theatre provides a stage for traditional opera, drama and ballet by the likes of Smetana, Shakespeare and Tchaikovsky, sharing the program alongside more modern works by composers and playwrights such as Philip Glass and John Osborne.

AUSTRIA, SWITZERLAND & THE CZECH REPUBLIC PRAGUE

Prague State Opera — Opera, Ballet

(Státní opera Praha; Map p698; 224 901 886; www.opera.cz; Wilsonova 4; opera tickets 100-1150Kč, ballet tickets 100-800Kč; box office 10am-5.30pm Mon-Fri, 10am-noon & 1-5.30pm Sat & Sun; M Muzeum) The impressive neo-rococo home of the Prague State Opera provides a glorious setting for perform-ances of classical, mostly Italian, opera and ballet.

Estates Theatre — Opera, Ballet

(Stavovské divadlo; Map p698; 224 902 322; www.narodni-divadlo.cz; Ovocný trh 1; tickets 30-1260Kč; box office 10am-6pm; M Můstek) The Estates Theatre (Stavovské divadlo; Map p698; 224 902 231; www.narodni-divadlo. cz; Ovocný trh 1; M Můstek) is the oldest theatre in Prague, famed as the place where Mozart conducted the premiere of *Don Giovanni* on 29 October 1787. The repertoire includes various opera, ballet and drama productions.

CLUBS

Roxy — Club, Performing Arts

(Map p698; 224 826 296; www.roxy.cz; Dlouhá 33; admission Fri & Sat free-300Kč; 7pm-midnight Mon-Thu, to 6am Fri & Sat; 5, 8, 14) Set in the ramshackle shell of an art deco cinema, the legendary Roxy is the place to see the country's top DJs and frequent live acts. On the 1st floor is NoD, an 'experimental space' that stages drama, dance, performance art, cinema and live music.

Sasazu — Club

(284 097 455; www.sasazu.com; block 25, Holešovice market, Bubenské nábřeží 306, Holešovice; admission 200-1000Kč; 9pm-5am; ; M Vltavská, 1, 3, 5, 25) One of the most popular dance clubs in the city, Sasazu attracts the fashionable elite and hangers-on in equal measure.

LIVE MUSIC

Palác Akropolis — Live Music, Club

(296 330 911; www.palacakropolis.cz; Kube-likova 27, Žižkov; admission free-50Kč; club 7pm-5am; 5, 9, 26 to Lipanska) The Akropo-lis is a Prague institution, a labyrinthine, sticky-floored shrine to alternative music and drama.

Lucerna Music Bar — Live Music

(Map p698; 224 217 108; www.musicbar. cz; Palác Lucerna, Vodičkova 36; admission 100-500Kč; 8pm-4am; M Můstek, 3, 9, 14, 24) Nostalgia reigns supreme at this atmospheric old theatre, now looking a lit-tle dog-eared, with anything from Beatles tribute bands to mainly Czech artists playing jazz, blues, pop, rock and more on midweek nights.

JazzDock — Jazz

(774 058 838; www.jazzdock.cz; Janáčkovo nábřeží 2, Smíchov; admission 90-150Kč; 4pm-3am; M Anděl, 7, 9, 12, 14) Most of Prague's jazz clubs are smoky cellar affairs. This riverside club is a definite step up, with a clean, modern decor and a decidedly romantic view out over the Vltava.

Shopping

Near Old Town Sq, explore the antique shops of Týnská and Týnská ulička.

Kubista — Homewares

(Map p698; 224 236 378; www.kubista.cz; Ovocný trh 19; 10am-6pm Tue-Sun; M Náměstí Republiky) Appropriately located in the Museum of Czech Cubism in Prague's finest cubist building, this shop special-ises in limited-edition reproductions of distinctive cubist furniture and ceramics, and designs by masters of the form such as Josef Gočár and Pavel Janák.

Moser — Glass

(Map p698; 224 211 293; www.moser-glass.com; Na Příkopě 12; 10am-8pm; M Můstek) One of the most exclusive and respected of Bohe-mian glassmakers, Moser was founded in Karlovy Vary in 1857 and is famous for its rich and flamboyant designs.

Pivní Galerie — Food, Drink

(220 870 613; www.pivnigalerie.cz; U Průhonu 9, Holešovice; noon-7pm Tue-Fri; 1, 3, 5, 25) Here you can sample and purchase a huge range of Bohemian and Moravian beers – nearly 150 varieties from 30 dif-ferent breweries.

ℹ Information

Dangers & Annoyances

Pickpockets work the crowds at the Astronomical Clock, Prague Castle and Charles Bridge, and on the central metro and tramlines, especially crowded trams 9 and 22.

Most taxi drivers are honest, but some operating from tourist areas overcharge their customers. Phone a reputable taxi company or look for the red and yellow signs for the 'Taxi Fair Place' scheme, indicating authorised taxi stands.

The park outside the main train station is a hang-out for dodgy types and worth avoiding late at night.

Emergency

If your passport or valuables are stolen, obtain a police report and crime number. You'll need this for an insurance claim. There's usually an English-speaker on hand. The emergency phone number for the police is 📞158.

Money

The major banks are best for changing cash, but using a debit card in an ATM gives a better rate of exchange. Avoid *směnárna* (private exchange booths), which advertise misleading rates and have exorbitant charges.

Tourist Information

Prague Welcome (Map p698; 📞221 714 444; www.praguewelcome.cz; Old Town Hall, Staroměstské náměstí 5; ⏱9am-7pm; Ⓜ Staroměstská) is the city's tourist information office, with branches at **Staré Město** (Map p698; 📞221 714 444; www.praguewelcome. cz; Rytířská 31, Staré Město; ⏱10am-7pm Mon-Sat; Ⓜ Můstek), the **Malá Strana Bridge Tower** (📞221 714 444; www.praguewelcome.cz; Malá Strana Bridge Tower, Mostecká ; ⏱10am-6pm Apr-Oct; 🚊12, 20, 22) as well as at Prague airport and the **main train station** (Map p698; 📞221 714 444; www.praguewelcome.cz; Wilsonova 8 , Nové Město; ⏱10am-6pm Mon-Sat; Ⓜ Hlavní Nádraží). The offices stock maps and brochures, all free.

ℹ Getting There & Away

Train

Prague is integrated into European rail networks and if you're arriving from somewhere in Europe, chances are you're coming by train. The Czech rail network is operated by **České dráhy** (ČD; Czech Railways; 📞840 112 113; www.cd.cz). Timetable information is available online at www.vlak-bus.cz.

Most trains arrive at **Praha hlavní nádraží** (Main Train Station; 📞840 112 113; www. cd.cz; Wilsonova 8, Nové Město). Some trains, particularly from Berlin, Vienna and Budapest, also stop at **Praha-Holešovice** (📞840 112 113; www.cd.cz; Vrbenského, Holešovice), north of the city centre. Both stations have their own stops on the metro line C (red).

International

Berlin 737Kč, five hours, daily

Dresden 483Kč, 2¼ hours, several daily

Frankfurt 1245Kč, eight hours, 2 daily

Munich 737Kč, five hours, four daily

Vienna 483Kč, four to five hours, several daily

National Theatre (p710), Prague
RICHARD NEBESKY/GETTY IMAGES ©

Domestic

Brno 210Kč, three hours, frequent

České Budějovice 220Kč, 2¾ hours, several daily

Olomouc 220Kč, 2¾ hours, several daily

Plzeň 100Kč, 1½ hours, hourly

ℹ Getting Around

To/From the Airport

To get into town from the airport, buy a full-price public transport ticket (32Kč) from the Prague Public Transport Authority (p713) desk in the arrivals hall and take bus 119 (20 minutes; every 10 minutes, 4am to midnight) to the end of metro line A (Dejvická), then continue by metro into the city centre (another 10 to 15 minutes; no new ticket needed).

Note you'll need a half-fare (16Kč) ticket for your bag or suitcase (per piece) if it's larger than 25cm x 45cm x 70cm.

There's also an **Airport Express** (tickets 50Kč; ⊘5am-10pm) bus which takes 35 minutes and runs every 30 minutes. It goes to Praha hlavní nádraží (main train station), where you can connect to metro line C (buy a ticket from the driver, luggage goes free).

AAA Radio Taxi (p714) operates a 24-hour taxi service, charging around 500Kč to 700Kč to get to the centre of Prague. Drivers usually speak some English and accept credit cards.

Car & Motorcycle

Challenges to driving in Prague include cobblestones, trams and one-way streets. Try not to arrive or leave on a Friday or Sunday afternoon or evening, when Prague folk are travelling to and from their weekend houses.

Central Prague has many pedestrian-only streets, marked with *pěší zóna* (pedestrian zone) signs, where only service vehicles and taxis are allowed; parking can be a nightmare. Meter time limits range from two to six hours at around 50Kč per hour. Parking in one-way streets is normally only allowed on the right-hand side.

Public Transport

Prague's excellent public-transport system combines tram, metro and bus services. It's operated by the **Prague Public Transport Authority** (DPP; ☎800 191 817; www.dpp.cz) (DPP) which has information desks at Prague airport (7am to 10pm) and in several metro

♥ If You Like…
Czech Castles

The magnificent castles in Prague and Český Krumlov (p718) draw the most visitors, but there are many more fortresses sprinkled across the Czech countryside.

1 KARLŠTEJN CASTLE
(Hrad Karlštejn; ☎311 681 617; www.hradkarlstejn.cz; adult/child Tour 1 270/180Kč, Tour 2 300/200Kč, Tour 3 120/60Kč; ⊘9am-6.30pm Jul & Aug, to 5.30pm Tue-Sun May, Jun & Sep, to 4.30pm Tue-Sun Apr & Oct, reduced hours Nov-Mar) This castle, 30km southwest of Prague, would look right at home in Disneyworld. It was built in 1348 as a hideaway for the crown jewels and treasury of the Holy Roman Emperor. Visits are by guided tour: look out for the Knight's Hall, Charles IV's bedchamber and the Jewel House, which contains a replica of the St Wenceslas Crown. Regular trains run from Prague.

2 HLUBOKÁ CHATEAU
(☎387 843 911; www.zamek-hluboka.eu; Zámek; adult/concession Tour 1 250/160Kč, Tour 2 230/160Kč, Tour 3 170/80Kč; ⊘9am-5pm Tue-Sun May-Jun, to 6pm Jul & Aug, shorter hours Sep-Feb, closed Mar) Crowned with crenellations and surrounded by a dainty garden, Hluboká Chateau is the second-most visited chateau in Bohemia after Karlštejn. Built by the Přemysl rulers in the latter half of the 13th century, the castle was later given a Tudor/Gothic overhaul based on Britain's Windsor Castle. It's in Hluboká nad Vltavou, an easy day trip from České Budějovice.

3 KONOPIŠTĚ CHATEAU
(Zámek Konopiště; ☎317 721 366; www.zamek-konopiste.cz; adult/child Tour 1 or 2 210/130Kč, Tour 3 310/210Kč; ⊘10am-noon & 1-5pm Tue-Sun Jun-Aug, to 4pm Apr, May & Sep, 10am-noon & 1-3pm Sat & Sun Oct & Nov, closed Dec-Mar) Konopiště Chateau was the country retreat of Archduke Franz Ferdinand, heir to the Austro-Hungarian empire. It featured all the latest technology – including electricity, central heating, flushing toilets, showers and a lift – and is decorated with more than 100,000 animal trophies supposedly shot by the archduke himself. The castle is 3km west of Benešov, from where there are trains to Prague.

stations, including Muzeum, Můstek, Anděl and Nádraží Holešovice. The metro operates daily from 5am to midnight.

The metro has three lines: line A (shown on transport maps in green) runs from the northwestern side of the city at Dejvická to the east at Depo Hostivař; line B (yellow) runs from the southwest at Zličín to the northeast at Černý Most; and line C (red) runs from the north at Letňany to the southeast at Háje. Convenient stops for visitors include Staroměstská (closest to Old Town Sq), Malostranská (Malá Strana), Můstek (Wenceslas Sq), Muzeum (National Museum), and Hlavní nádraží (main train station).

After the metro closes, night trams (51 to 58) rumble across the city about every 40 minutes through the night (only full-price 32Kč tickets are valid on these services). If you're planning a late evening, find out if one of these lines passes near where you are staying.

Tickets

Tickets are sold from machines at metro stations and some tram stops (coins only), as well as at DPP information offices and many newsstands and kiosks. Tickets are valid on all metros, trams and buses.

A full-price individual ticket costs 32/16Kč per adult/child aged six to 15 years and senior

aged 65 to 70 (kids under six ride free) and is valid for 90 minutes of unlimited travel, including transfers. For shorter journeys, buy short-term tickets that are valid for 30 minutes of unlimited travel. These cost 24/12Kč per adult/child and senior.

One-day passes cost 110/55Kč per adult/child and senior; three-day passes cost 310Kč (no discounts available for children or seniors).

Taxi

The official rate for licensed cabs is 40Kč flagfall plus 28Kč per kilometre and 6Kč per minute while waiting. On this basis, any trip within the city centre – say, from Wenceslas Sq to Malá Strana – should cost around 170Kč. A trip to the suburbs, depending on the distance, should run from around 200Kč to 400Kč, and to the airport between 500Kč and 700Kč.

Instead of hailing cabs off the street, call a radio taxi, as they're better regulated and more responsible. From our experience the following companies have honest drivers and offer 24-hour service and English-speaking operators.

AAA Radio Taxi (222 333 222, 14014; www.aaataxi.cz)

City Taxi (257 257 257; www.citytaxi.cz)

ProfiTaxi (14015; www.profitaxi.cz)

Grand Cafe Orient (p710)

Detour:
Mariánské Lázně & Chodová Planá

Mariánské Lázně (known abroad as Marienbad) is smaller, less urban and arguably prettier than Karlovy Vary. In the resort's heyday, Mariánské Lázně drew such luminaries as Goethe, Thomas Edison, Britain's King Edward VII and even author Mark Twain. The restored cast-iron **Colonnade** (Lázeňská kolonáda; Lázeňská kolonáda; ⏱ daily 6am-6pm) FREE is the spa's striking centrepiece, with a whitewashed pavilion that houses taps for the various springs. Notices on the walls (in English too) describe the various properties of the spa waters. In the evening, there's a **singing fountain**, where lights and water sashay to the sounds of Bach and Chopin. Half a dozen trains a day run from Prague (250Kč, three hours), passing through Plzeň en route.

If you prefer your spas with suds, so to speak, not far from Mariánské Lázně, in the village of **Planá**, you'll find a unique beer spa, **Beer Wellness Land**, at the **Chodovar Brewery** (☎ 374 617 100; www.chodovar.cz; Pivovarská 107; treatments from 660Kc). As the name implies, it's similar to a water bath, but here the liquid is heated beer, complete with confetti-sized fragments of hops.

Bohemia

The Czech Republic's western province boasts surprising variety. Český Krumlov, with its riverside setting and dramatic Renaissance castle, is in a class by itself, but lesser-known towns like Loket exude unexpected charm. Big cities like České Budějovice and Plzeň offer urban attractions like great museums and restaurants. The spa towns of western Bohemia were world famous in the 19th century and retain old-world lustre.

PLZEŇ

POP 173,000

Plzeň, the regional capital of western Bohemia and the second-biggest city in Bohemia after Prague, is best known as the home of the Pilsner Urquell brewery, but it has a handful of other interesting sights and enough good restaurants and night-time pursuits to justify an overnight stay.

 Sights

Pilsner Urquell Brewery   Brewery
(Prazdroj; ☎ 377 062 888; www.prazdroj.cz; U Prazdroje 7; guided tour adult/child 150/80Kč; ⏱ 8.30am-6pm Apr-Sep, to 5pm Oct-Mar; tours in English 12.45pm, 2.15pm & 4.15pm) Plzeň's most popular attraction is the tour of the Pisner Urquell Brewery, in operation since 1842 and arguably home to the world's best beer. Tour highlights include a trip to the old cellars (dress warmly) and a glass of unpasteurised nectar at the end.

Brewery Museum   Museum
(☎ 377 235 574; www.prazdroj.cz; Veleslavínova 6; adult/child guided tour 120/90Kč, English text 90/60Kč; ⏱ 10am-6pm Apr-Dec, 10am-5pm Jan-Mar) The Brewery Museum offers an insight into how beer was made (and drunk) in the days before Prazdroj was founded. Highlights include a mock-up of a 19th-century pub, a huge wooden beer tankard from Siberia and a collection of beer mats.

Underground Plzeň   Underground
(Plzeňské historické podzemí; ☎ 377 235 574; www.plzenskepodzemi.cz; Veleslavínova 6; adult/child 90/70Kč; ⏱ 10am-6pm Apr-Dec, 10am-5pm Feb-Mar, closed Jan; English tour 1pm daily) This extraordinary tour explores the passageways below the old city. The earliest were probably dug in the 14th century, perhaps for beer production or defence; the latest date from the 19th century. Of an estimated 11km that have been excavated,

If You Like…
Czech Architecture

Prague is justly famous for its architecture, but the crowds can take the shine off things. These little-visited towns are off the tourist radar, and make great places to experience the real Czech Republic.

1 OLOMOUC

Olomouc is a surprisingly majestic city, perhaps the most beautiful and authentic outside Prague. Around its stately streets you'll find an impressive castle, a Unesco-protected trinity column and one of the country's finest public squares. It's also famous for its cheese, *Olomoucký sýr*, reputedly the smelliest in the country. There are frequent trains from Prague and Brno.

2 TELČ

There are two reasons to visit Telč: its massive main square, lined by Renaissance and baroque burgers' houses, and its beautifully preserved Renaissance chateau, which can be visited on a guided tour. There's no train line, but around half-a-dozen buses run daily from Prague's Florenc bus station.

3 MIKULOV

In the heart of Moravian wine country, Mikulov is a wonderfully atmospheric town; surrounded by hills, adorned with an amazing hilltop Renaissance chateau and featuring a carefully restored Jewish Quarter. Little wonder that Czech poet Jan Skácel described it as a 'piece of Italy moved to Moravia by God's hand'. It's also an ideal base for sampling the local wines. Trains run to Brno and Bratislava.

some 500m of tunnels are open to the public. Bring extra clothing (it's a chilly 10°C underground).

Sleeping

Pension Stará Plzeň   Pension €
(377 259 901; www.pension-sp.cz; Na Roudné 12; s 600-1000Kč; d 800-1200Kč; P 🕐 @ 🛜) The pension 'Old Pilsen' offers light-and-

sunny rooms with skylights, wooden floors and comfy beds. The more expensive rooms offer antique-style beds, Persian rugs and exposed, wood-beam ceilings.

Courtyard By Marriott   Hotel €€
(373 370 100; www.marriott.com; sady 5 května 57; r 2000-2600Kč; P 🕐 ❄ @ 🛜) This handsome branch of the Marriott has a good location, near the Brewery Museum and central sights. The rooms are relatively spacious, clean and bright, with all of the conveniences you'd expect. The reception desk is particularly helpful and can arrange brewery tours and sightseeing options. Expect sizable discounts on weekends.

Eating

Aberdeen Angus Steakhouse   Steakhouse €€
(725 555 631; www.angusfarm.cz; Pražská 23; mains 180-400Kč) For our money, this may be the best steakhouse in all of the Czech Republic. The meats hail from the nearby Angus Farm, where the livestock is raised organically.

Na Parkánu   Czech €
(377 324 485; www.naparkanu.com; Veleslavínova 4; mains 80-180Kč; 🛜) Don't overlook this pleasant pub-restaurant, attached to the Brewery Museum. It may look a bit touristy, but the traditional Czech food is top rate, and the beer, naturally, could hardly be better. Try to snag a spot in the summer garden. Don't leave without trying the *nefiltrované pivo* (unfiltered beer).

Groll Pivovar   Czech €€
(602 596 161; www.pivovargroll.cz; Truhlářska 10; mains 129-259Kč) If you've come to Plzeň on a beer pilgrimage, then another essential visit is for a beer-garden lunch at this spiffy microbrewery. Meals include well-priced steaks and salads. The highlight is the drinks menu: homemade light and dark beers, complemented by an excellent (and still relatively rare) yeast beer.

ℹ️ Getting There & Away

Train

From Prague, eight trains (150Kč, 1½ hours) leave daily from the main station, *hlavní nádraží*.

ČESKÉ BUDĚJOVICE

POP 96,000

České Budějovice (pronounced chesky bood-yo-vit-zah) is the provincial capital of southern Bohemia and a natural base for exploring the region. Transport connections to nearby Český Krumlov are good, meaning you could easily spend the day there and evenings here. While České Budějovice lacks top sights, it does have one of Europe's largest main squares (the biggest in the Czech Republic) and a charming labyrinth of narrow lanes and winding alleyways. It's also the home of 'Budvar' beer (aka Czech 'Budweiser'), and a brewery tour usually tops the 'must-do' list.

◎ Sights

Budweiser Budvar Brewery   Brewery
(www.budvar.cz; cnr Pražská & K Světlé; adult/child 100/50Kč; ☺9am-5pm Mar-Dec, closed Sun & Mon Jan-Feb) The Budweiser Budvar Brewery is 3km north of the main square. Group tours run every day and the 2pm tour (Monday to Friday only) is open to individual travellers. The highlight is a glass of real-deal Budvar deep in the brewery's chilly cellars. Catch bus 2 to the Budvar stop.

Náměstí Přemysla Otakara II   Square
(náměstí Přemysla Otakara II) This mix of arcaded buildings centred on **Samson's Fountain** (Samsonova kašna; 1727) is the broadest plaza in the country, spanning 133m.

ℹ️ Getting There & Away

Train

From Prague, there's a frequent train service (222Kč, 2½ hours, hourly). Regular (slow) trains trundle to Český Krumlov (32Kč, 45 minutes). From the train station it's a 10-minute walk west

down Lannova třída, then Kanovnická, to nám Přemysla Otakara II, the main square.

ČESKÝ KRUMLOV

POP 14,100

Outside of Prague, Český Krumlov is arguably the Czech Republic's only other world-class sight and must-see. From a distance, the town looks like any other in the Czech countryside, but once you get closer and see the Renaissance castle towering over the undisturbed 17th-century townscape, you'll feel the appeal; this really is that fairy tale town the tourist brochures promised.

◎ Sights

Egon Schiele Art Centrum   Museum
(☎380 704 011; www.schieleartcentrum.cz; Široká 71; adult/concession 120/70Kč; ☺10am-6pm Tue-Sun) This excellent private gallery houses a small retrospective of the controversial Viennese painter Egon Schiele (1890–1918), who lived in Krumlov in 1911, and raised the ire of townsfolk by hiring young girls as nude models. For this and other sins he was eventually driven out. The centre also houses interesting temporary exhibitions.

🛏️ Sleeping

Castle Apartments   Apartment €€
(☎380 725 110; www.zameckaapartma.cz; Latrán 45-47; apt 1800-3800Kč; ☺🛜) Three adjoining houses near the castle district have been transformed into comfortable private apartments that offer wooden floors, and modern kitchenettes and bathrooms (no additional charge for the romantic views).

U Malého Vítka   Hotel €€
(☎380 711 925; www.vitekhotel.cz; Radniční 27; d 1600Kč; P🛜) We really like this small hotel in the heart of the Old Town. The room furnishings are of high-quality, hand-crafted wood, and each room is named after a traditional Czech fairy tale character. The downstairs restaurant and cafe are very good too.

GAVIN HELLIER/GETTY IMAGES ©

Don't Miss
Český Krumlov Castle

Český Krumlov's striking Renaissance castle, occupying a promontory high above the town, began life in the 13th century. It acquired its present appearance in the 16th to 18th centuries under the stewardship of the noble Rožmberk and Schwarzenberg families. The interiors are accessible by guided tour only, though you can stroll the grounds and climb the tower on your own.

Three main tours are offered: Tour I takes in the opulent Renaissance rooms, including the chapel, baroque suite, picture gallery and masquerade hall, while Tour II visits the Schwarzenberg portrait galleries and their apartments used in the 19th century; and the Theatre Tour explores the chateau's remarkable rococo theatre, complete with original stage machinery.

NEED TO KNOW

📞380 704 711; www.castle.ckrumlov.cz; Zámek; adult/concession Tour 1 250/160Kč, Tour 2 240/140Kč, Theatre Tour 380/220Kč, tower 50/30Kč; ⏰9am-6pm Tue-Sun Jun-Aug, 9am-5pm Apr, May, Sep & Oct

---

 Eating

Laibon   Vegetarian €
(📞728 676 654; www.laibon.cz; Parkán 105; mains 90-180Kč; 📶🍴) Candles and vaulted ceilings create a great boho ambience in the best little vegetarian teahouse in Bohemia. The riverside setting's pretty fine as well.

Krčma v Šatlavské   Czech €€
(📞380 713 344; www.satlava.cz; Horní 157; mains 150-260Kč) Nirvana for meat-lovers, this medieval barbecue cellar serves sizzling platters in a funky labyrinth illuminated by candles and the flickering flames of open grills. Booking ahead is es-

sential. Be forewarned: summer months bring tour-bus crowds.

Hospoda Na Louži　　Czech €

(☏ 380 711 280; www.nalouzi.cz; Kájovská 66; mains 90-170Kč) Nothing's changed in this wood-panelled *pivo* (beer) parlour for almost a century. Locals and tourists pack Na Louži for huge meals and tasty dark (and light) beer from the Eggenberg brewery.

ℹ Information

Infocentrum (☏ 380 704 622; www.ckrumlov. info; náměstí Svornosti 1; ⏱9am-7pm Jun-Aug, 9am-6pm Apr, May, Sep & Oct, 9am-5pm Nov-Mar) Transport and accommodation info, maps, internet access (5Kč per five minutes) and audio guides (100Kč per hour). A guide for disabled visitors is available.

ℹ Getting There & Away

Train

From Prague, the train journey (260Kč, 3½ hours) requires a change in České Budějovice. Buses are usually quicker and cheaper. There's a regular train service between České Budějovice and Český Krumlov (32Kč, 45 minutes).

SURVIVAL GUIDE

ℹ Directory A–Z

Accommodation

Austria

From simple mountain huts to five-star hotels fit for kings – you'll find the lot in Austria.

- ● It's wise to book ahead at all times, particularly during the high seasons: July and August and December to April (in ski resorts).
- ● Be aware that confirmed reservations in writing are considered binding, and cancellations within several days of arrival often involve a fee or full payment.
- ● Very often a hotel won't have lifts; if this is important, always check ahead.
- ● In mountain resorts, high-season prices can be up to double the prices charged in the low season (May to June and October to November).

- ● In some resorts (not often in cities), a *Gästekarte* (guest card) is issued if you stay overnight, which offers discounts on things such as cable cars and admission.
- ● Locally, always check the city or region website, as many (such as in Vienna, Salzburg and Graz) have an excellent booking function.

Some useful websites:

Austrian Hotelreservation (www.austrian-hotelreservation.at)

Austrian National Tourist Office (www.austria.info)

Booking.com (www.booking.com)

Hostelling International (HI; www.hihostels.com)

Hostelworld (www.hostelworld.com)

Our reviews refer to double rooms with private bathrooms, except in hostels or where otherwise specified. Quoted rates are for the high season: December to April in the Alps, June and August everywhere else.

€ less than €80

€€ €80 to €200

€€€ more than €200

Switzerland

From palatial palaces and castles to mountain refuges, nuclear bunkers, icy igloos or simple hay lofts, Switzerland sports traditional and creative accommodation in every price range.

- ● The prices may seem steep – even the most inexpensive places are pricey compared with other parts of Europe. The upside is that standards are usually quite high.
- ● In Switzerland, many budget hotels have cheaper rooms with shared toilet and shower facilities. From there the sky is truly the limit. Breakfast buffets can be extensive and tasty but are not always included in room rates.

Rates in cities and towns stay constant most of the year. In mountain resorts prices are seasonal (and can fall by 50% or more outside high season):

Low season mid-September to mid-December, mid-April to mid-June

Mid-season January to mid-February, mid-June to early July, September

High season July to August, Christmas, mid-February to Easter

The following price ranges refer to a double room with a private bathroom, except in hostels or where otherwise specified. Quoted rates are for the high season and don't include breakfast unless otherwise noted.

$ less than Sfr150

$$ Sfr150 to Sfr350

$$$ more than Sfr350

Czech Republic

Outside the peak summer season, hotel rates can fall by up to 40%. Booking ahead – especially in Prague – is recommended for summer and around Christmas and Easter. Many hotels are now completely or mostly nonsmoking.

Prices quoted here are for rooms with a private bathroom and a simple breakfast, unless otherwise stated. The following price indicators apply (for a high-season double room):

€ less than 1600Kč

€€ 1600Kč to 3700Kč

€€€ more than 3700Kč

Business Hours

The reviews in this chapter don't list hours unless they differ from the hours listed here. Hours are given for the high season and tend to decrease in the low season.

Austria

Banks 8am-3pm Mon-Fri, to 5.30pm Thu

Clubs 10pm to late

Post offices 8am-noon & 2-6pm Mon-Fri, 8am-noon Sat

Pubs 6pm-1am

Cafes 7.30am-8pm; hours vary widely

Restaurants noon-3pm, 7-11pm

Shops 9am-6.30pm Mon-Fri, 9am-5pm Sat

Supermarkets 9am-8pm Mon-Sat

Switzerland

Banks 8.30am-4.30pm Mon-Fri, usually with late opening hours one day a week

Offices 8am-noon & 2-5pm Mon-Fri

Post Offices 7.30am-noon & 2-6.30pm Mon-Fri, to 11am Sat (typically; however, opening times vary)

Restaurants noon-2pm & 6-10pm

Shops 9am-7pm Mon-Fri (sometimes with a one- to two-hour break for lunch at noon in small towns), 9am-6pm Sat. In cities, there's often shopping until 9pm on Thursday or Friday. Sunday sees some souvenir shops and supermarkets at some train stations open.

Czech Republic

Banks 8.30am to 4.30pm Mon-Fri

Bars 11am to midnight

Museums & Castles Usually closed Mon year-round

Restaurants 11am to 11pm

Shops 8.30am to 6pm Mon-Fri 8.30am to noon Sat

Food

Austria

The following price ranges refer to a two-course meal excluding drinks.

€ less than €15

€€ €15 to €30

€€€ more than €30

Switzerland

The following price ranges refer to a two-course meal.

$ less than Sfr25

$$ Sfr25 to Sfr45

$$$ more than Sfr45

Czech Republic

Restaurants open as early as 11am and carry on till midnight; some take a break between lunch and dinner. The following price ranges refer to a main meal.

€ less than 200Kč

€€ 200Kč to 500Kč

€€€ more than 500Kč

Gay & Lesbian Travellers

Switzerland

Attitudes towards homosexuality are reasonably tolerant in Switzerland. Zürich and Geneva have particularly lively gay scenes.

Cruiser Magazine (www.cruiser.ch)

Pink Cross (www.pinkcross.ch)

Czech Republic

Homosexuality is legal in the Czech Republic, but Czechs are not yet used to seeing public displays of affection; it's best to be discreet. For online information including links to accommodation and bars, see the **Prague Gay Guide** (www.prague.gayguide.net).

Money

Austria

ATMs Some *Bankomaten* (ATMs) are 24 hours. Most accept at the very least Maestro debit cards and Visa and MasterCard credit cards.

Credit Cards Visa and MasterCard (Eurocard) are accepted a little more widely than American Express (Amex) and Diners Club.

Taxes *Mehrwertsteuer* (MWST; value-added tax) is set at 20% for most goods.

Tipping It's customary to tip about 10% in restaurants, bars and cafes, and in taxis; hand over the bill and the tip together.

Switzerland

ATMs Automated teller machines (ATMs) – called Bancomats in banks and Postomats in post offices – are common.

Cash Swiss francs are divided into 100 centimes (*Rappen* in German-speaking Switzerland). There are notes for 10, 20, 50, 100, 200 and 1000 francs, and coins for 5, 10, 20 and 50 centimes, as well as for one, two and five francs. Euros are accepted by many tourism businesses.

Credit Cards The use of credit cards is slightly less widespread than in the UK or USA and not all shops, hotels or restaurants accept them.

Tipping Not necessary, given that hotels, restaurants, bars and even some taxis are legally required to include a 15% service charge in bills. You can round up the bill after a meal for good service, as locals do.

Czech Republic

ATMs ATMs linked to the most common global banking networks can be easily located in all major cities, and smaller towns and villages.

Cash Keep small change handy for use in public toilets, telephones and tram-ticket machines, and try to keep some small-denomination notes for shops, cafes and restaurants. Changing larger notes from ATMs can be a problem. Beware of *směnárna* (private exchange offices), especially in Prague – they advertise misleading

Train travelling through the Bernese Oberland (p685), Switzerland

GLENN VAN DER KNIJFF/GETTY IMAGES ©

rates, and often charge exorbitant commissions or 'handling fees'. There is no blackmarket for currency exchange, and anyone who offers to change money in the street is dodgy.

Credit Cards Credit cards are widely accepted in petrol stations, midrange and top-end hotels, restaurants and shops.

Tipping Leave small change as a tip in bars. It is optional in restaurants and taxis, but increasingly expected in Prague; round the bill up the next 20Kč or 30Kč (5% to 10%).

Public Holidays
Austria

New Year's Day (Neujahr) 1 January

Epiphany (Heilige Drei Könige) 6 January

Easter Monday (Ostermontag) March/April

Labour Day (Tag der Arbeit) 1 May

Whit Monday (Pfingstmontag) Sixth Monday after Easter

Ascension Day (Christi Himmelfahrt) Sixth Thursday after Easter

Corpus Christi (Fronleichnam) Second Thursday after Whitsunday

Assumption (Maria Himmelfahrt) 15 August

National Day (Nationalfeiertag) 26 October

All Saints' Day (Allerheiligen) 1 November

Immaculate Conception (Mariä Empfängnis) 8 December

Christmas Day (Christfest) 25 December

St Stephen's Day (Stephanitag) 26 December

Switzerland

New Year's Day 1 January

Easter March/April (Good Friday, Easter Sunday and Monday)

Ascension Day 40th day after Easter

Whit Sunday & Monday Seventh week after Easter

National Day 1 August

Christmas Day 25 December

St Stephen's Day 26 December

Czech Republic

New Year's Day 1 January

Easter Monday March/April

Labour Day 1 May

Liberation Day 8 May

SS Cyril & Methodius Day 5 July

Jan Hus Day 6 July

Czech Statehood Day 28 September

Republic Day 28 October

Freedom & Democracy Day 17 November

Christmas 24 to 26 December

Telephone
Austria

Austrian telephone numbers consist of an area code followed by the local number.

Country code ☎43

International access code ☎00

Mobiles The network works on GSM 1800 and is compatible with GSM 900

Náměstí Přemysla Otakara II (p717), Prague
STEPHEN SAKS/GETTY IMAGES ©

phones. Phone shops sell prepaid SIM cards for about €10.

Public telephones Phone-cards in different denominations are sold at post offices and *Tabak* (tobacconist) shops. Call centres are widespread in cities, and many internet cafes are geared for Skype calls.

Switzerland

Country code ☏ 41

International access code ☏ 00

Telephone numbers Numbers with the code ☏ 0800 are toll-free; those with ☏ 0848 are charged at the local rate. Numbers beginning with ☏ 156 or ☏ 157 are charged at the premium rate.

Mobiles Mobile phone numbers start with the code ☏ 076, ☏ 078 or ☏ 079. SIM cards are widely available from train station ticket counters, exchange bureaus and mobile telephone shops. Several providers offer the same good deal: €20 for a SIM card that comes with €20 credit.

Czech Republic

Country code ☏ 420

Telephone numbers All Czech phone numbers have nine digits; dial all nine for any call, local or long distance.

Mobiles Mobile-phone coverage (GSM 900/1800) is excellent. If you're from Europe, Australia or New Zealand, your own mobile phone should be compatible. Purchase a Czech SIM card from any mobile-phone shop for around 500Kč (including 300Kč of calling credit). Local mobile phone numbers start with the following; ☏ 601–608 and ☏ 720–779.

Public telephones Buy phonecards for public telephones from post offices and newsstands from 100Kč.

Tourist Information

Austria

Tourist offices, which are dispersed far and wide in Austria, tend to adjust their hours from one year to the next, so business hours may have changed slightly by the time you arrive.

The **Austrian National Tourist Office** (www. austria.info) has a number of overseas offices.

There is a comprehensive listing on the ANTO website.

Switzerland

Make the Swiss tourist board **Switzerland Tourism** (www.myswitzerland.com) your first port of call. Local tourist offices are extremely helpful and have reams of literature to give out, including maps (nearly always free). There are several useful tourist passes available:

Swiss Museum Pass (www.museumspass. ch; adult/family Sfr144/255) Regular or long-term visitors to Switzerland may want to buy this pass which covers entry to the permanent collection (only) of 450 museums.

Visitors' Cards In many resorts and cities there's a visitors' card (*Gästekarte*), which provides various benefits such as reduced prices for museums, swimming pools, public transport or cable cars. Cards are issued by your accommodation.

Czech Republic

Czech Tourism (Map p698; www.czechtourism. com) Official tourist information.

IDOS (www.idos.cz) Train and bus timetables.

Mapy (www.mapy.cz) Online maps.

Visas

Austria, Switzerland and the Czech Republic are all part of the Schengen Agreement, and citizens of most countries can spend up to 90 days in those countries in a six-month period without a visa. For travellers from some other countries, a Schengen Visa is required; you can only get this from your country of residence.

❶ Getting There & Away

Air

Austria

Vienna is the main transport hub for Austria, but Graz, Linz, Klagenfurt, Salzburg and Innsbruck all receive international flights. Flights to these cities are often a cheaper option than those to the capital, as are flights to Airport Letisko (Bratislava Airport), 85km east of Vienna in Slovakia.

Among the low-cost airlines, Ryanair and Air Berlin fly to Graz, Innsbruck, Klagenfurt, Linz, Salzburg and Vienna (Ryanair to Bratislava for Vienna).

Below: Ski lift in Tirol (p666), Austria;
Right: Traditional houses, Hallstatt (p665), Austria
(BELOW) RICHARD NEBESKY/GETTY IMAGES ©; (RIGHT) WESTEND61/GETTY IMAGES ©

Switzerland

The main international airports:

Aéroport International de Genève (GVA; ☎0900 571 500; www.gva.ch) The country's second airport has decent international links.

Zürich airport (ZRH; ☎043 816 22 11; www.zurich-airport.com) Switzerland's main airport has flights to/from destinations worldwide. For flight information, SMS ZHR plus your flight number to ☎92 92.

Czech Republic

Nearly all international flights arrive at **Václav Havel Airport Prague** (Letiště Praha; ☎220 111 888; www.prg.aero). Flights to and from destinations outside the EU's Schengen zone use the airport's Terminal 1, which has standard passport and customs checks. Flights within the Schengen zone use Terminal 2 and are treated as domestic flights.

The national carrier **Czech Airlines** (www.czechairlines.com) has a good safety record and is a member of the Skyteam airline alliance.

Car & Motorcycle

Austria

There are numerous entry points into Austria by road from Germany, the Czech Republic, Slovakia, Hungary, Slovenia, Italy and Switzerland. All border-crossing points are open 24 hours.

Standard European insurance and paperwork rules apply.

Switzerland

There are fast, well-maintained highways to Switzerland through all bordering countries. The Alps present a natural barrier to entering Switzerland, so main roads generally head through tunnels. Smaller roads are more scenically interesting, but special care is needed when negotiating mountain passes.

Czech Republic

The Czech Republic has border crossings with Germany, Poland, Slovakia and Austria. These are all EU member states within the Schengen zone, meaning there are no longer any passport or customs checks.

The Czech Republic lies along major European highways. On entering the country, motorists are

required to display on their windscreen a special prepaid sticker *(dálniční známka)*, purchased at petrol stations and kiosks near the border. A sticker valid for 10 days costs 310Kč, for 30 days 440Kč, and for a year 1500Kč.

Train

Austria

Austria has excellent rail connections. The main services in and out of the country from the west normally pass through Bregenz, Innsbruck or Salzburg en route to Vienna. Trains to Eastern Europe leave from Vienna. Express services to Italy go via Innsbruck or Villach; trains to Slovenia are routed through Graz.

Express & High-Speed Trains Express trains are identified by the symbols EC (EuroCity; serving international routes) or IC (InterCity; serving national routes).

Online Timetables ÖBB (Austrian National Railways; www.oebb.at) Austrian National Railways, with national and international connections. Only national connections have prices online.

Reservations Extra charges can apply on fast trains and international trains, and it is a good idea (sometimes obligatory) to make seat reservations for peak times.

SparSchiene (discounted ÖBB tickets) These are often available when you book online in advance and can cost as little as a third of the standard train fare.

Switzerland

Located in the heart of Europe, Switzerland is a hub of train connections to the rest of the Continent. Zürich is the busiest international terminus, with service to all neighbouring countries. Destinations include Milan (4¼ hours), Munich (four hours) and Vienna (eight hours).

There are numerous TGV trains daily from Paris to several cities, including Geneva (three hours), Lausanne (3¾ hours), Basel (three hours) and Zürich (four hours). Basel is a hub for services to Germany: fast ICE trains serve most major German cities. An easy way into Germany from Zürich is via medieval Constance (Sfr31, 1¼ hours).

Czech Republic

Prague's Praha hlavní nádraží (p712), is the country's international train gateway, with frequent service to and from Germany, Poland, Slovakia and Austria. Trains to/from the south and east, including from Bratislava, Vienna and Budapest, normally stop at Brno's main train station as well.

In Prague, buy international train tickets in advance from **ČD Travel** (☎ 972 241 861; www. cdtravel.cz; Wilsonova 8) agency, which has a large ticketing office on the lower level of Praha hlavní nádraží and a **city centre office** (☎ 972 233 930; V Celnici 6) not far from náměstí Republiky. Sales counters are divided into those selling domestic tickets *(vnitrostátní jízdenky)* and international tickets *(mezinárodní jízdenky)*, so make sure you're in the right line. The windows also sell seat reservations. Credit cards are accepted.

Both InterRail and Eurail passes are valid on the Czech rail network.

River & Lake

Hydrofoils run to Bratislava and Budapest from Vienna; slower boats cruise the Danube between the capital and Passau. The **Danube Tourist Commission** (www.danube-river.org) has a country-by-country list of operators and agents who can book tours. Germany and Switzerland can be reached from Bregenz.

🛈 Getting Around

Boat
Austria

The Danube serves as a thoroughfare between Vienna and Lower and Upper Austria. Services are generally slow, scenic excursions rather than functional means of transport.

Switzerland

Ferries and steamers link towns and cities on many lakes, including Constance, Geneva, Lucerne, Lugano, Murten and Zürich.

Bus
Austria

Postbus services usually depart from outside train stations. In remote regions, there are fewer services on Saturday and often none on Sunday. Generally, you can only buy tickets from the drivers. For information inside Austria, call ☎ 0810 222 333 (6am to 8pm); from outside Austria, call ☎ +43 1 71101, or visit the website, www.postbus.at.

Switzerland

Yellow postal buses are a supplement to the rail network, following postal routes and linking towns to the more inaccessible regions in the mountains. In all, routes cover some 8000km of terrain. Services are regular, and departures link to train schedules. Postbus stations are next to train stations and offer destination and timetable information.

Czech Republic

Within the Czech Republic, buses are often faster, cheaper and more convenient than trains. Many bus routes have reduced frequency (or none) at weekends. Buses occasionally leave early so get to the station at least 15 minutes before the official departure time. Check bus timetables and prices at www.idos.cz.

ČSAD (☎ information line 900 144 444) The national bus company links cities and smaller towns.

Car & Motorcycle

Autobahns ('A') and *Bundesstrassen* ('B') are major roads, while *Landstrassen* ('L') let you enjoy the ride and are usually good for cyclists. A daily motorail service links Vienna to Innsbruck, Salzburg and Villach.

Austria

Multinational car-hire firms **Avis** (☎ 0800 0800 87 57, in Vienna 60187-0; www.avis.at), **Budget** (www.budget.at), **Europcar** (www.europcar. co.at) and **Hertz** (www.hertz.at) all have offices in major cities; ask at tourist offices for details. The minimum age for hiring small cars is 19 years, or 25 years for larger, 'prestige' cars. Customers must have held a driving licence for at least a year. Many contracts forbid customers to take cars outside Austria, particularly into Eastern Europe.

A *Vignette* (toll sticker) is imposed on all motorways; charges for cars/motorbikes are €8.30/4.80 for 10 days and €24.20/12.10 for two months. *Vignette* can be purchased at border crossings, petrol stations and *Tabak* shops. There are additional tolls (usually €2.50 to €10) for some mountain tunnels.

The following road rules apply in Austria:
- The minimum driving age is 18.
- Drive on the right, overtake on the left.
- Give way to the right at all times except when a priority road sign indicates otherwise. Trams always have priority.
- An international driving licence should always be carried.

Old Town Square (p700), Prague

FRANCESCO IACOBELLI/GETTY IMAGES ©

- Seat belts are compulsory.
- The speed limit is 50km/h in built-up areas, 130km/h on motorways and 100km/h on other roads. Except for the A1 (Vienna–Salzburg) and the A2 (Vienna–Villach), the speed limit is 110km/h on the autobahn from 10pm to 5am.
- The penalty for drink-driving – over 0.05% – is a hefty on-the-spot fine and confiscation of your driving licence.
- Crash helmets are compulsory for motorcyclists and their passengers, not for cyclists.
- Children under the age of 14 who are shorter than 1.5m must have a special seat or restraint.
- Carrying a warning triangle, safety vest and first-aid kit in your vehicle is compulsory.
- Winter tyres and/or snow chains are compulsory from November to mid-April.
- It's illegal to hitchhike on Austrian motorways.

Switzerland

The **Swiss Touring Club** (Touring Club der Schweiz; ☎ 022 417 24 24; www.tcs.ch), Switzerland's largest motoring organisation, has reciprocal agreements with motoring organisations worldwide.

- You do not need an International Driving Permit to operate a vehicle in Switzerland. A licence from your home country is sufficient.

- Be prepared for winding roads, high passes and long tunnels.
- Normal speed limits are 50km/h in towns, 120km/h on motorways, 100km/h on semimotorways (designated by roadside rectangular pictograms showing a white car on a green background) and 80km/h on other roads.
- Mountain roads are well maintained. Some minor Alpine passes are closed from November to May – check with the local tourist offices before setting off.

Czech Republic

Small local car-hire companies tend to offer better prices, but are less likely to have fluent, English-speaking staff than large companies. It's often easier to book by email than by phone. Typical rates for a Škoda Fabia are around 800Kč a day, including unlimited kilometres, collision-damage waiver and value-added tax (VAT). Bring your credit card as a deposit. A motorway tax coupon is included with most rental cars. One reliable rental outfit is **Secco Car** (☎ 220 802 361; www.seccocar.cz; Přístavní 39, Holešovice).

Unleaded petrol is available as *natural* (95 octane) or *natural plus* (98 octane). The Czech for diesel is *nafta* or just *diesel*. *Autoplyn* (LPG gas) is available in every major town but at very few outlets.

Foreign driving licences are valid for up to 90 days. Strictly speaking, licences that do not include photo identification need an International Driving Permit as well, although this rule is rarely enforced.

The minimum driving age is 18. Traffic moves on the right. The following road rules apply in the Czech Republic:

- The use of seat belts is compulsory for front- and rear-seat passengers.
- Children under 12 or shorter than 1.5m (4ft 9in) are prohibited from sitting in the front seat and must use a child-safety seat.
- Headlights must always be on, even in bright daylight.
- The legal blood-alcohol limit is zero; if the police pull you over for any reason, they are required to administer a breathalyser.

Train

Austria

Austria has a clean, efficient rail system, and if you use a discount card it's very inexpensive.

Disabled Passengers Use the 24-hour ☎05-17 17 customer number for special travel assistance; do this at least 24 hours ahead of travel (48 hours ahead for international services). Staff at stations will help with boarding and alighting.

Fares Fares quoted here are for 2nd-class tickets.

Information ÖBB (www.oebb.at) is the main operator, supplemented with a handful of private lines. Tickets and timetables are available online.

RailJet It's worth seeking out RailJet train services connecting Vienna, Graz, Villach, Salzburg, Innsbruck, Linz and Klagenfurt, as they travel up to 200km/h.

Reservations In 2nd class within Austria this costs €3.50 for most express services; recommended for travel on weekends.

Depending on the amount of travelling you intend to do in Austria, rail passes can be a good deal. The following rail passes are available:

Eurail Austria Pass This handy pass is available to non-EU residents; prices start at €123 for three days' unlimited 2nd-class travel within one month, and youths under 26 receive substantial discounts. See the website at www.eurail.com for all options.

Interrail Passes are for European citizens and include One Country Pass Austria (three/four/six/eight days €181/205/267/311). Youths under 26 receive substantial discounts. See www.interrailnet.com for all options.

Vorteilscard Reduces fares by at least 45% and is valid for a year, but not on buses. Bring a photo and your passport or ID. It costs adult/under 26 years/senior €100/20/27.

Switzerland

The Swiss rail network combines state-run and private operations. The **Swiss Federal Railway** (www.rail.ch) is abbreviated to SBB in German, CFF in French and FFS in Italian.

- All major train stations are connected to each other by hourly departures, at least between 6am and midnight, and most long-distance trains have a dining car.

Cable car, Mt Pilatus (p687), Switzerland
PERMANENT TOURIST/GETTY IMAGES ©

- Second-class seats are perfectly acceptable, but cars are often close to full. First-class carriages are more comfortable, spacious and have fewer passengers.
- Powerpoints for laptops let you work aboard and some seats are in wi-fi hotspots – look for the insignia on the carriage.
- Ticket vending machines accept most major credit cards from around the world.
- The SBB smartphone app is an excellent resource and can be used to store your tickets electronically.
- Check the SBB website for cheap Supersaver tickets on major routes.
- Most stations have 24-hour lockers (small/large locker Sfr6/9), usually accessible from 6am to midnight.
- Seat reservations (Sfr5) are advisable for longer journeys, particularly in the high season.

Convenient discount passes make the Swiss transport system even more appealing. On extensive travel within Switzerland the following national travel passes generally offer better savings than Eurail or InterRail passes:

Swiss Pass The Swiss Pass entitles the holder to unlimited travel on almost every train, boat and bus service in the country, and on trams and buses in 41 towns, plus free entry to 400-odd museums. Reductions of 50% apply on funiculars, cable cars and private railways. Different passes are available, valid between four days (1st/2nd class US$460/288) and one month.

Swiss Flexi Pass This pass allows you to nominate a certain number of days (anywhere from three to six) during a month when you can enjoy unlimited travel.

Half-Fare Card Almost every Swiss owns one of these. As the name suggests, you pay only half the fare on trains with this card, plus you get some discounts on local-network buses, trams and cable cars. An adult one-year Half-Fare Card costs Sfr175 (photo necessary).

Swiss Card A variation on the Half-Fare Card that includes a round-trip ticket to/from a border area and is good for 30 days. It is sold abroad for US$300/200 1st/2nd class.

Junior Card The Sfr30 card gets free travel (on trains, buses and boats, even on some cable cars) for those aged six to 16 years when travelling with at least one of their parents. Children within that age bracket travelling with an adult who is not a relative get 50% off.

Regional Passes Network passes valid only within a particular region are available in several parts of the country. Such passes are available from train stations in the region.

Czech Republic

Czech Railways provides efficient train services to almost every part of the country. See www.idos.cz and www.cd.cz for fares and timetables.

Several different categories of train run on Czech rails, differing mainly in speed and comfort.

EC (EuroCity) Fast, comfortable international trains, stopping at main stations only, with 1st- and 2nd-class coaches; supplementary charge of 60Kč; reservations recommended. Includes 1st-class only SC Pendolino trains that run from Prague to Olomouc, Brno and Ostrava, with links to Vienna and Bratislava.

IC (InterCity) Long-distance and international trains with 1st- and 2nd-class coaches; supplement of 40Kč; reservations recommended.

Ex (express) Similar to IC trains, but no supplementary charge.

R (rychlík) The main domestic network of fast trains with 1st- and 2nd-class coaches and sleeper services; no supplement except for sleepers; express and rychlík trains are usually marked in red on timetables.

Os (osobní) Slow trains using older rolling stock that stop in every one-horse town; 2nd-class only.

Greece

Greece is an absolutely essential stop on any European trip, despite its well-publicised money troubles. The economy may be in a mess, but the elements that have always drawn people here are still very much in evidence: gorgeous beaches, paradisaical islands, great food and, of course, several thousand years' worth of ancient history.

Athens is the inevitable starting point, home to the nation's greatest Grecian monuments including the Acropolis and its landmark new museum. You'll find plenty of ancient history to explore further afield, from oracle's caves to abandoned amphitheatres. But the past is far from Greece's only selling point. Wanderers can island-hop to their hearts content, from Santorini to the faraway Aegean Islands, while gastronomes feast on ouzo and octopus, and beach addicts dive into the sapphire blue waters of the Mediterranean. There are many different sides to Greece – the hard part is deciding which one to experience first.

Ancient Delphi (p755)

ANTHONY PIDGEON/GETTY IMAGES ©

Greece

Prilep
Kavadarci
MACEDONIA
Lake Ohrid
Ohrid
Ljubojno
Sidirokastro
Drama
Strymnas (Struma)
Seres
Kilkis
E75
E79
Prespa Lakes
Florina
Edessa
Gianitsa
Thessaloniki
E90
Naoussa
Kristalopigi
Veria
Alexandria
Sazan Island
ALBANIA
Kastoria
Ptolemaida
Katerini
Kozani
Mt Olympus (2917m)

Meteora 3
E90
E65
Ionian Sea
Corfu
Meteora
Tirnavos-x
Corfu Town (Kerkyra)
Paxos
Ioannina
E92
Kalambaka
Larisa
Igoumenitsa
Trikala
Volos
Alonnisos
Arahthos
Karditsa
E75
Skiathos
Skopelos
E951
Arta
Loutra Edipsou
Strofylia
Preveza
Lamia
Kymi
Lefkada
Lefkada
E952
Agios Kostantinos
Evia
Mytikas
Astakos
Agrinio
Halkida
Ithaki
Acheloos
Messolongi
Mt Parnassos
E75
Kefallonia
Delphi
Argostoli
Patra
ATHENS
Kyllini
E55
Corinth
Piraeus
1 2
Zakynthos
Amaliada
Mycenae
Aegina
Lavrio
Zakynthos
Pyrgos
Olympia
Epidaurus
Methana
Nafplio
Galatas
Ionian Sea
E65
Hydra
Spetses
Sparta
Kalamata
Geraki
Pylos
Mystras
Gythio
Monemvasia
Areopoli
Gefyra
Neapoli
Kythira

1 Acropolis
2 Acropolis Museum
3 Meteora
4 Knossos
5 Santorini

Antikythira

MEDITERRANEAN SEA

Kastelli
Hania
Paleohora

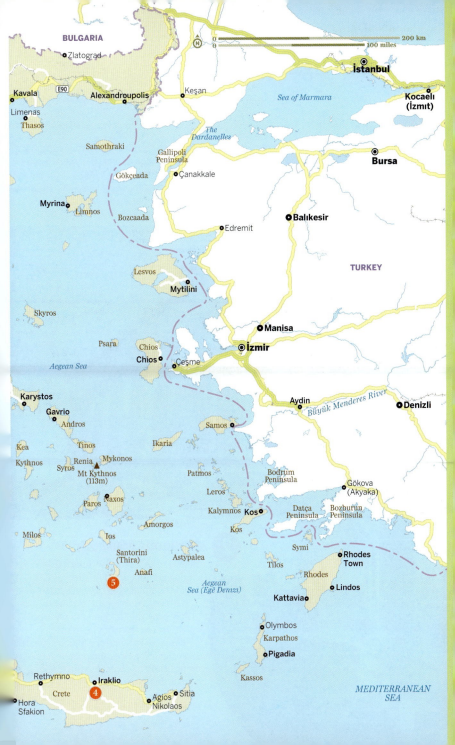

Greece Highlights

Acropolis

The Acropolis (p742) is a masterpiece of classical architecture and an absolutely essential item on any Athens itinerary. The complex was largely developed during the rule of Pericles, and even experiencing its part-ruined state will transport you back into the glory of Greece from long ago. Parthenon

1

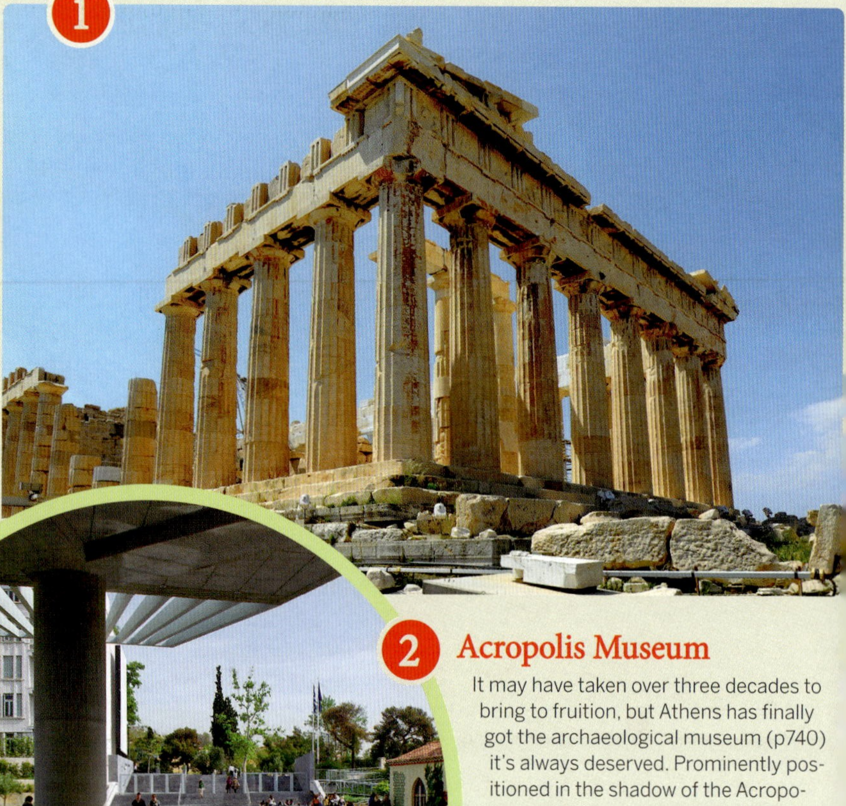

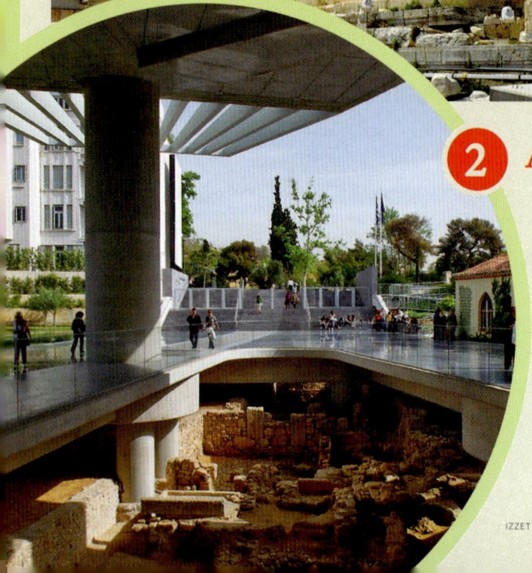

2 Acropolis Museum

It may have taken over three decades to bring to fruition, but Athens has finally got the archaeological museum (p740) it's always deserved. Prominently positioned in the shadow of the Acropolis, the museum has been specially designed to house the nation's greatest ancient treasures and provide fascinating historical context to the real-life ruins themselves.

IZZET KERIBAR/GETTY IMAGES ©

Meteora

The dramatic rock pinnacles at Meteora (p757) grace many a Grecian postcard, but nothing compares to seeing them for yourself. Inhabited by monks since the 11th century, these rocky spires are still home to a string of peaceful monasteries, best seen in the light of the setting sun. You can travel between them by road, but hiking the ancient paths provides a much more authentic pilgrimage. Agias Triados monastery

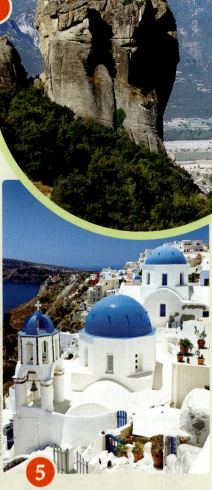

GEORGE TSAFOS/GETTY IMAGES ©

MBBIRDY/GETTY IMAGES ©

Knossos

The capital of Minoan Crete, Knossos (p766) is another essential attraction for aficionados of ancient history. According to legend, the city was once the site of the infamous Labyrinth inhabited by the beastly half-man, half-bull known as the Minotaur. Whatever the truth of the story, it's still a stunning sight – but you'll need to get there early to avoid the crowds. Palace of Knossos

Santorini

With its ancient ruins, seaside ports and rugged hillsides, Greece is irresistibly photogenic – but nowhere quite compares to Santorini (p761) in the scenery stakes. This idyllic island overlooks a glittering lagoon formed by a prehistoric volcanic explosion, and its clifftop churches, stark white buildings and azure waters are a photographer's dream come true. Oia (p763), Santorini

735

Greece's Best...

Ancient Sites

○ **Parthenon, Athens** (p743) The mother of all Doric structures, completed in 438 BC.

○ **Temple of Zeus, Ancient Olympia** (p741) The spiritual home of the Olympic Games.

○ **Temple of Athena, Delphi** (p743) Where ancient Greeks once consulted the Oracle.

○ **Knossos, Crete** (p766) The legendary lair of the Minotaur was rediscovered in 1900.

○ **Mycenae** (p750)This ancient cityscape is a must for archaeology buffs.

Old-World Towns

○ **Athens Old Town** (p740) Plaka and Monastiraki are brimming with antiquated atmosphere.

○ **Nafplio, Peloponnese** (p756) Elegant houses and seaside mansions; Nafplio is made for wandering.

○ **Rhodes Town** (p771) Protected by massive 12m-thick walls, this is a medieval gem.

○ **Corfu Town** (p774) A tangle of winding alleyways and hidden plazas, overlooked by fortresses.

○ **Hania** (p767) Crete's most picturesque town is a photographer's dream.

Island Getaways

○ **Paros** (p776) Sparkling beaches and marbled hills make for one of the loveliest islands of the Cyclades.

○ **Samos** (p776) The jewel of the Aegean archipelago was once an important centre of Hellenic culture.

○ **Kefallonia** (p775) Explore the island immortalised in Louis de Bernières' novel *Captain Corelli's Mandolin*.

○ **Ithaki** (p777) Escape to the legendary home of the Greek hero Odysseus.

○ **Santorini** (p761) Fall for the cliffside houses and azure waters of this vivid, volcanic island.

Geological Sights

o **Santorini's black beaches** (p763) Santorini's ink-black sand is a reminder of the island's volcanic origins.

o **Samaria Gorge** (p770) Hike through this spectacular canyon on the island of Crete.

o **Mt Olympus** (p750) The home of the gods, and now a hikers' paradise.

o **Meteora's pinnacles** (p757) A strange formation of rock spires, now topped by medieval monasteries.

ADVANCE PLANNING

o **As far as possible ahead** Book popular ferry routes, especially in high summer.

o **At least a month ahead** Top hotels are generally booked out in the high season, so reserve as early as you can.

o **When you arrive** The €12 Acropolis ticket covers entry to several other Athens ancient sites.

RESOURCES

o **Greek National Tourist Organisation** (www.gnto.gr) Known as EOT within Greece.

o **Ministry of Culture** (www.culture.gr) Crammed with cultural information.

o **Ancient Greece** (www.ancientgreece.com) Handy online guide to the ancient world.

o **Greek Ferries** (www.greekferries.gr) Essential resource for island-hoppers.

GETTING AROUND

o **Boat** Nearly every island has a boat service, but timetables are notoriously erratic –

sailings can be cancelled at short notice due to bad weather.

o **Bus** Often the only option for reaching smaller towns and villages.

o **Car** Allows for maximum freedom, but Greece's roads require nerves of steel. Scooters are a good option on many islands.

o **Train** Greece's train network is limited to two main lines (connecting Athens with the Peloponnese and northern Greece), plus a few small branch lines.

BE FOREWARNED

o **Theft** Watch out for pickpockets in crowded spots, especially in big cities such as Athens, at markets and in popular tourist areas. Never leave your belongings unattended on the beach.

o **Toilets** Public toilets in Greece are rare, and many can't handle toilet paper!

o **Driving** Take extra care – Greece has the highest road-fatality rate in Europe.

o **Ferries** Sailings are extremely weather dependent, so it pays to be flexible with your travel plans.

Left: Temple of Zeus, Ancient Olympia;
Above: Old town square of Rhodes
(LEFT) DIANA MAYFIELD/GETTY IMAGES ©
(ABOVE) CHRISTOPHER GROENHOUT/GETTY IMAGES ©

Greece Itineraries

With its mystic temples and magnificent ruins, travelling through Greece often feels like a journey through time. This wonderful country allows your imagination to truly wander.

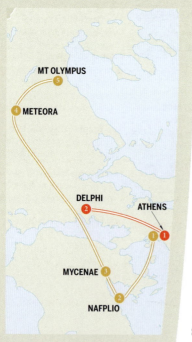

3 DAYS

ANCIENT WONDERS
Athens to Delphi

For an introduction to the world of ancient Greece, nowhere compares with ❶ **Athens** (p740). Magnificent monuments are scattered across the city, but for the historical background it's sensible to start at the Acropolis Museum, which brings together the surviving art treasures unearthed at the nearby Acropolis. In the afternoon, hike up to the Parthenon and Ancient Agora, and spend the evening exploring some of Athens' atmospheric tavernas. Spend the following day seeing the rest of Athens, including the National Archaeological and Benaki Museums, and finish with a tour of the Temple of Olympian Zeus.

On day three, take a trip north to ❷ **Delphi** (p755) and feel the potent spirit on the slopes of Mt Parnassos. The ancient Greeks considered this the centre of the world. You can follow in the pilgrims' footsteps along the Sacred Way, which leads uphill to the Temple of Apollo. Nearby is another impressive ruin, the 20-column Sanctuary of Athena.

Top Left: Statues at Ancient Agora (p741), Athens;
Top Right: Climbing stairs to a monastery at Meteora (p757)

5 DAYS

MANSIONS & MONASTERIES

Athens to Thessaloniki

With five days at your disposal, you can venture out from ❶ **Athens** (p740) on some fantastic day trips. A couple of hours west is ❷ **Nafplio** (p756) and its smart hillside mansions tumbling down towards the sparkling Mediterranean. The best views are from the Venetian Palamidi Fortress, which dates back to the early 18th century.

An hour from Nafplio is another unmissable relic of the ancient world, the ruined city of ❸ **Mycenae** (p750), once one of the most powerful in ancient Greece. Try to imagine the sights and sounds that would have greeted you as you walk through the monumental Lion's Gate, the city's main entrance, and one of the largest surviving ancient sculptures in Greece.

On day three, head back towards Athens for a pilgrimage to the bewitchingly beautiful rock-top monasteries of ❹ **Meteora** (p757). Take a bus up to the summit and work your way back down or walk the ancient paths; you can usually visit at least four of the religious communities in a day.

Spend the last couple of days exploring the sacred home of the gods, ❺ **Mt Olympus** (p750), which is criss-crossed by stunning hiking trails.

Discover Greece

At a Glance

- **Athens** (p740) Ancient history awaits in Greece's capital.

- **Cyclades** (p758) From buzzy beaches to volcanic Santorini.

- **Crete** (p764) Greece's largest island feels rugged and traditional.

- **Dodecanese** (p770) More idyllic beaches and hilltop villages in this popular archipelago.

- **Ionian Islands** (p774) Island getaways to daydream about.

Statue, Museum of the Ancient Agora (p741)
DENNIS K. JOHNSON/GETTY IMAGES ©

ATHENS AΘHNA
POP 3.8 MILLION

Ancient and modern, with equal measures of grunge and grace, bustling Athens is a heady mix of history and edginess. Iconic monuments mingle with first-rate museums, lively cafes and alfresco dining, and it's downright fun. With Greece's financial difficulties Athens has revealed its more restive aspect, but take the time to look beneath the surface and you'll discover a complex metropolis full of vibrant subcultures.

History

Athens' golden age, the pinnacle of the classical era under Pericles (r 461–429 BC), came after the Persian Empire was repulsed at the battles of Salamis and Plataea (480–479 BC). The city has passed through many hands and cast off myriad invaders, from Sparta to Philip II of Macedon, the Roman and Byzantine Empires, and, most recently, the Ottoman Empire. In 1834 Athens superseded Nafplio as the capital of independent Greece.

⊚ Sights

Due to the financial difficulties in Greece, which became acute starting in 2010, opening hours, prices and even the existence of some establishments have fluctuated much more than usual.

Acropolis Museum Museum
(☏ 210 900 0901; www.theacropolismuseum. gr; Dionysiou Areopagitou 15, Makrygianni; adult/ concession €5/3; ☻8am-8pm Tue-Sun, to 10pm Fri Apr-Oct, 9am-5pm Mon-Thu, to 10pm Fri, 9am-8pm Sat & Sun Nov-Mar; Ⓜ Akropoli) Don't miss this

superb museum on the southern base of the hill, and magnificently reflecting the **Parthenon** on its glass facade; it houses the surviving treasures of the Acropolis.

Bathed in natural light, the 1st-floor **Archaic Gallery** is a forest of statues, including stunning examples of 6th-century *kore* (maidens).

The museum's crowning glory is the top-floor **Parthenon Gallery**, a glass hall built in alignment with the Parthenon, which is visible through the windows. It showcases the temple's metopes and 160m frieze shown in sequence for the first time in over 200 years. Interspersed between the golden-hued originals, white plaster replicates the controversial Parthenon Marbles removed by Lord Elgin in 1801 and later sold to the British Museum.

Other highlights include five **Caryatids**, the maiden columns that held up the **Erechtheion** (the sixth is in the British Museum), a giant floral acroterion and a **movie** illustrating the history of the Acropolis.

Ancient Agora   Historic Site
(210 321 0185; http://odysseus.culture.gr; Adrianou; adult/child €4/free, free with Acropolis pass; 8am-3pm, museum closed 8-11am Mon; M Monastiraki) The Ancient Agora was the marketplace of early Athens and the focal point of civic and social life; Socrates spent time here expounding his philosophy. The main monuments of the Agora are the well-preserved **Temple of Hephaestus** (Monastiraki), the 11th-century **Church of the Holy Apostles** (Monastiraki) and the reconstructed **Stoa of Attalos**, which houses the site's excellent **museum**.

Roman Agora   Historic Site
(210 324 5220; cnr Pelopida & Eolou, Monastiraki; adult/child €2/1, free with Acropolis pass; 8.30am-3pm; M Monastiraki) The Romans built their agora just east of the ancient Athenian Agora. The wonderful **Tower of the Winds** (Roman Agora) was built in the 1st century BC by Syrian astronomer Andronicus. Each side represents a point

of the compass and has a relief carving depicting the associated wind.

National Archaeological Museum   Antiquities Museum
(210 821 7717; www.namuseum.gr; 28 Oktovriou-Patision 44, Exarhia; adult/concession €7/3; 1-8pm Mon, 8am-8pm Tue-Sat, 8am-3pm Sun; M Viktoria, 2, 4, 5, 9 or 11 Polytechnio stop) One of the world's great museums, the National Archaeological Museum contains significant finds from major archaeological sites throughout Greece. The vast collections of Greek art masterpieces include exquisite **Mycenaean gold artefacts**, **Minoan frescos** from Santorini and stunning, enormous statues.

Temple of Olympian Zeus   Landmark, Ruin
(210 922 6330; adult/child €2/free, free with Acropolis pass; 8am-3pm; M Syntagma, Akropoli) Begun in the 6th century BC, Greece's largest temple is impressive for the sheer size of its Corinthian columns: 17m high with a base diameter of 1.7m. It took more than 700 years to build, with Emperor Hadrian overseeing its completion in AD 131, and sits behind **Hadrian's Arch** (cnr Leoforos Vasilissis Olgas & Leoforos Vasilissis Amalias; M Syntagma) FREE.

Don't Miss
Acropolis

No monument encapsulates the glory and mystery of the ancient world better than the Acropolis, which stands on the top of a hill high above Athens and is visible right across the city. For many scholars, it's the most important ancient monument in the Western world.

☎ 210 321 0219

http://odysseus.culture.gr

adult/concession/child €12/6/free

🕐 8am-8pm, reduced in low season

Ⓜ Akropoli

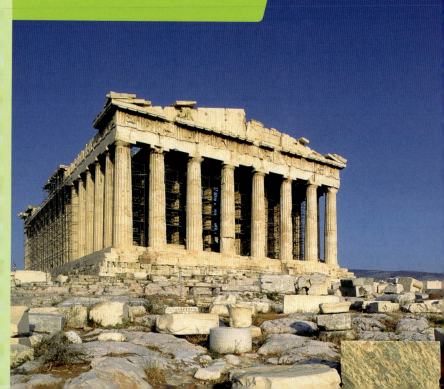

History

People lived on the Acropolis until the late 6th century BC, but in 510 BC the Delphic oracle declared that the Acropolis should be the province of the gods. When all the buildings were reduced to ashes by the Persians on the eve of the Battle of Salamis (480 BC), Pericles set about rebuilding a city purely of temples. The present-day Acropolis is what remains of this great project; although much has been lost, it still offers a wonderfully atmospheric glimpse into the world of the ancient Greeks.

Parthenon

The Parthenon epitomises the glory of ancient Greece. Completed in 438 BC, it's unsurpassed in grace and harmony. To achieve the appearance of perfect form, columns become narrower towards the top and the bases curve upward slightly towards the ends – effects that make them look straight when viewed from below. It's a demonstration of the truly remarkable understanding the ancient Greeks had of the fundamental rules of geometry, and how they could be applied in the real world.

Theatre of Dionysos

On the southern slope of the Acropolis, the importance of theatre in the everyday lives of ancient Athenians is made manifest in the enormous Theatre of Dionysos. Built between 340 and 330 BC on the site of an earlier theatre dating to the 6th century BC, it held 17,000 people.

Acropolis

RECOMMENDATIONS FROM
CATHERINE TRIANTIS,
PROFESSIONAL TOURIST GUIDE

1 PARTHENON
This is the crowning achievement of Greek architecture. Walk around the temple to get a feel for its geometry. Stop at the northeastern corner to see the curves of the building. By looking at the eastern steps, you can see them gradually ascend and then descend, forming a curve.

2 THE ERECHTHEION
Have a look at each side of this ornate and architecturally unique temple, characterised by elegance, grace and elaborate decoration. The most interesting side is the porch of the caryatids with six female Korae statues. Although the statues are copies, the artists' craftsmanship is evident in the transparency of the clothing and unique hairstyles.

3 VIEWS OF ATHENS
The Acropolis offers an aerial view of the city. To the north you'll see Plaka and Ancient Agora; to the east, the Temple of Olympian Zeus, Hadrian's Arch and the National Gardens; to the south, the new Acropolis Museum and Filopappou Hill; and to the west, the Athenian Observatory.

4 THE MONUMENT'S PAST
Built to protect the Acropolis after the Persian Wars in 479 BC, the massive northern fortification walls were made from columns taken from the sites of earlier temples. Look closely to spot hints of colour on these columns – almost everything was rendered with colour in the past.

5 TEMPLE OF ATHENA NIKE
An absolute jewel, this temple was dedicated to the victory goddess, Athena Nike, and contained a wingless statue of her to keep her from flying away from Athens and therefore keeping the city victorious.

The Acropolis

Cast your imagination back in time, two and a half millennia ago, and envision the majesty of the Acropolis. Its famed and hallowed monument, the Parthenon, dedicated to the goddess Athena, stood proudly over a small city, dwarfing the population with its graceful grandeur. In the Acropolis' heyday in the 5th century BC, pilgrims and priests worshipped at the temples illustrated here (most of which still stand in varying states of restoration). Many were painted brilliant colours and were abundantly adorned with sculptural masterpieces crafted from ivory, gold and semiprecious stones.

As you enter the site today, elevated on the right, perches one of the Acropolis' best-restored buildings: the diminutive **Temple of Athena Nike** ❶. Follow the Panathenaic Way through the Propylaia and up the slope toward the Parthenon – icon of the Western world. Its **majestic columns** ❷ sweep up to some of what were the finest carvings of their time: wraparound **pediments, metopes and a frieze** ❸. Stroll around the temple's exterior and take in the spectacular views over Athens and Piraeus below.

As you circle back to the centre of the site, you will encounter those renowned lovely ladies, the **Caryatids** ❹ of the Erechtheion. On the Erechtheion's northern face, the oft-forgotten **Temple of Poseidon** ❺ sits alongside ingenious **Themistocles' Wall** ❻. Wander to the Erechtheion's western side to find Athena's gift to the city: **the olive tree** ❼.

Sanctuary of Pandion

Themistocles' Wall
Crafty general Themistocles (524–459 BC) hastened to build a protective wall around the Acropolis and in so doing incorporated elements from archaic temples on the site. Look for the column drums built into the wall.

Sanctuary of Zeus Polieus

Erechtheion

Temple of Poseidon
Though he didn't win patronage of the city, Poseidon was worshipped on the northern side of the Erechtheion which still bears the mark of his trident-strike. Imagine the finely decorated coffered porch painted in rich colours, as it was before.

ALEXIS AVERBUCK ©

Porch of the Caryatids

Perhaps the most recognisable sculptural elements at the Acropolis are the majestic Caryatids (circa 415 BC). Modelled on women from Karyai (modern-day Karyes, in Lakonia) the maidens are thought to have held a libation bowl in one hand, and to be drawing up their dresses with the other.

Parthenon Pediments, Metopes & Frieze

The Parthenon's pediments (the triangular elements topping the east and west facades) were filled with elaborately carved three-dimensional sculptures. The west side depicted Athena and Poseidon in their contest for the city's patronage, the east Athena's birth from Zeus's head. The metopes are square carved panels set between channelled triglyphs. They depicted battle scenes, including the sacking of Troy and the clash between the Lapiths and the Centaurs. The cella was topped by the Ionic frieze, a continuous sculptured band depicting the Panathenaic Procession.

Parthenon

3

2

Chalkotheke

Panathenaic Way

Sanctuary of Artemis Brauronia

Statue of Athena Promachos

Arrephorion

Propylaia

Pinakothiki

Entrance

1

Spring of Klepsydra

Parthenon Columns

The Parthenon's fluted Doric columns achieve perfect form. Their lines were ingeniously curved to create an optical illusion: the foundations (like all the 'horizontal' surfaces of the temple) are slightly concave and the columns are slightly convex making both appear straight.

Temple of Athena Nike

Recently restored, this precious tiny Pentelic marble temple was designed by Kallicrates and built around 425 BC. The cella housed a wooden statue of Athena as Victory (Nike) and the exterior friezes illustrated Athenian battle triumphs.

Athena's Olive Tree

The flourishing olive tree next to the Erechtheion is meant to be the sacred tree that Athena produced to seize victory in the contest for Athens.

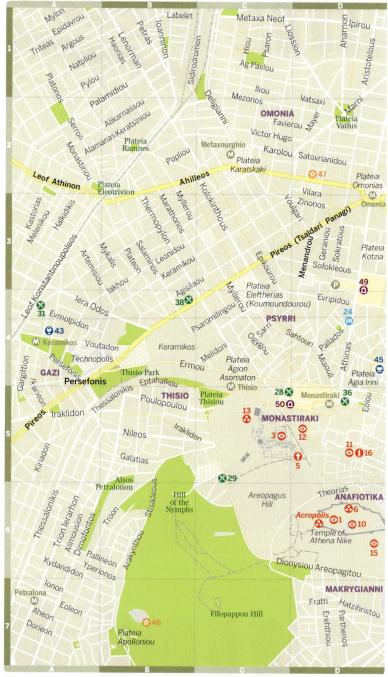

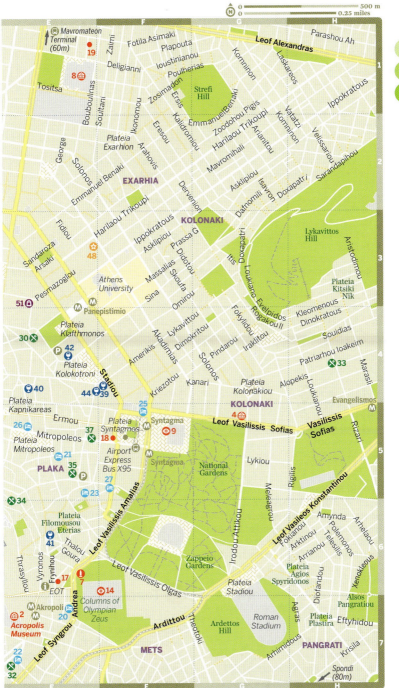

0   500 m
0   0.25 miles

Parashou Ah

Leof Alexandras

Komninon
Laskareos
Ippokratous

Fotila Asimaki
Plapouta
Zaimi
Ioustinianou
Deligianni
Poulherias

19

Tositsa
Bouboulinas
Soultani
Ikonomou
Zosimadon
Ersis
Kalidromiou
Emmanuel Benaki

Strefi
Hill

8

Zoodohou Pigis

Harilaou Trikoupi
Mavromihali

Vatatzi
Komninon
Arianitou

Velissariou
Sarandapihou

George
Solonos
Emmanuel Benaki
Arahovis
Eresou
Dervenion

Plateia
Exarhion

Asklipiou
Isavron
Dafnomili
Doxapatri

EXARHIA

Fidiou
Harilaou Trikoupi
Ippokratous
Asklipiou
Prassa G
Didotou

KOLONAKI

Doxapatri
Ittis
Loukianou
Evelpidos
Rogakou II

Lykavittos
Hill

Aristodimou

Sandaroza
Arsaki
Pesmazoglou

Massalias
Skoufa
Sina

Plateia
Kitsiki
Nik

48

Athens
University

Omirou
Lykavittou
Fokylidou

Kleomenous
Dinokratous

51

M Panepistimio

Akadimias
Dimokritou

Iraklitou

Souidias

Plateia
Klafthmonos

Amerikis
Pindarou

Patriarhou Ioakeim

30

42
Plateia
Kolokotroni

Kriezotou
Solonos

Plateia
Kolonakiou

Alopekis

33

Marasli

Stadiou

40

44 **39**

Kanari

KOLONAKI

Loukianou

Evangelismos

M

Plateia
Kapnikareas
Ermou

25

Syntagma

4

Leof Vasilissis Sofias

Vasilissis
Sofias

Rizari

26
Mitropoleos

37

Plateia
Syntagmos

18

9

Lykiou

21
Plateia
Mitropoleos

PLAKA
35

Airport
Express
Bus X95

Syntagma

National
Gardens

Meleagrou

Leof Vasileos Konstantinou

27

23

34

Leof Vasilissis Amalias

Irodou Attikou

Amynda
Polemonos

Plateia
Filomousou
Eterias

41

Fokianou
Arktinou
Arrianou

Telesilis
Arheliaou

Thalou
Goura

Zappeio
Gardens

Xenokleous

Thrasylou
Vyronos
Frynihou
Andrea

17

7

14

Leof Vasilissis Olgas

Plateia
Agios
Spyridonos

Diofandou

Alsos
Pangratiou

EOT
M Akropoli

20

Columns of
Olympian
Zeus

Plateia
Stadiou

Roman
Stadium

Agras

Plateia
Plastira
Eftyhidou

2
Acropolis
Museum

Ardittou

Theotoki

Ardettos
Hill

Arhimidous

PANGRATI

Krisila

22

32

Leof Syngrou

METS

Spondi
(80m)

Central Athens

◉ Don't Miss Sights
1 Acropolis D6
2 Acropolis Museum E7

◎ Sights
3 Ancient Agora C5
4 Benaki Museum G5
5 Church of the Holy Apostles D5
6 Erechtheion D6
7 Hadrian's Arch E6
8 National Archaeological
   Museum E1
9 Parliament & Changing of the
   Guard F5
10 Parthenon D6
11 Roman Agora D5
12 Stoa of Attalos D5
13 Temple of Hephaestus C5
14 Temple of Olympian Zeus F6
15 Theatre of Dionysos D6
16 Tower of the Winds D5

◉ Activities, Courses & Tours
17 Athens Segway Tours E6
18 CitySightseeing Athens F5
19 Trekking Hellas E1

⬡ Sleeping
20 Athens Gate E7
21 Central Hotel E5
22 Hera Hotel E7
23 Hotel Adonis E5
24 Hotel Cecil D4
25 Hotel Grande Bretagne F5
26 Magna Grecia E5
27 NEW Hotel F5

⊗ Eating
28 Café Avyssinia C5
29 Filistron C5
30 Kalnterimi E4
31 Kanella A4
32 Mani Mani E7
33 Oikeio H4
34 Palia Taverna Tou
   Psara E6
35 Paradosiako E5
36 Thanasis D5
37 Tzitzikas & Mermingas E5
38 Varoulko B4

⊖ Drinking & Nightlife
39 42 Bar F4
40 Baba Au Rum E4
41 Brettos E6
42 Gin Joint E4
43 Hoxton A4
44 Seven Jokers E4
45 Tailor Made D4

✪ Entertainment
46 Dora Stratou Dance
   Theatre B7
   Greek National Opera .... (see 48)
47 National Theatre D2
48 Olympia Theatre E3

⊙ Shopping
49 Athens Central Market D3
50 Monastiraki Flea
   Market C5
51 To Pantopoleion E3

Benaki Museum Cultural Museum
(☏ 210 367 1000; www.benaki.gr; Koumbari 1, cnr Leoforos Vasilissis Sofias, Kolonaki; adult/concession €7/5, free Thu; ⊙ 9am-5pm Wed & Fri, to midnight Thu & Sat, to 3pm Sun; M Syntagma, Evangelismos) This superb museum houses an extravagant collection, including ancient sculpture, Persian, Byzantine and Coptic objects, Chinese ceramics, icons, El Greco paintings, and fabulous traditional costumes.

Parliament & Changing of the Guard Ceremony
(Plateia Syntagmatos; M Syntagma) FREE
In front of the parliament building on Plateia Syntagmatos , the traditionally costumed *evzones* (guards) of the **Tomb of the Unknown Soldier** change every hour on the hour. On Sunday at 11am, a whole platoon marches down Vasilissis Sofias to the tomb, accompanied by a band.

🗘 Tours

The usual city tours exist like open-bus **CitySightseeing Athens** (☏ 210 922 0604; www.city-sightseeing.com; Plateia Syntagmatos, Syntagma; adult/child €15/6.50; ⊙ every 30min 9am-8pm; M Syntagma), **Athens Segway Tours** (☏ 210 322 2500; www.athenssegwaytours.com; Eschinou 9, Plaka; **M** Akropoli) or the volunteer **This is My Athens** (www. thisisathens.org). Get out of town on the cheap with **Athens: Adventures** (☎ 210 922 4044; www.athensadventures.gr). Hike or kayak with **Trekking Hellas** (☎ 210 331 0323; www.trekking.gr; Saripolou 10, Exarhia; **M** Viktoria).

🎪 Festivals & Events

Hellenic Festival   Performing Arts
(www.greekfestival.gr; 🕑 late May-Oct) Top line-up of local and international music, dance and theatre in venues across Athens and Epidavros' ancient theatre.

🛏 Sleeping

Book well ahead for July and August.

Plaka

Central Hotel   Boutique Hotel **€€**
(☎ 210 323 4357; www.centralhotel.gr; Apollonos 21, Plaka; d incl breakfast from €90; ❄ @;
M Syntagma) Pass through the sleek lobby and by the attentive staff to spacious white rooms hung with original art and decked out with all the mod cons. Some balconies have Acropolis views, as does the rooftop, where you can sunbake and relax in the Jacuzzi.

NEW Hotel
Boutique Hotel **€€**
(☎ 210 628 4565; www.yes-hotels.gr; Filellinon 16, Plaka; d incl breakfast from €123;
P ❄ 🛜; **M** Syntagma)
Smart New is the latest entry on the high-end Athens scene. Whether you dig the groovy, designer furniture or the pillow menu (tell 'em how you like it!), you'll find some sort of decadent treat to tickle your fancy.

Hotel Adonis   Hotel **€€**
(☎ 210 324 9737; www.hotel-adonis.gr; 3 Kodrou St, Plaka; s/d/tr incl breakfast €60/70/85;
❄ @ 🛜; **M** Syntagma) Comfortable rooms, newly renovated bathrooms, conscientious staff and Acropolis views from the break-fast room/bar keep folks coming back.

Monastiraki

Magna Grecia   Boutique Hotel **€€**
(☎ 210 324 0314; www.magnagreciahotel.com; Mitropoleos 54, Monastiraki; d incl breakfast €90-140, tr from €120; ❄ 🛜; **M** Monastiraki) Enjoy Acropolis views from the front rooms and rooftop terrace in a historic building opposite the cathedral. Imaginative, luxe rooms sport comfortable mattresses.

Hotel Cecil   Hotel **€€**
(☎ 210 321 7079; www.cecilhotel.gr; Athinas 39, Monastiraki; s/d/tr/q incl breakfast from €60/75/120/155; ❄ @ 🛜; **M** Monastiraki) Aromatic spices waft into the lobby from nearby Asian markets, but double-pane windows keep the high-ceilinged rooms in this classical building quiet.

View of the Acropolis (p742), Athens
THOMAS STANKIEWICZ/GETTY IMAGES ©

If You Like...
Ancient Greece

The Acropolis (p742) might be Greece's most famous ancient ruin, but there are hundreds more sites to uncover, from tumbledown temples to abandoned cities.

1 **EPIDAVROS** ΕΠΙΔΑΥΡΟΣ
(☎27530 22009; admission €6; ⏰8am-8pm Apr-Oct, to 5pm Nov-Mar) World Heritage–listed Epidavros was the sanctuary of Asclepius, god of medicine. The magnificent **theatre** is still used during the Hellenic Festival. The **Sanctuary of Asclepius** was an ancient healing centre. The site is 36km east of Nafplio.

2 **ANCIENT MYCENAE** ΑΡΧΑΙΕΣ ΜΥΚΗΝΕΣ
(☎27510 76585; admission €8; ⏰8am-6pm Mon-Fri, to 3pm Sat & Sun [winter]) Ancient Mycenae was at its most powerful from 1600 to 1200 BC. Its grand entrance, the **Lion's Gate**, is Europe's oldest monumental sculpture. It's 25km north of Nafplio.

3 **MYSTRAS** ΜΥΣΤΡΑΣ
(☎23315 25363; adult €5; ⏰8.30am-5.30pm Mon-Sat, to 3pm Sun, sometimes longer in summer) Magical Mystras was once the effective capital of the Byzantine Empire. Ruins of palaces, monasteries and churches, most of them dating from between 1271 and 1460, nestle at the base of the Taÿgetos Mountains. It's 7km from Sparta.

4 **ANCIENT OLYMPIA** ΟΛΥΜΠΙΑ
(☎26240 22517; adult/child €6/3, site & museum €9/5; ⏰8am-5pm Apr-Oct, 8am-3pm Nov-Mar) This ruined site was where the first Olympics were staged in 776 BC, and every four years thereafter until AD 394. Among the sights are the **Temple of Zeus**, to whom the games were dedicated. It's 20km east of Pyrgos.

5 **MT OLYMPUS** ΟΛΥΜΠΟΣ ΟΡΟΣ
Just as it did for the ancients, Greece's highest mountain still fires the imagination. The highest of Olympus' eight peaks is **Mytikas** (2917m), popular with trekkers, who use **Litohoro** (elevation 305m) as their base. The main route up takes two days, with a stay overnight at one of the refuges.

Syntagma
Hotel Grande Bretagne   Luxury Hotel €€€
(☎210 333 0000; www.grandebretagne.gr; Vasileos Georgiou 1, Syntagma; r/ste from €295/600; P ✳ @ 🛜; M Syntagma)Dripping with elegance and old-world charm, *the* place to stay in Athens has always been these deluxe digs. Built in 1862 to accommodate visiting heads of state, it ranks among the great hotels of the world. From the decadent, chandeliered lobby, to the exquisite guestrooms, divine spa and rooftop restaurant, this place is built for pampering.

Makrygianni & Koukaki
Athens Gate   Business Hotel €€
(☎210 923 8302; www.athensgate.gr; Leoforos Syngrou Andrea 10, Makrygianni; dinclbreakfast€125-165; ✳ @ 🛜; M Akropoli) With stunning views over the Temple of Olympian Zeus from the spacious front rooms, and a central (if busy) location, this totally refurbished hotel is a great find. Stylish, immaculate rooms have all the mod cons, staff are friendly and breakfast is served on the superb rooftop terrace with 360-degree Athens views.

Hera Hotel   Boutique Hotel €€
(☎210 923 6682; www.herahotel.gr; Falirou 9, Makrygianni; d from incl breakfast €130-160, ste €225; ✳ @ 🛜; M Akropoli) The ornate interior complements the hotel's lovely neoclassical facade. The rooftop garden, restaurant and bar boast spectacular views and it is a short walk to the Acropolis and Plaka.

Eating

In addition to mainstay tavernas, Athens has upscale eateries (wear your most stylish togs at night). Eat streets include Mitropoleos, Adrianou and Navarchou Apostoli in Monastiraki, the area around Plateia Psyrri, and Gazi, near Keramikos metro.

Evzones (guards) at the Tomb of the Unknown Soldier (p748)

PAOLO CORDELLI/GETTY IMAGES ©

The fruit and vegetable market, **Athens Central Market** (Varvakios Agora; Athinas, btwn Sofokleous & Evripidou; ⊙7am-3pm Mon-Sat; Ⓜ Monastiraki, Panepistimio, Omonia), on Athinas is opposite the meat market.

Syntagma & Monastiraki

Café Avyssinia   Mezedhes €€

(☏210 321 7047; www.avissinia.gr; Kynetou 7, Monastiraki; mains €10-16; ⊙11am-1am Tue-Sat, to 7pm Sun; Ⓜ Monastiraki) Hidden away on the edge of grungy Plateia Avyssinias in the middle of the flea market, this *mezedhopoleio* (mezedhes restaurant) gets top marks for atmosphere, and the food is not far behind. Often has live music on weekends.

Tzitzikas & Mermingas   Mezedhes €

(☏210 324 7607; Mitropoleos 12-14, Syntagma; mezedhes €6-11; ⊙lunch & dinner; Ⓜ Syntagma) Greek merchandise lines the walls of this cheery, modern *mezedhopoleio*. The great range of delicious and creative *mezedhes* draws a bustling local crowd. Don't miss the decadent honey-coated fried cheese with ham...it's the kind of special dish that will haunt your future dreams.

Kalnterimi   Taverna €

(☏210 331 0049; www.kalnterimi.gr; Plateia Agion Theodoron, cnr Skouleniou, Monastiraki; mains €5-8; ⊙lunch & dinner; Ⓜ Panepistimio) Find your way back behind the Church of Agii Theodori to this open-air taverna offering Greek food at its most authentic.

Thanasis   Souvlaki €

(☏210 324 4705; Mitropoleos 69, Monastiraki; gyros €2.50; ⊙8.30am-2.30am; Ⓜ Monastiraki) In the heart of Athens' souvlaki hub, Thanasis is known for its kebabs on *pitta* with grilled tomato and onions. Live music, grill aromas and crowds give the area an almost permanently festive air.

Plaka & Makrygianni

Mani Mani   Regional Cuisine €€

(☏210 921 8180; www.manimani.com.gr; Falirou 10, Makrygianni; mains €10-16, mezedhes €7.50; ⊙3pm-12.30am Tue-Fri, from 1pm Sat, 1-5.30pm Sun, closed Jul & Aug; Ⓜ Akropoli) Sample cuisine from Mani in the Peloponnese, such as tangy sausage with orange. Most dishes can be ordered as half-serves (at half-price), allowing you to try a wide range.

751

Paradosiako   Taverna €
(210 321 4121; Voulis 44a, Plaka; mains €5-12; lunch & dinner; ; Syntagma) For great traditional fare, you can't beat this inconspicuous, no-frills taverna on the periphery of Plaka. Choose from daily specials such as delicious shrimp *saganaki*.

Palia Taverna
Tou Psara   Taverna, Seafood €€
(210 321 8734; www.psaras-taverna.gr; Erehtheos 16, Plaka; mains €12-24; 11am-12.30pm Wed-Mon; Akropoli) On a path leading up towards the Acropolis, this gem of a taverna is one of Plaka's best, serving scrumptious mezedhes and excellent fish and meat classics on a tree-lined terrace.

Keramikos, Thissio & Gazi
Varoulko   Seafood €€€
(210 522 8400; www.varoulko.gr; Pireos 80, Keramikos; mains €35-60; from 8.30pm Mon-Sat; Thisio, Keramikos) For a magical Greek dining experience, you can't beat the winning combination of Acropolis views and delicious seafood by celebrated Michelin-starred chef Lefteris Lazarou. Athenian celebrities feast in an airy, glass-fronted dining room.

Kanella   Taverna €
(210 347 6320; Leoforos Konstantinoupoleos 70, Gazi; dishes €7-10; 1.30pm-late; Keramikos) Homemade village-style bread, mismatched retro crockery and brown-paper tablecloths set the tone for this trendy, modern taverna serving regional Greek cuisine.

Filistron   Mezedhes €
(210 346 7554; Apostolou Pavlou 23, Thisio; mezedhes €8-14; lunch & dinner Tue-Sun; Thisio) Book a prized table on the rooftop terrace of this excellent *mezedhopoleio*, which enjoys breathtaking Acropolis and Lykavittos views.

Kolonaki & Pangrati
Spondi   Mediterranean, French €€€
(210 756 4021; www.spondi.gr; Pyrronos 5, Pangrati; mains €35-50; 8pm-late) Dining in this superb restaurant's gorgeous vaulted cellar or in its bougainvillea-draped courtyard in summer is quite an understatedly elegant affair. Chef Arnaud Bignon has won two Michelin stars, creating extravagant seasonal menus adhering to French technique but embodying vibrant Greek flavours.

Oikeio   Taverna €
(210 725 9216; Ploutarhou 15, Kolonaki; mains €7-13; 1pm-2.30am Mon-Sat; Evangelismos) With excellent home-style cooking, this modern taverna lives up to its name ('Homey'). The intimate bistro atmosphere spills out to tables on the pavement for glitterati-watching without the usual high Kolonaki bill. Reservations recommended.

Lion's Gate, Mycenae (p750)
DEA/D. DAGLI ORTI/GETTY IMAGES ©

🍷 Drinking & Nightlife

Hoxton
Bar

(Voutadon 42, Gazi; M Keramikos) Kick back on overstuffed leather couches under modern art in this industrial space that fills up late with bohemians, ruggers and the occasional pop star.

Seven Jokers
Bar

(Voulis 7, Syntagma; M Syntagma) Lively and central Seven Jokers anchors the party block, also shared by spacious **42 Bar** (Kolokotroni 3, Syntagma) around the corner, for cocktails in wood-panelled splendour, with **Baba Au Rum** (Klitiou 6, Syntagma; M Syntagma) and **Gin Joint** (Lada 1, Syntagma; M Syntagma) nearby.

Brettos
Bar

(Kydathineon 41, Plaka; M Akropoli) This bar-distillery is back-lit by an eye-catching collection of coloured bottles.

Tailor Made
Cafe, Bar

(📞 213 004 9645; www.tailormade.gr; Plateia Agia Irini 2, Monastiraki; M Monastiraki) Cheerful Athenians spill from the mod art-festooned micro-roastery to tables alongside the flower market. At night it turns into a happening cocktail and wine bar.

⭐ Entertainment

For comprehensive events listings, with links to online ticket sales points, try: www.breathtakingathens.gr, www.elculture.gr, www.tickethour.com, www.tickethouse.gr, www.ticketservices.gr. The *Kathimerini* supplement inside the *International Herald Tribune* contains event listings and a cinema guide.

In summer, the excellent Hellenic Festival (p749) swings into action.

National Theatre
Theatre

(📞 210 528 8100; www.n-t.gr; Agiou Konstantinou 22-24, Omonia; M Omonia) Contemporary plays and ancient theatre on the main stage and other venues.

Olympia Theatre
Performing Arts

(📞 210 361 2461; Akadimias 59, Exarhia; M Panepistimio) November to June: ballet,

symphony and the **Greek National Opera** (Ethniki Lyriki Skini; 📞 210 366 2100; www.nationalopera.gr).

Dora Stratou Dance Theatre
Traditional Dance

(📞 210 324 4395; www.grdance.org; Filopappou Hill; adult/child €15/5; ⊙ performances 9.30pm Wed-Fri, 8.15pm Sat & Sun Jun-Sep; M Petralona, Akropoli) Traditional folk-dancing shows feature more than 75 musicians and dancers in an open-air amphitheatre.

🔒 Shopping

Shop for cool jewellery, clothes, shoes, and souvenirs such as backgammon sets, hand-woven textiles, olive-oil beauty products, worry beads and ceramics. Find boutiques around Syntagma, from the Attica department store past Voukourestiou and on Ermou; designer brands and cool shops in Kolonaki; and souvenirs, folk art and leather in Plaka and Monastiraki.

Monastiraki Flea Market
Market

(Adrianou, Monastiraki; ⊙ daily; M Monastiraki) Enthralling; spreads daily from Plateia Monastirakiou.

To Pantopoleion
Food, Drink

(📞 210 323 4612; Sofokleous 1, Omonia; M Panepistimio) Expansive store selling traditional food products from all over Greece.

ℹ️ Information

Dangers & Annoyances

- Though violent street crime remains relatively rare, travellers should be alert on the streets, especially at night, and beware the traps listed here.

- Streets surrounding Omonia have become markedly seedier, with an increase in prostitutes and junkies; avoid the area, especially at night.

- Watch for pickpockets on the metro and at the markets.

- When taking taxis, ask the driver to use the meter or negotiate a price in advance. Ignore stories that the hotel you've chosen is closed or full: they're angling for a commission from another hotel.

- Bar scams are commonplace, particularly in Plaka and Syntagma. They go something like this: friendly Greek approaches solo male traveller, discovers traveller is new to Athens, and reveals that he, too, is from out of town. However, friendly Greek knows a great bar where they order drinks and equally friendly owner offers another drink. Women appear and more drinks are served; at the end of the night the traveller is hit with an exorbitant bill.

Emergency

Tourist police (📞210 920 0724, 24hr 171; Veïkou 43-45, Koukaki; ⏰8am-10pm; Ⓜ Syngrou-Fix)

Police station (📞210 725 7000; Plateia Syntagmatos; Ⓜ Syntagma) Phone 📞100 for the police.

Money

Banks surround Plateia Syntagmatos.

Eurochange (📞210 331 2462; Karageorgi Servias 2, Syntagma; ⏰8am-9pm; Ⓜ Syntagma)

Tourist Information

EOT (Greek National Tourist Organisation; 📞210 331 0347, 210 331 0716; www.visitgreece. gr; Dionysiou Areopagitou 18-20, Makrygianni; ⏰8am-8pm Mon-Fri, 10am-4pm Sat & Sun May-Sep, 9am-7pm Mon-Fri Oct-Apr; Ⓜ Akropoli)

Sanctuary of Athena, Ancient Delphi

🛈 Getting There & Away

Air

Modern **Eleftherios Venizelos International Airport** (ATH; 📞210 353 0000; www.aia.gr), 27km east of Athens.

Boat

Most ferries, hydrofoils and high-speed catamarans leave from the massive port at Piraeus. Some depart from smaller ports at Rafina and Lavrio.

Bus

Athens has two main intercity **KTEL** (📞14505; www.ktel.org) bus stations, one 5km and one 7km to the north of Omonia. Tourist offices have timetables.

Buses for destinations in southern Attica leave from the **Mavromateon Terminal** (📞210 880 8000, 210 822 5148; cnr Leoforos Alexandras & 28 Oktovriou-Patision, Pedion Areos; Ⓜ Viktoria), about 250m north of the National Archaeological Museum.

Car & Motorcycle

The airport has car rental, and Syngrou, just south of the Temple of Olympian Zeus, is dotted with car-hire firms, though driving in Athens is treacherous.

Detour:
Delphi Δελφοί

Modern Delphi and its adjoining ruins hang stunningly on the slopes of Mt Parnassos overlooking the shimmering Gulf of Corinth.

According to mythology, Zeus released two eagles at opposite ends of the world and they met here, thus making Delphi the centre of the world. By the 6th century BC, **Ancient Delphi** (📞 22650 82312; www.culture.gr; site or museum €6, combined adult/concession €9/5; 🕐 8am-3pm winter, 7.30am-8pm summer) had become the Sanctuary of Apollo. Thousands of pilgrims flocked here to consult the middle-aged female oracle who sat at the mouth of a fume-emitting chasm. Wars, voyages and business transactions were undertaken on the strength of these prophecies. From the entrance, take the **Sacred Way** up to the **Temple of Apollo**, where the oracle sat. From here the path continues to the well-preserved **theatre** and **stadium**.

Opposite the main site and down the hill some 100m, don't miss the **Sanctuary of Athena** and the much-photographed **Tholos**, a 4th-century-BC columned rotunda of Pentelic marble.

Six buses a day go to Athens (€15.50, three hours).

Train

Intercity trains to central and northern Greece depart from the central **Larisis train station**, about 1km northwest of Plateia Omonias. For the Peloponnese, take the suburban rail to Kiato and change for other OSE services, or check for available lines at the Larisis station. International trains have been discontinued.

OSE office (📞 210 529 7005, in English 1110; www.ose.gr; Karolou 1, Omonia; 🕐 8am-3pm Mon-Fri; Ⓜ Metaxourghio)

ⓘ Getting Around

To/From the Airport

Bus

Tickets cost €5. Twenty-four-hour services:

Plateia Syntagmatos Bus X95, 60 to 90 minutes, every 15 minutes (the Syntagma stop is on Othonos)

Piraeus Port Bus X96, 1½ hours, every 20 minutes

Terminal A (Kifissos) Bus Station Bus X93, 35 minutes, every 30 minutes

Metro

Blue line 3 links the airport to the city centre in around 40 minutes; it operates from Monastiraki from 5.50am to midnight, and from the airport from 5.30am to 11.30pm. Tickets (€8) are valid for all public transport for 90 minutes. Fare for two or more passengers is €14 total.

Taxi

Fares vary according to the time of day and level of traffic; expect at least €35 from the airport to the centre, and €50 to Piraeus. Both trips can take up to an hour, more in heavy traffic.

Public Transport

The metro, tram and bus system makes getting around central Athens and to Piraeus easy. Athens' road traffic can be horrendous. Get maps and timetables at the tourist offices or **Athens Urban Transport Organisation** (OASA; 📞 185; www.oasa.gr; 🕐 6.30am-11.30pm Mon-Fri, 7.30am-10.30pm Sat & Sun).

Tickets & Passes

Tickets good for 90 minutes (€1.40), a 24-hour travel pass (€4) and a weekly ticket (€14) are valid for all forms of public transport except for airport services. Bus/trolleybus-only tickets (€1.20) cannot be used on the metro. Children under six travel free; people under 18 and over 65 pay half-fare. Buy tickets in metro stations, transport kiosks, or most *periptera*. Validate the ticket in the machine as you board your transport of choice.

Bus & Trolleybus

Buses and electric trolleybuses operate every 15 minutes from 5am to midnight.

Piraeus From Syntagma and Filellinon to Akti Xaveriou catch bus 040; from Omonia end of Athinas to Plateia Themistokleous, catch bus 049.

Metro

Trains operate from 5am to midnight (Friday and Saturday to around 2am), every three to 10 minutes.

Taxi

Flag fall is €1.16 with an additional surcharge of €1.05 from ports and train and bus stations, and €3.77 from the airport; then the day rate (tariff 1 on the meter) is €0.66 per kilometre. The night rate (tariff 2 on the meter, from midnight to 5am) is €1.16 per kilometre. Baggage costs €0.38 per item over 10kg. Minimum fare is €3.10. Booking a radio taxi costs €1.88 extra. Fixed rates are posted at the airport.

Train

Fast suburban rail (✆1110; www.trainose. gr) links Athens with the airport, Piraeus, the outer regions and the northern Peloponnese. It connects to the metro at Larisis, Doukissis Plakentias and Nerantziotissa stations, and goes from the airport to Kiato.

PELOPONNESE

Nafplio Ναύπλιο

POP 14,000

Elegant Venetian houses and neoclassical mansions dripping with crimson bougainvillea cascade down Nafplio's hillside to the azure sea. Vibrant cafes, shops and restaurants fill winding pedestrian streets. Crenulated Palamidi Fortress perches above it all. What's not to love?

🎯 Sights

Palamidi Fortress   Fort
(✆27520 28036; admission €4; ⏱8am-7.30pm May–mid-Oct, to 3pm mid-Oct–Apr) Enjoy spectacular views of the town and surrounding coast from the magnificent hilltop fortress built by the Venetians between 1711 and 1714.

Archaeological Museum   Museum
(✆27520 27502; Plateia Syntagmatos; adult/concession €3/2; ⏱noon-4pm Mon, 9am-4pm Tue-Sun) Fine exhibits include fire middens from 32,000 BC and bronze armour from near Mycenae (12th to 13th centuries BC).

Peloponnese Folklore Foundation Museum   Museum
(✆27520 28379; www.pli.gr; Vas Alexandrou 1; admission €2; ⏱9am-2.30pm Wed-Mon, 10am-3pm Sun Mar-Jan) One of Greece's best small museums, with displays of vibrant regional costumes and rotating exhibitions.

🛏 Sleeping

The Old Town is *the* place to stay, but it has few budget options. Friday to Sunday the town fills and prices rise; book ahead.

Pension Marianna   Hotel €€
(✆27520 24256; www.pensionmarianna.gr; Potamianou 9; s €50, d €65-75, tr €85, q €100 incl breakfast; P✳🖧) Welcoming owners epitomise Greek *filoxenia* (hospitality) and serve delicious organic breakfasts. Up a steep set of stairs, and tucked under the fortress walls, a dizzying array of rooms intermix with sea-view terraces.

Adiandi   Boutique Hotel €€
(✆27520 22073; www.hotel-adiandi.com; Othonos 31; r incl breakfast €70-110; ✳🖧) Rooms in this fun and upmarket place are quirkily decorated with artistic bedheads fashioned from doors and contemporary decor. Fantastic farm-fresh breakfasts.

Hotel Grande Bretagne   Luxury Hotel €€
(✆27520 96200; www.grandebretagne.com.gr; Plateia Filellinon; s/d/tr incl breakfast €95/130/145; ✳🖧) In the heart of Nafplio's cafe action and overlooking the sea, this splendidly restored hotel with high ceilings, antiques and chandeliers radiates plush opulence.

🍴 Eating

Alaloum   Greek €€
(✆27520 29883; Papanikolaou 10; mains €10-18) Heaping creative interpretations of tra-

PAOLO CORDELLI/GETTY IMAGES ©

★ Don't Miss
Meteora Μετέωρα

Meteora (meh-*teh*-o-rah) should be a certified Wonder of the World with its
magnificent late-14th-century monasteries perched dramatically atop enormous rocky
pinnacles. Try not to miss it. The tranquil village of **Kastraki**, 2km from Kalambaka, is
the best base for visiting.

While there were once monasteries on all 24 pinnacles, only six are still occupied:
Megalou Meteorou (Grand Meteoron; ☏ 24320 22278; ⊙ 9am-5pm Wed-Mon Apr-Oct, to 4pm Thu-
Mon Nov-Mar), **Varlaam** (☏ 24320 22277; ⊙ 9am-4pm Sat-Thu Apr-Oct, to 3pm Sat-Wed Nov-Mar),
Agiou Stefanou (☏ 24320 22279; ⊙ 9am-1.30pm & 3.30-5.30pm Tue-Sun Apr-Oct, 9.30am-1pm &
3-5pm Nov-Mar), **Agias Triados** (Holy Trinity; ☏ 24320 22220; ⊙ 9am-5pm Fri-Wed Apr-Oct, 10am-
3pm Nov-Mar), **Agiou Nikolaou Anapafsa** (☏ 24320 22375; ⊙ 9am-3.30pm Sat-Thu) and **Agias
Varvaras Rousanou** (⊙ 9am-6pm Thu-Tue Apr-Oct, to 2pm Nov-Mar). Admission is €2 for
each monastery and strict dress codes apply (no bare shoulders or knees and women
must wear skirts; borrow a long skirt at the door if you don't have one). Walk the
footpaths between monasteries, drive the back asphalt road, or take the bus (€1.20,
20 minutes) that departs from Kalambaka and Kastraki at 9am, and returns at 1pm.

From Kalambaka **train station** (☏ 24320 22451), trains run to Athens (regular/IC
€15/25, 5½/4½ hours, both twice daily) and Thessaloniki (€13, four hours, three
daily).

ditional dishes like rooster, veal or homemade pasta can be shared. Everything is
made from scratch and salads are a meal
in their own right.

Antica Gelateria di
Roma   Gelateria €
(☏ 27520 23520; www.anticagelateria.gr; cnr
Farmakopoulou & Komninou; snacks from €2)
The best (yes, best) traditional gelati
outside Italy.

Arapakos · Seafood €€

(📞 27520 27675; www.arapakos.gr; Bouboulinas 81; fish per kilo €35-65) The best of the boardwalk catch for fresh seafood.

🍷 Drinking & Nightlife

Wander the old town to cafe- and bar-hop the lively scene. You could start at newcomer **O Mavros Gatos** (Sofroni 1; ⏱8.30am-late), or creative stalwarts near Plateia Syntagmatos like **Cafe Rosso** (Komninou 5), where every table is different.

⭐ Entertainment

Fougaro · Cultural Centre

(📞 27520 96005; www.fougaro.gr; Asklipiou 98) Nafplio's arts and cultural centre opened with fanfare in 2012 in an impeccably renovated factory that now houses an art shop, library, cafe and exhibition spaces, and holds performing arts programs.

ℹ Getting There & Away

KTEL Argolis Bus Station (📞 27520 27323; www.ktel-argolidas.gr; Syngrou 8) has the following services:

Athens €13.10, 2½ hours, hourly (via Corinth)

Epidavros €2.90, 45 minutes, two Mon-Sat

Mycenae €2.90, one hour, three daily

CYCLADES ΚΥΚΛΑΔΕΣ

The Cyclades (kih-*klah*-dez) are Greek islands to dream about. Named after the rough *kyklos* (circle) they form around the island of Delos, they are rugged outcrops of rock in the azure Aegean, speckled with white cubist buildings and blue-domed Byzantine churches.

Some of the islands, such as Mykonos, Ios and Santorini, have seized tourism with great enthusiasm. Prepare to battle the crowds if you turn up at the height of summer.

Mykonos Μύκονος

POP 8000

Sophisticated Mykonos glitters happily under the Aegean sun, shamelessly surviving on tourism. The island has something for everyone, with marvellous beaches, romantic sunsets, chic boutiques, excellent restaurants and bars, and its long-held reputation as a mecca for gay travellers.

🎯 Sights & Activities

The island's most popular beaches are on the southern coast. **Platys Gialos** has wall-to-wall sun lounges, while nudity is not uncommon at **Paradise Beach**, **Super Paradise**, **Agrari** and gay-friendly **Elia**.

Mykonos Town · Neighbourhood

A stroll around Mykonos Town, shuffling through snaking streets with blinding white walls and balconies of flowers is a must for any visitor. **Little Venice**, where the sea laps up to the edge of the restaurants and bars, and Mykonos' famous hilltop row of **windmills** should be included in the spots-to-see list. You're bound to run into one of Mykonos' famous resident pelicans on your walk.

🛏 Sleeping

Carbonaki Hotel · Boutique Hotel €€

(📞 22890 24124; www.carbonaki.gr; 23 Panahrantou; s/d/tr/q €110/122/170/196; ❄🛜) This family-run place on the edge of the old town has bright and comfortable rooms dotted around a sunny central courtyard. Throw in a Jacuzzi, sauna and delightful ambience and this is a top place to stay.

Hotel Philippi · Pension €€

(📞 22890 22294; www.philippihotel.com; Kalogera 25; s/d from €70/90; ⏱Apr-Oct; ❄🛜) In the heart of the *hora*, Philippi, one of Mykonos' few budget options, has spacious and clean rooms that open onto a railed veranda overlooking a lush garden. An extremely peaceful, pleasant place to stay. Free wi-fi.

🍴 Eating

Fato a Mano · Mediterranean €

(Plateia Meletopoulou; mains €8-15) In the middle of the maze, this place is worth taking the effort to find. It serves up tasty

Mykonos

AEGEAN SEA

Dragonisi

Cape Evros

Cape Goni

Profitis Ilias Anomeritis (351m) ▲

Merchias Bay

Lia Beach

Kalafatis Beach

Cape Kalafatis

Mersini Bay

Fokos Beach

Kalo Livadi Beach

Cape Mavros

Mersini Beach

Cape Mavrokefalas

Ano Mera

Moni Panagias Tourlianis

Elia

Ftelia Beach

Elia Beach

Panormos Bay

Agrari Beach

Agios Sostis Beach

Panormos Beach

Lake Marathi

▲ (275m)

Super Paradise Beach

Paradise Beach

▲ (372m)

Vothonas

Airport

Platys Gialos

Marathi

Tourlos

Malaliamos Beach

Paraga Beach

Tourlos Beach

Hora (Mykonos Town)

Vrissi

Psarou

Platys Gialos

Agios Stefanos

Houlakia Beach

Agios Stefanos Beach

Psarou Beach

Platys Gialos

Ornos

Cape Armenistis

Korfos

Kapari

Agios Ioannis Beach

Nea Mykonos

Cape Algomandra

Delos

Excursion Boat

Tinos; Syros; Rafina; Kythnos; Piraeus; Thessaloniki

Ikaria; Samos; Patmos; Lipsi

Donousa; Amorgos

Naxos; Paros; Shinousa; Iraklio; Ios; Santorini; Amorgos

2 miles — 4 km

N

759

Mediterranean and traditional Greek dishes with pride.

Katerina's
Modern Greek €€

(Agion Anargyron; mains €11-25) Long a legendary bar in Little Venice with breath-taking views out over the water, Katerina's has added an excellent restaurant offering up Greek dishes.

ℹ️ Getting There & Around

Air

There are daily flights connecting Mykonos airport (JMK) to Athens, plus a growing number of international flights winging in directly from May to September. The airport is 3km southeast of the town centre; €1.60 by bus from the southern bus station.

Boat

Daily ferries (€32, five hours) and catamarans (€50, three hours) arrive from Piraeus. From Mykonos, there are daily ferries and hydrofoils to most major Cycladic islands, daily services to Crete, and less-frequent services to the northeastern Aegean Islands and the Dodecanese.

Naxos Νάξος

pop 12,000

The largest of the Cyclades islands, Naxos could probably survive without tourism – unlike many of its neighbouring islands. Green and fertile, Naxos produces olives, grapes, figs, citrus, corn and potatoes. **Naxos Town**, on the west coast, is the island's capital and port.

🎯 Sights & Activities

The popular beach of **Agios Georgios** is just a 10-minute walk south from the main waterfront. Beyond it, wonderful sandy beaches stretch as far south as **Pyrgaki Beach**. **Agia Anna Beach**, 6km from town, and **Plaka Beach** are lined with accommodation and packed in summer.

A hire car or scooter will help reveal Naxos' dramatic and rugged landscape. The **Tragaea** region has tranquil villages, churches atop rocky crags and huge olive groves. **Filoti**, the largest inland settlement, perches on the slopes of **Mt Zeus** (1004m), the highest peak in the Cyclades. The historic village of **Halki**, one-time centre of Naxian commerce, is well worth a visit.

Kastro
Castle

Behind the waterfront in Naxos Town, narrow alleyways scramble up to the spectacular hilltop 13th-century *kastro,* where the Venetian Catholics lived. The *kastro* looks out over the town, and has a well-stocked **archaeological museum** (admission €3; ⏰8am-3pm Tue-Sun).

Temple of Apollo
Archaeological Site

From the ferry quay it's a short stroll to the unfinished Temple of Apollo, Naxos' most famous landmark.

Paradise Beach (p758), Mykonos
GRAHAME MCCONNELL/GETTY IMAGES ©

Detour:
Delos Δήλος

Southwest of Mykonos, the island of **Delos** (sites & museum €5; ⏱8.30am-3pm Tue-Sun) is the Cyclades' archaeological jewel.

According to mythology, Delos was the birthplace of Apollo – the god of light, poetry, music, healing and prophecy. The island flourished as an important religious and commercial centre from the 3rd millennium BC, reaching its apex of power in the 5th century BC.

Ruins include the **Sanctuary of Apollo**, containing temples dedicated to him, and the **Terrace of the Lions**. These proud beasts were carved in the early 6th century BC using marble from Naxos to guard the sacred area. The original lions are in the island's **museum**, with replicas on the original site. The **Sacred Lake** (dry since 1926) is where Leto supposedly gave birth to Apollo, while the **Theatre Quarter** is where private houses were built around the **Theatre of Delos**.

Numerous boat companies offer trips from Mykonos to Delos (€18 return, 30 minutes) between 9am and 1pm. The return boats leave Delos between noon and 3pm. There is also a €5 per person entry fee on arrival at Delos.

🛏 Sleeping

Pension Sofi   Pension €€

(📞22850 23077; www.pensionsofi.gr; r €30-90; ⏱year-round; ❄🛜) Run by members of the Koufopoulos family, Pension Sofi is in Naxos Town, while their **Studios Panos** (📞22850 26078; www.studiospanos.com; Agios Georgios Beach; r €30-75; ❄🛜) is a 10-minute walk away near Agios Georgios Beach. Guests are met with family-made wine. Immaculate rooms come with bathroom and kitchen. Call ahead for pick-up at the port.

Hotel Grotta   Hotel €€

(📞22850 22215; www.hotelgrotta.gr; s/d incl breakfast €70/85; 🅿❄@🛜🏊) Overlooking Grotta Beach at the northern end of town, this modern hotel has comfortable and immaculate rooms, a Jacuzzi and minipool, and offers great sea views.

🍴 Eating

Picasso   Tex-Mex €

(www.picassoismexican.com; Agiou Arseniou; dishes €6-18; ⏱all day Jun-Sep, dinner only Oct-May) Definitely the best Mexican fare in Greece (and possibly in Europe!). Just off Main Square, Picasso boasts that it serves 'extraordinary Mexican food' and it does.

Metaximas   Taverna €

(Market St; dishes €8-20) Tucked away in the little maze that is Market St, Metaximas serves Naxian seafood at its best.

ℹ Getting There & Around

Air

Naxos airport (JNX) has daily flight connections with Athens. The airport is 3km south of town; no buses – a taxi costs €15.

Boat

There are daily ferries (€31, five hours) and catamarans (€48, 3¾ hours) from Naxos to Piraeus, and good ferry and hydrofoil connections to most Cycladic islands and Crete.

Car & Motorcycle

Having your own wheels is a good option on Naxos. Car and motorcycle rentals are readily available in Naxos Town.

Santorini (Thira)
Σαντορίνη (Θήρα)

POP 13,500

Stunning Santorini is unique and should not be missed. The startling sight of the submerged caldera almost encircled by sheer lava-layered cliffs – topped off by

N 0 ——————————— 4 km
   0 ——————————— 2 miles

Ios; Naxos; Paros;
Mykonos; Syros; Tinos;
Piraeus; Thessaloniki

Baxedes ● Paradise Beach

Pori Beach

AEGEAN SEA

Oia ● Finikia

Cape Riva
Ammoudi *Armeni Port*

Potamos Beach
● Potamos
Agrilla
● Manolas

Thirasia

Imerovigli ● Vourvoulos

Firostefani ●
Fira Skala ● ● Fira

Gialos Beach
Karterados Beach
Monolithos
Karterados
Monolithos Beach

Cape Trypiti

Nea Kameni

Messaria

Airport

Vothonas
Palia Kameni
Hot Springs
Santo Wines
Exo Gonia
Mesa Gonia

Aspronisi

Athinios ●

Pyrgos ●
Kamari

Crete

Megalohori ●

Mt Profitis Ilias (567m)

Kamari Beach

Cape Akrotiri
● Akrotiri
Black Beach
White Beach
Red Beach
Ancient Akrotiri
Akrotiri Beach

Emporio ●

Moni Profiti Ilia *Ancient Thira*

Perissa
Cape Mesa Vouno

Perivolos Beach
Vlihada Beach
Agios Georgios Beach
Cape Evo Mytis

clifftop towns that look like a dusting of icing sugar – will grab your attention. If you turn up in high season, though, be prepared for relentless crowds and commercialism – Santorini survives on tourism.

Sights & Activities

FIRA

Santorini's vibrant main town with its snaking narrow streets full of shops and restaurants perches on top of the caldera; the stunning caldera views from Fira are unparalleled.

The exceptional **Museum of Prehistoric Thira** (admission €3; 8.30am-3pm Tue-Sun), which has wonderful displays of artefacts predominantly from ancient Akrotiri, is two blocks south of the main square. **Megaron Gyzi Museum** (admission €3.50; 10.30am-1.30pm & 5-8pm Mon-Sat, 10.30am-4.30pm Sun), behind the Catholic cathedral, houses local memorabilia, including photographs of Fira before and after the 1956 earthquake.

AROUND THE ISLAND

At the north of the island, the intriguing village of **Oia** (ee-ah), famed for its postcard sunsets, is less hectic than Fira and a must-visit. Its caldera-facing tavernas are superb spots for brunch. There's a path from Fira to Oia along the top of the caldera that takes three to four hours to walk; otherwise take a taxi or bus.

Excavations in 1967 uncovered the remarkably well-preserved Minoan settlement of **Akrotiri** at the south of the island, with its remains of two- and three-storey buildings. Akrotiri has recently reopened to the public after a seven-year hiatus.

Santorini's black-sand **beaches** of **Perissa** and **Kamari** sizzle – beach mats are essential. Sitting on a mountain between the two are the atmospheric ruins of **Ancient Thira**, first settled in the 9th century BC.

Of the surrounding islets, only **Thirasia** is inhabited. Visitors can clamber around on volcanic lava on **Nea Kameni** then swim into warm springs in the sea at **Palia Kameni**; there are various excursions available to get you there.

 Sleeping

Hotel Keti   Hotel €€
(22860 22324; www.hotelketi.gr; Agiou Mina, Fira; d/tr €95/120; ❄ 🤍) Overlooking the caldera, with views to die for, Hotel Keti is a smaller place with traditional rooms carved into the cliffs. Some rooms have Jacuzzis. Head down next to Hotel Atlantis and follow the signs.

Aroma Suites
Boutique Hotel €€€
(6945026038, 22860 24112; www.aromas-uites.com; Agiou Mina; d €160-270; ❄ @ 🤍) At the southern end of

Fira on the caldera edge, this delightful boutique hotel has charming owners to match. Stylish modern facilities enhance traditional caldera interiors. Rates are substantially reduced in low season.

🍴 Eating

Selene   Greek €€
(22860 22249; www.selene.gr; Pyrgos; dishes €15-30) Out in the lovely hill-top village of Pyrgos, Selene is in the heart of Santorinian farming and culinary culture and special-ises in creative cuisine based on Cycladic produce and unique local ingredients, such as small tomatoes and fava beans.

Fanari   Greek €€
(22860 25107; www.fanari-restaurant.gr; Fira; dishes €7-20) In Fira, on the street leading down to the old port, Fanari serves up both tasty traditional dishes and superlative views.

ℹ️ Information

There is no tourist office. Try the website www.santorini.net for more information.

Fira, Santorini
DAVID C TOMLINSON/GETTY IMAGES ©

ℹ️ Getting There & Around

Air

Santorini airport (JTR) has daily flight connections with Athens, plus a growing number of domestic destinations and direct international flights from all over Europe. The airport is 5km southeast of Fira; frequent buses (€1.50) and taxis (€12).

Boat

There are daily ferries (€33.50, nine hours) and fast boats (€60, 5¼ hours) to Piraeus; daily connections in summer to Mykonos, Ios, Naxos, Paros and Iraklio; and ferries to the smaller islands in the Cyclades. Large ferries use Athinios port, where they are met by buses and taxis.

Car & Motorcycle

A car or scooter is a great option. There are plenty of places to rent them (from €30 per day).

CRETE ΚΡΗΤΗ

POP 550,000

Crete is Greece's largest and most southerly island and its size and distance from the rest of Greece give it the feel of a different country. The rugged mountainous interior, dotted with caves and sliced by dramatic gorges, offers rigorous hiking and climbing.

While Crete's proud, friendly and hospitable people have enthusiastically embraced tourism, they continue to fiercely protect their traditions and culture – and it is the people that remain a major part of the island's appeal.

Crete was the birthplace of Minoan culture, Europe's first advanced civilisation, which flourished between 2800 and 1450 BC.

Iraklio Ηράκλειο

POP 138,000

Iraklio (ee-*rah*-klee-oh; often spelt Heraklion), Crete's capital and economic hub, is a bustling modern city and the fifth-largest in Greece.

🎯 Sights

Archaeological Museum   Museum
(odysseus.culture.gr; Xanthoudidou 2; adult/student €4/2; ⏲ 8.30am-3pm Nov-Mar) The

Crete

outstanding Minoan collection here is second only to that of the national museum in Athens. The museum was under long-term reconstruction at the time of research, but its key exhibits are beautifully displayed in an annex.

Koules Venetian Fortress   Fortress
(Venetian Harbour) Protecting the old harbour, this impressive fortress is also known as Rocca al Mare, which, like the city walls, was built by the Venetians in the 16th century. It stopped the Turks for 21 years and later became a Turkish prison for Cretan rebels.

City Walls   Fortress
Iraklio burst out of its city walls long ago, but these massive Venetian fortifications, with seven bastions and four gates, are still very conspicuous, dwarfing the concrete structures of the 20th century.

Morosini Fountain   Fountain
(Plateia Venizelou) Iraklio's much loved 'lion fountain', built in 1628 by the Venetians, spurts water from four lions into eight ornate U-shaped marble troughs.

🛏 Sleeping

Lato Boutique
Hotel   Boutique Hotel €€
(☎2810 228103; www.lato.gr; Epimenidou 15; d incl breakfast €89-136; P❄@🛜) This stylish boutique hotel overlooking the waterfront is a top place to stay. The contemporary interior design extends to the bar, breakfast restaurant and **Brillant** (☎28102 28103; www.brillantrestaurant. gr; mains €10-25), the superb fine-dining restaurant on the ground floor. From May to October, the restaurant renames itself **Herb's Garden** and moves to the hotel rooftop for alfresco dining with harbour views.

Kronos Hotel   Hotel €
(☎2810 282240; www.kronoshotel.gr; Sofokli Venizelou 2; s/d €44/57; ❄@🛜) After a thorough makeover, this waterfront hotel has pole-vaulted to the top of the budget hotel category. The comfortable rooms have double-glazed windows and balconies. Ask for one of the rooms with sea views.

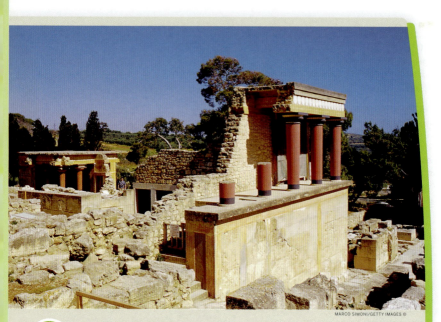

MARCO SIMONI/GETTY IMAGES ©

⭐ Don't Miss
Knossos Κνωσσός

Five kilometres south of Iraklio, Knossos was the capital of Minoan Crete, and is now the island's major tourist attraction. According to legend, King Minos of Knossos was given a magnificent white bull to sacrifice to the god Poseidon, but decided to keep it. This enraged Poseidon, who punished the king by causing his wife Pasiphae to fall in love with the animal. The result of this odd union was the Minotaur – half-man and half-bull – who lived in a labyrinth beneath the king's palace, munching on youths and maidens.

In 1900 Arthur Evans uncovered the ruins of Knossos. Although archaeologists tend to disparage Evans' reconstruction, the buildings – incorporating an immense palace, courtyards, private apartments, baths, lively frescos and more – give a fine idea of what a Minoan palace might have looked like.

Buses to Knossos (€1.50, 20 minutes, three per hour) leave from Bus Station A.

NEED TO KNOW
📞 28102 31940; admission €6; 🕐 8am-7pm Jun-Oct, to 3pm Nov-May

🍴 Eating

Giakoumis   Greek €
(€6-9; 🕐 lunch & dinner) Among the tavernas clustered around the 1866 market side streets, this is a favourite. There's a full menu of Cretan specialities and vegetarian options.

Ippokambos Ouzerie   Seafood €
Many locals come to this classic Iraklio haunt at the edge of the tourist-driven waterfront dining strip. Take a peek inside at the fresh trays and pots of *mayirefta* such as baked cuttlefish, and dine at one of the sidewalk tables or on the promenade across the road.

ℹ️ Getting There & Around

Air

Flights depart daily from Iraklio's Nikos Kazantzakis airport (HER) for Athens and there are regular flights to Thessaloniki and Rhodes. The airport is 5km east of town. Bus 1 travels between the airport and city centre (€1.20) every 15 minutes from 6am to 11pm.

Boat

Daily ferries service Piraeus (€37, seven hours), and catamarans head daily to Santorini and continue on to other Cycladic islands. Ferries sail east to Rhodes (€28, 12 hours) via Agios Nikolaos, Sitia, Kasos, Karpathos and Halki.

Phaestos & Other Minoan Sites Φαιστός

Phaestos (📞 29820 42315; admission €6; 🕐 8am-7pm May-Oct, to 5pm Nov-Apr), 63km southwest of Iraklio, is Crete's second-most important Minoan site. While not as impressive as Knossos, Phaestos (fes-*tos*) is still worth a visit for its stunning views of the surrounding Mesara plain and Mt Psiloritis (2456m; also known as Mt Ida). Eight buses a day head to Phaestos from Iraklio's Bus Station B (€6.30, 1½ hours).

Other important Minoan sites can be found at **Malia**, 34km east of Iraklio, where there's a palace complex and adjoining town, and **Zakros**, 40km southeast of Sitia, the last Minoan palace to have been discovered, in 1962.

Hania Χανιά

POP 54,000

Crete's most romantic, evocative and alluring town, Hania (hahn-*yah*; often spelt Chania) is the former capital and the island's second-largest city. There is a rich mosaic of Venetian and Ottoman architecture, particularly in the area of the old harbour, which lures tourists in droves.

⊙ Sights

Venetian Harbour   Historic Site
From Plateia 1866 in the middle of town, the old harbour is a short walk down

Halidon. A stroll around here is a must for any visitor to Hania. It is worth the 1.5km walk around the sea wall to get to the Venetian **lighthouse** at the entrance to the harbour.

Venetian Fortifications   Fortress
Part of a defensive system built by the Venetians from 1538, Hania's massive fortifications remain impressive.

Archaeological Museum   Museum
(Halidon 30; admission €2; 🕐 8.30am-3pm Tue-Sun) The museum is housed in a 16th-century Venetian church that the Turks made into a mosque.

Food Market   Market
Hania's covered food market, in a massive cross-shaped building 400m southeast of the Old Harbour, is definitely worth an inspection.

🛏️ Sleeping

Pension Lena   Pension €
(📞 28210 86860; www.lenachania.gr; Ritsou 5; s/d €35/55; ❄️ 🛜) For some real character in where you stay, Lena's pension (in an old Turkish building near the mouth of the old harbour) is the place to go. Help yourself to one of the appealing rooms if proprietor Lena isn't there – pick from the available ones on the list on the blackboard.

Amphora Hotel   Hotel €€
(📞 28210 93224; www.amphora.gr; Parodos Theotokopoulou 20; s €95, d €110-130; ❄️ 🛜) Most easily found from the waterfront, this is Hania's most historically evocative hotel. Amphora is in an impressively restored Venetian mansion with elegantly decorated rooms around a courtyard.

🍴 Eating

The entire waterfront of the old harbour is lined with restaurants and tavernas, many of which qualify as tourist traps. There are a number of good options one street back.

Michelas   Greek €
(📞 28210 90026; mains €4-12; 🕐 10am-4pm Mon-Sat) Serving up authentic Cretan

Palace of Knossos

The Highlights in Two Hours

The Palace of Knossos is Crete's busiest tourist attraction, and for good reason. A spin around the partially reconstructed complex delivers an eye-opening peek into the remarkably sophisticated society of the Minoans, who dominated southern Europe some 4000 years ago.

From the ticket booth, follow the marked trail to the **North Entrance** ❶ where the Charging Bull fresco gives you a first taste of Minoan artistry. Continue to the Central Court and join the queue waiting to glimpse the mystical **Throne Room** ❷, which probably hosted religious rituals. Turn right as you exit and follow the stairs up to the so-called Piano Nobile, where replicas of the palace's most famous artworks conveniently cluster in the **Fresco Room** ❸. Walk the length of the Piano Nobile, pausing to look at the clay storage vessels in the West Magazines, to a staircase descending to the **South Portico** ❹, beautifully decorated with the Cup Bearer fresco. Make your way back to the Central Court and head to the palace's eastern wing to admire the architecture of the **Grand Staircase** ❺ that led to the royal family's private quarters. For a closer look at some rooms, walk to the south end of the courtyard, stopping for a peek at the **Prince of the Lilies fresco** ❻, and head down to the lower floor. A highlight here is the **Queen's Megaron** ❼ (bedroom), playfully adorned with a fresco of frolicking dolphins. Stay on the lower level and make your way to the **Giant Pithoi** ❽, huge clay jars used for storage.

South Portico

Fine frescoes, most famously the Cup Bearer, embellish this palace entrance anchored by a massive open staircase leading to the Piano Nobile. The Horns of Consecration recreated nearby once topped the entire south facade.

Fresco Room

Take in sweeping views of the palace grounds from the west wing's upper floor, the Piano Nobile, before studying copies of the palace's most famous art works in its Fresco Room.

West Court

West Magazines

❹ **Horns of Consecration**

Food Tip

Save your appetite for a meal in the nearby Iraklio Wine Country, amid sunbaked slopes and lush valleys. It's just south of Knossos.

Prince of the Lilies Fresco

One of Knossos' most beloved frescoes was controversially cobbled together from various fragments and shows a young man adorned in lilies and peacock feathers.

Planning

To beat the crowds and avoid the heat, arrive before 10am. Budget several hours to explore the site thoroughly.

Throne Room

Sir Arthur Evans who discovered the Palace of Knossos in 1900, imagined the mythical King Minos himself holding court seated on the alabaster throne of this beautifully proportioned room. However, the lustral basin and griffin frescoes suggest a religious purpose, possibly under a priestess.

North Entrance

Bulls held a special status in Minoan society as evidenced by the famous relief fresco of a charging beast gracing the columned west bastion of the north palace, which harboured workshops and storage rooms.

Grand Staircase

The royal apartments in the eastern wing were accessed via this monumental staircase sporting four flights of gypsum steps supported by columns. The lower two flights are original. It's closed to the public.

Piano Nobile

Central Court

Royal Apartments

❸ ❶ ❺ ❷ ❻ ❼ ❽

Queen's Megaron

The queen's bedroom is among the prettiest in the residential eastern wing thanks to the playful Dolphin Fresco. The adjacent bathroom (with clay tub) and toilet are evidence of a sophisticated drainage system.

Giant Pithoi

These massive clay jars are rare remnants from the Old Palace period and were used to store wine, oil and grain. The jars were transported by slinging ropes through a series of handles.

specialities at reasonable prices for 75 years, this family-run place in the Food Market uses only local ingredients and cooks up a great selection each day that you can peruse, then choose from.

❶ Information

For more information visit the Hania website (www.chania.gr).
Tourist information office (☎ 28210 36155; Kydonias 29; ⏰8am-2.30pm)

❶ Getting There & Away

Air

There are several flights a day between Hania airport (CHQ) and Athens, plus a number of flights to Thessaloniki each week. The airport is 14km east of town on the Akrotiri Peninsula. Taxis to town cost €20; buses cost €2.30.

Samaria Gorge Φαράγγι της Σαμαριάς

The **Samaria Gorge** (☎ 28210 45570; www.samariagorge.eu; adult/child €5/2.50; ⏰7am-sunset May-late Oct) is one of Europe's most spectacular gorges and a superb hike. Walkers should take rugged footwear, food, drinks and sun protection for this strenuous five- to six-hour trek.

You can do the walk as part of an excursion tour, or independently by taking the Omalos bus from the main bus station in Hania (€6.90, one hour) to the head of the gorge at Xyloskalo (1230m). It's a 16.7km walk (all downhill) to Agia Roumeli on the coast, from where you take a boat to Hora Sfakion (€10, 1¼ hours) and then a bus back to Hania (€7.60, 1½ hours). You are not allowed to spend the night in the gorge, so you need to complete the walk in a day.

Boat

Daily ferries sail between Piraeus (€35, nine hours) and the port of Souda, 9km southeast of Hania. Frequent buses (€1.65) and taxis (€10) connect town and Souda.

DODECANESE ΔΩΔΕΚΑΝΗΣΑ

Strung out along the coast of western Turkey, the 12 main islands of the Dodecanese (*dodeca* means 12) have suffered a turbulent past of invasions and occupations that have endowed them with a fascinating diversity.

The islands themselves range from the verdant and mountainous to the rocky and dry. While Rhodes and Kos host highly developed tourism, the more remote islands await those in search of traditional island life.

Rhodes Ρόδος

POP 98,000

Rhodes (Rodos in Greek) is the largest island in the Dodecanese. According to mythology, the sun god Helios chose Rhodes as his bride and bestowed light, warmth and vegetation upon her. The blessing seems to have paid off, for Rhodes produces more flowers and sunny days than most Greek islands.

❶ Getting There & Away

Air

There are plenty of flights daily between Rhodes' **Diagoras airport** (RHO) and Athens, plus less-regular flights to Karpathos, Kastellorizo, Thessaloniki, Iraklio and Samos. The airport is on the west coast, 16km southwest of Rhodes Town; 25 minutes and €2.20 by bus.

Boat

There are daily ferries from Rhodes to Piraeus (€59, 13 hours). Most sail via the Dodecanese north of Rhodes, but at least twice a week there is a service via Karpathos, Crete and the Cyclades.

Palace of the Grand Masters, Rhodes

IAN CUMMING/GETTY IMAGES ©

GREECE RHODES

In summer, catamaran services run up and down the Dodecanese daily from Rhodes to Symi, Kos, Kalymnos, Nisyros, Tilos, Patmos and Leros.

RHODES TOWN

POP 56,000

Rhodes' capital is Rhodes Town, on the northern tip of the island. Its **Old Town**, the largest inhabited medieval town in Europe, is enclosed within massive walls and is a joy to explore. To the north is **New Town**, the commercial centre.

⊙ Sights

A wander around Rhodes' World Heritage–listed Old Town is a must. It is reputedly the world's finest surviving example of medieval fortification, with 12m-thick walls.

The Knights of St John lived in the Knights' Quarter in the northern end of the Old Town.

The cobbled **Odos Ippoton** (Ave of the Knights) is lined with magnificent medieval buildings, the most imposing of which is the **Palace of the Grand Masters** (✆22410 23359; admission €6; ⊗8.30am-3pm Tue-Sun), which was restored, but never used, as a holiday home for Mussolini.

The 15th-century Knight's Hospital now houses the **Archaeological Museum** (✆22410 27657; Plateia Mousiou; admission €3; ⊗8am-4pm Tue-Sun).

The pink-domed **Mosque of Süleyman**, at the top of Sokratous, was built in 1522 to commemorate the Ottoman victory against the knights, then rebuilt in 1808.

🛏 Sleeping

Marco Polo Mansion
Boutique Hotel €€

(✆22410 25562; www.marcopolomansion.gr; Agiou Fanouriou 40, Old Town; d incl breakfast from €90-180; ❄🛜) In a 15th-century building in the Turkish quarter of the Old Town, this place is rich in Ottoman-era colours and features in glossy European magazines. In the secluded garden is the highly recommended Marco Polo Café.

Mango Rooms
Rooms €

(✆22410 24877; www.mango.gr; Plateia Dorieos 3, Old Town; s/d/tr €44/58/66; ❄@🛜) A good-value, friendly one-stop shop near the back of the Old Town, Mango has an outdoor restaurant, bar and internet cafe down below, six well-kept rooms above, and a sunny terrace on top.

771

Hotel Andreas   Pension €€€

(☏22410 34156; www.hotelandreas.com; Omirou 28d, Old Town; s/d/tr €45/70/85; ❄@☎) Tasteful Hotel Andreas has individually decorated rooms and terrific views from its terrace.

🍴 Eating

Inside the walls, Old Town has it all in terms of touts and over-priced tavernas trying to separate less-savvy tourists from their euro. The back alleys tend to throw up better-quality eateries and prices.

To Meltemi   Taverna €

(Kountourioti 8; mains €10-15; P❄♿) At the northern end of Mandraki Harbour, To Meltemi is one place worth heading to. Try the grilled calamari stuffed with tomato and feta, and inspect the old photos of Rhodes.

Marco Polo Café   Mediterranean

(☏22410 25562; www.marcopolomansion.gr; Agiou Fanouriou 40, Old Town) A top spot to eat in Rhodes, Marco Polo Café is worth finding in the backstreets of the Old Town. Owner Efi is as tastefully colourful as her mansion and garden restaurant.

ℹ️ Information

For more information, visit the Rodos website (www.rodos.gr).

Tourist information office (EOT; ☏22410 35226; cnr Makariou & Papagou; ⏰8am-2.45pm Mon-Fri)

Kos Κως

POP 17,900

Captivating Kos, only 5km from the Turkish peninsula of Bodrum, is popular with history buffs as the birthplace of Hippocrates (460–377 BC), the father of medicine. The island also attracts an entirely different crowd – sun-worshipping beach lovers from northern Europe who flock here during summer.

🎯 Sights

Castle of the Knights   Castle

(☏22420 27927; admission €3; ⏰8am-2.30pm Tue-Sun; ♿) Built in the 14th century, this impressive castle protected the knights from the encroaching Ottomans, and was originally separated from town by a moat. That moat is now Finikon, a major street. Entrance to the castle is over the stone bridge behind the Hippocrates Tree.

Asklipieion   Archaeological Site

(☏22420 28763; adult/student €4/3; ⏰8am-7.30pm Tue-Sun) On a pine-clad hill 4km southwest of Kos Town stand the extensive ruins of the renowned healing centre where Hippocrates practised medicine. Groups of doctors come from all over the world to visit.

Hippocrates Plane Tree, Kos
INGOLF POMPE/GETTY IMAGES ©

Ancient Agora Ruin

The ancient agora, with the ruins of the **Shrine of Aphrodite** and **Temple of Hercules**, is just off Plateia Eleftherias. North of the agora is the **Hippocrates Plane Tree**, under which the man himself is said to have taught his pupils.

🛏 Sleeping

Hotel Afendoulis Hotel €

(☏ 22420 25321; www.afendoulishotel.com; Evripilou 1; s/d €30/50; ☼Mar-Nov; ❄ @ 🛜) In a pleasant, quiet area about 500m south of the ferry quay, this well-kept hotel won't disappoint. Run by the charismatic English-speaking Alexis, this is a great place to relax and enjoy Kos. Port and bus station transfers are complimentary, and you can get your laundry done here.

Hotel Sonia Hotel €€

(☏ 22420 28798; www.hotelsonia.gr; Irodotou 9; s/d/tr €45/60/75; ❄ 🛜) Recently refurbished, Sonia's place has long been a popular spot to stay in Kos. It has large rooms and a relaxing veranda and garden. They'll pick you up at the port or bus station for free and there are laundry facilities on site.

🍴 Eating

Stadium Restaurant Seafood €€

(☏ 22420 27880; mains €10-18) On the long waterfront 500m southeast of the castle, Stadium serves succulent seafood at good prices, along with excellent views of Turkey.

ℹ Information

Municipal Tourist Office (☏ 22420 24460; www.kosinfo.gr; Vasileos Georgiou 1; ☼8am-2.30pm & 3-10pm Mon-Fri, 9am-2pm Sat May-Oct)

ℹ Getting There & Around

Air

There are daily flights to Athens from Kos' Ippokratis airport (KGS), which is 28km southwest of Kos Town. Get to/from the airport by bus (€4) or taxi (€30).

Boat

There are frequent ferries from Rhodes to Kos that continue on to Piraeus (€53, 10 hours), as well as ferries heading the opposite way. Daily fast-boat connections head north to Patmos and Samos, and south to Symi and Rhodes.

Patmos Πάτμος

POP 3050

Patmos has a sense of 'spirit of place', and with its great beaches and relaxed atmosphere, it's a superb place to unwind.

The main town and port of Skala is about halfway down the east coast of Patmos, with a protected harbour. Towering above Skala to the south is the *hora*, crowned by the immense Monastery of St John the Theologian.

🎯 Sights

Beaches Beaches

Patmos' coastline provides secluded coves, mostly with pebble beaches. The best is **Psili Ammos**, in the south, reached by excursion boat from Skala port. **Lambi Beach**, on the north coast, is a pebble-beach-lover's dream come true.

🛏 Sleeping

Pension Maria Pascalidis Pension €

(☏ 22470 32152; s/d/tr €20/35/45; 🛜) Maria has cosy rooms in a fragrant citrus-tree garden on the road heading up to the Hora and Monastery. A travellers' favourite, guests share a communal bathroom and kitchen.

Blue Bay Hotel Hotel €€

(☏ 22470 31165; www.bluebaypatmos.gr; s/d/tr incl breakfast €85/100/145; ❄ @ 🛜) South of the harbour in Skala, this waterfront hotel has superb rooms, internet access, and breakfast included in its rates (which tumble outside of high season).

ℹ Information

See the websites www.patmosweb.gr, and www.patmos-island.com for more information.

Tourist office (☏ 22470 31666; ☼8am-6pm Mon-Fri Jun-Sep)

Beach at Paleokastritsa, Corfu

IAN WEST/GETTY IMAGES ©

ⓘ Getting There & Away

Patmos is well connected, with ferries to Piraeus (€37, seven hours) and south to Rhodes (€32, six hours). In summer daily high-speed services head south to Kos and Rhodes, and north to Samos.

IONIAN ISLANDS
ΤΑ ΕΠΤΑΝΗΣΑ

The idyllic cypress- and fir-covered Ionian Islands stretch down the western coast of Greece from Corfu in the north to Kythira, off the southern tip of the Peloponnese. Mountainous, with dramatic cliff-backed beaches, soft light and turquoise water, they're more Italian in feel, offering a contrasting experience to other Greek islands. Invest in a hire car to get to small villages tucked along quiet back roads.

Corfu Κέρκυρα

POP 122,700

Many consider Corfu, or Kerkyra (ker-kih-rah) in Greek, to be Greece's most beautiful island – the unfortunate consequence of which is that it's overbuilt and often overrun with crowds.

ⓘ Getting There & Away

Ioannis Kapodistrias Airport (CFU; ☏ 26610 89600; www.corfu-airport.com) is 3km from Corfu Town. **Olympic Air** (☏ 801 801 0101) and **Aegean Airlines** (☏ 26610 27100) fly daily to Athens and a few times a week to Thessaloniki.

A taxi from the airport to the centre costs around €12. Buses 6 and 10 stop 800m from the airport.

CORFU TOWN

POP 28,800

Built on a promontory and wedged between two fortresses, Corfu's Old Town is a tangle of narrow walking streets through gorgeous Venetian buildings.

◎ Sights

Museum of Asian Art   Museum
(☏ 26610 30443; www.matk.gr; adult/child incl audioguide €3/2; ◷ 8.30am-3.30pm Tue-Sun) Housed in the **Palace of St Michael & St George** this art collection is expertly curated with extensive English-language placards. Approximately 10,000 artefacts collected from China, Japan, India, Tibet and Thailand include priceless prehistoric bronzes, ceramics, jade figurines, and coins.

Palaio Frourio Fortress

(📞26610 48310; adult/concession €4/2; ⏰8am-5pm Apr-Oct, 8.30am-3pm Nov-Mar) Constructed by the Venetians in the 15th century on the remains of a Byzantine castle and further altered by the British, the Palaio Frourio stands on an eastern promontory; the Neo Frourio (New Fortress) lies to the northwest.

Antivouniotissa Museum Museum

(📞26610 38313; off Arseniou; adult/child €2/1; ⏰9am-4pm Tue-Sun) Exquisite basilica with an outstanding collection of Byzantine icons and artefacts dating from the 13th to the 17th centuries.

Archaeological Museum Museum

(📞26610 30680; P Vraïla 5; admission €3; ⏰8.30am-3pm Tue-Sun) Houses a collection of finds from Mycenaean to classical times.

Sleeping

Bella Venezia Boutique Hotel €€

(📞26610 46500; www.bellaveneziahotel.com; N Zambeli 4; s/d incl breakfast from €100/120; ❄🌐) Impeccable and understated; contemporary rooms are decked out in cream linens and marbles.

City Marina Hotel Hotel €€

(📞26610 39505; www.citymarina.gr; Donzelot 15; r incl breakfast €80; ❄🌐) Recently renovated and with some sea views, light-filled rooms are managed by friendly staff.

Hermes Hotel Hotel €€

(📞26610 39268; www.hermes-hotel.gr; Markora 12; s/d/tr €50/70/90; ❄🌐) Completely refurbished, pleasant, well-appointed rooms in the New Town.

Eating

La Cucina Italian €€

(📞26610 45029; Guilford 17; mains €10-25; ⏰dinner) Every detail is cared for at this intimate bistro (and its annex down the street), from the hand-rolled tortellini to the inventive pizzas and murals on the walls.

Rex Mediterranean €€

(📞26610 39649; www.rexrestaurant.gr; Kapodistriou 66; mains €12-18; ⏰lunch & dinner) Set back from the Liston, this elegant restaurant elevates Greek home cooking to fine dining.

Chrisomalis Taverna €

(📞26610 30342; N Theotoki 6; mains €8-13; ⏰lunch & dinner) In the heart of the Old Town, this ma and pa operation dishes out the classics.

AROUND THE ISLAND

To explore fully all regions of the island your own transport is best. Much of the coast just north of Corfu Town is overwhelmed with beach resorts, the south is quieter, and the west has beautiful, if popular, coastline. The **Corfu Trail** (www.thecorfutrail.com) traverses the island north to south.

In **Kassiopi**, **Manessis Apartments** (📞26610 34990; http://manessiskassiopi.com; Kassiopi; 4-person apt €70-100; ❄🌐) offers water-view apartments. In Sgombou, **Casa Lucia** (📞26610 91419; www.casa-lucia-corfu.com; Sgombou; studios & cottages €70-120; ⏰Apr-Oct; P🐕) 🖋 is a garden complex of lovely cottages with a strong alternative ethos. Don't miss a dinner at one of the island's best tavernas, **Klimataria** (Bellos; 📞26610 71201; mains €8-14; ⏰dinner) in Benitses.

For an aerial view of the cypress-backed bays around **Paleokastritsa**, the west coast's main resort, go to the quiet village of **Lakones**. Further south, good beaches surround tiny **Agios Gordios**.

Kefallonia
Κεφαλλονιά

POP 37,800

Tranquil cypress- and fir-covered Kefallonia, the largest Ionian island, is breathtakingly beautiful with rugged mountain ranges, rich vineyards, soaring coastal cliffs and golden beaches. It has not succumbed to package tourism to the extent that some of the other Ionian Islands have and remains low-key outside resort areas. Due to the widespread destruction of an earthquake in 1953,

If You Like...
Island Hopping

If you've fallen for the laid-back pace of life on the Ionian Islands, then you're in luck – Greece has plenty more island archipelagos to explore.

1 AEGEAN ISLANDS
These far-flung islands are strewn across the northeastern Aegean. **Samos** was an important centre of Hellenic culture. **Lesvos**, or Mytilini as it is often called, is the third-largest of the Greek Islands, and produces half the world's ouzo, while little **Chios** is ideal if you want to escape the crowds. There are regular flights from Athens, plus seasonal boats from the Cyclades and Dodecanese.

2 CYCLADES
Most people never make it beyond Mykonos and Santorini, but the Cyclades have lots of other fascinating islands. **Naxos** is the largest and lushest; **Paros** is known for its beaches and terraced hills; **Ios** is the island for party animals. All can be reached by ferry from Piraeus on the mainland and Iraklio on Crete.

3 DODECANESE
Beyond the main islands, traditional Greek culture still holds sway. To the north of Rhodes, **Symi** is home to the ancient Monastery of Panormitis, while the mountainous island of **Karpathos**, midway between Crete and Rhodes, is a scenic island with a cosy port and more than 40 unspoilt villages. Tourism remains low-key except in July and August, when the island goes mad. Both can be easily reached from Rhodes.

much of the island's historic architecture was levelled; Assos and Fiskardo are exceptions.

ℹ️ Getting There & Around

Air
Olympic Air (📞 26710 41511; www.olympicair. com) flies to Athens, and **Sky Express** serves the Ionians and Crete, from **Kefallonia airport** (EFL; 📞 26710 41511), 9km south of Argostoli.

Car
A car is best for exploring. **Pama Travel** (📞 26740 41033; www.pamatravel.com; Fiskardo) rents cars and boats. **Karavomilos** (📞 26740 22779; Sami) delivers cars.

FISKARDO

Pretty Fiskardo, with its pastel-coloured Venetian buildings set around a picturesque bay, is popular with European yachties but it's still peaceful enough to appeal to independent travellers. Take lovely walks to sheltered coves for swimming.

Eating

Fiskardo has no shortage of excellent waterside restaurants.

Tassia Mediterranean €€
(📞 26740 41205; mains €7-25; ⏱lunch & dinner May-Oct) This unassuming but famous Fiskardo institution run by Tassia Dendrinou, celebrated chef and writer, serves up excellent seafood and Greek dishes.

Café Tselenti Italian €€
(📞 26740 41344; mains €10-23; ⏱lunch & dinner May-Oct) Enjoy outstanding Italian classics served by friendly waiters; tucked back in a romantic plaza.

🛏️ Sleeping

Archontiko Pension €€
(📞 26740 41342; www.archontiko-fiskardo.gr; d without/with sea view €50/70; ❄️) Overlooking the harbour, people-watch from the balconies of luxurious rooms in a restored stone mansion.

Regina's Rooms Pension €
(📞 26740 41125; www.regina-studios-boats.gr; d/tr €50/60; ❄️🛜) Some of its colourful, breezy rooms have bay views or kitchenettes.

AROUND THE ISLAND

In **Argostoli**, the capital, stay over at **Vivian Villa** (📞 26710 23396; www. kefalonia-vivianvilla.gr; Deladetsima 11; d/studio

€45/55; ❄ 📶) with its big, bright rooms and friendly owners. Sample inventive Mediterranean cooking at **Casa Grec** (📞26710 24091; S Metaxa 12; ⏰dinner nightly, reduced in low season) or top Kefallonian cuisine at **Arhontiko** (📞26710 27213; Risospaston 5; mains €7-17; ⏰breakfast, lunch & dinner).

Straddling a slender isthmus on the northwest coast, the petite pastel-coloured village of **Assos** watches over the ruins of a Venetian fortress perched upon a pine-covered peninsula. Eat at **Platanos** (mains €6-15; ⏰breakfast, lunch & dinner Easter-Oct) for home-cooked food at its best. Splendid **Myrtos Beach**, 13km south of Assos, is spellbinding from above, with postcard views from the precarious roadway.

Near **Sami**, eat at **Paradise Beach** (Dendrinos; 📞26740 61392; Agia Evfymia; mains €6-13; ⏰lunch & dinner mid-May–mid-Oct), a renowned Kefallonian taverna.

The interior **Omala Valley** is home to **Robola wines** (www.robola.gr). **Paliki Peninsula** is filled with under-explored beauty.

Ithaki Ιθάκη

POP 1550

Odysseus' long-lost home in Homer's *Odyssey*, Ithaki (ancient Ithaca) remains a verdant, pristine island blessed with cypress-covered hills and beautiful turquoise coves.

❶ Getting There & Away

Strintzis Lines (www.strintzisferries.gr) has two ferries daily connecting Vathy or Piso Aetos with Patra (Peloponnese) via Sami (Kefallonia).

Ionian Pelagos (📞26450 31520) goes daily in high season between Piso Aetos, Sami and Astakos (mainland).

Check routes and schedules at **Delas Tours** (📞26740 32104) or **Polyctor Tours** (📞26740 33120; www.ithakiholidays.com), in Vathy.

KIONI

Tucked in a tiny, tranquil bay, Kioni is a wonderful place to chill for a few days.

Individuals rent rooms and **Captain's Apartments** (📞26740 31481; www.captains-apartments.gr; Kioni; 2-/4-person apt €70/95; ❄ 📶) has shipshape, spacious apartments with kitchens, satellite TV

Myrtos Beach, Kefallonia

TADEJ ZUPANCIC/GETTY IMAGES ©

and balconies overlooking the valley and village. **Mythos** (☎26740 31122; Kioni; mains €6-10; ⏱lunch & dinner) taverna on the harbour has excellent *pastitsio* (a thick noodle and ground beef casserole). Comfy **Cafe Spavento** (per hr €2) has internet.

AROUND THE ISLAND

The dusty port of **Frikes**, where some ferries dock, is a funkier alternative to Kioni and has rooms to rent.

Vathy, Ithaki's small, bustling capital, is the spot for hiring cars and getting cash (no banks in Kioni). Elegant mansions rise from around its bay and **Hotel Perantzada** (☎26740 33496; www.arthotel.gr/perantzada; Odyssea Androutsou; s/d incl breakfast from €135/170; ⏱Easter–mid-Oct; ❄@🛜🏊) occupies two with sensational rooms. **Odyssey Apartments** (☎26740 33400; www.odysseyapartments.gr; studio €100, 1-/2-bedroom apt €130/160; P❄🏊) overlooks town (500m up) and the sea with spotless studios and a pool.

SURVIVAL GUIDE

ℹ️ Directory A–Z

Accommodation

Hotels Classified as deluxe, or A, B, C, D or E class; ratings seldom seem to have much bearing on the price, which is determined more by season and location.

Domatia Greek equivalent of a B&B, minus the breakfast; don't worry about finding them – owners will find you as they greet ferries and buses shouting 'room!'.

Youth hostels In most major towns and on some islands; Greek Youth Hostel Organisation (☎21075 19530; www.athens-yhostel.com).

Camping grounds Generally open from April to October; standard facilities include hot showers, kitchens, restaurants and minimarkets – and often a swimming pool; Panhellenic Camping Association (☎21036 21560; www.panhellenic-camping-union.gr).

Mountain refuges Listed in *Greece Mountain Refuges & Ski Centres*, available free of charge at EOT and EOS (Ellinikos Orivatikos Syndesmos, the Greek Alpine Club) offices.

Price Ranges

'High season' is usually in July and August. If you turn up in the 'middle' or 'shoulder seasons' (May and June; September and October) expect to pay significantly less. During 'low season' (late October to late April) prices can be up to 50% cheaper, but a lot of places, especially on the islands, virtually close their shutters for winter.

Prices quoted in listings are for high season (usually July and August) and include a private bathroom.

€ less than €60

€€ €60 to €150

€€€ more than €150

Business Hours

Banks 8am-2.30pm Mon-Thu, 8am-2pm Fri (in cities, also: 3.30-6.30pm Mon-Fri, 8am-1.30pm Sat)

Cafes 10am-midnight

Post offices 7.30am-2pm Mon-Fri (in cities 7.30am-8pm Mon-Fri, 7.30am-2pm Sat)

Restaurants 11am-3pm & 7pm-1am (varies greatly)

Supermarkets 8am-8pm Mon-Fri, 8am-3pm Sat

Street kiosks *(Periptera)* early-late Mon-Sun

Food

Price ranges for Eating are as follows:

€ less than €15

€€ €15 to €40

€€€ more than €40

Gay & Lesbian Travellers

The church plays a significant role in shaping society's views on issues such as sexuality, and homosexuality is generally frowned-upon.

It is wise to be discreet and to avoid open displays of togetherness. That said, Greece is a popular destination for gay travellers.

Athens has a busy gay scene that packs up and heads to the islands for summer, with Mykonos famous for its bars, beaches and hedonism, and Eresos on Lesvos something of a pilgrimage for lesbians.

Fishing boats, Ithaki

GEORGE TSAFOS/GETTY IMAGES ©

Money

ATMs Everywhere except the smallest villages.

Bargaining While souvenir shops will generally bargain, prices in other shops are normally clearly marked and non-negotiable; accommodation is nearly always negotiable outside peak season, especially for longer stays.

Cash Currency is king at street kiosks and small shops, and especially in the countryside.

Changing currency Banks, post offices and currency exchange offices are all over the places; exchange all major currencies.

Credit cards Generally accepted, but may not be on smaller islands or in small villages.

Tipping The service charge is included on the bill in restaurants, but it is the custom to 'round up the bill'; same for taxis.

Public Holidays

New Year's Day 1 January

Epiphany 6 January

First Sunday in Lent February

Greek Independence Day 25 March

Good Friday/Easter Sunday March/April

May Day (Protomagia) 1 May

Feast of the Assumption 15 August

Ohi Day 28 October

Christmas Day 25 December

St Stephen's Day 26 December

Telephone

Maintained by Organismos Tilepikoinonion Ellados, known as OTE (o-*teh*). Public phones are everywhere, take all phonecards and are easy to use; pressing the 'i' button brings up the operating instructions in English.

For directory inquiries within Greece, call ☎131 or ☎132; for international directory inquiries, it's ☎161 or ☎162.

Mobile Phones

Mobile phones are a must-have in Greece. If you have a compatible GSM phone from a country with a global roaming agreement with Greece, you'll be able to use your phone there.

There are several mobile service providers in Greece; **CosmOTE** (www.cosmote.gr) has the best coverage. You can purchase a Greek SIM card for around €20.

Phone Codes

Telephone codes are part of the 10-digit number within Greece.

The landline prefix is 2 and for mobiles it's 6.

Phonecards

All public phones use OTE phonecards; sold at OTE offices and street kiosks. Phonecards come in €3, €5 and €10 versions; local calls cost €0.30 for three minutes. Discount-card schemes are available, offering much better value for money.

Time

There's one time zone throughout Greece, which is two hours ahead of GMT/UTC and three hours ahead on daylight-savings time (from the last Sunday in March to the last Sunday in October).

Toilets

Public toilets are rare, except at airports and bus and train stations.

Most places have Western-style toilets, but some public toilets may be Asian-style squat toilets.

Greek plumbing can't handle toilet paper: anything larger than a postage stamp will cause a blockage. Put your used toilet paper, sanitary napkins and tampons in the small bin provided next to every toilet.

Tourist Information

Greek National Tourist Organisation (GNTO; www.gnto.gr)

Travellers with Disabilities

Most hotels, museums and ancient sites are not wheelchair accessible; the uneven terrain is an issue even for able-bodied people. Few facilities exist for the visually or hearing impaired. Check out www.greecetravel.com/handicapped.

Visas

Visitors from most countries don't need a visa for Greece. Countries whose nationals can stay in Greece for up to three months include Australia, Canada, all EU countries, Iceland, Israel, Japan, New Zealand and the USA.

🛈 Getting There & Away

Air

Most visitors arrive by air, mostly into Athens. There are 17 international airports in Greece; most handle only summer charter flights to the islands.

Olympic Air (OA; www.olympicair.com)
Privatised version of former Olympic Airlines.

Aegean Airlines (A3; www.aegeanair.com)

Sea

Check out ferry routes, schedules and services online at www.greekferries.gr.

If you are travelling on a rail pass, check to see if ferry travel between Italy and Greece is included. Some ferries are free, others give a discount.

🛈 Getting Around

Boat

Ferry

Ferries come in all shapes and sizes, from state-of-the-art 'superferries' that run on the major routes, to ageing open ferries that operate local services to outlying islands.

Newer high-speed ferries are slashing travel times, but cost much more.

'Classes' on ferries are largely a thing of the past; you have the option of 'deck class', which is the cheapest ticket, or 'cabin class' with air-con cabins and a decent lounge and restaurant.

Venetian Lighthouse (p767), Hania, Crete

Tickets can be bought at the last minute at the dock, but in high season, some boats may be full – plan ahead.

The Greek Ships app for smartphones can be used for real-time tracking to see if your ferry is going to turn up on time – search for 'Greek Ships' in your app store.

Catamaran

High-speed catamarans have become an important part of the island travel scene and are much less prone to cancellation in rough weather.

Catamaran fares are generally more expensive than ferries and about the same as hydrofoils.

Hydrofoil

Hydrofoils are a faster alternative to ferries on some routes, take half the time, but cost twice as much. Most routes will operate only during the high season.

Tickets for hydrofoils must be bought in advance and they are often sold with seat allocation.

Car & Motorcycle

A great way to explore areas in Greece that are off the beaten track, but be careful – Greece has the highest road-fatality rate in Europe.

The Greek automobile club, **ELPA** (www.elpa.gr), generally offers reciprocal services to members of other national motoring associations. If your vehicle breaks down, dial 📞104.

EU-registered vehicles are allowed free entry into Greece for six months without road taxes being due; a green card (international third party insurance) is all that's required.

Rental Cars

Available just about anywhere in Greece, you'll get better rates with local rental-car companies than with the big multinational outfits. Check the insurance waivers closely; check how they can assist in case of a breakdown.

High-season weekly rates start at about €280 for the smallest models, dropping to €200 in winter – add tax and extras. Major companies will request a credit-card deposit.

Minimum driving age in Greece is 18, but most car-hire firms require a driver of 21 or over.

Mopeds & Motorcycles

These are available for hire everywhere. Regulations stipulate that you need a valid motorcycle licence stating proficiency for the size of motorcycle you wish to rent – from 50cc upwards.

Mopeds and 50cc motorcycles range from €10 to €25 per day or from €25 per day for a 250cc motorcycle. Outside high season, rates drop considerably.

Ensure that the bike is in good working order and the brakes work well, and check that your travel insurance covers you for injury resulting from motorcycle accidents.

Road Rules

- Drive on the right.
- Overtake on the left (not all Greeks do this!).
- Compulsory to wear seatbelts in the front seats, and in the back if they are fitted.
- Drink-driving laws are strict; a blood alcohol content of 0.05% incurs a fine of around €150 and over 0.08% is a criminal offence.

Public Transport

Taxi

Taxis are widely available and reasonably priced. Yellow city cabs are metered; rates double between midnight and 5am. Grey rural taxis do not have meters; settle on a price before you get in.

Athens taxi drivers are gifted in their ability to somehow make a little bit extra with every fare. If you have a complaint, note the cab number and contact the Tourist Police.

Train

Greece's train services were in a precarious state at the time of research. Check the Greek Railways Organisation website (www.ose.gr) for the latest. Greece has only two main lines: Athens north to Thessaloniki and Alexandroupolis, and Athens to the Peloponnese.

Europe
In Focus

Europe Today   784
The last few years have been a rocky ride for the Eurozone. Is the upturn in sight?

History   786
There's nowhere on earth with quite as complex and convoluted a history as Europe.

Family Travel   793
Travelling *en famille* can be testing at the best of times. Find out how to keep your trip on track.

Visual Arts   795
Europe has been the crucible for some of the most important artistic movements in history. Time to get clued up.

Architecture   798
From ancient churches to iconic skyscrapers, Europe's architecture is a window into its past, present and future.

Food & Drink   801
The sweetest crêpes, the tastiest tapas, the greatest pizzas – eating out is always an experience to remember.

Sports & Activities   808
Nothing stirs up passions in Europe quite as much as sport – whether it's catching a football match or cheering on the Tour de France.

European Landscapes   812
Whether you're inspired by mighty mountains or golden beaches, you'll find a European landscape to suit.

View of San Giorgio Maggiore, Venice, Italy
PHOTOGRAPHER: CHRISTOPHER GROENHOUT/GETTY IMAGES ©

Europe Today

growth throughout the EU has been sluggish or non-existent, with many countries dipping in and out of recession

European Parliament building, Brussels

belief systems
(% of population)

35	27	18	14	5	1
Catholic	Orthodox	No Religion	Protestant	Muslim	Other

if the EU were 100 people

15 would be 0-14
12 would be 15-24
42 would be 25-54
13 would be 55-64
18 would be 65 and over

population per sq km

≈ 7 people

EUROPE   AFRICA   NORTH AMERICA

Financial Fallout

Several years on, the effects of the 2008 financial crash continue to echo throughout Europe. A sustained recovery has proved elusive; growth throughout the EU has been sluggish or non-existent, with many countries dipping in and out of recession. More seriously, unemployment figures across many European nations have reached record highs, especially in Spain and Greece, where more than one in four people are currently without work, rising to around six in 10 people aged under 25.

On a more positive note, the Euro itself seems to have been stabilised, at least for now. Following a series of multibillion euro rescue packages for Greece, Ireland, Portugal and Spain, in July 2012 the President of the European Central Bank Mario Draghi declared that the ECB was 'ready to do whatever it takes to preserve the euro'. This statement of support seems to have reassured markets and investors alike, and no more bailouts have since been necessary.

ZIUTOGRAF/GETTY IMAGES ©

be headed as a political entity. In order to address its problems, a process of deeper integration seems inevitable, but this will involve individual nations having to relinquish further powers to the EU parliament – a controversial proposition, especially in Euro-sceptic countries such as the UK.

It also raises questions about democratic representation: in exchange for their financial bailouts, financially strapped countries such as Greece, Spain and Italy have been forced to follow the political will of Brussels, often in direct contradiction to the wishes of their own constituents. Inevitably, this has caused widespread unrest, with street protests and anti-EU demonstrations breaking out in many places from Madrid to Athens.

But the underlying problems still remain: slow growth, competition from emerging markets, rapidly ageing populations and, most importantly, the difficulty of reconciling the needs of divergent economies within the unified Eurozone. These are tough problems to solve, and for now the EU seems content to fight the fires rather than address the underlying causes.

Whither the EU?

Perhaps as a result of Europe's economic problems, the swing to the right has continued in many nations. The majority of Western Europe is now governed by right-of-centre parties, with the notable exception of France, who elected the staunchly socialist François Hollande to power in 2012.

While this is a predictable response in times of economic uncertainty, the shift hints at deeper issues – particularly the question of where Europe should

The Eurovision Issue

Every May, Europe's international song contest sparks the same old debates. Is the voting system rigged? Should countries sing in English or in their own language? And most importantly of all: why are the songs always so awful? This musical marathon has been screened every year since 1956, making it the longest-running television show of its kind, and allegedly Europe's most-watched non-sporting event.

Each country is allowed to enter one song, and is then allowed to pick their favourites from the songs submitted by their competitors. Inevitably this leads to accusations of 'block voting': Sweden, Norway and Finland all tend to vote for each other, for example, while the Eastern European nations usually show similar solidarity. Perhaps more confusing is the fact that several countries are allowed to enter which aren't officially members of Europe, including Israel, Morocco, Turkey and Russia.

History

Caryatids of the Erechtheion (p743) at the Acropolis, Greece

JEAN-PIERRE LESCOURRET/GETTY IMAGES ©

Europe is a place where history seems to seep into every corner. It's literally everywhere you look: in the tumbledown remains of Greek temples and Roman bathhouses, in the fabulously ostentatious architecture of French chateaux and Austrian castles, and in the winding streets and broad boulevards of its many stately cities. Understanding Europe's long and often troubled history is a crucial part of figuring out what makes this continent tick.

Prehistory

The first settlers arrived in Europe around two million years ago, but it wasn't until the end of the last major ice age between 12,000 BC and 8000 BC that humans really took hold. As the glaciers and ice sheets retreated, hunter-gatherer tribes extended their reach northwards in search of new land. Some of Europe's earliest human settlements were left behind by Neolithic tribes.

4500–2500 BC

Neolithic tribes build burial tombs, barrows, stone circles and alignments across Europe, including Stonehenge and Carnac.

Greeks & Romans

Europe's first great civilisations developed in Mycenae (about 90km southwest of Athens) and ancient Crete, but it was the Greeks and the Romans who left the most enduring mark. The civilisation of ancient Greece emerged around 2000 BC and made huge leaps forward in science, technology, architecture, philosophy and democratic principles. Many of the writers, thinkers and mathematicians of ancient Greece, from Pythagoras to Plato, still exert a profound influence to this day.

Then came the Romans, who set about conquering most of Europe and devised the world's first republic. At its height, Roman power extended all the way from Celtic Britain to ancient Persia (Iran). The Romans' myriad achievements are almost too numerous to mention: they founded cities, raised aqueducts, constructed roads, laid sewers and built baths all over the continent, and produced a string of brilliant writers, orators, politicians, philosophers and military leaders.

The Dark Ages

By the 4th century AD, the Greek and Roman Empires had seen their golden ages come and go. Greece had been swallowed by Macedonia, led by Alexander the Great, then by Rome itself in AD 146. Meanwhile, Rome's empire-building ambitions eventually proved too much, and a series of political troubles and military disasters resulted in the sacking of Rome (in 410) by the Goths. Although Roman emperors clung onto their eastern Byzantine empire for another thousand years, founding a new capital at Constantinople, Rome's dominance over Western Europe was over. A new era, the Dark Ages, had begun.

The next few centuries were marked by a series of conflicts in which the various kingdoms of the European mainland sought to gain political and strategic control. Eventually in 768, Charlemagne, King of the Franks, brought together much of Western Europe under what would become known as the Holy Roman Empire. Meanwhile, an alliance of Christian nations sent troops to reclaim the Holy Land from Islamic control in a series of campaigns known as the Crusades.

Renaissance & Reformation

Europe's troubles rumbled on into the 14th and 15th centuries. In the wake of further conflicts and political upheavals, as well as the devastating outbreak of the Black Death (estimated to have wiped out somewhere between a third and half of Europe's population), control over the Holy Roman Empire passed into the hands of the Austrian Habsburgs, a political dynasty that was to become one of the continent's

---

2500–500 BC

Ancient Greeks break new ground in technology, science, art and architecture.

1st century BC–4 AD

The Romans conquer much of Europe. The Roman Empire flourishes under Augustus and his successors.

410

The sacking of Rome by the Goths brings an end to Roman dominance.

The Best...
Ancient Ruins

1 Acropolis (p742), Greece

2 Colosseum (p394), Italy

3 Stonehenge (p104), England

4 Pompeii (p469), Italy

5 Alignements de Carnac (p230), France

dominant powers. Meanwhile, the Italian city-states of Genoa, Venice, Pisa and Amalfi consolidated their control over the Mediterranean, establishing trading links with much of the rest of Europe and the Far East, and embarking on some of the first journeys in search of the New World.

In the mid-15th century, a new age of artistic and philosophical development broke out across the continent. The Renaissance encouraged writers, artists and thinkers to challenge the accepted doctrines of theology, philosophy, architecture and art. The centre of this artistic tsunami was Florence, Italy, where such inspirational figures as Michelangelo and Leonardo da Vinci made great strides in art and architecture. Another epoch-changing development was under way in Germany, thanks to the invention of the printing press by Johannes Gutenburg in around 1440. The advent of 'movable type' made printed books available to the masses for the first time.

While the Renaissance challenged artistic ideas, the Reformation dealt with questions of religion. Challenging Catholic 'corruption' and the divine authority of the Pope, the German theologian Martin Luther established his own breakaway branch of the Church, to which he gave the name 'Protestantism', in 1517. Luther's stance was soon echoed by the English monarch Henry VIII, who cut ties with Rome in 1534 and went on to found his own (Protestant) Church of England, sowing the seeds for centuries of conflict between Catholics and Protestants.

The New World

The schisms of the Church weren't the only source of tension. The discovery of the 'New World' in the mid-16th century led to a colonial arms race between the major European nations, in which each country battled to lay claim to the newly discovered lands – often enslaving or killing the local populace in the process.

More trouble followed during the Thirty Years' War (1618–48), which began as a conflict between Catholics and Protestants and eventually sucked in most of Europe's principal powers. The war was ended by the Peace of Westphalia in 1648, and Europe entered a period of comparative stability.

1066
William the Conqueror defeats the English King Harold at the Battle of Hastings.

1340s
The Black Death reaches its peak in Europe, killing between 30% and 50% of Europe's population.

15th century
The Italian Renaissance brings about a revolution in art, architecture and science.

The Enlightenment

The Enlightenment (sometimes known as 'The Age of Reason') is the name given to a philosophical movement that spread throughout European society during the mid- to late-17th century. It emphasised the importance of logic, reason and science over the doctrines of religion. Key figures included the philosophers Baruch Spinoza, John Locke, Immanuel Kant and Voltaire, as well as scientists such as Isaac Newton.

The Enlightenment also questioned the political status quo. Since the Middle Ages, the majority of Europe's wealth and power had been concentrated in the hands of an all-powerful elite, largely made up of monarchs and aristocrats. This stood in direct contradiction to one of the core values of the Enlightenment – equality. Many thinkers believed it was an impasse that could only be solved by revolution.

Things came to a head in 1789 when armed mobs stormed the Bastille prison in Paris, thus kick-starting the French Revolution. The Revolution began with high ideals, inspired by its iconic slogan of *liberté, egalité, fraternité* (liberty, equality, brotherhood; a phrase that still graces French banknotes). Before long things turned sour and heads began to roll. Hardline republicans seized control and demanded retribution for centuries of oppression. Scores of aristocrats met their end under the guillotine's blade, including

Piazza Navona (p403), Rome

1517

Martin Luther nails his demands to the church door in Wittenburg, sparking the Reformation.
Martin Luther statue, Wittenburg

1789

France becomes a republic following the French Revolution. Thousands of aristocrats are executed by guillotine.

The Best...
Royal Palaces

1 Windsor Castle (p96), England

2 Château de Versailles (p218), France

3 Hofburg (p643), Austria

4 Palacio Real (p303), Madrid

5 Prague Castle (p701), Czech Republic

the French monarch Louis XVI and his wife Marie Antoinette, who were publicly executed in January 1793 in Paris' Place de la Concorde.

The Reign of Terror between September 1793 and July 1794 saw religious freedoms revoked, churches closed, cathedrals turned into 'Temples of Reason' and thousands beheaded. In the chaos, a dashing young Corsican general named Napoleon Bonaparte (1769–1821) seized his chance.

Napoleon assumed power in 1799 and in 1804 was crowned Emperor. He fought a series of campaigns across Europe and conquered vast swathes of territory for the French empire but, following a disastrous campaign to conquer Russia in 1812, his grip on power faltered and he was defeated by a coalition of British and Prussian forces at the Battle of Waterloo in 1815.

Industry, Empire & WWI

Having vanquished Napoleon, Britain emerged as Europe's predominant power. With such innovations as the steam engine, the railway and the factory, Britain unleashed the Industrial Revolution and, like many of Europe's major powers (including France, Spain, Belgium and the Austro-Hungarian empire), set about developing its colonies across much of Africa, Australasia and the Middle and Far East.

Before long these competing empires clashed again, with predictably catastrophic consequences. The assassination of the heir to the Austro-Hungarian Empire Franz Ferdinand in 1914 led to the outbreak of the Great War, or WWI, as it came to be known. By the end of hostilities in 1918, huge tracts of northern France and Belgium had been razed and over 16 million people across Europe had been killed.

In the Treaty of Versailles, the defeated powers of Austro-Hungary and Germany lost large areas of territory and found themselves crippled with a massive bill for reparations, sowing seeds of discontent that would be exploited a decade later by a young Austrian painter by the name of Adolf Hitler.

WWII

Hitler's rise to power was astonishingly swift. By 1936 he had become Chancellor and, as the head of the Nazi Party, assumed total control of Germany. Having spent much of the 1930s building up a formidable war machine, assisting General Franco's nationalist

18th & 19th centuries
The Industrial Revolution transforms European society.

1914
The assassination of Archduke Franz Ferdinand leads to the outbreak of WWI (1914–18).

1939–45
WWII rages across Europe, devastating many cities. After peace is declared, much of Eastern Europe falls under communist rule.

forces during the Spanish Civil War, Hitler annexed former German territories in Austria and parts of Czechoslovakia, before extending his reach onwards into Poland in 1939.

The occupation of Poland proved the final straw. Britain, France and its Commonwealth allies declared war on Germany, which had formed its own alliance of convenience with the Axis powers of Italy and Japan. Hitler unleashed his blitzkrieg on an unsuspecting Europe, and within a few short months had conquered huge areas of territory across Eastern and central Europe, forcing the French into submission and driving the British forces to a humiliating retreat at Dunkirk. Europe was to remain under Nazi occupation for the next four years.

The Axis retained the upper hand until the Japanese attack on Pearl Harbor forced a reluctant USA into the war in 1941. Hitler's subsequent decision to invade Russia in 1941 proved to be a catastrophic error, resulting in devastating German losses that opened the door for the Allied invasion of Normandy in June 1944.

After several months of bitter fighting, Hitler's remaining forces were pushed back towards Berlin. Hitler committed suicide on 30 April 1945 and the Russians took the city, crushing the last pockets of German resistance. By 8 May Germany and Italy had unconditionally surrendered to the Allied powers, bringing the war in Europe to an end.

Château de Versailles' Galerie des Glaces (p219), France

1957
The European Economic Community (EEC) is formed by a collection of Western European countries.

1989
The fall of the Berlin Wall heralds the downfall of oppressive regimes across much of Eastern Europe.

1993
The Maastricht Treaty leads to the formation of the EU.

The Best...
Historic Landmarks

1 Nelson's Column (p61), London

2 Place de la Bastille (p198), Paris

3 Berlin Wall (p564)

4 Alhambra (p372), Granada

5 D-Day Beaches (p224), France

The Iron Curtain

The cessation of hostilities was not the end of Europe's troubles. Differences of opinion between the Western powers and the communist Soviet Union soon led to a stand-off. The USSR closed off its assigned sectors, including East Berlin, East Germany and much of Eastern Europe, which heralded the descent of the Iron Curtain and the beginning of the Cold War. This period of political tension and social division in Europe lasted for 40 years.

The Cold War era came to an end in 1989, when popular unrest in Germany resulted in the fall of the Berlin Wall. Germany was reunified in 1990; a year later the USSR was dissolved. Shortly afterwards Romania, Bulgaria, Poland, Hungary and Albania had implemented multiparty democracy. In Czechoslovakia, the so-called Velvet Revolution brought about the downfall of the communist government through mass demonstrations and other nonviolent means.

Europe United

Elsewhere in Europe, the process of political and economic integration has continued apace since the end of WWII. The formation of the European Economic Community (EEC) in 1957 began as a loose trade alliance between six nations, but since its rebranding as the European Union (EU) at the Treaty of Maastricht in 1993 its core membership has expanded to 27 countries. Croatia is set to become the EU's 28th member sometime in 2013, while five other countries – Iceland, Macedonia, Montenegro, Serbia and Turkey – are slated for admission over the next few years. The 2009 Treaty of Lisbon also paved the way for the EU's first fixed-term president in 2009; it's a largely symbolic role at present. Another key development was the implementation of the Schengen Agreement in 1995, which abolished border checks and allowed EU citizens to travel freely throughout member states (with the notable exceptions of Britain and Ireland).

Even more momentous was the adoption of the single currency of the euro in 2000. To date, 17 countries have joined the Eurozone, while Britain, Norway, Denmark and Sweden have chosen to retain their national currencies. There seems little prospect of any of them being persuaded to join any time soon, but in future any new states joining the EU will be required to adopt the euro as a condition of entry. It's a hot topic, especially since the financial crash in countries including Greece and Spain, which has required richer nations (principally France and Germany) being called on to bail out several of their more indebted European neighbours.

2002
Twelve member states of the EU ditch their national currencies in favour of the euro.

2009–11
Europe is rocked by a series of financial crises, leading to costly bailouts for Ireland, Greece, Portugal and Spain.

Family Travel

Museo Guggenheim (p354), Spain

DOMINIC BONUCCELLI/GETTY IMAGES ©

Travelling with kids can be one long adventure or a nonstop nightmare. The key to fun and rewarding family travel is planning – organising your European trip together is not just an excellent way to avoid any unwelcome surprises on the road, it will also get everyone excited about the adventure ahead.

Travel

In general, Europe is an incredibly family-friendly place to travel, but distances can be long, so it's a good idea to break up the trip with things to see and do en route. Traffic is at its worst during holiday seasons, especially between June and August, and journey times are likely to be much longer during this period. Trains can be a great option for family travel – kids will have more space to move around, and you can pack books, puzzles and computer games to keep them entertained.

Children and young people qualify for cheap travel on most public transport in Europe (usually around 50% of the adult fare). Look out for railcards and passes that open up extra discounts – many cities offer passes that combine entry to sights and attractions with travel on public transport.

The Best...
Kids' Experiences

1 Disneyland Paris (p217)

2 Natural History Museum (p73), London

3 Park Güell (p345), Barcelona

4 Jungfraujoch (p688), Switzerland

5 Kinderdijk (p516), the Netherlands

Sights & Attractions

Most attractions offer discounted entry for children (generally for 12 years and under, although this varies). If you can, try to mix up educational activities with fun excursions they're guaranteed to enjoy – balance that visit to the Tate Modern or the Louvre with a trip to the London Aquarium or a day at Disneyland Paris, for example. The number one rule is to avoid packing too much in – you'll get tired, the kids will get irritable and tantrums are sure to follow. Plan carefully and you'll enjoy your time much more.

Hotels & Restaurants

It's always worth asking in advance whether hotels are happy to accept kids. Many are fully geared for family travel, with children's activities, child-minding services and the like, but others may impose a minimum age limit to deter guests with kids. Family-friendly hotels will usually be able to offer a large room with two or three beds to accommodate families, or at least neighbouring rooms with an adjoining door.

Dining out *en famille* is generally great fun, but again, it's always worth checking to see whether kids are welcome – generally the posher or more prestigious the establishment, the less kid-friendly they're likely to be. Many restaurants offer cheaper children's menus, usually based around simple staples such as steak, pasta, burgers and chicken. Most will also offer smaller portions of adult meals.

If your kids are fussy, buying your own ingredients at a local market can encourage them to experiment – they can choose their own food while simultaneously practising the local lingo.

Need to Know

- **Changing facilities** Found at most supermarkets and major attractions.
- **Cots and highchairs** Available in many restaurants and hotels, but ask ahead.
- **Health** Generally good, but pack your own first-aid kit to avoid language difficulties.
- **Kids' menus** Widely available.
- **Nappies (diapers)** Sold everywhere, including pharmacies and supermarkets.
- **Strollers** It's easiest to bring your own.
- **Transport** Children usually qualify for discounts; young kids often travel free.

Visual Arts

Galleria degli Uffizi (p447), Florence

JEAN-PIERRE LESCOURRET/GETTY IMAGES ©

If there were a global league table measuring artistic importance, Europe would surely take top prize. Many of the major art movements of the last millennium began in Europe, and you'll find some of the world's top artistic institutions dotted across the continent.

Ancient Art

Art was a crucial part of everyday life for ancient civilisations: decorative objects were a sign of status and prestige, while statues were used to venerate and honour the dead, and monuments and temples lavishly decorated in an attempt to appease the gods.

You'll find sculptures and artefacts from early civilisations in all Europe's top art museums, including the British Museum, the Louvre in Paris and the Acropolis Museum in Athens. Perhaps the most famous ancient artwork is the *Venus de Milo* at the Louvre, thought to have been created between 130 BC and 100 BC by the master sculptor Alexandros of Antioch.

Medieval Art

During the Middle Ages, the power of the Church and its importance as an artistic patron meant that the majority of medieval

The Best...
Modern Art Galleries

1 Tate Modern (p67), London

2 Museu Picasso (p337), Barcelona

3 Museo Guggenheim (p354), Bilbao

4 Louvre-Lens (p236), France

5 SMAK (p535), Ghent

art dealt with religious subjects. The Old Testament, the crucifixion, the apostles and the Last Judgment were common topics. Some of the finest medieval artworks are actually woven into the fabric of Europe's churches in the form of frescos painted onto panels or walls.

Flemish and German painting produced several important figures during the period, including Jan van Eyck (c1390–1441) and Hans Memling (c1430–94), known for their lifelike oils, and Hieronymus Bosch (1450–1516), known for his use of fantastic imagery and allegorical concepts.

The Renaissance

The Renaissance marked Europe's golden age of art. Artists such as Leonardo da Vinci (1452–1519), Michelangelo (1475–1564), Raphael (1483–1520), Titian (1487–1576) and Botticelli (1445–1510) introduced new techniques, colours and forms into the artistic lexicon, drawing inspiration from the sculptors and artists of the classical world.

Landscape and the human form gained increasing importance during the Renaissance. Michelangelo's masterpiece, *David,* is often cited as the perfect representation of the human figure (despite the fact that the artist deliberately distorted its proportions to make it more pleasing to the eye). The sculpture is now displayed at the Galleria dell'Accademia in Florence.

In the wake of the Renaissance came the great names of the baroque period, epitomised by the Italian artist Caravaggio (1573–1610) and the Dutch artists Rembrandt (1606–99), Rubens (1577–1640) and Johannes Vermeer (1632–75). The baroque artists employed light and shadow *(chiaroscuro)* to heighten the drama of a scene and give their work a photographic intensity.

Romanticism & Impressionism

During the 18th century, Romantic artists such as Caspar David Friedrich (1774–1840) and JMW Turner (1775–1851) explored the drama of the natural landscape – cloud-capped mountains, lonely hilltops, peaceful meadows and moody sunsets. Other artists, such as Théodore Géricault (1791–1824) and Eugène Délacroix (1798–1863), drew inspiration from French history and prominent people of the day. One of Spain's most important artists, Francisco Goya (1746–1828), covered everything from royal portraits to war scenes, bullfight etchings and tapestry designs.

During the late 19th century, artists such as Claude Monet (1840–1926), Edgar Degas (1834–1917), Camille Pissarro (1830–1903), Edouard Manet (1832–83) and Pierre-Auguste Renoir (1841–1919) aimed to capture the general 'impression' of a scene rather than its naturalistic representation (hence the name of their movement, 'Impressionism').

Their bold experiments with light, colour and form segued into that of their successors, the post-Impressionists such as Paul Cézanne (1839–1906), Vincent van Gogh (1853–90) and Paul Gauguin (1848–1903).

From Fauvism to Conceptual Art

The upheavals of the 20th century inspired many new artistic movements. The fauvists were fascinated by colour, typified by Henri Matisse (1869–1954), while the cubists, such as Georges Braque (1882–1963) and Pablo Picasso (1881–1973), broke their work down into abstract forms, taking inspiration from everything from primitive art to psychoanalysis.

The dadaists and surrealists took these ideas to their illogical extreme, exploring dreams and the subconscious: key figures include Réné Magritte (1898–1967) from Belgium, Max Ernst (1891–1976) from Germany, and Joan Miró (1893–1983) and Salvador Dalí (1904–89) from Spain.

After 1945 abstract art became a mainstay of the West German scene, with key figures such as Joseph Beuys, Monica Bonvicini and Anselm Kiefer enjoying worldwide reputations. After reunification, the New Leipzig School achieved success at home and abroad with figurative painters such as Neo Rauch generating much acclaim.

The late 20th century has introduced many more artistic movements: abstract expressionism, neoplasticism, minimalism, formalism and pop art, to name a few. One of the most controversial movements has been conceptual art, which stresses the importance of the idea behind a work rather than its aesthetic value. Britain has a particularly vibrant conceptual art scene: key names such as Tracy Emin, the Chapman Brothers, Rachel Whiteread, Mark Wallinger and Damien Hirst (famous for his pickled sharks and diamond-encrusted skulls) continue to provoke controversy.

Several exciting new modern art museums have also opened across Europe in recent decades. Particularly noteworthy are the Tate Modern in London, installed in a former power station beside the Thames, and the Louvre-Lens and Centre Pompidou-Metz in France, both offshoots of landmark Parisian museums.

The Best...
National Art Museums

1 National Gallery (p61), London

2 Musée du Louvre (p194), Paris

3 Galleria degli Uffizi (p447), Florence

4 Rijksmuseum (p496), Amsterdam

5 Museo del Prado (p302), Madrid

IN FOCUS VISUAL ARTS

Architecture

Erechtheion, the Acropolis (p743), Athens

DENNIS K. JOHNSON/GETTY IMAGES ©

With an architectural heritage stretching back seven millennia, Europe is one long textbook for building buffs. From Greek temples to venerable mosques and modern skyscrapers, this fascinating and complex architectural environment is bound to be one of the main highlights of your visit.

The Ancient World

Europe's oldest examples of architecture are the many hundreds of stone circles, henges, barrows, burial chambers and alignments built by Neolithic people between 4500 BC and 1500 BC. The most impressive examples of these ancient structures are at Brú Na Bóinne in Ireland, Carnac in Brittany and, of course, Stonehenge in the southwest of England.

No one is quite sure what the purpose of these structures was, although theories abound. Some say they could be celestial calendars, burial monuments or tribal meeting places, although it's generally agreed these days that they served some sort of religious function.

Greek & Roman Architecture

Several ancient cultures have left their mark around the shores of the Mediterranean, including the Minoans (in Crete), the Etruscans (in present-day Tuscany), the Mycenaeans (in the northeast Peloponnese) and, of course, the ancient Greeks and Romans. Athens is the best place to appreciate Greece's golden age: the dramatic monuments of the Acropolis illustrate the ancient Greeks' sophisticated understanding of geometry, shape and form, and set the blueprint for many of the architectural principles that have endured to the present day.

The Romans were even more ambitious, and built a host of monumental structures designed to project the might and majesty of the Roman Empire. Roman architecture was driven by a combination of form and function – structures such as the Pont du Gard in southern France show how the Romans valued architecture that looked beautiful but also served a practical purpose. Rome has the greatest concentration of architectural treasures, including the famous Colosseum, but remains of Roman buildings are scattered all over the continent.

The Best...
Gothic Landmarks

1 Cathédrale de Notre Dame (p190), Paris

2 Chartres Cathedral (p216), France

3 Cologne Cathedral (p616), Germany

4 Canterbury Cathedral (p97), Britain

5 St Vitus Cathedral (p696), Prague

IN FOCUS ARCHITECTURE

Romanesque & Gothic Architecture

The solidity and elegance of ancient Roman architecture echoed through the 10th and 11th centuries in buildings constructed during the Romanesque period. Many of Europe's earliest churches are classic examples of Romanesque construction, using rounded arches, vaulted roofs, and massive columns and walls.

Even more influential was the development of Gothic architecture, which gave rise to many of Europe's most spectacular cathedrals. Tell-tale characteristics include the use of pointed arches, ribbed vaulting, great showpiece windows and flying buttresses. The famous cathedrals situated in Chartres, Cologne, Reims and Notre-Dame in Paris are ideal places to see Gothic architecture in action.

Renaissance & Baroque Architecture

The Renaissance led to a huge range of architectural experiments. Pioneering Italian architects such as Brunelleschi, Michelangelo and Palladio shifted the emphasis away from Gothic austerity towards a more human approach. They combined elements of classical architecture with new building materials, and specially commissioned sculptures and decorative artworks. Florence and Venice are particularly rich in Renaissance buildings, but the movement's influence can be felt right across Europe – the showy chateaux in France's Loire Valley, for example, bear many hallmarks of the Renaissance movement.

Architectural showiness reached its zenith during the baroque period, when architects pulled out all the stops to show off the wealth and prestige of their clients. Baroque buildings are all about creating drama, and architects often employed swathes of craftsmen and used the most expensive materials available to create the desired effect.

The Best...
Modern Buildings

1 Museo Guggenheim (p354), Bilbao

2 The Shard (p72), London

3 Louvre-Lens (p236), near Lens

4 Reichstag Dome (p563), Berlin

5 Eden Project (p109), Cornwall

The lavish country estate of Castle Howard in northern England, Paris' Hôtel des Invalides and practically all of Salzburg's buildings showcase the ostentation and expense that underpinned baroque architecture.

The Industrial Age

The 19th century was the great age of urban planning, when the chaotic streets and squalid slums of many of Europe's cities were swept away in favour of grand squares and ruler-straight boulevards. This was partly driven by an attempt to clean up the urban environment, but it also allowed architects to redesign the urban landscape to suit the industrial age, merging factories, public buildings, museums and residential suburbs into a seamless whole. One of the most obvious examples of urban remodelling was Baron Haussmann's reinvention of Paris during the late 19th century, which resulted in the construction of the city's great boulevards and many of its landmark buildings.

Nineteenth-century architects began to move away from the showiness of the baroque and rococo periods in favour of new materials such as brick, iron and glass. Neo-Gothic architecture was designed to emphasise permanence, solidity and power, reflecting the confidence of the industrial age. It was an era that gave rise to many of Europe's great public buildings, including many landmark museums, libraries, city halls and train stations.

The 20th Century

By the turn of the 20th century, the worlds of art and architecture had both begun to experiment with new approaches to shape and form. The flowing shapes and natural forms of art nouveau had a profound influence on the work of Charles Rennie Mackintosh in Glasgow, the Belgian architect Victor Horta and the Modernista buildings of Antonio Gaudí. Meanwhile, other architects stripped their buildings back to the bare essentials, emphasising strict function over form: Le Corbusier, Ludwig Mies van der Rohe and Walter Gropius are among the most influential figures of the period.

Functional architecture continued to dominate much of mid-20th-century architecture, especially in the rush to reconstruct Europe's shattered cities in the wake of two world wars, although the 'concrete box' style of architecture has largely fallen out of fashion over recent decades. Europeans may have something of a love-hate relationship with modern architecture, but the best buildings eventually find their place – a good example is the inside-out Centre Pompidou in Paris, which initially drew howls of protest but is now considered one of the icons of 20th-century architecture.

More recently, the fashion for sky-high skyscrapers seems to have caught on in several European cities, especially London, where a rash of multistorey buildings is currently under construction, all with their own nickname (the Walkie Talkie, the Cheesegrater and so on). Topping them all is The Shard, which became Europe's highest building at 309.6m when it was completed in 2013 (although if you count Russia as part of Europe, it's already been beaten by Moscow's Mercury City tower at 339m).

Regardless of whether you approve of the more recent additions to Europe's architectural landscape, one thing's for sure – you won't find them boring.

Food & Drink

Spaghetti alla Vongole, Italy

LONELY PLANET/GETTY IMAGES ©

If there's one thing that unites Europe, it's a passion for food. Every country has its own unique flavours, from rich French cheeses and spicy German wurst to Italian pasta, Spanish tapas and Swiss fondues. The ingredients might not always be familiar, but you won't know till you try – so open your mind, swallow your preconceptions and tuck in. Bon appétit!

Britain & Ireland

Britain might not have a distinctive cuisine, but it does have a thriving food culture, with a host of celebrity chefs and big-name restaurants. Britain's colonial legacy has also left it with a taste for curry – a recent poll suggested the nation's favourite food was chicken tikka masala.

Traditional Dishes

The Brits love a good roast, traditionally eaten on a Sunday and accompanied by roast potatoes, vegetables and gravy. The classic is roast beef with Yorkshire pudding (a crisp batter puff), but lamb, pork and chicken are equally popular. 'Bangers and mash' (sausages and mashed potato) and fish and chips (battered cod served with thick-cut fried potatoes) are also old favourites.

Specialities in Scotland include haggis served with 'tatties and neeps' (potato and turnip). Traditional Welsh dishes include *cawl* (broth, usually with lamb and leeks) and *bara lafwr* (savoury scones made with oatmeal and seaweed).

Ireland's traditional dishes reflect the country's rustic past: look out for colcannon (mashed potato with cabbage), coddle (sliced sausages with bacon, potato and onion) and boxty (potato pancake), plus classic Irish stew (usually made with lamb or mutton).

Cheese

Britain's favourite cheese is cheddar – a matured hard cheese with a pungent flavour – but there are many others, including Wensleydale, Red Leicester and Stilton.

Drinks

The traditional British brew is ale, served warm and flat in order to bring out the hoppy flavours. It's an acquired taste, especially if you're used to cold, fizzy lagers.

Ireland's trademark ale is stout – usually Guinness, although in Cork stout can mean a Murphy's or a Beamish, too.

Scotland and Ireland are both known for whisky-making, with many distilleries open for tours and tasting sessions. Note that in Scotland it's always spelled whisky; it's only in Ireland that you add the 'e'.

France

Each French region has its distinctive dishes. Broadly, the hot south favours dishes based around olive oil, garlic and tomatoes, while the cooler north tends towards root vegetables, earthy flavours and creamy or buttery sauces. The French are famously unfussy about which bits of the animal they eat – kidney, liver, cheek and tongue are as much of a delicacy as a fillet steak or a prime rib.

Traditional Dishes

Bouillabaisse is the signature southern dish; it's a saffron-scented fish stew that's best eaten in Marseille. *Soupe de poissons* (fish soup) is thinner and served with spicy rouille sauce, gruyère cheese and croutons.

A European Breakfast

Frühstuck, desayuno, petit déjeuner – every country has its own take on breakfast.

In Britain and Ireland, the classic cooked breakfast ('fry-up') consists of eggs, bacon, sausages, mushroom, black pudding (blood sausage), fried bread, beans and tomatoes.

The Mediterranean approach is lighter. Spaniards usually start the day with coffee and a *tostada* (piece of toast) or *pastel/bollo* (pastry), while the French opt for coffee and a baguette with jam, a croissant or a *pain au chocolat*. Italians prefer a cappuccino and *cornetto* (Italian croissant) at a cafe.

The biggest breakfasts are served in Germany, Austria and Switzerland, where you could survive for the entire day purely on what's served up on the breakfast table – breads, cakes, pastries, cold meats, cheeses, cereals and fruit. *Gut essen* indeed!

The Alps are the place to try fondue, hunks of toasted bread dipped into cheese sauces. Brittany and Normandy are big on seafood, especially mussels and oysters. Lyon's small local restaurants *(bouchons)* are renowned for their piggy dishes, particularly *andouillette,* a sausage made from pig intestines.

Central France prides itself on its hearty cuisine, including *foie gras* (goose liver), *boeuf bourgignon* (beef cooked in red wine), *confit de canard* (duck cooked in preserved fat) and *truffes* (black truffles).

Cheese

Charles de Gaulle's famous quip that it was impossible to 'govern a country which has two hundred and forty-six varieties of cheese' speaks volumes about how much the French love their *fromages*. The big names are camembert, brie, Livarot, Pont l'Évêque and Époisses (all soft cheeses); Roquefort and Bleu d'Auvergne (blue cheeses); and Comté, cantal and gruyère (hard cheeses).

Drinks

France is Europe's biggest wine producer. The principal regions are Alsace, Bordeaux, Burgundy, Languedoc, the Loire and the Rhône, all of which produce reds, whites and rosés. Then, of course, there's Champagne – home to the world's favourite bubbly, aged in centuries-old cellars beneath Reims and Épernay.

The Best...
Foodie Experiences

1 Tucking into a Sunday roast in a British pub (p86)

2 Trying French cheeses in a Parisian food market (p209)

3 Choosing tapas on Madrid's Calle de Cava Baja (p314)

4 Eating crispy pizza in a real Roman pizzeria (p413)

5 Indulging in coffee and cake in a Vienna cafe (p647)

IN FOCUS FOOD & DRINK

Italy

Italian cuisine is dominated by the twin staples of pizza and pasta, which have been eaten in Italy since Roman times. A full meal comprises an antipasto (starter), *primo* (pasta or rice dish), *secondo* (usually meat or fish), *contorno* (vegetable side dish or salad), *dolce* (dessert) and coffee. When eating out it's OK to mix and match any combination.

Traditional Dishes

Italian pasta comes in numerous shapes, from bow-shaped *farfalle* to twisty *fusilli,* ribbed *rigatoni* and long *pappardelle*. Italian pasta is made with durum flour, which gives it a distinctive *al dente* bite; the type of pasta used is usually dictated by the type of dish being served (ribbed or shaped pastas hold sauce better, for example).

Italian pizza comes in two varieties: the Roman pizza with a thin crispy base, and the Neapolitan pizza, which has a higher, doughier base. The best are always prepared in a *forno a legna* (wood-fired oven). Flavours are generally kept simple – the best pizza restaurants often serve only a couple of toppings, such as *margherita* (tomato and mozzarella) and *marinara* (tomato, garlic and oregano).

Cheese

Like the French, the Italians pride themselves on their cheeses, especially prestigious varieties such as Parmesan, ricotta and mozzarella.

803

Drinks

Italy's wines run the gamut from big-bodied reds such as Piedmont's Barolo, to light white wines from Sardinia and sparkling *prosecco* from the Veneto.

The Netherlands & Belgium

Traditional Dishes

The Netherlands' colonial legacy has given the Dutch a taste for Indonesian and Surinamese-inspired meals like *rijsttafel* (rice table): an array of spicy dishes such as braised beef, pork satay and ribs, all served with white rice.

Other Dutch dishes to look out for are *erwertensoep* (pea soup with onions, carrots, sausage and bacon), *krokotten* (filled dough balls that are crumbed and deep-fried) and, of course, *friet* (fries), which the Dutch like to claim they invented. Here they're thin, crispy and eaten with mayonnaise rather than ketchup (tomato sauce).

The iconic Belgian dish is *mosselen moules* – a steaming cauldron of shell-on mussels, typically accompanied by *frites* (fries) and cold beer. Other dishes include *balekkes/bouletten* (meatballs), *vlaamse stoverij/carbonade flamande* (beer-based beef casserole) and *waterzooi* (creamy chicken or fish stew), often accompanied by *stoemp* (veg-and-potato mash).

Cheese

The Dutch are keen on cheese: the best known varieties are edam and gouda, sometimes served as bar snacks with mustard.

Drinks

Beer is the tipple of choice. Small Dutch brewers like Gulpen, Haarlem's Jopen, Bavaria, Drie Ringen, Leeuw and Utrecht are all excellent. You'll find an even bigger choice

Sweet Treats

From pralines to puddings, Europe specialises in foods that are sweet, sticky and sinful. Germans and Austrians have a particularly sweet tooth – treats include *Salzburger nockerl* (a fluffy soufflé) and *Schwarzwälder kirschtorte* (Black Forest cherry cake), plus many types of *apfeltasche* (apple pastry) and *strudel* (filled filo pastry). The Brits are another big cake-eating nation – a slice of cake or a dunked biscuit is an essential teatime ritual.

The Italians are famous for their *gelaterie* (ice-cream stalls; the best will be labelled *produzione propria,* indicating that it's handmade on the premises). Most Greek desserts are variations on pastry soaked in honey, such as *baklava* (thin layers of pastry filled with honey and nuts).

But it's the French who have really turned dessert into a fine art. Stroll past the window of any *boulangerie* (bakery) or patisserie and you'll be assaulted by temptations, from creamy *éclairs* (filled choux buns) and crunchy *macarons* (macaroons) to fluffy *madeleines* (shell-shaped sponge cakes) and wicked *gâteaux* (cakes).

Go on – you know you want to.

in Belgium: look out for dark Trappist beers, golden beers such as Duuvel and the champagne-style lambic beers brewed around Brussels.

Jenever is a spirit commonly drunk in the Netherlands.

Spain

Spain's cuisine is typical of the flavours of Mediterranean cooking, making extensive use of herbs, tomatoes, onions, garlic, spices and lashings of olive oil.

Traditional Dishes

The nation's signature dish is *paella,* consisting of rice, seafood and sometimes chicken or meat, simmered with saffron in a large pan. Valencia is considered the spiritual home of *paella*.

Spain also prides itself on its ham (especially *jamón serrano,* a cured ham similar to Italian Parma ham) and spicy sausages (including *chorizo, lomo* and *salchichón*). These are often used in making the bite-size Spanish dishes known as tapas (or *pintxos* in the Basque region). Tapas is usually a snack, but it can also be a main meal – three or four dishes is generally enough for one person.

Cheese

Spain has fewer world-famous cheeses than its neighbours in France and Italy, but there are still plenty worth trying. *Manchego* is perhaps the best known, a semi-hard sheep's cheese with a buttery flavour, often used in tapas.

Drinks

Spain boasts the largest area (1.2 million hectares) of wine cultivation in the world. La Rioja and Ribera del Duero are the principal wine-growing regions.

Cakes in a patisserie, Paris, France
PHOTOGRAPHER: JODIE WALLIS/GETTY IMAGES ©

Greece

Greece is known for its seafood. As with its Mediterranean neighbours, garlic, tomatoes and olives (either whole or as olive oil) feature heavily.

Traditional Dishes

The Greek form of tapas is *mezedhes:* common dishes include grilled octopus, kalamata olives, meatballs, fried sausages and fava beans, served with dips such as hummus (chickpeas), taramasalata (cod roe) and tzatziki (yoghurt, garlic and cucumber).

In Greece, large kebabs are known as *gyros,* while *souvlaki* is made from small cubes of meat cooked on a skewer; both are served in pitta bread with salad and sauces. Falafel (chickpea balls) are another much-loved Greek snack.

Cheese

Greece's main cheese is feta. Its strong, salty flavour is a key ingredient in many dishes and salads. *Halloumi* is a chewy cheese that is often cooked.

Drinks

The potent aniseed-flavoured spirit of ouzo is traditionally mixed with water and ice (turning it a cloudy white). Similar traditions exist in the south of France (where *pastis* is the tipple) and Spain *(grappa)*.

Germany, Austria and Switzerland

The Germanic nations are all about big flavours and big portions. *Wurst* (sausage) comes in hundreds of forms, and is often served with *sauerkraut* (fermented cabbage).

Traditional Dishes

The most common types of *wurst* include *bratwurst* (spiced sausage), *weissewurst* (veal sausage), *blutwurst* (blood sausage) and many forms of schnitzel (breaded pork or veal cutlet, the key ingredient in Austria's signature dish, *Wiener schnitzel*).

Other popular mains include *Rippenspeer* (spare ribs), *Rotwurst* (black pudding), *Rostbrätl* (grilled meat) and *Putenbrust* (turkey breast). Potatoes are served as *Bratkartoffeln* (fried), *Kartoffelpüree* (mashed), Swiss-style *rösti* (grated then fried) or *Pommes Frites* (French fries).

The Swiss are known for their love of fondue and the similar dish of *raclette* (melted cheese with potatoes).

Cheese

Gouda, Emmental and gruyère are the best-known Swiss cheeses, while the Germans are known for their hard cheeses – especially *Allgäu Emmentaler* and *Bergkäse* (mountain cheese).

Drinks

Beer is the national beverage. *Pils* is the crisp pilsner Germany is famous for, often slightly bitter. *Alt* is darker and more full bodied. *Weizenbier* is made with wheat

The Art of the Sandwich

There's no such thing as a simple sandwich in Europe. In the UK, a sandwich is usually made with two square slices of bread; across the Channel in France and Belgium, they make their sandwiches using a long baton-shaped baguette.

The Italians favour the *panini*, a pocket-shaped bread served piping hot. The pitta, a flat bread served widely in Greece, is a close relation.

Vegetarians & Vegans

Vegetarians will have a tough time in many areas of Europe – meat eating is still the norm, and fish is often seen as a vegetarian option. However, you'll usually find something meat-free on most menus, though don't expect much choice. Vegans will have an even tougher time – cheese, cream and milk are an integral ingredient in most European cuisines.

Vegetable-based *antipasti* (starters), tapas, meze, pastas, side dishes and salads are good ways of providing a meat-free meal. Shopping for yourself in markets is a good way of trying local flavours without having to compromise your principles.

instead of barley malt and served in a tall, 500mL glass. *Helles bier* is light beer, while *Dunkles bier* is dark.

Germany is principally known for white wines – inexpensive, light and intensely fruity. The Rhine and Moselle Valleys are the largest wine-growing regions.

Czech Republic

Traditional Dishes

Like many nations in Eastern Europe, Czech cuisine revolves around meat, potatoes and root vegetables, dished up in stews, goulashes and casseroles. *Pečená kachna* (roast duck) is the quintessential Czech restaurant dish, while *klobása* (sausage) is a common beer snack. A common side dish is *knedliky,* boiled dumplings made from wheat or potato flour.

Cheese

The Czechs are not renowned for their cheese, though you'll probably try *nakládaný hermelín,* a soft cheese covered in a white rind, at least once.

Drinks

The Czechs have a big beer culture, with some of Europe's best *pivo* (beer), usually lager style. The Moravian region is the up-and-coming area for Czech wines.

Sports & Activities

Glacier hiking, Jungfrau (p688), Switzerland

BRUCE YUANYUE BI/GETTY IMAGES ©

With decades of sporting prowess under its belt and a landscape taking in everything from snow-flecked mountains to sapphire seas, Europe offers endless ways to get active. Hardcore hikers, cyclists, diving devotees and adrenaline junkies will all find plenty to keep them occupied. And if you really want to get under a nation's skin, you could do a lot worse than head for the nearest football ground...

Football

Football (*not* soccer, please) is Europe's number-one spectator sport, and tantamount to a religion in many corners of the continent. Europe's big nations battle it out every four years in the knockout European Championships. The most recent winner was Spain, which beat France 4-0 in the 2012 finals in Poland – and became the first nation to win three major international cups in succession (following their triumphs at Euro 2008 and the World Cup in 2010). The next championships will be held in France in 2016, when the competition will be expanded from 16 to 24 teams.

Each country has it own top-flight domestic league (the Premier League in Britain, the Bundesliga in Germany, Serie A in Italy, La Liga in Spain, and so on) plus several lower divisions. The top teams from each league battle it out in the Champions

League in a bid to be crowned European champions, while lower-placed teams contest the UEFA Europa League. The football season varies from country to country, but it generally runs from sometime in August or September to anytime between May and July. Tickets for top sides such as Manchester United, Chelsea, Barcelona, Real Madrid, Bayern Munich, Juventus and Inter Milan are seriously expensive (if you can get hold of one) – if you're desperate to catch a match you'll have more luck seeing one of the lesser-ranked sides.

Cycling

Europe's hills and mountains don't seem to put people off getting into the saddle. Cycling is very popular in many areas of Europe, especially France, Italy and Austria: these countries have collectively produced some of the finest competitive cyclists the world has seen. Avid cyclists and fans stay glued to their TVs or turn out to cheer along the roadside during the annual Tour de France, a gruelling long-distance road race that's been held (nearly) every year since 1903. In 2012, Bradley Wiggins became the first British cyclist to win the Tour de France.

Road bikes tend to be the most popular form of cycling in Europe, although mountain bikes are catching up fast, especially in mountainous areas such as the Alps, the Pyrenees and the Dolomites. For a more sedate pace (and a lot fewer hills), Belgium, the Netherlands and Luxembourg are all fantastic countries to explore in the saddle, with large areas of flat, rolling countryside and a welcoming, bike-friendly attitude.

The Best...
Places to Explore by Bicycle

1 Kinderdijk (p516), the Netherlands

2 Flanders (p530), Belgium

3 The Loire Valley (p237), France

4 Tuscany (p446), Italy

5 The Lake District (p132), England

IN FOCUS SPORTS & ACTIVITIES

Hiking

Keen hikers can spend a lifetime exploring Western Europe's many exciting trails. Probably the most spectacular are to be found in the Alps and the Italian Dolomites, which are crisscrossed with well-marked trails; food and accommodation are available along the way in season. The equally sensational Pyrenees are less developed, which can add to the experience as you'll often rely on remote mountain villages for rest and sustenance. Hiking areas that are less well known, but still stunning, are Corsica and Sardinia. The Picos de Europa range in Spain is also rewarding, while the Lake District, the Yorkshire Dales and the Scottish Highlands are among the UK's top hiking spots.

The best months for hiking are generally June to September, although the weather can be unpredictable at any time of year. Be prepared: check the weather forecast before you head out and wear appropriate clothing, especially if you're planning on hiking through remote areas – if you get into trouble, help can be a long way away.

Most countries in Europe have a network of national parks that are ideal for hiking. Guided hikes are often available for those who aren't sure about their physical abilities or simply don't know what to look for. Local tourist offices can provide all the info you need.

For really hardcore hikers, Europe has several long-distance paths covering various countries, mostly making use of existing GR (grande randonnée) trails.

Skiing & Snowboarding

Winter sports are a way of life for residents of many European nations. The Austrians, Swiss, Germans and French are particularly snow-mad – between them they have produced many of the great names in skiing and snowboarding over the last century.

If you fancy taking to the pistes, you'll find hundreds of resorts in the Alps and Pyrenees for downhill skiing and snowboarding. Cross-country skiing is very popular in some areas, especially the Jura Mountains. Many resorts also offer other snowbound activities such as luging, bobsleighing and ice-climbing.

A skiing holiday can be expensive once you've added up the costs of ski lifts, accommodation and the inevitable après-ski sessions. Equipment hire, on the other hand, can be relatively cheap, and the hassle of bringing your own skis may not be worth it.

The ski season generally lasts from early December to late March, though at higher altitudes it may extend an extra month either side. Snow conditions can vary greatly from one year to the next and from region to region, but January and February tend to be the best (and busiest) months.

Ski resorts in the French and Swiss Alps offer great skiing and facilities, but are also by far the most expensive. Expect high prices in the German Alps, too, though Germany has some cheaper options available in the Black Forest and Harz Mountains. Austria is generally better value than France and Switzerland, especially in Carinthia. Prices in the Italian Alps are similar to those in Austria (although there are some upmarket exceptions), and can be relatively cheap given the right package.

Possibly the cheapest skiing in Western Europe is to be found in the Pyrenees in Spain and Andorra, and in the Sierra Nevada range in the south of Spain.

Water Sports

With the Mediterranean, the Atlantic, the Adriatic and the English Channel right on the doorstep, you won't be surprised to discover that messing about on the water is a popular European pastime.

Long-Distance Walking Trails

- **Camino de Santiago** (St James' Way; www.santiago-compostela.net) Spain's best-known long-distance trail traces the old pilgrimage route to Santiago de Compostela.
- **Grand Italian Trail** Hiking trail that cuts 6166km across Italy.
- **Haute Randonnée Pyrénéenne** High-altitude hiking through the Pyrenees.
- **South West Coast Path** (www.swcp.org.uk) Most of Britain's stunning southwest coastline is accessible via this 630km trail.
- **Via Alpina** (www.via-alpina.org) Network of five long-distance routes across the alpine regions of Slovenia, Austria, Germany, Liechtenstein, Switzerland, Italy, France and Monaco.
- **West Highland Way** (www.west-highland-way.co.uk) Classic route through southern Scotland.

Diving

It's not tropical, but that doesn't mean Europe isn't a great place to dive. Topaz waters and a spiky, volcanic geology make for spectacular diving all along the Mediterranean coast, while the clear waters and varied underwater life of the Adriatic have led to a flourishing dive industry, especially in Croatia. Wreck-diving is a particular highlight – Europe's long maritime history, as well as its war-torn past, mean the coastline is littered with underwater vessels. The many islands of the Mediterranean offer some of Europe's finest diving – Sicily's Aeolian Islands, Sardinia, Corsica and the Greek Islands all provide fantastic opportunities for underwater exploring.

If you're a novice diver, diving schools offering introductory dives and longer courses are available in many areas; make sure they're accredited by PADI or one of the equivalent organisations. If you're an experienced diver, remember to bring your accreditation certificates and any other relevant paperwork if you're planning on renting equipment or undertaking more complex dives.

The Best...
Ski Resorts

1 Chamonix (p249), France

2 Zermatt (p680), Switzerland

3 Innsbruck and Tirol (p666), Austria

4 The Dolomites (p445), Italy

IN FOCUS SPORTS & ACTIVITIES

Boating, Canoeing & Kayaking

Europe's lakes, rivers and diverse coastlines offer a variety of boating options unmatched anywhere in the world. You can kayak in Switzerland, row on a peaceful Alpine lake, join a Danube River cruise from Amsterdam to Vienna, rent a sailing boat on the Côte d'Azur or putter along the extraordinary canal networks of Britain, Ireland or France – the possibilities are endless.

Surfing & Windsurfing

The best surfing in Europe is on the Atlantic coastline. Top spots include the Atlantic Coast in France (especially around Biarritz), the west coasts of Wales, Ireland, Scotland and southwest England, and Spain's Basque Country (San Sebastián, Zarautz and Mundaka).

Windsurfing is less dependent on geography, so you'll be able to catch a break anywhere there's some wind and open water. With its long beaches and ceaseless wind, Tarifa, near Cádiz in Spain, is considered to be Europe's windsurfing capital, but you'll find windsurfing spots all over the Med and the Adriatic.

Sailing

Sailing is a brilliant way to see Europe's coastline. Sailing between the Mediterranean's coast and islands is hugely popular, especially in Greece. Sailing courses are widely available, although renting your own boat can be an expensive option, so you may need a few seagoing friends to make the expense worthwhile.

European Landscapes

Upper Grindelwald Glacier, Switzerland

Upper Grindelwald Glacier, Switzerland

DAVID C TOMLINSON/GETTY IMAGES

One of the great pleasures of travelling in Europe is the sheer diversity of its landscapes. A single day's journey can carry you from the glittering beaches of the Mediterranean to the icy glaciers of the Alps, from snow-capped mountains and rolling hills to patchwork fields and azure seas. Europe is a place where it's simply impossible not to feel inspired by the scenery.

Mountains

In terms of sheer scale, there's one mountain range in Europe that's impossible to ignore, and that's the Alps. This jagged chain of peaks covers over 1200km between Nice and Vienna, straddling the borders of France, Italy, Germany, Austria and Switzerland en route. With a total area of almost 192,000 sq km, the Alps are not just Europe's largest mountain range, they're one of the largest mountain systems on earth. They're also home to Europe's highest peak, moody Mont Blanc (4810m), which looms above the France–Italy border and remains snow-capped most of the year.

While the Alps might look like an untouched wilderness, they're actually not as pristine as they appear. In contrast to many mountain ranges in North America, for example, heavy industry and urban development are permitted in many areas of the Alps (albeit under strict controls). Tourism is also seriously big business, with several hundred ski resorts now dotted across the Alpine peaks, collectively clocking up over 201 million skier days every year.

Many areas have been protected from development by being designated national parks. Among the largest areas are the Parc Nacional de la Vanois and the Parc Nacional des Écrins in France, the Swiss National Park in Switzerland and Parco Nazionale del Gran Paradiso in Italy. Here you'll still be able to spot some of Europe's rarest wildlife, including ibexes, wolves, brown bears, lynxes, golden eagles, chamois and mouflons (a curly horned wild sheep).

To the east of the Alps lies one of Europe's other great mountain ranges, the Carpathians, which sprawl for 1500km across much of the Czech Republic and Eastern Europe. Slightly smaller in stature but no less spectacular are the Pyrenees, which stretch for just over 490km across the France–Spain border; the 300km-long Cantabria Mountains of northern Spain; and the various mountain ranges of Scotland, including the Grampians, Cairngorms and Highlands.

Coastlines & Beaches

Since Europe is surrounded on three sides by the sea, it's hardly surprising that the continent is home to some spectacular coastlines.

The Mediterranean draws the majority of visitors, thanks to its sparkling beaches and balmy summer temperatures. Spain, France, Greece and Italy all offer glorious stretches of coastline, but each area has a markedly different character: while package holidaymakers flock to the high-rise hotels sprawling along Spain's Costa Brava, for example, Italy's Amalfi Coast and the French Riviera are dotted with the kind of pretty coastal villages and picturesque harbours that hardly seem to have changed in the last hundred years.

Out to the west, Europe's Atlantic coast receives fewer visitors than the Med, mainly due to its chillier sea temperatures and less reliable weather. But while it might not always be the place for lounging around on the beach, the Atlantic swells are a boon for surfers: the west coasts of Spain, France, Ireland and southwest England offer some of the best surfing conditions anywhere in Europe.

But if it's coastline that floats your boat, it's hard to beat Britain. This sea-fringed island boasts the longest stretch of continuous coastline in Europe (over 17,000km in all), and is home to some of its most impressive scenery: from the craggy cliffs of Cornwall to the wide open beaches of the Gower Peninsula and the stately rock stacks of western and northern Scotland. The only drawback is the water temperature: it stays pretty chilly even in high summer, so you'll need to be made of stern stuff.

There is one advantage to Britain's Atlantic-facing position, however, and that's the surf: the coastlines of Wales, Cornwall and Ireland have some of the most reliable surf in Europe. These are closely followed by the Biarritz area in southwest France and Spain's Basque Country.

The Best...
Mountain Experiences

1 Riding the cable car to the Aiguille du Midi (p251)

2 Taking a train to Europe's highest station, Jungfraujoch (p688)

3 Catching your first sight of the Matterhorn (p680)

4 Hiking the Picos de Europa (p356)

5 Gazing over Grindelwald's glaciers (p687)

The Best...
Beach Destinations

1 Côte d'Azur (p272), France

2 Amalfi Coast (p476), Italy

3 Aegean Islands (p776), Greece

4 Atlantic Coast (p255), France

5 Southwest England (p102)

Forests

Europe was once covered by a vast forest that stretched all the way from the Arctic Ocean to the Mediterranean Sea; it's thought that forest probably covered around 80% of the continent. But since the Industrial Revolution somewhere between a half and two-thirds of the original tree cover has been lost. Large areas of forest have since been replanted, often with fast-growing non-native species such as pine, fir and conifer; around 5% of Europe's total forested area is now collectively protected by national agencies.

Outside eastern and Scandinavian Europe, the largest area of 'old growth' woodland is the Black Forest, covering around 12,000 sq km in the Baden-Württemberg region of southwest Germany. Other notable woodlands include the Landes Forest in southwest France, the forests of the Carpathian Mountains, and the New Forest in southern England.

Islands

Europe's seas are studded with countless islands. The highest concentration can be found in Greece, which is effectively a nation made up of numerous islands, including the Peloponnese, Cyclades and Dodecanese. Somewhat less frequented are the far-flung Ionian and Aegean Islands, each defined by its own unique character and decorated with a smattering of sandy beaches, secluded bays and hidden coves.

Many Mediterranean islands are volcanic in origin. The Greek island of Santorini is all that remains of a vast volcano that exploded sometime between 1700 BC and 1500 BC. Others, such as Sicily and the nearby Aeolian Islands, remain highly active – Mt Etna and Mt Stromboli both regularly blow their tops, with Etna thought to be overdue for a major eruption (the last serious explosion is estimated to have occurred around 2000 years ago).

The largest islands in the Mediterranean are Sardinia (governed by Italy) and Corsica (governed by France). Both of these popular destinations are packed with French and Italian holidaymakers, and their beaches are busiest between July and September. Time your visit for the shoulder months, however, and you might well have the islands all to yourself.

Further afield, Britain has a string of islands that make ideal places for escaping the crowds. Forty-five kilometres off the tip of southwest Britain are the tiny Isles of Scilly, only five of which are inhabited on a permanent basis. Off Scotland's west coast are the rocky Inner and Outer Hebrides, while further north are the Orkneys, home to some of Britain's most ancient settlements, and the isolated Shetland Islands, which mark the most northerly point in the British Isles.

Survival
Guide

DIRECTORY   816

Accommodation   816
Business Hours   816
Customs Regulations   816
Discount Cards   817
Electricity   817
Gay & Lesbian Travellers   818
Health   818

Insurance   818
Internet Access   819
Legal Matters   819
Money   819
Safe Travel   820
Telephone   821
Time   821
Tourist Information   821

Visas   821
Weights & Measures   822

TRANSPORT   822

Getting There & Away   822
Getting Around   822

LANGUAGE   827

St Peter's Square (p403), The Vatican
PHOTOGRAPHER: RUTH EASTHAM & MAX PAOLI/GETTY IMAGES ©

A-Z

Directory

Accommodation

Where you stay in Europe may be one of the highlights of your trip. Quirky family-run inns, manic city hostels, languid and low-key beach resorts are just some of the places where you'll make both new memories and, more than likely, new friends.

During peak holiday periods, accommodation can be hard to find, and it's advisable to book ahead.

B&Bs & Guest Houses

In the UK and Ireland myriad B&Bs are real bargains in this field, where you get bed and breakfast in a private home.

In other countries, similar private accommodation – though often without breakfast – may go under the name of pension, guest house, *Gasthaus, Zimmerfrei, chambre d'hôte* and so on.

Hotels

You'll often find inexpensive hotels clustered around the bus and train station areas, which are always good places to start hunting; however, these areas can be charmless and scruffy. Look for moderately priced places closer to the interesting parts of town. Ask about breakfast; sometimes it's included, sometimes it's not.

Besides big booking sites such as **Hotels.com** (www. hotels.com), we've had good luck with the following discount booking sites:

DHR (www.dhr.com)

Direct Rooms (www. directrooms.com)

Hotel Club (www.hotelclub. net)

Hotel Info (www.hotel.info)

HRS (www.hrs.com)

LateRooms (www.laterooms. com)

Rental Accommodation

Rentals can be both advantageous and fun for families travelling together or for those staying in one place for a few nights.

HolidayHavens (www. holidayhavens.co.uk)

Holiday-Rentals (www. holiday-rentals.com)

Homelidays (www. homelidays.com)

Vacations-Abroad (www. vacations-abroad.com)

VacationRentalsByOwner (www.vrbo.com)

Business Hours

Standard business hours vary hugely in Western Europe, where dinner means midnight in Madrid and 7pm in the Netherlands. Some countries have embraced Sunday shopping and others haven't.

Customs Regulations

Duty-free goods are not sold to those travelling from one EU country to another. For goods purchased at airports or on ferries *outside* the EU, the usual allowances apply for tobacco (200 cigarettes, 50 cigars or 250g of loose tobacco) – although some countries have reduced this to curb smoking – and alcohol (1L of spirits or 2L of liquor with less than 22% alcohol by volume; 4L of wine). The total value of these goods cannot exceed €300.

Book Your Stay Online

For more accommodation reviews by Lonely Planet authors, check out lonelyplanet.com/hotels. You'll find independent reviews, as well as recommendations on the best places to stay. Best of all, you can book online.

Climate

London

°C/°F **Temp**
- 40/104
- 30/86
- 20/68
- 10/50
- 0/32
- -10/14

J F M A M J J A S O N D

Rainfall inches/mm
- 4.9/125
- 3.9/100
- 2.9/75
- 2/50
- 1/25
- 0

Madrid

°C/°F **Temp**
- 40/104
- 30/86
- 20/68
- 10/50
- 0/32
- -10/14

J F M A M J J A S O N D

Rainfall inches/mm
- 4.9/125
- 3.9/100
- 2.9/75
- 2/50
- 1/25
- 0

Prague

°C/°F **Temp**
- 40/104
- 30/86
- 20/68
- 10/50
- 0/32
- -10/14

J F M A M J J A S O N D

Rainfall inches/mm
- 4.9/125
- 3.9/100
- 2.9/75
- 2/50
- 1/25
- 0

Discount Cards

Senior Cards

Museums and various other sights and attractions (including public swimming pools and spas), as well as transport companies, frequently offer discounts to retired people, old-age pensioners and/or those aged over 60.

Make sure you bring proof of age; that suave signor in Italy or that polite Parisian mademoiselle is not going to believe you're a day over 39.

Student & Youth Cards

The **International Student Travel Confederation** (ISTC; www.istc.org) issues three cards for students, teachers and under-26s, offering thousands of worldwide discounts on transport, museum entry, youth hostels and even some restaurants. These cards are: the ISIC (International Student Identity Card), the ITIC (International Teacher Identity Card) and the IYTC (International Youth Travel Card). You can check the full list of discounts and where to apply for the cards on the ISTC website. Issuing offices include **STA Travel** (www.statravel.com).

For people aged under 30, there's also the **European Youth Card** (www.euro26. org), which has scores of discounts.

Electricity

EU & Continental Europe

230V/50Hz

UK & Ireland

230V/50Hz

Emergency Number

The EU-wide general emergency number is 📞112 (but 📞999 in the UK).

Voltages & Cycles

Most of Europe runs on 220-240V, 50Hz AC (as opposed to say, North America, where the electricity is 120V, 60 Hz AC). Chargers for phones, iPods and laptops *usually* can handle any type of electricity. If in doubt, read the small print. What you'll need are plug converters.

Plugs & Sockets

If your plugs are of a different design from the UK/Ireland and EU plugs, you'll need an adaptor. If you don't get one before travelling, shops in airports and train stations often have a selection of adaptors.

Gay & Lesbian Travellers

In cosmopolitan centres in Western Europe you'll find very liberal attitudes towards homosexuality. Belgium, the Netherlands and Spain have legalised full same-sex marriages. Many other countries allow civil partnerships that grant all or most of the rights of marriage.

London, Paris, Berlin, Madrid, Lisbon and Amsterdam have thriving gay communities and pride events. The Greek islands of Mykonos and Lesvos are popular gay beach destinations.

Damron (www.damron.com) The USA's leading gay publisher offers guides to world cities.

Gay Journey (www.gayjourney.com) A mishmash of travel-related information, including lists of gay-friendly hotels in Europe.

International Lesbian and Gay Association (www.ilga.org) Campaigning group with some country-specific information on homosexual issues (not always up-to-date) and a conference calendar.

Spartacus International Gay Guide (www.spartacusworld.com) A male-only directory of gay entertainment venues in Europe.

Health

It is unlikely that you will encounter unusual health problems in Western Europe, and if you do, standards of care are world class.

- Bring medications in their original, clearly labelled containers.

- Bring a list of your prescriptions (photocopies of the containers are good) including generic names, so you can get replacements if your bags go on holiday – carry this info separately.

- If you have health problems that may need treatment, bring a signed and dated letter from your physician describing your medical conditions and medications.

- If carrying syringes or needles, have a physician's letter documenting their medical necessity.

- If you need vision correction, carry a spare pair of contact lenses or glasses, and/or bring your optical prescription with you.

Insurance

If you're an EU citizen, the European Health Insurance Card (EHIC) covers you for most medical care. EHIC will not cover you for nonemergencies or emergency repatriation. Citizens of other countries should find out if there is a reciprocal arrangement for free medical care between their country and the country visited. Find out in advance if your insurance plan will make payments directly to providers or reimburse you later for overseas health expenditures.

Recommended Vaccinations

No jabs are necessary for Western Europe. However, the World Health Organization (WHO) recommends that all travellers should be covered for diphtheria, tetanus, measles, mumps, rubella and polio, regardless of their destination.

Insurance

It's foolhardy to travel without insurance to cover theft, loss and medical problems. Start by seeing what your own insurance covers, be it medical, for home owners or renters. You may find that many aspects of travel in Western Europe are covered. If you need to purchase coverage, there's a wide variety of policies, so check the small print. Some policies specifically exclude 'dangerous activities', which can include scuba diving, motorcycling, winter sports, adventure sports or even hiking. Some pay doctors or hospitals directly, but most require you to pay upfront, save the documentation and then claim later. Check that the policy covers ambulances or an emergency flight home.

Internet Access

The number of internet cafes is plummeting. You'll may still find them in tourist areas and around big train stations.

o Hostels, hotels and other accommodation usually have wi-fi.

o Wi-fi (WLAN in Germany) access is best the further north in Western Europe you go (Greece and Portugal are laggards).

o Internet access places may add a surcharge of €1 to €5 per hour for using Skype.

Legal Matters

You are required by law to prove your identity if asked by police, so always carry your passport, or an identity card if you're an EU citizen.

You can generally purchase alcohol (beer and wine) between 16 and 18 years (usually 18 for spirits) but, if in doubt, ask. Although you can drive at 17 or 18 years, you might not be able to hire a car until you reach 25 years of age.

Illegal Drugs

Narcotics are sometimes openly available in Europe, but that doesn't mean they're legal. The Netherlands is most famed for its liberal attitudes, with 'coffee shops' openly selling cannabis. However, even there, it's a case of the police turning a blind eye.

Equally, in Belgium, the possession of up to 5g of cannabis is legal but selling the drug isn't, so if you get caught at the point of sale you could be in trouble.

Smoking

Although outdoor seating has long been a tradition outside European cafes, it's had new impetus given that most Western European countries have banned smoking in public places, including restaurants and bars.

Money

For security and flexibility, diversify your source of funds. Carry an ATM card, credit card and cash.

ATMs

Most countries in Europe have international ATMs that allow you to withdraw cash directly from your home account, and this is the most common way European travellers access their money. You should always have a back-up option, however, as some readers have reported glitches with ATMs in various countries, even when their card worked elsewhere across Europe.

When you withdraw money from an ATM the amounts are converted and dispensed in local currency. However, there will be fees. If you're uncertain, ask your bank to explain.

Finally, remember to always cover the keypad when entering your PIN and make sure that there are no unusual devices attached to the machine; these can copy your card's details or cause it to stick in the machine.

Cash

Nothing beats cash for convenience...or risk. If you lose it, it's gone forever and very few travel insurers will come to your rescue. Those that do will limit the amount to somewhere around €300 or £200.

There is no reason to get local currency before arriving in Europe, especially as exchange rates for doing so in your home country are likely to be abysmal.

Credit Cards

Credit cards are handy for major purchases such as air or rail tickets, and offer a lifeline in certain emergencies.

Visa and MasterCard/ Eurocard are more widely accepted in Europe than Amex and Diners Club.

As with ATM cards, banks have loaded up credit cards with hidden charges for foreign purchases. Cash withdrawals on a credit card are almost always a much worse idea than using an ATM

The Euro

A common currency, the euro is the official currency used in 16 of the 27 EU states: Austria, Belgium, Cyprus, Finland, France, Germany, Greece, Ireland, Italy, Luxembourg, Malta, the Netherlands, Portugal, Slovakia, Slovenia and Spain. Denmark, Britain, Switzerland and Sweden have held out against adopting the euro for political reasons.

The euro has the same value in all EU member countries. The euro is divided into 100 cents. There are seven euro notes (five, 10, 20, 50, 100, 200 and 500 euros) and eight euro coins (one and two euros, then one, two, five, 10, 20 and 50 cents). One side is standard for all euro coins and the other side bears a national emblem of participating countries.

card due to the fees and high interest rates. Your best bet is to check these things before leaving and try to use a card that offers the best deal.

Money Exchange

In general, US dollars and UK pounds are the easiest currencies to exchange in Western Europe. Get rid of Scottish and Welsh pounds before leaving the UK; nobody outside Britain will touch them.

Most airports, central train stations, big hotels and many border posts have banking facilities outside regular business hours, at times on a 24-hour basis. Post offices in Europe often perform banking tasks, tend to be open longer hours and outnumber banks in remote places.

The best exchange rates are usually at banks. *Bureaux de changes* usually – but not always – offer worse rates or charge higher commissions.

Taxes & Refunds

Sales tax applies to many goods and services in Western Europe (although the amount – 10% to 20% – is already built into the price of the item). Luckily, when non-EU residents spend more than a certain amount (around €75) they can usually reclaim that tax when leaving the country.

Tipping

Adding another 5% to 10% to a bill for a meal for good service is common across Western Europe.

Travellers Cheques

Travellers cheques have been replaced by international ATMs and it's often difficult to find places that cash them.

Safe Travel

On the whole, you should experience few problems travelling in Western Europe –

even alone – as the region is well developed and relatively safe. But do exercise common sense.

Also, leave a record (ie a photocopy) of your passport, credit and ATM cards and other important documents in a safe place. You can scan your documents and credit cards and post the file somewhere safe online, perhaps by emailing it to yourself. If things are stolen or lost, replacement is much easier when you have the vital details available.

Theft

Theft happens in Europe, and you have to be wary of theft by other travellers. The most important things to guard are your passport, papers, tickets and money – in that order.

You can lessen the risks further by being careful of snatch thieves. Cameras or shoulder bags are an open invitation for these people, who sometimes operate from motorcycles or scooters and expertly slash the strap before you have a chance to react. Be very careful at cafes and bars; loop the strap of your bag around your leg while seated.

Pickpockets are most active in dense crowds, especially in busy train stations and on public transport during peak hours. A common ploy is for one person to distract you while another zips through your pockets. Beware of gangs of kids – who can look either dishevelled or well dressed – madly waving newspapers and demanding attention. In the blink of an eye, a wallet or camera can go missing.

Telephone

Treat your hotel phone and its often hidden and outrageous rates the same way you'd treat a thief. Using wi-fi in the room for Skype is the most common way to connect.

Mobile Phones

Travellers can easily purchase prepaid mobile phones (from €30/£20) or SIM cards (from €10/£5). GSM cellular phones are compatible throughout all the countries in Western Europe.

If you bring your mobile phone from home:

○ Check international roaming rates in advance; often they are extortionate.

○ Check roaming fees for data usage for email and web connections; users of smart phones such as the iPhone can get socked with huge fees.

You can bring your mobile phone from home and buy a local SIM card to enjoy cheap local calling rates if it is (a) unlocked, and (b) compatible with European GSM networks.

Time

○ **GMT/UTC** Britain, Ireland

○ **Central European Time** (GMT/UTC +1) Andorra, Austria, Belgium, France, Germany, Greece, Italy, Liechtenstein, Luxembourg, Netherlands, Portugal, Spain, Switzerland

○ **East European Time** (GMT/UTC +2) Greece

○ **Daylight Saving Time/ Summer Time** Last Sunday in March to the last Sunday in October.

Tourist Information

Tourist offices in Western Europe are common and almost universally helpful. They can find accommodation, issue maps, advise on sights and activities, and help with more obscure queries such as 'Where can I wash my clothes?'.

Visas

With a valid passport you should be able to visit all countries in Western Europe for up to three months, provided you have some sort of onward or return ticket and/or 'sufficient means of support' (money).

In line with the Schengen Agreement, there are no passport controls at borders between Andorra, Austria, Belgium, Denmark, Finland, France, Germany, Greece, Iceland, Italy, Liechtenstein, Luxembourg, the Netherlands, Norway, Portugal, Spain, Sweden, Switzerland and many of the Eastern European EU members such as the Czech Republic.

Border procedures between EU and non-EU countries can still be thorough, though citizens of Australia, Canada, New Zealand and the USA don't need visas for tourist visits to any Schengen country or the UK.

Minimising ATM Charges

When you withdraw cash from an ATM overseas there are several ways you can get hit. Firstly, most banks add a hidden 2.75% loading to what's called the 'Visa/MasterCard wholesale' or 'interbank' exchange rate. In short, they're giving you a worse exchange rate than strictly necessary. Additionally, some banks charge their customers a cash withdrawal fee (usually 2% with a minimum €2 or more). If you're really unlucky, the bank at the foreign end might charge you as well. Triple whammy. If you use a credit card in ATMs you'll also pay interest – usually quite high interest – on the cash withdrawn.

Most experts agree that having the right bankcard is still cheaper than exchanging cash directly. If your bank levies fees, then making larger, less frequent withdrawals is better. It's also worth seeing if your bank has reciprocal agreements with banks where you are going that minimise ATM fees.

Weights & Measures

The metric system is in use throughout most Western European countries. Be aware that in Britain, however, nonmetric equivalents are common (for example: distances continue to be given in miles and beer is sold in pints not litres).

Transport

Getting There & Away

Major gateways to Western Europe include airports in London, Paris, Amsterdam, Frankfurt and Rome; however, with connections you can reach scores of airports across the continent.

Getting Around

✈ Air

Getting around Western Europe by air is very popular thanks to the proliferation of discount carriers and cheap fares. But with cheap fares come many caveats. First, some of the barebones carriers are just that. Discount leader Ryanair prides itself on nonreclining seats, nonexistent legroom and nonexistent window shades. At some of its far-flung airports customer service will also be nonexistent. Scores of other discount airlines are following this model.

A second caveat involves the airports. If you really want to go to Carcassonne in the south of France, then getting a €20 Ryanair ticket from London will be a dream come true. But if you want to go to Frankfurt in Germany and end up buying a ticket to 'Frankfurt-Hahn', you'll find yourself at a small airport 70km west of Frankfurt and two hours away by bus.

Although many people first think of budget carriers when they consider a cheap ticket in Western Europe, you should compare all carriers, including established ones like British Airways and Lufthansa, which serve major airports close to main destinations.

Bicycle

It is easy to hire bicycles in Western Europe and you can often negotiate good deals. Local tourist offices, hostels and hotels will have information on rental outlets. Occasionally you can drop off the bicycle at a different location so you don't have to double back on your route.

Urban bike-hire schemes where you check out a bike from one stand and return it to another after brief use have taken off in cities as huge as London and Paris.

Within Western Europe, bikes can sometimes be brought with you onto a train, subject to a small supplementary fee.

🚢 Boat

Most ferry companies adjust prices according to the level of demand (so-called fluid or dynamic pricing), so it may pay to offer alternative travel dates.

Some of the main areas of ferry service for Europe are between:

- Ireland and the UK
- Ireland and France
- The UK and the continent (especially France but also Belgium, the Netherlands and Spain)
- Italy and Greece

Compare fares and routes using **Ferry Savers** (www.ferrysavers.com).

🚌 Bus

Buses sometimes have the edge in terms of costs, but are generally slower and much less comfortable than trains and not as quick or sometimes as cheap as airlines.

Europe's largest network of international buses is provided by a consortium of bus companies that operates under the name **Eurolines** (www.eurolines.com).

Car & Motorcycle

Travelling with your own vehicle allows increased flexibility and the option to get off the beaten track. Unfortunately, cars can be the proverbial ball and chain in city centres when you have to negotiate one-way streets or find somewhere to park amid a confusing concrete jungle and a welter of expensive parking options.

Driving Licence

Proof of ownership of a private vehicle should always be carried (a Vehicle Registration Document for British-registered cars) when driving in Europe. An EU driving licence is acceptable.

Many non-European driving licences are valid in Europe. Some travel websites and auto clubs advise carrying an International Driving Permit (IDP), but this costly multilingual document sold by national auto clubs is not necessary in Europe – especially to rent a car.

Fuel

Fuel prices can vary enormously from country to country (though it's always more expensive than in North America or Australia) and may bear little relation to the general cost of living.

Unleaded petrol and diesel are available across Western Europe.

Hire

The big international rental firms will give you reliable service and a good standard of vehicle. Usually you will have the option of returning the car to a different outlet at the end of the rental period. Rates vary widely but expect to pay somewhere between €25 and €70 per day.

No matter where you rent from, it is imperative to understand exactly what is included in your rental agreement (collision damage waiver, unlimited mileage etc). Make sure you are covered with an adequate insurance

policy. And Americans should take note: less than 4% of European cars have automatic transmissions, so if you're afraid of a stick, you'll pay more than double for your car.

The minimum rental age is usually 21 or even 23, and you'll need a credit card.

Motorcycle and moped rental is easy to obtain in countries such as Italy, Spain, Greece and in the south of France.

Insurance

Third-party motor insurance is compulsory in Europe if you're driving your own car (rental cars usually come with insurance). Most UK motor-insurance policies automatically provide this for EU countries. Get your insurer to issue a Green Card (may cost extra): an internationally recognised proof of insurance, and check that it lists all the countries you intend to visit. Also ask your insurer for a European Accident Statement form. Never sign statements you can't read or understand – insist on a translation.

It's a good investment to take out a European motoring-assistance policy, such as the AA Five Star Service or the RAC European Motoring Assistance. Expect to pay about £50 for 14 days' cover, with a 10% discount for association members. Non-Europeans might find it cheaper to arrange international coverage with their national motoring organisation before leaving home. Ask your motoring

Climate Change & Travel

Every form of transport that relies on carbon-based fuel generates CO_2, the main cause of human-induced climate change. Modern travel is dependent on aeroplanes, which might use less fuel per kilometre per person than most cars but travel much greater distances. The altitude at which aircraft emit gases (including CO_2) and particles also contributes to their climate change impact. Many websites offer 'carbon calculators' that allow people to estimate the carbon emissions generated by their journey and, for those who wish to do so, to offset the impact of the greenhouse gases emitted with contributions to portfolios of climate-friendly initiatives throughout the world. Lonely Planet offsets the carbon footprint of all staff and author travel.

organisation for details about free services offered by affiliated organisations around Western Europe.

Every vehicle travelling across an international border should display a sticker showing its country of registration.

Road Conditions

Conditions and types of roads vary across Western Europe, but it is possible to make some generalisations. The fastest routes are four- or six-lane dual carriageways/highways, ie two or three lanes either side (motorway, autobahn, *autoroute, autostrada* etc). These roads are

Discount Train Tickets Online

The railways offer many cheap ticket deals through their websites.

Actually getting discount train tickets you've purchased online varies. Common methods include the following:

○ Reservation number issued with the reservation, which you use at a station ticket-vending machine (some UK lines).

○ Credit card you used to purchase the tickets used at a station ticket-vending machine (France, but non-French credit card holders must retrieve their tickets at a ticket window).

○ Ticket is emailed to buyer, who then prints it out (Germany).

○ Nonlocal credit cards aren't accepted online and you can't buy the discounted fares at the station (the Netherlands).

great for speed and comfort but driving can be dull, with little or no interesting scenery. Some of these roads incur expensive tolls (eg in Italy, France and Spain) or have a general tax for usage (Switzerland and Austria), but there will usually be an alternative route you can take. Motorways and other primary routes are almost always in good condition.

Road surfaces on minor routes are not perfect in some countries (eg Greece), although normally they will be more than adequate. These roads are narrower and progress is generally much slower.

Road Rules

With the exception of Britain and Ireland, driving is on the right-hand side of the road.

Take care with speed limits, as they vary from country to country. You may be surprised at the apparent disregard of traffic regulations in some places (particularly in Italy and Greece), but as a visitor it is always best to be cautious. In many countries, driving infringements are subject to an on-the-spot fine. Always ask for a receipt.

European drink-driving laws are particularly strict. The blood-alcohol concentration (BAC) limit when driving is between 0.05% and 0.08%, but in certain areas it can be *zero* per cent.

Public Transport

Most Western European cities have excellent public transport systems, which comprise some combination of subways, trains, trams and buses. Major airports generally have fast-train or subway links to the city centre.

Taxi

Taxis in Western Europe are metered and rates are generally high. There might also be supplements (depending on the country) for things such as luggage, the time of day, the location from which you boarded and for extra passengers. Good public transport networks make the use of taxis almost unnecessary, but if you need one in a hurry they can usually be found idling near train stations or outside big hotels. Spain, Greece and Portugal have lower fares, which makes taking a taxi more viable.

Train

Trains are a popular way of getting around: they are comfortable, frequent and generally on time. The Channel Tunnel makes it possible to get from Britain to continental Europe using **Eurostar** (www.eurostar.com).

Information

Every national rail company has a website with schedule and fare information. Recommended sites:

Deutsche Bahn (DB; www.bahn.de) Excellent schedule and fare information in English for trains not just in Germany but across Europe.

The Man in Seat 61 (www.seat61.com) Invaluable train descriptions and details of journeys to the far reaches of the continent.

If you plan to travel extensively by train, you might enjoy the *Thomas Cook European Timetable,* which gives a cleverly condensed listing of train schedules and indicates where supplements apply or where reservations are necessary. The timetable is updated monthly and is available from **Thomas Cook** (www.thomascookpublishing.com) outlets and bookshops in the UK (order online elsewhere in the world).

Note that European trains sometimes split en route in order to service two destinations, so even if you know you're on the right train, make sure you're in the correct carriage, too.

Highspeed Trains

Western European trains (outside Greece and Portugal) are often fast, frequent and usually comfortable. Highspeed networks (300km/h or more) continue to expand.

Major highspeed trains that cross borders include the following:

Eurostar (www.eurostar.com) Links beautiful St Pancras station in London to Brussels and Paris in about two hours.

ICE (www.db.de) The fast trains of the German railways span the country and extend to Paris, Brussels, Amsterdam, Vienna and Switzerland.

TGV (www.sncf.com) The legendary fast trains of France reach into Belgium, Luxembourg, Germany, Switzerland and Italy (Milan).

Thalys (www.thalys.com) Links Paris with Brussels, Amsterdam and Cologne.

Some sample travel times include the following:

ROUTE	DURATION
Amsterdam–Paris	3hr
Barcelona–Madrid	3hr
Brussels–Cologne	2¼hr
London–Paris	2¼hr
Milan–Rome	4hr
Nuremberg–Munich	1hr
Paris–Frankfurt	3¾hr
Paris–Marseille	3hr
Zürich–Milan	3¾hr

Night Trains

The romantic image of the European night train is becoming a lot less common with the popularity of budget airlines; however, you can still find a good network of routes that run from the north to Italy.

Artesia (www.artesia.eu) Runs services between Paris and Rome and points in between.

Caledonian Sleeper (www.scotrail.co.uk) Links London overnight with Scotland (as far north as Inverness and Aberdeen).

City Nightline (www.citynightline.de) Operates night trains from Germany and the Netherlands south through Switzerland and Austria into Italy as well as France.

Express Trains

Slower but still reasonably fast trains that cross borders are often called EuroCity (EC) or InterCity (IC). Reaching speeds of up to 200km/h or more, they are comfortable and frequent. A good example is the Railjet service of Austria that reaches Munich and Zürich.

Reservations

On weekends and during holidays and the summer, it's a good idea to reserve seats on trains (which costs about €3 to €5). You can usually reserve ahead of time using a ticket machine in stations or at a ticket window.

On many highspeed trains, such as France's TGVs, reservations are mandatory.

Rail Passes

Think carefully about purchasing a rail pass. Spend a little time online on the national railways sites and determine what it would cost to do your trip by buying the tickets separately. More often than not, you'll find that you'll spend less than if you buy a Eurail pass.

InterRail Pass Types

	ADULT 1ST CLASS	ADULT 2ND CLASS	UNDER 26 2ND CLASS
5 days of travel within 10 days	€374	€249	€159
10 days of travel within 22 days	€439	€359	€239
unlimited travel for 1 month	€899	€599	€399

Shop around, as pass prices can vary between different outlets. Once purchased, take care of your pass as it cannot be replaced or refunded if lost or stolen. Passes get reductions on Eurostar through the Channel Tunnel and on certain ferry routes (eg between France and Ireland). In the USA, **Rail Europe** (www.raileurope.com) sells a variety of rail passes (note that its individual train tickets tend to be more expensive than what you'll pay if buying from railways online or in stations).

Eurail

There are so many different **Eurail** (www.eurail.com) passes to choose from that you need to have a good idea of your itinerary before purchasing one. These passes can be bought only by residents of non-European countries, and are supposed to be purchased before arriving in Europe. There are also two options: adults and people under 26 years.

Eurail passes are valid for unlimited travel on national railways and some private lines in Austria, Belgium, France, Germany, Greece, Ireland, Italy, the Netherlands, Spain and Switzerland (including Liechtenstein), plus several more neighbouring ones, and for some ferries between Italy and Greece. The UK is *not* covered by Eurail;

it has its own Britrail pass. Reductions are given on some other ferry routes and on river/lake steamer services in various countries and on the Eurostar to/from the UK.

Eurail Global All the European countries (despite the much grander-sounding name) for a set number of consecutive days.

Eurail Flexi Offers travel for a set number of days within a period of time.

Eurail Saver Two to five people *always* travelling together can save about 15% on the previously discussed pass types.

Eurail Selectpass Buyers choose which neighbouring countries it covers and for how long. Use the Eurail website to calculate these.

Extra Fees

Eurail likes to promote the hop-on, hop-off aspect of its passes. But while German ICE trains may be used at will, French TGVs require a seat reservation and the catch

is that these are not always available to pass holders on all trains. In addition, some of the highspeed services like Thalys trains require a fairly hefty surcharge from pass users: 1st class/2nd class €41/€26.

InterRail

The **InterRail pass** (www.interrailnet.com) is available to European residents of more than six months standing (passport ID required). Terms and conditions vary slightly from country to country, but in the country of origin there is a discount of around 50% on the normal fares. The pass covers up to 30 countries.

InterRail passes are generally cheaper than Eurail, but most fast trains require you to buy a seat reservation and pay a supplement of €3 to €40 depending on the route. InterRail passes are also available for individual countries. Compare these to passes offered by the national railways.

National Rail Passes

If you're intending to travel extensively within one country, check what national rail passes are available as these can sometimes save you a lot of money. In a large country such as Germany where you might be covering long distances, a pass can make sense, whereas in a small country such as the Netherlands it won't.

Eurail Flexi

	10 DAYS IN 2 MONTHS	15 DAYS IN 2 MONTHS
Adult 1st class	US$832	US$1093
Under 26 2nd class	US$543	US$711

Eurail Global

	15 DAYS	1 MONTH
Adult 1st class	US$705	US$1135
Under 26 2nd class	US$458	US$739

A-Z

Language

Don't let the language barrier get in the way of your travel experience. This section offers basic phrases and pronunciation guides to help you negotiate your way around Europe. Note that in our pronunciation guides, the stressed syllables in words are indicated with italics.

To enhance your trip with a phrasebook (covering all of these languages in much greater detail), visit **lonelyplanet.com**. Lonely Planet iPhone phrasebooks are available through the Apple App store.

CZECH

Hello.	*Ahoj.*	uh·hoy
Goodbye.	*Na shledanou.*	nuh·skhle·duh·noh
Yes./No.	*Ano./Ne.*	uh·no/ne
Please.	*Prosím.*	pro·seem
Thank you.	*Děkuji.*	dye·ku·yi
Excuse me.	*Promiňte.*	pro·min'·te
Help!	*Pomoc!*	po·mots

Do you speak English?
Mluvíte anglicky?   mlu·vee·te uhn·glits·ki
I don't understand.
Nerozumím.   ne·ro·zu·meem
How much is this?
Kolik to stojí?   ko·lik to sto·yee
I'd like ..., please.
Chtěl/Chtěla bych ...,   khtyel/khtye·luh bikh ...
prosím. (m/f)   pro·seem
Where's (the toilet)?
Kde je (záchod)?   gde ye (za·khod)
I'm lost.
Zabloudil/   zuh·bloh·dyil/
Zabloudila jsem. (m/f)   zuh·bloh·dyi·luh ysem

DUTCH

Hello.	*Dag.*	dakh
Goodbye.	*Dag.*	dakh
Yes.	*Ja.*	yaa
No.	*Nee.*	ney
Please.	*Alstublieft.*	al·stew·*bleeft*
Thank you.	*Dank u.*	dangk ew
Excuse me.	*Excuseer mij.*	eks·kew·*zeyr* mey
Help!	*Help!*	help

Do you speak English?
Spreekt u Engels?   spreykt ew *eng*·uhls
I don't understand.
Ik begrijp het niet.   ik buh·*khreyp* huht neet
How much is this?
Hoeveel kost het?   hoo·*veyl* kost huht
I'd like ..., please.
Ik wil graag ...   ik wil khraakh ...
Where's (the toilet)?
Waar zijn   waar zeyn
(de toiletten)?   (duh twa·*le*·tuhn)
I'm lost.
Ik ben verdwaald.   ik ben vuhr·*dwaalt*

FRENCH

Hello.	*Bonjour.*	bon·zhoor
Goodbye.	*Au revoir.*	o·rer·vwa
Yes.	*Oui.*	wee
No.	*Non.*	non
Please.	*S'il vous plaît.*	seel voo play
Thank you.	*Merci.*	mair·see
Excuse me.	*Excusez-moi.*	ek·skew·zay·mwa
Help!	*Au secours!*	o skoor

Do you speak English?
Parlez-vous anglais?   par·lay·voo ong·glay
I don't understand.
Je ne comprends pas.   zher ner kom·pron pa
How much is this?
C'est combien?   say kom·byun
I'd like ..., please.
Je voudrais ...,   zher voo·dray ...
s'il vous plaît.   seel voo play
Where's (the toilet)?
Où sont   oo son
(les toilettes)?   (lay twa·let)
I'm lost.
Je suis perdu(e). (m/f)   zhe swee·pair·dew

GERMAN

Hello.	*Guten Tag.*	*goo*·ten taak
Goodbye.	*Auf Wiedersehen.*	owf *vee*·der·zey·en
Yes.	*Ja.*	yaa
No.	*Nein.*	nain
Please.	*Bitte.*	*bi*·te
Thank you.	*Danke.*	*dang*·ke
Excuse me.	*Entschuldigung.*	ent·*shul*·di·gung
Help!	*Hilfe!*	*hil*·fe

Do you speak English?
Sprechen Sie Englisch? — *shpre*·khen zee *eng*·lish
I don't understand.
Ich verstehe nicht. — ikh fer·*shtey*·e nikht
How much is this?
Was kostet das? — vas *kos*·tet das
I'd like ..., please.
Ich hätte gern ..., bitte. — ikh *he*·te gern ... *bi*·te
Where's (the toilet)?
Wo ist — vaw ist
(die Toilette)? — (dee to·*a*·*le*·te)
I'm lost.
Ich habe mich verirrt. — ikh *haa*·be mikh fer·*irt*

ITALIAN

Hello.	*Buongiorno.*	bwon·*jor*·no
Goodbye.	*Arrivederci.*	a·ree·ve·*der*·chee
Yes.	*Sì.*	see
No.	*No.*	no
Please.	*Per favore.*	per fa·*vo*·re
Thank you.	*Grazie.*	*gra*·tsye
Excuse me.	*Mi scusi.*	mee *skoo*·zee
Help!	*Aiuto!*	a·*yoo*·to

Do you speak English?
Parla inglese? — *par*·la een·*gle*·ze
I don't understand.
Non capisco. — non ka·*pee*·sko
How much is this?
Quanto costa? — *kwan*·to *ko*·sta
I'd like ..., please.
Vorrei ..., per favore. — vo·*ray* ... per fa·*vo*·re
Where's (the toilet)?
Dove sono — *do*·ve *so*·no
(i gabinetti)? — (ee ga·bee·*ne*·ti)
I'm lost.
Mi sono perso/a. (m/f) — mee *so*·no per·*so*/a

GREEK

Hello.	Γεια σου.	*yia* su
Goodbye.	Αντίο.	a·*di*·o
Yes.	Ναι.	ne
No.	Οχι.	*o*·hi
Please.	Παρακαλώ.	pa·ra·ka·*lo*
Thank you.	Ευχαριστώ.	ef·kha·ri·*sto*
Excuse me.	Με συγχωρείτε.	me sing·kho·*ri*·te
Help!	Βοήθεια!	vo·*i*·thia

Do you speak English?
Μιλάς Αγγλικά; — mi·*las* ang·gli·*ka*
I don't understand.
Δεν καταλαβαίνω. — dhen ka·ta·la·*ve*·no
How much is this?
Πόσο κάνει; — *po*·so *ka*·ni
I'd like ..., please.
Θα ήθελα ..., — tha *i*·the·la ...
παρακαλώ. — pa·ra·ka·*lo*
Where's (the toilet)?
Που είναι (η τουαλέτα); — pu *i*·ne (i tu·a·*le*·ta)
I'm lost.
Έχω χαθεί. — e·kho kha·*thi*

SPANISH

Hello.	*Hola.*	*o*·la
Goodbye.	*Adiós.*	a·*dyos*
Yes.	*Sí.*	see
No.	*No.*	no
Please.	*Por favor.*	por fa·*vor*
Thank you.	*Gracias.*	*gra*·thyas
Excuse me.	*Disculpe.*	dees·*kool*·pe
Help!	*¡Socorro!*	so·*ko*·ro

Do you speak English?
¿Habla inglés? — a·bla een·*gles*
I don't understand.
No entiendo. — no en·*tyen*·do
How much is this?
¿Cuánto cuesta? — *kwan*·to *kwes*·ta
I'd like ..., please.
Quisiera ..., por favor. — kee·*sye*·ra ... por fa·*vor*
Where's (the toilet)?
¿Dónde están — *don*·de es·*tan*
(los servicios)? — (los ser·*vee*·thyos)
I'm lost.
Estoy perdido/a. (m/f) — es·*toy* per·*dee*·do/a

Behind the Scenes

This Book

This 3rd edition of Lonely Planet's Discover Europe guidebook was coordinated by Oliver Berry, and was written and researched by Alexis Averbuck, Oliver Berry, Mark Baker, Kerry Christiani, Mark Elliott, Duncan Garwood, Anthony Ham, Virginia Maxwell, Craig McLachlan, Andrea Schulte-Peevers, Ryan Ver Berkmoes, Nicola Williams and Neil Wilson. This guidebook was commissioned in Lonely Planet's London office, and produced by the following:

Commissioning Editors Jo Cooke, Lucie Monie Hall, James Smart, Sam Trafford
Coordinating Editor Briohny Hooper
Senior Cartographers Valentina Kremenchutskaya, Anthony Phelan
Coordinating Layout Designer Nicholas Colicchia
Managing Editors Annelies Mertens, Angela Tinson
Managing Layout Designer Chris Girdler
Assisting Editors Carly Hall, Anne Mulvaney, Jeanette Wall, Amanda Williamson, Helen Yeates
Cover Research Naomi Parker
Internal Image Research Aude Vauconsant
Language Content Branislava Vladisavljevic
Thanks to Sasha Baskett, Barbara Delissen, Ryan Evans, Larissa Frost, Jane Hart, Martin Heng, Genesys India, Jouve India, Catherine Naghten, Trent Paton, Martine Power, Dianne Schallmeiner, Luna Soo, Kerrianne Southway, Gina Tsarouhas, Gerard Walker

Author Thanks

OLIVER BERRY

Thanks to Susie, Molly and Gracie Berry, Dana Hammett in Salzburg, Pieter Roelofs and Willemijn van Drunen in Amsterdam, Alan Kingshott and Pat Shelley. Thanks also to James Smart and Annelies Mertens for steering the ship from brief to book.

Acknowledgments

Climate map data adapted from Peel MC, Finlayson BL & McMahon TA (2007) 'Updated World Map of the Köppen-Geiger Climate Classification', *Hydrology and Earth System Sciences,* 11, 163344.

Illustrations pp70-1, pp80-1, pp124-5, pp140-1, pp144-5, pp148-9, pp192-3, pp196-7, pp220-1, pp228-9, pp266-7, pp284-5, pp304-5, pp334-5, pp338-9, pp362-3, pp368-9, pp374-5, pp396-7, pp430-1, pp448-9, pp470-1, pp744-5 and pp768-9 by Javier Zarracina.

Cover Photographs: Front: Alcázar, Segovia, Spain, Calle Montes, Corbis; Back: Colosseum, Rome, Italy, Maurizio Rellini, 4corners.

Our Readers

Many thanks to the travellers who used the last edition and wrote to us with helpful hints, useful advice and interesting anecdotes:

Bill Robinson, Dalibor Malek, Dom Van Abbe, Domain Jacques, Don Farrell, Emma White, Geoff Mackay, Jeff Goodhartz, Joe Jansson, John Mandeville, Katrien Goossens, Linda Dive, Mariola Kacwin, Nadezhda Petrova, Rebecca Graper, Renata Buarque, Sain Alizada, Sophie Beckwith, Stuart Keenan, Suzannah Conway, Taisto Leinonen, Tami Harmony Panik Vibberstoft

SEND US YOUR FEEDBACK

We love to hear from travellers – your comments keep us on our toes and help make our books better. Our well-travelled team reads every word on what you loved or loathed about this book. Although we cannot reply individually to postal submissions, we always guarantee that your feedback goes straight to the appropriate authors, in time for the next edition. Each person who sends us information is thanked in the next edition, the most useful submissions are rewarded with a selection of digital PDF chapters.

Visit **lonelyplanet.com/contact** to submit your updates and suggestions or to ask for help. Our award-winning website also features inspirational travel stories, news and discussions.

Note: We may edit, reproduce and incorporate your comments in Lonely Planet products such as guidebooks, websites and digital products, so let us know if you don't want your comments reproduced or your name acknowledged. For a copy of our privacy policy visit lonelyplanet.com/privacy.

Index

A

accommodation 49, 816, *see also individual locations*
Acropolis 24, 734, 742-5
Acropolis Museum 734, 740-1
activities 808-11, *see also individual activities*
Aegean Islands 776
Aeolian Islands 473
Aiguille du Midi 251
air travel 822
    Austria 723
    Belgium 548
    Britain 170-1, 171
    Czech Republic 724
    France 288, 289
    Germany 624
    Greece 780
    Ireland 170, 171
    Italy 481
    Netherlands, the 548
    Spain 379, 380
    Switzerland 724
Alhambra 19, 297, 372, 374-5
Alkmaar 508
Alps 812-13
    French 249-53
    German 597-608
Alsace 234-7
Altamira 366
Amalfi 477-8
Amalfi Coast 387, 474-8
Amboise 239-41

Amsterdam 17, 488, 494-508, **498-9**
    accommodation 501-2
    drinking 504-5
    entertainment 505
    food 502-4
    shopping 506, 507
    sights 494-501
    tourist information 506
    tours 501
    travel to/within 507-8
Andalucía 359-77
Angel of the North 126
Annecy 252-3
Antwerp 530-4
Arc de Triomphe 194-5
archaeological museums
    Acropolis Museum (Athens) 734, 740-1
    Corfu Archaeological Museum 775
    Hania Archaeological Museum 767
    Iraklio Archaeological Museum 764-5
    Jorvik Viking Centre (York) 118
    Mercati di Traiano Museo dei Fori Imperiali (Rome) 401
    Museo Civico Archeologico (Bologna) 444
    Nafplio Archaeological Museum 756
    National Archaeological Museum (Athens) 741
    National Museum of Ireland — Archaeology (Dublin) 151
archaeological sites & ruins 21, 388, 736, 788, 798-9
    Acropolis 24, 734, 742-5
    Akrotiri 763
    Amphitheater, Trier 613
    Ancient Agora 741, 773
    Ancient Delphi 755
    Ancient Mycenae 750
    Ancient Olympia 750
    Asklipieion 772

    Brú na Bóinne 159
    Colosseum 386, 394-5
    Delos 761
    Epidavros 750
    Fort National 225
    Hadrian's Wall 122-3, 124-5
    Hall of the Red Earl 163
    Herculaneum 469
    Kaiserthermen 613
    Knossos 735, 766
    Les Arènes 261
    Maison Carrée 261
    Morbihan Megaliths 230
    Mt Olympus 750
    Mystras 750
    Palatino 393
    Pantheon 403
    Parthenon 743
    Phaestos 767
    Pompeii 387, 469, 470-1
    Pont du Gard 179, 265
    Porta Nigra 613
    Roman Agora 741
    Roman Baths, Bath 106
    Roman Forum 11, 393, 396-7, 400
    Sanctuary of Apollo 761
    Scavi Archeologici di Ostia Antica 410
    Stonehenge 46, 55, 104-5
    Temple of Apollo 760
    Temple of Olympian Zeus 741
    Terme di Caracalla 410-11
    Terrace of the Lions 761
    Theatre of Dionysos 743
    Vaison-la-Romaine 272
    Vézère Valley 257
    Via Appia Antica 410
    Villa Adriana 410
    Villa Jovis 468
architecture 30, 798-800
    Belgium 490
    Britain 19, 72, 128
    Czech Republic 716
    France 180, 278
    Germany 558

Netherlands, the 490, 514-15
Spain 21, 322
Argostoli 776-7
art galleries
Albertina (Vienna) 637
Albertinum (Dresden) 584
Alte Pinakothek (Munich) 592
Bonnefantenmuseum (Maastricht) 514
Collezione Peggy Guggenheim (Venice) 434
East Side Gallery (Berlin) 570
Egon Schiele Art Centrum (Český Krumlov) 717
FOAM (Amsterdam) 495
Galleria degli Uffizi (Florence) 46, 447, 448-9
Galleria dell'Accademia (Florence) 454
Galleria Doria Pamphilj (Rome) 405
Galleria Nazionale d'Arte Antica: Palazzo Barberini (Rome) 405
Galleria Nazionale d'Arte Moderna (Rome) 408
Gallerie dell'Accademia (Venice) 434
Gemäldegalerie (Berlin) 568-9
Gemeentemuseum (Den Haag) 514
Groeningemuseum (Bruges) 537
Holburne Museum (Bath) 107
Kröller-Müller Museum (Hoge Veluwe) 514
Kunsthalle (Krems an der Donau) 653
Kunsthaus Graz (Graz) 654
Louvre, the (Paris) 194, 196-7
Louvre-Lens (Lens) 46, 236
MACBA (Barcelona) 330-1
MAMAC (Nice) 272-3
MAMbo (Bologna) 444
Manchester Art Gallery (Manchester) 126
Mauritshuis (Den Haag) 514

Musée d'Art Moderne et Contemporain (Strasbourg) 235
Musée de l'Annonciade (St-Tropez) 280
Musée des Beaux-Arts (Nancy) 237
Musée des Beaux-Arts (Rouen) 222
Musée d'Orsay (Paris) 185
Musée du Louvre (Paris) 194, 196-7
Musée Matisse (Nice) 273
Musée National Marc Chagall (Nice) 273
Musée Picasso (Paris) 198
Musée Rodin (Paris) 185
Musées Royaux des Beaux-Arts (Brussels) 520-1
Museo de Bellas Artes (Valencia) 352
Museo del Bargello (Florence) 453
Museo Oteiza (Alzuza) 352
Museo Picasso Málaga (Málaga) 352
Museu Nacional d'Art de Catalunya (Barcelona) 336
Museu Picasso (Barcelona) 337
Museum der Moderne (Salzburg) 660
Museum Ludwig (Cologne) 614
Museum of Asian Art (Corfu) 774
Museum Sammlung Rosengart (Lucerne) 685-6
National Gallery (Dublin) 153
National Gallery (London) 61
National Portrait Gallery (London) 61
Neue Galerie Graz Joanneumsviertel (Graz) 654
Neue Nationalgalerie (Berlin) 568
Neue Pinakothek (Munich) 592

Pinacoteca di Brera (Milan) 425
Pinakothek der Moderne (Munich) 592
Scottish National Gallery (Edinburgh) 138-9
SMAK (Ghent) 535
Šternberg Palace (Prague) 696
Tate Britain (London) 64
Tate Liverpool (Liverpool) 129-30
Tate Modern (London) 67
Tate St Ives (St Ives) 109
Teatre-Museu Dalí (Figueres) 352
Walker Art Gallery (Liverpool) 129
arts 795, see also indiviudal arts
Assisi 458
Assos 777
Athens 24, 740-56, **746-7**
accommodation 749-50
discount cards 741
drinking 753
entertainment 753
festivals & events 749
food 750-2
shopping 753
sights 740-8
tourist information 753-4
tours 748-9
travel to/from 754-5
travel within 755-6
Atlantic Coast (France) 255-60
ATMs 48, 819, 821
Augsburg 600-1
Austen, Jane 102, 107
Austria 627-72, 719-29, **629**, **638-9**
accommodation 719
drinking 806-7
food 720, 806
highlights 630-1
internet resources 633
itineraries 634-5
money 721

Austria *continued*
  opening hours 720
  planning 633
  public holidays 722
  tourist information 723
  travel to/from 46, 723-6
  travel within 633, 726-9
  visas 723
Avignon 269-71

B

Bacharach 611
Bad Ischl 664-5
Baden-Baden 609
Bamberg 610
Barcelona 327-50, **328-9**, **342-3**
  accommodation 337-41
  drinking 346
  entertainment 346-8
  festivals & events 336-7
  food 341-6
  shopping 348
  sights 327-36, 337, 345
  tourist information 348-9
  tours 336
  transport to/from 349
  transport within 349-50
Basque Country 350-5
Bastille Day 43
Bath 19, 55, 102-8, **103**
Bavaria 589-97
Bayeux 222-4
beaches 813, 814
  Biarritz 258
  Cádiz 376
  Cannes 278
  Corfu 775
  Kefallonia 777
  Mykonos 758
  Naxos 760
  Nice 273
  Patmos 773
  San Sebastián 350

Santorini (Thira) 763
Sorrento 473-4
St-Tropez 280
Beatles, the 129, 130
Beaune 241-4
beer 801-7, *see also* breweries
  Belgium 28
  Germany 557, 591, 596
  Oktoberfest 44, 592-4
Beilstein 613
Belgium 28, 485-93, 520-51,
  486-7
  accommodation 545-6
  drinking 804-5
  food 804
  highlights 488-9
  internet resources 491
  itineraries 492-3
  money 547
  opening hours 546
  planning 491
  public holidays 547
  telephone services 547
  travel to/from 547-50
  travel within 491, 550-1
  visas 547
Ben Nevis 151
Berchtesgaden 597-600
Berlin 16, 556, 562-82, **564-5**,
  574-5
  accommodation 573-6
  discount cards 567
  drinking 578
  entertainment 578-80
  food 576-8
  shopping 580
  sights 562-71, 572
  tourist information 580-1
  tours 571-2
  transport to/from 581
  transport within 581-2
Berlin Wall 16, 46, 570
Bern 682-4
Bernese Oberland 685-9
Bernkastel-Kues 613
Berthillon 207

Biarritz 258-60
bicycle tours
  Austria 660
  France 199
  Germany 572
bicycle travel, *see* cycling
Bilbao 352-5
biographical museums
  Anne Frank Huis
    (Amsterdam) 495
  Barbara Hepworth Museum
    (St Ives) 109
  Beatles Story (Liverpool) 129
  Brontë Parsonage Museum
    (Haworth) 118
  Charles Dickens Museum
    (London) 67
  Dr Johnson's House
    (London) 65
  Einstein Museum (Bern) 683
  Goethe Haus & National-
    museum (Weimar) 587
  James Joyce Museum (Dun
    Laoghaire) 158
  Jane Austen Centre (Bath)
    107
  Jane Austen's House
    Museum (Winchester) 102
  Karl Marx Haus (Trier) 614
  Maison et Jardins de Claude
    Monet (Giverny) 271
  Mozarts Geburtshaus
    (Salzburg) 659
  Mozart-Wohnhaus
    (Salzburg) 659
  Rubenshuis (Antwerp) 531
  Schiller Haus (Weimar) 587-8
  Shakespeare Houses
    (Stratford-upon-Avon) 114
  Sigmund Freud Museum
    (Vienna) 645
  Sir John Soane's Museum
    (London) 67
  Vermeer Centrum Delft
    (Delft) 512
Black Forest 608-9
Blarney 161
Blenheim Palace 113

Blois 238-9
boat travel 822
    Austria 726
    Belgium 550
    Britain 170
    France 289, 380
    Greece 780-1
    Ireland 170
    Italy 481, 482, 483
    Netherlands, the 549-50
    Spain 380
    Switzerland 726
boat trips 811
    Amsterdam 501
    Dingle Peninsula 162
    London 65
    Moselle Valley 545
    Oxford 111
    Rhine River 27
    Salzburg 660
Bohemia 715-19
Bologna 443-6
books 47
Bordeaux 255-8
breakfast 802
breweries
    Austria 650, 662
    Belgium 539
    Czech Republic 709, 715, 717
    England 127
    France 286
    Ireland 153, 160
    Netherlands, the 500
Brighton & Hove 98-101
Britain 51-9, 60-149, **52-3**
    accommodation 164-5
    drinking 802
    food 166, 801-2
    highlights 54-5
    internet resources 57
    itineraries 58-9
    language 167
    money 167
    planning 57
    public holidays 168
    telephone services 168

tourist information 169
travel to/from 170-1
travel within 57, 171-3
visas 169
British Museum 78
Brittany 225-7
Brú na Bóinne 159
Bruges 489, 537-42, **538**
Brussels 489, 520-30, **522-3**
    accommodation 525-6
    drinking 528-9
    food 526-8
    shopping 529
    sights 520-5
    tourist information 529
    travel to/within 530
Buchenwald 588
Buckingham Palace 64-5
budget 49
Burg Eltz 612-13
Burgundy 241-9
bus travel 822
    Austria 726
    Britain 171
    Czech Republic 726
    France 289
    Germany 624
    Ireland 171
    Italy 482
    Spain 380
    Switzerland 726
business hours 816, *see also*
    individual locations

C

Cádiz 376-7
Caerphilly 134
cakes 647, 804
Cambridge 116-18
Cancale 227
Cannes 278-80
canoeing 811
Canterbury 97-8
Capri 468-9, 472-73
car travel 49, 822-4

Austria 724, 726-7
Belgium 551
Britain 171
Czech Republic 724-5, 727-8
France 288, 290-1, 380
Germany 624, 625
Greece 781
Ireland 171-2
Italy 481, 482-3
Netherlands, the 550-1
Spain 380-1
Switzerland 724, 727
Carcassonne 260-1
Cardiff 131-4
Carnac 230
Carpentras 272
Castilla y León 321-4
Castilla-La Mancha 324-6
castles & chateaux 56, 632,
    see also palaces
    Alcázar 361-4
    Alcázar de los Reyes
        Cristianos 370
    Blarney Castle 161
    Burg Eltz 612
    Burg Hasegg 672
    Burg Landshut 613
    Burg Rheinfels 610
    Cardiff Castle 132
    Castello Sforzesco 425
    Castle Howard 121-2
    Castle of the Knights 772
    Český Krumlov Castle 718
    Château d'Azay-le-Rideau 238
    Château de Chambord 179,
        240
    Château de Chaumont-
        sur-Loire 238
    Château de Chenonceau 238
    Château de Cheverny 239
    Château de Versailles 178,
        218-21
    Château de Villandry 238
    Château d'If 264
    Château Royal d'Amboise 240
    Château Royal de Blois 238
    Conwy Castle 135

INDEX C

castles & chateaux *continued*
Dover Castle 97
Edinburgh Castle 55, 135, 138
Gravensteen 534-5
Grevenburg 613
Hluboká Chateau 713
Hohensalzburg 661
Hohenschwangau Castle 557, 602
Kaiserburg 605-6
Karlštejn Castle 713
Kastro 760
Konopiště Chateau 713
Leeds Castle 97
Malahide Castle 158
Neuschwanstein Castle 557, 602
Prague Castle 631, 701, 705
Schloss Ambras 668
Schloss Heidelberg 605
Schloss Nymphenburg 605
Schloss Schwerin 605
Skipton Castle 97
Stirling Castle 146-7, 148-9
Versailles 178, 218-21
Vyšehrad 705
Wartburg 605
Warwick Castle 97
Windsor Castle 96-7
Catalonia 327-50
Cathédrale Notre Dame 192-3, 216
cathedrals, *see also* **churches**
Barcelona La Catedral 330
Burgos Catedral 325
Cádiz Catedral 376
Canterbury Cathedral 97-8
Catedral de Nuestra Señora de la Almudena 308
Catedral de Santiago de Compostela 325
Cathédrale de Monaco 283
Cathédrale de Notre Dame de Paris (Paris) 190-1

Cathédrale Notre Dame (Paris) 192-3, 216
Cathédrale Notre Dame (Reims) 230
Cathédrale Notre Dame (Rouen) 222
Cathédrale Notre-Dame (Strasbourg) 235
Cathédrale St-André 255-6
Cathédrale St-Jean 245
Cathédrale St-Vincent 225
Cattedrale di San Martino 466
Christ Church Cathedral 153
Durham Cathedral 122
Ely Cathedral 122
Florence Duomo 446-7, 452
Girona Catedral 325
Kölner Dom 557, 616
La Sagrada Família 21, 296, 332-5
León Catedral 325
Liverpool Cathedral 129
Milan Duomo 424
Münster 683
Onze-Lieve-Vrouwekathedraal 531
Pamplona Cathedral 355
Salamanca Catedral Nueva 322
Salisbury Cathedral 122
Seville Cathedral 361, 362-3
Siena Duomo 463
St Fin Barre's Cathedral 159
St Paul's Cathedral 66
St Vitus Cathedral 696
St-Baafskathedraal 534
Toledo Catedral 324
Wells Cathedral 122
Westminster Cathedral 61, 64
Winchester Cathedral 101-2
York Minster 118
caves
Grotta Azzurra 468
Grotta dello Smeraldo 477
Grotte de la Mer de Glace 250
Vézère Valley 257
cell phones 48, 821

České Budějovice 717
Český Krumlov 717-19
Cézanne, Paul 271
Chagall, Marc 273
Chambord 179
Chamonix 26, 249-52
Champagne 20, 227-34
Charles Bridge 703, 705
chateaux, *see* **castles & chateaux**
Checkpoint Charlie 563-4, 571
cheese 508, 801-7
Chester 127-8
children, travel with 793-4
chocolate 28, 316, 529, 615
Chocolatería de San Ginés 316
Chodová Planá 715
Christmas markets 45
Nuremberg 606
Prague 706
Vienna 646
churches 18, 298, *see also* **cathedrals**
Abbaye du Mont St-Michel 226, 228-9
Amsterdam Nieuwe Kerk 494-5
Amsterdam Oude Kerk 495
Basilica di San Clemente 410
Basilica di San Giovanni in Laterano 410
Basilica di San Lorenzo 454
Basilica di San Marco 435
Basilica di San Pietro in Vincoli 409
Basilica di San Zeno Maggiore 428
Basilica di Santa Cecilia in Trastevere 409
Basilica di Santa Maria della Salute 436
Basilica di Santa Maria Gloriosa dei Frari 436
Basilica di Santa Maria in Trastevere 409
Basilica di Santa Maria Maggiore 409-10
Basilica of St George 696

Basilique du Sacré-Cœur 195
Basilique Notre Dame de Fourvière (Lyon) 245
Basilique Notre Dame de la Garde (Marseille) 264
Basilique St-Rémi 230-1
Bath Abbey 107
Battistero di San Giovanni 463
Berliner Dom 566-7
Catedral Vieja 322
Chiesa di Santa Maria del Popolo 407
Chiesa e Battistero dei SS Giovanni e Reparata 466
Church of Our Lady Before Týn 700-1
Delft Nieuwe Kerk 512
Delft Oude Kerk 512
Église Jeanne d'Arc 217
Église St-Germain des Prés 189
Église St-Sulpice 190
Església de Santa Maria del Mar 331
Frauenkirche (Dresden) 582
Frauenkirche (Munich) 591
Fraumünster (Zürich) 691
Grote Kerk van St Bavo 508-9
Heilig-Bloedbasiliek 538
Hofkirche 667
Holy Trinity Church 114
Iglesia de Santo Tomé 325
Jakobskirche 602
Kaisergruft 637
King's College Chapel 116
Museo di San Marco 455
Pantheon 403
Rosslyn Chapel 143, 144-5
Sistine Chapel 402
St Michael's Mount 110
St Nicholas Church 703
St Peter's Basilica 403
St Peterskirche (Munich) 591
St Peterskirche (Zürich) 691-2
Ste-Chapelle 191
Stephansdom 637

Stift Melk 654
Westminster Abbey 61
Wieskirche 599
Cinque Terre 422-3
Cliffs of Moher 162-3
climate 42-5, 48, 817
coffee 631, 649
Cold War 556, 558, 563, 792
Cologne 614-17
Colosseum 386, 394-5
Connemara 164
Córdoba 367-71
Corfu 774-5
Cork 158-60
Corsica 283
Côte d'Azur 179, 272-86
Cotswolds, the 114
Covent Garden 61
credit cards 48, 819-20
Crete 764-70, **764-5**
Cuenca 297, 327
culture 784-5
currency 48, 820
customs regulations 816
Cyclades 758-64, 776
cycling 809, 822, see also bicycle tours
    Belgium 550
    France 289
    Italy 482
    Netherlands, the 550
    Spain 380
Czech language 827
Czech Republic 627-35, 696-729, **629**, **697**
    accommodation 720
    drinking 807
    food 720, 807
    highlights 630-1
    internet resources 633
    itineraries 634-5
    language 827
    money 721-2
    opening hours 720
    planning 633
    public holidays 722

telephone services 723
tourist information 723
travel to/from 723-6
travel within 633, 726-9
visas 723

D

Damme 542
dangers 820
Danube Valley 652-3
D-Day Beaches 224-5
Delft 512-13
Delos 761
Delphi 755
Dingle Peninsula 162
disabilities, travellers with 481, 623, 780
discount cards 817
    France 291
    Germany 622
    Greece 741
Disneyland Resort Paris 217
diving 811
Dodecanese 770-4, 776
Dolomites 445
Dordogne 253-5
Dover 99
Dresden 582-7
drinking 17, 801-7, see also individual locations
driving, see car travel
Dublin 16, 151-8, **152**
Dun Laoghaire 158
Dune du Pilat 260
Duomo (Florence) 446-7, 452
Dutch language 827

E

Eagle's Nest 598
economy 784-5
Eden Project 109
Edinburgh 29, 135-46, **136-7**
    accommodation 142
    drinking 143
    festivals & events 139

Edinburgh *continued*
    food 142-3
    sights 135-9
    tourist information 143
    tours 139-42
    travel to/from 146
Edinburgh Castle 55, 135, 138
Eiffel Tower 12, 178, 189
electricity 817-18
emergencies 818
England 60-131, *see also* Britain
Enlightenment, the 789-90
Épernay 232-4
Eton 96-7
European Union 785, 792
events, *see* festivals & events
exchange rates 49

F

family travel 793-4
festivals & events 42-5, 298, 388, *see also individual locations,* film festivals, music festivals, sporting events
    Bienal de Flamenco 365
    Brighton Festival 99
    Carnaval de Nice 276
    Carnevale (Venice) 437
    Christmas markets 45, 606, 646, 706
    De Gentse Feesten 44
    Dia de Sant Joan 337
    Edinburgh Festival Fringe 139
    Edinburgh International Festival 44, 139
    Edinburgh Military Tattoo 139
    Escalade 676-7
    Feria de Abril 43, 365
    Festa de'Noantri 411
    Festa di San Giovanni 455
    Festes de la Mercè 45, 336-7
    Festival d'Avignon 270
    Fête des Lumières 247
    Fêtes de Genève 676
    Fiesta de San Isidro 308
    Galway Arts Festival 163
    Galway Oyster Festival 163
    Guy Fawkes Night 45
    Hay Festival 134-5
    Hellenic Festival 749
    Il Palio 43
    Koninginnedag 43
    Natale 45
    Natale di Roma 411
    Notting Hill Carnival 44, 83
    Oktoberfest 44, 594-6
    Opernball 646
    Palio 464
    Prague Fringe Festival 706
    Running of the Bulls 43
    Sanfermines 43, 355
    Scoppio del Carro 455
    Semana Santa 42, 365
    Settimana della Cultura 411
    Settimana Santa 43
    St Patrick's Day 42
    Suma Flamenca 308
    Trooping the Colour 83
    Venice Biennale 437
    Venice Carnevale 42
film festivals
    Cannes Film Festival 43
    Festival Internazionale del Film di Roma 411
    Venice International Film Festival 44, 437
    Viennale Film Festival 646
films 47
Fira 762
Fiskardo 776
flamenco 297, 318
Flanders 530-44
Florence 386, 446-60, **450-1**
    accommodation 455-7
    drinking 459-60
    festivals & events 455
    food 457-9
    sights 446-55
    tourist information 460
    tours 455

    travel to/from 460
    travel within 460
food 632, 801-7, *see also individual foods*
football 808-9
forests 814
forts
    Alcázar 324
    Castell de Montjuïc 336
    Ciudadela 355
    Festung Ehrenbreitstein 612
    Festung Hohensalzburg 658
    Festung Marienberg 604
    Koules Venetian Fortress 765
    Palaio Frourio 775
    Palamidi Fortress 756
    Venetian Fortifications 767
France 175-291, **176-7**
    accommodation 286
    drinking 803
    food 287, 802-3, 804
    highlights 178-9
    internet resources 181
    itineraries 182-3
    language 827
    money 287
    opening hours 181, 287
    planning 181
    public holidays 287-8
    shopping 181
    telephone services 288
    travel to/from 288-9, 380
    travel within 181, 289-91
    visas 288
French language 827
French Revolution 789-90
French Riviera 179, 272-86
Frikes 778

G

Galleria degli Uffizi 46, 447, 448-9
galleries, *see* art galleries
Galway 163-4

gardens, *see* parks & gardens
Gaudí, Antoni 21
gay travellers 167, 287, 377, 478-9, 505, 622-3, 720-1, 778, 818
gelato 413, 804
Geneva 672-80, **676**
    accommodation 677
    drinking 678-9
    festivals & events 676-7
    food 677-8
    shopping 679
    sights 673-6
    tourist information 679
    travel to/from 679
    travel within 679-80
German language 828
Germany 553-625, **554-5**
    accommodation 559, 622
    discount cards 622
    drinking 559, 806-7
    food 622, 806
    highlights 556-7
    internet resources 559
    itineraries 560-1
    language 828
    money 623
    opening hours 622
    planning 559
    public holidays 623
    telephone services 623
    travel to/from 623-4
    travel within 559, 624-5
    visas 623
Ghent 534-7
Giant's Causeway 25, 165
Giverny 271
Glastonbury 109
Glen Coe 147
Granada 371-3
Grand Canal, Venice 430-1
Grand Place, Brussels 521
Grasse 280
Graz 654-6
Greece 731-81, **732-3**
    accommodation 778

drinking 806
food 778, 806
highlights 734-5
internet resources 737
itineraries 738-9
language 828
money 779
opening hours 778
planning 737
public holidays 779
telephone services 779-80
tourist information 780
travel to/from 780
travel within 737, 780-1
visas 780
Greek language 828
Guinness 153

H

Haarlem 508-10
Hadrian's Wall 122-3, 124-5
Hallstatt 665-6
Hamburg 617-22
hamburgers 620
Hamelin 610
Hania 767-70
Haworth 118
Hay-on-Wye 134-5
health 818
Heiligenblut 671
Herculaneum 469
heritage organisations (UK) 167
hiking 809, 810
    Cinque Terre 422
    Corfu 775
    Dolomites 445
    France 250
    Samaria Gorge 770
history 180, 786-92
    Cold War 556, 558, 563, 792
    WWI 790
    WWII 224-5, 558, 563, 588, 790-1
Hofburg, Vienna 643
Hoge Veluwe National Park 519

Hohe Tauern National Park 671
Hohenschwangau Castle 557, 602
Hyde Park 77

I

ice cream 207, 804
immigration 821
Impressionism 796
Innsbruck 666-72
insurance 818-19, 823
Interlaken 687-9
internet access 48, 819
Ionian Islands 774-8
Iraklio 764-7
Ireland 51-9, 150-73, **52-3**
    accommodation 165
    drinking 802
    food 166, 801-2
    highlights 54-5
    internet resources 57
    itineraries 58-9
    language 167
    money 168-9
    opening hours 166
    planning 57
    public holidays 168
    telephone services 169-70
    tourist information 169
    travel to/from 170
    travel within 57, 171-3
    visas 169
Iron Curtain 792
islands 736, 814
    Aegean Islands 776
    Aeolian Islands 473
    Burano 436
    Capri 468-9, 472-73
    Château d'If 264
    Chios 776
    Corfu 774-5
    Crete 764-70, **764-5**
    Cyclades 758-64, 776
    Delos 761
    Dodecanese 770-4, 776

islands continued
  Îles de Lérins 278
  Ionian Islands 774-8
  Ios 776
  Isle of Skye 150
  Ithaki 777-8
  Karpathos 776
  Kefallonia 775-7
  Lesvos 776
  Murano 436
  Mykonos 758-60, **759**
  Naxos 760-1, 776
  Orkney 150
  Paros 776
  Rhodes 770-3
  Samos 776
  Santorini 30, 735, 761-4, **762**
  Sardinia 473
  Sicily 473
  St Michael's Mount 110-11
  Symi 776
  Torcello 436
Isle of Skye 150
Italian language 828
Italy 383-483, **384-5**
  accommodation 478
  drinking 804
  food 478, 803
  highlights 386-7
  internet resources 389
  itineraries 390-1
  language 828
  money 479
  opening hours 478
  planning 389
  public holidays 479-80
  telephone services 480-1
  tourist information 481
  travel to/from 481, 483
  travel within 389, 482-3
  visas 481
Ithaki 777-8
itineraries 32-41, see also
  individual locations

J

John O'Groats 150
Jungfraujoch 20, 631, 688
Jura 249-53, 254

K

Kastraki 757
kayaking 811
Kefallonia 775-7
Kensington Palace 46
Keukenhof Gardens 512
Kinderdijk 489, 516
Kioni 777-8
Knossos 735, 766
Koblenz 612
Kölner Dom 557, 616
Kos 772-3
Krems an der Donau 653

L

La Sagrada Família 21, 296,
  332-5
Lake Constance 608-9
Lake District 132
Lake Geneva 673
Lakones 775
Land's End 111
languages 48, 678, 827-8
Languedoc-Roussillon 260-3
Leaning Tower (Pisa) 461
Lecce 458
legal matters 819
Leiden 510-12
Les Baux de Provence 272
Les Calanques 268
Les Eyzies-de-Tayac-Sireuil
  255
lesbian travellers 167, 287, 377,
  478-9, 505, 622-3, 720-1,
  778, 818
Liverpool 128-31
Loch Lomond 146
Loch Ness 147
Loire Valley 237-41

London 13, 54, 60-96, **62-3,
  74-5**
  accommodation 83-6
  drinking 89-91
  entertainment 54, 91-3
  festivals & events 83
  food 86-9
  shopping 93-4
  sights 61-82
  tourist information 94
  tours 82-3
  travel to/from 94
  travel within 94-6
London Eye 67
Lorraine 234-7
Louvre, the 194, 196-7
Louvre-Lens 46, 236
Lucca 465-7
Lucerne 685-7
Lüneburg 610
Lyon 244-9

M

Madrid 302-21, **306-7, 310-11**
  accommodation 308-13
  drinking 315-16
  entertainment 316-19
  festivals 308
  food 313-15, 316
  shopping 319-20
  sights 302-8, 309
  tourist information 320-1
  tours 308
  travel to/from 321
  travel within 321
Mainz 611
Malahide Castle 158
Malia 767
Manchester 123-7
Mariánské Lázně 715
Marienbad 715
markets 45, see also
  Christmas markets
  Alkmaar 508
  Amsterdam 507
  Athens 753

000 Map pages

Barcelona 327, 331
Carpentras 272
Cork 159
Hamburg 618
Hania 767
London 93
Madrid 319-20
Marseille 268
Munich 591
Nuremberg 605, 606
Paris 209, 213
St-Tropez 281
Vaison-la-Romaine 272
Valencia 357
Vienna 646, 650
Marseille 263-9
Matera 475
Matisse, Henri 273
Matterhorn 23, 630, 680, 681
Meissen 587
Melk 654
Meteora 735, 757
Mezquita, Córdoba 367-70
Mikulov 716
Milan 423-7, **424**
mobile phones 48, 821
modern art 796
Monaco 282-6
monasteries 325, 349, 757
Monestir de Montserrat 349
Monet, Claude 271
money 48, 49, 819-20, 821
Mont St-Michel 226, 228-9
Monte Carlo Casino 282, 284-5
Montjuïc 338-9
Morbihan Megaliths 230
Moselle Valley 545, 611-14
mosques 18, 325, 367, 370
motorcycle travel 822-4
    Austria 724, 726-7
    Belgium 551
    Britain 171
    Czech Republic 724-5, 727-8
    France 288, 290-1, 380
    Germany 624, 625
    Greece 781

Ireland 171-2
Italy 481, 482-3
Netherlands, the 550-1
Spain 380-1
Switzerland 724, 727
Moulin Rouge 211
mountains 22, 812-13
    Aiguille du Midi 251
    Ben Nevis 151
    Dolomites 445
    Eiger 688
    Grossglockner 671
    Jungfrau 688
    Matterhorn 23, 630, 680, 681
    Mönch 688
    Mont Blanc 812
    Monte Igueldo 350
    Mt Pilatus 687
    Mt Rigi 687
    Mt Titlis 687
    Picos de Europa 356
    Schlossberg 655
Munich 589-97, **590**
    accommodation 594
    drinking 28, 557, 595
    festivals & events 592-4
    food 594-5
    sights 591-2, 593
    tourist information 596
    tours 592
    travel to/from 596-7
    travel within 597
Murcia 356-9
museums 194, 388, 797, see
    also archaeological
    museums, art galleries,
    biographical museums
    Alcázar (Toledo) 324-5
    Amsterdam Museum
        (Amsterdam) 495
    Antivouniotissa Museum
        (Corfu) 775
    Archivo de Indias (Seville)
        364
    Ashmolean Museum
        (Oxford) 112
    Atomium (Brussels) 525

Bauhaus Archiv (Berlin) 569
Bauhaus Museum (Weimar)
    588
Benaki Museum (Athens) 748
Bier & Oktoberfestmuseum
    (Munich) 592
British Museum (London) 78
Buchenwald Concentration
    Camp (Buchenwald) 588
Caixa Forum (Madrid) 303
Capitoline Museums (Rome)
    400-1
Carré d'Art (Nîmes) 261
Casa di Giulietta (Verona) 427
Centraal Museum (Utrecht)
    518
Centre d'Histoire de la
    Résistance et de la Dépor-
    tation (Lyon) 246-7
Centre Pompidou (Paris) 195
Centre Pompidou-Metz
    Museum (Metz) 271
Centro de Arte Reina Sofía
    (Madrid) 303
Charles Bridge Museum
    (Prague) 705
Chocolate Museum
    (Cologne) 615
Choco-Story (Bruges) 539
Churchill War Rooms
    (London) 64
Cité de l'Océan (Biarritz)
    258-9
Cork City Gaol (Cork) 159
DDR Museum (Berlin) 567,
    571
De Valk (Leiden) 511
Deutsches Historisches
    Museum (Berlin) 563
Dokumentation Obersalz-
    berg (Berchtesgaden) 598
Dublin Writers Museum
    (Dublin) 154
Euskal Museoa (Bilbao) 353
Fashion Museum (Bath) 107
Fitzwilliam Museum
    (Cambridge) 117
Frans Hals Museum
    (Haarlem) 509

museums *continued*

Fundació Joan Miró (Barcelona) 336

Galway City Museum (Galway) 163

Germanisches National-museum (Nuremberg) 606

Goldenes Dachl & Museum (Innsbruck) 667

Guinness Storehouse (Dublin) 153

Hamburger Kunsthalle (Hamburg) 619

Haus der Musik (Vienna) 645

Historium (Bruges) 539

Humboldt-Box (Berlin) 567

Imperial War Museum (London) 67, 72

Imperial War Museum North (Manchester) 126

International Red Cross & Red Crescent Museum (Geneva) 673

International Slavery Museum (Liverpool) 129

Internationales Maritimes Museum (Hamburg) 619

Joods Historisch Museum (Amsterdam) 501

Jüdisches Museum (Berlin) 570

Kilmainham Gaol (Dublin) 153

Kolumba (Cologne) 614-15

Kunsthaus (Zürich) 692

KunstHausWien (Vienna) 644

Kunsthistorisches Museum (Vienna) 637

Kunstmuseum (Bern) 684

Lakenhal (Leiden) 510

Landeszeughaus (Graz) 655

Lobkowicz Palace (Prague) 696

Madame Tussauds (London) 79

Maison de la Magie (Blois) 238

Matterhorn Museum (Zermatt) 680

Memorial Museum Passchen-daele 1917 (Ypres) 543

Militärhistorisches Museum Dresden (Dresden) 584

Mucha Museum (Prague) 704

Musée Angladon (Avignon) 270

Musée Calvet (Avignon) 270

Musée d'Art et d'Histoire (Geneva) 673

Musée de Montmartre (Paris) 199

Musée des Égouts de Paris (Paris) 185

Musée du Château (St-Malo) 225

Musée du Quai Branly (Paris) 184-5

Musée Horta (Brussels) 524

Musée Lumière (Lyon) 246

Musée Magritte (Brussels) 521

Musée Mémorial de la Bataille de Normandie (Bayeux) 223

Museo Altamira (Altamira) 366

Museo Chillida Leku (San Sebastián) 350

Museo Civico (Siena) 463

Museo de Bellas Artes (Bilbao) 352-3

Museo de Cádiz (Cádiz) 376

Museo de Navarra (Pamplona) 355

Museo del Baile Flamenco (Seville) 364-5

Museo del Prado (Madrid) 296, 302-3, 304-5

Museo dell'Ara Pacis (Rome) 407

Museo di San Marco (Florence) 455

Museo e Galleria Borghese (Rome) 408

Museo Guggenheim (Bilbao) 354

Museo Nazionale Etrusco di Villa Giulia (Rome) 408

Museo Nazionale Romano (Rome) 408

Museo Thyssen-Bornemisza (Madrid) 303

Museu d'Història de Barce-lona (Barcelona) 330

Museum Boijmans van Beu-ningen (Rotterdam) 514

Museum Catharijneconvent (Utrecht) 518

Museum für Film und Fernsehen (Berlin) 568

Museum het Rembrandthuis (Amsterdam) 501

Museum of Communism (Prague) 704-5

Museum of Liverpool (Liverpool) 130

Museum of Science & Indus-try (Manchester) 123

Museum Rotterdam (Rotterdam) 515

Museumsinsel (Berlin) 565-6

MuseumsQuartier (Vienna) 642

National Football Museum (Manchester) 126

National Maritime Museum (London) 79

National Museum (Prague) 704

National Museum Cardiff 132

National Railway Museum (York) 120

Natural History Museum (Dublin) 153-4

Natural History Museum (London) 73

Old Jameson Distillery (Dublin) 154

Palais du Tau (Reims) 230

Palazzo Ducale (Venice) 429, 434

Palazzo Grassi (Venice) 434-5

Palazzo Pitti (Florence) 453-4

Palazzo Vecchio (Florence) 452

Patek Phillipe Museum (Geneva) 673
Paul Klee Centre (Bern) 683
Peloponnese Folklore Foundation Museum (Nafplio) 756
People's History Museum (Manchester) 123
Prague City Museum (Prague) 704
Prague Jewish Museum (Prague) 701-3
Residenzmuseum (Munich) 593
Rijksmuseum (Amsterdam) 46, 488, 496-7
Rijksmuseum van Oudheden (Leiden) 510-11
Römisch-Germanisches Museum (Cologne) 614
Salzburg Museum (Salzburg) 658-9
Schweizerisches Landesmuseum (Zürich) 692
Science Museum (London) 77
Stasimuseum (Berlin) 570
Stedelijk Museum (Amsterdam) 495
Topographie des Terrors (Berlin) 569
Tränenpalast (Berlin) 564-5
Trinity College & Book of Kells (Dublin) 151
Van Gogh Museum (Amsterdam) 46, 495
Vatican Museums (Rome) 402
Verkehrshaus (Lucerne) 686
Victoria & Albert Museum (London) 73
Volkskunstmuseum (Innsbruck) 667
Wallraf-Richartz-Museum & Fondation Corboud (Cologne) 615
World Museum (Liverpool) 129
Zwinger (Dresden) 584
music 47

music festivals
  Brussels Jazz Marathon 43
  Glastonbury Festival 43, 109
  Maggio Musicale Fiorentino 455
  Nice Jazz Festival 276
  Prague Spring 706
  Puccini Festival 465
  Salzburg Festival 44, 660-1
Mykonos 758-60, **759**

N

Nafplio 756-8
Nancy 237
national parks & reserves
  Hoge Veluwe 519
  Hohe Tauern 671
  Lake District 132
  Les Calanques 268
  Peak District 115-16
  Snowdonia 135
National Trust (UK) 167
Navarra 355-6
Naxos 760-1, 776
Netherlands, the 485-519, 545-51, **486-7**
  accommodation 545
  drinking 804-5
  food 804
  highlights 488-9
  internet resources 491
  itineraries 492-3
  language 827
  money 547
  opening hours 546
  planning 491
  public holidays 547
  telephone services 547
  travel to/from 547-50
  travel within 491, 550-1
  visas 547
Neuschwanstein Castle 557, 602
Nice 272-80, **274-5**
  accommodation 276
  drinking 277

festivals 276
food 276-7
sights 272-3
tourist information 278
tours 273, 276
travel to/from 278
Nîmes 261-3
Normandy 217-25
North Rhine-Westphalia 614-17
Notre Dame cathedral 190-1, 192-3, 216
Notting Hill Carnival 44
Nuremberg 605-8

O

Oia 763
Oktoberfest 44, 592-4
Olomouc 716
Olympic Park, London 83
opening hours 816, see also individual locations
Orvieto 458
Oxford 111-13
Oyster Card 95

P

Padua 458
painting 795-7
palaces 14, 56, 632, see also castles & chateaux
  Alhambra 19, 297, 372, 374-5
  Blenheim Palace 113
  Buckingham Palace 64-5
  Hampton Court Palace 82
  Hofburg (Innsbruck) 667
  Hofburg (Vienna) 643
  Kaiservilla 664
  Kensington Palace 46, 77
  Lobkowicz Palace 696
  Old Royal Palace (Prague) 696
  Palace of Holyroodhouse 138
  Palacio Real 303
  Palais des Papes 270
  Palais Rohan 235

palaces *continued*
  Residenz (Munich) 593
  Residenz (Salzburg) 659
  Residenz (Würzburg) 603-4
  Residenzschloss (Dresden) 582, 584
  Royal Palace (Amsterdam) 494
  Royal Pavilion (Brighton) 98-9
  Schloss Belvedere 642, 644
  Schloss Charlottenburg 571
  Schloss Eggenberg 654
  Schloss Hellbrunn 661, 665
  Schloss Mirabell 659, 661
  Schloss Sanssouci 583
  Schloss Schönbrunn 637
  Šternberg Palace 696
Paleokastritsa 775
Pamplona 355-6
Pantheon 403
Paris 184-217, **186-7**, **200-1**
  accommodation 199-204
  drinking 208-11
  entertainment 211-13
  food 204-8
  shopping 213
  sights 184-99, 216
  tourist information 213
  tours 199
  travel to/within 213-15, 217
parks & gardens
  Backs, the 117
  Bains des Pâquis 673
  Castell de Montjuïc 336
  Ciudadela 355
  Englischer Garten 592
  Giardini di Augusto 468
  Holyrood Park 138
  Hyde Park 77
  Jardin Botanique (Geneva) 673
  Jardin des Plantes 188
  Jardin du Luxembourg 185
  Keukenhof Gardens 512
  Kew Gardens 79, 82

Musée Rodin 185
Parc de la Perle du Lac 673
Parc de la Tête d'Or 246
Parc des Bastions 673
Park an der Ilm 588
Park Güell 345
Park Sanssouci 583
Parque del Buen Retiro 309
Prater 644-5
Regent's Park 77-8
St James's Park 65
Tiergarten 556, 572
Villa Borghese 407-8
Vondelpark 500
Vrtbov Garden 704
Parque del Buen Retiro 309
Parthenon 743
passports 821
Patmos 773-4
Peloponnese 756-8
Phaestos 767
Piazza dei Miracoli 461
Picos de Europa 356
Pisa 460-2
planning
  budgeting 49
  calendar of events 42-5
  children, travel with 793-4
  Europe basics 48-9
  itineraries 32-41
  repeat visitors 46
  resources 47
  travel seasons 42-5, 48, 49
Plzeň 715-17
politics 784-5
Pompeii 387, 469, 470-1
Pont du Gard 179, 265
population 784
Positano 475-7
Potsdam 583
Prague 18, 696-715, **698-9**, **702**
  accommodation 706-7
  drinking 708-10
  entertainment 710-11
  festivals & events 706
  food 707-8

  shopping 711
  sights 696-705
  tourist information 712
  tours 705
  travel to/within 712-14
Prague Castle 631, 701, 705
Provence 263-72
public transport 824
punting (Oxford) 111

R

rail passes 824-6
Randstad 508-20
Ravenna 458
Reformation 787-8
Reign of Terror 790
Reims 230-2
religion 784
reserves, *see* national parks & reserves
Residenz, Munich 593
Rhine River 27
Rhine Valley 609-11
Rhodes 770-3
Rhône Valley 241-9
Rijksmuseum 46, 488, 496-7
Ring of Kerry 161-2
River Thames 80-1
road rules, *see* car travel
Rock of Cashel 160-1
Roman Forum 11, 393, 396-7, 400
Romantic Road 600-5
Romanticism 796
Rome 392-422, **398-9**, **404-5**
  accommodation 411-13
  drinking 416-17
  entertainment 417-18
  festivals & events 411
  food 413-16
  history 392-3
  shopping 418
  sights 393-411
  tourist information 418-19
  travel to/within 419-22
Rosslyn Chapel 143, 144-5

000 Map pages

Rothenburg ob der Tauber 601-3
Rotterdam 513-17
Rouen 217, 222
Royal Mile, Edinburgh 140-1
ruins, see archaeological sites & ruins
Running of the Bulls 43

S

safety 820
sailing 811
Salamanca 321-4
Salzburg 24, 630, 656-64, **658**
Salzkammergut 664-6
Samaria Gorge 770
San Gimignano 466
San Sebastián 350-2
Sanfermines 43, 355
Santorini (Thira) 30, 735, 761-4, **762**
Sardinia 473
Sarlat-La-Canéda 253-5
Saxony 582-7
Schiltach 610
Schloss Hellbrunn 661, 665
Schloss Schönbrunn 637
Schlösser, see castles & chateaux, palaces
Scotland 135-50
sculpture 795-7
Seville 359-67, **360-1**
Shakespeare's Globe 67
Shard, the 46, 72
shopping 29, see also individual locations
Sicily 473
Siena 462-5
Sistine Chapel 402
skiing & snowboarding 445, 810, 811
Chamonix 26
France 250, 254
Innsbruck 667-8, 669
Zermatt 680
soccer 808-9

Sorrento 473-4
Sound of Music, the 661, 662
Spain 293-381, **294-5**
accommodation 377
drinking 805
food 299, 377, 805
highlights 296-7
internet resources 299
itineraries 300-1
language 828
money 378
opening hours 377
planning 299
public holidays 378-9
telephone services 379
tourist information 379
travel to/from 379
travel within 299, 380-1
visas 379
Spanische Hofreitschule 652
Spanish language 828
sports 808-11
sporting events
Formula One Grand Prix 283
London Marathon 83
Regata Storica 437
University Boat Race 83
Wimbledon Lawn Tennis Championships 83
St Gallen 694
St Goar 610
St Goarshausen 610
St Ives 109-10
St Michael's Mount 110-11
St Paul's Cathedral 66
Stiftsbibliothek 694
Stirling 146-7
Stirling Castle 146-7, 148-9
St-Malo 225-7
Stonehenge 46, 55, 104-5
Strasbourg 235-7
Stratford-upon-Avon 113-15
St-Tropez 280-1
Switzerland 627-35, 672-95, 719-29, **629**, **674-5**
accommodation 719-20

drinking 806-7
food 720, 806
highlights 630-1
internet resources 633
itineraries 634-5
money 721
opening hours 720
planning 633
public holidays 722
telephone services 723
tourist information 723
travel to/from 723-6
travel within 633, 726-9
visas 723

T

tapas 314
taxes 820
taxi travel 824
Telč 716
telephone services 48, 821
Thames, the 80-1
Thira, see Santorini (Thira)
Thuringia 587-9
Tiergarten 556, 572
time 821
tipping 820
Tirol 666-72
Tivoli 421
Toledo 324-6
tourist information 821, see also individual locations
tours, see individual locations, bicycle tours, boat trips, walking tours
Tower Bridge 65
Tower of London 54, 68-71
Traben-Trarbach 613
Trafalgar Square 61
train travel 46, 824-6
Austria 46, 725, 728
Belgium 549, 551
Britain 170, 172-3
Czech Republic 726, 729
France 289, 291, 380
Germany 624, 625

Greece 781
Ireland 173
Italy 481, 483
Netherlands, the 548-9, 551
Spain 379-80, 380, 381
Switzerland 725, 728-9
travellers cheques 820
travel to/from Europe 822
travel within Europe 49, 822-6
Trevi Fountain 405
Trier 613-14
Tuscany 31, 446-67

U

Uffizi, see Galleria degli Uffizi
Unesco World Heritage Sites
Albert Dock 129-30
Basilique St-Rémi 230-1
Belfort, Ghent 534
Bern's Old Town 682-3
Blenheim Palace 113
Cathédrale St-André 255-6
Conwy Castle 135
Cuenca 297, 327
Dolomites 445
Durham Cathedral 122
Epidavros 750
Giant's Causeway 25, 165
Grande Île, Strasbourg 235
Greenwich 79
Herculaneum 469
Kinderdijk 516
Palais des Papes 270
Palais du Tau 230
Place Stanislas 237
Pompeii 387, 469, 470-1
Pont du Gard 179, 265
Ravenna mosaics 458
Residenz, Würzburg 603-4
Rhodes Old Town 771
Rietveld-Schröderhuis 518
Salzburg's Old Town 657
Schloss Eggenberg 654

Schloss Schönbrunn 637
Stiftsbibliothek 694
Vieux Lyon 245
Wieskirche 599
Utrecht 517-20

V

Vaison-la-Romaine 272
Valais 680-2
Valencia 356-9, **358**
Van Gogh Museum 46
Vathy 778
Vatican Museums 402
vegetarian travellers 807
Venice 15, 387, 429-43, **432-3**
accommodation 437-9
discount cards 436
drinking 441-2
entertainment 442
festivals & events 437
food 439-41
sights 429-36
tourist information 442
tours 437
travel to/within 438, 442-3
Venice Carnevale 42
Verona 427-9
Versailles 178, 218-21
Vienna 15, 636-52, **640-1**
accommodation 646-7
drinking 631, 649-50
entertainment 650, 652
festivals & events 646
food 647-9
shopping 650-1
sights 637-45
tourist information 651
tours 645
travel to/within 651-2
Vienna Boys' Choir 652
Vieux Port, Marseille 266-7
Villa d'Este 421
vineyards, see wine & vineyards
visas 48, 821
visual arts 25, 180, 257, 271, 352, 795-7

W

Wales 131-5
walking, see hiking
walking tours
Berlin 571
Dublin 154
Edinburgh 139-42
Florence 455
London 82-3
Nice 273
Paris 199
Prague 705
Vienna 645
York 120
weather 42-5, 48, 817
Weimar 587-9
Wieskirche 599
wi-fi 48, 819
Winchester 101-2
windmills 510, 516
Windsor 96-7
windsurfing 811
wine & vineyards 801-7
France 20, 227, 231, 232-3, 234-5, 235, 242, 258
Germany 604
Luxembourg 545
Wolfgangsee 668
Würzburg 603-5
WWI 790
WWII 224-5, 558, 563, 588, 790-1

Y

York 118-21, **119**
Ypres 542-4

Z

Zaanse Schans 510
Zakros 767
Zermatt 23, 680-2
Zürich 689-95, **690-1**